A New Choice for You!

Help today's students become tomorrow's expert teachers!

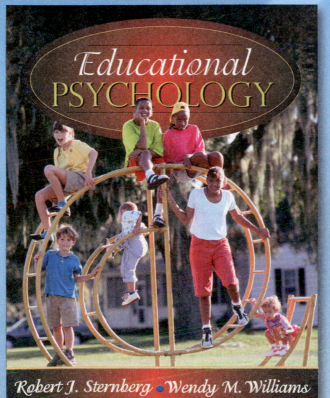

Educational Psychology

Robert J. Sternberg, *Yale University*
Wendy M. Williams, *Cornell University*

ALLYN & BACON
A Pearson Education Company

What does it take to become an expert teacher?

Robert Sternberg and Wendy Williams address this question throughout their new textbook. This renowned author team helps readers understand and develop expertise in both teaching and learning by offering a crystal-clear, in-depth presentation of both the science of educational psychology and art of teaching. Principles are illustrated through the practice of expert teachers and through personal reflection by the reader. By helping readers discover what it takes to become expert students, as well as expert teachers, this book gives a unique insight into the teaching-learning process.

"...the three main strengths of this [book] include the following: 1) focus on the practical with real world examples in the classroom, 2) variety of pedagogical features to help with student attention and facilitate student understanding, and 3) writing that keeps the student in mind – fast moving with many examples integrated into theoretical discussions."

–Katherine F. Wickstrom,
Eastern Illinois University

Meet the Authors

Robert J. Sternberg

is IBM Professor of Psychology and Education in the Department of Psychology at Yale University. He received his Ph.D. from Stanford University in 1975 and his B.A. summa cum laude, Phi Beta Kappa, from Yale University in 1972. Sternberg is the author of over 800 journal articles, book chapters, and books, and has received about $15 million in government grants and contracts for his research. The central focus of his research is on intelligence and cognitive development. Sternberg is a Fellow of the American Academy of Arts and Sciences, the American Association for the Advancement of Science, the American Psychological Association (in 12 divisions), and the American Psychological Society.

Sternberg has won many awards from APA, AERA, APS, and other organizations. He has been president of the Divisions of General Psychology, Educational Psychology, Psychology and the Arts, and Theoretical and Philosophical Psychology of the APA and has served as Editor of the *Psychological Bulletin* and is Editor of *Contemporary Psychology*. He is most well-known for his theory of successful intelligence, investment theory of creativity (developed with Todd Lubart), theory of mental self-government, balance theory of wisdom, and for his triangular theory of love and his theory of love as a story. Sternberg is a member of the Trustees Research Committee of the College Board and has served on a Research Advisory Committee for ETS.

Wendy M. Williams

is an Associate Professor in the Department of Human Development at Cornell University, where she studies the development, assessment, training, and societal implications of intelligence and related abilities. She holds Ph.D. and Master's degrees in psychology from Yale University, a Master's in physical anthropology from Yale, and a B.A. in English and biology from Columbia University. Williams directed the joint Harvard-Yale Practical and Creative Intelligence for School Project, and she was Co-Principal Investigator for a six-year, $1.4 million Army Research Institute grant to study practical intelligence and success at leadership. In addition to dozens of articles and chapters on her research, Williams has authored eight books and edited three volumes.

Williams is a Fellow of three divisions of the American Psychological Association (general psychology, developmental psychology, and media psychology), and she is currently serving a second consecutive term as Member-at-Large of the executive committee of the Society for General Psychology (division 1 of APA). She was also program chair and dissertation award committee chair for both divisions 1 and 15 (educational psychology) of APA. Williams received the 1996 Early Career Contribution Award from Division 15 of APA, and both the 1997 and 1999 Mensa Awards for Excellence in Research to a Senior Investigator. Williams also received the 2001 Robert Fantz Award for an Early Career Contribution to Psychology, given annually by the American Psychological Association to one individual in recognition of outstanding contributions to research in the first decade following receipt of the Ph.D.

Pedagogy that Works!

The introductory educational psychology course must convey vast amounts of material. To aid students in learning this material, this book includes various types of pedagogy to help them both master the content and apply it in their future teaching experiences.

Chapter Opener Pedagogy

Chapter Outline

A brief chapter outline including major headings provides students with a chapter organizer and study tool.

The Big Picture

A set of chapter objectives in question format also helps readers approach the content of the chapter.

Opening Vignette

Each chapter opens with a vignette showing reflective practitioners in action. The vignette highlights a major topic of the chapter, shows its relevance to experiences in the classroom, and is referenced throughout the chapter.

Chapter Overview

Following the vignette is a brief overview of what the chapter will cover and why it is relevant to the classroom. It provides students with an immediate link between the concepts of the chapter and the classroom.

Text Pedagogy

"Thinking" Questions (C.A.P.)

Research has shown that simply memorizing text is one of the least effective ways of learning. Rather, students learn more effectively when they process the information they need to learn in diverse ways and think deeply about it. The authors help them to do so by including questions integrated into the text that will encourage students to think creatively, analytically, and practically about what they are learning. Three types of questions—**Thinking Creatively, Thinking Analytically, and Thinking Practically**—appear throughout each chapter. This framework, based on the Sternberg triarchic theory of human intelligence, helps ensure that students will think about what they are learning, rather than merely processing it at a superficial level. Suggested responses are printed in the text so students can think about their own answers and then consider the modeled suggestions. (See Image #1)

The Flexible Expert

In each chapter, "The Flexible Expert" introduces readers to concise, specific strategies—practical, analytical, and creative—used by both expert teachers and expert students to approach the daily challenges of the classroom. (See Image #2)

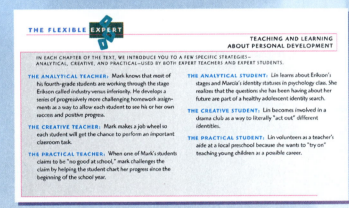

THINKING **CREATIVELY**

If you were to design a gifted program for a school where you were teaching, what form would the program take?

SUGGESTION: Each student must answer for himself or herself.

Image #1

THE FLEXIBLE EXPERT

TEACHING AND LEARNING
ABOUT PERSONAL DEVELOPMENT

IN EACH CHAPTER OF THE TEXT, WE INTRODUCE YOU TO A FEW SPECIFIC STRATEGIES—
ANALYTICAL, CREATIVE, AND PRACTICAL—USED BY BOTH EXPERT TEACHERS AND EXPERT STUDENTS.

THE ANALYTICAL TEACHER: Mark knows that most of his fourth-grade students are working through the stage Erikson called industry versus inferiority. He develops a series of progressively more challenging homework assignments as a way to allow each student to see his or her own success and positive progress.

THE CREATIVE TEACHER: Mark makes a job wheel so each student will get the chance to perform an important classroom task.

THE PRACTICAL TEACHER: When one of Mark's students claims to be "no good at school," mark challenges the claim by helping the student chart her progress since the beginning of the school year.

THE ANALYTICAL STUDENT: Lin learns about Erikson's stages and Marcia's identity statuses in psychology class. She realizes that the questions she has been having about her future are part of a healthy adolescent identity search.

THE CREATIVE STUDENT: Lin becomes involved in a drama club as a way to literally "act out" different identities.

THE PRACTICAL STUDENT: Lin volunteers as a teacher's aide at a local preschool because she wants to "try on" teaching young children as a possible career.

Image #2

"[This book] is very attractive to professors as well as students who have the mission of becoming expert teachers. I think that this text uses excellent pedagogical aids that support the need to respect and teach to individuals' diverse learning needs."

–Dr. Suzanne Morin,
Shippensburg University of Pennsylvania

FORUM

IS SPEED OF INFORMATION PROCESSING IMPORTANT TO INTELLIGENCE?

Terms that describe speed are often used to indicate intelligence as well. When people say, "She is a quick thinker," or "He is fast on his feet," they are implying the person is somehow more intelligent than a person who takes longer to come up with answers. What is the relationship between speed and intelligence?

FIRST VIEW: *Intelligence is closely linked to speed of information processing.* Some investigators have proposed to understand intelligence in terms of sheer speed of information processing, and they have used the simplest tasks they could devise to measure pure mental speed uncontaminated by other variables. These researchers (Jensen, 1982, 2000; Jensen & Munro, 1979) have suggested that the time it takes a person to decide which of two or more buttons to push in response to a given stimulus can be used as an indicator of that person's level of intelligence. According to

Image #3

EXPERT TEACHER INTERVIEW

FOCUS ON: EARLY ADOLESCENT IDENTITY DEVELOPMENT

GREGORY BOULJON: BETTENDORF MIDDLE SCHOOL, BETTENDORF, IOWA—GRADE 8, LANGUAGE ARTS

Gregory Bouljon has been teaching for thirty years. In 2000, he was certified by the National Board for Professional Teaching Standards as a teacher of English Language Arts for Early Adolescence.

Would you say that your students are at the personality development stage Erikson called "Identity versus Role Confusion"?

This definitely describes many of my eighth graders. Some are obvious, like a girl I taught last year, whom I'll call "Stephanie." Stephanie had a checkered past of numerous school disciplinary actions as well as police involvements with her "friends" in the community. She arrived the first day in total Goth attire: white makeup, black lip and eye color, all black clothes and demon figure jewelry. She sat in the back of the room with arms folded across her chest with a look of "Go ahead and try, but I'm not doing anything in here."

Over the next few weeks, we did a Writers' Workshop in which students self-select their own topics and genres. Fortunately (for all of us), Stephanie liked to write. Her first pieces were profanity-laced angry diatribes meant to offend us. The profanity turned out to be forced, but the anger for her parents was real—and deep. My student teacher and I listened, read, responded to the ideas and ignored the profanity.

Stephanie used her writing as a way to understand her anger. She began to realize that she had been reacting to her parents and an abusive relative and was not being herself. Once that began to happen, she changed. By October, she had apologized for her early work. She promised to rewrite it so that she could read it to the class and put it up in the room and in our display case. She began to wear other colors, and the makeup was gone. By December, she had new friends. The old ones, she told the two of us and the class, just wanted to use her. Some of her new friends were in our class and welcomed her insightful writing about herself that also seemed to capture their own identity struggles.

Once the student opens himself or herself to what you're teaching, miracles can happen in a very short time.

Not all students suffer with finding themselves as visibly as Stephanie did. For most it is a much more quiet, personal struggle to balance the expectations of parents, family, peers, coaches, and the perceived community in which they live. But in the course of a year, all my eighth graders begin, or continue, or set their concepts of themselves in relation to all the forces that push and tug and make demands on them.

Some theorists describe a process of "trying on" different identities during early adolescence. Your students seem to show they are in this process through their choices in clothing.

In the process of finding their identity, students' choices in clothing can change and do, regularly. It is not uncommon to see girls in the course of a single week dress in mini skirts and tight tops one day, loose jeans the next, and sweats another day. Holidays (especially Halloween) bring out the most bizarre attire allowed by our school codes. Often students will bring an extra, more acceptable outfit in case their first choice turns out to be too bizarre, revealing, or inappropriate.

Students also want their clothes to signify their membership in various peer groups. Most groups have a uniform of the day, or at least limits of what the student can wear and still be okay with his or her group.

Brand names are important. Either you have the "right" line of clothes on, or you don't, if you want people to know you are "your own person" and are not swayed by fashion.

Image #4

TECHNOLOGY TOOLS YOU CAN USE

Connecting Theory and Research to Practice

How are teachers putting constructivist theory into practice? In addition to the examples in this chapter, you can find many others on the Web. In their article, "Constructivist Learning Design," George Gagnon and Michelle Collay outline a method for instructional design that focuses on the constructivist concept of "designing for learning and not planning for teaching." In their article, available at *http://www.prainbow.com/cld/cldp.html*, they describe and illustrate a 6-point model for effectively incorporating constructivist principles in classroom and instructional design, provide a brief discussion regarding assessment, and present proposed applications of their model.

In a related Web site, located at *http://www.prainbow.com/cld/clds* ... paper, Gagnon and Collary discuss the responses of the classroom teachers, highlight teacher testimonials, and provide new insights and educational implications about effectively implementing constructivism in the classroom.

Another example of constructivist theory in practice is evident in the design for The Regents' Center for Early Developmental Education. The Center was created in 1988 as a means of infusing Piaget's constructivist perspectives on learning, knowledge, and intelligence in early childhood education. Their site (*http://www.uni.edu/coe/regentsctr/index.html*), which is devoted to developing, implementing, and disseminating information regarding constructivist education, also contains a wide variety of resources, links, and information.

The Schools for Thought (SFT) project in Nashville, Tennessee, is another example of how principles derived from constructivist views of learning can be implemented in classrooms. The SFT program was designed in conjunction with Vanderbilt University to promote instructional strategies that take advantage of constructivist principles such as creating communities of learners through social interaction, fostering a deep level of understanding of domain-specific knowledge, exploring cross-curricular and situated learning activities, and encouraging student-based inquiry. The Schools for Thought Web site, located at *http://peabody.vanderbilt.edu/projects/funded/sft/overview/welcome.html*, provides information about the background of the project, the curriculum, testimonials about the project, and resources for learning communities.

Building Your Self-Portrait as an Educator

Do you have problems or encounter difficulties remembering names, dates, or telephone numbers? Do you think there is a link between learning styles (discussed in Chapter 4) and memory? Visit Mind Tools at *http://www.demon.co.uk/mindtool/memory.html* to learn more. This site provides an overview of mne-

Image #5

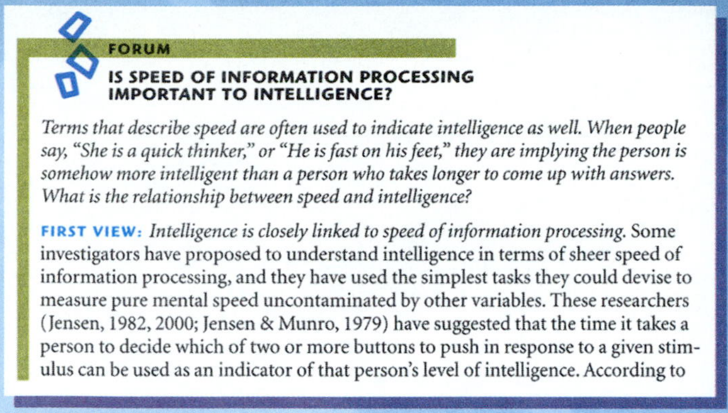

Implications for Teaching

These highlighted lists appear periodically throughout each chapter, following main sections. They provide students with practical implications of specific concepts of educational psychology by showing them how expert teachers apply these concepts in the classroom.

Constructing Your Own Learning

These in-text activities in each chapter help students understand constructivism by using the theory themselves to build upon what they have read in the text.

Forum

Each chapter includes a three-way debate about an important educational issue. Educators often discuss issues—like homogeneous versus heterogeneous grouping, or traditional versus multicultural classrooms—as though there is no middle ground. But educational issues are not as simple as a pro-con debate—there are no panaceas in education. Rather, we need intelligent combinations of techniques in order to be effective. Thus, in these Forum debates, the authors show that there are middle-ground positions between the extremes of the issues.
(See Image #3)

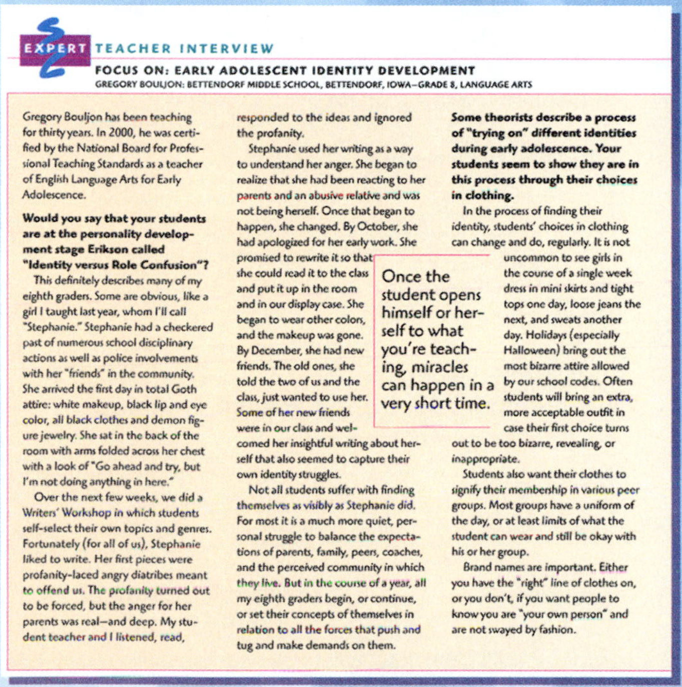

Expert Teacher Interviews

Each chapter contains an interview with a classroom teacher. These insights from an expert teacher show how he or she has applied in the classroom—often in a unique way—some of the material covered in the chapter. (See Image #4)

End-of-Chapter Pedagogy

Summing It Up

A comprehensive summary of key points, including classroom applications, is provided at the end of each chapter.

Key Terms and Definitions

Boldfaced terms in the chapter are here defined, accompanied by text page references.

Becoming an Expert: Questions and Problems

These activities, grouped for elementary, middle, and high school settings, invite readers to apply chapter concepts to the problems of classroom practice.

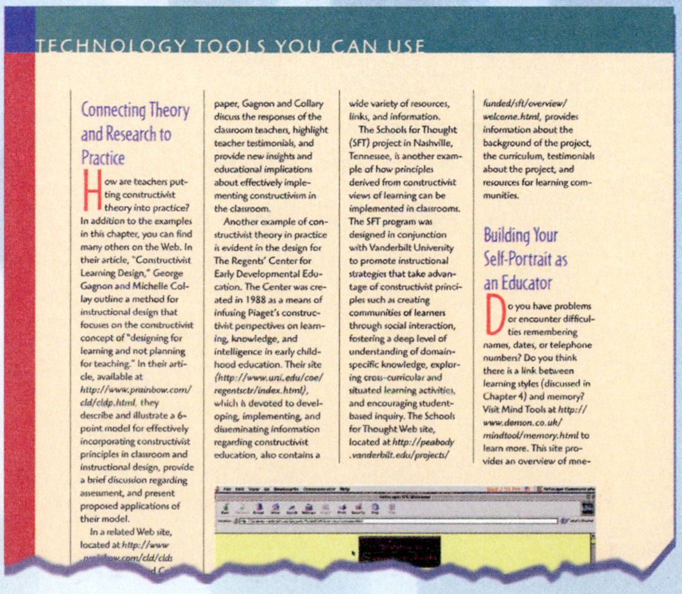

Technology Tools You Can Use

This feature helps students connect theory and research to practice, build a self-portrait as an educator, and connect with communities of learners and teachers by using the resources of the World Wide Web.
(See Image #5)

Optimize Student Learning

For the Student

■ **Grade Aid**

(Jada Kearns, Valencia Community College)
This vastly enhanced study guide features "Before You Read" chapter overviews and learning objectives, "As You Read" activities for each major chapter section, and "After You Read" practice tests. An answer key is included.

■ **Creative Intelligence for Schools Workbook**

(Wendy M. Williams, Faith Markle, Melanie Brigokas, and Robert J. Sternberg)
This workbook gives preservice and in-service teachers a useful tool to enrich their classroom teaching and help their students become more creative.

■ **Companion Website with Online Practice Tests**
http://www.ablongman.com/sternberg
(See description to the right.)

For the Instructor

■ **Instructor's Resource Manual**

(Mary Ann Rafoth, Indiana University of Pennsylvania)
This resource correlates all the text supplements with chapter learning objectives, and provides detailed lecture outlines, reproducible classroom activities, online and video resource references, and more!

■ **Test Bank**

(Jada Kearns, Valencia Community College)
This resource provides multiple choice, true-false, and short answer test items correlated to chapter learning objectives, plus correct answers and text page references. The Test Bank is also available on a cross-platform CD-ROM.

■ **PowerPoint™ Presentations**

(Jeff Swartwood, SUNY-Cortland)
This resource features chapter-by-chapter presentations with extensive lecture notes that can be easily used or adapted to convert your lectures to accompany this text.

■ **The Flexible Expert:**
Practical, Analytical, and Creative Teaching with *Educational Psychology*

This two-hour video features classroom footage and interviews with classroom teachers on topics related to each chapter of the text.

■ **Transparencies—Educational Psychology III**

This transparency package provides 100 full-color transparencies related to text topics for classroom use.

■ **Allyn & Bacon Digital Media Archive CD-ROM for Education, 2001 Edition**
(See description to the right.)

■ **CourseCompass™**
(See description to the right.)

■ **Computerized Test Bank**
(Windows CD-ROM and disk; MAC disk.)

Technology Advantage

Companion Website with Online Practice Tests
http://www.ablongman.com/sternberg

The Companion Website for Sternberg is available to all users of the text, and features online practice tests, links to websites related to topics in the book, author comments for each chapter, case studies, and a discussion area. Visit **http://www.ablongman.com/sternberg** for continuous updates about this exciting new textbook!

CourseCompass™

Allyn and Bacon's online course management tool powered by Blackboard helps instructors manage all aspects of teaching the course and includes preloaded content such as the instructor's Test Bank.
Visit **http://www.ablongman.com/coursecompass** for more information!

Allyn & Bacon Digital Media Archive
CD-ROM for Education, 2001 Edition

Allyn & Bacon provides an array of media products to help liven up your classroom presentations. The Digital Media Archive electronically provides charts, graphs, tables and figures on one cross-platform CD-ROM. The Digital Media Archive also provides video and audio clips along with the electronic images that can be easily integrated into your lectures. This helpful resource extends the coverage found on the Sternberg Powerpoint™ Presentation CD-ROM. Visit our DMA website at **http://www.ablongman.com/dma** for more information!

Make our technology work for you!

Allyn & Bacon's technology training services show you how to use our technology products, and, even more importantly, how to integrate them into your curriculum – all at your pace and comfort level. Best of all, our training resources are **FREE** to qualified adopters! We've helped numerous colleges and universities – let us help you next! Visit **http://www.ablongman.com/techsolutions** or contact your publisher's representative to find out more about our commitment to technology in the classroom.

www.ablongman.com/sternberg

Case Studies to Help Your Students Become Expert Teachers

The "typical" educational setting is anything but typical. The diverse situations and individual differences that comprise the richness—and uniqueness—of the "typical" classroom make the development of expert teachers particularly challenging. While there has always been concern about providing solid, applied examples for students of educational psychology, the need for quality, realistic experiences continues to grow. In recent years, prominent people in the field of educational psychology have responded to that call by introducing the use of cases and case-based teaching into preservice and inservice coursework.

For decades, case studies have been used in the professions of law, medicine, and business to hone problem-solving skills and provide opportunities for students to experience different perspectives on real-life issues and situations. In moving this time-honored pedagogy into preservice and inservice coursework, experts believe that opportunities to interact with well-written accounts of the classroom will better prepare teachers for the challenges they face in the 21st century.

Interactive Case Studies on the Companion Website for *Educational Psychology* (http://www.ablongman.com/sternberg) present just such real-life situations for exploring the implications of educational psychology theory as it is put into practice. There, students can read cases that correspond to each chapter of *Educational Psychology* and then e-mail their responses to each case study's follow-up questions to you for feedback. The following table lists cases available on the Website.

The following abstracts of the cases listed on the preceding table will help you integrate the cases with your instruction and introduce them to students. Also included are the Discussion Questions that follow each complete case on the Companion Website.

■ *Breadth versus Depth: Curriculum Conflicts in a Secondary Classroom* by J. Merrel Hansen

Mr. Benson, a caring and responsible professional, is perplexed by the content demands of his subject area. He loves history and senses its importance, but the volume and depth of the subject are overwhelming. He knows that the students object to the endless and hurried approach to the subject. He feels pressure from the administration and the state curriculum guidelines. His professional experiences heighten this problem. Mr. Benson has to make the decision of how best to use his limited time with a subject that seems endless and encyclopedic. He acknowledges the professional frustration and dilemma he has to face, and asks the question, to cover, or not to cover?

DISCUSSION QUESTIONS

1. Do you think Mr. Benson relied too heavily on the textbook for his class? Why or why not?

2. Did Mr. Benson's methods foster thinking? How could he have restructured his classes to teach for transfer?

3. Can you suggest some role-playing or group exercises to encourage thinking?

4. Do you believe teachers should "teach to the test" so that the school will have a higher test average? Why or why not?

5. Do you agree with Mr. Benson's feeling that students must learn about all aspects of a concept (the "depth") in order to fully appreciate and understand it? Why or why not?

6. Would you alter the weekly teaching plan for this class? Why or why not?

■ *Can You Hear Me? A Case of Racism* by Christianna Alger

The case occurs in an 8th grade English/History Core course where the teacher had chosen to study the Holocaust to show students that oppression and prejudice happen to many people and to provide a vehicle for discussing the parallels between the plight of the Jewish people and black/white racism. Her selected curriculum materials included two films and *The Diary of Anne Frank.*

In response to the first film shown, the students wanted to know why there were no African Americans in the film. This question leads to a discussion about segregation in the armed forces and social change. Later in the week, when the teacher was about to show the second film, the question about African American representation in this film was raised again—and this time sparked a confrontation and serious semantic misunderstanding.

DISCUSSION QUESTIONS

1. What are the important issues in this case?

2. Do you agree with the strategy of showing the parallels between the plight of the Jews and black/white racism?

3. Should the teacher talk to the whole class about the incident? If so, explain what she should say. If not, explain why you feel that way.

4. What could the teacher have done to avoid this problem?

5. What should she do now?

6. What did the students learn from the videos? How do you know?

7. Is this a case of racism? Why or why not?

■ *Dealing with Dishonesty* by Pamela Monk

This case takes place in an alternative middle school environment that allows students a level of freedom not found in traditional schools. The environment is also established to foster close personal relationships between teachers and their "family group"—a group of middle-schoolers assigned to the particular teacher. Pam is a new teacher at the middle school and loves her experience in this unconventional learning setting.

The theft of a twenty-dollar bill brings this case to a head as Pam makes the decision to confront Alicia, one of her family group members suspected of the theft. Armed with nothing but circumstantial evidence, Pam wrestles with the options for dealing with the theft and the impact on her relationship with Alicia—as well as other members of the family group—if she is wrong.

She decides to confront Alicia, who at first denies having anything to do with the theft. Finally, Alicia admits guilt and returns the money. The dialogue between Alicia and Pam during the confrontation is included in the case.

This case explores a teacher's role and responsibilities in relation to issues of lying and stealing, methods of confrontation, and issues of trust and boundaries between teachers and students.

1. What are the risks of a stand-off?

2. What if the teacher is wrong and the student is telling the truth? What damage does this cause? How can a teacher prepare for this possibility?

3. Why did this teacher bring up the issue of assumptions about group differences? Can you describe how those assumptions could backfire in this situation?

4. How much obligation does a teacher have to become involved with moral issues such as lying and cheating? Where is the line drawn? What interaction should there be with parents?

5. What classroom management techniques or guidelines could the teacher have employed?

6. The teacher is responsible for the well-being of each individual in the classroom as well as that of the entire class. What must be considered when deciding which to favor?

7. Do you agree with the "progression of behaviors" in lying described by this teacher?

8. Would you have handled Alicia in a different way? Explain.

9. How would you follow up with Alicia in the days and weeks after she "confessed" to lying?

■ *A Different Child* by Raymond H. Witte and Judy Steele

This case study examines how Ashleigh, a fifth grader who suffered a Traumatic Brain Injury (TBI), successfully returned to school with the help and assistance of her classroom teacher. No special education services were sought in this case and all of Ashleigh's instruction was provided in the regular classroom setting. Thankfully, her teacher was knowledgeable about TBI and developed a comprehensive education plan. In particular, key aspects of Mrs. Smith's action plan, including parental involvement, the formation of a school team, personal contact, individualized instructional planning, and classroom structure, are discussed.

Interventions designed to help Ashleigh are described along with the Structure, Organization, and Strategies (SOS) model that was followed in this case. A best practices approach is encouraged with all TBI cases, and Discussion Questions and practical Professional References are provided in order to help educators become more informed and more effective in teaching children with TBI.

DISCUSSION QUESTIONS

1. Ashleigh required a different learning environment with a variety of implications for the teacher. What were these additional implications?

2. How would you rate Mrs. Smith's instructional approach with Ashleigh in her classroom? Did Mrs. Smith act as an Expert Teacher?

3. If faced with the reality of teaching a child with TBI what would you do? What steps would you follow? Why?

4. How can the school team best address the educational needs of a student with TBI?

5. What do you think Ashleigh will have to do in order to maintain her progress in school?

■ *Educational Theory in the Classroom: An Eighth Grade in Action* by Nancy Kaczmarek

An eighth grade classroom is the setting for this case, in which students are working in small groups on an activity that is part of a unit on probability. In the activity, the students are trying to see how many different combinations they can make with four colored chips. As the teacher, Julie Green, monitors the groups, she notices some combining the chips at random, some doing the combinations in an orderly way, and one or two groups on the verge of moving out of random combining, sensing that there is a better way to solve the problem but not quite sure what it is.

The activity time draws near its end, and groups get into other conversations—the necessity of obeying school rules all the time, the relevance of this particular activity, their plans for the future, the sense of inferiority that resulted when one student compared himself with others in the class.

As the scenario ends, Julie calls her class together to analyze the activity on probability, wondering as she does so how she will be able to address all their needs—cognitive, psychosocial, ethical—in the limited time she has to teach them.

The case alludes to Piagetian cognitive theory in the group activity, which can indicate those moving from concrete operations into formal operations by showing which groups use an orderly process for determining the number of combinations (formal operations). Julie's scaffolding one group into seeing the value of an orderly approach exemplifies Vygotsky's theory. Erikson's psychosocial theory is reflected in Adam's discouragement when he compares his math scores with others' and Nora's insight into why their science projects are different, as well as in the students' future plans. Kohlberg's moral theory is alluded to in Terry's group giving their reasons for the acceptability of being late to class or the necessity of coming on time.

DISCUSSION QUESTIONS

1. Julie's use of cooperative learning leads into areas that she did not expect. Should she be concerned about her students' off-task behavior in this cooperative-group

work setting? Does it make a difference that her students are eighth-graders—that is, should she be more or less concerned than if they were older or younger? Are there ages when it is more appropriate to let students get off task?

2. Which of the overheard conversations do you think is most important? If you were Julie, which ones would you respond to in a small-group setting? Which ones do you think merit some time to address with the whole class?

3. How else might Julie use the information she overheard in the discussions? How might she use the information she got from seeing how the students addressed the problem of how many arrangements they could make from four chips of different colors?

4. What learning strategies were students using in this case? Where they acting responsibly and positively?

5. Julie learned a lot about her students, both academically and developmentally, in this lesson. Based on the information in Chapter 1, would you consider Julie an Expert Teacher? Why or why not? What kind of lesson could you create in your subject area that would give you the same kind of information? If you decide it is not a good use of teaching time, how else would you get that information?

■ *Eric's Last Stand* by Linda K. Elksnin, Linda Hardin, and Susan P. Gurganus

Mrs. Garver, an elementary resource teacher, is brought into a situation involving seven-year-old Eric Glover, his parents' domestic turmoil, and his problems in Mrs. Lang's second grade class. The assistant principal and principal are also involved as Eric's behavior problems escalate. This case should provoke discussion about crisis intervention, school-home relationships, referral procedures, the role of administrators in special education, and characteristics of children with behavior disorders.

DISCUSSION QUESTIONS

1. Identify the responses from all adults to Eric's behavior. What are the different ideas for handling Eric and how does Eric respond to them?

2. Discuss this case from Eric's point of view. How is it different from the original case? What is different?

3. Identify antecedents, behaviors, and consequences for Eric's outbursts. What crisis management techniques could both the classroom teacher and Ms. Garver use?

4. Recommend a behavior management program for Eric involving home and school. Note what legal rights and responsibilities need to be observed.

5. Identify the needs behind Eric's behavior. Determine how the teachers could help Eric meet his needs in a positive manner.

6. Identify how the home information affects the school situation. Determine alternative ways the school can use this information to help Eric and his mom.

7. Was Mrs. Lang acting ethically in discussing Mrs. Glover's information with Mrs. Garver? Why or why not? Who else needed to know that information? Who does not need to know that information?

8. Mr. Shapiro and Mrs. Garver evidently do not agree on how to handle Eric when he misbehaves. How does Mrs. Garver feel Eric and his behavior should be managed? Mr. Shapiro? What would be best for Eric? Are they both working toward this?

■ *Fireworks in the City* by Kathleen Halley

In this case, a kindergarten teacher in a city school has initiated an inclusion program with two other teachers. The extra work involved in collaborative curriculum development has begun to yield rewards, but suddenly she finds herself in conflict with other school colleagues. The case encourages students to think about how this teacher should approach the various demands or problems found in this situation.

DISCUSSION QUESTIONS

1. What steps is Kathie taking to become an Expert Teacher?

2. What is inclusion and what are its strengths and weaknesses?

3. What are IEPs and how are they affected by inclusion?

4. What are Monique's concerns? The speech pathologist's concerns? Kathie's concerns?

5. How well does the blended approach used by these three teachers suit the needs of their inner city children?

6. How are specific speech needs of individual students best met in a blended classroom?

7. Is Kathie's teaching position defensible, given the terms of inclusion?

■ *A Look Inside: A Student Teacher's Dilemma* by Julia MacMillan

"A Look Inside: A Student Teacher's Dilemma" is a series of student teacher journal entries dealing with the student-teaching experience from a student teacher-centered, first-person perspective. This student teacher's journal of her student-teaching experience focuses on one student in particular, a developmentally delayed student who was placed in the student teacher's full inclusion classroom. Throughout the student teacher's placement, this student began to exhibit progressively more violent reactions to authority/rules, teachers, and other students. This case also focuses on how the student teacher chose to deal with the many challenges that arise from working with a child with special needs.

Throughout the case, issues arise that the student teacher must address. These include her tendency to take things personally, her difficulty dealing with the developmentally delayed student, her difficulty dividing time fairly between this student and the other students, and her student teacher/clinical instructor relationship. This case also addresses the safety of the other students and teachers when a violent student disrupts the classroom, and the responsibilities and dilemmas of a student teacher in such a situation. This case deals specifically with this student teacher's lack of a support system, her lack of special needs training, and her difficulties managing the situation on her own.

DISCUSSION QUESTIONS

1. How would you describe Aaron's cognitive development? Describe any of Piaget's or Vygotsky's stages or zones that fit for Aaron.

2. Do you relate to the student teacher's difficulty in understanding Aaron? In what ways, if any, do you think she could have tried harder to understand Aaron and/or to help the other students understand him?

3. How much information should a classroom teacher share with her student teacher in regards to special needs students? Should the student teacher have had to ask her clinical instructor for such information, or should she have been provided with it from the beginning? What differences do you see arising in the classroom as a result of these two possible situations?

4. In what ways do you think this student teacher's tendency to take things personally will affect her teaching ability, interactions with the students, and interactions with other teachers?

5. How could this student teacher have dealt with the lack of special-education background and training? Should she have been placed in this particular inclusive classroom situation without any special training? Why or why not?

6. In your opinion, what should the characteristics of an ideal clinical instructor/student teacher relationship be for the maximum benefit to both parties? Comment on the rights and responsibilities of both parties.

7. Should the student teacher allow herself to concentrate on Aaron? Is she ignoring the needs of the other students in doing so? What could be the drawbacks of denying herself the experience of interacting with the other students?

8. After reading about how the student teacher reacted to the initial screaming incident, how do you think you would have reacted? Differently? Similarly? Why?

9. When considering Diane Rice's suggestions, do you think that she correctly analyzed the situation? What would you do differently, if anything?

10. In the last two entries of her journal, the student teacher talks about her relief and her guilt about wanting to leave. Did you perceive her thoughts as selfish the way she did, or do you think she was justified in her feelings?

■ Multicultural Education: Parents as (Subversive) Partners by Joan Armon

Multicultural education is a controversial endeavor. While teachers are encouraged by university and school district representatives to explore issues of race, gender, and ethnicity with students in public school classrooms, parents are not always in agreement that such topics are appropriate.

Where parents are actively involved in schools, they may work to prevent teachers' implementation of multicultural education. As is clear in this case, a teacher cannot assume that she has the support to include information in the curriculum about the contributions, struggles, and beliefs of people of color.

Susan is a second-grade teacher who was placed in a school where textbooks, district curriculum guides, and the school library featured materials that did not include people of color. Susan decided to work with her principal and colleagues to enrich a social studies/science unit that called for students to cooperatively construct a wood structure. Rather than creating only one project devoid of cultural context, Susan and her colleagues asked students to construct models of homes from around the world. Consequently, the expanded unit increased children's knowledge of diverse cultures.

The first year went smoothly, but during her second year, when Susan further expanded the curriculum to include people of color, two parents tried to undermine her efforts by enlisting other parents' involvement in a formal complaint against Susan. They accused her of spending too much time studying black people and not enough time studying "important" Americans. Two thematic units fueled parents' anger: Susan enriched a district unit on plants to feature the life and work of George Washington Carver, and months later, spent a week studying Martin Luther King, Jr. The parents' reactions, as well as the principal's warning, prompted Susan to question how extensively she should integrate her own commitments to democracy, diversity, and freedom into the curriculum.

1. What are the important issues in this case?

2. What are the likely cognitive, emotional, and social developmental characteristics of children in early primary grades? How might these characteristics influence a teacher's decisions about addressing the topics in Susan's class?

3. Do you agree with Susan's approach to making the curriculum more inclusive? Debate the issue.

4. What constructivist approaches is Susan using? What are their advantages and disadvantages?

5. Should Susan talk to Mrs. Woods and Mrs. Myers? If so, how should she approach the conversation? Should Susan talk again with her principal? Explain your answers.

6. What, if anything, could Susan have done to avoid this problem?

7. What should she do now?

8. What are Susan's students learning from her units on Carver and King? How do you know?

9. What formal or informal assessments are being used? Can you suggest other assessments?

10. How might Susan's curriculum innovations be adapted for older (5th or 6th grade) students?

■ *No Time for Emily: An Early Childhood Teaching Case* by Jenine M. Pedersen

When four-year-old Emily, a "problem child," lashes out physically against a playmate, a series of confrontational exchanges take place with day-care staff. Disciplinary actions such as time out and sending her to the office don't have much effect on her kicking and pinching behavior. No one has time to listen to Emily. Her mother is busy, her father works, and her day-care center is understaffed. This case asks: Would Emily's behavior be different if someone were there to listen to her?

DISCUSSION QUESTIONS

1. How would you assess the teacher's skills in dealing with Emily?

2. What developmental risks is Emily facing as a result of her situation?

3. What needs to happen for Emily in this class?

4. What evaluation instruments might the teacher use for assessing Emily?

5. What out-of-class support services could the teacher use to assist with children like Emily? What are the barriers that prevent schools from obtaining such services?

6. How should the teacher communicate with Emily's parents?

7. From a classroom management standpoint, how does the teacher contribute to Emily's behavior?

8. What would you do if you were the teacher?

■ *What Do I Do with Tim Now?* By Hollace Abrams, Mary Anne Lecos, Shirly Raines, Lucille Sorenson, Kenena Spaulding, Paula Treiber, and Pamela von Bredow

This case examines one teacher's efforts to manage a newly inherited classroom of first-graders. Mary is on her first assignment, taking over for a teacher on maternity leave who has left behind a legacy of children with poor behavior. Mary knows she must instill change in this classroom for the educational good of the children and for her own survival. Mary begins to firmly but gently enforce classroom rules and introduce age-appropriate activities. Attentive to their needs, Mary notices that a few of the children have learning disabilities but have never been referred for any special evaluation. Among these children is Tim, who has a difficult home life and little self-confidence, and whose self-pity slowly turns to anger. He lashed out at her and the other students, disrupting class with his often violent behavior. When she refers him for special-needs services, his parents are not supportive and lay the blame instead on Mary.

Through the support of her principal, who is a perceptive administrator, and the evaluation of a screening committee, Mary is able to convince Tim and his parents to face his misbehavior. Through her hard work, perseverance, and genuine care, Mary slowly begins to break through to Tim and the other children, and they begin to bond with her. Other children are also screened for particular needs and are found eligible for special services delivered within the classroom.

This case demonstrates the importance of a supportive administration and the teamwork of dedicated counselors, specialists, and, of course, teachers, in the effort to build a positive, enthusiastic classroom community that has concern and respect for each other and the learning environment.

DISCUSSION QUESTIONS

1. What behavioral approaches did Mary try with her classroom and Tim?

2. What other behavioral approaches would you suggest for this classroom? Make a list of suggestions.

3. What might have happened if Mary had allowed Tim to attend the party?

4. List the responsibilities of each of the following in preparation for the screening committee meeting: Mary, counselor, principal, parents.

5. What effect does Mary's teaching style have on the way she handles her new class? On the way she handles Tim?

6. How would you handle a situation where a parent refused to recognize that his or her child had a discipline issue?

■ *Whose Curriculum Is It? Conflict in the English Classroom* by Steve Rose

This case is designed to help preservice and inservice teachers grapple with issues of curriculum, censorship, and school governance. It is primarily aimed at teachers and possibly administrators at the middle-school and secondary levels, and especially those most likely to be involved with controversial materials.

Basically, this case dramatizes a situation in which a high school English teacher struggles with a member of the community who feels that the novel in question, *Flowers for Algernon,* is unfit for "required" reading in a high school English class. The teacher seems to deal successfully with this concern, but subterfuge on the part of the school administration basically removes the novel from the teacher's and his/her students' hands. It is worth pointing out that this novel is still widely used in many middle school and high school English/language arts classes.

This case attempts to focus its readers' attention on three interrelated issues:

1. How does a teacher deal with concerns that parents and communities have regarding potentially objectionable materials?

2. How does a teacher deal with a lack of building-level administrative support?

3. How should a teacher bring an administrator to task when the administrator unethically strips the teacher of instructional materials valued by the teacher?

It is worth pointing out that this case could actually be divided into three "sub-cases." The first would deal with the issue of dealing with parental/community concerns. The second raises questions about timing: should a teacher or school allow a "cooling off" period before using such materials again? Third, how does a teacher deal with unethical, or at least cowardly, administrators?

DISCUSSION QUESTIONS

1. Who legally has the right to determine curricular content in the classroom?

2. How should a teacher deal with concerns that parents and communities have regarding potentially objectionable materials?

3. How can a teacher deal with a lack of building-level administrative support?

4. What freedom should teachers as professionals have in determining the curriculum?

5. What rights do parents have in deciding what their children should read and learn?

6. What mechanisms should be in place to resolve conflicts among parents, teachers, and administrators when they occur?

7. What should teachers do if they disagree with the curriculum they are assigned to teach?

Educational Psychology

ROBERT J. STERNBERG

Yale University

WENDY M. WILLIAMS

Cornell University

ALLYN AND BACON

Boston   London   Toronto   Sydney   Tokyo   Singapore

Editor-in Chief, Education: *Paul Smith*

Series Editor: *Arnis E. Burvikovs*

Senior Development Editor: *Linda Bieze*

Editorial Assistant: *Matthew Forster*

Editorial Production Manager: *Elaine Ober*

Editorial Production Service: *Kathy Smith*

Marketing Manager: *Kathleen Morgan*

Photo Researchers: *PhotoSearch, Inc. and Kathy Smith*

Composition and Prepress Buyer: *Linda Cox*

Manufacturing Buyer: *Megan Cochran*

Cover Administrator: *Linda Knowles*

Interior Design: *Seventeenth Street Studios*

Electronic Composition: *Seventeenth Street Studios*

Between the time Website information is gathered and then published, it is not
unusual for some sites to have closed. Also, the transcription of URLs can result
in unintended typographical errors. The publisher would appreciate notification where these occur so that they may be corrected in subsequent editions.

Library of Congress Cataloging-in-Publication Data

Sternberg, Robert J.
  Educational psychology / Robert J. Sternberg, Wendy M. Williams.
    p. cm.
  Includes bibliographical references and index.
  ISBN 0-321-01184-8
Educational psychology. I. Williams, Wendy M. (Wendy Melissa), 1960–
  II. Title.

LB1051.S7394 2002
370.15—dc21   2001045101

Printed in the United States of America

10 9 8 7 6 5 4 3 2 1   VHP   06 05 04 03 02 01

$\mathcal{B}$RIEF CONTENTS

FEATURES

THE FLEXIBLE EXPERT

FORUM

IMPLICATIONS FOR TEACHING

TECHNOLOGY TOOLS YOU CAN USE

"THINKING" QUESTIONS

*Thinking Analytically, Thinking Creatively, and Thinking Practically questions
are found throughout each chapter.*
*See, for example, pages 5, 7, 9, 10, 11, 15, 16, 17, 19, 22, 24, 27, 28, 29, 31, and 32
in Chapter 1, "Becoming an Expert Teacher; Becoming an Expert Student."*

ONTENTS

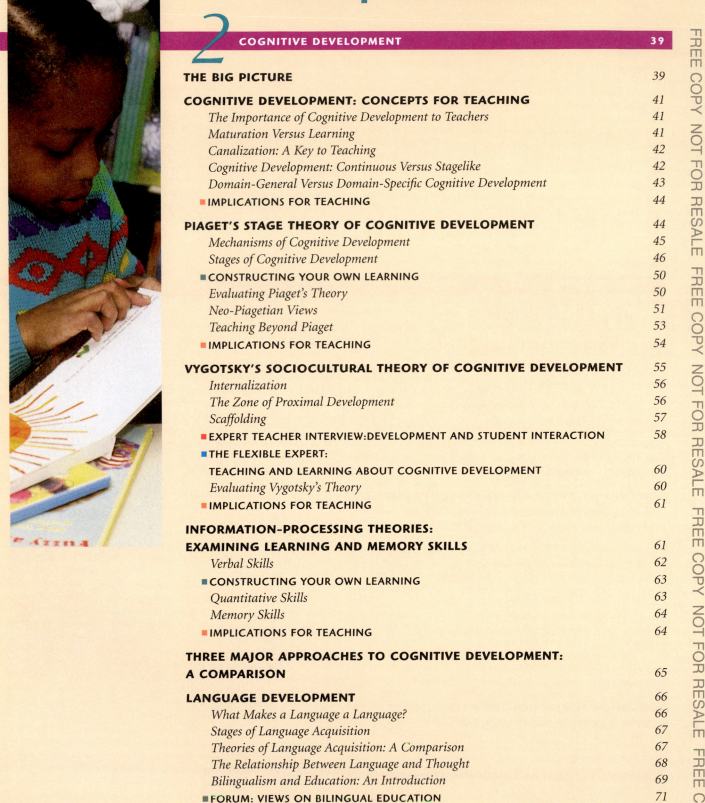

PART ONE | HUMAN DEVELOPMENT

PART TWO **|** HUMAN DIVERSITY

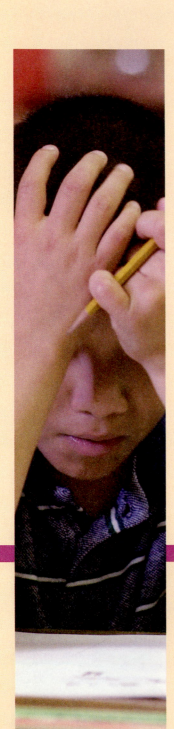

PART THREE | THINKING, LEARNING, AND MEMORY

8   COGNITIVE APPROACHES TO LEARNING   267

PART FIVE | ASSESSMENT

PREFACE

 With so many educational psychology textbooks available, why have we written yet another?

EMPHASES OF THE TEXT

We set two goals as we wrote this textbook. First, we wanted to give students a detailed view of what the field of educational psychology should and can accomplish. Second, we sought to imbue the text with a single, unifying vision to help students better understand this view. In short, we wanted to give students an understanding of both the art and the science of educational psychology. Specifically, we emphasize:

■ THE EXPERT TEACHER AND THE EXPERT STUDENT

We believe that the overarching goal of the field of educational psychology is to understand and develop expertise in teaching and learning, and that an educational psychology text should be organized around how each of the topics in the course relates to the development of expertise in teaching and learning. This text reflects our commitment to this goal. Chapter 1: Becoming an Expert Teacher; Becoming an Expert Student defines the expert teacher and expert student. This theme—the goal of becoming an expert—appears in all subsequent chapters, and the text's pedagogy is oriented around this theme as well.

■ A FOCUS ON THE PRACTICAL

Many educational psychology students are preservice or inservice teachers; hence, it is particularly important that the text express a practical emphasis. Throughout the book, we focus on the real world, showing readers how to use in the classroom what they are learning in the text. At the same time, we do not give long checklists of instructions, because such lists actually impede good teaching and learning. More important than memorizing lists is developing the hallmark of expertise: to be a reflective practitioner. We accomplish this goal by giving students useful tips and, more importantly, by showing them when and how to use these tips. Our research has shown that the hardest thing about practice is not learning effective procedures, but knowing when and how to use them.

In addition to these two major emphases, throughout the text we also emphasize:

■ MULTICULTURALISM AND GENDER DIFFERENCES

We make a special effort to prepare teachers for the classrooms of both today and the future. More and more frequently, teachers find themselves challenged by multicultural and multilingual classrooms. They must be prepared, for example, for the special needs of students who have limited English-proficiency skills. They also need to recognize how gender stereotypes limit educational opportunities for boys as well as for girls. These topics are covered especially in Chapter 6: Group Differences: Socioeconomic Status, Ethnicity, Gender, and Language.

■ INDIVIDUAL DIFFERENCES: EXCEPTIONAL CHILDREN

Also important to today's educators is an understanding of giftedness, disability, and learning disorders and how to approach these differences in the classroom. Notably in Chapter 5: Individual Differences: Exceptional Children, we present ways to challenge gifted students who are learning within the boundaries of traditional classrooms. In the same chapter, we also emphasize that students with disabilities can become expert learners just as students without disabilities can and offer guidelines for providing the help and support these students need to achieve their potential.

■ A BALANCED PERSPECTIVE

In organizing the text, we have maintained the standard scope and sequence of chapters. At the same time, we have included the most current and significant theory and research that students need to learn. In addition, while we have presented our own points of view throughout the text, we have carefully avoided presenting only single points of view, because we believe it is essential for students to make up their own minds on the issues in educational psychology. In that respect, this book is unique.

 ## PEDAGOGICAL FEATURES OF THE TEXT

The introductory educational psychology course must convey vast amounts of material. To aid students in learning this material, we have included various types of pedagogy to help them both master the content and apply it in their future teaching experiences.

■ CHAPTER OPENER PEDAGOGY

CHAPTER OUTLINE. A brief chapter outline including major headings provides students with a chapter organizer and study tool.

THE BIG PICTURE. A set of chapter objectives in question format also helps readers approach the content of the chapter.

OPENING VIGNETTE. Each chapter opens with a vignette showing reflective practitioners in action. The vignette highlights a major topic of the chapter, shows its relevance to experiences in the classroom, and is referenced throughout the chapter.

CHAPTER OVERVIEW. Following the vignette is a brief overview of what the chapter will cover and why it is relevant to the classroom. This section is titled, for example, "Why Understanding Thinking Is Important to Teachers" or "Why Understanding Motivation Is Important to Teachers." This introductory section provides students with an immediate link between the concepts of the chapter and the classroom.

■ TEXT PEDAGOGY

"THINKING" QUESTIONS. Research has shown that simply memorizing text is one of the least effective ways of learning. Rather, students learn more effectively when they process the information they need to learn in diverse ways and think deeply about it. We help them to do so by including questions integrated into the text that will encourage students to think analytically, creatively, and practically about what they are learning. Three types of questions—Thinking Analytically, Thinking Creatively, and Thinking Practically—appear throughout each chapter. This framework, based on the Sternberg triarchic theory of human intelligence, helps ensure that students will think about what they are learning, rather than merely process it at a superficial level. Suggested responses are printed in the text so students can think about their own answers and then consider the modeled suggestions.

THE FLEXIBLE EXPERT. Like the "Thinking" Questions, the suggestions in this feature prompt students to think in different ways—analytically, creatively, and practically—about a single topic. They describe the ways in which both teachers and students approach the daily challenges of the classroom.

IMPLICATIONS FOR TEACHING. These highlighted lists appear periodically throughout each chapter, following main sections. They provide students with practical implications of specific concepts of educational psychology by showing them how expert teachers apply these concepts in the classroom.

CONSTRUCTING YOUR OWN LEARNING. These in-text activities in each chapter help students understand constructivism by using the theory themselves to build upon what they have read in the text.

FORUM. Each chapter includes a three-way debate about an important educational issue. Educators often discuss issues—such as homogeneous versus heterogeneous grouping, or traditional versus multicultural classrooms—as though there is no middle ground. But educational issues are not as simple as a pro-con debate; there are no panaceas in education. Rather, we need intelligent combinations of techniques in order to be effective. Thus, in these Forum debates, we show that there are middle-ground positions between the extremes of the issues.

EXPERT TEACHER INTERVIEWS. Each chapter contains an interview with a classroom teacher. These insights from an expert teacher show how he or she has applied in the classroom—often in a unique way—some of the material covered in the chapter.

■ END-OF-CHAPTER PEDAGOGY

SUMMING IT UP. A comprehensive summary of key points, including classroom applications, is provided at the end of each chapter.

KEY TERMS AND CONCEPTS. Boldfaced terms in the chapter are defined here, accompanied by text page references.

BECOMING AN EXPERT: QUESTIONS AND PROBLEMS. These activities, grouped by elementary, middle, and high school settings, invite readers to apply chapter concepts to the problems of classroom practice.

TECHNOLOGY TOOLS YOU CAN USE. This between-chapters feature developed by Julia Matuga of Bowling Green State University helps students connect theory and research to practice, build a self-portrait as an educator, and connect with communities of learners and teachers by using the resources of the World Wide Web.

■ SUPPLEMENTS TO THE TEXT

For students an assortment of learning tools is available:

■ *Grade Aid,* written by Jada Kearns, Valencia Community College, is a vastly enhanced study guide that features "Before You Read" chapter overviews and learning objectives, "As You Read" activities for each major chapter section, and "After You Read" practice tests. An answer key is included.

■ *Creative Intelligence for School (CISS): 21 Lessons to Enhance Creativity in Middle and High School Students* by Wendy M. Williams, Faith Markle, Melanie Brigockas, and Robert J. Sternberg, gives preservice and inservice teachers a useful tool to enrich their classroom teaching and help their students become more creative.

■ Companion Website with Online Practice Tests, *http://www.ablongman.com/sternberg,* developed by Robert Hohn, University of Kansas, which is available to all users of the text, features online practice tests, links to websites related to topics in the book, cases and audio reflections on chapter topics by the authors, and a discussion area.

For instructors, the following supplements assist in teaching and managing the educational psychology course:

- *Instructor's Resource Manual,* written by Mary Ann Rafoth, Indiana University of Pennsylvania, correlates all the text supplements with chapter learning objectives, and provides detailed lecture outlines, reproducible classroom activities and handout masters, and online and video resource references.

- *Test Bank,* written by Jada Kearns, Valencia Community College, provides multiple choice, true–false, and short answer test items correlated to chapter learning objectives, plus correct answers and text page references. The Test Bank is also available on a cross-platform CD-ROM.

- *PowerPoint Presentations,* prepared by Jeff Swartwood, SUNY-Cortland, feature chapter-by-chapter presentations with extensive lecture notes that can be easily used or adapted to convert your lectures to accompany this text.

- *The Flexible Expert: Practical, Analytical, and Creative Teaching with Educational Psychology,* a two-hour video, features classroom footage and interviews with classroom teachers on topics related to each chapter of the text.

- *Acetate Transparencies*—Educational Psychology III provides 100 full-color transparencies related to text topics for classroom use.

- *Allyn & Bacon Digital Media Archive CD-ROM for Education,* 2001 Edition provides color images, video and audio clips, and weblinks to enhance your in-class presentations on text concepts.

- CourseCompass™, Allyn and Bacon's online course management tool powered by Blackboard™, helps instructors manage all aspects of teaching the course and includes preloaded content such as the Test Bank.

ACKNOWLEDGMENTS

Julia Matuga of Bowling Green State University deserves special thanks for her excellent work in developing and writing each chapter's Technology Tools You Can Use feature. Her contribution is truly appreciated.

We also thank the following reviewers whose insights assisted us at all stages in the development of this book:

Keith Allred
  Brigham Young University
Christopher Atang
Douglas A. Beed
  University of Montana
Sally Bing
  University of Maryland
  Eastern Shore
Frank E. Bowers
  Grace University
Kay S. Bull
  Oklahoma State University
Stephen Burgess
  South Western Oklahoma State
  University
Theodore Coladarci
  University of Maine
Peggy Dettmar
  Kansas State University

Beverly J. Dretzke
  University of Wisconsin–Eau Claire
Joanne Engel
  Oregon State University
William R. Fisk
  Clemson University
Hal Fletcher
  Florida State University
Marlynn M. Griffin
  Georgia Southern University
Grady E. Harlan
  University of Mississippi
Jan M. Heinitz
  Concordia University
Sharon Lee Hiett
  University of Central Florida
Robert L. Hohn
  University of Kansas

Susan Hupp
University of Minnesota
Nancy Johnson
University of Sioux Falls
Mitchell Kelly
University of Iowa
Suzanne Morin
Shippensburg University
David Morse
Mississippi State University
Linda W. Morse
Mississippi State University
Karen Nelson
Austin College
Regena F. Nelson
Western Michigan University
Mary Ann Rafoth
Indiana University of Pennsylvania

Rich Robbins
Washburn University
Ruth A. Sandlin
*California State University
at San Bernardino*
G. H. Budd Sapp
Fairmont State College
Carol A. Takacs
Cleveland State University
Anthony L. Truog
University of Wisconsin–Whitewater
James Martin Webb
Kent State University
Katherine F. Wickstrom
Eastern Illinois University
Jane A. Wolfe
Bowling Green State University

We are also grateful to the Education Team at Allyn and Bacon who helped bring this book to fruition: Paul A. Smith, Vice President and Editorial Director; Arnis E. Burvikovs, Series Editor for Educational Psychology; Linda M. Bieze, Senior Development Editor; Kathleen Morgan, Marketing Manager; Elaine Ober, Production Manager; Linda Knowles, Cover Administrator; and Matthew Forster, Editorial Assistant.

—R. J. S.
—W. M. W.

Educational Psychology

Becoming an Expert Teacher; Becoming an Expert Student

THE BIG PICTURE

To help you see the big picture, keep the following questions in mind as you read this introductory chapter. The chapters that follow will help you explore further the answers to these questions.

- What does it mean to be an expert teacher? What are the ingredients a person needs to maximize the likelihood of becoming an expert teacher? What is the best way to gain teaching expertise?

- What does it mean to be an expert student? How can you be an expert student today, as you read this and other textbooks and prepare for classes? How can you spot expert students in your classes in the future? What is involved in *becoming* an expert student, and how can you help every student you teach become an expert learner?

- Why are the topics covered in this book important for teachers? What can you expect to learn from each topic? How will you be able to *use* what you learn from this book and from your training in educational psychology in general?

◄ *Surrounded by colorful visual displays, a fifth-grade teacher discusses how to write a paper with her attentive class.* (Bob Daemmrich, The Image Works)

Sandy was afraid she was going to be sick. It was her first day of teaching, and she wanted to be and do her absolute best. Sandy had prepared as well as any novice teacher could—she had studied hard in school and read widely on the topic of education. Just as important, Sandy was as motivated as a person could be; she had wanted to be a teacher since she was a child.

"Why am I so nervous?" Sandy wondered, as she watched students file into the first of her several science classes. She greeted each one with a hello and a smile. The students took seats and looked around expectantly. Someone in the back row snickered—a boy who looked a couple of years older than his classmates. In the first row, two students were dressed as if they were going to a party. Their notebooks were open, and they sat still, looking like well-behaved soldiers. But behind them, in the next three rows, others were dressed more like high school students than seventh graders: These girls were talking to one another, and one of them passed a pack of cigarettes across her desk. Sandy took a deep breath, squared the papers on her desk, and began the speech she had rehearsed ten times during August as part of her preparation for the challenge of her new job.

By 3:30 P.M. that day, Sandy looked like the poorer twin of her 8 A.M. self. She was exhausted and confused, and the classroom looked like a college dorm after an all-night party. Four classes of students had filed into that room—120 in all—and each class seemed to contain more monsters and fewer children. And Sandy wanted to learn all their names, know their strengths and weaknesses, and teach them science. At this point, Sandy thought, it was a cruel joke that someone had played on her—these weren't actual seventh graders, they were actors hired by everyone in her life who had ever told Sandy she was crazy to want to teach 12-year-olds.

In the teacher's lounge, Sandy slipped off her shoes and rubbed her feet. Danielle, a 20-year veteran of middle school teaching, took the next seat and introduced herself. Sandy was eager to make friends among her colleagues, but right now she was too beat to be outgoing. She said hi and smiled, hoping this would suffice. Danielle wasn't put off—in fact, she had Sandy figured out. Like any expert teacher, Danielle appreciated what Sandy was experiencing as she began a new and challenging career.

Danielle was willing to help, and she offered Sandy advice, information, a shoulder to lean on, whatever she needed. "I think I just have to learn this stuff for myself—the hard way," Sandy replied. Danielle laughed. "I hope you're wrong," she answered. "Teaching is a tough business, and if you can't learn from seasoned colleagues it'll be a long road." "You're probably right," Sandy responded. "Thanks!"

Over the school year Sandy faced many difficult situations. Luckily, she had Danielle to lean on. The discipline problems, testing worries, parent-teacher conference anxiety, and daily instructional challenges of making science interesting to a bunch of kids entering puberty (who also had other things on their minds) were made much easier as a result of her sage advice. In Danielle's 20 years of teaching, she had been through just about every tough teaching situation you can imagine: She was a gold mine of information. By June 15, Sandy felt like donating one month's salary to Danielle. At that point, she felt more in control and much wiser about the ins and outs of teaching than she had so long ago—in September. Sandy was one year into a promising and rewarding career.

Sandy was experiencing a situation that every teacher has faced: beginning a demanding profession, wanting to do a good job, but not knowing exactly how to accomplish this goal. Many of you may find yourselves in this position in the near future, while others of you may have read about Sandy and smiled knowingly, having already been in her shoes. Stop for a moment and ask yourself, What do you expect from a career in teaching? What challenges are you likely to encounter? What obstacles will you face? And what strategies will you use to organize your work, get through to the students, and still feel energized when you return home after a long hard day?

Like Sandy, you probably share the goal of becoming an expert teacher like Danielle. **Expert teachers** use a broad base of organized knowledge and experience efficiently and creatively to solve the many kinds of problems that occur in educational settings. When we think about the Danielles of the teaching world, a variety of individual people come to mind—people linked to one another by their expertise as teachers, even though their styles, approaches, and attitudes may differ. Although expert teachers share certain characteristics—such as being able to motivate students to learn complex information, deal with test anxiety in students, and handle discipline problems effectively—they have many different methods for achieving these goals. Indeed, there is not just one way to be an expert teacher, but many ways that fit many different personalities. The key is that expert teachers solve problems effectively and get things done in the classroom. Your goal should be to find the best way for *you* to become an expert teacher by capitalizing on your strengths and compensating for your weaknesses. The purpose of this book is to help you on your journey.

Remember, some expert teachers are young. Twenty years of teaching experience does not always make an expert, nor are many years of experience necessary to become an expert teacher. Some teachers become expert relatively early in their careers by capitalizing on and learning from both their experiences and those of other teachers. Other teachers may have 20 years' experience at the front of a classroom, but they may not have learned and developed as much as they could have. This textbook will help you acquire the knowledge base you will need to profit from your teaching experiences and develop into an expert as early in your career as possible.

THINKING ANALYTICALLY

Evaluate three expert teachers you have known. In what ways were these teachers alike? In what ways did they differ? Were they more alike than different, or vice versa? *(Hint: Refresh your memory about how to answer these questions, which appear throughout this text, by rereading the section in the Preface that describes this feature of the book.)*

SUGGESTION: Some ways expert teachers are alike include sharing a love of and devotion to teaching, having clear objectives and goals, and using novel and creative approaches in the classroom to communicate their ideas. Expert teachers can differ in their presentation style (some may prefer lecturing, while others prefer discussion and dialogue), their friendliness and degree of nurture (some may prefer to challenge students, while others support them), and the importance they place on homework and tests. There are many ways to be an expert teacher.

The "Thinking" Triangle

To understand the exercises you'll find interspersed throughout the chapters in this book, you'll need to know a new term. *Triarchic* means having three parts, like the three sides of a triangle. This term refers to a theory of intelligence developed by Robert Sternberg in which intelligence is viewed as having three major aspects: analytical, creative, and practical abilities. The triarchic theory is explained in detail in Chapter 4, but the idea of a triangle of thinking is used throughout the text to encourage you to consider concepts and problems in these three different ways. Three kinds of questions are used:

- **Thinking Analytically** questions ask you to analyze, compare and contrast, or evaluate concepts or information.

- **Thinking Creatively** questions encourage you to invent, discover, or design. You are asked to stretch your thinking—to go beyond what you already know.

- **Thinking Practically** questions help you learn how to apply in everyday life what you already know.

Let's also consider the steps involved in becoming an expert student. **Expert students** use strategies to help them learn efficiently and are open to challenges and willing to overcome problems to achieve learning goals. Of course, as you read this book and attend classes in educational psychology, you are also a student. The more expert you are at being a student, the more you will learn and the better you will be able to *use* what you have learned in your career. Later, when you teach a class, knowing the fundamentals of what makes an expert student will also be critical. You will want to know which students are experts—which students are primed to learn and ready to benefit most from the learning experience.

THINKING CREATIVELY

It is often said that early in the life of every great person was a teacher who helped launch that person on the path to greatness. What might you do as a teacher to help a talented student onto such a path?

SUGGESTION: Encourage and support the student's interests—help the student obtain extra materials and resources to broaden her understanding. Challenge the student to do extra, advanced work. Introduce the talented student to an adult with expertise in the same domain. If necessary, meet with parents to suggest an environment for success. Encourage the student to develop a positive attitude about mistakes and failures.

You will also want to know which students are having trouble learning in the context of the school and classroom environments, so you can help these nonexpert students develop expertise.

Try to develop a list of ten behaviors that consistently distinguished your own best teachers. Recall two or three excellent teachers from your past, and two or three teachers you consider less effective. Think back to what the talented teachers did on a daily basis: What types of assignments did they give? How did they structure their classrooms? What types of activities did they choose? How did they keep the material interesting? How did they encourage you and how did they provide effective feedback? In contrast, in response to these same questions, think about what the ineffective teachers did poorly. Write down the ten key behaviors that characterize the excellent teachers, and distinguish these behaviors from those of the ineffective teachers. What does your list say about the types of instruction you, as a student, found most appealing? What does your list say about what may or may not work with the students you teach?

What Is an *Expert Teacher?*

The question of what it means to be an expert teacher is central to many of society's goals, and, presumably, to your personal goals as a reader of this book. If schools are to be first rate, their most important human resources—their teachers and students—must be fully developed. But how do we educators know what we should be developing teachers to become? To know where we are headed, we must understand what makes a teacher an expert. We must understand what distinguishes expert teachers from average teachers and develop ways to help novice teachers acquire expertise as smoothly and as early in their careers as possible. The goal is to help beginning teachers like Sandy become expert teachers like Danielle as quickly and smoothly as possible.

Sometimes, novice teachers have difficulty keeping order in their classes. As they become more expert, they will use a variety of strategies and techniques, efficiently and with growing insight, to arrive at solutions for such problems. (Will Faller)

You can consider teaching expertise in two important ways, both of which will be helpful to you as a student of educational psychology who wants to learn the principles of how to be an effective teacher (Sternberg & Horvath, 1995, 1998, 1999). First, think in terms of *how experts differ from nonexperts:* For example, what did your three best teachers do that was different from the rest of your teachers? What did your best teachers have in common? Second, think in terms of *how people view expertise in daily life:* For example, how can students be motivated when they are already burdened with work from other subjects? How do expert teachers handle teaching gifted students in the same classroom with average students and students with learning problems?

You can use these two ways to think about teaching expertise practically in day-to-day teaching to improve your performance. First, reflect on your progress at teaching, and attempt to understand what you are doing right and doing wrong and why. This type of **reflective thinking** has been shown to contribute to the development of expertise. Second, develop a personal and informal list of differences between experienced and less experienced teachers: For example, Nancy (an expert teacher) always raises her finger in the air to signal her class that she is going to say something important for them to write down; Dominic (an average teacher) mixes important definitions with less important information, so his students do not always know what is important to write down.

Both of these ways of thinking about teaching expertise—as a tendency toward reflective thinking and as a practice of developing a list of behaviors used by successful teachers—are useful, although neither one alone provides the entire picture. Clearly, teaching expertise is more than simply "a tendency to reflect on what works." Teaching expertise is also more than just a catch-all list of behaviors that work in the classroom. Being effective as a teacher does not happen simply because you sit down at the end of each school day and think about what it means to be an effective teacher. Reflecting on how to be an expert is essential, but it is not the whole story. You also need practical strategies for teaching and accurate, comprehensive content knowledge so that students see you as "knowing your stuff." However, neither is simply copying the behaviors of the most effective teachers a magic recipe. You must understand and reflect on what works and what does not. Integrate teaching techniques into your own approach, remembering that what works for Maria Campos in Room 211 might not work for you. Each teacher has a unique style, and part of capitalizing on this style is knowing what you do best—and worst—and playing to your strengths as you lead a class.

For example, imagine you sometimes lose the main point when you lecture for more than ten minutes. You know you go off on tangents until the students' eyes glaze over, and only the sound of snoring jolts you back into reality. If lecturing at length is not your strength, you can compensate for this shortcoming. To keep yourself on track, speak from main outline points you write on the board or concentrate on demonstrations or activities that require student participation to keep the class involved while you still get your point across. Or imagine you become flustered when students whisper or pass notes while you are teaching. Reflect on how the students' behavior unsettles you and select two or three calming strategies, such as correcting the misbehavior as soon as it occurs and smiling at the rest of the class to show appreciation for their good behavior and attentiveness.

Throughout this book, we focus on developing expertise in teaching—the gradual accumulation of knowledge that prepares teachers to do their jobs effectively and solve the daily problems of the job. We want to show you how to *become* an expert teacher, and the word *become* is critical. As Sandy in the opening vignette learned, becoming an expert teacher is a process, not a sudden insight or "aha" experience. This book will give you the tools you need to develop expertise as you participate in this process.

What are the characteristics of expert teachers? How do they differ from novice teachers? What made Danielle different from Sandy? Research has shown that expert teachers share three qualities. First, experts have expert *knowledge:* Expert teachers know more strategies and techniques for teaching, and they use their knowledge more effectively to solve problems than do novices. Second, experts are *efficient:* Expert teachers do more in less time than do novices. Third, experts have creative *insight:* Expert teachers are more likely to arrive at novel and appropriate solutions to problems than are novices.

Let us consider each of these distinctive characteristics in detail, so you have more specific ideas about what you are working to develop in your quest to become an expert teacher.

Experts have and use more knowledge to solve problems on the job than do novices. Experts also solve these problems more effectively. This difference may seem obvious, but it is worth exploring exactly what this "expert knowledge" consists of and how experts use this knowledge to perform successfully on the job.

When you have the good fortune to work alongside an expert teacher, or even when you are being taught by one, you may think to yourself, "Jim is just so much smarter than I am. He knows everything—he must have a better memory than I do. I could never remember all that stuff." But is this true? Are expert teachers blessed with better memories and more intelligence in general? Is there hope for all of us whose memories are not stellar and who are not the best students in our classes?

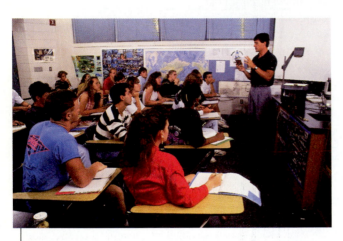

An expert in complete control of his class, this high school teacher lectures on a biology topic as students listen in rapt attention. (Bill Bachmann, PhotoEdit)

A classic study in psychology provides some answers to these questions. This study looked at differences between expert and novice chess players in memory for particular configurations of chess pieces on chess boards (Chase & Simon, 1973; Gobet & Simon, 1998). The researchers showed different configurations to both experts and novices, then assessed memory for the configurations. As expected, experts showed superior memory—but only when the chess pieces were arranged in a sensible configuration (i.e., a configuration that might logically evolve during the course of a game). When chess pieces were placed on the board in *random* configurations, both experts and novices showed *poor* memory for these configurations.

What does this finding mean? First, it shows that the advantage of chess experts over novices was related to chess *configurations* and did not reflect superiority in general memory or thinking ability. Experts' advantage was in having more knowledge: The chess experts had stored thousands of sensible configurations in memory, and this stored knowledge allowed them to memorize the chess pieces' patterns more easily, giving them an advantage over novices. Expert performance has been studied in a number of domains, including the memorization of restaurant orders, computer programming, judicial decision making, medical diagnosis (Lesgold, Rubinson, Feltovich, Glaser, Klopfer, & Wang, 1988; Petre & Blackwell, 1999), and even racetrack handicapping (Ceci & Liker, 1986). As a group, these studies have yielded the same general findings as the studies of chess experts—namely, that experts' main advantage over novices is in having more knowledge about their domain of expertise (Chi, Glaser, & Farr, 1988; Ericsson & Charness, 1999; Glaser, 1996; Glaser & Chi, 1988).

Expert teachers are not necessarily superior to novices in general, in regard to biologically based memory or thinking skills. However, expert teachers have extensive knowledge, acquired from experience, that they use to understand and act on problems. It is not simply genetics or what you were born with—it is knowledge you can acquire if you are willing to work to become an expert teacher.

■**TYPES OF EXPERT KNOWLEDGE** What are the specific types of knowledge necessary for expert teaching? First, and most obviously, expert teachers must have *content knowledge*—knowledge of the subject matter to be taught. You will develop content knowledge from taking content-based courses and from experiences outside of school. For example, if you intend to teach math, your content knowledge will come from your experience in math courses, as well as from using math, reading about math, and talking about math with others outside school.

Second, expert teachers need *pedagogical knowledge*—knowledge of how to teach. Pedagogical knowledge of the general variety includes knowledge of how to enhance student motivation, how to manage groups of students in a classroom setting, and how to design and administer tests. The purpose of this book and of your educational psychology course is to provide you with pedagogical knowledge.

Third, expert teachers need *pedagogical-content knowledge*—knowledge of how to teach what is specific to what is being taught, such as knowledge of how to explain particular concepts (for example, negative numbers), how to demonstrate and explain procedures and methods (Leinhardt, 1987; Marion, Hewson, Tabachnick, & Blomker, 1999), and how to correct students' naive theories and misconceptions about subject matter (Gardner, 1991; Liggitt-Fox, 1997). You will develop pedagogical-content knowledge as you apply the pedagogical knowledge you learn from this book and from your course to your particular content area of focus (for example, math).

■ **ORGANIZATION OF EXPERT KNOWLEDGE** Do experts and novices differ in how they organize and store knowledge? This question may at first seem unanswerable, because the knowledge is mental and its organization cannot easily be seen. Psychologists can study how experts and novices use knowledge during problem solving and see what differences emerge. For example, numerous studies detail how experts and novices solve physics problems (Chi, Feltovich, & Glaser, 1981; Chi, Glaser, & Farr, 1988; Chi, Glaser, & Rees, 1982; Chi & Van Lehn, 1991; Kozhevnikov, Hegarty, & Mayer, 1999; Larkin, McDermott, Simon, & Simon, 1980; Rochelle, 1998; Slotta, Chi, & Joram, 1995).

One study found that expert and novice problem solvers sorted the same physics problems differently (Chi, Feltovich, & Glaser, 1981). In general, experts were sensitive to the *deep structures* of the problems they sorted—they grouped problems together according to the physics principles that were relevant to problem solution (for example, conservation of momentum). By contrast, novices were more sensitive to *surface structure*—they sorted problems according to things mentioned in the problem (for example, inclined planes). These results suggest that experts and novices differ not only in the amount of knowledge they have but also in how they organize that knowledge in memory.

For a teacher, being sensitive to deep structure might mean recognizing that a poor child with a speech impediment and a more affluent and inappropriately outspoken child share feelings of low self-worth that lead to different types of undesirable classroom behavior. A teacher tuned in only to surface structure might see the children's problems as due entirely to more obvious causes (the speech impediment and a lack of discipline, for example), and this teacher might fail to solve the problems effectively.

LESSON PLANS. Several studies of expert teaching have concluded that expert and novice teachers differ in the organization of their teaching knowledge (Berliner, 1991; Borko & Livingston, 1989; Borko, Livingston, & Shavelson, 1990; Leinhardt & Greeno, 1986, 1991; Livingston & Borko, 1990; Moallem, 1998; Sabers, Cushing, & Berliner, 1991; Strauss, Ravid, Magen, & Berliner, 1998). These studies suggest that the knowledge of expert teachers is more thoroughly integrated (with bits and pieces of knowledge being more interrelated) than the knowledge of novices. How can we tell that experts' knowledge is more integrated? To answer this question, psychologists have looked at teachers' lesson plans (Berliner, 1991; Borko & Livingston, 1989; Collins & Stevens, 1991; Leinhardt, 1987; Leinhardt & Greeno, 1986; Sanchex & Valcarcel, 1999). The lesson plan integrates knowledge of content to be taught with knowledge of teaching methods.

According to Leinhardt and Greeno (1986), a lesson plan includes *global plans* not related to specific lesson content or subject matter (for example, "Begin with an example that shows the importance of the lesson topic to students' lives outside of school"), *local plans* related to content and subject matter (for example, "Before discussing the specifics of the Civil War, ask the students to brainstorm what it would have been like to be an African American child or a white child around 1860"), and *decision elements* that make the lesson plan responsive to expected and unexpected events (for example, "If the

What knowledge do you possess that you will be able to apply in your teaching?

SUGGESTION: Think of activities in which you have excelled, outside of school interests and hobbies. Think of subjects and topics you know the best. All of this knowledge and information will be useful in your teaching.

Describe a situation in which you were able to analyze the deep structure of a problem.

SUGGESTION: Your best friend starts doing poorly in school, blaming his failure on the fact that he is just not smart enough. However, you are able to understand that problems in the home are causing him stress and are in fact responsible for his poor performance.

students do not want to move forward with the lesson, start reading the Civil War diary passage to engage them in the next step," "If the students do not seem interested in the passage, ask them to imagine what soldiers' lives were like").

Global parts of the lesson plan might include routines for checking homework, presenting new material, and supervising guided practice. These global parts of the lesson plan apply regardless of the content being taught. Local parts of the plan might include routines for presenting particular concepts or for assessing student understanding of particular concepts. Local parts of the plan are tailored to the content being taught. Decision elements in the plan tell the teacher what to do when typical types of questions are asked, and they allow for unanticipated circumstances, for example, times when students do not understand the material as quickly as usual.

EXPERT VERSUS NOVICE PLANS. A good lesson plan enables the expert teacher to teach effectively and efficiently (see Figure 1.1a on page 12). General teaching knowledge, such as knowledge of class-management routines, maximizes the amount of time that students spend learning (rather than locating materials and supplies or switching activities, for example). Knowledge related to teaching content, such as explanations keyed to specific student questions, enables the expert teacher to connect student feedback to lesson objectives, thus keeping the lesson on track.

By contrast, novice teachers have less complex, less interconnected lesson plans. Because they lack knowledge of general routines, novice teachers tend to spend more time with their classes off-task—getting organized, accessing materials, and trying to discipline students and capture their attention (Leinhardt & Greeno, 1986). Because their content-related teaching knowledge is not as developed as that of experts, novice teachers tend to have difficulty generating examples and explanations if the examples and explanations have not been prepared in advance (Borko & Livingston, 1989). Because their plans are less likely to anticipate student misconceptions, novice teachers tend to have difficulty relating student questions to lesson objectives (Borko & Livingston, 1989). Novices' teaching plans often do not include the types of examples and explanations they need to teach effectively (see Figure 1.1b on page 13).

For example, in a lesson on photosynthesis, if a student asks why green plants need soil in order to survive, an expert teacher answers that soil supplies only water and minerals, but the food that plants need is made within them as plant cells transform sunlight into chemical energy. The expert teacher thus refocuses the student's misconception—that plants get food from soil—into a more appropriate conception, in other words, that plants get food from photosynthesis. Novice teachers, in contrast, are more likely to answer the same student question by saying simply that plants get necessary minerals from soil. Novices would not be as likely to refocus the question back onto the main lesson theme of photosynthesis.

THINKING PRACTICALLY

In day-to-day classroom teaching, how important do you believe teachers' *knowledge* is in accomplishing their goals? How important do you believe teachers' level of *commitment* is in daily teaching? Finally, how important do you believe teachers' *motivation* is to their classroom performance?

SUGGESTION: Knowledge of subject matter and teaching strategies is absolutely essential. But commitment to the daily tasks of teaching is what keeps a teacher coming back to the classroom day in and day out. Motivation is what gives a teacher a spark and the energy for teaching that students respond to.

■ **KNOWLEDGE ABOUT THE TEACHING CONTEXT** In addition to well-organized and interrelated knowledge of content and pedagogy, expert teachers need knowledge of the social and political context in which teaching occurs. In fact, knowing how to work effectively with others is an essential part of being an expert teacher, often just as important as knowledge of how to teach.

For example, expert teachers need to know how to package curricular innovations in order to convince other teachers, parents, and administrators of the worth of these innovations. Expert teachers also need to know how to compete effectively for limited school resources so their own students get necessary materials, supplies, equipment, and other tools. Frequently, in an era of shrinking school budgets, expert teachers need to be proficient at "working the system" to obtain needed services for their students. For instance, the expert teacher might befriend other teachers and administrators by serving on committees and by doing others favors when asked in anticipation of reaping later rewards. These rewards might

include loyalty of co-workers and the promise of help when the expert teacher needed it. Such practical ability, or savvy, is an essential part of teaching expertise.

In summary, expert teachers have extensive, well-organized knowledge that they can draw on readily during teaching. In addition to knowledge of subject matter and of how to teach, experts also have knowledge of the political and social context in which teaching occurs. This knowledge allows expert teachers to adapt to practical constraints in their field, including the need to become recognized as expert teachers.

The school environment can vary enormously, from a highly sophisticated classroom equipped with computers, VCRs, and other technical aids in the United States, to a simple classroom with few such aids in Mali. Expert teaching can take place in any of these environments. (Will Hart; Steve McCurry, Magnum Photos Inc.)

EXPERT TEACHERS ARE EFFICIENT

The second important difference between experts and novices is that experts are able to solve problems more efficiently than novices. Experts can do more in less time (and usually with less effort) than novices. (This is why it was *Sandy* who was exhausted after one day on the job, and not Danielle.) How do experts accomplish this? First, experts **automatize** well-learned skills. By automatize, we mean that experts develop the ability to perform important tasks without thinking much about them—like the way experienced adults drive (under normal weather and traffic conditions), and the way experienced teachers know how to silence a student who is talking in the back row during a lesson without disrupting other students' concentration. Second, experts effectively plan, monitor, and revise their approach to problems.

■AUTOMATIZING WELL-LEARNED SKILLS How do experts perform better than novices, and with less effort? People's mental resources are limited, but experts seem to stretch these limits—they seem to do more than novices, but with the same or even less expenditure of energy. The accepted explanation for this difference is that mental processes may be divided into those that take up a lot of thought and energy and those that are relatively easy and **automatic** (Schneider, 1999; Schneider & Shiffrin, 1985). Automatic mental processes are processes that have become well learned and, consequently, require little effort. Certain types of mental skills may become automatic with extensive practice: What is initially difficult becomes, with practice, second nature and relatively untaxing of one's resources (Anderson, 1982; Schneider, 1999). Thus, by virtue of their extensive experience, experts are able to perform tasks effortlessly that novices can perform only with effort.

The expert driver does not need to think about fundamental driving skills such as steering, shifting, and braking. Most adults who have been driving for a few years are expert drivers and can plan their day while they drive to work. The novice driver, however, can apply driving skills only with conscious effort—to let one's thoughts turn to another event could add new complications to the day's schedule, such as completing police accident reports and filing insurance claims!

THINKING PRACTICALLY

What automatic skills do you possess that you might apply to teaching?

SUGGESTION: Examples include driving, cooking, typing or word processing, athletic activities, dancing, drawing, and speaking different languages.

Lesson Title: The Importance of Using a Variety of Resources

What

An activity and discussion designed to show students the diversity in available sources of information, the fact that many sources are interesting and fun to pursue, and the relevance of specific sources to specific subjects.

What to Do

1. Ask the students to name as many different sources of information as they can. If they need help, start them off by suggesting that a textbook is a source of information. List responses on the board.

2. As a class, determine how many different kinds of sources have been listed. Some (perhaps most) will be printed matter (books, newspapers, magazines, etc.) or sources of printed matter (libraries, bookstores, etc.); others might be the World Wide Web, television, and movies.

3. Now lead students to consider more unusual resources:

    -   Does this list include any people? What kind of person could be a source of information? Does a person have to be a "certified expert" to be a source of information? (Polling and oral histories are two important sources precisely because they do not consult "experts.")

    -   Does this list include any places? What kind of place might be a source of information (e.g., travel destinations, museums, stores, factories, historical sites, etc.)? Does a place have to offer or have printed materials in order to be a source of information?

    -   Does this list include any "things" that are not printed matter or other modern media? What kinds of things can be considered a source of information (e.g., any artifact, such as an arrowhead or a collection of old photos)?

4. As a class, brainstorm another list of sources of information. This time try to focus on sources that are not composed largely of printed matter. The list might include:

    -   your mom
    -   an old graveyard
    -   an archaeologist at the local college
    -   a moon rock
    -   a foreign embassy or consulate
    -   an old record album
    -   your oldest living relative
    -   a neighbor who immigrated to the United States
    -   any museum (e.g., natural history, art, sports, transportation)

5. Once the brainstorm is over, go over the list and ask students to explain why they think the items are sources: What can you find out from each (e.g., your mom might be a source of information about what life was like when she was your age; a really old graveyard might be a source of information about how long average lives used to be and what kinds of names were popular years ago)?

6. To make the point more forcefully, ask students to reflect on times when they actually encountered alternative sources of information:

    -   Who in the class remembers a field trip she took someplace?
    -   Where was it, and how was that place a source of information?
    -   Does anyone ever remember having a guest speaker in the classroom?
    -   How was that person a source of information?
    -   Has anyone ever brought an object into class to use as a source of information (an aquarium, an exotic pet)? What was it, and what did it provide information about?

7. Explain to the students that using alternative sources requires information-gathering techniques that might be different from what they are used to. When you get information from the encyclopedia, you just look up the subject and read the articles that discuss it. Not much of a challenge. But getting information from other sources is more like detective work—you have to poke around a little, ask a lot of questions, jot down clues, and consult as many different sources as you can. It takes more

imagination than just reading one article, but it is also a lot more interesting. The encyclopedia is not a waste of time, though—often it is the first place to look to find out about *other* possible sources of information.

8. Choose a current topic on which a written assignment will be based. Have each student think of or locate three possible sources of information, and write how they would realistically go about getting information from these sources. For example:
   - Schedule an interview with a local person or expert.
   - Write to a distant person or organization and ask for a written or taped response to a written interview.
   - Visit a local site and take pictures and gather available literature.
   - Write for information about a distant site.
   - Consult a reference librarian.
   - Conduct searches using the World Wide Web.
   - Rent a pertinent video and take notes.
9. As a class, share ideas and discuss other ways of getting information from a variety of resources.

Questions to Consider:
- What if you are studying an ancient civilization? Because what you are studying happened so long ago, are you restricted to sources such as books and articles? What kinds of people, places, or things can you consult if your topic is ancient?
- If you do schedule an interview with a person, what will you need to think about or do before actually conducting the interview? Examples: Is the person just going to talk? Are there any questions you specifically want answered? How will you remember what the person says—will you take notes? Tape the interview? What if you cannot get to the person? Could a telephone interview work?
10. Finish the lesson by asking the students to help you list the benefits and problems of using a variety of sources. Talk with students about how to solve or minimize the problems students anticipate.

Novice Teacher's Lesson Plan

Lesson Title: Using Resources

1. Ask the students what types of information they usually use to do their schoolwork, projects, and assignments.
2. Discuss with the class the range of types of information that are available. Mention the three types of information teachers most often use when researching a topic for a lecture.
3. Ask the students to suggest some unusual and not frequently used types and sources of information. Sort these into categories on the chalkboard. Ask students how they have used these sources in the past, and what they have done specifically with these sources.
4. Choose a topic for the day's assignment. Students can contribute their ideas about what topic should be chosen. Once a specific topic has been agreed on, ask each student to gather three different types of information on the topic. Stress that at least one of the types of information should be as unusual as possible. Ask students to do the assignment at home and be prepared to present their results in class tomorrow.

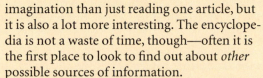

FIGURE 1.1a and 1.1b

Two examples of lesson plans, one by an expert teacher and one by a novice teacher, with numerous differences showing the advantages of expertise. *Source:* From *Practical Intelligence for School* by W.M.Williams, T. Blythe, N. White, J. Li, R.J. Sternberg, and H.I. Gardner. Copyright © 1996. Reprinted by permission of Addison–Wesley Educational Publishers, Inc.

Expert teachers instruct their students in classroom routines so the students are able to begin working as soon as they arrive in class. (Stone)

Expert teachers routinely deal with potential discipline problems before they erupt: Almost without realizing it, they mention students' names as they notice the students' attention drifting. The students' attention is thereby refocused on the lesson, but no one else even notices. In contrast, novice teachers may not perceive a problem until it becomes disruptive—as when drifting students begin talking about last night's game. By this point, the teacher has to divert time and energy from the lesson to correct the problem; the students whose attention has drifted feel exposed and possibly humiliated; and the rest of the class has been interrupted.

In considering the importance of automatic skills for expert teaching, we must remember that the ability to automatize well-learned routines does not exist independently from the possession of organized teaching knowledge. Consider the study of expert and novice teachers' monitoring of ongoing classroom events (Sabers, Cushing, & Berliner, 1991). Expert teachers in this study did a better job than novices of monitoring fast-paced classroom events. Experts also interpreted what happened in the class in a richer, more insightful, and more meaningful way than did novices. Expert teachers made proportionately more interpretations and evaluations of what they saw and made more coherent interpretations and evaluations. For example, consider one expert's interpretation of a videotaped lesson: "I haven't heard a bell, but the students are already at their desks and seem to be doing purposeful activity, and [so] they must be an accelerated group because they came into the room and started something rather than just sitting down and socializing" (Sabers et al., 1991, pp. 72–73). By contrast, a novice's interpretation was "I can't tell what they're doing. They're getting ready for class, but I can't tell what they're doing." What might explain the superior performance by the expert teacher?

Imagine that we want to emphasize the role of *automatic skills* in experts' superior performance. We could argue that the experiences of the expert teachers enabled them (1) to handle more information per unit time than did novices, or (2) to handle the information with less effort, or (3) both. This freeing up of mental energy would explain the experts' superior ability to see meaningful patterns in the events. Imagine that, on the other hand, we want to emphasize the role of *organization of knowledge.* We could argue that the experts' experience provided them with a store of meaningful patterns, corresponding to classroom situations, and that having these patterns stored in their minds made recognizing similar patterns easier for expert teachers. For example, in the Sabers et al. study excerpted here, the expert teachers may have had mental patterns and images of how students in an accelerated program behave when they arrive at class. Thus these experts were better able than novices to recognize what was happening in the videotape. Obviously, having both well-organized knowledge and well-learned automatic routines is helpful to a teacher who is in charge of 25 or more students.

■**PLANNING, MONITORING, AND EVALUATING** Experts also differ from novices in experts' tendency and ability to plan what to do, monitor their progress, and evaluate their performance. These types of thinking processes are sometimes called **metacognitive processes,** processes in which one "thinks about thinking." When expert teachers confront a problem, they *think about thinking* before jumping in and starting to solve the problem: They might think about which plan or approach is more likely to work, or they might think about how one plan compares to another one they had tried that failed. An expert social studies teacher deciding on a topic to assign for a book report would be likely to review past years' choices and evaluate how these choices worked, asking questions such as these: Which topics got students most interested? Which led to the best reports, and why? What can I do to make this year's reports the best ever? This expert teacher might also ask other teachers for their input and read teaching magazines for ideas and advice on spicing up the book-report-writing process.

Research on expertise has shown that experts and novices differ in metacognitive control of thinking—in other words, experts and novices "think about thinking" differently as they solve problems on the job. How? For one thing, experts spend more time trying to understand the problem to be solved. Novices, in contrast, invest less time in trying to understand the problem and more time in actually *trying out* different solutions (Lesgold, 1984; Sternberg, 1981). Experts are more likely to monitor their ongoing solution attempts, checking for accuracy ("Am I getting closer to the correct answer?") (Ertmer & Newby, 1996; Larkin, 1985; Larkin & Rainard, 1984; Sternberg, 1998). Experts are also more likely to update or elaborate problem representations as new constraints emerge ("I didn't realize that would happen—that changes things . . .") (Sternberg, 1998; Voss & Post, 1988).

In one study, expert teachers were found to plan their approach to classroom discipline problems in greater depth than novices. Experts tended to emphasize the definition of discipline problems and the evaluation of alternative explanations for the problems, whereas novices tended to be more solution oriented and less concerned with understanding the discipline problems (Swanson, O'Connor, & Cooney, 1990). Borko and Livingston (1989) studied how expert and novice mathematics teachers plan their lessons. In this study, the expert teachers did much more long-term planning than the novices, and the experts' plans fit the day's teaching into the overall goals and organization of a given chapter and the course in general. Experts' plans were more flexible and responsive to the different directions the class discussion might take, whereas novices' plans were more rigid—with the result that novices became more flustered when events in the classroom did not exactly follow their plans.

A great deal of interest has been expressed in "reflective practice in teaching" and its role in the process of becoming an expert teacher (Copeland, Birmingham, de la Cruz, & Lewin, 1993; Dinkelman, 2000). This focus on reflective practice in teaching is actually a focus on *thinking about thinking*. Researchers describe expert teachers as having a disposition toward reflection, which is defined as "continuous learning through experience" (Schon, 1983). Reflective teachers are considered to be those who use new problems as opportunities to expand their knowledge and competence. A number of studies have reported beneficial effects of fostering a "reflective stance" in teachers (Bean & Zulich, 1989, 1993; Bolin, 1988, 1990; see also Pollard, 1996).

The experience of one expert teacher illustrates reflective practice in teaching. When this teacher, who headed the students' school magazine, forbade students to publish artwork, poems, and stories he considered in bad taste, students protested and challenged the school. Students believed their right to free speech had been violated and that the school was engaging in censorship. Parents even came in to complain. Instead of digging in his heels, this expert teacher reflected on the situation and turned

When was the last time you "thought about thinking" as you debated in your own mind about how to solve a problem? Did it help?

SUGGESTION: Perhaps you recognized your own tendency to focus on negative outcomes of a situation. By noting this mechanism in your thinking, you became able to redirect negative thoughts. Thus thinking about thinking allowed you to improve problem solving.

Expert teachers use every situation as a learning opportunity. Here, students debate an issue about which both sides have strong feelings. (Will Hart)

it around, using the situation to advantage. He set up a series of debates for which students prepared in social studies class. He also set up an election to decide the issue, and had students practice opinion polling for credit as math projects. When it became clear his views on morality were not shared by the majority, he allowed a second school magazine to be created, giving each student the choice of whether to see and read the material he considered offensive. Had this teacher not reflected on the problem before him, extremely valuable learning opportunities would have been lost for all of the students.

■ **THE RELATIONSHIP BETWEEN AUTOMATIZING WELL-LEARNED SKILLS AND PLANNING, MONITORING, AND EVALUATING** The ability of experts to make skills automatic is related to their ability to be reflective and to think about thinking during problem solving. The mental resources that are saved when skills become automatic do not simply make problem solving easier for the expert. The saved resources are not lost; instead, they are available for higher level thinking that is beyond the capacity of the novice. Scardamalia and Bereiter (1996) believe this "reinvestment" of energy and mental resources is essential to being and becoming an expert. They believe true experts differ from experienced nonexperts because true experts *reinvest mental resources* to better understand problems. Whereas novices and experienced non-experts seek to reduce problems to fit what they already know, true experts are undaunted by complications, viewing them, instead, as challenges that allow them to work on the leading edge of their knowledge and skill.

THINKING PRACTICALLY

Name three ways a teacher's efficiency—or lack thereof—can affect her or his performance. Now name three ways a teacher might become more efficient.

SUGGESTION: Ways you might include, but are not limited to: time management in the classroom, quality of lesson preparation, scheduling of activities and hands-on work, and personal organization of notes, grade books, and materials.

Consider an example of an expert and a novice fourth-grade teacher confronted in September with students who seemingly will do anything to avoid math. The novice teacher may analyze the problem and conclude that the third-grade teacher last year disliked teaching math and, consequently, the students were not given much practice in math and were not shown that math can be enjoyable. The novice teacher's analysis of the problem might end here, and she or he would then use all available personal energy to review math and try to coerce the students to pay attention. The expert teacher, however, would perform a far richer analysis, made possible by his or her ability to deal quickly and easily with what was obvious about the math problem (for example, that the kids hated math) while reinvesting mental energy to think more deeply about the causes for the problem.

The expert teacher would review second- and third-grade math to determine how far behind the students were. At the same time, the expert teacher would assess individual students' progress to see if everyone was far behind, or whether only the most vocal students were far behind. The expert would see that three children apparently had learning disabilities in math, and others were actually ahead for their age but too embarrassed to show it for fear of being labeled "math nerds." The expert would also notice that the students talented in math apparently had not been complimented on this ability in the past, possibly because last year's teacher did not sufficiently emphasize math. This far richer and deeper analysis happens because the expert teacher is able automatically to teach her or his subject with less effort, thus having mental resources freed to develop a more complete picture of the problem, and ultimately, a more effective solution.

In summary, expert teachers are efficient in solving problems. By virtue of extensive experience, experts are able to perform many of the activities of teaching rapidly and with little cognitive effort. These automatic skills enable experts to devote attention to high-level reasoning and problem solving. In particular, experts plan and are self-aware in approaching problems—they do not jump into solution attempts prematurely. Beginning teachers must *learn* these behaviors with practice, just as Sandy had to learn from Danielle.

Both experts and novices apply knowledge and analysis to solve problems. Yet somehow experts are more likely to arrive at *creative* solutions to these problems—solutions that are both novel and appropriate.

■ **REDEFINING PROBLEMS** Experts do not simply solve the problem at hand; they often redefine the problem—that is, they do not take the problem at face value but instead cast the problem in a new light or see it from a new perspective. By redefining problems, experts reach ingenious and insightful solutions that somehow do not occur to others. These solutions are called *insightful* because they see into a problem deeply (Davidson, 1995; Mayer, 1995; Sternberg, 1996; Sternberg & Davidson, 1995).

Consider an example of an expert math teacher in a high-pressure high school in New York City. Dan repeatedly caught a small number of students cheating on class tests. He warned the cheaters at first, but he then caught others cheating. Most teachers would probably have thought about discipline-oriented methods for stopping the cheating, or ways to make tests more cheat-proof. But Dan redefined the problem. He asked himself, and the students, why they believed the cheating was going on. The answers surprised him. It turned out that parental pressure and competitiveness among students were increasing as the need to get scholarships to colleges was becoming more acute. Parents sometimes put unreasonable levels of pressure on their kids, who became pitted against one another in an "only 20 percent of us can get A's in math" game.

What did Dan do? He changed his grading system. He formulated a performance standard that he believed merited an A in his subject, and he cleared this standard with the principal and other math teachers. He announced that he did not care if every student in the class earned an A: What mattered was that the students showed mastery of the material at the level he defined. In other words, there would be no more grading on a curve. Although the students still had to know their math, Dan's strategy reduced competitiveness and increased students' tendencies to work collaboratively and study in groups for their tests. The new policy also encouraged students to ask more candid questions in class, because they no longer feared "giving away the answers and insights" to their peers. Cheating was no longer endemic in the classroom.

Thus by redefining the problem, Dan helped shift the emphasis in his classroom away from beating out the other kids, and onto meeting a performance standard by achieving highly as a group. Compared to previous years, a higher percentage of students ended up earning A's in the class, and the average level of performance was higher than in the past. Furthermore, when the class took the statewide math examination in June, it outperformed the other classes in the school. Thus by redefining the problem, this expert teacher had a positive impact on every student in his class.

■ **THREE KEY WAYS EXPERTS THINK ABOUT PROBLEMS** How and what do experts think about problems that makes their solutions more insightful than novices' solutions? Research has shown that three aspects contribute to experts' arriving at more insightful solutions than do novices (Davidson & Sternberg, 1984, 1998). First, experts distinguish information relevant to solving a problem from information that is not relevant. For example, an expert sees that a given piece of information—which others deem unimportant—is in fact important. Or the opposite: An expert sees that information everyone else thinks is important really does not matter.

For example, an expert teacher can distinguish lines of discussion that will help students learn the material from lines of discussion that will only complicate matters, or take everyone on a tangent. The expert teacher lecturing

THINKING CREATIVELY

Describe a recent time when you had a meaningful insight.

SUGGESTION: Perhaps you recall an occasion when the solution to a problem came to you all at once—for example, noting the price per square yard for carpeting, you remembered from math class how to compute the area of your bedroom floor and were able to compute the cost of new carpet.

THINKING CREATIVELY

Where do you think experts' insightful ideas come from? Might certain activities help teachers develop inventive ideas? What activities might hinder the development of insight in a teacher?

SUGGESTION: Experts report obtaining insights in multiple ways: from reading unrelated materials across a range of subjects, from seeing movies, from talking to other teachers, friends, or family, and so on. Activities that place a person into a new situation or context can stimulate insightful ideas, such as taking a course on a totally new topic, whereas those that are boring or overly repetitive can hinder insights by shutting down creative thoughts.

about photosynthesis sees a question about why plants need soil as an opportunity to point out that plants do not get food from soil, but rather from leaves; however, this same teacher sees a question about why plants have flowers and fruits as off-track for present purposes. This ability to know what really matters and what does not when solving problems is one reason experts tend to have more insightful solutions to problems than do novices.

Second, experts combine information in ways that are useful for problem solving. Experts can see that two pieces of information that seem irrelevant when considered separately can become relevant if combined. For example, an expert teacher recognizes

AT EVERY SCHOOL LEVEL, TEACHERS FACE SPECIAL CHALLENGES.

Elementary teachers teach basic skills such as reading, but they also must know about arts and crafts and other types of activities that appeal to young children. A kindergarten teacher explains calendar concepts to her class. (Elizabeth Crews)

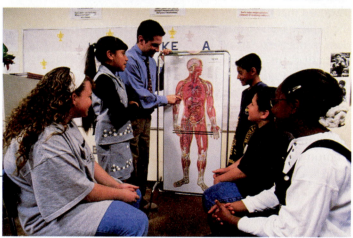

Middle-school teachers deal with adolescents, so they must understand the confusion of growing into an adult in a challenging society. This middle-school teacher explains anatomy to his biology class. (Will Hart, PhotoEdit)

High-school teachers must be able to motivate students for the world beyond school—helping them to choose among different vocations, careers, or colleges. A teacher and a small group of students discuss newspaper coverage of a current event. (Charles Gupton, Stock Boston)

that expensive new clothes, when combined with a drop in grades, may signal that a student is working too many hours at an after-school job. This ability to combine information to get new meaning from it is another reason experts have more insightful solutions to problems.

Third, experts apply to a teaching problem information acquired in another context. Obviously, in order to *apply* acquired knowledge, you have to have *acquired* it. Thus this aspect of expert thinking shows why having more and better organized knowledge is essential to being an expert. Expert teachers are adept at observing and applying an analogy in order to solve a problem. For example, an expert teacher may notice a similarity between a current classroom problem, such as managing a group of bright but disruptive students, and a problem she has seen solved earlier— perhaps in a business magazine article on the shareholder rights movement. The article may have noted that heads of corporations sometimes try to assuage volatile shareholders by listing the reasons why the corporate leaders are better equipped to make decisions about the organization's future than are the average shareholders, ultimately stressing that everyone comes out ahead if the best interests of the corporation are served.

The expert teacher remembering this article borrows a few suggestions. She asks the class to brainstorm why having someone in charge of the class is helpful to each one of them—particularly if they want to be admitted to college one day and must pass yearly examinations and get good grades. Or she asks the class to nominate the person they believe is best prepared to decide what the class should learn, with the person's qualifications listed in terms of training and experience. Or she stresses that she and her class members all share a common interest and that by working together they can best achieve their goals.

Expert teachers frequently exploit analogies between things that are *familiar* to their students (for example, a crowd of people moving through a set of turnstiles), and things that are *new* to their students (for example, electrical resistance in DC circuits). Expert teachers are able to explore the analogy between the two, and their ability to explore the analogy means they can come up with insightful solutions that would never occur to a novice. Again, having a lot of knowledge that is well organized is essential to an expert's ability: The more knowledge a teacher has, and the better this knowledge is organized, the more likely the teacher is to see meaningful analogies between problems and to arrive at more insightful solutions.

 ## ADVANTAGES OF EXPERTISE

In summary, expert teachers are insightful in solving problems. When solving a problem they are able to identify information that is promising and can combine that information effectively. Expert teachers are also able to develop and refine their thinking about a problem by observing and applying relevant analogies. As a result of these types of processes, expert teachers gain an advantage over novice teachers. Expert teachers are thus able to arrive at solutions to problems that are both novel and appropriate.

There are as many different ways to be an expert teacher as there are expert teachers themselves: Expert teachers differ in their personalities and specific gifts. However, *all* expert teachers have more knowledge, are generally more efficient, and have more insights than novice teachers. To become an expert teacher, you will need to develop knowledge, efficiency, and insights into problems. You will develop these three skills through your work in your educational psychology course, through your work in your other courses, and through hands-on practice in teaching and especially in student teaching working alongside experienced role models.

As you develop these three expert attributes, you will become better able to show and build on your personal strengths in the context of the classroom. Depending on the level of students you will teach, the exact skills you will require may differ: An expert

THINKING ANALYTICALLY

Drawing on your own experiences as a student, suggest three ways an expert teacher for elementary school differs from an expert teacher for high school or middle school. What do you remember about your own teachers that is relevant to your answer?

SUGGESTION: Expert elementary teachers have to know about arts and crafts and the types of activities that appeal to young children. They need to know how to teach basic skills such as reading. Expert middle school teachers must deal with adolescents; they need to understand the confusion of growing into an adult in a challenging society. Expert high school teachers must be able to motivate students for the world beyond school— possibly helping them choose among different careers, vocations, or colleges. High school teachers must handle students who are becoming independent of their parents.

Expert teachers can mentor novice teachers by giving them advice, information, and support. (Will Hart)

teacher of elementary school students may differ from an expert teacher of middle or high school students. Similarly, in the later grades and in postsecondary education, experts may differ as a function of subject taught. The social studies teacher, the art teacher, and the mathematics teacher may need to use somewhat different strategies to be expert. But all teachers, regardless of level or subject, need the features of expert teachers just discussed.

Expert teachers differ from novice teachers in their amount and depth of knowledge, their efficiency, and their insights into problems on the job. This book will help you develop these three attributes so you will become an expert teacher. We will help you learn important background knowledge that you can apply daily in the classroom. We will review techniques for effective teaching that will make you an efficient teacher and equip you with the tools to develop your own insights into the problems you face. As we wrote this book, we focused on your needs as a developing teacher. As we covered topics in psychology that are relevant to education, we concentrated on how you can apply what you are learning to the ultimate challenges you will encounter when you begin teaching.

After you have read this book, you will be well on your way to becoming an expert teacher. Like Sandy, the teacher in the opening vignette, you will have acquired wisdom from other experienced teachers, whose lessons and advice fill these pages. This book can help you in much the same way as a friend who is an experienced teacher: You will acquire wisdom by reading and thinking about the material contained here, which is based on research in psychology that can help you teach more effectively. Think of this book as your own personal mentor or expert teacher who is willing to share knowledge you will need to develop into an expert teacher yourself.

Implications for Teaching

- *Teachers become expert by learning from experience about the content of the subjects they teach, about general methods for teaching, and about specific methods that work to teach their content areas.* There is no one magic recipe for becoming an expert: Instead, many pieces of a large puzzle must be assembled individually by each person wishing to become an expert.

- *Teachers become expert by growing in efficiency as they "think about thinking" and learn to make daily tasks and routines automatic.* Most important skills start out seeming harder than they will seem in the future. Expertise grows over time.

■ *Teachers become expert by developing their insight and ability to solve problems by understanding the important aspects of problems, understanding how other solutions in the past can be used to solve problems in the present, and understanding how to reorganize problems to make them easier to solve.* These are skills you can develop, as long as you are willing to put in the work.

What Do We Know About *Expert Students?*

The discussion of what it takes to become an expert teacher is incomplete without our considering the other side of the equation—what it takes to be an expert student. Right now, as you read this book, you are striving to be an expert student. Later, as you lead a class, you will want to help each of your students be as expert at learning as possible. What does research in educational psychology say about the characteristics of expert students and learners?

USE OF EFFECTIVE LEARNING STRATEGIES

One important attribute of expert students is their use of strategies to help them learn, remember, and use information. They may acquire these strategies through direct instruction from their classroom teachers. Or expert students may learn strategies from other students and friends by studying in groups. Parents can provide a source of strategies, as can other adults, such as librarians, tutors, and even child-care professionals. Often, expert students even invent strategies on their own.

■**MEMORIZATION STRATEGIES** You have probably heard of the memorization strategy. Table 1.1 presents some of the memorization strategies found most helpful by college students. Research has shown that memorization and other learning strategies

TABLE 1.1 **Memory Strategies and Their Use**

■ **Categorical clustering:** Organize a list of items into a set of categories (for example, memorizing the dairy items separately from the fruits on a grocery list).

■ **Interactive images:** Create images that link the isolated words in a list (for example, to remember the words *car, blister, tornado,* picture a car with blistering paint being blown by a tornado).

■ **Pegwords:** Associate words with words on a previously memorized list, using interactive images (for example, the nursery rhyme, "one is a bun, two is a shoe, three is a tree," etc.).

■ **Method of loci:** Link well-known landmarks in an area to items to be remembered (for example, visualize a car in your driveway, a tornado on the edge of your yard, and a blister in the porch paint).

■ **Acronym:** Create an abbreviation (for example, people in therapy are counseled not to allow themselves to become HALT: hungry, angry, lonely, or tired).

■ **Acrostic:** Form a whole sentence made out of words beginning with the letters that start the words you wish to remember (for example, Hang And Look Tough).

■ **Keywords:** Form an interactive image linking the sound and meaning of a foreign word with the sound and meaning of the familiar word (for example, the Spanish word for cat is *gato*—you might picture a cat sitting on a gate, and later when you hear *gato* you will think of the cat sitting by the gate and remember that *gato* means cat).

FOCUS ON: BECOMING AN EXPERT TEACHER

JANET L. PINKERTON: EASLEY ELEMENTARY SCHOOL, DURHAM, NORTH CAROLINA — GRADE 2

Jan Pinkerton has 24 years of experience teaching second grade. She received board certification as an Early Childhood Educator in 1998 from the National Board for Professional Teaching Standards, and now advises and supports other teachers as they complete the challenging certification process.

What are some characteristics of an expert teacher?

The teachers I've always looked up to have a lot of knowledge. They know children and child development, and they use age-appropriate strategies to teach. They know their curriculum well. They also know the process of learning. Elementary school teachers, for example, need to know how students learn to read and write. Expert teachers use all this knowledge to teach at the right level for the students.

The expert teachers I've known also freely display affection and kindness to the students. I believe it's important to treat students the way you would want to be treated. I still give my students

hugs, although some teachers are not very comfortable doing that. I believe school should be a safe, warm, loving, encouraging place for children. The academic learning will come, but first students need to feel welcome in school.

Expert teachers model good academic behavior to their students, as well as appropriate personal and social behavior. They always behave professionally. As a board-certified teacher, I've also come to believe that it's important for teachers to be leaders in their communities, and advocates for their profession. Expert teachers make the time to talk to and encourage future teachers and to supervise student teachers, for example.

Have you noticed any characteristics that distinguish expert from novice teachers?

One of the key characteristics of an expert teacher seems to be efficient organization. Efficiency involves several aspects. First, teachers need to be constantly watching and assessing students'

progress in all areas. If they are efficient, teachers find a way to record and reflect on these observations regularly. If a parent or another teacher asks a question about a student, the expert teacher has the information she needs at her fingertips.

Efficiency also means making wise use of time. Efficient teachers organize the day so that students transition easily from one activity to another. There are not a lot of ten-minute "down" times, when the teacher has nothing planned for the children to do.

These kinds of efficiency did not come naturally to me, and I don't think they come naturally for most teachers. I recommend that new teachers do everything they can to learn organizational "tricks of the trade" from experienced mentors.

What can readers of this textbook do to become expert students and preservice teachers?

There are several ways students might begin preparing for their teaching

THINKING PRACTICALLY

Name three learning strategies you have used in the past, and evaluate how well each one worked and why.

SUGGESTION: Mnemonic devices are successful tools to aid memorization. Underlining key terms helps in processing information and in studying for exams. Think-aloud protocols help in developing understanding of processes and aid in avoiding errors in reasoning.

are *learned* in the first place; thus you can learn more and more effective strategies today for use in your adult life (Carr, Kurtz, Schneider, Turner, & Borkowski, 1989; Schneider & Sodian, 1997). If your own memory skills are not what you would like, you might consider a brief study skills course. These are offered at many colleges. Or you might consult a textbook such as *Teaching Study Skills: A Guide for Teachers* (Devine, 1987), which reviews many effective study skills.

When you learn a new strategy for studying, through whatever means, you must work to maintain the strategy. In other words, you must use the strategy to remember it. If you are preparing for a test in history, actually use a couple of the memory strategies in Table 1.1 in order to learn these strategies thoroughly and keep them fresh. Another goal of the expert student is to watch for ways to transfer strategies by using them with new material and in new contexts. Thus memory strategies you use to remember history facts can help you remember foreign language words. Memory strategies can also help you keep track of guests' names the next time you are at a party, or remember what you need at the grocery store so you do not have to make a list.

■ **EVALUATING STRATEGIES** A key point for expert students is that they will use strategies more effectively and more often if they know the strategies work (Borkowski, Levers, & Gruenenfelder, 1976; Ringel & Springer, 1980). Expert students monitor the

careers. First, collect *every* bit of information that comes your way. Experience will tell you later what you can safely discard, but in the meantime, you should prepare for anything. For example, I would recommend that elementary school teachers read all the children's literature they can find. Get the American Library Association's list of award-winning books, and read them.

College is also the best time to study the experts in the field where you'd like to work. It's vital to understand theories of learning, and read the most recent research available in your field. As a practicing teacher, you may not have as much time to study the research in detail, so it's important to have thorough background knowledge that will help you follow new directions in education.

Finally, keep an open mind about what kind of school you want to go to. Don't be biased by preconceived ideas. You may have heard a lot about the difficulties of teaching in underfunded schools, or in inner-city schools, but an inner-city school may actually end up being a wonderful teaching experience for you.

What other advice do you have for new teachers?

I would advise new teachers to seek out their colleagues. There is a big danger of isolation in the first year. New teachers may feel that they are all alone in their classroom and that only the principal knows if they are sinking or swimming. This is a horrible situation to be in. Other teachers are usually willing to help you, but they have a lot to do. They may not come to you, so you have to go to them. Don't be afraid to do it.

Even more important is how you relate to the children. Sometimes, teachers start their first year with a very idealistic feeling that they will love every child they teach. Then, they may be distressed when they find a child that they just do not like. It can be difficult to love a child who misbehaves a lot or one who is socially awkward. Teachers need to know that they won't love every child, and that it's OK to feel that way. But they also need to learn to ignore those feelings. Teachers must go into the classroom committed to treating every child fairly and justly. I also strive to find something positive about every child, something special that makes that child stand out from the others. A teacher can build on that. My hope at the end of the year is that every child feels it has been a special year with a teacher who thinks they were wonderful in some way.

> My hope at the end of the year is that every child feels it has been a special year with a teacher who thinks they were wonderful in some way.

effectiveness of their strategies by testing them to see which ones lead to increases in performance. For example, one study compared the performance of adults and children using two different strategies while learning foreign vocabulary words (Pressley, Ross, Levin, & Ghatala, 1984; see also Pressley, Levin, & Ghatala, 1988). Only after being tested on their ability to remember the words, and after being given feedback on how well they did, did the adults and children truly recognize the value of the better of the two strategies. Once they knew a given strategy worked well, these individuals continued to use it in the future. Thus the expert student must be attentive and keep tabs on gains in performance associated with different strategies. In general, students who become expert learners frequently ask themselves, "How is my current approach to studying working, and how could it be improved?" (Pressley, Ross, Levin, & Ghatala, 1984).

An important benefit of using learning strategies is that they can sometimes help compensate for lack of knowledge. For example, beginning readers who lack a knowledge base of vocabulary words must rely more heavily on strategies such as sounding out words than do advanced readers (Forsyth, Forbes, Scheitler, & Schwade, 1998; Pressley & Afflerbach, 1995). For the college-level student who is working to build a knowledge base, effective study skills and strategies can also be helpful in overcoming a temporary lack of knowledge and in acquiring needed knowledge.

One way you can tell what strategies you are now using is through **think-aloud protocols.** Think-aloud protocols are just what they sound like: You think aloud and methodically state your steps in solving a problem or doing a task. By thinking aloud and

Expert students use a variety of strategies to excel. This expert high school student works in a dedicated home environment in which she can study without distraction, enhancing her use of these strategies and thus her learning. (Elizabeth Crews)

verbalizing your steps and reasoning, you may find places where your reasoning is not sound or your strategy could be improved. Pritchard (1990) used the think-aloud technique to show that students reread and paraphrase more when they try to understand texts with unfamiliar versus familiar material. Presumably, these strategies (rereading and paraphrasing) helped students process and understand unfamiliar material. Even when students have knowledge relevant to a task, use of strategies can improve their performance. Prior knowledge definitely enhances learning on a topic, but strategy use can enhance learning still more (Woloshyn, Pressley, & Schneider, 1992).

Some helpful general learning strategies are described in Table 1.2, adapted from research by Williams, Blythe, White, Li, Sternberg, and Gardner (1996).

 INCREMENTAL VIEW OF INTELLIGENCE

Many students believe that intelligence is something they are born with, some students have more of it than others, and there is not much they can do to increase their intelligence. (Maybe you are one of these students.) Fortunately, research has shown that intelligence can be increased (Nickerson, 1994; Nickerson, Perkins, & Smith, 1985; Sternberg, 1997a, 1997b, 1998a, 1998b, 1999; Wagner & Sternberg, 1984). It is not hard to see that becoming an expert student is easier if one believes that intelligence can be increased through training and effort. In fact, some researchers have shown that motivation to achieve is linked to *the belief that intelligence can be increased*—an **incremental view**— as opposed to *the belief that intelligence is fixed*—an **entity view** (Brophy, 1998; Dweck & Leggett, 1988; Henderson & Dweck, 1990).

Why is an entity view unproductive for students? Students who believe intelligence is fixed tend to take negative evaluations of their abilities and performance very personally, seeing these evaluations as signs that they simply are not intelligent enough to succeed. Students with an entity view therefore tend to avoid situations in which they might get negative feedback, and thus tend to avoid challenges. Failure is often debilitating for these students. They are left feeling, "Why bother? I'm just not smart enough to do any better." Consider, however, the perceptions of students with an incremental view. These students see corrective feedback as an indication that more work and effort are needed to remediate the weakness. They respond to failure by working harder in the future. They seek out challenges because these challenges represent learning experiences. This pattern of findings about the consequences

THINKING ANALYTICALLY

What type of evidence would you require in order to believe your own intelligence in an area had improved?

SUGGESTION: Higher test scores, better understanding of teachers' and other students' classroom comments, enhanced interest in subject matter, improved writing about the topic, recognition from teachers and peers that performance has improved.

TABLE 1.2　General Strategies for Improving Learning and Performance

1. Knowing Why

Why does school exist? Why should students learn to read, write, do homework, or take tests? In order to succeed in school, students need to know the purposes of various school tasks, how learning is relevant to their lives now, and how they can use it to improve their lives later. Students and teachers should ask:

- What are the purposes of reading in and out of school?

- How is reading more or less effective than other ways of getting information?

- What are the purposes of writing in and out of school?

- What are the differences between written information and other types of information?

- What is the purpose of homework?

- How does homework relate to other work in and out of school, now and later?

- What are the roles of tests in and out of school?

- How does testing relate to other class work?

2. Knowing Self

What are the student's personal strengths, weaknesses, habits, and interests? Self-assessment techniques can help students understand their own work habits and intellectual preferences, and then focus on how to capitalize on strengths and compensate for weaknesses. Students should:

- Recognize current reading patterns and preferences.

- Identify personal strengths and weaknesses in terms of reading.

- Recognize current reading practices.

- Recognize current writing practices.

- Identify personal strengths and weaknesses in terms of writing.

- Know how to incorporate personal interests and expertise into writing assignments.

- Recognize current homework practice.

- Identify personal strengths and weaknesses in terms of homework.

- Recognize current study strategies and test-taking practices.

- Identify personal strengths and weaknesses in terms of testing.

3. Knowing Differences

How do school subjects differ from one another in content, learning process, and typical testing format? How is studying for a math test, for example, different from studying for social studies? How are the demands of schools similar to and different from life outside of school? As students recognize the connections and distinctions among these different kinds of work, they can begin to vary their strategies and working styles appropriately. Students should:

- Understand the different kinds of written material, and their different purposes, and know reading approaches that are appropriate for each.

- Know how to write for different types of assignments and audiences.

- Know different styles of and strategies for writing.

- Know the homework requirements for different classes.

- Understand the different kinds of homework and the different approaches that are appropriate for each.

- Recognize different kinds of tests and test questions, within and across subjects.

- Know what each test can and cannot determine about the test taker.

- Know different strategies that are appropriate for each test.

4. Knowing Process

What should a student do when stymied? What steps (such as making plans and using resources) are involved in completing school tasks? As students focus on process, recognizing and defining problems for themselves, they can plan effective strategies, locate and allocate resources, and use what they know to accomplish their work. Students should:

- Know strategies for reading actively.

- Know how to get unstuck.

- Understand how writing involves planning and organization.

- Know strategies and resources to overcome difficulties in writing.

- Get organized.

- Know and use resources.

- Incorporate personal interests, talents, and past experience into the work.

- Understand that long-term preparation is necessary to prepare for tests.

- Know both long-term and short-term strategies for test preparation, as well as strategies for solving problems during actual test taking.

5. Reworking

Is the first draft of an assignment the best one? Probably not. Taking time to go over work does not always seem worth it, but successful students recognize the importance of self-monitoring and reflection. Reworking pays off. Students should:

- Understand the purpose of rereading.

- Develop strategies for rereading effectively.

- Understand the importance of revision.

- Know how to revise.

- Understand the purpose of reworking homework.

- Develop strategies for going over homework and checking for errors.

- Use the results of tests as an opportunity for self-reflection and a stepping-stone toward more productive learning and test taking.

Source: From *Practical Intelligence for School* by W.M. Williams, T. Blythe, N. White, J. Li, R.J. Sternberg and H.I. Gardner. Copyright © 1996. Reprinted by permission of Addison-Wesley Educational Publishers, Inc.

of entity versus incremental views of intelligence has emerged from the work of many researchers (Dweck, 1999; Dweck & Leggett, 1988; Elliott & Dweck, 1988; Henderson & Dweck, 1990; Meece, Blumenfeld, & Hoyle, 1988; Wood & Bandura, 1989).

One particularly interesting study of the role of students' conceptions of intelligence in their performance was conducted by Ames and Archer (1988). Ames and Archer called incremental beliefs **mastery-oriented beliefs,** because the *students with these beliefs were concerned with mastering material.* Entity beliefs were called **performance-oriented beliefs** because *students with these beliefs were concerned with performing well.* Students with mastery-oriented beliefs, as compared with students having performance-oriented beliefs, used more strategies and more effective strategies in their schoolwork, were more open to challenging tasks, had a more positive attitude, and were more likely to believe that effort was the key to improvement in performance. Thus mastery-oriented beliefs were clearly superior to performance-oriented beliefs.

Consider some of the statements mastery-oriented students agreed with: "Making mistakes is a part of learning"; "I work hard to learn"; and "Students are given a chance to correct mistakes." Now consider some of the statements performance-oriented students agreed with: "Only a few students can get top marks"; "I really do not like to make mistakes"; and "I work hard to get a high grade" (Ames & Archer, 1988, p. 262). A substantial body of research indicates that focusing on effort and hard work as a route to mastering material is the hallmark of the expert student. From the point of view of the teacher, success for all students is only possible in a learning environment focused on mastery of material.

HIGH ASPIRATIONS

Markus and Nurius (1986) have pointed out that our beliefs about what we can become in life are important motivators that propel us toward future accomplishments, or, conversely, limit our efforts and accomplishments. Expert students have high aspirations: They believe they can achieve highly in life, and they work to make these achievements happen. Expert students believe they can succeed in life if they work hard. Although it is true that aspirations have to be realistic—not all of us can become astronauts or star professional athletes, for example—high aspirations tend to be positive motivators in students' lives.

Even when discrimination, poverty, or immigration status might limit students' participation in education, students can be encouraged to develop realistically high aspirations to increase their chances for success (see, e.g., Day, Borkowski, Dietmeyer, Howsepian, & Saenz, 1994). In this study, researchers stressed to Mexican American students the steps involved in making it through the educational process, as well as the rewards, such as good jobs and steady income, that result from completing school. The researchers taught the students that paths to success are always full of obstacles that must be overcome. The students in this study earned higher grades and had greater expectations of future success than did students not in the study. Thus teachers need to stress to their students the many steps involved in making it through school. Students especially need to know that paths to success are always full of obstacles. In addition, they should know the rewards of completing school, such as good jobs and income.

HIGH PERCEIVED SELF-EFFICACY

Expert students have high perceived **self-efficacy:** *They believe they are capable of succeeding in school* (Bandura, 1986, 1995; Bandura et al., 1996; Schunk, 1991). Students who believe they are capable of succeeding in school attempt more challenging tasks and achieve more academically as they progress through school (Schunk, 1998; Zimmerman, Bandura, & Martinez-Pons, 1992). As you would expect, previous success at an activity increases perceived self-efficacy—nothing succeeds like success. In addition, positive social role models can have an effect on perceived self-efficacy, especially encouraging role models who demonstrate how to succeed at a given activity (Schunk, 1990, 1991).

DEVELOPING TEACHING AND
LEARNING EXPERTISE

IN EACH CHAPTER OF THE TEXT, WE INTRODUCE YOU TO A FEW SPECIFIC STRATEGIES—
ANALYTICAL, CREATIVE, AND PRACTICAL—USED BY BOTH EXPERT TEACHERS AND EXPERT STUDENTS.

THE ANALYTICAL TEACHER: Sam sits down at the end of the week and evaluates which lessons worked the best for his students, which did not work well, and why.

THE CREATIVE TEACHER: Sam cuts the teacher of the week profile out of his teaching newsletter, and he adapts three ideas from the profile to use in his own classroom.

THE PRACTICAL TEACHER: Sam watches and listens to his colleagues, and listens to what students say about his colleagues, in order to learn from his colleagues' accomplishments and mistakes.

THE ANALYTICAL STUDENT: When Jamal recognizes his work is slipping, he reviews a list of key study habits (handed out by his teacher) in order to determine what he is doing wrong.

THE CREATIVE STUDENT: Jamal challenges himself by writing down and striving to meet different goals on a day-to-day basis to keep his study time from becoming boring and repetitive.

THE PRACTICAL STUDENT: Jamal organizes study groups with his friends, in which they help one another and push each other to work harder.

But self-efficacy tends to be found in particular domains. It is not usually experienced for everything one might possibly attempt. For example, students often have high self-efficacy in one subject (such as math) and low self-efficacy in another subject (such as English), and this self-knowledge tends to be accurate and reflective of students' areas of strong and weak performance (Marsh, 1992; Marsh & Craven, 1991; Wolters & Pintrich, 1998). A practical suggestion for students seeking to become more expert in an area is to focus on good performances in areas already mastered to bolster confidence and enhance effort when confronting a weaker area.

Another important finding about self-efficacy is that people tend to tolerate failures better when they have a previous record of success in an area—but that failure can be devastating to self-efficacy when it accompanies a first try at a new goal (Bandura, 1986; Schunk, 1991). These findings about self-efficacy make sense; students tend to be more vulnerable to failure and criticism when they try something new compared with when they try to move up a level in doing something they can already do well. Thus it is important to create a record of success for yourself when you work at developing proficiency in an area. Taking on too much too soon can lead to early failure and the belief that you just are not capable of succeeding, when in fact, if you had taken on a smaller portion of the task, you would have succeeded.

THINKING PRACTICALLY

Name three things you can do to improve your perceived self-efficacy.

SUGGESTION: Study, work hard, achieve more. Keep records of achievements. Seek out feedback—work for good results, and keep reminding yourself of past successes.

PURSUIT OF A TASK TO COMPLETION

We have just finished explaining that expert students have high perceived self-efficacy. One reason is that they see tasks through to completion: These students get things done without getting stuck in the middle. Often, students know how to get started on a task, but then, in the middle of the task, they lose momentum—because of frustration, inability to find necessary information, slow rates of progress, and other factors—and fail to finish. Expert students, however, use many different methods to help them through stumbling blocks and see tasks through. Let us consider some of these methods.

Lyn Corno (1994) studied student **volition,** which she defined as the tendency *to continue to pursue a goal* once the student began to take action to reach that goal. Corno studied how students could increase their rate of completion of tasks to ensure that they met their goals. She noted that, to increase their volition, students need to know

WHAT DO WE KNOW ABOUT *EXPERT STUDENTS*?

Name five strategies you can use to increase your ability to see tasks through to completion.

SUGGESTION: Make a list of all steps necessary to complete the task; set aside a specific amount of time each day to work on the task; visualize yourself being successful; gain motivation by talking to others who have done the task before; decide on a tangible reward you will allow yourself once the task is completed.

how to control and monitor their attention to tasks and to eliminate distractions. One way for students to control attention and eliminate distractions is to generate their own verbal self-instructions to keep on task (Pressley, 1979; see also Rath, 1998): For example, students can tell themselves to ignore distractions at the first sign of these distractions. Expert students must also know how to manage their study time: They must know when to take breaks and when to push on (Corno, 1989). Knowing when a break is needed to improve effectiveness of learning comes with experience; however, it is important for students not to confuse needing a break with laziness.

To see tasks through, expert students must also know how to control anxiety. Students can control anxiety by reminding themselves to remain calm and focused on a given task (Corno, 1989). Another skill expert students need is to know how to motivate themselves. Self-motivation is enhanced if students visualize successful completion of a task and focus on the rewards successful completion will bring. Students can also rehearse positively affirming statements, such as "I know this material, and I'll succeed next time," "I am capable of doing well on this task," "I can do as well as anyone else if I try hard," and so on.

In general, to become expert learners, students must develop strategies for improving performance and then try out these strategies. If we ask expert students about the types of learning strategies they use, we find these strategies share certain aspects, such as knowing oneself and, particularly, knowing one's preferred working conditions; knowing how to motivate oneself; knowing how to overcome roadblocks and obtain assistance from others when necessary; knowing how to locate information and resources; and knowing how to gauge when work is ready to be handed in. Expert students must also learn to control their environments as much as possible and to remove or reduce distractions—even creating specific environments explicitly designed to enhance their learning and use of strategies (Corno, 1989, 1992; Pressley, 1995). In summary, expert students can learn strategies to help them succeed, and by applying these strategies, expert students can increase their ability to see tasks through to completion.

 RESPONSIBILITY FOR SELF AND ACTIONS

Part of being an expert student is to take responsibility for yourself—both for your successes and for your failures. Expert students must be willing to take control of a task, to criticize themselves, and, conversely, to take pride in their best work. Unfortunately, many students fail to become expert learners because they always look for outside causes for their failures (for example, teachers, other students, or illnesses).

THINKING **ANALYTICALLY**

Do you have a more *internal* or a more *external* responsibility pattern?

SUGGESTION: Ask yourself if you tend to respond better to others' demands and expectations and to outside forces such as school deadlines, or, rather, to your own push to excel and succeed and your own list of goals.

People differ widely in the extent to which they take responsibility for the causes and consequences of their actions. Rotter (1966) has distinguished between two personality patterns, which he refers to as **internal** and **external.** Internals are people who tend to take responsibility for their lives. When things go well for them, they take credit for their efforts, but when things do not go well, they tend to take responsibility and try to make things go better. Externals, in contrast, tend to place responsibility outside themselves, especially when things do not go well. They are quick to blame circumstances for their failures (and often to attribute their successes to external circumstances as well). Expert students tend to be more oriented toward the internal side of Rotter's continuum.

Of course, almost no one is purely internal or external. Moreover, all of us know people who accept credit for their successes but who blame others for their failures, or who never credit themselves for their successes but who do blame themselves for their failures. The most realistic people recognize that both success and failure come about as an interaction between our own contributions and those of others.

Part of being an expert student is being able to work on a project or task for a long time without immediate rewards. Students must learn that rewards do not always come immediately: To be expert, students must learn to delay gratification, because there are clear benefits of doing so. Many students believe they should be rewarded immediately for good performance. However, the greatest rewards in life are often those that come in the distant future, and expert students understand this fact.

In a series of studies extending over many years, Walter Mischel has found that children who are better able to delay gratification are more successful in various aspects of their lives, including their academic performance (see, e.g., Mischel, Shoda, & Rodriguez, 1989). In a typical study, Mischel places young children in a room and gives them a choice between an immediate but smaller reward and a later but larger reward. He puts various temptations in their paths. It is harder to resist temptation if the immediate reward (for example, a chocolate bar) is visible than if it is hidden. The ability of children to delay gratification can even predict their scores on the *Scholastic Assessment Test (SAT)* when they are much older. Thus we see that rewards for delaying gratification can sometimes surface years in the future. The lesson for expert students is clear: It is essential to learn to see tasks through without immediate rewards.

THINKING CREATIVELY

How good are you at delaying gratification? What inventive strategies might you use to help?

SUGGESTION: Ask yourself how long you can wait for a reward—whether a chocolate bar if you are hungry and crave candy, a new pair of athletic shoes once your best friend buys some, or a merit recognition award from your school that requires months of work to earn.

Implications for Teaching

■ *Expert teachers work to help their students become expert learners.* These teachers recognize that development of expertise in any area is a process that takes time, patience, and hard work.

■ *Expert students use strategies to help them learn, know that intelligence can be increased, have high aspirations and see themselves as capable of achieving these aspirations, see tasks through to completion, take responsibility for themselves and their actions, and understand the value of delaying gratification.* These are some of the many characteristics that distinguish the most effective from less effective students.

Educational Psychology Helps Create Expert Teachers and Students

The goal of the science of **educational psychology** is to take knowledge from the discipline of psychology that is relevant to education and to apply this knowledge in order to improve the quality and outcome of the educational process. Research in educational psychology seeks to find scientific answers to questions about the best ways to educate people. For example, educational psychologists might study whether special classes for talented and gifted students are the best way to educate these students, or they might study whether peer tutoring (when one student helps another) improves the performance of the students. Thus research in educational psychology answers questions of teachers and other education professionals about the best way to do their jobs.

Through the process of finding answers to individual questions, educational psychologists develop guiding principles that answer groups of questions on the same topic. **Principles** describe well-known and established relationships between events. For example, a principle you are probably familiar with is that home preparation and study time are important to reinforce material learned in the classroom. Once several principles have been uncovered regarding a particular topic, researchers sometimes develop a **theory** from these principles. Theories are scientific explanations for why events happen the way they do; theories also allow us to predict events in the future. An example of a theory in educational psychology is the idea that external rewards and punishments are important in shaping students' studying behavior and subsequent performance on tests.

Theories developed by different researchers may disagree in their explanations and predictions. Thus one person might believe rewards and punishments are what makes a student work hard, whereas another person might believe the student's inner need to achieve and excel are what makes the student work hard. Theories are different ways of seeing the world and explaining events, and competing theories often explain the same events, but do so in different ways.

Some educational psychologists conduct individual studies that answer specific questions. Other educational psychologists synthesize the results of many such studies and try to unite the outcomes of these studies into a coherent whole with a unified explanation. Conducting individual studies and compiling overviews of other scientists' studies are both important mechanisms in the development of effective principles and theories.

 DESCRIPTIVE RESEARCH

Educational psychologists conduct directly two types of studies to answer specific questions. The first is called **descriptive research.** Here, the scientist observes and describes what is happening in a situation without changing the dynamics of the situation. For example, a researcher observes a class of students with learning disabilities who are receiving specialized instruction in reading in an attempt to uncover which specific approaches by the teacher result in better learning, and whether students with mild, moderate, or severe learning disabilities benefit similarly or differently from the various teaching approaches. The researcher watches the class one day per week over a period of several months. Descriptions of individual students' disabilities and progress, the students' test scores, and information about what programs the teachers used can then be analyzed to determine if any patterns or relationships exist.

The researcher might be interested in whether students with severe learning disabilities respond to specialized instruction differently from those with mild learning disabilities. To answer this question, the researcher assesses if a **correlation** exists between the student's degree of learning disability (mild, moderate, or severe) and his or her score in reading. A correlation is a relationship between two measured things. A **positive correlation** means that when one of the things increases, the other also increases. A **negative correlation** means that when one of the things increases, the other decreases.

In the example of the children with learning disabilities, a positive correlation would indicate that as a child's degree of learning disability increases so does her score in reading (in other words, a student with a severe learning disability would score *higher* in reading than would a student with a mild learning disability). A (more likely) negative correlation would indicate that as a child's degree of learning disability increases, his score in reading decreases (in other words, students with severe learning disabilities would score *lower* in reading than would students with mild learning disabilities). When researchers compute correlations on the data they collect, they try to determine whether the results are **statistically significant;** that is, the results are unlikely if only random or chance variation were operative.

Some descriptive research can take the form of a **case study,** an in-depth observation of one individual. For example, many classic case studies describe highly gifted inner-city teachers who, despite a lack of money and resources, nevertheless consistently produce outstanding and highly motivated students who go on to great achievements.

EXPERIMENTAL RESEARCH

The second type of study conducted directly by a researcher is called **experimental research,** which differs from descriptive research in that the scientist designs a test to answer a question and actually *changes* what happens to people so the effects can be observed. For example, a researcher might separate the students with learning disabilities at random into two groups, and ask the teacher to use one approach with one group and another approach with the other group. By comparing the test scores of the students in the two groups, the researcher learns if one method of instruction has worked better than the other.

FORUM

CONTENT KNOWLEDGE OR KNOWLEDGE ABOUT TEACHING?

Is in-depth content knowledge the most important skill for expert teachers to possess? Or is detailed knowledge of teaching and motivational strategies more important than content knowledge?

FIRST VIEW: *Content knowledge is more important for the expert teacher.* According to this view, detailed and thorough knowledge of the area they teach is what makes teachers experts. This detailed knowledge enables teachers to plan creative lessons that motivate and illuminate the subject matter for their students. Thorough knowledge also allows teachers to answer student questions accurately and to link clearly various subtopics within the area they teach, showing students the overarching themes in the area. Content knowledge enables teachers to plan classroom activities that extend what they are learning to other disciplines. Equally importantly, thorough content knowledge makes a teacher appear to be an expert in the eyes of students, which helps create and maintain an atmosphere of leadership in which students respect the teacher's knowledge and authority.

SECOND VIEW: *Knowledge about teaching is more important for the expert teacher.* This view states that no matter how well a teacher knows the area being taught, the teacher will be ineffective without direct knowledge about how to teach, also called pedagogical knowledge. Many experts in a content area are unable to give a lecture to novice students on what the experts do for a living— these experts may be unable to explain to beginners the importance of their domain. Good teaching requires the ability to capture students' attention, motivate students to learn, and distill the subject matter to reveal key points and issues for the beginner. Good teaching also entails knowing how to structure assignments to be challenging but not overwhelming, and knowing how to assess students' progress so the right balance and amount of material are presented. No amount of expert content knowledge provides teachers with these insights.

THIRD VIEW: A SYNTHESIS: *Both content knowledge and knowledge about teaching are essential to the expert teacher.* Research has shown that not only are both content knowledge and pedagogical knowledge important for effective teaching, a combined type of knowledge called pedagogical-content knowledge is also important (Shulman, 1987; Warren & Ogonowski, 1998). It is difficult for a teacher to become truly expert without thorough knowledge of the area being taught. It would also be difficult for a teacher to instruct and control

THINKING ANALYTICALLY

How would you study the effects of students' aspirations on their ultimate success? What are the important factors to consider in studying the effects of students' aspirations on what happens to these students later in life?

SUGGESTION: Chart the progress of a large group of students while regularly having them complete questionnaires about their aspirations and goals. Assess whether students with high aspirations are more successful. Remember that high aspirations may be the result of early success and demonstrated ability, which in turn leads to further success. Thus looking at the future success of students who have been equally successful so far but who have different levels of aspirations will tell more about the role of aspirations in the future.

a class without knowledge of teaching strategies and methods. In addition, however, specific knowledge about how to teach a given subject—pedagogical-content knowledge—is essential in the development of teaching expertise. For example, a math teacher may need to know specific strategies that work to teach math. These strategies might not work to teach English—an English teacher would need a separate set of specific content-area-related strategies. Thus expert teachers require *each one* of these *three* basic types of knowledge.

To say one method worked better, the two groups of students must be roughly equivalent, or subject to **random assignment.** Thus a student's likelihood of ending up in one group is equal to her or his likelihood of ending up in the other group. The students or people in experiments are sometimes called **subjects** (or *participants*). The important thing to remember about experimental research is that scientists get actively involved and *change* what happens to people in order to assess the effects of these changes. The groups of people who undergo such change by researchers are sometimes called **experimental groups.** Groups of people for whom nothing experimentally relevant is changed are called **control groups.** The purpose of control groups is to use their outcomes in comparison with those of the people in experimental groups (for whom something experimentally relevant was changed).

Both descriptive research and experimental research provide answers to questions about how best to educate students, and both types of research are valuable and important ways to gain information about how to become an expert teacher and how to help students become expert learners.

THINKING ANALYTICALLY

What types of questions are better answered by descriptive research? By experimental research?

SUGGESTION: Experiments work best when it is both ethical and feasible to assign subjects—in the case of educational psychology, students—to different classrooms, methods of instruction, textbooks, activities, and so on. Then the students' progress can be compared. Descriptive research works best when we wish to understand the subtleties and methods of a single great teacher or other working system that cannot be manipulated.

Implications for Teaching

- *Educational psychology uses science to uncover information that helps teachers solve problems and teach effectively.* Educational psychology is not simply folk wisdom or people's intuitions about teaching.

- *Educational psychology uncovers trends in how teachers teach and how students learn, and develops explanations for these trends so teachers can understand what happens in the classroom and why.* It can be a powerful tool for anyone wishing to develop teaching expertise.

- *Teachers can learn from descriptive research and case studies as well as from experimental research performed by educational psychologists and other scientists.* Many useful sources of valuable information are available about how to teach.

SUMMING IT UP

WHAT IS AN *EXPERT TEACHER?*

- We know a lot about what makes teachers expert. Expert teachers use reflective thinking to understand what they do right and wrong and how to improve. They have expert knowledge and more insight, although they do not necessarily have better memories or greater intelligence than novice teachers. Expert teachers also identify pertinent information that can help in solving a problem, and they combine this information effectively and use analogies to develop and refine their thinking.

- Three types of knowledge are important to expert teachers: content, pedagogical, and pedagogical-content knowledge. Also essential is the ability to automatize well-learned skills; having automatic skills allows teachers to get more done in less time and with less conscious thought. Finally, teachers who are expert plan what to do, monitor their progress, and evaluate their performance toward a goal.

WHAT DO WE KNOW ABOUT EXPERT STUDENTS?

- We also know something about what makes students expert. Expert students use and evaluate learning strategies to help them achieve their learning goals. Students with high self-efficacy believe they are capable of succeeding in school.

- According to the incremental view of intelligence, intelligence can be increased. In contrast, the entity view claims that intelligence is fixed or unchangeable. Expert students believe intelligence can be increased, and they focus on mastering material instead of on performing well by pleasing the teacher and getting high grades. These students' beliefs are called mastery-oriented beliefs. Students whose main concern is performing well on tests and in class are said to have performance-oriented beliefs.

- Expert students have high aspirations and high expectations of their ability to succeed in school. They also have volition: They see tasks through to completion. In addition, expert students are characterized by a responsibility pattern called internal, in which they take responsibility for themselves and their actions. This pattern contrasts with the external pattern, in which people blame circumstances for their failures. Finally, students called expert understand that they must delay gratification and work to achieve goals in the future.

HOW EDUCATIONAL PSYCHOLOGY HELPS CREATE EXPERT TEACHERS AND STUDENTS

- Educational psychology draws from the general discipline of psychology to improve the quality and outcome of the educational process. As a science, educational psychology develops principles and theories about learning and instruction.

- Descriptive and experimental research are both important ways to collect information. Subjects are the people who participate in scientific experiments. In sound scientific experiments, the subjects for each group or condition are chosen at random.

- Correlations show relationships between measured things. Statistically significant means the relationship is unlikely if only chance variation is operative. In a positive correlation, when one of two things increases, the other also increases. In a negative correlation, when one of the things increases, the other decreases. Control groups and experimental groups enable a researcher to test the effect of a specific change in the teaching environment.

KEY TERMS AND DEFINITIONS

- **Automatic** Mental processes that have become well learned and require little effort. Page 11

- **Automatize** Learn to perform important tasks without devoting much thought to them. Page 11

- **Case study** In-depth observation of one individual. Page 30

- **Control groups** Groups of people in an experiment for whom nothing experimentally relevant is changed. Page 32

- **Correlation** Relationship between two measured things or attributes; more exactly, the extent to which two or more measurements tend to vary together. Page 30

■ **Descriptive research** Research in which the scientist observes and describes what is happening in a situation without changing the dynamics of the situation. Page 30

■ **Educational psychology** Science that draws from psychology knowledge that is relevant to education and applies this knowledge to improving the quality and outcome of the educational process. Page 29

■ **Entity view** Belief that intelligence is fixed. Page 24

■ **Experimental groups** Groups of people for whom the scientist changes what happens. Page 32

■ **Experimental research** Research in which the scientist gets actively involved and changes what happens to people in order to assess the effects of these changes. Page 31

■ **Expert student** Student who uses strategies to learn efficiently and who is open to challenges and willing to overcome problems to achieve learning goals. Page 5

■ **Expert teacher** Teacher who uses a broad base of organized knowledge and experience efficiently and creatively to solve the many kinds of problems that occur in educational settings. Page 4

■ **External personality pattern** Tendency to place responsibility outside of oneself (i.e., to blame outside circumstances). Page 28

■ **Incremental view** Belief that intelligence can be increased. Page 24

■ **Internal personality pattern** Tendency to take personal responsibility for events. Page 28

■ **Mastery-oriented beliefs** Focus on meaningful learning and understanding of material. Page 26

■ **Metacognitive processes** Processes used in deliberately thinking about how one thinks, often in an effort to improve one's thinking. Page 14

■ **Negative correlation** Relationship between two measured things such that as one increases, the other decreases. Page 30

■ **Performance-oriented beliefs** Beliefs that focus on performing well and obtaining good grades on tests and in class. Page 26

■ **Positive correlation** Relationship between two measured things such that as one increases, the other also increases. Page 30

■ **Principles** Well-known and established relationships between events. Page 30

■ **Random assignment** Process in which experimental subjects are placed in groups with every person having an equivalent chance of being placed into a given group. Page 32

■ **Reflective thinking** Thinking about one's actions and attempting to understand what one is doing right and wrong and why. Page 6

■ **Self-efficacy** Belief that one can accomplish what one desires to accomplish. Page 26

■ **Statistically significant** Relationship between measured quantities that is unlikely if only chance variation is operative. Page 30

■ **Subjects** People who participate in scientific experiments. Page 32

■ **Theory** Systematic statement of general principles that explains known facts or events. Theories state the relations among sets of events so one can predict events in the future. Page 30

■ **Think-aloud protocols** Output of a procedure in which a person thinks aloud and methodically states the steps in solving a problem or doing a task. Page 23

■ **Volition** Motivation to continue to pursue a goal. Page 27

BECOMING AN EXPERT: QUESTIONS AND PROBLEMS

Apply the concepts you have learned in this chapter to the following problems of classroom practice.

IN ELEMENTARY SCHOOL

1. You are in charge of a class of 18 first graders. How important do you believe each of the three types of teaching knowledge (content knowledge, pedagogical knowledge, and pedagogical-content knowledge) will be in your teaching? Which type of knowledge will be the most (least) important to you?

2. You are teaching a fourth-grade class. Your students are basically bright and do well in school. What skills should you attempt to automatize to make your daily life on the job easier?

3. Several students in your third-grade class seem to believe they were born too stupid to do well in school. How can you show these students that their intelligence can be increased? What is the advantage of convincing these students that intelligence increases as a result of effort?

4. Your sixth-grade class is filled with students who set their sights low when it comes to accomplishments and expectations of themselves. You believe many of the parents of these students do not provide much encouragement in the home. What steps can you take to encourage your students to have high aspirations? Why should you work to raise students' aspirations?

5. Your second-grade students tend to blame outside events for their failures on tests and poor grades on assignments. What steps can you take to encourage your students to develop more internal responsibility patterns?

IN MIDDLE SCHOOL

1. Students in your class of eighth graders often complain about having poor memories, and they act as if they can do nothing about it. How can you encourage these students to use memory strategies? How can you convince these students of the value of memory strategies? Which strategies will be likely to work best with students of this age?

2. A troubled boy in your ninth-grade class refuses even to try to do his schoolwork. He believes nothing he does will make any difference, and sees himself as doomed to fail in school. What steps can you take to help him?

3. You are a new teacher preparing for your first day of class in middle school. What special challenges might you face with students of this age? What strategies can you use to deal with these challenges?

4. Your ninth-grade class does not grasp the meaning of the term *insight*. What exercises or activities can you use to make them appreciate what insight is and why it is important in learning?

5. How do you conceptualize the relative importance in your middle school teaching of content knowledge versus pedagogical knowledge? Explain your answer.

IN HIGH SCHOOL

1. You are excited about trying a new teaching technique with your twelfth-grade classes, but you wonder whether the technique will get through to the students. How can you tell whether the new teaching technique is working? Be specific.

2. Your tenth graders are obsessed with performance-oriented goals, such as getting an A, instead of with accomplishing meaningful learning. You want them to focus on mastery of important concepts and material. How can you show your students the shortcomings of having performance goals and the benefits of mastery-oriented goals?

3. Name three situations in which you can use an analogy when teaching ninth-grade biology.

4. How do you envision the role of reflective thinking in the life of a high school teacher? What situations in a tenth-grade class might result in a need for a teacher to think reflectively?

5. Your eleventh-grade class does not seem to understand the benefits of delaying gratification. They are often unable to muster the energy to work on assignments that are due in the future: They all want grades and positive feedback in response to the effort they invest every day. Why is it important to communicate with high school students the value of delaying gratification? What specific examples can you use to do so?

Becoming An Expert Teacher

About This Feature

Appearing at the end of each chapter, "Technology Tools You Can Use" focuses on four types of resources on the World Wide Web that can help you become an expert teacher and expert student:

1. *Connecting Theory and Research to Practice* provides resources in educational psychology theory and research that have practical implications for classroom practice, along with examples of how theory and research are being implemented by classroom teachers.

2. *Building Your Self-Portrait as an Educator* gives you a variety of reflective activities and tools to help you become an expert teacher.

3. *Communities of Learners/Teachers* offers resources on the World Wide Web for discussing pertinent issues in educational psychology with other learners and teachers already in the field.

4. *Online Resources* highlights organizations and publications that every educator should know about—a virtual library of professional resources.

Connecting Theory and Research to Practice

Is it possible to conduct descriptive or experimental research online? While that question is being discussed and debated by scientists all over the world, some researchers are already making use of the Web to conduct psychological experiments. For example, Dr. Bem Allen, professor of psychology at Western Illinois University (WIU), has created an online experiment investigating memory *(http://www.wiu.edu/users/mfbpa/slideshow.html)*. Another site is maintained by Purdue University's Department of Cognitive Psychology's Online Laboratory *(http://coglab.psych.purdue.edu/coglab)*. These sites are being used to collect data regarding such things as memory, perception, and learning. Both are secure sites, meaning you need special permission to enter the site and you must grant them permission to use your responses as data. There are other interesting sites that provide psychological experiments online but do not necessarily collect data.

The "Internet Psychology Laboratory" *(http://kahuna.psych.uiuc.edu/ipl/index.html)* is an Internet site that contains online psychological experiments. Visitors to the site can participate in a wide variety of psychological experiments investigating visual and auditory perception, memory and learning, and cognition. Each area contains a tutorial providing background information about each experiment, online interactive experiments, and an explanation of the experiment procedure and analysis of data.

One experiment investigating visual perception concerns the Müller-Lyer Illusion *(http://kahuna.psych.uiuc.edu/ipl/vis/muller_ly/level_3.html)*. After a brief tutorial explaining the illusion, individuals can participate in an interactive demonstration. The site also takes you through a tutorial explaining the independent and dependent variables in the experiment, data presentation and analysis, and interpretation of the results of the experiment.

While sites such as "The Internet Psychology Laboratory" provide very interesting interactive activities and experiments, they require a fast Internet connection and you may have to adjust your browser for the experiments to work properly. Luckily, "The Internet Psychology Laboratory" site presents simple, step-by-step instructions on how to set your browser so that the experiments are as effective as possible.

Several sites give information regarding the advantages and disadvantages of conducting psychological experiments online. For example, *http://www.psych.unizh.ch/genpsy/Ulf/Lab/WWWExpMethod.html* is a German site that discusses the pros and cons of online experiments and provides a listing of current research activities. Also, The American Psychological Society has a Web page called "Psychological Research on the Net" *(http://psych.hanover.edu/APS/exponnet.html)* that contains a list of the numerous psychological experiments available on the Web.

Building Your Self-Portrait as an Educator

One of the most powerful tools beginning teachers can arm themselves with is information, and one of the most informative educational organizations in the United States is the National Education Association (NEA). Founded in 1857, the NEA currently has an estimated 2.5 million members. The NEA provides a variety of services to its members including negotiating teacher contracts and rights at the local and state level, lobbying for legislation, and advocating for issues related to public education from preschool to graduate school.

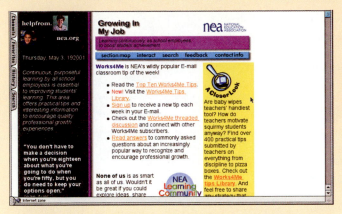

NEA's Web site, located at *www.nea.org*, provides a wide variety of information and tools pertinent to teacher education and teaching. On the site you can look at the top news stories that affect public education or view reports such as the 1997 NEA Report on the Individuals with Disabilities Education Act (IDEA). You can also gain information regarding important statistics such as the national average salary for a K–12 teacher, the number of children attending public schools who live in poverty, and the number of males entering the teaching profession. Information regarding important dates and educational events such as Read Across America are also available on the site's event calendar.

There is an area on the site entitled "Growing in My Job" (*www.nea.org/ helpfrom/growing/index .html*), which is devoted to helping new teachers. A feature called "Works 4 Me" and written by veteran teachers presents helpful classroom hints for new teachers. This feature also allows teachers to sign up to receive teaching tips and hints via e-mail. Another helpful tool available at this site is subject-based learning communities in which a teacher can sign up and join discussions focusing on a particular subject area.

Communities of Learners/Teachers

Are you interested in finding out what the first year of teaching is like? *Education World*, an online resource for teachers, has a featured article entitled "The First 180 Days: First-Year Teacher Diaries" (*www.education-world .com/a_curr/curr262 .shtml*). In the diaries, two first-year teachers describe the successes and challenges of being a teacher. These stories highlight a number of experiences that will be discussed throughout this text, such as student learning, classroom management, and student motivation. Additionally, these stories illustrate the professional development of a teacher and how to communicate effectively with colleagues, parents, and school administrators. *Education World* has also created a message board to discuss the diaries and to provide first-year and veteran teachers with a place to exchange stories and advice.

Online Resources

One valuable online resource for beginning teachers is "Education Week on the Web" (*http://www.edweek.org/*). Articles, special features, job postings, and a variety of information regarding the teaching profession are available.

"The Teacher's Guide to the U.S. Department of Education," located at *www.ed.gov/pubs/ TeachersGuide*, provides a textual reference for teachers to help navigate the various resources and programs available from the government agency.

The National Center for Research on Teacher Learning located at the School of Education at Michigan State University has an informative Web site at *http://ncrtl.msu.edu*. This site provides an overview of initiatives and reports that have looked at teacher learning and preparation. For example, in the annotated bibliography for the report "Findings on Learning to Teach" you can find research and bibliographic resources that address six myths about teacher education. (You will need a PDF [Acrobat Reader] on your computer to read the reports, but a link to download the free Acrobat Reader is on the site, and the program is easy to install on your computer.)

Cognitive Development

CHAPTER OUTLINE

THE BIG PICTURE

To help you see the big picture, keep the following questions in mind as you read this chapter:

■ Why do children seem to struggle at a certain level for months, and then show a big jump in performance over a couple of weeks? What can teachers do to hasten these jumps in performance?

■ Why do some children at a certain age pick up skills easily, while others work hard but just do not get it?

■ Why do children who have picked up a skill in one area have trouble doing similar tasks in other areas?

◄ *This little girl is obviously enjoying learning to read.*
(Robert Brenner, PhotoEdit)

39

Joan Carlin sat grading what seemed to be the 500th paper in her foot-tall stack. "Another C–!" she thought, worrying about the number of usually good students who had done poorly on the test. "What's going on with these kids?" she wondered. Ever since September, when she had left teaching at an elementary school and had begun teaching at a middle school, Joan had realized that teaching her seventh-grade math class would not be easy. Some of the students who paid attention in class and worked hard just didn't seem to get a lot of the material. Others caught on more quickly—even though they seemed not to care. And when it came to tests, some kids breezed through them while others struggled. Joan had taught math for eight years, but she had never seen such a mixture of kids at different levels of performance, all in the same classroom. This move from elementary to middle school teaching was proving to be a real eye-opener.

It was not until she attended a refresher course during the November in-service day that Joan gained insight into her problem. The workshop was entitled "Is Age Appropriate Always Appropriate? How to Assess Cognitive Readiness." The classes that Joan had sat through in college, with the instructor droning on about Piaget and Vygotsky and other people, flooded back to her mind and suddenly seemed relevant. "It has to do with their minds, with how they think and what they are able to think about at this age," she mused. "I am following the textbook, but some seventh graders are not yet fully able to think abstractly. They work hard, but they cannot make the leap from numbers on a chalkboard to word problems about ladders leaning against walls and trains traveling in opposite directions at different speeds. Others are able to think in terms of my examples, even though they do not study or do their homework. This was not a problem for me with my fourth-grade classes because those students were more similar in their levels of cognitive development. It is not just motivation and practice that's important at this age—it is whether or not the students are able to think about the problems the way we do."

Joan still had to figure out how she was going to put her newly remembered knowledge into practice. "It drives me crazy that they are at many different cognitive levels," Joan confided to an expert high school teacher during the coffee break at the workshop. "Some of my students sit and talk to themselves as they draw little pictures of the word problems in the margin. During tests it makes me wonder if they are cheating! Meanwhile, others do not even know where to start with the word problems. When their grades go down, their parents want conferences with me, and I don't know what to say! Most difficult are the ones who do not pay attention and do not do their homework but seem to pick up the material anyway. I want to grade fairly, but I do not know how to." "Believe me, I know," replied the expert instructor. "Welcome to the world of high school teaching! Let me tell you about some of the strategies I have tried with my classes. They made a big difference for me and I think they will for you too. . . ."

Joan Carlin was frustrated, and with good reason. What would you do in her situation? You were quite good, something of an expert, at teaching children at one grade level, but you are floundering with students who are just a little different in age. You are doing your best to teach a large class, but it seems as though each pupil is from a different planet, as far as his or her readiness to tackle the material is concerned. You are motivated to do a good job, but you are not at all sure what you can do to help your students.

Educational psychology can help answer many of these questions, such as why some of your students get it and others who work hard do not. Educational psychology can also give you ideas for dealing with the type of class Joan was facing. The part of educational psychology that deals with these issues is called the study of **cognitive development,** the changes in mental skills that occur through increasing maturity and experience.

Cognitive Development: Concepts for Teaching

THE IMPORTANCE OF COGNITIVE DEVELOPMENT TO TEACHERS

If you are training to be a teacher or a researcher, or if you just want to understand how children, and even adults, learn, knowing the basics of cognitive development is essential. Expert teachers know what level of cognitive development they can expect from most of the students in their classes. They use that knowledge to plan lessons, activities, and assessment, as well as to manage the classroom on a daily basis. Understanding the general level of thinking that can be expected from their students helps expert teachers recognize when a student is lagging behind in cognitive development or needs extra help. Expert teachers know how to challenge their students in ways that spur cognitive development rather than frustration. This is the lesson that Joan Carlin, the teacher described at the beginning of the chapter, is just starting to learn.

To understand cognitive development and to apply your new knowledge to teaching, you should be acquainted with a number of key concepts about cognitive development. The important differences among some of the major theories of cognitive development are often based on how the theorists viewed development in terms of these key concepts.

MATURATION VERSUS LEARNING

Cognitive development can take place through maturation, through learning, or through a combination of the two. **Maturation** is any relatively permanent change—be it cognitive, emotional, or physical—that occurs as a result of biological aging, regardless of personal experience. Here, we primarily discuss cognitive development. Maturation is preprogrammed—that is, it occurs regardless of the interactions a child has with the environment. For example, an infant knows how to cry at birth without the benefit of any experiences or instruction in how to cry. Expert teachers know that no matter how hard they work or how good they are, they cannot force a student to think or to do what he or she is not biologically old enough to do. Thus, as a teacher, you must know how old is old enough for the skills you need to teach. For example, Joan Carlin, the middle school math teacher, must determine whether her students have the cognitive maturity to understand the math problem hidden in a description of a ladder leaning against a wall. (We return to this point later, when we discuss different researchers' ideas about cognitive development.)

But what about changes in thought or behavior that do not happen automatically? These changes are the result of learning. **Learning** is any relatively permanent change in thought or behavior that occurs as a result of experience. Learning is not preprogrammed: It cannot occur in the absence of stimulation. For example, you know your name and the name of the country you live in, but only because you have learned these facts. You were not born with this knowledge. Indeed, learning is what education is all about. The theme of this entire book is how to go about teaching so students are able to learn as much as possible.

Clarifying the distinction between maturation and learning is important because as a teacher you need to know what kinds of abilities and behavior you can expect from children, regardless of their particular childhood experiences. Teachers also need to know what kinds of abilities and behavior depend on experience. Knowing what almost all children of a certain age can be expected to do helps a teacher plan good lessons and know when to push. However, understanding the role of learning allows an expert teacher

THINKING ANALYTICALLY

How might you tell whether a child's ability to distinguish faces from other kinds of visually presented stimuli is a result of maturation or of learning?

SUGGESTION: See whether infants just a few days (or even hours) old show discrimination between faces and other kinds of visually presented stimuli. If so, face discrimination is probably a result of maturation because the infant would not yet have had the opportunity to learn to make this discrimination.

to recognize when a child's experiences have not prepared him or her for a lesson. In this case, pushing will do little good—for the child needs more experiences to become ready to move forward.

CANALIZATION: A KEY TO TEACHING

The difference between maturation and learning is not as clear as it might seem. In the world around us, much of the development of behavior depends on the environment. The concept of **canalization** refers to the extent to which a behavior or an underlying ability develops *without* respect to the environment (Waddington, 1956). A highly canalized ability develops in nearly all children, despite widely varying environments. For example, perceptual abilities, such as the ability to see and to hear, are relatively highly canalized (Bertenthal & Clifton, 1998; Kellman & Banks, 1998). So are simple memory abilities, such as those used in learning a list of vocabulary words (Perlmutter & Lange, 1978; Woodward & Markman, 1998). We develop simple memory abilities in almost any environment, whether or not we are urged to do so (Schneider & Bjorklund, 1998).

Conversely, a weakly canalized ability develops only with a supportive environment. The interpersonal skills children use in their interactions with each other and teachers are relatively weakly canalized (Gardner, 1983, 1999); children need support and direction from parents, teachers, and their peers in order to learn how to deal with others in an appropriate way. Thus a child's environment affects social skills more strongly than it affects simple memory skills. Teachers are most easily able to help students develop weakly canalized skills.

The concept of canalization is key to teaching because children come into classrooms with widely differing experiences. It is helpful for teachers to know how much these different experiences have influenced the various kinds of academic and social behavior expected in the classroom. Almost all your students can be expected to show highly canalized abilities, such as simple memory skills, but only some will be likely to show weakly canalized abilities, such as working cooperatively on a team project (Rogoff, 1998). Within the context of their overall objectives, expert teachers match their expectations to what is possible and what is likely for their students to accomplish, while bearing in mind the difference.

How do children's abilities, whether strongly or weakly canalized, develop? Developmental theorists tend to be divided into two different camps regarding this question, as we see in the next section.

COGNITIVE DEVELOPMENT: CONTINUOUS VERSUS STAGELIKE

Is cognitive development continuous, occurring in a smooth, ever-increasing pattern of increments in cognitive skill? Or is it discrete, occurring in discontinuous, stagelike patterns with sharp gains at some points of development and virtually no increments at others?

Theories suggesting that development proceeds continuously assume cognitive abilities are acquired gradually, in increments, such that each new accomplishment builds directly on those that came before it. Continuous-development theories propose that a person's thinking is not fundamentally different at any one age or level of development than it is at any other age. As Figure 2.1 shows, the process of development proposed by these theories can be compared to the progress of a person walking up a slope or ramp. Just as the person on a ramp gradually gets to a higher level of ground, continuous-development theories propose that people gradually progress to higher levels of cognitive ability.

In contrast, stage theories make three major assumptions about development (Amsel & Renninger, 1997; Brainerd, 1978; Flavell, 1971). First, each stage is associated with a qualitatively distinct set of *cognitive structures,* or mental patterns of organization that influence our ways of dealing with the world. For example, in Piaget's stage theory, which

(a)   (b)

FIGURE 2.1

Continuity theories contrasted with stage theories. (a) *Continuous-development theories propose that a person's thinking is not fundamentally different at any one age or level of development than it is at any other age. Just as the person on a ramp gradually gets to a higher level of ground, continuous-development theories propose that people gradually progress to higher levels of cognitive ability.* (b) *A frequently used metaphor for stagelike development is climbing a staircase. At each step on the staircase, a person is at a different height. Similarly, a person's level of development at each stage is assumed to be clearly different from his or her level at any other stage.*

we explore later, older children are able to arrange their mental patterns, and to interact with the world, in certain ways not available to younger children, who are still in earlier stages of cognitive development. That is, the thinking of children in later stages of cognitive development is said to be fundamentally different from the thinking of children in earlier stages. Second, behavior unfolds in a one-directional, invariable sequence. In other words, development always moves forward, never backward; and it always moves in the same way for everyone, although the rate at which the stages unfold may differ from one person to another. A frequently used metaphor for stagelike development is climbing a staircase, as shown in Figure 2.1. At each step on the staircase, a person is at a different height. Similarly, a person's level of development at each stage proposed by a stage theory is assumed to be clearly different from his or her level of development at any other stage. Third, later stages build on earlier stages. As the child grows older, he or she consolidates previously developed skills and develops new ones.

DOMAIN-GENERAL VERSUS DOMAIN-SPECIFIC COGNITIVE DEVELOPMENT

Theorists of cognitive development also differ as to whether they believe such development is domain general or domain specific (Frensch & Buchner, 1999; Gelman & Williams, 1998). **Domain-general development** occurs more or less simultaneously in multiple areas. **Domain-specific development** occurs at different rates in different areas. If cognitive development proceeds in a domain-general way, for example, arithmetic and language abilities develop in synchrony. In contrast, if cognitive development is domain specific, arithmetic and language abilities may develop independently of each other. In sports, for example, if we expect domain-general development we can expect Little League baseball players to learn the skills of throwing, hitting, and catching all at about the same rate. If we support domain-specific development, we expect a Little Leaguer to learn to throw, hit, and catch at different rates. Throwing might come before catching, for example.

   The domain distinction is very relevant to you as a teacher: Can you expect a child with strong writing skills to perform well in math? What does it mean if a child does not perform well in both? Should you push the student harder? Is it possible that the child's weak performance in math may be due not to lack of effort but rather to a slower rate of development

THINKING CREATIVELY

Give an example of one highly canalized skill and one weakly canalized skill that would be important in the classroom. How might you help children develop these skills?

SUGGESTION: Highly canalized: perceptual-motor skills such as hand-eye coordination in inputting text into a computer. Weakly canalized: number skills. You might help children develop perceptual-motor skills by giving them opportunities to interact with their physical environment—for example, in after-school computer classes or clubs. You might help children develop number skills by creating games that involve using numbers in various ways.

THINKING PRACTICALLY

In what ways is the issue of domain generality versus specificity important to the teacher of young children? How might a teacher's approach be affected by the one kind of development or the other?

SUGGESTION: The teacher needs to know whether the level of performance shown in one subject matter area can be expected to generalize to another subject matter area. The teacher needs to teach at a more basic level if skills shown in one area are not necessarily shown in the area now being taught.

in the mathematical area? According to the domain-specific view, a child can be an expert in one domain of schoolwork and a novice in another.

For example, a child can get an A in art but be failing English, or vice versa, showing domain-specific development. But a child is unlikely to get an A in reading and an F in English, an example of domain-general development. The skills used in some sets of domains overlap weakly (they are domain specific), but in other sets of domains they overlap strongly (they are domain general).

Implications for Teaching

An understanding of the concepts of cognitive development helps effective teachers to better understand the development of their students' skills:

- ■ *A number of skills, including many academic and interpersonal skills, develop only with respect to the environment. Expert teachers are able to recognize these weakly canalized abilities in order to provide support and direction for them.* They also know what to expect of their students by understanding their environmental experiences.

- ■ *Some expert teachers subscribe to stagelike views of development, in which it is assumed that largely inborn factors determine the unfolding of a child's abilities over time. Thus they do not push students into development or force them to skip a stage, for development is established largely by nonenvironmental forces.* Other expert teachers, supporting a continuous view of development, expect children to have at least the rudiments of adult thinking at relatively early ages.

- ■ *The concept of domains helps expert teachers assess why a student's performance in one area, such as math, is not up to par with that in another area, such as reading.* According to the domain-specific view, differences in development can be expected because learning rates vary from one area to another.

Piaget's Stage Theory of Cognitive Development

Jean Piaget (1896–1980), a Swiss psychologist, proposed what is still considered the most influential single theory of cognitive development that has been offered. Piaget's theory is based on the premise of "the child as scientist." That is, at younger ages, the child's *scientific* exploration is limited by cognitive abilities that have yet to develop; but at all ages, children actively seek to explore the world and to come to terms with it. In some respects the theory is incomplete, and in other respects it has been shown to be incorrect. However, despite its flaws, Piaget's theory remains the most nearly complete (Bennett, 1999), influential theory to date, although not the only one (e.g., Demetriou, Efklides, & Platsidou, 1993; Keil, 1999; Siegler, 1996).

Piaget's theory is a stage theory of cognitive development specifying qualitative changes in cognitive development with each successive stage. Although the accomplishments characterizing a child at each stage build on those in the previous stage, these accomplishments are also distinct from the ones the child demonstrated at the previous stage. Thus those individuals who accept this theory believe teachers should expect sudden bursts in the development of cognitive abilities rather than a smooth

The Swiss psychologist Jean Piaget observing children in a classroom. Piaget's influential stage theory of cognitive development specifies qualitative changes in cognitive development at each successive stage. Piaget performed much of his research on his own children. (Monkmeyer/ Anderson, Monkmeyer Press)

progression of development over time. Piaget's theory is also largely domain general. It predicts that children who show cognitive development in one area generally should show comparable cognitive development in other areas.

However, children do not seem to develop expertise evenly in all of their abilities. Thus Piaget proposed that although abilities in all areas generally develop concurrently, the spread of an ability to various areas of performance takes place over time. Piaget called this concept **horizontal décalage,** the temporary difference in levels of performance that a child shows between various cognitive domains or activities within a given stage of development. In other words, development is domain general—almost. The child who has the capacity to perform at comparable levels in arithmetic and language may nevertheless lag slightly behind in one of these areas until the developed ability has had time to catch up. Thus teachers cannot expect students to show exactly comparable performance when what appears to be the same cognitive skill—such as understanding differences between concepts—is applied to different domains, such as words and numbers.

Piaget's theory contains many aspects—in fact, too many to be described here. However, we will consider three key concepts that describe specific mechanisms of cognitive development: equilibration, assimilation, and accommodation.

THINKING ANALYTICALLY

To what extent might horizontal décalage be viewed as a fudge factor in Piaget's theory—that is, an attempt to account, after the fact, for data showing an unevenness in domain development that do not really fit the domain-general theory?

SUGGESTION: It does appear to be a fudge factor, to some extent. Nevertheless, it is plausible to expect the existence of some level of horizontal décalage in a stage theory.

MECHANISMS OF COGNITIVE DEVELOPMENT

According to Piaget, the main mechanism by which cognitive development occurs is called **equilibration,** which is the balancing of cognitive structures with the needs of the environment (see Rogoff, 1998). As children interact with the world, they encounter situations that do not match their preconceived notion of the way the world is or should be. For example, an adult may use the word *cat* to refer to an animal that the child thinks is a *dog*. Piaget called this mismatch between the state of the world and one's preconceived notions as a state of **disequilibrium** and suggested it is good for children because it is the impetus for developing expertise. Thus teachers should not hesitate to provide novel situations for children, as long as the children are just about to reach the point where they can make sense of that novelty (Kuhn, Garcia-Mila, Zohar, & Anderson, 1995). For example, a child who has recently acquired a solid understanding of addition is likely to be ready to understand subtraction, but is less likely to be ready to understand division. Children, like everyone else, are uncomfortable with disequilibrium, and they attempt to restore equilibrium.

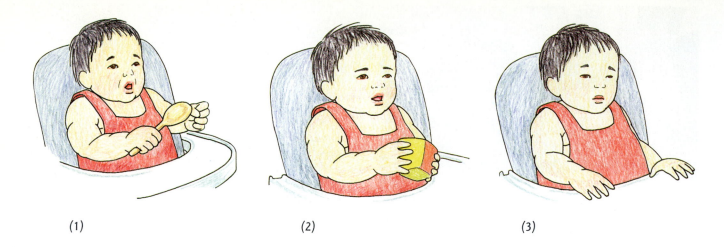

(1)   (2)   (3)

FIGURE 2.2

How the processes of assimilation and accommodation combine in the mechanism of equilibration.
(1) Banging as a scheme. (2) Assimilation occurs when the child includes the new object in the
scheme. (3) Accommodation occurs when the child cannot fit the new object into the scheme.

Equilibration can be achieved by either of two processes (see Figure 2.2). Both involve changes in the child's cognitive **schemas,** or cognitive frameworks, that provide a way to understand and organize new knowledge. For example, a child's schema about a dog may include facts such as that it is an animal, has four legs, and barks. In the first process, called **assimilation,** the child attempts to fit new information into the schemas he or she has already formed. If, for example, a young child has a schema for dog, and sees a previously unknown dog, such as a cocker spaniel, the child is assimilating the experience when she incorporates the cocker spaniel into the schema for dogs. In the second process, called **accommodation,** the child creates new schemas to organize information that he or she cannot assimilate into existing schemas. The child therefore needs to create an entirely new schema. For example, if the child sees a raccoon, and realizes it is like a dog in being alive and walking on four legs, but unlike a dog in being wild and a creature of the night, the child may create a new schema representing her accommodation of this information.

THINKING CREATIVELY

How might a teacher create disequilibrium for a child who does not yet understand that a bat is not just another kind of bird?

SUGGESTION: Think about the types of questions the teacher might ask to encourage the child to recognize the differences between a bat and a bird. For example, Which one sleeps at night? Which one sleeps hanging from its feet?

 STAGES OF COGNITIVE DEVELOPMENT

Piaget (1969, 1972) proposed four stages of cognitive development: sensorimotor, preoperational, concrete operational, and formal operational. Much of his description of these stages emerged from his observations of his own children. As with other stage theories of development, Piaget's theory posits that children pass through all four stages in a fixed, one-directional order. In other words, all children pass through the stages in the same order, and once they enter a stage, they never go back to a previous one. Subsequent stages build on previous ones, so full development of one stage becomes the basis for the equilibrations that lead to the next stage. Consider each stage in turn.

■**SENSORIMOTOR STAGE**   The **sensorimotor stage,** occurring between birth and about age 2, is primarily characterized by the development of sensory (simple input) and motor (simple output) functions. Sensory input includes, for example, seeing and hearing; motor output includes moving and experimenting—grasping at or playing—with

objects in the environment. During this stage, infants respond largely in reflexive, or inborn, ways, but as they develop, they modify these reflexes to suit the demands of the environment.

The two main accomplishments of this stage are object permanence and representational thought. **Object permanence** is the realization that an object continues to exist even when it is not immediately visible. For example, if you show a 5-month-old infant a rattle and then hide the rattle behind a cardboard barrier, the infant is likely to gaze at the rattle while it is being shown. But once the rattle is hidden, the child will act as though the rattle never existed. For the young infant, out of sight truly means out of mind. At about 9 months, however, a transition takes place. Thus, if you were to show an 11-month-old infant the rattle and then hide it, the infant would be likely to look for the rattle behind the barrier. If you move the rattle from one location to another while the infant is not looking, an 18-month-old will look for the rattle even in places he or she has never seen it before. The rattle has acquired a permanent identity for the infant—its existence continues even after it is out of sight.

The second major accomplishment of this stage is **representational thought,** the well-formed mental representations, or ideas, of external stimuli (Mandler, 1998). For example, an infant with representational thought might have in her head a well-formed image of a favorite toy rattle. She can call the rattle to mind, or think about it, whether it is visible to her or not. This accomplishment is associated with the end of the sensorimotor stage, usually after the eighteenth month of age and not later than the twenty-fourth month.

■ **PREOPERATIONAL STAGE** In the **preoperational stage,** which occurs for most children between approximately 24 months and 7 years of age, the child begins to actively develop the mental representations that were just starting to form near the end of the sensorimotor stage. During this stage, children begin to communicate by way of words, both with each other and with parents. Their use of words opens up many new possibilities for them. The use of words as symbols for concrete objects is made possible by the children's ability to think about the objects. The communication of preoperational children is often **egocentric,** centered on the self without understanding how other people perceive a situation. For example, the preoperational child does not understand that someone else looking at an object from a different point of view sees the object (such as a toy) differently (e.g., from the back rather than the front of the toy).

Children in the preoperational stage often also seem to be unaware of the art of conversation: They speak their minds without taking into account what the other party or parties to a conversation have said. The teacher of a child in this stage might get a response such as "I went to a restaurant last night" when asking whether the child would like blue or brown paper for an art project.

As children grow older, they become less egocentric and more focused on others. This development begins largely during the preoperational stage, although even in the sensorimotor stage, we can see the bare beginnings of movement away from egocentrism. Taking into consideration what others have to say then continues to develop throughout childhood and even into adulthood. The emergence of the ability to take others' points of view develops gradually, over a lengthy period of time.

■ **CONCRETE OPERATIONAL STAGE**   In the **concrete operational stage,** generally occurring from about ages 7 (or even 6) to 12 years, children become able to manipulate mentally the internal representations they started to form in the previous stage. In other words, they now not only have mental representations but also can act on and modify these representations. They can think logically as long as the logical thinking applies to concrete objects (such as blocks) rather than to abstractions (such as the concept of truth).

The best example of how children in this stage acquire the ability to manipulate internal representations is probably through their development of **conservation,** the recognition that even when the physical appearance of something changes, its underlying quantity (how much there is of it—number, size, or volume) remains the same—or in other words, is conserved.

The several different types of conservation occur at slightly different ages during the stage of concrete operations. Probably the most well known is the *conservation of liquid quantity.* In this type of conservation, a child recognizes that an amount of liquid quantity remains the same, even when the form the liquid takes is varied.

In a typical experiment, a child is shown two short, stout beakers with equal amounts of liquid in them. The child is asked to verify that the amounts of liquid are indeed the same. Then, with the child watching, an experimenter pours the liquid from one of the short, stout beakers into a third beaker, which is tall and thin. The shape of this third beaker produces a column of liquid that reaches a higher level than the liquid did in the short, stout beaker. The experimenter asks the child whether the same amount of liquid is in each of the two beakers. Whereas the preoperational child will report more liquid in the tall, thin beaker—where the liquid has reached a higher level—the concrete operational child will report that both beakers contain the same amount of liquid. (See Figure 2.3a.)

THINKING CREATIVELY

Can you think of another object to use to measure conservation, in addition to those mentioned here?

SUGGESTION: You might pack together a stack of cotton balls so they appear smaller than the original pile. Children who conserve will realize the same amount of cotton is in the second, denser pile.

FIGURE 2.3

Conservation is the recognition that even when the physical appearance of something changes, its underlying quantity remains the same. According to Piaget, this ability develops at the concrete operational stage. (Beaura Katherine Ringrose; Will Hart)

(a)

(b)

In general, the concrete operational child has reached a level at which thinking is **reversible**—that is, the child can mentally reverse a physical operation. For example, the concrete operational child sees the higher level of liquid in the tall, thin beaker. By reversing, in his or her mind, the set of actions performed by the experimenter, the child can go back to the original point before the pouring, when the amounts of liquid in the two short, stout beakers were the same. In the *conservation of mass,* a clay snake can be rolled into a ball and then back into a snake. (See Figure 2.3b.) Similarly, the concrete operational child can understand subtraction as the inverse of addition or division as the inverse of multiplication; the preoperational child cannot. At the same time, however, the operations are still concrete, because what is reversed is a concrete physical operation, such as pouring liquid from one beaker to another, rather than an abstract formal operation, such as giving people freedom or taking it away from them.

THINKING PRACTICALLY

Suppose you had to divide a single candy bar between two children. Why might a child who has not yet developed conservation believe that if the candy bar is cut in half "the long way," along the length of the bar, he or she would get more candy than if it is cut "the short way," dividing the width of the bar?

SUGGESTION: The child who has not yet mastered conservation may believe that the longer the piece he or she gets, the more candy there is, with little or no regard for width.

■ **FORMAL OPERATIONAL STAGE**   The **formal operational stage** begins at about 11 or 12 years of age and extends through adulthood. Individuals in this stage form and operate on—that is, reverse—abstract as well as concrete mental representations (Inhelder & Piaget, 1958). In this stage, for example, children can see **second-order relations,** or relations between relations, as required by analogical reasoning. Analogical reasoning is based on the perception of the similarity of like features of two things (DeLoache, Miller, & Pierroutsakos, 1998). An example of a second-order relation is this question: In what ways that a cat and dog are alike are a robin and sparrow also alike? Joan Carlin, the middle school math teacher described at the beginning of the chapter, realized that one reason many of her students had trouble was that they had not yet developed formal operational reasoning abilities. These students had trouble recognizing the geometry problem posed in the description of a ladder leaning against a wall because they were not able to see the similarities between the triangle made by the ladder and a triangle in a math problem.

Students perform an experiment in a physics lab, displaying their formal-operational skills. (Bob Daemmrich, Stock Boston)

Another important ability that develops during the formal operations stage is the ability to think abstractly, to think about concepts, such as *justice* or *inner peace*, that do not have any concrete, physical equivalents (Lutz & Sternberg, 1999). Formal operational children can also think systematically. For example, if told that some unknown subset of four colored chemicals will be clear in color when combined, the children systematically can go through all possible subsets to find the one that produces the solution that is clear in color. Obviously, formal operational thinking is important for both scientific and mathematical expertise, as well as for other kinds of expertise (Kuhn, Schauble, & Garcia-Mila, 1992).

Piaget's theory makes a number of predictions about cognitive development from birth through adulthood. There are many ways for you as a teacher to make use of your knowledge about the level of cognitive development of your students.

CONSTRUCTING YOUR OWN LEARNING

Now try a problem yourself that is sometimes used to assess whether someone has become formal operational: List all possible orderings (permutations) of the numbers 1, 2, 3, and 4. How many different ways can you find to arrange these 4 digits? If you are currently working in a practicum, you might also ask some of the children you are working with to try this same test. (Be sure to discuss this first with your cooperating teacher.) Observe their strategies for solving the problem. We will reveal the number of possible arrangements, as well as the implications of tests such as these, in the next section when we evaluate Piaget's theory.

EVALUATING PIAGET'S THEORY

What are the strengths and weaknesses of Piaget's theory? Let us consider some of the main aspects of each.

Piaget's theory is the most nearly complete theory of cognitive development to date, although it is heavily oriented toward developing expertise in scientific modes of thinking. The theory offers fewer ideas about the development of expertise in other modes, for example, aesthetic modes as would apply in the arts. Piaget's theory has also been useful in generating a tremendous amount of research and in suggesting to teachers what children at given ages can and cannot do.

THINKING ANALYTICALLY

Before reading the next section, evaluate (1) the strengths and weaknesses of Piaget's theory, and (2) how you might apply Piaget's theory in the classroom.

SUGGESTION: You will be given answers to these questions in the next section!

However, the *validity* of Piaget's theory—the extent to which it is accurate in describing children's cognitive development—has been questioned for a number of reasons (e.g., Gelman & Williams, 1998; Lutz & Sternberg, 1999): (1) the limitations of the stagelike nature of development, (2) questions regarding the ages at which children can first perform various kinds of tasks, (3) doubts whether children's failures to perform certain tasks are actually due to the reasons Piaget gave, (4) doubts whether all adults ever do become fully formal operational, and (5) concerns whether the theory is cross-culturally generalizable.

Consider the stagelike nature of development. Charles Brainerd (1978) has argued that the available evidence does not support the stagelike characterization of development proposed by Piaget. The concept of horizontal décalage that Piaget added to the theory suggests at least some continuity to development. In fact, no full consensus has been reached among cognitive developmentalists as to whether development is stagelike (i.e., discrete) or continuous. Some theorists, such as Robbie Case (1984; Case & Okamoto, 1996) and Kurt Fischer (1980; Fischer & Grannott, 1995), have continued to argue for the existence of stages.

Consider next the ages at which children can first perform tasks. Piaget seems to have underestimated the ages at which children are really capable of performing various kinds of cognitive tasks (Chen & Siegler, 2000; Siegler, 1998). The general trend of research (e.g., Baillargeon, 1993; Goswami & Brown, 1990) has been to suggest that children can do many tasks at ages earlier than Piaget thought, as long as the children are familiar with the content domain in which they are working. For example, children can solve analogies well before they are 11 or 12, the age at which formal operational thinking supposedly begins (see, e.g., Goswami & Brown, 1990; Sternberg & Rifkin, 1979). Expert teachers do not assume their students are unable to perform sophisticated reasoning tasks. They know that, in their ability to reason, children sometimes surprise not only researchers but also teachers (Sternberg & Grigorenko, 2000).

Now consider why children failed some of the tasks Piaget gave them. Bryant and Trabasso (1971) showed that in one task, called *transitive inference*, what Piaget had taken to be a reasoning failure was actually a memory failure. For example, if you tell children in an arithmetic lesson that a first object costs more than a second object, and the second object costs more than a third object, children will often be able to solve the problem if they can remember the original premises—here, the cost relations. In other words, their failure to solve the problem is more likely due to forgetting the relations described by the premises than to inability to reason with the givens of the premises. Thus, when children fail in a reasoning task, teachers should not immediately conclude that the children lack reasoning ability. It may be that the children cannot remember the givens of the problem.

Now consider the cross-cultural generalizability of the theory. Sometimes, children from diverse cultures do not even understand tests developed in Western cultures (Greenfield, 1997; Serpell, 2000; Suzuki & Valencia, 1997). A review by Werner (1972) of more than 50 studies suggests that infants in non-Western societies such as sub-Saharan Africa can often perform certain psychomotor accomplishments before Piaget postulated they could. However, cross-cultural research also suggests that many adolescents and even adults in non-Western cultures never acquire formal operations (Dasen & Heron, 1981). When you teach culturally diverse children, therefore, do not make assumptions about the cognitive readiness of members of one group on the basis of knowledge about the cognitive readiness of members of another group. Also be careful in testing. Some children accept and respond better to testing situations than do others. (We discuss testing in detail in Chapter 13, "Standardized Testing.")

Many adolescents and adults in Western cultures also may not reach formal operations. Consider, for example, a test in which you try to determine the number of possible permutations of order for the numbers 1, 2, 3, and 4. If you are fully formal operational, you probably devise a systematic strategy for listing the possible orderings, for example, starting with 1, 2, 3, 4; then reversing the last two digits to produce 1, 2, 4, 3; then reversing the middle two digits to produce 1, 3, 2, 4; and so on. If you are not fully formal operational, you are probably relatively unsystematic in listing the possible orderings, rather than using a system that guarantees you will list all 24 possible orderings. Tests such as this one typically show that many adults are not fully formal operational. In fact, Piaget (1972) eventually modified his theory to recognize that formal operations may be more a function of domain-specific expertise (e.g., practice with the various types of thinking that are involved) than of general cognitive maturation. In other words, a child's accomplishments in reasoning in one domain, such as language arts, do not guarantee comparable accomplishments in reasoning in other domains.

The weaknesses of Piaget's theory do not render it useless for educators. However, the challenges to Piagetian theory do indicate that teachers must be cautious in their attempts to apply the theory in their classrooms. So what can you gain from Piaget's theory for your classroom use?

 ## NEO-PIAGETIAN VIEWS

When theorists recognize that a theory is wrong in some respects or incomplete in others, they have two options. The first option is to reject the theory as a whole and seek to understand things in a completely different way. The second option is to build on the

In a typical performance, a seven-year-old boy practices the piano at home (left). In an optimal performance, young students practice together for an orchestra concert (right). (Stone; © Telegraph Colour Library. FPG International)

strengths of the theory and to let go of its weaker parts. *Neo-Piagetians* are a group of psychologists and educators who have built on Piaget's theory while disowning the parts of the theory that have not held up to close scrutiny. Although the label *neo-Piagetian* suggests these psychologists have similar views, individual psychologists have taken a variety of approaches to build on Piaget's work.

One neo-Piagetian approach is to propose alternative sets of stages (e.g., Demetriou & Valanides, 1998; Fischer, 1980; Fischer & Pipp, 1984; Parziale & Fischer, 1998). Fischer and Pipp have suggested somewhat different stages from those of Piaget. These psychologists have also made the useful distinction between optimal and typical levels of performance. The *optimal level* is the best performance an individual is capable of making on a given task. Fischer's theory builds on that of Piaget by showing that just because people are *optimally* capable of performing at a certain level (e.g., Piaget's formal operations) does not mean they will *typically* perform at that level in their everyday lives.

Another approach that neo-Piagetians have taken is to propose one or more stages beyond the four originally suggested by Piaget. Theorists who believe in such stages are basically suggesting the possibility of **postformal thinking,** or thinking that goes beyond that of formal operations in some way. Theories of postformal thinking suggest that cognitive development does not stop at age 12. A great deal of cognitive development goes on during adolescence and adulthood. As more and more adult students become involved in various aspects of education—going back to finish high school or college degrees, doing advanced graduate work, and becoming involved in on-the-job training—it is important to consider the cognitive development of adults (Baltes, 1997; Baltes & Staudinger, 2001; Berg, 2000; Brody, 1997; Ceci & Williams, 1997; Moshman, 1998; Schaie, 1996; Sternberg, 1997a).

For example, Patricia Arlin (1975, 1990) has suggested that a fifth stage of cognitive development is one of **problem finding,** in which an individual becomes able not just to solve problems, but also to identify the important problems to solve. In this view, as adolescents grow into adults, their development is not so much in how well they solve problems, but in how well they recognize which problems are worth solving.

THINKING PRACTICALLY

When in the course of doing schoolwork do you think you were performing at your own optimal level? What were the circumstances that induced you to work at that level?

SUGGESTION: Working at the optimal level involves performing a task at an appropriate level of challenge.

Klaus Riegel (1973), Gisela Labouve-Vief (1980, 1990), Juan Pascual-Leone (1984, 1990), Robert Sternberg (1998a), and others have proposed a stage beyond formal operations called **dialectical thinking** (see also Moshman, 1998). According to these investigators, as we mature through adolescence and into early adulthood, we recognize that most real-life problems do not have a unique solution that is fully correct while other solutions are incorrect. Rather, our thinking about problems evolves so we first propose some kind of **thesis** as a solution to a problem. Sooner or later, we or someone else proposes an **antithesis** that directly contradicts the thesis. Eventually, someone proposes a **synthesis** that somehow integrates what had appeared to be two opposing and even irreconcilable points of view. Truly expert thinking in any domain requires an appreciation of the dialectic.

For example, consider the issue of grouping in the classroom by ability levels. In the 1950s and 1960s, grouping was widely practiced and hardly questioned (thesis). There then came a period in which many argued that grouping was always wrong and was an injustice to all children (antithesis). Some still argue this way. Today, though, many educators believe that grouping, such as putting good readers together in one group and slower readers together in another, can be helpful if it is used selectively and in limited and flexible ways (synthesis) (see, e.g., Spear-Swerling & Sternberg, 1996; Sternberg & Grigorenko, 1999). To provide you with practice in this form of thinking, the Forum feature in each chapter of this text presents the dialectical progress of research or public opinion about a key topic in education.

TEACHING BEYOND PIAGET

Piaget's theory was sometimes off the mark. Here we consider related ideas that go beyond Piaget on the basis of current information (Kuhn & Siegler, 1998).

Piaget defined some of his stages, especially the preoperational stage and to a lesser extent the stage of concrete operations, in terms of what children *cannot* do. For example, preoperational children cannot conserve; concrete operational children cannot think in highly abstract ways. In fact, Piaget underestimated the ages at which children can do things. But, beyond such underestimation, a focus on what children cannot do may set up negative expectations, which in turn can become self-fulfilling prophecies. We recommend a focus on what children can do. For example, a teacher should not focus on a 5-year-old's inability to conserve. Instead, the teacher should give the child as many opportunities as possible to strengthen her or his quickly developing communication abilities.

Piaget was concerned with what he referred to as the "American problem"—the desire to hurry along the child's development. Indeed, David Elkind (1981), in *The Hurried Child*, wrote of just this obsession among Americans. We now know that often children's inability to think at a high level is due not to immaturity of higher order cognitive operations, but to lack of an experiential knowledge base. For example, students cannot design good experiments to study the effects of gravity if they do not have a rudimentary understanding of what gravity is. Once children acquire a knowledge base in an area, they can often think at a higher level in that area than in other areas in which they do not have the same amount of knowledge (Wellman & Gelman, 1998).

Again, we should not assume too much about what children cannot do. With knowledge, they can often do more than we suspect. Expert teachers know they can expect, and ask for, students to show higher levels of thinking in subjects in which the students have expertise. For example, a 9-year-old may be very active in a competitive sport. If the 9-year-old's coach

THINKING PRACTICALLY

What are some criteria you can use to decide whether a problem in education—such as whether to group children by ability levels—is an important problem?

SUGGESTION: You might ask whether solving the problem will have an impact on the lives of many students rather than just a few, and whether the impact itself is a major rather than a minor one.

THINKING CREATIVELY

How might you measure a person's ability to see the importance of problems, whether educational or otherwise?

SUGGESTION: You might ask students to judge the importance of a specific problem and then compare their responses to those of experts.

THINKING PRACTICALLY

Give an example of a thesis, antithesis, and synthesis in the development of your or others' thinking about an educational practice (e.g., homework, testing, teaching, reading, or grade retention).

SUGGESTION: Here is an example. Thesis: IQ is the only measure of ability that matters. Antithesis: IQ does not matter at all. Synthesis: IQ matters, but so do other measures of ability.

shows the team many examples of what it means to display good sportsmanship, the 9-year-old may be able to understand this abstract concept—even though he is still in the concrete operational stage of development. An important thing for children to learn is what they are capable of doing. They need to understand their own minds (Perner, 1999).

Finally, Piaget perhaps overemphasized the scientific side of development at the expense of other sides of development, such as the aesthetic. A balanced education means teaching children to think in many different modes, not just in the scientific mode that Piaget tended to emphasize in his theory of cognitive development. Artistic skills and appreciation of their importance, for example, should not be neglected in the school.

Implications for Teaching

PIAGET'S THEORY
Educators have been highly influenced by Piaget's theory. Indeed, the theory suggests many sound ideas for instruction and assessment:

- *Mix assimilations and accommodations.* Expert teachers balance assimilation and accommodation to help their students develop the schemas they have as well as create new schemas. In particular, you want to provide instruction that goes just a little bit beyond the level of children's thinking at a given point.

- *Take into account children's level of cognitive development.* A thorough introduction to Piaget's theory may help you develop expertise in recognizing the signs that students have reached the necessary cognitive level to master certain content, such as algebra. An expert teacher does not set expectations that students are developmentally unable to meet.

- *Teach children in a way that reflects their nature as natural-born scientists.* Expert teachers respond to and celebrate children's need to discover and master the mysteries of nature, such as the importance of photosynthesis for the development of plants.

- *Pay as much attention to understanding and correcting the bases of children's errors as to rewarding their correct answers.* Rather than simply putting a big "X" next to errors, a teacher needs to understand why students make the errors they do and how he or she can help the children correct the thinking that led to these errors.

- *New cognitive structures always build on old ones.* Piaget's theory stresses the cumulative nature of cognitive development. In teaching, you need to build carefully on what students already know. It is only in this way that students can integrate new knowledge with the old, and see in some cases how to correct misconceptions they may have had. For example, teaching of decimals can build on what children already have learned about fractions.

NEO-PIAGETIAN VIEWS
The work of the neo-Piagetians has implications for instruction and assessment that go beyond those of Piaget's original theory. A general implication of neo-Piagetian views for education is that cognitive development does not stop with formal operations. Thus we can expect more sophisticated forms of thinking in, say, college students than we can in middle school students. Consider the following teaching ideas that come from the work of neo-Piagetians.

(In this discussion of the implications of neo-Piagetian views for education, we are drawing on a variety of neo-Piagetian views held by researchers.)

■ ***Problem finding is at least as important as problem solving, and becomes more important in adolescence and beyond.*** Arlin (1990) and others have shown that students need to develop good judgment in the selection of problems (see also Sternberg, 1997b). Expert teachers do not always give students the problems to solve. Rather, the older students get, the more these teachers assume the role of guide or mentor, urging students to develop their own sense of what problems are worth solving (Rogoff, 1990).

■ ***Students, as they become adolescents, need to learn to think dialectically.*** Dialectical thinking, you will recall, is the recognition that in many issues of importance, we do not have final answers. Students need to come to appreciate knowledge not only as a product, but as part of a process of development that is ever ongoing.

BEYOND PIAGET
Recent work updating the views of Piaget suggests the following teaching techniques:

■ ***Expert teachers focus on what children of a given age <u>can</u> do.***

■ ***Children can be pushed just a bit beyond their current level of cognitive development.***

■ ***Children should be taught as multifaceted human beings, not just as developing scientists.***

Vygotsky's Sociocultural Theory of Cognitive Development

We have seen how important the thinking of Piaget and of the neo-Piagetians has been to our understanding of cognitive development and its interface with education. In Piaget's theory, development takes place largely from the inside, outward. In other words, abilities mature, and these are then applied by the child to the tasks he or she faces in the world. An alternative theory, however, has emphasized exactly the opposite direction of development.

In the theory of Lev Vygotsky, cognitive development is largely from the outside, inward (Vygotsky, 1978). Vygotsky's major premise was that a person's intrapersonal, or internal processes have their roots in interactions with others. In other words, children watch the interactions between the people in their world, interact with others themselves, and then make use of all these interactions to further their own development. This theory is sometimes referred to as a **sociocultural theory.**

Although he lived in the early part of the twentieth century, dying of tuberculosis at the age of only 38 in 1934, for many cognitive developmentalists Lev Vygotsky is among the most influential of theorists. Whereas the thinking of Piaget dominated the field of cognitive development in the 1960s and 1970s—leading to a spate of books on how to apply Piaget's theory to education—the theory of Vygotsky dominated the thinking of the field in the 1980s and 1990s. The increasing dominance of Vygotsky's thinking is due largely to Vygotsky's recognition that developmental accomplishments depend as much on the influence of the social and other environments as they do on sheer maturation.

As he watches his brother do his homework, this young boy is internalizing the knowledge he will need to perform many skills in school. (PhotoDisc)

In general, Vygotsky's theory is more limited than Piaget's, but it appears to be valid in many of its main assertions. Vygotsky formulated three particularly important ideas about cognitive development—the concepts of internalization, the zone of proximal development, and scaffolding.

 ## INTERNALIZATION

Internalization is the absorption, or taking in, of knowledge from the social contexts in which it is observed, so that one can use it for oneself (see Vygotsky, 1962, 1978). For example, imagine a child who is watching two adults argue for their respective beliefs (for example, on religion, politics, the relative merits of chocolate and vanilla ice cream, or which television program to watch). Through this observation, the child can learn how to argue for her own beliefs, both in the context of discussions with others and in the context of thinking through issues for herself. In school, a first grader might learn how to get a playground game started by watching how the third graders play. A high school freshman might begin to form sexual mores by observing the male-female interactions between seniors in the hallways and after school. In essence, children recreate within themselves the kinds of interactions they observe in the world so they can profit from the interactions they have observed. The more interactions a child observes, the more expert he or she becomes at extracting information from them.

Vygotsky believed thought and language are closely related. Language development is key to being able to internalize complex ideas (Vygotsky, 1962). Developing children's language skills helps children develop their thought. For example, if their language skills are strong, children can understand adult conversations better, and learn more from those conversations, than they can if they do not understand many of the words the adults are using.

 ## THE ZONE OF PROXIMAL DEVELOPMENT

Vygotsky's second major contribution is an idea termed the **zone of proximal development** (also called the **zone of potential development**), or **ZPD.** The ZPD is the range between a child's level of independent performance and the level of performance a child

THINKING ANALYTICALLY

If internalization is key to learning, to what extent are interactions in school—students questioning their teachers, for example, or waiting in line at a water fountain—critical to learning?

SUGGESTION: From a Vygotskian point of view, interaction is key because it is the basis of internalization. By listening to other students, students can learn how to ask questions when they are unsure of the meaning of a concept being taught. They can learn patience and civility (or the lack of these) by waiting with others in a line.

can reach with expert guidance. In conventional assessments of children's ability, we typically observe what children can do on their own. What they can do is based on the experiences they have had, and the interaction of the effects of these experiences with the children's inherited characteristics. Vygotsky's idea was to provide a way to measure the distance between this independent performance and the child's guided performance. This difference in turn can give educators an idea of the level of performance a child is ready to reach on his or her own.

Vygotsky argued that the ZPD could be assessed by testing children via a **dynamic assessment environment,** a testing situation in which the examiner not only gives the child problems to solve, but also gives the child a graded series of hints when the child is unable to solve the problems. The examiner then observes the child's ability to profit from this systematic instruction (Sternberg & Grigorenko, 2001). Suppose a child's reading comprehension is being tested in a dynamic assessment environment. One of the questions might require the child to figure out the meaning of a word in the reading passage. If the child cannot figure out the meaning of the word, the tester provides the first in a series of hints. For example, the examiner might give a hint about the part of speech, or about a function the underlying concept performs, or about a related word nearby in the reading passage. In each case, the examiner observes whether the child is able to profit from the hint (Lidz & Elliott, 2000). Thus, for Vygotsky, the key to understanding what a child is truly capable of is through the examiner's serving not only as a tester, but as a teacher as well.

In contrast to the dynamic assessment environment is the conventional testing situation, or *static assessment environment,* with which you are probably familiar from the many such tests you have taken. A **static assessment environment** is a testing situation in which the examiner gives the child problems to solve, but provides little or no feedback about the child's performance. The last thing the examiner wants to do is to give hints: To do so would be viewed as invalidating the conventional test.

Tests of the zone of proximal development have been devised (see, e.g., Brown & Ferrara, 1985; Day, Engelhardt, Maxwell, & Bolig, 1997; Feuerstein, 1979; Grigorenko & Sternberg, 1998), and they do seem to measure something other than general cognitive abilities. These tests have promise for helping teachers understand children's readiness to profit from instruction.

THINKING CREATIVELY

How can aspects of the theories of Piaget and Vygotsky be synthesized to better account for the whole picture of a child's cognitive development?

SUGGESTION: Both maturation and interactions with the environment through internalization are key aspects of cognitive development.

THINKING PRACTICALLY

What risks would you run in trying to assign a number or a score to a student's zone of proximal development?

SUGGESTION: Your evaluation might set a spurious limit on the student's perceived ability to profit from experience.

SCAFFOLDING

Many psychologists have extended the ideas of Vygotsky to better understand how children learn and think. For example, Reuven Feuerstein (1980) has suggested that children learn primarily in two different ways, through direct instruction or through mediated learning experiences. **Direct instruction** is the teaching situation in which a teacher, parent, or other authority imparts knowledge to a child by teaching it. When a middle school teacher says, "Today, we'll be learning about Brazil," he or she is embarking on direct instruction. A **mediated learning experience** (MLE) is a learning situation in which an adult or older child indirectly helps a child learn by explaining events in the environment, but without directly teaching some lesson. Mediated learning experience is a form of **scaffolding**—competent assistance or support, usually provided through mediation of the environment by a parent or teacher, by which cognitive, socioemotional, and behavioral forms of development can occur. For example, an adult might go with a child to a museum and explain what the exhibits mean; or the adult might watch a television program with a child and explain what is happening. The adult thus serves as an expert model for the child. Feuerstein believes MLE is the stronger of the two kinds of learning for the development of advanced cognitive skills.

FOCUS ON: DEVELOPMENT AND STUDENT INTERACTION
GRETCHEN MURPHY: UNIVERSITY PARK ELEMENTARY SCHOOL, FAIRBANKS, AK – GRADES K–6

Gretchen Murphy has been teaching for twenty-two years. She often uses Vygotsky's zone of proximal development to encourage her students' progress to the next level of understanding.

What do you consider to be a sound educational foundation?

Students need basic understanding in the primary grades: reading, writing, number sense, problem solving, spelling, and geography. These are things we all need to know.

Teaching children how to ask and research their own questions is critical because children need affirmation that life is dynamic, not static. Finding answers to their own questions is very empowering for learners.

How do you guide students to the next level of learning?

I keep in mind zones of proximal development, as described in Vygotsky's theory. Learning must have a comfortable foothold in what the learner already knows. Each of us learns through her or his strengths, and a teacher's job is to identify students' strengths to facilitate their learning.

The art of teaching is to open learning pathways for students.

The decision of what methods to use is determined by the needs of my students. I enjoy investigations and open-ended activities, so there is no limit to where our learning can go. I like to let the children discover rules for themselves, rather than plopping them down "from the top." I encourage students to reach out to more complex ideas. A child's curiosity is boundless.

For example, after learning the strategy of a favorite board game, some of my fourth-grade students wanted to create their own smaller, travel-sized versions of the game to take home. I saw this as an excellent opportunity for them to learn about proportions, so I asked groups of students to reduce the rectangular game board size without changing its shape.

Each group discovered a different way, not all of which were successful. After listening to each other's proposed methods, they realized that they needed to modify their investigations to discover a workable pattern rule. My students were not discouraged by a "wrong"

answer. They realized that they learned from their first incorrect methods and were anxious to keep searching for different patterns.

They need my guidance to reach a correct solution, so I developed a set of lessons using cubes, graph paper, and a blank factor chart. The original game board was a 30-inch by 42-inch rectangle. Since the children had not studied formal division, they used the cubes to find factors of 30 and 42 that "fit" the patterns we were developing. Choosing pairs that "fit," the students drew arrays on graph paper and cut them out so they had a visual representation with which to compare their new shape to that of the original game board. The smallest possible rectangle represented the ratio, so all the rectangles in that set "grew" by the same pattern. Experimenting with different rectangular proportions and "growing" rectangles with specific ratios led my students to discover the importance of proportion.

This is just one example of a lesson that grew with the students so that they created their own meaning and discovered principles of mathematics for

---

Teachers can create MLEs for students by explaining ideas or events, but allowing the *students* to see for themselves the connections among the ideas and their logical conclusions. A teacher might say, "As you can see, polar bears are white. They live in the Arctic, which is covered with snow." The students might then have the insight that being a white animal in a white environment is an integral aspect of the situation. If the students bring up this point, the teacher could offer further ideas, such as "Being white and blending in makes the polar bear hard to see. The polar bear must hunt seals for food," from which the students may conclude, "It is easier for a camouflaged animal to capture food."

Joan Carlin, the math teacher profiled at the beginning of the chapter, might say to her students, "When a ladder leans against a wall, it forms one side of a triangle. Can you see the triangle in this picture?" She might then add, "The formula we learned for calculating the size of one of the angles of a triangle works for all triangles." At this point, students might be able to see the relationship between the triangles in the math book and the triangle made by a ladder leaning against a wall.

In general, scaffolding is an excellent and key technique for stimulating cognitive development. The main element in many programs designed to facilitate early cognitive development is teaching parents to respond to their infants and young children in

themselves. I guided them to make discoveries for themselves at higher levels of understanding.

How does communicating their ideas help your students construct their own knowledge?

Communication validates learning and helps students construct their own knowledge. Visualizations that students create in their minds deserve an appropriate communication path, such as drawing, writing, acting, or talking. Communicating allows students to revisit their own thinking as well as share their ideas with others.

Explain how learning takes place between the students.

Learning is active. It demands attention and respect for other people and for the process of learning. I listen to the students and they listen to each other. It's important for kids to listen to each other.

When we do a school-wide graphing project, students talk math on their own. The younger students talk to the older ones, and the older ones mentor the younger ones. Peer groups compare data and discuss the graphs. One student said she thought that teachers sometimes got in the way of learning. I think that she has a good point. A lot of learning takes place between students.

We built a large dome in our classroom. Students worked together in small groups to construct miniature domes before we built our big one together. Within each group, students watched and listened to each other and helped each other build domes, offering each other suggestions and help. Children can understand one another's learning problems much better than I do. I often rely on peer tutoring to help a child who is having trouble.

What advice would you give to new teachers?

A teacher is a lifelong learner. The longer I teach, the more important I realize it is to collect best lessons from others (and from my own experience), to determine my own students' learning

> Learning is active. It demands attention and respect for other people and for the process of learning.

styles, and to keep up with current trends in learning and brain research. A teacher's job is to meld all of these into a classroom environment. Go slowly, one step at a time in a determined direction, and always follow your heart.

You can follow someone else's lead, such as the directions in a teacher's guide, until you have modified a lesson to suit yourself and your students. Use the standards to guide *what* you teach; use your students' learning styles to guide *how* you teach.

Listen to your students. Listen to what they say and how they say it; read their body language. Determine how each student learns. Include visual, kinesthetic, and aural techniques in each lesson, simultaneously if possible. Encourage your students to learn with all of their senses. Listen and learn with your students.

---

ways that provide scaffolding for the children (Anderson & Sawin, 1983; Barrera, Rosenbaum, & Cunningham, 1986; Sternberg & Grigorenko, 1997). Teachers using scaffolding can respond not only to the developed and developing cognitive abilities of children, but also to their developed and developing socioemotional needs and behavioral repertoire. This chapter's Flexible Expert feature shows how expert analytical, creative, and practical teachers and students make use of scaffolding.

Three converging lines of evidence demonstrate the importance of scaffolding for cognitive development. First, cognitive, socioemotional, and behavioral scaffolding adequate for a child's development are significantly associated with subsequent outcomes of cognitive development (Sternberg, Grigorenko, & Nokes, 1997). A child whose parents provide appropriate early scaffolding, for example, may be more likely to develop the cognitive abilities needed to succeed later in school.

Second, scaffolding is a crucial part in planning **intervention,** action taken to improve a child's cognitive, socioemotional, or behavioral development. Its importance here is twofold. Scaffolding is important for intervention programs targeting families, for it targets the parent-child instead of just the child. Parents need to respond to their children's needs. Scaffolding requires parents to provide carefully designed guidance.

IN EACH CHAPTER OF THE TEXT, WE INTRODUCE YOU TO A FEW SPECIFIC STRATEGIES—
ANALYTICAL, CREATIVE, AND PRACTICAL—USED BY BOTH EXPERT TEACHERS AND EXPERT STUDENTS.

THE ANALYTICAL TEACHER: Maria knows her high school chemistry students will need different levels of help on the upcoming lab assignment. She assigns students to groups that match more advanced students with those who need more help, so the advanced students can share their expertise as needed.

THE CREATIVE TEACHER: Maria uses her computer to make colorful posters and handouts that remind students of the steps for setting up the lab equipment. For the first few lab assignments, Maria requires students to check off each step as they complete it. Later, the posters and handouts serve as reminders. Eventually, all the students perform each step without even referring to the reminders.

THE PRACTICAL TEACHER: Maria works one on one with Betsy to teach her how to get a solid precipitate to form in a certain liquid compound. First Maria models the steps herself. Then she talks Betsy through the steps, providing reminders and directions as Betsy does the work herself. Finally, Maria leaves Betsy to do the experiment on her own.

THE ANALYTICAL STUDENT: Jacob plans to do all problems he can on his geometry assignment before he asks the teacher for help on the problems he cannot complete.

THE CREATIVE STUDENT: Jacob draws an illustrated checklist to help him remember the steps for solving his geometry problems.

THE PRACTICAL STUDENT: Jacob forms a study group with three other geometry students. Each member can call, e-mail, or get together with someone else in the group whenever he or she has trouble figuring out an assignment.

THINKING CREATIVELY

How might you apply mediated learning experience to help a child understand mathematical concepts used in everyday life?

SUGGESTION: You might work with the child by modeling the processes of deciding whether the purchase of a toy is worth the price.

This guidance is based on a child's actualized capacity, targeted to a child's potential gains, and unique and sensitive to a given child's needs. Many expensive intervention studies where parents were additional interventionists did not show any positive effects of intervention because parents were taught what to do but were not taught how to respond to their child's needs, how to read behavioral and socioemotional clues, or how to deliver adequate interventions without overstimulating their child.

Scaffolding also is important for interventions that target education, where the intervention is delivered in a centralized manner by professionals. Such programs focus on the teacher-student pair. Because scaffolding, especially that supporting the socioemotional needs of a child, is crucial within the family, the most effective intervention programs for developing cognitive expertise intertwine active educational intervention at preschools with adequate scaffolding at home.

Third, studies of the long-term effects of intervention indicate that without adequate duration of a program and without adequate scaffolding after the program, cognitive gains tend to disappear (Grotzer & Perkins, 2000; Sternberg & Williams, 1998). Inadequate scaffolding minimizes treatment effects and shrinks the window of educational opportunity for children in need of services. To foster and ensure long-term effects of early intervention, scaffolding should be present within families and schools.

 ### EVALUATING VYGOTSKY'S THEORY

Vygotsky's theory is a major contribution, but it seems to deal only with limited aspects of cognitive development. The zone of proximal development is an interesting construct, but it is difficult to know whether any instrument truly measures it. Most likely, internalization accounts for part of, but not all of, how children as well as adults learn. Information-processing theories provide more details on learning.

A teacher mediates a learning experience for her students at the New Mexico Museum of Natural History, as she points out the various species living in an aquarium. (Bob Daemmrich)

Implications for Teaching

Vygotsky's theory has at least three key implications for instruction and assessment:

■ ***Children learn by internalizing external dialogue.*** Children learn to think critically and well by observing those around them doing it. One of the most important aspects of being a teacher is serving as a role model for students. Other, more expert students also can serve as role models, although as with any such models, they can do so for good or for ill.

■ ***Children almost never operate at the peak of their capacity.*** Obviously, teachers can expect too much of children. But at least as often, they expect too little. Vygotsky's theory points out that children have a zone of proximal development, and that with proper guidance, children can be helped to develop further within the range of this zone.

■ ***Language and thought are intimately and inextricably related.*** The view that language is key to both direct instruction and mediated learning experience has direct implications for everyone, but especially for students who come to school speaking a language that is not the principal language of the school. Teachers need to build rather than destroy children's native languages when they do not correspond to the language of the school (Bialystock & Hakuta, 1994).

Information-Processing Theories: Examining Learning and Memory Skills

Information-processing theorists seek to understand cognitive development in terms of how people of various ages process information and represent it mentally (Klahr & MacWhinney, 1998). Information processing is not a theory, per se. Rather, it is an approach that has generated a number of different theories about cognitive development (see Amsel & Renninger, 1997; Kuhn & Siegler, 1998; Sternberg, 1984; Sternberg & Berg, 1990), most of them specific to particular domains of information-processing. Information-processing theorists are interested, for example, in the mental processes and strategies children use when they solve arithmetic problems, write essays, draw pictures, or engage in any of a number of other tasks. Although the same mental processes may occur in a variety of domains, the way they are used varies across domains.

For example, consider mathematical processing and verbal processing. Two key processes of cognitive development, *encoding* and *combination,* are used in thinking about both numbers and words. *Encoding* is the process by which we take in new information and make sense of the world, and *combination* is the process by which we put together the pieces of information we have encoded (Davidson, 1995; Siegler, 1984, 1998). The way we combine numbers, however, may have little in common with the way we combine words. For this reason we need to study cognitive processes in two ways: a *domain-general* way, identifying processes used in a variety of cognitive tasks; and a *domain-specific* way, identifying how the processes are used in each kind of task. Three key domains—verbal skills, quantitative skills, and memory—have been subject to extensive research by information-processing theorists and are discussed here. Researchers also have considered other intellectual abilities as well.

 ## VERBAL SKILLS

One verbal skill that has been studied in some detail is **verbal comprehension,** the ability to understand written and spoken material. Researchers have studied verbal comprehension at various levels.

One level is that of the comprehension of words in sentences. How do children learn what words mean? Robert Sternberg and several other researchers have suggested that most vocabulary is learned from context (Sternberg, 1987a; Sternberg & Powell, 1983; Werner & Kaplan, 1963; Woodward & Markman, 1998). These researchers suggest that children as well as adults use various cues to figure out word meanings. For example, read this sentence: "The teacher's instructions were ambiguous, with the result that the children just couldn't figure out what they were expected to do." A child might try to figure out what *ambiguous* means by noting it is something that can apply to instructions and it results in uncertainty. Sternberg and colleagues found that the amount of difficulty children would have in learning a word could be predicted by the kinds and numbers of cues available for figuring out the word's meaning. They also found, as predicted, that a student's ability to figure out word meanings was a good predictor of her vocabulary. This finding suggests a link between the ability to use verbal contexts and the level of vocabulary one develops. Indeed, one of the best ways for children to increase their vocabulary is simply to read a lot and thus have many opportunities to learn words in their natural contexts.

Ellen Markman (1977, 1979; Woodward & Markman, 1998) has studied verbal comprehension at the level of paragraph understanding. She asked children to read a passage such as the following:

> *To make it they put the ice cream in a very hot oven. The ice cream in Baked Alaska melts when it gets that hot. Then they take the ice cream out of the oven and serve it right away. When they make Baked Alaska, the ice cream stays firm and does not melt. (Markman, 1979, p. 656)*

As you may have noticed, this brief paragraph contradicts itself. In one place, it says the ice cream in Baked Alaska melts when it gets hot; in another place, it says the ice cream stays firm and does not melt. Amazingly, almost half of the children between 8 and 11 years of age that Markman tested did not notice the contradiction, even when warned in advance that such contradictions might exist. As a teacher, therefore, do not be surprised to discover that children may read and even accept two contradictory statements as though they did not contradict each other.

CONSTRUCTING YOUR OWN LEARNING

Read the following paragraph and see whether you can detect the contradiction embedded within it. If possible, you might also ask some of the children you are working with in a practicum to try this same test. What is it that makes a contradiction more or less difficult to detect? What could you, as a teacher, do to help your students learn to detect contradictions and improve their reading comprehension?

Janet was glad finally to be home after a hard day at school. Her English teacher had yelled at her, she had gotten a low grade on her math test, and she had struck out in baseball during gym class. Now she could relax and watch TV for a couple of hours before she started her homework. The TV shows were boring, though, so Janet decided to stop watching TV and call her friend Susie. She was not sure what to talk about though. Janet changed her mind again and decided to start working on studying for her first math test of the term.

QUANTITATIVE SKILLS

Investigators have taken a variety of approaches to understanding the development of quantitative skills. For example, Brown and Burton (1978) have found that children's errors in arithmetic can often be accounted for by *buggy algorithms,* or erroneous strategies the children consistently use when they add, subtract, multiply, or divide. Children may reason well but come to wrong answers because they are using algorithms that do not work (Ben-Zeev, 1995, 1998; see also Sternberg & Ben-Zeev, 1996). For example, one of Joan Carlin's middle school math students may consistently arrive at the wrong answer when asked to find the area of a circle. When she sees the student's homework, Joan notices that the student inserts the diameter, rather than the radius, of the circle into the formula for finding area. The student's algorithm, or set of steps, for finding the area of a circle has a "bug" that needs to be fixed if the student is to solve circle problems correctly.

Buggy algorithms are common in addition and subtraction of fractions. A student adding $\frac{1}{3} + \frac{1}{2}$ may come up with $\frac{2}{5}$, believing the correct algorithm is to add numerators and denominators separately. Because students often do not check whether their answers make sense, their buggy algorithms persist. In the case of this example, the sum is actually less than $\frac{1}{2}$, a senseless result, but one that the student may offer as correct nevertheless.

Groen and Parkman (1972) studied the processes of addition and subtraction. With addition, for example, they found that people tend to count upward from the larger addend the amount of the smaller addend when they add two numbers. For example, in $8 + 3$ they would count 3 up from 8. Siegler and Shrager (1984) proposed that when children do arithmetic, they first try to solve the problems by direct retrieval of the correct answer. If their attempt at direct retrieval fails, they then use backup strategies to see whether they can reach a solution in another way, for example, by counting up from the larger of two numbers in an addition problem (Siegler, 1996).

One of the more interesting studies of mathematical thinking was done by Paige and Simon (1966). They gave students algebra word problems to solve and looked not only at whether children made errors but also at the kinds of errors the students made. They found that students were surprisingly willing to supply problem solutions that simply made no sense, for example, that involved receiving "negative" change from a purchase. One of the most useful skills a teacher can offer his or her students, apparently, is

THINKING PRACTICALLY

As a teacher, how might you instill in students the strategy of always checking answers to problems in mathematics to ensure the answers are sensible, given the terms of the problems?

SUGGESTION: Show students how answers to math problems can sometimes be wrong simply because they do not make sense, such as in the case of negative change for a dollar.

to teach them to question whether the answers they arrive at when they solve problems, in arithmetic or otherwise, make sense.

MEMORY SKILLS

As you would predict, children's memory skills improve with age (Kail, 1986; Schneider & Bjorklund, 1998). Two factors that influence this improvement are knowledge about the domain in which people are learning and remembering, and people's understanding of their own memory.

Chi and Koeske (1983) found that our ability to remember is enhanced if we are knowledgeable about the domain in which we are recalling. Thus memory skills lead to increased knowledge, which in turn leads to better memory. Children will learn better, generally speaking, in domains about which they already have more knowledge.

The ability of people of any age to remember material depends in part on prior experiences. For example, Guatemalan and Australian aboriginal children from rural regions, even at the grade school level, are generally more expert than children in a typical urban or suburban U.S. environment at generating memory-enhancing strategies for spatial locations and arrangements of objects (Kearins, 1981; Rogoff, 1986). The greater skill of the Guatemalan and Australian aboriginal children is presumably due to their greater reliance on spatial skills in their environment. Typical U.S. children, however, usually are better at generating strategies for learning isolated bits of information, as they are often required to do in the schools they attend.

As these cross-cultural results suggest, understanding and control of one's own memory can also affect memory performance (Flavell, 1976, 1981; Flavell, Green, & Flavell, 1995; Flavell & Wellman, 1977; Nelson, 1996, 1999; Wellman & Gelman, 1998). In general, understanding and control of memory seem to develop as children age; children become more expert at using their own memories. Younger children, for example, greatly overestimate their own memory abilities. They are less likely than older children or adults to use recall strategies even if they are aware of them. When asked to recall information, for example, they often do not spontaneously rehearse the information. **Rehearsal** is a memory strategy in which a person, either mentally or aloud, recites information over and over again in order to remember it. Thus rehearsal allows an individual to gain some control of what information gets stored in memory over the long term. A young child may simply assume he will remember his new e-mail address, even though the child does not repeat the new address, either mentally or aloud. Students often rehearse what they learn to study for a test, as, for example, when they repeat to themselves an English word and its Spanish equivalent in an attempt to commit the pairing to memory. When taught strategies in one domain, younger children often fail to *transfer* them to another domain: For example, they do not apply what they learned in the art domain to the new history domain.

The information-processing approach to cognitive development helps explain how children and adults develop strategies for solving cognitive problems in a variety of domains. What are some of the implications of this approach for educators?

THINKING CREATIVELY

On what kind of memory test might you expect people from a rural region to do better than people from a city? On what kind of test might you expect the reverse?

SUGGESTION: Rural people might do better on problems involving animals or grains; city people, on problems involving street addresses or train schedules.

Implications for Teaching

Consider the following implications of the information-processing approach for instruction and assessment:

■ *We need to understand not just the answers children provide, but how they arrived at these answers.* By trying to understand children's thought processes and not just their final answers to problems, teachers can help students develop correct strategies and change incorrect ones. Expert teachers often ask students to explain how they came up with an answer or to "show their work" on tests and homework problems.

- ■ *Teach strategies for learning.* Teach the material of interest, but also teach children *how to learn and use* the material to best make use of their pattern of abilities. Do not just assume that students will acquire those strategies on their own.

- ■ *Knowledge as well as strategy is key to expertise.* We now recognize that both knowledge and strategy are key to expertise. Students cannot learn to think effectively in the absence of either knowledge or strategies for effectively utilizing that knowledge.

- ■ *How students represent information can be a key to their learning and problem solving.* The key to solving a mathematical word problem, a physics problem, or even a problem in social policy can be in the way information is represented. Often an error is not in the computation, but in how the problem is set up in the first place.

Three Major Approaches to Cognitive Development: A Comparison

We have considered three main approaches to cognitive development—that of Piaget, that of Vygotsky, and the general information-processing approach— as well as an offshoot of Piaget's approach called the *neo-Piagetian approach.* How are ways of understanding cognitive development similar and how are they different?

Piaget considered cognitive development to be largely a function of maturation. Children would reach cognitive milestones, such as the development of object permanence or the ability to reverse operations and recognize conservation, when they became cognitively mature enough to do so. Piaget did not encourage trying to hurry children through the process of cognitive development. Piaget's theory is based on stages of development. Piaget also proposed that, in general, development proceeds at the same rate across cognitive domains. He did, however, create the concept of horizontal décalage to make minor allowances for differences in the speed at which children show development in different domains.

Neo-Piagetian theorists tend to agree with many of Piaget's basic ideas about cognitive development. They also see development largely as a function of cognitive maturation, rather than as based on learning. Like Piaget, most neo-Piagetians propose stages of cognitive development. The main area of difference is that several neo-Piagetian theorists have suggested stages beyond Piaget's final stage of formal operations. In addition, neo-Piagetians tend to agree with Piaget's view of cognitive development as domain general.

The theory of Lev Vygotsky contrasts in several basic ways with the theories of Piaget and the neo-Piagetians. Vygotsky proposed that cognitive development results from children's internalization of information from their environment. In other words, children learn from the people around them. Vygotsky also viewed internalization as occurring continuously, without distinct stages in cognitive development. The importance of the child's surroundings in Vygotsky's theory also suggests he believed that development can occur at different rates in different cognitive domains, depending on the information available to a child and the amount of encouragement the child was provided.

Information-processing theorists also tend to see cognitive development partly as a result of learning and partly as a result of the child's level of maturation (e.g., Keil,

1989). Development typically is viewed as a continuous process with no obvious stages. Information-processing theorists suggest certain domain-general cognitive abilities such as encoding and combining pieces of information. However, these abilities may be used differently in different cognitive domains. Therefore, information-processing theorists also study domain-specific cognitive development.

These three major approaches each take slightly different views of the development of cognitive expertise, but they should not be considered entirely contradictory. Instead, they can be viewed as complementing each other, with some theories addressing aspects of cognitive development that others do not consider. All of these approaches provide us with valuable insights into the development of children's thinking abilities. Each approach also suggests several important implications for the way children are educated.

Although these approaches tell us a great deal about how children's thinking develops, we need to go beyond these approaches to understand one more particularly crucial part of development: the development of language.

Language Development

As Vygotsky and others have recognized, language is crucial to cognitive development (Nelson, 1999). Language appears to comprise a special set of abilities (Bloom, 1998). Virtually everyone is able to learn a language, regardless of the environment the person is in, unless the person is subject to extreme deprivation. Evidence even indicates there is a critical period in children's development when they are particularly receptive to learning language.

WHAT MAKES A LANGUAGE A LANGUAGE?

What, exactly, makes a language? Five properties seem to be key (Brown, 1965; Clark & Clark, 1977):

1. **Communication.** Language provides a means for one individual to understand the thoughts of another. It enables students to understand what the teacher is saying, and vice versa.

2. **Arbitrariness.** With few exceptions, the relation between a word and what it refers to is arbitrary. *Dog, chien,* and *perro* all provide equally usable ways of referring to the same animal, as would the equivalent words in other languages. Similarly, terms such as *subtract, take away,* and *minus* are arbitrary ways of saying essentially the same thing.

3. **Meaningful structure.** All languages are patterned so larger structures build in a sensible way on smaller ones: words on sounds, sentences on words, paragraphs on sentences, and so on. Children speaking *any* language are equally capable of creating meaningfully structured expressions.

4. **Multiplicity of structure.** All meaningful utterances can be analyzed at many levels. For example, we can analyze a sentence in terms of its grammar or its meaning. To appreciate language fully and expertly, children must learn about all these different types of structure.

5. **Productivity.** Any language can produce an infinite number of sentences. Every day, many new strings of words are being created that have never before been created in the history of the world. In other words, children are using language creatively every day of their lives, from a very early age.

Language is often viewed as developing in seven basic stages. As children pass through each of the following stages, they develop increasing expertise in speaking their native language (Jusczyk, 1997):

1. **Prenatal responsivity to the human voice.** It now appears that fetuses can hear their mothers' voices. Within days after birth, newborns show a preference for voices (e.g., their mothers') they have heard over voices they have not heard prenatally (e.g., DeCasper & Fifer, 1980).

2. **Cooing.** This is the earliest postnatal step in language acquisition. *Cooing* is the production of sounds by an infant. These sounds potentially include all sounds humans can produce. The cooing of infants is virtually the same all over the world, even among the deaf.

3. **Babbling.** *Babbling* is an infant's preferential production of sounds that are characteristic of the infant's to-be-learned first language. At this stage, the infant begins to lose the ability spontaneously to make sounds outside his or her own language system. Babbling thus differs among babies around the world.

4. **One-word utterances.** During this stage, the infant utters his first word. By 18 months of age, infants typically have vocabularies ranging from 3 to 100 words (Siegler, 1996). Children are likely at this stage to make great use of their limited vocabularies. In doing so they often make **overextension errors,** applications of a word beyond its legitimate use. For example, any man may come to be referred to as "Dada." Children sometimes make **underextension errors** as well, which involve using words too specifically—for example, fruit is only a banana.

5. **Two-word utterances.** At roughly 2.5 years of age, children may produce their first two-word utterances. During this stage, children first acquire the most rudimentary understanding of **syntax,** or the rules for combining words.

6. **Telegraphic speech.** At this stage, children of roughly age 3 become able to express **telegraphic speech,** speech that uses simple syntax in utterances of two or three words that impart simple meaning. Children's vocabulary is now expanding rapidly, typically reaching about three hundred words at age 2 and about a thousand words at age 3.

7. **Basic adult sentence structure.** This stage, which children typically enter by about 4 years of age, involves their speaking in much the manner of an adult, although in a format that may be simplified. However, by about age 10, the structure of children's language differs little from that of a typical adult, although their vocabulary is likely to be lesser and their knowledge of formal grammar still lacking. Thus, at a young age, children have all the ingredients for linguistic expertise.

THEORIES OF LANGUAGE ACQUISITION: A COMPARISON

There are several theories as to how children acquire language. These theories differ in several ways, most notably with respect to their claims regarding the role of nature (genetic programming) versus nurture (upbringing and interactions with the environment).

One theory, sometimes called a behavioral one, holds that acquisition is largely by imitation. This theory emphasizes the role of nurture in language acquisition. Indeed, we know that, to some extent, children imitate the speech patterns they hear in others. B. F. Skinner (1957) believed language acquisition goes beyond imitation: Children learn language through a system of reinforcements whereby they are consistently rewarded for correct but not for incorrect language use. Moreover, parents often use *child-directed speech,* which is a simplified way of speaking to children so the children will understand. It has been shown that children prefer listening to such speech over other kinds of speech (Fernald, Taeschner, Dunn, Papousek, DeBoysson-Bardies, & Fukui, 1989).

We must consider some drawbacks to a theory that suggests children learn language by imitation alone. One of the biggest ones is that children are constantly producing new sentences different from any they have ever heard. In producing such sentences, they are going beyond, rather than imitating, what they have heard. Moreover, children frequently **overregularize,** that is, use word forms that follow a rule rather than recognize an exception to it. For example, a child may overregularize the rule that says past tense words end in -*ed,* by saying "I goed home." Yet children typically have never heard the overregularizations they produce. Although this imitation theory may be incomplete, it correctly suggests that children will learn to speak and write better if they are given good models to learn from.

Another theory emphasizes nature. In this view, humans possess a **language acquisition device,** or **LAD,** an innate predisposition or ability to acquire language expertise (Chomsky, 1965, 1972; Pinker, 1994, 1998). Children are preprogrammed to learn language, and the environment merely serves as a catalyst for language development. Many language theorists who take this point of view believe that children exhibit **critical periods,** certain points in their development during which they are particularly attuned for various aspects of language development. Such critical periods may be behind the phenomenon of accents. Generally, if children learn a second language in an environment of native speakers, they acquire the accent of a native speaker. Adults, however, typically demonstrate an accent identifying them as speakers of another first language, whether or not they learn the second language from native speakers. Even when they become expert in the structure and vocabulary of a language, adults are still likely to speak with an accent identifying them as non-native speakers.

A consensus view is that both nature and nurture play interactive roles in stages of language development (Locke, 1994). On the one hand, humans do appear to be preprogrammed to learn their first language during childhood. On the other hand, the stimuli presented in the environment—the kind of speech, the amount of reading material, and so forth—can affect how well people acquire that language. Children seem to learn language, at least in part, through active **hypothesis testing,** forming hypotheses about language and linguistic forms and trying them out in their environments (Bloom, 1998; Slobin, 1971, 1985). Parents, teachers, and others who are responsive to the children's tests can facilitate the children's acquisition of language.

THINKING CREATIVELY

Suppose language did determine thought. Would people who have grown up speaking different languages be able to communicate effectively? Why or why not?

SUGGESTION: If language determined thought, the more different the languages, the harder people would find it to communicate with each other. The reason is that the greater the divergence of their languages, the more different will be their conceptual systems.

Hypothesis testing is illustrated in children's acquisition of the meaning of words. For example, meanings of many words are learned in context, as described earlier, through hypothesis testing. Suppose a student sees the sentence, "Tanith peered at Tobar through the oam of the bubbling stew" (Sternberg & Powell, 1983). A child reading this sentence can use hypothesis testing to figure out the meaning of *oam.* We know it is something translucent or transparent and connected with a bubbling stew, perhaps arising from it. A plausible meaning, and the correct one, is that *oam* means steam. Sternberg and Powell (1983) found a high correlation between students' ability to figure out meanings of words and the context, suggesting this ability is crucial to the formation of vocabulary.

THE RELATIONSHIP BETWEEN LANGUAGE AND THOUGHT

As children develop language, what effect is the language having on the children's thought processes? Again, there are competing views.

Edward Sapir (1941/1964) and Benjamin Lee Whorf (1956) have proposed what is usually considered an extreme view, namely, **linguistic determinism.** In this view, the structure of our language shapes our thought processes. Is there a difference in how you

Language and thought are related and interactive. The teaching of language becomes particularly important in a multicultural or bilingual classroom. Here, a group of students speaking a variety of languages at home work together on a school poster. Although different languages have different color terms and different numbers of them, speakers of these languages are nevertheless all able to identify the same colors. (David Young-Wolff, PhotoEdit)

think about the words "I am" in the two sentences "I am tired" and "I am a woman (or man)"? In Spanish, the words used to mean "I am" in these two sentences are different. Thus, for someone who believes in linguistic determinism, Spanish-speaking individuals will think of states of being differently from English-speaking individuals—because English speakers have just one form of the verb "to be," whereas Spanish speakers have two: *ser* and *estar*. Although there are several differences between the two forms, in general, *ser* is used for relatively permanent states, *estar* for more temporary ones (Sera, 1992). This point of view is intriguing, but not fully supported, because almost all languages permit us to communicate basically the same thoughts (Gerrig & Banaji, 1994). Moreover, although different languages have different color terms, and different numbers of them, speakers of these various languages are nevertheless all able to identify the same various colors (Heider & Olivier, 1972).

A related version of this point of view is called **linguistic relativity,** which suggests that language influences but does not determine thought (Lucy, 1997). For example, people familiar with all the different kinds of grass found in a lawn are likely to think about grass in a different way from people who simply view grass as "the green stuff that makes a lawn"—that is, they will have many more specific words for the generic word *grass*. Many theorists of language today accept the idea that language can influence thought, without absolutely determining it.

To conclude, language and thought are related and interactive. It is important to teach language well because language can facilitate thought. Moreover, adding a second language to a well-developed first language seems to enhance cognitive functioning (Bialystock & Hakuta, 1994; Hakuta, 1986). But language does not determine thought, nor thought, language. Moreover, language is related not only to thought but also to the social context of its use, as we discuss in Chapter 3 on social development.

BILINGUALISM AND EDUCATION: AN INTRODUCTION

Language is not only related to thought but, also in complex ways, to culture and educational and social functioning. In the United States, especially since the late 1970s, there has been a rise in the number of immigrants and refugees, especially from Latin America and Asia, adding to America's linguistic and cultural diversity. These demographic changes have had an impact on education and society. In this context, some groups have insisted that members of non-English-speaking communities learn English to function well in U.S. society. For children, this means learning English in school as early as possible and devoting a significant amount of school time to that second-language learning. Others, however, prefer to value and preserve linguistic diversity

THINKING CREATIVELY

Would an Inuit child from northern Alaska think about snow differently from a child growing up in southern Arizona? Why or why not?

SUGGESTION: The linguistic-determinism hypothesis would say yes. In reality, however, the difference may not be large, especially if the child from southern Arizona has visited snow-covered mountains.

and to use students' first language as a key resource for learning in school and performing in society in general.

The simplest definition of **bilingualism** is the ability to speak two languages. However, included with this definition should be an awareness of the social and cultural conditions that can make it difficult for a child speaking in a first language to learn a second and that can impede that learning as well as other kinds of learning and functioning in school and outside.

A Vietnamese-speaking child, or a child who knows for the most part only Spanish or Haitian Creole, experiences problems in school and society that students who speak English as a first language are spared. For example, moving between the social circle of one's English-speaking classmates and one's parents, who speak the native language and practice their immigrant culture at home, presents difficulties in adjustment. Some children may also be devastated by the name calling they suffer as a result of stumbling over English, even though they have acquired an age-appropriate mastery of their native language. In addition, these students may be pressured to learn English, yet not always have access to it. Access will depend on several circumstances. Clearly the age at which English as a second language is learned (usually, the earlier the better) and the context in which it is learned are going to be important factors. So will the presence or absence of English in the child's community.

Also critical to both English-language acquisition and other learning is the relative status of the languages: When the student's native language, such as Spanish or Chinese, is valued as much or virtually as much as English, then the bilingual experience will be a positive one. The individual's cultural identity will not suffer, nor will cognitive development and learning. In fact, when students are not pressured to give up their native language and bilingualism is accepted in the community, abilities in concept formation, creativity, and other cognitive functions actually appear to be enhanced (Garcia, 1992; Ricciardelli, 1992). Unfortunately, however, this is not always the case in the United States, where language diversity is not always tolerated and young people may experience discrimination as a result of speaking a "foreign" language. Even teachers may view students who have learned a first language other than English as being "handicapped" or "disadvantaged" or suffering a "deficit."

Negative thinking about non-English languages can cause teachers to ignore the first language as a resource for learning and thus rob students of access to that essential educational foundation. When this happens, the child's essential prior learning—the acquisition of the first language as a basis for future learning—cannot be tapped. On the significance of prior learning, Jim Cummins (1996, p. 75) writes, "There is general agreement among cognitive psychologists that we learn by integrating new input into our existing cognitive structures or schemata. Our prior experience provides the foundation for interpreting new information. No learner is a blank slate."

Studies in **bilingual education,** in which two languages are used as the medium of instruction, have indicated that recognizing and affirming students' native languages can be beneficial to learning in the classroom (Nieto, 2000). Where teachers understand and appreciate the process of learning a second language and how to teach to those who are just acquiring it, learning can be successful. Cummins (1976), Hakuta (1986), and others have shown that **additive bilingualism,** the addition of a second language that builds on an already well-developed first language, seems to enhance thinking ability. This contrasts with **subtractive bilingualism,** the learning of a second language that starts to replace a first language that has not yet been fully formed. In subtractive bilingual education, cognitive abilities tend to decrease. The additive—or English-*plus*—notion, however, helps not only to enrich cognitive development but also to avoid the psychological costs of abandoning one's first language.

Although educational psychology has increasingly affirmed the need to build on first-language learning for students' success in school, hot debate continues about how speakers of languages other than English are to learn. This debate is broken down and reevaluated in the Forum: Bilingual Education.

What is the best way for non-native speakers of English to learn in American schools? Although the research on this topic is explored in depth in Chapter 6, this chapter's introduction to the topic provides an excellent basis for a discussion of this controversial question. The issue is important because the number of children whose primary language is not English increased over 20 percent between 1990 and 1995, to approximately 3 million students, and has grown even more since.

FIRST VIEW: *The most widespread method now used to teach students whose first language is not English is through special bilingual education programs, which have been in use in many American schools since 1968.* In these programs, students receive instruction in core academic topics, as well as English lessons, in their primary language. Supporters of this method believe it allows children to keep up with their peers in critical academic subjects while they learn sufficient English eventually to become able to join English-only classes. According to this view, students placed in English-language classes fail to learn academic topics sufficiently because of language barriers. These children are then at risk for failure or for dropping out of school. In addition, proponents of bilingual education suggest that increasing knowledge in other areas of the curriculum may help students learn English. Alfredo Schifini states this position succinctly: "The more students know in their first language, the easier it will be to acquire a second" (Bozzone, 1995). In addition, the notion of additive bilingualism (Hakuta, 1986), discussed in this chapter, suggests that adding English to a first language that has become well developed through use in school as well as at home may enhance thinking skills.

SECOND VIEW: *There is growing public opposition to bilingual education as it is practiced in many large school districts (Hornblower, 1995; "Separate and Unequal," 1997).* Critics are concerned that students participating in bilingual education are not receiving enough English instruction to enable them to join English-language classes within a reasonable amount of time. Rather, they contend that bilingual classes have become an "educational ghetto" for children whose first language is not English, with children sometimes "stuck" in bilingual education for eight or nine years without developing English competency (Headden, 1995). They also point out that the shortage of qualified bilingual teachers often leads to inferior teaching of core academic topics, and sometimes of English, in bilingual programs (Headden, 1995; "Separate and Unequal," 1997). Opponents of bilingual instruction propose placing all children in English-language classes throughout the school day, for all topics. Children who do not speak English as their first language would be offered English tutoring (or classes in English as a Second Language, ESL) for part of the day to help them understand the instruction they receive in other subjects. Proponents of ESL instruction contend that students learn just as effectively as in bilingual classes and develop valuable English skills sooner. They also point out that English-language classes are often less expensive and that children with a variety of first languages can be taught using the English-language method, whereas bilingual education programs can usually serve only students whose first languages are rather common, such as Spanish speakers.

THIRD VIEW: A SYNTHESIS: *A small, but growing number of schools are developing immersion programs, also known as two-way or dual-language programs.* In these programs, all students, no matter what their primary languages, learn in English for part of the day and in the target immersion language for the rest of the day. Academic subjects are taught in both languages. The goal is "to create fully bilingual individuals, whether they be black, white, Hispanic, or Asian," says Elena Izquierdo, developer of one such program (Rodriguez, 1996). One of the pioneer schools in this form of instruction is the Oyster Elementary School in Washington, D.C. Another is the Dool Elementary School in Calexico, California. Both offer two-way Spanish-English programs. One of these schools is in an affluent area, and the other in a poorer area; however, students in the two-way programs at both schools have tested well above the national average in English, as well as in other academic subjects (Hornblower, 1995; Rodriguez, 1996). Although not all schools can afford to develop this option, it is one viable option, not only for teaching non-native speakers of English, but also for developing students' competence in a global economy, no matter what their native tongue.

Implications for Teaching

The study of language development and its interaction with thought harbors several implications for instruction:

- ***Ensure that children understand the language in which new material is presented.*** Sometimes children fail to learn not because they are incapable of understanding the concepts, but rather because the use of language in which the concepts are presented is above their level of sophistication. For example, telling an 8-year-old that antibiotics can help *ameliorate* their health is not an effective way of communicating that such drugs can help improve health.

- ***How you say something affects but does not determine how children think about that thing.*** Language affects, but does not determine thought. If you show through your use of language, for example, a negative attitude toward a group, children are likely to pick up on that negative attitude and possibly adopt it.

- ***Show respect for all languages, regardless of the language in which you teach.*** Language and culture are often closely bound. By showing respect for languages other than the one in which you teach, you also show respect for the cultures that use that language.

- ***Developing additive bilingualism enriches cognitive skills, whereas developing subtractive bilingualism detracts from them.*** Students benefit from a second language when that language builds on rather than replaces the first language. It is essential that all students learn to communicate well in at least one language, rather than to communicate poorly in multiple languages.

COGNITIVE DEVELOPMENT: CONCEPTS FOR TEACHING

- The study of cognitive development deals with questions such as when children first acquire various kinds of cognitive skills, whether the form that cognitive development takes is continuous or in stages, and whether it is domain specific or domain general.

- Psychologists distinguish between maturation, development that occurs without much regard to the environment, and learning, the acquisition of information and skills from interactions with the environment. Behavior is highly canalized when it develops without regard to the environment.

PIAGET'S STAGE THEORY OF COGNITIVE DEVELOPMENT

- The most nearly complete theory of cognitive development is that of Jean Piaget. This theory stresses the role of the development of new schemas, via accommodation, and the elaboration of old ones, via assimilation of new information, in a process of equilibration, an effort to achieve balance between cognitive capacities and the demands of the environment.

- Piaget proposed a series of four stages that he believed always occur in the same order, and at roughly the same ages, in all children: the sensorimotor stage, preoperational stage, concrete operational stage, and formal operational stage. He focused on the domain-general aspects of cognitive development, explaining temporary differences in domains in terms of horizontal décalage.

- Neo-Piagetians have elaborated on and refined Piaget's theory, often suggesting one or more stages of cognitive development that go beyond the fourth stage proposed by Piaget, such as a problem-finding stage, or the development of postformal thought. Dialectical thought, another possible fifth stage of cognitive development, involves the use of a thesis and an antithesis to create a synthesis.

VYGOTSKY'S SOCIOCULTURAL THEORY OF COGNITIVE DEVELOPMENT

- Vygotsky's sociocultural theory emphasized how interactions in the external environment are internalized by the child. He believed we also ought to consider the zone of proximal development (ZPD), the difference between what has been developed in the child and what might be developed with intervention from the environment, by testing via a dynamic-assessment environment.

- Scaffolding, such as through mediated learning experiences (MLE), indirectly helps children's learning; it can be seen in contrast to direct instruction.

INFORMATION-PROCESSING THEORIES: EXAMINING LEARNING AND MEMORY SKILLS

- Information-processing theorists emphasize the role of cognitive processing in development, and have provided fairly detailed models of how children of different ages solve various kinds of cognitive tasks. In recent years, these theorists have stressed the extent to which development is domain specific or domain general, and the importance of knowledge in cognitive development.

- Language develops in a series of seven stages: prenatal receptivity to voices, cooing, babbling, one-word utterances, two-word utterances, telegraphic speech, and, finally, basic adult sentence structure.

LANGUAGE DEVELOPMENT

- There seems to be an innately preprogrammed language acquisition device (LAD), as seen when children overregularize. Many language theorists believe in the existence of critical periods in language development. However, experiences in the environment also have an effect on language development, as seen when children use hypothesis testing as they learn language.

- The theory of linguistic determinism holds that the structure of language shapes thought processes. A related idea, linguistic relativity, proposes that language influences, but does not determine, thought processes. People speaking any language are generally able to express any thought, although the expression may be simpler in one language and more complex in another.

- Studies of bilingualism have shown that a student's first language, one other than English, can effectively be used as a resource for learning in schools. Research indicates that additive bilingualism, in which the student learns English by building on an already established first language, can enhance thinking abilities.

■ **Accommodation** Process of creating new schemas, or mental frameworks, to organize information that cannot be assimilated into existing schemas. Page 46

■ **Additive bilingualism** Addition of a second language that builds on an already well-developed first language. Page 70

■ **Antithesis** Proposed solution to a problem that directly contradicts an existing thesis. Page 53

■ **Assimilation** Revision of existing cognitive schemas to incorporate new information. Page 46

■ **Bilingual education** Schooling in which two languages are used as the medium of instruction. Page 70

■ **Bilingualism** Ability to communicate in two languages. Page 70

■ **Canalization** Extent to which a behavior or an underlying ability develops *without* respect to the environment. Page 42

■ **Cognitive development** Changes in mental skills that occur through increasing maturity and experience. Page 40

■ **Concrete operational stage** Piaget's third stage of cognitive development, occurring from about ages 7 to 12 years. During this stage, children become able to mentally manipulate internal representations of concrete objects. Page 48

■ **Conservation** Recognition that even when the physical appearance of something changes, its underlying quantity remains the same. Page 48

■ **Critical periods** Certain points during development when individuals are particularly tuned to various aspects of language, or other, development. Page 68

■ **Dialectical thinking** Recognition, usually occurring during late adolescence or early adulthood, that most real-life problems do not have a unique solution that is fully correct, with other solutions being incorrect; involves thesis, antithesis, and synthesis. Page 53

■ **Direct instruction** Learning situation in which a teacher, parent, or other authority imparts knowledge to a child by teaching it. Page 57

■ **Disequilibrium** State of confusion encountered when a situation does not match a preconceived notion of the way the world is or should be. Piaget suggested that disequilibrium is good for children, because it is the impetus for the development of expertise. Page 45

■ **Domain-general development** Development that occurs more or less simultaneously in multiple areas. Page 43

■ **Domain-specific development** Development that occurs at different rates in different areas. Page 43

■ **Dynamic assessment environment** Testing situation, designed to assess a child's zone of proximal development, in which the examiner not only gives the child problems to solve, but also gives the child a graded series of hints when the child is unable to solve the problems. Page 57

■ **Egocentric** Centered on the self without understanding of how other people perceive a situation. Page 47

■ **Equilibration** Balancing of cognitive structures with the needs of the environment. Page 45

■ **Formal operational stage** Piaget's final stage of cognitive development, occurring at about 11 or 12 years of age and extending through adulthood. Individuals in this stage form and operate on (e.g., reverse) abstract as well as concrete mental representations. Page 49

■ **Horizontal décalage** Jean Piaget's term for the temporary difference in performance that a child shows between various cognitive domains or activities, within a given stage of development. Page 45

■ **Hypothesis testing** As specific to this chapter, children's learning of language by forming hypotheses about language and linguistic forms and then testing those hypotheses in their environments. Page 68

■ **Internalization** Absorption, or taking in, of knowledge from the social contexts in which it is observed, so that one can use it for oneself. Page 56

■ **Intervention** Action undertaken to improve a child's cognitive, socioemotional, or behavioral development. Page 59

■ **Learning** Any relatively permanent change in thought or behavior that occurs as a result of experience. Page 41

■ **Language acquisition device,** or **LAD** Innate predisposition or ability to acquire language. Page 68

■ **Linguistic determinism** Theory of the relationship between language and thought that suggests the structure of our language shapes our thought processes. Page 68

■ **Linguistic relativity** Theory of the relationship between language and thought that suggests language influences, but does not determine, thought. Page 69

■ **Maturation** Any relatively permanent change in thought or behavior that occurs as a result of biological aging, regardless of personal experience. Page 41

■ **Mediated learning experience** (**MLE**) Learning situation in which an adult or older child indirectly helps a child learn by explaining events in the environment, but without directly teaching some lesson. Page 57

■ **Object permanence** Realization that an object continues to exist even when it is not immediately visible. Page 47

■ **Overextension errors** Applications of a word beyond its legitimate use. Page 67

■ **Overregularize** To use word forms that follow a rule rather than recognize an exception to it. Page 68

■ **Postformal thinking** Thinking that goes beyond that of formal operations in some way. Page 52

■ **Preoperational stage** Piaget's second stage of cognitive development, occurring between approximately 2 and 7 years of age. During this stage, the child actively begins to develop mental representations and learns to use words. Page 47

- **Problem finding** Stage of cognitive development proposed by Patricia Arlin, in which an individual becomes able not just to solve problems, but to find important problems to solve. Page 52

- **Rehearsal** Memory strategy in which a person, either mentally or aloud, recites information over and over again to remember it. Page 64

- **Representational thought** Well-formed mental representations, or ideas, of external stimuli. Page 47

- **Reversible thinking** Ability mentally to reverse a physical operation. According to Jean Piaget, this ability develops during the concrete operational stage of cognitive development. Page 49

- **Scaffolding** Competent assistance or support, usually provided through mediation of the environment by a parent or teacher, in which cognitive, socioemotional, and behavioral development can occur. Page 57

- **Schema** Cognitive framework that provides a way to understand and organize new knowledge. Page 46

- **Second-order relations** Relations between relations, as required by analogical reasoning. Page 49

- **Sensorimotor stage** Piaget's first stage of cognitive development, occurring between birth and about age 2. The sensorimotor stage is characterized by the development of sensory (simple input) and motor (simple output) functions. During this stage, infants respond largely in reflexive, or inborn, ways, but as they develop, they modify these reflexes to suit the demands of the environment. Page 46

- **Sociocultural theory** Vygotsky's major premise that cognitive development is largely from the outside, inward. Children reflect on the interactions between the people in their world and others, including themselves, and then make use of these interactions to further their own development. Page 55

- **Static assessment environment** Testing situation in which the examiner gives the child problems to solve, but provides little or no feedback about the child's performance. Page 57

- **Subtractive bilingualism** Learning of a second language that starts to replace a first language that has not yet been fully formed. Page 70

- **Syntax** Rules for combining words. Page 67

- **Synthesis** Proposed solution to a problem that reconciles two opposing points of view (the thesis and the antithesis). Page 53

- **Telegraphic speech** Speech that uses simple syntax in utterances of two or three words to impart a simple meaning. Children begin to develop this form of speech at about age 3. Page 67

- **Thesis** Proposed solution to a problem. Page 53

- **Underextension error** Limiting the applications of a word so the word's proposed meaning has too narrow a range of possible examples. Page 67

- **Verbal comprehension** Ability to understand spoken and written material. Page 62

- **Zone of proximal development** (also called the **zone of potential development**), or **ZPD** Range between a child's level of independent performance and the level of performance a child can reach with expert guidance. Page 56

BECOMING AN EXPERT: QUESTIONS AND PROBLEMS

Apply the concepts you have learned in this chapter to the following problems of classroom practice.

IN ELEMENTARY SCHOOL

1. In your fourth-grade class, almost all students are operating at Piaget's concrete operational level. How might you design a unit on the cycle of rain and evaporation that takes advantage of the concrete operational students' understanding of conservation?

2. How would you teach a class of first graders, all of whom are thinking at Piaget's preoperational level, about the water cycle? Could you design activities that take advantage of the egocentric thought that characterizes the preoperational stage?

3. What aspects of a unit on poetry would you emphasize for fifth graders?

4. How could you use Vygotsky's concept of internalization and Feuerstein's idea of the mediated learning experience to help a child who is having vocabulary and pronunciation problems?

5. How could you model or teach ways to figure out the meanings of unfamiliar words that your fifth graders encounter when they are reading the newspaper for social studies class?

IN MIDDLE SCHOOL

1. How could you use a unit on South American countries to encourage eighth graders to start using formal operational thinking?

2. Design a game or contest that might induce seventh graders to perform at their optimal level in an American government class.

3. What are some stories, poems, books, or plays you might assign to your eighth-grade English class to start a discussion of the importance of metacognition, being aware of one's own mental processes?

4. What kinds of mediating answers could you give to questions during a field trip to a sewage treatment plan to encourage learning about the chemical processes involved in treating wastewater?

5. Some of your sixth-grade English students seem to have very limited vocabularies. What are some interesting and fun ways you could help them expand their repertoire of words?

IN HIGH SCHOOL

1. What assignments could you make to encourage problem finding in a junior-level history class? What about a personal health class?

2. How would you balance the lessons of a physics unit on energy that introduces new ideas (which stu-dents must change their current cognitive schemas to accommodate) with lessons that focus on filling gaps in knowledge (facts the students need only assimilate into current cognitive structures)?

3. How would you design a peer tutoring program to encourage math achievement? How could you avoid frustrating students who use the tutoring program, but who have not yet achieved formal operational thinking abilities?

4. How could you use a unit on grocery shopping in a life-skills class to strengthen verbal-comprehension skills, especially noticing contradictions in written material?

5. What kinds of activities would you include in a literature class to encourage students to think dialectically?

Connecting Theory and Research to Practice

Every day in classrooms, you can see examples of Piaget's and Vygotsky's contributions to views of cognitive development. Several Web sites present specific instructional initiatives to illustrate their theories in practice.

For example, at *www.bestpraceduc.org* you will find "Best Practices in Education," which is devoted to disseminating information regarding Vygotsky's influence on educational practice. This site provides a brief

overview of several ongoing national and international educational initiatives that are based on Vygotskian theory and research. International projects include the French-U.S. Preschool Literacy Project, the Bulgarian Transformational Geometry Project, and Physics as a Way of Thinking, a collaborative project between educators in the United States and Russia. Also listed on this site are U.S. initiatives taking place in classrooms around the country.

One such program, called "Tools of the Mind" *(http://www.bestpraceduc.org/TOTM/)* was developed by Metropolitan State College of Denver psychology professors Dr. Deborah J. Leong and Dr. Elena Bodrova. The primary purpose of the "Tools of the Mind" program is to improve the reading and writing skills of at-risk elementary students. Based on Vygotskian views of learning and instruction, this program encourages the development of children as life-long, self-regulated learners. The site also includes a list of resources, including different techniques and strategies used for the program, and learning outcomes achieved by students.

Another site investigating Vygotskian theory in practice is the "Knowledge Integration Environment (KIE)" *(http://www.kie.berkeley.edu/KIE.html)* created and maintained by the Graduate School of Education at University of California, Berkeley. The primary purpose of this site is to present innovative uses of technology in teaching science to middle and high school students, by using scaffolded learning. The site also includes a curriculum library, information on how to become involved in the project, and a teacher center to help address questions about KIE.

Communities of Learners/Teachers

Sometimes the work of a psychologist is recognized by other psychologists and teachers to have a tremendous impact on how people think about thinking, learning, and teaching. Many Web pages are devoted to the scholarship of such influential psychologists. Often, these Web pages are created and maintained by special societies, groups of individuals who share a common research interest, or educators who feel that the psychologist has generated concepts and ideas applicable to the classroom that increase the effectiveness of teaching and learning.

One such Web site is devoted to developmental psychologist Jean Piaget *(http://www.piaget.org)*. The Jean Piaget Society was established in 1970 to promote Piaget's ideas and provide a forum for the discussion of his work among teachers, researchers, and scholars from all over the world. While this site is geared mainly toward

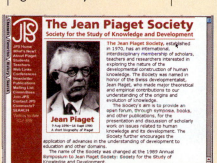

research scholars, it also provides excellent biographical material on Piaget and a variety of links and lists of text resources. It is an excellent example of how technological tools can facilitate a community of scholars, teachers, and researchers.

Online Resources

Dr. Margaret D. Anderson of Cortland College has created and designed excellent tutorials on a variety of educational psychology topics. A tutorial on Piaget's theory of cognitive development explaining his stages and biological view of development is available at: *http://snycorva.cortland.edu/~ANDESMD/ PIAGET/ PIAGET.HTML.* A tutorial on Vygotsky and his theory of sociocultural development is available at *http://snycorva.cortland.edu/~ANDESMD/VYG/VYG.HTML.*

Another interesting resource available at *http://www.iconceptual.com/ Siggraph.html* is a paper written by Robert Edgar (1995) entitled "PC is to Piaget as WWW is to Vygotsky." This humorous analogy compares the two influential developmental psychologists to technological advances.

Personal, Gender, Social, and Moral Development

THE BIG PICTURE

To help you see the big picture, keep the following questions in mind as you read this chapter:

- How does a child's personality develop, and what types of problems do children face as their personalities mature?

- How do students develop a sense of who they are and what they want to accomplish in life?

- How do children develop a sense of their roles as males or females?

- How is the progression of students' social development reflected in the classroom?

- What is moral reasoning, and how do children learn to think about morality? Can teachers help students develop a sense of moral values?

- How do expert teachers help students cope with risks to their personal development, such as eating disorders, depression, suicide, drug use, or pregnancy?

◄ *A group of teenage junior-high school students socially interact during recess. The social aspects of development are particularly relevant to teenagers.* (Mary Kate Denny, PhotoEdit)

79

Carla bit her lip to keep it from quivering. She knew the answer to the question her teacher, Mr. Conto, had just asked her, but her nervousness kept her from answering out loud. Tommy and Kim, the most popular boy and girl in the class, turned around to make faces at Carla. She could see them laughing, and all she wanted was to slink under the table and forget that school existed. Most of the time in class Carla tuned out, embarrassed just to be there. She was taller than the other girls in the fifth grade, and worst of all, she was taller than all of the boys! Her facial breakouts made her feel even

worse. Her only friend, Tanya, was also unpopular—in fact, this is what the two had most in common. They sat around after school and fantasized about what it would be like never to have to go back to the pit of despair school had become.

Carla's teacher, Jim Conto, wanted to help. He was very frustrated. He would like to have thrown out of the class the nasty kids who made fun of Carla. Carla was a bright young woman, but she was becoming less and less involved in school, and soon this reduced involvement would translate into failure. Jim had tried explaining logically to the other kids why they should be kinder to Carla. He had tried

disciplining the other kids when they disobeyed. He had also tried counseling Carla to help her improve her sense of self-esteem. None of these approaches had solved the problem. He could not understand why the other kids were so mean-spirited: Didn't they see that they could just as easily be in Carla's shoes? Nor could he understand why Carla caved in so easily. Sometimes he thought she almost enjoyed being a victim! Carla seemed headed for a life scarred by a deep sense of inferiority and an inability to socialize with other people. *Jim decided to read about theories of social development to get some help. He got it.*

Jim Conto is facing an inevitable teaching problem. He is finding out that teaching is not just about imparting knowledge; it is about dealing with children and adolescents as they confront the problems—sometimes, life-threatening problems—involved in growing up and attaining adult identities (Eisenberg, 1998). Sooner or later every teacher must try to help a student who is having problems with personal or social development. What would you do if you were Jim Conto? This chapter will give you some ideas to use when you are in his situation. Chapter 2 outlined the ways children's thinking changes as they develop. Here, you will learn what kinds of changes in personality, gender development, social interactions, and reasoning about right and wrong you can expect from your students at various points in their development.

Why Understanding Personal, Gender, Social, and Moral Development Is Important to Teachers

Many of the challenges and difficulties teachers face concern how to cope with their students' development changes and how to help them grow up as soundly and as trouble free as possible (Eisenberg & Fabes, 1998). Knowing your subject area and understanding methods of instruction will not be enough. To be an expert teacher, you also have to understand the processes of personal, social, and moral development. *Personal development* is the process of human development in which individuals acquire the set of attributes that makes them unique. *Social development* is the process of human development in which individuals learn how to interact with others and understand themselves as social beings. *Moral development* is the process of human development in which individuals acquire a sense of right and wrong, to use in evaluating their own actions and the actions of others.

Knowing what kinds of personal achievements, social skills, and ideas about right and wrong you can expect from most of your students will help you plan developmentally appropriate lessons that challenge but do not frustrate students. For example, very young students who are still seeking to establish their autonomy and demonstrate their individual abilities may not be ready effectively to take on cooperative group projects. Expert teachers also use a knowledge of typical personal, social, and moral development to help them see when students, such as Carla, are having problems in one or more areas. Before he can decide what kind of help Carla needs, Mr. Conto needs to know whether her shyness is merely an expression of normal developmental processes or a sign of a serious developmental problem. Normal shyness is nothing to worry about and even can have advantages. Children who are shy at age 3 are less likely to be aggressive and are more likely to avoid dangerous situations when they become adolescents (Caspi & Silva, 1995).

Although we examine each aspect of development separately, of course they interact. For example, as children's sense of morality develops, their interactions with peers change. Interactions with peers can also affect aspects of personal development, such as self-esteem. The section of the chapter on *sexual and gender development,* the growth of children's sense of themselves as male or female, may provide you with the clearest examples of the ways in which the domains of development overlap. For example, girls and boys often go through a period when they prefer to interact almost exclusively with members of their own gender. When designing lessons and activities, teachers need to keep in mind the overlapping nature of domains of student development and to remember that development in all areas contributes to the growth of a mature individual.

Personal Development: Becoming Unique

How does an individual's personality develop? One of the most thorough theories of personal development is that of Erik Erikson. Erikson's theory provides a way to think about how a child's personality develops that can be helpful to teachers, especially when a student seems to be having trouble in developing a healthy personality—as was the case with Carla, in the opening example.

ERIKSON'S THEORY OF PSYCHOSOCIAL DEVELOPMENT

Erik Erikson (1902–1994) proposed what he called a **psychosocial theory** of personal development (1950, 1968), a theory that explicitly acknowledges that individual development takes place in a social context. The theory was an unusual one at the time, because it recognized that development is a lifelong process rather than one that ends in early adulthood. Like Piaget's theory of cognitive development (discussed in Chapter 2), Erikson's theory is a stage theory. It contains eight stages. At every stage, one issue of psychosocial development comes to the forefront of an individual's development. Erikson framed these issues as **developmental crises**—that is, an individual has an opportunity to take a significant step in his or her development. Erikson theorized that each stage is framed in terms of what happens if the crisis of that stage is dealt with successfully or unsuccessfully. Although the focus in each stage is on only one issue of development, developmental steps taken at earlier stages can affect a person's ongoing development. Unsuccessful resolution of a previous stage can affect a person's later development negatively, but later stages also can provide an individual with the chance to overcome earlier problems. During any stage, the individual may bounce back and forth between states, such as between autonomy, on the one hand, and shame and doubt, on the other. As most people do not *totally* resolve a crisis, throughout their lives they may still have to struggle with feelings of shame and doubt. The eight stages of Erikson's theory can be summarized as follows:

1. **Trust Versus Mistrust** (birth to 1 year). According to Erikson, if infants pass through this stage successfully, they learn to trust that their basic needs will be met. They also develop a hopeful attitude toward life. If infants do not pass through this stage successfully, they come to mistrust others. Thus the outcome of this stage determines in part whether a person will come to view the world as basically supportive and friendly or as basically unsupportive and even hostile. The child's trust or mistrust of classmates may be traced to this stage. Caregivers who are consistently responsive to infants' needs for food and care demonstrate to the infants that they can depend on the world around them (Thompson, 1998).

2. **Autonomy Versus Shame and Doubt** (1 to 3 years). Children learn during this stage to be relatively self-sufficient—in walking, in talking, in eating, in using the toilet, and so forth. Erikson thought that successful passage through this stage results in a sense of autonomy, or independence, and a sense of will, or mastery over one's thoughts, emotions, and behavior. Unsuccessful passage leaves children doubting themselves and potentially feeling a sense of shame about themselves and about their ability to cope with the environment. Children who pass successfully through the stage are more likely to have confidence in their ability to succeed in their relations with their peers in school. Such confidence can breed success (Eccles, Wigfield & Schiefele, 1998). Caregivers should allow children opportunities to make choices, to feed themselves, and to exert their own self-control through toilet training. In this way, the caregivers support the children as the children practice their new physical and thinking abilities in ways that foster a sense of self-confidence. Thus in this stage it is important that caregivers be tolerant of accidents and mistakes.

3. **Initiative Versus Guilt** (3 to 6 years). In this stage, Erikson believed children learn to assert themselves in ways that are considered socially acceptable, and learn how to take the initiative in their dealings with people and tasks. Successful passage through this stage results in a sense of purpose in life. In contrast, unsuccessful passage results in feelings of guilt, and ultimately in difficulties in taking initiative in one's life endeavors. Children who master this stage are more likely to be able to set directions for themselves in their schoolwork, and later, in their careers. Caregivers should provide ways for children in this stage to try new things and to engage in some activities on their own, while helping them understand rules and limitations.

4. **Industry Versus Inferiority** (6 to 12 years). Here, according to Erikson, children acquire a sense of competency and industriousness in their work, particularly schoolwork. Successful passage means the development of a sense of competence, whereas unsuccessful passage results in feelings of inferiority. Children who master this stage are more likely to show engagement and industry in their schoolwork. Providing opportunities for children to set goals that are challenging but that the children can meet encourages the children's sense and attainment of success (Dweck, 1999). Caregivers also foster children's sense of industry by giving them tasks for which they are regularly responsible, and that they can carry out independently. The Flexible Expert: Teaching and Learning about Personal Development presents some examples of how expert teachers and students might facilitate the transition through this and the next of Erikson's stages.

5. **Identity Versus Role Confusion** (adolescence). During this stage, adolescents are figuring out who they are, what is and is not important to them, what their values are, and who they will become as they grow up. They try to integrate various aspects of themselves—intellectual, social, sexual, and moral—into a unified sense of self-identity (Harter, 1998). Those who succeed in their passage through this stage develop a sense of fidelity to themselves, whereas those who do not

IN EACH CHAPTER OF THE TEXT, WE INTRODUCE YOU TO A FEW SPECIFIC STRATEGIES—ANALYTICAL, CREATIVE, AND PRACTICAL—USED BY BOTH EXPERT TEACHERS AND EXPERT STUDENTS.

THE ANALYTICAL TEACHER: Mark knows that most of his fourth-grade students are working through the stage Erikson called industry versus inferiority. He develops a series of progressively more challenging homework assignments as a way to allow each student to see his or her own success and positive progress.

THE CREATIVE TEACHER: Mark makes a job wheel so each student will get the chance to perform an important classroom task.

THE PRACTICAL TEACHER: When one of Mark's students claims to be "no good at school," mark challenges the claim by helping the student chart her progress since the beginning of the school year.

THE ANALYTICAL STUDENT: Lin learns about Erikson's stages and Marcia's identity statuses in psychology class. She realizes that the questions she has been having about her future are part of a healthy adolescent identity search.

THE CREATIVE STUDENT: Lin becomes involved in a drama club as a way to literally "act out" different identities.

THE PRACTICAL STUDENT: Lin volunteers as a teacher's aide at a local preschool because she wants to "try on" teaching young children as a possible career.

---

remain confused about who they are, what they can become, and what they should do with their lives. Children who master this stage are more likely to view success in school as consistent rather than inconsistent with their image of who they are and who they want to become. Adults should show their appreciation of many models of problem solving, and of diverse careers, religions, and other ideologies. They even can show tolerance of diverse fashion as they help adolescents struggle to achieve their own identity.

6. **Intimacy Versus Isolation** (early adulthood). In this stage, Erikson believed the young adult seeks intimate relationships with others, including but not limited to a significant other. Success at this stage results in the person's learning nonselfish love—love that involves give-and-take. Failure results in a sense of isolation and in an inability to achieve intimacy with others (Berscheid & Reis, 1998; Sternberg, 1998). Adults who master this stage are more likely, as teachers, to be giving of themselves to their students without always expecting something in return. They serve as good role models for the students in developing their own relationships (Parke & O'Neill, 1997).

7. **Generativity Versus Stagnation** (middle adulthood). Adults who successfully meet this crisis feel a need to nurture and provide for the generation that follows them. They try not only to achieve for themselves, but to pass on to the next generation the fruits of what they have accomplished, often through child rearing or mentorship (Smetana, 1997). Adults who do not meet the challenges of this stage feel a sense of stagnation in their lives—as though they have not made a meaningful contribution to the world through their careers or raising of children. Adults who master this stage are more likely, as teachers, to take pride in the success they have had in molding their students' lives.

8. **Integrity versus Despair** (late adulthood/old age). At this stage, people try to make sense of and give meaning to the lives they have led, and in particular, to the choices and decisions they have made in their lives. Erikson thought that those who

THINKING CREATIVELY

Think about your years of childhood and adolescence. Do your experiences reflect the early stages of Erikson's theory? Would you add any stages to the theory? Why or why not?

SUGGESTION: Answers will vary. Many people find Erikson's stages useful in understanding at least some of the developmental challenges they have confronted.

What do you see as the greatest strength and the greatest weakness of Erikson's theory?

SUGGESTION: A strength is that the theory encompasses the entire human life span. A weakness is that the theory has not been adequately tested empirically.

succeed in this stage gain the wisdom of older age: Although they may not believe they have always made the right decisions, they come to terms with their mistakes (Baltes & Staudinger, 2001). Adults who do not successfully complete this stage feel a sense of despair over the mistakes they have made and the opportunities they have missed. Adults who master this stage look back over their lives with a sense of accomplishment and of a job well done, whatever those jobs may have been.

The eight stages of Erikson's theory are summarized in Figure 3.1.

FIGURE 3.1 Erikson's Psychosocial Theory of Development

Stage	Approximate Ages	What Happens in this Stage?	What Can be Done to Help a Person Pass Through the Stage Successfully?
I Trust versus Mistrust	Birth to 1 year	Infants either come to believe that their world is a safe and predictable place or that the world is undependable or even hostile.	Parents or child-care providers should respond promptly and consistently to an infant's needs.
II Autonomy versus Shame and Doubt	1 to 3 years	Children who pass through this stage successfully develop a sense of mastery over their thoughts, emotions, and behavior. Those who are not successful come to feel doubt about their ability to cope with their environment.	Parents or preschool teachers should provide young children with opportunities to perform tasks independently, including eating, dressing, and toilet use. Reward children's attempts and successes; avoid humiliating a child when he or she experiences setbacks or difficulties.
III Initiative versus Guilt	3 to 6 years	Children either learn to take control of their actions and situations, developing a sense of purpose, or they come to feel guilt and a lack of purpose.	Teachers or parents can offer children opportunities to make their own decisions when possible. For example, children can choose the colors of their own name tags or paper for art projects, decide which of two books should be read during story time, or choose from three or four different options for using free play time.
IV Industry versus Inferiority	6 to 12 years	Children either develop a sense of their own competence at a variety of tasks, especially schoolwork, or they come to believe they are not capable of success.	Teachers can arrange learning units in a series of steps, and reward or praise children for completing each step of a unit. Encourage children to compare their current level of performance with their own earlier levels, rather than with the performance of classmates.
V Identity versus Role Confusion	Adolescence	Adolescents explore various aspects of identity and either develop a unified sense of who they are or remain confused about who they are and what they want from life.	Teachers of adolescents can provide reassurance and examples of the normalcy of identity searches.
VI Intimacy versus Isolation	Early adulthood	Young adults either learn how to give and take love nonselfishly in relationships, or fail to connect with others in a meaningful way.	Teachers may themselves be in this stage. Consciously developing a network of colleagues can help provide not only practical support, but a sense of belonging. Teachers can help students who are in this stage by providing examples of successful relationships in subjects such as literature, or by encouraging students to develop their own networks, including study groups or organizations in students' fields of career interest.
VII Generativity versus Stagnation	Middle adulthood	Adults either develop the sense that they are somehow caring for or contributing to the well-being of the next generation of people, or they come to feel their efforts and accomplishments will have little meaning in the future.	Teachers can build their own sense of generativity by continuing to learn and practice innovative ways of teaching. They may also be able to help other adults, and their students, by inviting adults into the classroom as speakers about their career or other choices or as tutors.
VIII Integrity versus Despair	Late adulthood/old age	Evaluation of one's previous actions either leads to a feeling that one's life has unfolded in an inevitable, meaningful pattern, or to despair and a consciousness of missed opportunities.	Teachers who are themselves engaging in this evaluation may want to seek out news of successful former students. Teachers may also want to encourage students who are at earlier stages to keep journals or to "practice" evaluating their choices from the perspective of their future selves.

Source: Table "Erikson's Stages of Personal and Social Development" from *Identity and the Life Cycle* by Erik H. Erikson. Copyright © 1980 by W. W. Norton & Company. Copyright © 1959 by International Universities Press, Inc. Used by permission of W. W. Norton & Company.

FIGURE 3.2 Four Statuses of Identity

Has the person engaged in an active search for identity?	Has the person made commitments to values?	
	YES	**NO**
YES	**IDENTITY ACHIEVEMENT** ■ firm and secure sense of self ■ commitments to occupation, religion, beliefs about sex roles, and the like ■ the views, beliefs, and values of others have been considered, but own resolution has been reached by branching out	**MORATORIUM** ■ currently experiencing an identity crisis, or turning point ■ no clear commitments to society ■ no clear sense of identity ■ actively trying to achieve identity
NO	**FORECLOSURE** ■ commitments to occupation and various ideological positions ■ little evidence of the process of self-construction; adopted the values of others without seriously searching and questioning ■ foreclosed on the possibility of achieving own identity	**IDENTITY DIFFUSION** ■ lacking direction ■ unconcerned about political, religious, moral, or even occupational issues ■ does things without questioning why ■ unconcerned why others do what they are doing

MARCIA'S THEORY OF THE ACHIEVEMENT OF A PERSONAL IDENTITY

Erik Erikson wrote more about the search for identity than about any other crisis he proposed. His attention to this phase of development has inspired other psychologists, such as James Marcia, whose ideas we consider next, to think about the search for identity as well.

James Marcia has suggested that four main kinds of statuses can emerge during adolescence from the conflicts faced and the decisions made by adolescents (Marcia, 1966, 1980, 1991): identity achievement, foreclosure, identity diffusion, and moratorium. The four kinds of identities are possible combinations of yes-no answers to two questions: Has the person engaged in an active search for identity? And has the person made commitments (for example, to values, to school, to a job or career path, to who he or she wants to be as a person, or to other aspects of his or her identity)? An individual who answers yes to both questions is in the status of **identity achievement.** This individual has searched for his or her identity and, based on the results of this search, has made an educational, vocational, or other personal commitment. For example, Marla has decided on a career in medicine after careful reflection because she believes it will enable her to help people, use her talents, and make a good living besides.

Someone who answers no to both of the questions just posed is classified as experiencing **identity diffusion.** This person has neither engaged in a search for identity nor committed to any significant aspects of an identity. For example, Jethro has been living for the moment, doing more or less whatever feels good at the time, and has not taken the time to think about who he is or what he wants out of life.

A person who answers yes to the first question and no to the second is in **identity moratorium.** He or she has made a search for an identity, but has not yet made commitments. For example, Bert has gone from one religious group to another, in the hope of finding himself, but feels no closer to self-understanding than he did before he started his quest.

Answering no to the first question and yes to the second leads to foreclosure. An individual in **identity foreclosure** status has made commitments to a job, school, or other aspect of his or her identity without first engaging in a search process. For example,

FOCUS ON: EARLY ADOLESCENT IDENTITY DEVELOPMENT

GREGORY BOULJON: BETTENDORF MIDDLE SCHOOL, BETTENDORF, IOWA—GRADE 8, LANGUAGE ARTS

Gregory Bouljon has been teaching for thirty years. In 2000, he was certified by the National Board for Professional Teaching Standards as a teacher of English Language Arts for Early Adolescence.

Would you say that your students are at the personality development stage Erikson called "Identity versus Role Confusion"?

This definitely describes many of my eighth graders. Some are obvious, like a girl I taught last year, whom I'll call "Stephanie." Stephanie had a checkered past of numerous school disciplinary actions as well as police involvements with her "friends" in the community. She arrived the first day in total Goth attire: white makeup, black lip and eye color, all black clothes and demon figure jewelry. She sat in the back of the room with arms folded across her chest with a look of "Go ahead and try, but I'm not doing anything in here."

Over the next few weeks, we did a Writers' Workshop in which students self-select their own topics and genres. Fortunately (for all of us), Stephanie liked to write. Her first pieces were profanity-laced angry diatribes meant to offend us. The profanity turned out to be forced, but the anger for her parents was real—and deep. My student teacher and I listened, read, responded to the ideas and ignored the profanity.

Stephanie used her writing as a way to understand her anger. She began to realize that she had been reacting to her parents and an abusive relative and was not being herself. Once that began to happen, she changed. By October, she had apologized for her early work. She promised to rewrite it so that she could read it to the class and put it up in the room and in our display case. She began to wear other colors, and the makeup was gone. By December, she had new friends. The old ones, she told the two of us and the class, just wanted to use her. Some of her new friends were in our class and welcomed her insightful writing about herself that also seemed to capture their own identity struggles.

Not all students suffer with finding themselves as visibly as Stephanie did. For most it is a much more quiet, personal struggle to balance the expectations of parents, family, peers, coaches, and the perceived community in which they live. But in the course of a year, all my eighth graders begin, or continue, or set their concepts of themselves in relation to all the forces that push and tug and make demands on them.

> Once the student opens himself or herself to what you're teaching, miracles can happen in a very short time.

Some theorists describe a process of "trying on" different identities during early adolescence. Your students seem to show they are in this process through their choices in clothing.

In the process of finding their identity, students' choices in clothing can change and do, regularly. It is not uncommon to see girls in the course of a single week dress in mini skirts and tight tops one day, loose jeans the next, and sweats another day. Holidays (especially Halloween) bring out the most bizarre attire allowed by our school codes. Often students will bring an extra, more acceptable outfit in case their first choice turns out to be too bizarre, revealing, or inappropriate.

Students also want their clothes to signify their membership in various peer groups. Most groups have a uniform of the day, or at least limits of what the student can wear and still be okay with his or her group.

Brand names are important. Either you have the "right" line of clothes on, or you don't, if you want people to know you are "your own person" and are not swayed by fashion.

Bertha, like Marla, is premed, but only because she is following in the footsteps of her mother without adequately reflecting on whether she is choosing the right path for herself. Such individuals often have made commitments at the urging of their parents. These four kinds of identities are reviewed in Figure 3.2.

Both Erikson (1968) and Marcia believed that healthy adolescence can include a moratorium period, a time of searching for an appropriate identity while avoiding firm commitments. A moratorium period may be especially important to adolescents in a socially diverse, urbanized society who must choose from among many options for how to live their lives. In fact, the complexity of many societies may be one reason why identity issues take a long time to resolve. By the time they are seniors in high school, only about 20 percent of students are likely either to be actively searching for an identity or to have reached identity achievement status

THINKING PRACTICALLY

Which of Marcia's types of identities best characterizes you? Why?

SUGGESTION: Each student must answer for himself or herself.

Is sexual development and dating a big concern for your students?

I do not believe that many of my students are sexually active during their eighth grade year. Most of our students seem to be in the early stages of exploring their sexuality. Students talk and write disparagingly about their friends who are sexually active. They feel the others are wasting themselves on something meant for later in life. What is done is mostly "experimental."

Most of our students socialize in large, mixed gender groups at school functions (of which we have many) and in their private social lives. We encourage parents to create events and places where kids can "hang out" under supervision. Relationships change often, and few become serious in terms of sexual experimentation.

What about students who may be gay or bisexual?

It is very hard for kids who are asking questions about their sexual orientation. Not only do they have to sort out their school and personality identities, they have the sexual identity issues to deal with as well. In the last few years, it was not uncommon to hear students call others *gay* as a put-down for almost any offense to an individual or group. As a result of a near crusade on my part, I've gotten many faculty members to add the word *gay* to the list of other unacceptable epithets and to help put a stop to its use *in that way*. Many students caught saying it in the halls will tell you that they don't "mean it as a put-down," but, for all of us who see respect as a crucial element of school, it is when used inappropriately. Especially for those students who are desperately trying to sort out their sexual orientation.

Does your school have any character-education initiatives, such as service learning projects, to encourage moral development?

Our school is divided into interdisciplinary houses, and service learning projects are central. We do a wide variety of fundraising for families and organizations, read and write to younger students, and volunteer time at nursing homes and senior centers. We initially tried to make everyone participate in these projects in our school, but soon realized that each student must be allowed to participate at the level at which it is most comfortable for that student at that time. Service learning projects give students an opportunity to explore and develop another dimension of their personal identities. Often, the very kids who are usually talented "work avoiders," will do the most in these projects. Last year, it was about the only time that one boy wrote for my class at all. He took great care in writing stories for his elementary school pen pal. He also led other students to involvement with our charitable fundraising.

What advice would you have for new teachers?

Be slow to judge and quick to accept. Some students are so involved with finding out who they are, and with what their friends and family are demanding, that they have little left for your class. Start with where each student is, establish a friendly (and humorous) relationship, and gradually work your agenda into theirs.

I really believe that until a person "opens" herself or himself up to a topic, person, idea, or text, she or he cannot learn of it or from it. But to open yourself up when you are fourteen and not really sure of who you are is tough. There is a way to reach every student, if you can be patient enough to wait for that student to open the door enough for you to come in. It may not happen today, or next week, or next month, but it will happen, and you must be ready to seize that moment using the relationship of acceptance and understanding that you have built up in all your previous encounters. Once the student opens himself or herself to what you're teaching, miracles can happen in a very short time.

(Archer, 1982). The goal of an adolescent identity search, no matter how prolonged, is that the adolescent emerge with a firm and relatively secure sense of **self,** how she identifies her own characteristics, abilities, and behaviors (Harter, 1998). The adolescent's **self-esteem** (and everyone else's, for that matter) is the value she places on herself. The adolescent's view of herself is referred to as her **self-concept** (see Chapter 10). The adolescent's identity search may potentially affect her self-concept *and* self-esteem in a very profound way. Good friendships can help in the development of a sense of self and a positive self-concept (Hartup, 1996; Newcomb & Bagwell, 1995; Rubin, Bukowski, & Parker, 1998; Rubin, Coplan, Nelson, Cheah, & Lagace-Seguin, 1999).

It may seem from the foregoing description that identity achievement is the best of the four main identity statuses. Indeed, in Western societies

THINKING ANALYTICALLY

What is a way that schools tend to socialize children toward independence? Toward interdependence? How might teaching practices in part represent cultural norms that favor independence versus interdependence?

SUGGESTION: For independence, students primarily work on their own. For interdependence, they do some work in cooperative learning groups. However, individual activities tend to predominate in most U.S. classrooms.

THINKING PRACTICALLY

Describe a strategy you might try if you were Carla's teacher, if your goal was to help Carla feel better about herself.

SUGGESTION: You might help Carla form a list of her own strengths and of ways to make the most of these strengths.

that emphasize individual achievement and responsibility, many psychologists agree that moratorium and identity achievement reflect greater developmental maturity than do identity diffusion or foreclosure (Archer, 1982). However, many non-Western cultures place more emphasis on the interdependence of family and community members than do Western nations (Markus & Kitayama, 1991; Matsumoto, 1994, 1996). In these societies, parents or community leaders may be seen as the appropriate persons to choose an adolescent's career or marriage partner. Major decisions may be group-based rather than based exclusively on the desires of the individual (Markus, Kitayama, & Heiman, 1996). Identity foreclosure status would be considered more mature than an identity moratorium or search.

EVALUATING THE THEORIES OF ERIKSON AND MARCIA

The theories of Erikson and Marcia make valuable contributions to our understanding of children's personal development. At the same time, like all theories, they have some limitations. One limitation is the lack of solid empirical data supporting them. Neither theory has been adequately tested scientifically. Because of the many changes in society since the theories first were proposed, there is a specially pressing need for the theories to be tested. Marcia's theory, of course, applies only to a very limited aspect of the life span, thereby not taking fully into account the lifetime process of identity formation.

Normal adolescent uncertainty about identity, coupled with the complexities of modern society, can put teens at risk for certain psychological and behavioral problems. However, as we see next, the risk is certainly not limited to adolescents.

Implications for Teaching

ERIKSON'S THEORY OF PSYCHOSOCIAL DEVELOPMENT

■ *Expert preschool teachers provide young children with opportunities to perform tasks independently.* Basic skills such as eating, dressing, and toilet use can all be practiced at school, as can art and drama, helping children who are passing through the autonomy versus shame and doubt stage develop a sense of self-sufficiency.

■ *Expert teachers foster children's ability to assert themselves by allowing them to make as many of their own decisions as possible about schoolwork.* These teachers, whenever possible, incorporate children's suggestions about various activities into the classroom. By encouraging activities that involve a range of abilities, expert teachers give children more opportunities to experience success and thus to gain confidence to try new things.

■ *Expert teachers foster feelings of competence in students by noticing and praising students' successes.* Teachers arrange learning units in a series of steps, and reward or praise children as they complete each step of a unit. By encouraging students to make comparisons with their own earlier performance rather than with the performance of classmates, they help students see their developing expertise. In fact, in some cases, teachers may wish to provide positive feedback privately to discourage unfavorable comparisons between classmates.

■ *Expert teachers of adolescents reassure themselves and students by pointing out examples of the normalcy of identity searches.* These teachers may present role models in various subjects—famous scientists, mathematicians, or writers, for example. Teachers may even discuss with the students the paths these individuals took to achieve their success, including any searching or changes in identity that the role models underwent.

MARCIA'S THEORY OF IDENTITY ACHIEVEMENT

■ *Demonstrate role models for identity achievement.* Although expert teachers do not discourage students from engaging in their own identity searches, they do emphasize the value of eventually making the commitments that result in a firm sense of one's self. It may help to point out examples of people who have found success through keeping their commitments—literary characters, or real people in relevant subjects, such as scientists, local leaders, or celebrities. Most important, teachers and other adults need to be solid adult role models, not substitutes for childhood friends (Baumrind, 1991; Emmer, Evertson, Clements, & Worsham, 1997; Lamb, 1996).

■ *Facilitate exploration of alternative value systems, and the advantages and disadvantages of each.* In classes such as English or history, historical figures or literary characters can represent models that students can consider and emulate. In science, students can learn about scientific values by becoming involved in research or by reading about the discoveries of great scientists. Foreign language classes promote learning about another culture and how it is similar to and different from their own.

■ *Encourage students to make commitments that are sensible for their age level.* These commitments may be through students' doing their best in school, completing chores in the home, being loyal to friends and family, following religious teachings, or exploring one or more hobbies or fields of special interest. Learning how to make and keep commitments may be as valuable as fulfilling the particular commitments made.

■ *Consider cultural differences.* Many students come from cultural backgrounds in which foreclosure is more widely accepted than it is in the United States. Pushing students from such a background to engage in an identity search may cause them conflict with their families and with their own deeply held cultural convictions.

■ *Be aware of the ongoing nature of identity formation.* Marcia's theory is relevant primarily to individuals during adolescence, and potentially young adulthood. However, identity formation in a certain sense lasts a lifetime. People often must assess and reassess who they are, what they have become, and whether what they have become is what they want to remain.

THINKING PRACTICALLY

Can you think of one other educational implication of Erikson's theory? What is it?

SUGGESTION: Teachers themselves are developing, just as are their students. Expert teachers are generative through their contributions to the next generation.

THINKING PRACTICALLY

Have you searched for your identity? If so, how?

SUGGESTION: Each student must answer for himself or herself. Often, people search for their identity by trying out various roles and seeing which roles work for them and which do not.

Sexual and Gender Development: Acquiring Gender Roles

Psychologists typically distinguish between *sex* and *gender*. A person's sex is physiologically determined; a person's gender is psychologically determined and culturally influenced (Deaux, 1993). **Sexual development** refers to increasing awareness of the characteristics of each of the sexes, of the differences between the sexes, and of changing perceptions of one's own sexuality. **Gender identification** is a person's acquisition of sex-related roles, regardless of whether they correspond to one's physiological sex. For most people, sex and gender identifications correspond, but there are many exceptions to this generalization.

The culture in which an individual is raised shapes *gender roles,* behavior considered appropriate for males or for females (Brody, 1996; Eccles et al., 1993). Sandra Bem (1985, 1993) has described the typical feminine gender role in some societies as comprising what she refers to as expressive behavior, such as nurturing children, and traits, such as passivity. The typical masculine role is made up of what Bem calls instrumental behavior, such as sports participation, and traits, such as aggressiveness. However, these patterns do not hold true for all societies, and even where they do, there may be great overlap in behavior. Many women may display aggressive behavior, for example, and many men may be nurturant or passive. Also, many gender roles are actually sex neutral—that is, they could be performed equally well by males or females. This fact, in addition to the great variability in the way individual males and females perform their gender roles, makes it difficult to generalize about being "male" or "female" (Levy, Taylor, & Gelman, 1995). Bem (1981) has defined a state in which an individual feels comfortable displaying both expressive and instrumental qualities as **androgyny.**

The distinction between sex and gender is a vital one for teachers to keep in mind. Expert teachers do not make assumptions about their students' abilities based on biological sex. They know that researchers have found relatively few consistent sex differences in academic ability or personality (Halpern, 2000). In contrast, as we discuss in detail in Chapter 6, research has shown a great deal of overlap in males' and females' scores on most tests of ability or personality (Feingold, 1992; Fennema, 1987; Grossman & Grossman, 1994). However, it is clear to most teachers that many male and female students behave very differently in certain contexts. Most of these differences are likely results of differential socialization; others may be due to biological factors, including differing levels of hormones, such as testosterone. By the time they enter kindergarten, most children have a clear understanding, and usually acceptance, of their society's gender roles (Wynn & Fletcher, 1987).

THEORIES OF SEXUAL AND GENDER DEVELOPMENT

How do children come to recognize and, generally, to accept the gender roles that are deemed appropriate in their cultures? Are any differences between males and females consistent around the world? There are several points of view on these questions.

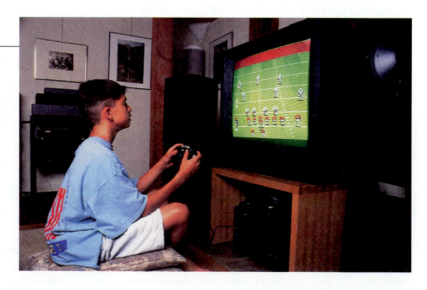

Male students consistently perform better than female students on tests of certain spatial abilities, including mental rotation of figures and predicting the paths of moving objects. Although there may be little difference between the potential abilities of males and females, it seems that boys and girls have inborn predispositions to develop their abilities in different ways. However, researchers disagree as to whether these differences are biological, social, or a mix of both. (Stone/Neurath, Stock Boston)

■BIOLOGICAL PERSPECTIVES Biological theorists argue that differences between the sexes are rooted in the physiological differences between men and women, and that boys and girls acquire different gender roles because they are biologically predisposed to do so (e.g., Benbow & Stanley, 1980; Berenbaum & Hines, 1992; Berenbaum & Snyder, 1995; Kagan, 1998).

Some theorists (e.g., Buss, 1996; Buss & Kenrick, 1998; Kenrick & Trost, 1993) emphasize the role of evolution in determining sexual behavior. For example, male students consistently perform better than do female students on tests of certain spatial abilities, including mental rotation of figures and predicting the paths of moving objects (Halpern, 2000). Evolutionary theorists suggest that these differences may be lingering adaptations from the hunting role that the students' male ancestors played long ago (Buss, 1995; Geary, 1995).

Biological theories seem to suggest that, although there may be little difference between the potential abilities of males and females, boys and girls may have inborn predispositions to develop their abilities in different ways. Biological differences between boys and girls may also trigger different treatment from parents and others in their environments. Sigmund Freud developed a theory of psychosexual development that is based, in part, on the assumption that males and females have inborn tendencies to develop in different ways.

■FREUD'S THEORY OF PSYCHOSEXUAL DEVELOPMENT Sigmund Freud (1856–1939) suggested that psychosexual development—the psychological development of one's sexuality—begins immediately after birth (1905/1964b). However, gender-role identification arises primarily from psychological crises faced during a stage of development that lasts from about 4 to 7 years of age. During this stage, children become susceptible to conflict, in which they start to have sexual feelings for the parent of the opposite sex. For boys, this conflict is called the *Oedipal conflict,* named after Oedipus, from Greek mythology, who killed his father and (unknowingly) married his mother. In particular, boys may in some ways desire their mothers but simultaneously fear the anger of their fathers. Eventually, boys realize they cannot express sexual desire for their mothers and look for an appropriate partner of the other sex.

The comparable reaction in girls—attraction to the father but fear of the mother—is sometimes referred to as the *Electra conflict,* after the myth of Electra, who hated her mother for having betrayed and then killed her husband, Electra's father. As they mature, girls realize they cannot express sexual desire for fathers and look for an appropriate partner of the opposite sex. Thus Freud believed these conflicts eventually cause children to identify with the same-sex parent and to internalize that parent's gender role as their own. Freud believed, as do many modern psychologists, that how parents treat their children has a large effect on their development (Bugental & Goodnow, 1998). Children end up perpetuating the stereotypes foisted on them by adults.

THINKING CREATIVELY

How do you think sex typing occurs?

SUGGESTION: Children may imitate behavior of older persons who seem most like them, which usually, but not always, would be the same-sex parent.

■BEHAVIORISM A behaviorist view emphasizes the importance of environmental forces. Boys and girls are treated differently from the moment they are born (Jacklin, DiPietro, & Maccoby, 1984; Ruble & Martin, 1998). Most parents of preschool and school-age children continue to treat boys differently from girls, rewarding assertive behavior on the part of boys and emotional sensitivity in girls (Fagot & Hagan, 1991; Lytton & Romney, 1991). Research has shown that teachers also treat boys and girls differently. Boys generally receive more teacher attention, both positive and negative, than do girls (Bailey, 1993; Sadker & Sadker, 1994). These differences in treatment can lead to different behavior. In particular, female students tend to become more passive in school, showing less and less class participation in relation to male students as they progress from elementary school through college (Sadker, Sadker, & Klein, 1991). In addition to rewarding or punishing children directly for gender-related behavior, parents and teachers often reinforce gender roles simply by acting as models of what men or women are like.

■ **SOCIAL LEARNING THEORY** **Social learning theory** holds that people come to think and behave as they do by observing others and then by imitating behavior they have seen reap rewards. This theory may be applied to gender-role learning, in which people observe and learn from role models as they follow those thought and behavioral patterns they see being rewarded (Bandura, 1977). Television, for example, provides many children with a way to observe a variety of models, including gender-role models. Television programs, however, may be demonstrating inaccurate gender stereotypes (Furnham & Skae, 1997; Signorielli; McLeod, & Healy, 1994). For example, about twice as many men as women appear on television, despite the fact that slightly more than half the real-world population is female (Calvert & Huston, 1987). In addition, males are frequently shown in aggressive roles, and women are more often portrayed as helpless, not just in the United States, but around the world (Mwangi, 1996; Zuckerman & Zuckerman, 1985). By modeling these roles, children end up perpetuating the stereotypes foisted on them by adults.

■ **SCHEMA THEORY** **Schema theory** suggests that everyone possesses organized mental systems of information (*schemas*) that help them make sense of and organize their experiences (S. Bem, 1981). Gender schema theory holds that people acquire schemas that guide their interpretations of what are and are not appropriate gender roles. For example, *gender stereotypes* are examples of schemas that are widely shared—views explaining that certain behavior is appropriate for males, and other behavior for females (Yzerbyt, Rocher, & Schadron, 1996). Schema theorists would suggest that many of these factors contribute to the development of a person's gender schema. For example, consider how a girl might form a gender schema that includes an emphasis on physical appearance. Perhaps she has seen that the women in her environment are more interested in their personal appearance than are the men. In addition, she herself may have been praised for looking pretty in new clothing. She may conclude that women are supposed to be more appearance-conscious than men, and thereafter pay great attention to her own appearance. Television and movies often strengthen these stereotypes.

As this seven-year-old boy helps his father knead bread dough, he's also forming ideas about gender roles. In gender-role learning, people observe and learn from role models as they follow those thought and behavioral patterns they see being rewarded. (John Fortunato, Stone)

FORUM

SINGLE-GENDER VERSUS MIXED-GENDER SCHOOLS

Several states have begun to introduce single-gender classes in their public schools. For example, in 1997, California began a pilot program offering single-gender academies within its public school system. Either boys or girls could enroll in a single-gender alternative to mixed-gender public schools. Is separating the genders the wisest way to make sure that boys and girls receive the best possible education?

FIRST VIEW: IN FAVOR OF SINGLE-GENDER SCHOOLS

Advocates of single-gender schools suggest that boys and girls learn differently. For example, some studies suggest that girls prefer cooperative learning, and boys prefer competition. In addition, advocates of single-gender classes point out studies showing that boys dominate mixed-gender classrooms, receiving a disproportionate share of teacher attention (Bailey, 1993; Sadker, Sadker, & Klein, 1991). Girls are more likely to speak out in class if there are only girls in the room than if the room contains members of both sexes. Further, research suggests that participation in all-girl classes fosters positive attitudes about learning, even in subjects where female students typically lack self-confidence, such as math (Streitmatter, 1997). High levels of self-confidence may be linked to better academic performance (Bandura, 1986; Norem & Cantor, 1990).

SECOND VIEW: IN OPPOSITION TO SINGLE-GENDER SCHOOLS

Opponents view single-gender schools as an unfair form of segregation. Several states have already discontinued experiments with single-gender public schools because of lawsuits contending that such schools violate laws entitling all students to have equal access to educational opportunities. For example, a boy who dislikes competitive learning and does not perform well under competitive pressure would not be allowed access to cooperative learning-style classes that could further his achievement if those classes only admitted girls. In addition, opponents believe that single-gender public schools do little to prepare students for the mixed-gender world they will encounter outside of school.

THIRD VIEW: A SYNTHESIS

Entirely separate schools for boys and girls may be unnecessary. Many of the studies conducted in the last two decades have shown evidence of declining differences between test scores of male and female students (Feingold, 1988; Linn & Hyde, 1989). Some psychologists and educators conclude that social developments in the same time period, including increasing awareness of teachers' different treatment of boys and girls, and efforts to equalize that treatment, have helped narrow performance gaps (Linn & Hyde, 1989).

Achievement differences still do exist between male and female students in math and science, however. Research suggests that these differences may be linked to differences in the levels of encouragement girls and boys receive for taking advanced science and math classes (American Association of University Women, 1992; Pallas & Alexander, 1983) and to different treatment of boys and girls by math and science teachers (American Association of University Women, 1992; Sadker, Sadker, & Klein, 1991). In response to these difficult-to-eradicate differences, some public school systems have offered single-gender classes in math and science. Girls and boys have the opportunity to enroll in classes that cover the same academic content, and with many of the same methods, but are limited to students of their own gender. At the same time, students also have the benefits of mixing with the other gender in other classes and in school activities. Such limited use of single-gender classes may help promote equal achievement in math and science until schools and teachers are able to develop effective ways of achieving the same goals in mixed-gender math and science classes.

THINKING PRACTICALLY

Think of ways you have interacted with students, either as a teacher or as a fellow student. In what ways, if any, have you encouraged sex-role stereotyping? How might you have done things differently?

SUGGESTION: Each student must answer for himself or herself. Sometimes teachers hold different expectations for girls and boys, depending on the subject. Teachers should try to overcome this stereotyping. One way to do so is by calling equally on boys in literature classes and on girls in math and science classes.

■ **HOMOSEXUALITY** **Homosexuality** describes a person's tendency to direct sexual attention toward members of the same sex. Homosexuality is not viewed as a form of mental illness (Hooker, 1993). Neither is it a "lifestyle"—gay and lesbian people occupy a full range of occupations and social classes, nor a "choice" or "preference" of sexuality. Rather, it is a sexual and affectional orientation and identity, probably most rooted in psychosexual development. Sexuality may be thought of as a continuum. People who have an exclusively heterosexual orientation are at one end of the continuum, and people who have an exclusively homosexual orientation are at the other end. Those people who fall in between may be considered *bisexual,* or people who direct their sexual attention toward members of both sexes. Research has shown that approximately 10 percent of men and a slightly lower proportion of women identify themselves as having predominantly homosexual orientations (e.g., see Fay, Turner, Klassen, & Gagnon, 1989; Rogers & Turner, 1991).

Many explanations have been proposed for the origins of homosexuality. The biological theory is a fairly strongly supported theory (Byrne, 1995). However, the expression of a biological predisposition toward a homosexual orientation (or heterosexual or bisexual orientation, for that matter) may depend on social learning and other environmental factors (D. Bem, 1996; Wade & Cirese, 1991). Other explanations of homosexuality stem from clinical and cognitive theories. These explanations are not well supported by data, and are not as widely accepted as is the biological theory of homosexuality. In fact, studies on identical male twins indicate that when one twin has a homosexual orientation, the other will be three times more likely to have the same orientation as when the twins are not identical (Bailey & Pillard, 1991). Expert teachers make a conscious effort to understand current research on homosexuality and to refrain from stereotyping or discriminating against students (or parents) who have a homosexual orientation.

Implications for Teaching

■ *Model and reward gender behavior desired of students.* Although teachers must be sensitive to parental or community standards regarding gender roles, teachers who wish, say, to encourage androgyny can do so by modeling it themselves and by rewarding it in their students. Teachers should model respect for all sexual orientations on the continuum, as well as respect for the abilities of both sexes.

TABLE 3.1   Educational Implications of Gender Development Theories

How Teachers Might Apply the Implications at Different Educational Levels

Implications	Preschool and Primary Grades	Elementary School	Middle School	High School
Model and reward the gender behavior desired of students.	Preschool and elementary school teachers may want to use gender-neutral terms, such as firefighter or mail carrier, when discussing potential occupations or dramatic play roles so that children of both genders feel free to play roles that interest them.	Children in the upper elementary grades generally prefer to play and work with same-sex peer groups. Teachers may wish to remind students of the value of working with the other gender by providing examples of boys and girls, or men and women, who have worked together to solve a problem, finish a job, or invent something.	Teachers of both genders should model respect for the other gender. Teachers should prohibit sexually harassing comments.	Female teachers may wish to demonstrate their own competence or interest in math and science, areas in which high school girls have been shown to lack confidence in their abilities. Teachers of both genders can point out examples, in daily life or the media, of the need to use math and science concepts.
Acknowledge and strive to overcome limiting gender stereotypes.	Teachers of young children will quickly notice that both girls and boys are very energetic and need opportunities to exercise large muscles in vigorous activities.	Teachers should avoid communicating expectations that either groups of boys or groups of girls will cause more "trouble" in class or on the playground. Correct misbehavior from individuals of both genders when it occurs.	Teachers may have been led by recent research to expect all middle school girls to develop low self-esteem. However, teachers should be alert for changes in the self-esteem of both male and female students, and avoid giving members of either gender special treatment unless needed.	High school teachers and counselors should avoid making assumptions about the level of interest and ability that male and female students have for various subjects or careers. Some male college-bound students may be planning to study traditionally "female" subjects, such as early childhood education.
Check learning materials for damaging gender stereotypes.	Check storybooks and picture books to see if male and female characters are equally represented.	Avoid literature that reinforces helpless female or aggressive male stereotypes.	Provide additional examples of female accomplishments in relevant subjects if they are not included in text or other materials.	Examine science and math for gender inclusion. Math word problems should not humorously reinforce male or female stereotypes, for example.

- *Acknowledge and strive to overcome gender stereotypes.* Expert teachers face up to their own gender stereotypes in analyzing how they interact with students. They learn to be aware, for example, of whether they are calling on boys in class more often than girls or avoiding interaction with students who may have a homosexual orientation. Some public schools have introduced single-sex classes in order to reduce gender stereotyping. This development has turned out to be somewhat controversial, as described in this chapter's Forum: Single-Gender versus Mixed-Gender Schools.

- *Check learning materials for damaging gender stereotypes.* Expert teachers compensate for a lack of gender equity in curriculum materials by adding examples or discussing different possibilities. Expert teachers also check reading material for fairness when the material discusses homosexuality. Table 3.1 suggests ways in which the teacher might apply these implications at different educational levels.

Social Development: Learning to Interact with Others

Whereas personal development concerns the development of the individual in relation to the self, social (interpersonal) development concerns the relationships of the individual with others, and how these relationships change over time. Several concepts of social development are relevant to the concerns of educational psychologists, one of which is attachment.

ATTACHMENT

Attachment refers to the strength and kind of emotional bond that exists between two people (Colin, 1996; Sroufe, 1996). Early work by John Bowlby (1951, 1969) claimed that the way an infant is attached to the mother has long-term effects on the child's interpersonal development.

Mary Ainsworth (Ainsworth, Bell, & Stayton, 1971; Ainsworth, Blehar, Waters, & Wall, 1978) proposed three basic modes of attachment. Although the three attachment patterns are described in terms of mother-child bonds, keep in mind that children are certainly capable of forming attachments with fathers and other significant people in their lives. Ainsworth assesses attachment style through infants' reactions to the **strange situation,** an experimental procedure in which the attachment of an infant to the parent is observed after the parent has left the infant with a stranger, and has then returned.

The mother is with the child. A stranger enters and starts playing with the child. The mother steps away and the child notices that she is gone. The mother then returns.

In the first pattern, **avoidant** (sometimes called "type A") **attachment,** the child generally avoids or ignores the mother when she returns after leaving the child with the stranger. These children pay little attention to the mother even when she is in the room, and they show minimal distress when she leaves. Children (and adults) with an avoidant attachment style sometimes are further subdivided in terms of whether they seem not to care about attaching themselves or actively avoid attachments (Main & Solomon, 1990). In **secure** ("type B") **attachment,** the child shows distress when the mother departs. When the mother returns, the child immediately goes to her, showing pleasure at being reunited. The secure child is friendly with the stranger but shows an obvious preference for the mother. Finally, in **resistant** ("type C") **attachment,** the child is ambivalent toward the mother. Upon reunion with the mother, the resistant child both seeks and resists physical contact. For example, the child might run to the mother when she returns, but then try to get away when held.

In same-sex classrooms, girls often volunteer answers more readily than they would in a mixed-sex classroom. (Jonathan Novrok, PhotoEdit)

The psychologist Mary Ainsworth proposed three basic modes of attachment, the strength and kind of emotional bond that exists between two people—in Ainsworth's research, between a mother and a child.

In her research, Ainsworth found that among American middle-class children in the 1970s, roughly 20 to 25 percent tended to be avoidant, about 65 percent were secure, and about 12 percent were resistant. However, patterns of attachment differ across socioeconomic class and family situation. For example, it appears that in unstable or nonintact American families of lower socioeconomic status, the chances of a child's being resistant are somewhat higher (Egeland & Sroufe, 1981; Vaughn, Gove, & Egeland, 1980).

Patterns of attachment also differ by cultures. There are more avoidant children in Western Europe, and more resistant children among Israelis and Japanese (Bretherton & Waters, 1985; Miyake, Chen, & Campos, 1985; Morelli, Rogoff, Oppenheim, & Goldsmith, 1992). However, these patterns suggest that the labels traditionally used are probably culturally biased. After all, had German people, who have a higher proportion of avoidant children, labeled the types of attachment, they would have been unlikely to have used the label "avoidant" to characterize their children's more common pattern of attachment, and unlikely to have used "secure" to characterize the more common pattern in the United States. It is important to avoid sociocultural biases that can lead people to label behavior as somehow "better" if it is indigenous to their own culture or country.

THINKING PRACTICALLY

How would you characterize the effects of your own early modes of attachment to significant others on your personal relationships?

SUGGESTION: Answers will vary. Adult relationships with teachers, employers, or friends often reflect patterns of attachment formed during infancy.

Does attachment have a long-term effect on children's patterns of development, as Bowlby claimed? It appears so. For example, securely attached children at the nursery school level tend to be more active, more likely to be sought out by other children, and rated by their teachers as more eager to learn than are other children (Waters, Wippman, & Sroufe, 1979). Several researchers have found evidence that an adolescent's security of attachment to his or her parents may be related to his or her competence and well-being (Allen & Kuperminc, 1995; Armsden & Greenberg, 1987; Black & McCartney, 1995; Kobak & Sceery, 1988; Torquati & Vazsonyi, 1994). Shaver, Hazan, and Bradshaw (1988) have even found what seems to be a relation between infantile patterns of attachment and the kinds of attachments one forms to friends and lovers during adulthood. Thus attachment styles first formed during infancy may persist in one form or another throughout the life span (Shaver, Collins, & Clark, 1996).

 FRIENDSHIP AND PLAY

Some of the most important, and potentially satisfying, attachments students form are those with their friends. An important aspect of children's social development is their play, both by themselves and with peers. Most of the interaction between young children occurs in the context of play (Hughes, 1995) and it is a way for children to begin forming friendships. Both play and friendship development seem to reflect cognitive development (described in Chapter 2).

■STAGES OF PLAY One classic developmental model of play defines six kinds of behavior (Parten, 1932). (1) *Unoccupied* children seem unable to decide what to do with themselves; often they watch other children, perhaps looking for clues. (2) In *solitary* play, the child plays by herself or himself with things that are available in the environment. (3) A step beyond is when the child is an *onlooker,* watching other children play but still playing alone. (4) In *parallel* play, the child plays with the same toys as other children, but the child does not directly interact with the others. (5) In *associative* play, the child shares toys and interacts to some extent with other children, but still basically plays on his or her own. (6) Finally, in *cooperative* play, the child fully cooperates with others in joint play efforts.

As they grow older, children tend to progress from the simpler and more solitary forms of play to more interactive and complex forms (Howes & Matheson, 1992; Roopnarine et al., 1992). In elementary school, children begin to progress toward playing games with rules, including organized sports, perhaps because they are entering Piaget's concrete operational stage of cognitive development, when rules become more comprehensible (Pellegrini, 1988; Rubenstein, 1993). Game playing seems to peak around ages 10 to 12. At later ages, games lose favor to organized sports or conversations (Bergin, 1988; Eiferman, 1971).

■TRENDS IN THE DEVELOPMENT OF FRIENDSHIPS Children show the same trends in their friendships with others that they show in their play, increasing their interactions with others as they develop. Until about 1 year of age, children's interactions are usually limited to single exchanges, rather than ongoing relations, but in the next few years, interactions increase dramatically (Vandell & Mueller, 1980).

During most of childhood, mutual play is the most common activity in and is sometimes the basis for friendships. During preschool and the primary grades, children generally form friendships based on shared activities. Between the ages of 3 and 9, children show increasing sharing of thoughts and feelings, learn better how to resolve conflicts, and discover how to please (as well as annoy!) each other (Gottman, 1983, 1986). Friendships may change rapidly between children at these ages (Berndt & Perry, 1986; Guralnick, 1986). Teachers may find it fairly easy to help young students who seem isolated by involving them in a group activity. In this way, teachers also help these students improve their self-esteem (Berndt, 1996).

In middle childhood, friendships become more stable, and students may have a more or less permanent best friend. Children usually choose friends of the same sex, on the basis of personality traits and on mutual give-and-take (Berndt & Perry, 1986; Hartup, 1989; Mitchell, 1990).

Expert teachers of students in the upper elementary grades or middle school often notice that some students are more popular than others. Children may be neglected or actively rejected by peers for a variety of reasons. Isolated children may be very shy, may be of a cultural group different from the other children, may have difficulty speaking the language the other children use among themselves, or may have a physical or mental handicap. Carla, the student described at the beginning of the chapter, is isolated from most of her peers, perhaps because of her early physical development or because of her shyness.

Today, with the trend toward full inclusion, the kinds of problems just mentioned occur, if anything, more than ever before. Two of the most common reasons children are rejected are that they lack prosocial, or helpful, skills and that they behave aggressively (Newcomb & Bukowski, 1984). Research has suggested that children who are isolated because they are neglected or rejected by their peers are more at risk for emotional and psychological problems, such as those described earlier in the chapter, than are children who have more friends (Kupersmidt & Coie, 1990; Morison & Masten, 1991).

Teachers may try to encourage more prosocial skills for isolated children by gradually involving them in group activities, possibly increasing the size of the group and target children's participation in the group in a slow, stable manner. Teachers also need to ensure that the children are treated fairly by others and not isolated within such groups.

Taking care to avoid gender stereotyping, expert teachers encourage boys and girls to play together. Here, second- and third-graders share a tire swing at recess. (Bob Daemmrich Photos, Inc.)

Friendships become very important in adolescence. Adolescents in middle school and high school rely on their friends for emotional support and intimacy, as well as for norms regarding dress and social behavior (Berndt, 1996; Hill, 1987). Abstract personal qualities, such as loyalty and shared outlook on life, become important as students become better able to think in abstractions (Furman & Bierman, 1984).

Boys and girls show somewhat different patterns in the nature and development of their friendships during childhood and adolescence. Most children of both sexes prefer friendships with same-sex peers during these periods. But boys are more likely to play in groups and to engage in competitive activities, whereas girls are more likely to prefer cooperative activities that they can do in pairs.

In adolescence, the friendships of girls pass through three stages (Douvan & Adelson, 1966). From the ages of about 11 to 13 years, the girls tend to engage in joint activities, where the central theme is to have fun together. From about 14 to 16, there is more emphasis on sharing secrets, especially about other friends (whether male or female). Trust becomes especially meaningful at this age level and girls may feel very possessive of their female friends. In later adolescence, shared personalities, shared interests, and general compatibility become more important. By this time, girls may have developed some relationship expertise with their female friends. They may begin to transfer onto males some of the trust, disclosure of secrets, and even possessiveness that they earlier shared with females.

At all ages, including adulthood, females emphasize emotional closeness and shared intimacies more than do males (Berndt, 1982, 1986; Rubin, 1980; Sternberg, 1998), although the extent of the difference may be decreasing (Peplau, 1983). Boys' friendships tend to be more oriented toward achievement and autonomy rather than intimacy. Perhaps unsurprisingly, male adults typically have far fewer close friends than do female adults.

 ### DEVELOPMENT OF PERSPECTIVE TAKING

As children grow older, their ability to form meaningful friendships increases because they become better able to take the perspectives of other people, understanding that people have different experiences and feelings (Eisenberg & Fabes, 1998; Knight, Johnson, Carlo, & Eisenberg, 1994). Robert Selman (1981) has developed a theory of the development of children's **perspective-taking abilities:**

Stage 1: Undifferentiated perspective taking (3–6 years). In this stage children recognize that others may have perspectives that differ from their own, but they tend to confuse their own thoughts and feelings with those of other people. For example, at this age Von cannot quite understand why his mother will not allow him to go out to play at night when he wants to play.

Stage 2: Social-informational perspective (5–9 years). In this stage children realize that others may have different perspectives, because these others may have access to different information. For example, Von understands that teachers may know better than children what is good for the children because the teachers know things about children that the children themselves do not know.

Stage 3: Self-reflective perspective taking (7–12 years). In this stage children become able to see themselves as others see them. In other words, they can step into other people's shoes. They further understand that

THINKING ANALYTICALLY

What effect might the different patterns of male and female development in boys' and girls' relations toward peers have on group work during middle childhood and later, during adolescence?

SUGGESTION: Young adults may act toward fellow students in ways that reflect the patterns they established during childhood.

others have this ability too. For example, Von now can understand that the talking he does with other students while the teacher is speaking is viewed by his teacher as disruptive.

Stage 4: Third-party perspective taking (10–15 years). In this stage children come to understand how their interaction with another person may be viewed by a third party outside their interaction. For example, Von and a friend throw play punches at each other, but Von suddenly realizes that a teacher observing them is viewing their playful interaction as a fight.

Stage 5: Societal perspective taking (14 years–adulthood). In this stage individuals come to understand that third-party perspective taking is influenced by larger systems of societal values. Thus Von realizes that a teacher may wish to stop his throwing play punches with friends because such behavior is viewed by society as inappropriate in school settings, even if it is well intentioned.

Implications for Teaching

ATTACHMENT

- ***Students can form attachments to teachers.*** Carollee Howes and her colleagues (Howes & Hamilton, 1993; Howes, Hamilton, & Matheson, 1994; Howes, Matheson, & Hamilton, 1994) have found that children's attachment to their day-care or preschool teachers was related to how the children got along with their peers. In addition, Howes and colleagues found that a change of teacher or a change in the child's relationship with the teacher was associated with changes in the child's relations with peers. This research suggests that teachers of young students should strive to establish as consistently positive a relationship as possible with each student.

- ***Students' infantile attachments to their parents can serve as templates for later interactions with teachers and classmates.*** Attachment style can affect students' abilities to make transitions, such as the transition to middle school. Teachers should provide extra help during transitions to children who seem to be having problems.

- ***Children who have experienced attachment difficulties can later experience problems in school.*** Disruptions in infantile attachment potentially can have severe effects on social, emotional, and even cognitive development later on (Belsky & Cassidy, 1994). Children with dysfunctional parent-child relationships are likely to have substantial problems of adjustment as they grow up, and are at considerable risk for antisocial behavior (Patterson, DeBarsyshe, & Ramsey, 1989). In addition, less severe attachment disruptions, such as those that occur when a student's parents divorce, can also affect school performance (Hetherington, 1993; McLanahan & Sandefur, 1994). Expert teachers make themselves aware of students who may be experiencing problems at home, and they are prepared to provide extra help to students who may be experiencing such problems.

- ***Teachers need to watch for signs of children who are neglected and abused.*** Teachers need to be on the lookout for children who show possible signs of physical abuse, such as wounds, open sores, or damage to limbs, as well as of psychological abuse, such as extreme withdrawal or extreme aggression.

■ *Monitor patterns of friendship among students, providing help to isolated students if necessary.* The main concern of expert teachers is not with styles of friendship, but with whether children are forming friendships at all. Expert teachers encourage, but do not pressure, isolated children to form friendships.

■ *Children's preferred play styles may be related to their preferred ways of learning.* Younger students who prefer solitary play may lack the skills or desire to study in groups. Group activities may need to be carefully structured until most students have reached the cognitive level necessary to take the perspective of other children and to understand rules. By the time students reach upper elementary school and middle school, they may be interested in games with rules.

■ *Gender differences in play styles and friendship patterns may affect learning activities.* Because they may be reluctant to participate in learn-

---

TABLE 3.2   Educational Implications of Attachment Theory

| Implications | **How Teachers Might Apply the Implications at Different Educational Levels** | | | |
	Preschool and Primary Grades	**Elementary School**	**Middle School**	**High School**
Students can form attachments with teachers.	Positive and consistent relationships with teachers may help children develop effective social skills.		Teachers should remain aware that they may serve, in many ways, as role models for students.	
Students' infantile attachments to their parents can serve as templates for later interactions with teachers and classmates.	Children who have formed avoidant attachments to parents may also avoid peers and teachers. Such children may need a slow introduction to group processes or may prefer independent learning.	Students with ambivalent attachment patterns may behave inconsistently with schoolmates. Teachers can help by setting and enforcing clear rules for acceptable conduct.	Students whose attachments to parents are secure may experience easier transition to the first year of middle school than do students with other attachment styles. Teachers can help students by providing engaging projects early in the school year, and asking students to compare their experiences in elementary school with those in middle school.	Adolescents with insecure attachments to parents may suffer from lower self-esteem and difficulty establishing friendship and romantic attachments. Teachers should look for ways to involve or interest these students in school activities so that they do not seek emotional satisfaction in socially unacceptable activity.
Children who have experienced attachment difficulties can later experience problems in school.	Extreme language difficulties and resistance or avoidance of all social contact may be signs of severe attachment disruptions, including abuse. Teachers who notice these and other signs of abuse, such as physical damage, must report their suspicions to their principal.	Students' attachment to parents can be disrupted at any age by parental divorce. Teachers should try to know if any of their students are experiencing parental separation and divorce, so that they may be alert for any difficulties the child might experience in school.	Students experience high pressure to conform to peers in middle school and children who have insecure attachments with parents may be at risk for conforming to self-destructive norms, such as drug or alcohol use. Consider adding discussions about making individual choices to classwork by pointing out, for example, historical, literary, or scientific personalities who have profited from non-conformism.	Insecure attachment to parents can be related to low self-esteem in adolescence. Encourage students to develop independent self-esteem by setting their own goals and comparing their performance to their own earlier work, rather than to the work of their peers.

ing activities that "only boys do" or "only girls do," teachers may want to strive for gender-neutral class activities. Teachers may want to assign children to mixed-gender project groups, at least sometimes, to allow a chance for boys and girls to interact positively with one another.

■ **Children's behavior reflects their ability to take perspectives.** Expert teachers realize that young children may behave inappropriately because the children do not realize how others perceive the behavior. Nevertheless, children must learn to behave appropriately, even if they do not yet fully understand why such behavior is appropriate.

Tables 3.2 and 3.3 offer examples of how teachers might apply the implications of attachment theory and play and friendship development at different educational levels.

At all educational levels, expert teachers often need to help children through the difficulties of adjustment the children face as they try to integrate themselves academically and socially in the classroom environment. Teachers need also to help children confront moral issues, which we consider next.

TABLE 3.3 Educational Implications of Theories of Play and Friendship Development

| Implications | How Teachers Might Apply the Implications at Different Educational Levels | | | |
	Preschool and Primary Grades	Elementary School	Middle School	High School
Monitor patterns of friendship among students, providing help to isolated students if necessary.	Because friendships between children in this age range can easily be formed on the basis of shared activities, teachers may find it fairly easy to help isolated children by assigning them to groups with other children for games or projects.	Students at these ages who have trouble making friends may need some practice with basic social skills. Teachers could hold class meetings so that all students could discuss, without naming specific students, ways for everyone to become more expert at making friends.	The physical changes of puberty may make some middle school students feel conspicuous and uncomfortable. These students may also be teased or rejected. Teachers should not allow teasing or harassment. They may wish to initiate classroom discussions about the actual importance of appearances, or the temporary nature of appearance in junior high school.	Friendships are often fairly well defined by the time students are in high school, and teachers may experience difficulty helping isolated or rejected students. Classroom groups may need to be assigned by the teacher to avoid arrangements based on friendship cliques and to assure all students a chance to join a group.
Children's preferred play styles may be related to their preferred learning styles.	Very young students may not be able to share play or learning materials, so teachers should make sure enough supplies are available for all students.	Students may still have some difficulties with fully cooperative play and learning activities. Teachers may need to provide clear guidelines for cooperative activities or structure group activities so each group member is assigned his or her own part of a complete project.	Middle school students may enjoy working as cooperative teams who compete against other teams in learning games. Students may enjoy helping define the rules for these games, but game structure should not be allowed to overwhelm academic content.	Students should be well able to work together in cooperative groups.
Gender differences in play styles and friendship patterns may affect learning activities.	Gender roles are apparent in younger children's preferred play activities. Learning activities that are gender neutral should interest all students.	Throughout elementary school, students generally prefer to interact with and form friendships with members of the same gender. Encourage mixed-gender learning groups, at least occasionally. Avoid unfavorable comparisons between genders.	Girls' and boys' friendship patterns begin to diverge in middle school. Rifts in intense female friendships could temporarily disrupt some students' academic performance.	Males' preference for competition may discourage female students from classroom participation. Consider including some cooperative learning activities.

Moral Development: Acquiring a Sense of Right and Wrong

Teachers and parents generally want children to obey adults' rules, but they also hope for children eventually to develop their own abilities to distinguish between what is right and wrong. They want children to develop a sense of morality. As we mentioned at the beginning of the chapter, *moral development* is the process by which individuals acquire a sense of right and wrong, to use in evaluating their own actions and the actions of others (Turiel, 1998). Moral development begins early, and continues throughout the life span. One of the earliest theories of moral development was proposed by Jean Piaget (1932/1965).

PIAGET'S THEORY OF MORAL DEVELOPMENT

According to Piaget, young children are egocentric and have difficulty taking the perspective of other people until roughly the age of 7. Up to this age, children generally believe that rules are inflexible mandates provided by some higher authority. Breaking a rule will automatically lead to punishment. Young children tend to make moral judgments on the basis of how much harm their actions will cause. For example, someone who breaks 15 glasses (by accident) while trying to sneak into the cookie jar will be judged more harshly than someone who breaks just one cup. Piaget called this first phase of moral development *heteronomous morality,* or morality that is subject to rules imposed by others. It is also called the stage of **moral realism** or the morality of constraint, characterized by the view that rules are absolute. Children pay attention to the actions of others but not to the intentions underlying their actions. After about age 8, however, children are able to understand that rules and laws are not absolute, but rather, are formed by the agreement of groups of people; rules can be changed in the same way if people agree a new rule is needed. In the case of a broken rule, older children are now capable of considering whether the individual acted intentionally. Piaget referred to this second stage of moral development as *autonomous morality,* the level at which children understand that people both make up rules and can change the rules, which are now seen as the products of people's agreements. He also referred to this level as moral relativism or the **morality of cooperation.**

THINKING CREATIVELY

How might you try to show young children the importance of intentionality in judging the relative guilt or innocence of a child who has been caught stealing?

SUGGESTION: The children might be asked to think of a time when other people misinterpreted the intentions behind their own actions.

More research has suggested that, as with Piaget's theory of cognitive development, children's abilities, in this case to judge intentions, may start to take form earlier than age 8 (Schultz, Wright, & Schleifer, 1986). In addition, moral development, like cognitive development, can be influenced by a child's social environment. For example, authoritarian parenting and teaching styles, which stress unquestioning obedience to adult rules, may tend to restrain children's moral reasoning from developing to the second, autonomous morality level (DeVries & Zan, 1995).

As did his theory of moral development, Piaget's theory of cognitive development has motivated others to develop their own ideas. Psychologist Lawrence Kohlberg used Piaget's theory as one of the starting points in developing his own, detailed theory of morality, which we consider next.

KOHLBERG'S THEORY OF MORAL DEVELOPMENT: LEVELS AND STAGES

Students encounter moral dilemmas constantly. Should they cheat on a test? Should they report a student whom they observed cheating? Should they violate a confidence, such as a confession of a crime made to them in confidence?

In Europe, a woman was near death from a rare form of cancer. The doctors thought that one drug might save her: a form of radium a druggist in the same town had recently discovered. The drug was expensive to make, but the druggist was also charging ten times his cost; having paid $400 for the radium, he charged $4,000 for a small dose. The sick woman's husband, Heinz, went to everyone he knew to borrow the money, but he could collect only $2,000. He begged the druggist to sell the drug more cheaply or to let him pay the balance later, but the druggist refused. So, having tried every legal means, Heinz desperately considered breaking into the drugstore to steal the drug for his wife. (Adapted from Kohlberg, 1963, 1983, 1984)

Lawrence Kohlberg (1963, 1983, 1984) used **moral dilemmas**—problems such as the one just described that because of their ambiguity require difficult ethical choice—to assess what he believed to be three levels and six stages of moral development in children. Kohlberg was not especially interested in the specific choices students made—in this case, whether they said Heinz should steal the radium or he should not. What interested Kohlberg was the reasoning students gave for their choices. He believed students' reasoning revealed their underlying moral reasoning, or thought processes about moral issues. The three levels and six stages of Kohlberg's theory of moral development are summarized in Table 3.4.

CONSTRUCTING YOUR OWN LEARNING

Before reading on, answer the Heinz dilemma for yourself and then try it on some of your friends. If you are currently working in a practicum, you might also ask some of the children you are working with how they would answer the dilemma. (Be sure to discuss this first with your cooperating teacher.) Then consider the scoring logic described in Table 3.4, and characterize where each of you would fall on this particular problem, according to Kohlberg's theory.

TABLE 3.4   Kohlberg's Levels of Moral Development

Level I—Preconventional Morality		Level II—Conventional Morality		Level III—Postconventional Morality	
Stage 1: Punishment and obedience are an individual's main concerns. Rules are obeyed because of the threat of punishment for infractions.	**Stage 2:** Individual adopts an orientation of individualism and exchange. Rules are followed if they are in the individual's best interest. Deals and compromises with others are sometimes used to solve problems.	**Stage 3:** Moral reasoning is guided by mutual interpersonal expectations and conformity. People try to do what is expected of them.	**Stage 4:** Individuals place importance on the social system, including laws, and on fulfilling obligations.	**Stage 5:** People recognize and try to balance the importance of both social contracts and individual rights.	**Stage 6:** Individuals adopt an orientation toward universal principles of justice, which exist regardless of a particular society's rules.
Sample Answer to Heinz Dilemma: "No, Heinz shouldn't take the radium because he might get caught and thrown into jail."	**Sample Answer to Heinz Dilemma:** "Yes, Heinz should take the radium, because the druggist is refusing to make a deal that will benefit both people."	**Sample Answer to Heinz Dilemma:** "Yes, Heinz should steal the drug. A good husband takes care of his wife. He would seem cold and heartless if he wasn't willing to risk a little jail time to help his wife live."	**Sample Answer to Heinz Dilemma:** "Heinz should not steal the drug. If everyone disobeyed the laws against theft, society would be in chaos."	**Sample Answer to Heinz Dilemma:** "Yes, Heinz should take the drug, because the value of human life outweighs the druggist's individual right to own property."	**Sample Answer to Heinz Dilemma:** "Yes, Heinz should take the drug, because the value of human life outweighs any other considerations."

Lawrence Kohlberg used moral dilemmas—ambiguous problems requiring difficult ethical choices—to assess what he identified as three levels and six stages of moral development in children. He believed that children's reasoning reveals their thought processes about moral issues. (Harvard University Office of News and Public Affairs)

Level I involves **preconventional morality,** a level of moral reasoning based primarily on egocentric concerns. Kohlberg suggested that this level of moral reasoning characterizes children between about ages 7 and 10. Some studies have found, however, that as many as 20 percent of U.S. teenagers function at the preconventional morality level (Turiel, 1973).

In stage 1 of this level, an individual behaves in one way or another primarily to obtain rewards and to avoid punishments. Thus *obedience* and *punishment* are the main issues for the individual. An authority is viewed as correct because if it is not obeyed, punishment will follow. The popular students in Jim Conto's class, described at the beginning of the chapter, seem to be functioning at a preconventional level, reserving their attacks on Carla for times they believe they will not be caught.

In stage 2, the orientation of the individual shifts to *individualism* and *exchange.* Stage 2 individuals follow rules, but only when they view such behavior as being to their benefit. Realizing that other people have other interests, a stage 2 individual will strike deals in order to compromise. For individuals in this stage, a sense of morality is relative, in that they view as right what they will be rewarded for doing. Tommy, an elementary school student, obeys his teachers because he has learned that his teachers will reward him for obedience.

At *level II* individuals think in terms of **conventional morality,** a level of moral reasoning that reflects a person's internalization of social rules. An individual conforms to social rules because he or she believes it is right to do so. Kohlberg suggested this level might apply primarily to people between the ages of 10 and 16, although many adults also reason primarily at the conventional morality level. Later in his career, Kohlberg realized his estimate of ages 10 to 16 for this stage may have been optimistic. Betty, age 13, helps her friends not because she gets rewards from them, but because she believes it is the right thing to do. The Flexible Expert: Moving from Preconventional to Conventional Moral Reasoning provides some examples of expert teachers and students who are making the transition from Kohlberg's preconventional level of moral reasoning to his conventional level.

THE FLEXIBLE EXPERT

MOVING FROM PRECONVENTIONAL TO CONVENTIONAL MORAL REASONING

IN EACH CHAPTER OF THE TEXT, WE INTRODUCE YOU TO A FEW SPECIFIC STRATEGIES—ANALYTICAL, CREATIVE, AND PRACTICAL—USED BY BOTH EXPERT TEACHERS AND EXPERT STUDENTS.

THE ANALYTICAL TEACHER: Sue observes that some of her sixth-grade students have begun to show signs of reasoning at Kohlberg's conventional level. She decides to hold class discussions of moral dilemmas so the students who still reason at the preconventional level can hear and learn from the ideas of the students using conventional-level reasoning.

THE CREATIVE TEACHER: Sue writes a play in which the characters must decide what to do with a large sum of cash they have found in a wallet. Each character's idea about what to do with the money reflects a different level of moral reasoning.

THE PRACTICAL TEACHER: Whenever students face a day-to-day moral dilemma, such as a problem negotiating cleanup duties, Sue leads a brief class discussion in which the students consider several alternative ideas for solving the dilemma. If students do not bring up potential solu-

tions that reflect the conventional level of reasoning, Sue suggests them.

THE ANALYTICAL STUDENT: Dale thinks about the reasons he chooses to go to school every day. He concludes that the main reasons are because his friends would be sad if he didn't show up and his parents would be disappointed because they have sacrificed their time to help him succeed in school.

THE CREATIVE STUDENT: Dale writes a song called "Give-and-Take" about what he believes to be an immoral attitude of showing kindness only in return for kindness already given.

THE PRACTICAL STUDENT: Dale tells his friends he won't shoplift music CDs with them, asking, "How would we feel if it was our store and some kids came in and took stuff without paying?"

In stage 3, the first stage at this level, people's reasoning is guided by *mutual interpersonal expectations* and *interpersonal conformity.* Stage 3 children try to meet the expectations of others who are important in their lives. Being good means having good motives underlying actions. Children recognize that the needs of a group often have to take precedence over the needs of the individual, and we need to live by the Golden Rule, doing unto others as we would have them do unto us. Kerji almost always asks himself not only how his actions will affect himself, but also, how they will affect others.

At stage 4 of level II, adolescents realize the importance of *conscience* and of the *social system.* They see the relevance of obeying laws and of fulfilling obligations, except in those rare cases where these obligations violate some higher social obligations. The adolescent distinguishes between the point of view of society and that of individual members of the society. Two or more people may agree on something that is nevertheless to society's detriment. Marvin opposes a war even though his friends and the government support it.

Level III involves **postconventional morality,** a level of moral reasoning based primarily on an internal set of moral absolutes, which may or may not agree with social rules. Leila has decided to commit civil disobedience because she is convinced that the death penalty, though legal, is immoral. Along with others, she chains herself to a fence in front of the courtroom where a death-penalty verdict has been handed down. Here, society's rules serve as the basis for most behavior, but a set of internal moral principles may outweigh the rules of society if a conflict arises between the two. This is a level reached by few people; if attained, it is generally not reached before the age of 16.

In stage 5, individuals recognize the importance both of *social contracts* and of *individual rights.* They realize that people hold many different values, most of which are relative, but that are upheld because they are part of a social contract to which the people have agreed. Nevertheless, certain values, such as the right of the individual to life and liberty, hold regardless of what the majority of people within a society may think. Stage 5 individuals recognize that, in theory, laws are enacted to provide the greatest good for the greatest number, but that, in practice, sometimes these laws violate moral principles. In such cases, there is no easy resolution. Only about one-fifth of adolescents actually reach this stage. Damon decides to try to fight against a totalitarian government in the society in which he lives, despite opposition from friends, family, and government.

In stage 6 of level III, individuals are oriented toward *universal principles of justice.* They believe they should uphold universal principles, and they are committed to these principles, whether other people in their society are or not. In his later writings, Kohlberg suggested that stage 6 is rarely, if ever, reached by real people, and it might be more of an ideal than a distinct moral stage. Mother Theresa battled conditions of extreme poverty because she felt a moral imperative to do so.

GILLIGAN'S ALTERNATIVE TO KOHLBERG'S THEORY

Carol Gilligan (1982; Gilligan, Hamner, & Lyons, 1990) has proposed one alternative model. She has suggested that women tend to have a different conception of morality than do men. According to Gilligan, whereas men tend to focus on abstract, rational principles such as justice and respect for the rights of others, women tend to view morality more in terms of caring and compassion. They are more concerned with issues of general human welfare and how relationships can contribute to it. In particular, women seem better able to show **empathy,** or the ability to understand how another person feels, when interacting with others. They are especially sensitive to the obligations of close relationships. In general, men tend to have a more competitive orientation; women, a more cooperative orientation.

Some researchers have found support for the kinds of claims made by Gilligan (e.g., Baumrind, 1986; Gibbs, Arnold, Ahlborn, & Chessman, 1984; Gilligan & Attanucci, 1988), whereas others have found that men as well as women seem to take into account considerations of caring in their moral judgments. Although women were more likely than men to express caring, girls were no more likely to do so than were boys (Walker, 1989; Walker, Pitts, Hennig, & Matsuba, 1995).

Carol Gilligan has proposed that women and men perceive morality differently. (Harvard Graduate School of Education)

CONSTRUCTING YOUR OWN LEARNING

reate three or four scenarios that you believe can allow responses that suggest either an orientation more directed toward abstract principles of justice or an orientation of concern with caring for another individual. Then try out your scenarios on friends, asking them their solutions to the dilemmas. If you are currently working on a practicum, you might also try out your scenarios with some of the children. Were males or females more likely to show a caring orientation?

EVALUATING KOHLBERG'S THEORY

Kohlberg's theory has generated enormous interest. It is the most nearly complete theory of moral development, and psychologists have found that moral development in many situations seems to proceed roughly along the lines Kohlberg suggested (Nisan & Kohlberg, 1982; Rest, 1983; Snarey, Reimer, & Kohlberg, 1985a, 1985b), even in other cultures, such as Turkey and Israel. But the theory has been criticized on various grounds.

First, the scoring of the scenarios is somewhat subjective, and can lead to errors of interpretation. James Rest (1979, 1983) has constructed an alternative test, the Defining Issues Test (DIT), which measures the stages of Kohlberg's theory somewhat less subjectively.

Second, stages of moral development seem to be less domain general than Kohlberg's theory suggests (Kurtines & Greif, 1974). The level of people's responses may vary, depending on the particular scenario to which they respond (Holstein, 1976). Further, evidence indicates that, contrary to the assumptions of stage theories, people may regress to earlier stages of moral reasoning under certain circumstances, such as when they are under stress (see Kohlberg & Kramer, 1969). Kohlberg's reply to this criticism was that even if an individual regresses, he or she still understands the higher level of reasoning.

Third, Kohlberg's own finding that people can regress in their behavior points out the weak link that often exists between thought and action (Kurtines & Greif, 1974). Someone may indeed understand higher levels of moral development, but not act in ways consistent with that understanding.

Finally, the theory was originally validated on a relatively small sample of white, middle-class American males under 17 years of age. Although some investigators have found cross-cultural support for Kohlberg's theory (e.g., Snarey, 1985), others have found that in certain circumstances, such as the lifestyle of the communal Israeli kibbutz, what is viewed as a "higher" level of morality differs from the value system Kohlberg suggested. The various criticisms of Kohlberg's theory have prompted some theorists to suggest alternative systems of valuing just what is "moral" (e.g., Etzioni, 1993; Wilson, 1993; Wright, 1994).

Implications for Teaching

■ *Teachers need to expect a level of moral thought and behavior that is appropriate to the child's age.* By setting expectations either too high or too low, expert teachers know they can fail to challenge students at a level appropriate to their development (see Table 3.5).

■ *Having classroom discussion of moral dilemmas helps challenge students' moral reasoning.* These can arise from the academic subject matter or from events inside or outside the classroom. Kohlberg and Kramer (1969) believed discussion of moral dilemmas could help a child develop expertise in moral reasoning by exposing the child to thinking at higher stages.

TABLE 3.5   Educational Implications of Morality Theories

How Teachers Might Apply the Implications at Different Educational Levels

Implications	Preschool and Primary Grades	Elementary School	Middle School	High School
Expect a level of moral thought and behavior that is appropriate to the child's age.	Young children often consider consequences more important than intentions in judging others. Teachers might use everyday examples, such as spills or playground accidents, to help point out to students that causing some damage on purpose is different than doing so unintentionally.	Students in the upper elementary grades and in middle school are often in the second of Kohlberg's moral levels, using conventional moral reasoning. They may enjoy setting some of the rules of the classroom "society" in class meetings.		High school teachers can challenge students to consider whether there are any universal principles. Subjects such as literature and social science make an easy context for moral discussion, but even science classes, for example, offer students opportunities to ponder the existence of global rules.
Discussions of moral dilemmas might help children develop their moral reasoning skills.	Younger children's decisions are generally based on egocentric concerns about their own punishment or rewards. Teachers should challenge young students to sometimes see how individual actions affect other people. Stories or real-life examples from the classroom could be used to provide opportunities for taking another's perspective.	Class meetings provide opportunities to bring up moral dilemmas students are actually facing and encourage discussion of possible choices.	In some school districts, it may be acceptable to encourage students to discuss issues that are being brought to their minds by the changes of puberty, such as personal sexual standards. Be sure to check the district's guidelines before initiating any discussions of sensitive topics.	Current events in many subjects, such as scientific advances leading to cloning or discoveries about the "true" nature of historical figures or events, can provide the basis for discussions of values and ethics in many different classes.
Teachers should be aware of cultural and gender influences on morality.	Children whose cultural backgrounds value interdependence may be uncomfortable away from their families for the first time. Teachers may be able to help by encouraging family members to visit, or even volunteer regularly, at school and by initiating frequent contact with families, designed to promote cooperation in helping the child adjust to school.	Cooperative learning tasks, such as team science or social science projects, encourage students who are oriented to independent achievement to also learn to value working for the sake of the group.	Some classes may wish to participate in civic projects that show students how their individual knowledge could be used to help their whole community. For example, one junior high school science class, on learning that bats eat biting insects, installed bat houses in a local park to make the park more comfortable for the whole community (Schukar, 1997).	In some schools, competition for grades may become fierce as students strive to impress college acceptance committees. Teachers may wish to point out the value of study groups for cooperatively boosting the achievements of all members.

- *Self-assessment will help teachers assess their own level of moral development to better understand how they perceive the thinking and behavior of their students.* Teachers need to understand themselves and their own thinking.

- *Teachers need to realize that no one theory of moral development is universally accepted.* All of the theories appear to apply only to some rather than to all individuals.

- *Teachers need to encourage and develop thinking that is not just moral, but also, wise.* Such thinking has as its aim the attainment of a common good—what is ultimately in everyone's best interests (Sternberg, 1999).

Cultural and sexual differences can often affect children's moral development. See Chapter 6 for a detailed discussion of these differences.

Identifying, Understanding, and Managing Developmental Risks

Children and adolescents today are at risk for certain problems. These challenges include increased risk for psychological problems, such as eating disorders and depression; behavioral problems, such as drug use; and unwanted consequences of sexual activity. Because these problems can threaten the success of students in school and in society—in some cases even threaten their lives—teachers must know how to identify and handle them.

AT RISK FOR EATING DISORDERS

Anorexia and bulimia are eating disorders that typically do not directly affect learning. However, because they are sufficiently common among adolescents and younger students, and especially female students, teachers need to be aware of them.

■ANOREXIA NERVOSA **Anorexia nervosa** is a life-threatening ailment characterized by a distorted self-image and the resulting severe fear of gaining weight. As a result of their fear, people with anorexia refuse to eat sufficient food to maintain adequate body weight and nutrition. Anorexics may also take laxatives and exercise extensively in a desperate effort to lose weight (Davison & Neale, 1994). Anorexia is far more common in women than in men. It occurs in about 0.3 percent of young women in grades 9 through 12 (Whitaker et al., 1990); thus the chances that a high school teacher will encounter at least one case every year or two is quite high. Ages 15 to 19 are the peak years for anorexia (Frombonne, 1995), but middle school and elementary school teachers should be aware of an increase in the number of cases of anorexia among 8- to 13-year-olds in the past 20 years (Lask & Bryant-Waugh, 1992).

THINKING ANALYTICALLY

Anorexia nervosa has been recognized only relatively recently as a disorder, and appears to be much more prevalent now than in the past. Why might the prevalence of anorexia nervosa have increased in recent times?

SUGGESTION: There is a great emphasis on thinness in many contemporary cultures—particularly in the United States.

Anorexics tend to be young women who are well behaved, conscientious, quiet, and even perfectionistic. A preoccupation with appearance, such as that of Carla, the girl at the beginning of the chapter, may lead to anorexia if it is severe and focused on thinness. Teachers may notice that students with anorexia are becoming extremely thin. In fact, anorexics often grow emaciated, with skull-like faces and protruding ribs. A student with anorexia will nevertheless persist in believing that he or she is too fat (Davison & Neale, 1994). Additional signs are dry, cracking skin, fine downy hair on the face and neck, brittle fingernails, yellowish discoloration of the skin, increased heart rate, reduced body temperature, and muscular weakness (Kaplan & Woodside, 1987). The self-starving that results from anorexia can bring on irreversible physiological changes, including heart and muscle damage. As many as 10 percent of people with anorexia die from complications of the disorder (American Psychiatric Association, 1993).

Because of the seriousness of the condition, a teacher who suspects a student has anorexia should act immediately, first by advising the student to seek counseling and treatment, and then by contacting the student's parents or school authorities if necessary to help the student get treatment. Anorexics sometimes require hospitalization to ensure weight gain, and follow-up treatment includes psychotherapy.

■BULIMIA NERVOSA **Bulimia nervosa** is an eating disorder characterized by food bingeing, followed by purging (Polivy & Herman, 1993). The sufferer may grossly overeat, usually in a short amount of time, and then either vomit the food or else take large amounts of laxatives in order to rid the body of the ingested food.

Estimates of the incidence of bulimia are hard to come by. No reliable statistics exist at the high school level, but estimates of the number of people in the general U.S. population who have bulimia range from 2 to 4 percent (Kendler, MacLean, Neale, Kessler, Heath, & Eaves, 1991). These numbers are likely to be conservative, however, because bulimia is much more easily hidden than is anorexia. As in the case of anorexia, the disorder is far more common in women than in men.

Teachers may find it difficult to recognize bulimia in their students. Although bulimics share the concern of anorexics about becoming too fat, students with bulimia do not necessarily show low body weight (Davison & Neale, 1994). Bulimic students may be depressed (Piran, Kennedy, Garfield, & Owens, 1985). Slipping grades or failing interpersonal relationships may also be signals of bulimia, because the eating and purging can use up time that might otherwise be spent on either schoolwork or social relationships. Bulimics may also have dental problems as their teeth become discolored or damaged because of the effects of acid from their repeated purging. Because bulimia, like anorexia, is unlikely to go away spontaneously unless treated, teachers should take steps to ensure that students with the disorder seek help. Bulimia is more easily treatable than anorexia, usually by a combination of therapy and *re-education* (Fairburn, Norman, Welch, O'Connor, Doll, & Peveler, 1995).

AT RISK FOR MAJOR DEPRESSION

A person with **major depression** is affected by feelings of hopelessness that significantly interfere with his or her life. Major depression is distinguished, by its severity and length, from the mood swings we all have so that sometimes we feel happy and other times we feel sad or depressed. Although depression does not usually produce notable physical or other impairments, it can sometimes be deadly, because of its link with suicide.

■**DEPRESSION** Depression is quite common among adolescents. Clinical levels of depression have been found in approximately 7 percent of adolescents sampled from the general U.S. population (Petersen, Compas, Brooks-Gunn, Stemmler, Ey, & Grant, 1993). Childhood depression is also more common than many teachers may know. One longitudinal study found that between 5 and 10 percent of third graders scored at a "serious" level of depression (Nolen-Hoeksema, Girgus, & Seligman, 1992). How do depressed children and adolescents act?

Young children, in preschool or the primary grades, may express feelings of sadness verbally, but mainly show depression through physical symptoms, for example, loss of appetite, sleep difficulties, fatigue, and somatic complaints such as stomachaches (Kashani & Carlson, 1987). Older children and adolescents are likely to have similar physical problems. In addition, depressed adolescents show many of the same characteristics as depressed adults, which usually fall into one of two patterns.

The first pattern, *agitated depression,* is characterized by a person's being unable to stay still, being constantly on the go, speaking loudly or rapidly, and complaining a lot. This form of depression is relatively rare. The other pattern, *retarded depression,* is more common. Persons with this type of depression feel profoundly sad and hopeless. They generally experience low levels of energy and may speak or act slowly. They are likely to lose weight and may seek to sleep as much of the time as possible.

Because of their feelings of hopelessness and discouragement, students suffering from major depression—whether agitated or retarded—are likely to show school performance well below that of which they are capable, as well as to show problems in their interpersonal relationships, especially loss of interest. Individuals with major depression are likely to show distorted patterns of thinking (Beck, 1967, 1985, 1997). They may magnify the importance of small errors they commit, minimize the importance of their accomplishments, take personal responsibility for things that go wrong for reasons over which

THINKING ANALYTICALLY

Why is it more difficult to determine the prevalence of bulimia than of anorexia?

SUGGESTION: The symptoms of anorexia are more readily apparent.

This depressed teenager is being comforted by her mother. (Bob Daemmrich Photos, Inc.)

Why it is important for teachers to be alert for major depression in their students as well as in themselves?

SUGGESTION: Depression can result in flagging quality of work and personal well-being, whether a teacher or a learner.

they have no control, and make arbitrary inferences. For example, a depressed student may believe a glance from a teacher means the teacher does not like the student.

Depression in children and adolescents is often related to disruptions in the student's life, such as homelessness, child abuse, or parental divorce. Teachers should be aware of students' home life and any risks for psychological problems that the home situation may create. Major depression, unlike the occasional mild depressions we all experience, needs treatment. Students showing signs of such depression need social support (Henderson, 1992) and should be encouraged to seek help, which usually consists of psychotherapy and sometimes therapy in combination with drugs. Teachers must act immediately to get help for depressed students who communicate ideas of suicide.

■ **SUICIDE**   The suicide rate for young people ages 15 to 24 has roughly tripled over the past 30 years, reaching almost 18 per 100,000 individuals, or 3,000 people each year. Suicide is now the second leading cause of death among teenagers, surpassed only by automobile accidents, and some "accidents" actually may be suicides as well (Douglas, 1967; Garland & Zigler, 1993; Gibbs, 1968; National Center for Health Statistics [NCHS], 1991). The rate of attempted suicide also has tripled, and one national poll found that 6 percent of U.S. teenagers have tried to kill themselves (Freiberg, 1991). Suicide, like depression, is not limited to older students (Diekstra, 1996). The NCHS (1993) estimates that as many as a quarter million U.S. children between the ages of 5 and 14 attempt suicide each year.

About three times as many females as males attempt suicide, often by overdosing on sleeping pills or other drugs. However, males, because they more often choose effective methods, such as shooting or hanging themselves, are about three times more likely than females to complete a suicide attempt.

A common myth about suicide is that people who talk about committing suicide do not actually go ahead and do it. In fact, nearly 80 percent of people who commit suicide have given some warning beforehand. For this reason it is critical that teachers take students' threats or discussion of suicide seriously. Some teachers may believe that talking about suicide with a student who has brought up the idea will encourage the student to act. Expert teachers know that talking can be a first step to getting help for the student (Range, 1993). Find out how much the student has thought about suicide and whether he or she has made plans or preparations for committing suicide. A student who has made a definite plan, or obtained the means to kill himself or herself is in immediate peril, and needs professional help immediately. Many schools have suicide prevention programs in place to provide students with counseling services or refer them for further help (Freiberg, 1991).

Expert teachers are also aware that the death of a student by suicide tremendously increases the risk of further student suicides (Lewinsohn, Rohde, & Seeley, 1994). For this reason, many schools arrange to make special counseling available to all surviving students if a student in the school or community dies by suicide. Suicide attempts may also become more likely following highly publicized suicide deaths, such as those of young celebrities (Stack, 1987).

THINKING ANALYTICALLY

Why should suicide threats always be taken seriously?

SUGGESTION: There is no certain way of knowing how likely a threat is to lead to an actual suicide attempt.

AT RISK FOR VIOLENT BEHAVIOR

In the past ten years there has been an alarming increase of violence in schools throughout the United States—whether urban, suburban, or rural. Schools and communities are actively working on ways to make schools safer through a variety of programs that involve protective as well as preventative measures. Among the many protective measures are closed-circuit TVs, "zero-tolerance policies" for weapons possession, safe havens for students, locker searches, metal detectors, phones in classrooms, and security personnel. However, equally if not more important are preventative measures such as conflict resolution and peer mediation training, safety teams, 24-hour student hot lines, multicultural sensitivity training, staff development, and home–school linkages.

DRUG USE: A PREVALENT PROBLEM

Drug use has become so prevalent that teachers simply cannot ignore it. For example, nearly half the high school seniors in one national survey (46 percent) reported that they had used an illicit drug at least once in their lifetimes, and almost one-third (31 percent) of students surveyed said they had used marijuana in the past year (SAMHSA, 1995). Alcohol use is also rampant, and it begins at early ages. Twenty-five percent of eighth graders and 40 percent of tenth graders in one survey reported that they had used alcohol just in the past month (SAMHSA, 1995). Like alcohol, use of inhalants such as glue is widespread, leading to the development of tolerance and withdrawal symptoms, and even to death.

Teachers must become expert at recognizing the effects of drug use in students, which can vary depending on the particular drug. General indicators of drug use include changes in behavior or academic performance; frequent absences or "illnesses"; weight loss; unusually lethargic or active behavior; involvement in criminal activities; possession of drug-using paraphernalia, such as needles; or traces and smells of marijuana, tobacco, or alcohol. Students who are using drugs risk addiction, particularly in the case of narcotic drugs, such as heroin, or stimulants, such as cocaine—especially crack cocaine. Expert teachers know that even the so-called legal drugs, alcohol and nicotine, can be highly addictive. Use of some drugs, even at relatively low doses, also can cause permanent damage to brain cells involved in learning and memory (Darley, Tinklenberg, Roth, Hollister, & Atkinson, 1973).

Many schools have alcohol and drug abuse and prevention programs in place, and teachers should encourage students who show signs of drug use to seek help through these or other programs. Such programs help students with severe drug problems find medical help or rehabilitation if needed. Prevention programs concentrate on teaching students to avoid situations that may encourage drug use and helping them practice the social skills needed to resist offers or peer pressure to use drugs (Hittner, 1997; Newcomb & Bentler, 1989). Teachers also may be able to help prevent drug use by modeling abstinence from drugs themselves, or pointing out positive role models, and by mentioning in the course of everyday classwork the negative consequences of drug use. Drug use is usually, but not always, intentional. For example, some women, without their knowledge, have been given drugs such as Rohyprol in order to render them nonresistant to and unaware of their being raped. Both the drug and its hidden administration are illegal.

THINKING ANALYTICALLY

Psychoactive drugs are addictive, expensive, and potentially life threatening. Why do so many children as well as adults start using them?

SUGGESTION: People often fail adequately to weigh long-term losses against what appear (often falsely) to be short-term gains.

THINKING PRACTICALLY

Some people have argued that the use of psychoactive drugs is the biggest problem our society is facing today. Why does use of illegal psychoactive drugs pose such a large potential threat?

SUGGESTION: Besides the economic costs, the costs of illegal psychoactive drugs in terms of wasted and even lost lives is incalculable.

THINKING PRACTICALLY

Can you think of an additional element that might be a part of an effective school program to combat student drug use?

SUGGESTION: Students might design posters to encourage abstinence from the use of illegal drugs.

UNWANTED CONSEQUENCES OF SEXUAL ACTIVITY

By the age of 19, about 80 percent of American men and 75 percent of American women have had sexual intercourse (Guttmacher Institute, 1994). Many students are becoming sexually active at even younger ages. One study, for example, found that nearly one in ten 13-year-olds had already experienced sexual intercourse (Mott, Fondell, Hu, Kowalski-Jones, & Menaghan, 1996). Unfortunately, for many students sex has unwanted consequences, such as sexually transmitted diseases and teenage pregnancy.

■ SEXUALLY TRANSMITTED DISEASES Three million U.S. teenagers contract a sexually transmitted disease (STD) every year (Tanfer, Cubbins, & Billy, 1995). Adolescents are at risk for contracting acquired immune deficiency syndrome (AIDS) and other STDs because of ignorance about means of sexual transmission and because of the

Do you believe condoms should be distributed on request to high school students? Why or why not?

SUGGESTION: An advantage is disease prevention. A disadvantage is inconsistency with the religious beliefs of some students.

illusions of invulnerability that frequently accompany the adolescent years. Teenagers may believe, for example, that STDs are something that happens to "someone else."

Although many STDs are curable, some are not. Syphilis and gonorrhea can both be treated by antibiotics, for example. However, if not treated, they can have grave consequences. Syphilis can lead over the long term to dementia and even death, and gonorrhea can lead to sterility. Chlamydia is also treatable, but it can result in pelvic inflammatory disease in women if not treated. Genital herpes can be treated but not cured. Venereal warts can be treated, but are associated with later risk in women for cervical cancer. Of special concern is AIDS, a usually and, in the long term, possibly always fatal disease contracted through exchange of bodily fluids, primarily blood and semen that contain the human immunodeficiency virus (HIV). Although new forms of drug treatment have extended the lives of those with AIDS, there is at present no known cure.

About one-fifth of AIDS cases in the United States occur in people between the ages of 20 to 29 (Berk, 1996). Because it can take ten years or longer for an HIV-infected person to develop the full-blown symptoms of AIDS, it is likely that many of the people who develop AIDS in their twenties were first infected with HIV as teenagers. AIDS is totally preventable through behavioral intervention, and adolescents should be taught how to reduce their risk of infection. In regard to sexual transmission, abstinence is obviously the safest course, followed by diligent use of condoms. Teachers should also make clear the risk to those who take drugs—particularly those who use needles. Besides the risks and modes of transmission of AIDS, teachers should make known how it is *not* transmitted—through saliva, routine physical contact with a friend or relative who has the disease, or coughing or sneezing. Research consistently indicates that increased knowledge about HIV and AIDS is related to safer behavior (Fisher & Fisher, 1992; Mickler, 1993).

■**TEEN PREGNANCY** More than a million U.S. teenage girls become pregnant each year (DeRidder, 1993). Although teen pregnancy is found in all socioeconomic groups, it is more prevalent among those who grow up in lower income homes (Morrison, 1985). Teenage motherhood is likely to lead young women to drop out of school early and to enter into a cycle of poverty that will affect the child or children as well as the mother.

Some of the factors contributing to the high rate of teen pregnancy are the same as those related to high rates of adolescent STDs. One key factor is ignorance about sexual and reproductive facts, such as when in the menstrual cycle a woman can become pregnant. Adolescent girls may also harbor illusions that they are somehow unlikely to become pregnant. In addition, some adolescent girls may feel that preparing for sexual intercourse by obtaining methods of contraception makes them appear promiscuous.

Teachers may view teen pregnancy in a largely or wholly negative light, but they need to be aware that not all teens do. Some adolescent girls do not view becoming a parent while young or unmarried as an unwanted situation at all. Indeed, the adolescent may actually wish for the responsibility, or thereby to be viewed by others as an "adult." Having a baby may make a girl feel more like a woman, or more nearly self-fulfilled. Sometimes accurate information about the day-to-day life of a teen mother can discourage teens who wish to become parents.

Some teachers and schools are reluctant to provide contraceptive information for fear of encouraging teenage sexual activity. However, research suggests that formal contraceptive education programs increase the likelihood that adolescents will use birth control methods (Mauldon & Luker, 1996). Providing teens with accurate information about sex and contraception seems to be related to fewer unwanted pregnancies (DeRidder, 1993; Mauldon & Luker, 1996).

What is a specific measure a school could take in order to try to reduce the incidence of teen pregnancy?

SUGGESTION: One measure would be the distribution of condoms. Another would be the encouragement of abstinence from sexual relations.

WHY UNDERSTANDING PERSONAL, GENDER, SOCIAL, AND MORAL DEVELOPMENT IS IMPORTANT TO TEACHERS

- This chapter considers the issues of personal, gender, social, and moral development. Although each aspect of development was considered separately, of course they interact. For example, as children's morality develops, their interactions with peers change.

PERSONAL DEVELOPMENT: BECOMING UNIQUE

- Erikson's theory of psychosocial development posits a series of eight developmental crises: trust vs. mistrust, autonomy vs. shame and doubt, initiative vs. guilt, industry vs. inferiority, identity vs. role confusion, intimacy vs. isolation, generativity vs. stagnation, and integrity vs. despair.

- Marcia has distinguished among identity achievement, in which people have made their own decisions and have a clear sense of who they are; identity foreclosure, in which people have chosen their path through life with little reflection; identity moratorium, in which people are still seeking an identity; and identity diffusion, in which people lack any clear direction or commitment.

SEXUAL AND GENDER DEVELOPMENT: ACQUIRING GENDER ROLES

- Theories regarding the development of gender identification have considered the roles of biology and evolution, role modeling (social learning theory), and schemas that help people make sense of their experiences. Gender schemas that are widely shared are called gender stereotypes. The development of gender identification is different from one's biological sexual development.

SOCIAL DEVELOPMENT: LEARNING TO INTERACT WITH OTHERS

- Attachment is an emotional tie with another person. The first such tie is usually with the mother. Avoidant children seem distant emotionally from others; secure children seem to bond naturally and comfortably with others; resistant children tend simulta-

neously to be both aloof and in need of closeness. Children who do not attach normally to one or more parental figures are at risk for disrupted behavior later on.

- Theorists of play and friendship have suggested various stages in the formation of strategies of play and of types of friendships. For example, Robert Selman proposed five stages in the development of children's perspective-taking abilities. In general, older children connect more with each other than do younger children, and girls seem to show more intimacy in their friendships than do boys.

MORAL DEVELOPMENT: ACQUIRING A SENSE OF RIGHT AND WRONG

- Various theories of moral development have been proposed, most notably those of Piaget, Kohlberg, and Gilligan. Piaget proposed two phases of moral development, moral realism and the morality of cooperation. Kohlberg's theory of moral development is the most nearly complete. It posits three levels of moral reasoning: preconventional morality, conventional morality, and postconventional morality, each divided into substages. One way that Kohlberg tested moral reasoning was through the use of moral dilemmas.

- Kohlberg's theory of moral development may be biased toward certain cultural groups and even toward men over women. Gilligan's theory attempts to correct this shortcoming by emphasizing the caring orientation of women, particularly their capacity for empathy.

IDENTIFYING, UNDERSTANDING, AND MANAGING DEVELOPMENTAL RISKS

- The risks to personal development that students face today include eating disorders, such as anorexia nervosa and bulimia nervosa; major depression and suicide; drug use; and unwanted consequences of sexual activity, including sexually transmitted diseases and teen pregnancy.

KEY TERMS AND DEFINITIONS

Androgyny State in which individuals feel free to display behavior that is stereotypical of both genders, rather than restricting themselves to behavior considered appropriate to their own gender. Page 90

Anorexia nervosa Life-threatening eating disorder characterized by minimal food intake, a distorted self-image, and a severe fear of gaining weight. Page 108

Attachment Strength and kind of emotional bond that exists between two people. Page 95

Autonomy versus shame and doubt Second stage in Erikson's psychosocial theory, during which, if passed successfully, toddlers gain a sense of mastery of their thoughts, emotions, and behavior. Page 82

Avoidant attachment Form of emotional bond, characterized by the child's avoiding or ignoring the parent or other attachment figure after a separation. Page 95

Bulimia nervosa Eating disorder characterized by bingeing on food, followed by purging. Page 108

Conventional morality Second level of moral development proposed by Kohlberg. Individual behavior and moral decisions are guided by interpersonal expectations and conformity to internalized social rules. Page 104

Developmental crises Issues within developmental stages that must be resolved in order successfully to prepare for the next stage. Page 81

Empathy Ability to feel how another person feels. Page 105

Gender identification Person's acquisition of sex-related roles, regardless of whether they correspond to one's physiological sex. Page 90

Generativity versus stagnation Sixth stage of psychosocial development, as proposed by Erik Erikson. In middle adulthood, adults must develop a sense of helping the next generation of people. This sense is often acquired through child rearing, but generativity can result from work or other efforts as well. Page 83

Homosexuality Person's tendency to direct sexual attention toward members of the same sex; it is a sexual and attentional orientation and identity, usually deeply rooted in psychosexual development. Page 93

Identity achievement One of four possible adolescent identity statuses proposed by James Marcia. Individuals in achievement status have engaged in a period of active search for an identity and have made firm commitments to at least some aspects of identity. Page 85

Identity diffusion One of four possible adolescent identity statuses proposed by James Marcia. Individuals in diffusion status have neither engaged in a period of active search for an identity nor made firm commitments to any aspects of identity. Page 85

Identity foreclosure One of four possible adolescent identity statuses proposed by James Marcia. Individuals in foreclosure status have not searched for an identity, but have nonetheless made firm commitments to at least some aspects of identity, often in accordance with the wishes of their parents. Page 85

Identity moratorium One of four possible adolescent identity statuses proposed by James Marcia. Individuals in achievement status have searched for an identity, but have not yet made any firm commitments to a choice of identity. Page 85

Identity versus role confusion Fourth stage of psychosocial development, as proposed by Erik Erikson. Adolescents try, during this stage, to determine who they are and what is important to them. Page 82

Industry versus inferiority Fourth stage in Erikson's psychosocial theory. Successful passage through this stage results in a sense of competence and industriousness in a variety of tasks. If not successful, children may come to believe they are incompetent. Page 82

Initiative versus guilt Third stage in Erikson's psychosocial theory. Successful passage through this stage results in a sense of purpose in life. If not successful, children may develop feelings of guilt and experience difficulty taking initiative. Page 82

Integrity versus despair Final stage of psychosocial development, as proposed by Erik Erikson. Older adults review their lives and either feel a sense of rightness about the way they have lived or sadness over mistakes it is too late to correct. Page 84

Intimacy versus isolation Sixth stage of psychosocial development, as proposed by Erik Erikson. To successfully complete this stage, a young adult must commit to an intimate relationship and learn to love in a way that is nonselfish. Page 83

Major depression Disorder characterized by feelings of hopelessness that significantly interfere with a person's life. Page 109

Moral dilemmas Ambiguous situations in which no one decision is clearly, morally right. Page 103

Morality of cooperation Piaget's second developmental phase of morality, at which children understand that people both make up rules and can change them. Page 102

Moral realism Piaget's first developmental phase of morality, at which children see rules as absolute. Page 102

Perspective-taking ability Ability to understand that people have different experiences and feelings. Page 98

Postconventional morality Third level of moral development proposed by Kohlberg. Individual behavior and moral decisions are based on an internal set of moral absolutes, which may or may not agree with social rules. Page 105

Preconventional morality First level of moral development, as proposed by Kohlberg. Individual behavior and moral decisions are based primarily on egocentric concerns—expectations of reward or punishment. Page 104

Psychosocial theory Theory that explicitly acknowledges that individual development takes place in a social context. Erik Erikson's psychosocial theory of development suggests that people gain important personal qualities and interpersonal skills through successfully meeting a series of crises throughout the life span. Page 81

■ **Resistant attachment** Form of emotional bond, characterized by the child's demonstrating ambivalence toward the parent after a separation. Page 95

■ **Schema theory** Theory that proposes the existence of organized mental systems of information, called *schemas,* that help people make sense of and organize their experiences. Page 92

■ **Secure attachment** Form of emotional bond, characterized by the child's showing distress when separated from a parent, and then displaying pleasure when reunited. Page 95

■ **Self** How an individual identifies her or his own characteristics, abilities, and behaviors. Page 87

■ **Self-concept** Individual's view of himself or herself. Page 87

■ **Self-esteem** Value that an individual places on himself or herself. Page 87

■ **Sexual development** Individual's increasing awareness of the characteristics of each of the sexes, of the differences between the sexes, and of changing perceptions of one's own sexuality. Page 89

■ **Social learning theory** Theory suggesting that people come to think and behave as they do by observing the behavior of others and imitating it. Page 92

■ **Strange situation** Experimental procedure in which the emotional attachment of an infant to the parent is observed after the parent has left the infant with a stranger and has then returned. Page 95

■ **Trust versus mistrust** First stage in Erikson's psychosocial theory, in which infants come to either believe or doubt the world is supportive and friendly. Page 82

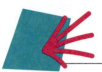

BECOMING AN EXPERT: QUESTIONS AND PROBLEMS

Apply the concepts you have learned in this chapter to the following problems of classroom practice.

IN ELEMENTARY SCHOOL

1. How could you help students develop a sense of their own capabilities, the quality that Erikson referred to as *industry?*

2. What are some values you would choose to model for elementary school students? How would you go about presenting yourself as a model of these values?

3. What is a book you might choose to have students read that would provide models of males and females in nonstereotypical gender roles?

4. How would you use team sports to encourage fifth graders to move from a preconventional, exchange-based level of moral reasoning to a conventional, social expectation–based level?

5. What is an opportunity you could make available to help kindergarten and first-grade students develop a sense of initiative, or control of their actions and choices?

IN MIDDLE SCHOOL

1. What are some ways a junior high biology teacher could build discussions of scientific values and ethics into a standard unit on mammals?

2. One of your sixth-grade science students comes to class with red eyes and smelling of marijuana. The student gives disjointed answers to questions you ask during class. What would you do?

3. How could you help a student who is experiencing friendship difficulties upon entering middle school?

4. After reading Salinger's *Catcher in the Rye* in your eighth-grade English class, a student comes to you and tells you that, like Holden Caulfield, he too wishes to kill himself. How should you respond?

5. Several of the students in your sixth-grade math class are picking on a student because she always gets the highest math scores and likes to spend a lot of time on the computer. You suspect the student is lonely and rejected in other classes as well. What can you do to help?

1. What are some ways a high school science teacher could allow or encourage adolescents in his or her class to explore different identities?

2. If you were a high school counselor or math teacher, how would you go about encouraging qualified female students to enroll in advanced math classes? How would you retain their participation in the mathematics program?

3. How could you use an American history unit on the Civil War to encourage students to explore their current status of identity achievement, focusing on the two key issues proposed by Marcia: seeking an identity and making a commitment to a choice of identity?

4. After school, you come across two members of the wrestling team purging in the bathroom so they can wrestle at their assigned weights in the upcoming meet. What will you do?

5. Two of the girls in your freshman English class started the term as good friends, but now they have had a fight. The friendship problem is interfering with both students' work, and now other students are beginning to get involved, taking sides and forming cliques. What can you do to make the classroom climate more productive?

Connecting Theory and Research to Practice

An educational movement that has moved from theory to practice in recent years is the promotion of character development. The foundation of this movement is prosocial and moral development. Many Web sites promote character development with listings of schools that are implementing character education in their classrooms, information on various character education programs, resources for implementing character education, and research results from successful character education programs.

One such Web site features the Center for the Fourth and Fifth R's: Respect and Responsibility *(http://www.cortland.edu/www/c4n5rs/CONTENTS.htm)*, directed by Dr. Thomas Lickona, a Professor of Education at the State University of New York at Cortland. The Center for the Fourth and Fifth R's provides a comprehensive model for incorporating character education that includes strategies for implementation at both the classroom and school levels. This site also contains information on how to receive a character education newsletter, a history of character education, principles of effective character education, and a survey that researchers, teachers, and school administrators can use to assess the effectiveness of character education.

Online Resources

One of the fastest growing movements in education is the use of service-learning in K-12 classrooms. Service-learning is an instructional method by which students learn prosocial, academic, and citizenship skills by providing a service that is needed and defined by the community. Many public schools are requiring some form of service-learning or community service for high school graduation. Sites that provide information and instructional strategies regarding service-learning are The National Service-Learning Clearinghouse *(www.nicsl.coled.umn.edu/home.htm)*, The Big Dummy's Guide to Service-Learning *(http://www.fiu.edu/~time4chg/Library/bigdummy.html)*, The Indiana Department of Education's Service-Learning site *(http://doe.state.in.us/opd/srvlrn/)*, and The International Partnership for Service-Learning *(http://www.ipsl.org/)*.

What exactly is a moral dilemma? A brief discussion of the origin of the moral dilemma and of differing views of the effectiveness of moral dilemmas as reasoning tools is found in "The Internet Encyclopedia of Philosophy" *(http://www.utm.edu/research/iep/m/m-dilemm.htm)*.

Have you wondered how real children would respond to moral dilemmas? Go to *http://www.mcps.k12.md.us/schools/chevychasees/dilemmas.html* to see what the students in Ms. Marley's fifth grade class at Chevy Chase Elementary School in Rockville, Maryland, have to say about moral dilemmas. This Web site provides six examples of moral dilemmas created by students as part of their character education curriculum.

Additional Reading

DeVries, R., & Zan, B. (1994). *Moral classrooms, moral children: Creating a constructivist atmosphere in early education.* New York: Teachers College Press.

Jackson, P.W., Boostrom, R.E., & Hansen, D.T. (1993). *The moral life of schools.* San Francisco: Jossey-Bass.

Likona, T. (1991). *Educating for character: How our schools can teach respect and responsibility.* New York: Bantam Books.

Nucci, L. (2001). *Education in the moral domain.* Cambridge, MA: Harvard University Press.

Nucci, L. (1989). *Moral development and character education: A dialogue.* Berkeley, CA: McCutchan.

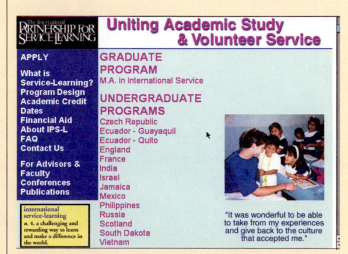

Copyright 1998, The Partnership for International Service-Learning.

Individual Differences

INTELLIGENCE, COGNITIVE AND LEARNING STYLES, AND CREATIVITY

THE BIG PICTURE

To help you see the big picture, keep the following questions in mind as you read through this chapter.

- What is intelligence?

- Is intelligence caused by genes or environment—or both? Can people increase their intelligence?

- What can a teacher do to make students more intelligent? Should teachers adapt to differences in intelligence by grouping students according to ability level?

- What are cognitive styles and learning styles? How can teachers use knowledge about styles to improve instruction and assessment?

- What is creativity, and how does it differ from intelligence? How can teachers encourage and develop creativity in their students and in themselves?

◄ *Teachers who encourage their students to display creativity often discover that some of them possess abilities the teachers had never before noticed. In addition, teachers are preparing their students to think and act in novel ways to solve problems they'll face throughout their lives.* (Charles Thatcher, Stone)

Tony Garcia sat at home grading math tests, fueled by a cup of strong coffee. As usual, there were no big surprises. It never escaped Tony's notice that the same students always excelled on classroom tests. And it was equally true that another group—again always the same—generally bombed on tests. It seemed no matter what Tony did, some students seemed to get it, and others did not. He had tried review sections, practice tests, extra homework, and about everything else he could think of to help the low scorers, but their performance simply wasn't up to the level he expected from his students.

Later that semester, Tony's way of thinking changed abruptly, and no one was more surprised than he. One day Tony read some articles about the value of independent projects for helping students get more excited about math. An open-minded teacher, Tony decided to add a new requirement to his algebra and geometry courses: a math project. Students were more or less free to do what they wanted, as long as the projects made use of the concepts he had taught in class. Students could apply the math to practical problems, come up with a creative

proof, write a paper on some aspect of the history of mathematics, or pursue other options.

To his amazement, Tony discovered on the day the projects were due that some of the most creative and exciting math projects had been done by students he thought were in the less skilled group! Their projects showed that they both understood the concepts and could apply them in novel ways. Tony now saw that he needed to view math achievement much more broadly than simply in terms of scores on his math tests.

Tony Garcia is not alone in his discovery. More and more teachers are finding that the differences among their students are not always what they first appear. Students are far more diverse, and often far more able, than conventional tests show. The goal of Chapter 2 on cognitive development and Chapter 3 on social and personal development was to help you understand diversity *across* age groups—to answer questions about the similar ways in which nearly all children change as they mature. The goal of this chapter is to help you understand diversity *within* an age group, the ways in which every child is different. This chapter describes some of the ways in which students in the same class differ from one another, and what you as a teacher should know about these differences.

Why Understanding Individual Differences Is Important to Teachers

When you walk into your classroom on the first day of school, you will probably be greeted by a sea of unfamiliar faces. You may have read other teachers' files and notes about the students, but in many ways these students are still strangers to you. How will you get to know each one as an individual? How can you determine what each of your students is capable of achieving in the upcoming school year? What qualities will you focus on in your efforts to teach each child expertly?

These questions are the focus of this chapter. We will cover research and theories about individual differences of several kinds. For teachers, one of the most important student attributes is intelligence. Teachers who wish to place students in ability groups start by informally assessing their students' intelligence. The teachers also may hope that higher intelligence will lead to higher scores on statewide or national standardized tests of achievement. We will present in this chapter various ideas, including the most current and comprehensive ones, about the nature of intelligence. We will also discuss some of the educational controversies generated by various theories of intelligence: the source of intelligence, the modifiability of intelligence, and ways that teachers can respond to differences in intelligence levels among students.

Expert teachers have learned that students all have different personalities. Particular combinations of personality and intelligence are often referred to as *cognitive styles,* or personal ways of using one's intelligence. Students' cognitive styles and learning styles can also affect their interactions with teachers. We will uncover some of the key differences in cognitive and learning styles and provide some suggestions for tailoring education to a variety of styles. Finally, teachers will notice that students differ in their expressions of creativity. We will discuss various views regarding creativity, as well as what the various views mean to you as a teacher.

Understanding Individual Differences in Intelligence

Much of the modern study of intelligence can be traced back to the work of the Frenchman Alfred Binet (1857–1911) (Brody, 2000). In 1904 the French minister of public instruction formed a commission to develop ways of determining which children should be placed in special classes because they were unable to learn at the average pace or level in classes offered in ordinary schools (Binet & Simon, 1916). To answer the need of the French schools, Binet and a colleague, Théodore Simon, created the first intelligence test (Binet & Simon, 1916).

Today many psychologists use an updated version of the test Binet and Simon developed (Thorndike, Hagen, & Sattler, 1986). The test produces a numerical score, known now as an **intelligence quotient,** or **IQ,** that compares the test performance of each student with an average, or standard, performance. We defer discussion of tests of intelligence, as well as detailed discussion of the IQ and various other types of scores from these tests, until Chapter 14 (on standardized tests; see also Kaufman, 2000). In this chapter, we will consider different ideas about the nature of intelligence and what these ideas mean for teachers.

WHAT IS INTELLIGENCE?

The idea that people vary in intelligence is widely accepted (Sternberg, 1994, 2000). Nearly all of us can name some individuals we consider to be smart, or more intelligent, as well as individuals we consider less intelligent. However, it is difficult to find agreement on just what is meant by *intelligent.* When he began assigning math projects, Tony Garcia realized he had been defining intelligence in a very narrow way, based only on test performance. Some people would consider a high school math student who is able to work with college-level differential equations intelligent, even if the student could not carry on a conversation with another person using any more than three sentences. In contrast, some people would describe as intelligent a high school student who is extremely well liked and runs for class president on a platform that is highly popular with students, even if that student was unable to calculate correctly the tip in a restaurant. Indeed, some people suggest that both the math student and the popular student are intelligent, just in different ways. Even experts are not immune to disagreements about what constitutes intelligence.

In 1921 and again in 1986, two groups of experts were asked to define *intelligence* ("Intelligence and Its Measurement," 1921; Sternberg & Detterman, 1986). Both groups of experts generated many different definitions. Some common themes did emerge, however. Both sets of experts defined **intelligence** in terms of (1) the ability to learn

Even experts disagree about what constitutes intelligence. Is it exhibited by the student on the left, who is able to do college-level math yet finds it difficult to carry on a conversation with his peers? Or is it displayed by the student on the right, who is the extremely popular president of a senior class yet has difficulty calculating a simple formula? Some people suggest that both the intellectual student and the popular student are intelligent, just in different ways. (Elizabeth Crews; Bob Daemmrich, Stock Boston)

from experience, and (2) the ability to adapt to the surrounding environment. In the later survey, experts also emphasized **metacognition**—people's understanding and control of their own thinking processes. For example, knowing your strengths and weaknesses would be an important part of metacognition (Nelson, 1999).

Although the experts did not fully agree with one another, based on their areas of agreement we define intelligence here as goal-directed, adaptive behavior. This broad definition leaves room for a lot of different ideas about the specifics of intelligence. For instance, is intelligence a single, broad ability, or is it actually a set of capabilities? This is a primary issue dealt with by the different theories of intelligence.

PSYCHOMETRIC THEORIES OF INTELLIGENCE

Psychometric theories of intelligence are based on statistical analyses of conventional tests of intelligence, requiring students to show basic vocabulary, mathematical ability, and reasoning as well as other skills (Brody, 2000). Earlier in the chapter, we mentioned that some people would consider both an advanced math student and a highly popular student to be intelligent, but in different ways. This kind of statement suggests that the quality known as intelligence might actually be a combination of several specific, component abilities.

The idea of multiple abilities is clear in the writings of intelligence-testing pioneer Alfred Binet. Binet (Binet & Simon, 1916) suggested three main elements of intelligence: (1) *direction*, which involves knowing what has to be done and how to do it; (2) *adaptation*, which involves figuring out how to perform a task and then monitoring the strategy you come up with while you are actually doing the task; and (3) *criticism*, or the ability to critique your own thoughts and actions. For example, in writing a book report, students would have to know (1) what to include (and not to include) in the book report (direction), (2) how to go about actually writing the book report and making sure it fits within the guidelines given by the teacher (adaptation), and (3) how to critique their own work so that they can turn in the best possible product (criticism).

Since the time of Binet, however, intelligence theorists have offered a number of different ideas about intelligence.

■ **A GENERAL INTELLIGENCE FACTOR** British psychologist Charles Spearman (1904, 1927) suggested that intelligence can be understood in terms of two kinds of underlying mental dimensions, or factors. The first is a single **general factor,** which Spearman labeled *g*, a hypothetical single intelligence ability thought to apply to many different tasks, thus influencing performance on all mental tests. Second are specific factors, each of which he labeled an **s.** Spearman believed these **s** factors are involved in performance on only a single type of mental ability test (such as a test of vocabulary, or arithmetic computation, or memory). Spearman believed the specific factors were not relevant to intelligence because they do not provide information that generalizes beyond a student's performance on a single test. But the general factor is relevant to intelligence, Spearman believed, precisely because it is general. Spearman suggested this factor is the key to intelligence and comes from individual differences in mental activity. Many investigators still believe in the existence of the *g* factor (e.g., Gottfredson, 2001; Jensen, 1998, 2001; Kyllonen, 2001; Petrill, 2001).

■ **PRIMARY MENTAL ABILITIES: MANY, NOT ONE** The American psychologist Louis Thurstone (1938) concluded that Spearman was wrong (Brody, 2000; Sternberg, 1990). Thurstone suggested that the core of intelligence resides not in one factor, but rather in seven basic interrelated factors, or primary mental abilities. This **theory of primary mental abilities** proposes that students' achievement in school can be understood partly in terms of their relative amounts of these different abilities. For example, a student high in verbal comprehension and verbal fluency might excel in English class; a student high in numbers might excel in math. Thurstone's seven primary mental abilities are as follows:

1. *verbal comprehension,* measured by tests such as vocabulary and general information;

2. *verbal fluency,* measured by tests requiring the test taker quickly to think of as many words as possible that begin with a given letter;

3. *inductive reasoning,* measured by tests such as analogies (lawyer : client:: doctor : <u>?</u>) and series completions (2, 5, 8, 11, <u>?</u>);

4. *spatial visualization,* measured by tests requiring mental rotations of pictures of objects;

5. *number,* measured by computation and simple mathematical problem-solving tests;

6. *memory,* measured by picture and word recall tests; and

7. *perceptual speed,* measured by tests that require the individual to recognize small differences, as in pairs of pictures, names, or numbers.

■ **HIERARCHICAL MODELS** In general, Thurstone's theory of primary mental abilities was more popular in its country of origin (the United States), and Spearman's general factor theory in its country of origin (Great Britain). But is

THINKING ANALYTICALLY

Do you know students who have unusually strong abilities to figure out computer programming problems or who quickly learn their ways around new technology? Do teachers and other students tend to regard these students as highly intelligent even though they may be weak in other areas, such as history or English? How would you assess these students' general intelligence?

SUGGESTION: In a society or school system that ranks technological learning high among skills, a student who excels with computers is likely to be perceived as generally more intelligent than one who does better at history or English, even though that student is weak in other areas.

An early elementary school student works on a picture arrangement test. (Laura Dwight, PhotoEdit)

A master glassblower demonstrates his skill to a student helper. His accumulation of knowledge about his craft, or crystallized intelligence, would be expected to surpass that of a younger person or at least to surpass the crystallized intelligence he had when younger. (Ron Sherman, Stock Boston)

there some way of combining the theories that would retain the best aspects of each?

Such a proposal was made in the form of hierarchical theories (e.g., Carroll, 1993; Cattell, 1971; Gustafsson, 1984; Gustafsson & Undheim, 1996; Vernon, 1971). The intent of these models was to combine the idea of a general factor with the idea of more narrowly defined subfactors that apply across classes of tasks, which are referred to as **group factors.**

Raymond Cattell and John Horn (Cattell, 1971; Horn, 1968), for example, have suggested that we can view general ability, or *g*, as the top of the hierarchy. Below that are two major subfactors, group factors that Cattell and Horn refer to as *fluid intelligence* and *crystallized intelligence.*

Fluid intelligence is the ability to understand abstract and often novel concepts. It requires us to think flexibly and to seek out new patterns (Lohman, 1995). For example, solving a series completion such as 1, 4, 9, 16, 25, ? would require fluid intelligence. **Crystallized intelligence** represents the accumulation of knowledge and is measured by tests of vocabulary and general information. An older person, for example, would be expected to surpass the crystallized intelligence he or she had when much younger (except in cases of mental incapacitation).

THINKING CREATIVELY

What might a teacher do to help students build crystallized intelligence? Explain.

SUGGESTION: One way is to have students do a lot of reading for understanding.

■ **TIME CONSTRAINTS: HOW FAST IS SMART?** As we have seen, even among contemporary researchers working on precise quantitative measurements of intelligence, there are still differences of opinion regarding intelligence. It is difficult to define and analyze this phenomenon. In fact, there are probably aspects of intelligence that no available test can fully capture. One element common to many tests of intelligence is the existence of time constraints. This chapter's Forum feature explores whether there really is a need for strict timing of performance on tests of intelligence.

FORUM

IS SPEED OF INFORMATION PROCESSING IMPORTANT TO INTELLIGENCE?

Terms that describe speed are often used to indicate intelligence as well. When people say, "She is a quick thinker," or "He is fast on his feet," they are implying the person is somehow more intelligent than a person who takes longer to come up with answers. What is the relationship between speed and intelligence?

FIRST VIEW: *Intelligence is closely linked to speed of information processing.* Some investigators have proposed to understand intelligence in terms of sheer speed of information processing, and they have used the simplest tasks they could devise to measure pure mental speed uncontaminated by other variables. These researchers (Jensen, 1982, 2000; Jensen & Munro, 1979) have suggested that the time it takes a person to decide which of two or more buttons to push in response to a given stimulus can be used as an indicator of that person's level of intelligence. According to this view, the ability to speed up simple tasks pays off in increased efficiency of processing new information. For example, students who are able to retrieve basic information about words from long-term memory very quickly are able to read and comprehend text faster (Hunt, 1978; Hunt, Lunneborg, & Lewis, 1975). Because most tests of intelligence are timed, and schools often require children to think quickly, more efficient processing of even the most simple information can lead to higher school grades and intelligence test scores.

Robert Sternberg (1977, 1999) suggested that speed might also be important for more complex types of problems, such as analogies. Consider, for example, the analogy, LAWYER : CLIENT :: DOCTOR : <u>?</u> (a. PATIENT, b. MEDICINE). Some of the processes that might be involved in solving this analogy would be to *encode* each of the basic analogy terms (to perceive the terms and retrieve the appropriate concepts from long-term memory), to *infer* the relation between LAWYER and CLIENT, and to *apply* this relation to DOCTOR. People who are faster and more accurate in using these processes, and who devise more efficient strategies for accomplishing them, might be viewed by this theory as more intelligent.

SECOND VIEW: *Faster is not always smarter; smarter is not always faster.* As we discuss later in this chapter, impulsive students who rush to give answers or complete work do not necessarily give the correct answers or do the work well the first time they try. In contrast, reflective students, who ponder questions or think before acting, may be correct or do good work more often.

For example, Robert Sternberg (1981; Wagner & Sternberg, 1985) found that, when asked to perform complex reasoning and reading tasks, more intelligent students actually spent more time before beginning a task than did less intelligent ones. The bright students spent the up-front time deciding how to do a task as a whole, what Sternberg referred to as *global planning.* The less intelligent students, in contrast, spent more time in *local planning,* that is, the micro-planning needed along the way to accomplish a task. As a result, the less intelligent students often blundered and had to keep going back. Years earlier, Bloom and Broder (1950) found similar results in comparing better with worse students, and Larkin, McDermott, Simon, and Simon (1980) found similar results in a comparison of expert and novice physics problem solvers.

Because many important tasks in everyday life—such as deciding on a course of study or on a job—are not necessarily ones that should be rushed, people who seem slower because they take more time for planning may actually be the ones who perform better when it counts.

THIRD VIEW: A SYNTHESIS. *Good information processing is not just a matter of being fast, but also a matter of knowing when to be fast.* Teachers who wish to help students develop their intelligence need to help them develop both speed and planning skills. Teachers can help students learn to perform simple processes more quickly by helping students automatize their information processing, as when they read. Some educational computer software also lets students practice speed. Just as importantly, teachers should encourage students to spend sufficient time in global planning before beginning a task. Expert teachers model global planning for their students whenever they have the chance, by planning aloud with the class different approaches to tasks and assignments. Teachers can also encourage students to do their own global planning by describing to students the value of global planning, and by telling them specific steps to follow, tailored to the project at hand. For example, a teacher might tell students to think through a project before beginning, and collect all the materials they will need to do it successfully before they start. The teacher might also suggest thinking through two or more ways of approaching the project before beginning to help students select an optimal method. Teachers should provide students the time necessary to engage in global planning.

Implications for Teaching

What can teachers learn from the ongoing theoretical debate over the number and structure of abilities that comprise intelligence?

■ *Accommodate multiple abilities.* Teachers must be open to the different forms of abilities that intelligence takes. An expert teacher assigns activities that involve understanding written prose and poetry (verbal comprehension), writing essays (verbal fluency), recalling main events in a story (memory), understanding the spatial layout presented in a description of a house, town, or nation (spatial visualization), comparing the personalities of two characters in a novel (inductive reasoning), and so on.

■ *Help students find and use their strengths.* Having more of one ability can sometimes compensate for having less of another (Salthouse, 1996; Salthouse & Somberg, 1982; Sternberg, 1999). Students use their strengths to compensate for their weaknesses.

CRITIQUE OF PSYCHOMETRIC THEORIES OF INTELLIGENCE

Although psychometric theories dominate current testing of intelligence, their validity has also been questioned. Some investigators believe the statistical methods used to test psychometric theories have been inadequate in showing the flaws of these theories (Sternberg, 1997b). Psychometric theories also tend to be somewhat narrower than contemporary theories in their conception of intelligence, although there are exceptions (e.g., Guilford, 1967).

CONTEMPORARY SYSTEMS THEORIES OF INTELLIGENCE

Some contemporary theorists tend to view intelligence as a complex system. In this section, we look at two widely studied contemporary theories of intelligence. The systems theories of intelligence tend to be broader than the other theories we have described, incorporating some of the major aspects of the other approaches. Systems theories have been criticized by some for being overinclusive—that is, for trying to capture too much in the concept of intelligence. Nevertheless, the general trend in psychology seems to be toward broader rather than narrower conceptions of intelligence, in recognition of the fact that children and adults can be intelligent in many different ways. The first theory we examine is Howard Gardner's theory of multiple intelligences.

■**MULTIPLE INTELLIGENCES.** Howard Gardner (1983, 1993, 1999) has proposed a **theory of multiple intelligences,** in which there are eight distinct and relatively independent intelligences. Each is a separate system of functioning, although the various systems can interact to produce overall intelligent performance:

1. *Linguistic intelligence.* Used in reading a novel, writing an essay or a poem, speaking coherently, and understanding lectures.

2. *Logical-mathematical intelligence.* Used in solving mathematical word or computation problems, balancing a checkbook, and doing a mathematical or logical proof.

3. *Spatial intelligence.* Used in walking or driving from one place to another, reading a map, packing suitcases in the trunk of a car so they will all fit, and deciding whether you can fit your automobile into a small parking space.

THINKING ANALYTICALLY

Gardner's theory specifies eight distinct and important multiple intelligences, whereas Spearman's theory specifies just a single important general ability (and unimportant specific abilities). As a teacher, which theory appeals to you more, and why? Which theory would lend itself better to being used in the classroom?

SUGGESTION: Each person must answer for herself or himself.

TABLE 4.1 The Theory of Multiple Intelligences

Intelligence	Core Components of the Intelligence	Example of a Person Who Uses This Intelligence Heavily	School Activities to Develop the Intelligence
1. Linguistic	Sensitivity to the sounds, rhythms, and meanings of words; understanding of the different functions of language.	Poet, journalist	Discussion of metaphor and onomatopoeia
2. Logical/ Mathematical	Sensitivity to, and capacity to discern, logical or numerical patterns; ability to handle long chains of reasoning.	Scientist, mathematician	Calculating the distance from one corner of a building diagonally to the other by knowing the formula for the area of a triangle
3. Spatial	Capacities to perceive the visual-spatial world accurately and to perform transformations on one's initial perceptions.	Navigator, sculptor	Using perspective in drawing pictures
4. Musical	Abilities to produce and appreciate rhythm, pitch, and timbre; appreciation of the forms of musical expressiveness.	Composer, violinist	Determining the melody or tempo of a song
5. Bodily/ kinesthetic	Abilities to control one's body movements and to handle objects skillfully.	Dancer, athlete	Playing pin-the-tail-on-the-donkey; square dancing
6. Interpersonal	Capacities to discern and respond appropriately to the moods, temperaments, motivations, and desires of other people.	Therapist, salesperson	Listening to both sides of an argument between classmates
7. Intrapersonal	Access to one's own feelings and the ability to discriminate among them and draw on them to guide behavior; knowledge of one's own strengths, weaknesses, desires, and intelligences.	Actor, novelist	Role playing a literary character to gain insight into one's own frustrations
8. Naturalist	Ability to spot and understand patterns in nature.	Geologist, explorer	Observation of patterns in the kinds of plant life in a forest setting

Source: Figure from p. 6 of "Multiple Intelligences Go to School" by H. Gardner and T. Hatch, *Educational Researcher,* vol. 18, no. 8, 1989. Reprinted by permission of American Educational Research Association.

4. *Musical intelligence.* Used in singing a song, playing the violin, composing a concerto, and understanding and appreciating the structure of a symphony.

5. *Bodily-kinesthetic intelligence.* Used in playing football, dancing, running a race, bowling, or shooting baskets.

6. *Interpersonal intelligence.* Used in understanding why other people behave as they do, deciding how to react to a person's comments in an appropriate way, and making a good impression during a job interview.

7. *Intrapersonal intelligence.* Used in understanding ourselves—why we think, feel, and act the ways we do—and knowing our strengths and our limitations.

8. *Naturalist intelligence.* Used in discerning patterns in nature, such as how different species are related or what kinds of weather we might expect on different days.

Table 4.1 describes users of each type of intelligence and recommends school activities that teachers can use to develop each type.

Gardner (1999) also has speculated on the possibility of an additional intelligence: existential. People high in existential intelligence find meaning in their lives and have success in contemplating fundamental questions of existence.

EXPERT TEACHER INTERVIEW

FOCUS ON: DIFFERENT LEARNING STYLES
BARBARA GILMAN: JOHN F. KENNEDY HIGH SCHOOL, TAMUNING, GUAM—GRADES 9–12 PHYSICAL EDUCATION

Barbara Gilman teaches physical education, elective dance classes, and ballroom dance classes at a high school in Guam. The high school also offers a program for the deaf, and deaf students frequently take her dance classes. Some of the dances she teaches are the cha-cha, foxtrot, swing, paso doble, tango, rumba, and Viennese waltz. It's common that each of the students in a dance pair uses a different technique to learn the same dance.

Why is dance class a more positive experience for your students than some of their other classes?

The students genuinely feel a part of the whole class; they don't feel isolated. In other classes, exceptional students are often isolated by their classmates. Dance partnering places the exceptional child in a situation in which he or she can be an integral part of a team. In dance, students are partnered all the time, so they have to find a way to communicate with each other for the dance to work. Each partner, whether an exceptional or general education student, must take an active role in communicating with each other. The burden is not left with only one child.

How is cultural and ethnic diversity represented in your classroom?

We have a mix of students from the United States, Guam, Micronesia, Taiwan, Japan, Korea, and the Philippines. While it is not verbalized, it is apparent that some cultural groups are ignored by others. If allowed, students will not select these children as partners. However, because partners in dance class change often, students of all cultures and abilities spend a great deal of time working together. As the students work closely together, they learn to appreciate one another's abilities and differences. By the end of the year, a special bond has developed among the dance students. As we conclude the year, everyone is hugging one another.

What are some of the different learning styles you work with in your classes, particularly those for exceptional and general education students?

Every student has areas of strength and areas of challenge. Some of my deaf students find that rhythm comes easily, while their hearing counterparts may struggle. Although dance is very visual, some students are not visual learners; they need tactile and/or auditory techniques to learn. I try to use a variety of ways of teaching a dance: counting verbally, as well as with my fingers, visually demonstrating, physically guiding students, repeating and practicing, partnering students with those who have stronger skills. I tack the dance routines on all four walls so students can see them as they change direction in the dance. Everyone learns differently—it's not necessarily the disability that makes the difference.

What are some ways you have adapted your instruction to accommodate the needs of students with physical disabilities?

To accommodate the needs of students with physical disabilities, I use a variety of teaching techniques. I sometimes modify a skill to allow a student with a disability access to the activity. Modifications may be very minor or very extreme, from adjusting footwork to accommodate a student with a limp to moving a wheelchair in time to the music. The exceptional students I've had the most experience with have been deaf or blind.

When working with deaf students, I assure that they are always partnered

Gardner used work done with several modern research methods in developing the theory of multiple intelligences. For example, he reviewed the distinctive effects of localized brain damage on specific kinds of intelligences, distinctive patterns of development in each kind of intelligence across the life span, evidence from exceptional children (both gifted and low achieving), and the possible evolutionary history of the eight intelligences.

In a way, Gardner's theory is reminiscent of multiple-factor theories, such as Thurstone's, because it specifies a list of abilities believed to be fundamental sources of individual differences. However, Gardner believes each intelligence to be truly a separate intelligence, not just another separate ability. Different intelligences, unlike abilities, use different symbol systems. For example, linguistic intelligence uses words in various combinations; logical-mathematical intelligence uses numbers and logical symbols; musical intelligence can use various kinds of musical notation. Moreover, Gardner views each intelligence as *modular*—that is, each intelligence originates from a distinctive portion of the brain.

with hearing students. The interpreter helps both partners, hearing and deaf, learn signs for various steps. This helps the couple communicate if the interpreter is busy with another student. I encourage hearing partners to develop signals with their deaf partners. The hearing student might gently tap the rhythm as a signal to begin dancing or if the couple gets off beat. I keep my instructions as visual as possible by demonstrating footwork or sequences from various positions. I find that my deaf students have very good memories when learning new sequences or routines.

I often ask blind students what will help them. One blind student found it helpful to place his hands on the tops of my feet to feel the footwork. I try to assure that they have physical contact with someone when the class is learning new footwork. I have found these students have excellent listening skills and good memories so I make every attempt to give clear verbal instructions. They learn faster than many of my sighted students because they accurately follow the verbal instructions.

Which experiences have been the most gratifying?

I believe the most gratifying experience I have working with exceptional students is when I watch them shine on the dance floor. I see smiles on their faces, bright eyes, and satisfaction in their accomplishments. I truly feel a sense of pride in their success and enjoy seeing the amazement of the audience as they watch these talented students. More often than not, the audience is unaware that the student has any disability.

All of my deaf students have successfully competed in our schoolwide ballroom dance competition. One young woman who is totally deaf participated in numerous presentations as well as competing in our top level of competition. It amazes people to find out she is deaf.

> Design projects and activities to involve the exceptional student; they are too often left out. Being in class by law doesn't make them a part of the class.

A blind student who, at his prior school had students take his cane and point him in the wrong direction, found enjoyment and satisfaction in dance class. He developed friendships and bonded with his classmates. During a class performance, he did such an outstanding job that the head of our school system was totally unaware that he was blind.

What advice do you have for new teachers to help them address different learning styles in their classes?

Get to know your students and help them all realize their full potential. Design projects and activities to involve the exceptional student; they are too often left out. Being in class by law doesn't make them a part of the class. The teacher must set up situations that include these children, making them feel they are contributing members of the class and demanding their best.

Implications for Teaching

Gardner's theory has several implications for teachers who wish to apply the theory in their classrooms:

- **Take a broad view of what constitutes intelligence.** The theory of multiple intelligences would view the highly musical or athletic child not just as talented in a specific way, but as intelligent in a way that formerly would not have been thought of as representing intelligence. An expert teacher might also appreciate the physical skills and quick judgment needed to play on a competitive varsity basketball team.

- **Include instruction that addresses underrepresented intelligences.** Multiple intelligences theory suggests that instruction probably needs to be diversified more than it currently is. Traditional education tends to focus heavily on linguistic and logical-mathematical abilities. Teachers who recognize an imbalance in their instructional priorities can add activities to develop a variety of students' intelligences (see also Goodrich, Andrade, & Perkins, 1998; Krechevsky & Seidel, 1998; Parziale & Fischer, 1998).

■ *Remember, not every topic can be approached through all eight intelligences.* Teachers implementing multiple intelligences theory should usually avoid trying to address each of the eight intelligences in every topic unit (Hoerr, 1996). For example, it just may not be feasible to build much bodily-kinesthetic content into most math lessons.

■**THE TRIARCHIC THEORY OF HUMAN INTELLIGENCE** Whereas Gardner's theory of multiple intelligences has emphasized a set of relatively independent structures, Robert Sternberg's (1985, 1988a, 1988b, 1997a) **triarchic theory of human intelligence** has emphasized a set of relatively interdependent processes. According to the triarchic theory, there are three related aspects of intelligence—*analytical ability, creative ability,* and *practical ability*—each capturing a different subtheory of the theory as a whole. The subtheories and their interrelation are summarized in Figure 4.1.

The first subtheory is referred to as a *componential subtheory* because it deals with the basic information processes, or *components,* underlying intelligent performance. According to Sternberg, there are three main kinds of processes:

1. *Metacomponents*—higher order executive (metacognitive) processes used to plan what you are going to do, monitor it while you are doing it, and evaluate it after it is done. For example, to do their math projects, Tony Garcia's students need to decide on a topic and plan a strategy for getting the project done; make sure that the project is working out—that they are finding enough information or have access to necessary materials, that they organize the information and materials in a coherent way, and that their projects are related closely enough to the content of the class; and make sure, after they are done, that their projects show what they want them to show.

FIGURE 4.1   The Triarchic Theory of Intelligence

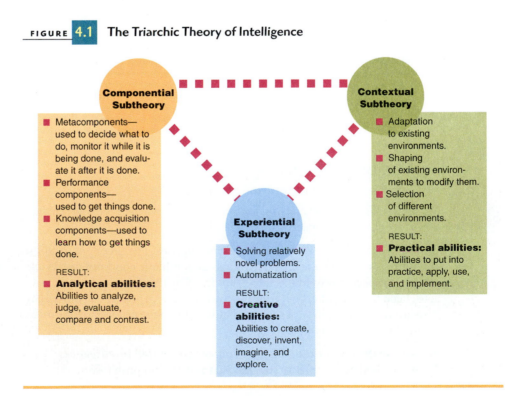

2. *Performance components*—processes used for implementing the commands of the metacomponents. For example, actually reading the books or articles about math, actually gathering the materials needed for the project, and actually writing or assembling the project once it has been planned.

3. *Knowledge-acquisition components*—processes used for learning how to solve problems in the first place. For example, learning how to do research in the library or on the Internet, learning how to organize such a project, and learning how to write or present visual materials in a way that is coherent and interesting.

The three kinds of information-processing components are interrelated. Metacomponents allow us to decide what to do, and in turn activate the performance components and knowledge-acquisition components. The latter kinds of components, in turn, provide feedback to the metacomponents, enabling the metacomponents to adjust representations of information and strategies for processing information. For example, a student may originally plan to write a term paper on a certain topic (metacomponent); learn about the topic (knowledge-acquisition components); try to write it (performance components); decide that the paper is not going well (metacomponents); and then decide on a new topic (metacomponents).

Sternberg's second subtheory, the *experiential subtheory*, suggests that intelligence is related to experience. Clearly, information-processing components are applied by people with varying prior levels of experience with a task. According to this subtheory, a task best measures intelligence when the task is either relatively novel or is in the process of being automatized, or becoming more familiar.

A relatively novel task is one that is unfamiliar but not totally outside the scope of a person's experience. For example, most 7-year-olds are probably not able to use their intelligence to solve advanced calculus problems, because the problems are just too far outside the range of their experience. They would be challenged more appropriately by novel kinds of addition or subtraction tasks. Students who are able to solve relatively novel problems would be considered more intelligent than those who are slower to adapt to novelty.

Automatization is the process by which a task becomes increasingly familiar, requiring less effort in information processing and less explicit consciousness of the way it is performed. For example, 7-year-olds are in the process of automatizing reading. They are evolving from *novices,* performing in an effortful, highly conscious way, into *experts,* performing in an effortless way in which much of their information processing is beneath consciousness and hardly noticed at all. In Sternberg's view, more intelligent students can more quickly and effectively automatize tasks, thus freeing attention for more learning.

The third subtheory, the *contextual subtheory*, relates intelligence to the everyday contexts, or settings, in which we live. According to this subtheory, there are three basic processes of making contact with everyday surroundings (Sternberg et al., 2000).

In *adaptation,* people modify themselves to fit their environment. For example, when teachers start teaching in a new school, they need to adapt themselves to the environment, figuring out how to fit into the norms and job demands of the school.

Eventually, as people accustom themselves to the environment, they may start to engage in *shaping,* whereby they modify the environment to fit themselves. For example, teachers who care about teaching thinking skills may try to make some changes not only in their own classrooms, but in the overall value systems of their schools. Thus teachers who do not believe in work sheets not only may limit their own use of these but may try to discourage their use by other teachers.

THINKING **PRACTICALLY**

What strategies might you use to encourage children to plan more thoroughly before doing tasks, monitor their performance on tasks more carefully, and check their work more diligently after they are finished?

SUGGESTION: One way is to tell students you especially value work that is carefully planned and, after it is completed, checked.

THINKING **PRACTICALLY**

Drawing on your own experiences as a student or as a teacher, give three examples of how students try to shape their classroom environments to suit themselves better.

SUGGESTION: They might choose their own paper or project topics, indicate pleasure or displeasure at the way they are being taught or tested, and raise their hand to give their point of view on an issue.

A high school student taking a driver's education course. As he becomes increasingly familiar with the skills of driving, the process of automatization takes place. According to Sternberg, a more intelligent student can more quickly and effectively automatize tasks, thus freeing attention for further learning. (Bob Daemmrich Photos, Inc.)

IN EACH CHAPTER OF THE TEXT, WE INTRODUCE YOU TO A FEW SPECIFIC STRATEGIES—ANALYTICAL, CREATIVE, AND PRACTICAL—USED BY BOTH EXPERT TEACHERS AND EXPERT STUDENTS.

THE ANALYTICAL TEACHER: Tam analyzes different forms of poetry to decide whether poems in each style would provide his tenth-grade English students with an appropriate level of novelty and challenge, or whether the forms would be just too new to the students to provoke their interest at all.

THE CREATIVE TEACHER: Tam has been assigned to a windowless, unattractive classroom for the remainder of the academic year. In order to shape the environment into one that is more stimulating and pleasant for himself and students, he puts up posters from the local Shakespeare company and designs a bulletin board where he can share a rotating selection of his favorite literary quotes.

THE PRACTICAL TEACHER: Tam assigns several short research papers, only about one to two pages each, rather than one long paper, so his students will get the chance to practice the process of preparing a research paper several times. In this way, he hopes that research and writing will become more automatized for the students.

THE ANALYTICAL STUDENT: Every time Betsy reads a book, story, or play for English class, she considers how well she would fit into the role of one of the main characters, comparing her personality and strengths to those of the character.

THE CREATIVE STUDENT: Whenever Tam assigns the English class to write another short research paper, Betsy chooses a topic that will work as a chapter or episode in the novel she hopes to write someday. By the time she is ready to write a book, she hopes to have gathered a great deal of information and become an expert researcher.

THE PRACTICAL STUDENT: Betsy spent last summer in a South American rain forest with her parents, an environment in which she quickly realized that most of what she had previously known would not be very useful to her. She soon adapted to the environment, however, by learning several skills that were useful, such as navigating in the deep jungle and learning to avoid poisonous plants and animals.

Sometimes, however, shaping does not work. You may find you are able neither to adapt to an environment nor to shape it in a way that satisfies you. In such instances, you may simply have to *select* another environment. For example, teachers sometimes leave schools when they find the practices in the school contradict their own personal educational philosophy. The bottom line is that intelligence in everyday life requires a balance among adaptation to, shaping of, and selection of environments. The most intelligent people are the ones who most effectively balance the processes of adaptation, shaping, and selection to ensure a good fit between their own strengths and the demands of their environment.

The multifaceted subtheories may make the triarchic theory seem complex, but the theory can be put to use fairly easily to teach and learn, as the Flexible Expert feature demonstrates. See if you can match each expert teaching and learning behavior with the subtheory it demonstrates.

Implications for Teaching

The triarchic theory is rich in educational implications. Some of the main ones are listed here. We consider others later in the section on helping children develop their intelligence (see also Sternberg & Grigorenko, 2000; Sternberg & Spear-Swerling, 1996).

■ ***Focus on the practical as well as the academic aspects of intelligence.***
Some subjects, such as geography or social studies, provide natural opportunities to encourage students to apply contextual intelligence—to think about how they might fit into a different environment. Biology teachers can discuss parallels between the ways adaptation, shaping, and selection occur in humans and other animals.

- *Consider the various ways students' cultural backgrounds contribute to their definitions and expressions of intelligence.* What is considered intelligent behavior can vary, depending on cultural context (see also Serpell, 2000). Some students' cultures set priorities for behavior, such as practical or social skills, different from the priorities set in the classroom, where the emphasis is on academic skills. Rather than denigrating the students' cultural values, expert teachers help students understand what behavior is considered intelligent in the classroom that may or may not be considered intelligent at home. The expert teacher then encourages the students to behave intelligently in both environments.

- *Help students capitalize on their strengths.* People need to figure out what they do well, and make the most of it. They also must figure out what they do not do well, and either make themselves good enough to get by (remediation) or find ways around what they don't do well (compensation). Students have at least some options in a school setting (e.g., programs of study), and by choosing their options wisely, they can maximize the use of their intelligence and accomplish their goals.

Remember that experts are generally not good at everything; rather, they make the most of what they are good at. They also increase their utilization of their abilities, as we discuss next.

CRITIQUE OF CONTEMPORARY SYSTEMS THEORIES OF INTELLIGENCE

Contemporary systems theories of intelligence attempt to go beyond the scope of conventional psychometric theories in explaining intelligence. They are successful in doing so to some extent, but they are not without limitations. Since it was proposed in 1983, there have been no published empirical tests of the whole of Gardner's theory of multiple intelligences. Such tests are needed to verify the claims of the theory. Moreover, the claim that the multiple intelligences are independent is suspect because so many studies have found intercorrelations among abilities (see Carroll, 1993; Jensen, 1998; Sternberg, 2000). Sternberg's theory of intelligence has been tested (e.g., Sternberg, Grigorenko, Ferrari, & Clinkenbeard, 1999; Sternberg, Castejón, Prieto, Hautamäki, & Grigorenko, 2001), but is very broad. Some researchers and educators may prefer to view creative and practical skills as being beyond rather than within the domain of intelligence. Thus contemporary theories have advanced educators' thinking about intelligence, but as they have answered some questions, they have raised others.

CONSTRUCTING YOUR OWN LEARNING

Now that you have read about the various theories of intelligence, take a few moments to integrate what you have read with ideas of your own. Choose one of the theories. How would you teach students a concept in a way that takes key aspects of that theory into account? How would you teach students that same concept if you were including the ideas of a different theory of intelligence?

Current Educational Controversies in Intelligence

The sheer number of theories of intelligence presented in the preceding section makes it obvious that theorists and researchers disagree about the nature of intelligence and what behavior reflects it. There are also some major disagreements regarding other aspects of intelligence. Because the position teachers take on some of these issues can affect how they approach their students in the classroom, we cover three of these controversies in some detail.

The first controversy regards the *source* of intelligence—the extent to which it is inherited versus the extent to which it develops in response to a person's environment. A second disagreement regards the extent to which a student's level of intelligence can be *modified*. Finally, there are differences of opinion regarding how teachers should best cope with *varying levels* of intelligence among their students. One common, but controversial, method is to group students according to ability level; another method is to have no grouping at all.

 HERITABILITY AND MODIFIABILITY OF INTELLIGENCE

Many aspects of intelligence are at least partially inherited, and teachers need to understand the educational implications of this fact. At the base of some controversies over the source and stability of intelligence are disagreements about the extent of genetic versus environmental influences on people. Thus it is essential to understand clearly the concepts of genetic and environmental influences.

Genetic influences are biologically coded—programmed at the moment of conception. Each individual has myriad genes, which express their many influences—on skin color, body shape, and even intelligence, for example—in complex and interactive ways. Environmental influences, in contrast, are solely a product of experience. Usually, when people think about environment, they think about family, educational, economic, political, and similar influences, but environmental experience begins even before birth. Prenatal nutrition is an environmental influence, for example; so is prenatal exposure to toxic substances. A child born to a mother addicted to drugs, or whose mother has consumed even moderate quantities of alcohol, has experienced a harmful environment *before* birth.

■ TO WHAT EXTENT ARE DIFFERENCES DETERMINED BY GENES? Heritability refers to the extent to which individual differences in an attribute, or a specific characteristic of a person, are genetically determined, strictly speaking, independently of any environmental influences (Sternberg & Grigorenko, 1997). Heritability is often expressed in terms of a **heritability coefficient,** which is a number on a 0 to 1 scale. A coefficient of 0 indicates that heredity has no influence at all on variation among people, and a coefficient of 1 means that only heredity—nothing else—has an influence on such variation. Heritability measures the extent to which *individual differences in* intelligence are inherited, not the extent to which intelligence *itself* is inherited. In certain aspects of intelligence there are no or only trivial individual differences (e.g., the speaking of a native language), and the coefficient of heritability does not take these aspects into account. An attribute can be genetic and yet not show up in the heritability coefficient if that attribute is not a source of meaningful individual differences.

THINKING ANALYTICALLY

What do you think is more important in leading someone to achieve good grades in school—genes or environment? Why?

SUGGESTION: Both genes and environment are important, and their interaction should be considered. But the classroom, family, and community are all important environmental influences, and only they can be changed.

A variety of methods have been used to estimate the heritability of intelligence; most involve some analysis of kinship patterns (Loehlin, Horn, & Willerman, 1997; Scarr, 1997). For example, one method involves the study of identical twins separated at or shortly after birth. The idea is that such identical twins will share identical heredities (because they have the same genes), but not the same environment (because they have been raised apart), so that one can separate the effects of heredity from those of the environment. A second method involves comparing identical twins, who share all their genes, with fraternal twins, who share half their genes, but who are raised in what are assumed to be strictly comparable environments. A third method involves looking at adopted children, and comparing attributes of these children with the attributes of both their biological parents and their adoptive parents. The idea behind this method is that the children will share genes but not environment with the biological parents, and environment but not genes with the adoptive parents.

All these methods can be useful for determining the heritability of intelligence, but none is conclusive (Grigorenko, 2000). The world does not usually lend itself to perfectly controlled natural experiments. For example, all the separated identical twins spent at least nine months together—in the intrauterine environment—and most also spent at least some time together after birth. Moreover, adoption agencies do not really place adoptees at random. The agencies generally look for a good home environment, and one that is roughly comparable to the environment from which the child originated. For these and a variety of technical reasons, we need to be cautious in interpreting the results of heritability studies. We also need to remember that the studies tend to use conventional tests of intelligence based on conventional theories. Today, there are many broader theories not represented well by the conventional tests that might yield different results.

Many of the early theorists of intelligence simply assumed that intelligence is largely or entirely genetically determined (e.g., Terman, 1930). Thus intelligence tests were thought by many such theorists to measure largely an inborn, unchangeable trait. However, many estimates made using the methods we have described suggest that intelligence is not entirely controlled by genes (Grigorenko, 2000). Different studies give somewhat different estimates of heritability. Studies of twins reared apart (e.g., Bouchard & McGue, 1981; Juel-Nielsen, 1965; Newman, Freeman, & Holzinger, 1937; Shields, 1962) suggest a heritability coefficient in roughly the 0.6 to 0.8 range. Studies of identical versus fraternal twins suggest a heritability of roughly 0.7 to 0.8 (Bouchard, 1997; Bouchard & McGue, 1981). These numbers indicate that genetic influences affect individual differences in intelligence, but that these influences are not the only determining factor. Moreover, these results hold only for the populations under study, at the times they were studied, with the measures being used, and with the assumptions about intelligence and methodology made in the studies. An interesting finding is that the heritability of intelligence appears to increase with age (Plomin, 1997)—that is, early individual differences in environments have less of an effect as individuals grow older.

The key implication of this discussion for teachers is that, although genetics certainly play a role in determining intelligence, a significant part of students' performance is attributable to environmental influences. School environment is a major aspect of these influences. In fact, greater and longer attendance at school is almost always associated with higher scores on intelligence tests (Ceci & Williams, 1997). Expert teaching definitely does make a difference. Next we discuss the ways in which teaching and other environmental forces can affect intelligence.

■ **CAN INTELLIGENCE BE MODIFIED?** At one time, virtually all psychologists believed that intelligence is fixed—what we are born with is what we have for life. Today, some psychologists still believe this notion, but many, including the authors of this text, do not. The key concept in the debate over the stability of intelligence is the idea of **modifiability,** or the extent to which an attribute is susceptible to change. Even after it was determined that intelligence is not entirely inherited, many psychologists and educators believed that intelligence is a fixed attribute. Most attributes are modifiable, however. That there may be genetic influence on these attributes does not change this fact.

For example, consider height. With a heritability coefficient of about 0.9, height is one of the most highly heritable attributes of all. Despite this fact, over the past several generations heights have increased dramatically in the United States, and even more in other countries such as Japan. People's genetic codes for height have not changed in the last two or three generations, but heights have increased. What does this fact mean? Obviously, environmental factors such as nutrition and disease prevention have influenced the expression of the genes for height. If children receive inadequate nutrition and contract diseases, they are less likely to reach the

THINKING ANALYTICALLY

Explain how environment can affect an attribute, such as height, even if that attribute is highly heritable.

SUGGESTION: Heritability refers to patterns of individual differences, not levels of attributes. Height might be highly heritable both in Japan and in the United States, so that parents' heights predict children's heights. However, the heights of children may fluctuate more in Japan than in the United States, because of major changes in diet in Japan over the past 30 years.

full potential height their genes would allow (Sternberg & Grigorenko, 1997). Nutrition and other environmental factors can have a large effect on development, whether or not an attribute is highly heritable (Sternberg, Grigorenko, & Nokes, 1997). The same logic applies to other attributes as well, including intelligence (Grotzer & Perkins, 2000; Mayer, 2000).

Another major concept is called **gene–environment interaction,** the idea that genetic and environmental influences can combine to produce results that might be unexpected on the basis of either factor alone (Grigorenko, 2000). Genes do not produce individual differences on their own. How they express themselves depends on the influence of the environment. Some theorists have proposed models of gene–environment reaction that include a **reaction range,** a spectrum of ways that an attribute can be expressed in the environment, bounded by genetic possibilities. A reaction range for intelligence would suggest that the upper and possibly lower limits of a person's intellectual abilities are determined by genetics. Within the range between the person's upper and lower limits, however, environmental forces determine exactly what level of intelligence the person will attain. For example, a student who has a genetic predisposition toward only moderate intelligence, but who is raised in a stimulating home atmosphere and who receives sensitive, appropriate instruction at school, might have a higher IQ than a student who inherits genes for high intelligence but who is raised in a deprived environment without a stimulating home or school life. Exactly what kinds of environmental influences make a difference in intelligence levels?

■**HOW ENVIRONMENTAL INFLUENCES MAKE A DIFFERENCE: LESSONS FOR TEACHERS** Robert Bradley and Bettye Caldwell (1984) have argued that a child's home environment during the preschool years is particularly crucial to intellectual development. They found that high scores on tests of intelligence were associated with (1) emotional and verbal responsivity of the primary caregiver and the caregiver's *involvement* with the child; (2) *avoidance of restriction* and punishment; (3) *organization* of the physical environment and activity schedule; (4) provision of appropriate play *materials;* and (5) opportunities for *variety* in daily stimulation. Bradley and Caldwell found that these factors predicted intelligence test scores better than did either socioeconomic variables or family structure variables. These results have clear implications for structuring a preschool, or even a primary grade, environment that would foster children's intelligence. For example, teachers of young children need to be as involved and responsive to each student as possible. Small class sizes, if possible, foster teacher-child involvement.

Positive interaction between teachers and students is immediately apparent in this preschool grade classroom. (Brian Smith)

One preschool program that includes many of the intellectually stimulating qualities defined by Bradley and Caldwell is Head Start. Head Start, initiated in the 1960s, is probably the most well-known program for developing intelligence. Head Start was designed to provide preschoolers with an advantage both in their intellectual abilities and in their school achievements when they started school. Research reveals that children who were in this program in its early years tended, on average, to score higher on a variety of scholastic achievement tests, to need less remedial attention, and to show fewer behavioral problems (Lazar & Darlington, 1982; Ramey & Landesman Ramey, 2000; Zigler & Berman, 1983). There is some debate as to how well these effects have held up over time and whether the programs are worth their cost.

Some analysts (e.g., Herrnstein & Murray, 1994), using the argument that intelligence is partially genetically based, have argued that programs such as Head Start are likely not to be very successful. They have suggested that improvements in performance are temporary, in any case, and they do not represent true changes in ability. But there may be other reasons why they are temporary. If an intervention is started but then a child is thrown back into an environment that does not carry through on the intervention, the effects of the intervention will almost inevitably be weakened. As an analogy, consider a diet. The diet can help you lose weight, but you can keep the weight off only if you change your way of eating afterward, not just during the diet!

Head Start was created to accomplish several different goals. Other programs have been developed for the sole purpose of improving intelligence. One of the more notable programs is the *Instrumental Enrichment* program of Reuven Feuerstein (1980), which is designed to remedy deficiencies in cognitive processing and to increase students' internal motivation and feelings of self-worth. Another is the *Odyssey* program, constructed by a team of investigators at Harvard University and Bolt, Beranek, and Newman (Adams, 1986). Both programs have been shown to improve children's thinking (Feuerstein, 1980; Herrnstein, Nickerson, de Sanchez, & Swets, 1986). Other programs, such as *The IDEAL Problem Solver* (Bransford & Stein, 1984, 1993), which aims to teach problem-solving abilities, and *Intelligence Applied* (Sternberg, 1986; Sternberg & Grigorenko, 2002), which includes the three subtheories of Sternberg's triarchic theory, are also based on modern cognitive theories, but have been less extensively tested.

Not all programs attempt to develop all aspects of intelligence. For example, *Practical Intelligence for School* (Williams, Blythe, White, Li, Steinberg, & Gardner, 1996), a joint effort between Harvard and Yale that combines aspects of the theory of multiple intelligences with aspects of the triarchic theory of intelligence, has been found to be successful at improving the adaptability of middle school children to the intellectual demands of reading, writing, homework, and test taking (Gardner, Krechevsky, Sternberg, & Okagaki, 1994; Sternberg, Okagaki, & Jackson, 1990). Sternberg (1987b) has also found that aspects of his componential subtheory, such as the ability to learn meanings of words from context, can be taught successfully. So can aspects of his experiential theory, including the ability to think insightfully about novel problems (Davidson & Sternberg, 1984). The processes of the triarchic theory can also be infused into regular school instruction in order to increase performance (Sternberg, Ferrari, Clinkenbeard, & Grigorenko, 1996; Sternberg & Grigorenko, 2000; Sternberg, Torff, & Grigorenko, 1998).

In conclusion, good evidence indicates that we can have some effects on children's intellectual functioning through carefully constructed interventions.

THINKING CREATIVELY

Suppose you want to improve your students' attitudes toward schoolwork. What might you do to help students feel more positive about themselves and their performance?

SUGGESTION: Ask students to identify strengths in their work. Then help them apply these strengths to other skills.

Implications for Teaching

■ *Allow children to play and learn without too many limitations.* Small class sizes, if possible, foster teacher-child involvement. Expert teachers provide a clearly organized classroom with hazardous materials removed or locked, so children can safely learn and play without too many physical restrictions. They also provide plenty of toys and materials for all students, so that each child can have a variety of experiences.

■ *Focus on each student's potential for improvement.* Embrace the concept that intelligence is modifiable. When students feel that they have no potential, their enthusiasm for learning diminishes. Expert teachers emphasize their students' potentials and thus encourage the students to improve on their abilities. Although the effects are not always dramatic, expert teachers can help improve the intelligence of any student.

- **Provide opportunities to practice skills that are part of intelligent behavior.** Many programs for improving intelligence include exercises designed to help students develop the skills that are part of overall intelligence. Students may improve their overall intellectual functioning if they are able to improve even one aspect, such as the ability to monitor their performance while solving problems. A formal program might explain why self-monitoring skills are important, and how to check answers to math problems, for example. Even without a formal program, though, teachers can provide similar instruction and practice.

- **Help students link skills to real-world needs.** The *Practical Intelligence for School* program emphasizes not only being "smart," but knowing how and when to apply intelligence. Teachers who can help students see ways to effectively use their skills may help those students improve their chances of achieving their goals in life (Sternberg, 1996).

TEACHING STUDENTS OF VARYING LEVELS: ABILITY GROUPING

Expert teachers know that people are malleable in their abilities. They are open to experience and change, not fixed at an immutable level set at conception. Improvements in intelligence do take time, as well as careful planning. Many teachers, however, face an immediate question of how to teach students who are currently functioning at a variety of different levels.

As a teacher, you may encounter some substantial differences in your students' patterns of abilities. For example, if you ask the class to read a passage of text, and you then question the students about the material, you may notice that some students can answer your questions with such ease that they seem bored. Other students seem to be truly provoked into thought by your questions. Meanwhile, still others are struggling to make out many of the words. How can you effectively teach students at varying levels of ability?

One method that has been widely used is **ability grouping,** the practice of assigning students to separate instructional groups on the basis of similar levels of achievement or ability in a subject. Ability grouping is very common at all educational levels in U.S. schools (Oakes, Quartz, Gong, Guiton, & Lipton, 1993; Wheelock, 1994). A variety of methods for grouping students according to ability have been developed.

■ **METHODS OF GROUPING BY ABILITY** There are three main types of ability groups. The first is **within-class grouping,** in which a single class of students is divided into two or three groups for instruction in certain subjects. For example, an individual fourth-grade teacher may keep his or her entire class together for most of the day, but divide the class into three different groups for reading lessons. Within-class grouping is most common at the elementary school level (Goodlad, 1984; McPartland, Coldiron, & Braddock, 1987), where ability groups are often used for reading and sometimes for math (Slavin, 1993).

In a first-grade open classroom, a teacher meets with a reading group as the rest of the class works on other projects. Within-class grouping allows a single class of students to be divided into two or three ability groups for instruction, particularly in reading and math. (Elizabeth Crews)

A second method of ability grouping is **between-class grouping.** In this method, students are assigned to separate classes according to ability. Assignments are often made on the basis of standardized intelligence or achievement tests. Using this plan, for example, seventh-grade students, such as Tony Garcia's, might be assigned to a lower level, mid-level, or high-level math course on the basis of their previous math performance or their standardized test scores. Between-class ability grouping is more common at the middle school and high school levels than at the elementary school level (McPartland et al., 1987).

Between-class ability grouping can be expanded into a practice known as **tracking,** or making assignments to all or almost all classes based on variations in ability levels and possibly interests. Often, students are assigned to a given track and then stay in that track for all classes. For example, many high schools have separate college preparation and vocational preparation tracks (Braddock, 1990).

A third major method is known as **regrouping,** an ability-grouping plan in which students are members of two or more classes or groups at once. Students are assigned to a general, mixed-ability class for most of the day, but regroup, or switch to ability-based groups, for certain subjects. Under a regrouping plan, for example, a fourth-grade student stays with his or her main class group for social studies, English, art, music, and physical education, but studies math with a different group of students during part of each day. Regrouping is often used in elementary schools, and there are several variations on the general regrouping idea. Ability groups in a regrouping plan can be made up of children who are all at the same age or grade level, or they can be composed of students from a range of ages and grade levels.

A regrouping plan in which students of various ages are assigned to the same ability-based group is known as the **Joplin Plan.** Nongraded, or cross-age elementary schools are those in which students are not assigned to grade levels, such as first or second grade, but rather are grouped according to broad age categories, such as ages 5 to 7. Within the broad groups of nongraded schools, students of various ages may be grouped by ability for instruction in some subjects, as in the Joplin Plan (Guitiérrez & Slavin, 1992).

 ADVANTAGES AND DISADVANTAGES OF ABILITY GROUPING

Ability grouping has several advantages for teachers and students. The practice can help teachers meet the need to adjust teaching techniques to the varying levels of their students. For example, teachers can cover topics faster or slower, depending on students' needs. They can also match textbooks and other teaching materials more closely to students' abilities than they could in a mixed-ability classroom. Adjusting instruction to groups of students, rather than individualizing instruction for each pupil, also helps teachers make effective use of their limited time (Cotton & Cavard, 1981). In addition, students may be helped in some subjects by being in groups with peers at similar achievement levels. In reading, math, and foreign languages, for instance, skills are acquired sequentially, with more advanced skills building on the foundation of basic skills. Students who are at various points in skill building can be grouped and taught the skills they currently need (Slavin, 1993).

The disadvantages of ability grouping may outweigh the advantages, however. Between-class ability grouping has the most problems. First, students in between-class groups or tracks are often trapped in their assigned group for an entire school year, or longer, even if their skills have changed and the placement is no longer appropriate (Good & Marshall, 1984; Oakes, 1992). A less obvious problem is that students from lower socioeconomic levels and ethnic minority groups tend to be overrepresented in lower ability groups, and higher ability groups have higher percentages of white and higher socioeconomic level students (Braddock & Dawkins, 1993; Dornbush, 1994). Second, students in the lower ability classes often receive lower quality instruction, with less instruction on critical thinking skills and more emphasis on drills and routines, than do students in higher ability classes (Gamoran, Nystrand, Berends, & LePore, 1995). Third, placement in a low-ability group can stigmatize students socially and lower their self-esteem (Oakes & Guiton, 1995; Page, 1991). Perhaps these disadvantages contribute to the greater likelihood of students in lower ability tracks, compared with other students, to drop out of school (Goodlad, 1984). Fourth, between-class grouping may not be effective. Some studies have found that lower ability students who were placed in mixed-ability classes performed better than did low-ability students who were assigned to homogeneous low-ability classes (Good & Brophy, 1994). Finally, certain forms of ability grouping, and certainly tracking, are inconsistent with modern notions of cognitive expertise as comprising multiple abilities or even intelligences.

Within-class and regrouping plans are generally more successful (Slavin, 1987). These plans usually have more flexibility for moving students to new groups as the students' abilities develop than do between-class grouping plans (Mason & Good, 1993). Also, ability groups in within-class and regrouping plans are typically limited to one or two subjects—students remain in mixed-ability classes the rest of the school day. Within-class plans can cause difficulties for teachers, who must plan and monitor independent activities for some students while working in a group with others (Good & Brophy, 1994; Oakes, 1992).

Expert teachers take into account both the advantages and the disadvantages when deciding whether to use ability groups. Teachers who decide to use ability grouping, or are assigned to ability-tracked classes, can also use some techniques to make their teaching more effective. Often, simple group activities work just fine, without the need for grouping by abilities for the groups to be effective (Slavin, 1995).

Implications for Teaching

- *Target ability grouping carefully.* People often have stronger abilities in some areas than in others. Group assignments should therefore be made on a subject-by-subject basis. Assignments should also be based on multiple measures, including not only test scores, but also past performance, teacher observations, and other sources of information (Corno & Snow, 1986; Gamoran, Nystrand, Berends, & LePore, 1995).

- *Assess student progress frequently and adjust group assignments according to progress.* Group assignments should be changed with students' changing skill levels. Elementary school teachers who use within-class reading or math groups can easily switch students to different groups. At the secondary level, where students may be tracked into an entire sequence of classes, teachers must be prepared to accommodate different ability levels, even within supposedly homogeneous groups.

- *Avoid comparisons between groups.* Discourage unfavorable remarks about lower ability groups. If such comparisons do arise, you may wish to point out to students the compensatory nature of abilities, or the flexible nature of the groups. A student who is feeling discouraged about being assigned to the prealgebra class instead of the algebra class might be reminded of his or her other strengths.

- *Keep quality of instruction high for all students.* Lower ability students may be learning earlier steps in the acquisition of subjects than higher ability students. Teachers should not, however, reduce their enthusiasm or expectations for students in the lower groups. Plan lessons carefully for groups at all levels to encourage participation, creativity, and critical thinking. Explain to students that they can go quite far just on the basis of their commitment to learning.

Cognitive Styles and Learning Styles

Despite the importance of responding to students' differing ability levels, expert teachers know that other factors besides intelligence can also affect students' levels of achievement. Styles of thinking and learning often affect how students will behave in school, and what kind of teaching and learning situations will be most effective for those students.

The combination of personality with intelligence has been called *cognitive style* (Sternberg & Zhang, 2000). Two students may be equally capable, but one may prefer to work on her own ideas and to write essays on topics she generates, whereas the other may await explicit direction from a teacher before attempting schoolwork. In Tony Garcia's class, for example, some students were content to do the homework problems and take the tests Tony assigned. Others relished the opportunity to think of their own ideas for class projects.

Similarly, one student may enjoy the details of an assignment, and the other may prefer thinking about the conclusions and what they mean rather than getting bogged down in details. One student may easily prioritize a list of tasks in a manner that matches the teacher's expectations; the other is unable to see which tasks are more important and so jumps from task to task. In addition, two students may have differences in their preferred *learning styles*—the ways they like to learn. One may enjoy a noisy classroom, with lots of talk and group action, and the other likes quiet and solitude. Again, these two students may have similar levels of intelligence or even of multiple intelligences, but the expression of their intelligence is affected by their differing personalities, leading to their different cognitive and learning styles.

COGNITIVE STYLES

A **cognitive style** (sometimes also called **thinking style**) refers to an individual's preferred way of mentally processing information. Several differences in cognitive style have been explored. We briefly review a few of the main ones here (for more detailed reviews, see Grigorenko & Sternberg, 1995; Messick, 1984; Sternberg, 1997a; Sternberg & Grigorenko, 2000a; Sternberg & Zhang, 2000), along with their implications for teachers.

■ FIELD INDEPENDENCE VERSUS FIELD DEPENDENCE

A **field-independent** person is able to separate self, or objects viewed, from the surrounding context. For example, a field-independent person might be better able to read text upside down than a field-dependent person. A **field-dependent** person has trouble separating self, or objects, from the surrounding field. A typical test for field independence asks a person to detect a particular shape embedded in the context of other, surrounding shapes, such as a hidden triangle in a set of intersecting lines. Field-independent people can separate the target shapes from the background, or field, more quickly and easily than field-dependent people (Witkin, 1973; Witkin, Dyk, Faterson, Goodenough, & Karp, 1962; Witkin, Oltman, Raskin, & Karp, 1971).

Students' level of field independence can be related to their performance in school (Davis, 1991). Field-dependent students tend to be more attuned to the social aspects of school situations, and may perform better at group tasks than field-independent students, for example. They may prefer academic subjects, such as literature and history, that require them to perceive broad patterns. Teachers may sometimes need to help field-dependent students see the key elements of a problem or set their priorities for an unstructured task. Field-independent students, in contrast, are able to separate and analyze components, or parts, of a larger pattern by ignoring irrelevant details. Field-independent students may

An impulsive student quickly offers an answer to the teacher's question, while a reflective classmate ponders a solution. Students' levels of impulsivity often affect their performance in school. Impulsive children, for example, frequently offer incorrect solutions to reasoning problems and visual discrimination. With expert teaching, these students can learn to be more reflective without losing their enthusiasm. (Myrleen Ferguson, PhotoEdit)

prefer subjects such as math or science that require their analytical abilities (Wapner & Demick, 1991). Field-independent students may need help seeing how their actions affect the group as a whole or perceiving how several isolated facts can fit together into a larger pattern. Because teachers are unlikely to know their students' styles, they must plan to teach in diverse ways to all students.

Field independence was formulated as a cognitive style. However, higher levels of it are associated with higher levels of spatial ability—meaning that it does not quite function the way a style should (see Ferrari & Sternberg, 1998; Sternberg, 1997a).

■ **REFLECTIVITY VERSUS IMPULSIVITY**   A **reflective** person tends to consider alternative solutions before reaching a decision. An **impulsive** person tends to produce quick answers without carefully thinking about them first (Kagan, 1965, 1966). A person's level of reflectivity or impulsiveness seems to be a general stylistic trait that appears early in life and affects his or her behavior in a variety of situations.

Students' levels of impulsivity can affect their performance in school. Impulsive children tend to make more errors in reading and memory tasks, and more frequently offer incorrect solutions to reasoning problems and visual discrimination tasks (Stahl, Erickson, & Rayman, 1986). With expert teaching, students can learn to be more reflective. To keep impulsive students from cutting short the thoughts of more reflective students, you may want to consider using turn-taking systems for group question-and-answer sessions. During individual tasks, encourage impulsive students to talk to themselves mentally as they are working on problems. For example, on multiple-choice tests, students can remind themselves to cross off each answer choice as they consider it, to avoid making a premature answer choice. Teach students how to check their work on math or science problems, and consider rewarding evidence of self-checking when grading papers and tests.

■ **MENTAL SELF-GOVERNMENT**   Sternberg (1988b, 1994a, 1994b, 1997b) has proposed a **theory of mental self-government.** In this theory, people, like towns or countries, need to organize and govern themselves. The theory distinguishes among 13 main learning styles. Three of the styles are listed in Table 4.2, along with the kinds of instructional and assessment activities that tend to be oriented toward each of the styles. These three styles are as follows:

Legislative: A student who enjoys creating, formulating, and planning problem solutions and likes to do things his or her own way.

Executive: A student who likes to implement plans, follow rules, and choose from established options.

Judicial: A student who enjoys evaluating rules, procedures, or products.

A major implication of this theory is that some ways of teaching and assessing students tend consistently to benefit students with certain styles at the expense of students with other styles. Thus, whenever possible, try to include methods and activities that appeal to a broader variety of self-government styles. The idea is not to label students, but to teach to all styles. Research shows that teachers tend to give better evaluations to students whose styles more closely match their own. This tendency may be due to teachers' tendencies to overestimate the extent to which students share their own styles of thinking. However, not all schools value the same styles; in fact, large differences have been found in which styles are preferred in which schools (Sternberg & Grigorenko, 1997b).

TABLE 4.2   Three Styles of Mental Self-Government

Style Name	Description of a Student Who Works in This Style	Teaching Implications
Legislative	Enjoys creating, formulating, and planning problem solutions. Likes to do things his or her own way.	Legislative students enjoy the opportunity to choose their own topics for papers or projects, devise their own experiments, or organize their own study time.
Executive	Likes to implement plans, follow rules, and choose from established options. Prefers structured problems.	Executive students would prefer to choose from a set of suggestions for paper topics, or to take multiple-choice exams, rather than generate their own paper topics or essay answers.
Judicial	Enjoys evaluating rules, procedures, or products.	Judicial students would likely welcome papers or exam questions that require them to compare and contrast two things, or to analyze a single point of view.

LEARNING STYLES

Students' individual preferences or needs for different learning conditions are called **learning styles,** or **learning preferences.** Learning styles can range from straightforward preferences for physical surroundings to more fundamental differences that may be rooted in culture or personality. We examine some key aspects of learning styles here, starting with the basics.

Uncomfortable physical surroundings can distract students from their subject matter. Students vary, for example, in preferences for aspects of the classroom environment such as lighting, hard or soft seating, or level of noise (Dunn & Dunn, 1987). A quiet corner with soft furniture might be some students' ideal reading environment. Others might prefer bright lighting and a desk on which to lay out their work. You may not be able to provide each student with his or her ideal physical environment, but you can often offer a variety of study and learning conditions, all within a single classroom. For example, you might provide headphones so that some students can listen to music or audiotaped books without disturbing those who wish to work quietly. To help students develop flexibility, provide some instruction that fits students' learning styles but other instruction that challenges them to adjust the way they learn.

Some of the styles expressed as physical preferences may actually be culturally related differences in learning (Watkins, 2001). For example, some Native American, African American, and rural students may come from families that favor spoken over written learning. These students might learn better by listening to a book on tape as they read it, rather than just reading it alone (Bennett, 1995). Some Asian American and African American students may have a cultural background that encourages *interdependence between people,* rather than the independent achievements traditionally encouraged by American schools. (For more about cultural differences in learning styles, see Chapter 6.) To meet all their students' needs, expert teachers provide opportunities for students to learn in groups, or through cooperative projects, as well as independently.

Individual differences in personality, as well as cultural background, can affect the way different students approach the same learning task. One personality difference in learning style is the depth to which students prefer to process information (Snow, Corno, & Jackson, 1996). Some students take a *deep-processing approach,* seeking the underlying concepts, or meaning, of activities or lessons. Others take a *surface-processing approach,* focusing on memorization rather than analysis and understanding. Some researchers have found that students' preferences for depth of processing are more likely to be stable across situations and subjects (Biggs, 2001; Boulton-Lewis, Marton, & Wilss, 2001; Entwistle, McCune, & Walker, 2001; Pintrich & Schrauben, 1992). Students who take a surface approach tend to be motivated by grades and other external rewards, whereas those who take a deep approach seem to enjoy learning for the sake of learning and are less concerned with external evaluations (Marton & Booth, 1997).

As with cognitive styles, such as impulsivity, teachers can encourage students toward taking a deeper or more surface approach. For example, designing tests that emphasize key concepts of lessons, rather than just surface features, such as key terms, can encourage deeper processing. As Tony Garcia discovered, projects that require students to apply the ideas from a lesson to another context also encourage deeper processing. For example, a teacher might ask students to apply the idea of *hubris,* or excessive pride, learned from studying Shakespeare, by finding examples of hubris demonstrated in current events or movies.

Students who process information more deeply may also be able to produce more creative work than can surface processors. We explore individual differences in creativity next.

Understanding Individual Differences in Creativity

Creativity is the ability to produce work that is novel, high in quality, and appropriate (Barron, 1968; Jackson & Messick, 1965; MacKinnon, 1962; Ochse, 1990; Sternberg & Lubart, 1999). A product is novel when it is original and not expected. A product is appropriate when it fulfills a certain set of constraints on what constitutes a usable solution to a task.

Creativity, your own as well as that of your students, is very important to you as a teacher. As this chapter on individual differences has demonstrated, you sometimes must become experts in inventiveness to effectively teach each of your students. You will also find it very rewarding to develop your students' creativity. On an immediate level, grading projects can become more fun and interesting, as Tony Garcia, the math teacher described at the beginning of the chapter, noticed! Teachers who encourage students to display their creativity discover that some of those students possess abilities the teachers had never noticed before. On a deeper level, you win the reward of knowing you are preparing your students to think and act in novel and appropriate ways to solve problems they'll face throughout their lives—problems we may not even be able to imagine today. To help your students be as creative as possible, first broaden your own understanding of creativity. There have been several different approaches to creativity (Albert & Runco, 1999; Runco & Pritzker, 1999; Sternberg & Lubart, 1996). We consider four such approaches next.

THE MYSTICAL APPROACH

In the mystical, and oldest, approach to creativity, creativity is seen as the result either of divine intervention or of other unexplainable forces. For example, Plato argued that a poet creates only as his or her muse, a goddess who presides over the arts, dictates, and the writer Rudyard Kipling referred to a "Daemon" as guiding his pen (1937/1985). To this day, many people believe their creative ideas are somehow divinely inspired, under the control of forces that are supernatural, or at least not understandable through scientific means. The problem with this approach is that it lends itself neither to scientific investigation nor to educational interventions.

THE PSYCHOMETRIC APPROACH

In the psychometric approach to creativity, the central emphasis is on measuring creative abilities in much the same ways as other abilities, such as intelligence, are measured (Plucker & Renzulli, 1999). This approach to creativity is best exemplified by the Torrance Tests of Creative Thinking (Torrance, 1974), which are fairly widely used in assessing creativity. Examples of exercises in the Torrance tests include thinking of questions one could ask about a scene that is depicted, thinking of ways to change a toy monkey so children will have more fun playing with it, and expanding empty circles into different drawings and then titling these drawings.

J. P. Guilford (1950) especially emphasized the role played in creativity by **divergent thinking,** or the ability to generate many different ideas in response to a problem. The opposite of divergent thinking is called **convergent thinking,** the process of finding a single correct answer. Convergent thinking is the more common kind of thinking required in schools. Like others who take a psychometric approach, Guilford attempted to measure individuals' divergent thinking abilities. For example, in one of Guilford's creativity tests, called "Unusual Uses," a test taker has to think of as many unusual uses as possible for fairly common objects, such as a brick or paper clip. Guilford (1967) was also well known for his theory of intelligence.

 ### SOCIAL-PSYCHOLOGICAL APPROACHES

Social-psychological approaches to creativity focus on environmental variables that influence creative thinking. For example, Teresa Amabile (1983, 1996) as well as others (Crutchfield, 1962; Golann, 1962) have emphasized the relevance to creative thinking of **intrinsic motivation**—a desire to do something because you really want to do it, not for the sake of any external rewards. The opposite of intrinsic motivation is **extrinsic motivation,** doing something in order to achieve rewards, such as praise, good grades, or a paycheck, from an external source. Creative people are generally people who love what they are doing. Helping children find what they love to do is one of the single best ways teachers can enhance their creativity. Creative people often generate ways to find extrinsic rewards for what they are intrinsically motivated to do.

Dean Simonton (1984, 1988, 1994, 1999) has analyzed the role of society in the development of creative thought. For example, Simonton (1988) has shown that the odds of an eminent creative person emerging in a given generation increase with the number of creatively eminent figures in the preceding two generations. Simonton has also argued that people who are thoroughly exposed to two or more cultures have a creative advantage over those who are fully exposed to just a single culture.

Mihalyi Csikszentmihalyi (1988, 1996, 1999) is another theorist who has argued for the importance of social context. He emphasizes the significance of the social organization of knowledge (the *field*) in fostering or inhibiting creativity as people pursue a given endeavor. He distinguishes the field from the *domain,* which is the cognitive organization of knowledge. What we call creativity is never the result of just one person acting alone: It is an interaction between what an individual produces and what others label as "creative." The importance of social context is shown by the varied reactions elicited by some of the graffiti artists who spray-paint walls and subways in large cities. Some art critics praise their work as raw and authentic masterpieces. At the same time, police and property owners condemn the painters as nothing more than common law breakers. The reaction that the graffiti makers perceive as predominant may affect whether they continue painting.

 ### A CONFLUENCE APPROACH

Robert Sternberg and Todd Lubart (1991, 1995, 1996, 1999) have attempted to integrate many of the ideas just discussed in their **investment theory of creativity.** This theory describes creative people as good investors in the world of ideas who "buy low and sell high." That is, the creative individual finds an idea that is undervalued by contemporaries ("buys low"), then develops that idea into a meaningful, significant creative

How might the school environment either facilitate or impede creative work on the part of students or teachers?

SUGGESTION: Schools facilitate creativity when they encourage students to take intellectual risks, and they impede creativity when they discourage such risks.

contribution. Once the creator has convinced other people of the worth of that idea, he or she then moves on to the next unpopular idea ("sells high").

The investment view of creativity represents a coming together, or *confluence,* of a number of research and theoretical strands to fashion a composite picture of creativity (see also Amabile, 1996; Barron, 1988; Collins & Amabile, 1999; Costa & McCrae, 1985; Frensch & Sternberg, 1989; Ghiselin, 1952/1985; Golann, 1962; Hayes, 1989; Mayer, 1999; McClelland, 1953; McCrae, 1987; Roe, 1953). Creative people, according to this theory, (1) do not accept traditional ways of seeing problems, but rather, try to see problems in new ways; (2) know something about the field to which they wish to contribute, but are usually not "walking encyclopedias" of knowledge in the area or at least do not allow their knowledge to interfere with their seeing things in new ways; (3) like being creative; (4) persevere in the face of obstacles; (5) are open to new experiences; (6) are willing to take sensible risks; (7) are intrinsically motivated; and (8) find environments that support and reward their creative work.

Implications for Teaching

■ *Model creativity.* Provide students with profiles of creative individuals in different fields, including artists, writers, scientists, historians, and mathematicians (see, e.g., Gardner, 1993; Gruber & Wallace, 1999; Policastro & Gardner, 1999). Expert teachers actually demonstrate creativity themselves. Other ways of bringing creativity into the classroom include involving students in writing, in acting in plays, or in storylike demonstrations that illustrate a concept covered in class.

■ *Encourage students to question assumptions.* Ask questions that provoke students to question common assumptions or to imagine someone else's viewpoint. Let students work together in groups on some projects, so they have the benefit of hearing several viewpoints on a single problem.

■ *Encourage sensible risk taking.* Expert teachers take steps to counter thinking that is wholly risk avoidant. Train students to distinguish sensible risks, such as an unusual choice of topic or approach for a paper, from senseless risks, such as dropping out of school or taking drugs. Encourage sensible risk taking by praising the effort, even when you must provide negative feedback on the result.

■ *Promote persistence.* Creative thinkers need to develop an attitude toward objections to new and unpopular ideas as normal responses to creative thinking. You can help by modeling persistence and by pointing out other models who triumphed through perseverance. You can also reward persistence through encouragement and even grading practices such as "second chances"—opportunities to resubmit assignments after improvements have been made.

■ *Allow mistakes.* Children who have developed a tolerance for risk and are willing to face the possibility of failure actually choose to attempt to solve harder problems, and score higher on standardized tests, than do those who are less willing to risk (Clifford, 1988). Expert teachers can use mistakes to reinforce creativity. Discuss students' mistakes to help them see how a good idea may have gotten off-track or what could be improved in their next effort.

TABLE 4.3   Teaching for Creativity

Implication	Example at Preschool/ Primary Level	Example at Elementary School Level	Example at Middle School Level	Example at High School Level
Model creativity	Feel free to use "unrealistic" colors or pictures for bulletin boards, handouts, or computer programs.	Demonstrate ways to combine ideas from subjects that are usually covered in the school day. For example, use chemical reactions to produce a musical instrument of some kind.	Provide examples of creative individuals in different subjects. Use your desk or office space to express your own creativity. Publicly acknowledge students who dress, eat, play, or work creatively.	Model divergent thinking by brainstorming with students to list a number of possible solutions to demonstration problems.
Encourage students to question assumptions	Imagine with students what classic stories would be like if the main characters' roles were changed. For example, what if a little "goldy-bear" came into the house of three people.	Consider assigning students to read "wacky" children's books that question common ideas, such as *Cloudy with a Chance of Meatballs,* about a town where food falls from the sky.	Ask students to write alternative endings or alternative versions of assigned stories, or books.	Consider assigning students to develop spoofs or current adaptations of classic literature.
Encourage sensible risk taking	Provide a safe environment for young children to try new physical skills.	Help children distinguish sensible from dangerous risks. To help students decide if the idea is too risky, for example, discuss "what is the worst thing that could happen?" if the class decided to implement the idea.	Encourage students to develop ideas for creative paper topics or projects, and help them evaluate which ideas present acceptable creative risks.	Encourage students to attempt seemingly difficult courses or projects.
Promote persistence	Model persistence when your own first attempts fail. Praise students when they are noticeably trying hard to learn new skills.	Encourage students to try again if they give a wrong answer during a question-and-answer session.	Point out instances of persistence by creative role models in various fields. For instance, describe how hard professional athletes must train and practice in order to make their movements seem beautifully effortless.	Consider allowing "second chances" on homework or projects—opportunities to re-submit improved work for a potentially higher grade.
Allow mistakes	Encourage young children to try new activities, even though they may not be good at them.	Praise students for trying to answer a question or work on a problem in class, even if the solution is not correct.	To avoid unduly penalizing students for creative risk taking, consider grading schemes that allow students to drop their worst quiz, project, or assignment from their overall grade.	Help students learn from mistakes by providing specific feedback on how an unsuccessful essay, project, or assignment could be improved.
Provide time and opportunities for creative thinking	Whenever possible, let children use toys and classroom materials, like popsicle sticks and construction paper, in novel ways—such as building three-dimensional shapes or new toys like kites.	Allow students to experiment with classroom materials, such as computer graphics programs or art supplies, during free time.	Allow free time for global planning before beginning a class experiment or project.	Encourage students to take responsibility for planning their own creative time, by scheduling free time periods into their school days.
Reward creativity	Praise creative efforts on art or other projects, as well as technical accomplishments.	Display creative work and recognize students' creative successes publicly when possible.	Consider adding a creativity component to the grade for some projects or assignments.	Help students see the possibilities of tangible rewards for some creative efforts. For example, encourage students to submit particularly creative essays or poetry to magazines and newspapers.

- **Model and encourage divergent thinking.** Ask the class to predict the results of a scientific experiment before they conduct it. Brainstorm ideas for alternative conclusions when discussing current events, historical events, or story plots (Richards, 1999). It may soon become clear to students that the more they learn about a subject, the more ideas they are able to generate when a question or problem arises.

- **Allow time and opportunities for creative thinking.** Allow students to experiment with using classroom materials, or combining subjects, in novel ways. Expert teachers do not assume that students who seem to be doing nothing are actually unoccupied. Instead, the students may be planning or thinking about a problem.

- **Reward creativity.** Although intrinsic motivation is important in creativity, teachers can sometimes reward students' creative work without damaging their desire to continue. Praise students for the diversity of ideas shared in a class brainstorming session, or include a grading component for creativity on some projects. Create an environment in which creativity is allowed to flourish (Sternberg & Lubart, 1995).

There are many ways to teach creativity. Steps people can take to enhance the creativity of their work are shown in Table 4.3 on Page 147.

SUMMING IT UP

WHY UNDERSTANDING INDIVIDUAL DIFFERENCES IS IMPORTANT TO TEACHERS

- Various kinds of individual differences contribute to human diversity. From a teacher's viewpoint, some of the most important are differences in intelligence, in cognitive styles, and in creativity.

UNDERSTANDING INDIVIDUAL DIFFERENCES IN INTELLIGENCE

- The modern study of intelligence dates to the work of Alfred Binet, who developed the intelligence test used for determining which schoolchildren should be placed in special classes. An updated version of Binet's test is still used today for measuring people's intelligence quotients, or IQs.

- Researchers have disagreed about what intelligence actually is. Spearman suggested the existence of a general factor of intelligence. Thurstone proposed a theory of seven primary mental abilities, and Guilford proposed as many as 180 different abilities based on the crossing of processes, contents, and products.

- Hierarchical theories of intelligence, which propose both a general factor and varying numbers of group factors that apply to limited ranges of tests, represent a widely accepted current view. Cattell suggested fluid intelligence and crystallized intelligence as two important group factors.

- Systems theories of intelligence attempt to integrate psychometric and information-processing approaches. Gardner's theory of multiple intelligences posits eight distinct and relatively independent intelligences, whereas Sternberg's triarchic theory of human intelligence suggests that intelligence involves, in part, applying component processes to relatively novel tasks for the purposes of adaptation to, shaping of, and selection of environments.

CURRENT EDUCATIONAL CONTROVERSIES IN INTELLIGENCE

- Controversial issues in intelligence include the extent to which intelligence is heritable, and the extent to which it is modifiable. Intelligence seems to be at least partly genetically transmitted. The influence of genes on individual differences in intelligence or other attributes is stated by means of a heritability coefficient. However, environment affects an individual's actual expression of intelligence through gene–environment interaction, often within a given reaction range. Several programs, including Head Start, have been successful in modifying students' intelligence test scores, at least modestly and sometimes only temporarily.

■ Another controversial issue in intelligence is the effectiveness of grouping students by ability level. Teachers often rely on ability-based grouping to improve efficiency in instruction. Students can be grouped by abilities in a variety of ways, including between-class grouping, within-class grouping, and various regrouping plans such as the Joplin Plan and ungraded elementary schools. Between-class ability grouping has several disadvantages. For example, tracking causes some students to become trapped within a group that may no longer be appropriate. Within-class and regrouping plans are usually more flexible than between-class grouping plans and may therefore be more successful. Careful and flexible placement, along with high-quality teaching and frequent evaluation, seems to be key in using ability groups successfully.

COGNITIVE STYLES AND LEARNING STYLES

■ Cognitive (or thinking) styles and learning styles are relevant to how students perform in school. Cognitive

styles that have been studied include field dependence versus field independence and reflectivity versus impulsivity. Sternberg's theory of mental government proposes a variety of different thinking styles.

■ Learning styles range from preferences for certain physical environments to cultural and personality-based styles, such as a preference for group learning, or for surface versus deep processing of information and materials. Teachers can often structure lessons and classrooms to meet the variety of learning preferences of their students.

UNDERSTANDING INDIVIDUAL DIFFERENCES IN CREATIVITY

■ Creativity, the ability to produce work that is novel, high in quality, and appropriate, is an essential attribute for success in today's world. Early mystical approaches to creativity have been replaced by analyses of the cognitive, personality, and social variables that affect creative functioning, such as divergent versus convergent thinking or intrinsic versus extrinsic motivation. The investment theory emphasizes that creative people are ones who go against the crowd.

■ Teachers can enhance their own creativity as well as that of their students by finding models of creativity, trying alternative viewpoints, taking sensible risks, practicing divergent thinking, allowing time for creative thinking, and rewarding creative efforts.

KEY TERMS AND DEFINITIONS

■ **Ability grouping** Practice of assigning students to separate instructional groups on the basis of similar levels of achievement or ability. Page 138

■ **Between-class grouping** Method of ability grouping in which students are assigned to separate classes according to ability. Page 139

■ **Cognitive style (or thinking style)** Individual's preferred way of mentally processing information. Page 141

■ **Convergent thinking** Ability to generate a single correct solution to a problem. Page 145

■ **Creativity** Ability to produce work that is novel, high in quality, and appropriate. Page 144

■ **Crystallized intelligence** Accumulation of knowledge, measured by tests of vocabulary and general information. Page 124

■ **Divergent thinking** Ability to generate many different ideas in response to a problem. Page 145

■ **Extrinsic motivation** Desire to do something in order to achieve rewards from an external source. Page 145

■ **Field dependent** Inability to separate oneself, or objects viewed, from the surrounding context. Page 141

■ **Field independent** Ability to separate oneself, or objects viewed, from the surrounding context. Page 141

■ **Fluid intelligence** Ability to understand abstract and novel concepts. Page 124

■ **Gene–environment interaction** Idea that genetic and environmental influences can combine to produce results that might be unexpected on the basis of either factor alone. Page 136

■ **General factor** (or **g**) Hypothetical single intelligence ability that applies to many different tasks; first suggested by Charles Spearman, who theorized that general ability is supplemented by a number of specific abilities, each applying to a different task. Page 123

■ **Group factors** Subfactors of Spearman's general factor (g) of intelligence that apply across classes of tasks. These subfactors include fluid intelligence and crystallized intelligence. Page 124

Heritability Extent to which individual differences in an attribute are genetically determined, strictly speaking, independently of any environmental influences. Page 134

Heritability coefficient Number between 0 and 1, used to describe the extent to which individual differences in an attribute are due to genetic factors. A coefficient of 0 indicates that heredity has no influence at all on variation among people, and a coefficient of 1 means that nothing but heredity has any influence. Page 134

Impulsive Cognitive style characterized by the tendency to produce quick answers without first carefully thinking them through. Page 142

Intelligence Ability to produce goal-directed, adaptive behavior. Components of intelligence include the ability to learn from experience, the ability to adapt to one's surroundings and metacognition—the ability to understand and control one's own thinking processes. Page 122

Intelligence quotient (or **IQ**) Numerical score that compares the intelligence test performance of each student with an average, or standard, performance. Page 121

Intrinsic motivation Desire to do something simply for the reward of doing it, rather than for the sake of external rewards. Page 145

Investment theory of creativity Theory that describes creative people as those who find an idea undervalued by contemporaries ("buys low") and then develop that idea into a meaningful, significant creative contribution. Page 145

Joplin Plan Regrouping plan in which students of various ages are assigned to the same ability-based group. Page 139

Learning styles (also called **learning preferences**) Students' individual preferences or needs for different learning conditions. Page 143

Metacognition People's understanding and control of their own thinking processes. Page 122

Modifiability Extent to which an attribute is susceptible to change. Page 135

Psychometric theories of intelligence Views of intelligence based on statistical analyses of the results obtained on conventional tests of intelligence, requiring students to show a knowledge of basic vocabulary, mathematical ability, and reasoning skills. Page 122

Reaction range Spectrum of ways that an attribute can be expressed in the environment, bounded by genetic possibilities. Page 136

Reflective Cognitive style characterized by the tendency to consider alternative solutions before reaching a decision. Page 142

Regrouping Ability-grouping plan in which students are members of two or more classes or groups at once. Students are assigned to a general, mixed-ability class for most of the day, but regroup, or switch to ability-based groups, for certain subjects. Page 139

Theory of mental self-government Robert Sternberg's theory of thinking styles. This theory suggests there are 13 different main styles that people use to organize and govern themselves in order to learn and think. Page 142

Theory of multiple intelligences Howard Gardner's theory suggesting the existence of at least eight distinct and relatively independent intelligences: linguistic, logical-mathematical, spatial, musical, bodily-kinesthetic, interpersonal, intrapersonal, and naturalist. Page 126

Theory of primary mental abilities Louis Thurstone's theory that seven basic interrelated factors, or mental abilities, make up the core of intelligence. These primary abilities are verbal comprehension, verbal fluency, inductive reasoning, spatial visualization, number skills, memory, and perceptual speed. Page 123

Tracking Practice of making assignments to entire sets of classes based on variations in ability levels and interests. Page 139

Triarchic theory of human intelligence Robert Sternberg's theory of intelligence that emphasizes relatively interdependent processes. The theory suggests the existence of three related aspects of intelligence: analytic, creative, and practical abilities. Each aspect is described in its own subtheory: the componential subtheory, the experiential subtheory, and the contextual subtheory. Page 130

Within-class grouping Method of ability grouping in which a single class of students is divided into two or three groups for instruction in certain subjects. Page 138

Apply the concepts you have learned in this chapter to the following problems of classroom practice.

IN ELEMENTARY SCHOOL

1. How could you develop students' awareness of their problem-solving strategies—in Sternberg's terms, their metacognition—in the course of a math unit on multiplication?

2. What are some methods you would use to encourage students in the primary grades to become more reflective in general, and to engage in more global planning before starting projects, tests, or assignments?

3. How could you encourage student creativity during a fifth-grade unit on electricity?

4. What are some ways you could include Gardner's musical and bodily-kinesthetic intelligences in a second-grade math unit?

5. What are some criteria you would choose for deciding when to switch students to different reading ability groups in your fourth-grade classroom?

IN MIDDLE SCHOOL

1. Design a unit on the Revolutionary War that includes activities using as many as possible of Gardner's eight intelligences.

2. According to Sternberg's triarchic theory of intelligence, students should begin to automatize familiar tasks. How can a middle school math teacher assess the extent to which students have automatized multiplication and division? How can the teacher help students who have not automatized multiplication or division?

3. How could a unit on cellular biology be structured for students who have a field-dependent cognitive style? Could the same unit be designed for field-independent students as well?

4. What are some ways you could encourage divergent thinking in an eighth-grade Spanish-language class?

5. Most of the students in your higher track seventh-grade English class seem to be highly extrinsically motivated, or perhaps only interested in surface processing of the class information. Every time you discuss a topic, it seems the first question is, "Will this be on the test?" How can you present the material in a way that makes learning it more intrinsically rewarding for students?

IN HIGH SCHOOL

1. If you were assigned to teach the lower track math class, what are some strategies you would use to make sure quality of instruction equaled that of the fast trackers in the school?

2. Design a unit on the branches of the U.S. government that would include activities to appeal to the three styles of mental self-government described by Sternberg's theory.

3. What are some ways a high school math teacher can model and encourage creativity in a physics class?

4. How could you provide opportunities for students in your world governments class to use Gardner's interpersonal and intrapersonal intelligences? Do you think this class would provide appropriate opportunities for using musical, bodily-kinesthetic, or naturalist intelligences? Why or why not?

5. Several of the students in your tenth-grade chemistry class seem to be rather impulsive, and you are concerned they may leap too quickly into activities that could be dangerous in the lab. How could you get them to slow down and plan their laboratory work with safety in mind?

Connecting Theory and Research to Practice

Are you interested in finding out more about different theories of intelligence or the history of intelligence testing? Try connecting to the "History of Influences in the Development of Intelligence Theory and Testing" Web site at *http://www .indiana.edu/~intell/index. html*. This Web site, created and maintained by Dr. Jonathan Plucker from Indiana University, provides a visual map of the history of intelligence theory and testing from Plato's (428 B.C.) perspective to those of psychologists of today.

The site is searchable in two ways: by the name of contributor or by the time period index representing different schools of thought. The biographical information and contributions of over 60 philosophers and psychologists who have made contributions to the field of intelligence and intelligence testing are featured on this site. The biography of each individual provides a wealth of information including major contributions to the field of intelligence, intellectual history, quotes, publications, and summaries of ideas and theories associated with intelligence.

The site is divided into six historical schools of thought regarding intelligence and intelligence testing, starting with the historical foundations of intelligence before 1690 and culminating with current efforts. A brief explanation of each school of thought provides an overview of the prevalent ideas regarding intelligence and intelligence testing at that time as well as a historical context for the individuals who contributed during that period.

Building Your Self-Portrait as an Educator

Interested in finding out your strengths with regard to Gardner's multiple intelligences? Your IQ? Your level of creativity? The Internet offers a variety of online tests you can take to give you an idea of how intelligence, cognitive and learning styles, and creativity can be assessed:

- One multiple intelligence survey, created by Walter McKenzie, is available at *http:// surfaquarium.com/ Mlinvent.htm*. The survey, as well as methods of scoring and interpreting the results are available from this site.

- Diana Bohmer created a series of questions that parents and teachers can ask themselves *(http:// familyeducation.com/ article/0%2C1120%2 C43201%2C00.html)* about the learning preferences of individual children to diagnose their strengths and weaknesses regarding multiple intelligences.

- An Index of Learning Styles Questionnaire, created by Barbara Soloman and Richard Felder of North Carolina State

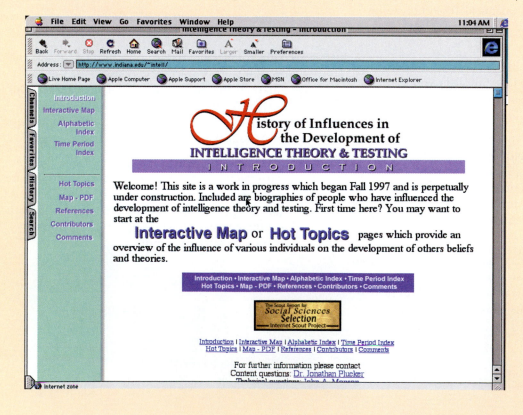

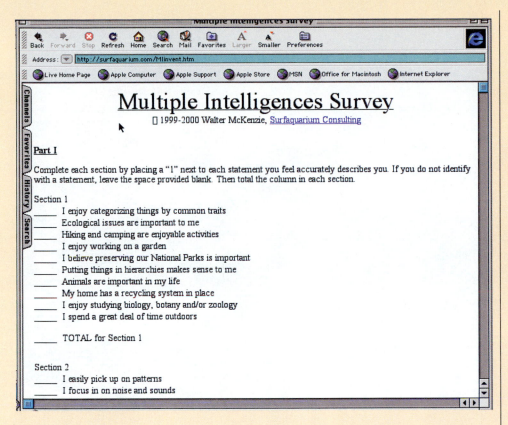

Multiple Intelligences Survey

☐ 1999-2000 Walter McKenzie, <u>Surfaquarium Consulting</u>

<u>Part I</u>

Complete each section by placing a "1" next to each statement you feel accurately describes you. If you do not identify with a statement, leave the space provided blank. Then total the column in each section.

Section 1

_____ I enjoy categorizing things by common traits
_____ Ecological issues are important to me
_____ Hiking and camping are enjoyable activities
_____ I enjoy working on a garden
_____ I believe preserving our National Parks is important
_____ Putting things in hierarchies makes sense to me
_____ Animals are important in my life
_____ My home has a recycling system in place
_____ I enjoy studying biology, botany and/or zoology
_____ I spend a great deal of time outdoors

_____ TOTAL for Section 1

Section 2

_____ I easily pick up on patterns
_____ I focus in on noise and sounds

University, contains 44 questions regarding learning preferences, automatically scores responses, and provides immediate feedback to the questionnaire. Also available at this site is an explanation by Soloman and Richard about different dimensions of learning styles and effective learning strategies for each dimension or type of learner. The site is located at *http://www2 .ncsu.edu/unity/lockers/ users/f/felder/public/ ILSdir/ilsweb.html.*

■ "The Creativity Test," available at *http:// www.personality.com/*

Tests/Create/index.html, is one of the few attempts at an online creativity test. This test asks a series of questions regarding preferences for work, and includes a personality index or questionnaire. It was most likely constructed by asking creative individuals how they worked or what they did when they were creating something.

■ Queendom.com has compiled a list of several online intelligence tests that individuals can take at *http://www.queendom .com/tests/iq/index .html.*

It is important to note that tests available on the Internet are, more often than not, quite different than those used by researchers, and the results of such tests cannot be taken seriously. For example, tests usually used for research purposes are carefully designed to ensure their reliability and validity (see Chapter 13). Therefore, one important word of caution is necessary when you take a test online: Most tests that are available on the Web have not been shown to be reliable or valid. However, taking these tests and reflecting on them may change how

you view them or provide you with a different perspective on individual differences.

Online Resources

One controversial topic in recent years that raises questions regarding individual differences and intelligence is the issue of emotional intelligence. While the validity of emotional intelligence is still debated by many psychologists, there are efforts to measure it and understand its role in learning. One emotional intelligence site that provides information, references, and suggestions for testing and research in this area is located at *http://trochim.human .cornell.edu/gallery/young/ emotion.htm* and is maintained by Cheri Young.

Individual Differences

EXCEPTIONAL CHILDREN

THE BIG PICTURE

To help you see the big picture, keep the following questions in mind as you read this chapter:

- Who are exceptional children, why do they have special needs, and why do teachers need to be aware of and responsive to these needs?

- What laws protect children with special needs, and how have these laws been implemented?

- How can children with special needs best be served in schools, and what kinds of resources are currently available to them?

- What is meant by a *gifted child*, and what are the means by which we can respond to the needs of gifted children?

- What is meant by *mental retardation?* What defines children as having mental retardation, and can we improve the school performance of these children?

- What does *learning disability* mean? How can teachers help children who have learning disabilities?

- What is *attention deficit hyperactivity disorder?* What are the problems that teachers are likely to encounter with such children in the classroom?

- What special knowledge is needed by teachers of children who have physical conditions and illnesses that require attention in the classroom?

◄ *Today, nearly every classroom includes at least one or two students with special needs. As specifically defined in this text, an exceptional child is a child who is unusual in one or more ways, and whose unusual characteristics—whether of giftedness or of disability—create special needs with respect to identification, instruction, or assessment. (Willl Hart)*

Karen Schultz watched as the students filed into her third-grade classroom. "This certainly wasn't what I expected during teacher training," she thought. Only a few years ago, Karen's view of teaching was that if she knew effective teaching techniques and the content of what she was supposed to cover—and if she enjoyed young people—she would have what it takes to become a good teacher. But the reality of her situation proved very different. Karen's class included many different types of children: one student who participated in the school's program for gifted children, one student with mild mental retardation, one with a hearing impairment, one student who had a reading disability, and another who had been diagnosed with attention deficit hyperactivity disorder (ADHD).

Instead of using straightforward teaching tips to present content, Karen found herself dealing with children whose abilities and needs required her to understand a lot more than how to teach typical students. She had to know how to challenge gifted students working alongside students with mental disabilities. She had to know how to help the child with a reading disability keep up with the increasing amount of reading children encounter in third grade, and she even hoped to help her overcome her disability. Karen had to know what to do when the student showing ADHD just could not sit still in class, and she had to help her student with a hearing impairment compensate for a physical challenge.

After a number of years of classroom experience, Karen had learned that succeeding as a teacher meant acquiring broad knowledge and skills. Karen also had realized that the psychological theories she had studied in her preparation as a teacher were now useful to her in dealing with her diverse students.

Exceptional children present you with many perplexing challenges, particularly if you are new to teaching. To develop into an expert teacher, you need to know the content and subject matter of the subjects you teach, plus techniques designed to help you communicate this material to your students. And, like Karen Schultz, you also need specific knowledge and techniques for dealing with the exceptional students you encounter. The goal of this chapter is to show you that exceptional students can become expert learners just as typical students can—and to show you how you can provide the help and support they need to actualize their potential.

Why Understanding Exceptional Children Is Important to Teachers

At one time most teachers did not need to be as aware as they must be today of how to meet the challenges of children with disabilities. Formerly, these children—whether diagnosed with mental retardation, learning disabilities, physical handicaps, or a variety of other conditions—were placed in so-called *special classes* (Detterman & Thompson, 1997). Today, special education teachers are not the only ones who work with exceptional children. A trend toward *full inclusion* of all children in the regular classroom has resulted in almost every teacher's becoming a teacher of children with special educational needs. The result is that all teachers need to know how to handle the challenges these children provide.

Every child is *exceptional* in multiple ways. Some children are exceptional athletes, others exceptional musicians or artists, others exceptional interpersonally, others exceptional in their appearance, and others exceptional because they seem so unexceptional that they are unusual in being so undistinctive! However, in this text, we define *excep-*

tional more specifically. An **exceptional child** is a child who is unusual in one or more ways, and whose unusual characteristic(s) create special needs with respect to identification, instruction, or assessment. In other words, exceptional children—whether with gifts or disabilities—are ones who for educational reasons, and sometimes for legal reasons, need to be identified and educated as such.

Unless exceptional children with disabilities receive appropriate instruction, they are in danger of failing to gain the skills they will need to succeed—not only in school, but in life in general. This group of **at-risk children** includes children with all of the exceptionalities described in this chapter, as well as other exceptionalities such as emotional and physical problems, and special forms of learning disabilities. They need special kinds of interventions inside or outside the classroom to help them reach their potential. And they may need special kinds of assessments (for example, in the case of individuals with visual handicaps or with hearing impairments) to allow them to show what they have learned.

In this chapter we provide an overview of the main types of exceptionalities that can affect the children you teach. First, we highlight the legal implications of working with exceptional children, along with strategies for teaching them effectively.

Teaching Exceptional Children

Special education refers to any program that provides distinctive services for children identified as having special needs. During the first half of the twentieth century, special education as we have come to know it hardly existed at all. Exceptional children received few or no services in the schools. Children with sufficiently severe problems to cause discomfort to those educating them were placed into institutions that varied greatly in quality and quantity of services provided.

By the late 1960s, critics argued that children with a variety of disabilities were being shut away in institutions that often did not provide adequately for them. These critics said the institutions often left children without the skills they would later need to become an integral part of society (e.g., Dunn, 1968). Clearly, change was needed. In the 1970s, the first of a series of major special education laws was enacted.

MAJOR LAWS AND LEGAL RIGHTS

In 1975 the U.S. Congress passed **Public Law 94-142,** "The Education for All Handicapped Children Act," which required states to provide "a free, appropriate public education for every child between the ages of three and twenty-one (unless state law does not provide free public education to children three to five or eighteen to twenty-one years of age) regardless of how, or how seriously he may be handicapped." Because schools were already educating most children, the impact of this law mostly concerned those in need of special education. The law meant that states could no longer hide from the issues of dealing with children having special needs, because the law applied to *all* children, regardless of how or how seriously the children might be challenged.

In 1986 **Public Law 99-457** extended these rights to all children ages 3 to 5, regardless of state laws, and added programs addressing the needs of infants with serious disabilities. In 1990 **Public Law 101-476** changed the name of Public Law 94-142 to the **Individuals with Disabilities Education Act,** or **IDEA,** and required that schools plan for the transition of adolescents with disabilities into either further education or employment at age 16.

IDEA also replaced the term *handicapped* with the term *disabled.* "Handicapped" as a label had acquired a stigma, and lawmakers apparently felt "disabled" would be less negatively stereotypic. However, in time the word *disabled* came to be seen as stigmatizing,

IDEA enabled children with disabilities to participate fully in the public school experience, including riding on a school bus. (Robin L. Sachs, PhotoEdit)

and many individuals formerly called disabled chose to term themselves "physically challenged" or "differently abled" or as "having a disability." But it is difficult to create a term that prevents people who are not members of the group previously termed handicapped from drawing negative and prejudicial conclusions about the capabilities of people in the group. No matter how tactfully chosen, a label can become a stereotype.

In your own work as a teacher—and particularly when you speak to your class—you need to underscore that people with disabilities, whatever we call these disabilities, are human beings. Expert teachers know that each of us has strengths and each of us has weaknesses, although some people's weaknesses are physically easier to observe. Individual children are just that—individuals—and should be described as individuals and treated as individuals, not as bearers of a label.

Collectively, special education laws have given children with disabilities and their parents a number of legal rights that they did not previously enjoy. For example, parents must be notified about all conferences and decisions regarding the child's placement, and may file a grievance against a school district if they believe the child's special educational needs have been improperly handled. In addition to expanded legal rights for students and parents, the special education laws include two other provisions that are particularly relevant for classroom teachers: *least restrictive placement* and *individualized educational programs.*

■**LEAST RESTRICTIVE PLACEMENT**   The first provision, **least restrictive placement,** means a child must be placed in a setting that is as normal as possible. Partly as a result of this provision, and partly as a result of evolving educational philosophies, exceptional students have increasingly been included in regular classrooms, such as Karen Schultz's class. This inclusion is accomplished in various ways. One method, known as **mainstreaming,** places exceptional students in regular classes as soon as they are able to meet fundamentally the same requirements as typical students (Friend & Bursuck, 1996). Students with more severe disabilities may be mainstreamed part of the time, and put in special classes for the rest of the time to provide services that cannot be provided in the regular classroom.

In another method, known as **full inclusion,** schools place students, even those with severe disabilities, into regular classes, making accommodations as necessary to enable the exceptional students to succeed. There are many politically and educationally based arguments both for and against full inclusion. Advocates of full inclusion argue that students with disabilities benefit because they learn how best to interact with their peers without disabilities and because their peers learn in turn how to interact with them (e.g., Stainback & Stainback, 1992). Opponents, however, argue that in severe cases, no one's interests are served: Students who have severe disabilities are never really able to interact well or be accepted by their peers without such disabilities; and the needs of other children are not met because so much attention must be devoted to those children with disabilities—often with the addition of extra personnel and special procedures in the classroom.

Sometimes education goes from one extreme to another, without trying to find a sensible and balanced middle ground. For example, until the 1970s, students with severe disabilities were routinely excluded from regular classes. Today, however, some experts argue that all students can be served in regular classrooms. A more balanced approach to inclusion of students with severe disabilities is to make decisions on a case-by-case basis, taking into account the needs of all students (including but not limited to the ones with disabilities in the classroom), the needs of the teacher in order to teach effectively, and the available resources in the school. Moreover, decisions need to be reviewed regularly, as what is the right decision at one point in time may not remain the right decision as a result of changing circumstances.

THINKING PRACTICALLY

Name one advantage and one disadvantage of full inclusion.

SUGGESTION: An advantage is that the student with special needs is less likely to receive a watered-down curriculum. A disadvantage is that other students may receive less attention.

IN EACH CHAPTER OF THE TEXT, WE INTRODUCE YOU TO A FEW SPECIFIC STRATEGIES—ANALYTICAL, CREATIVE, AND PRACTICAL—USED BY BOTH EXPERT TEACHERS AND EXPERT STUDENTS.

THE ANALYTICAL TEACHER: Because Aisha will have a student with mild retardation in her class next term, she is taking time now to plan how class assignments can be divided into small, manageable steps that will not exceed the student's attention span or frustration level.

THE CREATIVE TEACHER: Aisha develops a private "sign language" system so she can let a student with attention deficit hyperactivity disorder know when he needs to return to his seat or be more quiet, without disrupting the whole class to correct the student's behavior.

THE PRACTICAL TEACHER: Aisha assigns students to project groups based on an alphabetical rotation so every student gets the chance to be in a group with every other student, regardless of individual differences.

THE ANALYTICAL STUDENT: Because Ronald already knows the material his math classmates are learning, he develops a plan for working ahead, and asks his teacher if they can work together to implement the plan.

THE CREATIVE STUDENT: Josie's cerebral palsy affects her ability to speak clearly; thus she uses the computer to make animated thank-you notes for the peer aides who help her get around the school building every day.

THE PRACTICAL STUDENT: Because Wyeth knows his reading disability means he needs extra time for homework, he plans fewer after-school activities on days he has a lot of reading to do.

Even in schools that do not try to achieve full inclusion, many students with special needs are included in regular classes. The Flexible Expert: Teaching and Learning in Inclusive Classrooms shows how some expert teachers and students adjust to a classroom that includes students with a variety of abilities and disabilities.

■ **THE INDIVIDUALIZED EDUCATION PROGRAM (IEP)** The special education laws require that each student with special needs have an **individualized education program,** or **IEP,** which specifies the goals and objectives set to improve the student's level of achievement and how these goals and objectives will be achieved. The IEP is written by a team consisting minimally of the student's teacher or teachers, a qualified school psychologist or special education supervisor, the parent(s) or guardian(s), and, where possible, the individual student. Typically, school principals—and, where they are available, guidance counselors—also become involved. Karen Schultz, the teacher described at the beginning of the chapter, probably participates in planning the IEPs for her students with special needs. Figure 5.1 on page 160 includes an example of part of an IEP. The individualized education program must be updated annually and, as the figure shows, must state in writing all of the following:

- The student's current level of achievement.

- Annual goals and short-term measurable instructional objectives that will result in the attainment of these goals.

- Specific services to be provided to the student, including when the services will be initiated.

- A specification of how and how fully the student will participate in the regular instructional program of the school.

- A description of how long the special services will be needed.

- A statement of how progress toward objectives will be evaluated for those children age 16 and older, a description of needed services to provide a transition to either further education or work.

THINKING ANALYTICALLY

How might a school draw up a rational policy that protects the rights of all students, including both those with and those without exceptional needs?

SUGGESTION: A rational policy would recognize that inclusion is desirable up to the point that it encroaches on the needs of students other than the ones with the disability.

THINKING ANALYTICALLY

Why are IEPs a useful resource in guiding and evaluating the special education program for a child having exceptional needs?

SUGGESTION: The IEPs provide a clear set of procedures for educating the students so as to eliminate ambiguities as much as possible.

FIGURE **5.1** **Example of an Individualized Education Program**

Excerpt from an Individualized Education Program

IEP was developed for a 9-year-old girl. This section of the plan focuses on following the teacher's directions and on reading.

STUDENT: Amy North   AGE: 9   GRADE: 1   DATE: Oct. 17, 1995

---

1. UNIQUE CHARACTERISTICS OR NEEDS: NONCOMPLIANCE

PRESENT LEVELS OF PERFORMANCE

1. *Frequently noncompliant with teacher's instructions.*
   Complies with about 50% of teacher requests/commands.

2. SPECIAL EDUCATION, RELATED SERVICES, AND MODIFICATIONS

   Implemented immediately, strong reinforcement for compliance with teacher's instructions (Example "Sure I will" plan including precision requests and reinforcer menu for points earned for compliance, as described in The Tough Kid Book, *by Rhode, Jenson, and Reavis, 1992); within 3 weeks, training of parents by school psychologist to use precision requests and reinforcement at home.*

3. OBJECTIVES (INCLUDING PROCEDURES, CRITERIA, AND SCHEDULE)

   Within one month, will comply with teacher requests/commands 90% of the time; compliance monitored weekly by the teacher.

4. ANNUAL GOALS

   Will become compliant with teacher's requests/commands.

---

2. UNIQUE CHARACTERISTICS OR NEEDS: READING

   2a. *Very slow reading rate*

   2b. *Poor comprehension*

   2c. *Limited phonics skills*

   2d. *Limited sight-word vocabulary*

1. PRESENT LEVELS OF PERFORMANCE

   2a. *Reads stories of approximately 100 words of first-grade level at approximately 40 words per minute.*

   2b. *Seldom can recall factual information about stories immediately after reading them.*

   2c. *Consistently confuses vowel sounds, often misidentifies consonants, and does not blend sounds.*

   2d. *Has sight-word vocabulary of approximately 150 words.*

2. SPECIAL EDUCATION, RELATED SERVICES, AND MODIFICATIONS

   2a–2c. *Direct instruction 30 minutes daily in vowel discrimination, consonant identification, and sound blending: begin immediately, continue throughout schoolyear.*

   2a & 2d. *Sight word drill 10 minutes daily in addition to phonics instruction and daily practice; 10 minutes practice in using phonics and sight-word skills in reading story at her level; begin immediately, continue for schoolyear.*

3. OBJECTIVES (INCLUDING PROCEDURES, CRITERIA, AND SCHEDULE)

   2a. *Within 3 months, will read stories on her level at 60 words per minute with 2 or fewer errors per story; within six months, 80 words with 2 or fewer errors; performance monitored daily by teacher or aide.*

   2b. *Within 3 months will answer oral and written comprehension questions requiring recall of information from stories she has just read with 90% accuracy (e.g., Who is in the story? What happened? When? Why?) and be able to predict probable outcomes with 80% accuracy; performance monitored daily by teacher or aide.*

   2c. *Within 3 months, will increase sight-word vocabulary to 200 words, within 6 months to 250 words, assessed by flashcard presentation.*

4. ANNUAL GOALS

   2a–2c. *Will read fluently and with comprehension at beginning-second-grade level.*

Source: From figure 1–6 (p. 37) in *Exceptional Learners: Introduction to Special Education,* 7/e by Daniel P. Hallahan & James M. Kauffman. Copyright © 1995 by Allyn & Bacon. Reprinted by permission.

What types of special education services are available to exceptional children in U.S. schools? Schools typically provide a variety of special education services for those who need them. These services can be viewed as forming a hierarchy based on the amount of extra help or service provided. Services range from simple teaching consultations all the way to providing entirely special schools, and include the following:

- Special education teachers, trained in teaching students who have various kinds of learning challenges, often consult on a one-to-one basis with regular classroom teachers. They may suggest ideas to regular teachers who are working with students with mild disabilities or other learning problems.

- Many school districts provide resources that meet special needs, for students without as well as with disabilities. For example, mathematics or reading resource rooms are common across the United States. These resource rooms are staffed by resource teachers who specialize in teaching one subject matter area, such as math or reading, to a variety of children.

- Students with special needs may be assigned fixed times to work with teachers who are subject matter specialists, whether or not in special resource rooms, to help meet their special needs.

In a well-equipped resource room, a specialist for students with learning disabilities works on letter sounds with students. (Elizabeth Crews)

- Special education teachers or teachers who are subject matter specialists may join a regular teacher daily to teach a class in which some of the students have special needs and others do not. Special education and regular teachers may team teach, each leading part of the lessons, or a special education teacher may provide extra help to exceptional students while the regular classroom teacher leads lessons.

- Exceptional students may be placed in special education classes, taught by subject matter specialists or general special education teachers, for part of the day. In some cases, students may need to attend special education classes for all subjects. Some districts place special education classes in the same buildings as regular classes, and other districts use separate facilities.

Quantity and quality of services differ substantially across schools and school districts. Teachers who are seeking special services for one or more of their students should investigate the opportunities available in their own schools.

An observant teacher is always on the lookout for children with special needs. Referrals for diagnosis usually originate with teachers' recognition that the relatively poor performance of a student has no readily apparent explanation. In today's world—for legal, educational, and ethical reasons—teachers must be sensitive to the needs of all students, including those with exceptionalities that place them at risk for being underserved. How do you, as a teacher, initiate special services when you believe one or more of your students has needs that are currently not being met? Pullen and Kaufman (1987) have made several suggestions for such referrals, which are summarized in Figure 5.2.

Step 1.

Contact the student's parents or guardians. Discuss the student's problems with the parents before you refer.

Step 2.

Before making a referral, check all the student's school records.

Has the student ever:

- qualified for special services?
- been included in other special programs (for example, for disadvantaged children, or speech and language therapy)?
- scored far below average on standardized tests?
- been retained?

Do the records indicate:

- good progress in some areas, poor progress in others?
- a medical or physical problem?
- that the student is taking medication?

Step 3.

Talk to the student's other teachers and professional support personnel about your concern for the student.

- Have other teachers also had difficulty with the student?
- Have they found ways of dealing successfully with the student?

Document the strategies you have used in your class to meet the student's educational needs. Your documentation will be used as evidence that will be helpful to or required by the committee of professionals who will evaluate the student. Demonstrate your concern by keeping written records. Your notes should include items such as:

- exactly what you are concerned about
- why you are concerned about it
- dates, places, and times you have observed the problem
- precisely what you have done to try to resolve the problem
- who, if anyone, helped you devise the plans or strategies you have used
- evidence that the strategies have been successful or unsuccessful

Remember: Refer a student only if you can make a convincing case that the student may have a handicapping condition and probably cannot be served appropriately without special education. Referral for special education begins a time–consuming, costly, and stressful process that is potentially damaging to the student and has many legal ramifications.

Source: "Referring a Child for Special Services: An Example of a Procedure" from *What Should I Know About Special Education? Answers for Classroom Teachers* by P. L. Pullen and James M. Kauffman, Pro-Ed, 1986. Reprinted by permission of James M. Kauffman.

As Figure 5.2 shows, the first step is to contact the student's parent(s) or guardian(s). Parents may be able to provide information that can help the teacher meet the student's needs. Even if they cannot provide helpful information, parents must—for legal reasons—be notified of, and preferably involved in, all further steps in a referral. Next, make a thorough check of all the student's school records, looking for indications of previous problems and the results of any earlier testing of the student. Third, talk with other teachers who have worked with the child. Double-check your perceptions of the child and discuss ideas for working successfully with him or her. Finally, before making a referral, document the strategies you have used with the student. Not only is this a legal requirement, but it can be helpful to the team of professionals who will evaluate, and perhaps work further, with the child.

Who are children with special needs? What exactly should teachers be observing when they are trying to decide whether to refer a child for special services? Exceptional children may have unusually high levels of intellectual ability, or unusually low. They may also be confronted by any of a variety of learning challenges. We first examine children who function at the extremes of intellectual capacity: the gifted and the mentally disabled.

Extremes of Intellectual Functioning: Giftedness

A **gifted child** is one with exceptional abilities or talents (Callahan, 2000). Estimates of the number of gifted children in U.S. schools vary, but it is likely that about 3 to 5 percent of students are gifted (Mitchell & Erickson, 1980). Thus, if you are a high school teacher who teaches 100 students per day, 3 to 5 of your students are likely to qualify as gifted.

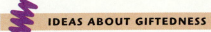

IDEAS ABOUT GIFTEDNESS

Some scholars differentiate among levels as well as kinds of giftedness. These differentiations can be made on the basis of level of intelligence, level of accomplishments, or kind of accomplishments. For example, Joseph Renzulli (1986, 1994) believes that traditional notions of giftedness deal with *schoolhouse giftedness,* unusually high performance in areas such as language skills and math, that are prized in traditional educational settings. Renzulli distinguishes between schoolhouse giftedness and *creative-productive giftedness,* the kind of giftedness observed in adults as well as children who actually produce works of art or literature, theater, scientific research, or other accomplishments that are valued in the world beyond the school (Renzulli & Reis, 2000). He argues that those who are schoolhouse gifted are not necessarily creative-productively gifted, and vice versa. Thus identifying children as gifted only in the schoolhouse manner may miss those children who could sooner or later make major creative contributions.

Other experts (Sternberg, 1993; Sternberg & Zhang, 1995; Tannenbaum, 1986) have pointed out how much sociocultural values shape our conceptions of giftedness: What one sociocultural group values as gifted, another may not. For example, whereas schools in the United States may value conventional intelligence tests and the kinds of abilities measured in them, other societies do not use these tests and may not value as highly the abilities they emphasize (Sorlano de Alencar, Blumen & Castellanos-Simon, 2000; Taylor & Kokot, 2000). One society may value the exceptional hunter; another, the person with exceptional physical strength. Even within our own society, work such as that by Lynn Okagaki and Robert Sternberg (1991, 1993), by Shirley Brice Heath (1983), and by Wade Boykin (1994; Serpell & Boykin, 1994) has shown how different sociocultural groups within U.S. society may have different ideas about giftedness (see also Chapter 6). Thus we need to be aware of how and how much our own cultural values may shape our notions of what giftedness is all about.

IDENTIFYING GIFTED STUDENTS

Many schools seek to identify gifted children, and in some states identification is mandated by the state department of education. The methods teachers and schools use to identify gifted students depend on the ways they conceptualize giftedness. Various conceptions of giftedness have been proposed.

One view suggests that intelligence, as it is traditionally measured, is the central attribute of giftedness (e.g., Gallagher & Courtright, 1986; Gallagher & Gallagher, 1994; Humphreys, 1986; Terman, 1925). Advocates of this viewpoint usually place considerable reliance on the results of conventional intelligence tests, believing that, although there are abilities other than those measured by such tests, the abilities measured by such tests are probably the most important (see Jensen, 1980). Schools that follow this line of reasoning use conventional tests of intelligence as their exclusive or primary ways to identify the gifted. Schools might, for example, identify as gifted those children in the top 1 or 2 percent on certain intelligence tests.

Such identification, however, is based on a fairly narrow view of what it means to be gifted (Tannenbaum, 2000). It also tends to identify what some educators view as a relatively high proportion of white middle-class students relative to members of other groups. In the early 1970s, a government commission headed by then U.S. Commissioner of Education Sidney Marland, Jr., proposed a broader view of giftedness (Marland, 1972). The **Marland Report** outlined six areas as worthy of consideration in identifying gifted children: (1) general intellectual ability, (2) specific academic aptitude, (3) creative or productive thinking, (4) leadership ability, (5) visual and performing arts, and (6) psychomotor ability. The report emphasized that children who are exceptional in one or more of these areas should be identified and provided with special services. Although the last category, psychomotor ability, was dropped soon after the report was published, the *Marland Report* became a guide used by many school districts as a basis for deciding what abilities to identify.

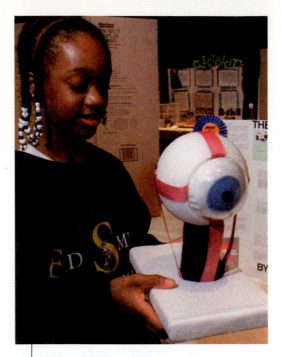

Demonstrating how the eye works and how people see, a gifted student displays a model of the human eye that she has made from household objects. If gifted children are given instruction that is tailored to their particular form of giftedness, they will often do even better than if they are merely identified as "gifted" and placed in a special program. (Gary Walts, The Image Works)

THINKING ANALYTICALLY

How would you conceptualize giftedness? What do you believe "gifted" means? Be as specific as possible.

SUGGESTION: Each student must answer for himself or herself.

Today, most schools use at least some other kind of assessment in addition to intelligence tests, such as school performance measured by grades or achievement test scores, teacher recommendations, tests of creativity, or signs of unusual motivation. Some schools are now using Howard Gardner's (1983, 1993, 1999) theory of multiple intelligences (see Chapter 4) as a basis for identifying the gifted. In this case gifted children are identified as those who show exceptionally high levels of linguistic, logical-mathematical, spatial, musical, bodily-kinesthetic, naturalist, interpersonal, or intrapersonal intelligence, or some combination of these intelligences. The triarchic theory (Sternberg, 1985, 1988b, 1997b, 1999) also has been used to identify analytically, creatively, and practically gifted students.

Another widely used conception of giftedness is based on the *three-ring model* of Joseph Renzulli (1977, 1986, 1994). According to Renzulli, giftedness occurs at the intersection of three attributes, as shown in Figure 5.3: (1) above-average ability, (2) creativity, and (3) task commitment. According to this model, a gifted individual has above-average, but not necessarily exceptional levels of traditional kinds of abilities, both general and specific. Renzulli (1986) believes that being in the top 15 to 20 percent of individuals is sufficient to satisfy this criterion. Beyond these abilities, however, a gifted person needs to show a fairly high level of creativity as well as task commitment or motivation to follow particular pursuits. One also might use a broader conception of abilities in implementing this model.

What do these guidelines mean to you as a teacher? How can you identify gifted children among the students you teach? What will these students be like? Pressley (1995) has reviewed a wide number of studies on how gifted children differ from their average counterparts in the classroom. He concluded that gifted children are experts in a number of respects: They have more and better learning strategies, metacognition (the ability to think about and organize one's own thinking and problem solving), knowledge about other people, and motivation to learn and excel. They process information more quickly and efficiently. Gifted students more readily transfer to new situations what they know how to do. They also have more and better insights during problem solving (Schneider, 2000). Perhaps most importantly, gifted students do not simply solve problems defined by others—they create new problems to solve and ask new types of questions. For example, a gifted student in a middle school biology class might go beyond learning about the way that water quality affects fish to explore the quality of water in the area of his or her own school, or even to look for ways to improve the water quality of local fish habitats.

Teachers can look for other signs of giftedness and talent as well—unusual accomplishments in writing, mathematics, music, art, athletics, dance, or other domains. Unusual creative or practical accomplishments of any kind are also signs of giftedness. One should not rely only on formal tests for the identification of gifted and talented students. Accomplishments may tell teachers as much or more.

These characteristics of gifted students may exhaust a teacher who struggles to keep up as the gifted student races ahead of the other students in the class. A variety of special education techniques have been developed to try to meet the needs of gifted children. In addition, we offer some ideas for working with gifted students in regular classes.

TEACHING GIFTED STUDENTS

Gifted students are not covered by the federal special education laws. That is, schools are not legally required to provide special education to help gifted students reach their potential. Nevertheless, many school districts do provide special education programs for the gifted. Several different types of programs for gifted and talented students have met with varying degrees of success.

Probably the most well known—and perhaps the most widely used technique—is the *pull-out program.* In this approach, gifted children are placed in a normal classroom but are taken out of the classroom at regular intervals for special instruction by a teacher, often one with special training in gifted education. For example, the gifted student in Karen Schultz's third-grade class might go to special classes for an hour or two on three days of the week. Such programs allow gifted children to have time to interact both with their regular classroom peers and with their gifted peers. However, the programs usually give gifted children very limited amounts of special instruction, and the children often have to make up the instruction they missed in their regular classroom while they were in special classes.

Another kind of program for the gifted is *acceleration,* which has been strongly advocated by Julian Stanley (1996; Stanley & Benbow, 1982, 1986a, 1986b). Here, students are given a normal course or program, but the presentation of material is speeded up. As a result, gifted children cover basically the same material that would be covered in a normal course, but in much less time. For example, a gifted student might cover both the third- and fourth-grade math curricula during the time span of a single academic year. A related idea is *curriculum compacting* (Renzulli, Smith, & Reis, 1982), which also involves teaching an essentially normal course, but deleting redundant material—what students already know. Compacting a math curriculum for a gifted third grader, for example, might involve pretesting the student to determine what he or she already knows, then assigning lessons that cover only those parts of the third-grade math curriculum the student has not already learned. Research shows that gifted students can learn a whole course worth of material in much less time simply by not being burdened with material that is merely review of what they have already learned. The time gained can then be used for acceleration or enrichment activities.

In the *enrichment* approach, children are taught a normal course, but activities are added to enhance the understanding and application of what they have learned. Enrichment is sometimes depicted as a contrasting, "either-or" alternative to acceleration programs. In truth, however, the two approaches are complementary and can be used at the same time. Renzulli (1986) has described three specific types of enrichment. *Type I enrichment* involves invitations to more advanced levels of involvement in a topic, and is thus designed to interest students in pursuing a topic further. *Type II enrichment* consists of activities designed to develop higher level thinking skills, as well as research skills, reference-using skills, and personal and social skills. *Type III enrichment* involves individual and small-group investigations of real problems drawing on what the students have learned. For example, students in a literature class are reading a book by Charles Dickens. Type I enrichment involves asking gifted students to read some of Dickens's other works. Type II enrichment includes assigning gifted students to find out more about the times in which Dickens lived. Type III enrichment involves a student, or group of students, investigating current social conditions in inner cities to see how they compare to those of nineteenth-century London. This type of enrichment enables students especially to apply their creative skills.

Renzulli advocates using the three types of enrichment in conjunction with what he refers to as a *revolving-door model* of identification and instruction (Renzulli, 1994), in which enrichment is provided to different students at different

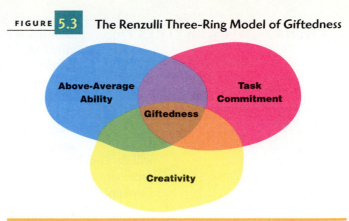

FIGURE 5.3 **The Renzulli Three-Ring Model of Giftedness**

Source: Fig. 3.1, p. 66 from "The Three-Ring Conception of Giftedness: A Developmental Model for Creative Productivity" by J. S. Renzulli in *Conceptions of Giftedness* ed. by R. J. Sternberg and J. E. Davidson. Copyright © 1996. Reprinted by permission of Cambridge University Press.

Steve Lu was ten years old when he enrolled at Cal Sate University. (Mingasson/Liaison)

If you were to design a gifted program for a school where you were teaching, what form would the program take?

SUGGESTION: Each student must answer for himself or herself.

times according to their particular strengths. In this model, rather than identifying just a single group as gifted, multiple groups are identified as gifted in different areas and are given opportunities as appropriate to develop the skills in which they have particular gifts.

Do gifted children actually benefit from special identification and assessment? The preponderance of research suggests that they do (see, e.g., Feldhusen & Jarwan, 2000; Fetterman, 1994; Horowitz & O'Brien, 1986; Sternberg & Davidson, 1986). There is even evidence that if gifted children are given instruction tailored to their particular form of giftedness, they will do even better than if they are merely identified as "gifted" and placed in a special program (Sternberg, 1994b; Sternberg & Clinkenbeard, 1995; Sternberg, Ferrari, Clinkenbeard, & Grigorenko, 1996).

CONSTRUCTING YOUR OWN LEARNING

You may not be an expert teacher of the gifted, but you already know enough to begin to evaluate programs for identifying and teaching the gifted. Try out your skills. Evaluate the program described in the following scenario as if you were a consultant to the school district. What you would change, if anything, about the way gifted students in this district are identified and taught?

A school district in a suburban town with a population of 35,000 has implemented a program in which all first-grade children are screened for giftedness. They are given an intelligence test comprising only pictures, because some of the children are not yet readers. The test is given to children in large groups. The children must follow directions, and make appropriate Xs on pages where the pictures have certain attributes. The district then selects for its gifted program children in the top 2 percent of the national sample that was administered the test. The cutoff is uniformly and strictly enforced to avoid complaints from parents of favoritism on the basis of less objective criteria.

The children thus selected become a part of the gifted program, which consists of a pull-out program once a week for two hours at a time. This program will continue until grade three, after which the district provides no special services for the gifted. The program consists of a variety of mind-challenging games, taken from books and other sources, that are intended to encourage the children to think. Children seem to like the program, and parents are happy to have their children in a gifted program. Because the program pulls out children only for limited amounts of time, there have been few complaints from teachers.

Implications for Teaching

- *Reward gifted students' motivation to learn more.* Allow gifted students freedom to go further than their classmates—to read extra books and write reports on them, to seek out additional sources, and to cover higher level work. Allowing gifted students to work ahead during review sessions reinforces their desire to learn and do more.

- *Help gifted students find problems to solve.* Suggest some ways gifted students could find more information by themselves and guide them to problems in their less developed as well as more developed areas of strength.

- *Keep gifted students challenged.* Try to help gifted students gain access to the most challenging activities and instruction available. Peers with the same or greater abilities may challenge the gifted students to perform even better. A network of gifted children's programs may provide help to a teacher who feels overwhelmed by her students' needs.

■ **Work with families of gifted students.** At times, you may encounter parents of gifted students who do not accept or reinforce their children's positive behaviors. In dealing with the parents of gifted children, expert teachers stress that the children need environmental reinforcement, support, and challenge if they are to develop to their potential. When family support is lacking, a teacher may ask the school guidance counselor to play a more active role in supporting a gifted student.

■ **Reinforce gifted students' self-esteem.** It might seem that gifted students would be the last to need bolstering of their self-esteem. But that is not the case. Expert teachers can support gifted students' self-esteem by helping them compare their current levels of achievement with their own past performance, rather than relying on comparisons to classmates, which can make gifted students feel conspicuously "brainy." Avoid making gifted students feel embarrassed about being different or allowing them to be teased because of their exceptionalities.

THINKING ANALYTICALLY

Why might gifted girls develop lower self-esteem than gifted boys? What steps could teachers take to improve the self-esteem of gifted girls?

SUGGESTION: Gifted girls may be more frequent targets of teasing and negative stereotypes. Teachers should give adequate recognition and praise to gifted girls.

Extremes of Intellectual Functioning: Mental Retardation

Mental retardation refers to low levels of mental competence in general (Detterman, Gabriel, & Ruthsatz, 2000). The American Association on Mental Retardation (AAMR) (1992) defines mental retardation as involving substantial limitations in present functioning. The definition includes three main components: (1) significantly below-average intellectual functioning; (2) low adaptive competence, as reflected by limitations in two or more of the following areas: communication, self-care, home living, social skills, community use, self-direction, health and safety, functional academics, leisure, and work; and (3) manifestation of these difficulties before the age of 18.

THINKING ANALYTICALLY

What are the advantages and disadvantages of labeling a child as having "mental retardation"?

SUGGESTION: One advantage is being able to identify who needs special services of a given kind. A disadvantage is possible stigmatization.

Including adaptive competence in this definition of mental retardation is essential. Children can show "schoolhouse retardation," with deficits in academic skills, and yet adapt quite well to everyday life (see, e.g., Campione, Brown, & Ferrara, 1982). Because of stigmatization, most schools are careful these days in applying the label *mental retardation,* and apply it only when practical competence as well as academic or IQ deficits are shown. As a teacher, bear in mind that doing well in school is only one part of functioning effectively in life. When evaluating a child whom you suspect may have mental retardation, be sure to consider the student's ability to get along in the world at large—not just the world inside your classroom (Luckasson, 1992).

In this section, we look at the causes and degrees of mental retardation. We also consider how students with retardation differ from their classmates.

CAUSES OF MENTAL RETARDATION

The causes of mental retardation are not all known. Those that are known can be divided into two groups: *familial* and *organic* (Hodapp & Zigler, 1999; Zigler, 1982, 1999). *Familial retardation,* as the name implies, tends to run in families. If one child in a family shows it, another child in that family is more likely to show it than a child selected at random. *Organic* cases are associated with traumatic events or abnormalities, and do not run in families (see also Hodapp, 1994). These include chromosomal disorders, such as Down syndrome; metabolic disorders; prenatal developmental abnormalities; prenatal exposure to toxins such as alcohol or cocaine consumed by the mother; brain diseases, birth trauma, or other birthing problems; and poisoning, malnutrition, or trauma during early childhood. Perhaps as many as half of all cases of mental retardation could be prevented if organic causes were eliminated (Campbell & Ramey, 1994; Hardman, Drew, & Egan, 1996; Smith & Luckasson, 1995). Poor living environments, whether caused by poverty, environmental toxins, poor nutrition, or other factors, can reduce performance beyond what it might otherwise be in a more adequate environment.

LEVELS OF MENTAL RETARDATION

Almost without regard to how it is defined, mental retardation is a matter of degree. There are different ways of determining a student's level of mental retardation. One widely used classification includes four levels of retardation—mild, moderate, severe, and profound—based on individual IQ scores. Individuals with different levels of mental retardation perform, on average, at very different levels.

Individuals with mild retardation have IQs in the 50 to 70 range (the average person's IQ is 100). These people represent 80 to 85 percent of those with retardation and roughly 2 percent of the general population. The vast majority of students with retardation who are mainstreamed fall into this category, and these are often the only students with retardation non–special education teachers are likely to have in their classes. For example, the student in Karen Schultz's class has a mild level of retardation. Given special educational assistance, these students may eventually master academic skills at or below the sixth-grade level. With suitable training and a supportive environment, these students can often acquire various vocation-related skills.

Individuals with moderate retardation have IQs in the 35 to 50 range; they represent 10 percent of persons with retardation and about 0.1 percent of the general population. These students require considerable educational assistance, and with it they may eventually master academic skills at the fourth-grade level. With highly structured environmental support and supervision, these people may be able to complete unskilled or, possibly, highly routinized, semiskilled vocational activities.

The remaining 5 percent of individuals with mental retardation suffer from severe or profound retardation; they have IQs below 35. People with severe retardation are unlikely to benefit from vocational training, and people with profound retardation are generally able to respond to training only for very limited tasks, such as walking or using

With structural environmental support and supervision, individuals with moderate retardation can often complete unskilled or highly routinized, semi-skilled vocational activities. This teenager with Down syndrome displays obvious joy at working in a local bakery. (Greenlar, The Image Works)

Level	Description	Example
Intermittent	Supports are provided on an "as needed basis." Characterized by episodic nature, the person not always needing the support(s), or short-term supports are needed during life-span transitions (such as job loss or an acute medical crisis). Intermittent supports may be high or low intensity when provided.	A student may need extra help coping with academic demands after a medical absence from school.
Limited	Characterized by consistency over time and how it is time limited but not of an intermittent nature. May require fewer staff members and less cost than more intense levels of support.	A student may need help making the transition from school to work.
Extensive	Supports characterized by regular involvement (perhaps daily) in at least some environments (such as work or home) and not time limited.	Long-term home living support or daily instruction from a special education teacher.
Pervasive	Supports characterized by their constancy, high intensity, and provision across environments. Potential life-sustaining nature. Pervasive supports typically involve more staff members and intrusiveness than do extensive or time-limited supports.	Full-time help needed for feeding, dressing, toileting, and other tasks of daily living.

Source: Table "Levels of Support for Persons with Mental Retardation" from *Mental Retardation:* Definition, Classification, and Systems of Support by AAMR Ad Hoc Committee on Terminology and Classification, 1992, Washington, DC: Copyright 1992 by AAMR.

a spoon. Most teachers will not encounter children with severe or profound retardation in their classes.

Note that an IQ of 70 is used in this classification (which is incomplete because it does not take adaptive skills into account) as the cutoff point to determine who has retardation. Expert teachers realize, however, that people with IQs from 70 to 85 are at greater risk for failure in school than average-intelligence individuals (Zetlin & Murtaugh, 1990). There are four times more people with IQs of 70 to 85 than with IQs below 70. Thus you will encounter these students with lower IQs, also sometimes called *slow learners* (Petrus, 1997), in your teaching, and you will likely encounter a fair number of them. Students with lower-than-average IQs (70 to 85) can be helped with many of the same teaching techniques that help children with mental retardation.

Other classifications have also been developed. Because, as we have seen, retardation is more than a matter of low IQ score alone, the AAMR has developed a classification based on the amount and types of *support,* or help from others, an individual needs to function. This system is summarized in Table 5.1. As the table shows, levels of support include *intermittent support,* provided only occasionally during times of stress; *limited support,* which is provided on a regular, but perhaps not daily, basis; *extensive support,* provided daily to allow the person to function at work, school, or home; and *pervasive support,* constant help in accomplishing basic tasks, such as eating and toileting.

CHARACTERIZATIONS OF MENTAL RETARDATION

How do students with mental retardation differ from average-IQ classmates? Researchers have proposed several ways of how best to characterize mental retardation. These theorists' ideas about mental retardation have, in some cases, also influenced training programs, designed to help children with mental retardation better develop their cognitive skills.

Zigler (1982, 1999) argued that individuals with familial retardation simply show slower mental growth than do individuals of normal intelligence. For example, Karen Schultz might find that her student is still working on the prereading skills the rest of the third-grade students learned in kindergarten or first grade. Zigler contrasted his theory of developmental delay with *difference theories:* Difference theories state that individuals with mental retardation are not merely slower in development than are other individuals but are different in some way.

Several different theories have been proposed. For example, one theory has suggested that individuals with mental retardation are more rigid in their thinking (Kounin, 1941); another, that they show deficits primarily in learning and memory (Ellis, 1963). Earl Butterfield and John Belmont (1977) have emphasized the importance of *executive functioning*. In this view, people with mental retardation have particular trouble in higher order processes such as planning, monitoring, and evaluating their cognitive strategies (Campione, Brown, & Ferrara, 1982). In the absence of instruction, individuals with mental retardation are less likely to develop a variety of strategies for use during learning and problem solving (Ellis, 1979; Pressley, 1995). For example, children with mental retardation do not spontaneously rehearse lists of words (say the words over and over to themselves) when they are asked to memorize them (Brown, Campione, Bray, & Wilcox, 1973). Even when such children are trained to memorize a given kind of list, they do not transfer that strategy to memorizing other kinds of lists (Butterfield, Wambold, & Belmont, 1973).

Another view, proposed by Robert Sternberg and Louise Spear (1985), is that children with mental retardation show deficits not only in executive processing, but also in coping with novelty and in adaptive competence in everyday life. For example, when a child with mental retardation is given a new toy to play with, he is not able to figure out what to do with it, and he also may not enjoy receiving a strange object.

Those who believe in the importance of executive processes have concentrated on training at this higher order cognitive level. For example, Ann Brown and Joseph Campione (1977, Campione & Brown, 1978) concentrated on teaching higher order executive processing strategies for learning, such as thoughtfully rehearsing what one has learned, as well as for monitoring and evaluating performance. John Belmont, Earl Butterfield, and John Borkowski (1978) took a similar approach. These programs have had at least some success in helping children with mental retardation perform better, although it has often been difficult to get the children to transfer what they learn from one domain to another.

Not all definitions of mental retardation view it as a trait, or permanent characteristic of a person. Reuven Feuerstein (1979, 1980) has viewed it as a *state*, or temporary status, and thus has referred to "retarded performers" rather than to "retarded people." He believes retardation is a result of lack of *mediated learning experience* (see Chapter 2) of the environment by parents for children; in other words, the children have not had the environment sufficiently interpreted for them as they have grown up. Thus Feuerstein's (1980) program of *Instrumental Enrichment* concentrates on mediation.

Implications for Teaching

■ *Teach learning strategies.* Students with mental retardation can be taught learning and problem-solving strategies successfully. Simple checklists that students help to create could serve as reminders of these strategies.

■ *Divide lessons into small, clearly defined steps.* With step-by-step guidelines and teacher support, students with mental retardation can improve the regulation of their use of strategies. For example, expert teachers encourage students to think of a goal, make a plan to attain it, try the plan, and ask themselves if the plan worked.

■ *Help students learn self-regulation.* Expert teachers teach students with mental retardation to self-regulate, monitor their progress, and correct themselves when necessary. Expert teachers strongly encourage their students to plan as much as possible.

- *Make lessons concrete and applicable to daily life.* Lessons that allow students to see the connection to concrete objects help. Pressley (1995) also has recommended using material that is functionally important to the daily lives of people with retardation to make instruction and learning "real" to them.

- *Help students raise their self-esteem.* Expert teachers repeat the message that "you can succeed, you are competent, and with effort you can overcome difficulties." In your teaching, help students with mental retardation to focus on effort more than on outcome, and reward them with praise and recognition for even small steps in the right direction. Bolster their low sense of self-esteem, and make them feel competent and in control of their own learning and performance.

Challenges to Learning

A variety of specific conditions can make learning difficult for students. These conditions include learning disabilities; attention deficit hyperactivity disorder; emotional and behavioral disorders and related problems such as autistic disorder; health disorders, including seizure and cerebral palsy; sensory impairments, such as vision and hearing difficulties; and communication disorders. Of these disorders, the ones involving language skills are typically the most common.

We describe these challenges next, from the most commonly encountered to the least. Then we suggest some ways in which teachers can help students who are trying to overcome learning challenges.

LEARNING DISABILITIES

Some children show generally high levels of performance at the same time that they show a deficit, sometimes a glaring one, in a specific aspect of their school performance. Recognition of this fact led educators as well as scientists and parents to seek a diagnostic label that would distinguish such children from children whose performance was depressed in all areas of academic and other kinds of functioning. The result was a new kind of classification, that of *learning disabilities,* which first we need to define.

■**DEFINING LEARNING DISABILITIES** **Learning disabilities** (LD) typically are diagnosed when performance in a specific subject matter is substantially worse than would be expected from a child's overall level of measured intelligence. Although these disorders typically first manifest themselves during childhood, they can and often do occur throughout the life span (National Joint Committee on Learning Disabilities, 1999).

Learning disabilities have also been defined as "a subset of instances in which individuals cannot master skills important in school success, such as reading, spelling, mathematics, communication, or social skills" (Forster, 1994, p. 647). For example, a child with an average IQ but notably poor reading skills might be identified as having a **reading disability.**

The definition of learning disabilities has proved to be problematic in a number of respects (Spear-Swerling & Sternberg, 1996; Sternberg & Grigorenko, 1999). First, many educators question whether the tests used to assess general intelligence really provide an adequate measure (e.g., Gardner, 1999; Sternberg, 1999). If they do not, the discrepancies between intelligence and performance calculated on the basis of these scores will be flawed.

FOCUS ON: WORKING WITH INCLUSION STUDENTS

CATHY DOWNEY, STECK ELEMENTARY SCHOOL, DENVER, CO—GRADES K-6, SPECIAL EDUCATION

Cathy Downey has been teaching for 15 years. She was certified as an Exceptional Needs Specialist by the National Board for Professional Teaching Standards in 1999, the first year special education certification was available.

What are some of the challenges faced by your students?

The children I teach now are all included in the regular classrooms. I teach children who have learning disabilities and mild cognitive disabilities. The children with learning disabilities that I teach all have average or above-average intelligence, but something is preventing them from learning. I work with them to find out what it is. I test to see if they might have a problem with auditory or visual processing, difficulty making sense, or perceiving, what they physically hear or see. I also test to see if they might show symptoms of ADHD. Maybe they can't learn because they can't attend in class. Since ADHD is a medical diagnosis, I always suggest to the parents of a student who might show some signs of it, that the child be evaluated by a doctor.

I have some children who have mild to moderate emotional or behavioral disorders. I have one student now who has Asperger's Syndrome, a kind of high-functioning autism. He is absolutely the most delightful child in the world! He is extremely intelligent, and I work with him on the social problems caused by his Asperger's.

Can you describe the identification and Individual Education Plan process?

The process starts when a student's classroom teacher becomes concerned about something. The teacher will come to me to ask advice. We put together a Peer Assistance Team, including me, the referring teacher, and one other teacher. Parents are always involved, too. We develop some strategies the classroom teacher can try. I work with him or her to implement these strategies for four to six weeks. If the child is still having problems, we begin a more formal identification process, including thorough testing. A school psychologist does cognitive testing, a social worker takes a social history of the child's home environment, a school nurse checks for physical problems. After that, we meet to determine the child's eligibility for special education services. If the child needs special education, all these people—and, often, the child himself or herself—work together on an IEP. Special education works much more efficiently if everyone has a well-defined role, so my IEPs tend to be very lengthy and detailed.

How do you go about working with children with special needs included in regular classrooms?

I'm very involved at all stages of working with the children in my school, from helping identify children who might need special education, to developing IEPs, to teaching on a day-to-day-basis. I work with students in their regular classroom. I also pull students out for as long as 30 minutes at a time for special lessons with me.

I do a lot of different things with the children, depending on their needs, but I work with all of them on motivation and self-esteem. Self-esteem is a huge part of learning. Some students have failed so often at learning that they just see themselves as failures and won't even try anymore. I start by finding the highest level at which each child has learned in a subject, such as reading. Then I give them each an assignment that will be really easy, something that moves them forward, but builds in success. Once they feel they can succeed, they are much more motivated, and we continue to move forward in small, sequential steps.

I use a lot of ways to keep students motivated. I help them develop their

---

THINKING ANALYTICALLY

Why is it important to distinguish specific learning disabilities from mental retardation?

SUGGESTION: The problems are different and the needed interventions are different as well. Mental retardation produces a much more pervasive deficit in performance.

Second, discrepancy scores do not seem to serve equally well at all points along a continuum of abilities, even if one does accept the intelligence test scores as valid. For example, the learning problems of students whose IQs put them in the gifted range but whose reading scores merely put them in the above-average range do not seem comparable to the problems of students whose IQs put them in the below-average range and whose reading scores are still poorer.

Third, differences in scores are plagued by statistical problems, such as low reliability, although an explanation of these problems goes beyond the scope of this book. The statistical problems make some educators question the usefulness of information provided by these test scores.

Finally, there is sometimes an overlap between the skills required for intelligence tests (e.g., vocabulary) and the skills required on tests of specific skills (e.g., reading, which can require high levels of vocabulary). Thus the two scores being compared (e.g., an IQ score and a reading score) may not have measured entirely different things.

own learning strategies, so they can feel ownership and involvement in learning. Sometimes we play games. On Fridays, we have literacy games like Sight-Word Bingo. If I have to, I use tangible rewards to help get students motivated.

How do you coordinate with the classroom teachers?

I work with a lot of really great teachers, and all of them are interested in the learning of all their children. I like to work *very* closely with the classroom teachers. I encourage informal consultations in the hallway at any time. Of course we work together on IEPs. I also coordinate my lessons so that what I'm doing with students reinforces what their classroom teacher is doing. I also develop strategies and lessons a student's classroom teacher can use. I always try to keep the whole class in mind and suggest things that the whole class could benefit from. I also work with students when they're in their regular classes.

What do you do when you work with students in their classrooms?

I work differently with the different teachers, depending on their needs. For example, one teacher here is in her first year. She is teaching a combined fifth and sixth grade, and seven of her sixth graders need special education. Since she has so many students who need extra help, I play a fairly large role when I'm in the room with this teacher. When she divides the class for reading groups, for example, I'll take one of the groups, the one with the special education kids. I've also taught the whole class a lesson on note-taking. This is a skill that students at this age need, and it was a big problem for my students. It turned out several students had difficulties learning to take notes, so I adapted my lesson for that whole class.

Other teachers have different needs. I also work with one highly experienced third-grade teacher whose class is very well organized and structured. My student with Asperger's is in her class, and the predictability makes it a great place for him. I don't need to play a big role. I go and sit with my student in this teacher's class, to work with him as she teaches. I also consult with the teacher on areas of his behavior that are puzzling or cause concern.

What advice would you give to new teachers?

Well, I love what I do. I think it's an under-recognized field and certainly under-staffed, so I always try to encourage teachers to consider special education. We joke that you don't go into special education for the glamour and the money, but it can be very rewarding. I get letters from children I taught who have now grown up and had children of their own, and are making their way in the world.

My advice to students who want to be regular classroom teachers would be to take special education electives in college. The numbers of students who need special education services are rising, and it will really help you to develop an awareness of children with special needs.

Classroom teachers should feel comfortable consulting a special education teacher when children have problems that concern them. Don't be afraid to ask the special education teacher. He or she may be able to develop interventions even for kids who are do not need special education. You just can't have too many people helping kids.

> Self-esteem is a huge part of learning. Some students have failed so often at learning that they just see themselves as failures and won't even try anymore.

■ **PROBLEMS WITH SPECIAL SERVICES** The exact criteria used to identify children as having a learning disability can differ substantially from one state or even community to another, substantially reducing evenhandedness in who is identified as having a disability. This issue becomes particularly problematical when parents view the "disability" as the only way to get special services for their children, whom they may view as needing but not receiving such services. Thus parents who can afford to may seek a diagnosis from a private diagnostician or actually may move from one school district to another in order to facilitate the child's receiving special services.

The special services themselves can create issues of equity (Kelman & Lester, 1997). Children identified as having disabilities may get special accommodations, such as substantial extra time for taking tests as well as a distraction-free special room in which to take these tests (see Forum: What Is the Best Way to Teach Students with Learning Disabilities?). But because other students also would benefit from such measures, society must decide how it can fairly allocate them.

An additional problem is that LD-related services are not the same for all students. In some districts, especially wealthy ones, the LD label may lead to substantial benefits. In other districts (and especially some impoverished ones that lack adequate funds), students labeled as having learning or other disabilities may be dumped into special classes featuring a watered-down, inadequate curriculum that causes these students to fall further behind.

Although all these problems are probably not insurmountable, they pose a serious challenge for society, school districts, and individuals. Until these problems are sufficiently resolved, society will not be able to provide an adequate education for all individuals.

■**MAKING SENSE OF READING DISABILITIES**   Reading disabilities are by far the most commonly recognized kind of learning disability (Sternberg & Spear-Swerling, 1999). Several different theories of reading disability have been proposed. One of the earliest views—that reading disability is due to deficits in visual perception (Orton, 1937)—is still widely believed, despite its having been thoroughly discredited (see Vellutino, 1978). A second view is that individuals with reading disabilities have difficulty in phonemic processing, that is, in being able to sound out letters and letter combinations (Liberman, Mann, Shankweiler, & Werfelman, 1981; Mann, 1991; Torgesen, 1999; Wagner & Garon, 1999). For example, a child with a reading disability might have difficulty sounding out the artificial word *gleak,* whereas a normal reader would not. The child with a reading disability might also have difficulty in answering the question of how *blanket* would be pronounced if the first consonant was removed.

Still another, third view, emphasizes problems in automatization (LaBerge & Samuels, 1974; Samuels, 1988, 1999; Sternberg & Wagner, 1982). Here, students with reading disabilities may have trouble making the skills of reading—which at first are applied consciously, deliberately, and rather slowly—become largely unconscious and rapid. According to this view, children with reading disabilities never get beyond the stage where reading is highly labored and in need of their full attention and effort.

A fourth view is that "reading disability" is a label that society has created in order to explain its own failure in teaching some children to read. According to this view, the problem is not in the individual, but in the society (Christensen, 1999; Skrtic, 1997). Some believe that reading level expectations may have risen too high. For example, a child who has not yet reached the expected reading level for her age group might be considered as having a reading disability, despite her steady reading progress.

A teacher helps an elementary school student with a learning handicap try to connect words with concepts and colors. (Elizabeth Crews)

Overall, evidence suggests that reading disability is not a single phenomenon, but rather one with multiple causes. For example, the reading disability of the student in Karen Schultz's class might stem from a very different cause than the reading disability of the child in another teacher's class. Reading disabilities can result from problems at very low levels of processing, as in recognition of visual cues and words, all the way up to problems at very high processing levels, as required for strategic reading (Spear-Swerling & Sternberg, 1994, 1996; Sternberg & Grigorenko, 1999). Both biological and environmental factors may play a role in the development of reading disabilities, and typically these two factors interact. Whatever the cause, children with reading disabilities are typically taught in the same manner as other poor readers, although there seems to an emphasis on training in phonics for many individuals with learning disabilities.

Although reading disability is by far the most common categorization among the specific learning disabilities, it is not the only one. Some children are identified as having mathematical disabilities. These students do well in many areas of functioning but have great difficulty in dealing with numbers and problems that require various types of mathematical thinking.

Other kinds of disabilities have also been suggested; however, there is substantially more disagreement regarding their nature and the specifics of their identification. For example, some diagnosticians believe in the existence of specific foreign language or reasoning disabilities, whereas others do not (Kelman & Lester, 1997). The issues regarding just what kinds of discrepancies should be regarded as genuine disabilities in learning or other processes still need to be resolved.

Some dispute focuses on whether education for students with learning disabilities should focus on *remediation,* or correcting the student's areas of weakness, or on *compensation,* helping the student find ways to work around his or her areas of disability. A combination of both approaches seems to make sense. Students who have difficulty forming letters when they write by hand, but who can think and compose papers clearly, can use a computer word processing program so they are not penalized unnecessarily for illegible handwriting. At the same time, of course, these students should practice their handwriting skills. The techniques described in Chapter 4 for helping all students focus on their learning strengths are especially important when teaching students with learning disabilities.

Sometimes the students' strengths lie outside the classroom. It may be hard to use excellent social skills or athletic abilities to compensate for a mathematical disability. Remember that labeling of children can be inconsistent and sometimes confusing, so pay attention to actual weaknesses in performance, not ones you might assume exist (perhaps falsely) on the basis of a label.

Federal laws, as described earlier in this chapter, apply to teaching students with learning disabilities. Teachers may need to work with a team to prepare an individualized learning program (IEP) for their students who have specific learning disabilities. In many cases, the laws have been interpreted to require that schools and teachers adapt assignments or teaching methods to accommodate the needs of students who have learning disabilities. As the Forum feature in this chapter points out, however, accommodations can have unintended results.

FORUM

WHAT IS THE BEST WAY TO TEACH STUDENTS WITH LEARNING DISABILITIES?

Students with learning disabilities are covered under IDEA and other federal and state special education laws. This means that federal funding is available for special education for these students. Instruction and assessment must also be adapted, if necessary, to accommodate the special needs of students with learning disabilities. However, adaptations may be bringing about their own problems.

FIRST VIEW: TOO MUCH HELP. *Some people assert that students with learning disabilities are getting too much help.* In fact, they claim, the accommodations made for students with learning disabilities are so attractive that parents have lied about their children's disability status in order to give them advantages, such as extra time on the standardized tests used by many colleges, law schools, and medical schools as part of their acceptance criteria (Borow, 1996). Although students who have trouble learning need extra training to surmount their difficulties, they must also face the challenge of obtaining the basic skills they need to get along in the world. Generous accommodations may help students gain better grades and test scores in the short run, but students are harmed in the long term if they finish their education without ever gaining the skills they will need to succeed outside of school.

SECOND VIEW: THE NEED FOR EXTRA HELP. *Supporters of special accommodations argue that adapted tests and lessons are needed to determine the true extent of students' abilities.* Students with learning disabilities may have mastered the material tested by the Scholastic Assessment Test (SAT), for example, and may be able to do well in college. However, they cannot demonstrate their mastery under ordinary testing conditions, which include the pressure of limited time and the possible distractions created by the presence of perhaps hundreds of other test takers. Rather than setting students up to fail, accommodations for their disabilities are allowing them to succeed. In addition, accommodations may be the only strategy to keep many students with learning disabilities in school. Repeated failure at lessons that have not been adapted to accommodate their disabilities puts such students at high risk for developing low self-esteem, low motivation for attending classes, and eventually dropping out of school (Hallahan, Kauffman, & Lloyd, 1995).

THIRD VIEW: A SYNTHESIS. *As in many other areas of education, the key to teaching students is flexibility.* Each student's individual needs must be thoroughly and regularly evaluated. Students who have a learning disability at one time may not need to receive extra help for the rest of their academic careers. They may learn to use cognitive and learning strategies well enough to overcome the disability, or they may develop strengths that let them compensate for any limitations caused by their specific disabilities. Sternberg (1997a) argues that accommodations in testing and instruction should be used to help students find their strengths and make the most of them. Teachers must communicate their high expectations to all students, including those with learning disabilities, and find ways to motivate them to work at the peak of their abilities.

Implications for Teaching

- *Learning disabilities are specific.* Expert teachers are conscious of the fact that students who have learning disabilities are usually of similar intelligence, overall, to typical students. They do not have mental retardation. In fact, even otherwise gifted students can have specific learning disabilities, and some schools have started special programs to teach these "twice-exceptional" children (Wright, 1997). Teaching strategies therefore need to be relevant to specific needs, such as helping certain children with reading disabilities improve their phonological awareness (understanding of mapping between written letters and their sounds).

- *Teach learning strategies, and encourage students to plan and monitor learning.* Students with learning disabilities are, like students with mental retardation, less likely to use helpful strategies during learning and problem solving. Expert teachers explain and stress the use of strategies to ensure that students who have learning disabilities understand and actually put the strategies into action. They remind students with learning disabilities to think about what they are doing, step by step, in advance if possible, and to focus on which path to the solution will be best for a given problem.

- *Foster self-esteem and provide motivation for learning.* Teachers need to improve the motivation of students with learning disabilities. These students tend to lack self-esteem and to consider themselves failures at school. Expert teachers know that they must help these students see success or failure not as inevitable outcomes of who the students are as people, but rather as results of the strategies, approaches, and amount of work the students invest. It is essential to stress and reward effort and improvement relative to one's past performances rather than to one's peers. A teacher's enthusiasm is especially vital for students with learning disabilities.

■ *Help students find their learning strengths and use those strengths to compensate for their weaknesses.* An expert teacher can call on these strengths when helping students work on their weaknesses. For example, mathematics can be used to compute batting averages or proportions of wins by a particular football team.

ATTENTION DEFICIT HYPERACTIVITY DISORDER (ADHD)

The term **attention deficit hyperactivity disorder (ADHD)** applies to children who show a significant problem with attention, impulsivity of behavior, and hyperactivity. In other words, these children have trouble focusing on important things, such as the teacher's words; often seem to act without thinking first; and show what is considered excess physical activity. As Karen Schultz has noticed, students with ADHD often cannot stay in their seats at school. They may constantly fidget or twist in their chairs, tap their fingers, or simply seem very restless. They also have trouble finishing what they start and may be disorganized.

Symptoms tend to wax and wane in intensity, and the exact symptoms may change with age. As with learning disabilities, researchers have recently found evidence that, in as many as two-thirds of the people who have it, ADHD can continue into adulthood (Khouzam, 1997). Signs of a significant problem are usually identified by age 7 or 8, sometimes much sooner. Teachers are often the first to notice signs of ADHD, because school requires more focused attention and self-control than many other situations. Academic and disciplinary problems in school are common. Signs of learning difficulties become more apparent and seem to worsen as the material to be learned becomes more complex (Ward, 1994). Students with ADHD may also experience social problems, since impulsive behavior can make it hard to form friendships.

Recent years have seen a large increase in the number of children diagnosed with ADHD. Current estimates indicate this disorder occurs in 6 to 9 percent of all school-age children, and 5 to 7 percent of the general population (Ward, 1994). Boys are about five to nine times as likely to be diagnosed with ADHD as girls. The disparity between boys and girls may be a result of boys being more likely to display the hyperactive and impulsive behaviors characterizing the disorder and girls being more likely to show inattentive behavior (Livingston, 1997). Expert teachers are aware of the gender differences in ADHD diagnoses, and they strive to evaluate fairly the behavior shown by all students.

Children with mild cases of ADHD are generally treated through a combination of counseling and special educational assistance. Moderate and severe cases are typically treated with a combination of behavioral intervention and stimulant drugs. The drugs administered to children with ADHD tend to result in decreased motor activity and increased attention (Rapoport et al., 1980). Among the most commonly used stimulants are Ritalin, followed by Dexedrine and Cylert (Ward, 1994). Stimulant drugs can have negative side effects, including increased heart rate and blood pressure, nausea, insomnia, and interference with growth and weight gain (Livingston, 1997). A number of writers and parents' groups have expressed concern that stimulant drugs are overprescribed and that other techniques should be emphasized in the treatment of ADHD (Livingston, 1997; Price, 1996; Smelter, Rasch, Fleming, Nazos, & Baranowski, 1996). Another problem is the illegal use of these drugs when they are obtained other than by a doctor's prescription.

Even the most expert teachers may find it challenging to teach students with ADHD. The following techniques may help (adapted from Hogan, 1997, and "How to Manage your Students with ADD/ADHD," 1997):

1. *Carefully structure the classroom environment.* Seat students with ADHD as far from distractions such as the door, windows, and pencil sharpener, as possible. It may help to seat a child with ADHD next to students who are good workers.

THINKING ANALYTICALLY

Have you encountered any children diagnosed with ADHD in your classes, either as a teacher or as a student? If so, how was their behavior distinctive from that of other students?

SUGGESTION: The children tend to have trouble paying attention and sitting still.

Children with ADHD sometimes have trouble staying organized. Elementary school teachers, such as Karen Schultz, can help by providing a clearly organized classroom, with materials and the places where they belong color coded or labeled. Help students set up their own organization systems as well.

2. *Structure activities.* Students with ADHD can become impatient if they do not know what is expected of them. Creating a daily routine helps students know what is coming next. In addition, teachers should state rules clearly, and even post visual reminders of expected behavior. Provide some sort of structured escape for students who easily tire of routine. Some teachers allow students to choose to stand in the back of the class, if standing helps them to pay better attention than when they are sitting. Such methods should be used only if they do not distract the other students.

3. *Help students focus attention.* Some teachers work with their students with ADHD to devise private signals that are used to bring attention back to the classroom. For example, a teacher might touch the student on the shoulder as he or she passes, to ensure the student stays focused on the teacher's words. Nonverbal cues, such as clapping hands or holding up an index finger before beginning to speak, help attract attention from all students. Clapping of hands should be used sparingly, however, or it loses its effect.

4. *Help students develop awareness of their behavior.* Checklists of steps for assignments; charts of target behaviors, whether good or bad; and clear feedback all help students become aware of what they are doing and whether their behavior is appropriate for the situation.

5. *Provide opportunities to use excess energy.* Elementary school teachers, such as Karen Schultz, might alternate highly physical activities with sedate lessons. Even in middle school and high school, teachers may want to allow some movement in classes. For example, science classes can be set up with exploration centers; literature classes can include occasional opportunities to dramatize the works that are studied.

Also keep in mind that inattentive or hyperactive behavior may be a signal of something other than ADHD, for example an emotional or behavioral disorder. Be aware that some students show attention deficit without hyperactivity (ADD).

 EMOTIONAL AND BEHAVIORAL DISORDERS

During your teaching career, you will probably encounter students who show symptoms of emotional and behavioral disorders. In this section, we define and discuss the kinds of disorders that teachers need to understand to help students succeed in school.

■**DEFINING AND CATEGORIZING BEHAVIORAL DISORDERS** Emotional and **behavioral disorders** are defined in the Individuals with Disabilities Education Act (IDEA), or Public Law 101-476, as problems, such as behavior inappropriate to the circumstances or pervasive unhappy moods, that adversely affect a child's education performance and cannot be explained by intellectual, sensory, or health factors. Several names are used interchangeably for emotional and behavior disorders, including *emotional disturbance* or *social maladjustment.* Many teachers and schools prefer to use the term *behavioral disorder* because it focuses attention on a student's behavioral problems, rather than his or her general character.

The IDEA definition of behavioral disorders leaves room for uncertainty. For example, "normal circumstances" for one student may be highly unusual circumstances for a different student. Another problem with this definition is that it is so vague it describes the behavior of nearly all students at one time or another (Bower, 1982). Generally, however, a behavioral disorder is diagnosed only when a student's behavior becomes a problem because it is unusually severe, displayed frequently, and chronic, or long lasting (Coleman, 1996). A teacher who believes a student may have a behavioral disorder should seek the help of a school psychologist or other professional to make a diagnosis. Teachers also need to realize that dull or overly restrictive environments can incite acting-out behavior in children whose behavior might be acceptable in a more interesting or less restrictive environment.

Differing definitions of emotional and behavioral disorders are probably the reason for the wide range of estimates of the number of children affected. The U.S. Department of Education (1994) has reported that about 1 percent of U.S. schoolchildren have a behavior disorder severe enough to require special education. Other estimates, however, range as high as 20 percent of all schoolchildren, with most experts suggesting the problem affects about 6 to 10 percent of students (Coleman, 1996). About three times as many boys as girls are diagnosed with behavioral disorders (U.S. Department of Education, 1994). The incidence of behavioral disorders also seems to be increasing.

Behavioral disorders can be divided into two main categories: *internalizing* and *externalizing* (Coleman, 1996). An *internalizing behavior disorder* is characterized by shyness, withdrawal, or depression. Students may be fearful and anxious, apathetic, sad, or overly self-conscious and self-criticizing. They may avoid group participation and may seem preoccupied and inattentive (Coleman, 1996). A teacher may not notice that a student has such a disorder, unless it disrupts the student's academic performance. For example, Lorraine seems merely shy to her teachers, when in fact, she dreads having to interact with others, whom she fears are going to criticize her. Teachers of students who have internalizing types of disorders may find it useful to include group projects as a natural and nonthreatening part of their lessons. Clarify rules for respectful treatment and inclusion of all group members before starting group projects. In addition, some children can be helped by lessons in specific social skills, such as joining groups, because their anxiety and timidity may have prevented them from picking up these skills earlier.

In contrast to those with internalizing disorders, a student who has an *externalizing* type of disorder is usually quite noticeable to teachers. Such students tend to demand teachers' attention because they are disruptive, disobey rules, and may be openly defiant of teachers. These students may engage in illegal or self-destructive behavior, such as lying, theft, or drug use. They may also be aggressive toward other students or destructive of school property (Coleman, 1996). One category of externalizing emotional disorder that has been clearly defined is **conduct disorder,** described as "a distinctive pattern of antisocial behavior that violates the rights of others" (Coleman, 1996). Students who have a conduct disorder are often aggressive and may get into physical fights with teachers and other students. They show little regard for rules, repeatedly disobeying instructions. Without intervention, they may go on to a life of crime (Brodkin & Coleman, 1996). Harry, for example, often does not show up for class, is a frequent troublemaker when he does show up, and constantly is picking fights with other students.

Most teachers will encounter students who show symptoms of emotional and behavioral disorders. Here, junior high students have a heated argument on a school playground. A teacher who believes a student may have a behavioral disorder should seek the help of a school psychologist or other professional to make a diagnosis. (Bob Daemmrich Photos, Inc.)

Students with externalizing disorders can be quite challenging for teachers. Teachers must take the time to structure the class to avoid the possibility of disruptive behavior. Seat students who are likely to act out where they can be easily seen by the teacher and are unlikely to hurt other students or themselves. Behavioral techniques, such as those explained in Chapter 7 (e.g., linking learning with positive emotions, shaping behavior, giving time-out), also may be helpful. Such tools as checklists of behavior, rewards for positive class behavior, and clearly stated penalties for negative behavior can help both student and teacher see progress.

■**MAKING SENSE OF AUTISTIC DISORDER**   One specific disorder often considered under the general category of behavior disorders is autism. **Autistic disorder,** also called *autism* or *Kanner's syndrome,* is a pervasive developmental disorder characterized by (1) marked lack of interest in other people accompanied by strong interest in the inanimate environment, (2) emotional distance and avoidance of eye contact, (3) failure in the development of peer relationships, (4) delayed or practically nonexistent development of language, (5) stereotyped, and often seemingly purposeless and repetitive movements, such as rocking of the body or flapping of the hands, (6) self-injurious behavior, and, often, (7) mental retardation, sometimes accompanied by isolated skills in which the autistic individual shows great talent (Kanner, 1943; Volkmar, 1996). Although not all children with autism have all the characteristics of the disorder, most have social and language impairments (Frith, 1993). Mel, for example, seems to live in a world of his own. He rarely interacts with others and has limited speech. He shows many repeated stereotyped movements that seem to have no instrumental value, and he is very concerned that objects be in their proper places. Nevertheless, he is a gifted watercolor artist.

Symptoms usually start to display themselves shortly after birth or at least within the first year of life, although many children are not diagnosed properly until past age 3. Autism has sometimes been confused with childhood schizophrenia but is distinct from it. The disorder is rare, occurring in about 2 out every 10,000 children, and is about four to five times more common in males than in females (Volkmar, 1996). There is no known cure for the disorder, and treatment usually consists of a combination of psychotherapy, especially behavior modification techniques, and special education.

THINKING ANALYTICALLY

How might having autism have predisposed Mel to develop his painting talents?

SUGGESTION: Mel concentrated heavily on developing this talent, often to the exclusion of many others.

Teachers who have children with autism in their classes might need to adapt assignments so these students can respond in nonverbal ways. Typically, only children with mild forms of autism are found in conventional classrooms, although there are exceptions. If a child with autism cannot interact with a group, a teacher may need to assign that student individual work in place of group assignments. Behavioral approaches to learning, covered in greater detail in Chapter 7, are often effective in helping children with autism learn appropriate social behavior and language skills, as well as helping them decrease inappropriate or self-injurious behavior (Lovaas, 1987).

HEALTH DISORDERS

Health disorders include physical conditions such as drug use and acquired immune deficiency syndrome (AIDS), which are discussed in Chapter 3; seizure disorders and cerebral palsy are discussed here. Some other relevant health disorders are:

1. *Diabetes mellitus,* a chronic disease caused by insufficient production of insulin by the body and resulting in abnormal metabolism.

2. *Spina bifida,* a congenital defect in which the spinal column is imperfectly closed and partly protrudes, and which can result in various neurological disorders.

3. *Muscular dystrophy,* any of a group of progressive and chronic muscle disorders caused by a genetic abnormality and resulting in gradual and irreversible wasting of skeletal muscles.

4. *Cystic fibrosis,* a genetically caused disease characterized by the production of abnormally dense mucus in the affected glands, and usually resulting in chronically impaired respiratory and pancreatic functioning.

5. Damage caused by parents' addictions to chemical substances, such as *fetal alcohol syndrome.*

There are many other health disorders, such as allergies, asthma, and various autoimmune disorders. Teachers need to be aware of all health disorders in students that may affect their adaptations to the classroom environment.

Teachers of children with physical exceptionalities should learn as much as they can about the children's conditions from parents and school medical personnel. Teachers need to know what to do in case a child has a health emergency. In addition, if a teacher is asked to administer medication or perform other necessary health care tasks, she or he must be thoroughly trained in the procedure. Teachers of children with physical conditions should be aware of the children's limitations; expert teachers keep their focus on each child's abilities so they can challenge children to perform to the best of their ability.

■**MAKING SENSE OF SEIZURE DISORDERS** Some of the most misunderstood physical conditions are seizure disorders. Teachers who are not informed of the causes and proper responses for seizures may be nervous or alarmed about teaching a child with a seizure disorder. With information and training, however, teachers can overcome any fears they may have.

Seizure disorders, collectively referred to as **epilepsy,** are characterized by abnormal discharges of electrical energy in parts of the brain (Hallahan & Kauffman, 1997). There are two main types of easily observable seizures, *generalized* (formerly called a *grand mal seizure*) and *partial* (formerly called a *petit mal seizure*), the former involving much of the brain and the latter involving only a small part of it. Partial, or petit mal, seizures are often unnoticeable, except to trained observers. In contrast, a generalized seizure is extremely noticeable.

A full-blown generalized seizure is typified by uncontrolled jerking movements that can last from two to five minutes, followed by deep sleep, or in rarer cases, coma. During the seizure, the child loses the normal state of consciousness, and may shake, jerk violently (which you will not be able to control), and appear very rigid. Upon waking, the individual may be confused or disoriented. If a child has such a seizure, you must take action, including the following steps (Hallahan & Kauffman, 1997; Heward & Orlansky, 1980):

■ Ease the child gently to the floor, away from furniture, other nearby objects that the child might strike, and walls.

■ Loosen the child's collar and any tight clothing.

■ Place something soft under the child's head.

■ Remove any hard or sharp objects nearby or on the child's person that might be sources of injury.

■ Gently turn the child's head to one side so saliva can be released.

■ Allow the child to rest upon regaining consciousness.

■ Call for medical help if the seizure lasts more than a few minutes or if there are multiple seizures in succession.

A third type of seizure, an *absence seizure,* is very brief, and may not even be observable. It also may appear as daydreaming followed by a period of disorientation and loss of memory for what happened during the time of the seizure. During such seizures, the individual may have a blank look and appear to stare. The child may not even be aware

A student with cerebral palsy is being helped by an infrared communication device. Teachers should always remember that, for such children, it is the body, not the mind, that is disadvantaged, and technology can help these students succeed. (Bob Daemmrich Photos, Inc.)

that the seizure occurred. Children who are prone to absence seizures may miss information presented during the time they are "absent." Teachers should double-check with these students to make sure they understand lessons and instructions, repeating information for them if necessary.

Seizures can be caused by various illnesses; hence, if they are unexpected, they must be brought to the attention of appropriate medical personnel. For example, they can be associated with hypoglycemia (reduction of blood glucose well below normal levels), which itself can be a complication of diabetes, especially if it is undiagnosed or not adequately treated.

When not subject to seizures, a child with epilepsy will show no particular signs of the condition. Seizures can be partially controlled through medication. Other children are not at risk—epilepsy is not contagious. Generalized seizures can be traumatic to see, however, especially in the case of young children, and can result in a child's being ostracized by her peers. An expert teacher knows that if a child with epilepsy is in class and likely to have seizures, it is better to confront the possibility in advance, both with that student and with other students so they will be informed and will not panic if a seizure occurs. The teacher may choose to discuss with students some of the reasons why seizures might scare them. The class can then plan ways to face seizures with courage and compassion.

Another frequently misunderstood physical condition is cerebral palsy.

■ **MAKING SENSE OF CEREBRAL PALSY** **Cerebral palsy** is a motor impairment caused by damage to the brain. Typically, the brain damage is a result of oxygen deprivation before, during, or shortly after birth. The child with cerebral palsy typically has difficulty in moving and coordinating the parts of the body and may have speech and hearing problems (Kirk, Gallagher, & Anastasiow, 1993). The impairment can but does not necessarily cause mental retardation. Teachers of children with cerebral palsy should keep this distinction in mind. Sometimes an excellent mind is caged in a dysfunctional body, and it can be freed with expert teaching.

Cerebral palsy is not progressive—although its symptoms may be progressive, it does not continuously get worse—nor is it contagious. The extent of the symptoms is highly variable, ranging from an almost undetectable lack of motor coordination, to severe difficulty in coordination, requiring use of a brace or a wheelchair, and in speaking. A variety of prosthetic devices and computer technology are available to help students who have severe movement and communication problems. Teachers should become familiar with the workings of any physical aids their students use, as they should in the case of devices that aid children who have sensory impairments, which we discuss next.

 SENSORY IMPAIRMENTS

Sensory impairments refer to difficulties in intake of information through the sensory systems of the body. These impairments are primarily visual and auditory—problems seeing and hearing.

■ **SEEING PROBLEMS** A **visual impairment** is a serious, uncorrectable problem of seeing. About 1 in 1000 U.S. children has a visual impairment. Children with such impairments can be helped by large-print books or by the use of special glasses, including, but not limited to, magnifying glasses. A smaller proportion, roughly 1 out every 2500 children, is educationally blind—that is, the child must make use of auditory and tactile (touch) sensory channels (as through *Braille,* a language for the blind that uses raised dots and is decoded through the sense of touch) in order to learn.

A variety of means are available to help students with visual impairments, including large-print and Braille books, books and lectures on audiotape, special calculators and typewriters, and special measurement devices. In gathering together and preparing materials for visually handicapped individuals, remember it is not only the size of the print that matters, but also the quality of print. Thus take special care with the quality of print in reproductions or other sources given to these children. Place children with visual impairments at the front of the room where they will best be able to see words on the blackboard or items shown from the front of the classroom. Lisa, for example, has a visual impairment. Despite her sitting in the first row of her fourth-grade classroom, she still has difficulty seeing what is written on the blackboard. For this reason, her teacher, Mrs. Robinson, is careful to write with large, dark, clear letters on the blackboard.

Be aware of signs of possible visual problems that may as yet be undiagnosed. Examples of such signs include (1) holding reading material very close to or very far from the eyes; (2) failing to pay attention when a chalkboard or other visual aid is used; (3) frequent questioning about things that have been presented via visual channels; (4) great sensitivity to glare; (5) physical problems with the eyes, such as swelling, redness, or crusting, or excessive rubbing of the eyes. If you suspect a visual problem, contact parents or school medical personnel to recommend the student receive a thorough vision examination.

■ **HEARING PROBLEMS** Hearing impairments are often correctable with a hearing aid, but such impairments can be corrected only if they are detected first. Moreover, some hearing impairments are not fully or even partially correctable, even through a hearing aid. Expert teachers are always on the lookout for children who indicate, in one way or another, that they are having hearing difficulties. Examples of ways children might indicate such difficulties are by their asking the teacher to repeat questions or statements, asking frequent questions about orally presented material and especially questions that were clearly answered, straining or frequently cocking their heads so as to improve their hearing, or asking the teacher to speak louder. Because children are often unaware of or hide hearing impairments, consider such impairments prior to inferring a nonexistent psychological problem.

When children with hearing impairments are in the classroom, several steps can be taken to help them. Seat a student with a hearing impairment in the front on the room, or on the side of a "good ear" if one ear hears better than the other; by facing the student(s) when speaking; and by speaking at the eye level of the students. Assist students with their hearing aids as necessary. For example, Luke's teacher, Mr. Shabazz, takes care to speak loudly, clearly, and slowly in class. Mr. Shabazz has discovered that such speech not only aids Luke, who has a hearing impairment, but also benefits the other students.

THINKING PRACTICALLY

Why are children with visual and hearing impairments at risk of false diagnoses for learning disabilities? What steps can be taken to prevent such false diagnoses?

SUGGESTION: Children with these impairments can be low achievers whose behavior resembles that of children with LDs or other psychological problems. Visual and hearing tests are essential to preventing misdiagnosis.

COMMUNICATION DISORDERS

Communication disorders are problems with speech in particular, or with language in general. Teachers are likely to encounter some common communication disorders, including stuttering, articulation disorders, and voicing problems.

Stuttering is characterized by repetitions, prolongations, or hesitations in articulation that disrupt the flow of speech. Stuttering typically appears around the ages of 3 or 4, and causes considerable embarrassment to the sufferer. It occurs in about 1 percent of students, and is four times more common in males than in females (Papalia & Wendkos-Olds, 1989). No one knows the exact cause. In roughly half of all cases, it spontaneously disappears during early adolescence (Wiig, 1982), but speech therapy is generally recommended as soon as possible to alleviate the problem as much as possible. Teachers of children who stutter must exercise patience, whenever possible allowing the child to finish his or her spoken thoughts without interruption.

Children with communication disorders may have trouble being fully accepted by their peers (Guralnick, Connor, Hammond, Gottman, & Kinnish, 1996). For example, Emil's tendency to stutter has led him to be an object of ridicule by some children in his class. To keep classmates from teasing students who stutter, expert teachers set clear rules, or lead class discussions on student differences and respectful treatment.

Articulation disorders involve substituting one sound for another, distorting sounds, adding sounds, or subtracting sounds. Most of these disorders disappear with age. Indeed, children are not typically able to pronounce fully all the sounds necessary for a normal conversation in English until they are 6 to 8 years old. Certain sounds, such as *l, r, sh,* and *th,* are particularly difficult. Children who grow up with a language other than English as their first language are at a special disadvantage, because the sounds of their language will be different from those in English. Adults who learn English as a second language are likely never to master the exact articulation of English, and thus will carry with them an accent that identifies them as native speakers of another language. Nonetheless, such adults can adapt successfully to the demands of life in the United States. Provide correct examples of articulation. Encourage students to try to pronounce sounds correctly, but remember that even those who never fully learn English articulation can do extremely well in society.

Voicing problems are characterized by hoarseness, inappropriate pitch, loudness, or intonation (as when someone speaks in a monotone) (Wiig, 1982). Often, children merely need to be made aware of such problems and with a little help from the teacher can correct them.

As we stated at the beginning of this chapter, all students are exceptional. Expert teachers become knowledgeable about the exceptionalities they are likely to encounter in their students and use this information to find ways to help each of their students achieve his or her potential.

THINKING PRACTICALLY

Speaking with poor articulation or in a monotone is not a problem limited to students. What can a teacher do to ensure that her speaking voice is both understandable to and engaging of students?

SUGGESTION: The teacher can tape her voice when teaching and then analyze it and invite others to do the same.

TEACHING EXCEPTIONAL CHILDREN

■ Exceptional children need special services in order to profit maximally from the educational experience provided by the schools. Special education refers to any program that provides special services for at-risk children.

■ Public laws require children with special needs access to least restrictive placement in an educational setting that is as normal as possible. Efforts to provide the least restrictive placement have included mainstreaming, or gradually placing special needs children into regular classes when they are able to meet mainstream requirements, and full inclusion, the placement of all children, even those with severe disabilities, in regular classes. Also in accordance with federal laws, individualized educational programs (or IEPs) are created and followed for each student with special needs.

EXTREMES OF INTELLECTUAL FUNCTIONING: GIFTEDNESS

■ Gifted children are those with exceptionally strong abilities or talents. Definitions of giftedness must take into account the context in which the child is being considered.

■ A high IQ in itself is not necessary or sufficient for identifying a child as gifted. The *Marland Report* distinguished six broad areas of ability that can be used to identify gifted children. The three-ring model of giftedness suggests that giftedness occurs at the intersection of ability, creativity, and task commitment.

■ A variety of educational alternatives, including pull-out programs, acceleration, curriculum compacting, and enrichment, as well as combinations of these approaches, such as a revolving-door model, have been used to teach gifted students. In addition, teachers should try to encourage and challenge gifted students regularly.

EXTREMES OF INTELLECTUAL FUNCTIONING: MENTAL RETARDATION

■ Teachers and other professionals must consider both academic and practical-competence aspects of performance before identifying a child as having mental retardation. Alternative conceptions of mental retardation include a developmental view and views that people with mental retardation are qualitatively different from people without it. Teachers can help students with mental retardation by teaching cognitive strategies directly, dividing lessons into steps, focusing on concrete and practical aspects of learning, and providing encouragement and support for self-esteem.

CHALLENGES TO LEARNING

■ Some children have specific learning disabilities. Most widely studied is reading disability, which may have multiple causes and manifestations. Although students with learning disabilities are not usually retarded, they can, like retarded students, often be helped by direct teaching of cognitive strategies.

■ Concern has been expressed about the growing number of children diagnosed with attention deficit hyperactivity disorder (ADHD), characterized by difficulties in paying attention, hyperactivity, and impulsive behavior. Treatment with stimulants, often combined with therapy, is common, and has provided another cause for concern. Teachers can help students with ADHD by structuring their classrooms and activities, and developing techniques to assist in focusing attention.

■ Emotional and behavioral disorders affect a growing number of children. Such disorders are marked either by internalizing behavior, such as shyness and anxiety, or externalizing behavior, including defiance and aggression. Pervasive developmental disorders, including autistic disorder, are rare but have severe symptoms.

■ Teachers are likely to encounter students with a variety of health disorders. Seizure disorders, also called epilepsy, and cerebral palsy are two of the more severe and most misunderstood. Teachers should learn all they can about any health disorders affecting their students and seek out proper training in case of emergencies.

■ Teachers also need to accommodate students with sensory impairments. Teachers need especially to be on the lookout for children with auditory and visual impairments. Such problems, when undiagnosed, can lead to poor performance in school that might be readily correctable.

■ Teachers can also help students with common communication disorders such as stuttering, problems of articulation, and problems of voicing.

■ **At-risk children** Exceptional children who are in danger of failing to gain the skills needed to succeed in school and in life in general. Page 157

■ **Attention deficit hyperactivity disorder (ADHD)** Disorder in which children have trouble paying attention, often seem to act without thinking first, and show what is considered excess physical activity. Page 177

■ **Autistic disorder** Also called *autism* or *Kanner's syndrome*. A form of pervasive developmental disorder involving severe social and language difficulties. Page 180

■ **Cerebral palsy** Motor impairment caused by damage to the brain. Page 182

■ **Communication disorders** Problems in language in general, or in speech, including stuttering, articulation disorders, and voicing problems. Page 183

■ **Conduct disorder** Type of behavioral disorder in which children display a pattern of disruptive, aggressive behavior that often violates the rights of others. Page 179

■ **Emotional and behavioral disorders** Group of disorders that cannot be explained by intellect, sensory, or health factors. May be marked by either internalizing symptoms, such as shyness and anxiety, or externalizing symptoms, including disobedience and aggression. Page 178

■ **Exceptional child** Child who is unusual in one or more ways, and whose unusual characteristic(s) creates special needs with respect to identification, instruction, or assessment. Page 157

■ **Full inclusion** Placement of all children, even those with severe disabilities, in regular classes. Page 158

■ **Gifted children** Children with exceptionally strong intellectual abilities or talents. Page 162

■ **Individualized educational program** (or **IEP**) Team-written educational plan updated annually to help a student with special needs attain certain specific goals. Page 159

■ **Learning disabilities** (or **LD**) Instances in which individuals perform more poorly in subject matter areas than would be expected, given average intelligence, or cannot master specific skills important in school success. Page 171

■ **Least restrictive placement** Legal requirement that every child must be taught in an educational setting that is as normal as possible. Page 158

■ **Mainstreaming** Placing special needs children into regular classes when they are able to meet the requirements of those classes. Page 158

■ **Marland Report** Government document issued in 1972 that distinguished six broad areas of ability that should be used to identify gifted children. Page 163

■ **Mental retardation** Overall low levels of mental competence, usually viewed as including low IQ and low adaptive competence. Page 167

■ **Public Law 94-142** Also known as the "Education for All Handicapped Children Act." A federal law passed in 1975 that requires states to provide a free, appropriate public education for every child between the ages of 3 and 21, regardless of how or how seriously the child is handicapped. Page 157

■ **Public Law 99-457** Federal law passed in 1986 that extended the age range covered by PL 94-142. Page 157

■ **Public Law 101-476** Also known as the **Individuals with Disabilities Education Act**, or **IDEA**. A federal law enacted in 1990 that expanded the requirements of Public Law 94-142 to include transition planning for adolescents with disabilities. Page 157

■ **Reading disability** Most commonly recognized kind of learning disability, characterized by reading performance that is substantially worse than would be expected from a child's overall level of measured intelligence. Page 171

■ **Seizure disorders** Collectively referred to as **epilepsy,** a condition in which abnormal discharges of electrical energy in parts of the brain cause seizures, ranging from convulsive to barely noticeable. Page 181

■ **Sensory impairments** Difficulties in intake of information through the sensory systems of the body, primarily visual and auditory. Page 182

■ **Special education** Any program that provides distinctive services for at-risk children. Page 157

■ **Visual impairment** Uncorrectable difficulties in seeing. Page 182

Apply the concepts you have learned in this chapter to the following problems of classroom practice.

IN ELEMENTARY SCHOOL

1. A student in your kindergarten class is already reading at the third-grade level. How would you go about determining whether this student should be included in your school's gifted and talented program? How will you keep the student challenged in kindergarten?

2. You have just caught one of your fourth-grade students brandishing a heavy stick on the playground. This student also frequently gets into fights and disrupts lessons in a variety of ingenious ways. What steps should you take to determine whether the student has a conduct disorder? How will you help the student control his or her behavior?

3. One of your second graders has been out of school with frequent ear infections. You have noticed the student, although normally quick and accurate with seatwork assignments, often has not started the assignment until you come around to check progress. The child also seems to be getting things wrong more frequently, almost as if he or she is not understanding the directions. What could be wrong? What can you do to help the student?

4. You have just learned that a student with mild retardation will be joining your fifth-grade class. How will you prepare your other students to accept this student?

5. How would you help a student with a hearing disability with the phonics work in second-grade reading lessons?

IN MIDDLE SCHOOL

1. How would you adapt a lesson on the U.S. government so it is meaningful and appropriate for a student with mild mental retardation in your social studies class?

2. What can you do to help a gifted seventh-grade student who is working on college-level math courses more advanced than any you ever took yourself?

3. What alternatives to a long term-paper project could you give to allow a student with a reading disability to demonstrate his or her mastery of the material taught in your English class?

4. One of your sixth-grade Spanish-class students is so timid he cannot bring himself to speak during pronunciation practices. As you review the student's records, you see that previous teachers have remarked on the student's shyness and withdrawal from social contact. You suspect the student may have an internalizing emotional disorder. What is your next step toward helping this student?

5. How could you adapt laboratory assignments so they could be performed by a seventh-grade science student who uses a wheelchair and has difficulty moving her hands?

IN HIGH SCHOOL

1. What would you do to help a student with ADHD, who is having problems sitting through your English literature class, be less disruptive to classmates?

2. What steps might you take to make sure a student with cerebral palsy could perform, or at least participate in, all the experiments you require for students in your advanced chemistry class?

3. As the math teacher for a student with mild retardation, you are part of the group working with the student's parents to prepare a transition-to-work plan. What math concepts do you consider vital for this student to learn, and how will you teach them?

4. What are some ways you could enrich your normal American government curriculum for a gifted student enrolled in the class?

5. One of your junior-level literature students has a reading disability and has asked to substitute books on audiotape for the required reading assignments. Should you allow this accommodation? Why or why not?

Connecting Theory and Research to Practice

The Council for Exceptional Children (CEC) *(http://www.cec.sped .org/index.html)* has created a very informative Web site for teachers, administrators, and parents regarding issues pertinent to the education of students who are exceptional, disabled, and gifted. While primarily an advocacy group for children with exceptionalities, this site also provides a wide variety of resources for classroom use including the online instructional magazine, *Teaching Exceptional Children.*

For example, do you wonder how you are going to handle discipline and management issues with a student in an inclusive classroom? Vera I. Daniels wrote and article for the March/April 2001 issue of *Teaching Exceptional Children* entitled, "How to Manage Disruptive Behavior in Inclusive Classrooms" *(http://www .cec.sped.org/bk/focus/ daniels.htm).* This article presents classroom teachers with 10 reflective questions about what may or may not contribute to disruptive behavior and also provides teachers with helpful tips on how to deal with this issue.

Building Your Self-Portrait as an Educator

Would you like to learn more about students with disabilities? Available at *http://curry.edschool .virginia.edu/go/specialed/* is the Office of Special Education: A Web Resource for Special Education. A wealth of information is available at this site, including links to sites providing information on different disabilities, resources for parents and teachers, and special reports about legislation regarding individuals with disabilities.

This site contains a directory of discussion list-servs, or e-mail discussion lists, for individuals who would like to exchange ideas and stories and to provide support to those who are teaching children with disabilities. Various discussion list-servs are available for teachers of children with autism, behavioral and emotional problems, deafness, or Down Syndrome. The directory of list-servs is available at *http://curry.edschool .virginia.edu/go/cise/ose/ resources/spedlists.html.* Also provided at this site is practical information about how to sign up for a list-serv.

Communities of Learners/Teachers

Sometimes students with a learning disability, physical disability, speech communication disorder, or a chronic illness fight feelings of social isolation and low self-esteem. One online community designed specifically for exceptional children is Ability OnLine *(www. ablelink.org/public/ default.htm).* This site was created in 1992 by the Ability OnLine Support Network, a nonprofit organization, as a simple online bulletin board.

Now, thanks to corporate sponsorship, Ability OnLine gives students with a wide range of exceptionalities a way to interact, generate, and maintain friendships in a safe, monitored environment. The goals of Ability OnLine are to promote respect for individual differences, to provide an opportunity for exceptional children to interact with others, and to build and support positive peer relationships.

In order to effectively educate students with exceptionalities, teachers and parents need to establish and nourish special relationships. One site devoted to providing information and resources to teachers and parents of children with exceptionalities is LD OnLine *(http://www.ldonline.org)*, which is a collaborative service project between The Learning Project and The Coordinated Campaign for Learning Disabilities. Available in multiple languages, this site offers teachers and parents a variety of resources regarding state and national legislation that affects the education of students with learning disabilities, information about valuable resources and programs, and a free e-mailed newsletter to keep members abreast of new developments concerning learning disabilities. One goal of the site is to promote collaboration and discussion among teachers and parents. For example, in the online article "Targeting Home-School Collaboration for Students with ADHD," authors Candace S. Bos, Maria L. Nahmias, and Magda A. Urban provide an action plan to help classroom teachers involve parents of children with ADHD in assessing appropriate behavior, monitoring medication, and helping with learning skills such as homework.

Online Resources

Students with Intellectual Disabilities: A Resource Guide for Teachers" is available at *www.bced.gov.bc.ca/specialed/sid/contents.htm* and includes tips for teachers, resources, case studies, and information for new teachers regarding intellectual disabilities.

Hood College, located in Frederick, Maryland, has a listing of resources for parents and teachers regarding learning disabilities and education. SERI, or Special Education Resources on the Internet, is available at *http://seriweb.com/*. Hundreds of resources are available and arranged logically (for easy searching) by topics, such as mental retardation, learning disabilities, inclusion resources, hearing impairment, behavioral disorders, and gifted and talented.

Group Differences

SOCIOECONOMIC STATUS, ETHNICITY, GENDER, AND LANGUAGE

THE BIG PICTURE

To help you see the big picture, keep the following questions in mind as you read this chapter:

- What are today's classrooms like compared to the classrooms of the past, and how are tomorrow's classrooms likely to compare with today's? What are the implications of these demographic trends for a developing teacher?

- How do differences in social class affect student performance and teacher responsibilities? How can teachers meet the needs of students from differing social classes when these students must be taught in the same groups?

- Why are ethnic and racial differences impor-tant for teachers to understand? How can we understand the challenges faced by students of different racial and ethnic groups?

- How do differences between the sexes affect classroom performance, student achievement, and learning patterns?

- How can teachers reach students who have a language barrier and help these students learn various subjects while the students are acquiring necessary language skills?

- How can teachers encourage students to overcome their reluc-tance, work together, and share projects and responsibilities with other students from dif-fering backgrounds?

◀ *The composition of American classrooms is becoming more and more heterogeneous. Today, expert teachers must understand the meaning of diversity and its implications for their daily teaching.* (Elizabeth Crews)

harlene Johnson had just moved to an urban area for the first time in her teaching career, and her class reminded her of a United Nations poster. Where Charlene used to teach, there were poor kids and well-off kids, but that was about it for diversity—everyone was white and from the same small town. But now it was a new story: Charlene's class of eleventh graders included African Americans, Asian Americans, Hispanics, and Caucasians; rich kids, poor kids, and the whole range in between; orthodox Jews, Catholics, Muslims, Buddhists, and Protestants. Charlene had never had experience with so many different types of people. However, she knew enough to ask the right questions, such as,

"What can I do when they start arguing among themselves and making jokes at one another's expense? How can I keep the peace and maintain high standards, but still show respect for their differences? How can I have fair and equal expectations of such dissimilar students?"

Within a few days, Charlene had learned something about how racial and ethnic differences in her classroom were important to consider in teaching and managing students. Students from similar backgrounds always sat together at lunch and during activities, and they would sometimes speak in their home languages, interacting only rarely with students from other backgrounds. Students from different backgrounds also had varying styles of interacting with

Charlene—she had to be aware of the expectations of the various groups of students in order to keep lines of communication open and to make sure she didn't offend anyone. Moreover, students of different backgrounds seemed to have different preferences for writing papers or doing projects or taking tests. Charlene noted that academic success was not equally important to students from different groups—or, if it was, the students did not show their dedication in comparable ways. Charlene wanted to be an effective teacher and reach all of her students. Her goal, then, was to learn to understand and teach all her students even though she shared so little background with so many of them.

harlene's situation is a common one today. The composition of classrooms is more heterogeneous now than when you began your schooling, and this trend will probably accelerate. Regardless of personal experiences and degree of exposure to people from different cultural, racial, and ethnic groups, each of us is more familiar with the values and norms of some cultures than we are with those of others. To be an expert teacher today, you must know what diversity means and understand its implications in your daily teaching. You must know how to solve the types of problems facing Charlene Johnson. This chapter will provide you with an overview of group differences so you can acquire some of the skills you will need to reach every one of your students and teach them effectively.

Why Understanding Group Differences Is Important to Teachers

Some teachers believe that all they have to do is teach well and their students will learn, regardless of the attributes of each specific student. These teachers may have been taught effective teaching techniques, and they may think a package of good teaching tools is all they need to succeed. Expert teachers, however, know that students differ—and they appreciate how some of these differences can affect how students learn. Each student has an identity that is a product of personal abilities and experiences, gender, social class, nationality, race, ethnic group, religion, and geographic region. Of course, within any racial, cultural, ethnic, or religious group, individuals vary widely on all sorts of characteristics. But there are *trends* that characterize the members of differ-

In the traditional Chinese classroom at the left, uniformed students sit quietly as they do a reading exercise, while in a typical U.S. classroom at the right, students enthusiastically raise their hands and often speak out all at the same time. (Paul Conklin, PhotoEdit; Mark Adams, FPG International)

ent groups, and these trends influence how much and how well students learn. Expert teachers appreciate group differences and know how to adjust their teaching styles to reach students of various groups. Charlene Johnson is striving for expertise.

For example, the home environments and cultural experiences of some Asian American students teach these students not to speak up quickly in groups, but rather, patiently to wait their turn. Interrupting is considered rude in their culture (Lee & Zane, 1998). But many urban middle-class children from other cultures in the United States grow up in an environment that encourages and rewards speaking up quickly and often loudly. In this environment, interrupting with enthusiasm is a sign that the listener is actively involved in the conversation. The forwardness of some of these children would be disturbing to an Asian American child of the same age. And the more controlled social-interaction style of some Asian American children might seem like a sign of detachment or lack of interest to children from other cultures. Indeed, teachers of Asian American children report that they often must provide clearer cues and opportunities to Asian American children (compared with other children) in order to encourage them to speak out in class.

Most of this textbook is concerned with providing you with the background, resources, and direct instructional techniques you need to build a generally effective teaching style. To teach, and reach, every student, you must understand the complex package of values, beliefs, cultural norms, expectations, and behaviors that each individual represents. This chapter, which focuses on group-related differences among students, prepares you to respond optimally to group-oriented differences that affect student learning and performance.

At the outset, let us review some relevant terms and their definitions.* **Culture** is the socially communicated behaviors, beliefs, values, knowledge, and other traits that characterize a particular time period or a particular class, community, or population of people. Cultures can differ within as well as between nations, and even can differ within communities. Another concept commonly talked about is *race*, but race is a culturally constructed concept, not a scientific one. **Ethnicity** refers to a distinct national, religious, linguistic, or cultural heritage shared by a sizable group of people. The term **minority group** originally was used to refer to a group that was smaller than the group

THINKING PRACTICALLY

What might happen to a typical U.S. student if he were transported to a typical classroom in a very different culture—say, for example, Japan or India?

SUGGESTION: A U.S. student might speak out too aggressively and too often in an Asian classroom, thus seeming undisciplined. He might behave in ways perceived as rude or inappropriate by teachers in other countries, although his behavior would be seen as normal in the United States.

*Dictionary entries adapted and reproduced from *The American Heritage Dictionary of the English Language*, Third Edition. Copyright © 1996 by Houghton Mifflin Company. Reprinted with permission.

What factors in the way children of different groups are raised might account for group differences among children?

SUGGESTION: The nature and extent of discipline used by parents—whether parents are very controlling versus very permissive, or highly critical versus encouraging and supportive—can contribute to group differences. Attitudes toward education—whether it is a primary focus of life or secondary to family life and family activities—can also be important. Exposure to books and higher education in the home might be a factor as well.

representing the dominant culture; now, however, the term often is used to refer to people from traditionally disadvantaged backgrounds. **Discrimination** is treatment or consideration—usually negative—based on perceived class or category rather than individual merit.

What will the composition of your classrooms be? How many ethnic and cultural groups are you likely to encounter? Consider the following facts about the changing composition of the U.S. population, and consequently, of the children who will populate your classrooms: By the year 2040, a majority of U.S. school students—51 percent—will be non-Caucasian. Today, about 33 percent of U.S. students are non-Caucasian (Hernandez, 1997). Thus the students now described as "minorities" will soon comprise the majority when aggregated and compared to the proportion of Caucasian students. In other words, in roughly 40 years, the combined proportion of African American, Asian American, Hispanic, and Native American students will outnumber Caucasian students. It is important to realize there is great diversity within each of these groups.

Socioeconomic Diversity

Socioeconomic status (SES) is usually defined by psychologists as a measure of a person's social class level based on income and educational level. The Hollingshead Index (Hollingshead & Redlich, 1958) was historically used by social scientists to give a score for a person's combined level of income and education. There is no single, set definition of socioeconomic status, however. Sociologists believe that in addition to how much money a person makes, another important factor in determining social class is the prestige of the person's job (Davis & Smith, 1994). In other words, two people who earn the same amount of money could have different socioeconomic statuses if their occupations differed in prestige. Hauser and Warren (1997) have developed an extensive socioeconomic status index for various occupations; these authors argue that the best measure of occupational SES is provided by calculating what percentage of the people in a given occupation have completed at least one year of college. We all have our own ideas about which occupations are more prestigious than others, and these ideas can be idiosyncratic. For example, it is common for teenagers to believe that rock stars have highly prestigious jobs, while their parents believe the opposite. The Nakao-Treas Prestige Scores (Hauser & Warren, 1997) provide one formal index of the prestige of various occupations (see Table 6.1 for an excerpt); Hauser and Warren provide a more complex table of occupational ratings that is beyond the scope of this text.

How could you develop a scientifically accurate measure of the prestige level of different jobs?

SUGGESTION: One method might involve asking large and diverse groups of people to rank the prestige of different jobs on a 1-to-100 scale; another method is to rank jobs on the basis of the average income earned by people employed in these jobs.

Most people believe that income and job prestige go hand-in-hand. Sometimes they do go hand-in-hand—with physicians and lawyers, for example—but other times they do not. Consider a professional gambler who regularly cleans up at the blackjack table. This person might have a high income, but would still have a job relatively low in prestige. The converse is also true: University professors are customarily thought to have high-prestige jobs, but their income is not extremely high (as the authors of this text can attest). And, of course, there are people whose income and job prestige level are both low, such as fast-food servers. Expert teachers know that, just as a book should not be judged by its cover, a student's SES should not be judged simply by the student's clothing and demeanor. Anyone who has been in a classroom lately knows that many students choose to dress in deliberately torn, baggy, and dirty clothes, all in the name of style, and much to their parents' dismay. The moral for the expert teacher is that determining a student's SES requires far more meaningful information than can be gathered by a glance.

TABLE 6.1	Samples of Occupations and Their Prestige Ratings				
Advertising	39.29	Insurance Salesperson	44.85	Registered Nurse	66.48
Air Traffic Controller	64.76	Janitor	22.33	Sales Worker, Apparel	30.22
Architect	73.15	Launderer	23.25	Sales Worker, Furniture	30.62
Author	63.05	Lawyer	74.77	Secretary	46.08
Auto Mechanic	39.64	Legal Assistant	56.53	Speech Therapist	60.76
Baker	34.86	Legislator	60.92	Tailor	42.48
Bank Teller	43.28	Librarian	54.42	Teacher, Biological Science	73.51
Bus Driver	32.07	Mail Carrier	47.04	Teacher, Chemistry	73.51
Cabinet Maker	43.81	News Vendor	19.38	Teacher, Elementary	64.08
Cashier	29.45	Nuclear Engineer	63.30	Teacher, Physics	73.51
Chief Executive Officer	70.45	Optometrist	67.16	Teacher, Postsecondary	73.51
Child Care Worker	29.25	Order Clerk	31.03	Teacher, Pre-kindergarten and Kindergarten	54.93
Computer Programmer	60.51	Painter, Sculptor	52.38	Teacher, Psychology	73.51
Construction	35.67	Pest Control	32.34	Teacher, Secondary	66.37
Dancer	53.49	Physician	86.05	Teacher, Special Education	65.06
Dentist	71.79	Police	59.99	Truck Driver	30.00
Farmer	40.39	Proofreader	43.14	Veterinarian	62.28
Firefighter	52.87	Psychologist	69.39	Waiter/waitress	28.08
Fisher	34.46	Real Estate Salesperson	48.82		
Hairdresser	36.08	Receptionist	39.02		

Source: Adapted from the Hauser-Warren Socioeconomic Index, 1997, Portraying 1989 Nakao-Treas Prestige Measures.

SES AND SCHOOL ACHIEVEMENT

Why are the concepts of socioeconomic status and social class important to you as a teacher? Isn't it your goal to teach every student equally, regardless of social class? Just as Charlene Johnson learned, meaningful differences in student achievement are related to SES. To teach effectively and to understand your students' needs, you must first understand the role social class plays in their educational experiences and performance.

■ PARENTS' INCOME AND CHILDREN'S SCHOLASTIC ASSESSMENT TEST *(SAT)* SCORES

The student from a low socioeconomic level presents an educational challenge. Consider the relationship between parents' income and their children's *Scholastic Assessment Test (SAT)* scores (see Figure 6.1 on page 196). The average *SAT* verbal and math scores for children of parents earning a combined income between $70,000 and $80,000 a year are 527 and 532, respectively, on a scale ranging from 200 to 800. The average verbal and math scores for children of parents earning between $30,000 and $40,000 a year are 495 and 497; those for parents earning under $10,000 a year are 427 and 446. Because *SAT* test scores are used to screen students for college admission, these scores are important in determining access to higher education. Students with lower *SATs* may not get equal access; consequently, they may earn less at their jobs because they lack the education to get better jobs. Education in and of itself results in higher earnings independently of a person's level of intelligence (see Figure 6.2 on page 197). Ultimately, when these low scorers become adults and have their own children, who are raised in lower income households, these children tend also to score low on the *SAT.* A cycle is created in which being of low SES is associated with low *SAT* and other standardized test scores, which in turn is associated with being of low SES, from one generation to the next.

FIGURE 6.1

Relationship Between *SAT* Scores
and Family Income, 1997–1998
Source: College Entrance
Examination Board

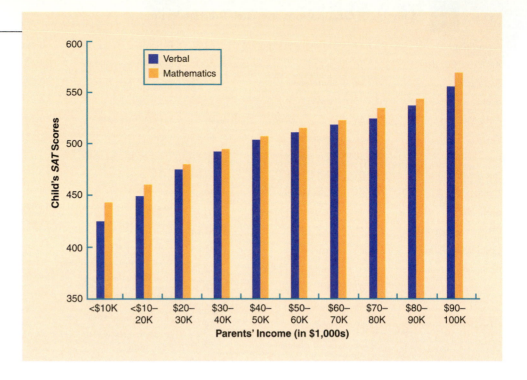

Various possible reasons for the relationship between *SAT*s and SES have been suggested. Lower income families often do not have access to the best schools and lack the funds for tutoring, out-of-school lessons, and summer camps. Also, lower income families may not possess as many computers, books, and other learning tools and games. Thus lower income children lack certain experiences that would help prepare them for standardized tests such as the *SAT*.

■ **WHAT DETERMINES CHILDREN'S SES?** Children's SES is partly determined by general societal trends in marriage, divorce, and single parenthood. Consider Figure 6.3 on page 198, which shows the trend toward more and more children being raised by one unmarried parent. In 1970 roughly 10 percent of children under 6 years of age were being raised by one unmarried parent (who was almost always divorced). By 1994 this number had risen to roughly 28 percent of children under 6, and these children were more likely than not being raised by a parent who was never married. A later study showed that by 1998, 27 percent of children under age 18 were living with a single parent, most often a mother, and 4 percent lived with neither parent. The implications for these children's educational attainment, and the resulting effects on their SES, are clear. Figure 6.4 on page 199 shows the percentage of children who graduate from high school as a function of whether they grew up with a never-married mother, a never-married father, a divorced parent, or two married parents. The figure shows the percentages separately for Hispanic, Black, and White children. Clearly, children perform differently in school—and have different high school graduation rates—depending on their home environments.

Although teachers cannot change the composition of a student's home environment, teachers can help students whose home environments do not provide all of the support and interaction they need. Extra help from a caring teacher can close the gap between what a student *does* accomplish and what a student *can* accomplish. This extra help can consist of daily words of praise and encouragement, extra feedback, meetings outside class time, and telephone calls to enlist parental support in meeting children's educational goals.

THINKING PRACTICALLY

How might an expert teacher help low-SES students score higher on the *SAT*?

SUGGESTION: Recommend extra preparation time, either in formal prep classes or by use of a preparation book to complete sample tests and exercises. Encourage students and bolster their belief that they have the ability to succeed on the test.

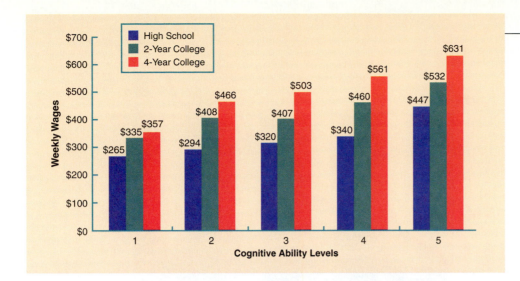

FIGURE 6.2

Wages by Levels of Schooling and Cognitive Ability
Source: From *The State of Americans: This Generation and the Next* by Urie Bronfenbrenner, Peter McClelland, Elaine Wetherington, Phyllis Moen, and Stephen J. Ceci. Copyright © 1996 by Urie Bronfenbrenner, Peter McClelland, Elaine Wetherington, Phyllis Moen, and Stephen J. Ceci. Reprinted by permission of The Free Press, a Division of Simon & Schuster, Inc.

The challenge for the expert teacher is to help the individual students she instructs to break the cycle of low SES leading to low education leading to low earnings leading to low SES. This textbook is filled with ideas about better teaching techniques that help students achieve to their optimal levels. If you use in your daily teaching what you have learned in this book (particularly in the Implications for Teaching sections), you can help your low-SES students escape the cycle of poverty and low achievement.

SES AND STUDENTS' DEVELOPMENT

Obviously, children grow up differently depending on the income and educational level of their parents and the prestige of their parents' jobs. For one thing, more income in the household may mean more resources: more books, better toys, enriched preschool programs, family trips and vacations, private music or athletic lessons, and so on. The resulting broader experiences provide developing children with opportunities for informal and formal learning outside the immediate school environment (Williams, 1998). When these children enter school, they often already know how to read and have a jump on their peers from less resource-rich environments.

But money in the household is not the whole story. When we look at a family's SES and draw conclusions about the children's likelihood of succeeding in school, we must remember to think critically about another key variable: family size. On average, today's families are smaller; there has been a general downward trend in number of children born per family for nonwelfare families. Today's families have fewer children, and fewer children overall means that each child has fewer siblings with whom she or he needs to share resources. Thus greater financial resources are available per child. Nonwelfare family income per child has increased (Ceci, 1996; Grissmer et al., 1994). Real income per family has not grown since 1971, but the dollars available to be spent on each child have increased. This trend toward families having more dollars per child is noteworthy, because even children who come from poor families will do better in school if they have fewer siblings and consequently have access to greater financial resources.

Expert teachers who learn that a student is from a large family, especially one from a lower SES level, are vigilant about recognizing cues that a student needs extra encouragement and support. These students may have parents who are working long hours and who are stretched thin among several children. Expert teachers help students compensate for resources lacking in the home by providing extra attention, additional academic challenges such as extra reading practice, and special feedback.

THINKING ANALYTICALLY

How many factors can you name to explain why having fewer children per family might influence how children grow up and how they do in school?

SUGGESTION: Fewer children can mean that more resources are available for each child: more parental attention, more time spent interacting with adults, and more money available for summer camp, enrichment experiences, music and art lessons, travel, vacation, and other opportunities.

FIGURE 6.3

Increase in Number of Children
Being Raised by One Unmarried
Parent
*Source: The State of Americans:
This Generation and the Next*
by Urie Bronfenbrenner, Peter
McClelland, Elaine Wetherington,
Phyllis Moen, and Stephen J. Ceci.
Copyright © 1996 by Urie Bron-
fenbrenner, Peter McClelland,
Elaine Wetherington, Phyllis Moen,
and Stephen J. Ceci. Reprinted by
permission of The Free Press, a
Division of Simon and Schuster, Inc.

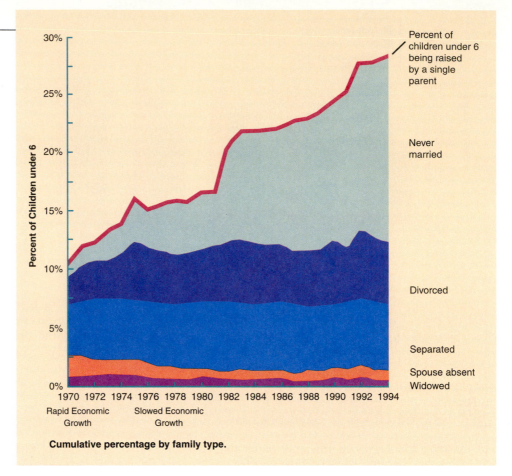

Cumulative percentage by family type.

SES, PARENTAL STYLE, AND EDUCATIONAL PERFORMANCE

A specific line of educational research has examined how parental attitudes and practices regarding child rearing affect children's success in school. This research has looked at parental attitudes that tend to be associated with social class level and with ethnic group. The purpose has been to determine whether systematic ways of parenting characterize different groups, and to learn whether, in turn, there are systematic differences in children's school achievement, depending on their parents' child-rearing attitudes and styles. This line of research has meaning for you as a developing teacher. To become an expert teacher, recognize your own style of interacting with students, and also the costs and benefits of this style for student achievement. You may even wish to modify your style to make it more effective in bringing about optimal student achievement.

Expert teachers are often aware from students' classroom behavior of the different types of parenting that students receive at home. Some parents' styles are more conducive to creating a child who benefits from school; other parents may discourage question asking and information seeking and may discipline children so harshly that the children respond by sitting still and keeping their mouths shut. Sensitivity to these potential home experiences helps teachers both to interact positively with students and to counteract negative influences in the home.

■ **PARENTAL STYLES** What do we know about the parenting styles of middle- versus lower-class parents today (Bronfenbrenner, 1985; Bronfenbrenner & Ceci, 1994; see also Hoffman & Youngblade, 1998 and Hughes & Perry-Jenkins, 1996)? Today's middle-class mothers tend to be more responsive to and less directive of their children than are lower class mothers. This pattern was reversed in the 1940s—back then, middle-class

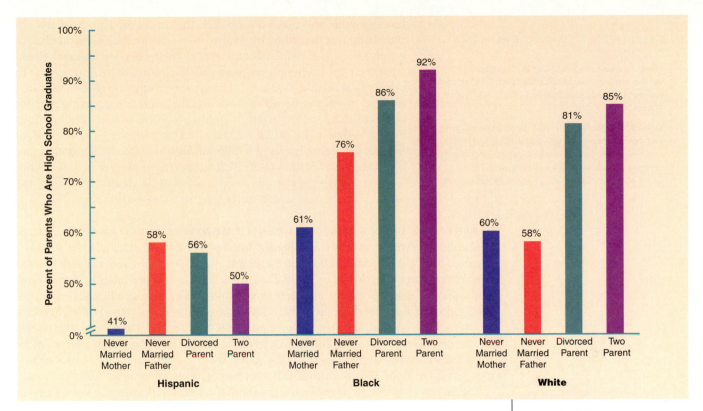

mothers were more rigid and controlling and lower class mothers were more permissive. Bronfenbrenner (1985) believes the literature on child rearing that first became popular in the 1960s and 1970s has changed the way middle-class mothers interact with their children, by making them more responsive and by encouraging them to let the child lead the way rather than by suggesting they try to control the child. Although a student's SES is not always a reliable indicator of the parental style in the student's home, there are tendencies among parents of a given social class and culture to treat children in certain ways. Expert teachers are attentive to these trends and their significance for the students' learning, development, and behavior in school.

As we discussed in Chapter 3, Diana Baumrind has developed a taxonomy to help researchers understand, describe, and study different parenting practices. Baumrind (1991) views parental behavior as fitting within three general types or patterns: *authoritarian, permissive,* and *authoritative.* Parents with an authoritarian style try to shape and control their children's behaviors, which they evaluate against a set of rigid standards. Authoritarian parents emphasize obedience, respect for authority, hard work, and traditional values, and discourage real communication in favor of the "listen and obey" mode. Baumrind (1971, 1973) saw authoritarian parents as being high in demandingness and low on responsiveness toward their children. The second parental style—the permissive style—refers to parents who give their children considerable freedom. Permissive parents have a tolerant and accepting attitude toward their children, rarely punish them, and make

FIGURE 6.4

Education Attained and Current Family Situation of Parents of Young Children
Source: From *The State of Americans: This Generation and the Next* by Urie Bronfenbrenner, Peter McClelland, Elaine Wetherington, Phyllis Moen, and Stephen J. Ceci. Copyright © 1996 by Urie Bronfenbrenner, Peter McClelland, Elaine Wetherington, Phyllis Moen, and Stephen J. Ceci. Reprinted by permission of The Free Press, a Division of Simon & Schuster, Inc.

Authoritative parents set clear standards and expect their children to meet them. However, they also encourage their children to develop independence and individuality and thus practice open communication in which they consider their children's points of view. Here, a mother does her best to listen to her son's version of their argument. The authoritarian-permissive-authoritative framework can also be used to describe teaching styles in the classroom. (Robert Brenner, PhotoEdit)

What style best describes your teaching approach (or the way you would naturally teach)? What could you do to modify your style to make it as effective as possible?

SUGGESTION: Are you basically a nondemanding and permissive person, or a demanding and critical one? As either, you can make a conscious choice to improve by behaving in a less extreme manner. Being open to student and peer feedback will help.

few demands and place few restrictions on them. The third style of parenting was described by Baumrind as authoritative. Authoritative parents set clear standards and expect their children to meet them, treat their children maturely, and use discipline where appropriate to ensure that rules are followed. These parents encourage their children to develop independence and individuality, and consequently practice open communication in which children's points of view and opinions are considered. In other words, children's rights as independent human beings are honored within the authoritative family system (see also Darling & Steinberg, 1993; Fletcher, Steinberg & Sellers, 1999). Teachers' styles in the classroom can also be described within the authoritarian–permissive–authoritative framework.

■**PARENTAL STYLES AND CHILDREN'S COGNITIVE PERFORMANCE** Baumrind conducted many studies exploring the interrelationship of parental style and children's cognitive and social competence. She began by studying preschool children to learn what effects parental style had on the children's intelligence and personality. Later, Baumrind and other researchers expanded their investigations to include middle and high school age children, children of different races and ethnic groups, and children of different socioeconomic backgrounds. In general, Baumrind (1989, 1991) found that parents who display an authoritative style of discipline and child rearing tend to raise children who are more cognitively competent. The lesson for the expert teacher is that an authoritative style is more effective in the classroom and leads to better learning outcomes.

Other researchers have investigated the mother–child relationship as a predictor of later IQ and language development in the child (Bee et al., 1982; Kelly, Morisset, Barnard, & Hammond, 1996; Landry, Smith, Swank, & Miller-Loncar, 2000). Helen Bee and her associates evaluated the effects on IQ and language development of two different sets of factors: infant physical status shortly after birth, early childhood performance, and family ecology (e.g., level of stress, social support, and maternal education), on the one hand, and various measures of mother–infant interaction, on the other hand. The authors found that the quality of mother–infant interaction was one of the best predictors at every age tested, and as good as actual child performance in predicting IQ and language development. Like mother–child interactions, teacher–student interactions can also be a significant force in the life of a developing child.

Another study evaluating the emotional quality of the mother–child relationship and its long-term consequences for children's cognitive performance found that the emotional quality of the mother–child relationship when the child was 4 years old was associated with mental ability at age 4, IQ at age 6, and school achievement at age 12 (Estrada, Arsenio, Hess, & Halloway, 1987). The associations remained significant even after the effects of mother's IQ, SES, and children's mental ability at age 4 were taken into account. The authors suggested that emotional relationships influence cognitive development through the parent's willingness to help children solve problems, through the development of children's social competence, and through the encouragement of children's exploratory tendencies.

One large study examined the relation of parenting style to adolescent school performance in a sample of 7836 high school students (Dornbusch et al., 1987). This study showed that both authoritarian and permissive styles were associated with lower grades, whereas *authoritative* parenting was associated with higher grades. The strongest effect on grades was in the negative direction for *authoritarian* parenting. Children of families with a purely authoritative style had the highest average grades, whereas children of families with mixed or inconsistent styles had the lowest grades. Again, expert teachers recognize the value of an authoritative style in helping students achieve in school.

A similar study investigating parenting practices and adolescent achievement focused on the impact of authoritative parenting, parental involvement in schooling, and parental encouragement to succeed on adolescent school achievement (Steinberg, Lamborn, Dornbusch, & Darling, 1992). The sample was ethnically and socioeconomically heterogeneous, involving 6400 American high school students. The authors found that authoritative parenting led to better school performance and stronger school engagement. They also found that parental involvement with schooling was a positive force in adolescents' lives when the parents had an authoritative style, but less so when the parents had other styles. It is not surprising that school involvement by demanding, rigid, critical parents does not have the positive impact of school involvement by parents who accept their children's interests and goals and assist them in achieving these goals!

What about the *processes* through which parental behavior affects a child's development? By watching 32 middle-class mothers preparing their 6- to 9-year-old children for a memory test, researchers found that the mothers guided the children in transferring relevant concepts from more familiar settings to the relatively novel laboratory task, thus assisting the children in mastering the task and in developing methods for completing similar future tasks (Rogoff, Ellis, & Gardner, 1984). These mothers acted like good teachers by helping their children borrow knowledge from one domain and apply it to another domain—something expert teachers do every day.

The main conclusion of these studies is that parental style tends to vary as a result of social class, and that parental style also predicts school achievement of children. As a teacher, you may find that children from lower social class families have been exposed to parental styles that are more authoritarian and directive (Bronfenbrenner, 1985). The consequences for these children's school performance may not be desirable. Children from higher SES families may have been exposed to parental styles that are more authoritative and more beneficial for school performance (Bronfenbrenner, 1985). Expert teachers know how to counteract some of the negative aspects of authoritarian parenting styles by allowing children more independence in the classroom so these children learn how to direct themselves instead of doing only exactly what they are told to do. For example, students who are tightly controlled at home and criticized by harsh or overly demanding parents can be given flexibility and freedom in choosing paper topics, reading materials, and activities. Teachers can make an extra effort not to react negatively to these students' mistakes, and to praise positive efforts in order to build students' self-worth.

SES, SELF-ESTEEM, AND ACHIEVEMENT

Many teachers believe that low-SES students also have low self-esteem. These teachers may think that if they can just help these students to think more of themselves and their abilities, their achievement will improve. Charlene Johnson thought often about how she might make her lowest SES students feel better about themselves, in the hope that this would help them do better in school. Although it is clearly worthwhile to help students develop positive self-images, surveys of low-achieving students have revealed that the self-esteem levels of these students are comparable to those of high-achieving students (Rosenberg, Schooler, & Schoenbach, 1989). In other words, a teacher cannot cure low achievement simply by raising students' self-esteem. Sometimes the *highest* achieving students have *more* self-doubts and *lower* self-esteem—they do not see themselves as being as good as they are (Kolligian & Sternberg, 1987). And, conversely, high school dropouts' self-esteem is just as high as that of high school graduates! Thus the data on self-esteem show that it is not the quick–fix route for enhancing achievement. Helping raise students' self-esteem may be a worthwhile goal, but real gains in achievement must be targeted, not merely gains in self-esteem.

THINKING CREATIVELY

How might you help a student whose parents have an authoritarian style to deal with her parents effectively and to develop positive relationships with adult mentors outside of the family?

SUGGESTION: Explain to her that her parents probably believe they are doing their best for her. Suggest that she obey her parents and behave respectfully to them while pointing out to them that she needs their support to do her best. Encourage her to seek out adults who are supportive and nurturing—perhaps meeting them through hobbies, religious organizations, after-school activities, or sports.

THINKING PRACTICALLY

Name three reasons why helping students to think more of themselves might not necessarily help the students to do better in school.

SUGGESTION: High self-esteem might make a student feel that he does not need to work and study hard to do well, because he is naturally brilliant. Students who think a lot of themselves might spend their time on activities other than studying. Students with high self-esteem might nevertheless lack basic study skills and knowledge of the material.

Within any single SES group, achievement is extremely variable. Many trends are associated with SES, and these trends have surfaced in study after study. But within each SES group are achievement stars and stragglers. When you look at any individual student's performance, you will find that often you could not have predicted it from the student's apparent SES level. Some lower class children come from homes in which education is stressed and achievement in school is prized, and these children can rank first in their classes. Also, upper class children who do not study or apply themselves and whose parents are completely uninvolved in their educational success can be among your worst performers.

This is the important message of this section: Never assume because students are from poor families that they are incapable of doing well. Students' SES is not their destiny. For any given person, it is what the person does, and not what the population as a whole tends to do, that matters. A large proportion of revolutionary ideas, medical discoveries, inventions, and other accomplishments that represent the best of our society's attainments have come from people from relatively modest or even poor backgrounds.

African American Mae Jemison, though from a modest family background, not only became a physician but also went on to be the first African American female astronaut. She was determined from childhood to explore space. She presently dedicates much of her time to encouraging women and minorities throughout the world to enter scientific fields. (Paul Howell, Liaison)

Implications for Teaching

- **Never judge a student's SES on the basis of superficial attributes such as clothing—work to develop a deeper understanding of each student's background.** Especially in today's society, affluent children may dress in torn clothes, and children living in poverty may dress neatly. Old standards for judging social class are no longer appropriate.

- **Recognize that lower-SES students must overcome greater obstacles to achieve equally to middle- and upper-SES students, and provide these lower-SES students with extra support and encouragement.** Teachers can help make up for the lack of advantages in the home by providing extra materials and direction regarding low-cost methods of enrichment (such as after-school programs).

- **Recognize that students from single-parent homes often have a parent who must work long hours and who cannot provide necessary support; provide extra scaffolding for these students.** When you assign work that a student needs a parent's help to complete, remember that you may unintentionally be disadvantaging some students, and offer alternatives to these students.

- **Work to develop an authoritative style to optimize interactions with students, especially students whose parents have authoritarian or permissive styles.** Offer these students project choices; encourage them and praise their work

- **Discourage a focus simply on "feeling good about ourselves"; instead, help students believe in their ability to accomplish meaningful tasks.** Stress accomplishments that reflect effort instead of self-esteem for its own sake.

- **Remember that SES is not destiny.** Great accomplishments have been achieved by people from low-SES backgrounds. Use examples of these people in your teaching to provide effective role models for students from lower SES backgrounds.

THINKING CREATIVELY

Why might people from humble backgrounds tend to develop unusual inventions or make discoveries? How might a poor background be helpful to an inventor?

SUGGESTION: Growing up and living without money may force a person to be creative by making or building things instead of buying them. Lacking money can make someone more resourceful and force the person to find alternate routes to goals. Poor people often come from backgrounds filled with numerous challenges that spurred them to become creative.

Ethnic and Socioeconomic Diversity

Unless you plan to teach in a remote rural region, you will likely be confronted by a diverse array of student backgrounds in your classrooms. Like Charlene Johnson, you may be amazed by the ethnic variety you find that first day of class. You will be expected to teach students of different cultural and ethnic groups right from the start. To teach these students effectively you must understand the significance of group differences to school achievement. Remember, though, that the trends in achievement patterns for different cultural and ethnic groups are just that—*trends*—and not labels that fit every individual. This said, there do appear to be significant and reliable differences among ethnic and other groups in academic performance and test scores. But what do these differences mean? What causes these differences?

We know that SES is associated with many variables affecting the lives of school-aged children. Socioeconomic status also is related to cultural and ethnic background—and it is difficult, if not impossible, to define exactly the effects on school achievement of being of a certain ethnic group and socioeconomic level. For example, proportionately more African American and Hispanic children live in poverty than do White children. Consequently, it is difficult to know if the lower scholastic achievement of African American and Hispanic children is due to a true difference between the two groups or to the economic conditions experienced by the children in the two groups. Although a few scientists believe that intrinsic differences in ability are related to ethnic group (e.g., Gordon, 1985; Gottfredson & Koper, 1997; Herrnstein & Murray, 1996; Jensen, 1997; Lynn, 1997; Rushton, 1997a, 1997b, 1997c), many other scientists believe the observed differences are more reflective of the lowered performance of children living in conditions of greater economic need and scarcity of other resources (e.g., Ceci, 1996; Gardner, 1995; Neisser, et al., 1996; Sowell, Bergwall, Zeigler, & Cartwright, 1990; Steele, 1997; Sternberg, 1995; Williams & Ceci, 1997).

> ### THINKING ANALYTICALLY
>
> How might living at or near the poverty level affect a child's scholastic performance?
>
> **SUGGESTION:** The child might lack a secure place to live, might not get adequate rest and nutrition, might not receive adequate parenting, might lack clothing, books, and other resources such as medical care. All of these factors can affect performance in school.

GROUP DIFFERENCES IN TEST SCORES

Let us examine some of the group differences in test scores and school performance by viewing these differences within a broad perspective that shows what has happened to these group differences in performance over the past 30 years or so. By tying our discussion of group differences to their changes over a relatively short period of time, you will see that these differences reflect numerous environmental factors. An argument that the performance gaps between the groups are intrinsic, biological, or genetic would not allow for dramatic changes in the patterns of differences over comparatively short periods (for example, 30 years)—genetic changes in groups take considerably longer to occur.

■**TRENDS IN TEST SCORES**   After a period of steady decline that began in the 1960s, American students' standardized test scores (based on National Assessment of Educational Progress results) have been headed upward for the past several years (Bronfenbrenner et al., 1996; Grissmer, Kirby, Berends, & Williamson, 1994; Neisser, 1998; Williams & Ceci, 1997). The biggest gains have been achieved by African American and Hispanic students; White students have remained at their 1970 level (Grissmer et al., 1994; Grissmer, Flanagan, & Williamson, 1998; Neisser, 1998). The 1970 gap in test scores between White and African American students was cut in half by 1988, although African American students still score lower than Whites do. But the gap was narrowed considerably between 1970 and 1988.

Why has the gap been closing? Reasons probably include the trend toward smaller family sizes and the greater resources per child made possible by smaller families; greater educational spending on minority and disadvantaged children; and increases in the educational levels of parents (Bronfenbrenner et al., 1996; Grissmer et al., 1994; Williams, 1998). Educational spending was up over 260 percent in inflation-controlled dollars during this time period (Grissmer et al., 1994), with increases in spending disproportionately targeted to educational programs serving minority youngsters (e.g., Title 1, Head Start, lunch programs). Many traditional "black schools" have been desegregated—a factor known to be associated with rising test scores for minority youngsters. African American parents' educational level and income increased over twice as fast as those of all other groups during the period from 1970 to 1990 (Bronfenbrenner et al., 1996).

THINKING ANALYTICALLY

Why is the education level of parents important to a child's school performance?

SUGGESTION: Better educated parents tend to encourage education in their children, discuss topics relevant to education, have better vocabularies and education-related values, have higher incomes and access to better schools, and have the ability to afford camps and special tutors.

FIGURE 6.5

School Attendance Rates of Members of Different Ethnic Groups
Source: Table "School Attendance Rates of Members of Different Racial Groups" from *An American Imperative: Accelerating Minority Educational Achievement* by S.L. Miller. Copyright © 1995 by S.L. Miller. Reprinted by permission of Yale University Press.

Parental educational attainment, which is linked to children's educational attainment, increased markedly between 1970 and 1990. The rate of college completion of African American parents increased far faster than that of White or Hispanic parents during this period—about 200 percent for African Americans versus 100 percent for Whites and 25 percent for Hispanics. The rates for mothers attending some college during this period increased 350 percent for African Americans versus 98 percent for White mothers and 95 percent for Hispanic mothers (Bronfenbrenner et al., 1996; Grissmer et al., 1994; Hernandez, 1997). In sum, the educational attainment of nonminority parents increased by 70 percent, and that of minority parents increased by 350 percent, from 1971 to 1990 (Grissmer et al., 1994). In 1920, 18 percent of mothers and 16 percent of fathers had an educational level of four years of high school or more. In 1983, 81 percent of mothers and 86 percent of fathers had an educational level of four years of high school or more (Hernandez, 1993). This upward trend is linear; the increase is enormous by any standard. This trend leveled out around the early 1970s. These trends mean that today's teachers have students whose parents are better educated than were parents of a generation or two ago. The trend toward more education provides testimony to the increasingly important role of teachers in people's lives. More people attaining higher levels of education means that teachers' ability to impact society continues to grow.

■**TRENDS IN EDUCATIONAL ATTAINMENT** During the past 30 years, all racial groups have made progress in terms of educational attainment: Consider the data in Figure 6.5 (Miller, 1995). These figures show that despite enormous gains for minorities

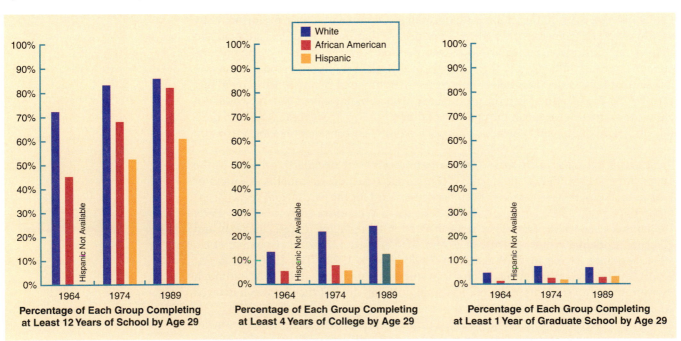

during the past 30 years, there are still large gaps in educational attainment. In some ways the most severe attainment gap difficulty is experienced by Hispanics/Latinos. Unlike the African American–White gap, which is now centered on college completion rates, the Hispanic–African American gap is evident even in high school graduation rates (Miller, 1995). Teachers of Hispanic/Latino students should therefore work extra hard to stress the value of completing high school.

■**TRENDS IN EDUCATIONAL PERFORMANCE** Beginning in the late 1960s, under the aegis of the Department of Education, the Educational Testing Service (ETS) undertook an assessment of educational progress of 9-, 13-, and 17-year-olds' math, reading, writing, and science achievement. This large-scale project, which continues today, is known as the National Assessment of Educational Progress (NAEP). If we look at NAEP scores for reading, we can divide them into five levels. Starting from the most rudimentary, these levels are

■ scores below 150—"can carry out simple, discrete reading tasks"

■ 150–199—"can comprehend specific or sequentially related information"

■ 200–249—"can search for specific information, interrelate ideas, and make generalizations"

■ 250–299—"can find, summarize, and explain relatively complicated information"

■ 300–500—"can synthesize and learn from specialized reading materials."
Figure 6.6 displays some NAEP scores by ethnicity.

Note the percentage of 9-year-olds in each ethnic group who score at each of the five levels described above: 94 percent of Whites surpass 150 (rudimentary reading skills); only 77 percent of African Americans and 84 percent of Hispanics do. At the other extreme, only 2.2 percent of Whites reach level 5 (called "Advanced readers" by NAEP), whereas

THINKING **ANALYTICALLY**

Why are the scholastic educational gains of minorities important from the point of view of teachers and school administrators?

SUGGESTION: These gains show that our society can successfully increase the education level of minorities through various methods; also, these education gains mean minorities get better jobs, have higher incomes, and do better in school.

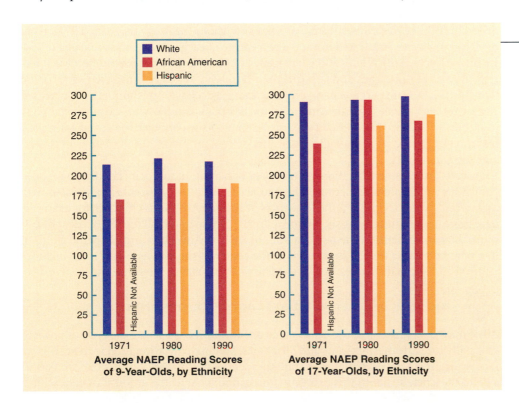

FIGURE 6.6

NAEP Scores as a Function of Ethnicity
Source: From "Are Americans Becoming More or Less Alike?" by W.M. Williams and S.J. Ceci, *American Psychologist*, vol. 52, no. 11, 1997, pp. 1226–1235. Copyright © 1997 by The American Psychological Association, Adapted with permission.

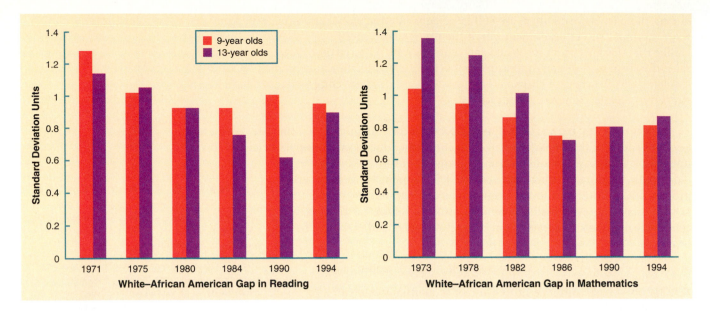

FIGURE 6.7

Narrowing of the White–African American gap in reading and mathematics between 1971 and 1994. *Source:* From "Are Americans Becoming More or Less Alike?" by W.M. Williams and S.J. Ceci, *American Psychologist,* vol. 52, no. 11, 1997, pp, 1226–1235. Copyright © 1997 by The American Psychological Association, Adapted with permission.

only 0.3 percent of African Americans and 0.2 percent of Hispanics do. For 17-year-olds, between 96 and 99 percent of each of the three groups surpass rudimentary levels, but for Advanced levels (350+), 8.7 percent of Whites, 1.5 percent of African Americans, and 2.4 percent of Hispanics do. Thus African Americans clearly made substantial progress in the 1970s, but their progress in this area leveled out by the mid-1980s and has remained there (Bronfenbrenner et al., 1996; Miller, 1995; Williams & Ceci, 1997).

The trends in math performance on the *SAT* mimic the trends for reading on the NAEP just described (Miller, 1995). The highest scorers on the math *SAT* (those with scores above 750) are distributed similarly to the highest scorers on the NAEP with regard to ethnicity—and students scoring above 750 are sought out by the nation's elite universities and are the students most often offered scholarships. Asian Americans accounted for more than 1 in 4 of those scoring above 750 in math on the *SATs* even though they comprised only 7.7 percent of test takers. Whites and Asians together constituted 97 percent of all scoring above 750. If we look at the percentage of each group who scored above 750, we find 1.1 percent of Whites and 4.0 percent of Asians; in contrast, we find only 0.1 percent of African Americans and 0.2 percent of Hispanics (College Entrance Examination Board, 1989, p. 9). Expert teachers recognize that extra classroom support and increased challenges can enable African American and Hispanic students to score substantially higher on standardized tests. Such support can include in-depth feedback and assistance, tutoring, extra reading and assignments, after-school programs, test preparation classes, and computer access.

In sum, increases in educational attainment of parents of minority children have been enormous and impressive. Because a high level of education of parents is associated with higher test scores of children, the test scores of African American children, for example, have gone up significantly, as shown in Figure 6.7. These trends all testify to real and substantial improvements in the performance of African American and Hispanic children in a relatively short time. Education is at the center of the answer, which also includes cultural and societal changes. You as a teacher can be part of the solution.

 THE ROLE OF MENTORING IN SCHOOL PERFORMANCE

All of these data make clear the importance of education in breaking the cycle of poverty, especially for African Americans and Hispanics. Parents' education level is critical; as we said earlier, it is a good predictor of children's school performance. But what can you, as a child's teacher, do about this problem? You cannot change the amount of education a child's parents have. However, you can practice mentoring, which will make a significant difference in the lives of your students.

Zena Blau (1981) has conducted extensive research focusing on the importance to a young and impressionable minority child of having one educated adult in her or his life. More than one educated and inspiring adult is better still, but one is enough to make a real difference. One educated adult in a developing child's life means the child has a mentor and role model who represents the doors that education can open. Blau found that the African American inner-city children who have better life outcomes have at least one adult in their lives with an educational orientation. This adult could be a parent, other relative, friend, teacher, and so on. Knowing one person with an educational focus is essential to the child's outcome. You as a teacher can be this adult—and you can make a real difference to a developing child. By serving as a mentor and role model you will help break the cycle of poverty, low school performance, and low education that has held back many youngsters of less advantaged groups.

To accomplish this goal, make clear that education and hard work matter to you, stress their values in your own life, and show students how they can benefit as a result of educational success. You can use a variety of techniques to meet these goals—analysis of real-life problems and issues education helped to solve, and discussions about famous individuals whose lives were changed by an educational focus—and generally be available to listen to students' opinions and to provide advice.

THINKING PRACTICALLY

Name three ways you can become an effective mentor and role model for your students.

SUGGESTION: Offer advice, support, and encouragement; discuss the obstacles you encountered and how you overcame them; listen to students and provide direction during troubled times.

Implications for Teaching

- **Do not assume that lower scores necessarily reflect lower levels of innate ability.** Lower test scores of students from certain racial and ethnic groups are likely the result of restricted resources. With improved resources, differences in scores among groups narrow considerably.

- **Recognize that the parents of today's students—particularly minority parents—are dramatically more educated today than they were a generation or two ago.** Do not stereotype minority parents unfairly.

- **Stress to all students, particularly those from traditionally disadvantaged groups, the lifetime value and rewards associated with completing high school and attending college.** Teachers can be effective vehicles of the message that education is the ultimate answer to many problems experienced by people of lower SES.

- **Never underestimate what one dedicated teacher can mean at a critical time in a student's life.** One teacher or other educated adult mentor can make an enormous difference in the life of a developing student.

Every Saturday, this African American teaching assistant helps an African American elementary school student with his math. Research has shown the enormous importance of mentoring, particularly to a young and impressionable minority child. Mentors and role models make clear the doors education can open. Expert teachers, too, can make a real difference to a developing child. (Randi Anglin, The Image Works)

Gender Diversity

Women and men are different, both in obvious and not-so-obvious ways. Boys and girls are also different, and regardless of the age of the students you teach, you will be confronted with sex and gender differences. Like all teachers, Charlene Johnson has had to deal with sex and gender differences in addition to SES and cultural differences. Unless you teach in a single-sex school, you will confront these differences, too. **Sex differences** are biologically controlled differences; **gender differences** are psychologically and socially controlled differences. Gender differences are related to how people express their biological sex in behavior. According to this definition, sex differences reflect biological factors, and gender differences reflect cultural factors in addition to biological ones.

Early in our writing of this textbook, we attended a professional education conference where we met other textbook authors. Upon meeting the two of us (and not knowing of our book), one of these authors asked if the second author of this book (a woman) was the new secretary assigned to the first author of this book (a man)! Many readers of this text can undoubtedly offer similar accounts of their own experiences with sexual stereotyping, ranging from amusing instances such as that just described, to more blatant and distressing cases of discrimination in which someone is denied employment or other opportunities solely because of sex. **Gender bias** exists when a person possesses unjustified views of female versus male competencies; these views often favor one gender over the other. Many traditional notions about gender and sex roles are changing, and concepts of gender and people's beliefs and expectations about it are influenced by numerous trends in modern society.

WHAT TEACHERS NEED TO KNOW ABOUT SEX DIFFERENCES

Given that a person's sex is almost always an immediately obvious trait, most people—teachers included—may process and act on this information without even realizing they are doing so. Examples are a teacher treating a 7-year-old girl differently from a 7-year-old boy when she returns an incomplete math test, a teacher calling more frequently on girls in literature courses and more frequently on boys in science courses, and a teacher encouraging boys to tough it out when they are scared and girls to withdraw from frightening situations. Because teachers have such a substantial influence on their developing students, and because their influence is exerted as students are developing their gender identities, they should be especially aware of their own biases and beliefs about the sexes. In this section we explore what is known about sex and gender differences, and—equally important—what remains speculative or unconfirmed.

Obviously, expert teachers should understand what is known, and what is not known, about sex differences. Armed with accurate knowledge, the expert teacher can ensure that all students are given the best possible chance to show what they know. Are there sex differences in intellectual abilities, scholastic performance, and achievement? Whether such sex differences really exist, and if they do, what causes them, has been a hot topic in the social sciences for many years. If as a society we are concerned with the low percentage of women who enter technical and highly scientific fields and seek to encourage more women to enter these fields, we should want to know whether women are biologically at a disadvantage for developing mathematical skills, for example. Early studies of sex differences, reviewed by Halpern (2000), were biased and based on samples of people that did not fairly represent the population as a whole. Recently, however, better meth-

THINKING ANALYTICALLY

Through what specific behaviors do you represent your gender to the world? What exactly do you do that defines you as male or female?

SUGGESTION: For example, think about how you behave in social situations, and how you dress—the jewelry and other accessories you wear, your hairstyle, and other aspects.

THINKING PRACTICALLY

Have you ever used a sexual stereotype to describe someone? Was your description fair and accurate?

SUGGESTION: Think of a time when you described someone (perhaps someone at school or in your family) as either stereotypically masculine or feminine—for example, "as strong as an ox," or "as pretty as a picture." Did your description capture what this individual is really like?

Despite both stringent legal guidelines and changes in social attitudes, in certain professions prejudice remains for both men and women. The female construction worker and the male nurse, for example, continue to face difficulties. (C.W. McKeen, The Image Works; Telegraph Colour Library, FPG International)

ods have been developed and more representative samples have been used to examine sex differences in abilities (Halpern, 2000; Hedges & Nowell, 1995; see also Garner & Engelhard, 1999; Marsh & Yeung, 1998).

 THE EVIDENCE FOR SEX DIFFERENCES IN COGNITIVE PERFORMANCE

Are there any true, fundamental differences between males and females in their ability to perform cognitive tasks? Are there biological differences (i.e., differences in brain function, for example) that underlie male/female differences in intellectual task performance?

■ **DIFFERENCES ARE SPECIFIC, NOT GENERAL** A substantial number of studies have found no overall difference in the performance of females and males on intelligence tests (Halpern, 1992, 2000; Flynn, 1998; see also Mackintosh, 1996). However, certain differences emerge when we examine patterns of scores on different types of performances. On average, females score higher than males in many aspects of verbal ability, which includes reading, vocabulary, spelling, grammatical knowledge, and oral comprehension. Males are far more likely than females to have problems with verbal abilities, for example, stuttering. Little girls already show their average verbal superiority over boys by mastering talking and language earlier than boys. These gender differences in verbal abilities tend to be small (Hyde, 1997; Hyde & Linn, 1988; Smedler & Torestad, 1996) but consistent, and they may be observable by you in your teaching.

On average, males are better than females in many visual-spatial tasks, including tasks such as rotating visual images mentally (Nordvik & Amponsah, 1998; Vederhus & Krekling, 1996). These differences in visual-spatial ability can be substantial. Regardless of practice and training, which improves performance of all children, sex differences persist (Ben-Chaim, Lappan, & Houang, 1986). Thus experience with the task helps, but there does seem to be an underlying biological component to males' overall superior performance on many visual-spatial tasks.

THINKING PRACTICALLY

How might teachers' values regarding sex differences influence their teaching, particularly those values and beliefs the teachers themselves do not realize they possess?

SUGGESTION: Teachers who believe girls are more cooperative and boys are more competitive might be quicker to criticize boys and praise girls. Teachers who feel girls are smarter in a subject might give girls higher grades on tests, homework, and overall.

THINKING ANALYTICALLY

Must differences between males and females have a biological root in order to exist?

SUGGESTION: No. If boys and girls are raised with different experiences and expectations they can grow up to possess different abilities and characteristics.

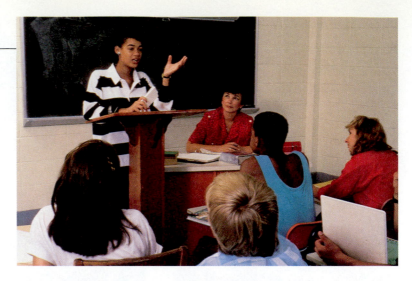

A young woman gives her presentation in a high school debating club. On average, females score higher on intelligence tests than males in many aspects of verbal ability. However, males are better than females, on average, at many visual-spatial tasks, including, for example, the mental rotation of visual images. (Billy Barnes, Stock Boston)

Males are also less influenced than females by context effects in perceptual tasks, differing in what is called *field dependence/independence*. Have you seen the cereal boxes and children's placemats with the "Find the 25 hidden faces" games? Boys perform better on these types of tasks, on average, than girls do. Quantitative skills of the type measured on standardized tests are another area where males tend to outperform females. These gender differences in quantitative abilities tend to be larger than the differences in verbal abilities. Males particularly outnumber females at the extreme end of high performance in math tests. For example, 13 times as many boys as girls score above 700 on the math Scholastic Assessment Test *(SAT)* (Benbow & Stanley, 1980; Lubinski & Benbow, 1992). Males' better overall math performance relative to females' does not start to appear until the high school years—before this point, girls outperform boys in general on math tests, although boys always do better at certain kinds of problem solving than do girls (Hyde, Fennema, & Lamon, 1990). We discuss this finding further in the section on the role of motivation.

■ **MALE PERFORMANCE IS MORE VARIABLE** What is interesting about the very large number of high-scoring males relative to females is that there is also a large group of very low-scoring males. The performance of males is simply more variable overall (Feingold, 1992; Hyde, 1997)—that is, males' scores are more widely distributed and more different from one another than are females' scores, which are more tightly clustered. Maccoby and Jacklin (1987) showed that males' scores were more widely distributed and more highly variable than women's scores for mathematical abilities and spatial abilities, but not for other abilities. Jensen (1985) reviewed the literature on sex differences in IQ and concluded that males' scores were more variable than females' scores. More recently, Feingold (1992) reviewed a large sample of summary statistics on tests and concluded that male scores were more variable than female scores for tests of quantitative and spatial ability but not for tests of verbal ability. What these results suggest is that teachers may see more very high-achieving boys than girls—but that these teachers may also see many more low-achieving boys than girls. The girls' scores will simply be less variable, overall. Thus, in your work as a teacher, your star math performers in high school may mostly be boys—but your worst math performers may also be boys.

■ **ROLE OF MOTIVATION** Despite these male/female differences, expert teachers know this list of sex differences in cognitive abilities is short relative to the large numbers of cognitive abilities for which no sex differences have been found. For example, no consistent sex differences are apparent on most types of memory tests. And when it comes to explain-

THINKING PRACTICALLY

How can a middle school teacher interact with the parents of a girl who is talented in math but who do not encourage their daughter to achieve in math, in order to encourage these parents to set higher standards for her?

SUGGESTION: The teacher might tell the parents about the girl's high scores relative to other students, to give them proof of her ability, and suggest to the parents that their attitude is holding their daughter back. The teacher might recommend an extra class or enrichment program for the girl, and explain to the parents why this is a good idea.

ing why males do better at math, we clearly have to consider the roles of motivation to do well in math and cultural values and support for math achievement. Ask yourself, did your parents, teachers, culture, and our society as a whole encourage you to excel in math? What about a young child of the opposite sex—would the support systems have been the same as they were for you?

Lubinski and Benbow (1992) believe that female motivation to do well in math is less than male motivation, even for the highest scoring females. They have investigated why even high-scoring women fail to choose careers in math and science: Men are 6 to 8 times as likely to pursue such careers. Why is it that these women do not seek careers as scientists as often as do men who score comparably in math? Lubinski and Benbow believe there are no simple explanations. Perhaps females are turned off by careers in science in part because the society as a whole does not support the entry of young females into the ranks of professional scientists. Encouraging your female students is another area in which you as an expert teacher can make a big difference in the life of these developing young women. By stressing that science and math achievement is something to strive for and be proud of—citing the achievements of famous women mathematicians, scientists, and engineers—you can help create a culture in which females seek scientific careers. It would be interesting to know how large the magnitude of male-female differences in math would be if girls and boys were given equal encouragement, rewards, and cultural and societal supports for math achievements.

THINKING CREATIVELY

In what ways did our culture encourage or discourage your own math achievement?

SUGGESTION: Were you made to feel competent in math as a child? Were you expected to succeed or to fail? Think about what cultural messages you received about your math ability.

ARE FEMALE-MALE DIFFERENCES BIOLOGICAL, CULTURAL, OR BOTH?

Observed differences between males and females may come about as a result of biological, genetically based factors or as a result of differences in how female and male children are raised in our culture. One study asked people to rate the behavior of a baby in terms of how exploratory and active the baby was (Condry, 1984; Condry & Condry, 1976; Condry & Ross, 1985). Some people rated a baby dressed in a blue outfit and others rated a baby dressed in pink. The blue-suited baby was rated as more active and exploratory and as exhibiting typically male behaviors. The catch was that all people rated exactly the same baby! Clearly, cultural expectations of male versus female behavior influenced how people perceived the baby's behavior. Teachers are as likely as anyone else to possess subtle gender-related expectations and biases. Understanding the basis of male-female differences helps the expert teacher to cope with differences in a positive manner.

■**BIOLOGICAL DIFFERENCES**   Evidence indicates that some sex differences may have a biological basis (Halpern, 1992, 2000). Prenatal sex hormones such as testosterone affect the development of gender differences in the brain. High levels of male hormones during fetal life have been shown to increase spatial abilities in females. Male fetuses that do not respond appropriately to male hormones develop certain female psychological characteristics, such as higher levels of verbal than spatial ability. Some researchers believe that gender differences may in part be explained by differential brain lateralization in males and females. Testosterone affects the development of the right and left hemispheres of the brain, and males have more lateralization of their brains than females do (Hiscock, Inch, Hawryluk, Lyon, & Perachio, 1999; Kee, Gottfried, Bathurst, & Brown, 1987; Meinschaefer, Hausmann, & Guentuerkuen, 1999). Verbal skills are more left hemisphere related for males than for females. For females, verbal skills more involve the use of both hemispheres, and many spatial abilities originate in the right hemisphere.

Another biological factor influencing females' performance is the pattern of hormonal changes during the menstrual cycle (Hampson & Kimura, 1988; McEwen, Alves, Bulloch, & Weiland, 1998). During menstruation, when female hormones are at their lowest all month, women do better on tasks on which males are usually superior, such as map problems, mazes, and visual-spatial problems. But when female hormones peak at midcycle, females do even better on tasks on which they are usually superior, such as verbal fluency (Hampson, 1990; Hampson & Kimura, 1988). Another observable biological difference between females and males is that the corpus callosum, a part of the brain that connects the two brain hemispheres, is larger in females than in males, meaning that females' brain hemispheres may be better able than males' to communicate back and forth. All in all, there are several potential biological bases for sex differences in cognitive performance. However, environmental and social factors that influence cognition are also important to consider, particularly because teachers can do nothing about biological differences but can have a substantial impact on the social environments of developing children.

■ **CULTURAL DIFFERENCES**　Cultural and social attitudes and stereotypes that shape how a girl grows into a woman and how a boy grows into a man are everywhere in our society. Little boys and girls are treated differently. They grow up exposed to different values, lessons, morals, encouragements, and expectations. Traditionally, in North American culture, females have been enculturated to have lowered expectations for scholastic performance and ultimate career success compared with males (Halpern, 1992, 2000; Stroh & Reilly, 1999). Men are shown occupying the positions of greatest income, prestige, and influence in magazines, newspapers, books, movies, television, and so on. As they grow up, boys are encouraged more to set their sights high and have high aspirations.

CONSTRUCTING YOUR OWN LEARNING

How have gender role expectations affected your own development? Ask yourself, and list the typical statements you remember hearing while growing up regarding your performance in school, what subjects you should study, what activities you should participate in, and what ultimate career plans you should make. Make two separate lists, one list containing the messages you received from your female teachers and caregivers, and the other containing messages from male teachers and caregivers. Were you encouraged to have different expectations for yourself as a result of the gender of the person who encouraged you? Now ask a member of the opposite sex about the messages about school performance and life goals that person received while growing up. Do you observe any differences in the messages given to women versus men, or in the messages given by women versus men? How might your life have turned out differently if you had heard the messages that were targeted at a member of the opposite sex? What messages will you try to send, or avoid sending, to the male and female students you teach?

Math and science classes in particular encourage boys more than girls—boys often ask more questions in these classes and receive more teacher attention, and boys generally dominate the math and science scene (Handley & Morse, 1984). Consider how math and science are usually taught in our culture: Competitive grading and solitary work encourage the male working style (Eccles, Wigfield, Harold, & Blumenfeld, 1993). Females often prefer socially cooperative styles of working and often would be likely to do better in science if it were taught from a perspective of group-project work and had fewer grading pressures. Little boys typically get more experience in competitive activities, beginning with the preschool years (Carpenter, Huston, & Holt, 1986; Carpenter & Huston-Stein, 1980; Tassi & Schneider, 1997). Despite the ability of many females to speak more fluently than males, males often dominate interactions with females as well as the decisions that are reached (Lockheed, 1986).

What specific cultural and social-cognitive influences might account for gender differences in cognition (Halpern, 1992)? Researchers have considered many factors. Some gender differences in spatial abilities might be related to the fact that more males play video games, which train these skills. Boys' toys and play activities might place greater developmental influences on spatial skills. Boys often are more encouraged by adults to explore their environments than girls are (Bornstein, Haynes, Pascual, Painter, & Galperin, 1999; Lindow, Wilkinson, & Peterson, 1985), and hence may develop visual-spatial skills more readily. Indeed, young girls with interests in stereotypically male activities grow up to have greater spatial abilities than other girls (Newcombe & Dubas, 1992).

In terms of math performance, our culture obviously encourages boys more than girls, as just described (Halpern, 1992, 2000; She, 2000; Tiedemann, 2000). Girls typically take fewer math courses than boys and are more likely to drop out of math. Most math teachers have higher expectations for boys than for girls. The society expects math to be tough for girls—a doll marketed in the early 1990s even said out loud, "Math classes are hard!" Think about how these messages affect little girls, who form notions about their math competence and attitudes toward math that may persist throughout their lives. However, expert teachers can make a substantial difference in providing equality of opportunity and experiences to both girls and boys by having the same high expectations for members of each sex (see the Implications for Teaching section). Other notable differences between the sexes include the following:

■ Boys are more likely than girls to be hyperactive and to show behavior problems. Boys are more likely than girls to be referred for reading disabilities; thus teachers often must focus more on reading skills with boys (Shaywitz et al., 1990; Willcutt & Pennington, 2000).

■ Females typically score higher than males in classroom grades in math (Kimball, 1989).

■ For boys, math achievement can be predicted from previous math achievement and expectations of success or failure in math (Ethington,1992). For girls, math achievement can be predicted from previous math achievement and expectations of future achievement. However, other interesting findings applied only to girls: Girls who were less likely to receive help from families in math suffered more than boys in the comparable situation, girls who viewed math as a male dominion achieved less than other girls, and girls who viewed math as difficult also had lower achievement.

■ According to a report by Stipek and Gralinski (1991), girls typically rate their math abilities lower than do boys, expect to do less well in math, and are less likely to attribute success in math to ability and failures to bad luck; elementary-aged girls are less likely to be confident that math success can be achieved through effort, and girls often take less pride in math success.

Most important, we note that male-female differences in U.S. math achievement have declined in recent years, possibly showing the impact of changing cultural values about girls' math achievement (Friedman, 1989; Hyde, Fennema, E., & Lamon, 1990). And, in some other cultures, males and females perform comparably on math assessments (Walberg, Harnisch, & Tsai, 1986).

THINKING PRACTICALLY

What can you do to encourage students at different grade levels who are "mathphobic," or afraid of math?

SUGGESTION: Give extra practice tests and quizzes to build confidence; play games with math concepts; give some untimed or ungraded tests; pair students with others not afraid of math on group projects; describe students who overcame math phobia and went on to achieve in math.

THINKING ANALYTICALLY

Why do females typically score higher than males in classroom math grades?

SUGGESTION: Teachers, who are often female, may prefer girls' typically more cooperative school attitudes and thus give girls higher grades. Girls may study more than boys. Girls may have more ability for classroom math than boys do. Girls may pay more attention in class.

THINKING PRACTICALLY

How might a teacher make use of the typical attitude differences between boys and girls in math?

SUGGESTION: Challenge competent girls to recognize they are capable in math. Point out to girls that they can do as well as boys in math, and they should recognize this fact and not be intimidated by boys. Tell boys that attentiveness, hard work, and studying—"the way the girls do it"—are necessary to bolster good performance.

Implications for Teaching

■ *Strive to eliminate gender bias from your thinking and teaching.* Even the slightest bias can harm students. Ask valued colleagues and other people you admire to critique your approach, looking for gender bias.

- *Biologically based sex differences do exist. However, do not judge any individual student because of trends that characterize the entire population.* None of us is "average" or typical in all of our attributes. Judge individuals as individuals, based on meaningful information.

- *Remember that most abilities do not vary between the sexes.* Even for those that do, hard work can overcome skill deficits. Differences between individual boys and girls will be greater than any population-based differences.

- *Cultural messages about gender-appropriate behaviors received by girls and boys can be destructive.* Do not add to the negative messages rampant in our society. Examine your own upbringing for hints, and eradicate any current behaviors that perpetuate negative or limiting gender messages.

- *Expect the same level of performance from girls and boys.* Call on both sexes equally often in every class, and do not vary your expectations of the sexes for different subjects. Do not limit any student by expecting less from her or him on the basis of gender or any stereotype.

Language Diversity

Standard English, the language of our schools, is most widely accepted as the spoken and written language of educated speakers in formal and informal contexts and is characterized by generally accepted conventions of spelling, grammar, and vocabulary. It is the English favored by most teachers and textbook writers as well as by journalists, speechwriters, and professionals, and it is the language people try to use when interviewing for a job. Although languages as spoken in everyday life evolve and change over time, formal use of languages is slower to catch up (for example, the word *fax* is only now starting to show up in dictionaries). Students are expected to speak and write Standard English in order to do well on tests and receive good grades. But, as Charlene Johnson learned, students have not all had equivalent exposure to Standard English.

What about the student who moves to the United States or Canada from another country and does not speak any English? What about the native-born student from the United States who speaks a **dialect** of English—a particular variety of a language distinguished by consistent pronunciation, grammar, or vocabulary that is spoken and understood by individuals from a certain region? And how about the student who is bilingual and does speak Standard English in addition to another language spoken in the home? More and more frequently, teachers find their classrooms filled with students who speak different languages, and the expert teacher must have a concrete plan for managing and teaching these students despite their language differences. The number of students from both Asia and Latin America is growing dramatically, and this growth translates into an enormous challenge for teachers.

THINKING ANALYTICALLY

What languages do you speak? Analyze the conditions under which you learned these languages—were these conditions favorable or unfavorable, and in what ways?

SUGGESTION: Did you learn any languages growing up in a house with relatives who spoke different languages? In special schools? From foreign travel or residence? Did everyone around you speak the same languages? Describe what you would change about your experiences if you could.

TEACHING NON-NATIVE SPEAKERS OF ENGLISH

Questions addressed by researchers studying linguistics and bilingual education center on how best to instruct children with varying language needs so these children learn optimally within the school environment (Hakuta, 1999; Hakuta & Mostafapour, 1996; Pintozzi & Valeri-Gold, 2000; Romaine, 1996). **Bilingual education** is education that to

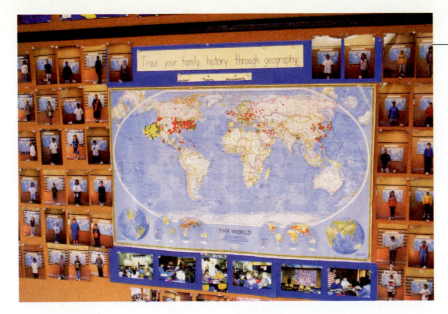

Given the growing diversity of American classrooms, it is becoming increasingly important that teachers give students opportunities to become aware and proud of their heritage. Students in this classroom have traced their family histories and positioned their photos on a world map. (David Young-Wolff, PhotoEdit)

a greater or lesser extent takes place in more than one language. **English as a Second Language (ESL)** (and also, English for Speakers of Other Languages, abbreviated ESOL) is the name used for instructional programs that teach English to students who do not speak English as their first language. Should children be allowed to speak their native language in school if it is not English? Should they be instructed in their home language if they are more proficient in it? Where will we find teachers capable of teaching in these foreign languages? Research has shown that although children can reach conversational proficiency in a second language within two years, becoming academically proficient can take up to six years (Fillmore, 1989, 1991). Not only must children learn Standard English, they must also learn social studies, math, science, and other courses at the same time. How can a teacher be expected to get the material across to a student who does not even understand the language?

Many children who enter school in the United States not speaking Standard English come from less affluent homes. These children are often from lower socioeconomic backgrounds and have parents who themselves never learned to speak Standard English, and consequently do not speak it in the home. These parents often have less formal education than the parents of native-English-speaking middle-class students. Children from higher socioeconomic levels tend to have been exposed to Standard English, either in the home or through schooling, and tend to have mastered Standard English at an earlier age than poorer children. Children who do not speak Standard English may have had little exposure to formal schooling and less parental support in the home for helping them with schoolwork. The challenge represented by these students is therefore magnified. For these reasons, some educators believe the best way to instruct these limited-English students is to teach in their home language (Hakuta & Garcia, 1989). They suggest that the children will more easily develop literacy skills in their native language than in a new language. These skills can then be transferred to the new language, English. In addition, instructing students in their native language keeps the children speaking their native language, which may be the only language these children share with their parents.

Jim Cummins (1976) distinguishes between additive versus subtractive bilingualism. In **additive bilingualism,** a second language is taught in addition to a relatively well-developed first language. In **subtractive bilingualism,** elements of a second language replace elements of the first language. Cummins believes that the additive form results in increased cognitive functioning, whereas the subtractive form results in decreased

THINKING PRACTICALLY

Name three ways a teacher might motivate a reluctant student to learn English.

SUGGESTION: Start with simple and entertaining books in an area of student interest. Try putting on a play to draw the students in. Offer to have assignments and papers that can be redone, instead of mostly relying on tests that may cause anxiety. Point out similarities between works of literature and the students' lives.

What are the advantages and disadvantages of having a national language and requiring students to learn to speak it exclusively in schools versus allowing teaching to take place in students' specific languages?

SUGGESTION: *ADVANTAGES OF A NATIONAL LANGUAGE:* Students are ensured of having language-appropriate best possible teachers, because everyone works in the same language; in addition, students are readied to compete in the work force. Students also experience more commonality and unity because of a shared language.

DISADVANTAGES OF A NATIONAL LANGUAGE: Some students might be left behind because they have not yet mastered the language. This ground might not easily be made up.

ADVANTAGES OF SPECIFIC-LANGUAGE INSTRUCTION: Students may more easily develop their literary skills. They may also receive greater support from their parents, who may not speak the national language.

DISADVANTAGES OF SPECIFIC-LANGUAGE INSTRUCTION: Teachers have to be trained in multiple languages and might not be effective in some of them. Students might leave school unprepared for the work force and for living in the dominant culture.

functioning. In fact, individuals may need to be at a relatively high level of competence in both languages to experience a positive effect of bilingualism. Children from lower socioeconomic backgrounds appear more likely to be subtractive bilinguals than middle-SES children.

Krashen and Biber (1988) have recommended that limited-English students at the elementary level be taught academic subjects in their primary language, with English taught as a second language. Instruction in English starts to replace instruction in the native language as the students master English. Gradually all instruction is conducted in English, usually by around the seventh grade. More commonly, however, bilingual programs give students only a year or two of instruction in their primary language—for just a short time each day (Ramirez, 1986).

Ramirez (1986) studied some different approaches for teaching students with limited English (in this case, Spanish-speaking students) and found that being taught in Spanish for only one or two years for a period of time each day led to performance similar to being taught only in English. But being taught in Spanish almost exclusively for many years led to better reading and math performance. Teaching students exclusively in their native language may work, but where are schools supposed to find the teachers to instruct their limited-English students? Obviously, qualified teachers are essential, and there are not enough bilingual teachers to go around: This is a point worth remembering for you as a developing teacher, inasmuch as you may want to refine and further develop any additional language capacity you already have. And what about schools, often in more urban areas, in which various children speak many different languages as their primary language? How can schools cope logistically with instructing children in all these languages, even if the schools can find qualified teachers?

A question raised by some researchers is whether too many years of instruction in the primary language may inhibit the full learning of English. To secure a good-paying job in the United States, a person usually must have mastered Standard English. Some have pointed out that Asian students seem to master English more easily than other students whose native languages are far more similar to English than are the Asian languages (Hakuta & Garcia, 1989). The implication is that if Asian students can learn English and function effectively in our schools, so can children from other racial and ethnic groups.

 SES AND LANGUAGE USE

Use of language differs for students from different SES backgrounds. Lower SES children often use language with a focus on the present; this language is more concrete, less descriptive and flowery, and more simple and basic (Bernstein, 1961, 1979). Fewer words overall are used to express the same things. Middle-class children often speak in more elaborate sentences, using more words overall. Their language is more playful and complex. They often enjoy talking and playing games with words. Middle-class children typically use more metaphorical expressions and speak in less concrete terms.

Influential early work on the differences in speaking styles associated with social class was conducted in England by Basil Bernstein (1961, 1979). Bernstein was an anthropological linguist who compared the use of language by gang members with that of middle-class students. He showed that the gang members, who were from lower SES backgrounds, tended to use what Bernstein called "restricted code language." This form of language was sparse and simple and tended to communicate in a compact way. The middle-class children typically used more elaborate language. Others have disagreed with Bernstein's analysis, however, pointing out that lower SES children can use more elaborate language under certain circumstances (Labov, 1997).

Thus the use of language varies among students partly because of the customary ways of using language in the students' homes. It may be easier and more natural for middle-class students to speak in elaborate sentences rich in detail. But lower SES students may find this type of self-expression to be a challenge, and you may have to encourage and guide them in developing more elaborate speaking styles. As with all types of group differences, language differences will raise many challenges for you as a developing teacher. Some of these challenges may be dealt with through a teaching approach known as *multicultural education*, which we discuss next.

THINKING PRACTICALLY

How was language used in your own family as you grew up? How has your use of language changed since you left home?

SUGGESTION: What languages did you speak growing up? Were the adults in the household very literate, with good vocabularies? How do you speak today, compared with during your childhood?

Implications for Teaching

- ■ *Work on developing a second language if possible.* It will be a substantial asset in the classroom, because more and more students are coming from homes in which English is not the first language. Take advantage of any languages you may have learned but since have forgotten—they may be easily relearned.

- ■ *Recognize that speaking habits, such as how descriptive students' language can be, are influenced by cultural values in the home.* Model for students the types of responses sought in school so students will understand the type of speaking rewarded in school. Remember that not all students come from homes that teach appropriate means for communicating in school. Do not assume students know what is expected.

Multicultural Education

Multicultural education exposes students to the values and norms of different cultures in an attempt to show them the diversity of the human experience. If you are like most people, you probably have some strong views on the subject of multicultural education, even though you may not be sure exactly what it is or how children are educated from this perspective. Right now, before you read any further, examine your own views on multicultural education. *Multicultural education* became a buzzword in the 1990s. The concept elicits strong reactions on all sides of the debate. Some people argue that schools must teach equally the values and customs of all cultures across the world, making absolutely no judgments about "better" or "worse" cultures or cultural practices. Others argue that only the cultures of the students in a particular school should be studied, and that the time devoted to each culture should reflect how many students in the school are members of that culture. Still other people believe that the United States is a country of Americans with a common, shared, dominant culture, and it is the job of schools to teach the values and customs of this dominant culture (although exactly what this culture consists of is often a source of controversy).

Regardless of your personal views, you may well be called on to teach a multicultural curriculum in the future. Charlene Johnson was expected to use a multicultural curriculum in her classroom even though she had little experience with diversity issues. Therefore, to be an expert teacher, you must understand what the multicultural approach represents and how teaching from this perspective will affect your preferred methods of instruction.

THINKING ANALYTICALLY

What are the strengths and weaknesses of each approach to teaching described here?

SUGGESTION: Teaching about many cultures can be extremely time consuming, and students may lack direct experience to appreciate these cultures. Teaching about the cultures in the school may fractionate the students and the community by emphasizing people's differences instead of similarities. Teaching only the dominant culture can leave students without an understanding of diversity that would broaden their attitudes and be helpful in today's world.

FOCUS ON: DIVERSITY IN HIGH SCHOOL

MARK H. SMITH, MEDFORD HIGH SCHOOL, MEDFORD, MASSACHUSETTS—GRADES 9–12, MATH

Mark Smith has been teaching for nineteen years. Enrollment of students who are members of minority groups has risen from 8 percent to approximately 20 percent of the student body at his school during the past decade.

What cultures and ethnic groups are represented in your class?

We have a pretty big population of black students, including many Haitian students. We also have a growing Hispanic population. We also have students who speak a lot of different languages. We have more and more students in our ESL (English as a Second Language) program.

How do language differences affect your teaching?

Initially, it's hard to know where to place ESL students. Local schools, and many American schools, follow a math sequence that progresses from pre-algebra to algebra to geometry and on up, perhaps to calculus. But other countries do not have the same sequences, and limited English can make it difficult for students to perform on placement tests. Sometimes, we find that a student has stronger or weaker math skills than we thought, and we need to move that student into a different math class.

Once they are enrolled in a class, the challenge is to figure out whether students are having problems with the language or with math skills. Many times students have great math skills, but the language blocks them. I have a girl who speaks Chinese in my class right now. She takes a long time to figure out what the problems are asking her to do because she has to understand the English. But once she understands the problem, she has the math skills to solve it.

ESL students also have a hard time with our state standardized tests. The new tests focus on problem solving that requires strong English skills.

What do you do to help English-language learners with math?

We try to get them extra help in ESL class or after school. For example, the ESL teachers often ask for the math words that we're using. In class, I have learned to be flexible and mix things up. I know that students won't understand things and I work on making them feel comfortable letting me know what they need and what they don't understand.

The kids also help tutor each other. Last year, I had three or four Spanish-speaking kids in one class. All of them were challenged by the English, but one girl had stronger math skills than the others and she would help the others, in Spanish, as soon as she understood a problem. This year, another Spanish-speaking student is helping the Chinese-speaking girl I mentioned.

Do you notice gender differences in math performance?

No, I've had the whole spectrum. Girls who do great, girls who do poorly, boys the same. More than half the students in my honors class this year are girls, for example. Again, I think you have to get to know students individually, and find out what they can do.

What about socioeconomic status? Do you find that higher SES students are higher achievers?

At our school, parental involvement seems to be more important than actual SES. Parents who value education and who have a strong educational background themselves pay attention to their children's education. They stay in contact with the school. They keep track of their kids, and keep on them. And these parents come from all economic levels. I've seen some very poor kids whose parents are very involved in their education do very well. I've also seen some very well-off students whose parents are not involved and who don't do very well.

We try hard to get parents involved. They get a lot of things sent in the mail to them. Teachers call home, and parents can call them. But it's still difficult for many parents. When students have two parents who are both working, it's hard to keep track, especially at the high-school level. And some parents just don't seem to be interested. We have low attendance at open houses, sometimes as few as thirty parents, and all of those are the parents of the top students. We have some parents who don't even know there are report cards.

What advice would you give to new teachers?

There are two big things new teachers need to know: First, be flexible. You need to be able to adjust to different situations. Don't be rigid with every single rule. Instead, you need to choose your battles, and not get upset when students forget their pencils or are a minute late.

Second, don't try to be everybody's friend. This is especially tempting for young teachers who are close to the age of high-school students. New teachers have to be professional. They can't be rigid about the rules, but they also can't let students do things that make them too comfortable, and hard to discipline later. Kids will adjust if you tell them your most important standards and enforce them from the beginning.

> I know that students won't understand things and I work on making them feel comfortable letting me know what they need and what they don't understand.

THE RATIONALE FOR MULTICULTURAL EDUCATION

The idea that underlies the trend toward multicultural education is that children from certain racial and ethnic groups tend to succeed more easily in typical schools than do children from other groups. Children who do not do as well often come from cultural groups with values that differ from the values stressed in school. For example, because U.S. schools often stress Western European values such as punctuality, future planning, solitary work, competition, goal orientation, and an emphasis on the individual, children from Western European backgrounds tend to match this dominant school culture. However, children from Latin American backgrounds, for example, tend to have a more team-oriented, collaborative, noncompetitive, present-oriented, and less rigid cultural orientation (Miller, 1995; Sensales & Greenfield, 1995). These children may not fit in as well with the scholastic environment and may fail to show what they know within the context of a typical school's demands. Indeed, students from different racial and ethnic groups may perceive aspects of the school day and typical instructional practices differently than white students do (Levy, Wubbels, Brekelmans, & Morganfield, 1997; Thorkildsen & Schmahl, 1997). Do schools have to emphasize a unique set of values? Some researchers think the answer is no: These researchers believe schools can take many different approaches to instruction, to match the values of diverse cultural groups.

COMPATIBILITY OF CULTURAL AND SCHOOL VALUES

Let us examine some of the ways the cultures of certain racial and ethnic groups may sometimes be incompatible with the cultures of the schools while simultaneously considering how schools can be modified to be more accommodating to children from these other cultures (for a review see Miller, 1995). One famous program of research was conducted by Roland Tharp, who in 1970 began a school improvement program for primary grade Native Hawaiian students. Tharp (1989; Tharp, Cutts, and Burkholder, 1970) focused on academic learning problems that might have originated in a poor match between the culture of the home and that of the school. Tharp's work resulted in a reading program and specific techniques for adapting the findings of his research to other minority group students. Tharp focused on increasing the match between students and the classroom in four areas: classroom dynamics and sociolinguistics, cognition, and motivation.

■**CULTURE AND CLASSROOM DYNAMICS: SOCIOLINGUISTICS** The typical U.S. classroom contains one teacher and many students; the teacher leads lessons and discussions; and the students listen, take notes, answer questions, and work independently at their desks. For children coming from affiliative, group-oriented cultures, this atmosphere may seem strange. These children may wish to work in groups, share resources, talk to one another, and draw on adult guidance when necessary. Tharp found that the children in his study spent half their time in peer interactions. These children sought their peers rather than their teacher for directions. Seizing on this natural inclination of the children, Tharp created small groups that worked on projects, sometimes with the teacher present in the group, and sometimes alone.

The normal manner of speaking in the classroom is for the teacher to lead and the students to follow. Students are not supposed to speak out of turn; they are supposed to wait until called on and then to speak one at a time. This style fits well with the upbringing and expectations of many white middle-class children, whose parents have taught them the same rules at home (Heath, 1982). But Tharp found that this type of interaction was uncommon for Native Hawaiian youngsters, who tended to speak to

THINKING CREATIVELY

How might you illustrate for a child (without offending her) why her way of behaving could alienate other members of the class who share a different cultural background?

SUGGESTION: An outspoken child who fails to raise her hand before offering an enthusiastic comment might be told that the other students are not getting a chance to contribute, or that her vocalizing of her answer reduces the opportunities for other students to think of the answer themselves.

adults as a group. Perhaps because they were unfamiliar with what the teacher expected, these youngsters did not do well when teachers asked them questions one on one. But when the teachers directed questions to everyone in a small group, allowing any child or children to respond, the children performed far better.

Shirley Heath's study of a working-class community of African Americans in the southern United States showed that adults usually talk in terms of stories. Children wishing to join in must initiate their own participation—adults do not invite children to participate. Imaginative and dramatic stories are highly regarded in this group. You can see how this type of training in the home environment might prepare a child to do exactly what teachers do not like—to interrupt and to launch into imaginative and dramatic stories instead of getting quickly to the point. Shade (1982) concluded that African American children may require a classroom environment promoting group instructional activities and active, verbally demonstrative activities.

■ **CULTURE AND COGNITION** Do members of different cultures actually *think* differently? If different cultural, ethnic, or racial groups do think and solve problems differently, then teachers must be aware of these differences in order to help all children succeed in the classroom. Doing well in the typical North American classroom requires analytical, abstract thinking and reasoning, often applied reflectively over a long period of attention to academic tasks that may have little real-world significance.

Do some racial and ethnic backgrounds lend themselves more to this type of thinking style? Tharp believes that white students find it easier to adopt a verbal/analytical thinking approach, whereas some minority group members tend to emphasize nonverbal thinking not geared toward breaking problems down into their component parts. Clearly, the more exposure a child has to formal schooling, the more accustomed the child will become to thinking in the way the school values (Ceci, 1991, 1996). Nonverbal styles are more likely in children who have had less schooling (Cole & Scribner, 1974). Thus, as a teacher, if you encounter students without much formal schooling, you may find they are not used to solving problems in the analytical and verbal style you seek. To reach these students, change your focus to enable them to show in other ways what they know, as they become accustomed to the demands of the school system. For example, allow students to do creative work to show what they know—write stories, plays, poems, skits, songs, cartoons, and so on. Students with difficulty writing can tape-record their story or poem and perform it for the class, or they can draw or sculpt or otherwise create a three-dimensional model that depicts the story. You might also allow students to do meaningful, practical work to show what they know, such as planning a small park cleanup and planting project, starting a small mock business, or mentoring younger students.

Native Hawaiian children learn things at home by watching an experienced person or by trying to do a task with verbal assistance. Thus Tharp designed a reading program that utilized small groups and emphasized comprehension of stories. The teachers tried to relate the stories to the children's lives. This approach helped the child learn to read far better, and their abilities even carried over to their performance on standardized reading tests. Matching the instructional style to the children's cultural style resulted in obvious gains in reading ability. As you prepare to teach children of different cultural and ethnic backgrounds, remember to modify your instruction to capitalize on students' culturally rehearsed favored methods of learning.

■ **CULTURE AND MOTIVATION** Motivation is the all-important push we all needed to get through school, and for minority children more than the average dose is often required so they can overcome the cultural obstacles that will restrain them from succeeding in the mainstream culture (Qian & Blair, 1999). There is no substitute for motivation. Do members of different racial and ethnic groups have differing patterns of motivation? Research suggests that Asian American children and their parents believe education is the answer, and that education will guarantee opportunity (Goyette & Xie, 1999; Hsia, 1988). But for African American children and their parents, there sometimes appears to be a perception that education will not lead to economic and employment opportunities (Miller, 1995).

To motivate students effectively, a teacher must understand and deal with the students' perceptions about what getting a good education is likely to bring them in life. For many Asian American students, relying on statements such as, "If you work hard on this assignment and others like it, you will get the type of job you want someday" may work well, because these statements are being echoed in the home environment and by the Asian American culture in general (Hsia & Peng, 1998). But for many African American students, promises of opportunity must be linked to concrete examples to overcome potential negative messages these students may have internalized from the media, their friends, and even their family members. In this case, concrete examples such as "If you score a 90 percent in this course you can attend the special summer math program and get college credit" may work better.

With regard to the more group-oriented structure of the Native Hawaiian society, Tharp (1989) found that praising the group as a whole for good work was more motivating than praising individuals from the group. In the typical classroom in North America, praise is given for individual and often competitive accomplishments—but for students from other cultures, this approach may not work optimally. It is up to the expert teacher to recognize these types of issues and respond to the children in a way that will motivate them most effectively. Expert teachers are flexible in their approach when dealing with students from different racial and ethnic groups: They use praise in the way that is most motivating (and not embarrassing) for the students, phrase and present challenges in a way that fits with students' cultural values (as just discussed), and are generally aware that subtle differences in classroom activities and structure can make a big difference to students.

AVOIDING GROUP STEREOTYPES

The point of the multicultural approach is to reach all students and to create a fair classroom environment for all students regardless of race, ethnicity, gender, culture, or other group differences. By discussing how ethnic and racial groups may vary, we do not wish to suggest that *all* members of each group share *any* characteristics. For example, not all Chinese American students are motivated to study, nor do all boys perform better than girls in math. Individuals are different from one another in every culture. Your students will differ in so many dimensions that their cultural or ethnic background may provide few clues to understanding systematic patterns of their behavior. We have provided this information in the hope that it will give you an appreciation of some cultural, social, and ethnic differences—not to give you a stereotype of a typical student from each culture.

Expert teachers never assume that a given student will behave in a manner expected for her or his culture. Remember that in our discussion of socioeconomic status, we pointed out that being from a certain social class may create distinct similarities in upbringing for students from very different cultures. In fact, students from the same cultural group but from different income-level households may have radically different upbringings. Expert teachers view each student as a unique individual and use information about group differences to illuminate their thinking and to help explain why students may learn differently in school.

MULTICULTURAL APPLICATIONS IN THE CLASSROOM

Now that we have discussed the concepts motivating the use of a multicultural curriculum and considered some examples illustrating how to change the standard curriculum to implement multicultural approaches, we review some general principles of multicultural instruction. One thing is certain: Multicultural education means different things to different people. Banks (1993, 1997) defines multicultural education in terms of providing educational equality for all students, regardless of gender, ethnicity, race, culture, social class, religion, or exceptionality (for example, high IQ, low IQ, or

IN EACH CHAPTER OF THE TEXT, WE INTRODUCE YOU TO A FEW SPECIFIC STRATEGIES—
ANALYTICAL, CREATIVE, AND PRACTICAL—USED BY BOTH EXPERT TEACHERS AND EXPERT STUDENTS.

THE ANALYTICAL TEACHER: Susan asks her students to critically examine the cultural values they grew up with and ask whether these values serve society's best interest.

THE CREATIVE TEACHER: Susan has her students dress in the style of their countries of origin (extending back as many generations as they wish) and bring in typical dishes eaten on holidays to help them understand each others' cultures.

THE PRACTICAL TEACHER: Susan recognizes that certain types of facial expressions and body language may mean one thing for one group of students, but something very different for another group of students.

THE ANALYTICAL STUDENT: José is able to contrast the styles of the criminal justice system in four countries and explain how the different cultures gave rise to different attitudes about crime and punishment.

THE CREATIVE STUDENT: José writes a play for literature class in which the characters are famous women and men throughout history from different countries, all of whom became great scientists.

THE PRACTICAL STUDENT: José settles disagreements between different groups of students by talking to them about how their cultural values caused them to interpret what was said in ways different from those the speakers intended.

physically limited). Researchers believing in a multicultural approach advocate specific methods for making existing curricula more multicultural. We review these recommendations here. (Note that not all researchers or teachers support this perspective, however, as we discuss later).

To teach multiculturally, you must first understand your students and their backgrounds: There is simply no substitute for getting to know your students' cultural backgrounds so you understand the context in which they are growing up. Once you possess this information, you can modify the curriculum to include presentations related to the cultures in the classroom, for example. You can discuss works of literature and art from each culture, political issues from the countries of origin of the students, geography and biology of the countries of origin of the students, and holidays from each culture in the classroom. When concepts are taught, provide examples from diverse sources across many cultures. These guidelines will help you reach every child.

Before using any curricular materials, review them to ensure they are free from stereotypes related to race, ethnicity, gender, and disability. Scrutinize books, illustrations, artwork, and plays chosen for production by the school, and choose culturally fair examples of these materials. When using pictures or verbal descriptions of individuals from different groups, including the two sexes, choose materials depicting these people in activities or jobs that are diverse and not associated with stereotypes. To help students overcome their stereotypes, discuss openly the current political and social status of different cultures. Use high-status individuals from various racial and ethnic groups, and from both sexes, as examples in classroom teaching, both through the use of case studies and through classroom visits or field trips if possible.

To achieve a multicultural perspective, take pains to avoid using sexist or racist language, such as referring to the girls as "girls" and the boys as "young men," and enacting any stereotypes in the class, such as calling on boys more frequently in math or girls more frequently in language arts. When supervising children in the gym or at play, assign boys and girls to activities without regard to gender, and encourage all children equally. When possible, ask members of the class from nondominant cultures to share descriptions of

THINKING CREATIVELY

How can your own cultural background provide examples for classroom teaching?

SUGGESTION: Think of the unique talents and customs of your culture. What can students learn from these characteristics? Teachers may develop lessons about the history of cultural groups—political history, geographic history, or art history. For example, an African American teacher might present a lesson about the underground railroad used to smuggle slaves to freedom.

their customs with the class—even bringing to the school samples of ethnic cuisines or costumes, and describing other celebrations. Draw examples of these customs from other cultures using the daily lives of the students in the class, and make the differences among cultures clear by talking in terms of how children from these different backgrounds spend family time, recreational time, and so on. Culture and religion are inextricably related in many holiday observances, life cycle observances, and even special foods. If your teaching environment does not permit discussion of religion, avoid discussions of ethnic customs that include a religious component or clear them first with the administration. Finally, teaching from a multicultural approach means encouraging all students to have high goals and aspirations for their futures, regardless of their race or ethnicity or gender.

As a teacher, you will need techniques to decide if your multicultural approach is working. See if your classroom permits and encourages the expressions of diverse opinions, even those negative toward the dominant and nondominant cultures, so these opinions and feelings can be examined and discussed in a nonconfrontational environment by the class as a whole. The classroom should *not* be a place where diverse views are discouraged by the teacher. The classroom that successfully integrates multicultural principles shows it in its artwork and displays. Anyone walking into the classroom should be able to tell that the values of different cultures are represented. Students are expected to intermingle and become friends across racial and ethnic lines—teachers then know they have been getting their points across.

Expert teachers respect the needs of different students to learn in different ways, and flexibility in the design of the curriculum enables all students to show what they know. Expert teachers make an honest attempt to understand different students' and groups' attitudes toward classroom success and the meaning of education. These teachers also try to involve the parents of culturally diverse students as often as they involve the parents of students from the dominant culture. All students who need extra help or special services should have access without regard to race, ethnicity, or gender. By checking regularly, teachers can tell if they have been successful in implementing a multicultural approach in daily teaching and thinking about educational issues.

In your future teaching career you will undoubtedly be expected to teach from a multicultural perspective. However, some educators believe the move toward multicultural education is misguided, that succeeding in North American society means becoming a member of the dominant culture of the United States or Canada. These people argue that students will ultimately be denied opportunities if they are not immersed by the school in the dominant culture and taught its values (see Forum: Multicultural Education—A Good Idea?).

Implications for Teaching

■ *Recognize that multicultural education is a contentious issue that evokes strong responses from people on both sides.* Treat discussions about multicultural education appropriately. Do not assume everyone around you shares your views, regardless of what they may be.

■ *Accept that, regardless of your personal views, you will probably be expected to teach from a multicultural perspective.* Do your best to be effective at your job, and make an effort to continue your own learning.

■ *Work to familiarize yourself with the range of cultures you are likely to encounter in the classroom.* Maintain an open mind and attempt to learn as much as possible about these cultures. Recognize your own cultural limitations and work to broaden your perspective on other cultures.

- *Adapt instruction and assessment for students of nonmainstream cultures to provide these students with varied opportunities to show what they know.* Never assume that just because students are "different," they have less to contribute.

- *Never equate different styles of speaking and interacting with differences in intelligence.* Intelligence is impossible to judge on the basis of superficial information and observations.

- *Avoid judging individuals on the basis of group stereotypes.* A few stereotypes may be accurate in general, but they will not predict what any one individual is like. No individual is simply "just like the group."

- *Accept diverse views in the classroom, and encourage students to elaborate on these views so everyone will understand them.* Be tolerant of dominant and nondominant views. Model for students the fact that diversity does not have to be threatening.

FORUM

MULTICULTURAL EDUCATION—A GOOD IDEA?

Is multicultural education, which stresses the diversity that characterizes human beings, a good idea? Or should education stress the dominant culture to better enable students to function and compete within that culture?

FIRST VIEW: *Education should stress the value of diversity and avoid portraying one culture or group as superior to others.* Proponents of this view believe that, for too many years, educational systems marginalized some groups of people and their values while teaching only the values of the dominant culture. Because of this emphasis, students were denied the opportunity to examine critically the assumptions of the dominant culture, or possibly to choose alternative paths through life. Teachers praised and rewarded students who looked and acted "mainstream"; students who did not resemble the standard cultural prototypes were viewed as different and were often encouraged to assimilate and become more like members of the more prevalent culture. By stressing the many ways in which human beings differ, education can show the range of possibilities available to everyone. Students can learn there are many "correct" approaches to life and to learning and performing in school.

SECOND VIEW: *Education should stress the values of the dominant culture to better enable students to understand and function effectively within that culture; an appreciation for diversity can be developed in students' lives outside of school.* According to this view, education's primary goal is to equip students to succeed in the real world. Understanding diversity is not the goal of education: Knowledge of what is expected in the world outside of school is. Students who are constantly taught about diversity may fail to see that our culture does label certain behaviors as appropriate and success oriented and others as unacceptable. By helping students assimilate, educational institutions can provide a link between the home worlds of students—which may vary dramatically in terms of what is expected and what values are stressed—and the public world of our society. Reminding students of their similarities to one another instead of talking only about their differences can help create a sense of community and a common set of goals among our youth. Stressing what binds us together instead of what draws us apart is a healthier emphasis for modern educational institutions.

THIRD VIEW: A SYNTHESIS: *Education can explain the values of the dominant culture so students know how to behave in order to succeed within that culture while simultaneously stressing the values of diversity.* The synthesis view recognizes the value of teaching students about the range of opportunities available to them and about the richness and diversity of the human experience. However, this view also recognizes that meaningful success usually derives from functioning successfully in the dominant culture, even if individuals choose to live their personal lives according to their own cultures. Thus a synthesis view recommends describing the many ways human beings live and work and raise their families while also describing what is needed to make it in the real world outside of school. Students can be told that individuality and self-expression are fine, but that they must also abide by society's rules, both fair and unfair, if they are to function effectively as members of that society.

SUMMING IT UP

WHY UNDERSTANDING GROUP DIFFERENCES IS IMPORTANT TO TEACHERS

■ To teach a student effectively, an expert teacher must first understand that student's identity, which is formed in relation to the many types of groups the student belongs to: cultural, ethnic, social class, gender, ability, nationality, religious, and so on.

SOCIOECONOMIC DIVERSITY

■ Socioeconomic status (SES) affects students' achievement. SES also affects parental styles of child rearing, and these styles (authoritative, authoritarian, and permissive) can in turn affect scholastic achievement. Low SES is related to low achievement and to low self-esteem; however, raising students' self-esteem does not necessarily enhance their school performance.

ETHNIC AND RACIAL DIVERSITY

■ Different ethnic groups score differently on average on standardized tests of intelligence and achievement. Genetic factors alone cannot account for the differences among the ethnic groups and the dramatic narrowing of the gap between the groups in test performance over the past 30 years.

■ Increases in parental educational attainment, which has soared in particular for parents of minority children, has contributed to children's school success. Research has shown that teachers can act as mentors and role models, and by doing so can effect significant positive changes in the lives of developing students.

GENDER DIVERSITY

■ Gender differences are defined as being psychologically based; sex differences, as being biologically based. Reliable sex differences exist in cognitive task performance. On average, females outperform males on many verbal ability measures, and males outperform females on many tests of visual-spatial ability and quantitative ability. Male scores are more variable overall than are female scores.

■ Differences in average test performance between females and males are thought to have both biological and cultural roots. Because findings are based on population averages, it is wrong to use gender bias to discriminate against individual members of one gender because of general trends in the performance of their gender.

LANGUAGE DIVERSITY

■ Today's teachers need to understand the best ways to instruct students who do not speak Standard English or even a dialect of Standard English. These students often are taught with an English as a Second Language (ESL) program. In additive bilingualism, a second language is taught in addition to a relatively well-developed first language. In subtractive bilingualism, the elements of a second language replace elements of the first language.

■ The best instructional methods and the best outcomes often differ, depending on the socioeconomic status of the students in a particular bilingual education program.

MULTICULTURAL EDUCATION

- Given the demographic changes in the United States, the need for teachers to reach students from nontraditional backgrounds and backgrounds unfamiliar to the teachers is growing rapidly, and teachers must be sensitive to the needs of these students.

- There is a mismatch between the values of certain cultural groups and the values of traditional North American schools. The social organization typical in schools differs from the social organization many children are familiar and comfortable with from their cultural backgrounds. Styles of communicating differ for traditional school environments and various cultural groups. It is important that teachers consider the ways of thinking and learning that are typical for various cultures and that might create problems for students from these cultures, and integrate these within the traditional school environment.

KEY TERMS AND DEFINITIONS

Additive bilingualism Situation in which a second language is taught in addition to a relatively well-developed first language. Page 215

Bilingual education Education that to a greater or lesser extent takes place in more than one language. Page 214

Culture Socially communicated behaviors, beliefs, values, knowledge, and other traits that characterize a particular time period or a particular class, community, or population of people. Page 193

English as a Second Language (ESL) Instructional programs that teach English to students who do not speak English as their first language. Page 215

Ethnicity Distinct national, religious, linguistic, or cultural heritage shared in common by a sizable group of people. Page 193

Dialect Variety of a language distinguished by consistent pronunciation, grammar, or vocabulary that is spoken and understood by individuals from a certain region. Page 214

Discrimination Treatment or consideration based on class or category rather than individual merit. Page 194

Gender bias Possessing different views of female versus male competencies, often favoring one gender over the other. Page 208

Gender differences Psychologically and socially controlled differences between women and men; how people express their gender in behavior. Page 208

Minority group Traditionally, a group smaller than the group representing the dominant culture; now, usually people from traditionally disadvantaged backgrounds. Page 193

Multicultural education Education that exposes students to the values and norms of different cultures in an attempt to show students the diversity that characterizes the human experience. Page 217

Sex differences Biologically controlled differences between men and women. Page 208

Socioeconomic status (SES) Measure of a person's social class level based on her or his income and educational level. Page 194

Standard English Variety of English most widely accepted as the spoken and written language of educated speakers in formal and informal contexts and characterized by generally accepted conventions of spelling, grammar, and vocabulary. Page 214

Subtractive bilingualism Situation in which elements of a second language replace elements of the first language, resulting in decreased cognitive functioning. Page 215

Apply the concepts you have learned in this chapter to the following problems of classroom practice:

IN ELEMENTARY SCHOOL

1. Most of your second-grade students avoid one student, who is from a lower social class than the rest of the group. You are concerned about the messages being received by the student, who is being shunned by peers. How can you convince your students that being from a different socioeconomic level does not mean a student cannot be their friend?

2. Several of your third-grade students are difficult to manage. You have spoken to their parents, and you have learned these parents are very permissive in the home. How can you convince these parents that their children are suffering because they do not pay attention—as well as hurting everyone in the class?

3. You are supervising your fourth-grade class at recess when three students begin using racial slurs while shouting at two other students. How can you handle this situation so your students see how destructive and inappropriate their behavior is? What classroom activities might help promote interracial understanding?

4. Several boys in your third-grade class never open their mouths during literature class. What can you do to encourage them to contribute and give them more confidence in their abilities?

5. Imagine you are a new teacher who grew up in a small, homogeneous town. You have little to no experience with racial, ethnic, and cultural diversity. Yet you are expected to teach from a multicultural perspective beginning on your first day in front of your sixth-grade class. What steps can you take to become more familiar with multiculturalism?

IN MIDDLE SCHOOL

1. You are concerned about one of your brightest eighth-grade students, because although she does well in nearly every subject she seems to have a phobia about math. When you call her mother, her mother seems unconcerned about her daughter's poor math performance, blaming it on her daughter's sex. What can you say to this parent to convince her to help?

2. How can you start off the year positively with a ninth-grade student who speaks virtually no English?

3. You are teaching a diverse group of seventh graders. How can you encourage tolerance and respect for people, cultures, and customs very far from your students' experience? What activities, projects, or discussions will help you get through to the students?

4. Sometimes you wonder whether your own behavior is completely free of damaging stereotypes that could hurt your eighth-grade students. What steps can you take to become aware of any racial or cultural stereotypes you may have adopted?

5. Your ethnically and racially diverse group of seventh graders seem reluctant to share their home and cultural experiences with others from different backgrounds. Yet you believe such openness would be good for all students. What steps can you take to encourage more sharing of cultural values?

IN HIGH SCHOOL

1. Your ninth-grade social studies class has students from two different socioeconomic levels—middle class and lower class. These students rarely interact with one another and do not seem to form any friendships outside of their own group. You want to encourage collaboration across socioeconomic lines. What steps can you take to encourage your students to work together productively?

2. What should your expectations be regarding the standardized test scores of children of different races? How might your expectations influence your students' performance?

3. Every day in your twelfth-grade math class, the same hands go up, mostly all boys' hands. What can you do to ensure that girls are getting equal access to learning and equal time?

4. A student earns low grades in all of his subjects because of his limited proficiency in English. You do not speak his language, yet you believe your tenth-grade science class might allow him opportunities to participate in project work that he could accomplish regardless of his limited English. What steps can you take to help this student to do well in your class?

5. In your eleventh-grade class are six students from foreign countries where communal learning rather than competitiveness is prized and encouraged. These students are having a difficult time adapting to your classroom's and school's expectations. What steps can you take to help them?

Connecting Theory and Research to Practice

Gender differences tend to be multidimensional and complex. One prevalent concept related to gender differences and cognitive abilities is that boys tend to do better than girls in math and science. A possible reason for this gender difference, as discussed in this chapter and researched by Lubinski and Benbow (1992), revolves around the idea that motivation plays a key role in the success of girls in the fields of math and science. One approach to this dilemma has been to provide extra encouragement and sup-

port to girls interested in math and science as a way to bolster self-esteem and motivation.

A three-year project, Voices *(www.ael.org/nsf/ voices/vocbrief.htm)*, conducted by the National Science Foundation, investigated the mathematical and scientific development of sixth-grade girls. In this study, investigators examined how girls felt about math and science, paired them with expert mentors, and had them tutor younger girls in math and science. This site contains information about the project, articles and information on women in math and science fields, curriculum materials, and online resources regarding gender equity in math and science.

Building Your Self-Portrait as an Educator

Many misunderstandings about group differences stem from a lack of communication between and among different groups of people. A Web site devoted to breaking the barriers between groups is Y? The National Forum on People's Differences *(http://www.yforum .com/index.html)*. The main goal of Y? is to bring people together to discuss and address the various questions, curiosities, and stereotypes individuals may have about one another. Specifically, Y? provides a moderated environment to

give individuals "a way to ask people from other ethnic or cultural backgrounds the questions you've always been too embarrassed or uncomfortable to ask them." While there are many guidelines that must be met prior to posting a question, the main purpose of this forum is to generate an open exchange of information regarding group differences to promote understanding and bridge cultural and ethnic communication barriers.

Another Web site that builds self-awareness regarding cultural issues is the Multicultural Pavilion, available at *http://curry .edschool.virginia.edu/go/ multicultural/* created by Dr. Paul Gorsky at the Curry School of Education at the University of Virginia. This site provides educators with an index of multicultural initiatives, references, and activities to promote multicultural awareness and education. One of the most interesting features, Awareness Activities, provides a variety of self-reflective exercises and activities that students and teachers can use to facilitate discussion about issues regarding multiculturalism, gender issues, or discrimination.

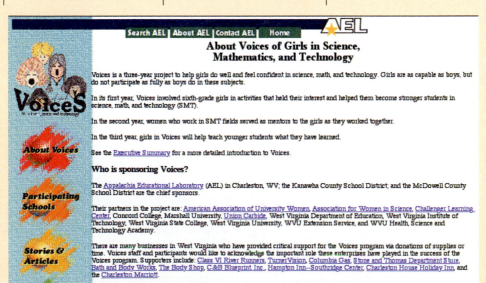

Online Resources

Are you interested in how your state compares to others within the United States with regard to money spent by the state per child for education, average class size, the number of children serviced by Head Start each year, or how many children are at or below the poverty level? The Children's Defense Fund is a private, nonprofit child advocacy group that investigates and reports on issues regarding poverty, diversity, and children with special needs.

The Children's Defense Fund's Web site *(www.childrensdefense.org/index.htm)* contains a variety of information including state data, parent resources, information about current programs, government news, and current events that impact the lives of children. As a teacher looking for a job, you may find it helpful to investigate the state in which you are applying for a teaching position to see how much that state pays per student for education, the average class size, the high school completion rate, and what kinds of teachers are needed within that state.

What is racism? Are all people inherently prejudiced against one group or another? What is the psychological foundation of racism or prejudice? The American Psychological Association has created a web site that focuses on the topic of racism and cultural and ethnic stereotypes. This site, located at *www.apa.org/pi/oema/racism/q16.html,* provides information about racism and psychology and poses critical questions about race and prejudice. This site also provides an invaluable resource for teachers, including the article "10 Things That Teachers Can Do To Fight Racism and Prejudice," plus contact information for groups who are actively fighting racism and prejudice and ways to contact them.

Designed and managed by Martha C. Phelps-Borrowman, The Gender Equity in Education Web site *(http://softlib.rice.edu/CRPC/GT/mborrow/GenderEquity/gendsite.html)* contains information and a list of resources regarding gender equity in public education.

For resources regarding multicultural education, click on The National Association for Multicultural Education at *www.nameorg.org.* On this Web site you will find lesson plans, discussion boards, and state-by-state resources for implementing multicultural education in classrooms.

Resources for Diversity, located at *http://alabanza.com/kabacoff/Inter-Links/diversity.html,* offers informative resources for various issues related to diversity including ethnicity and culture, gender, sexual orientation, and religious beliefs.

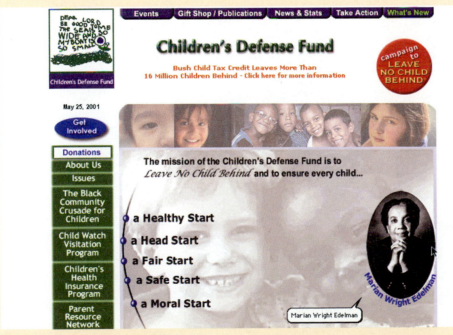

© Children's Defense Fund. Reprinted with permission.

Behavioral Approaches to Learning

THE BIG PICTURE

To help you see the big picture, keep the following questions in mind as you read this chapter:

■ What is learning? How does it differ from performance?

■ What is classical conditioning? What is the role of the learner who is being classically conditioned?

■ What is operant conditioning? What is the role of operant conditioning in classroom learning?

■ What is social learning? How can teachers use social learning to their advantage?

■ What is cognitive-behavioral modification, and how, when, and why does it work?

■ What are some ways behavioral techniques may be misused in the classroom, and what can be the consequences of such misuse?

◀ *Student looking apprehensive as he takes a test.* (Bob Daemmrich Photos, Inc.)

This week, Tom Douglass introduced a new teaching technique to his fifth-grade class that he had read about in his continuing education seminar. He asked students who were good at each subject to show the class how they worked through problems in their area of strength. Mara was the first student he selected. She got up, walked to the board, and worked through a tough math problem. She did a great job; the only trouble was that Jimmy kept starting disruptive conversations with his friends, which were soon followed by conversations among other students. Jimmy often did the same thing to Tom, and Tom had tried warning and disciplining Jimmy before. But this time Jimmy went too far. Tom could not allow one student to interrupt another student's presentation. He sent Jimmy to the hallway for a time-out—with directions to reconsider his inappropriate behavior. Mara completed her pres-

entation, and the students were visibly impressed. A number of hands went up when Tom asked for another volunteer.

Next, Tom called on Mark, a student who was particularly good at science. Tom asked Mark to talk about his science project, explaining how he chose his topic, how he collected the information he needed, and how he built the display. Mark turned as white as a sheet when he was asked to talk, and Tom could see his hands shaking as he walked to the front of the room. Mark started talking, but he was so nervous he couldn't continue. Mark was a shy kid—Tom knew Mark sometimes had trouble speaking in front of others. But Tom had thought that because Mark loved science and had done such a terrific project, he would be able to describe its basic steps. Tom was wrong: Mark ended up sitting down, feeling embarrassed. Suddenly none of the other students wanted to do a demonstration either. Each student Tom called on needed more time or made up an excuse.

Later that day, Tom decided he would try to draw Mark out in class and mend his self-esteem. He let Mark sit in his seat, but he coached him with some questions. He started out by saying that lots of students are nervous about talking in front of the class, and that he himself had been petrified when he started teaching. He then asked Mark a really easy question about his project. Mark answered tentatively. Tom said, "That's great, Mark. Then what did you do? How did you find those sources of information?" Mark was encouraged. Tom coached him again, telling him what a great project he had done and expressing confidence that Mark would do well in the science fair competition. Soon Mark was talking more about his project, describing how he had built the display and the various problems he had encountered. Tom's strategy had worked: He had encouraged Mark to speak out and had captured the interest of the other students, who were now fascinated by Mark's project.

In this chapter we consider **learning,** any relatively permanent change in the behavior, thoughts, or feelings of an organism that results from experience (Mazur, 1990; Reisberg, 1999; Rocklin, 1987). As we discussed in Chapter 2, on cognitive development, learning is distinguished from *maturation,* which is change that occurs as a result of genetic programming, given the normal range of environments. Learning is also distinguished from the moment-by-moment fluctuations in behavior that may occur as a result of environmental circumstances. For example, when you veer to the left on the sidewalk to avoid bumping into another pedestrian, you are not "learning." This type of action does not represent any true relatively permanent change in the way you think about, feel about, or do things.

In this chapter, we concentrate on **behavioral theories of learning,** which focus primarily on changes in observable behavior rather than on internal mental processes. Behavioral approaches to learning tend to emphasize the role of external events in the environment of the individual (DeGrandpré & Buskist, 2000). In Chapter 8, we consider internal cognitive, or mental states. As we shall see, the distinction between the behavioral approaches discussed in this chapter and the cognitive ones discussed in the next chapter is not always sharp. Indeed, cognitive-behavioral modification programs such as those discussed at the end of this chapter show that today what were once two distinct approaches are now often combined (Kendall, Krain, & Henin, 2000).

Why Understanding Behavioral Learning Is Important to Teachers

Every teacher needs to understand behavioral approaches to learning because students' behavior is what teachers deal with every day. Consider Tom. To manage and engage his class, he used the basic principles of behavioral learning, which you will learn about in this chapter. First, Tom called on a good student, Mara, to show the class how she went about solving a math problem. The class watched and was impressed, and other students then wanted to demonstrate their strengths. This is an example of social learning, in which people learn how to think or act by watching someone model certain behavior.

When Jimmy interrupted Mara, Tom sent Jimmy away from his friends for a time-out. Tom's goal was to make Jimmy think twice about interrupting lessons in the future. The effects of punishment on learning are also discussed in this chapter.

Then Tom called on Mark, who became too nervous to proceed. Mark had been embarrassed in the past when he tried to speak in front of the class, and this time the mere thought of doing so distressed him. His anxiety was the result of classical conditioning, a form of learning that sometimes involves emotions becoming linked with certain activities or situations. But Tom worked with Mark, little by little, to build his confidence and draw him out of his shell. Tom used a learning principle called *positive reinforcement* (Branch, 2000)—he rewarded Mark with deserved praise and encouraged Mark to talk about his project, which Mark ultimately did successfully.

In a single day in the classroom, you will need most if not all the principles of behavioral learning. Once you understand how these principles work, you will be able to use them effectively in your teaching.

Learning by Classical Conditioning

Do you get nervous when someone mentions the word *exam?* Does the sight of some kinds of food make you sick to your stomach? Do you shudder when you hear the sudden loud bark of a nearby dog? All of these common responses are the result of **classical conditioning,** a learning process in which an originally **neutral stimulus**—such as the word *exam,* or the food, or the bark of the dog—becomes associated with a particular physiological or emotional response—or both—that the stimulus did not originally produce (LoLordo, 2000). The anxiety about public speaking experienced by Mark, the student at the beginning of the chapter, was a result of classical conditioning.

THE DISCOVERY OF CLASSICAL CONDITIONING

Pavlov (1849–1936), a Russian physiologist, was studying digestion in dogs. To this end, Pavlov collected dogs' saliva in a container in order to measure the amount of salivation produced when the dogs smelled food (in this case, meat powder). But a curious and annoying thing was happening. The dogs were salivating even before they smelled the meat powder. Indeed, just the sight of the lab technician or even the sound of the lab technician's footsteps was enough to start them salivating. Pavlov's first response, of course, was to try to think of ways to stop this premature salivation, because it was ruining his research.

Eventually, however, Pavlov realized that what had appeared to be an irrelevant and confounding event was of interest in its own right. He inferred that some kind of learning

The Russian physiologist Ivan Pavlov, who understood that what had appeared to be an irrelevant and confounding event to other researchers—that dogs salivated before they smelled meat powder— was of interest in its own right. Thus came the discovery of classical, now called Pavlovian, conditioning. (Roger Viollet/Liaison)

must have taken place for the dogs to be able to salivate even before they smelled the meat powder. Thus came the discovery of classical, or Pavlovian, conditioning.

Phenomena such as that observed by Pavlov had been observed by others. Indeed, some people ridiculed Pavlov's discovery as trivial, because any horse owner would have observed the same phenomenon in various ways. What distinguished Pavlov was his recognition of the significance of what was happening. Pavlov made use of information whose importance was not appreciated by other people. As Louis Pasteur once said, "Chance favors the prepared mind."

 ### HOW DOES CLASSICAL CONDITIONING HAPPEN?

Pavlov (1955) developed a simple paradigm for studying classical conditioning, illustrated in Figure 7.1. The basic components of classical conditioning remain the same and can be seen in common classroom situations:

1. Start with a stimulus that elicits a physiological or emotional response (or both). In Pavlov's experiment, this stimulus was meat powder. For Tom Douglass's student, Mark, the original unconditioned stimulus might have been ridicule from his classmates. This stimulus is called the **unconditioned stimulus,** or **US,** because it elicits a response before any conditioning takes place. The response is produced automatically.

2. Note your participant's automatic physiological or other response to the stimulus. This response is called the **unconditioned response,** or **UR,** because the response is the natural one of the organism, which occurs without any conditioning procedure. The unconditioned response of Pavlov's dogs was to salivate when the meat powder was on their tongues. Mark's unconditioned response to his classmates' teasing might have been feelings of humiliation and anxiety.

3. Choose a stimulus that is originally neutral but that you wish later to elicit the desired response. This originally neutral stimulus is called the **conditioned stimulus,** or **CS,** because it is the stimulus that will come to elicit the response after the conditioning procedure takes place. Pavlov chose the sound of a buzzer. For Mark, the originally neutral stimulus was standing in the front of the room to give a class presentation.

4. Pair the CS and the US repeatedly, so the CS and the US become associated. Eventually, you will obtain from the CS a **conditioned response,** or **CR,** which is similar to the UR; it is elicited from the CS rather than from the US. Pavlov sounded the buzzer immediately before giving the dogs their meat powder. After a number of repetitions of this buzzer–meat powder pairing, the dogs' conditioned response was to salivate when the buzzer sounded, even though meat powder was not yet in their mouths. Perhaps the first several times Mark stood up in front of his classmates to talk, some of them ridiculed him. Eventually, Mark came to feel humiliated and anxious whenever he was asked to come to the front of the class, or even when he thought about giving a class presentation.

Before Conditioning

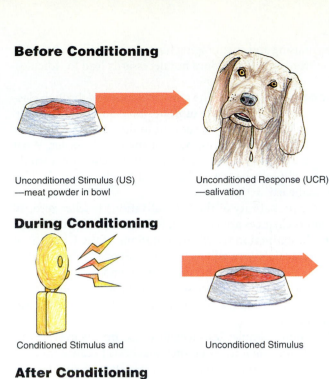

Unconditioned Stimulus (US) —meat powder in bowl

Unconditioned Response (UCR) —salivation

Neutral Stimulus (NS) which later will become Conditioned Stimulus (CS)

Neutral Stimulus (NS)—buzzer

No response

During Conditioning

Conditioned Stimulus and

Unconditioned Stimulus

Unconditioned Response

After Conditioning

Conditioned Stimulus

Conditioned Response—salivation

FIGURE 7.1

Pavlov's Procedure
Before conditioning, the dog's unconditioned response is to salivate in response to the unconditioned stimulus of meat powder. The dog has no response to the buzzer. During conditioning the buzzer is paired repeatedly with meat powder, eliciting the unconditioned salivation response. Finally after conditioning, the dog salivates in response to the sound of the buzzer alone, a conditioned response.

Why do organisms become classically conditioned? Over the years, several different explanations have been proposed. One explanation, dating back to the ancient Greek philosopher Aristotle, is that of **temporal contiguity.** According to this view, the mere closeness in time between the CS (the buzzer or the ridicule) and the US (meat powder or an upset feeling) explains conditioning (Guthrie, 1959). In fact, we know that temporal contiguity is necessary.

As in telling a joke, timing in classical conditioning is critical. Not only should the CS and the US occur close together in time, but the CS ideally should come right before the US. If the CS comes too much before the US, conditioning will be minimal or not occur at all. For example, if a student says to Mark a week after his presentation, "You are such a show-off when you get up in front of the class," the remark might not upset Mark as much as it would if the student said it right after Mark gave his presentation. Conditioning is also unlikely if the CS occurs simultaneously with, or after, the US.

But temporal contiguity alone is not enough to cause classical conditioning. Robert Rescorla (1967) believed that something more cognitive—more sophisticated and thoughtful—is involved, namely, contingency. *Contingency* is the dependence of one action or event on another event or on the presence of a stimulus. Rescorla showed that when the CS always predicts the US, learning occurs easily and quickly. But when the CS does not predict the US, learning does not occur—even if the CS and US are close in time. For example, what conditioned the dogs was not the proximity in time of stimuli—such as lab technicians to meat powder—but that the presence of the lab technicians *predicted* the appearance of the meat powder. According to Rescorla, people try to make sense of their environments by noting which stimuli can predict events that are important to them. Tom Douglass knew

In the upper-level classroom, if the school bell rings, students rush out of their classes. In other words, the bell predicts the students' "rushing-out behavior." What are some other examples of contingencies in the classroom?

SUGGESTION: Distributing "blue books" can be a contingency for the taking of an examination.

this and helped Mark realize, by praising and encouraging him when he talked about his science project, that speaking in front of the class does not necessarily lead to ridicule.

■**PHASES OF CLASSICAL CONDITIONING** The growth of learning through classical conditioning, just described, is called the phase of *acquisition*. Suppose, however, that in a conditioning situation the CS were to continue, but in the absence of the US: Say you continue to present the buzzer to the dogs, but not the meat powder. What would happen? Soon, the level of the CR would start to decline, and eventually, it would completely disappear. The dogs might salivate less and less, and finally, not at all. This phase of learning is referred to as the **extinction** phase.

You might think that when the probability of the CR (salivation) reaches zero, all the learning that took place is gone. Chances are, however, that it is not. If you give the organism a chance to rest after the extinction trials (presentations of the CS without the US) and you then resume these trials, you will typically observe a higher level of response than you observed right before the rest period. This phenomenon is called **spontaneous recovery.** The organism seems to recover some level of response spontaneously during the rest period, even though the US was absent during this period.

Consider a classroom example: Tests usually cause anxiety in students. Students learn to become anxious when they take tests because they are graded and evaluated (acquisition). But if a teacher starts giving tests in which students are given a second chance to improve their grades, test anxiety may diminish (extinction). After a vacation, however, the first self-graded test may elicit more nervousness from students than did the last self-graded test given before the vacation (spontaneous recovery).

During extinction, performance stops reflecting learning. Nevertheless, learning remains available to the individual.

■**GENERALIZATION AND DISCRIMINATION** A Bugandan proverb states, "He who is bitten by the snake fears the lizard." This proverb suggests, correctly, that when students become conditioned to respond to a particular stimuli, they can experience the same conditioned response to other, similar stimuli. The mechanism by which stimuli similar to the original CS can elicit the CR is referred to as **stimulus generalization.** Consider an example: Many students become anxious when the teacher announces "close your notebooks" and holds up a stack of papers for distribution—they know a test is coming. These students may also find themselves becoming anxious when the teacher says "close your notebooks" and holds up an activity sheet, despite the fact that the students actually enjoy the activity. The activity sheet is similar enough to the test papers to elicit the same conditioned anxiety.

What if the teacher says "close your notebooks" and, rather than papers of any kind, holds up art materials to distribute. In this case, students are unlikely to react with nervousness. The students are showing **stimulus discrimination,** a mechanism by which organisms are able to distinguish between the conditioned stimulus, which elicits a conditioned response, and other stimuli, which do not elicit the conditioned response.

■**HOW AVERSION OCCURS IN THE CLASSROOM** Classical conditioning can occur whether or not teachers are aware of it. As we mentioned at the beginning of our discussion of classical conditioning, physical and emotional responses are most susceptible to classical conditioning. In fact, the term **conditioned emotional response,** or **CER,** is used for emotional responses that have developed from classical conditioning. Stimuli that produce negative emotional responses are called **aversive stimuli.** One of the most common conditioned responses teachers will notice is *test anxiety,* a generalized feeling of dread in response to tests (Covington & Omelich, 1987). If severe, such anxiety can cripple a child's chances for success in the school environment. Students who have repeated aversive experiences in school also may develop a generalized aversion to schools and learning that can be a major cause of their dropping out of school at a later date. This aversion may even affect how they react to the schools their children attend. Teachers, however, can do a great deal to prevent and alleviate such negative conditioned responses if they remain conscious of the potential for controlling classical conditioning processes in their classrooms.

Relaxation training, in which students are taught to pair testing stimuli with a relaxation response that is incompatible with anxiety, is the basis of the success of many formal programs for reducing test anxiety (e.g., Sapp, 1996). In addition, a teacher can help a student with test anxiety get used to tests in small steps. For example, the teacher may have the student use the standard blue book or computer-grading sheet for everyday in-class assignments or even for art projects, helping diminish the student's conditioned link between seeing the familiar testing prop and feeling nervous. Tom Douglass was using this method to help Mark take small steps toward being able to talk in class, first by answering questions from his seat, and then by describing his project in some detail. A teacher could also give practice tests graded solely on the basis of the students' participation. A student who takes the entire test, grades the test for herself, and then corrects mistakes would receive full credit. These practice tests are good preparation for the real tests. They also help students become familiar with the testing environment without the usual accompanying pressure.

Classical conditioning can be important in people's lives. But in everyday life, a second kind of conditioning occurs with far greater frequency. We consider this kind of conditioning in the next section.

Implications for Teaching

Teachers who wish to put classical conditioning to work in their classrooms could try the following suggestions:

- *Avoid classically conditioned negative emotions.* Expert teachers learn to anticipate situations, such as this one, where negative feelings might be learned through classical conditioning, and try to prevent such situations (Tauber, 1990). If a student turns in a poor performance, rather than dwelling on the poor performance, tell the student that you expect better work next time.

- *Link learning with positive emotions.* One way to prevent classical conditioning of negative responses is to arrange repeated pairing of positive feelings with certain kinds of learning, especially subjects that are anxiety provoking. For example, teachers can let students who are having reading difficulties read in a comfortable, welcoming reading area. Students may come to associate the pleasure they feel from being in the reading area with the task of reading.

- *Teach students to generalize and discriminate appropriately.* Teachers need to help students determine which stimuli should be linked with responses. Poor performance on one project or test does not make the student an overall poor performer!

- *Help students cope with classically conditioned anxiety.* Students with severe test anxiety or other anxiety problems may need outside help, but teachers can help many students take steps to reduce milder cases of classically conditioned anxiety.

Learning by Operant Conditioning

Operant conditioning (also called *instrumental conditioning*) is learning produced by the rewards and punishments of active behavior (an *operant*) of a human or other organism interacting with the environment. This active behavior, called an **operant,** is the behavior the organism, or person, uses to "operate" on the environment. Thus, when Tom's student Mark finally began to talk about his science project, his talking was the operant, and Tom's praise, the reward. Operant conditioning results in either an increase or a decrease in the probability of an operant behavior in response to environmental events.

The differences between classical and operant conditioning are summarized in Table 7.1. As you can see in the table, the crucial difference between classical and operant conditioning is in the role of the individual. In classical conditioning, the individual is largely passive. The experimenter or the environment controls the repeated pairings of the CS with the US. In classical conditioning, therefore, the crucial relationship for conditioning is between the CS and the US. In operant conditioning, in contrast, the individual is largely active. The individual operates on the environment in order to bring about reinforcement. In fact, this key feature is what leads to the use of the term *operant* for the basic unit of behavior studied in operant conditioning. Thus the crucial relationship for operant conditioning is between environmental contingencies and the kinds of behavior (operants) an organism emits.

Scientists who believe that much and possibly all of behavior can be accounted for by operant conditioning are called *behaviorists*. The founding father of behaviorism was John Watson (1878–1958), who believed the principles of behaviorism can be applied to create virtually any behavior at all in a person, acceptable or unacceptable (Buckley, 2000). The most influential of modern behaviorists was Burrhus F. Skinner (1904–1990), who developed a theory and set of methods known as the *experimental analysis of behavior*. According to this point of view, all behavior should be studied in terms of the effects of environmental contingencies on behavior. Skinner believed the study of animals, such as rats and pigeons, is particularly useful for understanding the principles of learning (Coleman, 2000). The boxes into which he placed these animals in order to study conditioning have come to be called *Skinner boxes* in his honor.

Skinner believed the principles of conditioning can be applied widely in life, because to Skinner much of life involves learning to deal with the effects of the environment on our actions. At some level, Skinner was certainly right. Rewards and punishments certainly shape much of our daily behavior. How was such a powerful phenomenon first discovered?

TABLE **7.1** **Comparison of the Main Features of Classical and Operant Conditioning**

	Classical Conditioning	**Operant Conditioning**
Key relationship	Between conditioned stimulus and unconditioned stimulus.	Between operant behavior and its consequences (either reward or punishment).
Student's behavior	Involuntary. Behavior is elicited by the unconditioned or conditioned stimulus.	Voluntary. Behavior occurs; then its likelihood is increased or decreased by its consequences.
Sequence of events	At the start of conditioning: NS US UR / After conditioning is acquired: CS CR	Operant behavior: Reinforcement—increase in behavior or / Operant behavior: Punishment—decrease in behavior.
Example	Teacher repeatedly raises hand before shouting "Quiet." Unconditioned response of being quiet when shout is heard is similar to conditioned response of becoming quiet when hand is raised.	Reinforcement: Teacher praises students when they happen to be quiet. They are more likely to be quiet in the future. Punishment: Teacher ends students' free time when they get too noisy. They are less likely to be noisy during future free time.

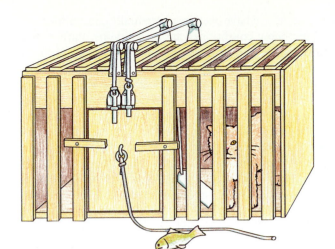

FIGURE **7.2**

Thorndike's Puzzle Box

Edward Thorndike observed that cats could learn to release themselves from puzzle boxes such as this one when they were rewarded for doing so. These experiments led him to develop the Law of Effect, which states that those actions that are rewarded will tend to be strengthened and will be more likely to occur in the future, whereas those actions that are punished will be weakened and thus will be less likely to occur in the future.

THE DISCOVERY OF OPERANT CONDITIONING

At some level, people have always known that organisms respond to rewards and punishments. Thus the discovery of operant conditioning was more identifying a phenomenon than it was an actual discovery. Edward Lee Thorndike (1898, 1911) studied cats placed in puzzle boxes (see Figure 7.2). The door to the puzzle box was held tightly shut by a latch. However, the latch could be easily opened when its fastening device (which was located inside the cage) was appropriately triggered. The cat inside the cage could see a delicious piece of fish in a dish, located just outside the cage. First, the cat would try to reach the fish by extending its paws through the slats of the cage, but it would not succeed. Then it would start scratching, bumping, and jumping around in its cage. Eventually, it would accidentally release the latch, simply through a process of trial and error. Once it did so, the door to the cage would open, and the cat would run to get the fish.

Later, the cat would again be placed in the cage, and the whole process would be repeated. But this time, the scratching and jumping around would not last very long. After many trials, the cat could be placed in the box, and it would immediately claw the button to release the latch and enable it to get to the fish. The cat had learned how to open the cage.

Thorndike proposed a mechanism to account for operant conditioning, which he referred to as the **law of effect,** a law stating that those actions that are rewarded—"the effect"—will tend to be strengthened and will be more likely to occur in the future, whereas those actions that are punished will be weakened and thus will be less likely to occur in the future. Thus, according to Thorndike, the crucial variable for operant conditioning is reward or punishment. In Thorndike's time, reward and punishment were viewed simply as having opposite effects. Today, educational psychologists know the situation is much more complicated, with punishment, especially, often having unintended related consequences.

Operant conditioning occurs in the classroom with great frequency. It happens to teachers as well as to students.

RECOGNIZING OPERANT CONDITIONING IN THE CLASSROOM

Suppose you teach two main kinds of lessons in an English class: literature and grammar. On the whole, the students love the literature but hate the grammar. When you teach literature, the students seem to light up: They smile, they respond actively, they are happy. When you teach grammar, they are, at best, silent and sulky, and at worst, noisy and disruptive. Slowly you may find yourself spending more and more time teaching literature

---

THINKING ANALYTICALLY

Think about the cat that learned to open the latch in Thorndike's puzzle box through a process that began with the cat inadvertently opening the latch. What might students perceive about learning classroom lessons through instrumental conditioning that is much like that experienced by the cat in the puzzle box?

SUGGESTION: They might understand that learning one lesson provides the key to learning the next. Also, they may realize that their own actions are important in learning each of those lessons.

and less and less time teaching grammar. You have been instrumentally conditioned! An expert teacher is on the lookout for being conditioned by his students. Rather than allowing himself to be conditioned, the expert teacher looks for ways to make more interesting the subjects that students are less responsive to, such as grammar.

Operant conditioning also occurs in interactions among the children you are teaching (or in your interactions with your peers). Suppose two girls want to work together in an art workshop, but one wants to work with paints, the other with clay. A heated discussion ensues. Eventually, one of the girls finally gives in, pointing out that although she wants to work with paints, she values the friendship more than the choice of art medium. She suggests, therefore, that they work with the clay. The other girl, embarrassed, looks the first girl straight in the eye and suggests they work with paints after all.

The next time the girls have an argument, whether about art media or something else, the argument may be briefer. The first girl again will give in, and thereby end up getting what she wants. She has been instrumentally conditioned, and has learned that, paradoxically, she can get her way by giving in. Many of us can remember similar situations in our daily lives with our families or spouses.

What are the key principles of operant conditioning? First, we examine how desired behavior can be increased, or even created, by using reinforcement.

HOW DOES OPERANT CONDITIONING HAPPEN?

As Thorndike's law of effect states, the consequences, or environmental responses to operant behaviors, are the key to operant conditioning. The consequences of behavior can be divided into two broad categories, rewards and punishments, which are also known as *reinforcers*. Let us explore each of these two options in some depth.

■ **REINFORCEMENT** A **reinforcer** is a stimulus that increases the probability the operant associated with it will happen again. The reinforcer typically occurs immediately or very soon after the behavior in question. If it does not occur soon thereafter, learning does not take place, or is weakened. Reinforcers are of two kinds: positive and negative.

A *positive reinforcer* is a reward that follows an operant and increases the likelihood of that operant occurring again. When a positive reinforcer occurs soon after an operant behavior, thereby strengthening the response, we refer to the pairing of the positive reinforcer with the response as **positive reinforcement.** Examples of positive reinforcers are a teacher's approval, as indicated by a smile or a favorable comment; an A on a test; or even the candy bar that comes out of a vending machine after you have put in your money. One positive reinforcer that teachers frequently use is praise. The Flexible Expert: Using Praise Effectively shows how some expert teachers and students use praise.

A *negative reinforcer* is an unpleasant stimulus that ceases or is removed following an operant behavior. The removal of an unpleasant stimulus that results in an increased

An eighth-grade teacher inappropriately reprimands a student while the rest of the class looks on. An expert teacher takes great care in punishing a student for inappropriate behavior—explaining the problem clearly, immediately instituting the punishment, punishing consistently, and coupling the punishment with positive reinforcement. (Will Hart)

IN EACH CHAPTER OF THE TEXT, WE INTRODUCE YOU TO A FEW SPECIFIC STRATEGIES—
ANALYTICAL, CREATIVE, AND PRACTICAL—USED BY BOTH EXPERT TEACHERS AND EXPERT STUDENTS.

THE ANALYTICAL TEACHER: Tanisha would like all her students to complete a term paper. She breaks the assignment into several steps, then praises and rewards students as they finish each step.

THE CREATIVE TEACHER: Tanisha practices several different ways she can provide encouragement—both verbally and nonverbally—without repeating herself too often.

THE PRACTICAL TEACHER: Tanisha keeps careful records and samples of students' past work, so she can always find something specific about which to offer genuine praise when she writes comments on homework papers.

THE ANALYTICAL STUDENT: Austin points out to the other members of his social studies project team that they have all really learned a lot about Brazil since they started the project, and lists the accomplishments of several students who deserve thanks.

THE CREATIVE STUDENT: Austin, realizing he has been paying more attention to achieving length than to coming up with good ideas for his term paper, decides to reward himself not by how much he writes, but by how original he thinks his ideas are for that day of work on the paper.

THE PRACTICAL STUDENT: Austin, realizing he has been hogging the soccer ball, starts praising himself each time he makes a pass to a teammate.

probability of the response's occurring is called **negative reinforcement.** *Negative* here refers not to something *bad,* but to *removal:* Negative reinforcement comes not from presenting of a stimulus, but from taking it away. Negative reinforcement and punishment are sometimes confused with each other, although they are completely different. The key difference is that punishment decreases the probability of a response, whereas negative reinforcement, like positive reinforcement, increases it. An example of a negative reinforcement is the way an annoying buzz or bell in a car stops when all the occupants have fastened their seat belts. The end of the sound is usually rewarding enough to increase the chances that you will fasten your seat belt the next time you enter the car.

An example of the use of negative reinforcement in the classroom occurs when an elementary school teacher says, "We will go outside for recess just as soon as you clean the classroom." The negative reinforcement is release from the cleaning of the classroom. The release from cleaning the classroom is likely to be rewarding enough that students will clean up the room more promptly the next time the teacher asks. Another example would be allowing students who get 100 percent on a practice spelling test to skip the later formal test. A problem with the deliberate use of negative reinforcement is it requires the introduction of some level of unpleasant stimulation that will be alleviated through the technique.

Teachers, too, are negatively reinforced on a regular basis. When a teacher gives in to students' whining requests to skip homework or a quiz, he or she is usually rewarded by a cessation of the whining requests. Such negative reinforcement could increase the chances that, the next time students beg for a reprieve, the teacher will give up even faster.

■**CHOOSING REINFORCERS** Psychologists distinguish between two main kinds of reinforcers. **Primary reinforcers** are rewards, such as food and shelter from the elements, that provide immediate satisfaction or enjoyment. **Secondary reinforcers** are rewards that gain reinforcement value through their association with primary reinforcers. They are not inherently reinforcing, or satisfying in a basic biological sense, as are primary reinforcers. Rather, they are learned to be reinforcing. Examples of secondary

THINKING PRACTICALLY

How might you positively reinforce your students? Now, how might students positively reinforce you?

SUGGESTION: You give praise to reinforce students. When students pay attention, they reinforce you.

Many schools overuse one kind of secondary reinforcer to a point that this reinforcer may not help students to develop as well as they might. What kind of reinforcer might this be?

SUGGESTION: Grades sometimes are overused. This process can lead students to place too much emphasis on grades rather than on what they are learning.

reinforcers are grades, money, and objects associated with status, such as clothing or fancy cars. Money, for example, is paper with no value in itself, but it can buy us food, shelter, and much more. Most of the reinforcers you will use as a teacher are secondary reinforcers.

One way some teachers use secondary reinforcers is by creating *token economies,* or systems in which token-based reinforcement is used to change behavior (Kazdin, 2000). The tokens are objects that in themselves have no value, such as a certificate or a star on a chart, but are exchanged for other things that do have value. Token economies are common in classrooms. In a typical arrangement, students will be rewarded for performing a desired behavior with a token. After accumulating a certain number of tokens, students can exchange them, or use them to "buy" desired rewards. For example, ten certificates may earn the student a chance to choose from a selection of small toys or school supplies. Ten stars may be worth ten minutes of free time on Friday.

Token economies have been used successfully to improve student conduct as well as academic performance (McLaughlin & Williams, 1988; Shook, LaBrie, Vallies, McLaughlin, & Williams, 1990). Some commentators, however, have raised questions about the ethics and long-term effectiveness of reward systems, and the use of behavioral learning methods in general. These questions are explored in the Forum: Are Behavioral Approaches Ethical?

FORUM

ARE BEHAVIORAL APPROACHES ETHICAL?

The research summarized in this chapter clearly indicates that behavioral approaches can be powerful tools to affect student learning. Some teachers and commentators, however, suggest that the use of behavioral learning approaches is ethically unacceptable and, perhaps, ineffective as well. Much of the debate has focused on operant conditioning, particularly rewarding students.

FIRST VIEW: *Against Behavioral Approaches.* Some scholars have suggested that behavioral techniques are too controlling, that they are "a way of doing things to children rather than working with them" (Kohn, 1993, p. 784). Teachers could easily misuse rewards and punishments. For example, as we saw in Chapter 6, a teacher may inadvertently reward boys more often than girls for raising their hands and speaking in class, teaching girls to avoid class participation. The dangers of punishment are detailed later in this chapter.

In addition, behavioral principles may backfire, becoming ineffective in the long run. Some schools, for example, have used rewards, including cash incentives, to reinforce attendance, reading, or good grades (Gorman, 1994). Critics of reward plans, however, warn that students may perform the tasks required to earn rewards or avoid punishment, but only as long as the rewards or punishments remain in effect. They may never make a commitment of their own to learning (Bracey, 1994; Kohn, 1993). Worse yet, some research has shown that rewarding behavior by which a student is already intrinsically motivated can actually decrease the student's intrinsic motivation (Sethi, Drake, Dialdin, & Lepper, 1995; Spence & Helmreich, 1983; Swanson, 1995). A student who enjoys reading, for example, may find that being required to read two books a week in order to earn reward points actually dims his or her pleasure in reading.

SECOND VIEW: *In Defense of Behavioral Approaches.* Defenders of behavioral learning approaches point out that students' actions are rewarded or punished all the time in various ways. Controlling behavioral consequences, they argue, actually provides for more fairness in education than leaving the possibility of rewards up to chance. For example, a math teacher can praise students as they learn each of the steps in subtraction, rather than letting students who learn faster be the only ones to earn rewards, in the form of the highest test scores. In addition, behavioral approaches provide feedback to students about their performance. According to Paul Chance (1993, p. 788), "[P]eople learn best in a responsive environment. Teachers who praise or otherwise reward student performance provide such an environment."

The effects of rewards on intrinsic motivation are not entirely clear, either, as you will learn in Chapter 10. A student may be highly intrinsically motivated, but also have high needs for extrinsic motivation. He or she may enjoy reading about people in other countries during social studies class, but also savor a teacher's praise for a good class presentation about Venezuela. In addition, the nature of the task may be related to the effectiveness of rewards. Some research has suggested, for example, that rewards can enhance creativity on difficult, but not on easy, tasks (Eisenberger & Selbst, 1994).

THIRD VIEW: A SYNTHESIS: *Behavioral approaches to learning, operant conditioning in particular, are here to stay.* The challenge for expert teachers is to use behavioral learning techniques wisely. Students need not be passive recipients of behavioral techniques. Teachers can involve students in plans for modifying the students' behavior and encourage students to reward themselves as they progress. External rewards, whether given by the teacher or self-rewarded, may help students overcome their initial difficulties or lack of interest in some subjects. In fact, some school districts have offered high school students incentives simply for attending school, based on the idea that, once the initial hurdle of showing up was passed, students might reap intrinsic rewards from their participation (Phillipps, 1995).

Some evidence indicates that once the initial stages are mastered, whether through the help of rewards or not, students' growing competence does become its own reward (Chance, 1992). For example, a student may need rewards for undertaking each of the component steps required in learning to write a short story, but once he or she becomes able to craft stories without help, the joy of writing may become intrinsically motivating. The goal of behavioral learning techniques, and of all teaching, is for students to master the desired behavior themselves—to move beyond their need for the teacher.

Is a primary or a secondary reinforcer more effective? What kinds of secondary reinforcers might work with your students? The answers to these questions are different for every student. Expert teachers realize that what is reinforcing for one person may not be for another; usually it requires some experimentation to find what works best with each student. This principle was demonstrated by David Premack (1959), who experimented with two different rewards, playing with a pinball machine and eating candy. Premack found that some children preferred one of the rewards; other children preferred the other reward. You may have noticed the same phenomenon yourself. Perhaps a good friend rewards himself or herself for a productive afternoon of studying by spending an hour in a lively pickup basketball game, an activity you would find unrewarding in the extreme, preferring to treat yourself to an hour-long nap. The idea that different people like different things is certainly useful to keep in mind. But an even more useful discovery came from Premack's research, a discovery called the *Premack principle.*

The **Premack principle** states that more preferred activities reinforce those that are less preferred (Premack, 1959). According to Premack, everyone has a reinforcement hierarchy, in which (1) reinforcers higher in the hierarchy are more likely to produce operant behaviors than are reinforcers lower in the hierarchy, and in which (2) activities higher in the hierarchy reinforce those lower in the hierarchy. Thus Premack found that, for children who preferred the candy, one could reinforce playing with the pinball machine by giving the children candy. For children who preferred playing with the pinball machine, one could reinforce eating the candy by allowing the children to play with the pinball machine. Like operant conditioning itself, the Premack principle has been

Think of a child you have taught or interacted with whose preferences you know quite well. How might you use the Premack principle to reinforce the kinds of behavior you desire in that child?

SUGGESTION: Find out what kinds of rewards will reinforce the behavior you want to see in that child. Then use those rewards.

known informally for a long time. In fact, some people refer to it as "Grandma's rule," based on the type of bargains made every day by some clever grandmothers, such as "You can go out to play after you finish eating your vegetables."

The Premack principle can be useful to people who want to become expert teachers. In effect, it means that to be an expert teacher who uses reinforcement effectively, you need to determine each of your student's reinforcement hierarchies. You can find out by observing what they like to do in varying degrees. You can then use your observations to provide appropriate reinforcements to the children—that is, applying the reinforcements that will work best for them (and are acceptable to you!), and reinforcing less desired behaviors (say, doing math for a given child) with more desired behaviors (say, playing at recess). Consider the active practice of the Premack principle in a classroom of first graders who love crafts: A teacher reinforces the increased use of correct grammar by bringing in special clay for students to play with during free time.

■**SCHEDULES OF REINFORCEMENT**   Neither you nor your students are always rewarded for good behavior, nor are you always punished for bad behavior. Yet you behave well, at least a good part of the time! Why is this so?

We are reinforced in life on a **schedule of reinforcement,** that is, a certain pattern by which reinforcements follow operants. In our preceding discussion, we actually assumed a schedule of **continuous reinforcement**—that a reinforcement always follows a particular desired behavior. For example, in the early Thorndike experiments, the cat got to eat the fish every time it was able to open the latch. But in everyday life, we are much more likely to encounter schedules of **partial reinforcement** (also called **intermittent reinforcement**). In these schedules, the desired behavior is reinforced only some of the time.

The two basic types of reinforcement schedules are *ratio schedules* and *interval schedules.* In a **ratio schedule** a certain number of the desired operants is reinforced, without regard to the passage of time. For example, if you pay a child something for every eight empty bottles she returns, the reinforced schedule is a ratio one. The critical variable here is the number of times the operant has occurred. In an **interval schedule,** reinforcement is a function of the time that has passed, regardless of the number of operants that have occurred (as long as there has been at least one operant). Being paid every two weeks is an example of delivering a reinforcement on an interval schedule. Furthermore, there are two types of both ratio and interval schedules: fixed and variable. How do the four partial reinforcement schedules work?

In a *fixed-ratio reinforcement schedule,* reinforcements always occur after a certain number of responses have occurred. For example, some libraries have summer book clubs and recognize children for having read a fixed numbers of books. Thus there might be some recognition for the child's having read five books, further recognition at ten books, and so on. If students must complete ten homework assignments over the course of an academic term to earn an A, again, this is a fixed-ratio schedule of reinforcement.

In a *variable-ratio schedule of reinforcement,* the individual is rewarded, on average, for a certain number of responses, but the exact number of responses needed to gain a reward can vary from one reinforcement to the next. Teachers usually reinforce students on a variable-ratio schedule for raising their hands to answer questions in class. The teacher may call on each student an average of once out of every four hand raises, for example, but the actual number of times a student must raise his or hand before being called on varies.

In a *fixed-interval schedule of reinforcement,* individuals are always reinforced for the first response that occurs after the passage of a fixed amount of time, regardless of how many operant responses have taken place after that time interval. Fixed-interval reinforcements are fairly common in our lives. When schools have fixed marking periods, after which grades are assigned for a given period of time (perhaps every six weeks or quarterly), the grades can serve as fixed-interval reinforcements.

Finally, in a *variable-interval schedule of reinforcement,* individuals are reinforced for the first response after the passage of an average interval of time, regardless of how many operant responses have taken place after that time interval. The specific amount of time between reinforcements can change from one reinforcement to the next. For example, in some countries, people who are supposed to be paid on a fixed-interval schedule actually are paid on a variable interval schedule!

Table 7.2 shows the patterns of behavior that each of the schedules of reinforcement tends to produce. As you can see, the various schedules tend to produce different patterns of behavior. Continuous reinforcement tends to produce behavior more quickly, but also to eliminate behavior more quickly if the reinforcement stops. With regard to partial schedules, ratio schedules generally produce more of the desired behavior than do interval schedules. For fixed schedules, there tends to be a pause in behavior right after reinforcement is administered: Variable schedules maintain a more nearly constant rate of responding than do fixed schedules.

In everyday life, schedules of reinforcement are often much more complex than our discussion suggests. For example, certain kinds of rewards and recognitions are given out according to a system that contains aspects of both variable-ratio and variable-interval schedules of reinforcement. Awards for good teaching, in places where they are given, might represent systems that combine ratio and interval schedules. Moreover, schedules of reinforcement can change. A teaching technique that worked almost all the time in your early years of teaching may start working less frequently in your later years, because of societal changes in the behavior patterns of the children.

THINKING CREATIVELY

Give one example, in addition to those in the text, of one of the four kinds of partial reinforcement schedules as it occurs in a school setting.

SUGGESTION: Teachers call on children who raise their hands on (roughly) a variable-ratio schedule. The more the children raise their hands, the more they are called on, but they are not called on every time.

TABLE 7.2   Schedules of Reinforcement

Schedule	Description When Reinforcement Starts	Example	Pattern of Response		
			During Reinforcement	When Reinforcement Stops	After Reinforcement Stops
Continuous	Every operant is reinforced.	Gold star for every paper turned in.	Rapid increase in operants.	Steady response as long as reinforcer is desired.	Operants rapidly stop.
Fixed ratio	Reinforcement occurs for first response after a certain fixed number of operants.	Gold star for every five papers turned in.	Fairly rapid increase in operants, but not as fast as under continuous reinforcement.	Usually high response rate, but with a pause after each reinforcer.	Operants stop rapidly if reinforcement does not occur after expected number of operants.
Variable ratio	Reinforcement occurs after varying numbers of operants.	Teacher picks a different "magic number" every day for number of papers to be turned in to earn a gold star.	Slow increase in operants.	Steady and high—less pause after each reinforcer.	Operants stop slowly.
Fixed interval	Reinforcement occurs for first response after a certain fixed period of time.	Gold star every week after weekly paper is turned in.	Somewhat faster increase in operants than in variable schedules, slower than under continuous reinforcement.	High, but response rate often increases as time for reinforcement approaches, then drops after each reinforcement.	Operants stop rapidly if reinforcement does not occur after expected amount of time.
Variable interval	Reinforcement occurs for first response after varying amounts of time.	Surprise "Gold Star Days" when turning in paper earns gold star.	Slow increase in operants.	Constant high response rate with little pause after each reinforcement.	Operants decrease slowly and gradually.

■ **ANTECEDENTS OF BEHAVIOR**   Expert teachers know that if they wait for a desired behavior to occur before providing reinforcement, they may end up waiting a long time. Similarly, if they wait for an undesired behavior to occur before punishing it, frustration and unhappiness may result for both student and teacher. The solution for both these problems is to prepare students with some idea of what kind of behavior is expected of them. *Antecedent stimuli,* or *cues,* are events that precede an operant behavior and serve to predict the consequences of that behavior. Antecedent stimuli demonstrate the role that cognitive processes can play in operant conditioning.

Students can act on their knowledge about potential consequences either to achieve promised rewards or to avoid threatened punishment. Teachers can use several ways to cue students about the potential consequences of their acts. Teachers can simply tell students what will happen. For example, a teacher may say, "If you hand in all ten homework assignments on time over the course of the semester, you will earn fifty points toward your final grade." Tom Douglass might have given his student Jimmy a cue about the upcoming punishment for interrupting Mara by saying, "Jimmy, if you interrupt Mara once more, I will send you to the hallway for a time-out." Teachers can also create written or visual reminders, such as posters of class rules or checklists for projects or activities (Sulzer-Azaroff & Mayer, 1986). A formal method of informing students about the consequences of their behavior is to draw up a **contingency contract,** a written or oral agreement between student and teacher specifying desired behavior and promised reward.

■ **PUNISHMENT**   Mr. Clemens believes in very strict discipline in his classroom. He seeks to establish order and control on the very first day of class. By making an example of any transgressors, he believes he can quickly get the students in line. This year, the first one to get out of line was Ricky. Ricky had taunted another student for being stupid. After scolding Ricky for taunting the other student and then pointing out to Ricky that by his actions he had shown himself to be the head of the stupidity department, Mr. Clemens put Ricky in a corner for the rest of the day. Ricky was facing the wall and unable to see or interact with other children. Mr. Clemens made assorted jibes at Ricky during the day, noting that the only way he seemed to learn how to behave with others was to be by himself, and he didn't look so tough with his back facing the class.

Mr. Clemens seems to have established an orderly classroom. As always, the principal is impressed when she comes to observe. But other teachers have complained that Mr. Clemens's students are far more aggressive than are the other students at recess. They cause trouble on the playground when anyone but Mr. Clemens is supervising them. Also, a disproportionate number of antisocial events outside the school have involved Mr. Clemens's students. Worse, Ricky has become a hero to some of the students in Mr. Clemens's classroom, and the student Ricky taunted has been ostracized by these children. Moreover, Mr. Clemens has modeled the very behavior he criticized, and now has lost the respect of many of his students.

Mr. Clemens has reached his main goal: Through frequent and harsh use of punishment, he has established order in his classroom, and as a result he rarely has classroom incidents. Were that his only goal, he might be viewed as successful. But to the extent that his behavior has been aimed at reducing aggression in his students, his policies not only seem to have been unsuccessful, but have backfired. Other teachers find his students to be the most aggressive of all outside the classroom. Such patterns are not uncommon: Highly punitive parents often find they are able to achieve discipline in the home at the cost of producing a bully in the outside world. What exactly is happening here? Might there be other ways Mr. Clemens can teach children good behavior? How much should a teacher depend on punishment?

Punishment is the use of a stimulus that decreases the probability of a response (Steinberg, 2000). A response can be discouraged through **presentation punishment,** the application of an aversive, or unpleasant stimulus. Examples of aversive stimuli are failing grades, being yelled at, or, in the case of Ricky, feeling humiliated. A response can also be discouraged through **removal punishment,** taking away a pleasant stimulus.

Removal of a pleasant stimulus is also referred to as a *penalty*. Common examples of penalties are losing recess privileges or having a desired toy or book taken away.

In some situations, teachers cannot avoid using punishment. For example, if a student or other child has done something that places herself or another student in danger, punishment may be called for. Or if attempts to use reinforcement have failed, punishment may be advisable. If you decide to use punishment to correct errant behavior, a number of guidelines can help you use it more effectively (Parke & Walters, 1967; Walters & Grusec, 1977). In particular, the person administering the punishment should consider the following options:

- **Provide alternative responses.** Make available alternative responses to replace those being punished. If the student does not see what else can be done instead of what he or she is doing, it is difficult to change the behavior. For example, assume that Ricky wanted praise for his science skills. Mr. Clemens could have sent Ricky to the corner to think about why he taunted another student but then taken Ricky aside after class and helped him create a special science project. Once Ricky finished the project, Mr. Clemens could allow Ricky to present his work to the class. This alternative way of gaining peers' attention has many benefits, including Ricky's change from a negative role model into a positive one.

- **Couple punishment with positive reinforcement.** Complement the punishment with positive reinforcement that rewards the behavior you desire instead. For example, Mr. Clemens could have reinforced Ricky's interest in science by giving Ricky many opportunities to exhibit his science skills. Homework is one commonly used opportunity. In instances of aggression, a teacher should reward students when they are gentle and considerate, even if those are times when students are not interacting much with others.

- **Explain the problem.** Ensure that the student being punished understands just what behavior is being punished, and why. Do not assume that because it is obvious to you why punishment is called for, it will be obvious to the student as well.

- **Punish immediately.** Administer the punishment immediately after the undesirable operant behavior, or as soon as possible thereafter.

- **Use appropriate intensity.** Administer punishment that is appropriate for the infraction, neither greater nor longer than necessary to make the point.

- **Punish consistently.** The inappropriate behavior *always* should be punished.

- **Make escape impossible.** Try to make sure it is impossible for the student to escape the punishment if the behavior is demonstrated.

- **Use penalties.** Use removal punishment (withholding of rewards or other desired things), wherever possible, in preference to presentation punishment. For example, preferably Mr. Clemens would have removed attention from Ricky because attention seemed to be what Ricky was seeking.

- **Ensure appropriateness.** Above all, make sure the punishment is appropriate in the first place and that it will not backfire. Assigning English compositions as a punishment, for example, may lead to an aversion to doing such compositions. Emotional abuse may damage a child's psychological well-being. After the time Ricky spent in the corner, a public apology from him to the taunted student would have been much more appropriate than the emotional abuse that Mr. Clemens inflicted on him.

In the case at the beginning of this chapter, fifth-grade teacher Tom Douglass followed the guidelines outlined here when he punished Jimmy,

THINKING ANALYTICALLY

Think of a situation in which you have used punishment. Using the principles described here, state how you might have made the punishment more effective.

SUGGESTION: You can make a punishment more effective by rendering it immediately after the provocative act.

who was interrupting another student's presentation to the class. Tom promptly applied a punishment that was appropriate for the situation—a time-out—along with instructions for an alternative behavior—Jimmy's quietly thinking about how he could behave better when he returned. **Time-out,** a brief period of social isolation, not only serves as a punishment, depriving a student of pleasant social stimulation, but also removes a reward that the student may have been receiving for his or her unacceptable behavior, the attention and approval of classmates (O'Leary & O'Leary, 1977). It seems to be effective in changing behavior.

Another effective form of punishment is a **response cost,** a small penalty imposed for each instance of the undesirable behavior. If Tom had told Jimmy that, for each time he interrupted Mara, he would lose one minute of recess, he would have been using response cost. Although only of use in a few situations, another technique that can some-times effectively decrease the likelihood of an undesirable behavior is **satiation,** compelling students to continue a behavior until they are tired of it. If Jimmy had been interrupting Mara by flying a paper airplane across the room while she was talking, Tom Douglass could have used satiation by presenting Jimmy with 100 sheets of paper and telling him to make paper airplanes from every sheet. The chore of making dozens of paper airplanes might cause Jimmy to be less interested in making them in the future. Some educators have sug-gested the use of *assertive discipline* to control behavior. Such discipline involves carefully stating rules and describing specific reinforcements and punishments that will follow from obedience or disobedience (Canter & Canter, 1992). Such discipline has the advantage that the consequences of behavior are clearly spelled out. Nevertheless, this method of disci-pline has been criticized for putting teachers and students into antagonistic roles, and for stressing obedience at the expense of learning (e.g., McLaughlin, 1994). Thus the program is controversial but is still widely used. Table 7.3 reviews the four most common forms of operant conditioning—positive and neg-ative reinforcement, presentation punishment, and removal punishment— and their effects on operant behavior.

THINKING CREATIVELY

A teacher yells at her students for talking during her lectures. How might she instead use reinforcement to change that behavior?

SUGGESTION: Instead of punishing students' talking, she could reward their silence.

In spite of its effectiveness in certain classroom situations, punishment should never be used for retribution or retaliation. Expert teachers know that punishment can be less effective for achieving behavioral change than reinforcement. Ultimately, punishment should be used to produce posi-tive behavior, which can then be rewarded. Moreover, as described in Table 7.4, punish-ment can lead to unfortunate side effects, such as escape attempts, backfires, increased aggressiveness, decreased self-esteem, or even injury (Bates, 1987; Bongiovanni, 1977). Corporal punishment, or hitting, is likely to lead to the last of these dangers, injury to students. The risks of injury, as well as all the other dangers inherent in the use of pun-ishment, indicate that teachers should refrain from using corporal punishment. In fact, the practice is banned in over half of U.S. states (Evans & Richardson, 1995).

TABLE 7.3   Consequences of Operant Behavior

Name of Consequence	Description	Effect of Consequence on Future Operant Behavior	Example
Positive reinforcement	A *pleasant* stimulus is *presented* fol-lowing operant behavior.	*Increases* likelihood.	Student receives a gold star for handing in assignment on time.
Negative reinforcement	An *unpleasant* stimulus is *removed* following operant behavior.	*Increases* likelihood.	Student goes to recess only after assignment is completed.
Presentation punishment	An *unpleasant* stimulus is *presented* following operant behavior.	*Decreases* likelihood.	Student is scolded for failing to turn in assignment.
Removal punishment (penalty)	A *pleasant* stimulus is *removed* following operant behavior.	*Decreases* likelihood.	Student loses gerbil-feeding privilege for failing to turn in assignment.

TABLE 7.4	The Dangers of Punishment	
Danger	**Description**	**Example**
Escape attempts	Students try to continue with the behavior being punished, but to find a way of continuing without being punished (such as by hiding the behavior).	Ricky may continue to taunt other students, being careful to do so only when Mr. Clemens has his back turned or is out of the room.
Backfiring	Punishment, especially when harsh, may cause unintended, or even the direct opposite of intended, results.	Mr. Clemens's punishment of Ricky may cause Ricky to become so afraid of being punished that he starts skipping class in order to avoid Mr. Clemens.
Increased aggressiveness	Punishment can increase aggressive behavior on the part of the person being punished. Sometimes the behavior of the individual will improve in interactions with the person administering the punishment, but the individual will then show the same or similar punishing behavior with others.	Mr. Clemens used punishment to elicit compliance, and gained it, but at the expense of his students' acting out aggressive behavior outside the classroom.
Loss of self-esteem	Even when behavioral change is achieved, it sometimes occurs at the expense of a severe loss of self-esteem, which can be more damaging, in the long run, than the behavior that was punished.	Mr. Clemens's taunts may have convinced Ricky that he is, indeed, stupid and ill behaved, an image he will now reflect in his future behavior.
Injury	Punishment can result in inadvertent (or occasionally, intentional) injury. Punishment becomes child abuse when a child is physically or psychologically harmed as a result of the punishment.	Ricky may develop depression as a result of his low self-esteem and subsequent poor relations with teachers, classmates, and parents.

CONSTRUCTING YOUR OWN LEARNING

Practice shaping techniques using yourself as a subject. Think of a goal that you would like to reach such as losing 20 pounds or getting in shape to run a 10K race. Make a list of small steps that you could take that would lead to the goal. The steps should be ones that you will carry out over a period of days, weeks, or even months, not all ones you can do right away. Plot out a plan for reaching the goal, ensuring that each of the steps along the way is sufficiently realistic that you could attain it without giving up on the whole plan along the way. Decide how you could reinforce yourself for attaining each of those steps. Consider how, if you falter at some point, you could get back on the plan. You might share your plan with others, to see whether they have suggestions as to how better to reach your goal. You might also want to commit yourself to the plan publicly, in order to increase your incentive to follow through on it. Now, go ahead and, over whatever time period it takes, execute the plan. Be sure to keep a record of your progress. What, if anything, would you do differently if you were planning to shape the behavior of students you taught, instead of your own?

BEHAVIORAL MODIFICATION: CHANGING STUDENTS' BEHAVIOR

When teachers use operant conditioning in the classroom, they are generally interested in **behavioral modification,** or changing students' behavior by managing the contingencies, or consequences, of that behavior. Teachers may be interested in increasing such desired behavior as the completion of homework or expressions of respect toward fellow students. Or they may need to decrease incidents of unwanted behavior, such as disruption of a class by talking out of turn or acts of aggression toward classmates. The ultimate goal of any behavioral modification program is to produce self-regulated learners who will be able to control and modify their own behavior.

In using behavioral modification, keep in mind that you are dealing with people, not rats or pigeons. Expert teachers show respect for their students' humanity and carefully consider the ethical issues involved, such as whether it truly is the teacher's prerogative

Scott Turner uses conditioning and reinforcements to encourage students to respect each other and remain on task. The atmosphere in his classroom is relaxed and nonpunitive. Students often view the behavioral methods as fun or helpful.

Do you use behavioral methods with your second-grade students?

Yes. For example, when I need to say something important. I ring a bell and students are supposed to freeze. We practiced it in the beginning of the school year. It works well. Sometimes I need to ring the bell twice. If there are a few kids who are not standing still, they feel self-conscious because all the other kids are frozen. They quickly get the point.

What methods do you use to reinforce good behavior?

I reinforce good behavior from the class, as a whole, with a handful of marbles. I have an empty glass jar, and when the students are well mannered I put a handful of marbles in the jar. For example, if another teacher comes to my class to teach a lesson or if we go to the library and the students are quiet and good listeners, I give them a handful of marbles. My one rule is that they can't ask for the marbles. I tell them that these are things they should be doing anyway, like walking in a straight line and not talking during a fire drill. I probably give the class a handful of marbles two or three times a week; it's a variable schedule. When

the jar is full, they get a class party. We watch a short video cartoon, and I bring in ice cream or pizza.

To reward individual students, each day I give a starfish card to one student who shows a positive attitude—cooperation, dependability, sharing, responsibility. This is a big deal for the kids. For example, one student continued to write on his paper even after I called "time." When I was correcting his paper, I noticed that he had erased some writing. He told me, "I realized I shouldn't have kept writing, so I erased that part." He received a starfish card for dependability.

How do you discourage inappropriate behavior? Do you ever use punishments?

Yes. We have a pocket chart in the classroom. Each kid has a card in the chart that is green on one side, yellow on the other. If a child misbehaves, I give him or her a verbal warning. If they do the same thing a second time, they have to turn their card to yellow on the chart. For a third offense, they lose recess time. The final stage, which I've never used, is a note to the child's parent. We've talked about this system ahead of time, and students know the consequences if they misbehave.

I also pair this system with rewards for good behavior. I use money that I've invented, called "Turner dollars." Students can earn Turner dollars by keeping their card on the green side and by turning in their homework. They collect the dollars

> Students are not trying to make your life difficult when they misbehave. Instead, they are showing how much they need your help in learning appropriate behaviors.

and, at the end of every month, they can use them to go "shopping." They shop at a treasure chest I've stocked with small toys and candies.

Do students ever become able to reinforce or monitor their own behavior?

I try to help students learn to change their own behaviors. For example, quiet time is critically important during writing; students shouldn't be chatting. Students are aware of this rule. If they are talking, they tend to look at me, because they know they are not behaving appropriately.

When these distractions happen—about two or three times a week—I give students the opportunity to choose a different behavior. I provide choices that let them be the decision makers. For example, I have a desk for students who are distracted or who are bothering their neighbors. I call it "Australia." Students can volunteer to move over there. I make it clear they volunteer to move; it's not a punishment. I'll say something like, "Oh, why don't you go to Australia, maybe you can work better there." With this method, it's not a big stigma.

What advice would you give to new teachers?

Don't take students' misbehavior personally. When I first started teaching, I was frustrated by student misbehavior. Eventually, I came to realize that the cause of the behavior might not be obvious. I now see misbehavior as almost a plea for help. Students are not trying to make your life difficult when they misbehave. Instead, they are showing how much they need your help in learning appropriate behaviors.

to shape a particular kind of behavior, and if so, how it is appropriate to shape it. The techniques are justifiable only when used with full respect for the student's well-being.

■INCREASING DESIRED BEHAVIOR Many of the aspects of reinforcement we have described, including the use of various schedules and types of reinforcers, can help you increase the frequency of desired behavior that students already are performing. In addition, you can use antecedent cues to get students to perform new behavior, if the students already understand how to perform the new behavior. But what about behavior students don't yet know how to do? Helping students acquire complex new behavior, such as solving algebra problems or writing persuasive papers, is the core of teaching.

One very effective method of teaching complex behavior is the method of **successive approximations,** which involves rewarding behavior that comes closer and closer to the desired behavior. This is the method animal trainers use when they teach whales, lions, and other show business animals to perform elaborate tricks. You or anyone else can *shape* behavior by first rewarding a very crude approximation to the behavior that is desired as the result. After you have succeeded in establishing that behavior, you reward only behavior that represents a closer approximation to what you want. You then stop rewarding this behavior, and again reward only a still closer approximation. Although it may sometimes take years of training, eventually the organism reaches the desired behavior, whether aiding in naval tactics (dolphins) or solving algebra problems (students).

A coach shouts encouraging words to elementary school soccer players. Reinforcement is frequently apparent on the playing field, but classroom teachers, too, should recognize and reward their students. (Cindy Charles, PhotoEdit)

Parents and teachers often shape the behavior of their charges without even realizing what they are doing. For example, when toilet training a child, no reasonable parent expects perfection right away. Rather, parents may first reward the child even if he or she makes it to the toilet only once in several tries. Then the parents' expectations increase, and rewards may be doled out only if the child makes it most of the time. Eventually, of course, the parents expect the child to make it all the time.

Similarly, teachers instructing children in writing do not expect perfectly formed letters the first time. Rather, expert teachers first praise when a letter has some of the main features that distinguish it from others. Then, like the toilet-training parents, teachers gradually raise their expectations. They require students to have the correct number of horizontal lines, three, in an E, then to make the E "stand up straight" with right angles between the vertical and horizontal lines, and so on, until the student makes a perfect E every time. In the vignette at the beginning of the chapter, Tom Douglass used shaping techniques to help Mark speak in class about his science project. Tom first rewarded Mark for answering a really easy question. Then Tom continued to ask increasingly in-depth questions, praising and encouraging Mark as he gave longer and more elaborate answers, until finally Mark was able to describe the project without any prompting.

Teachers' classroom shaping of student behavior includes a number of specific steps (Walker & Shea, 1991):

1. Select the target behavior they wish students eventually to perform.

2. Determine how often the target behavior occurs before shaping.

3. Choose the reinforcers to be used.

4. Reinforce successive approximations of the target behavior on a continuous schedule, that is, every time they occur.

5. Reinforce the target behavior, when it first appears, on a continuous schedule.

6. Switch to variable reinforcement to maintain the target behavior.

Rewarding small successive approximations is an essential part of the expert teacher's behavioral modification plans. Expert teachers have learned that people who expect total change typically become disappointed very quickly. When these people do not see total change right away, they often give up. The method of successive approximations allows both student and teacher to see progress as it occurs.

As you know by now, one of the most effective ways of shaping behavior is through the use of praise and the avoidance of harsh or destructive feedback (Pintrich & Schunk, 1996). Research (Brophy, 1981) shows that teachers use praise considerably less than most people think. On average, they use it less than five times per class session. It also tends to decrease in upper versus lower levels of schooling. This pattern may be in part a result of a tendency of older students to discount praise, particularly when it is received for a relatively easy task (Emmer, 1988; Good, 1987). Teachers often praise students not because of particular work or responses, but because of the teachers' perception of the kinds of students with whom they are dealing. Thus students who are perceived by teachers as high achieving, well behaved, and highly motivated, tend to receive praise, often independent of any particular work they do. Praise is most effective when it is (1) genuine, (2) immediate, (3) specific, (4) judicious, and (5) in response to effort (Brophy, 1981). For example, consider the student who has just mastered copying the shapes of the letters in cursive. Another student in her class has just mastered writing whole words in cursive. The expert teacher would recognize that both students deserve equal praise for their accomplishments, despite the difference in the levels achieved.

Implications for Teaching

- **First, try to avoid punishment.** Reinforce desirable behavior that is incompatible with the target behavior. For example, try praising and rewarding students for raising their hands in class, before considering punishment for shouting out answers.

- **Try ignoring the behavior.** For example, if you do not accept answers that students call out, ignoring them until the same answer is offered by a student who has raised his or her hand, students may be less likely to call out answers in the future. Sometimes, however, classmates will provide the reinforcement that a disruptive student is seeking. In these cases, teachers must act to decrease the disruptive behavior.

- **Provide warning cues before applying punishment.** For example, if a teacher says the next student who shouts out an answer will give up one gold star on the class reward chart, students may become very careful to raise their hands.

- **Consider appropriate modifications of the environment.** For example, if children are wiggling and bumping each other as they sit on the floor during story time, try letting them sit on chairs. Perhaps you will need to do nothing more.

When all these tactics have been tried, you may need to incorporate punishment into a behavior modification plan. Behavior modification plans based on operant conditioning principles modify the behavior of each student directly by changing the consequences he or she experiences. Expert teachers are aware, however, that students can also learn from the consequences of their classmates' behavior, a form of learning we discuss next.

Social Learning

Social learning takes place when we learn from observing the behavior of others and the environmental outcomes of their behavior (Bandura, 2000). For example, when a child watches a parent act aggressively, and then starts to act the same way, the child has engaged in social learning. Note that social learning is, in a sense, indirect. It occurs by observing others. For this reason, it is sometimes called *observational learning* or even *vicarious learning*.

Albert Bandura, who explored the concept of social learning with colleagues in the Bobo doll experiments. (Archives of the History of American Psychology)

THE DISCOVERY OF SOCIAL LEARNING

The concept of social learning first came to prominence through the work of Albert Bandura (1965, 1969), who, along with a number of colleagues, studied children who watched films featuring an adult interacting with an inflatable toy known as a Bobo doll. The adult was highly aggressive, hitting, kicking, punching, and throwing things at the doll. The film then ended in one of three ways, depending on the group to which a given child was assigned. In one group, the adult was rewarded for behaving aggressively; in another (the control group), the adult was punished; in a third, there were no consequences at all.

After watching the film, the children were themselves allowed to play with a Bobo doll. The results were simple and clear cut: Children who had seen the adult rewarded for aggressive behavior were more likely than children in the control group to behave aggressively toward the doll, whereas children who had seen the adult be punished for the aggressive behavior were less likely than the controls to behave aggressively. In other words, children had learned merely through observation, without any active participation on their own part.

Subsequent work showed that children do not even have to see aggressive behavior being rewarded to **model** it, that is, behave as the role model did. In one such subsequent study (Bandura, Ross, & Ross, 1963), children watched an adult model either sit quietly next to a Bobo doll or attack the doll. No rewards or punishments of any kind were given to either adult. Children who had seen the adult attack the doll were later more likely to behave aggressively with it than were children who had not seen the aggressive behavior.

Social learning constitutes much of the learning that children and adults do as they develop. For example, much of gender development occurs through watching the role modeling provided by the same-sex parent (Thompson, 1975). As teachers, our goal is to serve as positive role models to help children. However, it is likely that your students are exposed to a tremendous amount of negative role modeling as well. For example, many children and adolescents spend several hours a day watching television, during which they

After watching a film of adults interacting with a Bobo doll, children who had seen the adult rewarded for aggressive behavior were more likely to behave aggressively toward the doll than were children who had seen the adult punished for the aggressive behavior. (Albert Bandura)

THINKING ANALYTICALLY

What do you see as the main positive and the main negative effects of television on children? What is one change you would most like to see to improve children's television programming?

SUGGESTION: One positive effect of television is increasing everyday vocabulary. One negative effect of television is massive exposure to violence. This exposure should be reduced.

view countless acts of violence. Bandura's early experiments suggested that television could be a powerful medium for observational learning.

Indeed, strong evidence indicates that exposure to violent activity on television can lead to aggressive behavior on the part of those who watch television (e.g., Friedrich-Cofer & Huston, 1986; Huesmann, Lagerspetz, & Eron, 1984; Parke, Berkowitz, Leyens, West, & Sebastian, 1977). Even worse, many children are exposed to large amounts of violent behavior on their streets or in their backyards. Teachers have to overcome a lot of negative role modeling. Expert teachers use the principles of social learning described in the next section to encourage what they see as positive modeling.

HOW DOES SOCIAL LEARNING HAPPEN?

Teachers often want their students to engage in observational learning. In having them do so, teachers must make sure the following four necessary conditions are met (Bandura, 1977):

1. **Attention.** For learning to take place, the individual needs to be paying attention to the behavior to be learned. *Attention* refers to that information we actively attend to—it is the filter between the vast amounts of information that assail our senses to the relatively limited amount of information we actually perceive. Some modern theories of attention suggest that people have one or more fixed pools of attentional resources, which they can allocate as various tasks require (e.g., Kahneman, 1973). For example, in the classroom, a student may be dividing attention among your lesson, another student's classroom antics, and a pounding headache that is making it hard to concentrate on what you are saying. Expert teachers attempt to reduce distractions in the classroom so as much as possible of each student's attention is focused on the teacher rather than on lesson-irrelevant stimuli.

THINKING PRACTICALLY

Describe one way you could get students' attention.

SUGGESTION: One strategy to get students' attention is to start a class period with a joke.

In addition to reducing distractions, teachers sometimes have to grab students' attention to focus it on the lesson at hand. Some of the common and useful devices teachers can use include the showing of enthusiasm, being passionate about what they teach, and varying the types of activities they do. If a teacher wants students to learn to recycle paper, for example, he or she might attract students' attention by mentioning aloud that he or she is about to put a piece of paper in the recycling bin, instead of just silently placing the paper in the bin.

This enthusiastic teacher obviously has the attention of all her young students. (F. Pedrick, The Image Works)

2. **Retention.** The individual has to remember what he or she observed when later given the opportunity to act in the same way. To help your pupils better retain the positive behavior you want them to model, encourage them to use active memory techniques. The more clearly students are able to state what they observed, and the deeper they understand it, the more likely the behavior will be retained in memory. Ask students to recall and describe how you handled a certain kind of task for which you served as a role model. Encourage them to figure out why you handled the task as you did. You might even quiz them to ensure that they remember. If the behavior to be learned is paper recycling, a teacher might ask students to recall what they saw him or her do with the empty paper milk cartons at lunchtime. The teacher might then ask students what they thought would eventually happen to the paper milk cartons that were sorted into a separate bin.

3. **Motivation.** The individual has to be motivated to model the observed behavior. One way to motivate students to behave in a certain way is to give them reasons to behave that way. Another is to reinforce them. Reinforcement can be (1) **direct reinforcement,** as when you reward students for behaving the way you wish them to, (2) **vicarious reinforcement,** which occurs when children watch someone else being reinforced (as in real life or on TV), or (3) **self-reinforcement,** rewards people deliver to themselves for showing desired behavior. Children need to learn to reinforce themselves so they can become self-regulated learners.

   The teacher who wants to teach environmentally responsible habits, for example, might point out to students the general environmental benefits of paper recycling, such as more space in landfills and inexpensive recycled paper products. He or she could praise students when they remember to put paper in the recycling bin instead of the trash. Showing videos or movies in which children are rewarded for recycling activities would provide vicarious reinforcement. Students could even be allowed to reinforce themselves, perhaps by putting stickers onto a class recycling chart, whenever they put their papers into the correct bin.

4. **Potential for modeling.** Can the students actually do what you want them to? For example, you could show lots of films of star racers running a 4-minute mile, but the chances are that none of your students would be able to imitate this behavior. The children need to be not only physically, but also mentally and emotionally capable of doing what you wish them to do. As we saw in Chapter 2 in the discussion of moral development, you might want young children to understand universal principles of justice and how these principles apply to their lives, but the children are unlikely to be ready to understand. Sometimes external factors stand in the way of a student's reproducing the desired behavior. The teacher who wishes to teach paper recycling may increase classroom recycling, for example, but if students' parents refuse to institute paper recycling at home, the students cannot reproduce their new behavior outside of the classroom.

   The likelihood that a behavior will be modeled is also affected by the nature of the model, or person performing the behavior. As detailed in Table 7.5, the salience of the model—that is, how the model stands out in relation to the other models, the degree to which the student likes and respects the model, the amount of similarity between model and student, and the consequences the model is seen as experiencing—all affect the chances that the behavior will be imitated (Schunk,

> ### THINKING PRACTICALLY
>
> Given what you have just read, what is one specific thing you can do to increase the likelihood that your students will model behavior you wish them to model?
>
> **SUGGESTION:** Be very clear about what the behavior is you want the students to model.

TABLE 7.5 What Makes a Good Model for Social Learning?

Characteristic	Why It Works	Example
Salience: the model stands out in relation to competing models.	The behavior of a salient adult (parent or teacher), or of a salient age-mate (best friend), is more likely to be imitated than is the behavior of a random adult or child.	A high school math teacher demonstrates the correct way of solving a problem, knowing that, as teacher, he or she is a salient model for some students.
Liking and respect: the model is liked and respected by the individual.	A child is more likely to model the behavior of a respected teacher or friend than of a stranger or someone who is disliked.	To provide another model who is liked and respected, the math teacher asks a popular student to be the first student to solve a problem at the chalkboard.
Similarity: the individual views the model and herself or himself as being alike in key ways.	Again, a parent or best friend is more likely to serve as a role model because of perceived similarity to the individual who is doing the learning.	The math teacher asks several students to come up and solve problems, so each student begins to envision himself or herself as the next one at the chalkboard.
Reinforcement: the consequences of a model's behavior are observed.	An individual is more likely to imitate a model's behavior if the model is rewarded for his or her acts.	The math teacher liberally praises each student, not only stepping up in front of the class, but also for each step leading to a correct problem solution.

1996; Sulzer-Azaroff & Mayer, 1986). A student is likely to imitate a person who stands out from the crowd, especially if the student likes or respects the person and believes he or she actually stands a chance of experiencing rewards similar to those the model receives.

The ultimate goal of social learning is to teach students **self-regulation,** the ability to control their own behavior (Pressley, 1995; Winne, 1995; Zimmerman, 1995). Recall from Chapter 2 Vygotsky's (1978) notion of *internalization,* the idea that children learn by first seeing things happen socially, or watching someone with more expertise perform a task, then taking what they see and making it a part of themselves. Internalization is really what social learning is about. It is teaching children to take what they see—not only academic knowledge, but all kinds of desirable behavior—and make it theirs. Your students will not always have you, or other adults, looking over their shoulders. They must learn, the sooner the better, how to look over their own shoulders. Social learning can help them do so.

THINKING CREATIVELY

What is one behavior you think is really important for your students to show that most of them have not shown in the past? How might you use social learning to help them acquire that behavior?

SUGGESTION: Each individual must answer for himself or herself.

Implications for Teaching

Social learning can be used to help you and your students accomplish the objectives outlined here (see Bandura, 1986; Schunk, 1987):

- *Acquire new behavior.* As an instructor, one of your main goals will be to teach students behavior you want them to acquire: how to interact with peers and adults, how to read effectively, how to think critically and creatively, or how to write clear sentences, for example. Serving as a role model is one of the most effective means you have for teaching your students (Schunk, 1987, 1996).

- *Manifest already learned behavior.* Often, your students will know what they need to do, but will need your role modeling to compel them to do it or to do it more often. By showing respect for others, for example, you encourage students to manifest the behavior they already have available but may not quite be ready to display.

- *Strengthen or weaken inhibitions to action.* Inhibitions can prevent someone from doing something he or she ought not to do, such as taking drugs. Inhibitions, however, can also prevent someone from doing something she or he should do, such as learning math or science. As a teacher, you can serve as a model for inhibiting certain behavior and for diminishing the inhibition of other behavior.

- *Direct attention toward what is important.* In the classroom, in reading, and in life more generally, children need to learn what is important and what is not. Some teachers seem to pay attention to the smallest details of students' behavior or work, without seeing either in a larger context. Your behavior can provide the larger context, as well as suggest which of the details are the important ones.

- *Arouse appropriate emotions.* Enthusiasm is contagious. Expert teachers convey the enthusiasm they have for subject matter and the repulsion they feel toward inappropriate behavior such as cheating. In this way, they help students learn both how to behave and how to feel about the way they behave.

Cognitive-behavioral modification techniques, considered next, have been developed with the goal of teaching students self-regulation.

Cognitive-Behavioral Modification

Throughout the chapter, we have talked about applications of behavioral principles. We have also pointed out the role of cognitive processes in each of the forms of behavioral learning. Some researchers suggest, for example, that predicting contingencies of conditioned stimuli involves cognitive processes. The effectiveness of antecedents in operant conditioning, such as behavioral cues or contracts, depends heavily on a student's cognitive activity. Bandura's ideas about social learning emphasized that cognitive processes are as important as observable behavior. In discussing further applications, we again find that the division between behavioral and cognitive perspectives is a fuzzy one, because many techniques use a combination of the two perspectives to produce the most effective possible means for shaping behavior.

Cognitive-behavioral modification techniques use a combination of cognitive and behavioral learning principles to shape and encourage desired behavior. In cognitive-behavioral techniques, learners' thoughts become either discriminating stimuli to which the learners respond, or reinforcing stimuli, as in the case of self-reinforcement (Schunk, 1996). Not surprisingly, instructions to students based on cognitive and behavioral principles of learning work better than instructions based only on behavioral principles. One idea that has had very promising results is self-instruction.

Donald Meichenbaum (1977) has suggested a set of steps that students can use to engage in **self-instruction,** that is, teaching themselves. Meichenbaum's work was based on a large body of research showing that self-speech could be used to organize behavior. In Chapter 2, we described Vygotsky's (1962) idea that mature thinking is basically inner speech and that children develop the capacity for inner speech by learning external

Teachers can serve as role models to increase inhibitions against undesirable behavior. (Smith/Monkmeyer)

A teacher guides one of her students in solving a difficult mathematics problem. (Young-Wolff, PhotoEdit)

speech through talking with others. Since Vygotsky's time, researchers have demonstrated that, indeed, people do engage in self-speech when they are given difficult problems to solve. Meichenbaum built on the same social learning ideas we described earlier in this chapter to develop the following set of steps for teaching people to use self-speech as part of self-instruction:

1. **Demonstration by model.** A model demonstrates the performance to be modeled. Models are typically adults, but expert students can also serve as models. For example, consider a teacher demonstrating how to solve addition with carrying. The teacher speaks aloud while he or she is performing the task, so the student can become aware of the thought processes the model engages in while carrying out the needed steps.

2. **Modeling with overt adult guidance.** The learner then performs the same actions while talking aloud while the model supervises the learner's performance. For example, a student might solve the addition problem, talking aloud while doing so. The teacher guides the student on what he or she is doing correctly and incorrectly.

3. **Modeling with overt self-guidance.** The learner now performs the task while instructing himself aloud, without the guidance of the model. In essence, the learner is guiding himself. For example, the student solves the addition problem with carrying, saying to himself to carry over from the ones to the tens column the tens digit, and to do the same from the tens to the hundreds column for the hundreds digit.

4. **Modeling with faded self-guidance.** The learner does the same as above, except now whispering the self-instructions rather than saying them aloud.

5. **Modeling with covert self-guidance.** Finally, the learner again models the behavior, but by speaking silently to himself or herself. The behavior has now been internalized through this inner speech.

Brenda Manning (1991) suggests that teachers consistently model self-instruction by talking through the steps of doing tasks aloud. For example, a teacher demonstrating the steps of writing a research paper might say,

Okay, how should I start? Get my notes. Get the materials. Before writing I should look at this stuff, organize my ideas. As I read, I will jot down the main points, then make them into an outline that makes sense. I need some other information—let me find it now before I start writing. At last, I am ready to plan the composition. What would be a good way to open the paper to catch the teacher's attention? What did he like and dislike about my last paper? What should I do differently this time?

In an experiment comparing the behavior of children given training in self-instruction with children given other training, Manning (1988) showed that teachers perceived students who had received self-instruction training as more self-controlled and on task more of the time than students who were not trained in self-instruction. Students who received the training also believed themselves to be more in control of their behaviors. In further research, Manning (1990) described one girl who went from being on-task 15 percent of the time before receiving training in self-instruction to being on-task 80 percent of the time after training. This gain persisted for three months after training had ended.

Self-instruction can be used effectively on a variety of populations. Children as young as preschoolers have been taught to use self-speech, including self-questioning, to resist temptations and to improve their performance on intellectual tasks (Fjellstrom, Born, & Baer, 1988; Patterson & Mischel, 1976). Research has also explored using self-instruction techniques to help students with special needs. The techniques have been useful in helping impulsive children become more reflective, enhancing the reading comprehension of students with learning disabilities, and improving the ability of retarded students to apply problem-solving skills in new situations (Graham & Wong, 1993; Meichenbaum & Goodman, 1971).

The principles of operant conditioning, as well as those of social learning, can be utilized in self-instruction. An important part of many self-instruction programs, for example, is training students to become more expert in self-reinforcement, or in providing their own rewards and punishments, and not always have them provided by others. In fact, one study concluded that two of the most effective self-instruction techniques for hyperactive children are to use self-talk to interrupt impulsive behavior and to give themselves reinforcement for regaining control (Zentall, 1989).

Self-instruction training can provide lasting benefits for teachers as well as for students. This training gives students their own internalized set of rules and procedures to get things done. Systems based on reinforcement and punishment take a lot of the teacher's energy to maintain, because when the reinforcements or punishments are not forthcoming, the desired behavior may not be forthcoming either. But self-instruction training gives students the internal understanding of what they're doing and why, and the motivation to keep on doing it, even long after a particular teacher or class is just a picture on the wall. All in all, self-instruction is one of the more exciting and promising approaches being used in education today.

WHY UNDERSTANDING BEHAVIORAL LEARNING IS IMPORTANT TO TEACHERS

■ Learning is a relatively permanent change in the behavior, thoughts, or feelings of an organism that results from experience. Behavioral theories of learning deal with the causes of and changes in observable behavior. Cognitive learning theories, in contrast, deal with mental processes.

LEARNING BY CLASSICAL CONDITIONING

■ Classical conditioning is one of the two main types of conditioning. In classical conditioning, an unconditioned stimulus, which produces an unconditioned response, is paired with a conditioned stimulus, which originally does not produce such a response. After repeated pairings, the conditioned stimulus may come to elicit a conditioned response. The CS and US must occur with close temporal contiguity. Despite appearances, classical conditioning is largely a cognitive phenomenon that occurs as a result of learning contingencies between stimuli and responses.

■ Once learning has been acquired, it can be extinguished—that is, it is no longer demonstrated. But the phenomenon of spontaneous recovery illustrates that learning has taken place or been maintained even though performance does not reflect it. Also, although learning typically takes place in response to a particular stimulus, we show both stimulus generalization and stimulus discrimination in our ability to respond appropriately to different stimuli.

LEARNING BY OPERANT CONDITIONING

■ Operant conditioning, unlike classical conditioning, is largely learner controlled. Behaviorists, such as B. F. Skinner, have studied humans and animals to determine how the consequences of a behavior affect the likelihood of the behavior recurring. The law of effect states the basic principle of operant conditioning: Responses are strengthened when rewarded. The particular behavior targeted in any operant conditioning procedure is called the *operant*.

■ Unwanted behavior can be reduced through punishment. Presentation punishment is the administration of an aversive, or unpleasant, stimulus; removal punishment is the withholding of a positive stimulus. Common classroom punishments include time-out, response cost, and satiation. Punishment easily can be misused or backfire, so teachers must use it only as a last resort and with care.

■ Positive and negative reinforcement both involve rewards, or reinforcers, but in the latter case, the reward is in the removal of the organism from an uncomfortable or even painful situation. The Premack principle can be used to produce desired behavior by taking into account the hierarchy into which reinforcements are organized. Teachers should also distinguish between primary reinforcements, such as food, and secondary reinforcements, such as grades.

■ People do not usually receive continuous reinforcement. Instead, reinforcement is usually partial, provided on some sort of intermittent schedule. Common schedules of reinforcement include ratio schedules, both fixed ratio and variable ratio, and interval schedules, both fixed interval and variable interval. Each schedule has a different effect on behavior.

■ Antecedent events, or cues, help alert students to the potential consequences of their behavior. A formal agreement regarding desired behavior and its consequences is called a *contingency contract*.

■ The principles of operant conditioning are often applied by teachers as part of behavioral modification plans for their students. Reinforcements can be used to shape desirable behavior through the method of successive approximations, in which reinforcement is progressively given for behavior that comes closer and closer to the behavior ultimately desired.

SOCIAL LEARNING

■ Social learning takes place when students learn from observing the behavior of others. Students then may model the behavior they have learned. The salience of the model may affect the amount of social learning that takes place. Social learning can be used to teach new behavior, encourage students to show or avoid showing behavior they already have learned, or to arouse emotions in students. Attention is a key to social learning.

■ The consequences observed along with a certain behavior may vicariously reinforce and therefore encourage learning, as can certain characteristics of the individuals demonstrating the behavior. Students also can learn self-reinforcement. These ways of receiving reinforcement are in addition to direct reinforcement.

COGNITIVE-BEHAVIORAL MODIFICATION

■ The goal of education, in general, and cognitive-behavioral modification, in particular, is to

encourage self-regulation in students. The idea of cognitive-behavioral modification shows once again how closely related the behavioral and cognitive approaches to learning can be. Teachers can use the techniques of cognitive-behavioral modification to help students learn self-instruction, whereby the students teach themselves.

KEY TERMS AND DEFINITIONS

■ **Aversive stimulus** Something unpleasant that can produce a negative emotional response. Page 236

■ **Behavioral modification** Changing students' behavior by managing the contingencies, or consequences, of that behavior. Page 249

■ **Behavioral theories of learning** Explanations of learning that focus primarily on changes in observable behavior, rather than on internal mental processes. Page 232

■ **Classical conditioning** Learning process in which an originally neutral stimulus becomes associated with a particular physiological or emotional response (or both) that the stimulus did not originally produce. Page 233

■ **Cognitive-behavioral modification** Learning techniques that use a combination of cognitive and behavioral learning principles to shape and encourage desired behavior. Page 257

■ **Conditioned emotional response (CER)** Emotional response that has developed through the process of classical conditioning. Page 236

■ **Conditioned response, or CR** Physiological or emotional response that is elicited from a conditioned stimulus as a result of classical conditioning. Page 234

■ **Conditioned stimulus, or CS** Originally neutral stimulus that comes to elicit a response as a result of classical conditioning procedures. Page 234

■ **Contingency contract** Written or oral agreement between student and teacher specifying desired behavior and promised reward. Page 246

■ **Continuous reinforcement** Operant conditioning schedule of reinforcement in which a reinforcement always follows a particular desired behavior. Page 244

■ **Direct reinforcement** Rewarding individuals for behaving the way you wish them to. Page 255

■ **Extinction** Phase of classical conditioning during which conditioned responses occur less and less frequently in response to a conditioned stimulus, and eventually stop. Page 236

■ **Interval schedule of reinforcement** Operant conditioning schedule of reinforcement in which reinforcement is given for the first response after a certain amount of time has passed. Page 244

■ **Law of effect** Thorndike's explanation for operant conditioning, which states that those actions that are rewarded tend to be strengthened and more likely to occur in the future, whereas those actions that are punished are weakened and thus less likely to occur in the future. Page 239

■ **Learning** Any relatively permanent change in the behavior, thoughts, or feelings of an organism that results from experience. Page 232

■ **Model** To behave as the role model has behaved. Page 253

■ **Negative reinforcement** Operant conditioning involving the removal of an aversive stimulus soon after an operant response, thereby strengthening the response. Page 240

■ **Neutral stimulus** Stimulus that does not evoke any particular response until it becomes linked with a conditioned response via classical conditioning. Page 233

■ **Operant** Active behavior that the organism uses to operate on the environment. The basic unit studied in operant conditioning. Page 238

■ **Operant conditioning** (also called **instrumental conditioning**) Learning produced by the rewards and punishments of active behavior (an operant) of a human or other organism interacting with the environment. Page 238

■ **Partial reinforcement** (also called **intermittent reinforcement**) Schedules of operant conditioning reinforcement in which desired behavior is reinforced only some of the time. Page 244

■ **Positive reinforcement** Operant conditioning in which a positive reinforcer is paired with an operant response, thereby strengthening the response. Page 240

■ **Premack principle** Law of operant conditioning that states that more preferred activities reinforce less preferred ones. Page 243

■ **Presentation punishment** Application of an unpleasant stimulus to discourage a response. Page 246

■ **Primary reinforcers** Operant conditioning rewards, such as food or shelter from the elements, that provide immediate satisfaction or enjoyment. Page 242

■ **Punishment** Use of a stimulus that decreases the probability of a response, either through the application of an unpleasant stimulus or through the removal of a pleasant one. Page 246

- **Ratio schedule of reinforcement** Operant conditioning schedule of reinforcement in which a certain number of desired operants are reinforced without respect to the passage of time. Page 244

- **Reinforcer** Stimulus that increases the probability that the operant associated with it will happen again. Page 240

- **Removal punishment** Taking away a pleasant stimulus to discourage a response. Page 247

- **Response cost** Form of punishment in which a small penalty is imposed for each instance of the undesirable behavior. Page 248

- **Satiation** Compelling individuals to continue a behavior until they are tired of it. Page 248

- **Schedule of reinforcement** Certain pattern by which reinforcements follow operants during operant conditioning procedures. Page 244

- **Secondary reinforcers** Operant conditioning rewards that gain reinforcement value through their association with primary reinforcers. Page 242

- **Self-instruction** Teaching of one's self. Page 257

- **Self-regulation** Control of one's behavior. Page 256

- **Self-reinforcement** Administration of reinforcers to oneself. Page 255

- **Social learning** (also called **observational learning** or **vicarious learning**) Learning that takes place when people learn from observing the behavior of others and the environmental outcomes of others' behavior. Page 252

- **Spontaneous recovery** Classical conditioning phenomenon in which a conditioned response returns after an extinction period. Page 236

- **Stimulus discrimination** Classical conditioning mechanism whereby an individual distinguishes between the conditioned stimulus and another stimulus that is sufficiently unlike it so as not to elicit the same (or possibly any) level of conditioning. Page 236

- **Stimulus generalization** Classical conditioning mechanism by which stimuli similar to the original conditioned stimulus can elicit the same conditioned response. Page 236

- **Successive approximation** Operant conditioning method of teaching complex behavior by rewarding behavior that comes closer and closer to the desired behavior. Page 251

- **Temporal contiguity** Principle of classical conditioning that states that the mere closeness in time between the conditioned stimulus and the unconditioned stimulus helps explain conditioning. Page 235

- **Time-out** Punishment by enforcing a brief period of social isolation. Page 248

- **Unconditioned response,** or **UR** Organism's natural response to a stimulus, which occurs without any conditioning. Page 234

- **Unconditioned stimulus,** or **US** Stimulus that elicits a physiological or emotional response (or both) before any conditioning takes place. Page 234

- **Vicarious reinforcement** Reinforcement that occurs through the observation of someone else's behavior being reinforced. Page 255

Apply the concepts you have learned in this chapter to the following problems of classroom practice.

IN ELEMENTARY SCHOOL

1. How could you use the principles of classical conditioning to start a lifelong love of reading in your second graders?

2. Describe how you could set up a token economy or other operant conditioning system that would reward fourth graders for cooperative behavior during group projects. Is there a way you could eventually phase out the reward program and still expect cooperative behavior from your students?

3. What are some ways you could avoid punishing your third-grade students, but still reduce the frequency of insults and name calling in class?

4. You have just witnessed several of your first graders during recess reenacting violent scenes from a popular movie. What are some ways you can counteract this negative example of social learning?

5. What kind of a cognitive-behavioral modification program would you set up to help fifth-grade students begin to check their own math homework?

IN MIDDLE SCHOOL

1. What steps could you take to reduce the anxiety of a student who becomes too nervous to speak when called on during pronunciation practice in your eighth-grade Spanish class?

2. Some of the students in your seventh-grade biology class have been making crude jokes and profane comments during the lab session on animal reproduction. How can you use operant conditioning principles to stop this behavior?

3. What are some ways you can use social learning principles to help students in your social studies class develop and internalize map-reading skills?

4. Who would you point out as a model of nonviolent behavior for students in your seventh-grade social studies class?

5. Your sixth-grade English students are used to receiving small rewards, such as stickers or pencil erasers, whenever they finish reading a book. How can you move them from this continuous reinforcement schedule, with rewards provided by you, to a partial reinforcement schedule, and, eventually, to a point at which they reinforce themselves for reading books?

IN HIGH SCHOOL

1. It is halfway through the academic year, but your first-year English students are still depending on you to give them instructions every time they have to do library or Internet research for a paper. How can you get them to internalize research skills?

2. You have been allowing students who have completed their physics homework by Friday fifteen minutes of "free exploration" time in the lab at the end of each Friday's class session. The students seem to like this opportunity and most of them turn in their papers, but you have recently noticed that the students seem to turn in homework only on Thursdays, leaving you with a pile of grading to do each weekend. How can you change your reinforcement schedule to get students to do homework all week long?

3. A number of students in your life-skills class will be seeking their first full-time jobs immediately after graduation. How could you use social learning principles to help these students learn effective job search and interview skills?

4. How could you help a student in your junior-level biology class who has become classically conditioned to feel queasy and faint whenever the class discusses animals of any kind?

5. What kinds of rewards do you think might be effective for increasing the amount of homework your remedial math students turn in on time?

Connecting Theory and Research to Practice

The North Central Regional Educational Laboratory has created a Web site entitled "Critical Issue: Working Toward Student Self-Direction and Personal Efficacy as Educational Goals" located at *http://www.ncrel.org/sdrs/areas/issues/students/learning/lr200.htm*. The primary focus of this site is to promote self-regulated learning as an educational goal.

The site offers many strategies for developing and supporting self-regulation and identifying characteristics of students who have developed effective self-regulatory skills. It also provides explanations of key terms and definitions, textual references, and strategies for administrators, teachers, and students to use that enhance self-regulatory skills. One especially interesting feature is the testimonials of several teachers (available on downloadable audio files) who have used these strategies in their classrooms. Also highlighted is a real-life school example of how self-regulated learning was used at Lake Okoboji High School in Milford, Iowa, providing an excellent example of how learning theory impacts educational practice.

Have you wondered how self-regulation would apply to specific disciplines? Gregory Schraw and David Brooks from the University of Nebraska-Lincoln investigated how to use self-regulation to increase proficiency in math and science. Their article, "Helping Students Self-Regulate in Math and Sciences Courses: Improving the Will and the Skill," is available at *http://www.cci.unl.edu/Chau/SR/Self_Reg.html*. This paper presents an overview of self-regulation and associated psychological concepts, an excellent visual model of the factors affecting self-regulation, and a discussion regarding effective self-regulation strategies for science and math teachers to employ. Many tips and suggestions are also presented in this online publication to promote the development of self-regulation in students.

Online Resources

One Web site that provides interesting information regarding the behaviorist perspective on learning is located at *http://www.brembs.net/learning/*. Hosted at the Universtity of Würzburg in Germany, the Biozentrum Center presents overviews of classical and operant conditioning, in addition to topics for discussion such as whether a snail or a fly can learn via classical or operant conditioning and how to design experiments to study such questions. Other features include a historical overview of classical and operant conditioning, learning in relatively simple animals, data presentation, analysis, and interpretation of results of current research supported by the Center. Another feature presents the historic "Nature" *versus* "Nurture" debate with regard to learning and a brief discussion of the role of neural networks in learning.

NCREL North Central Regional Educational Laboratory

Critical Issue: Working Toward Student Self-Direction and Personal Efficacy as Educational Goals

Pathways Home Page | Critical Issues for this Area

ISSUE: Because learning in schools is traditionally dominated and controlled by adults, students seldom make decisions about their own learning (Goodlad, 1984). Even though our philosophies of education purport to graduating students who are responsible citizens capable of participating thoughtfully in a democracy, our educational practices have a tendency to foster dependence, passivity and a "tell me what to do and think" attitude.

OVERVIEW: A touchstone of effective learning is that students are in charge of their own learning; essentially, they direct their own learning processes. In a discussion of indicators of engaged, effective learning, Jones, Valdez, Nowakowski, and Rasmussen (1995) describe characteristics of students who are responsible for their own learning. One characteristic is a student's ability to shape and manage change, in other words, self-directed. Covey (1989) recognizes the importance of self-directedness, which he calls proactivity, by including it as one of the habits characterizing highly-effective individuals: "It means more than merely taking initiative. It means that as human beings, we are responsible for our own lives. Our behavior is a function of our decisions, not our conditions. We can subordinate feelings to values. We have the initiative and the responsibility to make things happen" (p. 71).

We as educators can nurture student self-direction and personal efficacy by providing students with opportunities before, during and after instruction to exercise some control of their own learning. This does not mean students make all the decisions and it does not mean reverting to a curriculum of "personal relevance" of the '60s or the "child centered curriculum" of years ago. An emphasis on student self-direction and efficacy means that we teach and engage students in specific strategies that offer them opportunities to make decisions and solve problems on their own without being told what to do at all times. It means we provide them with strategies designed to help them process information effectively and to be self-confident, believing that they have the abilities to succeed. And perhaps most important, we help students become more reflective about their thinking and learning processes.

Specific strategies we can provide include encouraging students to set their own goals for personal development and instructional improvement, and planning ways to achieve these goals. According to Hom and Murphy (1983):

Another related Web site contains the work of R. W. Kentridge, and is devoted to exploring and presenting information about classical conditioning. Found at *http://www.brembs.net/ classical/classical.html,* this site offers information about the variables affecting classical conditioning, experiments and models of classical conditioning, and a discussion regarding associations made in classical conditioning.

To find out more about the history of operant conditioning go to *http:// www.biozentrum .uni-wuerzburg.de/ genetics/behavior/ learning/behaviorism.html.* This site provides links to brief biographies of three psychologists who greatly contributed to operant conditioning as a theory of learning: Edward Thorndike, John B. Watson, and B. F. Skinner. Also linked to the site is information about and a diagram of a Skinner Box.

"Operant Conditioning: How Reinforcement and Punishment Affects Children" by Maria E. Chapa is a Web-based document available at *http://www .hwi.com/tygger/edpsych/ Behavioral/OPERANT .html.* This site provides a nice overview of the various instructional implications of operant conditioning, including the effects of positive and negative reinforcements, instrumental conditioning, and examples of each. Also included is a brief list of resources to learn more about the topics highlighted on this Web site.

Encarta, an online encyclopedia reference service, has a site explaining behavior modification at *http://encarta.msn .com/find/Concise.asp ?ti=04C8E000#s1.* This site provides a brief introduction, historical background, and examples of behavior modification.

A very nice biography of Albert Bandura and an overview of his social learning theory is available at *http://www.ship.edu/ ~cgboeree/bandura.html.* The site was created and maintained by Dr. Boeree and contains information on modeling, self-regulation, various therapies derived from social learning theory, and a brief discussion of the impact Bandura's theory and work has had on cognitive psychology and personality theory. More biographical information on Albert Bandura can be found at the psychology resources site, The Psi Café, at *http://www.psy.pdx.edu/ PsiCafe/KeyTheorists/ Bandura.htm.*

As discussed in this chapter, self-regulation is a concept associated with Bandura's social learning theory. Several sites devoted to self-regulation include information and resources. To learn more about self-regulation go to:

http://www.apa.org/ monitor/jun00/howtolearn .html

http://www.oit.pdx.edu/ ~kerlinb/myresearch/srl/ self_reg_learn.html

http://www.lhbe.edu.on .ca/teach2000/onramp/ srl/self_reg_learn.html

Are you interested in the Bobo doll study conducted by Bandura that is discussed in this chapter? A research article by Bandura, Ross, and Ross (1961) entitled "Transmission of Aggression Through Imitation of Aggressive Models" in which the Bobo doll was used is available at *http:// psychclassics.yorku.ca/ Bandura/bobo.htm.*

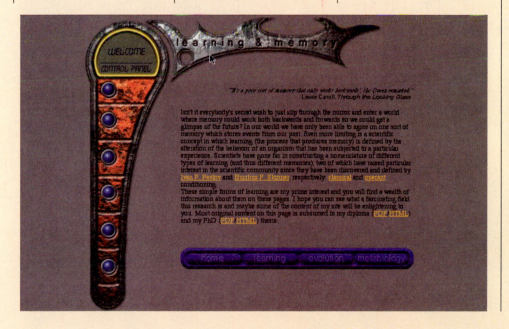

8

Cognitive Approaches to Learning

THE BIG PICTURE

To help you see the big picture, keep the following questions in mind as you read this chapter:

- How is information entered or encoded into memory? How do we go from seeing or hearing information, to learning the information, to putting it into memory?

- How is information stored in memory? What are the different kinds of memory storage that people use?

- What models have been proposed to account for how information is stored in memory?

- How do we retrieve information from memory? What factors influence remembering and forgetting?

- What can people do to improve their memories? What specific techniques can students and teachers use to enhance their memories?

- How do the conditions under which we learn something influence our likelihood of remembering and using the information?

◀ *Two first-graders test each other in telling-time skills.* (Elizabeth Crews, The Image Works)

ill Norton is pleased. He has finally found a way to help the eighth-grade pupils in his fifth-period English class remember their vocabulary words! On a recent vocabulary test, the average score was a discouraging 59 percent, even after Bill had spent a whole class period conducting a review drill with the students. He had said each word on the vocabulary list, and the class had then repeated the definition in unison. Bill reviewed the list with the students three times, noticing each time that the definitions seemed to come out a little more rapidly. He had been confident that the students were learning the words and their meanings. The test scores seemed to prove, however, that repetition drills were not the best way to teach vocabulary words.

Bill realized that he had to rethink his plan. He had read an article in a teaching magazine that described ways several expert teachers taught new concepts and terms by making them interesting and meaningful for students. Making the terms more interesting certainly made sense, based on Bill's own school experiences, and he decided to make the vocabulary words more meaningful to his own students. He began by introducing the vocabulary words in the context of the novel the class was reading. Before the class read the assigned chapters, Bill supplied each student with a worksheet listing the vocabulary words. However, this time Bill asked the students to supply the definition for each new term themselves, using their own words. In the review session, Bill read off each word and called on one of the students to read his or her definition of the word. He clarified any answers that seemed off-track, and then, for each word on the list, asked several students to use the word correctly in sentences they created about their own lives. The scores on the next test showed that Bill's new method worked a lot better—the average score was 82 percent!

learly, something was wrong with Bill Norton's original method of teaching vocabulary words. In terms of cognitive theories of learning, the subject of this chapter, Bill had made several mistakes. Here, we consider what the mistakes were, and why Bill's next plan to raise vocabulary scores was so successful.

In Chapter 7, on behavioral approaches to learning, we focused on changes in behavior. In this chapter, we discuss cognitive approaches to *learning*—that is, any relatively permanent change in thought or behavior that occurs as a result of experience. **Cognitive approaches** focus on the changes in thought that are part of learning. Cognitive approaches differ from behavioral approaches in that they emphasize the mental mechanisms underlying the processing and representation of information during learning. One cognitive function that plays a key role in learning is **memory,** the active mental mechanisms that enable people to retain and retrieve information about past experience (Baddeley, 1999; Crowder, 1976). For learning to take place—for any changes in thought or behavior to be "relatively permanent"—students must remember their experiences.

How do students learn and remember? We consider a number of models of memory in this chapter, along with the implications of each for how well students remember information and the usefulness of their memorized knowledge. We also discuss the importance of the **context,** or learning environment, to memory and learning.

Why Understanding Cognitive Approaches to Learning Is Important to Teachers

To get a feel for some of the topics of this chapter related to the nature of learning and how information gets committed to memory, read the following extract and see if you can figure out what it describes:

The procedure is actually quite simple. First you arrange items into different groups. Of course one pile may be sufficient depending on how much there is to do. If you have to go somewhere else due to lack of facilities that is the next step; otherwise, you are pretty well set. It is important not to overdo things. That is, it is better to do too few things at once than too many. In the short run this may not seem important but complications can easily arise. A mistake can be expensive as well. At first, the whole procedure will seem complicated. Soon, however, it will become just another facet of life. It is difficult to foresee any end to the necessity for this task in the immediate future, but then, one can never tell. After the procedure is completed one arranges the materials into different groups again. Then they can be put into their appropriate places. Eventually they will be used once more and the whole cycle will have to be repeated. However, that is part of life.

Most people find this passage (from Bransford & Johnson, 1972; cited in Bransford, 1979, pp. 134–135) difficult to understand and perhaps even meaningless. What makes the passage difficult is the lack of context for the passage and hence our inability to apply much of our prior knowledge. Suppose, however, you were told the title is "Washing Clothes." Now reread the passage, and you will find it makes perfect sense! The procedure described in the passage has been transformed from something nearly incomprehensible to a familiar, commonplace experience. You now have a *context,* which sets up expectations for what you are to read. It is easy to apply your prior knowledge. Cognitive approaches to learning have become popular among educators because they can be so directly applied to help students learn (Anderson, 1995; Bruer, 1993; Goodrich, Andrade, & Perkins, 1998).

This demonstration points out that learning is more complicated than simply seeing or hearing something and then committing it to memory. You can memorize the passage here word for word without ever knowing the topic, for example, but it will probably be of little use to you in the future. In fact, some psychologists have described knowledge committed to memory without adequate understanding as *inert,* or unavailable for full use (Bransford, Burns, Delcos, & Vye, 1986). These researchers suggest that, although memory is key to learning, memorizing information without knowing how to apply it represents incomplete learning.

Like researchers, teachers want students not only to remember the material they are taught but also to be able to use that material later. Expert teachers are always looking for ways to ensure that students are able to use what they learn—whether on tests and assignments, or in future classes, or outside school when students need to write a letter, balance their checkbooks, or build shelves for their home theater equipment. The teachers know that if there is a fundamental principle of teaching subject matter, it is to make the material meaningful to the students and, if possible, relevant to the students' lives (Schank & Joseph, 1998). Memory is an important part of the learning process. Expert teachers know that understanding what is known about the workings of memory can help them create memorable lessons that will be the foundation of complete learning.

The Standard Memory Model

Researchers have proposed a number of models to explain exactly what happens when information is stored in memory. Most of these models have in common three basic operations: encoding, storage, and retrieval. *Encoding* refers to how you transform a sensory input into some kind of representation that you can place into memory. *Storage* refers to how you retain encoded information in memory. **Retrieval** refers to how you gain access to information stored in memory.

For example, suppose a teacher wants his students to learn vocabulary words. The first thing the students need to do is to see the words on the printed page, and place the sensory information they absorb from the page into their memories (encoding). Next, they have to keep that information in memory (storage). Later, they have to get the information out when they are tested (retrieval).

Typically, encoding, storage, and retrieval are viewed as sequential stages: First you encode the information, then you store it, and later you retrieve it. However, the three processes are also interactive. For example, students trying to learn information usually learn it better if they test themselves periodically. In other words, contrary to Bill Norton's first procedure, students should not just repeat to themselves the definitions of vocabulary words. Rather, they should test themselves as they go along, thereby alternating encoding, storage, and retrieval. This procedure is more effective than just their doing only the encoding and storage and hoping that retrieval will work when they later take a test.

As illustrated in Figure 8.1, the standard model of memory assumes there are three basic kinds of memory storage (Atkinson & Shiffrin, 1968; see also Waugh & Norman, 1965, for a related model). For a student to remember something, the information must be encoded in three steps, going from one memory storage area to the next.

THINKING ANALYTICALLY

An English teacher presents a new vocabulary word and its meaning. The next week, the teacher gives a quiz that asks the students to write down the word's meaning. How might the concepts of encoding, storage, and retrieval apply to the learning of the vocabulary word? Be specific.

SUGGESTION: Encoding is involved in placing the word and its corresponding meaning into memory. Storage is involved in keeping them there. Retrieval is involved in taking them out of memory when they are needed.

ENCODING KNOWLEDGE INTO THREE MEMORY STORES

The first store of memory is a **sensory register,** where much information is first stored when it is sensed. It is capable of holding relatively small amounts of information for brief moments of time. The second store is **short-term memory,** which is capable of holding relatively limited amounts of information for a matter of seconds and, in some cases, up to two minutes. The third is **long-term memory,** which has very large, possibly unlimited capacity; it is capable of storing information for very long periods of time, possibly indefinitely.

As you can see, the three kinds of storage differ primarily in terms of the length of time information is held in them. They also differ in several other respects, including the form in which the information is represented, the amount of information that is lost or forgotten, and the way information is lost. For example, although information can be lost from the sensory register in less than one second, some researchers believe that, once knowledge makes it into long-term memory, it may remain there for the rest of a person's life.

FIGURE 8.1

Characteristics of Three Memory Stores in the Standard Memory Model

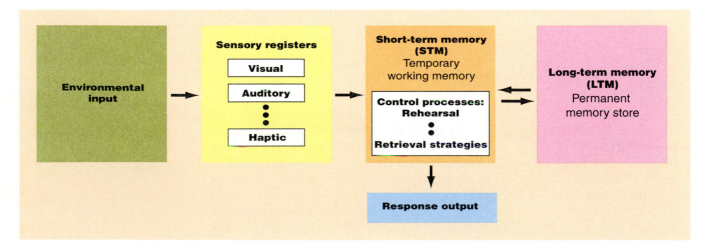

■**THE SENSORY REGISTER**   The sensory register, where much information is first stored when it is sensed, holds an accurate representation of everything that is sensed, but it holds information for only a very brief time (Crowder & Surprenant, 2000). When you first see something, the image of that thing is placed into sensory memory. In essence, you see in your mind an image of all or part of what you have seen on a page, or on a television screen, or elsewhere in the environment. Sensory memory is precategorical—it stores information we have not yet understood and categorized.

If you have ever "written" your name with a lighted sparkler on the Fourth of July, you have experienced the persistence of sensory memory. You briefly "see" your name, even though the sparkler leaves no physical trace. Visual sensory memory lasts for only about one second, and it can hold only about nine items in memory. Some researchers suggest the existence of an auditory sensory memory, but the evidence is inconclusive (Crowder & Surprenant, 2000; Darwin, Turvey, & Crowder, 1972; Greene & Crowder, 1984; Spoehr & Corin, 1978).

The sensory register gives students a chance to catch important information that they might otherwise have missed. Suppose, for example, that a student's attention wanders for a moment away from the teacher's notes on an overhead projector. Suddenly the student notices that the teacher is saying "and this term will be on the test." That student would have only about a second to shift attention and transfer the information to the next store, that of short-term memory.

■**SHORT-TERM MEMORY**   Whereas sensory memory holds information for only about a second, short-term memory can hold information for up to a minute or two. You use short-term memory when you look up a number in the phone book and try to hold it in memory long enough to enter it into the telephone. Similarly, when teachers say something, and then check whether the students have listened by immediately or almost immediately asking students what was just said, the teachers are checking whether the students have placed the information into their short-term memory.

Information will disappear rapidly from short-term memory unless you take action to ensure its survival. This action is typically **rehearsal,** the repeated recitation of an item. For example, if you repeat a phone number to yourself over and over again, you are more likely to remember it.

Rehearsal may seem like a natural, inborn process. You know to keep saying the number over and over again, and perhaps no one ever explicitly told you to do so. But rehearsal is actually a learned process. In fact, as we discussed in Chapter 2, a major difference between the learning of younger and older children is in the differential use of strategies, such as rehearsal, by the two groups (Flavell & Wellman, 1977; Moses & Baird, 1999; Schraw & Moshman, 1995). Younger children's knowledge and control of their memories—skills referred to as *metamemory skills*—are generally poorer than are those of older children; that is, older children have developed more expertise in using their memories. The strategies to assist memory described later in this chapter also make use of metamemory skills: They are learned ways in which we can improve our learning and memory.

For rehearsal to succeed, you need to do more than just mindlessly repeat words. You must make an active effort to encode and store the information. Indeed, rehearsal is the major way in which people can transfer information from short-term memory to a more nearly permanent form of storage, which we consider soon. Recall Bill Norton, the teacher described at the beginning of the chapter. In his first attempt to teach vocabulary words, Bill had his students repeat back definitions again and again. He did nothing to encourage his students to process actively the information they were repeating. The result was that little learning took place: Mere repetition of words is not sufficient to guarantee learning (Tulving, 1966).

What is the capacity of short-term memory? Research suggests that it holds roughly seven items, plus or minus two (Baddeley, 1994; Miller, 1956; Thompson, 2000). But the amount of information that short-term memory can hold depends, in part, on how the information is encoded. For example, if you simply try to remember as separate numbers 1-6-2-0-1-7-7-6, you probably cannot hold much more in memory than these eight digits. But suppose instead you reencode the digits as the year in which the Pilgrims landed and the year in which the Declaration of Independence was signed. Then you are storing these eight numbers as just two pieces of information, or chunks of information. **Chunking,** or grouping items of information, expands the amount of information you can store in short-term memory.

■**LONG-TERM MEMORY**   When people talk about memory, they typically are talking about long-term memory (also called the *long-term store*). Much of who you are is determined by your long-term memory. This form of memory can hold essentially unlimited amounts of information, and for extremely long periods of time, perhaps forever. How well information is encoded into long-term memory depends on how the information is learned.

An important principle of learning, called the **total-time hypothesis,** suggests that how much you learn typically depends on how much time you spend studying. Within a given study session, you can budget your study time in different ways, according to this hypothesis, with similar results. For example, if a student is learning vocabulary words, the student can study each word once for one minute, or each word twice for thirty seconds, and it will probably make little difference, because the total study time for each word within the session was the same.

There are three constraints on the total-time hypothesis, however (Cooper & Pantle, 1967). First, use the full amount of time allotted for study actually to study—daydreaming doesn't count! Second, encode the information in a way that is consistent with the way in which you are tested. For example, if you need to recall words in order, then you will do well on a test only if you memorized the order of the words as well as the words themselves. Third, **elaborate** the information as much as possible, thinking about it carefully and associating it with other things you know.

The third constraint is the basis for an important principle of learning. Learning psychologists distinguish between two kinds of rehearsal strategies: *maintenance rehearsal* and *elaborative rehearsal.* In **maintenance rehearsal,** you simply repeat items to be learned. This is what Bill Norton's students did before their first vocabulary test. Such rehearsal may be useful for keeping items in short-term memory for small amounts of time, but it is not as useful for transferring information to long-term memory. The other kind of rehearsal, **elaborative rehearsal,** involves taking the information to be learned and trying to associate it with other things you know, or trying to associate various items

A second-grade teacher explains contractions to her students, using flash cards. Research has shown that maintenance rehearsal, such as simply repeating the flash cards, is not as helpful for encoding long-term memory as elaborative rehearsal, such as thinking of a sentence, for each flash card. (Elizabeth Crews)

TABLE 8.1   The Three Memory Stores of the Standard Model

Name	Type of Information Stored	Amount of Information Stored	How Long Memories Last	Examples
Sensory Register	Visual (and possibly auditory)	About nine items	Up to one second	The image left after "writing" name with a sparkler, or after a teacher turns off an overhead projector
Short-Term Memory	Information that is being currently used	Five to nine items. Storage can be increased by chunking information into groups	Up to one minute without rehearsal	A telephone number; a list of vocabulary words
Long-Term Memory	Information that has been learned or encoded for long-term storage	Possibly unlimited	Possibly for life	The square root of 144 is 12; the name of your favorite candy bar; how to open your bicycle lock

of the to-be-learned information (Willoughby, Wood, & Khan, 1994). This kind of rehearsal is generally more useful if you want to retain information over time in long-term memory. Table 8.1 summarizes the characteristics of the three kinds of memory in the standard model.

Bill Norton's students improved their vocabulary scores when they used elaborative rehearsal to learn the vocabulary words—the words were more firmly implanted in their memories. To encourage the students to use elaborative rehearsal, Bill Norton related each word to the assigned reading. He also asked each student to craft a meaningful sentence for each word related to the student's own experience. He could have asked the students to write a sentence with a word they already know that means about the same thing as the new word being learned. Or, he could have asked them to say to what extent each word could be used to describe someone in their family. These techniques are all likely to lead to a deeper level of processing by the students.

Maintenance rehearsal, or learning through repetition with little attempt to add or find meaning in the information, is sometimes known as **rote learning.** This kind of learning was more prevalent in the past than it is today in U.S. schools (Johnson, 1994). It is also more common outside the United States. In fact, schools and students in Asian countries are often stereotypically portrayed as relying heavily on rote learning (Kember & Gow, 1991; Watkins, Reghi, & Astilla, 1991). The comparative advantage of Asian students on standardized tests in some academic areas is sometimes used as a basis for calls for a return to more rote learning in the United States. The Forum: Is There Ever a Need for Rote Memorization? explores whether there are some uses for which rote learning is, indeed, the most appropriate strategy.

THINKING PRACTICALLY

Suppose a student comes to you and says that she spent a lot of time studying for a history test, with disappointing results. She describes how she studied, and you recognize that she used maintenance rehearsal: She repeated several times each day a long list of facts, dates, and figures about World War II. How might you help her to improve her performance on the next test?

SUGGESTION: Encourage her to spend more time on elaborative rehearsal, associating the facts with each other, or with other information, and thus making the material more meaningful to her.

FORUM

IS THERE EVER A NEED FOR ROTE MEMORIZATION?

Much of the information covered in this chapter suggests that students learn better when information is meaningful to them. The standard model of memory suggests that elaborative rehearsal is more effective for encoding information in long-term memory. Constructivist approaches to memory suggest that new knowledge must build on previous knowledge. Are there ever times when students need just to memorize information by rote, or simple repetition without elaboration?

FIRST VIEW: *Rote memorization is unnecessary.* Many educators say there is never any need for students to subject themselves to the process of repetitive or rote memorization. Even information typically learned by rote can be learned in more meaningful ways. For example, one study found that theatrical lines, which are generally learned using repetition methods because they must be spoken word for word as written, were actually recalled better by actors who first got the meaning, or gist, of their lines (Noice, 1993).

Furthermore, some theorists suggest that information simply memorized without meaning is inert; students can never make full use of the information. One group of researchers compares inert knowledge to tools (Brown, Collins, & Duguid, 1989). Just as a person can acquire a tool and not be able to use it, so a person can acquire knowledge, such as facts or formulas, that he or she is not able to use. Many researchers claim that knowledge acquired through rote memorization is more likely to be inert than is knowledge which is learned in more meaningful ways.

Finally, proponents of meaningful learning methods point out that students prefer such methods over rote repetition methods (Yuen-Yee & Watkins, 1994). Students who enjoy the learning methods used in their classes are less vulnerable to boredom and other problems that can undermine learning and teaching.

SECOND VIEW: *Rote memorization can be useful.* Some educators believe that, although currently unpopular, rote memorization continues to be a valuable learning technique. They believe that learning "by heart" through repetition is the most efficient way to encode some information, such as vocabulary words in both native and foreign languages (Cook, 1994). Information learned by heart may also be less likely to be forgotten. One study, for example, found that students who learned foreign language words by rote remembered more words than those who used a mnemonic method to learn the words (Wang, Thomas, & Ouellette, 1992). Finally, proponents of rote learning suggest that a base of memorized facts helps students better develop complex thinking and problem-solving skills (Rist, 1992).

THIRD VIEW: A SYNTHESIS: *Teachers can combine the techniques of rote memorization, such as repetition and drilling, with more meaningful learning methods, to give their students the advantages of both methods.* For example, teachers can have students practice vocabulary words by drilling with flash cards of the words. However, the students might use flash card drills with a more meaningful twist. Each time a student sees a word, for example, he or she might try to make up a new sentence using the word.

Teachers of older students can also explicitly teach students about the advantages and disadvantages of different ways of learning or memorizing information, and let students choose the method that works best for them on given materials. Students may find that their improved awareness of their own memory and learning processes, or *metacognition,* will help them make more efficient use of their study time, by distinguishing information that needs more elaborative rehearsal from information that needs more repetitive rehearsal.

The total-time hypothesis applies within a single study session. If you look across sessions, however, the distribution of time becomes important. Suppose, now, that your students have to study for a test. In general, would they do better to cram as much as they can the night before, or to divide up the same amount of time across multiple study sessions? While studying people's learning of Spanish vocabulary words, Harry Bahrick and Elizabeth Phelps (1987) showed, as have others, that students generally do better to study via **distributed learning** (i.e., learning spaced out over several learning sessions) than via **massed learning** (i.e., learning that is crammed, occurring all at one time). Expert students and teachers know that cramming the day before a test, as Bill Norton's students originally did, is not a particularly effective way to learn. Moreover, even if you do remember the information for a test the next day, chances are you will forget it rather quickly thereafter. Bill Norton's new method of having students define the words as they read the novel, and then practice them again later, led to better test scores and improved the chance that they will remember the words for life.

TYPES OF STORAGE IN LONG-TERM MEMORY

We have talked about storage of information in long-term memory as though it were a singular phenomenon in all respects. But it is not. For example, there appear to be several different kinds of long-term storage, each of which is important to us in different ways. Table 8.2 depicts the types of knowledge stored in long-term memory. As you can see in the table, the two main categories of long-term memories are *declarative* and *procedural*. There may also be a third category, *conditional* knowledge.

Mental representations are the ways in which knowledge is stored in memory (Von Eckardt, 1999). These representations preserve certain information about as well as our interpretations of objects and events in the world, and they can be operated on by a variety of mental processes (McNamara, 1994). Concepts can be represented in multiple ways, which later may enhance recall. It thus is useful for teachers to present information in multiple ways, such as orally and visually (Mousavi, Low, & Sweller, 1995). Next, we look in detail at declarative and procedural knowledge and the ways each is represented in long-term memory.

■**DECLARATIVE KNOWLEDGE** **Declarative knowledge** comprises knowledge of facts stored in semantic or episodic memory. It is sometimes described as "knowing that" (Anderson, 2000; Sylvester, 1985). For example, you may know that the sun rises in the east and sets in the west. Category knowledge, such as that a cat is an animal, also is declarative (Gayne, Yekovich, & Yekovich, 1993). Memory researchers have suggested that declarative knowledge can be divided into two types: *semantic* and *episodic* (Tulving, 1983). Each type of memory involves somewhat different kinds of information.

Semantic memory comprises long-term memories that hold our general knowledge—what a zebra is, what the word *bitter* means, and what the color of leaves on trees

THINKING **ANALYTICALLY**

If, on one Friday, you introduce students to a list of vocabulary words or other facts to be learned, and you plan to test the students the following Friday, how would you suggest they study for the test?

SUGGESTION: They should distribute their learning rather than massing it. Cramming is relatively ineffective as a means of study.

TABLE 8.2   Types of Knowledge Stored in Long-Term Memory

	Declarative ("Knowing that")	Procedural ("Knowing how")	Conditional ("Knowing why" or "Knowing when")
Type of Memory Used for Storing It	Semantic memory: widely known facts Episodic memory: personal experiences	Procedural memory: ways to do things	Conditional memory: involves knowing when and how to apply the declarative and procedural knowledge you have
Form in Which It Is Stored	Hierarchies or other organized networks of representations, either: Analogical (images) or Symbolic (propositions)	Ordered sequences of productions (condition-action sequences)	Cognitive strategies: information about the conditions under which certain declarative or procedural knowledge is useful
Examples	Knowing what you did with your best friend yesterday (episodic), or planning for your best friend's birthday (semantic); can be stored as a mental picture of you and your friend at the movies (analogical representation), or as a set of propositions to indicate the birthday (propositional representation)	Knowing how to ride a bicycle or write a research paper	Knowing when to stop doing research for a research paper

is in the spring (Tulving, 2000). Such information is not unique to people as individuals, and people usually do not even remember when they first learned the information.

Episodic memory comprises long-term memories that hold knowledge of personally experienced events, or episodes (Tulving, 2000). People use this kind of memory when they learn lists of words or when they need to recall something they learned in a particular personal context. For example, suppose you saw a fellow teacher, named Tom Gordon, in the principal's office yesterday. Remembering that you saw Tom there yesterday is an episodic memory. Your knowledge of Tom's name, however, is a semantic memory. The experience of seeing him yesterday is a personal, time-tagged experience, whereas Gordon's name is a general semantic fact, known to all, with no attached time tag.

Although we believe the distinction between semantic and episodic memory is useful, not all investigators of memory accept the distinction (see, e.g., Anderson, 2000; Baddeley, 1984; Eysenck & Keane, 1990; Johnson & Hasher, 1987; McKoon & Ratcliff, 1986; Richardson-Klavehn & Bjork, 1988). Expert teachers know that students learn facts, or semantic information, in the course of their everyday experiences; that is, they encode semantic knowledge along with episodic knowledge. Some researchers have suggested that, if the experience or learning episode is memorable, students may be better able to recall the semantic knowledge (Martin, 1993). For example, if a chemistry teacher creates an explosion to demonstrate the body's metabolic processing of sugar, students may remember the facts about sugar metabolism more easily than they would if they had learned the facts from a lecture or textbook.

Declarative knowledge is represented in memory in two main ways, referred to as analogical and symbolic representations (Kosslyn, 1995; McNamara, 1994).

Analogical representations are declarative memories that preserve many of the aspects of the original stimulus, whether object or event (Anderson, 2000; Palmer, 1978). The most well-known analogical representation is *mental imagery,* or a mental picture that people believe looks like the objects or event they have seen. For example, if you see a beautiful sunset, and then imagine the sunset in your mind, you may well form a mental image of what the sunset looked like.

Symbolic representations are declarative memories that rely on arbitrary symbols that bear no obvious relation to whatever is being represented (Anderson, 2000; Palmer, 1978). The word *dog* bears no physical resemblance to a dog, despite the fact that it represents the concept of a dog. Similarly, nothing about the numeral *8* is reminiscent of "eightness," yet people use this numeral to represent the number eight. The most well-known symbolic representation is a *proposition,* an abstract way of representing the underlying (or "deep structural") relations among things. For example, the statement "John is heavier than Sam" might be represented in terms of the proposition *HEAVIER* (John, Sam), which is an abstract way of comparing the weights of the two individuals.

Both semantic and episodic memory can be represented in either analogue form, as images, or symbol form, as propositions. The *dual-trace theory* suggests that people can represent information both in the form of mental images and in the form of mental propositions (e.g., Paivio, 1971, 1986). The implication of dual-trace theory for teachers is that students are more likely to retain important information if it is presented to them both as words and as pictures (Small, Lovett, & Scher, 1993).

Propositions are combined through **propositional networks,** schematic integrations of interrelated propositions. Figure 8.2 shows an example of a propositional network about animals. Obviously, the figure is not intended to convey the full extent of people's knowledge about animals, but rather, only a small portion of it. What you can see, however, is that information about animals is interrelated in a roughly hierarchical fashion. For example, people have various pieces of information stored about animals in general, and then information stored about specific types of animals, such as birds and fish, and then information stored about specific types of birds and fish. What led researchers to believe that long-term memories might be stored in a hierarchical organization?

When this girl thinks about sunsets at another time, she will recall the mental image she formed while looking at this one. (Gary Conner, PhotoEdit)

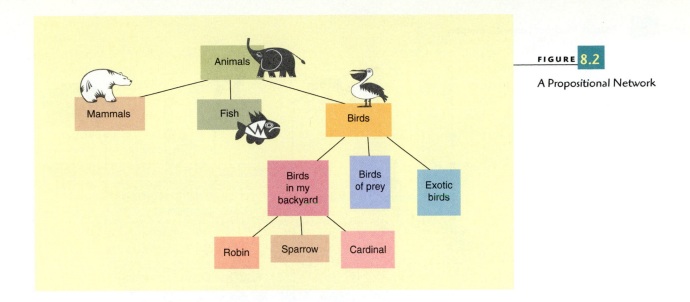

FIGURE 8.2

A Propositional Network

Until 1969, almost all experiments on memory had investigated episodic memory. People were given lists of words, numbers, or other items to remember and then quizzed on what they had learned. A landmark experiment investigating the structure of semantic memory was instigated by Allan Collins and Ross Quillian (1969), who timed people while they verified the truth or falsity of statements such as "A robin is a bird" and "A robin is an animal." Collins and Quillian found that the more remote the subject of the statement (e.g., robin) was from the conceptual category of the predicate (e.g., bird versus animal), the longer it took their research participants, on average, to verify the statement as true. These results demonstrated that it is possible to study the structure of semantic as well as of episodic memory. The results also provided one of the first suggestions that information is stored in memory in some kind of hierarchical form, as shown in Figure 8.2.

Researchers disagree about the basis people use to organize declarative knowledge. For example, Collins and Quillian (1969) noticed that it took people longer to verify that "A lion is a mammal" than to verify that "A lion is an animal," although *animal* is a more remote category with respect to lion than is *mammal*. This result suggested at least some important exceptions to the hierarchical rule. (Of course, it is possible that students did not recognize the word *mammal*.) Other researchers have proposed that people store information based on a comparison of semantic features, or the possible meanings of the target information (Smith, Shoben, & Rips, 1974). Still other researchers have proposed that people store information based on a combination of semantic features and hierarchical categories (Collins & Loftus, 1975).

Consider, for example, members of the set of mammal names. Mammal names could be represented in terms of three features: size, ferocity, and humanness (Henley, 1969). A lion, for example, would be high in all three, whereas an elephant would be particularly high in size but not so high in ferocity. A rat would be small in size but relatively high in ferocity, and so on. Figure 8.3 on page 278 shows how information might be stored and accessed in semantic memory if a feature-based theory of storage such as that of Smith, Shoben, and Rips were correct.

THINKING CREATIVELY

How might you use a network representation such as that shown in Figure 8.2 to help you teach children about dinosaurs?

SUGGESTION: Have children represent various dinosaurs in a network according to different principles of classifications—for example, land, air; carnivore, herbivore.

THINKING ANALYTICALLY

What other kinds of information might people be likely to store hierarchically? What are some kinds of information that do not seem to lend themselves to a hierarchical form of storage?

SUGGESTION: Types of plants may be stored hierarchically: trees, bushes, flowers, parts of flowers. Relatives among a group of friends would not be well represented hierarchically.

FIGURE **8.3** Feature Model of Semantic Memory

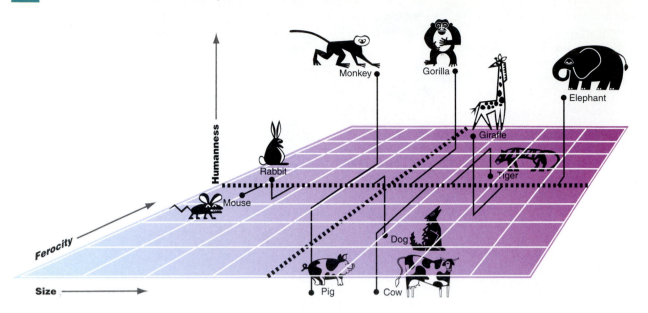

■**PROCEDURAL KNOWLEDGE** **Procedural knowledge,** or "knowing how" (Reed, 2000; Sylvester, 1985), is knowledge of how to do certain things. Knowing how to tell time according to the position of the sun is an example of procedural knowledge. Declarative and procedural knowledge appear to be held in distinct stores in long-term memory. In addition, each type of knowledge seems to be represented in memory in a different form. *Procedural memory* holds our knowledge of how to do things—drive a car, ride a bike, teach a class, and so on (see Cohen & Squire, 1980; Reed, 2000; Squire, 1987). Procedural knowledge appears to be distinct from declarative knowledge in long-term memory. Generally, procedural memories are also remarkably long lasting. For example, once a person has learned how to ride a bicycle, the person usually can remember how to do it for a long time after learning. Even if the person has not been on a bicycle for years, after a brief reorientation period, he or she can ride it as well as before. Part of what enables people to be procedurally expert is the development of *automaticity,* or the execution of procedures that is largely unconscious, effortless, and noninterfering with the performance of other unrelated or weakly related tasks (e.g., when you drive and listen to the radio at the same time).

Procedural knowledge appears to be represented in the form of what are called **productions,** or **condition-action sequences** (J. R. Anderson, 1976, 2000; Newell, 1973; Newell & Simon, 1972). These forms of storage tell us "If this, do that." An example of a production would be "If the teacher says *STOP,* then discontinue work on the test." When the "if" condition is met, the action is executed.

Productions are integrated through *production systems,* which are ordered sequences of productions (e.g., J. R. Anderson, 1976, 1983, 1993, 2000; Kintsch, 1988, 1998; Newell & Simon, 1972). In a production system, you go down a list of if–then statements until you find one whose condition (if statement) is satisfied. When you find such a statement, you execute the action, and then return to the top of the list. An example of a simple production system would be the following:

■ If the teacher says *START,* then begin work on the test.

■ If the teacher says nothing, then continue work on the test.

■ If the teacher says something to clarify a test item, then listen to what the teacher is saying while continuing working.

■ If the teacher says *STOP,* then discontinue work on the test.

■ **CONDITIONAL KNOWLEDGE** Are other types of knowledge stored in memory, besides declarative and procedural knowledge? Some researchers have suggested the possibility that higher order **metamemories,** that is, knowledge and control of your memory, might form a distinct kind of knowledge. Other theorists have spoken of **conditional knowledge,** or knowing when and how to apply the declarative and procedural knowledge you have learned (see Gagné, 1985; Paris & Cunningham, 1996; Paris, Lipson, & Wixson, 1983). Such information might be stored as *cognitive strategies,* or information about the conditions under which declarative and procedural knowledge is useful (Gagné, 1985). Whether such higher order knowledge really requires separate storage is ambiguous; but what is clear is the importance of such knowledge for success in school.

Students need to develop expertise in discerning when they should apply particular study strategies (Palincsar & Collins, 2000; Roediger, 1980). They must recognize, for example, the need to study facts and definitions for a multiple-choice test, or to practice summarizing and applying broad principles for an essay test measuring general understandings. Similarly, you do not read a mathematics textbook from cover to cover the same way you read a novel for pleasure.

Some students experience low levels of success in school because they fail to apply useful study strategies to the information they need to remember. If the teacher were to talk to these students, she would discover the students knew much more about the target information than they displayed on their tests. The problem for these students is not in their memory ability, but rather in their ability to apply appropriate study skills to the given information. For example, one student may study vocabulary words using a procedural memory strategy. This student may understand how to spell the words and use them in a sentence; however, when the student is required to list all the vocabulary words during her test, she might not remember many of the words. Had this student been tested on the meanings and uses of the vocabulary words provided on the test, she may have performed well. Given the way she was tested, this student should have used a declarative memory strategy to learn all of the vocabulary words.

Expert teachers look for this problem in students who seem to work hard in school but who perform poorly on measures of their knowledge. Several solutions are available for students who struggle to achieve conditional knowledge. Some teachers prefer to indicate directly how they expect their students to study. Other teachers prefer to assign other students who display good conditional knowledge as peer leaders of group study sessions in the classroom.

THINKING ANALYTICALLY

How would conditional knowledge be important to students when they do their homework?

SUGGESTION: The students need to know, for example, when to use which mathematical formula.

Implications for Teaching

THE THREE MEMORY STORES

Teachers can help students move information from sensory register through short-term memory into long-term memory. Some of the ways expert teachers use the standard model of memory to help students learn more effectively include the following:

■ ***Get students' attention.*** The standard memory model emphasizes getting students' attention so information in the sensory register will be transferred to short-term memory, where it will be processed further. A creative way of getting your students' attention is to use large, colorful visual aids to accompany the key points of a presentation. Identify particularly important concepts and information, and repeat for emphasis.

■ ***Help students develop metamemory.*** Teach students techniques such as chunking information (for example, French words by topic) by demonstrating the techniques in class and modeling them yourself. Help students identify which memory strategies work best for them. For example, if the class is quizzed on key terms every week, then for several weeks a teacher could prescribe a different memory strategy each week. After this trial period, the teacher could ask students to indicate their preferred strategies and explain why they believed these strategies worked.

■ *Allow time for rehearsal.* Presenting too much information or presenting information too quickly does not give students the opportunity to rehearse it. Expert teachers pause occasionally, maybe by asking if students have questions, to let students process their new knowledge.

■ *Help students elaborate.* Elaborative rehearsal is more effective than maintenance rehearsal in transferring information into long-term memory (it may also aid recall from long-term memory). Bill Norton helped students engage in elaborative rehearsal by having them define the vocabulary words in the context of the book they were reading and by asking them to make up a sentence about themselves. Teachers can reward students for elaborative rehearsal during practice tests.

■ *Schedule frequent practices of new information.* Expert teachers provide students several opportunities, spread out over time, to rehearse or elaborate on new information. For example, a biology teacher might present the parts of a cell one day, ask students to draw a cell and label the parts as homework, and schedule a review of the parts of the cell at the beginning of the next class before talking about the function of each part.

LONG-TERM MEMORY
The different models of how knowledge is stored in long-term memory have many implications for teachers who wish to enhance their students' memories. Among them are these:

■ *Arrange memorable learning experiences.* Expert teachers know that certain days or moments in class certainly do stand out in students' recollection. Research on the role of highly memorable experiences in increasing seman-

A teacher uses a poster to teach a science lesson to her class. (Jonathon Selig, Stone)

tic memory suggests that teachers should plan memorable learning experiences. For example, providing students with more opportunities to complete projects either on their own or in teams may increase their store of both episodic and semantic knowledge.

- ■ **Use pictures.** Expert teachers encourage the development of both analogical and semantic representations in their students' memories by visually demonstrating topics on the chalkboard or overhead projector or by using posters, time lines, or movies. They also encourage students to create their own mental pictures. For information that includes both pictures and meanings, students might draw models of their ideas, or the information they are trying to remember, to help them develop a dual memory trace.

- ■ **Organize information.** Provide students with *advance organizers,* such as outlines or lists of key points, before a lecture or reading assignment. Consider organizing information in ways that memory may be organized. For example, an English teacher can present information about parts of speech in a hierarchical fashion, from most to least important in a sentence.

- ■ **Teach conditional knowledge.** Include appropriate rules or guidelines for using newly acquired knowledge. When reading for English class, students might use a list of "questions that should be answered by the time the story is finished," to identify the important elements of a story.

- ■ **Encourage "learning by doing."** Procedural knowledge may best be learned by doing. Drivers' education is the ultimate example of the need for students to actually perform a procedure in order to learn it. Other procedural knowledge that is best learned by doing includes handwriting, math skills, science experiments, computer programming, and map reading. Sports and playing an instrument are also learned through lots of practice.

Alternative Models of Memory

As is often the case with scientific models, support for the standard model of memory is not definitive. Some of the researchers who disagree with the standard model have suggested other ways information enters into the brain and is stored. Because alternative models suggest several implications for teachers, we describe three of the major alternatives to the standard model: *connectionist models,* the *working-memory model,* and the *levels-of-processing model,* along with the major classroom implications of each.

CONNECTIONIST MODELS

For people to be able to use information in their memories, they clearly need some way to combine declarative and procedural knowledge. They need to know both about certain things and about how to use those things. One model of memory suggests how we are able to do so.

The **parallel distributed processing (PDP) model,** or **connectionist model,** focuses on the ways declarative and procedural knowledge are combined via a series of connections among elements (Smolensky, 2000). Consider how such models work.

In a network representation, such as a network of propositions, information is stored via a series of interconnected *nodes,* or slots in the network. Memory theorists differ as to the exact form their suggestions of networks of propositions take (e.g., Norman & Rumelhart, 1975, versus Schank, 1972), but the basic idea of a series of interconnected, labeled nodes is common to all of these representations. In connectionist models, however, the key to knowledge representation lies in the *connections* among nodes, not in the nodes themselves. An example of a connectionist model is shown in Figure 8.4.

In the model, nodes are activated by some kind of stimulus; that is, they come alive to a certain degree. More importantly, activation of one node may prompt activation of another, connected node, a phenomenon called **spreading activation** (Reisberg, 1997). A node that activates a connected node is termed a *prime,* and the resulting activation is termed a *priming effect* (Matlin, 1998). As shown in the figure, for example, if you hear the word *Senator,* the node for Senator is activated, and the activation is likely to spread to other, connected nodes, such as those for Representative and President. Perhaps there is some spread of activation to the nodes for White House and Capitol. Thus the activated node for Senator becomes a prime for the activation of the other nodes. An important feature of this model is that the spread of activation occurs *in parallel*—that is, activation spreads simultaneously across many interconnections in the network. For example, activation may spread simultaneously to Representative and President. Although there is considerable evidence of priming effects (e.g., McClelland & Rumelhart, 1985, 1988), researchers disagree on whether the priming is due to spreading activation (e.g., McKoon & Ratcliff, 1992). The details of this disagreement go beyond the scope of this text.

The important thing to remember about connectionist models is that your useful knowledge resides in the connections among nodes. For example, everything you know about dogs—that they are animals, that they bark, that they have fur, even that they exist—is stored in connections among nodes. Without connections, you would know nothing, and not even be able to retrieve the concept of "dog" itself.

Connectionist models also suggest that if you want students to learn about a topic, it helps to prime them—to prepare them with background information and concepts related to the topic. One way to conceptualize priming is through the use of a metaphor. A metaphor for the connectionist view of memory is the idea of a person's train of thought. Say a woman walks past a flower shop and sees a yellow tulip. This experience reminds her of her aunt, because the last time the woman visited her aunt, there was a

FIGURE **8.4**

A Connectionist Model of Memory

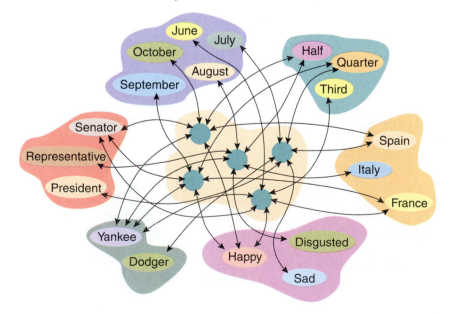

vase of yellow tulips in her aunt's window. After the woman thinks of her aunt, she starts wondering how her three cousins, the sons of this aunt, are doing since they moved to Boston. Then the woman starts thinking about Boston, and that it is on the way to Martha's Vineyard, where she spent a summer during college . . . and so her thoughts move on. The sight of the yellow tulip served as a prime, and the subsequent thought about her aunt further primed other thoughts. The way that the woman's thoughts went from one idea to another reflects what happens in spreading activation.

Connectionist models are appealing. Researchers have been able to build computer simulations based on the assumptions of connectionist models that react as humans would, a result suggesting that humans may, in fact, use parallel distributed processing (PDP). PDP models also make assumptions essentially identical to those used by psychologists who directly study how the brain functions via *neural networks,* or actual interconnections among neurons (nerve cells) in the brain (Hendry & King, 1994; Matlin, 1998; Solso, 1995). Thus connectionist models seem to have a certain direct tie to the biology of the brain that is less obvious in other models.

Priming can set the stage for introducing new information in class. Teachers can strengthen certain connections in their students' memory networks through reviews of information and concepts. A teacher might strengthen the connection between Spanish words and their pronunciations by having students conduct conversations in Spanish two days a week.

THINKING ANALYTICALLY

How might advance organizers function to prime students for learning the text they read?

SUGGESTION: The advance organizers—for example, summaries of text before the actual text—can organize related concepts and prime material that is to follow.

THINKING ANALYTICALLY

Why might it be important that a cognitive model of memory have direct links to what psychologists have learned from biological studies of the brain?

SUGGESTION: Each kind of model (cognitive and biological) can help explain the other. For example, biological processes place constraints on what cognitive processes are possible.

THE WORKING-MEMORY MODEL

Remember that the emphasis in the standard model is on three memory stores, among which there is a continual flow of information from the sensory register to short-term memory and then to the long-term memory. An alternative model places the emphasis on what is called **working memory,** which is an active part of long-term memory that also includes short-term memory. As you can see in Figure 8.5 (see, e.g., Baddeley, 1994; Cantor & Engle, 1993; Daneman & Carpenter, 1980; Daneman & Tardif, 1987; Engle, 1994; Engle, Cantor, & Carullo, 1992; Smith, 1999), working memory holds the most recently activated portion of long-term memory, and it moves these activated elements into and out of brief, temporary memory storage. Working memory may operate via at least some amount of parallel processing, as described earlier.

Thus working memory is an active form of storage. Table 8.3 shows that this is a key difference between the working-memory model and the standard model, in which the memory stores are more passive receptacles of information. The working-memory model even emphasizes the functions of working memory in governing other processes

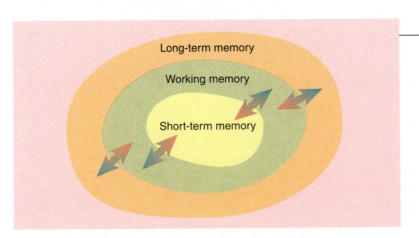

FIGURE 8.5

The Working-Memory Model

	Standard Memory Model	Working-Memory Model
Terminology	Short-term memory is sometimes called *working memory,* but it is distinct from long-term memory	Working memory includes both short-term memory *and* long-term memory
Relationship of Memory Stores	Short-term memory is distinct from long-term memory, although information may move between the two stores	Short-term memory is not entirely distinct from long-term memory; rather, it is a part of working memory along with whatever information in long-term memory is currently activated
Key Emphasis of Model	On the distinctions between different memory stores	On the role of activation in moving information into working memory and on the errors of working memory in memory processes

of memory, such as encoding and integrating information. Some functions of working memory may include integrating acoustic and visual information, organizing information into meaningful chunks, and linking new information to existing forms of knowledge representation in long-term memory.

Consider metaphors for these two alternative models of memory. The metaphor for the standard three-stores view can be a warehouse, in which information is passively stored and then called on as needed. In this metaphor, the sensory store is the loading dock and the short-term store is the area surrounding the loading dock where information is stored temporarily until it is moved to or from the proper location in the warehouse. In contrast, a metaphor for the working-memory model might be a multimedia production house, which continually generates and manipulates images and sounds, coordinating the integration of sights and sounds into meaningful arrangements. Once images, sounds, and other information are stored, they are still available for reformatting and reintegration in novel ways, as new demands and new information become available.

The concept of working memory reinforces the implication for teachers that activating, or getting students to recall, knowledge they already have helps the students integrate new knowledge into their long-term memories. The working-memory model further suggests the importance of integrating new, incoming information with information already stored in long-term memory. For example, an expert teacher who wants to correct students' misconceptions about people in another country can start by asking students what they know about people in the other country. Then the teacher shows a film or reads a story about the foreign land, and asks students to compare what they first thought about the people in that land with what the film or story suggests about the people. Students should alter their long-term memory preconceptions about the other country and its people based on the new information entered into working memory during the lesson. Table 8.3 summarizes the differences between the standard model and the working-memory model of memory.

THINKING ANALYTICALLY

In what ways would working memory be especially important to students when they are doing arithmetic computations?

SUGGESTION: Working memory could be important for holding in mind intermediate steps and results. For example, the Pythagorean theorem might already be in a student's long-term memory. When she sits down to do her geometry homework, she places this knowledge into her working memory and uses it as she completes her homework.

THE LEVELS-OF-PROCESSING MODEL

Another alternative model of memory is the **levels-of-processing model,** proposed originally by Fergus Craik and Robert Lockhart (1972). According to this model, memory does not comprise three or even any specific number of separate stores. Instead, as shown in Figure 8.6, storage varies along a continuous dimension in terms of depth of encoding. In other words, theoretically there are an infinite number of levels of processing (LOP) at which items can be encoded, with no distinct boundaries between one level and the next. The level at which information is stored will depend, in large part, on how it is encoded. Furthermore, the deeper the level at which an item is processed, the higher the probability that the item will be retrieved. There is an exception, however: If students encode information deeply, but are then tested in a superficial manner, they may do poorly on the test. For example, if students study deeper meanings in a history lesson and are then tested only on dates, their in-depth studying may actually hurt them.

Fergus Craik and Endel Tulving (1975) performed a set of experiments in order to support the LOP view. Participants were presented with a list of words, with each word preceded by a question. The questions, however, were not of a uniform kind. Rather, the questions were varied to encourage three different levels of processing, in progressive order of depth: *physical, acoustic,* and *semantic.* The results of the study seemed clear cut: The deeper the level of processing encouraged by the question, the higher the level of recall later achieved. Therefore, the way a word looks (its *physical appearance*) is only superficially processed in the brain. The way that word sounds (its *acoustic character*) helps the word to be processed more deeply in one's memory. However, the meaning of the word (its *semantic character*) is most deeply processed in the brain and thus provides the best way to commit that word to memory. Students' eyes and ears receive many sensations from the environment. When sensed objects become meaningful to students, students will better remember those objects.

According to the levels-of-processing model, teachers should help their students encode information at the deepest level possible. Return for a moment to Bill Norton, the teacher from the beginning of the chapter. When you consider the first task he had students do, you can see why, from the LOP point of view, his students would show relatively poor recall of the vocabulary words. Having students merely repeat words and definitions encourages them to process the words only at a shallow level. Bill's second try at teaching the vocabulary words used methods that encouraged deeper levels of processing. Of course, there are several ways he could have led students to deeper processing. For example, he might also have asked students to supply a synonym for each word, or to categorize the words in some meaningful way. Expert teachers remember that making ideas meaningful for students is the best way to help students learn.

The technique Bill Norton chose—asking students to give a sentence about themselves using each word—was especially effective in encouraging deeper levels of processing because it made use of the **self-reference effect,** by which people show very high levels of recall when asked to relate words meaningfully to themselves by determining whether the words describe themselves (Rogers, Kuiper, & Kirker, 1977; see also Bower & Gilligan, 1979; Brown, Keenan, & Potts, 1986; Ganellen & Carver, 1985; Katz, 1987; Reeder, McCormick, & Esselman, 1987). Even words that people decide are not very descriptive of themselves are recalled at high levels, merely because the person considered whether the words were self-descriptive. The best recall, however, results when the words actually do describe the

THINKING CREATIVELY

Suppose you want to encourage students to learn a set of facts about life in colonial America in a way that will maximize their recall. How might you use what you have learned about levels of processing in order to maximize their later recall?

SUGGESTION: Have the students relate each new concept to something meaningful that they already know. For example, have the students compare the time it took colonial women to make a meal to the time it takes us to make our meals today. Or have the students look for similarities between the town councils in colonial times and our own town councils.

FIGURE 8.6

The Levels of Processing Model

Level of Processing		Example
Bottom Level	Semantic Processing	"I like to pet the goats on my aunt's farm."
Middle Level	Acoustic Processing	"Goat rhymes with boat."
Top Level	Physical Processing	"Goat starts with the letter G."

person who evaluates them. For example, sixth graders assigned to learn about the turn of the century and the World's Fair in San Francisco could use self-referencing to study. Students could decide which exhibits at the fair they would have enjoyed most and which they would have enjoyed least. The students would be sure to remember the events that surrounded the World's Fair, and would probably remember more of the history related to the particular exhibits they believed they would have liked or disliked.

The self-reference effect has been interpreted as possible support for the LOP model. Each of us has a very well-developed *self-schema,* an organized system of internal information regarding ourselves, our attributes, and our personal experience (see Mills, 1983). Because this self-schema is so well developed, you can richly and elaborately encode information related to yourself—more so than you can when the information is related to other topics (Anderson, 2000; Bellezza, 1984, 1992). In terms of levels of processing, people process information about themselves at a very deep level.

The self-reference effect suggests that students better recall information to the extent that they can see its relevance to themselves. The information effectively becomes a part of the students as people. As teachers, we know that we listen better to and learn better from in-service lectures or workshops when we realize how we can use the information in our own lives. Students, of course, are no different. The more the information relates to them as people, the better they are likely to retain it. Encourage students to think actively about how new information relates to them personally. Indeed, people demonstrate higher levels of recall when they generate their own cues for later recall than when someone else generates the cues for them (Greenwald & Banaji, 1989).

Implications for Teaching

- ***Use the ideas of priming and spreading activation to help students learn.***
  For example, a teacher may review subtraction and multiplication as a way of priming students before teaching division.

- ***Help your students encode information at the deepest level possible.***
  Expert teachers know that making ideas meaningful for students is the best way to help the students learn.

Retrieving Information

The standard memory model and the alternatives to it that we discussed all focus primarily on encoding and storing information. Once you have stored information, what happens when you try to retrieve it? Sometimes it is very easy to retrieve a fact or procedure from long-term memory. Other times, try as you might, retrieval seems impossible. Retrieval is critical in school, because teachers generally base their evaluations of how well students have learned on students' demonstrations of retrieval, such as their performance on exams (Greeno, Collins, & Resnick, 1996). We will discuss what makes information easier to retrieve, and what makes it more difficult to retrieve, but first, consider the different ways teachers assess their students' memories.

 TASKS USED TO ASSESS STUDENTS' MEMORIES

There are two basic types of memory tasks you will undoubtedly use when you evaluate students' learning. These two types measure *recall* and *recognition* memory. We discuss recall and recognition memory tasks in detail.

■**RECALL TASKS** Perhaps the most common way to assess learning and memory is through a **recall task,** in which a person is asked to produce information from memory. The information might be a single word, fact, or picture, or a string of words, facts, pictures, or perhaps other symbols. Recall can be measured in various ways.

In **free recall,** students are presented with a list of items and must recite back the items in any order they prefer. For example, a teacher might ask students to list the names of important historical figures, or the names of the world's oceans, or to recall a list of important prepositions. In these cases, the teacher does not care what order the items are listed in, but rather, how many items are correctly listed.

In **serial recall,** students are presented with a list of items, and their task is to repeat the items back in the order they were presented. Serial recall is used as a subtest on a number of tests of intelligence, for example, when people are asked to repeat back (in forward or sometimes reverse order) a list of digits. Serial recall is sometimes used in school as well. For example, when students learn to recite a poem, they need to learn the words in order. Just repeating back all the words of the poem in random order will not do! Similarly, learning lines of a play means learning them in order, not just randomly ordering the words that need to be said.

In **paired-associates recall,** students are presented with items in pairs. When they are tested, students are given the first item of each pair, and they must repeat back the item with which the first item was paired. For example, vocabulary tests, where you present a word and ask students to define it (as in Bill Norton's vocabulary test), are paired-associates tests. Similarly, if you give your geography students the name of a state, and ask them to write down the capital, you are testing their paired-associates recall. If you teach chemistry, and ask students what element has an atomic number of 16, you are also giving a paired-associates test.

In schools, many learning and memory tasks require a combination of the various kinds of memory demands. For example, suppose you ask your students to write an essay recounting the main events leading up to Abraham Lincoln's Gettysburg Address, or to the beginning of the French Revolution. You are requiring students to use some combination of free and serial recall, as well as other higher order thinking processes (described in Chapter 9). On the one hand, you have not prescribed a fixed order of recall. On the other hand, you presumably expect students to know something of the chronology of events and would not be satisfied if they simply listed events in a random order.

■**RECOGNITION TASKS** Another kind of task used to assess memory is a **recognition task,** in which students have to select or identify something that they learned previously. Suppose Bill Norton tested vocabulary through a multiple-choice test. He would present a definition, and ask students which word corresponds to the definition; or he might present a word, and give alternative definitions. The students must recognize the correct answer from among the choices Bill presented. Of course, recognition can be measured in other ways. For example, in a matching test, in which you give the names of countries and the student has to match them with their appropriate continents, you are testing recognition as well.

Many multiple-choice tests and related tests measure more than straight recognition memory. Such tests often involve an element of reasoning as well (discussed in Chapter 9). Indeed, few teacher-made or standardized tests are pure measures of any one kind of memory.

Benton Underwood and his colleagues (Underwood, Boruch, & Mulmi, 1978) did a study comparing the various kinds of memory tests and found that performances on them are not very highly related. In other words, someone who does well on one kind of memory test does not necessarily do well on another. For this reason, expert teachers vary their forms of assessment, thereby allowing students with different kinds of memory and other skills to show what they know.

THINKING CREATIVELY

How can you measure free recall in the context of measuring learning of a science lesson? As an example, consider a science lesson about different animals or plants that live in the rain forest, or use an actual science lesson you have used or heard about.

SUGGESTION: You can have the students recall the names of the animals or plants.

THINKING ANALYTICALLY

Describe a recent example from your own experience as a student of the difference between recall and recognition memory.

SUGGESTION: Recall is primarily involved in short-answer, fill-in-the blanks, tests; recognition, in multiple-choice tests.

Psychologists studying retrieval distinguish between the *availability* and the *accessibility* of memories. Availability refers to whether information is actually stored in long-term memory. Accessibility refers to how easily stored information can be retrieved. In a study illustrating this point, Harry Bahrick, Phyllis Bahrick, and Roy Wittlinger (1975) tested people's memory for names and photographs of their high school classmates. Even after twenty-five years, the research participants had surprisingly good memory for the names and faces. Moreover, at times when participants seemed not to remember, further prompting enabled them to remember things they thought they had forgotten. The information about their classmates, in other words, was available—it was there in long-term memory. The difficulty was in retrieving it, or making it accessible. Similar findings have emerged from studying people's memory for what they learned of a foreign language many years earlier (Bahrick, 1984; Bahrick, Bahrick, Bahrick, & Bahrick, 1993). What makes some information more accessible and other information less accessible?

THINKING PRACTICALLY

How might you use the findings of Tulving to help children learn and later retrieve information about various kinds of rocks in a science class?

SUGGESTION: Have the students learn the identities of the rocks by categories (igneous, sedimentary, metamorphic), and then encourage the students during testing to retrieve the rocks by categories.

■**RETRIEVAL CUES** One of the best ways to make information easier to get out of mental storage is through **retrieval cues,** clues or reminders that can enhance the ability to retrieve stored information from memory. Endel Tulving and Zena Pearlstone (1966) asked participants in an experiment to memorize lists of categorized words. For example, the participants might hear the category "articles of clothing," followed by the words, "shirt, socks, pants, belt." Participants were later tested for their recall in one of two ways. In a free-recall condition, participants merely recalled as many words as they could in any order they could. In a cued-recall condition, participants were tested category by category. They were given each category label as a cue, and were then asked to recall as many words as they could from that category.

The critical result of this research was that cued recall was far better, on average, than free recall. Had the experimenters tested the participants only via free recall, they might have concluded that the participants had learned far fewer words than they had actually learned. In other words, difficulties in the free-recall condition were due not to availability difficulties, or lack of words stored, but to accessibility difficulties in retrieving the words. Once participants were given cues, they were better able to retrieve the memorized words.

An elementary school child uses a globe to visualize geographical terms she must learn and later retrieve from her memory. Retrieval is critical to school performance, particularly on exams. (Margaret Ross, Stock Boston)

This research suggests that teachers can greatly enhance students' learning of and subsequent memory for information if they provide some way for them to organize the information in advance. This way of organizing information is sometimes called an **advance organizer.** For example, at the beginning of this chapter, the title of the quoted passage "Washing Clothes" would serve as an advance organizer. Other examples of advance organizers can be found throughout this book. The title and outline of each chapter—as well as the lists of objectives—are designed to help you organize *in advance* the information in the chapter to make this information easier for you to learn.

The settings in which students learn information can also function as retrieval cues. According to the principle of **encoding specificity** (Tulving & Thomson, 1973), what is recalled depends on the context in which it is encoded. You recall best if the circumstances of recall match the circumstances of encoding. Even seemingly irrelevant aspects of the learning environment can be encoded along with class information, to function later as retrieval cues.

A particularly interesting demonstration of this effect was shown in an experiment in which 16 underwater divers were asked to learn a list of 40 unrelated words, either while they were on shore or while they were 20 feet beneath the surface (Godden & Baddeley, 1975). Later, when the divers were asked to recall the words either in the underwater environment or on shore, their retrieval was better if the retrieval environment was the same as the encoding environment at the time of learning. Divers who learned while underwater had better recall when tested underwater, whereas divers who learned while ashore remembered better when tested ashore.

Even people's moods can provide retrieval cues for later recall. That is, those things we encode during a particular mood are more easily retrieved if they are recalled when we are in the same mood (Bower, 1981). Thus, if students learn things when they are happy, they often will retrieve them better during a time when they are happy than a time when they are sad. Expert teachers are aware of the effect of context on their students' learning and make it a point to pay attention, not only to the material the students are to learn, but also to the context in which the students are to learn it.

■**MNEMONIC DEVICES** You can use or teach your students to use a number of **mnemonic devices,** or specific techniques for improving learning and memory. Most of the mnemonic devices are based on the general principles of encoding and retrieval suggested by current memory models described in this chapter, and most of them are easily taught. Here are seven of the main ones (Sternberg & Grigorenko, 2002).

1. **Categorical clustering.** Encourage your students to organize a list of items to be remembered into a set of categories. For example, suppose you want your students to learn the major exports of each of the major countries of Europe, but they have trouble memorizing lists of products. You might encourage them to group the products by categories, for example, names of fruits (apples, oranges, grapefruits), names of dairy products (yogurt, cheese, butter), names of industrial goods, and so on.

2. **Interactive images.** Create interactive images that link together items that would otherwise be isolated. For example, suppose, in the preceding example, you want your students to learn the names of major exports and to use another method to help them remember. Suppose further that the main exports of a given country are wine, cheese, automobiles, and designer dresses. You might ask students to imagine as vividly as possible a bottle of wine driving an automobile, wearing a designer dress, and eating a piece of cheese. Even better, you might suggest that students come up with their own images.

   Research discussed earlier shows that much of declarative knowledge is stored in images. Interactive imagery is one of the most useful ways to learn and remember material, and it can be used in a variety of circumstances. Some of the techniques described here make use of interactive imagery in particular ways.

3. **Pegwords.** Associate each word to be learned with a word on a list that has previously been memorized—a pegword—and form an interactive image between the two words. For example, a standard list that is frequently used is "one is a bun, two is a shoe, three is a tree, four is a door, five is a hive." The list can be extended in length indefinitely. For the pegword method to work, students must first memorize this list. Now suppose you want your students to learn the names of the presidents of the United States in chronological order. You ask them to imagine George Washington eating a bun, John Adams wearing an extremely large shoe, Thomas Jefferson climbing a tree, and so on. Or if you want students to learn the exports, again, you might have them imagine a bun with a gigantic slice of cheese in the middle, a designer dress attached to a shoe, an automobile ramming into a tree, and so on.

4. **Method of loci.** Visualize walking or driving along a familiar path that has distinctive landmarks, such as the roads or streets along which you travel to go to school. Reflect carefully on the distinctive landmarks. Now link each of the words or items to be remembered through an interactive image to each of the landmarks. To recall the words later, merely collect them from the landmarks. Suppose, for example, that some of the landmarks are a stop sign, a huge boulder, a traffic light, and a grocery store. In the export example, you might imagine a bottle of wine replacing the word *stop* on the sign, a designer dress wrapped around the huge boulder, an automobile stopped at the traffic light, and a large picture of a cheese adorning the grocery store. As you mentally walk or ride through the route, you pluck the products from each of the landmarks.

THINKING CREATIVELY

Take one of the mnemonics and describe how you can show students how to use the mnemonic in a way that will be relevant to whatever you are teaching them.

SUGGESTION: Each student must answer for himself or herself.

5. **Acronyms.** Form a word or expression whose letters each signify some other word or concept. Acronyms are very common as abbreviations; for example, O.R. can stand for operations research. But acronyms can also be used for learning concepts. For example, suppose you want to remember each of the mnemonics in this section. You might create the acronym, I AM PACK, where each letter stands for the first letter of one of the mnemonics (Interactive images, Acronyms, Method of loci, Pegwords, Acrostics, Categories, and Keywords). Both the acronym and the acrostic methods, described next, make use of levels of processing deeper than those required for rote learning, to generate the mnemonic devices.

6. **Acrostics.** Form a sentence in which the first letter of each word of the sentence is the first letter of one of the words to be remembered. For example, "**E**very **G**ood **B**oy **D**oes **F**ine" is an acrostic frequently used to memorize the notes on lines of the treble clef in music, and "**C**an **A** **W**oman **D**ance?" might be used to remember the four products mentioned earlier—cheese, automobiles, wine, and designer dresses. **M**other **V**ery **E**asily **M**akes **J**elly **S**andwiches **U**sing **N**o **P**eanut butter can be used to remember the names of the planets in the order of their distance from the sun.

A music teacher showing her student the "Every Good Boy Does Fine" acrostic, used as a memory device for remembering the lines of a treble staff. (Tony Freeman, PhotoEdit)

7. **Keywords.** Form an interactive image that links the sound and meaning of a foreign word with the sound and meaning of a familiar word. For example, suppose you want to learn that the French word for *butter* is *beurre*. You might observe that the French word sounds like "bear." So now associate the keyword "bear" with butter in an image or sentence. For example, you might imagine a bear eating a stick of butter. Later, the image of a bear will provide a retrieval cue for *beurre*.

Other general mnemonic devices can be used. One of the most well known is called **PQ4R,** which stands for *Preview, Question, Read, Reflect, Recite,* and *Review* (Thomas & Robinson, 1972). The PQ4R technique is designed to help you remember what you read (see Figure 8.7). To use the strategy, first preview the material to be read by skimming the main chapter headings, summaries, and any other organizing information the authors included. Next, write questions about each section of the material that relate the material to your reason for reading it ("Why does a teacher need to know about PQ4R?). Then, read the material, paying attention to details. While you are reading, reflect on the material and try to build your understanding by drawing conclusions from it. Next, recite to yourself the contents of what you just read, and answer the questions you wrote without looking back at the text. Finally, review what you read previously to build on it with the new information you have just read; this step is part of an ongoing, cumulative process.

FIGURE 8.7

Using PQ4R

Preview
"I will read all the headings in this chapter before I read the chapter."

Question
"Why would a teacher need to know about mnemonic devices?"

Read

Reflect
"I have used the acronym method lots of times. It really does help."

Recite
"As a teacher, I will need to know about mnemonic devices so I can help my students improve their recall for tests and assignments."

Review
"Mnemonics work because they build on the principles of the models of memory."

Indeed, a whole host of strategies can help students become expert learners: Some of these strategies were described in Chapter 1, where we discussed how to become an expert student.

CONSTRUCTING YOUR OWN LEARNING

Read "The War of the Ghosts," which follows.

One night two young men from Egulac went down to the river to hunt seals, and while they were there it became foggy and calm. Then they heard war-cries, and they thought: "Maybe this is a war-party." They escaped to the shore, and hid behind a log. Now canoes came up, and they heard the noise of paddles, and saw one canoe coming up to them. There were five men in the canoe, and they said: "What do you think? We wish to take you along. We are going up the river to make war on the people."

One of the young men said, "I have no arrows."

"Arrows are in the canoe," they said.

"I will not go along. I might be killed. My relatives do not know where I have gone. But you," he said, turning to the other, "may go with them."

So one of the young men went, but the other returned home. And the warriors went on up the river to a town on the other side of Kalama. The people came down to the water, and they began to fight, and many were killed. But presently the young man heard one of the warriors say: "Quick, let us go home; that Indian has been hit." Now he thought; "Oh, they are ghosts." He did not feel sick, but they said he had been shot.

So the canoes went back to Egulac, and the young man went ashore to his house, and made a fire. And he told everybody and said: "Behold I accompanied the ghosts, and we went to fight. Many of our fellows were killed, and many of those who attacked us were killed. They said I was hit, and I did not feel sick."

He told it all, and then he became quiet. When the sun rose he fell down. Something black came out of his mouth. His face became contorted. The people jumped up and cried.

He was dead.

After reading the story, do something else for fifteen minutes. Then try to recall as much of the story as possible. What kinds of errors in recall did you make?

If you are currently working in a practicum, you might also ask some of the students you are working with to try this same test, or a similar one with a story that you select. (Be sure to discuss this first with your cooperating teacher.)

Most people tend to commit errors that help make incomprehensible aspects of the text comprehensible to them. The reason is that the text is unfamiliar and difficult. More generally, when students read material that is difficult for them, they may distort what they read in ways that are consistent with their existing knowledge base. Giving students an advance organizer to help them understand what they are about to read may reduce or eliminate such distortion. Can you think of any other ways to reduce distortion?

 RETRIEVAL FAILURE

Of course, many attempts at retrieval fail. We commonly call our failure to retrieve information from memory, *forgetting*. Why do we forget information, whether from long-term memory or from short-term memory?

The two most well-known theories of forgetting from the short-term store are decay theory and interference theory. **Decay theory** posits that information is forgotten because of the gradual disappearance over time of an unusual memory trace. Although there is some evidence of decay (Reitman, 1971, 1974), it appears that decay plays a relatively little role, if any, in forgetting.

Interference theory asserts that we forget because competing information renders inaccessible (and possibly unavailable) the information we want to remember. There are two main kinds of interference. **Retroactive interference** (also called **retroactive inhibition**) is forgetting caused by activity *following* the time something is learned, but before we need to recall that thing (Sternberg, 1999). Thus new learning interferes with old learning. In other words, you learn something you will need to recall, then you learn something else, and then you are tested on the to-be-recalled material.

An example of retroactive interference occurs when a student studies for a world history test to take place the next day and afterward completes her American history homework. The information in the American history homework can retroactively interfere with her ability to remember what she studied for the world history test. Or consider the native Chinese speaker who has completed an advanced English class and is now studying French. He may have difficulty speaking English because of retroactive interference from what he is learning about French grammar and vocabulary.

In contrast, **proactive interference** (also called **proactive inhibition**) is forgetting what occurs when the interfering material *precedes* the to-be-remembered material (Sternberg, 1999). Here, old learning interferes with new learning. In other words, you learn something not related to what you will later need to recall, then you learn what you will need to recall, and finally you are tested on the to-be-recalled material.

THINKING ANALYTICALLY

Give an example of how you might experience proactive interference if you are taking two foreign language courses, one in French and one in Spanish. *Hint:* What if your French course meets at 9 A.M. and your Spanish course meets at 11 A.M.?

SUGGESTION: Your learning in the French class may proactively interfere with your learning in the later Spanish course.

An example of proactive interference is when a student completes her American history homework and then studies for the world history test the next day. American history information may proactively interfere with her ability to learn and recall the world history material. Or, after completing an advanced English class, a student who is a native Chinese speaker and is now taking a French class may have difficulty in French class because of proactive interference from what he has learned previously about English grammar and vocabulary.

When you learn a number of items at once, and later have to retrieve them, you are likely to be able to recall some items more easily than others. In particular, you tend better to remember items near the beginning and near the end of the list than you remember items from the middle of the list. For example, if you are asked to recall the numbers 4-8-6-1-9-8-2-7-3-5, you are more likely to recall well the first few and last few numbers, and to be less able to remember those in the middle. Better recall of items near the beginning of a list is sometimes referred to as a *primacy effect*. Better recall of items near the end of the list is sometimes referred to as a *recency effect*. The combination of the primacy and recency effects is referred to as the **serial-position curve;** it is shown in idealized form in Figure 8.8.

Why do you recall more items at the two ends? One interpretation is that items at the beginning of a list are subject only to retroactive interference, whereas items at the end of a list are subject only to proactive interference. Items in the middle of the list, however, are subject to both retroactive and proactive interference.

The serial-position curve has a practical implication for those who wish to become expert teachers. Suppose you have a lot of material to teach, and you do not expect students to remember every single thing you have taught. Place the most important material either at the beginning or at the end of the lesson, because material at the two extremes is most likely to be remembered.

As you can see, the context in which you learn things makes a large difference in how well you can retrieve those things. Moreover, competing contexts can interfere with later retrieval. In the next section we consider the effects of context in more detail.

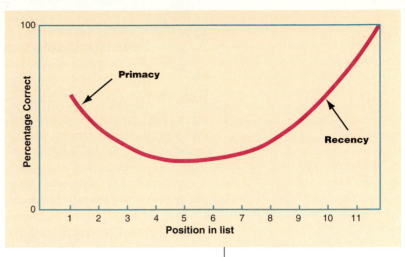

Primacy

Recency

Percentage Correct

Position in list

FIGURE 8.8

The Serial Position Curve

THINKING **PRACTICALLY**

If you plan to go job hunting, why might you want to be interviewed either at the beginning or at the end of the series of interviews of job applicants?

SUGGESTION: You might be more memorable to the interviewer.

Implications for Teaching

■ *Be aware of the effect of context on your students' learning and make it a point to pay attention not only to the material the students are to learn, but also to the context in which the students are to learn it.* For example, if posters were used as visual aids when the target information was presented, an expert teacher might decide not to remove these posters completely during the testing time. Instead, the teacher might cover parts of the posters that revealed too much information. Or the teacher can simply turn the posters away from the students, for the mere presence of the posters contributes to the contextual similarity between the information as presented and the information as tested. This similarity could result in better performance for some students.

■ *Make use of mnemonic devices to help your students study.* For example, have a group of students learn a list of unrelated words—*dwelling, underwear, cavalier, kinetic, warble, ambush, larvae,* and *kilowatt*—by using the acronym DUCK WALK.

Constructivist Approaches

We mentioned at the outset of this chapter that learning is more than just loading down students with memories, as you would a computer disk. **Constructivist approaches** to learning and memory are based on the idea that, unlike a computer disk or an empty container, children do not wait passively to be filled up with knowledge (Cobb, 2000). Rather, children actively build, or construct, their own knowledge. The constructivist approach to education stresses that, although teachers cannot entirely control their students' learning, expert teachers can do much to facilitate students' own active learning processes.

CONSTRUCTIVIST APPROACHES TO MEMORY

A constructivist approach to memory recognizes that prior experience and context affect the way we encode memories, how we recall things, and what we actually recall (Alexander, 1996; Greeno, Collins, & Resnick, 1996). Thus memory is *constructive*—it is something we build—rather than merely *reproductive,* or something we extract from our knowledge base. New knowledge is built on the memory foundation of prior experiences.

What do we mean when we say that memory is affected by prior experience and context? Consider the case of Bubbles P., a 33-year-old professional gambler, card dealer, and crap shooter, who also worked part time in a liquor store. Bubbles was studied extensively by Stephen Ceci and his associates (Ceci, DeSimone, & Johnson, 1992). Bubbles was known for his exceptional memory for cards—he could memorize the exact order of 52 cards in a deck in only 6 minutes! It took Bubbles only 9 minutes to memorize 50 numbers in order. But when it came to memorizing colors, faces, or words, Bubbles's memory was only average (as was his IQ of 103); for example, he could memorize only eight colors.

The key is that Bubbles's memory was affected by context. What Bubbles did for a living affected his motivation and his memory—he had trained his memory to count cards and remember numbers. Memory is not an entity or thing that exists independent of the person. Rather, memory depends on a person's knowledge, experiences, and motivations.

One of the first scientists to recognize the importance of a constructivist approach to memory was Frederic Bartlett (1932). Bartlett asked British university students to learn what must have seemed to them to be a strange and only poorly comprehensible North American Indian legend, "The War of the Ghosts." Bartlett found that people tended to distort their recall in order to render the story more comprehensible. For example, the British university students who participated in Bartlett's study often recalled two young men going on a fishing trip, rather than seal hunting, or recalled that the war party used a rowboat instead of a canoe. In other words, their prior knowledge, as well as the expectations they had based on this prior knowledge, had a large effect on how they recalled the text.

Bartlett suggested that people bring into a memory task **schemas,** or cognitive frameworks for organizing associated concepts, based on previous experience, which affect how we learn and remember. Recall from Chapter 2 that Jean Piaget also suggested the

Few players at blackjack tables share Bubbles's extraordinary ability to memorize the order of a deck of cards. (Donald Nussbaum, Stone)

existence of cognitive schemas. Piaget's theory, however, emphasized the ways that schemas change as children develop and must assimilate or accommodate new information. Bartlett's research suggests that not only does information change children's schemas, their schemas may also affect the information they learn. Students' prior knowledge and expectations may cause them to remember information in a distorted way that fits into their existing cognitive frameworks. Recall that, during his review session, Bill Norton asked several students to state their own definitions of the vocabulary words. Doing so enabled him to determine whether the students had interpreted the words in ways that, perhaps, fit with their own cognitive frameworks, but were distortions of the actual meanings.

Other research on eyewitness testimony, done by Elizabeth Loftus and colleagues (Loftus, 1975, 1977; Loftus & Ketcham, 1991; Loftus, Miller, & Burns, 1978, 1987; Loftus & Pickerall, 1995 and others [see, e.g., Thompson et al., 1998]) also suggests that people can be led to distort their memories. They use cognitive schemas to build, rather than merely take out, knowledge when they try to recall what they have learned. For example, when Mary is asked about her memory of the past Memorial Day, she remembers how much she enjoyed going to the beach. Yet a week after she was first questioned, Mary discovers (through a false report) that the past Memorial Day had broken the state's hot weather records. Now when asked, Mary remembers her time at the beach as less fun than she did at first. In particular, she begins to remember how hot the sand had been! Mary's memory of the past Memorial Day was shaped by the new information she learned, even though this information wasn't true. Memorial Day wasn't any hotter than usual, yet because Mary believed the new information, she incorporated it into her memory. Her perceptions thereby changed. Thus expert teachers are careful to look for distorted perceptions and memories on the part of students. Asking students to relate what they know about a subject may help teachers clear up distorted perceptions before these perceptions become problematic.

Roger Schank and Robert Abelson (1977) have taken the concept of schemas one step further, suggesting that people develop organized **scripts,** or stereotypical story outlines for how events typically proceed. A script for a typical test-taking session, for example, can include the following:

- Learn material.

- Participate or take notes in review session.

- Practice material the night before the exam.

- Walk into the classroom; take a seat.

- Teacher hands out exam papers.

- Answer questions that are easy.

- Check test time remaining.

- Return to hard questions; try to answer.

- Finish all the questions.

- Hand in exam to teacher.

We have similar scripts for activities such as going to a restaurant or going out on a date. Evidence indicates that scripts have psychological reality (Bower, Black, & Turner, 1979), although they are only one of many representations we use for complex sets of information. Scripts are useful for stereotyped sets of actions, such as going to a doctor's office, but they appear to be less useful in novel kinds of situations.

Research has shown that children have scripts that can affect their recall of events (Hudson, 1990; Hudson & Nelson, 1986). In other words, children tend to recall an event as though it corresponds with the script they have for the event. In one study, children who went regularly to a creative-movement workshop developed a script that included initial stretching and then certain exercises and activities. One day, the teacher omitted one typical event—for example, the stretching. Later, when the children were asked to recall what they did at the workshop that day, they reported having performed the omitted activity. For example, they said they had done the stretches that day. The children were script dependent—they truly believed the way the event had happened on a given day must have corresponded to their script.

As a teacher, you will see examples of students' scripts for events, such as how class activities should proceed, how tests should be written and graded, how book reports and projects should be completed, and so on. Expert teachers have discovered that they need to exercise patience if they wish students to do things differently from the way their script dictates. Scripts have a significant influence on students and it can be a challenge for students to violate their scripts. Initially, students may not be enthusiastic about a teacher's desire to change the way things are done!

CONSTRUCTIVIST APPROACHES TO LEARNING

Constructivist approaches to education are built on the same key ideas as constructivist approaches to memory, which are that learners must build their own knowledge—it cannot be given to them—and that new knowledge builds on current knowledge. Constructivist approaches to education are based, in part, on the theories of Lev Vygotsky (Karpov & Bransford, 1995). For example, as described in Chapter 2, Vygotsky (1978) believed that children internalize what they see in their surroundings (or contexts), building up their knowledge from what they observe around them. Vygotsky also recognized the essentially social nature of learning. Constructivists believe other people are a part of every learning situation—indeed, every context. Thus you cannot meaningfully study learning without taking into account the social situation in which the learning occurs.

Many educational approaches based on constructivist views emphasize the social contexts of learning. For example, some constructivists suggest that learning best takes place, not through direct instruction, but through *cognitive apprenticeships,* or partnerships between novice students and experts, such as teachers or more experienced students. The expert acts as a facilitator, advising and helping the novice student when he or she encounters problems while trying to master a task or concept (Collins, Brown, & Newman, 1989; Farnham-Diggory, 1992; Greene, Collins, & Resnick, 1996; Rogoff, 1990). In Vygotsky's terms, the expert provides the novice student with scaffolding, or gradually decreasing levels of support, as the novice internalizes the task. For example, a math or science teacher asks students to figure out how much water three different containers hold. The teacher does not directly teach students the formula for determining the volume of a container. Instead, he meets with groups of students to help them plan a strategy for solving the problem, and then makes himself available for questions or offers hints as students try to develop the formula on their own. Group projects increase the chances that students will learn from one another, as well as from the teacher. Thus group projects are an important part of many constructivist educational approaches.

Constructivist views have become increasingly important in schools. They have been used as the basis for the standards of teaching developed by education groups, including the National Council of Teachers of Mathematics' *Curriculum and Evaluation Standards for*

Group projects in school increase the chances that students will learn from one another, as well as from the teacher; thus, they are an important aspect of constructivist educational approaches. This group of high school students is working on a Habitat for Humanity project. (Mary Kate Denny, PhotoEdit)

FOCUS ON: AUTHENTIC LEARNING EXPERIENCES
RON FORESO: PARSIPPANY HIGH SCHOOL, PARSIPPANY, NEW JERSEY—GRADES 9–12, SOCIAL STUDIES

In December of 1991, as an alternative to their usual winter music program of Christmas and Hanukkah songs, the students of Parsippany High School performed a multimedia event commemorating the fiftieth anniversary of America's entry into World War II. Students at every grade and academic level, representing nearly every department in the high school, performed this tribute to the local veterans of World War II and their families.

Why did you choose World War II as the theme for this project?

The purpose of the program was not to celebrate a devastating war, but to honor those who fought in defense of our freedom. More than 292,000 young Americans died in combat, and nearly 300,000 factory workers were killed in accidents on the homefront. We shouldn't forget their sacrifice. "Those who don't remember are doomed to repeat it." We must also remember that out of the war experience came advancements in science, medicine, education, and technology that greatly improve our lives today.

How did this program address the students' different learning styles?

This program addressed the needs of many learning styles. There was an opportunity for diverse kids to shine, and to show their expertise. A powerful reason for entering into these programs is that they allow the students to excel at what they are good at, whether it's history, music, English, or art. Some students are not good test-takers, but they are excellent public speakers. These kids were the narrators for the evening's event. Some students are good musicians but not great in history or math. Their brilliance is in their music. Band students researched authentic music from the war years. They dug through libraries, grandmothers' attics. They went about this with a great sense of purpose. Art classes

painted banners; social studies classes researched war history; stagecraft students constructed realistic backdrops. For the performance, students wore World War II uniforms and clothing. The history and English classes researched and wrote the narrative material that was performed. The audio/visual and stagecraft students presented a slide show depicting the war.

Describe the night of the performance.

The night of the performance there were more than five hundred people in the audience. Nearly half were World War II veterans. The last part of the program was a medley of armed services songs played and sung by our band and choir. The veterans of each branch of the service were invited to stand to be acknowledged. As the Navy veterans stood for "Anchors Aweigh," one of the veterans near the front of the auditorium began to cry. His granddaughter, a choir member, saw him and began to cry. Soon, much of the choir and many in the audience were in tears. This event touched all of us on a deeper level than any typical classroom experience.

What did the students learn?

This authentic learning experience involved all areas of the curriculum. In addition, the students were emotionally involved with the learning experience.

Students put human faces to something they usually only read about in a history book or see in a film. A reception preceded the event. The students provided name tags for the veterans and offered refreshments. It was an epiphany for the kids to see that these were real people, who had participated in the making of history, standing right in front of them. Kids made the con-

nection. Spontaneously, several veterans came up to the stage at the end of the concert and had photos taken with the students.

Our students were truly satisfied by the result of their efforts. They received great feedback from the community. One student commented, "I learned more from preparing for this concert than in every history class I've ever taken."

Were the students graded for their participation in this event?

The choir and band classes were graded on their performance that night, as part of their normal grading procedure. They also wrote an essay critiquing the performance. The contributions of English, social studies, art, and stagecraft classes were all graded by their teachers in those subjects.

What is your advice to novice teachers who are planning authentic and multidisciplinary projects?

I told the music teachers at my school not to hide in their department but to go out and teach across the curriculum. Make contact with people in other areas. Get involved with each other's subjects. Students don't learn in a vacuum and neither do teachers.

I urge young teachers to be innovative, to create learning opportunities that engage your students' interest. Don't be afraid to try new things. Do your homework beforehand, but don't let this inhibit you. You have to dream as well as act. You need to have big ideas. We need leaders of inspired enthusiasm. If you allow yourself to think small, you won't create the educational opportunities kids need. Kids love spectaculars!

> I urge young teachers to be innovative, to create learning opportunities that engage your students' interest. Don't be afraid to try new things.

experiments. These experiments can be done by students working in groups and thus sharing the construction of knowledge. Foreign language teachers can invite a native speaker of the language to converse with the class.

Not all cognitive psychologists accept the situationist view. Many argue that general principles of learning apply in a variety of situations (e.g., Banaji & Crowder, 1989), although how they apply varies somewhat from one situation to another. We discuss this idea of *transfer* of knowledge in detail in Chapter 9. The situated-learning view is important for educators, however, because it points out that how well children will learn in the classroom depends in part not only on the teacher's specific instruction, but also on the general environment for learning and the role that the teacher takes in the classroom.

SUMMING IT UP

WHY UNDERSTANDING COGNITIVE APPROACHES TO LEARNING IS IMPORTANT TO TEACHERS

- This chapter discussed a cognitive approach to learning. Much of the chapter was devoted to describing the workings of memory, the mechanisms of which allow us to retain and retrieve information.

THE STANDARD MEMORY MODEL

- Three basic operations of memory are encoding of information, storage of information, and retrieval of information. According to the standard model of memory, information first enters a sensory register, then moves to short-term memory, and finally moves to long-term memory.

- Information can be moved into or held in short-term memory if there is rehearsal, a metamemory skill that can be learned. Information must be encoded into long-term memory. The total-time hypothesis suggests that spending a longer amount of time studying information in a single session increases the chances of that information's being remembered. However, distributed learning, via several learning sessions spaced out over time, is more effective for long-term memory than is massed learning, or cramming.

- Another way to encode information for long-term storage is to elaborate on it, or associate it with something already known. Elaborative rehearsal is more effective than maintenance rehearsal, which consists of simply repeating new information.

- Long-term memory also can be divided into declarative knowledge, or "knowing that," and procedural knowledge, or "knowing how." Conditional knowledge is "knowing when" to use information stored in long-term memory. Declarative knowledge can be divided into two types: semantic (our general knowledge of the world) and episodic (personally experienced events or episodes).

- Information is mentally represented in memory in several different ways. Declarative knowledge can be stored in analogical representations, such as mental imagery, or in symbolic representations, such as propositions. Propositions may be organized into propositional networks, consisting of a web of interlinked nodes.

ALTERNATIVE MODELS OF MEMORY

- There are various alternatives to the standard model of memory. For example, connectionist models integrate much of what we know about memory. They rely heavily on the idea of networks of stored information and the idea that activating one part of a network will lead to a spreading activation of related information. Another alternative model of memory emphasizes working memory, which is a temporarily activated part of long-term memory. A third model is that of levels of processing, which proposes continuous levels rather than discrete stores for holding information.

RETRIEVING INFORMATION

- Tasks used to assess students' memories generally can be divided into two groups: recall or recognition. Recall tasks, which require a person to produce information from memory, include free recall, serial recall, and paired-associates recall. In contrast, recognition tasks require that the person select or identify something he or she has learned.

Retrieval cues can enhance accessibility of stored information. Advance organizers provide one form of retrieval cue. The context in which something is encoded substantially affects how well that something is later retrieved. According to the encoding-specificity principle, what is encoded determines in large part what is later retrieved. Some mnemonic techniques that students or teachers can use in order to improve their learning and memory include categorical clustering, interactive images, pegwords, the method of loci, acronyms, acrostics, and keywords. Mnemonic devices, such as PQ4R, also can be used during studying.

Although decay may play some role in forgetting, interference appears to be more important. The two main kinds of interference are proactive and retroactive interference.

CONSTRUCTIVIST APPROACHES

Constructivist approaches suggest that memory is largely constructive, or built on prior experience and context, rather than merely reproductive. People often use existing cognitive frameworks, or schemas, to construct organizations for new information. Mental scripts, or stereotypical sequences of events, also can affect students' expectations and memories.

Proponents of situated learning suggest that social factors form an important part of the context responsible for how well people learn, and that learning must be studied and understood in the context in which it takes place. Learning takes place in and is relevant to a cultural context called *enculturation*. An important aspect of situated learning is people's metacognition, or the way they understand and control their own thinking.

KEY TERMS AND DEFINITIONS

Advance organizer Way of organizing information to be learned to enhance learning. Page 288

Analogical representations Declarative memories that preserve many aspects of the original stimulus. Page 276

Chunking Grouping items of information in order to expand the amount of information that can be stored in short-term memory. Page 272

Cognitive approaches Theories that emphasize the mental mechanisms underlying the processing and representation of information during learning. Page 268

Conditional knowledge Knowledge of when and how to apply the declarative and procedural knowledge you have. Page 279

Constructivist approach Approach to learning based on the idea that children actively build their own knowledge. It suggests that prior experience and the context of learning affect the way we encode memories, how we recall, and what we recall. Page 294

Context Environment in which learning takes place. Page 268

Decay theory Theory of memory suggesting that information is forgotten because of the gradual disappearance over time of an unused memory trace. Page 292

Declarative knowledge Knowledge of facts stored in semantic or episodic memory. It is sometimes described as "knowing that." Page 275

Distributed learning Learning done over several sessions spaced out over time. Page 274

Elaborate To learn by thinking carefully about information and associating it with other known information. Page 272

Elaborative rehearsal Learning strategy in which the person thinks carefully about new information, associating it with information already learned or associating various items of the to-be-learned information. Page 273

Encoding specificity Principle of memory suggesting that the context in which something is encoded substantially affects how well that something is later retrieved. Page 288

Enculturation Principle of situated learning suggesting that much of learning is achieved through "learning the situation" in a culturally relative context. Page 298

Episodic memory Long-term memories holding personally experienced events or episodes. Page 276

Free recall Type of memory test in which a person must recite back a list of learned items, in any order. Page 287

Interference theory Theory suggesting that forgetting is caused by competing information that renders the sought-after information inaccessible. Page 292

Levels-of-processing model Model of memory in which storage is seen as varying along a continuous dimension in terms of depth of encoding. It suggests that the deeper the level at which an item is processed, the higher the probability that the item later will be retrieved. Page 284

Long-term memory According to the standard model of memory, the third store of memory, which has a very large, possibly unlimited capacity; it is capable of storing information for very long periods of time, possibly indefinitely. Page 270

Maintenance rehearsal (or **rote learning**) Learning strategy that involves learning and memorizing new information by simply repeating it. Page 272

- **Massed learning** Learning that is crammed, occurring all at one time. Page 274

- **Memory** Active mental mechanisms that enable people to retain and retrieve information about past experience. Page 268

- **Mental representations** Ways in which knowledge is stored in memory. Page 275

- **Metacognition** Understanding and control of one's own cognition. Page 298

- **Metamemory** Knowledge and control of one's own memory. Page 279

- **Mnemonic devices** Specific techniques for improving learning and memory. Page 289

- **Paired-associates recall** Type of memory procedure in which a person learns pairs of words. When one word in the pair is presented, the person must respond with the correct matching word. Page 287

- **Parallel distributed processing (PDP) model,** or **connectionist models** Models of memory that focus on the ways declarative and procedural knowledge are combined via series of connections among elements. Page 281

- **PQ4R** Mnemonic device for the steps in a study method Preview, Question, Read, Reflect, Recite, and Review. Page 291

- **Proactive interference** (or **proactive inhibition**) Forgetting caused by activity that occurs before something is learned. Page 292

- **Procedural knowledge** Knowledge of how to do certain things, that is, "knowing how." Page 278

- **Productions** (or **condition-action sequences**) Way of storing procedural knowledge in memory as condition-action sequences that tell us "if this, then do that." Page 278

- **Propositional network** Schematic integration of interrelated propositions. Page 276

- **Recall tasks** Memory tasks that require a person to produce information from memory. Page 287

- **Recognition task** Memory test that requires a person to select or identify something he or she has learned previously. Page 287

- **Rehearsal** Repeated recitation of an item. Page 271

- **Retrieval** Gaining access to information stored in memory; one of three basic memory operations. Page 269

- **Retrieval cues** Clues or reminders that can enhance the ability to retrieve stored information from memory. Page 288

- **Retroactive interference** (or **retroactive inhibition**) Forgetting caused by activity that occurs after something is learned. Page 292

- **Rote learning** Learning by repetition with little or no attempt to add to or find meaning in the information. Page 273

- **Schemas** Cognitive frameworks for organizing associated concepts. Page 294

- **Script** Stereotypical story outline for how events typically proceed. Page 295

- **Self-reference effect** Effect whereby people show very high levels of recall when asked to relate words meaningfully to themselves by determining whether the words describe themselves. Page 285

- **Semantic memory** Long-term memories holding general knowledge of the world. Page 275

- **Sensory register** According to the standard model of memory, where much information is first stored when it is sensed. It is capable of holding relatively small amounts of information for brief moments of time. Page 270

- **Serial-position curve** Combination of phenomena in which items near the beginning of a list and near the end of a list are remembered well. Page 293

- **Serial recall** Type of memory procedure in which a person must recite back a list of learned items, in the same order that the items were originally presented. Page 287

- **Short-term memory** According to the standard model of memory, the second store of memory, which is capable of holding relatively limited amounts of information for a matter of seconds, and, in some instances, up to two minutes. Page 270

- **Situated learning** View suggesting that social factors and specific learning environments form an important part of the context responsible for how well people learn. Page 298

- **Spreading activation** According to the connectionist model of memory, a phenomenon whereby activation of one node may prompt activation of another, connected node. Page 282

- **Symbolic representations** Declarative memories that rely on arbitrary symbols that may bear no obvious relation to whatever it is being represented. Page 276

- **Total-time hypothesis** Principle of learning suggesting that how much you learn studying in a single session depends on how much time you spend studying. Page 272

- **Working memory** According to the working model of memory, an active part of long-term memory that also includes temporary, or short-term memory. Page 283

Apply the concepts introduced in this chapter to the following problems of teaching practice.

IN ELEMENTARY SCHOOL

1. How could you teach kindergartners to use elaborative rehearsal to remember the letters of the alphabet?

2. How would you prime second graders before teaching them subtraction? In other words, what previous knowledge do you think second graders would have on which to build an understanding of subtraction?

3. How would you create an authentic learning situation for a sixth-grade social studies unit on Japan?

4. What kind of assignment would you give your fifth graders to assess both their recognition and their recall of the names of countries in Africa?

5. How might you develop a lesson, based on the ideas of the working-memory model, to clear up first graders' misconceptions about the nature of electricity?

IN MIDDLE SCHOOL

1. What would you say to convince your eighth-grade Spanish students that rote memorization may not be the most effective way to learn Spanish?

2. How would you encourage your seventh-grade science students to process the names of the plant phyla at deeper, rather than surface, levels?

3. What are some mnemonic devices you could use to help students in your health class remember the names of vitamins that are important to include in their diets?

4. What kinds of advance organizers would you use to help sixth graders learn and remember the key points of a unit on structuring paragraphs?

5. How would you set up a unit on geometry that would let students work in groups, with you serving only as an expert resource, to discover the way to find the sizes of the angles in a triangle?

IN HIGH SCHOOL

1. How would you incorporate students' metamemory skills in your Chemistry I class curriculum?

2. What could you do to help students in your last-period English class avoid forgetting what you teach them, due to proactive interference from the information learned in all their previous classes on the same day?

3. How could you incorporate some of the principles of constructivist learning (student-constructed knowledge, building on previous knowledge, cognitive apprenticeships, group learning, and authentic learning situations) into first-semester algebra classes?

4. What are some ways you could get tenth-grade students today to elaborate via self-reference—that is, to think about their own resemblance and connection to—Shakespeare's *Macbeth*?

5. How would you prime the memories of the students in your world history class before beginning a unit on the Crusades?

Connecting Theory and Research to Practice

How are teachers putting constructivist theory into practice? In addition to the examples in this chapter, you can find many others on the Web. In their article, "Constructivist Learning Design," George Gagnon and Michelle Collay outline a method for instructional design that focuses on the constructivist concept of "designing for learning and not planning for teaching." In their article, available at *http://www.prainbow.com/cld/cldp.html*, they describe and illustrate a 6-point model for effectively incorporating constructivist principles in classroom and instructional design, provide a brief discussion regarding assessment, and present proposed applications of their model.

In a related Web site, located at *http://www.prainbow.com/cld/clds.html*, Gagnon and Collary discuss one study that they conducted to investigate the effectiveness of their 6-point model. In their research, entitled "Teachers' Perspectives on a Constructivist Learning Design," Gagnon and Collary interviewed four teachers who had used the 6-point model for constructivism for at least one year. The teachers' perceptions of student learning in their classrooms were addressed in a series of questions. In this paper, Gagnon and Collary discuss the responses of the classroom teachers, highlight teacher testimonials, and provide new insights and educational implications about effectively implementing constructivism in the classroom.

Another example of constructivist theory in practice is evident in the design for The Regents' Center for Early Developmental Education. The Center was created in 1988 as a means of infusing Piaget's constructivist perspectives on learning, knowledge, and intelligence in early childhood education. Their site *(http://www.uni.edu/coe/regentsctr/index.html)*, which is devoted to developing, implementing, and disseminating information regarding constructivist education, also contains a wide variety of resources, links, and information.

The Schools for Thought (SFT) project in Nashville, Tennessee, is another example of how principles derived from constructivist views of learning can be implemented in classrooms. The SFT program was designed in conjunction with Vanderbilt University to promote instructional strategies that take advantage of constructivist principles such as creating communities of learners through social interaction, fostering a deep level of understanding of domain-specific knowledge, exploring cross-curricular and situated learning activities, and encouraging student-based inquiry. The Schools for Thought Web site, located at *http://peabody.vanderbilt.edu/projects/funded/sft/overview/welcome.html*, provides information about the background of the project, the curriculum, testimonials about the project, and resources for learning communities.

Building Your Self-Portrait as an Educator

Do you have problems or encounter difficulties remembering names, dates, or telephone numbers? Do you think there is a link between learning styles (discussed in Chapter 4) and memory? Visit Mind Tools at *http://www.demon.co.uk/mindtool/memory.html* to learn more. This site provides an overview of mne-

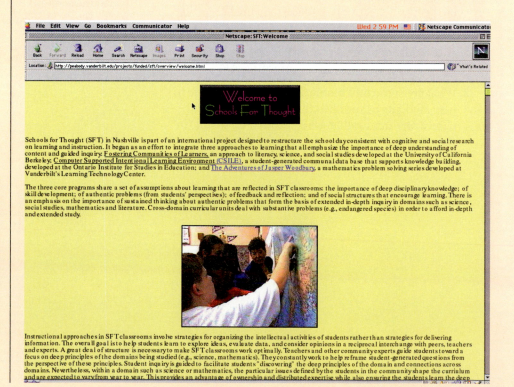

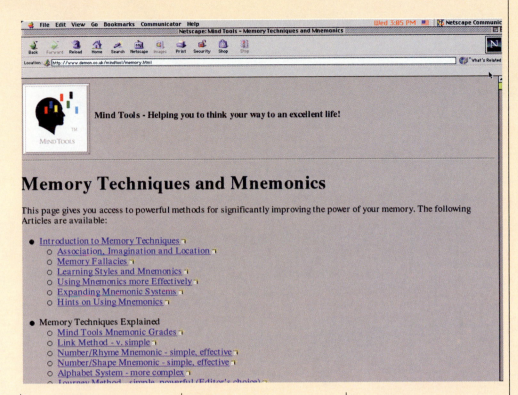

Memory Techniques and Mnemonics

This page gives you access to powerful methods for significantly improving the power of your memory. The following Articles are available:

- Introduction to Memory Techniques
  - Association, Imagination and Location
  - Memory Fallacies
  - Learning Styles and Mnemonics
  - Using Mnemonics more Effectively
  - Expanding Mnemonic Systems
  - Hints on Using Mnemonics

- Memory Techniques Explained
  - Mind Tools Mnemonic Grades
  - Link Method - v. simple
  - Number/Rhyme Mnemonic - simple, effective
  - Number/Shape Mnemonic - simple, effective
  - Alphabet System - more complex
  - Journey Method - simple, powerful (Editor's choice)

monic techniques and discusses how to effectively use them. It also presents some examples of simple and more complex mnemonic techniques, as well as mnemonics for specific purposes such as remembering dates or phone numbers. While helpful for students, this site can also provide techniques that teachers may also use when navigating through a busy school day.

Online Resources

The National Academy Press has published a textbook entitled "How People Learn" available for free on the Web (http://books.nap.edu/ catalog/6160.html). Edited by John D. Brans-

ford, Ann L. Brown, and Rodney R. Cocking, the book examines contemporary neuropsychological and cognitive research to address questions about learning, education, and the role of technology in each area.

Another resource for information regarding cognitive approaches to learning is available at The Learning Network. The Learning Network provides educational resources connecting Web sites organized under five different topics: K–12 education (e.g., curriculum materials and textual resources), Higher Education (e.g., information for college students and faculty), Professional Development (e.g., references for professional educators), Lifelong Learning (e.g.,

promoting self-regulated and lifelong learning skills), and the Reference Channel (e.g., online encyclopedia of educational topics, database, and educational publications). The Learning Network is available at http://www .learningnetwork.com/ resources/aboutLearning-Network.html.

Are you interested in the relationship between constructivism and technology? Many constructivists have also been interested in the role that technology plays in learning. The site http://www.uwm.edu/ ~bdaley/mwr2p/ is a tutorial and article by Mark and Simone Runlee entitled "Constructivist Learning Theory to Web-Based Course Design: An Instructional Design Approach."

An article available on the Web that addresses the underlying assumptions of constructivism was written by Yuan Feng from the University of Washington (available at http://www.coe.uh .edu/insite/elec_pub/ html1995/196.htm). While Feng's article is geared toward educational psychologists and researchers, those interested in constructivism may find "Some Thoughts About Applying Constructivist Theories of Learning to Guide Instruction" very informative as it provides a critical examination of the theory and its implementation in classrooms.

Another site that provides information and related Web resources on constructivism, "Constructivist Learning Environments" is available at http://www .stemnet.nf.ca/~elmurphy/ emurphy/constructivism .html. This site provides a brief overview of the goals of and instructional principles for constructivist instructional design, links to constructivist sites, and textual resources.

Some of the best-known educational psychologists within the field of situated cognition are John Brown, Allan Collins, and Paul Duguid. A version of their paper "Situated Cognition and the Culture of Learning" is available online at http://www.ilt.columbia .edu/ilt/papers/JohnBrown .html.

9

Thinking

CONCEPT FORMATION, REASONING, AND PROBLEM SOLVING

THE BIG PICTURE

To help you see the big picture, keep the following questions in mind as you read this chapter:

- How do students learn and organize their knowledge about concepts? What are the main approaches to understanding what concepts are and how they are used?

- What are the main kinds of reasoning? What kinds of errors in reasoning do students make, and how can they avoid these errors?

- What kinds of problems do students confront?

- What techniques can students use to improve their solving of both school and real-life problems? What makes a student an expert problem solver?

- How can you help students transfer knowledge and skills gained from solving one type of problem to other types of problems?

- What steps can you take to promote effective thinking, inside and outside the classroom? How can you help students develop insightful solutions to problems?

◄ *Students playing out how the various characters of a story would react in a new situation. Role-playing is an imaginative way for students to understand a point of view other than their own.* (Mary Kate Denny, PhotoEdit)

307

After taking a continuing education seminar over the summer on teaching for thinking, Joan Gracek decided to change the emphasis of instruction in her tenth-grade biology classes this fall. Joan had stressed a combination of memorizing basic concepts about plants and animals and learning to write good essays about biological principles such as evolution. This year, however, she decided to give students a more active role in which they are expected to examine, interpret, and judge critically several different theories about the natural world. Joan believed this new approach would help students become more active learners who know how to solve problems in biology and to reason more effectively with biological concepts.

The plan sounded great—that is, until the students heard it! They were not pleased. Joan had a reputation for being an easy teacher who gave mostly A's, and the students were expecting to slide through her course with little more than the basic textbook for support. The first test, on plant species, showed that the students had a long way to go before they would be able to think like scientists.

Joan realized the next unit, on animals, would require more effort on her part. She decided to change her approach to teaching concepts. She started by having students learn about groups of animals by judging, based on a number of examples of animals both in and out of the group, what the name and characteristics of a group, such as mammals or birds, might be. Then she gave them a "mystery animal" game to play. The students pretend to be biologists exploring an unknown island who have come across an undiscovered animal. They could draw clues about the animal, or about various animal groups, from a special deck of clue cards that Joan had prepared. For example, Lin drew a card that read, "Most mammals give birth to live young. Some reptiles and amphibians give birth to live young. This animal gives birth to live young." The students combined a number of such clues to solve the problem of how to classify and name the newly discovered animal. With such practice during the animal unit, the students were able to do much better when faced with similar problems on their second test.

Joan Gracek, like many teachers, has come to believe that the teaching of thinking skills should be a central and vital task in education. The overall goal of education is to help students gain knowledge they can use to help them succeed, not only in their schoolwork, but also throughout their lives. Knowledge that cannot be used or applied is often called *inert knowledge*. The ability to make active use of knowledge is what most of us consider to be thinking.

More formally defined, *thinking* involves the representation and processing of information in the mind. Thinking skills can and should be taught, and later in this chapter we cover the main methods for doing so. Most important, teachers need to establish a culture of thinking in the classroom whereby students learn that critical thinking and inquisitiveness are an integral part of all classroom activities, not add-ons that apply only on special occasions.

One important part of thinking is the formation of *concepts*, organizations or groupings of ideas in the mind (Barsalou, 2000; Hampton, 1997, 1999). Teachers can have a great influence on their students' abilities to form concepts effectively. Another thinking skill that is important both in and out of school is the ability to reason—to draw conclusions from evidence. In this chapter we discuss the two major types of reasoning. We also describe some common flaws in people's reasoning and some ways you and your students can avoid them.

Teachers are interested not only in how students think, or process information in their minds, but also in how they apply their thinking skills to problems they encounter, both inside and outside school. We will describe effective strategies for solving problems that you can teach to your students. We will also provide you with some key guidelines for teaching your students how to transfer their knowledge, or apply what they have learned appropriately in new settings.

Why Understanding Thinking Is Important to Teachers

Do students really need to be taught to think? Perhaps not. Raymond Nickerson (1987, p. 28) has pointed out that "with or without special training, everyone thinks." What people should be taught, Nickerson (1987, p. 28) has suggested, is "how to think more effectively—more critically, more coherently, more creatively, more deeply—than we often, perhaps typically, do." Nickerson (1994, p. 411) also has summarized the concerns of researchers and educators that "many students, at all levels of formal education, are unable to do the kind of thinking and problem solving that their schoolwork requires" (see also Grotzer & Perkins, 2000; Perkins & Grotzer, 1997). For example, some students may understand material they retrieve from the Internet without being able adequately to evaluate the credibility of the source of that material.

What is an effective thinker? Numerous activities are included under the broad definition of thinking. For example, students must be able to classify ideas or objects, place them in various orders, make estimates, extrapolate from limited data, weigh evidence and draw conclusions, and use analogies appropriately. Effective thinking not only is analytical, it also involves creative and practical modes.

One distinction often made in education is that between critical thinking and mindlessness. Educators are particularly interested in encouraging **critical thinking,** in which students consciously and purposefully direct their thoughts to find a solution to a problem (Halpern, 1998). In contrast, most teachers work hard to help their students avoid mindless thinking—routinely and automatically following a customary thought pattern without consciously directing their thoughts (Langer, 1993, 1997). For example, memorizing a list of pollutants and their sources in a local river may be more useful if students working together in groups also develop a plan to reduce the level of one of the pollutants.

Why is effective thinking so important? Nickerson (1994) suggests three key reasons: First, effective thinking is becoming increasingly important for success in school. Second, independent thinking and problem solving are becoming job requirements for careers that students may pursue after they leave school. Third, a thoughtful populace is better able to solve the complex problems facing society at all levels, from neighborhoods and towns, to nations and even the world community. The Flexible Expert: Teaching and Learning About Thinking provides examples of teachers and students who think effectively in analytical, creative, and practical modes.

Many students face the immediate need to develop effective thinking skills in order to succeed in school. In 1991, for example, the U.S. Department of Education's National Educational Goals Panel set a goal of demonstrating a substantial improvement in the critical thinking and problem-solving abilities of college graduates by the year 2000 (National Educational Goals Panel, 1991). As part of the effort to develop the thinking skills of today's students, statewide and national tests, as well as some tests given on a school-by-school basis, increasingly require students not only to remember material, but to analyze and evaluate it as well (Ennis, 1987).

For students to understand thoroughly what they are taught, they need to learn to think deeply about the material. They also need to understand their own thinking, and the kinds of errors they are likely to make. Thus *metacognition*—the understanding and control of one's cognitive processing—is as important to thinking as it is to learning and memory (Moses & Baird, 2000). What is involved in this type of thinking, and how can students be taught to think more effectively? This is the main question we address in this chapter.

THINKING PRACTICALLY

Critics of particular schools or teachers sometimes complain that students are forced to engage in mindless activities. What do you see as an example of a mindless activity that students pursue in some classrooms? Drawing on your own experience and imagination, can you identify an example of another activity students might pursue that will help them be more mindful?

SUGGESTION: Worksheets with many repetitive examples of the same kind of activity can become mind numbing. A better alternative or, at least, supplement is practice with simulations of real-world problems requiring the same operations.

IN EACH CHAPTER OF THE TEXT, WE INTRODUCE YOU TO A FEW SPECIFIC STRATEGIES—
ANALYTICAL, CREATIVE, AND PRACTICAL—USED BY BOTH EXPERT TEACHERS AND EXPERT STUDENTS.

THE ANALYTICAL TEACHER: Pat studies the thinking processes that lead to insightful problem solving and then brainstorms how he can apply these to his own teaching.

THE CREATIVE TEACHER: Pat creates a mystery story that the students must use creative thinking skills to solve.

THE PRACTICAL TEACHER: Pat suddenly realizes that students' low scores on math tests with word problems may be due to their inability to decide which information is relevant to the problem, not to an inability to perform the calculations. Pat hands out a checklist of steps for solving word problems, and he works through the steps with students when presenting new word problems in class.

THE ANALYTICAL STUDENT: Chris can point out fallacies in the reasoning of a character in a novel that led to the character's tragic demise.

THE CREATIVE STUDENT: Chris writes a story about what happens to a person who wrongly reasons that, because "everyone is doing drugs," she will not be harmed if she experiments with dangerous drugs.

THE PRACTICAL STUDENT: Whenever she thinks they are reasoning fallaciously, Chris asks her friends questions so they clarify their arguments.

Concept Formation

Let us begin by considering how students form **concepts,** mental abstractions or categories of similar objects, people, events, or ideas (Hampton, 2000). A key goal of teaching is conveying to students the nature of various concepts, such as odd numbers, longitude, tragedy, plural, and mass, to name just a few. At first, the topic of how concepts are formed may seem obvious to you—you learned many concepts when you first learned language as a child. But research on how people learn concepts suggests that not all concepts are learned in the same way (Keil, 1999; Ross, 2000). Thus expert teachers must know different methods for teaching concepts so they can reach more students with more effective instruction.

DEFINING FEATURES OF CONCEPTS

How do you know that two is an even number and three an odd number? Probably because some time ago you learned that an *even number* is defined as any integer that is divisible by two without a remainder, and that an *odd number* is one that is not evenly divisible by two. Other concepts can also be systematically defined. For example, a *bachelor* is an unmarried adult male.

Concepts such as that of an even number or a bachelor are easily understood in terms of **defining features,** that is, features necessary and sufficient for defining a concept (see Katz, 1972; Katz & Fodor, 1963; Medin, Proffitt, & Schwartz, 2000). What does it mean for a feature to be necessary and sufficient?

Consider an example. If an integer is evenly divisible by two, this feature is a *necessary* characteristic of an even number—you cannot find an even number without this property. Being divisible by two is also enough to *guarantee* that the integer is an even number; in other words, divisibility by two is *sufficient* for evenness of a number.

When students learn about concepts, it is useful for them to think about what features are necessary and what features are sufficient. In this way, they better learn the exact nature of the concept. For example, they might learn that a *widow* is a woman who has previously been married (a necessary but not sufficient feature—the woman might be divorced) and whose husband has died (a necessary and sufficient feature). As another example, because a *pair* always involves two of something and two of anything is always a pair, we can say that "twoness" is a necessary and sufficient feature of a pair. Similarly, *uranium* has an atomic number of 92, and any element with an atomic number of 92 is uranium, again yielding the atomic number as a necessary and sufficient feature of uranium.

CHARACTERISTIC FEATURES OF CONCEPTS

Defining a concept in terms of necessary and sufficient features works well for some but not for all concepts. For example, try listing the necessary or sufficient features of a bird. Most birds fly, but not all of them do. For instance, an ostrich is a bird, but it does not fly. And what are the necessary or sufficient features of a game (Wittgenstein, 1953)? Most games are enjoyable, but not all are. Most games are played by several people, but solitaire certainly is not. Because some concepts do not seem to be well described in terms of necessary and sufficient features, psychologists also think in terms of a second kind of feature, referred to as a *characteristic feature*.

A **characteristic feature** (Medin, Proffitt, & Schwartz, 2000; Rosch & Mervis, 1975) is a property typical of something represented in a concept, but not always associated with it. For example, the ability to fly is a characteristic rather than a defining feature of a bird. Having multiple players is a characteristic feature of games, but not a defining feature. Numbers are characteristic of mathematics problems, but they do not constitute defining features.

THINKING ANALYTICALLY

Are there any defining features of a teacher? In other words, do any attributions uniquely define someone as a teacher?

SUGGESTION: Imparting of knowledge to one or more students is a defining feature. (Note that to be a teacher, one need not be a professional. Parents are teachers, regardless of whether or not they are paid to teach.)

THINKING ANALYTICALLY

What are the characteristic features of a school?

SUGGESTION: Examples of characteristic features are the presence of classrooms, books, and students.

Although each of these three schoolhouses is distinctive in its look, all are schools that share certain typical features. It is important that students have a full understanding of a concept—here, the meaning of "school." (Bob Daemmrich, The Image Works; Lawrence Migdale, Stock Boston; J. Sohm, The Image Works)

Students should learn to understand the difference between characteristic and defining features. For example, in history class students need to distinguish between two kinds of features of a king. Being the titular head of a kingdom is a defining characteristic of being a king of a country. Inheriting the throne, however, is only a characteristic feature: In some countries, kings have come to power through other means, such as rebellion.

Obviously, some concepts have many and others have few characteristic features. For example, a robin seems to have a lot of the characteristic features of a bird, whereas an ostrich does not. Similarly, a cow is quite typical of a mammal, whereas bats and whales are not. The most representative instance of a given concept is referred to as a **prototype** (Hampton, 1995; Medin, Proffit, & Schwartz, 2000; Rosch, 1973; see also Smith & Medin, 1981). For most North American readers of this book, a robin would come close to being prototypical of a bird.

How do we actually represent concepts in our minds? Some concepts, such as that of an "odd number," seem to be organized primarily in terms of defining features. Others, such as "game," are organized primarily in terms of characteristic features. Still other concepts, such as "bird," seem to be organized in terms of both defining and characteristic features. We have described the characteristic features of a bird, but birds also have defining features, such as their warm-bloodedness. Thus teaching students about the meanings of concepts can involve teaching them about only defining features, only characteristic features, or about both defining and characteristic features.

Not everyone agrees that concepts described primarily in terms of characteristic features are mentally represented in terms of prototypes. It is difficult, for example, to think of just what the prototype for a dog would be—a German shepherd, perhaps? A cocker spaniel? For many people, no one kind of dog seems quite as typical of dogs as a robin does of birds. Some researchers have suggested instead that what people store are good **exemplars** of such concepts—that is, highly typical instances (see Barsalou, 1990, 2000; Medin, Proffitt, & Schwartz, 2000). In the case of a dog, a person might compare a new animal to exemplars such as a collie, a poodle, or other typical dogs, and decide whether the new animal is a dog by seeing whether it closely resembles any of these good exemplars (Ross & Spalding, 1994; see also Komatsu, 1992). When teaching new concepts, expert teachers start with highly typical exemplars, and then move on to ones that are less typical, at the same time helping students see the more and less typical features.

Mentioning a larger category may activate students' memories of related information, helping them fit the new concept into their schemas (Murphy & Allopena, 1994). Teachers can also draw a **concept map,** a picture or diagram, such as the hypothetical map of one student's concept of sports in Figure 9.1, to illustrate the relationships between different concepts (Novak & Musonda, 1991).

FIGURE 9.1

Example of a Concept Map

Implications for Teaching

Expert teachers use several different ways to teach concepts effectively. They include the following:

- *Use a lot of examples.* Examples help clarify the boundaries of a concept. Here are three general rules to keep in mind when presenting examples of concepts (Tennyson & Park, 1980, p. 59):

  - Rule 1: Present the examples in order from easiest to most difficult. Highly typical exemplars are likely to be the easiest for students to understand. A science teacher presenting examples of stars discusses the North Star before mentioning that our sun is also a star.

JoAnn Leonard has been teaching for 22 years. She introduces concepts to her first graders by accessing their prior knowledge, or she asks her students to relate the concept to a personal experience.

What concepts do you encourage your first-grade students to learn?

Teaching first grade is the best! Children enter this level with little or no knowledge of reading, writing, and math skills, and leave with a good basis to build on for their future schooling.

The students learn many new concepts in each subject. More specifically, in the area of mathematics, first graders are exposed to the concepts of addition, subtraction, time, money, simple geometry, and number sense, as dictated by the district curriculum.

How do you approach teaching these concepts to first-grade students?

It is important to begin the teaching of these concepts by accessing the prior knowledge of the students. Once a personal connection has been made, it is the role of the teacher to provide ways for students to comprehend and apply the subject matter. This is Vygotsky's Zone of Proximal Development. For example, in the kindergarten, students are introduced to the concept of time only to the hour. In first grade, I build on that knowledge by introducing the concept of the half hour. In second grade students learn time to the quarter hour, building further on the same concept.

When I present the concept of money, the students' experiences vary greatly. Some first graders haven't touched money because their parents are afraid they will swallow it. Other kids have much experience handling the coins. At Back-To-School Night, I ask the parents to let their child handle money so that as first graders they can begin to understand the concept. I further enhance these concepts by letting students use various manipulatives in the classroom.

Addition and subtraction are the primary concepts in the math curriculum. It is wonderful if they can add in their heads, but many students must use a number line or counters. Each student gets these concepts at different times. By the end of the school year, however, I want them to be less dependent on the concrete; I encourage them to add without the counter or number line. To reinforce this, we play "hot pencils." The students add numbers on paper, and when I say "hot pencils" they must drop their pencils. I give them enough time to add in their heads, but not to use counters or the number line. There is a prize at the end of the game—a shiny new pencil!

How do you know when students have mastered a concept?

There is so much growth at this age. When the light bulb goes on for these children, it is dynamic and rewarding!

Students who have mastered a math concept often complete their work without reaching for the manipulative. They can verbalize the skill they are

> In first grade, problem solving is primarily about social issues. For example, feeling accepted, following rules, tattle-taling, and making new friends.

completing, and they can complete their assignments without much teacher direction or assistance. In addition, when a student can use the concept and apply it to a different skill, it is apparent that the child has acquired the main idea.

How do you approach problem solving with your students?

In first grade, problem solving is primarily about social issues. For example, feeling accepted, following rules, tattle-taling, and making new friends. I often use books or videos to point out social issues as they are occurring in our classroom. After reading the books or watching the video, the class discusses the content and makes comparisons to activities surrounding them. The students are often aware that a certain issue is present in our classroom, although sometimes they cannot relate.

What advice would you give to new teachers?

Never assume that a child has experience in a skill. Always begin with the concrete and work toward the concept. Have manipulatives readily available for those students who need them longer than others do.

To experience teaching, you must be in the classroom. Theory assists you, but just like the students, you need hands-on, concrete time to experience what teaching is all about!

- Rule 2: Select examples that are different from one another. The science teacher presenting the stars includes examples of both new and old stars.

- Rule 3: Compare and contrast examples and nonexamples. Examples of objects in space that are not stars include planets, our moon, and meteors.

■ ***Combine examples with definitions to encourage full understanding of a concept (Joyce & Weil, 1996).*** Joan Gracek taught her biology students about animal groups by discussing examples before presenting definitions of the concept (Tennyson & Cocchiarella, 1986). Another method is to present the definition first, for example, defining *alliteration* as the repetition of initial consonant sounds in two or more neighboring words, offering examples such as "partridge in a pear tree" and "two turtle doves." A synthesis of the two approaches would involve presenting the definition, followed by examples, followed by a reinforcement of the definition.

■ ***Distinguish between defining and characteristic features.*** Some concepts are easily described by their defining features, but teachers may need to define other concepts using characteristic features. Discussion should focus on whether features are necessary, sufficient, or both. For example, a teacher might point out, through a discussion of bats and insects on the one hand, and of penguins, on the other, that the characteristic of flight is neither necessary nor sufficient to identify an animal as a bird.

■ ***Help students link new concepts to what they already know.*** For example, the teacher introducing alliteration might mention that it belongs to a larger group of word sounds that also includes rhyming and assonance.

Reasoning

Reasoning is the process of drawing conclusions from evidence (Sternberg, 2000; Sternberg & Ben Zeev, 2001; Wason & Johnson-Laird, 1972). By reasoning, students make sense of what they read and hear in class. Reasoning is a basic part of deep and thoughtful learning, and expert teachers encourage students to reason with concepts, rather than simply to memorize these concepts. Philosophers and psychologists alike typically divide reasoning into two basic kinds—deductive and inductive.

DEDUCTIVE AND INDUCTIVE REASONING

Deductive reasoning is the process of drawing specific, logically valid conclusions from one or more general premises, in other words, of going from the general to the specific (Johnson-Laird, 2000; Rips, 1999; Sternberg, 2000). By its nature, deductive reasoning leads to conclusions that are logically certain.

Some of the material students learn in school is presented first in terms of general concepts, and second in terms of specific points and conclusions that follow from these concepts. Examples are easy to find in science classes. A teacher explains that every liquid has a distinctive boiling point at which it turns into gaseous form, and then asks students to identify several different clear liquids based on their boiling points. The name of the liquid follows logically here from knowledge of the boiling point (assuming each liquid has a unique boiling point). In formal terms, we say, for example, "If a liquid boils at 212° F, it is water. This liquid boils at 212° F. Therefore, it is water." In the story at the beginning of the chapter, Joan Gracek had students deduce from several general clues in what group an unidentified animal might belong. If there is only one possible kind of animal it can be, the reasoning involved is deductive reasoning. The logical form might be: "If an animal is warm-blooded and feeds with milk secreted by the mammary glands of a female, then it is a mammal. This rabbit is warm-blooded and feeds with milk secreted by the mammary glands of the female. Therefore, it is a mammal."

Most real-world arguments do not involve the kind of certainty possible in deduction. In real life, we are not usually told the overarching rule that explains what will happen and why—often, there is no such rule. Most real-world arguments involve the process of making plausible inferences. For example, suppose a young child notices that every adult he or she has ever met talks. The child might reasonably conclude that all adults talk. But this inference is incorrect, and eventually the child is likely to encounter a person who is mute. The inference is thereby falsified, not by logic, but by experience.

Inductive reasoning is the process of drawing reasonable general conclusions from specific facts or observations, in other words, of going from the specific to the general (Johnson-Laird, 2000; Thagard, 1999). In induction, it is not possible to have logical certainty, because there is always the chance that the next observation you make will disconfirm what all the previous observations have confirmed. For example, an adult who is mute will disconfirm the inference that all adults talk, or a dog missing a leg might disconfirm the inference that all dogs have four legs. Expert teachers look for ways to challenge conclusions that students reach on the basis of inductive reasoning. In this manner teachers help students understand how alternative conclusions often can be based on the same set of facts. Teachers may discuss how inductive reasoning in scientific research is problematic. As soon as one part of a scientific theory is disconfirmed, scientists are forced to search for a different solution.

DEVELOPING REASONING SKILLS

Effective reasoning is something students will depend on for the rest of their lives. Reasoning is an important thinking skill, in and of itself, but it is also the foundation for several other thinking skills, including problem solving and making judgments, discussed in the next section. Expert teachers use many methods to help their students learn to reason, including the following.

■**USING SYLLOGISMS**   When children argue, they can often be "fast and loose" in monitoring the validity of their arguments. The same applies to adults. An argument is *deductively valid* only when its conclusions follow logically (with certainty) from its premises (Johnson-Laird & Byrne, 1991). One of the best ways to practice deductive arguments is to use **syllogism,** a deductive argument that permits a conclusion from a series of two statements or premises (Braine & O'Brien, 1998; Polk & Newell, 1995; Rips, 1994). Each of these two premises contains two terms, with one term common to both premises. Many of the "clue cards" that Joan Gracek prepared for her biology students contained syllogisms.

There are three general kinds of syllogism—linear, categorical, and conditional (Sternberg & Ben Zeev, 2001). Linear syllogisms relate terms to one another over a successive (linear) sequence expressed in a series of statements called *premises*. An example of a linear syllogism might include:

Premise A: You are taller than your best friend.

Premise B: Your best friend is taller than your sister.

Who is the tallest?

The logically consistent conclusion is that you are the tallest of the three. The linear syllogism makes apparent the fact that you are the tallest, because of the comparisons and rank ordering the syllogism presents. Note that linear syllogisms are valid only when the premises represent *transitive* relations: In other words, the fact that A exceeds B on some dimension and B exceeds C on that dimension guarantees that A exceeds C. As many tennis players have learned, not all linear relations are transitive. John might win over

Sandy and Sandy might win over Jason, but Jason can win over John because John finds himself powerless against Jason's powerful serve.

Young children (under about age 8) often have difficulty in transitive reasoning because they have trouble holding all the terms of the problem in their working memory (see Bryant & Trabasso, 1971). In other words, 6-year-old Jessica probably has forgotten that she is taller than her best friend (premise A) by the time that the question "Who is the tallest?" is asked. By this time, all that Jessica may remember is that her best friend is taller than her sister (premise B).

Categorical syllogisms typically involve relations where members of one category belong to another category as well. For example, the premises of a categorical syllogism might be "all robins are birds" and "all birds are animals." Questions that help students reason with a categorical syllogism such as this one might include "are all birds animals?" or "are some animals not birds?" Teachers might also encourage students to draw or represent the relationships in a categorical syllogism visually, in order to help them make logically valid deductions. Invalid syllogistic reasoning can hurt students in school. If a student learns that some educational psychology tests are easy and that some easy tests do not require much studying, the student *cannot* conclude that some educational psychology tests do not require the student to study much.

Conditional syllogisms involve determining the validity of a deduction based on conditions given in the premises of the syllogism. An example of a conditional syllogism might be "If an animal is a robin, then it is a bird. This animal is a robin. Is it a bird?" A good conditional syllogism for students to understand is that "If students work very hard, they succeed in school. X is a student who works very hard. Therefore X will almost always succeed in school." Children's reasoning tends to improve with age (Sternberg & Ben Zeev, 2001).

Two errors are commonly made in conditional reasoning. One is called *affirming the consequent*. Here we assume that if the conditional is true, the "if" and "then" statements can be reversed and the conditional will still remain true. However, although it is true that if an animal is a robin, then it is a bird, it is *not* true that if an animal is a bird, then it is a robin (affirming the consequent). The other error, *denying the antecedent*, assumes that if a conditional is true, it is also true with its antecedent negated. But it is *not* logically valid to conclude that "if an animal is a robin, then it is a bird" implies the validity of "if an animal is not a robin, then it is not a bird" (denying the antecedent). A pigeon, for example, is not a robin, but a pigeon is a bird.

Deductive validity applies only to whether a conclusion follows logically from its premises; it does not deal with the question of whether the premises and thus the conclusion are in fact true. Consider the following deductive argument: "All lawyers are professionals. All professionals work hard. Therefore, all lawyers work hard." This argument is deductively valid, but it is factually incorrect. In the argument, the second premise, that all professionals work hard, is false. Thus, although the argument is deductively valid, the conclusion is not empirically true. In evaluating arguments and in teaching your students to evaluate arguments, take into account not only whether the conclusions follow from the premises, but also whether the premises are all true. If they are not, then any conclusions that follow may well be factually wrong.

■**ENCOURAGING INDUCTIVE REASONING** Students need to be taught that it is important to make inductive inferences, but also important to be looking constantly for disconfirmations of these inferences (Popper, 1959; Sternberg & Grigorenko, 2000). In other words, they need to realize that inductions are only as good as the experience on which they are based.

Not only is inductive reasoning a natural way to learn; it is also a way in which students can sharpen their reasoning skills in everyday life (Gigerenzer, Todd, & the ABC Group, 1999). For example, students may come to believe that a subject is dull because they have studied it before and didn't find it interesting. This induction represents an error in thinking called a *hasty generalization*. In fact, a new approach to teaching or learning in that

Having students work in racially and sex-mixed study groups will help them avoid making hasty generalizations about their peers.
(Bob Daemmrich Photos, Inc.)

subject may make interesting a subject that previously was uninteresting. In much the same way, stereotypes often result when students hastily generalize about a group of people based on a small number of people they have met from the given group. By examining inductive inferences, we can become much better thinkers and avoid making fallacies. An expert teacher actively works to challenge the hasty generalizations of his or her students and encourages students to challenge their own hasty generalizations. A way to discredit negative hasty generalizations about race or sex might be to create racially and sex-mixed study groups that will work together to reach a common academic goal.

THINKING PRACTICALLY

Consider a hasty generalization you have made in your own past. What was the error, and how did you correct it? How might you help students correct their own hasty generalizations?

SUGGESTION: Each student will provide his or her own example. However, you can help students correct such errors by encouraging them to identify the errors and to think reflectively of alternative courses of action.

■**REPAIRING FALLACIOUS REASONING** Expert teachers are quick to point out underlying errors in students' arguments or to help students come to realize their own errors. By doing so these teachers help students improve their reasoning skills in ways that will be useful well beyond the immediate situation.

Although people can reason fallaciously in a large number of ways (see, e.g., Levy, 1997; Sternberg, 1986, for lists of common fallacies), certain fallacies tend to be particularly common. Fallacies tend to result from the incorrect application of **heuristics**—informal, intuitive, and often speculative shortcuts in thinking that may solve a problem but are not guaranteed to do so (Korf, 1999; Simon, 1999).

One of the most common fallacies is misuse of the **availability heuristic** (Tversky & Kahneman, 1973). People relying on this shortcut in thinking make judgments on the basis of how easily they are able to call to mind what they perceive as relevant instances of a phenomenon. Sometimes this heuristic works appropriately, but at others times, it leads people astray.

Most of us at least occasionally use the availability heuristic (Tversky & Kahneman, 1973), in which we make judgments on the basis of how easily we can call to mind what we perceive as relevant instances of a phenomenon. For example, consider the letter R. Are there more words in the English language that begin with the letter R or that have R as their third letter? Most respondents say there are more words beginning with the letter R (Tversky & Kahneman, 1973). Why? Because it is easier to generate words beginning with the letter R than it is to generate words having R as the third letter. In fact, there are more English language words with R as their third letter. The same happens to be true of some other letters as well, such as K, L, N, and V (Sternberg, 1999).

It is important to teach students about errors in reasoning such as the availability heuristic so they do not make inappropriate conclusions simply on the basis of whatever information quickly comes to mind. Students must learn that just because a practice is common, and thus "available," it is not necessarily desirable.

THINKING PRACTICALLY

Give an example from your own life of your use of the availability heuristic, and how it led you to an incorrect conclusion. What were the consequences at the time? What did you learn from the experience?

SUGGESTION: Each student must answer for himself or herself.

Teachers also can fall prey to the availability heuristic. For example, teaching in a way that emphasizes rote memory of concepts may be a strategy that is highly available to many teachers. Its easy availability does not make it the best strategy in all circumstances, however.

Another common fallacy is misuse of the **representativeness heuristic.** When people use this heuristic, they judge the probability that a particular event or object belongs to a certain category by how obviously it resembles or represents the population from which it comes (Kahneman & Tversky, 1971). Consider an example. For much of history, the notion that diseases are caused by microbes eluded laypeople and even medical practitioners. Although there were many reasons for this lack of understanding, one almost certainly was that microbes seem nothing at all like the diseases they cause: They seem not to be representative of diseases. Rather, many people considered evil spirits as somehow more akin to the diseases they allegedly caused. Students need to realize that causes (e.g., microbes) often bear no resemblance to their effects (e.g., symptoms of diseases).

Most people believe that if a coin is tossed six times, a sequence of HTHHTH (with H representing heads and T standing for tails) is more likely than a sequence of HHHHTH. In fact, however, each sequence is equally likely to be generated by a random process. The first sequence somehow seems to "represent" a random coin-tossing process better than the second sequence.

THINKING PRACTICALLY

When have you used the representativeness heuristic to reach a false conclusion? Describe the situation and the consequences.

SUGGESTION: Each student must answer for himself or herself.

Students and teachers alike misuse the representativeness heuristic when they rely on stereotypes or group memberships to judge individuals. For example, a teacher may wrongly assume that a student who is a member of a street gang has little motivation for school, just because other gang members do not seem to be motivated by school. Or some people may take it for granted that a well-disciplined classroom is one in which learning is taking place. They falsely assume that good discipline adequately represents the quality of learning taking place! Teachers also may falsely assume that because the students are having fun in the classroom, the students therefore are learning.

A third common heuristic is **overconfidence,** an overestimate of the likelihood of the correctness of a judgment. Try a little test. Do you believe that absinthe is (a) a liqueur, or (b) a precious stone? Baruch Fischhoff, Paul Slovic, and Sarah Lichtenstein (1977) gave 200 people two alternative statements such as this one, and found that people were strangely overconfident in their responses. In fact, when people were 100 percent confident of their answers, they were right in those answers only about 80 percent of the time. Overconfidence may explain why students are so reluctant to check their work, proofread their papers, and think before they talk. They overestimate the quality of what they have done. By warning students of the overconfidence heuristic, you may help them realize the importance of checking over (in particular, monitoring and evaluating) what they do. If possible, use strong past work to show a student how well he might have done, had he taken the time to go over his work. When the student realizes that small errors can reduce the quality of the grade on a well-thought-out project, he may begin to place more importance on doing a final check of his work.

THINKING CREATIVELY

Describe an activity you can do with students in which they use their own work to become aware of the prevalence and the danger of overconfidence.

SUGGESTION: An example might be rock climbing, where one may have confidence in oneself despite lack of training.

Of course, equally unsuccessful is **underconfidence,** a thought pattern in which people believe they are less likely to be correct than they actually are. As we discussed in Chapter 4, underconfidence seems to be more common in girls than in boys (Phillips & Zimmerman, 1990). Underconfidence can impair a person's willingness to undertake challenges that he or she is fully capable of meeting. Underconfidence also can leave students less willing to ask a teacher or peer for help when they are faced with challenges. Thus teachers need to be sensitive to both of these erroneous thought patterns.

Problem Solving

Students use concepts and reasoning to solve problems and, through this process, to learn about and make sense of the world. **Problem solving** is the process of moving from a situation in need of resolution to a solution, overcoming any obstacles along the way (Reed, 2000; Sternberg, 1997a). Here we consider several aspects of problem solving, asking first how students go about solving problems. The expert teacher needs to understand the problem-solving cycle in order to teach students how to use effective problem-solving techniques.

THE PROBLEM-SOLVING CYCLE

Various models have been proposed for the exact set of steps to use in solving problems (e.g., Bransford & Stein, 1993; Gick, 1986; Spear-Swerling & Sternberg, 1996; Sternberg, 1986; Sternberg & Grigorenko, 2000, 2001). In contemplating any set of steps, recognize that they represent a problem-solving *cycle,* not a linear progression of steps. When people use these steps, they almost never use them in the strict order presented here. Rather, they do some of the steps, then cycle back and do some of them over again. Even when a problem is solved, the solution to one problem often becomes the basis for the next problem. When you have earned an A in this course it may mean you are ready for a more advanced course next semester! Thus the problem-solving cycle starts anew when you take the next course.

The set of steps that follow is useful for characterizing problem solving (Sternberg & Grigorenko, 2001):

Step 1. Identify the existence of a problem. We cannot overemphasize the importance of this step. Students need to recognize, for example, if they are not understanding the material being taught, for without such understanding they cannot seek help when they need it. Teachers also need to identify students who are in trouble, whether academically or personally. For example, some students who appear attentive and well behaved may still be missing the point in class: They may be daydreaming while scribbling down mindless notes. Expert teachers recognize the existence of such a problem before it becomes a serious issue.

Step 2. Define the problem. It is one thing to know you have a problem, and another to figure out what the problem is. For example, students may recognize that they do not understand something, such as fractions, without being sure of exactly what it is that they do not understand ("some funny-looking numbers written one on top of another!"). Or students may identify a task, such as the need to write a paper on "World War I." Each student, however, must still define a particular issue to write about. Many students have trouble defining problems or topic issues for themselves. A teacher can help by providing questions that help define the problem. In this case, the teacher can ask students some defining questions such as "What do you think led to World War I?" or "What would have happened if some of the countries involved had been aligned on different sides?"

Problem definition is important to teachers as well. A novice teacher may consider a student's low score on a math test as a way to identify the existence of a problem. But the expert teacher will go beyond this identification to pinpoint exactly what it is that the student does not understand in the math lesson that has

THINKING CREATIVELY

Give an example of a problem that teachers face in which the solution to the one problem can serve as the basis for a new problem.

SUGGESTION: Using harsh discipline may temporarily suppress bad behavior, but it may result in other kinds of problems, such as displaced aggression and low self-esteem.

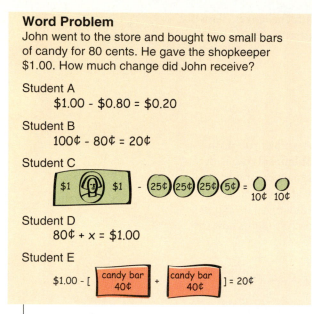

Word Problem

John went to the store and bought two small bars of candy for 80 cents. He gave the shopkeeper $1.00. How much change did John receive?

Student A

$1.00 - $0.80 = $0.20

Student B

100¢ - 80¢ = 20¢

Student C

$1 🪙 $1 - 25¢ 25¢ 25¢ 5¢ = ◯ ◯
                                  10¢ 10¢

Student D

80¢ + x = $1.00

Student E

$1.00 - [candy bar 40¢ + candy bar 40¢] = 20¢

FIGURE 9.2

Five students represent the same mathematics problem in their own way, with each way yielding a correct solution.

been taught. Teachers also must define problems in their own teaching. If a teacher realizes he or she is not holding students' attention, then that teacher has identified the existence of a problem. However, the teacher still needs to define what the problem is—why he or she is not holding the students' attention.

Step 3. Represent and organize information about a problem. How people represent information about a problem often determines whether they will solve it, or at least, solve it correctly (Hunt, 1994; Von Eckardt, 1999). For example, students often solve math problems more easily if they construct a diagram or other kind of sketch. There are often many different ways to represent the information in a math problem, as Figure 9.2 shows. Representing and organizing information is important in problem solving in every domain: Some students find it easier to organize their writing of a paper if they first organize their thinking with an outline.

Step 4. Create or select a strategy for problem solving. Students are far better problem solvers when they think strategically and plan for problem solving. Indeed, research shows that better student problem solvers spend more time in planning for problem solving up front; in contrast, poorer problem solvers often jump right in, only to find later that they are following a dead end and have to start again (Sternberg, 1981; see also Bloom & Broder, 1950; Larkin, McDermott, Simon, & Simon, 1980). Good readers, too, decide before they start to read how to read in a way that is appropriate for the material and the strategic goals they have set out. For example, good readers who are reading a novel for pleasure pursue a different strategy in reading from the one they use when they are reading a textbook to prepare for a multiple-choice test. In contrast, average and poor readers read almost everything in roughly the same way (Wagner & Sternberg, 1987). In summary, strategic planning pays off for students in their schoolwork.

Strategic planning is also important for teachers (Sternberg & Grigorenko, 2000). The well-planned lesson is almost always more successful than one that is impromptu. Teachers who have thought carefully about potential student reactions to, comments on, and questions about material find that anticipating these responses pays off. Of course, we can become paralyzed by overplanning, trying to predict every possible contingency. The expert teacher learns to plan, but also to know the limits of planning.

Step 5. Allocate resources for problem solving. Because neither teachers nor students have unlimited time for getting their work done, they need to budget their time effectively. The good problem solver decides how much time a problem is worth and then works within that time frame. On standardized tests in particular, research shows that students who devote too much or too little time to problems often do worse than effective time allocators, independent of their actual knowledge about or understanding of the material being tested (Sternberg, 1981). Of course, people have to be flexible, sometimes reallocating time when they discover they initially have allocated too little (or too much) time.

Time is only one of many resources on which students and teachers need to draw. A second resource is effort. How hard should one work before giving up, or seeking help? Able students not only understand things quickly or well but also know when they should seek help from the teacher. Less able students often seek help immediately without trying sufficiently hard on a problem, or they do not seek help even when their efforts clearly are getting them nowhere. Of course, there are many other resources—money, space, equipment, and materials. Wise allocation of these resources in the school creates an effective environment for learning and allows for flexibility.

Step 6. Monitor problem solving. As people are solving a problem, they must keep track of their problem solving. For example, students sometimes choose a research paper topic, only to find out not enough past research has been done on the topic to justify a review of that research. In such cases, the students are better off quickly moving on to another topic.

Expert teachers encourage students to clarify and even write out each step they take to solve a problem. This strategy works particularly well with mathematics but may be used in other classes too. When students reach an incorrect answer, the expert teacher may review with the students the steps they took to reach this answer. When the wrong step is found—preferably by the students themselves—the students can correct it and finish completing the problem, without having to rework the entire problem. Such a strategy can save time and frustration.

Step 7. Evaluate the solution to a problem. After you solve a problem, you need to evaluate your solution. Students need to check their work on a test, proofread a paper, or even ask themselves whether their answer to a problem makes sense. Paige and Simon (1966) found that students were willing to present, as final solutions to problems involving money, answers that involved negative amounts of change, that is, answers that made no sense. In our own experience, students often compromise the grades they receive on papers by not bothering to do even perfunctory proofreading. Similarly, teachers need to ask themselves questions such as whether a lesson has gone well, and if not, what they can do the next time to improve it.

A student carefully checks her answers to a homework assignment—an important problem-solving technique. Students often compromise their grades by not bothering to do even perfunctory proofreading of papers or tests. (David Young-Wolff, PhotoEdit)

Several models for solving problems have been proposed (Hayes, 1989; Simon, 1999). John Bransford and Barry Stein (1993) have proposed a model that includes most of the steps we describe, although with somewhat different names. Their model can easily be remembered by its handy acronym, IDEAL: **I**dentify problems and opportunities, **D**efine goals and represent the problem, **E**xplore possible strategies, **A**nticipate the outcomes and **A**ct, and **L**ook back and **L**earn. No matter what method you or your students choose, you can use the steps of the problem-solving cycle for many different types of problems. However, as we shall see, the type of problem *does* affect the ease or difficulty of reaching a solution.

TYPES OF PROBLEMS

No two problems are exactly alike, but many problems do share common characteristics. One dimension in which problems can vary is their structure. Problems can be either well structured or ill structured. Another characteristic of many problems is the type of thinking required to solve them. We look in depth at one type of problem, the insight problem, that requires the problem solver to think in novel types of ways.

■ **WELL-STRUCTURED AND ILL-STRUCTURED PROBLEMS** Many problems that students encounter in school are **well-structured problems,** that is, problems with clear paths to their solutions (Sternberg, 1999). For example, say a student is asked to subtract one number from another and to provide an answer, or to choose among several answer options on a vocabulary test, or even to solve a fairly difficult physics problem. These problems are considered well structured, because the student can use a well-defined path in order to reach a solution.

In contrast to well-structured problems are **ill-structured problems,** problems with no clear paths to a solution (Sternberg, 1999). Note that the term *ill structured* does not refer to something's being wrong or amiss with the problems. Rather, the term implies that the problems have no other obvious paths to solution. For example, when students are asked to write a term paper on a topic of their choice, they are being given an ill-structured problem, because no one obvious, correct, clear path will help them choose a good topic, research the topic, and actually write the paper. Similarly, planning an effective class presentation is to a large extent an ill-structured problem because there is no set of steps teachers can follow to guarantee a successful lesson.

Knowing the distinction between the two kinds of problems is useful for both students and teachers, if only so they will know whether they can expect a clear path to solving a given problem. For example, when students learn how to do scientific research, they often have the unrealistic expectation that research proceeds in close accord with an idealized scientific method they may have learned earlier: First, the scientist formulates an hypothesis, then the scientist tests the hypothesis, and so on. In real life, however, research is typically much less organized than the idealized scientific method implies. Indeed, research presents an ill-structured rather than a well-structured problem.

Teachers also need to learn when problems are well structured and when they are ill structured. For example, some teachers attend in-service workshops with the unrealistic hope that the workshop leader will provide them with a step-by-step recipe they can follow that will guarantee success in teaching. They are then disappointed when they learn that, whether the workshop leader admits it or not, no surefire recipe exists. Expert teachers know that becoming a successful teacher is an ill-structured problem and there is no single clear path to success.

■ **INSIGHT PROBLEMS**   Many, but not all, ill-structured problems are called **insight problems** (Sternberg, 1999). These are problems that require the problem solver to think in novel ways that are not obvious from the way in which the problem is presented (Sternberg & Davidson, 1995). For example, suppose students are asked, "If you have blue socks and brown socks in a drawer, mixed in a ratio of 4 to 5, how many socks do you have to take out of the drawer in order to be assured of having a match?" (see Sternberg & Davidson, 1982). The students may try complicated reasoning using the 4:5 ratio, or they may realize that, at worst, the first two socks they pull out of the drawer will be of different colors, so they need to pull out only one more sock in order to make a match. Here, as with many insight problems, the first path to solution that occurs to you is often the wrong path.

Do you remember the step of the problem-solving cycle called "defining the nature of the problem"? Insight problems typically require the problem solver to *redefine* the problem, sometimes many times. In other words, these problems require successive alternative definitions until a useful definition is found.

Consider an example. A junior high school student who was doing splendid work early in the term is suddenly doing work well below average. What has happened? A teacher who treats this situation as an insight problem may be able to help. It may be that the student's work is below average for a straightforward reason. The student worked hard early in the term, and simply has decided to slack off later on. There could, however, be less obvious reasons. For example, the student may be having trouble with his or her parents, may have a substance abuse problem, may be trying to do too much, or may have become friends with other students who discourage hard work. Seeing the problem as an insight problem open to alternative definitions may result in the teacher's being able to help the student in a way that otherwise would not be possible.

Janet Davidson and Robert Sternberg (1984; see also Davidson, 1995; Sternberg, 1985) have suggested three processes that are key to insightful thinking. These processes can help you or your students crack problems that require nonobvious insights. They can also be used for problems that do not require such insights.

The first process is *selective encoding,* used to distinguish relevant from irrelevant information. For example, a student listening to a lecture needs to recognize the important information worth noting. That same student writing a paper has to decide which information is worth including.

The second process is *selective combination*, used to put together information that is sometimes related in nonobvious ways. For example, a student listening to a lecture may see how to combine various points the teacher has made in order to go beyond what the teacher is saying. In a mathematics problem, the same student not only needs to recognize which information is relevant, but needs to decide how to combine it to yield a solution.

The third process is *selective comparison*, used to relate new information to old information already stored in memory. Selective comparison is essentially analogy formation, that is, seeing the relationship between two things or among a group of things. For example, a student may see a relation between something now being learned in physics and something that was learned earlier in math. Or the student may connect something learned in European history with something learned in American history.

Table 9.1 gives some well-known examples of insight problems. Each problem requires the use of selective encoding, selective combination, or selective comparison. You can use problems such as these in class to help your students develop their ability to think productively.

THINKING CREATIVELY

Give an example of a problem that requires selective encoding for its solution.

SUGGESTION: A minister in a certain town married nine women within a 3-month period. He never divorced but broke no laws. How was this possible?

TABLE **9.1**   Insight Problem

Insightful Thought Process Required	Selective Encoding	Selective Combination	Selective Comparison
Problem	A teacher had 23 pupils in class. All but 7 of them went on a museum trip and thus were away for the day. How many of them remained in class that day?	There were 100 politicians at a meeting. Each politician was either honest or dishonest. We know the following two facts: First at least one of the politicians was honest; second, for any two politicians at least one of the two was dishonest. How many of the politicians were honest and how many were dishonest, and what were the respective numbers of each?	Create a novel analogy by altering the normal state of something in the world: If villains are lovable, then *hero* is to *admiration* as *villain* is to: a. contempt b. affection c. cruel d. kind
Solution	Insightful problem solvers must realize that the number of students in the class, 23, is actually irrelevant in this problem. Instead they should notice the number of students who did not go on the trip, and therefore stayed in class: 7.	Problem solvers know there is at least one honest politician. That leaves 99 possibly dishonest politicians. Second, they know that, if you take any two politicians, one of them is guaranteed to be dishonest (and maybe both are). Insightful problem solvers must combine the two clues. If the honest politician is paired with any of the 99 other politicians, at least one of the pair must be dishonest. The insightful problem solver concludes there is one honest politician and 99 dishonest ones.	(Answer: b. affection) There are two processes at work. First, the problem solver must avoid being confused by the normal definition of a villain. Then the problem solver must see the relationship between the two other terms in the analogy (heroes receive admiration) and choose the word that creates a similar relationship with the newly defined term, *villain*.
Other Examples	An airplane crashes on the U.S.–Canadian border. In which country are the survivors buried? (Answer: *Survivors* are not buried at all) Fifteen percent of the people in a certain town have unlisted telephone numbers. You select 200 names at random from the local phone book. How many of these people can be expected to have unlisted telephone numbers? (Answer: None. If they are in the phone book, their number is *listed*.)	I bought one share of stock in the Sure-Fire corporation for $70. I sold that share for $80. I bought back the share for $90, but later sold it for $100. How much money did I make? (Answer: Combine the two purchase prices ($70 + $90) and combine the two selling prices ($80 + $100). Subtract total purchase price from total selling price ($180 - $160) = $20 profit.	If lakes are dry, then *trail* is to *hike* as *lake* is to: a. swim b. dust c. water d. walk (Answer: d. walk) If broomsticks are machines, then *jet is to pilot* as *broomstick* is to: a. house b. hermit c. witch d. garden (Answer: c. witch)

Source: Excerpted from pp. 215–216 and 221–222 from Intelligence Applied: Understanding and Increasing Your Intellectual Skills by Robert J. Sternberg. Copyright © 1986 by Robert J. Sternberg. Used by permission of the author.

By learning effective strategies for solving problems, you will become better able to teach these strategies to your students. Bright students often are unable to begin a problem because they do not know a relevant strategy to help them get started or do not know how to organize their thinking and to apply their knowledge. Today, when more and more students come from homes in which parents do not teach children basic learning and problem-solving strategies, it is up to teachers to fill in the gaps in students' knowledge. Students need to be able to develop strategies for exploring multiple ways of answering questions and solving problems.

■ **ALGORITHMS AND HEURISTICS**   We can use two basic approaches to solve problems (Korf, 1999; Newell & Simon, 1972). The first is to follow a clear and fixed set of steps that guarantees a solution to a problem, called an **algorithm.** Given the problem of multiplying 26 by 12, for example, you might use the following algorithm:

■ Multiply the right-most digits (6 × 2) to get their product;

■ Write down the ones digit (2) in the ones column and carry the tens digit (1);

■ Multiply the right-most digit of the second factor by the left-most digit of the first factor (2 × 2);

■ Add the carried number (1) to the product; and so on.

Eventually, if you follow the steps correctly, you are guaranteed to get the correct solution to the problem. You buy security—a guarantee of a correct solution—but often at the expense of efficiency. A fairly substantial portion of many teachers' time is spent teaching students how to choose and use algorithms, especially in subjects such as math or science.

Some problems, however, do not lend themselves to algorithms. Suppose, for example, you want to locate a friend. You know where she lives, and something about the kinds of places she is likely to be. You could specify an algorithm for solving this problem that would involve carefully searching every possible place in the world where she might be, but such an algorithm would be impractical. You need some other way to solve the problem. You are more likely to use a *heuristic,* an informal, intuitive, and often speculative strategy that might solve a problem but is not guaranteed to do so (Korf, 1999). For example, a heuristic for finding your friend is to start by asking her other friends where she is. You are not guaranteed to find her, but this plan is more practical than searching everywhere in the world. Heuristics yield efficiency, but at the expense of the security that you will definitely find the correct solution.

Psychologists have found that certain heuristics tend to be used again and again for a variety of problems. These are heuristics that can be taught to students as general means to aid them in their problem solving. People are most likely to rely on these domain-general strategies when they do not have domain-specific strategies available, or when the domain-specific strategies they have fail to work (Alexander, 1996; Perkins & Salomon, 1989). Here are four of the most common heuristics (Newell & Simon, 1972; see also Lesgold, 1988), and examples illustrating them:

1. **Means-ends analysis.** The problem solver analyzes the problem by viewing the goal and then tries to decrease the distance between the current state and the goal. A student who breaks down a problem, such as completing a complex term paper, into smaller problems or subgoals and works in turn on each subgoal (Schunk, 1996) is using means-ends analysis (Korf, 1999; Newell & Simon, 1972).

THINKING ANALYTICALLY

Specify an algorithm for checking whether you have a certain textbook on your bookshelf. How does the algorithm guarantee that you will find the book if it is really on your shelf?

SUGGESTION: You can go through every book on the shelf until you encounter the book that you seek.

THINKING CREATIVELY

Suggest a problem a teacher is likely to encounter that is best solved by a heuristic. Describe the heuristic as well as the problem.

SUGGESTION: At the beginning of a lesson, you can ask students some questions to get a sense of their current level of understanding for what you are about to teach.

---

2. **Working forward.** The problem solver begins with an analysis of the current state and tries to solve the problem from start to finish. The student who makes a list of all the steps needed to complete the term paper, before he or she begins it, is working forward.

3. **Working backward.** The problem solver starts at the end, or goal, and tries to work backward from there. A student who knows a final deadline for a complicated project and then writes reminders in his or her calendar about when to start each step so as to be done in time is working backward.

4. **Generate and test** (also known as **trial and error**). The problem solver simply generates alternative courses of action, not necessarily in a systematic way, and then considers whether each course of action works. A student using this heuristic might sit down and write the introduction of the term paper, before realizing that he or she needed to do research. Although this heuristic is generally regarded as ineffective, in a completely new situation it is sometimes better to use it to gather data that will let you move to a more methodical heuristic.

■**PROBLEM ISOMORPHS** Sometimes a problem may stump students, even though they already know exactly how to solve the problem when it is represented in a somewhat different form. For an example, consider the "monk problem":

A monk decides to pursue study, contemplation, and prayer in a place where he will not be disturbed. He decides that the best place to go is an isolated monastery at the top of a high mountain (as shown in Figure 9.3). The monk starts climbing the mountain at 8 A.M. and arrives at the top of the mountain at 4 P.M. of the same day. He varies his speed, of course, depending on just how steep a given part of the mountain is, and he also stops for lunch. The next week, the monk, feeling spiritually refreshed, decides to return. He starts his descent at 8 A.M. Feeling relaxed and peaceful, he descends the mountain slowly, not arriving at the bottom of the mountain until 4 P.M. Must there be a point on the mountain that the monk passes at exactly the same time of day on the two different days of his ascent and subsequent descent? Why or why not?

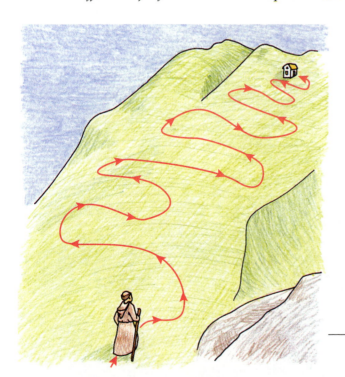

FIGURE 9.3

The Monk-on-the-Mountain Problem

It turns out that even grade school children know the answer to the monk problem when it is expressed in a slightly different form! The monk problem is a difficult one, and when the problem is described as it is here, very few people are able both to give the correct answer and to specify why that answer is correct. Yet the solution to the problem can be made relatively straightforward by changing the terms of the problem slightly. In this changed form, instead of imagining the same monk going both up and down the mountain on the separate days, you imagine two separate monks, one ascending the mountain and the other descending the mountain on the same day (see Sternberg, 1986). If one monk goes up and the other simultaneously goes down, clearly the two monks will have to pass each other at some time of the day, as shown in Figure 9.4.

The two forms of the problem have somewhat different verbal and even pictorial expressions, but they are exactly the same in terms of the constraints of the problem. They are **problem isomorphs,** problems that have the same formal structure, but different ways of expressing this structure (Hayes & Simon, 1974; Kotovsky, Hayes, & Simon, 1985).

The two problems described here have the same formal structure because if you simply imagine the second monk walking down the mountain path exactly one week later, the second monk becomes (formally speaking) the first monk. Thus the correct answer is that there must be a point the monk crosses at the same time on the two separate days. Here, as elsewhere, we cannot easily see that two forms of a problem are isomorphic.

The concept of problem isomorphism is important for teachers to understand. A given mathematics problem often can be represented (1) verbally, (2) algebraically, and (3) geometrically. The problem is the same; only the representation is different. Similarly, the grammar of a sentence can be represented verbally or diagrammatically. Students respond differently to different representations of information, however. By showing a student how to represent a problem in different isomorphic ways, you can help that student find a representation that works well. Instructions for tests and homework sometimes confuse students. Expert teachers may express the instructions in different isomorphic ways in order to help students better understand the tasks they must do. The ability to express a given idea in various ways is a sign that a teacher or a student thoroughly understands the idea.

FIGURE 9.4

Isomorph of the monk problem, showing two monks, one going up the mountain and the other simultaneously going down the mountain.

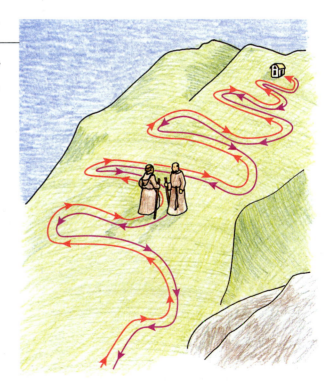

In teaching students to be effective problem solvers, teach them to consider looking for a problem isomorph when they find the original form in which a problem is presented to be very difficult. The problem need not be a formal one, as were the problems described earlier. The point is to make the solving of a given problem as easy as you possibly can. For example, when two elementary school students argue over the use of the classroom paper cutter, a teacher might point out the usefulness of having a problem isomorph, "This is a lot like the story we read the other day. What did the two children in the story decide to do when they both wanted the same thing?"

■ **INCUBATION** Sometimes we try and try to solve a problem requiring insight, but no matter how hard we try we don't succeed. At such times, a practice called incubation may help. **Incubation** involves temporarily ceasing to work actively on a problem (Wallas, 1926). Psychologists have found that incubating on a problem often helps us solve it, even though when we are incubating, we don't seem to be working on the problem (Anderson, 1985; Smith, 1995). Thus if you are baffled by a problem, putting it aside for a while may be the best thing you can do.

Hard-working students who become frustrated in their problem-solving efforts may believe that incubation means giving up. Teachers should help these students understand that incubation can be an important part of the problem-solving process that helps complete this process.

How can you best benefit from incubation? Craig Kaplan and Janet Davidson (1989) have suggested that you or your students are most likely to benefit from incubation if you invest enough time in the problem initially, so you have thought about it as fully as you can, and you allow sufficient incubation time to have an insight.

IMPEDIMENTS TO PROBLEM SOLVING

Sometimes people do not solve problems or have insights because they are blocked. Fortunately, by becoming aware of the reasons we sometimes get blocked during the problem-solving process, we can consciously overcome maladaptive thought processes and reach a solution.

That a person has a predisposition to think about a problem in a particular way is referred to as having a **mental set** (Luchins, 1942). Often, students have a mental set for how to complete a book report that involves a boring set of steps that yields a dull report. When they are shown more creative ways to approach the task—such as writing and acting out skits containing the book's characters, or designing costumes that might have been worn by the characters—these same students may approach the next book report assignment very differently.

Teachers can also acquire mental sets. For example, years ago, many teachers were trained to teach almost exclusively by rote memorization. In fact, some teachers are still trained this way. Consequently, the teachers have often formed a mental set that blocks them from teaching in a new and more effective way, even if the teachers are told that students will soon be tested in a new way that requires skills beyond memorization. These teachers have had to work hard to overcome these mental sets. Recent research shows that, under many circumstances, most students learn better—even in regard to memorizing for facts—when they think to learn rather than merely memorize by rote (Sternberg, Torff, & Grigorenko, 1998).

A particular kind of mental set in which a person is unable to invent a specific new use for something because the person is so used to seeing a conventional use for that thing is called **functional fixedness** (Duncker, 1945). For example, coat hangers are usually used for hanging coats and credit cards for charging purchases. However, when locked out, you can also use a coat hanger to open a car and a credit card to enter a locked door.

Some people are expert problem solvers in a given field of endeavor. We discussed at length in Chapter 1 the characteristics of an expert teacher and an expert student. This topic is particularly relevant in our current discussion of expert problem solving. What is it that distinguishes experts from novices at problem solving?

William Chase and Herbert Simon (1973) found that chess experts had better memory for chess pieces than novices, but only when the chess pieces were placed on the chessboard in a sensible configuration for the game of chess. If the pieces were arranged randomly on the board, experts could not recall their positions any better than novices could. Chase and Simon interpreted these results as suggesting that what distinguished the experts from the novices was the storage in their long-term memories of many thousands of configurations of pieces in actual chess games. The experts therefore could draw on this past knowledge in the memory task, but only when they were shown sensible configurations of pieces. Since that time, many other investigators have replicated this type of finding across a wide variety of fields of endeavor, including other games, physics, radiology, mathematics, chemistry, and sociology (see Chi, Glaser, & Farr, 1988; Ericsson, 1996, 1999; Reitman, 1976; Sternberg & Frensch, 1991).

The same observations that have been made with adult experts have been made with child experts as well. For example, one study showed that fourth-grade children who were experts in soccer learned and remembered more new soccer terms than nonexpert children, even though the children were considered equal in general learning and memory abilities (Schneider & Bjorklund, 1992).

A study of the advantages experts have over novices concludes they have five primary advantages (Chi, Glaser, & Farr, 1988):

1. They perceive large, meaningful patterns of information more readily than novices. In other words, they see the whole picture more easily than do novices, who may become fixated on details.

2. They perform tasks more quickly and with fewer errors than novices.

3. They deal with problems at a deeper level than novices. Therefore, they deal with the underlying meanings of problems, not just with the way the problems look or sound.

4. Their memory for information in their domain is superior to that of novices because of their ability to draw on more and better organized prior knowledge about their domain of expertise.

5. They take more time to analyze a problem before undertaking it, allowing them then to solve it more efficiently than novices.

In large part, what experts gain from the experience with large numbers of problems in their domain of expertise is **automaticity** in the solution of domain-relevant problems. Experts gain automaticity from having procedures they can execute with hardly any effort or even conscious awareness of what they are doing.

There can be costs to expertise (Frensch & Sternberg, 1989; see also Sternberg & Lubart, 1995, 1996). On the one hand, being an expert can facilitate problem solving through automaticity. On the other hand, expert problem solvers can become *entrenched*—so used to seeing problems in one way that they have difficulty seeing them in another (Adelson, 1984).

As teachers, you will need to be vigilant about your own expertise, to realize the same expertise that can make you a better teacher also can hinder your learning about and implementing new ways of teaching. You may encounter teachers who claim, "I've been doing the same thing for 30 years, so I can be sure I know what I'm doing." Expert teachers avoid this way of thinking. They know they need to be lifelong learners, constantly improving their own expertise.

THINKING PRACTICALLY

What are some steps you personally can take to avoid becoming entrenched in your teaching?

SUGGESTION: Attending in-services and professional meetings can help.

Implications for Teaching

In addition to furthering their own expertise in problem solving, expert teachers help their students learn effective problem-solving strategies. Some ways teachers can develop their students' problem-solving skills are suggested here.

- ■ **Define problems.** Teachers can practice defining problems using the content of lessons or naturally occurring opportunities. For example, an elementary school teacher might assemble the class to discuss a problem the teacher has identified: The room is not being cleaned up before students go to recess. Students need to know what kind of problem they face before they plan a solution strategy.

- ■ **Teach strategies for insightful problem solving.** In mathematics problems, a selective-encoding insight may be involved in distinguishing relevant from irrelevant information. For example, in the socks problem mentioned earlier, an insight needed to solve the problem is that the ratio information (socks mixed in a ratio of 4:5) is irrelevant. Expert teachers can develop creative curricula through selective combination of students' interests, materials, and assignments. For example, in preparing to work with twelfth-grade remedial English students who previously failed the class, a teacher might have the students read a newspaper article on an issue of interest (such as gun control), learn vocabulary based on the article, and write a letter to the editor about the issue. The teacher's selective-combination insight is the basis for a solution to the problem of how to motivate and reach a challenging group of students. Expert teachers may initially develop analogies to help their students solve problems, but then gradually require the students to suggest analogies of their own.

- ■ **Look for isomorphs.** An isomorph of a geometry problem that requires finding the perimeter of a rectangle might involve asking students to imagine walking the length and width of the school soccer field.

- ■ **Help students overcome impediments to problem solving.** Help students practice flexible thinking, by occasionally doing things in a slightly different way. For example, an elementary school teacher might read books that reverse common stories, such as *The Three Little Wolves and the Big Bad Pig;* in a physics lesson, a teacher might ask students to invent novel uses of a blank piece of notebook paper, for example, as a blindfold for a demonstration of the importance of the sense of sight.

Transfer

Students can become very effective at solving problems in school. Sometimes, however, they may not be able to use their knowledge when they encounter problems outside school: They cannot transfer their knowledge to a new situation. **Transfer** means carrying over knowledge from one problem or situation to a new problem (see Detterman & Sternberg, 1993, for alternative views of transfer). As we will see, transfer of knowledge gained from earlier problems can either help solve new problems or hinder their solution. In addition, researchers have identified different types of transfer, based on the ways transfer is achieved or planned.

Transfer can have either welcome or unwelcome effects (Mayer & Wittrock, 1996). **Positive transfer** occurs when the solution of an earlier problem facilitates solution of a later problem. **Negative transfer** occurs when the solution of an earlier problem impedes solution of a later problem.

Suppose, for example, that you teach grade school children the basic notion of decimals, and you also teach them how to do basic arithmetic operations with decimals. You are now ready to teach them the basic concepts and operations involving percentages. Percentages, of course, are conceptually similar to decimals; thus you would hope to attain positive transfer.

Often, the same prior learning that leads to positive transfer in some respects can lead to negative transfer in others. For example, having just learned decimals, some students may believe that 1 percent is written as .01 percent. Similarly, for the most part, knowing one language helps you learn a second language. But you may find yourself using the grammar or words from the first language to construct sentences in the second language, even though they are inappropriate in the second language. In such cases, both positive and negative transfer occur simultaneously. Figure 9.5 shows examples of positive and negative transfer as they apply to learning two different foreign languages.

Psychologists have studied the conditions under which transfer takes place. It is surprisingly hard to get positive transfer. As we discussed in Chapter 8, learning that is situated, or closely linked to a particular situation, is difficult to transfer. Mary Gick and Keith Holyoak (1980, 1983) found that positive transfer is more likely to occur if people are given more prior examples of how something works and if they are explicitly told to transfer what they learn. If you are teaching mathematics, you can increase the probability of transfer from one lesson to another by giving a lot of practice with different kinds of problems on a concept and telling students explicitly that they should look for instances of that concept in problems they will be solving.

Sometimes transfer is not symmetrical; it does not work equally well in both directions. For example, Bassok and Holyoak (1993) have reported that transfer of principles from math to physics is greater than that from physics to math—perhaps because people learn math with the expectation of having to transfer it to other courses, but do not learn physics with the same mental set.

Gavriel Salomon and David Perkins (1989) have suggested two kinds of transfer, which they refer to as *low-road transfer* and *high-road transfer*. These two types of transfer occur in different kinds of situations.

THINKING CREATIVELY

Give one example of positive transfer and another of negative transfer in the context of applying what students learn in school to the performance of work on the job.

SUGGESTION: An example of positive transfer is applying mathematics to shopping at a supermarket. An example of negative transfer is paying attention only to price and not quality.

FIGURE 9.5

Demonstration of both positive and negative transfer as they apply to the learning of vocabulary and grammar of one language as it is transferred to the learning of vocabulary and grammar of another.

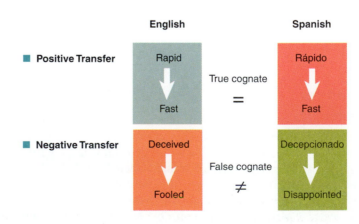

Low-road transfer is spontaneous and automatic. It occurs when a highly practiced skill is carried over from one situation to another, with little or no reflective thinking. For example, once you know how to ride a ten-speed bike, or to drive an automatic car, or to use a computer, you are likely to be able to transfer these skills relatively easily from one bike, car, or computer to another.

Low-road transfer is most likely to occur when the skills have been well practiced and used under diverse circumstances. Thus, the more you have driven and the more cars you have driven, the more likely you are to transfer driving skills easily from one car to another. Low-road transfer will be impeded, however, as the difference between situations increases. Thus, if you have learned how to drive using only an automatic shift, you are likely to get far less transfer to another car if it has a standard rather than an automatic shift. The student who has done lots of multiplication problems may not be able to solve a problem as quickly if it requires division.

High-road transfer occurs when you consciously apply abstract knowledge you have learned in one situation to another situation. For example, if you take a behind-the-wheel driver education course and use a school automobile, you will be using it with the goal of transferring what you learn about driving on it to your own car. If you are an education or psychology student and you learn statistics, it is usually with the explicit intention of applying it to your work.

In order to get high-road transfer, you need a meaningful abstraction of whatever principles need to be transferred. In other words, you need a good understanding of the concept at an abstract level so you can apply it later in another situation. For example, a teacher wants students to recognize the relevance of events that led to the Vietnam War as applied to the possible involvement of the United States in another war. In order for students appropriately to transfer what they have learned about the Vietnam War, they must have a good abstract idea of the circumstances leading up to that war that may (or may not) be applicable under other circumstances.

Mindless drilling practice leads to little improvement in anything. For a practice or drill of any kind to be effective, it should be mindful, or deliberate: Individuals should be attentive to what they are doing, watching for and correcting errors and working toward improvement (Ericsson, 1996).

We can distinguish kinds of transfer even further. In **forward-reaching transfer,** you intend the transfer at the time you are learning whatever you are learning. For example, when you take a statistics course, you may be purposely taking it in order to apply statistical techniques in your work. In **backward-reaching transfer,** you realize the applicability of what you learned in the past only after it becomes relevant. For example, perhaps you took the statistics course just for fun, before you even started studying psychology and education. If, later on, you find you can use the statistics in your work, you are engaging in backward-reaching transfer.

TEACHING FOR TRANSFER

How often do students actually transfer what they learn? Investigators have diverse viewpoints on this issue (see Detterman & Sternberg, 1993; Greeno, Smith, & Moore, 1993; Mayer & Wittrock, 1996). The consensus, however, is that teachers can help students achieve meaningful transfer if the teachers conscientiously follow principles such as those described here. The important thing from the teacher's point of view is not just to hope that students will transfer, but to follow procedures such as those described here actively to promote the transfer. Let us consider some of the ways teachers can promote students' transfer of knowledge and training.

■**MEANINGFULNESS** The teacher emphasizes tying whatever is being taught to whatever knowledge students already have and use a lot. Students are more likely to learn about the concept of transfer if they see how it can be a key to their own success in school or in life outside school.

■ENCODING SPECIFICITY As we discussed in Chapter 8, the ability to retrieve information can be helped or hindered by a number of circumstances. For example, students may tend to transfer learning only in conditions similar to those in which the original learning took place. Expert teachers help students overcome this tendency known as **encoding specificity** (Tulving & Thomson, 1973). They teach new information in a way that will help students retrieve the information more flexibly later on (Ceci & Howe, 1978). They explicitly show students how to apply information in various contexts, and they give students opportunities to practice doing so.

Expert teachers regularly ask students to suggest their own ideas regarding new contexts in which they can apply information (Mayer & Wittrock, 1996). For example, a social studies teacher is presenting a series of lessons on colonial American life. Suppose he or she lectures about "the way things were in colonial America" without linking this information to later cultural and political trends and without making any comparisons to life before and after the period under study. In this case, the students may be left with knowledge they will have trouble applying to contexts other than colonial America. But if the teacher begins the lessons by talking about how life in colonial America influenced later trends in American society, and then makes these kinds of connections throughout the lessons, the students will see the relevance of what they are learning to other contexts and they will be able to retrieve the information more flexibly in the future.

■ORGANIZATION The likelihood that students will be able to transfer information from one situation to another can sometimes be affected by the way the information was organized when it was first learned (Bower, Clark, Lesgold, & Winzenz, 1969). For example, it would be much more difficult for students to learn the correct use of commas in writing by memorizing hundreds of sentences in which commas are correctly placed than for them to learn a relatively small set of rules for correct placement of commas.

To help students overcome the limitations of the way they organize information, expert teachers present new information within a coherent, well-organized framework: The expert teacher makes clear to the students what the big idea is that underlies a lesson and also makes clear how the various concepts taught relate to that big idea. Each individual lesson is internally well organized, and each lesson also fits into an overarching scheme of information. As we have emphasized when we described ways to help students learn concepts, expert teachers also help students see how new information relates to old information students already know. They do this by explicitly stating the connections and also by encouraging students to suggest their own ideas regarding relevant connections.

For example, a science teacher intends to spend three months focusing on the characteristics of different types of animals. Suppose he or she presents the material in the format: "The first animal we will discuss is called a kangaroo. It lives in Australia. It is a marsupial. It eats leaves. Its young are born in a highly undeveloped state . . . ," and so on, into a discussion of the habits of kangaroos. The next day, the teacher presents the characteristics of another animal. In this case, the students will create a mental organization of knowledge in the form "animal—country of origin—biological name—diet—reproductive habits—etc." They will know many different types of animals by the end of the year, and they will have memorized details about the habits of each. However, the students may be limited by the way this information is organized.

The teacher can instead begin the series of lessons with an overview of the world's biological habitats and major types of animals. He or she focuses on types of diets (carnivores, herbivores, omnivores), types of animals (mammals, amphibians, reptiles, etc.), modes of reproduction (egg laying, live birthing), and so on. Through this teaching approach, the students develop a more flexibly organized base of knowledge that enables them to retrieve information in more ways and for more uses in the future. The beneficial effects of a highly organized knowledge base have been demonstrated repeatedly in empirical research (Ceci, 1980; Sternberg, 1999).

■ DISCRIMINATION Students also need to learn when information previously learned does not apply to a new situation. Expert teachers help students develop this ability, which is known as **discrimination,** so that students recognize more readily when old information is not relevant in new situations. The teachers may accomplish this goal by stating outright the types of situations to which new information does and does not apply. Also, teachers can ask students to speculate about situations in which new information is and is not relevant.

For example, the science teacher tells students that mammals are a group of animals distinguished by being warm-blooded, furry, and nursing their young with milk. The teacher also notes that the vast majority of mammals give birth to live young. However, this teacher states that giving birth to live young does not necessarily mean a creature is a mammal: Duck-billed platypi are mammals that lay eggs, and numerous species of amphibians and reptiles give birth to live young. By making these distinctions for students and by explaining what the new information about mammals does and does not apply to, the teacher is helping students develop the power to discriminate appropriately among different contexts and situations. Note the relevance of the discussion earlier in the chapter regarding necessary versus characteristic features: Giving birth to live young is a characteristic but not a necessary feature of a mammal.

Teaching for Thinking

Now that you have learned about concept formation, reasoning, and problem solving, we are ready to consider the important issue of how teachers can teach students to think more effectively. In Chapter 4, we discussed issues related to teaching to increase intelligence. Here, we consider some issues not presented in that chapter.

You can take two basic approaches to teach students how to think. One approach is to teach thinking via a **stand-alone program.** In such a program, thinking is taught as a separate unit or even a separate course. A number of such stand-alone programs have been used with some success (for examples, see Baron & Sternberg, 1987; Costa, 1985; for evaluations, see Perkins & Grotzer, 1997; Nickerson, Perkins, & Smith, 1985; Sternberg & Bhana, 1986; Sternberg & Spear-Swerling, 1996). Examples of stand-alone programs are Reuven Feuerstein's (1980) *Instrumental Enrichment,* Matthew Lipman's *Philosophy for Children* (Lipman, Sharp, & Oscanyan, 1980), and the *Odyssey* program (Adams, 1986). In these programs, students learn and practice specific thinking skills such as classifying items, forming different orders of items, or making comparisons between ideas or things; and reasoning skills such as making inferences.

The more commonly used approach is **infused instruction,** whereby teaching how to think is an integral part of a curriculum. Thus the teacher teaches thinking in the course of teaching other subjects, such as history, mathematics, English literature, or science. We examine the relative merits of stand-alone and infused instruction in Forum: What Is the Best Way to Teach Thinking?

FORUM

WHAT IS THE BEST WAY TO TEACH THINKING?

Which is better, a separate program for teaching thinking or one infused into regular instruction?

FIRST VIEW: *Thinking is best taught as a separate topic.* The advantage of separate instruction is that it tends to be more intensive. Sometimes, because of the press of other things teachers need to do, infused programs disintegrate gradually over time. The best intentions go awry as teachers find they just do not have the time or perhaps the know-how to do the infusion. Separate programs also increase the likelihood that the thinking skills will be taught in a systematic, logical manner, with one skill building on another. Most of these programs have been used in a large number of sites, so they have the benefit of having been developed and refined over of a number of years.

SECOND VIEW: *Thinking skills are best developed in concert with other skills as part of the standard curriculum.* The danger of separate programs to teach thinking is that what the student learns in them will not be transferred to other classes. A stand-alone program could result in stand-alone thinking. Students may come to believe that thinking is something they do in thinking class and then leave behind when they leave the class. For example, one team of researchers (Mayer & Wittrock, 1996) found that people often neglect to apply mathematical thinking skills learned in school to real-world situations such as grocery shopping. Moreover, when thinking is taught in a stand-alone way, the connections with other subject matter are often not obvious. In infused programs, however, the connection is made directly, so students can see how to apply thinking skills when and as they need them.

THIRD VIEW: A SYNTHESIS: *Separate thinking courses or programs allow students to see the links between different steps and thought processes and can be delivered by teachers who are well trained and experienced in teaching students thinking skills.* However, teachers in other courses must reinforce what is taught in the course on thinking. Although regular classroom teachers may not be experts in teaching thinking, they must have training so they become able to infuse thinking skills and practice into their day-to-day lessons. They should be thoroughly familiar with the content of the separate thinking classes, for example. A history teacher who knows that students in thinking class have been trained to look for connections between subjects could plan to include this skill in a unit on ancient history. The teacher might explore with students the relevance of ancient Greek and Roman mathematical and scientific accomplishments, relating them to modern-day math and science, as well as the more standard discussion of political, philosophical and artistic achievements.

Initially, infusion takes day-to-day effort, as well as training, for regular classroom teachers. Teachers must train themselves to use the skills they are trying to teach students, in order to plan creative and effective lessons. If they have been relying on more mindless activities, teachers may need to learn to plan their lessons in a different way. They should also take the time to become familiar with the content of students' other classes and their interests and activities outside of school, in order to help the students themselves make connections among these arenas. The goal of such effort, of course, is to develop the thinking expertise of students. As students become expert thinkers, teachers realize not only the rewards of helping the students develop self-regulation, but also the advantage of shouldering less of the responsibility for the development of students' thinking skills. Teachers should gradually ask students to take on the effort of infusing thinking skills for themselves. As students become expert thinkers, a history teacher may not need to point out the connections among math, science, and history as explicitly as when the students are novice thinkers. The teacher with expert students may be able to ask students to suggest ideas themselves.

A number of different approaches have been suggested for infusing thinking into the classroom. Robert Ennis (1987) has developed a taxonomy of abilities that he believes are part of critical thinking, which he defines as reasonable reflective thinking focused on deciding what to believe or do. Ennis believes these critical thinking skills can be taught. Table 9.2 lists some of the skills that Ennis believes to be key. We have discussed ideas for teaching many of the skills that Ennis identifies, including defining terms and concepts, making deductions and inductions, and deciding on courses of action.

TABLE 9.2   Essential and Teachable Thinking Skills

Ability	Definition	Example
Focusing on a question	Identifying or formulating the key question in a situation and keeping the question in mind.	A student proposes the central question of a term paper, "Was Hamlet sane?"
Analyzing arguments	Identifying the parts of an argument, conclusion and supporting reasons, and seeing the structure of an argument.	The student reads articles from literary scholars claiming that Hamlet suffered from hallucinations, when he saw the ghost of his father, and depression. The student summarizes the arguments in support of these diagnoses.
Asking and answering questions	Being able to ask and answer questions that clarify or challenge an argument.	The student asks himself or herself, "What do these writers mean by depression?" and "Does Hamlet really display all the symptoms of depression?"
Judging the credibility of a source	Rating the expertise, reputation, and motivations of a person making an argument.	The student notices that none of the literary scholars who claim Hamlet suffered from mental illness is a qualified psychologist or psychiatrist.
Observing and judging the reports of others' observations	Making careful notes and reports of observations without including judgments or rating the quality of others' observations.	The student notes several instances of Hamlet's well-adapted behavior throughout the course of the play.
Deducing and judging others' deductions	Using general logical rules to draw specific conclusions.	The student knows that not everyone who has hallucinations is mentally ill, and therefore deduces that whether or not the ghost of his father really existed, Hamlet could be sane.
Inducing and judging others' inductions	Drawing general rules based on specific instances, but always looking for an exception to the rule.	A key point in the arguments that Hamlet suffered from depression is the famous "to be or not to be" speech, which many scholars interpret as Hamlet considering suicide. However, the student notes that Hamlet does not consistently express an interest in dying throughout the play.
Making value judgments	Weighing and balancing alternative beliefs or plans.	The student compares the writings of those who claim Hamlet was depressed with articles that claim he was in full mental control.
Defining terms and judging others' definitions	Examining definitions closely to see how useful or well constructed they are.	The student carefully examines the definitions of sanity and insanity presented in the articles about Hamlet.
Identifying assumptions	Pointing out unstated reasons or assumptions.	The student notices that many of the writers who claim Hamlet was sane because he carried out complicated travel and other plans seem to assume that people with mental illnesses cannot do these things.
Deciding on an action	Based on the steps of the problem cycle, after identifying and defining the problem and generating alternative solutions, choosing one.	The student chooses a position on the question of Hamlet's mental health and prepares an outline for the term paper.
Interacting with others	Arguing, debating, or presenting a position.	The student writes the paper summarizing the evidence on both sides of the question, and the reasons for his or her own conclusions about Hamlet's sanity.

Source: Adapted from Table 1, pp. 12–15 from "A Taxonomy of Critical Thinking Dispositions and Abilities" by R. Ennis in *Teaching Thinking Skills* by Joan B. Baron and Robert J. Sternberg. Copyright © 1987 by W.H. Freeman and Company. Used with permission.

Note: Robert Ennis (1987) has developed a taxonomy of abilities that he believes are part of critical thinking, which he defines as *reasonable reflective thinking* focused on deciding what to believe or do. Ennis believes these critical thinking skills can be taught.

Richard Paul (1987) has emphasized the importance of what he refers to as **dialogical thinking,** which involves being able to see not only your own point of view, but also that of others. Robert Sternberg (1998a, 1998b) has emphasized the importance of **dialectical thinking,** a type of thinking proposed by nineteenth-century German philosopher Georg Hegel. This kind of thinking involves someone's first coming up with an idea, or *thesis;* then an *antithesis,* or opposing idea; and finally an integrating *synthesis.* Sometimes, it is the same person who comes up with the successive ideas. David

Perkins (1995) has proposed a set of dispositions that he believes are key for thinking, such as the propensity to think clearly and deeply about problems.

In each case, educational theorists have tried to provide guidelines for how teachers can enhance their teaching of thinking in the classroom. All these guidelines have one key point in common. They stress the importance of practicing the skills and dispositions of critical thinking often. At the beginning of the chapter, biology teacher Joan Gracek realized that her students needed more practice to develop the ability to think like scientists, and she provided it in the unit on animals. We describe some ways to include regular thinking practice next.

 USE ROLE PLAYING

Richard Paul (1987) has suggested that a good way truly to understand a point of view other than your own is to try using it. Teachers can build role playing into almost any subject. For example, students can play out how the various characters of a story would react in a new situation. They can enact the thinking of famous historical figures, or figures in current political controversies. They can even role-play persons of different cultures in social studies or foreign-language classes.

 USE GROUPS

Group projects provide students with natural opportunities to practice many important thinking skills. Students can work together in groups to learn concepts. For example, a science teacher labels a number of items as examples and nonexamples of a plant family, and asks groups of students to identify the family, or concept. Students may also work together to solve a mystery proposed by the teacher that requires deductive reasoning.

 MODEL AND EXPLICITLY TEACH THINKING SKILLS

Teachers should model effective thinking skills, including problem solving and reasoning, as they teach day-to-day content. Some researchers (e.g., Palincsar & Brown, 1984; Perkins, 1987; Schoenfeld, 1979), however, have concluded that modeling alone is not enough to help students learn to think effectively. Teachers must explicitly teach the thinking skills as well. A math teacher helps students learn to use the steps in the problem-solving cycle by posting a chart of the steps, and describing, as he or she works model problems on the chalkboard, which step of the problem-solving cycle is involved. For example, the teacher identifies a problem by writing it on the board. Then, he or she says, "Our next step is to define this problem. First, can anyone tell me what information is relevant?" and so forth through the remaining steps.

THINKING CREATIVELY

How might you plan a classroom lesson on alternative forms of government that systematically encourages children to engage in dialogical thinking?

SUGGESTION: Form a simulated alternative government in your classroom.

Expert teachers have automatized the habit of building practice in thinking into their everyday lessons. They know that with guided and focused practice, students can become expert thinkers. Using critical thinking skills can become a low-effort, automatized habit that helps students succeed in school and beyond.

 **CONSTRUCTING YOUR OWN LEARNING**

Taking into account all you have learned in this chapter, write down several ideas for specific ways you would infuse the teaching of thinking into a lesson on a subject with which you are familiar. Carefully consider the ages of students for which your ideas would be appropriate. Share your ideas with others, and have them comment or share their own ideas with you. In what ways are you now better equipped to teach for thinking than you were before you read this chapter?

WHY UNDERSTANDING THINKING IS IMPORTANT TO TEACHERS

■ Critical-thinking skills enable students to purposely search for solutions to problems. These skills are important to students' success both in and out of school.

CONCEPT FORMATION

■ Concepts are represented and organized in the mind by means of defining and characteristic features. Many concepts do not have defining features, and thus are best described in terms of either prototypes or multiple exemplars.

REASONING

■ Reasoning is of two basic kinds: deductive, which goes from the general to the specific; and inductive, which goes from the specific to the general. Teachers help students learn to reason by providing practice with syllogisms, encouraging thoughtful inductive reasoning, and teaching students to avoid common fallacies, including inappropriate use of the availability and representativeness heuristics, overconfidence, and underconfidence.

PROBLEM SOLVING

■ Many problems are solved via a problem-solving cycle, which is best used without sticking to a straight-line path from the beginning to the end of the sequence of steps. Problems can be divided into two categories: well structured and ill structured. It is often difficult to reach a reasonable solution for ill-defined problems. Some of the most challenging problems students and teachers alike confront are insight problems.

■ Algorithms, sets of steps that guarantee a solution to a problem, often work for well-defined problems. For many real-world problems, however, algorithms are either unavailable or too complex to be used successfully. In these cases, people use informal strategies known as *heuristics,* such as mean-ends analysis, working forward, working backward, or generate and test.

■ A problem that seems to be impossible to solve when presented in one way can become much easier to solve when a problem isomorph is presented, providing an alternative way of seeing the problem's formal structure. Often, incubation is the best way to reach an insight when persistent efforts to solve an insight problem have failed. The thinking required to solve insight problems includes (but is not limited to) three key processes: selective encoding, selective combination, and selective comparison. Old mental sets, including functional fixedness, can interfere with insightful thinking.

■ Expert thinkers differ from novices, primarily by knowing more and better organizing knowledge about their area of expertise. These advantages allow experts to develop a level of automaticity in solving problems. Although experts may be better problem solvers in their domain of expertise, entrenchment can creep in, thwarting flexible thinking. Teachers should encourage students to use both dialectical thinking and dialogical thinking to avoid entrenchment.

TRANSFER

■ Transfer occurs when previous learning affects current performance. Transfer can be either positive, when previous learning aids current performance, or negative, when previous learning interferes with current performance. Transfer can also be characterized as either high road or low road, depending on the circumstances under which it occurs. Forward-reaching transfer occurs when a person intends to transfer knowledge to a new situation. Backward-reaching transfer results when the applicability of previously learned knowledge is realized only at the time it is needed.

■ Teachers can facilitate transfer by helping students overcome the disadvantages of encoding limitations, poorly organized knowledge bases, and indiscriminate use of knowledge. For example, teachers can teach students to use organization and discrimination.

TEACHING FOR THINKING

■ The two common methods for teaching students how to think are stand-alone programs and infused programs. Each type of program has its advantages and disadvantages.

■ **Algorithm** Clear and fixed set of steps that guarantees a solution to a problem. Page 324

■ **Automaticity** Execution of mental procedures with hardly any effort or even conscious awareness of doing so. Page 328

■ **Availability heuristic** Shortcut in thinking by which people make judgments on the basis of how easily they are able to call to mind what they perceive as relevant instances of a phenomenon. Page 317

■ **Backward-reaching transfer** Realization of the applicability of what you learned in the past only after it becomes relevant. Page 331

■ **Characteristic features** Features typical of a thing represented in a concept, although not always associated with it. Page 311

■ **Concept** Mental abstraction or category of similar objects, people, events, or ideas. Page 310

■ **Concept map** Picture or diagram illustrating the relationships between different concepts. Page 312

■ **Critical thinking** Conscious and purposeful direction of thought toward finding a solution to a problem. Page 309

■ **Deductive reasoning** Process of drawing specific, logically valid conclusions from one or more general premises. Page 314

■ **Defining features** Features that are necessary and sufficient for defining a concept. Page 310

■ **Dialectical thinking** Thinking characterized by a progression in which first a thesis is proposed, then an opposing antithesis, and finally, an integrative synthesis. Page 335

■ **Dialogical thinking** Ability to see not only one's own point of view, but also that of others. Page 335

■ **Discrimination** Ability to recognize when information previously learned is not relevant in a new situation. Page 333

■ **Encoding specificity** Ability to transfer learning only in conditions similar to those in which the original learning took place. Page 332

■ **Exemplars** Highly typical instances of a concept. Page 312

■ **Forward-reaching transfer** Transfer that occurs when a person intends to bring knowledge to a new situation. Page 331

■ **Functional fixedness** Particular kind of mental set in which a person is unable to invent a specific new use for something because he or she is so used to seeing a conventional use for that thing. Page 327

■ **Generate and test strategy** (also known as **trial and error**) Way of solving a problem by generating alternative courses of action, not necessarily in a systematic way, and then seeing whether each course of action works. Page 325

■ **Heuristic** Informal, intuitive, and often speculative shortcut in thinking that may solve a problem, but is not guaranteed to do so. Page 317

■ **High-road transfer** Transfer that occurs when abstract knowledge learned in one situation is consciously applied to another situation. Page 331

■ **Ill-structured problems** Problems that have no clear path to a solution. Page 321

■ **Incubation** Temporarily ceasing to work actively on a problem in order to generate an insight. Page 327

■ **Inductive reasoning** Process of drawing reasonable general conclusions from specific facts or observations. Page 315

■ **Infused instruction** Teaching how to think as an integral part of a curriculum. Page 333

■ **Insight problems** Problems that require the problem solver to think in novel ways that are not obvious from the way in which the problems are presented. Page 322

■ **Low-road transfer** Transfer that occurs when a highly practiced skill is carried over from one situation to another, with little or no reflective thinking. Page 331

■ **Means-end analysis** Analysis of a problem by viewing the goal that is sought and then trying to decrease the distance between the current state and the goal. Page 324

■ **Mental set** Predisposition to think about a problem in a particular way. Page 327

■ **Negative transfer** Transfer that hinders the solution of a new problem as a result of experience with an earlier problem. Page 330

■ **Overconfidence** Heuristic described as an overestimate of the likelihood of the correctness of a judgment. Page 318

■ **Positive transfer** Transfer that facilitates the solution of a new problem as a result of experience with an earlier problem. Page 330

■ **Problem isomorphs** Problems that have the same formal structure, but different ways of expressing this structure. Page 326

■ **Problem solving** Process of moving from a situation in need of resolution to a solution, overcoming any obstacles along the way. Page 319

■ **Prototype** Most representative example of a given concept. Page 312

■ **Reasoning** Process of drawing conclusions from evidence. Page 314

■ **Representativeness heuristic** Shortcut in thinking by which people judge the probability that a particular event or object belongs to a certain category by how obviously it resembles, or represents the population from which it comes. Page 318

■ **Stand-alone program** Program in which thinking is taught as a separate unit or even a separate course. Page 333

■ **Syllogism** Deductive argument that permits a conclusion to be drawn from a series of two statements, or premises. Page 315

■ **Transfer** Carrying knowledge from one problem or situation over to a new problem or situation. It can either facilitate or hinder the solving of the new problem. Page 329

■ **Underconfidence** Thought pattern in which people believe they are less likely to be correct than they actually are. Page 318

■ **Well-structured problems** Problems with clear paths to their solutions. Page 321

■ **Working backward** Problem solving that begins with an analysis of the end state, proceeding from the end to the beginning to solve the problem. Page 325

■ **Working forward** Problem solving that begins with an analysis of the current state, proceeding from start to finish to solve the problem. Page 325

BECOMING AN EXPERT: QUESTIONS AND PROBLEMS

Apply the concepts you have learned in this chapter to the following problems of classroom practice.

IN ELEMENTARY SCHOOL

1. What kind of examples would you give to help second graders learn the concept of good citizenship?

2. How would you teach third graders to avoid inappropriate use of the availability heuristic during a social studies lesson on South America?

3. How would you teach your fifth-grade students to check regularly whether answers to math word problems make sense?

4. How would you conduct a lesson designed to help first graders move from relying on the generate-and-test heuristic for building a wooden skyscraper model of Popsicle sticks to using heuristics that involve more planning?

5. How can you help fourth-grade students organize their knowledge of the plants and animals common to your region so they are likely to transfer the knowledge to the problem of identifying different species they encounter on a class hike planned as a field trip next month?

IN MIDDLE SCHOOL

1. What personal characteristics do you suggest as being prototypical of the concept of "popularity" at the seventh-grade level? What would you avoid doing while teaching about the concept of popularity?

2. You are a new Spanish teacher. The previous teacher relied heavily on repetition and drill and, as a result, the eighth-grade students in your classes are convinced that Spanish is the most boring class in school. How will you demonstrate that their reasoning is faulty?

3. You have assigned your ninth-grade social science class a project to design a house in which a 65-year-old married couple will live after they retire. How can you help the students avoid the availability and representativeness heuristics in their assumptions about the needs of the home owners?

4. What are some exercises you can use in an eighth-grade poetry unit to help students overcome their functional fixedness about the ways words can be used?

5. How would you organize a unit on healthy eating so students in your seventh-grade health class are likely to transfer the knowledge to actually choosing their meals in the cafeteria?

IN HIGH SCHOOL

1. Develop a set of guidelines that will help students in your contemporary literature class use incubation effectively as they are completing their term papers.

2. What kind of analogies can you make to help students in your American government class understand the relationship between the rights of states and those of the federal government?

3. Develop some ideas for using popular movies to teach students to selectively combine what they have learned in science classes, such as physics or chemistry, with what they know about good movie plot lines.

4. How might you encourage students in your advanced biology class to transfer what they learned in the required prerequisite course, basic chemistry, to a lesson on metabolism and digestive processes?

5. Which topics would you choose to teach students in a senior-level history class the 12 critical-thinking skills defined by Ennis?

Connecting Theory and Research to Practice

Having students use concept maps is an excellent way of connecting theory and research to pedagogical practice. Concept maps, as stated in this chapter, provide a visual map of thought processes. Additional information regarding the creation and use of concept maps can be found on perhaps the largest concept map of all, the World Wide Web. For example, at *http://classes .aces.uiuc.edu/ACES100/ Mind/CMap.html* a classroom teacher can find information regarding the advantages of using concept maps as an instructional tool in the classroom, suggestions and tips for creating concept maps, a listing of the different types of concept maps, and example concept maps.

Another informative Web site on the topic of concept maps was created by Brian Gaines and Mildred Shaw of the Knowledge Science Institute at the University of Calgary. While the main focus of their online publication, "Concept Maps as Hypermedia Components" (available at *http://ksi.cpsc .ucalgary.ca/articles/ ConceptMaps/*), is the creation of concept maps using hypermedia, the article also provides information on the nature of concept maps, a few examples, and illustrations of their uses in education. Gaines and Shaw also have a related Web site illustrating the use of concept maps to support collaborative learning activities in electronic environments. Their article, entitled "Collaboration Through Concept Maps," is available at *http://ksi.cpsc.ucalgary.ca/ articles/CSCL95CM/.*

Communities of Learners/Teachers

Many universities around the world develop and support research and instruction by creating centers that focus on the study of a particular topic or subtopic within a discipline. Around the United States, centers studying problem-based learning (PBL) have formed to support the dissemination of information about this topic. For example, The Illinois Center of Mathematics and Science Academy's (IMSA) Center for Problem-Based Learning is available online at *http:// www.imsa.edu/team/ cpbl/cpbl.html.* This site provides teachers and researchers interested in problem-based learning in mathematics or the sciences with information, various resources, and notification of special events that may be of interest to them. While resources at this site are geared toward teaching in mathematics and the sciences, the site also contains information that is valuable for all teachers interested in designing, implementing, and evaluating problem-based learning in their classrooms. The Center for Problem-Based Learning located at Samford University, available online at *http://www.samford.edu/ pbl/aboutsu.html,* is another excellent resource for information on problem-based learning initiatives.

Online Resources

Critical thinking resources for primary and secondary educators are available from The Center for Critical Thinking at Sonoma State University and located online at

Copyright Illinois Mathematics and Science Academy. Reprinted by permission, The Center @ IMSA, Illinois Mathematics and Science Academy, Aurora, Illinois.

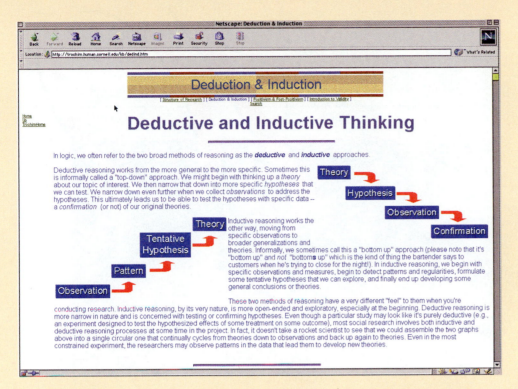

Deduction & Induction

[Structure of Research] [Deduction & Induction] [Positivism & Post-Positivism] [Introduction to Validity]
Search

Home
Up
TrochimHome

Deductive and Inductive Thinking

In logic, we often refer to the two broad methods of reasoning as the **deductive** and **inductive** approaches.

Deductive reasoning works from the more general to the more specific. Sometimes this is informally called a "top-down" approach. We might begin with thinking up a *theory* about our topic of interest. We then narrow that down into more specific *hypotheses* that we can test. We narrow down even further when we collect *observations* to address the hypotheses. This ultimately leads us to be able to test the hypotheses with specific data -- a *confirmation* (or not) of our original theories.

Inductive reasoning works the other way, moving from specific observations to broader generalizations and theories. Informally, we sometimes call this a "bottom up" approach (please note that it's "bottom up" and *not* "bottoms up" which is the kind of thing the bartender says to customers when he's trying to close for the night!). In inductive reasoning, we begin with specific observations and measures, begin to detect patterns and regularities, formulate some tentative hypotheses that we can explore, and finally end up developing some general conclusions or theories.

These two methods of reasoning have a very different "feel" to them when you're conducting research. Inductive reasoning, by its very nature, is more open-ended and exploratory, especially at the beginning. Deductive reasoning is more narrow in nature and is concerned with testing or confirming hypotheses. Even though a particular study may look like it's purely deductive (e.g., an experiment designed to test the hypothesized effects of some treatment on some outcome), most social research involves both inductive and deductive reasoning processes at some time in the project. In fact, it doesn't take a rocket scientist to see that we could assemble the two graphs above into a single circular one that continually cycles from theories down to observations and back up again to theories. Even in the most constrained experiment, the researchers may observe patterns in the data that lead them to develop new theories.

---

http://www.criticalthinking.org/K12/default.html. References, curriculum guidelines and activities, and special events concerning critical thinking are highlighted on this site.

"Critical Thinking On the Web: A Directory of Quality Online Resources," available at *http://www.philosophy.unimelb.edu.au/reason/critical/index.html,* provides a wide variety of Web resources related to critical thinking, reasoning skills, and problem solving. Hundreds of articles and publications are available online and cover a variety of topics. For example, the site presents articles about critical thinkers who have made outstanding contributions, theories of critical thinking, and approaches for assessing critical thinking. Additionally, it offers a short listing of fun activities related to critical thinking available on the Web.

The article "The Use of Concept Maps in the Teaching-Learning Process" presents a historical overview of the use of the concept map in education, primary uses of concept maps, and suggested steps for constructing concept maps. The article is available at *http://www.schoolnet.edu.mo/general/biology/temp/cmap/cmapguid.html.*

For information regarding the improvement of deductive reasoning skills in students grade 7–12, visit *http://unite.ukans.edu/explorer/explorer-db/html/783750187-447DED81.html.* Available on this site is a downloadable activity/lesson plan (in PDF and Acrobat format) geared toward improving deductive reasoning skills.

A nice Web site explaining the differences between deductive and inductive reasoning is available at *http://trochim.human.cornell.edu/kb/dedind.htm.*

A bibliography of textual resources on problem-based learning is available at *http://www.pbli.org/bibliography/* and is supported by Southern Illinois University.

10

Motivating Students

THE BIG PICTURE

To help you see the big picture, keep the following questions in mind as you read this chapter:

- Does motivation come from inside oneself or from the environment? What is the most effective type of motivation for a student—the internal push or the external reward?

- What are the implications of past and current research about the best ways to motivate students?

- How do the needs and goals of students determine their motivation level, and how can teachers use their knowledge of students' needs and goals to motivate students more effectively?

- How do students' beliefs about their own competence affect their level of motivation? Can students be taught to rethink negative beliefs and thus increase their achievement?

- How can teachers keep themselves motivated? What can we learn from expert teachers about how they motivate themselves while confronting one challenging class after another?

- How can a teacher motivate students with special needs? Does the teacher need special techniques, or do the same basic techniques work with all students?

- Should the parents of students be involved if the students are having trouble in school? What are the pros and cons of such involvement?

◀ *A student proudly shows her paper, with its positive and motivating remarks from her teacher.*
(Bob Daemmrich Photos, Inc.)

343

A frustrated Jim Jenson paced back and forth in front of his fourth-grade class. "Every one of these children has the potential ability to read and to read well," he thought. Jim had tried everything he could think of to get his class excited about reading. The techniques he used had all worked well in the suburban school where he had once taught. But his current students were hard to reach and hard to motivate: The pep talks about working hard today to prepare for a successful future, the threats to call parents when students slacked off, and the reading contests designed to stimulate interest didn't work. Jim's school was in a poor, inner-city community, where most of the students came from single-parent homes. Most parents were too busy working to spend time reading to their children, and the children were performing extremely poorly in reading.

At the beginning of the school year Jim had tried using an incentive program, awarding students gold stars for every reading attempt. But the students didn't seem to care about getting the stars: They threw the stars on the floor and showed no increase in reading time. Then Jim explained the power reading skills would have in the students' lives in order to convince them it was worth the effort to apply themselves. He talked about students who had discovered their life interests from reading (like the female astronaut whose interest in flying started with a book she received as a gift at age 7). But still his students remained unmotivated and basically uninterested. Their lives lacked positive reading role models and they could not relate to the examples of role models he described—mostly middle-class students who attended poetry workshops and went frequently to bookstores.

Finally, Jim decided to show his students that they could change their negative beliefs and attitudes about their reading ability by changing how they thought about reading—for example, by thinking about reading as a skill they could conquer. He used positive reinforcement and kept telling the students over and over that they had the power to read well if they could only see how their own negative beliefs were derailing their progress. These pep talks made the students feel that Jim cared about them and wanted to help, but the students still shied away from books.

Jim knows that reading ability is at the core of all academic performance, and he is determined to get through to his students. But nothing he tries seems to help. What else might he do to motivate them?

Jim's frustration is common among today's teachers. For students to learn and achieve in school, they must first be motivated to pay attention, read, write, take exams, and, in general, to apply themselves to the process of learning. Unmotivated students are the greatest challenge for many teachers. A teacher may have prepared a terrific in-class lesson and take-home assignment; however, if her students are not motivated to listen to her, she cannot simply present the lesson and reach them successfully.

Thirty years ago, almost all classrooms were orderly places in which students listened to teachers. Even if the students had motivational problems, at least the teachers could speak to them and be heard. Today's teachers complain that often their students are so disruptive and unruly that the teachers do not even know where to start. At the other extreme are quiet, well-behaved students. Some of these students believe they are not capable of succeeding in school, and they, too, produce work well below their ability level. How can a teacher convince all of these students that they are, in fact, competent? In this chapter we discuss how expert teachers motivate students of different ages and types to help them become successful learners.

Why Understanding Motivation Is Important to Teachers

Motivation is an internal state that arouses, directs, and maintains behavior. Think of motivation as internal psychic energy or as a mental force that helps a person achieve a goal. Motivation is important in many contexts: school, home, and the world at large. The key reason that motivation is important to teachers is the well-documented relationship between motivation and academic achievement. Students who are motivated tend to achieve more in school; they stay in school longer, learn more, and perform better on tests. Thus, as Jim Jenson recognized, teachers must foster motivation for learning before they can expect students to profit from instruction or from school in general (Dembo, 2000; McCombs, 1996, 1998).

To understand student motivation, remember that motivation is related to context. When students refuse to do something the teacher desires, there can be many reasons: The students may not actually lack motivation; rather, they may have motivation of the wrong type (as far as the teacher is concerned). Even very young students behave differently for different motives under different circumstances. For example, one study found that a 3-year-old child is highly motivated to protect a parent or loved one (Ceci, Leichtman, Nightingale, & Putnick, 1993). Close behind this motivating value is the desire to avoid pain or embarrassment. Gaining material rewards is somewhat less motivating for young students. Even less motivating, usually, is the desire to sustain a game with an adult.

An **incentive** is an object or event that encourages or discourages behavior. Not all incentives are equally motivating for students. A student may not respond to an incentive the teacher thinks is motivating if that incentive is not important to the student. For example, Jim Jenson found that his students were not motivated by receiving gold stars—a reward that works with some fourth graders. The right incentive for a person is one that is personally meaningful to her or him. Some students strive to earn praise; others work much harder for tangible rewards such as money, toys, or privileges.

Another important point about incentives is that sometimes incentives motivate behavior to meet undesirable goals. For example, the quest for peer group acceptance can motivate students to throw spitballs and write graffiti on desks. Some students are highly motivated—but their motivation is directed toward goals that are not compatible with success in school or in society at large. Assuming the values that lead to success in our culture are important to teachers and parents, a challenge for the expert teacher is redirecting student motivation toward goals that will lead to success, both in school and in the outside world.

Expert teachers know that motivation always exists in a context, and each child's situation is unique. These teachers also know that different groups may need to be treated differently to best develop their motivation. For example, research by Bronfenbrenner (1985) showed that girls and boys may need different types of assistance in order to develop motivation. When interviewed as successful adults and asked about valuable mentors from their formative years, boys more often cited people who challenged and pushed them as essential to their development of motivation. Girls, however, cited nurturant and supportive people, who encouraged them without being overly assertive, as being most important to their development of motivation. When girls and boys are assigned different types of mentors, the girls tend to blossom with somewhat more supportive mentors, and the boys to do better with more challenging mentors. We discussed the origin of these gender differences in

THINKING PRACTICALLY

Which current classroom contexts do you find most motivating? Least motivating? What can you do to increase your motivation when you are in a context you do not find motivating?

SUGGESTION: Perhaps you most enjoy classroom discussions, in which students question one another and the teacher, but you are bored by lectures, in which the teacher basically just talks for a half hour or more. To increase your motivation during lectures, you might jot down the questions that come into your mind during the lecture (pretending to yourself that it is a discussion). Later, you can have a discussion with classmates, friends, or the teacher about these points.

THINKING CREATIVELY

How might you determine what classroom context is most motivating for a particular student?

SUGGESTION: You can try several different teaching approaches over a two-week span—for example, straight lecture, discussion, demonstration, group activity—and watch the student closely to see which type of instruction is most motivating.

Name two unusual ways a teacher could motivate middle school students to do a book report project on ancient Egypt.

SUGGESTION: A teacher might ask the students to write a brief play based on the lives of people in ancient Egypt as a part of the book report project; or he could ask students to write about how ancient Egyptians spent their spare time compared to how the students spend theirs.

student development more fully in Chapter 6 on group differences; the key point here is that expert teachers must bear in mind gender and other group differences when they choose the best type of motivating mentorship.

Expert teachers also recognize that students' motivational issues and needs change over the years they spend in school. Research has examined the decline in motivation that often accompanies students' entry into middle school (Anderman, E., 1998; Anderman, L., 1999; Eccles, Lord, & Buchanan, 1996; Eccles, Lord, & Midgley, 1991; Henderson & Dweck, 1990; Midgley, Feldlaufer, & Eccles, 1989). When students enter middle school, their levels of school interest, self-confidence, and grades decline. They begin to show test anxiety and to miss school more often. Why does this decline in motivation occur at this point in students' careers, and what can teachers at the middle school level do about it?

The researchers found that middle school teachers are more likely than sixth-grade (grade school) teachers to emphasize classroom control and discipline, and to believe that students are untrustworthy. Middle school teachers generally felt less able to influence student learning; they often were less supportive, friendly, and fair to students than grade school teachers. The researchers believe that the observed trends are exactly the opposite of what students entering adolescence and puberty need. Expert teachers are aware of these general trends, and they recognize that these ways of thinking are erroneous. Armed with this knowledge, expert teachers take positive steps to give adolescent students the environment they need as they enter middle school. These teachers seek to provide their students with ample support and make an effort to treat students fairly at all times. Expert teachers make clear to middle school students that they are trustworthy and capable of learning and performing well, even though their transition into adolescence sometimes derails them from these goals. In essence, effective teachers help adolescents meet the challenges of puberty.

Everyone knows talented young people who have failed to achieve their potential because of lack of motivation. Everyone also knows people who seemed about average in ability, but who have had the motivation to push themselves and have infected those around them with almost contagious possibility thinking. Highly motivated people can

THE FLEXIBLE EXPERT

TEACHING AND LEARNING
ABOUT MOTIVATION

IN EACH CHAPTER OF THE TEXT, WE INTRODUCE YOU TO A FEW SPECIFIC STRATEGIES—ANALYTICAL, CREATIVE, AND PRACTICAL—USED BY BOTH EXPERT TEACHERS AND EXPERT STUDENTS.

THE ANALYTICAL TEACHER: Kami sees that the value of the rewards she's giving to get her high school students to do homework is decreasing, so she switches to showing her students why doing homework is important in developing real-world skills relevant to their future careers.

THE CREATIVE TEACHER: Kami has her students write a play in which the characters each express the students' negative beliefs about their ability in school, and other characters prove these beliefs wrong.

THE PRACTICAL TEACHER: Kami recognizes the facial expressions that mean her students are feeling insecure about their abilities, and she gives a pep talk reminding students of past successes and the future successes the students will enjoy if they apply themselves.

THE ANALYTICAL STUDENT: Jason is able to detail the differences among the four basic theories of motivation and to state the strengths and weaknesses of each.

THE CREATIVE STUDENT: Jason draws colorful signs with motivational slogans (such as "The hardest part is beginning" and "Do something now") and hangs them in the room where he studies.

THE PRACTICAL STUDENT: Jason can tell when his friends on the chess team are having trouble motivating themselves, and he knows just what to say to get them excited about competing again.

accomplish remarkable feats, and—regardless of how brilliant they may be—poorly motivated people tend to go nowhere. But what is known from the standpoint of psychological science about this elusive quality that so often makes the difference between success and failure? Where does motivation come from, what, exactly, causes it, and how can a teacher create it? These are our next topics of discussion.

Intrinsic and Extrinsic Motivation

Do you have friends who have tried on their own, unsuccessfully, to lose weight, and who have then joined a weight-loss program in which they participate in group meetings and are weighed in once a week? Many people unable to lose weight alone find themselves getting slimmer by the week when they join such weight-loss programs. Unfortunately, when they stop attending regular meetings, they tend gradually to regain the weight. This common phenomenon illustrates the difference between extrinsic and intrinsic motivation—and also explains why so many weight-loss programs do such a brisk business.

A dieter with **intrinsic motivation** gets the push to exercise and control food intake from within. Intrinsic motivation means that an individual has developed an internal desire to do something—in this case, to meet the challenge of getting and staying in shape. A dieter who succeeds while attending group meetings is relying on **extrinsic motivation,** or the motivation that comes from outside the individual, for example, from gaining the approval of others, meeting publicly stated goals, and performing behaviors valued by the group. Most dieters find it far easier to lose weight through a formal weight-loss program that provides some extrinsic motivation than through solitary dieting. However, over time, those who keep weight off tend to rely on intrinsic motivation.

THINKING ANALYTICALLY

Under what circumstances are you more likely to be motivated by intrinsic factors? Under what circumstances do extrinsic motivators work best for you?

SUGGESTION: Intrinsic factors motivate best when the activity is something you enjoy and have succeeded at in the past. Extrinsic factors work best when you dislike the activity, have failed at it in the past, and need an external push to get through the task.

RESEARCH ON INTRINSIC AND EXTRINSIC MOTIVATION

Researchers distinguish between intrinsic and extrinsic motivation in their studies of what motivates students most effectively (Covington, 2000). Intrinsic motivation is the push students give themselves; extrinsic motivation is the push students get from pursuing external rewards or incentives (Pintrich & Schunk, 1996). Extrinsic motivation works particularly well for young students, and teachers of grade school students recognize this fact when they create systems of rewards, such as gold stars, points, or tokens, to get students excited about learning. But as students grow older, they must develop intrinsic motivation. If they do not develop motivation from within, they will never experience or develop the joy of learning.

The issue of where a student gains motivation—intrinsically, extrinsically, or through some combination of the two—is a critical one for teachers to understand. Knowing which motivators work is often difficult, as Jim Jenson learned with his fourth graders. Expert teachers recognize that motivating students requires the use of both extrinsic and intrinsic motivators. Through experience, teachers also learn precisely which factors are most important, and hence most motivating, for each student. For example, if a high school student tells her teacher that she would much rather be exercising than writing an essay, the teacher might suggest that the student treat herself to a special workout if she writes for two hours (an extrinsic motivator). The teacher might also suggest that she choose a topic she is interested in and cares about—such as exercise or sports—and that she remind herself of how good it will feel to have accomplished the goal of writing the essay (intrinsic motivation). From experience with students and from trying different approaches with each student, expert teachers learn that for some students grades motivate best,

Most younger students are motivated by praise and gold stickers, whereas many older students thrive on self-motivation. (Michael Newman, PhotoEdit)

whereas for others the joy of self-discovery motivates best. These teachers may therefore try several different approaches to motivate each student.

Research on extrinsic and intrinsic motivation (e.g., Deci, 1975; Deci, Koestner, & Ryan, 1999; Deci & Ryan, 1985, 1987; Lepper, 1988; Lepper, Keavney, & Drake, 1996; Lepper, Sethi, Dialdin, & Drake, 1997) has evaluated which form of motivation is best in the long run for encouraging student learning. A key insight is that extrinsic and intrinsic motivation are not opposite points along the same continuum (Covington, 2000; Pintrich & Schunk, 1996). In fact, they vary independently of one another. A student may have a high need for teacher praise and a high desire to learn for its own sake, and thus be high both in extrinsic and intrinsic motivation. Or a student might be low in both needs, or high in one and low in the other. Expert teachers recognize this fact when they help students build every type of motivation, with special emphasis on fostering intrinsic motivation because this type of motivation is increasingly important as students progress through the grades.

Students can also be highly motivated in one subject or context, but poorly motivated in another—something we all have experienced when assigned to write a report on one of our least favorite subjects. An effective teacher uses motivators from a subject or context the student likes to motivate her in a subject she dislikes. For example, if Beth loves team projects in social studies and hates solitary studying in math class, her teacher might suggest she do a team project in math class. Her teacher might even ask Beth to try solitary work in social studies to show her that working alone can be a positive experience.

CONSTRUCTING YOUR OWN LEARNING

To better understand what motivates you and why, create a chart, such as the one on page 349, labeled with "high" and "low" intrinsic motivation along the top and "high" and "low" extrinsic motivation down the side. Now list as many activities as you can that you are able to characterize according to the amount and type of motivation you have for each activity. For example, a part-time job might rank high in extrinsic motivation because you do it for the money, and low in intrinsic motivation because you do not really enjoy it for its own sake. Cleaning your apartment might rank high in intrinsic motivation because you enjoy doing the cleaning, and high in extrinsic motivation, too, because your roommate praises and rewards you for doing the cleaning. See whether you can fill in each box in the chart with a few different behaviors. What does your chart reveal about the sources of your motivation?

Try filling out a similar chart to understand your motivation for different aspects of teaching. If you are currently working in a practicum, consider creating a motivation chart, based on what you know of one or more of the students. What do these charts tell you about yourself as a teacher? How do they affect your plans for motivating the students you teach?

	Intrinsic Motivation	
	High	Low
Extrinsic Motivation		
High		
Low		

MOTIVATION AND THE DEVELOPMENT OF EXCEPTIONAL ABILITIES

Intrinsic motivation can empower people to accomplish remarkable tasks. Consider the remarkable memory expert Rajan, who memorized the value of pi to the ten-thousandth decimal place. Rajan worked to develop his astounding memory ability without any external reinforcement; he received no external rewards. His self-professed desire was to be "the most outstanding mnemonist in the world." Regardless of whether Rajan strikes us as a success story, he is certainly an example of exceptional motivation. This type of internal push is very important in becoming successful: The world contains many successful individuals who developed a strong internal push early on in life and pursued their goals relentlessly.

Michael Howe (1999a, 1999b) has studied the origins of exceptional abilities and concluded that intrinsic motivation is often important in developing exceptional talents. One group Howe studied was autistic savants—students labeled as having functional retardation but who show exceptional levels of performance on certain tasks. Some of these students had the ability to memorize perpetual calendars: They could answer accurately when asked, "On what day of the week will August 15, 2008, fall?" Howe found that these children led basically bleak family lives because of their autism. One day, some crucial event happened in the lives of each of the children who later became savants. The event rewarded the children for memorizing something. For example, if a relative visited and the child remembered the date of the relative's previous visit, the family may have praised the child and showered him with attention. Building on this initial external and minor reinforcement, the child developed an obsessive desire to memorize calendars, or to pursue whatever the particular fixation was. From this point on, the strong and now internal push propelled the child to work obsessively on learning the material.

Howe (1992) also drew attention to children in an orphanage in eighteenth-century Venice. These children were completely immersed in the study of music from an early age. The orphanage in which they were raised had a reputation for developing young musicians, and all children who lived there felt a responsibility to do their best to measure up to the expectations of the adult mentors; excellence at music was part of the culture of the group of people in the orphanage. There is no reason to assume these children had, on average, any more or less musical talent than any other group of children. However, by age 8, not only had half the children

THINKING ANALYTICALLY

What might have happened if the children in the Venetian orphanage had been adolescents when they began the total immersion in the study of music?

SUGGESTION: Although both time and place are different from those in other studies we cite, adolescents might resist the adults' attempts to completely immerse them in the study of music; they might already have well-developed interests in another area. Also, some evidence suggests that very young children are better able to develop musical ability than are older children.

Tony DeBlois is a person who is blind, has autism, and is a prodigious musical savant. He plays fourteen musical instruments (including voice) and has been performing professionally since age nine. (Janice DeBlois)

THINKING CREATIVELY

How might a teacher encourage a student to develop intrinsic motivation for playing a musical instrument?

SUGGESTION: By telling the student he has natural talent (if at all true); or encouraging the love of music by sharing CDs and books about great musicians; and by pointing out and modeling the internal rewards that come from practice (ability to focus, belief in oneself, feelings of accomplishment).

played in a symphony orchestra, they were also described as creating extraordinary music. The case of these children, who were taught music by the Italian composer Antonio Vivaldi, reveals again the importance of motivation and hard work in developing talents. Expert teachers understand the importance of motivation in helping children maximize their potential.

The value of exceptional motivation is also clear in a study of expert race-track handicappers, who predict the winners in a horse race (Ceci & Liker, 1986). This study showed that expert, highly successful handicappers did not differ from nonexperts in intelligence, social class, or years of schooling. The difference was in their motivation to understand the outcomes of horse races: Once a race had been run, most handicappers turned the page of their race guide and began focusing on the next race. But the experts—the most successful handicappers—watched replays again and again, and continually analyzed and reanalyzed the race, in order to understand why the horses performed as they did. These experts were extremely motivated. They worked toward the external rewards represented by financial windfalls, but also, in large part, for internal reasons (their love of horse racing).

EXTRINSIC REWARDS MAY UNDERMINE MOTIVATION

Our society has created many extrinsic rewards to ensure that people accomplish what is in society's best interests. Much of our educational system is based on grades, diplomas, and other external manifestations of what a person has accomplished. These extrinsic rewards are examples of how society acknowledges the value of completing an educational program. But how much weight do *individuals* give to extrinsic rewards? In fact, people do their most creative work when they are *intrinsically* motivated (Amabile, 1996). If we look at the most creative writers, artists, scientists, or people in any other field, they are usually people who have done their work for the enjoyment of it. It is not that these individuals do not care about extrinsic rewards, such as money and fame. Rather, they are task focused—they work because they enjoy it, and the money, fame, and other extrinsic rewards are pleasant by-products.

Extrinsic motivators can sometimes undermine intrinsic motivation. Spence and Helmreich (1983) studied the motivation and achievement of thousands of college students, scientists, pilots, businesspeople, and athletes. They concluded that intrinsic motivation produces high achievement, and that extrinsic motivation often does not. These researchers identified three facets of people's intrinsic motivation: (1) quest for mastery, (2) drive to work, and (3) competitiveness. They found that, despite similar abilities, people oriented toward mastery and hard work typically achieve more than people not so oriented. However, those people who were the most competitive, and thereby showed a more extrinsic orientation, achieved less. People driven by a desire for meaningful learning, mastery of skills, and work—who are sometimes described as **mastery oriented**—achieved more if they were not also highly competitive.

Not all extrinsic rewards have a negative effect on intrinsic motivation, however. Three factors determine whether an extrinsic motivator will undermine intrinsic motivation. (In other words, when the following three conditions are met, extrinsic motivators will undermine intrinsic motivation.) First, the individual must expect to receive the reward upon completing the task. Second, the reward must be something important to the individual. Third, the reward usually must be tangible (a grade, money, a prize). Intangible rewards, such as praise or a smile, seem not to undermine intrinsic motivation (Deci, 1996).

How students *perceive* their teachers' motivation is also important to student learning (Wild, Enzle, & Hawkins, 1992). This study compared two groups of college students. In one class, the teacher was portrayed as being extrinsically motivated by a $25 payment. In a second class, the teacher was portrayed as being an intrinsically motivated volunteer. The teacher was the same throughout and not informed of what the students had been told. The students were taught the piano one at a time. Students who thought the teacher was a volunteer perceived the teacher as showing greater enjoyment, enthusiasm, and innovation than did students in the paid condition. Students in the volunteer condition also enjoyed the lesson more, reported a more positive mood, and were more interested in further learning. During an interval of playing on the piano in which students were free to play whatever they wished, subjects with the supposedly volunteer teacher were more exploratory and tried more new ways of playing than those with the paid teacher.

Do parents recognize that they should be promoting intrinsic motivation in their children? Barrett and Boggiano (1988) showed that the average parent or college student prefers using controlling strategies with children, and prefers using rewards and other methods for promoting extrinsic motivation, compared to alternatives that create intrinsic motivation. The average individual also thought that *teachers* prefer extrinsically motivated students to intrinsically motivated students, and believed that extrinsically motivated students derive more benefit from feedback. Teachers themselves often prefer extrinsic motivation to influence their students. In particular, teachers who themselves believe that individuals are best controlled by external forces prefer using extrinsic motivators with students. For example, one study found that teachers with an external **locus of control** preferred to use external motivation in teaching (Trice & Wood-Shuman, 1984). Locus of control refers to the location of the source of control for an individual, usually described as internal or external; thus teachers who see *themselves* as controlled by outside forces apply this same perspective when interacting with students.

Implications for Teaching

- **Consider student age when choosing motivators.** Extrinsic motivators, such as grades and pats on the back, tend to work best with younger students. Intrinsic motivators, including doing something for the enjoyment of it, tend to work best with older students. But do not overly limit your choices—at any age, students are individuals who do not necessarily fit general patterns.

- **Choose from a variety of techniques to motivate students.** Extrinsic motivators can cause rapid changes in behavior, but these changes are often short lived. Intrinsic motivators usually cause more gradual but longer term changes in behavior. For both short- and long-term results, a combination of motivators is useful. The best way to know and do what works to motivate students is to try several motivating approaches.

- **Don't underestimate the substantial value of intrinsic motivation.** Students with substantial intrinsic motivation can accomplish remarkable things.

- **Besides modeling intrinsic motivation, plan classes that stimulate students' curiosity.** Build their interest in learning by encouraging their sense of competence. Offering them some freedom to devise their own solutions to problems and to have a positive effect on their environment will give them a taste for challenges and a desire to overcome them.

- **Show your own love and enthusiasm for learning, and try novel methods that reflect your curiosity and interests.** If your interest is piqued by rain forests or the modern short story, your students are more likely to take notice and follow your example.

Are today's students less motivated than the students of previous generations? Or are today's students highly motivated, but simply to achieve goals that are not related to school?

FIRST VIEW: *Students are less motivated today.* Some educators believe that students today are simply less motivated and less disciplined than their parents were at their age. People adhering to this view note that students watch as much as seven hours of television per day. Their lives are filled with passive activities and forms of entertainment that have kept these students from learning the value of hard work. Parents today provide for most of their children's material needs without even requiring disciplined participation by children in family chores and without expecting their children to do meaningful work. These are signs of our times: Parents are overworked, and children are unsupervised and undisciplined by their parents. When in school, these students present teachers with major challenges, because the students do not arrive at school with the necessary backgrounds and values for teachers to capitalize on.

SECOND VIEW: *Students are highly motivated for activities they find meaningful— which often do not include schoolwork.* Other educators believe that students show great discipline and motivation—but that this effort is not expended on school-related tasks. This view sees students as plenty motivated, but for achieving nonacademic goals. For example, some students spend hours playing video games; thus, they have persistence, but lack the discipline to apply themselves to schoolwork. Parents may contribute to the focusing of their children's motivation on nonoptimal goals. According to this view, there is not much teachers can do, because students are already predisposed by the time they enter school to focus on the goals the students believe are important, and these goals are not the teacher's goals. With no common ground to stand on with their students, teachers can find themselves frustrated. Parents often respond to this problem by stating that it is the task of the schools to motivate their children to care about scholastic performance.

THIRD VIEW: A SYNTHESIS: *Students lack school motivation, but they are motivated; the challenge is to redirect their motivation toward goals that will bring more ultimate rewards in life.* According to this view, teachers face the challenge of determining what motivates their students outside of school, and then channeling the students' motivation into more appropriate school activities. The task for the teacher becomes one of harnessing students' natural motivation and redirecting it. Approaches teachers can use include asking students to describe their hobbies and how they like to spend their time, and then using this information to structure classwork and homework assignments to take advantage of natural interest areas. (For example, for a student who loves sports, a history project can focus on sports during different periods in history: who played, what games, when, and why.) Assignments can be given that demand hands-on participation in community events. Students can be given extra responsibility to encourage them to grow—perhaps publishing their own writing in the form of a newsletter. Members of the community whom the students would find motivating—such as athletes, businesspeople, and actors—can be used as role models; students can even write to these individuals. All of these strategies will help students mobilize their motivation and redirect it toward activities representing meaningful scholastic work. In addition, teachers can explain to parents that their children are directing their energies toward nonoptimal goals, and ask the parents for help in enforcing a focus on more appropriate goals, chosen to be as unobjectionable as possible to students.

Four Ways to Understand Motivation

Having considered how intrinsic and extrinsic motivation influence behavior, we are ready to review the major theories of motivation, which are based on the major theories of learning. Recall from Chapters 7 and 8 the description of behavioral and cognitive theories of learning. These approaches to learning also help explain motivation. Four theories of motivation follow from the learning theories.

BEHAVIORAL THEORIES

Behaviorists think that learning results from rewards and punishments experienced by a person. Similarly, behaviorists see motivation as the result of rewards and punishments that serve to mold behavior in the direction of seeking rewards and avoiding punishments. According to this view, students become motivated to do things that are reinforced. Recall from Chapter 7 that a reinforcer is a stimulus that increases the probability the behavior associated with it will happen again. The reinforcer typically occurs immediately or very soon after the behavior in question. If it does not occur soon thereafter, learning does not take place, or is weakened. To review, reinforcers are of two kinds: positive and negative. A positive reinforcer is a reward following a behavior that strengthens the behavior and leads to increased likelihood of future occurrence of the behavior. Examples of positive reinforcers are a teacher's approval, indicated by a smile or a favorable comment; an A on a test; or an award certificate recognizing excellent performance. The behavior that is increased is studying and achieving in school. A negative reinforcer is the removal or cessation of an unpleasant stimulus, which as a consequence increases the likelihood of future occurrence of the behavior. For example, leaving an extremely hot room or an uncomfortably noisy concert serves as a negative reinforcer. The behavior that is increased is leaving the hot or noisy room. The removal of an unpleasant stimulus that results in an increased probability of response is referred to as negative reinforcement.

In contrast to positive and negative reinforcement, punishment is a process that diminishes or suppresses behavior. Punishment can consist either of doing something aversive and unpleasant to a student who is not behaving appropriately, or of denying privileges and *not* doing what the student wants if the student is not behaving appropriately. In other words, punishment is a stimulus that *decreases* the probability of a response, either through the application of an unpleasant stimulus or through the removal of a pleasant one. Punishment and negative reinforcement are sometimes confused with each other; however, punishment decreases the probability of a response, whereas negative reinforcement increases it. Common examples of punishment are a failing grade, being yelled at, being hit, or being humiliated. (The behavior that is decreased is studying in the case of the failing grade used as a punisher.) Punishment tends to be less effective for achieving behavioral change than reinforcement.

Thus, as we discussed in Chapter 7, both positive and negative reinforcers increase behavior, and punishment decreases behavior. A student who wins high marks in spelling early in the term and gets praised by her teacher and her parents may continue to study spelling for months afterward in response to these rewards. She may even participate in the school spelling bee in an effort to gain further recognition for her skill. The student has been positively reinforced, or rewarded, for her spelling ability. However, if the same student does not do particularly well in social studies early in the term, and consequently receives no praise or other rewards, she may not study social studies because she has not experienced an incentive or reinforcement to continue. If the same student is ridiculed by her peers for earning high marks in spelling—and is thus, in effect, punished for working hard—she may work much less hard on the next spelling test so she does not perform as well.

Many parents pay their children for getting good grades in school. What are the pros and cons of paying children for grades?

SUGGESTION: Pros: This is a powerful motivator in the short run, shows that parents care about children's success, and produces a tangible reward. Cons: This undermines intrinsic motivation—children do not learn to value success for its own sake; over time, it encourages children to perceive that their parents are "buying" their success rather than showing sincere interest; it produces feelings of being used.

You can see that behavioral approaches to understanding motivation are closely linked to extrinsic motivation, because of the reliance on external rewards and incentives in producing certain behaviors. Jim Jenson used incentives based on behavioral principles when he offered his students gold stars for progress in reading.

What are the negative aspects of the behavioral theory of motivation, and of the use of rewards, incentives, and punishments to shape behavior in the classroom? First, ask yourself, how do you feel when teachers or mentors attempt to mold your behavior by using incentives, rewards, and punishments? Many younger students seem to respond well to a system of rewards and punishments, but as they grow up, they sometimes resent such systems and the external pressures they impose. One problem with using external rewards to motivate students to learn is that the students may never develop as much intrinsic motivation as they ideally need. In fact, researchers have found that offering rewards to children for doing tasks the children find naturally motivating actually decreases the children's desire to perform the tasks (Deci, Koestner, & Ryan, 1999; Deci & Ryan, 1987). Mark Lepper (Lepper & Chabay, 1985) has shown that giving students extrinsic rewards for working on problems they find interesting has the effect of decreasing the students' interest level—exactly the opposite of what the teacher intends. Expert teachers make their use of rewards more effective by offering rewards for effort and for meaningful progress on tasks, rather than simply for handing work in.

External rewards can also focus students on the rewards rather than on learning and growing though the learning experience. Our society supports the heavy emphasis that students place on grades as they develop. Expert teachers must confront this fact and remind students of the joys of learning through the teachers' example and of noting the unseen rewards down the line that come from developing intrinsic motivation (Mischel, Shoda, & Rodriguez, 1989). Another reason you may find rewards difficult to use is simply one of availability: There are not always enough rewards to go around. It is tough to keep students motivated all year in every subject through the use of rewards without running out of effective rewards.

Another problem with using external rewards to motivate students is that the system becomes less effective as students grow up. More mature students may sometimes perceive attempts to reward them as attempts to bribe them. What works for a 7-year-old can be sometimes be seen as manipulative by a 14-year-old. In addition, offering privileges or time without homework means that older students may not do the work they must do to succeed in school. Although bonus systems motivate many adults to work harder in order to meet deadlines, adults expect to perform work in exchange for financial compensation, whereas students are not usually compensated financially for doing schoolwork. Students are expected to do their schoolwork without being given constant extrinsic rewards. Thus something more appropriate to the schooling domain than a rewards-based approach is needed, and that something can be an appeal to the thoughts, pride, and feelings of self-efficacy and competence of a developing student.

COGNITIVE THEORIES

Cognitive theories of learning stress what goes on inside the student's head. This emphasis differs from one on the external environment so important in behavioral views. Like cognitive views of learning, cognitive views of motivation focus on what students think, how they think, and how their thoughts create or reduce motivation to act (Schunk, 1991, 1996, 1999). Thus cognitive theories of motivation emphasize the importance of intrinsic, as opposed to extrinsic, motivation. Jim Jenson took a cognitive perspective on motivation when he explained to his students the many benefits reading would confer in their lives. Research conducted by those with a cognitive emphasis has examined students' planning ability and how to improve it; the role of students' expectations of themselves, others, and their environment; the importance of goals (and how to craft effective goals); and ways in which students explain their successes and failures.

Part of what makes us human is our capacity for goal-directed, adaptive behavior. Cognitive theorists explain motivation by pointing to our human need to understand, strive, excel, succeed, advance, and continue to challenge ourselves. Some students sit for hours and work on a tough problem without even noticing the passage of time. Why do some people have such strong motivation? Why do people enjoy doing puzzles and making up limericks? Why do people push forward when it would be easier just to relax and enjoy life? Cognitive theorists examine questions such as these by exploring how students' thoughts influence their behavior.

SOCIAL LEARNING THEORIES

Recall from Chapter 8 that social learning theory combines behavioral and cognitive approaches. Similarly, the social learning approach to understanding motivation mixes the behavioral and cognitive approaches just described. From the social learning perspective, motivation results both from what goes on inside a person's head (the person's thoughts, plans, and belief in her or his abilities), and what goes on in the external environment (the likelihood of reaching a goal, and the payoff if that goal is reached). Thus social learning approaches to motivation combine extrinsic and intrinsic motivational factors.

The scientific name for this combination of internal thoughts and how the environment is perceived is **expectancy X value theory.** According to this theory, people work hard and are motivated when they believe they have a reasonable chance of succeeding, and when the goal is personally meaningful to them (see Table 10.1). Jim Jenson used this approach when he praised and encouraged his students about their reading progress and tried to convince them that reading would bring them meaningful rewards.

HUMANISTIC THEORIES

The humanistic approach to understanding motivation is a reaction to the behaviorist and cognitive approaches. Humanists believe that motivation results from more than just external rewards and internal conceptualizations of one's ability and performance. As the term *humanistic* suggests, humanistic views emphasize a higher order incentive to achieve and excel that comes from within the person. For a humanist, everything that affects the person, including thoughts, feelings, and aspects of the environment, can create or affect motivation. Humanists have used varied terms to express different

TABLE 10.1 Using Expectancy X Value Theory to Enhance Student Motivation

Motivating the Student Who Expects to Succeed	Motivating the Student Who Expects to Fail
■ *When goal is valued:* High motivation and effort; student successful.	■ *When goal is valued:* Student fails to try despite wanting the goal—teacher must encourage and reward effort and incremental progress, stressing the value of the goal to the student.
■ *When goal is not valued:* Normally high motivation must be harnessed—teacher must choose new goal that is more valued and student will succeed; teacher should recognize and praise normally high motivation.	■ *When goal is not valued:* Student does not care—teacher must first select a new, more valued goal, and must then encourage incremental effort and progress toward this new goal.

aspects of the inner drive to excel. For example, Abraham Maslow (1970) believed that humans have an inborn need for **self-actualization,** or making the most of oneself. Carl Rogers (Rogers & Freiberg, 1994) termed the inner source of motivation the *actualizing tendency;* Edward Deci (1994) has described a similar force as the need for self-determination.

How does the humanistic approach work in the classroom? The humanistic approach emphasizes the "whole student": in other words, the *emotional* and *social* aspects of a student's life, in addition to the intellectual aspects that are the focus of most instruction. This approach assumes students are naturally motivated to learn, provided the educational experience is meaningful and the students view themselves as capable of learning. An aspect of this approach is the frequent emphasis on helping students develop self-esteem. The humanistic approach also stresses the importance of teachers acting in a supportive and caring manner, and relying more on explaining why things must be done a certain way instead of on doling out discipline. Jim Jenson used a humanistic approach when he worked on enhancing his students' self-esteem.

One study looked at eighth graders in a nontraditional (nongraded self-selection) school considered to be "a humanistic student-centered environment" (Matthews, 1991). This school attempted to influence the positive feelings and motives of students. Students worked in a relaxed atmosphere with small classes; their input influenced decision making and the general functioning of the school. Students in this humanistic school had higher intrinsic motivation than students in a more structured environment. A summary of the four different theories of motivation for teachers appears in Table 10.2.

THINKING ANALYTICALLY

Would a nontraditional school be better for every student (for example, a school in which no grades are given, or no formal, timed classes are held, or in which all work is project and group based)? Why or why not?

SUGGESTION: No. Students have widely varying needs: Some flourish in the structured, disciplined atmosphere of a traditional school environment; others succeed best in a less structured setting.

TABLE 10.2 **The Four Theories of Motivation: Incentives to Enhance Motivation**

Behavioral

Extrinsic reinforcers in the form of rewards or punishments:

> High grades/low grades; praise/criticism; free time/detention; awards/demerits.

Cognitive

Intrinsic reinforcers based on beliefs, attributions, and expectations:

> Understanding the purposes of schoolwork and homework; believing in one's ability to succeed; attributing success to hard work; expecting to do well as a function of effort invested.

Social Learning

A mix of extrinsic and intrinsic reinforcers based on expectations and the personal value of goals:

> Understanding how to set workable, effective goals that can be attained; understanding the likelihood of reaching a goal and the payoff once the goal is reached; knowing how to choose goals with payoffs that are personally meaningful.

Humanistic

Intrinsic reinforcers based on the human needs to achieve, excel, and self-actualize:

> A meaningful educational environment in which students are encouraged to see themselves as capable; development of self-esteem; teachers acting warm and supportive; explaining why things must be done a certain way—no rules for the sake of rules.

FOCUS ON: ACROSS-THE-CURRICULUM MOTIVATION

PEGGY GARWOOD: OAK GROVE SCHOOL, GREEN OAKS, ILLINOIS—GRADE 8, ALGEBRA

Peggy Garwood has been teaching eighth-grade algebra for twenty-three years. She strongly believes that it's important to teach across the curriculum by linking math projects with art, social studies, and other subjects. Here, she describes one particularly successful undertaking—a fund-raising quilting project that requires students not only to use their math and algebra skills, but also to acquire business and social understanding.

What is the quilting project?

Students in the eighth-grade math classes used their geometry skills to design several quilts. The quilts were then raffled off. Students sold the raffle tickets, and the money that was raised went to benefit a local soup kitchen. The quilt project has grown enormously over the five years that we've been doing it. The first year 38 students made one quilt, which was raffled for $2700. This year, 117 students designed three quilts. The raffle raised $7000.

How does this project teach students math and geometry?

Creating the quilts incorporates math and geometry skills. I begin the project by spending one class period explaining the art of quilting. I discuss its history and specific methods, while I show examples of quilts and point out math applications. In the same week, I teach concepts of geometric construction using a straight edge, compass, and protractor. Then each student is asked to design a seven-inch square quilt block using these techniques. Sometimes I give students guidelines they need to follow. For example, this year each design had to be symmetric to a line or a point. As the students are making their quilt designs, they have to be precise so that all the quilt blocks will fit together.

Raffling the quilts also helps build math skills. The students are in great competition with each other when they sell the raffle tickets—the class that sells the most tickets gets a bag of candy.

They are competitive even for that little bag of candy. This level of competition provides a highly motivational opportunity for students to learn the concept of unit pricing. Class sizes range from 12 to 23 students. This year, a larger class raised the most money from the raffle tickets. When I asked the other classes, "Should I take their jar of money and say they win?" the students replied, "No, it's not fair. They have more students in their class." I guided them as they figured out a fair criterion, based on the amount of money raised per student.

How do projects like the quilt motivate students?

These projects are motivating to students because of the broad range of subjects and interests that are addressed. Every student can find something to enjoy. Having something to look forward to makes coming to class more fun. Every year, there are students who say they have heard about the projects I do, and that they can hardly wait until they can be in my class.

How does this project encourage students' social and moral development?

Giving the money to the soup kitchen helps students develop socially and personally. Staff members at the soup kitchen have pointed out to students that, because of the support from the quilt project, the kitchen is able to take care of many of its needs. The students are proud that every penny of each raffle ticket goes to the kitchen. A sewing center donates the material; the school pays for printing the raffle tickets and a few supplies. One year, the school board offered to buy the quilt, but selling tickets not only offers the potential of making more money for the soup kitchen, it gives students additional opportunities to do a service for the community.

> Look for ways to relate your topic to students' everyday lives and to other subjects. Don't just stick to the book.

Students also get a personal opportunity to serve. When the students visited the kitchen, they met one man who had been going there for sixteen years. Many students at my school are wealthy; they were stunned by this man's story. Some of the money we raised for the soup kitchen helped him. The kids were proud of this and were motivated to help even more. They noticed that forks and spoons were needed and brought them to the soup kitchen. My students have become better citizens in the community.

How do students of varying abilities approach this project?

All students have to participate in this project. And each student approaches it differently. One or two students designed their quilt blocks on the computer. One student with cerebral palsy found the drawing difficult, but she designed a quilt block herself with only a little help on the physical work of drawing. One boy had information processing difficulties. He made five designs and none of them worked, but he persisted. When he finally caught on, he was very proud of his work.

What advice would you give to new teachers?

When I was a beginning teacher, everything was done strictly out of the book. Now, every quarter, I have projects that relate to other subjects. I help students relate math to science, art, and poetry. Our projects have included creating a geometry collage, constructing a dual dodecahedron, and using origami to construct a polyhedron. During almost every project, I see a student who didn't really like math become much more excited about it because he or she is interested in the connection between math and another subject.

Implications for Teaching

■ *Try behavioral motivators—rewards and punishments—when you need motivational techniques that work quickly.* Behavioral motivators are often helpful in day-to-day life in the classroom. However, remember that behavioral motivations, although they influence students' behavior, do so without creating a deeper understanding on the part of students.

■ *Focus on cognitive motivators for the long-term changes in the way students think.* Cognitive motivators, including beliefs in the values of work and in one's own abilities, can be harder for teachers to develop in students. But in the long run they tend to create more substantial and long-lasting changes.

■ *Combine behavioral and cognitive motivators to give students the benefits of each.* Effective teachers have at their disposal numerous types of tools that work in multiple ways and at different rates. These teachers routinely use different types of approaches to motivate students.

■ *Stress the meaningful lifetime rewards and positive feelings of self-actualization that result from hard work in the present.* As students show increased motivation and readiness to learn, model the valuable results of hard work by describing your own successes and the efforts that led up to them. Plan lessons based on well-known and respected people whose life stories show the ultimate value and rewards of hard work.

The Role of Arousal Level

Any attempt to explain what motivates students must consider the students' level of attentiveness to learning in general. Let us now turn to a discussion of the role of student arousal in creating and maintaining motivation.

Arousal is an individual's level of alertness, wakefulness, and activation (Anderson, 1990). It is a state of physical and psychological readiness for action provoked by the activity of the central nervous system, including the brain. Most people are familiar with the sensations of arousal—sitting in the dentist's waiting room, walking out on the high diving board, waiting to go on stage, and those last few minutes before an important standardized test—all these situations tend to create a state of arousal. Too much arousal is often associated with **anxiety,** a sense of nervousness, worry, and self-doubt. If you think about your own arousal tendencies, you will realize that each individual responds differently to different situations as a function of unique experiences, capabilities, and goals. For example, someone who does not particularly care about going to college may not experience much arousal in the moments before an entrance examination, but someone who is determined to get into a competitive college may be literally overwhelmed with anxiety.

 AROUSAL LEVEL AND PERFORMANCE

In the early part of the twentieth century, Yerkes and Dodson (1908) showed that very low arousal and very high arousal are both associated with poor performance. A moderate level of arousal is associated with the best performance. People generally also feel their best when their level of arousal is moderate (Berlyne, 1960). Expert teachers habitually use a moderate level of arousal to their students' advantage. They capture their students' interest and provoke them with intriguing questions and problems to solve. But expert teachers do not create a high anxiety situation for their students by overly stressing performance on tests, for example. That is, instead of saying, "Your whole grade depends on how well you perform in the next hour!" an expert teacher might say, "You have one hour to show what you have learned about mitosis and meiosis. I am interested in seeing how you think about the problems we discussed in class." Effective teachers also provide opportunities for doing additional work to help compensate for poor test grades, which are sometimes due simply to nervousness rather than a lack of knowledge.

In an attempt to preserve discipline in the classroom, beginning teachers sometimes create too high a state of arousal and anxiety, thus hindering learning. The converse, creating too little arousal, results in a classroom in which students find themselves doodling, daydreaming, or even drifting off to sleep. Probably all of us can remember teachers who made the mistake of creating too much arousal or too little arousal in their students. In general, effective teachers strike an effective balance by using a variety of methods to assess students.

 ## CREATING OPTIMAL AROUSAL LEVELS

The optimal level of arousal for performance varies with the task as well as with the individual. For simple tasks, moderately high arousal is better, whereas for difficult tasks, moderately low arousal is better (Broadhurst, 1957). If students need to complete those fairly repetitive and mindless tasks that are sometimes necessary in the classroom, a higher level of arousal may be needed to create enough motivation. When students complete complex tasks, however, lower levels of arousal help them avoid the anxiety that may be associated with poor performance (see Table 10.3 on page 360). Students themselves also differ in terms of their optimal arousal level. Some students work well under deadlines and flourish when a lot is expected of them. Other students work best when there are few demanding standards; then they feel no anxiety and are able to focus on

THINKING PRACTICALLY

What techniques can students use to keep from becoming overly aroused before important tests?

SUGGESTION: They can focus on past successes, get enough rest the night before, eat a nutritious breakfast and lunch the day of the test, practice deep breathing, and remember there will be other opportunities if this test does not go well.

Study habits vary, especially among older students. On the left, a junior high school student studies quietly on the living room sofa, while on the right, another junior high school student does his homework as he watches television and snacks. (Myrleen Cate, PhotoEdit; Spencer Grant, Stock Boston)

TABLE 10.3   Helping Students Cope with Test Anxiety

Coping with Emotional Problems

- Role-play stressful pretest situations with the students. Have one student assume the teacher's role and give advice to an anxiety-ridden student played by the teacher.

- Role-play a positive self-image and a positive, confident attitude toward tests with the students. Emphasize the following attitudes:

  - Think about the test as an opportunity both to show what you know and to learn something about yourself.

  - Tell yourself, "I can and will perform well on this test." See yourself in control of your test performance.

  - Remember that no test is perfect. Some, for example, assess only a single ability. Simply do your best with the test before you.

- Acknowledge the expertise of the skillful test takers in your class by having them discuss and demonstrate what they do to stay calm and clear-headed in a testing situation. (If necessary, add to their discussion the techniques of focusing, relaxing, and positive thinking.)

Coping with Physical Problems
(of the "I was too hungry/tired to concentrate" variety)

- Tell students that, on the night before the test, they should eat and sleep as they normally do: They should get their usual amount of sleep, relaxation, exercise, and food.

- If remembering to do this is a problem, suggest that students use the buddy system: Have a friend call and remind them about bedtime, or wake them up in time for breakfast.

Coping with Intellectual Problems (not understanding the questions, forgetting information, getting stumped)

- Tell students to ask questions (another role-playing opportunity here).

- Suggest that students write immediately on the edge of their paper any facts/formulas they might forget.

- Suggest skipping hard questions (marking them so they will know to come back).

Coping with Situational Problems
(running out of time, not having notes or pencils)

- Tell students to check the time limit at the beginning and plan how much time to allot to each part.

- Suggest that students pack their book bags the night before.

learning instead of on getting high grades. For the average student, however, a moderate level of arousal is generally best.

What creates a moderate and effective level of arousal in students? One cause we are all familiar with is a student's curiosity. Students may wonder, "How does that work? Who invented that? Where does this lead? Can I learn how to do that?" Pique curiosity by asking students leading questions and by encouraging students to ask themselves these same questions when studying at home. Often, the right questions can raise arousal to an optimal level in which students are primed to learn and to pay attention, and are driven by the need to understand. Some students are naturally curious, perhaps because their home environments foster a curious, questioning perspective as they are growing up. Other students may have been punished for being curious in the past by adults who complained, "You ask too many questions!" For these students, who can be recognized by their timidity and nervousness during attempts at questioning, expert teachers extend a supportive welcome to ask more questions. To reach these students, respond to questions positively and listen fully to everything the students say.

What makes students curious about some things but not others? People tend to be curious about things that are moderately novel to them and are moderately complex

THINKING CREATIVELY

How can a teacher reduce test anxiety while simultaneously increasing students' desire to perform well on tests?

SUGGESTION: Give more frequent, smaller, less formal tests; on occasion allow students to retake tests if they score poorly; design tests that give students multiple ways to show what they know; recognize effort as well as achievement.

(Heyduk & Bahrick, 1977; Mark, 1998). If something is totally familiar to students, they often ignore it; and if something is totally novel or very complex, the students have no basis for understanding it. Something novel but within students' realm of understanding creates in them the curiosity to explore it.

Historically, some teachers and schools have viewed curiosity as disruptive. These schools have emphasized heavy-handed discipline under the assumption that learning is very serious business and that students must be kept under tight control. However, overemphasis on discipline can be shortsighted if it produces too high an arousal level. One study compared different versions of the same educational activity for third to fifth graders, identical in instructional content but different in motivational appeal. The results indicated that, at this level, making learning fun increased both learning and retention and subsequent interest in the subject matter (Lepper & Cordova, 1992). Thus neither too little nor too much stress on students is desirable; both conditions create nonoptimal arousal levels.

Implications for Teaching

■ *Work to create optimal arousal.* Underaroused and overaroused students perform below their ability level on assignments and tests. It takes practice and patience to develop a set of teaching techniques that creates optimal arousal. Experienced teachers can be an excellent source of ideas.

■ *Create optimal arousal levels in students by piquing their curiosity and getting them interested in learning.* Overly stressing performance on tests can put a damper on learning. Too much or too little arousal hinders student learning and test performance; aim to strike a balance that helps students show what they know.

■ *Learn what works best for each student.* Individual students vary in their optimal levels of arousal; in addition, a student often has a different optimal level for each subject. It takes time to learn your students' arousal problems. Meanwhile, aim for moderate levels of arousal; later, you can tailor individual comments and interactions to students' specific needs.

The Role of Student Goals

Once you prepare students to pay attention and learn by helping them develop an optimal level of arousal, you must proceed to the next step in channeling and maintaining student motivation: the effective use of goals. A *goal* is something an individual is working to accomplish. Setting effective goals can make the difference between a student who succeeds and one who falls short. Those students who persist in an activity often pursue a self-selected goal, whereas those who quit rarely have in mind any clear, desired goals for the activity.

WHY AND HOW GOALS ENHANCE MOTIVATION

Why are goals so effective as motivators of performance? According to Locke and Latham, there are four main reasons (1990):

1. *Goals help focus attention.* We pay more attention to tasks if we have clearly defined goals in executing them.

2. *Goals help mobilize resources.* They give us a sense of what we need to do to get where we want to be.

3. *Goals facilitate persistence.* If we know we want to read one extra book a week over and above our school requirements, keeping this goal in mind will constantly remind us of where we are versus where we want to be.

4. *Goals facilitate accomplishment.* Having goals helps us define and enact specific steps to reach the goals. Goals motivate us to keep on trying to succeed; if we find our first plan is not working, we can always create a second or third plan to help us achieve our goals.

Along with goals come *plans,* or strategies for getting from where we are to where we want to be (Miller, Galanter, & Pribram, 1960, 1986). Goals can help motivate behavior only if they are accompanied by one or more plans for reaching the goals. For example, if your goal is to become principal of your school, your first step should be to formulate a plan for achieving that goal. Set a series of subgoals and then calculate the differences between where you are and where you want to go. You can then take action to reach each of the subgoals, working within the broader scheme of reaching the final goal. A first step might consist of working over the summer for the state department of education to meet the people who control educational resources. A next step might be competing for a major teaching award to create name recognition and awareness of your accomplishments. A later step might consist of serving on several influential committees so you are seen as a person with educational and political strivings.

THINKING PRACTICALLY

Devise a plan for increasing the motivation of an underachieving student to work hard in school—to master academic tasks, study information, do homework, and so on. Indicate which of the theories of motivation are guiding your plan.

SUGGESTION: Consider a situation in which the student comes from an unsupportive or abusive home. The teacher can work with the student, enhancing her belief in herself, while providing positive feedback and reinforcement for efforts in the right direction. Guided by the humanistic theory of motivation, the teacher might also give hints on how to master academic tasks.

Having unrealistically high goals can be self-defeating for students. For example, some students are perfection oriented and consequently never attain their goals of doing perfect work. They feel worse than if they had never tried to do perfect work in the first place. Even when their grade is an A minus, they believe they have failed. Realistic and attainable goals are the answer, and expert teachers help students define and focus on realistic goals in their daily work. Based on their experiences with many students, these teachers help students define their goals in terms of what they can reasonably expect to accomplish with hard work and perseverance in the time allotted.

What about another type of goal—deadlines? Are deadlines effective? Researchers have studied the effects of externally imposed deadlines on students' task performance and subsequent interest in the task (Amabile, DeJong, & Lepper, 1976). Students given the deadline were less interested in the task than those not given a deadline. Thus expert teachers remember not to use deadlines all the time, with the goal of increasing students' interest in their tasks and students' intrinsic motivation.

Expert teachers know the value of the right types of goals. These teachers make tasks a slight stretch for students—neither too easy, nor too hard. Researchers since the early 1970s have known (e.g., Atkinson, 1972) that many people prefer tackling tasks on which they have about a 50–50 chance of succeeding. In other words, if you give individuals a choice of standing close to a target they are aiming at, they will prefer to stand at the point where they have a 50–50 chance of hitting the target. However, students with low **achievement motivation,** a drive to excel, will stand very close to the target because of a fear of failure. Another important point to bear in mind is that goals will not motivate students unless they are accompanied by clear feedback. If a child doesn't know how close she is to achieving a goal, she will not know when to work harder.

WHAT MAKES GOALS EFFECTIVE?

A study by Meece, Blumenfeld, and Hoyle (1988) examined whether students used high-effort or effort-minimizing strategies while completing science activities. The researchers found that students who emphasized **task-mastery goals,** which stress working to understand and succeed at a task, reported more active engagement in their tasks than students who did not emphasize task-mastery goals. In contrast, students motivated by gaining social recognition, pleasing the teacher, or avoiding work reported a lower level of engagement. Task-mastery goals helped focus the students' behaviors in a positive way.

Of course, students can have different types of goals: subgoals or portions of the overall task (e.g., breaking the task into ten steps), ultimate goals (e.g., the completion of the entire task), and time-oriented goals (e.g., spending three hours studying). Which types of goals are more effective? Morgan (1985) compared three different types of self-monitoring of private study to investigate the effects of these types of studying on academic performance and intrinsic motivation. **Self-monitoring** refers to students keeping track of their own progress. The participants were college students, assigned to four different study conditions: self-monitor subgoal condition—keeping track of their progress on each step in completing the task; self-monitor time-on-study condition—keeping track of time spent studying; self-monitor distal-goal condition—keeping track of whether they had achieved the overall goal; and control—studying the way they normally would.

In end-of-year exams, students who used self-monitored subgoals, or keeping track of their progress on each step in completing the task, outperformed students who used self-monitoring of either time spent studying or distal goals, such as doing well in the entire course. Students who self-monitored the duration of their study time actually spent longer studying than did control students, who did nothing special, but these self-monitors did not score better on exams. Besides the beneficial effects on learning, subgoal self-monitoring increased intrinsic interest in the course. Thus make clear for your students how to use self-monitoring of progress toward subgoals during studying, perhaps by talking students through your own way of studying with subgoals. Also, encourage and reward students who use this approach.

How about the effect of the overall goals students are aiming for in their learning? Benware and Deci (1984) studied whether learning with an active orientation would be more intrinsically motivating than learning with a passive orientation. They defined an active orientation as learning material with the expectation of teaching it to another student, and a passive orientation as learning with the expectation of being tested. For the college students in this study, learning in order to teach was more intrinsically motivating. In addition, students who learned with the goal of teaching what they learned had higher conceptual learning scores and perceived themselves as more engaged. However, the rote learning scores of students with active and passive orientations were equal.

THINKING ANALYTICALLY

Think of an assignment you must complete. Break the assignment down into a minimum of eight subgoals. Track your progress as you complete the assignment.

SUGGESTION: Perhaps you have a term paper due in your educational psychology course. Your subgoals can be as follows: (1) Brainstorm various topics, (2) Choose a topic and discuss with the teacher, (3) Gather sources and resources, (4) Review information and compose an outline, (5) Write the first draft, (6) Seek comments and feedback from others on the first draft, (7) Research areas that need work and add or correct material, and (8) Write the polished final draft.

THE IMPORTANCE OF TEACHER FEEDBACK AND TEACHER EXPECTATIONS

Think of how you feel when you read your teacher's feedback on your term paper. Feedback is of central importance in developing expert learners, because it is the vehicle through which students see themselves as others see them and learn to improve. What is the effect on students' motivation of receiving versus not receiving feedback? Butler and Nisan (1986) showed that intrinsic motivation was maintained after getting a nonthreatening, task-related evaluation. However, intrinsic motivation was undermined after repeatedly failing to receive feedback.

Teachers' expectations of students, and the feedback based on these expectations, are extremely important in creating or dampening student enthusiasm. Expert teachers recognize the importance of their own expectations in molding their reactions to students. The subject of how teachers' expectations affect students' motivation has been the focus of research dating back to a classic study by Rosenthal and Jacobson (1968). This study showed that student performance was influenced by teachers' expectations of students' ability levels, even when the information that teachers relied on to make their judgments was randomly generated by the researchers. In other words, teachers were told that some students were likely to blossom during the year, and these students did in fact do better. But the students named as likely to blossom were chosen at random. The effect of teachers' expectations on student performance was called the *Pygmalion effect.* Thus, the term Pygmalion effect refers to the growth in accomplishments that can result when a teacher believes in and encourages a student. The name comes from the ancient mythological King Pygmalion, who created a statue and then brought it to life.

Although this research has been criticized (e.g., Elashoff & Snow, 1971; Snow, 1995) and the findings have not always been replicated (e.g., Goldenberg, 1992), it is generally agreed that the Pygmalion effect does happen (Harris & Rosenthal, 1985; Rosenthal, 1995; Smith, Jussim, & Eccles, 1999; Smith, Jussim, Eccles, VanNoy, Madon, & Palumbo, 1998). The Pygmalion effect–inspired research has shown that teachers generally perceive their expectations of students to have been confirmed (Brophy, 1983, 1985a; Brophy & Good, 1974; Crano & Mellon, 1978; Humphreys & Stubbs, 1977; Rist, 1970; Williams, 1976). Other research has shown that inaccurate teacher expectations (given to teachers by researchers) also influence teacher behavior and student performance (Harris & Rosenthal, 1985; Jussim, 1991a, 1991b; Raudenbush, 1984). The Pygmalion effect has also been demonstrated for business managers and people in the military (McNatt, 2000).

THINKING PRACTICALLY

Have you ever had a teacher who had very high expectations of your ability? How did you perform in the class? How did the teacher convey these high expectations?

SUGGESTION: A supportive teacher who conveys high expectations along with suggestions for how the student can actualize them will likely be rewarded with good student performance, including yours.

In general, the lesson from this research is that high teacher expectations create better student performance, or at least, the perception of better performance. When teachers are told that certain students are very smart, these students tend to perform better—or, even if the students do not actually perform better, the teachers *think* they perform better. Positive teacher expectations and feedback can be highly motivating to a student. Expert teachers capitalize on this fact when they provide students with positive feedback whenever possible. Even if students make errors, expert teachers are able to find something to praise while at the same time showing students how to improve. Research has shown that students praised for effort and for what they succeed at doing perform better overall than students not praised in this way (Lepper, 1988). Realize also that low expectations may hurt student performance.

Implications for Teaching

- **Emphasize student goals of mastering tasks and completing meaningful learning.** Avoid or downplay goals of performing at specific levels or achieving specific scores. Focus on the essence of learning and the joy it brings, not on comparing one student with others.

- **Maintain positive expectations of all students.** Don't let preconceived notions about students' capabilities stop you from expecting their best efforts. Many students will perform better than you might have expected if held to a high standard.

- **Teach students to monitor and control their own rates of progress.** This is truly a life skill that will provide continual rewards in any endeavor.

The Role of Student Needs

Students' goals are only a part of what motivates students. Also important as controllers of and contributors to motivation are students' needs. Students have many and varied needs that can be used by expert teachers as motivators. Expert teachers understand the differing types of student needs so they can appeal to needs that will effectively motivate each student. Student needs include the need for power, the need for affiliation, and the need to achieve.

People who rank high in the **need for power** seek to control others. They try to make the world conform to their own image of what it should be. In groups, they want to be recognized (Winter, 1973). They are also concerned with their visibility among the general public (McClelland & Teague, 1975). Teachers can motivate students with this need by making them leaders of projects (as long as the students are reasonably competent), and by giving them public recognition.

People who rank high in the **need for achievement** have a strong drive to excel and succeed. The need for achievement has been studied extensively by David McClelland (1985) and his associates. People who rank high in the need for achievement, such as successful entrepreneurs, seek out moderately challenging tasks, persist at them, and are especially likely to pursue success at their occupations. Why do these people seek out tasks that are moderately challenging? Because in these tasks the people are likely both to succeed and to extend themselves. They do not pursue overly challenging tasks they have no hope of accomplishing, nor are they attracted to simple tasks that pose no challenge.

People who rank high in the **need for affiliation** like to form close connections with other people and be members of groups. They avoid arguments (Exline, 1962) as well as competitive games (Terhune, 1968). They also tend to become anxious when they feel they are being evaluated (Byrne, 1961). Expert teachers who wish to motivate students with a need for affiliation are attentive to creating a nurturing environment that is neither competitive nor evaluative. These environments might stress creative activities that are ungraded and group activities that are ungraded in which working together is encouraged.

 ## MASLOW'S HIERARCHY OF NEEDS

The needs for power, affiliation, and achievement all fit into the theory of motivation proposed by the humanist Abraham Maslow (1970). Maslow believed human needs form a kind of hierarchy. Individuals first need to satisfy needs at lower levels of the hierarchy before they seek satisfaction of higher level needs. Levels 1 through 4 refer to deficiency needs, and levels 5 through 7 to growth needs. Maslow's first level includes basic biological needs such as for food, water, and oxygen, which are necessary for continued survival. In fact, many homeless people face the challenge of getting these needs met every day. In some schools, there are students who also face these needs—students who do not have adequate nutrition, for example. Until their need for food is satisfied, such students may have a very difficult time learning in school.

Maslow's second level addresses needs for safety and security, in other words, for shelter, protection, and emotional safety. Safe schools provide such a secure environment for students, and Maslow's hierarchy demonstrates why schools must be free of violence. The third level is the need to belong, to feel that other people love and care about us and to be a part of a meaningful group. The importance of this need is illustrated by the bond between parents and their children, and also by the bond between members of peer groups at school and by the relationships that develop between expert teachers and their students. The fourth level is the need for self-esteem—to feel worthwhile as a person. Students gain self-esteem from successfully performing activities that are meaningful to them, and particularly from meeting challenges.

Levels 5 through 7 are growth needs. The fifth level is the need to know and understand; this need reflects the fact that ignorance and lack of insight into the world around us can be a debilitating condition, and that people generally seek to understand their surroundings and themselves. The sixth level represents aesthetic needs—the need for beauty and balance in the physical, intellectual, emotional, and spiritual world we occupy. The highest level, level 7, is the need for self-actualization, the need to fulfill our potential as human beings. We might consider athletes who compete in the Olympics as having

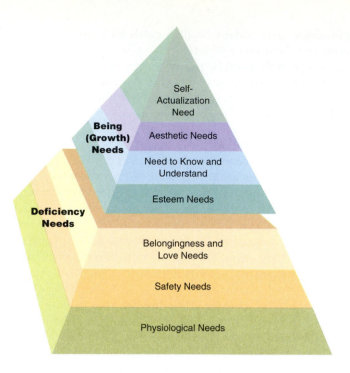

FIGURE 10.1

Maslow's Hierarchy of Needs

Source: Figure "Hierarchy of Needs" from *Motivation and Personality* by Abraham H. Maslow. Copyright © 1987 by Pearson Education. Reprinted by permission.

THINKING CREATIVELY

Propose an addition or modification to Maslow's hierarchy and defend your proposed change.

SUGGESTION: The need for independence and self-reliance might be added between levels 4 and 5, stressing the importance of belief in one's ability to get things done.

achieved their self-actualized athletic potential, and top-notch brain surgeons, astronauts, and Nobel-Prize-winning scientists as having achieved their self-actualized intellectual potential. For other people, achieving this level might be measured in different ways—for example, by running a soup kitchen that successfully feeds and shelters homeless people in the winter. Figure 10.1 illustrates the seven levels of Maslow's hierarchy of needs.

The level that a student occupies in Maslow's hierarchy gives teachers a clue about the motives that will work for the student. For example, if the student is at the most basic step (need for food and water), opportunities to alleviate hunger and thirst will motivate the student. If the student has met that need and has entered Maslow's next step (the need for safety), behaviors that provide opportunities for shelter and security will motivate the student. Expert teachers sense when a student is fixated at the third level, the need for love and affection, and use their ability to provide emotional warmth as a motivator for the student. It is only when a student has satisfied these three basic needs (food, safety, and affection) that he or she will crave respect from classmates and begin to develop a need for self-esteem. Maslow believed that self-actualization is the highest step in this motivational framework, but that few or no individuals ever truly reach it. Jim Jenson, the teacher in the chapter-opening vignette, worked in a poor, inner-city school; he had to ensure that his students had their basic needs met before he could expect them to make progress in reading.

 ## ACHIEVEMENT MOTIVATION

How do people with a high need for achievement motivate themselves? Researchers have found that people high in the need for achievement privately set goals for themselves (McClelland & Watson, 1973; see also Ablard & Lipschultz, 1998). Because these goals tend to be of intermediate difficulty, the people are likely to get a sense of personal accomplishment. The researchers also found that people high in need for *power* seek to stand out publicly, and do so (for example) by taking more extreme risks. Conversely, those high in need for *affiliation* try to avoid public competition by taking low risks.

Achievement motivation tends to be domain specific. Some students may be highly motivated to achieve at athletics, but not at academics. Other students reject school psychologically, and may join peer groups or even gangs in which school achievement is seen as undesirable. These students may have a high need to achieve, but the need may be directed toward nonschool-relevant goals, and sometimes toward goals that damage society, such as gang-related criminal behaviors.

How do students react to teachers' demands for achievement (see Alderman, 1999, for an overview)? Consider the situation in which a teacher knows a particular student is capable of doing far better work than she is currently doing. However, the student herself may not believe in her own competence. The teacher's demand for achievement may go unmet, not because the student is incapable, but because she is unaware of her capabilities. The perception of reality, rather than reality per se, is the more powerful predictor of how people, especially children, react to demands for achievement (Phillips, 1984). Unfortunately, girls—particularly as they grow older—often perceive their competence to be lower than boys' perceptions of their own competence. The result can be lesser expectations for achievement on the part of girls—*and, thus, lesser achievement* (Phillips & Zimmerman, 1990). This effect emerges as early as kindergarten (Frey & Ruble, 1987).

The motivation to achieve appears to be present in every culture that has been studied (Markus & Kitayama, 1991). The goal of one reasonably successful project in India was to raise the achievement motivation of Indian businesspeople and workers in their companies in order to help these people improve their lives. The employees attended an intense series of seminars designed to get them to think, talk, and act like achievement-oriented businesspeople (McClelland & Winter, 1969). The fact that the need to achieve could be strengthened through training is relevant to teachers. Expert teachers often use similar techniques to get their students to "think big" about their potential and their future lives. These teachers stop students from talking in a nonachievement-oriented manner and model achievement-oriented behaviors for their students, such as how to use positive self-talk and possibility thinking to motivate themselves. For example, they say aloud, "I wasn't sure how to solve this problem, and I felt stumped. But then I thought, 'You can do it! Think of the times you have been successful in the past. Brainstorm five ways to solve the problem and work from there ...'"

In the discussion of group differences in Chapter 6, we noted that achievement patterns vary for different ethnic and cultural groups. One study of achievement motivation in China showed that Chinese parents place great emphasis on achievement, but their focus is different from that of American parents (Ho, 1986). Whereas American children are motivated to achieve in order to become independent, Chinese children are motivated to please the family and community. Expert teachers remind themselves frequently that what motivates one child may be different from what motivates another child.

 SELF-DETERMINATION AND CONTROL

In everyday activities, people behave to some degree as a function of intrinsic motivation. People seek to be active, to observe and explore their surroundings, to manipulate aspects of and objects in their environments, and to gain mastery over their environments (White, 1959). People also seek **self-determination,** the ability to make things happen, to have control of oneself and one's environment. People prefer self-determination over determination by outside forces. Most people are unhappy when they feel controlled, whether by another person or by outside events. In short, we are motivated to be in charge of our own destiny.

Edward Deci and his colleagues (Deci, 1996; Deci, Vallerand, Pelletier, & Ryan, 1991) have proposed a theory of self-determination. According to this theory, humans need to feel competent, related, and autonomous. Deci suggests that intrinsically motivated activities satisfy both people's need for competence and need for autonomy. In contrast, many extrinsically motivated activities can undermine people's sense of autonomy because they attribute the control of their behavior to sources outside themselves, rather than to internal ones.

Deci and his colleagues found that students with self-determined motivation are more likely to stay in school, behave well, show conceptual understanding, and be well adjusted. Motivation is facilitated by *competence,* which is fostered by facing optimal challenges and receiving valuable performance feedback, and by *relatedness,* which is fostered by parental involvement and peer acceptance. The degree to which teachers encourage *autonomy* as opposed to retaining tight control also affects student motivation.

Implications for Teaching

- ■ *Help students with a need for power and achievement by giving them leadership opportunities and presenting them with challenges.* When possible, work with and not against student dispositions. Guide students to direct their natural dispositions toward meaningful, positive accomplishments.

- ■ *Help students with a need for affiliation by being nurturing and providing constructive criticism in a positive environment.* Be aware that these students may not perform well in an environment that stresses competitive games, argumentation, or judgments of their performance. Fulfill students' needs in order to free them to learn at their capacity and best demonstrate their knowledge.

- ■ *Motivate students to develop the need for self-determination by allowing them to earn autonomy.* Give students control over assignment topics and tasks whenever possible. Teach by example—share your own experiences about how you developed the need for self-determination and describe its positive effects in your life.

- ■ *Ensure that students' basic needs for food, shelter, and security are being met before challenging them to achieve at higher levels.* Enlist the support of the school administration and social agencies if necessary. Do not waste your own and the students' time by challenging them to achieve if their basic needs have not been met.

The Role of Student Attributions and Beliefs

Students' goals and needs intimately affect their motivation levels, but also important in the development and maintenance of motivation are students' *beliefs* about their own and others' behaviors. Students' motivation is often affected by how the students explain their own successes and failures, as well as those of their peers. The ways students understand the workings of the school environment also impact their motivation. Thus two important types of student understanding are *attributions* and *beliefs*.

ATTRIBUTION THEORY

An **attribution** is an explanation pointing to the cause of a particular behavior. For example, for Tomás to explain his newfound fondness for geometry, he might make an attribution regarding his perceptions of himself, telling himself that he is the type of person who likes geometry. Attribution theories clarify how people explain not only their own behavior, but also the behavior of others. People make attributions so they can

Success and Failure Viewed as Stable Traits

| | Success | | Failure | |
	Controllable	Uncontrollable	Controllable	Uncontrollable
Internal	"I am smart because I always study."	"I am smart and succeed no matter what I do."	"I never try."	"I am stupid."
External	"The teacher likes me."	"I got the easy version of the test."	"The teacher hates me."	"The cutoff grade for passing was too high."

Success and Failure Viewed as Unstable Traits

| | Success | | Failure | |
	Controllable	Uncontrollable	Controllable	Uncontrollable
Internal	"I worked really hard this time."	"Sometimes I am on, and sometimes I am not."	"I did not study enough."	"I got sick and could not think straight."
External	"I got the teacher a birthday card last week."	"I was really lucky."	"My parents did not quiz me at home."	"I had awful luck."

FIGURE 10.2

How Students Explain Success and Failure

Source: Figure "How Students Explain Success and Failure" from *Human Motivation: Metaphors, Theories, and Research* by B. Weiner. Copyright © 1992 by B. Weiner. Reprinted by permission of Sage Publications, Inc.

understand their social world and answer questions such as, "Why did I act that way?" and "Why did she do that?"

Fritz Heider (1958), who developed attribution theory, pointed out that people make two basic kinds of attributions. The first kind are personal, or **dispositional attributions,** explanations of behavior based on internal characteristics in a person—"My nervousness when taking tests and my poor memory made me fail." The second kind are **situational attributions,** caused by external factors such as settings, events, or other people—"The overcrowded, hot room and the noisy play rehearsal next door made me fail."

Bernard Weiner (1982, 1985) has shown that people use a variety of sources of information to explain the causes of their behavior in achievement-related contexts. The most important causes of success and failure are people's perceptions of their ability and effort. Other salient factors are the home environment and the teacher. Thus, in Weiner's theory of motivation and emotion, how people explain their behavior is of central importance (see Figure 10.2).

BELIEFS ABOUT ABILITY AND SELF-EFFICACY

The difference between those students who achieve in school and those who do not is due to more than the ability levels of the students. It is also related to students' perceptions of their ability (Dweck, 1983, 1999). Students who believe they are not capable but who have high ability generally perform less well than their ability would predict. Students who believe they are very capable often perform better than their ability would predict. Dweck's research on entity versus incremental views of intelligence is relevant to this point (see Chapter 1). Those who subscribe to the **entity view of intelligence** believe they are born with a fixed amount of intelligence that cannot be increased, whereas those who subscribe to the **incremental view of intelligence** believe they are born with a certain amount of intelligence that can be increased.

The entity view that "what you are born with is what you have got" contrasts with the incremental view of more successful students, who believe that improvement comes from effort and hard work. Students who see the value of effort and hard work at achieving their goals are more likely to be

THINKING CREATIVELY

Describe three ways a teacher could encourage a student to hold an incremental as opposed to an entity view of intelligence.

SUGGESTION: Provide examples of students and famous people who started out as failures and later succeeded. Reward effort and a positive attitude. Praise students who improve over past performance and encourage them to share their hints for success with other students.

motivated and to push themselves to excel—and thus to possess an internal rather than external locus of control, as we discussed earlier in this chapter. Expert teachers can help students develop an incremental view of their abilities and an "effort attitude" by stressing that improvement comes from effort and that everyone has the ability to improve through hard work. Expert teachers avoid making statements about how some children are simply born smarter or more talented; instead, they stress the role of hard work in becoming expert learners. Some schools may inadvertently encourage an entity view of intelligence by labeling certain children as gifted or outstanding students without stressing that they have worked harder than have lower achieving students.

■ **HOW STUDENTS RESPOND TO CHALLENGES** Researchers have uncovered two different response patterns by students working on very challenging tasks (Dweck, 1998; Dweck & Leggett, 1988; Nicholls, 1984). What happens to a child when he or she is no longer able to complete a task and fails? Some students, termed *helpless*, tend to give up easily or to show poor performance when confronting difficult problems. These helpless students seem not even to be trying at the level their ability would predict. Other students, called *mastery oriented*, keep trying just as hard or even harder when problems become more difficult. Helpless students often blame low ability for their poor performance; mastery-oriented students blame their poor performance on lack of effort and maintain these expectations for future success.

The researchers found that helpless and mastery-oriented students did not differ in ability. What separated these students was their attitude about ability and achievement (Dweck & Leggett, 1988; Nicholls, 1984). Helpless students tend to have **performance goals,** which are related to the judgments others make of their performance: They want to look smart, earn positive teacher comments, and avoid negative judgments of their ability. Mastery-oriented children have **learning goals**—they want to improve their skills and learn new things. These two types of students have very differing views of the nature of ability (see Table 10.4). Helpless students hold an entity view of intelligence, in which intelligence is seen as a fixed quantity that each of us is born with. Mastery-oriented students hold an incremental view of intelligence, which suggests that intelligence can be improved through effort.

The helpless view has been observed in children as young as 4 years old (Heyman, Dweck, & Cain, 1992). When children from the two groups are highly confident about their abilities, they may reach similar levels of achievement. However, when children lack confidence in their abilities, if they also see intelligence as something fixed rather than something that can be developed, they give up easily and fail, believing themselves capable of no more. This research carries an important lesson for expert teachers: Too much

TABLE 10.4 Recognizing Students with Learning Versus Performance Goals

Students with Learning Goals	Students with Performance Goals
■ Define success in terms of improvement and progress.	■ Define success in terms of recognition, high grades, and perfect scores.
■ Place intrinsic value on effort, hard work, challenges, and meaningful learning.	■ Place intrinsic value on outperforming others and consistently scoring highly.
■ View errors as a normal part of the learning process.	■ View errors as unacceptable and embarrassing.
■ Are oriented toward the process of learning.	■ Are oriented toward the product of learning.
■ Enjoy the act of learning something new.	■ Enjoy the act of performing well in comparison to others.
■ Measure their success against their own past performance.	■ Measure their success against others' performance.

emphasis on performance goals (such as praise, grades, and high scores) can undermine students' focus on mastery-oriented goals (such as learning new things and improving themselves) (see Table 10.4). The message of this research has also been shown to apply to college students (Strange, 1997), for whom an incremental view of intelligence is associated with mastery-oriented achievement attitudes and behaviors.

■**KEEPING STUDENTS FOCUSED ON LEARNING GOALS** Expert teachers must maintain a focus on the love of learning and skill building for their own sake, especially as children get older, so as not to allow children to become overly fixated on performance goals at the expense of learning goals. If a teacher stresses performance and grades, students will learn their lessons to please the teacher, not because the lessons hold students' interest. As these students grow older and move up through the grades, they will encounter more complex material; unless they are able to enjoy learning for its own sake they will become frustrated with the new experiences of challenges (Henderson & Dweck, 1990). Instead of seeking challenges and the learning they offer, they will avoid challenges to avoid failure.

In a class such as Jim Jenson's, you would focus on helping students adopt learning goals that represent meaningful mastery of material, rather than performance goals that will be undermined in this case by the students' beliefs that they cannot accomplish meaningful tasks. You can encourage learning goals by emphasizing meaningful understanding rather than by simply working through 20 sample problems, for example. Remember that teachers who are themselves intrinsically motivated are better at getting students to seek the intrinsic rewards of learning (Csikszentmihalyi, 1997).

How does receiving instruction affect students' motivation? One study answered this question by having students play a computer game (Sansone, Sachau, & Weir, 1989). The experimenters varied whether students received performance feedback. The game also gave students instruction on how to perform better. The study showed that receiving instruction actually lowered motivation, but only when no performance feedback was provided. When feedback was given, instruction did not decrease motivation; in this case, students remained interested and motivated. The lesson for the expert teacher is that *instruction must be coupled with meaningful feedback on performance*. In another study, the experimenters changed how meaningful the context was by describing the activity's goals as either skill related or fantasy related. Instruction decreased interest in the fantasy-emphasis context but increased interest in the skill-emphasis context. Thus, when instruction matched perceived goals, students experienced greater positive affect while performing the task.

■**PERCEPTIONS OF ABILITY AS INFLUENCES ON ACHIEVEMENT** As an example of the role of perceptions of ability in subsequent achievement, consider girls' and boys' *Scholastic Assessment Test (SAT)* math scores as a function of the students' attitudes about their competence in math. Girls and boys tend to have different perceptions about their abilities, with girls believing they are less capable and boys believing they are more capable. Research has shown that students who believe they are quite capable do better than predicted by their ability level, but students who believe they are not capable do less well than predicted by their ability level. In general, children with negative thoughts about their ability become distracted from learning, lose track of the details of their tasks, and sometimes become immobilized from further learning (Brown, Bransford, Ferrara, & Campione, 1983). Thus these children wind up getting less and less practice in the areas in which they need practice the most.

A program of research by Claude Steele (1995) has also looked at the issue of students' beliefs about their own competence. This research has focused on minority students' beliefs about their general academic competence, and female students' beliefs about their competence in mathematics. Steele has attempted to show that students' negative beliefs lower their performance. Before giving a tough math test to a group of boys and girls, he had the test taker tell one-half of the students that girls and boys perform equivalently on the test. The other half of the test-takers were given no information related to gender. Steele showed that girls' performance was substantially higher on the same test when they were told beforehand that girls perform the same as boys, compared to when girls were given no information about gender-related performance.

Steele explains the jump in girls' performance by saying that girls hold negative stereotypes about their mathematical ability. These stereotypes depress girls' performance on difficult math tests (only performance on difficult tests was assessed). But when girls are told that past research has shown that on the particular test they are taking, girls perform the same as boys, then girls do not suffer from their negative stereotype, and their performance shoots up (Steele, 1995). In this situation, Steele believes that because the girls are told that girls do as well as boys, they are not hindered by their negative stereotypes. Steele labels this phenomenon *stereotype threat.*

In one of his other studies on stereotype threat, Black and White students were given intellectual tests under two conditions: Diagnostic, in which they were told "This test is a genuine test of your verbal abilities and limitations . . . and will help us in an analysis of your verbal ability"; and Not Diagnostic, in which they were told "This study is designed to better understand the psychological factors involved in solving verbal problems . . . Try hard even though we will not be evaluating your ability." Results showed that with Scholastic Aptitude Test differences statistically controlled, Black subjects performed worse than White subjects when the test was presented as a measure of their ability, but improved dramatically, matching the performance of Whites, when the test was presented as less reflective of ability. Steele believes that when taking an intellectual test, Black students risk confirming as self-characteristic a negative stereotype of low intelligence. This vulnerability interferes with performance on tests because it causes anxiety, diverts attention to other concerns, and produces overcautiousness and self-indicting interpretations (in other words, "stereotype threat") (see Figure 10.3).

Researchers have looked at the role of perceived competence and control in students' preference for taking on a challenge (Boggiano, Main, & Katz, 1988). They investigated students' perceptions of their academic competence and their beliefs in their level of personal control over school-related performance. The researchers found that these perceptions and beliefs affected the students' intrinsic interest in and preference for challenge in an evaluative setting. Students with higher perceptions of their academic competence and personal control had more intrinsic interest in schoolwork and more preference for challenging school activities. When given an evaluative, controlling directive (such as, "Your last three answers are not correct—try another sample problem and let me check your work before you go on to Chapter 3"), students who had high perceptions of their own academic competence and control preferred a greater challenge than did students who had lower perceptions of their academic competence and control. No difference between the groups of students in terms of preference for challenge was evident when no controlling directive was presented. Thus students' belief in their academic competence is important, as is their belief in their ability to control their school performance.

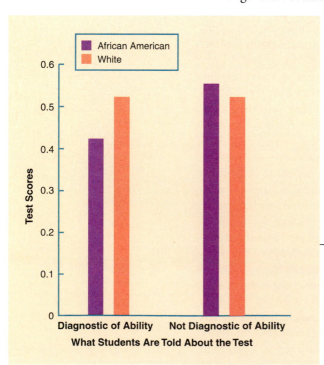

FIGURE 10.3

How Stereotype Threat Works
In the condition represented by the bars on the left, a group of African American and White students were told the intellectual test they were taking was diagnostic of their ability. In the condition represented by the bars on the right, another group of African American and White students were told the same test was *not* diagnostic of their ability. African American students' performance improved when they believed the test was not diagnostic of their ability. *Source: Steele, 1995.*

Self-esteem refers to the value a person places on himself or herself. Self-esteem is related to **self-concept,** or one's ideas about one's attributes and abilities. According to research by Harter (1990), people's self-concepts became increasingly differentiated over the course of development. As students explore their abilities and learn more skills, the self-concept becomes increasingly differentiated. They may think highly of themselves in one area, but not in another. Between the ages of 4 and 7, children can make reliable judgments about themselves in four personal domains: cognitive competence, physical ability, social ability, and behavioral conduct (Harter & Pike, 1984). By adulthood, people can rate themselves within 11 different domains of competency: intelligence, sense of humor, job competence, morality, athletic ability, physical appearance, sociability, intimacy, nurtu-rance, adequacy as a provider, and household management (Messer & Har-ter, 1985).

THINKING PRACTICALLY

Rate yourself in each of the 11 domains of compe-tency, on a 1–to–10 scale in which 1 = extremely poor, 5 = average, and 10 = outstanding.

SUGGESTION: Hint: Think of how you perform in different types of situations for each of the domains. Compare your ratings with a classmate's.

Not only do our own judgments of ourselves affect our self-esteem, it is also true that other people's judgments of us affect our self-esteem (Cooley, 1982). In general, children's perceptions of their ability become more mod-est and more accurate as they grow older (Frey & Ruble, 1987; Stipek, 1984). However, when self-perceptions are too modest and therefore inaccurate, problems result. Self-evaluations of low ability lead to motivational problems, especially in older children (Rholes, Jones, & Wade, 1980). Children who underestimate their abilities also seem to seek out less challenging tasks than do more realistic children (Harter, 1982, 1990). Chil-dren from low SES backgrounds have been shown to display less positive self-perceptions in a number of life domains compared to higher SES children (Muldoon, 2000).

Teachers cannot neglect the importance of self-perceptions, especially because inac-curate self-perceptions guide how children handle both schoolwork and life outside of school (Phillips, 1984, 1987). For example, children who seriously underestimate them-selves have low expectations for their success, believe that respected adults also take a dim view of their abilities, are reluctant to sustain effort in difficult tasks, and are more anxious about being evaluated than are other children (Phillips & Zimmerman, 1990). Often, the concept of self-esteem is described as though the effects of self-esteem are simple and straightforward; however, the converse is closer to the truth—in practice, self-esteem is multidimensional, complex, and influenced by numerous factors (DuBois & Hirsch, 2000).

Self-efficacy refers to a person's belief in his or her ability to get things done. How does our competence affect the likelihood that we will attain a particular goal? Self-efficacy theory emphasizes that *our ability to achieve a goal is based on our belief as to whether or not we can achieve the goal* (Bandura, 1986). People's expectations of self-efficacy can derive from a number of different sources: direct experience, interpreta-tions of the experiences of others, what people tell them they are able to do, and others' assessment of their emotional or motivational state. In general, if someone has a higher degree of self-efficacy she or he is more likely to attain the outcome desired.

Students' level of self-efficacy can lead to self-fulfilling prophecies. When students believe they are able to do something, they are more likely to expend the effort and resources to do it, and therefore eventually to achieve their objective. Indeed, Jim Jenson kept telling his students that they were capable of reading if only they applied them-selves. One success leads to another, helping students to view themselves as being con-tinually successful in maintaining the outcomes they desire. In contrast, if students have a low sense of self-efficacy, they may believe they are unable to succeed and, as a result, they may hardly try. The result is failure, which leads to the expectation of future failure. Expert teachers enhance students' self-efficacy by setting for the students realistic, highly specific, and attainable goals, and then helping them plan how to meet these goals (see Table 10.5 on page 374).

The goal of this lesson is to move students away from common misconceptions about intelligence and toward more productive attitudes. Although it can take a long time to change someone's attitude about intelligence, this lesson raises important questions and suggests the variety of ways that people can be talented.

Common Misconceptions

- Intelligence is a fixed thing that you either have or don't have.
- There is only one kind of intelligence—everyone who's smart is smart in the same way.

More Useful Conceptions

- Intelligence is something that you can improve through work, thinking about yourself, and monitoring your actions.
- There are many different ways to be intelligent—everyone is smart in some ways and not so smart in others.

What to Do

1. Introduce the importance of thinking about intelligence. One possible way:

   - Part of your (the students') job this year will be to show me (the teacher) how you are smart.
   - This job will be easy because each of you already is smart in many different ways.
   - This job will not be so easy because you may not know *how* you are smart, how to *demonstrate* your abilities, or how to *develop* them.
   - Part of my job is to help you figure out your strengths and how to use them.
   - A good place to start is to think about what *smart* or *intelligent* means. Our own personal definitions of intelligence can influence how we think of ourselves and what we do—both in and out of school.

2. Give students a chance to think individually about intelligence by writing in journals or simply having a moment to think quietly before class discussion.

3. For a class discussion, ask students to describe particular people they think are very good at something. If they have trouble, you might ask them to think of relatives, friends, famous people, heroes—people they would want to be.

4. Encourage diverse examples. If students focus mainly on academic talent, ask them to think of talented musicians, athletes, artists, actors, cooks, auto mechanics, and so on. Continuing for about ten minutes, ask students to talk about how each person is talented. What kind of intelligence does that person need to do what she or he does so well? You might keep track of the range of responses on a board.

5. Review their ideas and have the class think about what it means to be intelligent.

6. Encourage the notion that intelligence is an ability to do things that we value and there are many different ways to be productive and talented. Also encourage the notion that people's abilities change and *improve* over time.

   - Can you think of people who are smart at one thing and terrible at another?
   - Can you remember when you could not do something that you are very good at now?
   - If someone does well in school, will that person do well in anything she or he tries?

7. Sum up what the class has said. Inform students that they will spend much of the year thinking about their own talents and improving how they work in school.

Source: From *Practical Intelligence for School* by W.M. Williams, T. Blythe, N. White, R.J. Sternberg, and H.I. Gardner. Copyright © 1996. Reprinted by permission of Addison-Wesley Educational Publishers, Inc.

Implications for Teaching

- *Discourage students from blaming their failures on bad luck or other unfortunate situations. Instead, encourage students to blame failures on lack of hard work.* Model effective techniques by talking positively about your own school failures and their causes (and potential or actual solutions).

- *Encourage students to view success in school and in life as a result of hard work, not innate ability.* Point out that students who excel have often worked long and hard to earn their accomplishments. Make clear that this level of dedication applies also to all their favorite athletes, writers, or performers. Make examples of hard workers, and ask these students to share their secrets for success with the class.

- *Emphasize that students can feel good about themselves as a result of meaningful accomplishments, both within and outside of the traditional school domain.* Discourage the idea that "everyone should feel good about herself or himself regardless of what she or he does." Stress the role of concrete, effective action rather than simply thinking good thoughts.

Motivating Challenging Students

Once you have helped students set goals and develop effective self-concepts, these students will still face daily challenges in staying motivated. However, for some students, the typical and traditional methods of motivation aren't enough. There are many challenging students in today's classrooms, and you are likely to encounter these students and be expected to motivate them from your first day on the job.

Today's teachers face many students who come from backgrounds that may place these students at a disadvantage for developing motivation. For example, students from single-parent families often need more motivation than they now tend to have (Bronfenbrenner, McClelland, Wethington, & Moen, 1996). Compared with other students, those from single-parent homes miss school more often, and on average are more pessimistic about the value of schooling and the value of planning for later life. Children from single-parent homes tend to have a lower standard of living and greater economic and other types of stresses. Expert teachers are alert to the needs of students from single-parent families, who may require special assistance in developing motivation. Of course, children vary widely, and no one profile fits all children from single-parent families, just as no research findings predict the behavior of all children living in these families.

STUDENT MOTIVATION AND ACHIEVEMENT

Consider one finding regarding student motivation and achievement: Among high school seniors in the years 1990 to 1992, 22 percent of students coming from two-parent homes achieved an A grade point average, whereas only 16 percent of students coming from families headed by a single mother did so. In other words, there is a 38 percent increase in the number of students who earn an A average when we compare two-parent homes to single-parent homes. Thirty percent of students from two-parent families had skipped one or more days of school in a four-week period, 34 percent of students from families headed by a single mother had done so, and 37 percent of students from other nontraditional family structures had done so. In general, students' motivation to plan for the future has declined since 1980 (White & Wethington, 1996). This decline has been associated with a widening gap in which students from single-parent families are becoming even less motivated to plan for the future. However, the more education a student's mother has, the more likely that student is to believe in the value of planning for the future (White & Wethington, 1996).

Consider another finding showing the relationship between parental/family involvement and patterns of student motivation and achievement. Ginsburg and Bronstein (1993) looked at family factors related to students' intrinsic/extrinsic motivational orientation and academic performance. Students with an extrinsic motivational style who earned lower grades were likely to have parents who policed their homework. These students were also likely to have parents who maintained either too much or too little control over their children. These parents were often not involved meaningfully in students' school performances, and tended to

THINKING CREATIVELY

What *advantages* might students from single–parent households have compared to students from dual–parent households?

SUGGESTION: They might be more independent and self-reliant; they might be more mature and exhibit more adultlike behaviors and skills. They might therefore succeed better in school.

use extrinsic rewards to motivate their children. In contrast, students with an intrinsic style were likely to have received parental encouragement in response to their grades. Intrinsically motivated students were likely to have higher academic performance and to have parents who supported reasonable autonomy in their children. In general, expert teachers remember that there are numerous, complex, interacting factors that influence student motivation and achievement.

■ MOTIVATING STUDENTS FROM LOW SOCIOECONOMIC STATUS BACKGROUNDS

Antonio Roazzi (1988) examined which incentives work to motivate children from different socioeconomic groups. He gave children tough paper-and-pencil tasks to complete under one of three conditions: verbal reinforcement ("that's great!"), a modest financial reinforcement, or gustatory reinforcement (a chocolate bar). Roazzi found that the effects of incentives varied by social class: For middle-class students, the value of verbal reinforcement was just as salient as the value of the other two types of reinforcement. For lower socioeconomic status (SES) students, however, verbal reinforcement was not as effective. (It is possible that teachers from higher SES groups may have trouble choosing the most effective verbal reinforcements for lower SES students, and may also have trouble earning the respect of lower SES students in general.) The teacher of lower SES students must realize that the teaching tips that work to motivate middle-class students may sometimes need to be adjusted to motivate low-SES students. When working with hard-to-motivate students of any type, expert teachers know they must begin by determining what really matters to each student. Knowing what's most important to a student enables a teacher to choose the incentive or reward that is most motivating (McCombs & Pope, 1994).

Students from disadvantaged social, ethnic, and cultural groups may sometimes benefit from an extra dose of motivation to enable them to overcome obstacles that may keep them from succeeding in the mainstream culture. These students must often work harder than their nondisadvantaged counterparts to succeed equally well. A key finding about how to motivate minority children comes from work by Zena Blau (1981) with inner-city Chicago children. Blau found that the children motivated enough to escape the cycle of poverty had in common one educated adult in their lives—teacher, parent, friend, or other role model—with an educational focus (i.e., someone who heavily stressed the value of education). Even if the children's parents themselves were not well educated, this research showed that a single educated adult who provided mentoring and role modeling helped these children turn their lives around. Interacting with one person with an educational focus was essential to the child's outcome. Expert teachers remember this critical role they can play in their students' lives every day.

In order to improve their fine motor skills, a teacher encourages two young children with disabilities to finger-paint. Motivation is particularly important to children with mental and physical challenges. Expert teachers understand how important it is to use incremental goals to motivate such students and to make every task seem reachable. (Bob Daemmrich Photos, Inc.)

■ MOTIVATING STUDENTS IN SPECIAL EDUCATION PROGRAMS

As an illustration of how motivation can be increased through the use of incremental goals, consider the programs created for students with special needs. In Chapter 5 on exceptional children we discussed the use of IEPs (Individualized Educational Plans) mandated by Public Law 94-122, the Education for All Handicapped Children Act. These IEPs are created by the teacher in consultation with the child, and they specify the child's learning and performance goals. The plans begin with global statements about what the student will attempt to achieve in a given year. Next, the plans provide incremental and specific goals for achieving the plan. These goals are spelled out in sequential steps that specify individual behaviors and performances for each step. Once the student works through the steps, he or she has accomplished the overarching goals for the term or year.

The message for the expert teacher is clear: IEPs are used for students with learning challenges not only because they are required by law, but also because they work by focusing students on individual goals that lead to larger goals. In fact, expert teachers know the power of using incremental goals to motivate every student and to make every task, regardless of how daunting, seem within reach. And incremental goals do not work only in the school environment: One teacher recently expressed disbelief to the person painting her house that he could possibly paint the entire building working alone. He answered that he paints only one side at a time and does not think about the remaining sides.

Motivational orientation is particularly important for populations with learning challenges. One study looked at the motivational orientation and academic achievement of elementary and middle school students with behavior disorders compared to their peers without learning challenges (Schultz & Switzky, 1993). This study found that students with behavioral disorders showed significantly greater academic performance differences due to motivational orientation compared with peers without learning challenges. In addition, individual differences in motivational orientation appear to affect the academic performance of students with behavioral disorders more than their peers without learning challenges. Encouragingly, Rawson (1992) increased academic intrinsic motivation of boys with learning disabilities who had severe classroom behavior problems through a highly intensive academic remediation curriculum. Teachers of students with special needs must be particularly alert to helping these students develop optimal motivation.

Implications for Teaching

- **Recognize that students from single-parent homes may need extra encouragement, support, and direction.** In some situations, these students may not receive as much attention at home as do students from dual-parent households. Hook students up with older mentors and study partners if possible. Encourage students to join after-school programs to provide some of what they may be missing at home.

- **Behavioral motivators (rewards and punishments) are often the best way to start with students with learning disabilities or students from challenged groups.** Eventually, cognitive motivators may be phased in. Begin with small, incremental goals, and do not allow yourself to become easily frustrated by the challenges of teaching these students.

- **Teachers need to work harder to meet the needs of students from groups with learning challenges.** These students often depend more on their teachers than do students from other groups. Your dedication and experience may be tested, but remember that over time you will grow in your ability to meet such challenges. Often, the students who need you the most will provide the greatest rewards over time.

WHY UNDERSTANDING MOTIVATION IS IMPORTANT TO TEACHERS

■ Motivation is closely related to academic achievement, is influenced by context, and changes over time. Incentives are objects or events that encourage or discourage behavior.

INTRINSIC AND EXTRINSIC MOTIVATION

■ Intrinsic motivation comes from within the person—it is an internal push to do something. Extrinsic motivation, tied to the environment, comes from external factors, rewards, and incentives. Both intrinsic and extrinsic motivation are important in motivating students, although intrinsic motivation generally helps students accomplish more on their own.

FOUR WAYS TO UNDERSTAND MOTIVATION

■ According to behavioral theories, motivation results from rewards and punishments that serve to mold behavior. Cognitive theories of motivation focus on what students think, how they think, and how their thoughts create or reduce motivation to act. According to social learning theories, motivation results both from what goes on inside a person's head and from what goes on in the external environment: Social learning theories combine behavioral and cognitive theories. Humanistic theories of motivation propose that motivation results from a higher-order push to achieve and excel that comes from within a person.

THE ROLE OF AROUSAL LEVEL

■ Arousal, or alertness, is important to motivation—neither too much nor too little arousal is desirable for optimal learning and performance. Curiosity can be used to create a moderate level of arousal and interest in learning.

THE ROLE OF STUDENT GOALS

■ Goals are important to help students focus attention, mobilize resources, persist in achieving a goal, and see different methods for achieving a goal. Task-mastery goals—working to understand and succeed at a task—are best for students. Self-monitoring is the student's ability to keep track of his or her own progress; self-monitoring can help students achieve goals and follow through on plans.

THE ROLE OF STUDENT NEEDS

■ Maslow's hierarchy of needs suggests that students must be adequately sheltered and fed, and have adequate love and attention, before they can learn effectively. The need for achievement is an internal drive to excel. The need for self-determination is a drive to control our environment and our destiny.

THE ROLE OF STUDENT ATTRIBUTIONS AND BELIEFS

■ Students' attributions, or ways of explaining their own behavior, are important to their academic performance. There are internal, or dispositional attributions, and external, or situational attributions.

■ Those who hold an incremental view of intelligence believe that intelligence can be increased. Those who hold an entity view of intelligence believe that intelligence is fixed at an inborn level. Students with incremental views outperform students with entity views. Learning goals (the desire to improve skills) are better for student performance than performance goals (the desire to look smart and avoid negative judgments of ability).

■ Students' self-concepts become increasingly differentiated over the course of development—students come to think of themselves as good in some things but not in others. Self-efficacy, or belief in one's ability to get things done, is important to student achievement. It differs from self-esteem, which reflects the value we place on ourselves. Expectancy X value theory says that people work hard and are motivated when they have a reasonable chance of succeeding, and when the goal is personally meaningful to them.

MOTIVATING CHALLENGING STUDENTS

■ Students from nontraditional families sometimes need extra help with motivation so they will stay in school and perform well. Students from different socioeconomic levels often are motivated by different factors. Students in special education programs are especially in need of specific goals and plans to focus their actions.

KEY TERMS AND DEFINITIONS

■ **Achievement motivation** Drive to excel. Page 362

■ **Anxiety** Sense of nervousness, worry, and self-doubt. Page 358

■ **Arousal** Individual's level of alertness, wakefulness, and activation. Page 358

■ **Attribution** Explanation pointing to the cause of a particular behavior. Page 368

■ **Dispositional attributions** Explanations for behavior, based on internal characteristics of a person. Page 369

■ **Entity view of intelligence** Belief that intelligence consists of a fixed amount that a person is born with and cannot be increased. Page 369

■ **Expectancy X value theory** Theory proposing that people work hard and are motivated when they believe they have a reasonable chance of succeeding, and when the goal is personally meaningful to them. Page 355

■ **Extrinsic motivation** Motivation that comes from outside the individual, for example, from gaining the approval of others, meeting publicly stated goals, and performing behaviors valued by the group. Page 347

■ **Incentive** Object or event that encourages or discourages behavior; a reason to behave in a certain way. Page 345

■ **Incremental view of intelligence** Belief that intelligence can be increased. Page 369

■ **Intrinsic motivation** Motivation that comes from within the individual and can take the form of personal energy, drive, or ambition. Page 347

■ **Learning goals** Goals focused on improving skills and learning new things. Page 370

■ **Locus of control** Location of the source of control for an individual, usually described as internal or external. Page 351

■ **Mastery oriented** Being driven by a desire for meaningful learning, mastery of skills, and work. Page 350

■ **Motivation** Internal state that arouses, directs, and maintains behavior. Page 345

■ **Need for achievement** Drive to excel. Page 365

■ **Need for affiliation** Desire to form close connections with other people and to be a member of groups. Page 365

■ **Need for power** Desire to control others. Page 365

■ **Performance goals** Goals focused on the judgments others make of a performance. These involve "looking smart," earning positive teacher comments, and avoiding negative judgments of ability. Page 370

■ **Self-actualization** Need to make the most of oneself. Page 356

■ **Self-concept** Ideas about our attributes and abilities. Page 373

■ **Self-determination** Ability to make things happen, to have control of ourselves and our environment. Page 367

■ **Self-efficacy** Beliefs in our ability to get things done. Page 373

■ **Self-esteem** Value one assigns to one's own characteristics (for example, one's abilities, talents, and actions). Page 373

■ **Self-monitoring** Keeping track of our own progress. Page 363

■ **Situational attributions** Explanations for behavior based on external factors such as settings, events, or other people. Page 369

■ **Task-mastery goals** Goals that stress working to understand and succeed at a task. Page 362

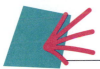

BECOMING AN EXPERT: QUESTIONS AND PROBLEMS

Apply the concepts you have learned in this chapter to the following problems of classroom practice.

IN ELEMENTARY SCHOOL

1. Your goal is to motivate first-grade students to listen attentively during reading class and not talk to one another or fidget. What types of incentives would be most motivating for these students? What steps would you take to introduce these students to the concept of incentives in an effective manner?

2. Why might a fourth-grade student lack motivation for mathematics? (Name as many reasons as you can.) Now, think of something you could do in response to each problem to help the student develop more motivation.

3. Imagine you are working with a gifted sixth grader. She is particularly capable in science, and you can see a bright future ahead for her. What could you do to help her capitalize on her talent in this area?

4. You are leading a class of fourteen second graders who are of mixed levels of ability. What types of goals would you want your students to define, and how would you help them do so?

5. Your class of fifth graders contains three students who suffer from severe test anxiety, which is inhibiting their performance on tests. How can you help these students approach tests more effectively and score more in line with their level of ability?

IN MIDDLE SCHOOL

1. Your class of seventh graders contains many students in the midst of puberty who are undergoing major developmental transitions. What problems might this create for you, and what steps would you take to solve these problems?

2. You have recently been transferred from a fourth-grade class to an eighth-grade class. Previously, with the younger students, you had success while using extrinsic motivators. Do you think this situation will change? Will your new students respond similarly? What role will intrinsic motivators play with the older students?

3. You are teaching seventh grade in an inner-city area. You have found that your students do not seem to set goals for themselves. How can you demonstrate the value of goal setting to these students in order to convince them that it is worthwhile to do so?

4. Your eighth-grade math class contains two students who claim they just are not smart enough to do well in math. What steps could you take to help these students?

5. Your seventh-grade students seem to have plenty of self-esteem, but they lack self-efficacy (the belief that they can accomplish what they wish). How can you build on their general positive feelings to help them develop more confidence in specific abilities—such as writing compositions or taking math tests?

IN HIGH SCHOOL

1. Your tenth-grade class writes essays that are deadly dull. You want to motivate these students to be more creative, but their other teachers tend to downplay the importance of creativity. What can you do to solve this problem?

2. Your ninth-grade class includes three students with learning disabilities who have substantial difficulties completing their mathematics assignments on time. These students already have extra tutoring in addition to your class. What can you do to help these students maintain their motivation to work through the obstacles they encounter?

3. You have recently begun teaching twelfth grade, and you are surprised by the large number of students with little or no school motivation in your classes. Your classes of ninth graders seemed far more motivated to do well in school. Why might this be happening with the older students, and what can you do about it?

4. Say that your goal is to promote rapid changes of behavior in your tenth-grade students—you want them to study more this week and complete the next two assignments on time, for example. Which type of motivation (extrinsic versus intrinsic) should you attempt to instill if you are looking for quick results? How about the situation in which you are seeking longer term changes in behavior—what approach would work best, and why?

5. Your ninth-grade students seem to be more motivated by the need for affiliation than by the need for achievement. What problems do you foresee developing for these students? What steps can you take to help these students develop more achievement orientation?

Building Your Self-Portrait as an Educator

Finding ways to motivate student learning is not the only challenge teachers face with regard to motivation. Sometimes, teachers need to find ways to motivate themselves. New teachers who find themselves somewhat isolated in the classroom may be vulnerable to teacher burn-out, a condition in which teachers lose the motivation to teach (Foehr, 1999). In "Avoiding Teacher Burn-Out: New Teachers Dialoguing with Experienced Teachers" *(http://www.ncte.org/notesplus/FoehrApr1999.html)*, Regina Foehr discusses the common problems facing beginning teachers that may lead to burn-out and ways to avoid it.

The focus of Foehr's paper is building relationships between new and veteran teachers to discuss problems that the new teacher may have and prevent feelings of isolation, as well as to provide professional mentoring. The article includes anecdotes from new teachers about motivation, tips for new teachers on how to avoid burn-out, and resources about burn-out. If you find yourself in a situation in which you start to feel isolated and anxious about teaching but have no one to ask for help, several online resources are available here to facilitate conversations with other teachers, share frustrations, and receive feedback and advice.

Communities of Learners/Teachers

Several Web sites provide help and community support for beginning teachers. For example, The Survival Guide for New Teachers, located at *www.ed.gov/pubs/survivalguide,* provides helpful tips on finding a mentor or working with parents and school administrators. This resource also provides a list of Web resources on professional development, educational organizations, and educational materials. Also available online is Teachers Net *(www.teachers.com),* a Web site devoted to providing resources for teachers, including chat rooms, lesson plans, and job information.

Online Resources

One of the most comprehensive and exhaustive lists of Web resources on self-efficacy is available at *www.emory.edu/EDUCATION/mfp/effpage.html.* This site, entitled "Information on Self-Efficacy," provides a wide range of information and resources in three different languages: English, Spanish, and Portuguese. This site includes links to thousands of Web sites on self-efficacy, Albert Bandura, social learning theory and social cognitive theory (see Chapter 8), books about self-efficacy, papers about self-efficacy available on the Web, information about instruments to measure self-efficacy, and a list of scholars and graduate students conducting research on self-efficacy in particular areas (i.e., self-efficacy and teacher education).

Are you interested in finding your own locus of control? How about your attribution style? An online quiz to test your locus of control and attribution style is currently available at *www.queendom.com/lc.html.*

Many Web sites address the issue of test anxiety. While some sites give more information than others about how to identify symptoms of test anxiety, all provide practical tips for how to curtail and combat it. A few sites are

> http://www.cmd.stthomas.edu/studyguides/tstprp8.htm
> http://www.umr.edu/~counsel/test.html
> http://www.shsu.edu/~counsel/test_anxiety.html.

Information about the life and contributions of Urie Bronfenbrenner, Professor of Human Development and of Psychology at Cornell University, is available at *http://www.people.cornell.edu/pages/ub11/.*

"Learning Theories and Models of Teaching" provides textual resources on many topics related to teaching and learning. One feature of this site, located at *http://chiron.valdosta.edu/whuitt/col/affsys/humed.html,* highlights the humanistic perspective of learning. This site provides an overview of the history of the humanistic perspective, goals and principles of humanistic education, and a list of textual references for learning more about the humanistic perspective of teaching and learning. Another, more compact site about the humanistic perspective of teaching and learning can be found at *http://curriculum.calstatela.edu/faculty/psparks/theorists/501human.htm.* This site provides an explanation of humanistic theory, briefly discusses implications for teaching and learning, and presents a few textual resources.

© Copyright by Martin Briner.

For Further Reading

Merseth, K. K. (1992). First aid for first-year teachers. *Phi Delta Kappan, 73* (9), 678–683.

Clement, M. C. (1997). *Bright ideas: A pocket mentor for beginning teachers.* Washington: National Education Association.

Classroom Management

THE BIG PICTURE

To help you see the big picture, keep the following questions in mind as you read this chapter:

- How can the science of educational psychology help teachers manage their classrooms? What practical information can a textbook such as this one provide to a teacher—information that will be useful in day-to-day teaching?

- How can good planning prevent classroom problems? Which is a more effective approach: planning to prevent problems before these problems occur, or waiting to deal only with problems that actually occur? Should a teacher place primary emphasis on teaching first and management second—or vice versa?

- What rules, regulations, policies, and procedures do expert teachers use to manage their classrooms? What is the appropriate role of rules and procedures in classroom management?

- Should a teacher's management goals and strategies vary, depending on the age of the students? What are the challenges of managing children with special needs, and how can a teacher meet these challenges?

- What are the characteristics of teachers who are especially effective at classroom management?

- How can the use of effective communication strategies assist teachers in becoming good classroom managers?

- How can a teacher create a classroom environment that is orderly and appropriate for learning when students place little value on school and seem not to care about learning? How much order and discipline are necessary in a class containing bright, motivated, and successful students?

◄ *A kindergarten teacher leads her attentive students in a game of "Simon Says." (Will Hart, PhotoEdit)*

Charlie Grenda was thrilled. He had just been hired to teach social studies at a suburban middle school. Charlie was a new teacher, and when he arrived at the school to meet with the principal he was filled with positive anticipation. The principal, Shirley Walker, began by giving Charlie some words of advice. "Middle school students are at a difficult transition point in their development. Many teachers find that classroom management is their toughest challenge with these students. I know you have had good preparation about how to teach, but I hope you have also thought about how to manage your classroom and your students. The other teachers can provide an invaluable resource." Charlie grinned and said he recognized that he was new, but he believed he could handle anything these kids might challenge him with.

Shirley suggested a tour of the school, and Charlie appreciated the escort as he learned about his new work environment. As Shirley led him through the building, Charlie was surprised to find a remarkable degree of variety from class to class. The first class they observed was a sixth-grade science class taught by a seasoned veteran. The students were carrying out a laboratory assignment that involved using elaborate equipment and working in groups; the room was orderly and the students appeared engrossed in their lesson. A student who needed assistance walked to the front of the room and waited patiently and without interrupting as the teacher helped another student. Charlie was very impressed.

The next room Charlie and Shirley visited was an eighth-grade language arts class. Although the students were supposed to be listening to the teacher as she read aloud to them and discussed a poem, they were acting up. Several boys in the last three rows were talking and throwing wads of chewing gum at one another. Two girls were passing notes. Other students were doodling aimlessly in their notebooks. Charlie was amazed that the teacher just kept reading and talking as if nothing were wrong. "See what I mean?" Shirley asked. "It can be tough to maintain discipline with kids at this age—but it can be done. Let me show you another example of a teacher who is really in control."

The third room Shirley led Charlie to was a seventh-grade social studies class. This class was filled with students busily taking notes, raising their hands, listening to one another, and obviously showing respect for their teacher. Again, Charlie was struck by the differences he observed among the classes. He saw clearly that if he failed to establish appropriate control over his students, little that he tried to teach would matter. Charlie also recognized that he was not particularly well prepared for dealing with the ins and outs of classroom management, since his formal training had not stressed such skills. He knew that being able to see and appreciate the differences from one classroom to the next did not mean he was ready to handle the situations that were causing trouble in the less well-managed classrooms. Obviously, one of his most important goals as he began his teaching career would be to consider and implement positive techniques for classroom management.

Charlie has recognized how important it is for teachers to be able to manage their students to create an orderly classroom where everyone is ready and able to learn. While at college, he had worked diligently to prepare himself to be an effective teacher; however, he did not yet possess much practical know-how about how to accomplish the goals of managing his students. **Classroom management** is defined as a set of techniques and skills that allow a teacher to control students effectively in order to create a positive learning environment for all students. This practical know-how can be learned from other experienced and effective teachers (Covino & Iwanicki, 1996); it can also be learned by reading about the techniques found through research to be useful in managing students.

Why Understanding Classroom Management Is Important to Teachers

His first day of teaching made clear to Charlie Grenda that he was not well prepared to effectively manage his students. Listen to a group of teachers talking about the problems they face at work, and you will find that at the heart of most of their problems is the issue of classroom management (Martin & Baldwin, 1996). When students are disruptive and off-task, learning ceases. When students ignore rules and challenge their teacher's authority, learning again takes a backseat. When students fight with one another and create a hostile environment filled with fear and uneasiness, learning is the last thing on anyone's mind. How often do these events happen?

Unfortunately, the answer is, more often than they should. Every year, a Gallup Poll is conducted to assess the public's perception of the biggest problems facing our schools. Every year, maintaining discipline is seen as a primary concern—led in recent years by the problems surrounding the use of drugs, which is itself another type of discipline problem (Elam & Rose, 1995). You are undoubtedly familiar with the term *discipline*. When used in the domain of classroom management, **discipline** refers specifically to teacher-initiated actions designed to minimize student behavior problems and distractions in order to create a maximally effective learning environment.

CHANGES IN OUR SOCIETY AND IN OUR SCHOOLS

Were schools always such undisciplined and seemingly unmanageable places? Have teachers historically had to fight such a tough battle every working day? The answer, as our parents and friends of generations past tell us, is no. For example, classrooms of the 1950s were more orderly than classrooms of today, and children in those classrooms were easier to manage (see Elam & Rose, 1995). A recent poll of top-ten concerns of teachers showed that in the 1950s, "gum chewing" and "littering" were top teacher concerns, whereas today teachers worry about "violence in school" and "drug use." How can we explain this major and significant shift in the types of behaviors characterizing students over the past half century?

■ **CHANGES IN FAMILIES AND ATTITUDES** To understand what has happened in our schools, we must first understand what has changed in our society. Families today are different from families a generation or two ago, and children consequently grow up in different environments than in the past. Most households of today do not stress the same types of values that were seen as important 50 years ago. As a result, most of today's students are different from their counterparts in previous generations. Consider some illustrative statistics, profiled in the book *The State of Americans* (Bronfenbrenner et al., 1996).

In 1969, 34 percent of high school students reported having cheated on tests; in 1989, this figure had risen to 68 percent (see Figure 11.1). In 1981, 31 percent of students agreed that "most people can be trusted," but by 1992, only 18 percent agreed with this statement. Over this same time period, teenagers' acceptance of out-of-wedlock births rose considerably. In addition, religious attendance declined from 41 percent of high school seniors in 1975 to 32 percent in 1992. The change in the American family has also played an important role in the attitudes of today's youth. The United States leads all other developed nations in rates of single parenthood and divorce; more and more children are being raised by one never-married parent. Twenty-two percent of students from two-parent households achieve grade point averages of A, whereas only 16 percent of students from mother-headed households, and 14 percent of students from father-headed households and households headed by other adults, do so.

FIGURE 11.1

Cheating and tolerance of cheating has increased over time.

Source: From *The State of Americans: This Generation and the Next* by Urie Bronfenbrenner, Peter McClelland, Elaine Wetherington, Phyllis Moen, and Stephen J. Ceci. Copyright © 1996 by Urie Bronfenbrenner, Peter McClelland, Elaine Wetherington, Phyllis Moen, and Stephen J. Ceci. Reprinted by permission of The Free Press, a Division of Simon & Schuster.

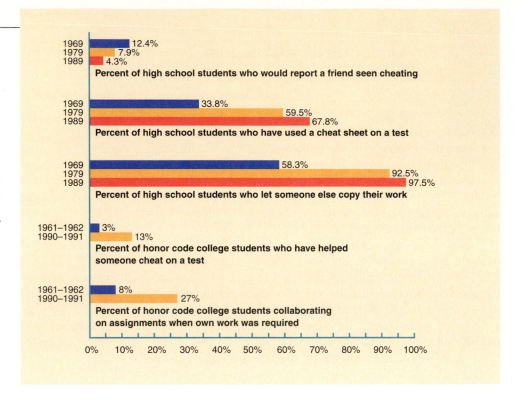

■ **INCREASE IN VIOLENCE** Consider also the data on violence in schools: In 1990, as many as 32 percent of male high school students reported carrying a weapon to school in the previous month; in 1992, 44 percent of students had taken part in a physical fight in the past year; in 1986, 34 percent of violent crimes against 12- to 15-year-olds took place in school, and another 20 percent took place on the way to school; in 1993, 56 percent of high school students did not feel very safe in school; and in 1994, 46 percent of high school students did not trust other students because of violence. In general, youth are more likely than adults to be victims of violent crime (see Figure 11.2). In 1995 and 1996, juveniles were twice as likely as adults to be victims of serious violent crime and three times as likely to be victims of simple assault. Younger juveniles (ages 12–14) were more likely than older juveniles to be victims of simple assault. In addition, the property crime victimization rate was greater for juveniles than for adults (Snyder & Sickmund, 1999). In a 1989 survey of youth aged 13 to 17 from Rochester, New York, 47 percent had used drugs and/or alcohol, 50 percent had committed a delinquent act, 55 percent had engaged in sexual intercourse, and 29 percent had done all three. In general, school violence is most likely in schools located in high-crime areas, in large schools with large classes, in schools containing a high percentage of male students, and in schools with weak administrators (Baker, 1985). In sum, since the 1960s, school crime and violence have become major concerns of teachers, administrators, parents, and our society as a whole (Hoffman, 1996).

Given these facts and figures, it is understandable that today's teachers report classroom management as their major concern and responsibility (Long, Biggs, & Hinson, 1999). We can sympathize with teachers who become exhausted and decide to go easy on discipline, as long as the students are not harming one another or damaging the classroom. Furthermore, teachers often must reconcile conflicting pieces of advice from fel-

THINKING ANALYTICALLY

Name three ways in which the students of today may be easier to manage than the students of a half century ago.

SUGGESTION: Today's students may be more independent because they spend more time alone, away from parents; they may be more mature at a younger age because of the effects of growing up in our society; and they may be more goal oriented and concerned about the future, given the pressures of modern life and its frequent emphasis on preparation for the future. Of course, they are also more technologically sophisticated.

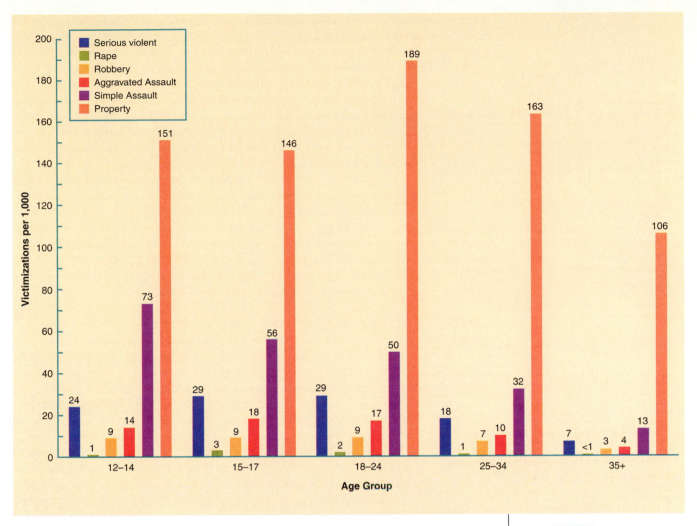

FIGURE 11.2

Youth are more likely than adults to be victims of violent crime. *Source:* Adapted from H. Snyder & M. Sickmund *Juvenile Offenders and Victims:* 1999 National Report, p. 26. Washington, DC: Office of Juvenile Justice and Delinquency Prevention, 1999.

low teachers, administrators, and even parents, each of whom has a different approach and solution to the teacher's daily problems. In this chapter we review what is known about effective classroom management, in order to help you develop and hone a collection of insights and strategies you can use in your own teaching to make your classrooms as open to learning as possible.

GOALS OF CLASSROOM MANAGEMENT

What are the specific goals of classroom management? The first goal is to create an environment that maximizes student learning. Therefore, good management techniques will lead to enhanced learning. Management techniques that lead only to quieter classrooms and classrooms with fewer student questions do not necessarily result in more learning. The students may have been managed into being quiet and orderly, but their docile behavior may not be in the service of learning. Thus teachers must ask themselves whether their management techniques are, in fact, contributing to a positive atmosphere of learning.

■ **ALLOCATED VERSUS ENGAGED TIME** One key way for you as a teacher to assess the outcome of classroom management techniques is to evaluate how much time students really have for learning. **Allocated time** is the time you earmark and plan to use for learning. **Engaged time** is the time that students actually spend on learning.

A surprising study showed that students are engaged in meaningful academic learning for only about one-third of the total instructional hours they are mandated to receive, which translates to about 333 hours of quality learning time per student per year (Weinstein & Mignano, 1993). Three hundred hours divided by 187 school days equals about 90 minutes per day of actual quality learning time. Studies that have examined the relation between students' opportunity to learn and time spent on learning have found the amount of content covered by the teacher predicts, to some degree, the amount students learned (Berliner, 1988, 1990).

Thus a well-managed classroom means more quality learning time, and more quality learning time means more actual learning can take place. Keeping track of the amount of time students spend in quality learning is one way that teachers can evaluate the success of their management techniques. Of course, the emphasis must be on *quality* learning—time in and of itself will not translate to greater learning if this time is not well spent. Teachers can increase quality learning time by minimizing downtime between activities and tasks, by being well prepared and highly organized, by effectively disciplining troublemakers, and by maintaining order and control in the classroom.

■**PROMOTING SELF-MANAGEMENT** Other important goals of classroom management are to help students gain in maturity so they learn how to manage themselves, and to show students how to internalize rules and procedures that enhance learning. As we discussed in Chapter 7 on behavioral approaches to learning, *self-management* is the control people maintain over their own learning. By assisting students in developing their ability to understand, control, and evaluate their own learning, teachers help students mature into lifelong learners (the same skills are highly valuable for teachers, as well [Kremer & Tillema, 1999]). Part of succeeding with the goal of helping students mature is knowing how to put the focus on developing a sense of responsibility regarding learning, rather than on developing obedience and conformity for their own sake. It may initially take extra time to explain to students how and why they should take responsibility for their own learning, but in the long run students who manage themselves are easier to teach and better equipped for life. The more mature students become, the better able they become to manage themselves effectively. The principles of cognitive development we discussed in Chapter 2 are thus again relevant to teachers, who must tailor their expectations to students' cognitive capacity.

THINKING PRACTICALLY

Describe three additional ways a high school teacher could increase the amount of quality time her students spent in learning activities over the course of a normal school day.

SUGGESTION: The teacher can make sure that tasks are well matched to students' level of competence—not too easy and not too difficult; create incentives and rewards for students who remain on-task longer; and make examples of students who spend more of their time on quality learning versus other activities.

THINKING CREATIVELY

How might a teacher convince his students that managing their own learning is a key to real-world success?

SUGGESTION: By bringing in stories of role models—successful people who attribute their achievements to good self-management; by demonstrating to students that they do better on a quiz following deliberate work at self-management, compared with a quiz taken without such preparation.

Implications for Teaching

■ *Encourage students to reflect about their behaviors and school performance.* To encourage self-reflection and analysis, ask students frequent questions regarding what they are doing and why.

■ *Recognize and reward meaningful effort.* Give verbal reinforcement and praise for students' positive attempts at self-management.

■ *Make an example of successful students' techniques.* Have students describe good techniques to the class. Review case studies of famous children—and adults—who used successful self-management strategies. Gather relevant material from news stories and biographies and by asking friends for examples.

- *Provided students are succeeding, allow diversity in methods of self-management.* Do not expect all students to conform to the same strategies.

- *Model good self-management techniques.* Talk about how to use them and explain the benefits that come from using them. Assign students to interview successful adults to learn their self-management strategies; have students prepare papers or projects and present them to the class on this theme.

How Effective Teachers Manage Their Students

An obvious first step in being a good classroom manager is to conduct well-planned and carefully thought-out instruction. The right lessons—ones that intrigue and challenge students—will help keep students on-task. Teachers' supervision and active leading of lessons also encourage student engagement. When students know what is expected of them and have the necessary materials and resources available to complete their tasks, their time spent on-task will increase. All these factors are aspects of good instruction, which is the topic of Chapter 12. However, Charlie Grenda *knew* how to plan effective instruction; nevertheless, he still found he was not equipped to manage his students. What about the issue of good classroom management independent of what is being taught? What is known about the characteristics of good classroom managers in general—regardless of exactly what they are teaching?

A PIONEERING STUDY OF CLASSROOM MANAGERS

What are the basics of being a good classroom manager? One of the first to study this question was Jacob Kounin (1970), who conducted a series of pioneering studies examining student reactions to various methods of teacher control. The key classroom management skills and behaviors Kounin uncovered are as useful today as they were in 1970. What are these key behaviors underlying expertise in classroom management?

■ **"WITH-IT-NESS"** According to Kounin, **with-it-ness** means that teachers are observant and attentive to everything going on around the teacher in the classroom. Teachers who show they are with it have fewer discipline problems than do teachers who are unaware of or do not react to what is going on. Effective teachers respond immediately to the very suggestion of a discipline problem. Less effective teachers either may not notice the potential discipline problem, or may not respond to the incipient problem once they do notice it, in the hope that it will disappear on its own.

Teachers can become more with it by monitoring the entire classroom every minute for signs of disruption or other problems, and by making frequent eye contact with students and calling them by name to show they are fully aware of what each student is doing. When multiple problems arise, with-it teachers always deal with the more serious problems first. You can increase your with-it-ness by making maximal use of your voice, eyes, and body language to remain simultaneously in contact with different students. In addition, aim to be aware of students' outside-of-class activities and interests, to have more common ground with them and to encourage students to see you as up to date on their lives. With-it teachers use the techniques for student management described throughout this chapter in order to keep students under control.

> **THINKING PRACTICALLY**
>
> What additional steps can a teacher take to become more with it more often?
>
> **SUGGESTION:** Participate in a youth group or youth organization outside of school; get plenty of rest and exercise to increase alertness; make an effort not to criticize youthful styles of clothing and music that the students enjoy.

■ **COPING SIMULTANEOUSLY WITH NUMEROUS SITUATIONS** Some people prefer to focus on just one thing at a time. This preference can be an asset if the person's occupation requires intense concentration in a solitary environment. For a teacher, however, this preference can be a major problem. Expert classroom managers must do several things at once: They must be aware of what's going on all around them (with-it-ness); they must be leading a lesson; they must be monitoring which students are comprehending the lesson and which students are getting lost; they must know how much time is left before the lunch bell rings; and they must even know that the open window in the back of the room is distracting a student who is sitting in front of it. **Overlapping** is supervising several activities at once: A teacher might find herself checking on the work of one group of students while simultaneously disciplining a student from another group. On top of all this, she might be watching the clock and timing what's going on in the classroom. Managing such overlapped activities can be quite demanding.

The teaching profession is a good match for people who are able and willing to cope with a lot of things going on all at once. If you are not one of these people, and if you are committed to a career in teaching, you can develop the skill to deal with numerous simultaneous events. The key is deliberate practice (Ericsson, 1996). A good way to develop this skill is to practice it during your student teaching assignment or to work in another environment that requires coping with simultaneous events (for example, being a food server in a restaurant, or working in a store or other environment in which you are expected to deal with a lot of information at once).

An expert teacher working with one group of children on their science projects simultaneously monitors all the other children in the room, ensuring that they, too, are working on their science projects. Despite a normal low-level drone of discussion, the students should all be actively engaged in the task. If a disagreement between two troublesome students breaks out across the room, the expert classroom manager spots it immediately and verbally admonishes the students. If words are not enough, the teacher might quickly walk over and stop the behavior—but first she tells the group of students she is working with to continue doing whatever they are doing. The mistake a novice teacher might make is to stop her work with the student group in midstream after the shouts from across the room have interrupted the work of all students and have brought the problem to the teacher's attention.

THINKING CREATIVELY

Devise a creative plan for improving your ability to deal with several things at once.

SUGGESTION: Turn on both a radio or television talk show and listen while also doing another task, such as reading or revising a paper, or talking on the telephone. Then assess your comprehension of the paper or of your conversation.

Even the most expert of teachers is often barraged by the multiple demands of her students.
(Elizabeth Crews)

■CREATING MOMENTUM AND ENSURING SMOOTH TRANSITIONS Less effective teachers often interrupt one activity or discussion to present something else, to admonish a student, or to redirect student behavior. These interruptions disrupt the natural flow of student behavior. Another mistake less effective teachers make is to follow their lesson plan relentlessly, without regard to the state of mind of their students. These teachers spend on each step precisely the amount of time they planned to spend, regardless of whether the students already know the material and are bored, or are lost and are absorbing nothing. Less effective teachers may also have trouble distinguishing the important from the trivial, thus boring their students and losing their attention.

In general, interruptions in the classroom detract from meaningful learning. Interruptions pull students off-task, and many students may have trouble getting engaged again. They may even give up on the task and resort to less productive behaviors, such as spitball fights and note passing. Even as adults, an interruption (such as a telephone call) can pry a person loose from a task, making it hard to get engaged in the task again. And the challenge of maintaining and reestablishing concentration is far greater for schoolchildren.

Expert classroom managers spend as much uninterrupted time on an activity as needed before switching children to another activity. They maintain an awareness of student interest and comprehension levels, and tailor their instruction to fit student strengths and limitations. For example, if usually attentive students are daydreaming, doodling, or passing notes, the expert teacher interprets the signs as indicating that the lesson has dragged on too long, failed to hold students' attention, or exceeded the students' comprehension level. Expert classroom managers plan their instruction ahead of time, but they also tailor their plans to students' reactions. For example, an expert teacher might make use of a particularly good student response to a lesson by extending the lesson for an extra half hour, either on the same day or on the next day, if the students change classes at a specified time.

Expert teachers also keep unnecessary activity changes and interruptions to a minimum. When something happens that requires the teacher to divert her attention, the teacher gives the students an activity to keep them busy ("do three problems in your workbook now") while she seamlessly attends to the other issue ("Carlos, open your book. Steve, move to the other side of the room now, please."). When a classroom is being managed smoothly and seamlessly, the teacher and the students (as well as any observers) can feel the classroom working and can see the positive results.

■INVOLVING EVERY STUDENT Even if expert teachers are helping an individual pupil or responding to a question, they remain attentive to other students' needs. One way teachers can succeed at involving every student is to call on students using a somewhat unpredictable order. If a teacher always calls on students in the same order, those students who know their turn is far in the future may drift off or, even worse, become disruptive. If a teacher surprises students by calling on them at random, she will hold their attention because they will be uncertain when their turn will come.

A mistake made by some teachers, particularly when teaching elementary and middle school students, is to engage a single child in a lengthy interaction, allowing other students to tune out the lesson. High school students who place an emphasis on school achievement may be less apt to drift off when another classmate is being queried. However, high school students not committed to doing well in school may be just as apt to tune out as first graders when the teacher does not include them directly in the lesson.

What specific techniques can you use to keep every student involved in classroom activities? In general, successful management techniques encourage all students to share in the responsibility for learning, foster participation by all students, and keep students alert and guessing when their turn will come.

THINKING ANALYTICALLY

Name three ways a teacher can tell if he is switching too frequently from one activity to the next.

SUGGESTION: If students act nervous or disoriented and lose track of what is happening; if the teacher feels overly stressed; if students keep asking off-point questions, showing they do not understand the topic of instruction.

THINKING CREATIVELY

How might a teacher ensure that she is involving all her students in a lesson? Describe two methods not mentioned in the text.

SUGGESTION: Surprise quizzes, either graded by students or teachers and either counted toward the class grade or not; confidential feedback sheets distributed to students on which students can indicate their level of involvement and satisfaction with instruction.

A sixth-grade science teacher holds the rapt attention of her students as she uses simple colorful balloons and blocks to demonstrate Newton's third law of motion. (R. Sidney, The Image Works)

Consider a few examples of effective techniques. Expert classroom managers engage the entire class in a problem being completed on the board by one student by asking all students to complete the problem in their notebooks. They break up material into parts and ask several different students to answer related questions about the material. Effective teachers call on several students in a row, using a random order to select students, and get all students to provide answers to the same open-ended problem. They ask a question first and then call on an individual student for an answer. In this way they send the message that all students need to listen in case they are called on.

Expert classroom managers also ask questions in a way that allows all students to display their answers. For example, a teacher might pose a question and say, "All those who disagree with this statement, raise one hand; all those who agree, raise both hands." (Next, the teacher might ask students why they agree or disagree.) Or a teacher might ask all students to complete a problem in their workbooks and to raise their hands as soon as they have answers—with one finger showing for choice A, two fingers showing for choice B, and so on. These methods encourage vigilance by a student who might otherwise have daydreamed instead of doing the problem.

■ **GENERATING ENTHUSIASM AND KEEPING LESSONS INTERESTING** Teachers generate enthusiasm and excitement when they use a variety of approaches and presentation styles. We have all met teachers who made clear that they were excited and interested by their work. Their attitude is usually contagious. Other teachers act bored by following the same monotonous procedures every day. When teachers are monotonous, students tune out. Not surprisingly, therefore, expert management requires the maintenance of students' interest levels. Enthusiastic teaching leads not only to better instruction, but also to fewer behavior problems in the classroom. As we discussed in Chapter 7 on behavioral approaches to learning, a teacher's appropriate use of praise and encouragement is also essential in maintaining a positive atmosphere of control in the classroom.

Interest levels can be maintained only within the limits of students' attention spans. Holding students' attention is in part a function of adept teaching, but limitations are imposed by students' developmental age. Younger children do not have the same attention spans as older children. It is rare for a young child to be willing or able to concentrate for a long period of time on any one thing.

Because children's needs differ as a function of age, techniques for effective classroom management differ for students of different ages. An elementary school teacher must watch for short attention spans and have new activities or appropriate distractions ready if children lose interest in a task. This loss of interest can occur in as little as ten minutes. The attention spans of middle school children are somewhat longer, but these students still do not have the attention span of a high school student or an adult. By high school, a teacher can expect motivated students to have attention spans comparable to their own. Regardless of the age of the student, expert teachers remember that attention span is not a fixed quantity; rather, it varies with the type of material and the way this material is presented, and also reflects what is going on in the student's life.

In general, expert classroom management of elementary school children requires the use of a variety of activities and teaching methods, because these children cannot be expected to remain on one task or engaged in one activity for very long. Teachers of more advanced students find that the variety appreciated by younger students might be perceived as disruptive once students' attention spans have developed and lengthened. A knowledge of cognitive development (see Chapter 2) is helpful to a teacher in deciding what she can expect from her students, and in choosing the best methods to keep them excited about learning.

■**CRITICIZING STUDENTS CONSTRUCTIVELY** Knowing how to give constructive criticism is essential for effective classroom management. Constructive criticism is specific and clear, and it focuses on inappropriate behaviors rather than on the person performing the behavior. For example, a teacher might say, "When you turn in a paper with misspellings, it makes it difficult for me to concentrate on your ideas," or "When you talk while I am lecturing, it distracts the other students and interferes with learning." Constructive criticism is also free of anger, yelling, shouting, sarcasm, or intentional mean-spiritedness. Students can sometimes try a teacher's patience, but expert classroom managers do not give in to their anger, and they never allow themselves to be controlled by it.

Constructive criticism is effective not only for the student to whom the criticism is directed: Other students who observe the misbehavior or outburst, and then observe the teacher's reaction to it, are also influenced positively by an atmosphere in which criticism is delivered constructively. On the other hand, a teacher who loses her temper and yells at a student delivers a negative message to every other student who sees or hears about the incident.

How do expert classroom managers respond to misbehavior? Kounin (1970) identified several techniques that work. First, state the name of the student who is misbehaving and clearly describe the undesirable behavior. Focus on the behavior and not on the person. In other words, state what was done that was unacceptable, rather than stating that the student himself or herself is unworthy, stupid, or incompetent. Second, provide a reason why the behavior was undesirable. Third, describe the desirable behavior that should replace the undesirable one. Fourth, be firm and in charge, and do not act in an overtly angry or threatening manner.

ADDITIONAL FINDINGS REGARDING CLASSROOM MANAGEMENT

Since the work of Kounin, other researchers have also studied how expert teachers manage their classrooms (for example, Brophy, 1979; Good, 1983a, 1983b; Good & Brophy, 1994). These studies have shown that well-managed classrooms are characterized by students who are actively engaged in lessons being led by their teacher. These students know exactly what is expected of them in the classroom. They have feelings of self-efficacy regarding their schoolwork—that is, they believe they are capable of accomplishing it. Well-managed classrooms are free of interruptions, confusion, and wasted time. There is a balanced atmosphere in which academic work is stressed; the classroom is not overly disciplined and controlled to the point that students are making more of an effort to keep quiet than to learn. Well-managed classrooms are a direct result of teachers' effective use of the management techniques such as the ones just described.

Educational psychologists at the University of Texas at Austin have conducted numerous studies of classroom management (e.g., Emmer, Evertson, Sanford, Clements, & Worsham, 1997; Evertson, 1988, 1989; Evertson, Emmer, Sanford, Clements, & Worsham, 1997). These researchers observed a large number of classrooms. The most and least effective classroom managers were identified by looking at the quality of classroom management as well as at student achievement in the classes. After observing the techniques of the more effective teachers, the researchers taught the techniques of the effective teachers to a new group of teachers. When these new teachers used the techniques, they found they had fewer behavior problems in their classes. Their students were less disruptive, spent more time on task, and had higher achievement.

Studies of student management in the elementary school (Evertson et al., 1997) and in the secondary school (Emmer et al., 1997) provided substantial detail regarding the best ways to manage students. Although there are differences between the management

THINKING PRACTICALLY

How might a teacher improve her level of enthusiasm on a day when she is feeling overwhelmed by the demands of her job?

SUGGESTION: Take a few minutes alone to unwind, and focus on examples of other people with far more stressful jobs or life experiences.

THINKING ANALYTICALLY

In your view, what are the greatest classroom management challenges (1) at the elementary level, and (2) at the secondary levels?

SUGGESTION: Challenges at the elementary level: neglected children who are tired, hungry, or ill equipped for school; children who have no idea what to expect from school and no idea what is expected of them. Challenges at the secondary level: sexual development leading to inappropriate behavior and attention; violence due to a sense of not belonging; students who become tuned out and less involved with school.

IN EACH CHAPTER OF THE TEXT, WE INTRODUCE YOU TO A FEW SPECIFIC STRATEGIES—ANALYTICAL, CREATIVE, AND PRACTICAL—USED BY BOTH EXPERT TEACHERS AND EXPERT STUDENTS.

THE ANALYTICAL TEACHER: Well in advance of the first day of school, Rita thinks carefully about the likely effects of the rules and procedures she will put into place.

THE CREATIVE TEACHER: Rita asks her students to draw comics and cartoons that show the consequences for students who break the rules—then, as a reminder, she displays this artwork prominently in the classroom.

THE PRACTICAL TEACHER: Rita asks misbehaving students to put themselves in the positions of their classmates and to give her three good reasons why they should change their disruptive behavior.

THE ANALYTICAL STUDENT: Lance keeps himself on-task by reminding himself of the extra points and privileges he will earn by behaving well.

THE CREATIVE STUDENT: Lance writes a report in which he describes ten ways for non-English-speaking students to become integrated into the classroom more quickly.

THE PRACTICAL STUDENT: As a part of an extra assignment, Lance meets with his friends and develops a list for his teacher of potential ways to improve the classroom's learning environment.

techniques that work best for elementary school students and those that work best for secondary school students, many general principles apply to students of all ages.

First, expert classroom managers are well prepared for the first day of class; they have developed ahead of time rules and procedures, which they explain to students on the first day of class. Second, for the first few weeks of a new school year, effective teachers work with the entire class at once. In other words, they avoid activities that separate students into small groups, so in the opening weeks all students feel included in the instruction. Once the school year is well under way, the best classroom managers continue to give students clear directions, regardless of the specific activity, and maintain the standards represented by the rules and procedures already announced. They also provide students with regular feedback on their performance. Table 11.1 offers guidelines to prepare you for your first day of teaching.

TABLE 11.1   A Plan to Ready Yourself for Your First Day of Teaching

- Have realistic expectations. Review these expectations, especially those for Day 1, with seasoned teachers.

- Find a mentor to help you right from the start—from the same or another school.

- Line up your friends and ask for their support; clean your house; and assume you will not have a minute of spare time for at least a month.

- Be overprepared; start off the year on a positive note, and expect the unexpected. Anticipate what might go wrong and develop a list of three strategies to deal with each problem.

- Bring well-thought-out lesson plans for each class, plus backup plans in case the primary plans fail.

- Develop a list of rules and procedures based on your own expectations and your school's normal policies and procedures, and present this list to your classes on the first day.

- Expect to have some unreasonable colleagues, and prepare for some unpleasant surprises on the job.

- Expect to be exhausted, frustrated, and overworked.

- Expect to be tested and evaluated by your students, who often can quickly detect your novice status.

- Expect difficult parents to challenge you on your decisions regarding their children.

- Maintain a sense of humor and recognize that every new teacher feels almost overwhelmed at first.

Implications for Teaching

■ *Show students you are with it.* Pay attention to everything going on in the classroom, maintain control of events, and promptly correct misbehaviors. Teachers seen by students as out of touch with what is going on in the classroom lose respect, and with it the ability to manage students effectively.

■ *Learn how to supervise numerous activities at once.* This skill can be honed through practice. Teachers cannot afford to be good at doing only one thing at a time; they must be able to do several things at once without becoming flustered. This is one of the reasons that teaching is such a demanding profession.

■ *Establish and preserve a natural flow of student activities.* Generate momentum, enthusiasm, excitement, and interest and ensure smooth transitions from one activity to the next. Teachers who "go with the flow" and maintain high energy stay more closely in touch with classroom rhythms.

■ *Involve every student in classroom activities and schoolwork.* Resist the tendency to call on the same students every time, even if it is easier than probing the more reluctant ones.

■ *Criticize students constructively to help them improve.* Provide specific suggestions for improvement, not simply warnings to "do better next time." Avoid statements about ability and focus instead on effort: "You must work harder to memorize your vocabulary lists—learning new words takes time and effort."

Developing and Implementing Rules and Procedures

A good recipe is important, but it does not always mean a good outcome. Similarly, a good plan for running a classroom is important, but it does not automatically translate to an orderly and attentive group of students. Developing and implementing management plans can be challenging—as Charlie Grenda learned, formal course work does not always prepare a teacher for the challenges of classroom management. What are the issues, factors, and concerns to take into account when you are developing and implementing rules and procedures for managing the classroom?

THE ROLE OF GOOD PLANNING

Given the omnipresent need for teachers to manage their classrooms effectively and efficiently in an era that would try any teacher's patience, the role of good planning has become increasingly important. Effective teachers use good planning to prevent classroom management problems from developing: By far the best way to handle classroom problems is to prevent them from happening in the first place. The effort involved in planning is always less substantial than the effort required to repair the damage done by lack of planning in the classroom.

Consider an example shared by a model teacher: Nancy noted that, in her early years of teaching, she was always a bit unprepared on the first day of school. In fact, the first few weeks found her always running to catch up. When her students filed in the first day, Nancy would be a bit nervous and would sit passively and wait until all of the students had stopped talking, taken seats, and settled down before announcing her name and describing the goals of her class. The message to the students was clear: Their teacher was nice, a bit disorganized, and not completely in charge. The students acted accordingly, and over the subsequent months Nancy had problems asserting her authority.

Today, Nancy reports that she learned the hard way that time spent in organizing and preparing for the first day of class is time well spent. Today, when a new group of students enters her class on the first day of school, she greets them individually and firmly directs them to take assigned seats (which they locate by looking at a chart with their names on it in front of the room). There is an assignment already handed out to them on their desks that they are expected to start immediately. When Nancy addresses the class, she speaks in a commanding voice and makes clear her expectations and the class rules and procedures. Her classrooms today are orderly and well managed.

■ **RESEARCH ON EFFECTIVE PLANNING** Research has borne out Nancy's observation about the importance of planning to prevent management problems (Kounin, 1970). Kounin found that expert and nonexpert teachers did not differ much in their methods for handling student misbehavior. What did distinguish these two types of teachers, however, was the expert teachers' use of strategies to prevent classroom disruptions from happening: in other words, good planning. But where do good plans come from? What management factors should you take into consideration while drafting rules and procedures?

STUDENTS' DEVELOPMENTAL AGE AND MATURITY LEVEL. In preparing effective plans, consider the developmental age and maturity level of the students. Plans and procedures that work well with fourth graders might be perceived as insulting by eleventh graders. Plans and procedures within the grasp of sixth graders might not be understandable by first graders. Earlier chapters in this book discussed cognitive, social, and moral development of children. In those chapters, you learned that children's ways of understanding the world around them change and mature as their cognitive capacity and reasoning ability develop. Expert teachers take such considerations into account when creating workable classroom management systems.

Although the techniques for effective classroom management covered in this chapter apply to all teaching situations, the secondary school classroom is a different kind of environment from the grade school classroom. Let us first consider the routine that students follow in primary versus secondary school, and the implications for their teachers. The elementary school teacher typically has just one class of, say, 15, 20, or even 30 students. This teacher will be responsible for teaching every or nearly every subject (although other teachers may handle special aspects of the curriculum such as music or art). The secondary school teacher typically teaches five different classes per day, each one containing at least 20 or 30 students. The secondary school teacher must remember the names and characteristics of at least 150 students and consequently has less detailed knowledge of any particular student than does the elementary school teacher.

THINKING CREATIVELY

We have discussed the differences between teaching elementary school and secondary school students. Now describe how the two kinds of teaching are similar.

SUGGESTION: Teachers must understand the age of students they teach and must prepare material that is appropriate.

The secondary school teacher is more likely to see a wide range of discipline problems and has only a limited amount of time each day with each student in order to deal with these problems. A difficult fourth-grade girl has one teacher all day, and this teacher will be more likely to develop effective ways to control the girl than would her five different teachers in eighth grade, each of whom has exposure to the girl for only fifty minutes a day. An additional challenge faced by secondary teachers is that they have only the forty- to fifty-minute class period in which both to seize the students' attention and to provide instruction. Discipline problems can thus be extremely upsetting to the secondary teacher's agenda. For all of these reasons, secondary teachers—even more than elementary teachers—must focus on preventing misbehavior from even developing in the first place.

The book *Classroom Management for Secondary Teachers* (Emmer et al., 1997) provides guidance for how secondary teachers can accomplish their goals in this challenging environment. First, Emmer and colleagues suggest careful attention to the physical environment of the classroom. Plan the layout of the furniture and the positioning of resources to facilitate instruction and learning. Organize the classroom so high traffic areas are kept free of congestion and teaching materials and supplies are within easy reach. Set up the room so you can see all the students and keep track of what they are doing, and so the students can see you and all displays, presentations, and visual aids.

Emmer and colleagues found that secondary students often misbehaved because rules and procedures were not clearly understood. Thus, emphasize rules and procedures at the start of the term and post them in a prominent place. High school students may also be given a handout listing the rules. Secondary students, even more than elementary students, may be more compliant to rules when they have been involved in establishing them. But there are pitfalls. Several teachers who teach the same subject may have very different rules because of student participation in rule setting. Even in smaller schools, it can be confusing and potentially unfair to students when some teachers have far more restrictive rules and procedures than other teachers. Thus as a secondary teacher, remain aware of your students' contacts with other teachers and check with other teachers and school administrators about their rules and guidelines.

Secondary classes sometimes require more elaborate procedures than elementary school classrooms. Effective procedures make it possible for you to accomplish your goals within the time constraints of a forty- to fifty-minute class period. For example, secondary teachers need effective procedures for getting the students into their seats, ready to work, and on time for class; for collecting and distributing assignment sheets, homework, and tests; for sharing materials and equipment; for handling in-class presentations and small-group work; and for monitoring classroom discussion. The secondary school environment can sometimes be less tolerant of poor teaching because of its greater regimentation and because of the greater demands of controlling adolescents. However, elementary school teachers must be highly organized too because they do not have timed class periods to impose external organization on them. Elementary teachers must ensure that students complete many different activities within unstructured blocks of time.

THE SCHOOL ENVIRONMENT. In preparing effective plans, also consider the general environment of the school. The word *environment* in this context has several meanings. Some schools have a generally permissive environment in which the norm is few rules and restrictions. Other schools resemble army training camps, and discipline is the word of the day, every day. You may believe the best way to reach students is with a relaxed and autonomy-oriented rule system; however, if the school has a rigidly controlled environment, you may not succeed with such a system. The principal, other administrators,

A high school chemistry teacher helps his students with an experiment. (Will Hart, PhotoEdit)

or other teachers may protest. For the students, the contrast of a tight rule-bound environment in all classrooms but one may be confusing. Thus, create rules consistent with your overall school environment. Alternatively, work to influence and change the school environment as you see fit.

Another aspect of the school environment relevant to your planning has to do with the physical characteristics of the school. Some schools are spacious and have few students; others are tiny and crowded. Some schools have computers and laboratory equipment for all students; others have little equipment and few supplies—or even none. In addition, the physical layout of classrooms can work to make your job either easier or more difficult. Work within these physical realities when developing rules and procedures (see Figure 11.3 a–b).

FIGURE **11.3a**

An Elementary Classroom Arrangement

This 4th-grade teacher has designed a space that allows teacher presentations and demonstrations, small group work, computer interactions, math manipulatives activities, informal reading, art, and other projects without requiring constant rearrangements.

Source: From *Elementary Classroom Management* (2nd ed.), by C. S. Weinstein and A. J. Mignano, Jr., 1997, New York: McGraw-Hill. Copyright © 1997 by The McGraw-Hill Companies. Reprinted with permission.

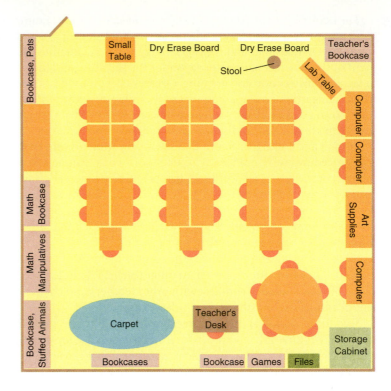

FIGURE **11.3b**

A High School Math Classroom

This high school teacher has designed a math classroom that allows teacher presentations and demonstrations as well as small group work. By moving 3 tables, the room can be transformed into 4 horizontal rows for independent work or testing.

Source: From *Elementary Classroom Management* (2nd ed.), by C. S. Weinstein and A. J. Mignano, Jr., 1997, New York: McGraw-Hill. Copyright © 1997 by The McGraw-Hill Companies. Reprinted with permission.

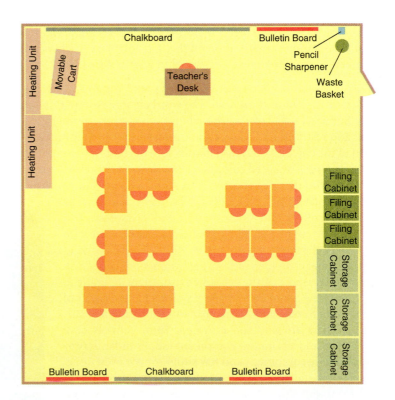

One more aspect of the school environment to consider when developing plans is the school administration's tolerance for new, unusual, or creative rules and procedures. Some school environments tolerate virtually no new rules and procedures; other school environments encourage teacher creativity. Savvy teachers check with other experienced teachers and with administrators before developing their classroom management system.

STUDENT CHARACTERISTICS AND HISTORIES. In preparing effective plans, also consider the relevant histories of the students in the class. Middle-class students in an upscale suburb may respond differently from lower socio-economic status (SES) rural students, who may themselves respond differently from urban students in general. Students from some socioeconomic and ethnic groups or from certain geographical areas may have had less adequate school preparation, and may be weaker in school achievement, than other students. Socioeconomic status and associated social factors are powerful influences on children's development (see Chapter 6). Remain sensitive to the needs and expectations of different groups of children, and be cautious when applying rules that worked on one group of children to another group of children from a different socioeconomic background. Children with a history of school success respond differently to a teacher's management plans than do students with a history of negative school experiences. Individual students each have their own unique scholastic history, and it is always helpful to become familiar with this background information as well.

One teacher began his career in a rural working-class community and found that the students were well behaved in school and readily accepted the rules he instituted and the teaching plan he implemented, as well as his authority, in general. When this teacher later began working in a relatively affluent suburban school, he found the students talked back frequently and mocked and challenged his rules and procedures. Whenever you change teaching environments, you must take stock of your new situation before creating new rules and new teaching plans. Generalizations are difficult, but one thing is certain: You must remain attentive to the differing needs and characteristics of students from different groups when developing and implementing rules and procedures.

THINKING PRACTICALLY

What type of school environment might make a teacher more likely to use restrictive rules and procedures?

SUGGESTION: A relatively unsafe or potentially violent school environment; an uncontrolled environment; or an environment in which the administration and other teachers strongly encourage and support restrictive rules and procedures.

THINKING CREATIVELY

How might you evaluate what type of students you have in your class so you can develop appropriate rules and procedures for your students?

SUGGESTION: Begin by watching and listening, in order to gather information; then try out some sample rules and procedures on a trial basis to see how students respond. Modify the plan as necessary.

PROCEDURES AND RULES

The terms *procedures* and *rules* have been mentioned often in this chapter. When Charlie Grenda started teaching, he suddenly realized how essential procedures and rules are. Let us take a closer look at procedures and rules, and how they are best used by expert teachers.

■**PROCEDURES** **Procedures** are the methods for accomplishing classroom activities in an orderly manner. Procedures are needed in order to specify how students will get things done and accomplish the activities necessary for learning. Procedures determine how students get their class folders from the side of the classroom, what library resources students will be allowed to use and how these resources will be accessed, and what students should do if they have to go to the rest room. To construct a procedure, first divide the activity into the individual steps required to accomplish it and enumerate these steps clearly. Ask yourself what might go wrong with each step and build in safeguards to prevent problems and misunderstandings and to maintain order. Seek student feedback and modify the procedures as appropriate. You can explain the procedures orally or write them and post in the classroom. Finally, review the procedures periodically to ensure that they are still accomplishing meaningful objectives as efficiently as possible.

Sometimes, members of one culture are familiar with a certain procedure as a result of growing up in a similar environment. However, when students from different cultures join the classroom, do not assume a knowledge of procedures. Explain to students the precise steps involved in classroom procedures so all are equally aware of these procedures. A student who is unaware may behave inappropriately without even knowing why. For example, a student from another country, or even from another region of the same country in which the school is located, may have previously been taught never to speak out unless called on by name. If the student's current teacher encourages students to speak out spontaneously—or gives extra credit to students who speak out with enthusiasm during open discussions, this procedure should be clearly explained to the student. Adjusting to new classroom procedures can take time. Some students may remain uncomfortable with fundamentally new procedures for many months. Teachers in schools located in areas in which families often move should be particularly sensitive to helping students learn the new procedures.

What types of classroom activities should be covered by procedures? Establish basic administrative procedures for taking attendance and ensuring that homework is completed; procedures governing students who wish to leave the room; procedures for maintaining a clean and orderly classroom environment; procedures for collecting and returning assignments, exams, and homework; and, finally, procedures governing how students should interact with one another, and how students should interact with you (Weinstein & Mignano, 1993, 1997).

■ **RULES** Procedures specify how things get done in the classroom, whereas **rules** are statements that specify acceptable and unacceptable behaviors in the classroom. Rules tend to be fewer in number and more explicit than procedures. In fact, effective classroom managers write down the class rules, post them, and hand them out (to older students). The nature of the rules in a classroom helps shape the learning environment that will exist. Thus carefully consider the rules, and even discuss them with colleagues and the principal, before implementing them. Think of rules as creating the necessary limits on student behavior that will lead to an optimal learning environment for all students.

Once again, when setting rules you must be aware of the general school rules. Confusion or resentment may result if one teacher allows students more freedom than the school rules or the rules of other teachers. Some teachers make the mistake of having too many or too detailed rules, and students in their classes spend more time trying to figure out what the rules are than they spend engaged in productive learning. In general, having a short list of clear and concise rules that apply to many different types of situations is preferable to having an exhaustive list of rules that no one—sometimes not even the teacher—can remember. Effective teachers often involve students in creating, reviewing, and reworking classroom rules and consequences for breaking them, while providing these students with input about administrative and general school requirements.

Evertson and colleagues (1997) list five types of general rules that are helpful for elementary school students:

1. Be polite and helpful.

2. Respect other people's property.

3. Listen quietly while others are speaking.

4. Do not hit, shove, or hurt others.

5. Obey all school rules.

The last rule is important because it clarifies for students that school rules are always to be followed, regardless of teacher.

Especially with elementary school students, provide clear examples of the behavior prohibited by each rule. Students need to discuss examples to ensure that everyone understands the concepts that underlie the rules. If you must replace or amend a rule, fully apprise the students and explain the reasons for the change. Posting written rules prominently in the classroom—in several spots—is an excellent idea.

Emmer and colleagues (1994) list six general rules helpful in managing secondary school students:

1. Bring all needed materials to class.

2. Be in your seat and ready to work when the bell rings.

3. Respect and be polite to everyone.

4. Respect other people's property.

5. Listen and stay seated while someone else is speaking.

6. Obey all school rules.

As with younger students, clearly explain the rules and give and discuss examples openly in the classroom. Figures 11.4 through 11.6 display some typical rules and procedures for elementary, middle, and high school students.

Consider cultural differences among children when developing and implementing rules. For example, as discussed in Chapter 6 on group differences, many teachers report that urban children tend to interrupt each other often while speaking and view such interruptions as a normal and natural aspect of communication. The urban culture may encourage this behavior. However, rural children tend to wait until others are finished speaking to begin speaking, and they tend to tolerate long pauses in conversations. These pauses can make urban children very uncomfortable.

THINKING PRACTICALLY

How might you convince a rule-resistant student that rules are in everyone's best interest?

SUGGESTION: One method is to explain how the rule-resistant student himself directly benefits from the rules. Another method is to review a situation in which the lack of rules ended up causing some kind of injury to a student or teacher.

FIGURE 11.4

School and Classroom Rules: Elementary School Students

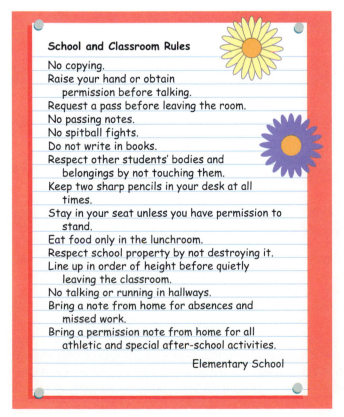

School and Classroom Rules

No copying.
Raise your hand or obtain
    permission before talking.
Request a pass before leaving the room.
No passing notes.
No spitball fights.
Do not write in books.
Respect other students' bodies and
    belongings by not touching them.
Keep two sharp pencils in your desk at all
    times.
Stay in your seat unless you have permission to
    stand.
Eat food only in the lunchroom.
Respect school property by not destroying it.
Line up in order of height before quietly
    leaving the classroom.
No talking or running in hallways.
Bring a note from home for absences and
    missed work.
Bring a permission note from home for all
    athletic and special after-school activities.

                        Elementary School

FIGURE 11.5

School and Classroom Rules: Middle School Students

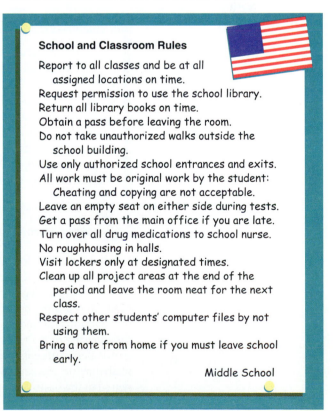

School and Classroom Rules

Report to all classes and be at all
    assigned locations on time.
Request permission to use the school library.
Return all library books on time.
Obtain a pass before leaving the room.
Do not take unauthorized walks outside the
    school building.
Use only authorized school entrances and exits.
All work must be original work by the student:
    Cheating and copying are not acceptable.
Leave an empty seat on either side during tests.
Get a pass from the main office if you are late.
Turn over all drug medications to school nurse.
No roughhousing in halls.
Visit lockers only at designated times.
Clean up all project areas at the end of the
    period and leave the room neat for the next
    class.
Respect other students' computer files by not
    using them.
Bring a note from home if you must leave school
    early.

                        Middle School

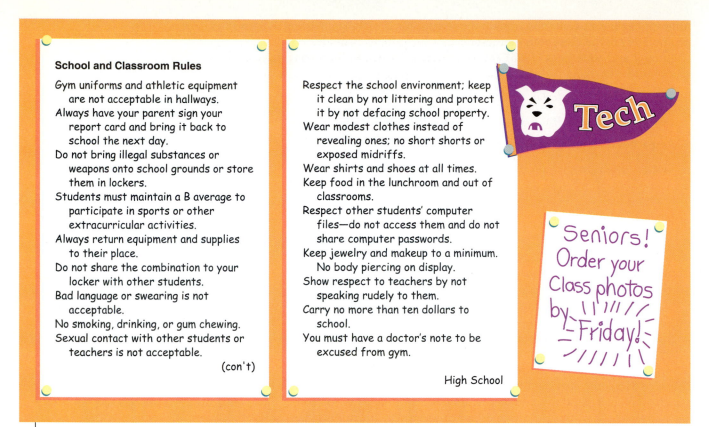

School and Classroom Rules

Gym uniforms and athletic equipment are not acceptable in hallways.

Always have your parent sign your report card and bring it back to school the next day.

Do not bring illegal substances or weapons onto school grounds or store them in lockers.

Students must maintain a B average to participate in sports or other extracurricular activities.

Always return equipment and supplies to their place.

Do not share the combination to your locker with other students.

Bad language or swearing is not acceptable.

No smoking, drinking, or gum chewing.

Sexual contact with other students or teachers is not acceptable.

(con't)

Respect the school environment; keep it clean by not littering and protect it by not defacing school property.

Wear modest clothes instead of revealing ones; no short shorts or exposed midriffs.

Wear shirts and shoes at all times.

Keep food in the lunchroom and out of classrooms.

Respect other students' computer files—do not access them and do not share computer passwords.

Keep jewelry and makeup to a minimum. No body piercing on display.

Show respect to teachers by not speaking rudely to them.

Carry no more than ten dollars to school.

You must have a doctor's note to be excused from gym.

High School

Seniors! Order your Class photos by Friday!

FIGURE 11.6

School and Classroom Rules: High School Students

The styles of these groups of children can be different enough so as to make you wish to change rules developed for use in one cultural group if you begin teaching children from another cultural group.

CONSTRUCTING YOUR OWN LEARNING

Choose one age-range on which to focus (elementary, middle school, or high school), and develop a list of class rules and procedures to use with students you teach. Think back to your own teachers and to teachers you may have observed in your field work. Consider the rules and procedures they used. Which ones worked best, and why? Which rules and procedures were less effective? Try to develop a workable and reasonable list for the age of student you have chosen. Once you have developed your list, ask one or two friends or classmates to read and comment on it. Try to defend your choices, but feel free to revise your list as you see fit. Keep your list handy for future reference.

 RESPONDING TO BROKEN RULES

What should you do when a student breaks a rule? For rules to be effective, broken rules must lead to specific and appropriate consequences. As we discussed in Chapter 7, consequences and privileges are quite useful in shaping behavior. For minor rule infractions, students may simply be required to repeat the activity or action, but to do it correctly. For more serious infractions, more serious consequences will be necessary in order to uphold the integrity of the rule system with all students. Many teachers find that a graduated system is best. Students can thus be managed by facing consequences appropriate to their misbehavior: You can ask yourself, "How serious was the infraction? How often has it happened in the past? What penalties were imposed in the past, and how well did they work?"

A minor first-time infraction may require only an expression of disappointment by the teacher. Next, a teacher can try removing some privilege valued by the student—for example, the student can lose a free period or recess break or have extra work to do in place of an otherwise pleasurable activity. Some students are controlled effectively by being excluded from the group. For these students, being ostracized or ignored represents an effective consequence. For students old enough to write a letter, an assignment to write a letter explaining and atoning for their misbehavior may deter future misbehavior. Especially if the written letter is placed in the student's file, this consequence can be motivation not to repeat a mistake.

If unacceptable behaviors persist, or a serious misbehavior takes place, you may wish to send a student to detention. An informal detention might be to require the student to stay in the classroom and do quiet work while you grade papers and the rest of the class is enjoying free time. Formal detentions are held by schools after the normal school day, during lunch period, or during other free periods.

THINKING CREATIVELY

What unusual but reasonable punishments can you think of that would encourage students to obey the rules?

SUGGESTION: No bakery-fresh cookies that the teacher brings to class for young students who do not follow the rules; no field trips and no substitution of more for less enjoyable assignments for older students who disobey the rules.

When rule infractions are serious, call in reinforcements to help manage the situation and the student. In some cases, you may need to involve the principal and/or the parents. A badly misbehaving student—for example, a student who has hit another student or stolen something—should be sent to the principal's office, where appropriate additional punishments will be meted out. Telephoning the student's parents is often a good idea, because they should be informed of any serious problems. If serious problems persist—such as when a knife or gun is carried to school—the student can be suspended from school or even expelled. These actions are taken by the principal.

The potential necessity of these extreme consequences shows why you must keep the school principal informed of serious misbehaviors. Sometimes, if you are convinced you can deal with the situation, you may fail to properly inform the principal. If the misbehavior then becomes more serious, you may require the principal's help and may need belatedly to inform the principal of the entire sequence of events. The principal at this point may justifiably feel she should have been informed sooner of potentially serious situations. Table 11.2 lists strategies for coping successfully with some common student behavior problems.

TABLE 11.2   Strategies for Coping with Student Behavior Problems

- Don't ignore problems: Try to create solutions before problems worsen. Don't overreact by making problems seem worse than they are.

- Reseat troublesome students to isolate them from others.

- Engage, rechannel, and redirect the energies of troublesome students: Assign peer tutoring and challenge students to help others; give problem students special tasks such as classroom pet care; challenge students to perform as well as others.

- Offer small rewards for good behavior; pay more attention to well-behaved students than to troublemakers; ignore troublemakers who seem to crave attention.

- Offer no homework on weekends, field trips, and other desired rewards for good behavior by the entire class—this will mean that peers will influence each other to behave well.

- Give time-outs to let students calm down and deescalate the situation.

- Be consistent in following through with rewards and punishments.

- Gain the cooperation of parents to help in managing major problems or issues. Send a brief, daily report card home to parents to keep them informed. Randomly call parents of well-behaving students to praise their children; this will secure parental cooperation in the future.

- Keep cool; avoid angry outbursts.

- Give praise for good behaviors; clarify for the class what the positive behaviors consist of so this information will be clear to the whole class.

- Try to assign work and lead instruction that is relevant to the students' lives. Avoid teaching boring material in a boring fashion.

- Ask the school psychologist for help with particularly difficult students; speak to other teachers and the principal and request assistance.

- Model positive behaviors to make sure students understand what these behaviors consist of; talk often about people who became successful after rough starts in school.

- Rule out medical causes such as illness, poor eyesight, or hearing or other disability.

- Have problem students evaluated to determine whether they are gifted or have other special needs.

- Use the rule of successive approximations to shape students' behavior in small steps to create more positive behaviors (see Chapter 7).

Even if you have almost no familiarity with managing a classroom, you know that managing 6-year-olds is very different from managing 18-year-olds. Brophy and Evertson (1978) believe that teachers need to use four different approaches to classroom management as a function of the students' age.

As children begin school and become accustomed to the school environment in kindergarten and grades 1 and 2, they need patient and constant immersion in and reminding of basic classroom rules and procedures. At this age, school is a frightening experience and students need to get used to going to school and dealing with the environment away from home.

By the middle elementary years students have become accustomed to going to school and following school rules and procedures. At this level, focus on teaching the specific rules that apply to each activity. Because the students will have developed more school savvy, they will be able to spend more time learning material and less time simply being introduced to the rules and procedures of the school.

As students finish elementary school and begin adolescence, their peers take on greater influence. The problems of adolescence and changes associated with puberty may cause students to care less about pleasing their teachers. Some students may become defiant and difficult to manage. As teachers of students at this age you must concern yourselves with motivating students who may be tuning out of school as the pressures of puberty place their minds on other concerns, and with handling disruptive and contentious students.

Once the biological aspects of adolescence are resolved and students have reached the last two years of high school, they often have a more adultlike focus and ability to discipline themselves. Many students are focused on academics and on their future education or careers after high school. Effective classroom management for these students involves teaching the right material to maximize learning, tailoring instruction to life and career goals, and helping students manage their own learning. Because students have developed elaborate scripts for rules and procedures by this point, much less time is devoted at this stage to teaching rules and procedures. Table 11.3 lists the developmental characteristics of students that impact teachers' management styles.

THINKING ANALYTICALLY

Why should a teacher who instructs only secondary school children need to be familiar with the demands of teaching elementary school?

SUGGESTION: Understanding past school experiences is essential for a teacher wishing to teach students at the secondary level.

TABLE 11.3 **Developmental Characteristics of Students That Influence Teachers' Management Styles**

Ask yourself the following questions before deciding which management techniques to use:

- Can the student feel and understand what the teacher feels? (Capacity for empathy)
- Can the student understand what the teacher expects? (Vocabulary and intellectual capacity)
- Can the student understand how his or her behavior affects others? (Knowledge of consequences)
- Can the student see her or his role in her or his behavior? (Knowledge of causality)
- Can the student appreciate how symbols can be used to represent ideas? (Understanding of metaphors)
- Can the student understand responsibility to a larger group—the peer group, the class, the school community, or society at large? (Capacity for altruism)
- Can the student understand the values and goals of the school environment? (Practical knowledge of school environment)
- Can the student understand that parents' goals, values, and behaviors may differ from school values and behaviors? (Perspective on one's culture)
- Can the student understand that criticism and punishment can be for the student's own benefit? (Knowledge of the necessity of consequences)
- Can the student understand that other people's goals, values, behaviors, and cultural views are important considerations? (Appreciation of the value of diversity)

WHO SHOULD LEAD AND WHO SHOULD FOLLOW?

Do middle school and high school students learn best in a tightly managed and highly disciplined environment in which the teacher is in control? Or does the best learning environment consist of an open classroom in which the teacher provides assistance to students but does not control events? How much discipline is necessary and desirable in order to bring about maximal learning?

Jefferson High School in Virginia has been the focus of a controversy regarding these questions. Jefferson graduates more National Merit Scholars than any other high school in the United States. Traditionally, students at Jefferson have had a significant amount of free time in which to talk informally about their work to other students and to teachers, and in which to work on projects of their own choice. Rigid discipline has not been stressed. But in late 1996, following the arrest of several Jefferson students for minor incidents of vandalism, there was a call for increased discipline at the school.

FIRST VIEW: *Students learn best in a structured and highly disciplined environment.* Proponents of this position argue that too much free time leads students astray from learning. According to this view, learning requires a disciplined mind, and a disciplined mind can be trained only through many hours of focused academic work over many years of schooling. Students must *learn* to enjoy academic work and must *learn* the pleasure of sticking with an activity and completing it—and they will learn these valuable lessons only if the school environment enforces strict discipline, rules, and procedures. In addition, too much freedom for students is seen as undermining the authority of teachers and other adult role models. Thus Jefferson students are seen as having been given too much of a say in how they spend their time, and the resulting discipline problems—albeit involving only a handful of students—are seen as the beginning of a more serious trend.

SECOND VIEW: *Students learn best in an unstructured environment.* People who believe that students prosper with less structure argue that the only learning that matters is active and engaged learning, initiated by the individual student. According to this view, enforced discipline causes only a perfunctory performance of academic tasks and does little good in the long run. An open and free learning environment encourages students to seek out those activities and subjects that interest them the most. By causing students to equate learning with rigid discipline, a controlled environment serves to teach students that learning is not fun, and that it is something they are forced to do. However, by equating learning with exploration, self-discovery, and fulfillment of personal influences, a student working in an unstructured environment internalizes the love of learning and carries this value into adult life. With this view, the success of so many students from Jefferson High School clearly shows that less structure is better.

THIRD VIEW: A SYNTHESIS: *Students need structure up to a point, but once they reach that point they will benefit from a less structured environment.* The middle-ground position argues that teachers will not lose their authority with students by relinquishing tight control once the students have earned the privilege of working within a less structured environment. When students begin their academic careers, they need to learn good work habits and learn how to interact positively with teachers and classmates. Once these basic skills are mastered, responsible students with personal ambition and drive to excel in school may then be given a reasonable amount of freedom and unstructured time. The majority of students at Jefferson have earned this privilege, and should thus be rewarded with a less structured learning environment. Students who excel academically and who love learning do not need to be pushed to be made to work; often they need to be told to stop working in order to eat meals and attend to other tasks. Teachers of academically motivated students are thus freed to lead students by providing support and access to resources. As always, the structure of a discipline system should be based in part on students' maturity and developmental level.

Implications for Teaching

■ *Before developing a management plan, consider the developmental age, maturity level, and background of the students.* Do not simply draw up a plan that sounds good to you; develop one that will work for the specific students in your classroom. To do this effectively, you must get to know your students.

■ *Set reasonable procedures and rules and make sure students are familiar with them.* Being overly punitive or overly lenient will backfire. Your goal is to manage students for optimal learning, not to control their every thought and movement, and not to allow the students to control you either.

■ *When drafting the procedures and rules, consider the school's physical and cultural environment, and the advantages and disadvantages of each.* Each school has its own particularities; get the facts before mapping your plan. Consider alternatives before settling on a final plan.

■ *Review other teachers' rules and procedures before drafting your own; discuss your plans with other teachers for input.* Never underestimate the value of peer feedback, particularly that of experienced and effective peers. Be willing to borrow the best techniques from your colleagues.

■ *Tailor punishments to the severity of the misbehaviors that motivated the punishments.* Retain perspective on how bad the misbehavior is and what punishment is deserved. Too lenient or too harsh an approach will not extinguish misbehavior as effectively as a more appropriate reaction.

Maintaining Control and Preventing Problems

So far in this chapter we have considered the role of classroom management in effective teaching, the importance of effective plans, rules, and procedures, and techniques for implementing these rules and procedures to make classrooms work. Thus most of our discussion has focused on getting started with a new class. But many teachers consider the hardest part of classroom management to be maintaining order and control for the long haul—between October and May. Even after Charlie Grenda figured out how to get in control of his students, he still faced the challenges of maintaining control for the rest of the year. Let us assume that a teacher has established effective rules and has a generally well-behaved class. Problems will still occur, and when they do, the expert teacher is prepared to deal with them and to prevent their recurrence. What are the key issues you must understand about maintaining control in the classroom?

In this text we have often emphasized good communication because it underlies successful teaching. Here we focus on good communication in terms of how it supports effective classroom management. Because rules and procedures are effective only if they are clearly understood, teachers who communicate effectively with students have better results in managing their students than do less effective communicators who implement the same rules and procedures. Communication with parents is also essential, because the students' home environment can either foster good study skills and appropriate classroom behavior or undermine the lessons you are working to get across. Much of being a good communicator consists of being a good listener who is able to empathize with others. Another important part of communicating effectively is practicing reflective thinking in which you mull over situations and work to understand them from each participant's perspective.

Communication is an intricate phenomenon. Much of what we communicate—whether intentionally or unintentionally—is nonverbal. What we say aloud is only a part of the story. Our body language, tone of voice, and gestures all contribute to the picture of what we really mean. To be an effective classroom manager—and to be an effective teacher in general—you must become an effective communicator. Part of this skill involves identifying the real message behind what is directly stated.

For example, students who are frustrated at their inability to complete a task may simply stop working. As you approach the desk of such a student, the student may respond that the assignment is meaningless, boring, repetitive, or stupid. Although you can easily interpret the message just as it sounds, the real underlying message—one picked up by the effective teacher—is that the student is upset by her own inability to accomplish the work. Getting to the root of why she had trouble starts with recognizing that what she says aloud does not tell the whole story. Her defiant stare, her body language, and her snippy tone might all signal that her emotions are out of control. Thus dealing with such situations effectively requires sensitivity to the range of emotions and thoughts that are sometimes buried beneath a simple verbal message.

THINKING PRACTICALLY

How can you improve your own communication skills?

SUGGESTION: Ask people you admire to critique your skills and suggest methods for improvement; listen to yourself on tape; take a course emphasizing communication skills; and practice in front of a mirror.

RESPONDING TO STUDENT MISBEHAVIOR

Expert teachers have a variety of strategies for dealing effectively with student misbehavior. Each student and each situation are unique, but in most situations certain strategies can be applied to correct the misbehavior and allow everyone to return to meaningful learning.

■ **"I" MESSAGES** One approach to handling student misbehavior is to use an "I" message (Ginott, 1972; Gordon, 1974). An **"I" message** is a clear, direct, assertive statement about exactly what a student did that constitutes misbehaving, how the misbehavior affects the teacher's ability to teach, and how the teacher feels about the misbehavior. An "I" message is thus a first line of defense against misbehavior, in that it does not immediately demand or require a change in behavior on the part of the student. The goal of an "I" message is to effect a voluntary change in the student's behavior by appealing to the student's conscience and desire to do the right thing. For example, a teacher says, "When you talk to another student during my lessons, it makes me feel as though you do not care about hearing

A teenage student shows anger by his defiant and hostile body language as his teacher discusses a low grade on a paper. (Cleve Bryant, PhotoEdit)

what I have to say," or "When you fail to hand in your assignments on time, it makes me think that you do not believe the work we are doing is important."

As Kounin suggested in his techniques for effective classroom management, an "I" message tells students what behaviors they are engaging in that they should change without becoming a personal attack on the character and personality of the student. The "I" message approach is based on the humanistic approach to education and motivation we discussed in Chapter 10—that is, that students who can be made to understand the consequences of their actions will voluntarily change these actions. The premise of the "I" message approach is that the teacher's authority and ability to punish students should be used only when other methods, such as the "I" message, have failed to modify students' behavior.

■**ASSERTIVE DISCIPLINE** Another approach for handling student misbehavior is known as the **assertive discipline** program developed by Lee Canter (1989a, 1989b, 1992). Assertive discipline is a method of responding to misbehavior that is clear, firm, and direct. As the word *assertive* suggests, teachers who use this style make their expectations clear and firmly state the consequences for misbehavior. They then follow through with these consequences if appropriate.

Canter believes that teachers who fail at classroom management do so because they have one of two ineffective styles. The first ineffective style is the *passive style*. Passive teachers fail to label the problem behavior firmly and directly and tell the student what should have been done. Passive teachers may also simply ignore inappropriate behavior or may fail to enforce the stated consequences. The second ineffective style is the *hostile style*. Teachers who act in a hostile manner may tell a misbehaving student that she is an inept or stupid person. Hostile teachers pronounce extreme punishments and then fail to follow through, or they attempt to undermine a student's sense of self-worth by telling the student that she seems to be incapable of performing better. Hostility can be communicated nonverbally as well as verbally—a hostile teacher can communicate through body language and other means that a student is inept or stupid without ever saying these words.

Canter advocates the assertive discipline approach as an effective method for dealing with student misbehavior. The program consists of three basic parts:

1. The teacher teaches students how to behave. To accomplish this, establish clear and specific directions for each activity and make sure the students know how to behave. To check if students know how to behave, rehearse the desired behaviors with the class, write the behaviors on the board, ask students to repeat the list, question students about what they are supposed to be doing, and watch carefully during the first few times a new activity is performed, to ensure that all students understand the rules.

2. The teacher provides positive reinforcement. Thus you might comment when a student is doing a good job of following the rules. By drawing all students' attention to a desirable behavior, you strengthen students' understanding of what desirable behaviors consist of and also strengthen their resolve to perform these behaviors.

3. The teacher invokes the discipline plan, which consists of the programmatic approach to discipline problems you have developed ahead of time. The discipline plan entails negative consequences if students refuse to perform the desired behaviors. It should include different levels of negative consequences for misbehavior, in which each level of response is more severe than the previous one. Canter advocates no more than five levels of negative consequences.

Many teachers and school administrators report that they use assertive discipline with success in their classrooms. However, researchers in the educational and psychological communities have pointed out that the efficacy of assertive discipline has not been adequately demonstrated. In an overview of the literature, Render, Padilla, and Krank (1989) found that anecdotal reports, as opposed to empirical studies, were the basis for people's opinions about the success of assertive discipline.

Assertive discipline takes a behavioral approach to modifying student misbehaviors (see Chapter 7), linking student behavior to specific positive and negative consequences. What may be lacking is a true understanding, on the part of the student, about the reasons for certain rules. Thus researchers taking a cognitive perspective (see Chapter 8 on cognitive approaches to learning) argue that students need to understand the reasons for the rules that are used to manage classroom learning, rather than simply being told that an escalating series of punishments will be the consequence of a lack of conformity to those rules.

What if neither an "I" message nor the use of assertive discipline produces the necessary behavioral change? You must retain control of the class while imposing control on the disruptive student (or students). Anger is your enemy here, although it is often easy to become angry with a defiant student. Instead of becoming angry, initiate a positive reaction to the discipline problem. At times, such as when safety is an issue, simply state what is going to happen—or, in other words, give a direct order. More often, however, attempt a reconciliation and joint solution.

■ **DECIDING WHO OWNS THE PROBLEM** Giving students choices is generally a very effective strategy. An analysis of how to proceed in this situation is provided by Gordon (1974, 1981). In his book *Teacher Effectiveness Training*, Gordon states that before deciding on a course of action in response to a problem, a teacher must decide who "owns the problem." Some student actions might trouble or even repel you, but they might still represent problems that are not your responsibility to solve. Start out by analyzing who owns the problem and why the problem is affecting you. If you own the problem, you must direct the student to solve the problem. If the student owns the problem, however, your role becomes one of providing a sympathetic ear and of helping the student find his or her own solution.

Let's assume that a student's misbehavior disrupts classroom instruction. In this case, you own the problem and must respond and take action to modify the student's behavior. In this case, you must confront the student and direct the solution of the problem. However, if a student becomes angry or upset about something that happens in school (such as losing the lead in a school play), the student owns the problem (unless, of course, the student's anger causes her or him to become disruptive). If you respond with discipline to a student-owned problem, the student may be less able to find a solution. The expert teacher understands that student-owned problems are the *student's* responsibility to solve—not the teacher's. Too much teacher direction prevents students from solving their own problems and learning the skills involved in doing so successfully.

The key is to consider whether the problem obstructs effective teaching and learning. If so, you own the problem. However, if the behavior simply annoys you but does not interfere with teaching or learning, the student probably owns the problem.

■ **WHEN THE STUDENT OWNS THE PROBLEM: ACTIVE LISTENING** But what should you do when a student is stuck on a problem that the student owns? Gordon recommends you try **active listening,** which consists of allotting the time to listen to a student in an active and concerned manner and encouraging the student to state the problem fully. This technique involves paraphrasing what the student says and encouraging the student to work through the problem. For example, the teacher says, in a concerned tone, "Sarah, I can see something is bothering you. I suspect you are upset about your parents' recent divorce. Your mother called to tell me that she is worried about you. How are you feeling about

THINKING PRACTICALLY

How can you tell *if* you are being too passive or too hostile in your management style?

SUGGESTION: By observing student reactions and charting student achievement; by asking colleagues for feedback; by taking courses and reading books to hone skills.

A teacher quietly disciplines an errant student—away from the classroom and his student peers. (Bob Daemmrich, Stock Boston)

the situation? Would you like to talk about it? If so, I am here to listen and to do what I can to make you feel better so you can concentrate again on your schoolwork."

Active listening does not entail your directing the student's words, telling the student how she should feel, or otherwise determining the outcome of the student's feelings about the problem. Your response is limited to acknowledging the student's feelings and opinions. During conversations with students, teachers often find it helpful to implement the **paraphrase rule,** designed to promote accurate communication. In following this rule, the teacher or student, before speaking, must first summarize in her or his own words what the other person said.

To be effective as an active listener, block out external stimuli—for example, do not take interruptions from other students—and listen carefully to both verbal and nonverbal messages being delivered by the student. Disentangle the emotional and intellectual content of the message and make appropriate inferences regarding the student speaker's

EXPERT TEACHER INTERVIEW

FOCUS ON: CLASSROOM MANAGEMENT STRATEGIES
TRACEY SABBATO: HICKORY MIDDLE SCHOOL, CHESAPEAKE, VIRGINIA—GRADE 8, ENGLISH

Tracey Sabbato has been teaching for four years. Before she gets to the subject matter, she has a routine in place and her eighth-grade students know exactly what to expect if they misbehave. This consistency is peppered with a good sense of humor to create a classroom atmosphere that works well for her and her students.

What are eighth-grade students like in the classroom?

In general, eighth graders are experiencing a highly emotional period in their young lives, and are in the process of learning how to manage these emotions. If something upsets them, they are quite vocal and/or reactionary. Many psychologists maintain that it is difficult during this period of young adolescence for eighth graders to concentrate on their studies for long periods of time.

Eighth-grade teachers frequently lament that daily they are confronted with young people in their classes who commonly disrupt class with excessive talking and bizarre noises. In order to cut down on these and other types of disciplinary issues, I establish a consistent classroom routine to follow. Without the predictability of a routine, student behavior may be more easily thrown off course.

What is the general routine you and your students follow? How do you introduce it to students at the beginning of the year?

One of the most difficult challenges is getting all students focused on the intended lesson at same time. Once they become fully engaged in an activity, they generally participate positively in their learning process. I spend the first five minutes of class focusing their attention with some type of activity. An example is a journal topic. I use the journal to give them an opportunity to express an opinion about what we are reading in class. I use this time to check homework, talk to students individually, and take care of some paper work. When they have had time to settle down and get prepared for the class we start the lesson. This routine starts on the first day of school. They begin to expect and rely on this opportunity to get focused.

What strategies do you use to manage an emotional situation for students?

Two years ago a middle-school student was killed in a car accident. My students had never experienced the death of a friend, so understandably,

they were very upset and were having difficulty in expressing their grief over what was, to some, a devastating loss.

Some of my teaching colleagues chose not to discuss the tragedy with their classes, but I felt that it needed to be verbalized in an open forum to give the students an outlet and sounding board on how they were feeling. Furthermore, I felt that if I didn't allow discussion about such an issue, the students would have remained very unproductive in class.

I gave them the opportunity to share funny anecdotes about the student who had been killed, and it resulted in not only a therapeutic practice for my students, but it also succeeded in redirecting them to more of a learning mode afterwards.

What strategies do you use to manage misbehavior?

The students in my class remain together for all their other classes—social studies, science, and math. The whole school works on the team concept model. A core team of four teachers works with a designated group of students. The teachers from my students' team decide on the discipline policy for the group. The approach ensures consis-

feelings (Sokolove, Garrett, Sadker, & Sadker, 1986). Empathize with the student by taking her position and showing her that you know how she feels. Sometimes being understood by an adult authority figure is all that is needed to make a student feel better.

■ **WHEN THE TEACHER OWNS THE PROBLEM: THE NO-LOSE METHOD**
When you own the problem and must therefore create a change in the student's behavior, Gordon advocates use of a **no-lose method** to resolve the problem. The concept behind the no-lose method is that resolving conflicts will be easier and more productive if neither you nor the student feel you are losing. For example, if you tell a boy passing notes in the back row to stop or else go to detention, and if you are successful in halting the bad behavior, the boy loses. If you fail to control the boy and the misbehavior continues, you lose. Gordon believes the right solution is that you and the boy come up with a compromise that represents a no-lose option—that is, a solution that allows neither

tency in behavior management for each class that the students are in.

We have four levels of response to misbehavior in class—verbal warning, parental contact, detention, and ultimately a visit to the principal's office. Students receive a verbal warning for excessive talking, disturbing the class (making inappropriate noises, for example), or make inappropriate comments (such as sexual remarks or profanity). Other behaviors warranting a verbal warning include picking on someone (for example, "Shut up, you are stupid!"), throwing things in class, or physically touching students to provoke them.

I hand out a detention when I've given a student a verbal warning but he or she continues the behavior. If a student leaves class without permission, he or she receives a detention without a verbal warning. However, if a student leaves class to diffuse anger, the student gets a warning, not a detention.

More serious behaviors such as kicking someone or injuring another student result in an immediate trip to the principal's office.

These methods for managing behavior in our team's classes have proven to be effective. I had 130 students this year, and I've written twenty referrals to the principal's office, which is a relatively small number when you take into account the number of students and the time frame in which the referrals were handed out. Fortunately, we have not had major ordeals.

What role does a sense of humor play in classroom management?

A sense of humor, I believe, is an enormously important attribute. I use humor to control or redirect students' negative behavior. For me, it may be as important as being consistent. I maintain a good rapport with my eighth-graders, even the "trouble-makers," because I can view some of their behavior with a sense of humor. I can laugh at some of what

> One of the most difficult challenges is getting all students focused on the intended lesson at same time. Once they become fully engaged in an activity, they generally participate positively in their learning process.

they do. As young teens, they experiment with all types of behavior, and some of what they do turns out to be quite funny, in my opinion. I believe that if I reacted very seriously and sternly to every little behavioral "blip," I would not be able to reach them as effectively as I currently do.

There are teachers who barely smile at their students throughout the entire school year because they cannot find humor in what they sometimes do. I don't think that these teachers like going to work as much as I do. In addition, they are more often the target of students' bad behavior.

What advice do you have for new teachers?

Students want to be your friend, but you need to *immediately* establish that this is not the role that you will play, although this may be hard to do. If you are in your twenties, you are still someone who could have a relationship with a young person based on friendship. However, I believe that new, especially younger teachers, need to quickly establish their roles as teacher and, whenever necessary, disciplinarian. There is a fine line between being friendly and being friends.

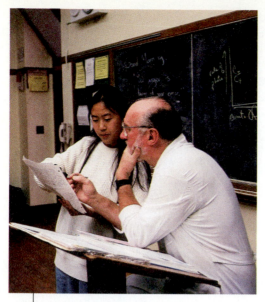

Engaged in active listening, a ninth-grade teacher reviews his student's work with her after class. (Elizabeth Crews)

party to lose. For example, you engage the boy in the class discussion by asking him a question you know he is able to answer, thus transferring the student's attention from note passing to learning. Later, you speak to the boy in private, stating that note passing is not acceptable and that you want him to remain actively involved in lessons. The specific six-step procedure advocated is the following:

1. Define the problem.

2. Generate possible solutions.

3. Evaluate the solutions.

4. Decide which solution is best.

5. Determine how to implement the solution.

6. Assess the success of the solution.

Consider an example of the use of the no-lose method. Suppose several students have been approaching their teacher repeatedly about wanting to have no homework on weekends. Because other teachers have instituted a no-homework-on-weekends policy, the students are resentful that their class does not have the policy. If the teacher simply says, "Too bad—in my class, there is homework on weekends," the students lose. If the teacher simply responds with, "OK— we won't have homework on weekends," the teacher loses because she knows the material must be covered if the students are to perform well on the mastery tests in two months. A no-lose method might involve a negotiated compromise such as the following: The teacher states, "Here is a compromise. What if I give 30 minutes extra homework on Monday through Thursday nights? If you all do your homework and no one complains about having more homework on weekdays, I will stop giving homework on weekends." Or the teacher asks the entire class to offer suggestions about how they can get the required amount of work done while still having no homework on weekends. There should also be a joint teacher/student-generated plan to evaluate the results.

One problem with the no-lose method is that negotiation is not appropriate in every situation, particularly with disruptive and unpredictable students who do not possess the goals of learning and achievement. If the student does not want to create a positive environment and is not motivated to learn and cooperate with the teacher, the no-lose method will probably not work.

GENERAL BEHAVIORAL INFLUENCE TECHNIQUES

In 1959 Redl and Wattenberg published a book that discussed techniques for influencing behavior. Although more than forty years old, teachers still find this list of techniques quite useful. More recent research (Walker & Shea, 1991) has built on and expanded on the earlier ideas. In addition, Emmer and colleagues (1997) also suggest methods for stopping student misbehavior. One technique advocated by this group of researchers is called *supporting self-control*; just as it sounds, it helps students develop self-control to minimize their misbehavior. You can help students develop self-control simply by ignoring inappropriate behaviors, as long as these behaviors are not disrupting other students' learning. You can also use proximity to the student as a cue to the student to halt the misbehavior. In this case, you simply stand close to the student and continue the lesson, or possibly even touch the student (for example, by placing your hand gently on the student's shoulder) if the behavior does not cease. You can also make eye contact with the student or give another nonverbal signal until the student stops the inappropriate behavior. Or you can help students develop self-control by using humor (not sarcasm) to halt the bad behavior.

THINKING ANALYTICALLY

Name three additional problems with the no-lose method.

SUGGESTION: The no-lose method can be too time consuming, can detract from the teacher's authority when used with some rebellious students, and can lead to solutions that the teacher feels compelled to endorse but that do not ultimately work.

Another general set of techniques for controlling a disruptive student involves *providing situational assistance*. First, you help the students over hurdles they are encountering. The idea of this technique is that students may not understand what they are supposed to do, or they may lack the ability to do it and therefore may have responded with poor behavior. Next, you can use rules and procedures to more effectively regiment and control what is going on in class. If the students are failing to follow a procedure correctly, restate the procedure and ask the students to start over. Or ask the misbehaving students to state the correct rule and then to follow it.

Yet another technique is to give misbehaving students a time-out. If there are objects in the room that seem to be distracting students or encouraging misbehaviors, remove the objects rather than continually fighting a losing battle.

A final set of techniques, referred to as *reality and value appraisal*, is also designed to redirect students' behavior toward more constructive, useful, and intelligent outcomes. To use these techniques, first restate the rule that was broken and note the reasons why the rule was developed in the first place, clearly explaining the limits on students' behavior implied by the rule. Then use criticism and encouragement. In this case, as we have already discussed, the criticism should be constructive and aimed at the inappropriate behavior rather than at the person. Ideally, follow the criticism by encouragement to change in the form of a statement describing the right behavior and explaining how the student could engage in the right behavior.

After discipline has been administered, there is sometimes a tense atmosphere in the classroom as well as potentially bad feelings between you and the disciplined student. In this case, you can speak to the student privately about the incident and improve the atmosphere between you. Or you can engage the class in a discussion about what happened and why, in an effort to put the event behind everyone. A teacher who is vigilant may even sense a situation that can become an opportunity for disruptive behavior. Sometimes, by commenting on the situation positively and by telling students what to expect, you can stop the misbehavior before it starts.

COPING WITH VIOLENCE IN SCHOOL

In addition to the typical types of management problems just discussed, teachers unfortunately also confront serious management problems (see the beginning of this chapter as well as Chapter 6 for an in-depth discussion of the condition of today's classrooms relative to the classrooms of days past). School violence is most likely in large schools located in high crime areas, in schools with weak administrators, and in schools with a high percentage of male students. Which students are more likely to engage in violent behaviors? Boys are more aggressive than girls on average (see Chapter 6), and consequently become involved in more violent acts and situations. Low-achieving students are also generally more likely to be violent, although the low achievement may not be a cause of the violent behavior but rather a consequence of a negative attitude about school and learning. Violent acts are twice as frequent in junior high schools as they are in senior high schools. In addition, some schools are poorly designed and administered, and the atmosphere in these schools often contributes to student violence.

What can you as an individual teacher do to reduce the chances that your pupils will become violent? Through the consistent use of clear and fair classroom management techniques, you can help direct students' energies more productively onto meaningful achievement (Rutter, 1983; Rutter et al., 1979). Students at risk for developing violent behavior do best in an environment that stresses incremental progress toward individual short-term goals—an environment that emphasizes improvement and hard work rather than absolute levels of achievement, as violence-prone students may not excel academically. Other tactics for reducing violence include inviting students to participate in developing the rules and procedures that will govern them, as well as in choosing the emphasis of their curriculum. When students have a role in deciding what they are taught and what rules they must obey, these students are more likely to return to the learning experience. And of course, all students benefit when teachers work to keep the material they teach both interesting and relevant to students' daily lives.

James Garbarino (1999), who has studied youthful offenders in and out of prison, believes that violence can best be prevented by coordinated efforts to make the school environment more responsive to the special needs of high-risk children and youth. These efforts include active mental health services, character education initiatives, conflict resolution programs, small schools to promote active participation by all students, and a strong and active adult presence in every aspect of the school environment. If the violent behaviors are displayed by members of racial and ethnic minorities, many researchers believe that these behaviors must be addressed within a context that is sensitive to the specific culture of these groups and that takes into consideration the multiple factors that uniquely affect these students (Cartledge & Johnson, 1997). In general, effective school violence prevention must involve a focus on the teacher and her or his skills and experiences, coupled with an emphasis on the supports available to teachers who deal with aggressive, challenging students (Keller & Tapasak, 1997).

THINKING PRACTICALLY

What can schools do to reduce school violence? Is a tough approach better than a go-easy approach?

SUGGESTION: Unfortunately, there are no easy answers to combating school violence. In some cases, a tough approach is necessary; in others, a more relaxed approach may work. If the neighborhood is violent and the students are afraid, a tougher approach is probably indicated. If the threats of violence are few, a less stringent approach might work.

Well-managed schools, free of violence, can be of many different types and can cater to diverse types of students. For example, researchers have studied effective alternative schools for at-risk, troubled students; successful magnet schools that mix gifted and talented students from widely ranging socioeconomic and ethnic backgrounds; and successful vocational schools for students who are learning career-relevant skills in place of an all-academic curricular focus (McLaughlin & Talbert, 1990). What these schools had in common was an emphasis on personalized instruction. Teachers met and interacted frequently with students outside of the traditional classroom setting. Students' views were heard, and a cooperative atmosphere was established and maintained through daily interactions, school rules and procedures, daily meetings between small groups of students and the teacher, and after-school activities in which teachers and students participated.

Implications for Teaching

- *Cultivate good communication skills that can be applied in diverse educational settings.* Tell other teachers what has worked and why. Read articles and books about good communication skills, take a course or workshop, watch videos, and so on.

- *Use "I" messages to explain the consequences of students' misbehaviors in a nonjudgmental manner.* If students feel attacked, they will respond by fighting back or withdrawing instead of by understanding their error and correcting it.

- *Be firm, clear, direct, and assertive when dealing with student misbehavior.* Do not allow yourself to be perceived as a pushover or a lightweight. But do not behave like an army drill sergeant, either.

- *Decide whether a problem is owned by you or the student before taking steps to solve it.* You cannot solve every problem students have: You are one individual doing a tough job, and you must learn to distinguish what is and what is not your responsibility.

- *When the student owns the problem, use active listening to express concern and to give support.* Some students may have no one in their lives who listens to them. You can help these students simply by caring enough to share your time and offer a sympathetic ear.

- **When you own the problem, use the no-lose method to achieve a solution.** This is one that makes every party feel positive about the situation. If time permits, involve students in the solution—the result will last longer and be more effective than your unilateral response would have been.

- **Respond immediately to potential threats of violence; involve other teachers and administrators or other appropriate authorities in solving the problem.** Never assume that you are overreacting when students' and teachers' safety is at issue. Never take risks with threats of violence.

Special Approaches to Classroom Management

Researchers and practitioners have developed several formal systems for classroom management (see Chapters 7 and 10). These systems are best suited to specific types of classrooms and situations.

GROUP CONSEQUENCE SYSTEMS

The first of these formal systems for classroom management is called a **group consequence system.** In this system, which also has been used with adults in business settings, the teacher keeps track of students' behaviors by adding points to a total. The class can work toward earning a desired privilege by trying to amass a given number of points. For example, the teacher may promise a field trip, extra free time, or a class party. Charlie Grenda used a group consequence system to encourage his students to accumulate points toward an overnight camping trip to a wildlife preserve.

The situations in which a group consequence system works best are those in which students are motivated to retain the approval of their peers. Sometimes, one wise-cracking student who is a real troublemaker can be quieted by pressure from his peers when they perceive he is losing points for the entire class toward a desired objective. Students in these situations may become more cooperative and may unite to reach a group goal. But there is another side to using a group consequence system, and it can lead to problems. If a class troublemaker does not care about the opinions of his peers, punishing the other well-mannered students on account of his behavior is unfair and can lead to resentment. This resentment can be directed by all the students toward the teacher, and by the well-behaving children toward the troublemaker, thus worsening her problems. For these reasons, when using a group consequence system, remain alert to the specific class dynamics and ensure that this system is fair and is helping to improve the students' behavior.

Also remember that young students often have trouble waiting a long time for desired rewards. As we discussed in Chapter 7, choose a schedule of reinforcement that provides rewards to students in a meaningful and effective way. Young students in particular can become frustrated if they have to wait more than a few days to receive a reward; such frustration can be counterproductive and can undermine motivation and hinder performance.

THINKING CREATIVELY

Design three group consequence systems for use in a second-, sixth-, and tenth-grade classroom.

SUGGESTION: *Second grade:* Students must amass points as a group to earn a day trip to a nearby zoo. *Sixth grade:* Students must earn "perfect attendance" points (with allowances made for illness documented by a doctor's note) for a class trip to an amusement park. *Tenth grade:* Students must raise money for muscular dystrophy or another charitable organization or cause by walking a designated number of miles (summed for the class) in a walkathon.

TOKEN REINFORCEMENT SYSTEMS

The second formal system for classroom management is a **token reinforcement system** in which students earn tokens—points, stars, or other tangible items—for good behavior or

Daily points for good behavior help motivate this teacher's students and encourage good classroom behavior. (Jim Pickerell, Stock Boston)

classroom achievement. The tokens are collected by the students and can later be exchanged for a reward, such as a gift or privilege. The rewards that work best depend in part on the age of the students. Young students can be motivated to receive stuffed animals or other small toys. Older students may value free time or the opportunity to substitute a paper topic of their choice for a teacher-generated topic.

To acquaint students with the token system, use it aggressively at the start, with tokens being given out often and with frequent opportunities for their redemption. Later, however, scale down the number of tokens given out and make the rewards somewhat harder to earn. By gradually scaling down the frequency of use of the system, the system will become more manageable in the long run. If parents are willing to help out, they can be involved in the token economy by providing rewards at home for tokens earned.

You may think that employing token economies is a lot of work for the teacher, and you are right. For this reason, use them only in specific and complex situations, such as when a group of students is entirely out of control, when students do not care at all about their work, or when students have had a history of failure. Token systems have sometimes worked well to shape behavior with challenged populations, such as students with learning disabilities, students with severe behavior problems, and students who have been out of the academic mindset for some time.

 **CONTINGENCY CONTRACT SYSTEMS**

The third type of formal classroom management system is the **contingency contract system,** an agreement between the teacher and each individual student regarding the exact goal the student must accomplish in order to earn a reward. Both students and teachers can decide on the behaviors to be tallied and on the nature of the rewards to be earned. For example, you might enter into a contract with a student regarding the student's promise to complete assignments at a certain rate over the school year. The reward for successful completion of assignments is a grade of A for a job well done, a positive note sent home to the parents, and even a special purchase or privilege provided by the parents in recognition of the child's good performance. You must be clear about the quality of work that constitutes the successful completion or performance of a task, and make such specific criteria a part of a contingency contract system.

These three types of formal management systems contain both advantages and pitfalls. Thus do not implement these systems without thorough attention to the possible negative consequences of their use. Remember from Chapter 7 that extrinsic motivators can undermine intrinsic motivation; in other words, children motivated to win points or tokens are often less apt to learn to enjoy the experience of learning. There are also other potential problems. For example, if the teacher cannot purchase small rewards for students with school reserve funds, or if parents do not hold up their end of the bargain by rewarding children at home, you can find yourself in possession of problems rather than happy students. For these reasons, if you are considering using a token economy or contingency system, speak to other teachers and your principal—and to the school or district psychologist, if available—to work out potential problems before they arise.

THINKING PRACTICALLY

How would you feel about participating in a contingency contract system for work in your educational psychology course? Place yourself in the role of a student participating in such a system, and ask yourself how you would perceive the experience.

SUGGESTION: Many students like the control that comes with such a system. It puts students in charge of their destiny in a course. Only you can answer how you would react to this approach, however.

Implications for Teaching

■ *Try group consequence systems.* These will help unite a class in achieving a common goal and harness the power of peer pressure to gain the coopera-

tion of every student. They will also help you instill an attitude of cooperation among students and an atmosphere of enthusiasm.

- ■ *For younger students, and for students with physical, behavioral, or learning challenges, use token reinforcement systems.* These will help to get students on-track. Have a variety of management techniques at your disposal and choose the ones that fit each situation. Be willing to switch if an approach is not working. Phase these systems out over time.

- ■ *For older students, use contingency contracts to keep motivation high and attention focused on meaningful learning goals.* By showing students they are in charge of their own learning and rate of progress, you can empower them to do their best.

SUMMING IT UP

WHY UNDERSTANDING CLASSROOM MANAGE-MENT IS IMPORTANT TO TEACHERS

- ■ Because of societal violence, drug use, teenage sex, and a decline in students' respect for authority, managing students has become increasingly difficult for teachers. Classroom management is defined as a set of techniques and skills that allow a teacher to control students effectively in order to create a positive learning environment for all students.

- ■ The key goal of classroom management—to create an environment that maximizes student learning—generally means creating as much quality learning time as possible and helping students gain in maturity so they learn how to manage themselves effectively. Allocated time is the time a teacher earmarks and plans to use for learning. Engaged time is the time that is actually spent on learning.

HOW EFFECTIVE TEACHERS MANAGER THEIR STUDENTS

- ■ The most effective teachers are "with it"—that is, they are attentive to everything going on around them in the classroom. They are also able to supervise several activities at once, and they create momentum in classroom activities, ensuring smooth transitions from one activity to the next. Effective teachers make an effort to involve every student in the class in what is going on and to generate enthusiasm for learning.

- ■ Effective teachers criticize constructively, focusing on inappropriate behaviors rather than criticizing the person performing them. Effective teachers also are well prepared the first day of class and develop rules and procedures ahead of time.

- ■ Good plans for classroom management take into account the developmental age and maturity level of the students. Elementary school students are less familiar with school demands, but generally are more compliant, than older children. Middle school children require special attention because of the biological and social ramifications of puberty. High school students are generally easier to manage because they have completed puberty and are familiar with the requirements of schooling.

DEVELOPING AND IMPLEMENTING RULES AND PROCEDURES

- ■ When drawing up rules and procedures, teachers should consider the general school environment as well as the relevant histories of the students. When students disregard the rules, teachers should respond with progressively more serious consequences.

MAINTAINING CONTROL AND PREVENTING PROBLEMS

- ■ Teachers should strive to develop communication skills and work to see themselves as their students see them. "I" messages are a method for responding to student misbehavior by stating how the misbehavior affects the teacher's ability to do her job and how the teacher feels about the misbehavior.

- ■ Assertive discipline is a technique for dealing with misbehavior in which teachers make their expectations clear and firmly state the consequences for misbehavior, and then follow through with these consequences. The assertive style is preferable to either a hostile or a passive style. To invoke assertive discipline, a teacher should make sure the students know how to behave, provide positive reinforcement for good behavior, and use a discipline plan to respond to misbehavior. The paraphrase rule involves summarizing in the person's own words what the previous speaker said.

- Before deciding on a course of action to a problem, a teacher must decide who owns the problem—the teacher or the student. Student-owned problems are not the teacher's responsibility to solve, but active listening by the teacher can help the student come to terms with the problem. Teacher-owned problems can be resolved through the use of the no-lose method, in which both student and teacher work out a compromise solution that blames neither party.

- Coping with violence in school is a major challenge for teachers. Use of fair and clear rules and procedures will help, as will allowing students input into setting rules and procedures.

SPECIAL APPROACHES TO CLASSROOM MANAGEMENT

- Group consequence systems can help with managing certain classes, particularly those containing children with physical, behavioral, or learning challenges. In this type of system, points are amassed by the entire class, based on the behavior of individuals, and the class wins a desired goal when a certain number of points is earned. Token reinforcement systems allow students to earn tokens individually and then exchange them for rewards. Contingency contract systems are agreements between students and teachers that promise specific rewards for a given set of accomplishments—such as an A for a certain quantity of work done well and on time.

KEY TERMS AND DEFINITIONS

- **Active listening** Type of listening in which a teacher encourages a student to state his or her problems fully and listens in an active and concerned manner. Page 409

- **Allocated time** Time a teacher earmarks and plans to use for learning. Page 387

- **Assertive discipline** Method of responding to misbehavior that is clear, firm, and direct; it involves stating the consequences for misbehaving and following through with those consequences as appropriate. Page 408

- **Classroom management** Set of techniques and skills that allows a teacher to control students effectively in order to create a positive learning environment for all students. Page 384

- **Contingency contract system** Agreement between a teacher and each individual student regarding exactly what the student must accomplish in order to earn a reward. Page 416

- **Discipline** Teacher-initiated actions designed to minimize student behavior problems and distractions in order to create a maximally effective learning environment. Page 385

- **Engaged time** Time that is actually spent on learning. Page 387

- **Group consequence system** System in which the teacher keeps track of students' behaviors by adding points to a total, or through some other method. Page 415

- **"I" message** Clear, direct, assertive statement about exactly what a student did that constitutes misbehaving, how the misbehavior affects the teacher's ability to teach, and how the teacher feels about the misbehavior. Page 407

- **No-lose method** Method of resolving conflicts in which teacher and student work out a compromise solution that allows neither party to lose. Page 411

- **Overlapping** Supervising several activities at once. Page 390

- **Paraphrase rule** System designed to promote accurate communication in which, before speaking, the teacher or student summarizes in her or his own words what the other person said. Page 410

- **Procedures** Methods for accomplishing classroom activities in an orderly manner. Page 399

- **Rules** Statements that specify acceptable and unacceptable behaviors in the classroom. Page 400

- **Token reinforcement system** System in which students earn tokens—points, stars, or other tangible items—for good behavior or classroom achievement. Page 415

- **With-it-ness** Quality of being observant and attentive to everything going on around the teacher in the classroom. Page 389

IN ELEMENTARY SCHOOL

1. How can you deal with a first-grade student who cries and acts distressed when his parents drop him off at school every morning? What steps can you take with the student and with his parents to make being left at school less traumatic for him?

2. You are a new fourth-grade teacher. When might a token economy be effective with your students? What types of tokens would you consider using? How would you determine which type of token and which types of reward would be most effective with your students?

3. One of your second-grade students is acting withdrawn and upset over her parents' divorce. What can you do to ensure that her schoolwork does not suffer?

4. Your room full of third graders is overly excited about a field trip, and you are having difficulty calming them so they can collect their belongings and board the bus. What specific steps might help in this situation?

5. You are a trained fifth-grade teacher who has been assigned unexpectedly to a first-grade class. You have a definite idea about the rules and procedures you would like to implement. What steps can you take to make implementation go smoothly?

IN MIDDLE SCHOOL

1. What should you do about a student who acts out often and threatens other children in your seventh-grade social studies class?

2. A girl in your seventh-grade language arts class has developed a disabling crush on another student and has started to daydream all of the time. You recognize that this behavior is normal, but you want to keep the girl on-track. What should you do?

3. How can you help a new entering class of sixth graders at your school, who must get used to switching classes for the first time? What steps can you take to make these students feel comfortable with this and other major changes in the school environment?

4. One of your classes of eighth graders contains a particularly belligerent and unruly student. How should you respond to defiant behavior by this student, after you have tried and failed on several previous occasions to control the student?

5. One of your seventh graders completely ignores his homework assignments for your foreign language class. Describe how you might use the no-lose method to deal with this student.

IN HIGH SCHOOL

1. You are teaching chemistry and physics to four classes of tenth graders. How might you use a contingency contract system to enhance the amount of time students spend studying and to increase their exam grades and frequency of participation in class?

2. Describe how you could use assertive discipline to cope with a belligerent student who continually talks out in your eleventh-grade social studies class.

3. You are a tenth-grade teacher with four classes of fairly tough students who cause you to be exhausted at the end of the day. Name three situations in which you should call your students' parents in response to student misbehavior. Name three situations that do not require parents to be called.

4. Your eleventh-grade science class contains three very bright students who are becoming bored and tuning out to school. How can you make your science instruction more challenging for these students? What steps can you take to help these students?

5. What steps can you take to help a group of urban twelfth-grade students whose lives are marked by violence at home and in their communities? What role can school play in breaking the cycle of poverty for these students?

Connecting Theory and Research to Practice

Are you thinking about or searching for creative strategies to deal with classroom management problems? Try connecting to *Teachnet*'s forum on classroom management *(www.teachnet.com/how -to/manage)*. On this Internet site, classroom teachers describe a number of innovative strategies and tactics that they have used to address classroom management problems and situations they have encountered.

For example, Brenda Dyck, of the Master's Academy College in Alberta, Canada, describes a technique called "Six Hats" (see de Bono, 1985). The "Six Hats" approach, in this example, is used to address, discuss, and generate solutions to classroom management problems (preferably with middle and high school students, but this particular approach could be modified for use with students in upper elementary grades). Using this approach, the teacher and students assume different perspectives, or metaphorical "hats," when discussing and seeking solutions to a particular classroom management problem. For example, one "hat" may deal with the emotions encountered by the students and the teacher in a particular situation while another "hat" may deal with aspects of the situation that negatively affected student learning. While this activity promotes the students' development of multiple perspective taking, the pros and cons of this approach are also briefly discussed from the teacher's perspective.

The *Teachnet* classroom management forum also allows teachers who have used these various approaches to comment on their own classroom experience in using a particular approach. You may want to see what other teachers have to say about a particular approach before trying it yourself, or you may wish to start and keep a file of innovative classroom management strategies for future use.

As you read through these different approaches on the Internet, ask yourself how they relate to principles and models of effective classroom management addressed in this chapter. For example, do these approaches address some of the suggested best practices for classroom management, such as promoting student involvement, providing constructive criticism, and using "I" messages? Do some of these approaches illustrate different models of classroom management such as a group consequence system?

Building Your Self-Portrait as an Educator

Are you worried about being too easy on your students or not being able to enforce the rules in your future classroom? Are you curious as to what kind of classroom manager you are or may be? Go to *Teacher Talk (http://education .indiana.edu/cas/tt/v1i2/ what.html)* to answer a series of questions that will help you determine your classroom management profile.

Four classroom management styles are profiled on this site: authoritarian, authoritative, laissez-faire, and indifferent (see Baumrind, 1971). These four styles are based upon two continuums: level of warmth (i.e., mutual respect, criticism, communication skills, etc.) and level of classroom control (i.e., with-it-ness, consistency in dealing with student misbehavior, etc.) (see Table 1). For example, an expert teacher is more likely to exhibit characteristics in line with the authoritative classroom management style. An authoritative classroom manager would exhibit a high degree of warmth with a high degree of control (e.g., a high degree of with-it-ness, the use of constructive criticism, consistent response to student misbehavior, and good communication skills). However, it is important to note that after taking this self-assessment, you will have a classroom management profile that encompasses all four classroom management styles. This could be helpful in providing you with some feedback and direction on what skills you may need to work on to become a more effective classroom manager.

Teacher Talk is an online journal and resource for teachers created and maintained by the Center for Adolescent Studies at Indiana University's School of Education. The home page *(education.indiana.edu/ cas/tt/tthmpg.html)* provides an index of the various

topics covered in *Teacher Talk*. The particular site featured here, detailing classroom management styles, is included in Volume 1, Issue 2 of *Teacher Talk*. Some other topics related to classroom management include: *Violence in the Schools* (Volume 2, Issue 3), *Building Rapport with Students* (Volume 3, Issue 1), and *Depression and Suicide* (Volume 3, Issue 2). However, a wide variety of interesting topics and sensitive issues are also featured in *Teacher Talk,* including *Dealing with Sex Issues in Any Classroom* (Volume 1, Issue 3) and *Cultural Diversity in the Classroom* (Volume 2, Issue 2), and *Common Concerns of Student Teachers* (Volume 3, Issue 1).

Communities of Learners/Teachers

One of the most challenging aspects of being a teacher is fighting the feeling of classroom and professional isolation. This is particularly troublesome given that feelings of isolation may contribute to lowered teacher self-efficacy (see Chapter 10), which, in turn, is likely to affect classroom management. When a teacher with low self-efficacy encounters a classroom management problem, the teacher, who already feels as if he or she has very little control within the classroom, is more likely to overreact to student mis-

behavior, thereby making the classroom situation worse. This creates a somewhat recursive, or unending, cycle of classroom management problems. One of the most powerful technological tools to combat feelings of classroom and professional isolation are the various discussion boards available on the Internet.

One such discussion board on which expert and novice teachers can discuss classroom management problems is available at *Teachers.Net (http:// www.teachers.net/ mentors/classroom_ management).* Classroom teachers (or anyone working with students or children) may post a message on this site and receive comments, feedback, or suggestions from other classroom teachers on how to deal with a wide variety of classroom management problems and concerns. Discussion topics range from how to handle a student who is biting others to how to deal with problematic parents. This site also gives classroom teachers an opportunity to reflect on their own classroom management practices. For example, one teacher posted the discussion topic "I'm losing i t . . ." and another posted "Am I unreasonable?" Both teachers then received encouragement, support, and alternative perspectives from others within the field.

Teacher Talk

What is your classroom management profile?

Answer these 12 questions and learn more about your classroom management profile. The steps are simple:

- Read each statement carefully.
- Write your response, from the scale below, on a sheet of paper.
- Respond to each statement based upon either actual or imagined classroom experience.
- Then, follow the scoring instructions below. It couldn't be easier!

1. = Strongly Disagree
2. = Disagree
3. = Neutral
4. = Agree
5. = Strongly Agree

(1) If a student is disruptive during class, I assign him/her to detention, without further discussion.

(2) I don't want to impose any rules on my students.

(3) The classroom must be quiet in order for students to learn.

(4) I am concerned about both what my students learn and how they learn.

Online Resources

An additional resource for classroom management issues can be found in a document entitled *Schoolwide and Classroom Discipline* from the School Improvement Research Series (SIRS) *(http://www.nwrel.org/ scpd/sirs/5/cu9.html).* This document provides a brief overview of research on various discipline problems facing American schools today, introductions to various classroom management programs, suggested schoolwide and classroom management guidelines, and a list of valuable text resources for

schoolwide and classroom management and discipline.

Additional Reading

Baumrind, D. (1971). Current patterns of parental authority. *Developmental Psychology Monographs, 4* (1, Part 2).

De Bono, E. (1985). *Six thinking hats.* Boston: Little, Brown, and Company. (Online material of Edward de Bono's work, including other instructional activities to stimulate students' thinking, can be found at *http://www.ozemail.com .au/~caveman/Creative/ Authors/ABono.htm).*

TABLE 1 **Classroom Management Styles**

Level of Control	Level of Warmth	
	■ Low	■ High
■ High	Authoritarian	Authoritative
■ Low	Laissez-Faire	Indifferent

12

Classroom Teaching

THE BIG PICTURE

To help you see the big picture, keep the following questions in mind as you read this chapter:

- How can the science of educational psychology help teachers decide how to present material most effectively? What practical information can a book like this provide to a teacher—information that will be useful in day-to-day teaching?

- How important to effective teaching are specific plans and learning objectives? What is the precise role of learning objectives in classroom teaching?

- What age-related considerations should teachers be aware of when planning their instruction?

- What are the strengths and weaknesses of the direct instruction approaches to teaching? When is the use of individual project work, small-group activities,

and whole-class discussion appropriate, and what are the strengths and weaknesses of each approach?

- How can a teacher use homework as an effective teaching tool? What are the differences in homework assignments for elementary, middle, and high school students?

- What role can computers play in effective instruction?

- What does the concept of student-centered or constructionist teaching really mean? What are the strengths and weaknesses of group discussions, whole-group activities, small-group work, and peer instruction?

- How can peer instruction be used effectively? How should peer instruction be structured for classes that contain a broad range of students—gifted, average, and disabled?

◄ *A middle school science teacher engages the attention of his class as he performs an experiment.* (Jim Cummins, FPG International)

Lauren Hodges contemplated the rough draft of her syllabus as she prepared for her first day in a new job as a high school language arts teacher. She understood what material she was supposed to cover, and she had a good idea of what the students were expected to know in order to do well on the statewide mastery tests, an important goal of their English instruction. However, she was not so sure about how to teach the students the material: Should she lead standard lectures, assign whole-class activities and discussions, or even break the students up into small groups to do their work? Most of her time in college and graduate school had been spent learning about the English language and literature. Although she had

taken a few courses that covered hands-on aspects of teaching, she was having trouble applying much of what she had learned. Now, as Lauren tried to recall how her teachers had presented material to their classes, she found it was tough to transform memories based on her own experiences as a student into a practical plan for teaching her own classes.

Lauren telephoned Amina, an experienced teacher from her school, and asked for advice. Amina suggested that Lauren start the first class with a group discussion and finish up with an individual activity that the students could start during class and finish for homework. She also recommended that, the next day, Lauren begin with a lecture and then assign small-group project work.

For each day of the week, Amina had another suggestion about how to structure the presentation of material in order to keep the class mentally involved in the learning experience. Lauren was impressed and asked Amina where she had gotten this invaluable information. Amina answered that, over the years, she had intentionally experimented with a variety of approaches in her high school and middle school classes, and she had found which ones work best for students of each age group. Although she was really confident about the content she was supposed to teach, Lauren realized she still had a lot to learn about how best to structure her teaching.

What would you do if you were Lauren? Deciding on the best way to present material to students can be a confusing prospect. The topics of this chapter will help you structure your teaching appropriately and creatively, so your students remain interested and motivated to learn. We review different teaching methods, explaining the strengths and weaknesses of each approach. When you have finished your study of the chapter, you will be acquainted with a whole array of techniques you can use in your own classroom teaching.

Why Understanding Classroom Teaching Is Important to Teachers

In our discussion in Chapter 1 about the characteristics of effective teachers, we noted that expert teachers share three qualities that differentiate them from novice teachers. First, experts have more *knowledge:* Expert teachers know more strategies and techniques for teaching, and compared to novices they use their knowledge more effectively to solve problems. Second, experts are more *efficient:* Expert teachers do more in less time than novices. Third, experts have more *insight:* Expert teachers are more likely to arrive at novel and appropriate solutions to problems than novices.

When you think about the characteristics of expert teachers you have known, most of the examples that come to your mind probably involve teachers leading a class. This is not surprising: After all, teaching classes is at the heart of what teachers do. In fact, most of the topics covered in this textbook have focused on how teachers can improve the processes involved in student learning and comprehension—and student learning begins with teachers teaching. As Lauren Hodges has learned, a key aspect of becoming an expert teacher is developing knowledge, efficiency, and insights relevant to classroom teaching.

A group of elementary school teachers discuss their lesson plans with one another. (Michael Newman, PhotoEdit)

A solid understanding of the many ways to conduct a class will improve your efficiency and flexibility, allowing you to accomplish more with students in less time. In addition, knowing a variety of teaching techniques will help you hone your instincts and develop more insightful solutions to problems. We also discuss the principles of learning presumed to underlie the success of different approaches. Teacher-centered learning approaches, such as direct lecturing and recitation (questioning of students), are related to a behavioral view of learning (see Chapter 7). According to this view, students are passive recipients of knowledge imparted to them by teachers. For some subjects and students, direct instruction works very effectively. Student-centered learning approaches, such as activity-based learning, project work, and peer instruction, are related to a cognitive view of learning (see Chapter 8). According to this view, students come to the learning experience with knowledge, ideas, and values that cause them to construct what they are learning in their own minds, and different students will learn different things from the same lesson. For some situations, student-based learning works best.

As you read this chapter, making mental lists of techniques you can use in planning your own instruction, remember that planning is wise, especially for novice teachers, but flexibility is also important in meeting student needs. An overly rigid instructional plan can be worse than no plan at all. An important characteristic of expert teachers is that they rely heavily on planning (see Chapter 1). Experts differ from novices in their tendency and ability to plan what to do, monitor their progress, and evaluate their performance. When expert teachers plan how to present a lesson, they think carefully before starting to solve the problem: They think about which approach is more likely to work, or about how one approach compares to another one they tried before that failed. An expert science teacher deciding on an approach for a lesson on photosynthesis is likely to review past years' approaches and evaluate how these approaches worked, asking questions such as these: Which approach got students most interested? Which led to the best understanding and performance, and why? What can I do to make this year's lesson the best ever?

In general, experts spend more time than novices on trying to understand the problem to be solved and then on planning effectively (Sternberg, 1981). In a study of how expert and novice mathematics teachers plan their lessons, the expert teachers did much more long-term planning than the novices, and the experts' plans fit the day's teaching into the overall goals and organization of a given chapter and the course in general (Borko & Livingston, 1989). Experts' plans were more flexible and responsive to the different directions the class discussion might take; novices' plans were more rigid. The result was that novices became flustered when events in the classroom did not exactly follow their plans. The lesson for the developing teacher is to understand the array of available techniques and to plan for their use while allowing room for changes when plans fall short.

Principles of Teacher-Centered Teaching

When most of us think about teaching and about our own experiences as students, we remember examples of teachers giving lectures, asking questions, leading discussions, and generally controlling events in the classroom. This traditional perspective on teaching views the teacher as the person with the knowledge to impart, and the students as the people who learn the knowledge imparted by the teacher. This approach is aptly referred to as **teacher-centered.** In this section, we first discuss how to organize and plan effective teacher-centered instruction and then consider specific teaching methods to use in the classroom.

THE ROLE OF PLANNING IN TEACHER-CENTERED INSTRUCTION

Exactly what do your teachers do as they sit at home, like Lauren Hodges, planning tomorrow's lesson? How do they know which topics to cover, and in what degree of depth? How do they decide what information to teach and what to leave out? Do they follow a syllabus, and if so, where does this semester-long instruction plan come from?

■ **INDIVIDUAL DIFFERENCES IN PLANNING** Good teaching depends on good planning done long before a teacher ever steps in front of a class to lead a discussion or give a demonstration. Individual teachers' preferences often influence how they plan their instruction. One teacher we know confided that he spends more than twice the allotted time on science with his sixth-grade class because he has always particularly loved science. His students may be getting terrific instruction in science, but they are losing out on language arts, a subject he has never enjoyed. Although it is human nature to enjoy teaching some subjects more than others, effective planning and time allocation help teachers avoid short-changing their students on certain subjects.

What time frames do teachers' plans occupy? First, you must decide what general topics to cover. Sometimes, schoolwide or districtwide policies about curricular content take precedence. At other times, you have more discretion in deciding what to cover. Once you decide on a general topic, you must develop teaching plans that chart instruction over the months and weeks of the school year. From this level of information, you then plan what to teach from Monday through Friday. Obviously, if the general plans at the semester or month level are ineffective, it is difficult to create coherent instruction on a day-by-day basis that serves the overarching goals of instruction in each discipline.

■ **LIMITATIONS OF PLANNING** Like Lauren Hodges, you may find yourself persuaded by the value of good planning. Before you plan your next year of teaching, however, bear in mind that expert teachers recognize the limitations of plans as well as their strengths. Say you have crafted a lesson plan that fits a lecture, a demonstration, and a group discussion into one class period. You know that as long as you make good progress with your plan, the students will make it through all of the material, just in time for next week's test. The pressure is on: You talk quickly, holding the students' attention as you introduce the topic and set up your demonstration. But several students in the back of the room start passing notes and whispering to one another. Students in the front row appear confused. Suddenly you realize your lesson plan is not working.

THINKING CREATIVELY

Can you think of any other ways to conceptualize the teaching and learning process, in addition to the teacher-centered approach?

SUGGESTION: One way is to consider how students can best comprehend what they learn and how they can become active creators of knowledge, such as during project-based and other student-centered learning approaches.

THINKING PRACTICALLY

How might students' preferences for some subjects over others influence what a teacher covers in class?

SUGGESTION: If students are interested and engaged in a topic, teachers often spend more time on it in class because the students actively participate in classroom discussions and are more motivated to learn.

Wise teachers change their tactics at this point, even if it means abandoning the plan. They might decide to cover only half the material in one lesson and spend more time elaborating the introduction. They might attempt to relate the topic to the students' daily lives, or ask a few open-ended questions about the topic to involve the students. Ineffective teachers tend either not to notice their plans are failing, or they press on with the plan anyway because they feel they must. The students become completely lost, but as long as the plan is accomplished the teacher feels successful. Research has shown that students learn more when their teachers are *flexible* in their planning and in their allocation of time instead of adhering rigidly to their plans (Schwartz, Lin, Brophy, & Bransford, 1999; Shavelson, 1987). The issue of flexibility is key. Effective teachers recognize this fact, regroup, and move on, rather than sticking with a plan that obviously is not working.

An imaginative first-year teacher explains complex DNA concepts to his high school students with the use of simple paper cut-outs. (Bob Daemmrich Photos, Inc.)

The process of planning instruction evolves as you grow in competence and experience. At the beginning, it tends to make you feel more secure to create detailed teaching plans. But expert teachers, who tend to create more succinct and flexible plans, draw on their extensive content knowledge, pedagogical knowledge, and pedagogical-content knowledge (as discussed in Chapter 1). There is no one right way to approach planning. Each person has her or his own approach, and there are many ways to plan successfully. We next review two types of planning approaches that you can use as the basis of your own instructional system.

■**LEARNING OBJECTIVES** Every chapter of this book has opened with a list of questions, specific learning objectives, to guide you as you study the chapter. **Learning objectives** are clear descriptions of educational goals. Like the list you carry to the supermarket or the chore list you draw up on Saturday morning, lists of learning objectives structure how the teacher and student will spend their time so as to accomplish what is on the list.

SPECIFIC OBJECTIVES. Robert Mager (1975) defined one popular system for teachers to use in writing instructional objectives. Mager's perspective is that instructional objectives should be action oriented and specific. He believed that objectives should describe, first, specifically what students should do to demonstrate their achievements, and second, how teachers can recognize student success in demonstrating their achievements. Mager conceptualized objectives as ideally containing three aspects: (1) The objective should describe the behavior the student is supposed to engage in—for example, "Memorize a list of 20 vocabulary words"; (2) the objective should describe the conditions under which the student will perform the behavior—for example, "Complete this assignment by next Monday morning"; and (3) the objective should define what behaviors constitute evidence that the objective has been mastered—for example, "Attain a score of 18 correct on the quiz." These specific types of objectives can take a long time to develop, but once defined they can assist motivated students in mastering the material.

THINKING CREATIVELY

Describe three different types of plans you might create for teaching the same lesson.

SUGGESTION: For a lesson on evolution, you can: (1) begin with pictures of museum specimens long since extinct, asking students what they think happened to the animals and why; (2) ask students to scan the Web for information on horse evolution because the fossil record for horses is unusually well preserved; or (3) bring to class plastic replicas of human skulls from various evolutionary stages and ask students to arrange them in order from oldest to most recent.

GENERAL OBJECTIVES. Norman Gronlund (1991, 1993) tackled the problem of defining good objectives from the opposite perspective. Instead of seeing good objectives as action oriented and specific, Gronlund sees them as general, focusing on cognitive goals such as "compare and contrast," "understand," and so on. The student should recognize that the goal is to understand and reason with overarching concepts and ideas. To make the goal more concrete, and to create a method for charting student progress toward the goal, the teacher describes what types of student behaviors demonstrate the

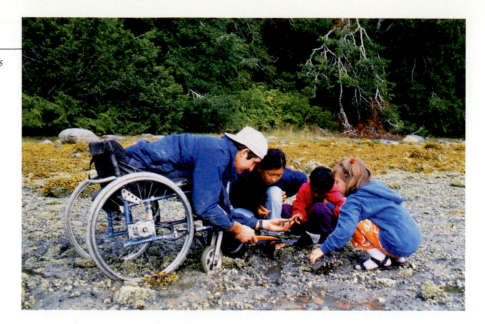

A teacher and group of elementary students on a field trip view an outdoor exhibit. (Derke/O'Hara, Stone)

essential understanding and reasoning. Students should understand that the specific tasks they are accomplishing are just a subset of many similar tasks they could tackle with the ability to think and reason in a new domain.

USING OBJECTIVES. The success of learning objectives depends, not surprisingly, on their appropriate use. Highly organized texts and teaching aids may reduce the need for teacher-defined objectives; the students will get all the objectives they need from the printed material. But what about a class trip to a museum? Here, the objective is far from obvious. If a teacher defines a specific objective, or a general objective with specific behaviors that demonstrate it, the fun experience can become a learning experience. Consider the case in which the teacher distributes a handout that asks students to find, sketch, and label at least two animals that display convergent evolution. A scientist we know was given just this assignment before a class trip to the American Museum of Natural History. The lessons learned about biology and evolution that followed remain clear 20 years later.

LIMITATIONS OF OBJECTIVES. Although objectives are useful, they are not without critics. Poorly written objectives can needlessly confuse students before they have a chance to master a concept: For example, "Use the following formula whenever you can to solve 20 mathematics problems" or "Write an essay about two eras in American history." Because it is easier to write short objectives describing basic tasks and learning goals, it is tempting to ignore the real goals of learning in favor of the simpler goals that more easily translate into objectives: "Memorize these 10 mathematical formulas" or "List all the main characters in *Moby-Dick.*" If students simply memorize lists of objectives and a few examples of each objective in action, they may accomplish little meaningful learning. Also, some students master the material quickly and will be ready to move past such objectives early on in the school year.

Whether objectives are specified or not, most teachers will have some guidelines about what constitutes acceptable, good, and excellent student performance. Students will infer their teachers' objectives by examining what types of classwork, seatwork, and homework they are assigned, what types of tests they are given, and how their grades are computed. Unfortunately, however, students often infer objectives too late to be optimally useful; thus always state your objectives early and often.

THINKING PRACTICALLY

What are your general and specific learning objectives for this course?

SUGGESTION: Think about your ultimate goals, this semester and over the next few years. How will you use what you are learning in this course? Think of your objectives in terms of your planned use of the material.

Objectives obviously play important roles in student learning. How can objectives be made as effective as possible? First, make sure students *understand* the objectives presented. Expert teachers ask students to repeat the intent of objectives and to provide examples of behaviors that indicate accomplishment of the objectives. Expert teachers work with students to make objectives authentic to the learning experience—and to ensure that measuring them focuses on meaningful behaviors. In writing objectives, experts avoid phrases that are trite or clichéd, such as "Students should do their best," "Students should work hard," and "Students should do what they are told by the teacher." And, as we discuss in the final two chapters of this book, expert teachers make sure that tests mirror the objectives. If they do not, students will question their use: "Why did I bother studying that? It wasn't even on the test!" Table 12.1 displays examples of well-written and poorly written objectives.

■TAXONOMIES **Taxonomies** are systematic or hierarchical classifications of learning objectives. The point of a taxonomy is to take a collection of learning objectives and organize or group them sensibly. Ideally, a taxonomy helps you understand the higher order concepts and skills represented by learning objectives. Benjamin Bloom developed an approach to organizing educational objectives that involves sorting these objectives into three domains, **cognitive** (focused on thinking), **affective** (focused on feeling and emotion), and **psychomotor** (focused on physical action). The cognitive domain is of primary interest to most teachers. We discussed Bloom's six objectives within the cognitive domain in Chapter 9 on thinking; this material is also relevant to lesson planning.

COGNITIVE OBJECTIVES. Bloom and his colleagues (Bloom, Engelhart, Frost, Hill, & Krathwohl, 1956) suggested that thinking occurs within six distinct levels, phrased in terms of cognitive objectives for education:

Level 1, *Knowledge,* consists of remembering or recognizing something, either with or without true understanding of it.

Level 2, *Comprehension,* consists of understanding something, without necessarily being able to relate it to other things.

Level 3, *Application,* consists of being able to use a general concept in the solution of a particular problem.

Level 4, *Analysis,* consists of breaking a concept down into its constituent parts.

Level 5, *Synthesis,* consists of creating a new idea by combining other ideas.

Level 6, *Evaluation,* consists of judging the worth or value of something, particularly as it applies in a particular situation.

TABLE **12.1**   **Examples of Well-Written and Poorly Written Learning Objectives**

Well Written	Poorly Written
Compute the volume of a sphere.	Know how big a sphere is inside.
Name the countries of Western Europe and describe their locations relative to one another	Know the countries in Europe.
Memorize 20 Spanish vocabulary words.	Learn more Spanish vocabulary words.
Describe the role of mythology in the development of the plot in Homer's *Odyssey.*	Describe the myths in Homer's *Odyssey.*
Describe five species of North American bat and state their habitats and habits.	Describe different types of bats.
Complete Chapter 12 of the text and work through the end-of-chapter questions.	Study educational psychology.

Teachers often think of these levels of learning as organized from least complex to most complex. However, they are not hierarchically related in a strict sense (see, e.g., Pring, 1971; Seddon, 1978), nor do they represent the only taxonomy that you might use for classifying aspects of thought. In fact, many teachers believe that younger children should be challenged to perform at relatively higher levels of mental operations in Bloom's taxonomy. Nevertheless, the taxonomy is useful for understanding the process of thinking, because its terminology is clear and it describes different types and goals of thinking. Table 12.2 shows how a social studies teacher can use this taxonomy to generate objectives for a course and to evaluate whether her test questions measure a range of different types of thinking about colonial America.

Today, Bloom's taxonomy is less influential than it used to be. Some teachers view it as being *suggestive* of how students think, rather than being a true psychological model of how students think. Other teachers believe that Bloom's taxonomy is still influential, but that now students must apply their understanding in ways different from those used by students of two or three decades ago—for example, by emphasizing integration of ideas, concepts, and material. There also exist other, newer, and more detailed taxonomies of thinking (Baron & Sternberg, 1987).

In 1995, a group of educational researchers began work on revising Bloom's taxonomy. The result of their thinking is a matrix of six cognitive processes (based on Bloom's six cognitive objectives)—remembering, understanding, applying, analyzing, evaluating, and creating—that can be applied to four kinds of knowledge—factual, conceptual, procedural, and metacognitive (Anderson & Krathwohl, 2001). Not only did these researchers slightly change the order of Bloom's terms, but they have also added a new emphasis on *what* each of the cognitive processes acts upon—specifically, any one of the four kinds of knowledge.

The social studies teacher mentioned above might use this revision of Bloom's taxonomy to generate objectives such as the following for her unit on colonial America:

After reading the historical novel My Brother Sam Is Dead *by James Lincoln Collier and Christopher Collier, students will be able to describe the emotional impact of the American Revolution.* Analyzing conceptual knowledge.

Each student will write a fictional account of an incident that occurred during the American Revolution. Creating conceptual knowledge.

TABLE 12.2 **Examples of Bloom's Taxonomy and Test Questions Assessing Each Element**

1. Knowledge
Betsy Ross sewed the first American flag in what year?
What was thrown overboard in protest at the Boston Tea Party?
What was the name of the monarch in England at the time of the American Revolution?

2. Comprehension
Why did Betsy Ross sew the first American flag?
Why did the Boston Tea Party take place?

3. Application
Describe the role of human feelings such as jealousy, loyalty, and desire for autonomy in the American Revolution.

4. Analysis
Describe each stage of the American Revolution and relate each stage to what happened before it and after it.

5. Synthesis
What did the French Revolution and the American Revolution have in common? How did they differ?

6. Evaluation
Analyze how the American Revolution helped and hindered the development of culture and daily life in the newly emerging country.

AFFECTIVE OBJECTIVES. Within the affective, or emotional, domain are five specific objectives that relate to different levels of commitment (Krathwohl, Bloom, & Masia, 1964):

Level 1, *Receiving*, consists only of being minimally aware of something going on in the environment (for example, listening begrudgingly).

Level 2, *Responding*, consists of displaying some new behavior as a result of experience (for example, smiling and laughing or otherwise showing interest).

Level 3, *Valuing*, consists of showing some involvement or commitment (for example, offering to participate in the activity).

Level 4, *Organization*, consists of changing one's value system to accommodate a new value (for example, joining a club or team).

Level 5, *Characterization by value*, consists of behaving consistently in keeping with the new value (for example, regularly attending an activity and discussing it openly with others).

Table 12.3 shows examples of behaviors that demonstrate each of the five affective objectives.

PSYCHOMOTOR OBJECTIVES. The last of the three domains, the psychomotor or physical ability domain, has not been as well studied as the cognitive and affective domains. Taxonomies do exist, however (Harrow, 1972; Simpson, 1972). These taxonomies progress from basic reflexive actions to highly skilled movements. Despite the fact that psychomotor objectives have not received the same attention as cognitive and affective taxonomies, the mastery of psychomotor skills is relevant to effective performance in many areas. Consider, for example, the rapid and skilled use of a modern computer and mouse, a laboratory apparatus, and a calligraphy pen or charcoal sketching crayon. All these types of physical actions require trained, skilled performances. Consider also the skills involved in playing

THINKING ANALYTICALLY

What are the advantages and disadvantages of taxonomies? How might you use taxonomies to improve your teaching? How might taxonomies interfere with good teaching?

SUGGESTION: Taxonomies organize teaching and learning; however, they may unnecessarily limit the way students naturally think about the material by creating artificial distinctions between different aspects of the same topic. Taxonomies can give students a useful idea of the breadth of what they are expected to master; however, they can also encourage students to learn only the stated aspects of the question, instead of exploring the topic more deeply and creatively.

TABLE 12.3 Examples of Behaviors Demonstrating Each of the Five Affective Objectives

Level 1: Receiving
Making occasional eye contact.
Showing slight changes in expression or response to the teacher's effort.
Continuing another activity (reading newspaper) while occasionally stopping to listen.

Level 2: Responding
Raising one's hand in response to a question.
Making verbal comments to another student.
Laughing or reacting at appropriate points.

Level 3: Valuing
Offering to participate or help.
Offering to tutor another student.
Requesting help or clarification; caring about one's grade.

Level 4: Organization
Changing school behavior, such as arriving earlier or staying later to participate in an activity.
Taking new courses or pursuing new subjects previously not pursued (joining drama, chorus, art club, etc.).
Encouraging other students to participate in activities.

Level 5: Characterization by value
Showing improvement in behaviors criticized in past.
Consistently showing up for activities and participating.
Making sacrifices to continue with activities (forgoing recess to practice an instrument).

tennis, skiing, soccer, and other sports. Skilled performances in the psychomotor domain are central to many life activities and accomplishments. For a teacher interested in helping students master psychomotor skills, it is important to focus on incremental improvements in skills over time.

Each of the types of objectives—cognitive, affective, and psychomotor—is relevant to instruction at every level. However, student differences may mean that for any individual student some types of objectives are more important than others. For example, affective objectives may be particularly important to a student experiencing an abusive home environment, or who is emotionally labile or disturbed. Affective objectives are also important for gifted students. Cognitive objectives may be most important for a gifted student, whereas psychomotor objectives may be most important for students who are highly adept at working with their hands but not as skilled at taking traditional tests. As a guide to planning students' instruction and assessing their learning, expert teachers think in terms of objectives within each of these domains, tailored to students' individual needs and learning profiles.

THINKING PRACTICALLY

Early in a course, which should you emphasize more heavily, affective objectives or cognitive objectives? Why?

SUGGESTION: If students are not affectively engaged in learning (or are tuned out completely), there is no point in stressing cognitive objectives.

DIRECT INSTRUCTION METHODS

Now that you have learned general approaches to planning what you are going to teach, the next question is, "Exactly how should I present the material?" Lauren Hodges grappled with precisely this issue in planning her lessons. Say your plan states that you must present a lesson on colonial America in social studies class tomorrow. How might you conduct this class? Methods of **direct instruction** include lecturing, recitation and questioning, and seatwork and homework. Expert teachers always use a combination of teaching techniques to vary their approach and keep their students actively involved in learning. We consider the strengths and weaknesses of each of these teaching techniques. But, first, let us review what research has shown about the success of direct instruction.

Barak Rosenshine (1979, 1986; Rosenshine & Stevens, 1986) studied the conditions associated with achievement gains in the classroom, with an emphasis on methods of direct instruction. Rosenshine believes that high levels of learning result when students spend more time on academic tasks and, consequently, cover more content (see also Bloom, 1976). Learning occurs best in classrooms that are academically focused and directed by a teacher who presents structured content. Rosenshine finds that high achievement is possible even when teachers lead large groups of students. He sees the ideal learning environment as one in which, first, the teacher is in charge; and second, there are clear goals, sufficient time for instruction, monitoring of student performance, questioning by the teacher with responding by students, immediate feedback, warmth, democracy, and an atmosphere of cooperation. By definition, expert teachers meet all of these criteria in their direct instruction; let us see how they accomplish this feat.

■**LECTURING AND EXPLAINING**   All of us have had the experience of listening in rapt attention to a wonderful lecture. We have also had the opposite experience—drifting off to sleep or counting the ceiling tiles as the teacher droned on.

STRENGTHS OF LECTURING. Lecturing is a good method to use to communicate an overview of a topic to students, to describe detailed examples, and in general to tell a story about a sequence of events. A good lecture piques students' interest. Students learn through practice to sit and listen attentively. However, for young students with shorter attention spans, keep lectures brief. For high school students, lectures can be far longer, even occupying an entire class period. During lectures, students are necessarily more passive than they are during other methods of instruction, such as discussions or group activities. Thus use lectures to introduce students to topics and ideas that they can then further explore with your assistance through other teaching techniques.

WEAKNESSES OF LECTURING. The drawbacks of lecturing are obvious: Some students find it difficult to sit and listen, and they may become disruptive. Lecturing can leave behind students who are less prepared and who are unable or unwilling to interrupt the teacher with questions, and lecturing requires you to speak convincingly and clearly for long stretches of time. Lectures also demand that you be well prepared and organized. If you cannot invest the necessary amount of time to prepare an effective lecture, consider other methods because badly presented lectures can turn off students to potentially interesting topics. Also, learning through listening to lectures is relatively passive.

SPECIFIC LECTURING TECHNIQUES. Always helpful are the big three rules of effective speaking: "Tell them what you are going to tell them, tell them, then tell them what you told them." First, in giving a good lecture, begin by stating your objectives in giving the lecture and providing necessary context (in other words, a solid introduction; Brophy, 1982). Second, present the content one step at a time, using body language that conveys enthusiasm, and using slides, overheads, or other tools to increase the students' interest level (Williams & Ceci, 1997). And, third, review what was presented and show how it relates to other material that students have studied or will study. Follow lectures with teacher-supervised practice, then independent practice (seatwork), and finally, appropriate homework. A study by Wendy Williams and Stephen Ceci (1997) demonstrated just how essential it is to lecture using an enthusiastic tone of voice. This study compared college student ratings of their instructor and the course as a whole for two groups of students taught identical material in an identical format, using the same textbook, and evaluated with the same tests. One group was taught with an "enthusiastic" tone; the second group was taught by the same instructor in a more subdued speaking style. Williams and Ceci found that student ratings of various aspects of the instructor and course increased considerably when the instructor used an enthusiastic tone of voice. Students gave higher ratings for the instructor's knowledge, tolerance, organization, and accessibility, as well as for the fairness of the grading policy, the clarity of the course's goals, and the quality of the (identical) textbook. Overall, the "enthusiastically" taught course was rated considerably higher and students reported that they learned much more in it. However, the test results showed nearly identical performance by both groups of students. Thus, even though students may learn from less enthusiastic teachers, they dramatically prefer more enthusiastic teachers and courses. Figure 12.1 shows the differences in student ratings for the two courses.

THINKING CREATIVELY

Based on personal experience and what you have learned in your educational psychology course, name four unusual or innovative ways a teacher can make a lecture more interesting.

SUGGESTION: Relate the lecture to current events; relate the lecture to students' daily lives; use creative props or visual aids; open with a reading from a work of fiction related to the topic.

FIGURE 12.1

Students' Evaluations as a Function of Professor's Voice Pitch

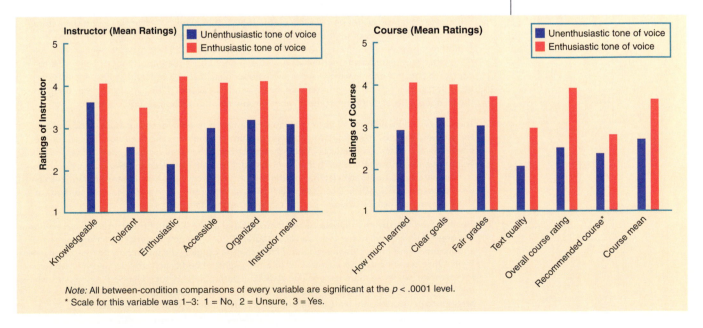

Note: All between-condition comparisons of every variable are significant at the $p < .0001$ level.
* Scale for this variable was 1–3: 1 = No, 2 = Unsure, 3 = Yes.

David Ausubel (1977) believes that meaningful verbal learning should be the goal of an effective lecture. His **expository teaching** approach suggests that well-presented verbal information and ideas, received and digested by the listener, result in meaningful learning. Ausubel advocates that teachers speak from the general to the specific—in other words, begin with the rule and proceed to examples. Lessons begin with advance organizers—such as the objectives we placed at the beginning of every chapter—to provide an overview of what is to come and to orient students in the right direction. Advance organizers should describe in clear language what is to come, so students can activate their relevant prior information and help themselves learn. Next, teachers describe the content they wish to cover, stressing similarities and differences between the new material and what students already know. Students themselves may be asked to supply examples of such similarities and differences. Teachers often repeat the goals of the lesson, linking these goals back to the advance organizers. Because of the types of information processing it requires, expository teaching works best with students at the fifth-grade level or above. Table 12.4 shows a direct instruction lesson plan based on the expository teaching approach.

Robert Gagné (1977) believes instruction should be based on the information processing model of learning (described in detail in Chapter 8). For present purposes, Gagné's views state that there are phases of learning and specific types of instructional events that support each phase. The period of *preparation for learning* involves three phases: attention and alertness, during which you as the teacher must seize students' attention; expectancy, during which you inform students of the objectives of the lesson and motivate the students; and retrieval to working memory, during which you encourage students to recall prior knowledge relevant to the lesson. The period of *acquisition and performance* includes four phases: selective perception of stimulus features, during which you present the new material and say what is new about it; encoding and storage in long-term memory, during which you scaffold students as they learn; retrieval and responding, during which you lead students to answer questions; and reinforcement, during which you provide meaningful feedback. Finally, the period of *transfer of learning* involves two phases: cueing retrieval and generalizing, during which you assess performance.

TABLE 12.4 Direct Instruction Lesson Plan Based on Expository Teaching

1. Tell students that today's lesson will focus on the theme of humankind's struggle against the natural world. Give an overview of what this struggle has meant, describing the challenges faced by early explorers in new lands as they vied with nature and tried to make a living for their families. Ask students what they remember from their social studies lessons about the importance of being able to cope with nature if people were to survive. Ask students if they have ever had any experiences of being at the mercy of nature—for example, being lost in the woods during a camping trip. Bring up the recent plights of hurricane, tornado, and volcanic eruption victims around the world.

2. Then, begin a discussion of the book students were assigned to read for today: *Moby-Dick.* Describe the plot and the characters, involving students as much as possible in the discussion. Talk about the similarities and differences between *Moby-Dick* and a book they read recently, such as *The Call of the Wild.* Have students generate a list of similarities and differences between the two books. Ask students to nominate other books the class has—or they alone have—read, and describe the similarities to and differences from *Moby-Dick.* Discuss Melville's goals in telling this story, and encourage students to think in terms of the main theme—people's struggle against nature.

3. Finally, revisit the advance organizers—the themes stated at the outset of the lesson. Ask students how the original description of the topic can be elaborated on. What new material have they learned about humankind's struggle against nature? How can the opening discussion now be recast into a new light? What new insights have been gained into the plights of hurricane, tornado, and volcano victims, for example? What can students conclude about the personalities of men involved in America's whaling industry a century and more ago? Open a broad discussion related to the original theme, and attempt to get students thinking along multiple lines that link up with the main theme.

ADAPTING LECTURING FOR DIFFERENT LEARNING STYLES. As we have emphasized, students have individual learning and thinking styles (see Chapter 4) that influence how well they learn from the lecture format. For some students, who are auditory learners, material presented in a spoken format works well. Visual learners prefer to take in information by reading it or by seeing it displayed in charts and graphs; these students do better in a lecture if the teacher uses visual aids. Some learners are kinesthetically oriented—that is, they learn best by touching, feeling, manipulating, and working with objects and props. These students tend to have more trouble learning from traditional lectures, even those with good visual aids. Such students do well in laboratories or in classes based on activities. Expert teachers are aware of the diversity of learning styles in their classrooms and do everything possible to broaden instruction in order to reach a range of students.

■RECITATION AND QUESTIONING Moving beyond pure lecturing to lecturing combined with discussion raises students' retention, develops higher order thinking, and enhances attitudes and motivation (McKeachie & Kulik, 1975)—one of the reasons that Lauren Hodges worked so hard to incorporate several different approaches in her teaching. Combining lecture and recitation gives students the best of both techniques. You may not recognize the term *recitation*, but you have actually been involved in recitation many times. **Recitation** is a teaching method in which teachers ask questions and students provide answers. Good teacher questions are organized or generally planned in advance to lead students to develop key understandings. When the students provide answers, the teacher responds to these answers with yet more questions to further develop the lesson.

Given their diverse learning styles, some students adapt better to the recitation and questioning approach. Some students learn as they verbalize their thoughts—ideas and concepts take shape as the students talk about them. Others are good speakers, comfortable thinking on their feet and speaking in front of others; here recitation and questioning are effective. However, recitation and questioning may be a poor fit for quiet or reticent students and students who prefer to absorb information through their eyes or by working with props. Expert teachers thus develop and diversify their instructional approaches to meet the needs of diverse students.

THINKING ANALYTICALLY

Name three aspects of effective versus ineffective recitation.

SUGGESTION: Well-defined versus poorly defined questions; an encouraging approach when asking questions versus a demoralizing one—"I know you will be able to figure this out if you think about it" versus "This is probably too tough for you"; the allotment of adequate versus inadequate time for students to think and answer.

■ASKING THE RIGHT QUESTIONS Although asking good and appropriate questions that develop students' thinking is both a skill and an art, you can certainly learn the technique through practice. Bloom's cognitive taxonomy—knowledge, comprehension, application, analysis, synthesis, and evaluation—can be used to categorize your questions. To be effective, think about distributing questioning across different objectives in order to create a well-rounded learning experience. For instance, consider our example of the teacher planning a lesson on colonial America. Table 12.2 lists the types of questions about colonial America that the teacher might ask to tap cognitive abilities and thinking relevant to each stage of Bloom's taxonomy.

What student-related factors should you consider when developing and asking questions? Lower level questions are obviously more appropriate for younger students and for more basic learning experiences, although even very young students can at times answer higher order questions. Higher level questions tend to be better for older students and for students ready to move beyond basic learning (Gall, 1984). In general, younger and lower ability students do best with simple questions that enable them to often answer correctly, so you can create an atmosphere of encouragement and success. For higher ability students, however, Berliner (1987) found that the best learning occurs when teachers use hard questions from each of the levels coupled with critical teacher feedback. However, all students need a variety of question types and a chance to use their higher level abilities at some point.

The more teachers communicate an interest in students' questions, the more students move toward analytical and creative learning. (Carolina Kroon, Impact Visuals)

METHODS OF QUESTIONING. We can all remember examples of fairly meaningless teacher questions from our own school experiences. One chemistry teacher asked the first student in each row to state the name, atomic number, and atomic weight of each of the elements in the row of the periodic table that matched the row in which the students were sitting. But even well-formulated questions can be poorly used—for example, if the teacher asks the question, calls on a student, grows frustrated at the lack of response or at an inadequate response, and blurts out the correct answer. **Wait time** is the period of silence both before and after a student answers a question that gives all students an opportunity to think. Appropriate wait times give students a chance to process questions and think about answers, and possibly even raise their hands.

As teachers, we should work hard at eliciting the correct answers from our students. We should allow students time to think and then call on several students and tolerate pauses if necessary to draw out reticent students (Berliner, 1987). Avoid calling on volunteers, as this approach gives other students encouragement not to listen because they know they will not be called on. In fact, call on every student at fairly regular intervals (Weinstein & Mignano, 1993). Sometimes, with adept questioning, even a student who believes he knows very little about a subject can be led to answer low-level questions accurately. This student may then experience growing feelings of competence and may pay more attention in class and work harder. In this way teachers promote positive expectations on the part of their students and themselves (Weinstein, 1998).

RESPONDING TO STUDENT QUESTIONS. Ask good questions, but also respond to student questions appropriately in order to encourage further learning and questioning. In fact, it is often more important that students learn what questions to ask, and how to ask them, than that they learn the answers to the questions (Sternberg, 1994). Sternberg believes that it can sometimes be a mistake for a teacher to encourage students to view the teacher as the one who should ask questions and the students as the ones to answer them. Teachers must realize—and make sure the students realize—that what matters most is not the "facts" students know, but rather their ability to *use* those facts. Often, schools tend to emphasize the *answering* of questions, rather than the *asking* of them. The good student is perceived as the one who usually furnishes the right answers, preferably rapidly. The expert in a field thus becomes the extension of the expert student—the one who knows a lot of information and can recite it from memory at will.

Contrary to this view, however, many cognitive and educational psychologists are returning to the thinking of John Dewey (1910), who realized that *how* we think is often more important than *what* we think. Dewey believed that teachers should place more emphasis on the teaching of *how to ask* questions, and *how to ask* the right questions (good,

THINKING PRACTICALLY

What might you do to monitor your ability to ask good questions that most benefit your students?

SUGGESTION: Ask students to complete anonymous feedback forms giving you comments; videotape or audiotape yourself and analyze the tape; ask a teacher you admire to observe you and critique your performance.

THINKING PRACTICALLY

At what level do your teachers respond to your questions? Describe seven examples of teacher-student interactions that can be characterized as representing each of the seven levels in Sternberg's model.

SUGGESTION: The teacher might state:

Level 1: "I do not have time for this now."

Level 2: "Because that's just the way it works."

Level 3: "That's a good question; I don't really know the answer offhand."

Level 4: "I'll check the Web for information tonight and get back to you tomorrow."

Level 5: "Let's think about it . . . several possibilities that come to mind include . . ."

Level 6: "Here are a few possibilities . . . we could test each one by doing the following . . . this way we could see which is most likely."

Level 7: "Here are a few possibilities . . . Let's make it a project to collect information about which one is most likely to be accurate . . . Why don't you do this by tomorrow, and I will do that, and we will compare notes and see what happens."

Consider a question a student might pose after visiting Holland, seeing a documentary about Holland on television, or reading a book about Holland: Why are people in Holland so tall? Consider various ways a teacher might respond to this question. The higher the level of the response, the more the teacher is doing to enhance the student's intellectual development.

Level 1: Rejection of questions: "Don't ask so many questions!"—"Don't bother me!"—"Don't ask stupid questions!"—and "Be quiet!"

When teachers respond at this level, the basic message to the student is to shut up. Questions are seen as inappropriate or irritating. Students learn to be seen and not heard, and to keep their place. The result of consistent punishment for question asking, of course, is that students learn not to ask questions, and hence, not to learn.

Level 2: Restatement of questions as responses: "Because they are Dutch, and Dutch people are very tall," or "Because they grow a lot."

At this level, teachers answer students' questions, but in a wholly empty way. Their response is nothing more than a restatement of the original question.

Level 3: Admission of ignorance or direct responses: "I don't know" or "Because . . . ," followed by a reasonable answer (say, about nutrition or genetics).

At this level, teachers either say they do not know or give a response based on what they do know. Students are given the opportunity to learn something new or to realize their teachers do not know everything. When teachers answer at this level, they can do so

either with or without "reinforcement": They can either reward students for asking the question or not reward them. Examples of rewards would be "That's a good question" or "I'm glad you asked that" or "That's a really interesting question." Such a response rewards question asking and is likely to increase its frequency, which fosters further opportunities for students to learn.

Level 4: Encouragement to seek response through authority: "I'll look it up in the encyclopedia" or "Why don't you look it up in the encyclopedia?"

At level 4, the question-answering process does not end just with an answer or admission of ignorance. Students are taught that information not possessed can and often *should* be sought out. Notice, however, the difference in the two responses. In the first, the teacher takes responsibility for seeking the information. Students thereby learn that information can be sought, but also there is someone else to do it for them. Thus the learning ultimately accomplished is *passive learning*. In the second response, the student is given the responsibility, and not only learns but learns how to learn—by means of *active learning*. Through active learning, students develop their own information-seeking skills, rather than becoming dependent on others.

Level 5: Consideration of alternative explanations: "People in Holland might be tall because of the food, the weather, genetics, hormone injections, killing of short children, wearing of elevator shoes, and so on."

Here, the teacher says she or he does not know, but suggests the student explore some possibilities. Ideally, the student and teacher generate possibilities together. The student

thus comes to realize that even simple questions can invite hypothesis formulation and testing.

Level 6: Consideration of explanations in addition to means of evaluating the explanations: "How might we go about deciding which of these explanations is correct?"

Here, teachers not only encourage alternative explanations, as in level 5, but also discuss ways of evaluating the validity of the alternative explanations. "For example, if genetics were responsible for the high average height of the Dutch, what might we expect to observe? How might we discern whether food or weather is responsible? How can we quickly rule out the possibility that the Dutch kill short children?" Students can learn via the responses of their teachers not only how to generate alternative hypotheses, as in level 5, but also how to test them.

Level 7: Consideration of explanations, in addition to means of evaluating them and follow-through in evaluations: "Let's try getting some of the information we need to help us decide among these explanations."

Here, the teacher actually encourages the student to perform the experiments by gathering information that could distinguish among the alternative explanations. Students learn not only how to think but how to act on their thoughts. Although it may not be possible to test every explanation of a phenomenon, it will often be possible to test several of them. For example, students can gather information about whether taller Dutch parents also tend to have taller children, whether there are reports of missing short children, and so on.

thought-provoking, and interesting ones), and less emphasis on the simple retrieval of the correct answers to whatever questions *we* might pose. The ability to ask good questions and to know how to ask them is an essential part of intelligence, and arguably, the most important part (Arlin, 1990; Getzels & Csikszentmihalyi, 1967; Sternberg & Spear-Swerling, 1996).

When students seek teacher engagement by asking questions, teachers have several different characteristic ways of responding. We believe that how teachers respond to children's questions is important because the types of responses are differentially helpful to children in developing their intelligence. Sternberg (1994) has proposed a seven-level model of teacher-child interaction in the questioning process. (The seven levels of responding are reviewed in Table 12.5.) The basic idea is that mediators who respond at higher levels better foster their children's intellectual development. As teachers move up the levels, they go from rejecting children's questions, at one extreme, to encouraging hypothesis formation and testing, at the other. Students move from no learning, to passive rote learning, to analytic and creative learning. The higher the teacher's level of response, the more they communicate an interest in students' questions. Teachers may not always have the time or resources to respond to children's questions according to level 7. Nor are higher levels of response equally appropriate for children of all ages—responses need to be developmentally appropriate to be maximally useful. However, the more teachers use the higher levels, the more they encourage students to develop their cognitive skills.

■ **SEATWORK AND HOMEWORK**   Students work independently when they do both homework and **seatwork,** the quiet independent work students do at their desks. Obviously, the uses of homework and seatwork are many and varied, and both types of work can be either effective or ineffective at helping children learn, depending on the types of work assigned. Ideally, seatwork gives students an opportunity to practice what they have just learned, generally by working through practice problems at increasing levels of difficulty. Do not use this type of work to teach students completely new material. Seatwork or homework may involve **programmed instruction,** consisting of structured lessons that students work on by themselves and at their own pace.

MAKING SEATWORK AND HOMEWORK EFFECTIVE.   For either type of assignment to be effective, be sure the students understand the directions and the task you are asking them to complete. Often, expert teachers work out a sample question or problem on the chalkboard to show students generally what is expected. This type of scaffolding is especially important in classes with students who may only recently have joined the class, the school, or even the country—although it certainly is helpful to all students. Express openly the many implicit rules for doing homework and seatwork to help children unfamiliar with the rules and to refresh other students' memories. For example, does using a calculator represent cheating on math seatwork or homework? Do students have to acknowledge written sources? Is checking each other's work permitted? Can they consult dictionaries or textbooks during exams? Table 12.6 shows a lesson plan for helping students overcome homework difficulties and for making homework assignments interesting and even enjoyable.

HOW MUCH HOMEWORK?   A recent composite analysis of many independent studies conducted around the world found no obvious relationship between the amount of homework assigned and the amount students learn, as measured on standardized tests (Third International Mathematics and Science Study [TIMSS], 1996). In some schools, much homework is assigned, but it does not appear to do much good. In other schools, a lot of homework is assigned and the students clearly benefit. In still other schools, little homework is assigned, and students do well, presumably because classwork and seatwork are effective and students' home lives foster good study habits and encourage reading. Then there are schools that assign little homework and shortchange their students.

Newmann (1991) found that homework coupled with high expectations for student performance were characteristic of the most effective secondary schools in the United States. There is no simple relationship between giving more homework and getting better performance out of your students: The homework you assign must be appropriate, challenging, and relevant to meaningful aspects of student performance. In general, frequent, smaller assignments are better than less frequent, larger ones (Cooper, 1989a, 1989b). Effective homework reinforces classroom learning, enables students to succeed (by not being too difficult), is used as a normal part of instruction, and is graded promptly and returned to students (Berliner, 1988; Berliner & Calfee, 1996).

An interesting finding about homework is that Japanese students actually spend *less* time doing math homework than do American students (TIMSS, 1996). Why, then, do

TABLE 12.6   Lesson Plan for Helping Students Overcome Homework Difficulties

Central Themes

Knowing Self

Knowing Process

Knowing Differences

Synopsis

An experience (three different possibilities are described) to expose students to the materials and methods available to help them with homework difficulties.

What To Do

Choose one of the following three activities.

A. Homework Fair

1. Designate a period of time as a "homework fair" devoted entirely to helping students figure out ways to overcome difficulties that they have with homework.

2. Ask students to identify important areas to consider by reviewing their homework questionnaires and their plans for improvement (from Lesson 2).

3. Set up (or have students set up) homework displays around the room. For example: exhibits of helpful homework materials (trapper keepers, daily-planner notebooks, pocket folders, etc.); motivational displays (a chart showing how many hours each basketball star practices free throws); demonstrations of personal progress (before-and-after stories). Because good displays require much preparation, you might rely on students to do the work. Preparation for the fair can be a class project; or you might ask individual students to prepare displays or presentations that explain their particularly successful ideas.

4. Walk students through the displays, explaining whatever may be unclear (or have students do so for displays they've created). Allow students to talk to each other about their reactions. If it is difficult to have students walking around the room, you might pass materials around as you discuss them.

5. Include a "workshop" as a part of the fair. Have a table or some space for students to make their own materials, or to personalize purchased materials.

6. Require that each student write down at least *two* new ideas he learned from the fair. At the end of the fair, have students read the ideas aloud and tell how they can be used to solve their own problems.

B. Field Trip to a Supply Store

1. Arrange for students to visit a school or office-supply store. If possible, arrange for a store representative to present some of the materials available there that can help students with homework (notebooks, resource books, thesaurus and dictionary, folders, pencils, pens, highlighters).

2. Let students know that they'll be going to a store to see some of the materials that can help them better handle homework. Ask students to prepare by reviewing their homework questionnaires (from Lesson 2) and lists for improvement.

3. Visit the store with your class.

4. Sometime around when you visit the store, include time in class for students to make their own materials or to personalize purchased materials.

5. Require that each student make a note of at least *two* new and useful things (strategies or materials) she learned. At the end of the trip, have each student share the things he noted (reading aloud) and tell how these things can be used to solve his own problems.

C. "Dear Abby"

1. Ask students to review their homework questionnaires (from Lesson 2) for ways in which they get stuck or have difficulty doing homework.

2. Have students write letters in the style of "Dear Abby" to ask for advice on how to handle a particular difficulty. For example, "Dear Abby, the teacher always tells us to show our work on math problems. So I do, but then she complains that she can't find my answers because the paper is too messy. Is this fair? What should I do?" Or, "Dear Abby, I always think I understand my writing assignment until I get home and try to do it. Then it doesn't make any sense. Help!"

3. Have students exchange letters and write responses to each other.

4. Have students read their letters aloud and comment on the advice they get from their partners: How useful is it? Will they try to use it?

Note

Whichever option you choose, make sure that students consider whether their solutions to homework difficulties are appropriate for different kinds of homework (long-range assignments, overnight math worksheets, defining vocabulary).

Follow-Up Activity

Have students record in journals the new and useful ideas, tips, or materials that they discover. Later they can revisit what they've written and consider how they've used what they learned or (if appropriate) why they *haven't* used what they learned.

Source: From *Practical Intelligence for School* by W.M. Williams, T. Blythe, N. White, J. Li, R.J. Sternberg, and H.I. Gardner. Copyright © 1996. Reprinted by permission of Addison-Wesley Publishers, Inc.

Japanese students outperform American students in math? The answer has to do with differences in the style of instruction in the two countries. Japanese teachers spend far less time on drill than do American teachers, and more time on helping students understand and explore both their errors and their correct answers. This more thoughtful approach to teaching improves math performance. Thus more homework alone is not the answer to improving performance; the entire teaching approach, homework included, must be evaluated.

Carefully and thoughtfully designed homework can be more than just a collection of exercises mirroring those done in class. Good homework piques the students' attention and causes them to reason with the concepts they learned in class. Good homework differs enough from classwork that students need to read and follow the directions carefully. And, as we dis-

THINKING CREATIVELY

Name five ways you might design an interesting homework assignment for your students.

SUGGESTION: Have students write a story or play about the material learned in class. Design a costume about a historical period studied in class. Interview a person knowledgeable about a topic under study. Create a folder of materials gathered from the Web. Write an exam that could be used to test the information covered in class.

Research has shown that assigned homework should be appropriate, challenging, and relevant to meaningful aspects of a student's performance. Frequent, small assignments allow students to reinforce their classroom learning and increase their success in the classroom. (Michael Newman, PhotoEdit)

cussed in Chapter 11 on classroom management, an expert teacher develops an appropriate system to ensure that students actually complete their homework on time. Consider the examples of creative and interesting types of homework assignments listed in Table 12.7.

ASSIGNING EFFECTIVE SEATWORK. Although you should define seatwork as carefully as homework, often it will have to resemble more closely what you actually taught in class: follow-up exercises, additional problems of the kind completed during instruction, and so on. Especially with young students, do not assign extended periods of seatwork; it is preferable to rotate between lecturing and demonstrating problems on the board and assigning five sample seatwork problems that help students process what they have just learned. While students are working quietly at their seats, expert teachers make themselves available by walking around the room. Students should not have to work hard to get your attention; otherwise, some students may be embarrassed to ask their questions. Expert teachers provide a few moments of contact to every child in the class, even if just to look over her or his shoulder and say, "Good work!" (Brophy & Good, 1986).

For both homework and seatwork, avoid creating situations in which students simply copy to finish work quickly. Sometimes students feel pressure solely to get the right answer, and ineffective teachers may give assignments that provide an easy way out for these students. If students are not expected to show their work and explain their reasoning, it may become tempting to take a shortcut by copying or even cheating. In such cases, little meaningful learning takes place. Tell students clearly the reasons for the work they are assigned, and hold them accountable for *displaying* actual understanding and

TABLE 12.7 Models of Effective Homework Assignments

1. **Grade 1:** Under adult supervision, using just the items in your refrigerator and cupboard, make a dye you could use to color clothes. Color a small kerchief or piece of cloth and bring it to class.

2. **Grade 3:** With the help of an adult, get a newspaper or magazine flyer and cut out the coupons for 20 items of different types (meat, canned goods, paper products, etc.). Figure the total savings if all coupons are used, and then figure out how much is saved on each category of item.

3. **Grade 5:** Inflate a round balloon, get a tape measure, and measure its circumference. Place the balloon in the freezer for an hour and measure it again. Place the balloon in warm water for a half hour and measure it again. Write an essay explaining your findings.

4. **Grade 8:** Take a stack of newspapers for an entire week and go through each front-page story. Record whether the story is about a man or woman, and record how many times men versus women are quoted or described. Rate the role played by each person mentioned in each story as positive or negative. Tally the results and explain.

5. **Grade 12:** Read Joseph Conrad's *The Secret Sharer* and write a new ending for the story.

Students can use home computers for exercises to reinforce classroom learning or to research class projects on the Internet. (Loren Santow, Stone)

the ability to reason with the concepts and information they learn. Effective teachers can also tailor homework and seatwork to different students' learning styles, so each student plays to her or his strengths: Auditory learners might be asked to listen to a tape and work through questions, visual learners might be asked to read and view diagrams, and kinesthetic learners might be asked to design models or projects or work with colorful manipulatives.

 MEETING THE NEEDS OF DIFFERENT STUDENTS

This book has returned often to issues of diversity among students and the resulting need for you to broaden instructional approaches to meet the needs of every student. As students become more ethnically and socioeconomically diverse, teachers face greater challenges in reaching their students. Lauren Hodges recognized these challenges and was determined to meet them by designing broad and interesting instructional approaches. In Chapter 5 on exceptional children and Chapter 6 on group differences we stressed the differing demands of teaching students from widely ranging backgrounds. We return briefly to this topic to stress the importance of teaching—and reaching—every student, regardless of her or his special needs.

THINKING ANALYTICALLY

How can you use seatwork to enrich the work assigned to a gifted child?

SUGGESTION: The student might tackle more advanced exercises while the rest of the class works at their own pace, or read additional materials or sources to gather more information about a topic.

■**APTITUDE-BY-TREATMENT INTERACTIONS** Years ago, researchers such as Richard Snow (1966, 1989) began to observe that children learn different things from instruction depending on their level of ability and their personality. This effect, called an **aptitude-by-treatment interaction,** indicates that individual students learn different things from the same instruction, as a result of background, abilities, and prior experiences. Understanding the nuances of why some students learn better than others in given situations is extremely complex. However, the effect is real, and we cannot expect all students to be able to learn from the same approach. That a child fails to perform may not be due to willfulness or stubbornness; rather, it may be a mismatch between the teaching method and the child's needs. In such cases, another approach is the best answer. Trying new ways to reach students who are not performing can yield impressive results.

Sternberg has studied the importance of a match between instruction and a student's pattern of abilities. In general, analytical abilities tend to be the most important in school performance, because of the emphasis of most instruction and assessment on factual recall. If courses are taught primarily to emphasize other abilities, such as creative and practical ones, these abilities will become more important in course performance

(Sternberg, 1994b, 1996; Sternberg & Clinkenbeard, 1995; Sternberg, Ferrari, Clinkenbeard, & Grigorenko, 1996). Sternberg designed an introductory, college-level psychology course that was taught and evaluated in a way that allowed for expression of creative and practical as well as analytical abilities. Students in this course performed at a higher level if their pattern of abilities was at least partially matched to the abilities emphasized in instruction and assessment.

In general, Sternberg has advocated teaching to promote the development of diverse types of abilities, and teaching from different perspectives to reach students with diverse types of learning styles (Sternberg, 1996; Sternberg & Spear-Swerling, 1996). He has focused on three abilities: *analytical abilities*—used to compare and contrast, analyze, and evaluate; *creative abilities*—used to invent, discover, and generate; and *practical abilities*—used to apply, utilize, and implement. Indeed, much of the pedagogy in this textbook is based on the analytical, creative, and practical focus, as you have probably noticed when you addressed the questions throughout each chapter. The abilities you have used to answer these questions differ, depending on the type of question—analytic, creative, or practical—you answer.

■ **ADAPTING INSTRUCTION FOR DIVERSE STUDENTS** Expert teachers remember that certain teaching approaches and activities benefit certain types of students. For example, a particularly artistic and creative student does better than other students with classroom discussion questions such as, "Imagine you wrote this poem—what might have motivated you to write it?" and with homework assignments to write alternative endings to poems. An analytically gifted student in the same class does better when classroom discussions ask, "Compare and contrast this poem to the poems we read last week," and when homework assignments ask students to diagram the form of a poem's rhyme and meter.

Students' differential patterns of abilities are an important, but often overlooked, aspect of teaching dynamics. A more commonly recognized distinction among students affecting how they learn concerns students' prior knowledge (Cronbach & Snow, 1977; Dochy, Segers, & Buehl, 1999). Students with the benefit of prior knowledge are able to profit from many forms of instruction. But students who lack prior knowledge often hit roadblocks in their learning and need more scaffolding and generally more responsive teaching (Rosenshine & Stevens, 1986). Richard Snow (1977, 1992, 1995) argued that when students lack necessary background knowledge, the learning process must be designed to assist them in recognizing and learning the most important points so their attention is focused on what matters most. Thus one way to understand the importance of matching teaching approaches to abilities is to think of the match as a way to help students capitalize on prior knowledge and strengths when learning new material.

THINKING CREATIVELY

Name three ways you might customize instruction for an ethnically diverse class. Name three ways that would work with a very intellectually diverse class.

SUGGESTION: Ethnically diverse: Each child does a project on the customs of his or her upbringing; each child writes a story about family life in his or her native culture; each child writes an essay describing how his or her parents or forebears came to the United States. Intellectually diverse: Students with more hands-on abilities build models or mobiles about the era in which a book was set; students with more creative abilities write poems, songs, or plays about the story; students with more analytic abilities write in-depth book reviews.

LIMITATIONS OF DIRECT INSTRUCTION

Direct instruction has been criticized as limiting the types of thinking students engage in (Marshall, 1992). Although in theory this need not be the case, in practice it often is. However, expert teachers can develop lecture and recitation plans that force students to integrate and think critically about material, and these teachers can assign seatwork and homework that demands higher order processing of what students have learned (see the examples in Table 12.7). But accomplishing these objectives is challenging and requires careful planning. It is easier merely to rely on a lower level approach that follows the textbook and workbook. One unfortunate result of direct instruction is that it sometimes emphasizes performance over understanding: If students give the right answers, you feel you have accomplished the goals of teaching the students, despite the students' lack of meaningful understanding of what they said or wrote (Stodolsky, 1988).

Direct instruction has also been criticized as placing students into passive roles (Marshall, 1992). Because students often remain passive as the teacher controls the learning events, deep cognitive engagement sometimes is lacking. Teachers may both praise and prefer students who sit and listen quietly and take good notes, and who are able on a test to repeat what the teacher originally said. Independent thinking or questioning of the teacher's views and assumptions is often not a part of direct instruction approaches.

THINKING ANALYTICALLY

What method of instruction best matches your abilities?

SUGGESTION: Ask yourself about past experiences in which you learned material quickly and easily—how was the material taught? This method of instruction undoubtedly well matches your abilities.

Some critics argue that direct instruction, which is grounded in a behavioral view of learning (see Chapter 7), views teaching and learning as a process of mechanical transmissions of knowledge from teacher to student. Knowledge is transferred from teacher to student in incremental portions, and the task of the student is to sit and absorb the knowledge, watch the teacher complete problems on the chalkboard, and then mimic these behaviors during seatwork and homework assignments. Just as cognitive views of learning began to replace behavioral ones, a view of learning as a student-centered activity has broadened traditional emphases on teacher-centered instruction.

Cognitive views of learning (see Chapter 8) stress what is going on *inside the mind of the learner:* These views see the learner as a complex package of prior learning and experiences that influence current learning. Similarly, student-centered views of instruction view the student as the creator of his or her own learning, and the teacher as the catalyst who enables and encourages that learning. We turn now to a consideration of methods of student-centered instruction.

Implications for Teaching

- *Carefully plan your instruction.* Expert teachers draw on the experiences of other effective teachers. They also recognize that plans must be flexible to adapt to students' changing needs. Although effective teachers know that planning is helpful, they also realize they cannot predict every situation that may arise. Sometimes plans must be abandoned and new approaches tried on the fly in the classroom.

- *Familiarize yourself with a wide range of direct instruction techniques.* These include lecturing, recitation and questioning, and seatwork and homework. Variety enables you to better cope with rapidly changing classroom environments and student needs. On the job, it can be difficult to master a teaching technique when you have little familiarity with it. Practice various techniques before leading a class, either during student teaching time or in mock teaching experiences with friends and fellow teachers.

- *Remain attentive to issues of diversity in learning styles.* Expert teachers make learning effective for all students by tailoring their approaches to students' different learning and thinking styles. Effective teachers rehearse ahead of time several ways of communicating a point they wish to make during a lesson: They may practice oral presentation (speaking in a traditional lecture format) and visual presentation (displaying relevant props); they may work to teach from analytic, creative, and practical perspectives (illustrated by the "Flexible Expert" feature that appears throughout the text).

Principles of Student-Centered or Constructivist Teaching

Researchers have shifted from viewing the *teacher* as belonging at the center of the learning process, to viewing the *student* as having a more central and active role (Davis, 1997; Manger & Wigle, 1997; Nuthall & Alton-Lee, 1992, 1993; Pintrich & Schunk, 1993). Consistent with the **student-centered approach** is a view sometimes called **constructivism,** because it sees students as constructing their own understanding (see Chapter 8). Lauren Hodges recognized the importance of the students' roles in learning and consequently planned to teach in a way that would both involve and excite her students.

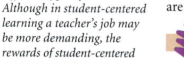

CONSTRUCTIVISM IN THE CLASSROOM

The most significant impact of student-centered approaches, at least in the eyes of teachers and students, is that these approaches involve very different types of classroom instruction and activities. With the constructivist perspective comes an increased awareness of the role of individual differences in learning—and this includes all of the different types of individual differences discussed in Chapters 5 and 6 of this book: ability level, learning style, ethnicity, gender, socioeconomic status, and so on. The constructivist perspective also brings with it a renewed emphasis in learning of the role of student motivation, prior experiences and knowledge, and interpersonal skills.

What does it mean to place students at the center of the learning process? In one regard, it means teachers' jobs are more demanding, because it is often harder to make student-centered approaches work than it is simply to stand at the front of the room and give a lecture. Student-centered approaches require thorough planning, tools and equipment, and in-depth knowledge of the students. Placing students at the center of the learning process also means your goal must be to teach for meaningful, useful, and deep understanding, rather than for the number of correct responses on a quiz. However, the rewards of student-centered approaches are many, and when implemented appropriately students can experience great benefits. Student-centered teaching has been the foundation of so-called **open schools,** a term often used to describe schools in which students are actively involved in deciding what and how they will study.

CREATING CONSTRUCTIVIST LEARNING ENVIRONMENTS

What are some of the ways expert teachers think about creating student-centered learning situations? First, teachers create *complex* learning environments instead of deliberately *simplified* ones, as is often the case for traditional methods of instruction. Student-centered teaching involves giving students real-world problems to solve, with all of the confusion inherent in such problems. The idea is that students should work on ecologically meaningful problems, the solutions for which represent workable real-world solutions, rather than simply being expected to memorize and then restate correct answers on tests.

Second, student-centered learning often involves social interactions with other students in varied formats, including **group instruction,** in which students learn, process, and discuss material in groups. **Group discussions** are conversations among students in which students pose and answer their own questions; the teacher does not play the dominant role. Thus learning becomes a socially mediated and facilitated activity. In Chapter 2 we discussed views of cognitive development that place social interactions at the center of a child's

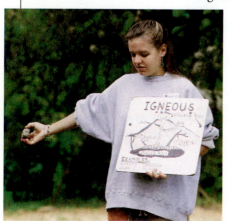

A fifth-grade student gives a science presentation on a group field trip to hunt for different types of rocks. Although in student-centered learning a teacher's job may be more demanding, the rewards of student-centered approaches are many. (Bob Daemmrich, Stock Boston)

developing representation of knowledge about the world. Student-centered teaching is in concert with this view, and many student-centered techniques require students to work effectively with others in order to succeed on tasks.

Third, student-centered approaches involve using multiple representations of content in order to help students generalize and transfer what they learn. This richer and more varied approach attempts to give students information they can *use*. It also attempts to help students develop realistic, flexible, and useful mental representations of knowledge that are not artificially limited as a function of having been learned in a particular context.

Fourth, student-centered teaching requires teachers to use the principles and findings of cognitive and educational psychology to structure instruction so it best enhances the intellectual development of the student. Teachers must be aware of what it really means to learn, and how the process of learning is affected by different factors. Thus, again, student-centered teaching is demanding on the teachers who use this approach.

One study found that teacher-guided discussions were a more efficient means of attaining higher levels of reasoning and higher quality explanations, but peer discussions tended to be more generative and exploratory (Hogan, Nastasi, & Pressley, 1999). Peer discussions also gave rise to more varied student discourse. Thus the benefits of peer discussions differ from the benefits of teacher-guided discussion; clearly, both teaching approaches have an important place in today's classrooms.

At first inspection, some novice teachers might be tempted to conclude, "This student-centered approach is great. Less work for the teacher—let the students teach themselves and each other." However, this assumption misses the main point. By giving students more leeway in their learning, you relinquish the tight control you have when standing before a group of 30 students who sit quietly and attentively taking notes. Now you must come up with activities and benchmarks for measuring performance, and must watch over students as they work in groups—still remaining available to handle difficult situations but not butting in too often. If you lack clear goals for instruction, the students will learn nothing from this approach, and you will be held responsible.

It is also difficult to recognize when meaningful learning is taking place—sometimes students may talk animatedly about a subject and be learning nothing. At other times, students take the opportunities of group work to gossip or joke around. You have less control, and it can be difficult to monitor what is going on. Thus the responsibilities for using student-centered methods are many and demanding. But the rewards are many, too, as we shall see.

Fortunately, a formal set of guidelines can help you use a student-centered perspective. Before describing actual in-class techniques, we first review these principles.

 ## LEARNER-CENTERED PSYCHOLOGICAL PRINCIPLES

Several years ago, the American Psychological Association assigned a task force the goal of developing a collection of learner-centered psychological principles. These principles were intended to serve as guidelines for school redesign and reform (Work Group of the American Psychological Association Board of Educational Affairs, 1997). The members of the task force created a list of 14 principles that describe the foundations of the student-centered learning approach. The 14 principles have not been uniformly well received; however, they effectively express the perspective of their authors, who are advocates of the learner-centered approach. Table 12.8 lists the 14 principles, which will provide you with an overview of the tenets of student-centered teaching. (Because of space limitations, we do not discuss these principles in the main text.)

THINKING ANALYTICALLY

Name three three similarities and three differences between teacher-centered and student-centered views of instruction.

SUGGESTION: Similarities: Involves organized learning; requires motivation in order to succeed; can result in long-term retention of material. Differences: In teacher-centered instruction, the teacher generally controls rate of learning, leads the direction of the lesson's development, and determines ending point of instruction in a lesson. In student-centered instruction, it is the student who determines these aspects.

THINKING ANALYTICALLY

Name three ways you can tell whether students are engaging in meaningful learning rather than simply having an animated discussion.

SUGGESTION: Clues to meaningful learning: If students are making connections between different topics, suggesting methods for researching and developing ideas, or critiquing each other's thinking.

The following 14 psychological principles pertain to the learner and the learning process. They focus on psychological factors that are primarily internal to and under the control of the learner rather than conditioned habits or physiological factors. However, the principles also attempt to acknowledge external environment or contextual factors that interact with these internal factors.

The principles are intended to deal holistically with learners in the context of real-world learning situations. Thus, they are best understood as an organized set of principles; no principle should be viewed in isolation. The 14 principles are divided into those referring to cognitive and metacognitive, motivational and affective, developmental and social, and individual difference factors influencing learners and learning. Finally, the principles are intended to apply to all learners—to children, to teachers, to administrators, to parents, and to community members involved in our educational system.

Cognitive and Metacognitive Factors

Principle 1. Nature of the learning process. The learning of complex subject matter is most effective when it is an intentional process of constructing meaning from information and experience.

There are different types of learning processes, for example, habit formation in motor learning; and learning that involves the generation of knowledge, or cognitive skills and learning strategies. Learning in schools emphasizes the use of intentional processes that students can use to construct meaning from information, experiences, and their own thoughts and beliefs. Successful learners are active, goal-directed, self-regulating, and assume personal responsibility for contributing to their own learning. The principles set forth in this document focus on this type of learning.

Principle 2. Goals of the learning process. The successful learner, over time and with support and instructional guidance, can create meaningful, coherent representations of knowledge.

The strategic nature of learning requires students to be goal directed. To construct useful representations of knowledge and to acquire the thinking and learning strategies necessary for continued learning success across the life span, students must generate and pursue personally relevant goals. Initially, students' short-term goals and learning may be sketchy in an area, but over time their understanding can be refined by filling gaps, resolving inconsistencies, and deepening their understanding of the subject matter so that they can reach

longer-term goals. Educators can assist learners in creating meaningful learning goals that are consistent with both personal and educational aspirations and interests.

Principle 3. Construction of knowledge. The successful learner can link new information with existing knowledge in meaningful ways.

Knowledge widens and deepens as students continue to build links between new information and experiences and their existing knowledge base. The nature of these links can take a variety of forms, such as adding to, modifying, or reorganizing existing knowledge or skills. How these links are made or develop may vary in different subject areas, and among students with varying talents, interests, and abilities. However, unless new knowledge becomes integrated with the learner's prior knowledge and understanding, this new knowledge remains isolated, cannot be used most effectively in new tasks, and does not transfer readily to new situations. Educators can assist learners in acquiring and integrating knowledge by a number of strategies that have been shown to be effective with learners of varying abilities, such as concept mapping and thematic organization or categorizing.

Principle 4. Strategic thinking. The successful learner can create and use a repertoire of thinking and reasoning strategies to achieve complex learning goals.

Successful learners use strategic thinking in their approach to learning, reasoning, problem solving, and concept learning. They understand and can use a variety of strategies to help them reach learning and performance goals, and to apply their knowledge in novel situations. They also continue to expand their repertoire of strategies by reflecting on the methods they use to see which work well for them, by receiving guided instruction and feedback, and by observing or interacting with appropriate models. Learning outcomes can be enhanced if educators assist learners in developing, applying, and assessing their strategic learning skills.

Principle 5. Thinking about thinking. Higher order strategies for selecting and monitoring mental operations facilitate creative and critical thinking.

Successful learners can reflect on how they think and learn, set reasonable learning or performance goals, select potentially appropriate learning strategies or methods, and monitor their progress toward these goals. In addition, successful learners know what to do if a problem occurs or if they are not making sufficient or timely progress toward a goal. They can generate alternative methods to

reach their goal (or reassess the appropriateness and utility of the goal). Instructional methods that focus on helping learners develop these higher order (metacognitive) strategies can enhance student learning and personal responsibility for learning.

Principle 6. Context of learning. Learning is influenced by environmental factors, including culture, technology, and instructional practices.

Learning does not occur in a vacuum. Teachers play a major interactive role with both the learner and the learning environment. Cultural or group influences on students can impact many educationally relevant variables, such as motivation, orientation toward learning, and ways of thinking. Technologies and instructional practices must be appropriate for learners' level of prior knowledge, cognitive abilities, and their learning and thinking strategies. The classroom environment, particularly the degree to which it is nurturing or not, can also have significant impacts on student learning.

Motivational and Affective Factors

Principle 7. Motivational and emotional influences on learning. What and how much is learned is influenced by the learner's motivation. Motivation to learn, in turn, is influenced by the individual's emotional states, beliefs, interests and goals, and habits of thinking.

The rich internal world of thoughts, beliefs, goals, and expectations for success or failure can enhance or interfere with the learner's quality of thinking and information processing. Students' beliefs about themselves as learners and the nature of learning have a marked influence on motivation. Motivational and emotional factors also influence both the quality of thinking and information processing as well as an individual's motivation to learn. Positive emotions, such as curiosity, generally enhance motivation and facilitate learning and performance. Mild anxiety can also enhance learning and performance by focusing the learner's attention on a particular task. However, intense negative emotions (e.g., anxiety, panic, rage, insecurity) and related thoughts (e.g., worrying about competence, ruminating about failure, fearing punishment, ridicule, or stigmatizing labels) generally detract from motivation, interfere with learning, and contribute to low performance.

Principle 8. Intrinsic motivation to learn. The learner's creativity, higher order thinking, and natural curiosity all contribute to motivation to learn. Intrinsic motivation is stimulated by tasks of optimal novelty and dif-

TABLE 12.8 **Learner-Centered Psychological Principles,** *continued*

ficulty, relevant to personal interests, and providing for personal choice and control.

Curiosity, flexible and insightful thinking, and creativity are major indicators of the learners' intrinsic motivation to learn, which is in large part a function of meeting basic needs to be competent and to exercise personal control. Intrinsic motivation is facilitated on tasks that learners perceive as interesting and personally relevant and meaningful, appropriate in complexity and difficulty to the learners' abilities, and on which they believe they can succeed. Intrinsic motivation is also facilitated on tasks that are comparable to real-world situations and meet needs for choice and control. Educators can encourage and support learners' natural curiosity and motivation to learn by attending to individual differences in learners' perceptions of optimal novelty and difficulty, relevance, and personal choice and control.

Principle 9. Effects of motivation on effort.
Acquisition of complex knowledge and skills requires extended learner effort and guided practice. Without learners' motivation to learn, the willingness to exert this effort is unlikely without coercion.

Effort is another major indicator of motivation to learn. The acquisition of complex knowledge and skills demands the investment of considerable learner energy and strategic effort, along with persistence over time. Educators need to be concerned with facilitating motivation by strategies that enhance learner effort and commitment to learning and to achieving high standards of comprehension and understanding. Effective strategies include purposeful learning activities, guided by practices that enhance positive emotions and intrinsic motivation to learn, and methods that increase learners' perceptions that a task is interesting and personally relevant.

Developmental and Social

Principle 10. Developmental influences on learning.
As individuals develop, there are different opportunities and constraints for learning. Learning is most effective when differential development within and across physical, intellectual, emotional, and social domains is taken into account.

Individuals learn best when material is appropriate to their developmental level and is presented in an enjoyable and interesting way. Because individual development varies across intellectual, social, emotional, and physical domains, achievement in different instructional domains may also vary. Overemphasis on one type of developmental readiness—such as reading readiness, for example—may preclude learners from demonstrating that they are more

capable in other areas of performance. The cognitive, emotional, and social development of individual learners and how they interpret life experiences are affected by prior schooling, home, culture, and community factors. Early and continuing parental involvement in schooling, and the quality of language interactions and two-way communications between adults and children, can influence these developmental areas. Awareness and understanding of developmental differences among children with and without emotional, physical, or intellectual disabilities, can facilitate the creation of optimal learning contexts.

Principle 11. Social influences on learning.
Learning is influenced by social interactions, interpersonal relations, and communication with others.

Learning can be enhanced when the learner has an opportunity to interact and to collaborate with others on instructional tasks. Learning settings that allow for social interactions, and that respect diversity, encourage flexible thinking and social competence. In interactive and collaborative instructional contexts, individuals have an opportunity for perspective taking and reflective thinking that may lead to higher levels of cognitive, social, and moral development, as well as self-esteem. Quality personal relationships that provide stability, trust, and caring can increase learners' sense of belonging, self-respect and self-acceptance, and provide a positive climate for learning. Family influences, positive interpersonal support, and instruction in self-motivation strategies can offset factors that interfere with optimal learning such as negative beliefs about competence in a particular subject, high levels of test anxiety, negative sex role expectations, and undue pressure to perform well. Positive learning climates can also help to establish the context for healthier levels of thinking, feeling, and behaving. Such contexts help learners feel safe to share ideas, actively participate in the learning process, and create a learning community.

Individual Differences

Principle 12. Individual differences in learning.
Learners have different strategies, approaches, and capabilities for learning that are a function of prior experience and heredity.

Individuals are born with and develop their own capabilities and talents. In addition, through learning and social acculturation, they have acquired their own preferences for how they like to learn and the pace at which they learn. However, these preferences are not always useful in helping learners reach their learning goals. Educators need to help

students examine their learning preferences and expand or modify them, if necessary. The interaction between learner differences and curricular and environmental conditions is another key factor affecting learning outcomes. Educators need to be sensitive to individual differences, in general. They also need to attend to learner perceptions of the degree to which these differences are accepted and adapted to by varying instructional methods and materials.

Principle 13. Learning and diversity.
Learning is most effective when differences in learners' linguistic, cultural, and social backgrounds are taken into account.

The same basic principles of learning, motivation, and effective instruction apply to all learners. However, language, ethnicity, race, beliefs, and socioeconomic status all can influence learning. Careful attention to these factors in the instructional setting enhances the possibilities for designing and implementing appropriate learning environments. When learners perceive that their individual differences in abilities, backgrounds, cultures, and experiences are valued, respected, and accommodated in learning tasks and contexts, levels of motivation and achievement are enhanced.

Principle 14. Standards and assessment.
Setting appropriately high and challenging standards and assessing the learner as well as learning progress—including diagnostic, process, and outcome assessment—are integral parts of the learning process.

Assessment provides important information to both the learner and teacher at all stages of the learning process. Effective learning takes place when learners feel challenged to work towards appropriately high goals; therefore, appraisal of the learner's cognitive strengths and weaknesses, as well as current knowledge and skills, is important for the selection of instructional materials of an optimal degree of difficulty. Ongoing assessment of the learner's understanding of the curricular material can provide valuable feedback to both learners and teachers about progress toward the learning goals. Standardized assessment of learner progress and outcomes assessment provides one type of information about achievement levels both within and across individuals that can inform various types of programmatic decisions. Performance assessments can provide other sources of information about the attainment of learning outcomes. Self-assessments of learning progress can also improve students' self-appraisal skills and enhance motivation and self-directed learning.

Good planning is always important to good teaching. But exactly what is being planned differs for student-centered methods of teaching as compared to teacher-centered methods? As we discussed in the previous section of this chapter, teacher-centered planning focuses on your overarching learning goals for your students and on the specific steps you plan to take to help students achieve these goals. The perspective is that the individual possessing the knowledge designs a process that best imparts this knowledge to the students.

Planning from a constructivist approach, however, has different goals. It is still necessary to define the main topic and overarching goals of the learning experience. But rather than drafting a precise lesson plan, teachers taking a student-centered approach may choose to involve the students in the process of planning instruction. The teacher and students can discuss issues such as these: What are the reasons for studying this topic? What information about the topic is relevant? How will the class learn the topic—what types of activities will take place? What will be the respective roles of the teacher and the students? How will students demonstrate their learning? What types of assignments or projects will they complete? How will these assignments be graded?

Expert teachers are adept at choosing, as the basis for these discussions, topics that lend themselves to broad and relevant learning by students. Expert teachers also define the starting point by stating the focal topic and area. There is both a skill and an art to selecting topics that energize and motivate students. For example, less effective teachers might ask students to participate in planning a unit on pollution. More effective teachers might ask students to design a project that measures pollution in the community around the school and alerts relevant agencies and the general public to areas in need of improvement. Carefully focused goals allow students considerable leeway in planning precise activities, but these goals ensure that certain types of learning experiences are included in instructional experiences—in this case, experiences such as experimental design and data collection, familiarity with the roles of governmental agencies, and persuasive communication and letter writing. Table 12.9 shows a sample teaching plan based on a constructivist perspective.

THINKING CREATIVELY

Design three questions that would lead to constructivist activities resulting in meaningful learning.

SUGGESTION: Conduct an experiment on animal behavior using your own or a friend's pet, and report on the results. Compare the weather forecasts of different news stations in your area for three days and comment on their variability and possible reasons for it. Write a new ending for the novel assigned in class and defend why your ending is more likely than the real ending.

TABLE 12.9   Sample Teaching Plan, Sixth-Grade Science Class: Constructivist Perspective

1. Open with a brief overview of the concept of plate tectonics. Ask students if they think the continents ever moved. Ask students why continents might move and what this move would mean to life on earth. Ask students what they find most interesting about the concept of plate tectonics.

2. Have students trace an outline of each major continent using a large globe. Next, ask students to use colored construction paper to make cutouts of each continent.

3. Ask students to form groups of three to four, and then work together to come up with various positions the continents may have once occupied. Ask the students to show their ideas to the others in their group and discuss why they think the continents might have been located in those positions.

4. Have a class discussion about the concept of plate tectonics. Show the class a large picture of how the continents did drift. Distribute a handout identifying the continents at different periods in geological history. Talk about climate trends and implications for animal and plant life. Ask students their ideas and opinions about what might have happened as the continents drifted. Encourage each student to contribute to the discussion and show her or his own representation of how the continents might have looked.

5. For homework, ask students to research and write an essay about the effects of plate tectonics on the evolution of animals living in the large landmasses when the continents were joined.

Some methods for teaching from a constructivist perspective are actually adaptations of more traditional, teacher-centered approaches. Other methods are new and unique in their applications and goals. As was the case with direct instruction, good teaching from a constructivist perspective depends on the effective *combination* of specific techniques to reach the widest possible audience. We review the most useful methods here, with tips for selecting and applying these methods in daily teaching.

■INDIVIDUALIZED INSTRUCTION   In Chapter 5 on exceptional children, we noted that by law, each student with special needs must have an individualized education program, or IEP. This program consists of a detailed description of the specific student's goals, educational activities and requirements, and incremental plans for meeting these requirements. The point of the IEP for a child with special needs is that the child's needs differ from the needs of the "average" child; or consequently, this child requires an educational program designed just for her or for him.

By recognizing that some children do not fit typical profiles of learning and ability, the response of education professionals who advocated the use of IEPs foreshadowed the student-centered teaching movement, which views each child as a special case. **Individualized instruction** is a form of instruction tailored to meet the needs of individual students. Note that expert teachers have always taken steps to individualize instruction—for example, by assigning different levels and numbers of math problems to students of different ability levels, by allowing artistic students to spend relatively more time than nonartistic students on drawing and painting, and by accelerating the pace of gifted students. Viewed by proponents of student-centered approaches to teaching, individualized instruction is what should be done for every student, to capitalize on individual patterns of strengths and interests.

MAKING INDIVIDUALIZED INSTRUCTION WORK.   How do expert teachers systematically create individualized instruction plans for their students? They use three basic aspects of instruction that can vary from student to student. First, the teacher gives

THINKING PRACTICALLY

How would an individualized instruction program you designed for yourself in this course differ from what you have actually done?

SUGGESTION: Ask yourself what rate of progress you would have made had you challenged yourself with goals and milestones personally meaningful to you and your career goals; also ask yourself what aspects of educational psychology interested you the most and thus might have been more heavily focused on.

This student is using a computer to analyze the data he has collected from his independent-study chemistry experiment. (David Young-Wolff, Stone)

the students differing amounts of time to complete learning objectives. In all classrooms, high-ability students tend to need less time than lower ability students to accomplish a learning objective. Teachers in the past dealt with this situation by providing extra challenges and by assigning extra work to higher achievers.

Second, the expert teacher varies the actual learning activities that students engage in from one student to the next. All teachers follow this principle of student-centered teaching when they allow students a choice not only of which specific topic to write about for a project but also of the mode the project will take—for example, a play or script, a short story, or a report comparing two works by the same author.

Third, teachers can vary the actual instructional materials used with each student. Some students can be taught with standard school books, others with relevant works of fiction, and still others with videos or computer programs. The precise materials would vary as a function of the specific student's needs and objectives.

LIMITATIONS OF INDIVIDUALIZED INSTRUCTION. Responses to individualization have varied, depending on who uses it, why, and how effectively. Like other educational approaches, individualized instruction can be done well or poorly. If frequent assessments are not built into the program, students may lack motivation to push themselves and may not learn as much as they ought to (Good & Brophy, 1994). Individualization also encourages students to pursue what they are already proficient in and enjoy, because these are the types of activities students tend to choose. Thus it is better for certain types of learning experiences than others: Complex thinking skills are unlikely to develop as students work on their own. Finally, individualized instruction (like most forms of instruction) is most effective for highly motivated students who are willing to push themselves (Bangert, Kulik, & Kulik, 1983).

■ **DISCOVERY APPROACHES** **Discovery learning** is a process in which students use information supplied to them to construct their own understanding (Bruner, 1971). **Unstructured discovery** occurs when students make discoveries on their own. **Guided discovery** occurs when the teacher assists the students in making the discoveries. Guided discovery is more practical and effective; unstructured discovery often leads students to become confused and frustrated and may result in students' drawing inappropriate conclusions (Brown & Campione, 1994). Guided discovery as a process is also in concert with research on children's cognitive development (Brown & Campione, 1994). During guided-discovery instruction, teachers and students tend to follow the 14 learner-centered principles of student-centered teaching discussed earlier (Work Group of the American Psychological Association's Board of Educational Affairs, 1997).

Guided discovery works well for science lessons, in which the students can be an integral part of the questioning and learning process and can construct knowledge for themselves with the assistance of their teacher. Different props and manipulatives can often be used to help students reason with newly learned concepts. Students can also explore the limitations of what they are learning by conducting small experiments with equipment or tools you provide. Always remain available and direct the process to make it as fruitful for the students as possible. Table 12.10 shows sample topics and questions on which guided-discovery lessons can be based.

■ **GROUP DISCUSSION** Group discussion from a student-centered approach elaborates on recitation from a teacher-centered approach. As we have discussed, recitation takes place when you lead the class by asking questions, tolerating pauses, and eliciting student answers, in order to build on basic student understanding to create more complex forms of understanding. Group discussion from the student-centered perspective, however, places you more on the sidelines as the students take center stage. In group discussions, students do not just respond to teacher-initiated questions, they respond to each other's questions in an open discussion format. Students can enter into animated

THINKING CREATIVELY

Propose a lesson that successfully uses guided discovery.

SUGGESTION: Use the examples in Table 12.8 to come up with a related idea for a lesson using guided discovery.

debates and even have heated exchanges in which they express opposing opinions. However, expert teachers remember to set up ground rules to create a workable atmosphere. For example, students are expected not to interrupt one another, which would undermine learning.

One of the advantages of group discussions is that they allow students to interact with one another directly, and thus to develop interpersonal skills. The general goals of effective group discussions are to encourage students to learn how to listen to and understand one another, to accept different points of view, and to evaluate the opinions, beliefs, and attitudes of themselves and others. How do expert teachers ensure that these goals are met?

First, expert teachers define specific enough questions to bring about a discussion in which students explore the issues deeply. They also assess whether students have the necessary prior knowledge to engage in a meaningful discussion: If not, another learning activity should precede the group discussion to even out students' levels of knowledge of the topic. One unfortunate outcome of discussions among students lacking necessary background is that students express opinions and take sides on issues they know little about. Discussions should never be allowed to turn into shouting matches, arguments, or other unproductive verbal exchanges

Expert teachers know how to keep discussions on-track by asking questions that keep students focused on central aspects of the issue or relevant controversial aspects of the issue. Discussions function best when they are used to encourage deep exploration of topics about which students already possess some basic knowledge and understanding. Discussions are perfect for taking on higher level learning objectives, such as evaluation and synthesis of ideas. In discussions, the cursory types of understanding that result from more shallow types of learning can evolve into deeper and more meaningful forms of understanding.

Effective discussions teach more than the content of the discussions: Properly held, they provide students with scripts for handling disagreements and for airing competing views in an open forum. Sometimes, students come from homes or family backgrounds in which such discussions do not take place. For these students in particular, the experience of participating in an open discussion can be a valuable growth experience.

Group discussions also allow students to see that their peers share certain questions and confusions about issues. By exploring these issues together, students may feel less isolated or somehow "different." Two problems that can arise are the situations in which one eager student dominates the entire discussion, and the converse situation in which some students say nary a word. In such situations, you must act to establish a better dynamic, by limiting the input of some students and soliciting more input from other students.

Other techniques for maintaining good dynamics in discussions are that you: (1) refrain from actually answering questions if there is a student who could do so, (2) help

THINKING ANALYTICALLY

Describe two situations in which you should interrupt a group discussion.

SUGGESTION: If students are shouting or using foul language, or making deliberately abusive or insulting statements, it's appropriate to interrupt.

TABLE 12.10 Guided-Discovery Science Lesson: Sample Topics/Questions

1. Give students a small seesaw and a set of weights. Ask them to stack five 1-pound weights 24 inches from the fulcrum. Then ask them to figure out how many weights placed at the end of the opposite side, 36 inches from the fulcrum, will balance the seesaw. The students' goal is to induce the rule for balancing the seesaw and write it down.

2. Give students various objects and a tank of water and ask them to determine the rules and principles that describe which objects float.

3. Give students five jars of brightly colored water (tinted with food coloring). Ask them to determine how much colored water from each jar is needed to create the new color in a jar on the teacher's desk.

4. Give students a selection of actual animal skulls, models of skulls, or pictures of skulls representing various small mammals. Ask students to determine each animal's diet and defend their answers by reference to the types, location, and shape of teeth.

---

students clarify their statements, (3) ask students to elaborate when it is possible that they have more of relevance to say, (4) keep the discussion on track, and (5) remain attentive to the reactions of other students and work constantly to monitor events.

■ **INQUIRY METHODS**   Earlier in this chapter we described how teachers can enhance student learning by encouraging students to ask the right kinds of questions. This approach is based on the work of John Dewey (1910), who stressed the importance of *how* students think in their intellectual development. Dewey advocated what is known as an **inquiry method** of teaching. Using an inquiry method consists of first asking students a question. Students then formulate various hypotheses that represent possible answers, gather actual information to evaluate the rival hypotheses, and come to appropriate conclusions. Finally, students revisit the processes they followed and evaluate them.

Table 12.5 on page 437 (Sternberg's Seven-Level Model), presents an example of the inquiry method (see level 7): The mediator encourages the child to perform the experiments by gathering information that can distinguish among the alternative explanations. To be effective, inquiry methods of teaching must be preceded by careful and thorough preparation. Although the experience of inquiry learning can be deeply meaningful for students, it will work only when you choose good starting questions and develop practical ways for the students to evaluate rival hypotheses.

■ **GROUPWORK**   Guided discovery, group discussions, and inquiry-based instruction often involve every student in the class. However, for some learning activities, it can be effective to break the class up into several smaller groups. These smaller groups allow for more in-depth communication between students. **Student groupwork** consists of small groups of students working together on tasks in relatively informal settings. One of the main advantages of student groupwork is that it forces every student to become an active participant—shy students do not easily fade into the background. By participating in small-group settings, reticent children can learn to gain confidence.

For the student groupwork experience to be effective, you must plan carefully when to use it. Specify goals of groupwork clearly and hold students accountable for reaching these goals. Choose tasks to ensure that two or more students work together to accomplish them; in particular, tasks should require student interaction. There must also be a finely tuned system for getting students smoothly into their groups without disruptions or arguments.

Expert teachers introduce their students to groupwork with a quick and simple task that takes only a short time to complete ("work together to build a dog out of the plastic body parts in your kit"). Expert teachers make the rules of participation clear, including the rules for assembling into groups. They describe tasks clearly and specify performance goals (resulting in meaningful products) as well as the amount of time students have to complete their tasks. Expert teachers also remember to watch students closely and remain available to answer questions while students are in groups. Table 12.11 describes some sample groupwork goals and shows examples of products demonstrating goal achievement.

■ **COOPERATIVE LEARNING**   A meta-analysis of 46 studies published between 1929 and 1993 concluded that members of cooperative teams outperform individuals competing with each other on four types of problems (linguistic, nonlinguistic, well-defined, and ill-defined) (Qin, Johnson, & Johnson, 1995). This strength in numbers effect is one idea behind **cooperative learning,** a teaching approach in which structured groups of students use specific strategies for enhancing learning and interpersonal development (Johnson & Johnson, 1985, 1991; Slavin, 1995a, 1995b; Slavin & Cooper, 1999). Cooperative learning is similar to groupwork, except that it is more highly structured by the teacher and the mechanisms involved are under tighter teacher control.

TABLE 12.11 Five Groupwork Goals, with Examples of Goal-Achievement Products

Goal	Product
1. Make a diorama of an event in ancient Greece (for example, the first Olympics).	1. Diorama and explanation by students who built it
2. Write a short story, with each group member contributing one portion.	2. Story
3. Design a computer environment or hyperstudio (series of computer screens on related topics often containing visual aids) on a science topic (for example, geothermal energy).	3. Computer environment and presentations by students about designing it
4. Design a large poster convincing teenagers not to smoke.	4. Poster and students' descriptions of why they made it the way they did
5. Write and perform a skit about good and bad study habits.	5. The skit, both written and performed

Groups usually contain three to five students; four is considered the best number (Slavin, 1995a, 1995b). Advocates of this approach suggest that groups be balanced with regard to gender, ethnicity, and ability factors. This balancing is supposed to increase cooperation among students who might not otherwise have had the opportunity to work with one another. Of course, with this intermixing can come interpersonal difficulties or failures in communication; thus you must remain vigilant as to what is going on in each group to prevent interpersonal problems.

EFFECTIVE COOPERATIVE LEARNING APPROACHES. Robert Slavin (1995a, 1995b) is a leading proponent of cooperative learning. He and other researchers have observed several important features of effective cooperative learning situations. First, cooperative learning groups develop students' interpersonal skills, and these skills are directly taught by the teacher. Interpersonal skills are a key aspect of why students are placed into cooperative learning activities in the first place. Second, when cooperative learning is successful, it increases the achievement of every student in the group. Third, effective cooperative learning situations require students to interact in order to accomplish the goal (the teacher ensures that the chosen and stated goal meets this condition). As a way to facilitate student interaction, students can be given different components or tools that must be combined or used in tandem to reach the final solution or create the final product. These force students to work together.

Slavin's (1995a, 1995b) research has demonstrated that cooperative learning increases students' tolerance for others from differing backgrounds and of the opposite gender. He has also shown that cooperative learning increases student achievement across content areas on both standardized tests and custom-designed assessments. Slavin's method is sometimes referred to as STAD, or **Student Teams Achievement Divisions.** STAD is a formalized system for cooperative learning that creates learning situations most likely to result in desired outcomes. Teachers using STAD begin with direct instruction and then follow it with team study. Students complete exercises and compare and discuss their answers, reconciling differences on their own. When all members of a team understand the completed questions, the team study concludes. Next, students take quizzes to assess their learning. Teams can be rewarded for total points amassed by all team members, a system that gives all team members the incentive to help one another to achieve. Teams do not necessarily compete with one another—rewards are sometimes given for points earned, even if every team earns the points.

Another cooperative learning approach is called **Jigsaw** (Aronson et al., 1978), a method that encourages the interdependence of group members. In the original method, Jigsaw I, the teacher assigned each group member one portion of the material to be learned. That team member would then attempt to become an expert on her or his topic, and group members would then teach each other, leading to everyone's learning about all team members' topics. More recently, Jigsaw II (Slavin 1995), incorporates the addition of expert meetings of all students in the class who have been assigned the same topic. At these expert meetings the students compare notes, go over material, and plan how to teach their group members. Back in their groups, the students teach others the material. Finally, students take individual tests to ensure that they have learned the material. Teams can compete for highest total points or for other types of rewards.

CRITICISMS OF COOPERATIVE LEARNING. A review of 122 studies of cooperative learning (Johnson & Johnson, 1991) supported the value of this approach. Some researchers, however, are not as positive about the value of cooperative learning, and believe this technique should always be used in conjunction with other teaching techniques. Some disadvantages of cooperative learning include the possibility that group interactions will negatively affect learning: For example, peer pressure may give popular group members unwarranted influence; controlling and dominant students may use group interactions to serve their own purposes rather than to create meaningful learning; and nonmainstream students may be ignored. According to McCaslin and Good (1996), cooperative learning can also encourage students to place more value on processes and procedures—doing it quickly, finishing the product—than on meaningful learning, which can result in reinforcement of student misconceptions, place peer relations and friendships in a more important role than learning, and encourage some students not to do their share of the work.

■ **RECIPROCAL TEACHING** **Reciprocal teaching** is a method to increase students' understanding of what they read (Brown & Campione, 1990; Brown & Palincsar, 1989; King & Johnson, 1999; Palincsar, 1986; Palincsar & Brown, 1984). One review of 16 studies of reciprocal teaching found that it is effective both when standardized tests are used to gauge learning and when customized comprehension tests are used to measure learning (Rosenshine & Meister, 1994). Students are taught four strategies to enhance reading understanding: First, they summarize what they have read; second, they ask a question about an important point in the text; third, they clarify the difficult portions of the material; and fourth, they predict what is likely to come next in the material. You describe these strategies to the students; then, over several days, you demonstrate how to use them, gradually building one on the others. You and the students complete a reading together and analyze it together, following the four steps. Finally, the students learn to follow the steps on their own, with your guidance. Students can take turns teaching and leading the class or their group.

Palincsar and Brown (1984) showed that reciprocal teaching works best with young adolescents who can read words accurately but who are not proficient in reading comprehension. However, reciprocal teaching works with students of all ages and has even been shown to be effective with students with learning disabilities (Lederer, 2000). Teachers wishing to use this approach must, first, shift gradually from showing the students how to use the techniques to having the students take control and work on their own; second, match the task difficulty to students' levels and abilities; and third, diagnose the students' thinking to reveal what types of further instruction would best serve each student. A review of the evidence on 19 studies of reciprocal teaching concluded that the approach works best when the comprehension strategies are taught explicitly before the actual reciprocal teaching begins (Rosenshine & Meister, 1992).

■ **THE ROLE OF COMPUTERS** The use of computers in the classroom, and by students at home, is growing faster than the statistics can show. For example, by 1995, 50

THINKING ANALYTICALLY

Why is it important to give quizzes to students individually when they have learned in a cooperative group?

SUGGESTION: Teachers must distinguish students who are really learning from those who just seem as though they are, in order to ensure that meaningful learning occurs for everyone. Individual quizzes are necessary to make such a judgment.

IN EACH CHAPTER OF THE TEXT, WE INTRODUCE YOU TO A FEW SPECIFIC STRATEGIES—
ANALYTICAL, CREATIVE, AND PRACTICAL—USED BY BOTH EXPERT TEACHERS AND EXPERT STUDENTS.

THE ANALYTICAL TEACHER: Before class, Amina carefully reviews the material she will cover and then chooses the ideal approach to use in presenting this material.

THE CREATIVE TEACHER: To vary her students' classroom experiences and maintain their interest level, Amina chooses a different teaching approach for each day of the week.

THE PRACTICAL TEACHER: Amina watches carefully to see if her students are becoming confused by or losing interest in their classroom lessons. When she senses a problem, she changes her approach to one that should work better.

THE ANALYTICAL STUDENT: Edward recognizes and understands the different methods he should use to prepare for class as a function of the teaching methods his teachers prefer.

THE CREATIVE STUDENT: Edward talks to his friends, and they all suggest to their teacher that she break the class up into small groups and give each group one portion of the overall assignment to complete.

THE PRACTICAL STUDENT: Edward peer-tutors his friend Larry in order to help Larry improve in math, and Edward finds that his own test performance increases as a result.

---

percent of public and 25 percent of private schools in the United States had Internet access, and this figure is growing rapidly. Students' attitudes toward computers vary, as do their results with computers: One study showed that even students who assert that a teacher provides better help than an artificially intelligent computer tutor nonetheless prefer using the computer tutor to learning from the teacher—and appear often to learn more while doing so (Schofield, Eurich-Fulcer, & Britt, 1994). In this case, the computers actually provided additional help and resources for students, the teachers were able to design programs tailored to each student's learning needs, and the students benefited from tailored help and avoided the possible embarrassment of asking questions in public. Numerous quality computer programs can target instruction to a student's level of understanding, and consequently can relieve you of much repetitive drill-based instruction.

Some students spend hours each day surfing the Internet or using sophisticated computer games and simulations. Recent programs have significant educational implications—some of these programs encourage students to develop cognitively sophisticated reasoning skills. For example, one program allows the student to design an entire urban city down to the smallest detail. Other types of software include old standbys of home-based research, such as encyclopedias, newly packaged on CD-ROMs with graphics and audio additions. Students call up a term—such as *polar bear*—and get not only the full description that appeared in the original encyclopedia, but also bear vocalizations, a video of bears fighting, panoramic shots of bear habitats, and interviews with zoo officials running captive breeding programs. Parents often become as engrossed in these programs as do their children.

EFFECTIVE VERSUS INEFFECTIVE USES OF COMPUTERS. A key aspect of the successful use of computers as educational tools is common sense. Sometimes, computers function as learning tools; other times, they function as expensive toys. A student who logs onto the Internet and reads the contents of chatrooms about a favorite television situation comedy, for example, is not engaging in an educationally relevant activity. A student who plays computer games involving shooting down as many monkeys as possible may be having fun, but she is not learning. Students who use e-mail to gossip about their classmates are not benefiting the same way as students who use e-mail to hear the perspective of students from different countries.

THINKING ANALYTICALLY

How might reciprocal teaching be used in an area other than reading instruction?

SUGGESTION: Students could borrow the techniques and apply them with slight modification to mathematics learning. In this case, the techniques might include basic computation, error checking, explanation of the process involved in determining correct answers, and generation of new sample problems.

EXPERT TEACHER INTERVIEW

FOCUS ON: INSTRUCTIONAL METHODS, INCLUDING TECHNOLOGY
BARBARA ROSEN: PUBLIC SCHOOL 145, DISTRICT 3, NEW YORK, NEW YORK—GRADES K–5, GEOGRAPHY

Barbara Rosen is a cluster teacher in geography at a Manhattan elementary school. She has been teaching social studies and geography for twenty years. Barbara discusses the importance of geography as a subject, how to teach geography, its impact on students with reading difficulties, and use of technology in the classroom.

Describe your role as a cluster teacher of geography.

As a cluster teacher, I have expertise in an area that the classroom teacher does not; these are very specialized positions. When I walk into a classroom to lead a geography lesson, the classroom teacher leaves for a preparation period. I teach geography in all grades, K–5, at our elementary school. In one day, I might teach a geography lesson to six different classrooms of students.

Geography is a much neglected subject area—one of the reasons I decided to focus on geography. For example, a study was conducted seven years ago that indicated that many American students couldn't recognize the United States on a world map.

You use a lot of hands-on methods and problem-based projects to teach geography. Can you describe a project?

Right now, the third graders are studying climates of the world. We've been studying climates in several ways. First, I defined global terms, such as

hemispheres and *equator*, explaining that the cooler climates tended to be further away from the equator. To help students with the new terms, we made an analogy to our bodies; the head as the North Pole, the feet as the South Pole, the waist as the Equator, and so on. Then we played a game. I would say, "Point to where a cold climate in the Northern Hemisphere would be," and students would point toward their heads. We followed this up with several activities, in which students colored pictures related to different climates. Now, they are dressing paper dolls. Each student will be randomly assigned a location on the globe. They need to draw and cut out clothes to dress their paper doll as though it were going to visit that place.

What are some of the benefits of project-based learning?

Hands-on projects take a long time, but there are great payoffs. Active engagement helps students really learn concepts in a way that is meaningful for them. High levels of engagement in projects also lead to fewer behavior problems in class. In addition, hands-on projects can often reduce the frustrations of students who have difficulties reading.

Can you recommend a basic geography project to classroom teachers?

When I do a workshop with teachers, I tell them that geography is a perspective on the world and understanding it. Get a globe and a map and use these when students are reading a story about another country. Point out the country to the kids; ask them how we'd get there. What do we have to cross? What separates us?

Human–environment interaction is one of the major concepts of geography. A great book to bring this across is Dr. Seuss's *The Lorax* (Random House, 1971). In the beginning of the book, there are animals living in a forest of trees, and then a factory is built. Ask students, "What happens to the environment? What has changed? How do these things resemble what's happening in our environment?" Fifth graders, who loved this book from their earlier childhood years, now read it from a new perspective. They learn about the human role in creating pollution, such as acid rain.

How do you reach students with different learning styles and abilities?

Geography is an alternate mode to reaching children—students who are

> I suggest trying to find a theme behind the material that needs to be learned, and incorporating instruction in several disciplines as you explore that theme with the students.

Teachers (and parents) should use common sense in deciding what types of computer use constitute meaningful learning. **Computer-assisted instruction** is a type of individualized instruction administered by a computer; it is an example of a meaningful learning activity enhanced through technology. Computer-assisted instruction can become part of a technology-enhanced student-centered learning environment that encourages the students' manipulation of information and that roots the learning process in concrete experience and extended investigation (Hannafin & Land, 1997).

Another important use of computers is the word processor, complete with spell checker and thesaurus. Productivity can soar when students learn to write on screen instead of using pencil and paper and then transcribing words. However, there is another side to

not word-oriented can still be very bright. It is a different way to learn. One of the lecturers for *National Geographic* is a brilliant Ph.D. He discovered geography because he has dyslexia and geography is not word-based. He excels at what he does. His story proves that there is another avenue, another way to shine.

Especially in elementary school, many children are concrete learners. Hands-on projects, with materials students can manipulate, help them learn. For example, the fourth graders were recently learning some words for different geographical formations: island, river, peninsula, and so on. We worked through three different methods before I really felt the students understood these words. First, students read the words and their definitions. Then, we tried an activity in which students matched the geographical term to a picture. I could tell that students just were not getting it. So, I got some blue construction paper and some brown paper bags. We cut shapes out of the bags to represent land and out of the blue paper to represent water. Students glued these together in ways that showed the various geographical features. It wasn't until we did this activity that I finally felt the students comfortably understood these words.

How do you use technology to teach geography?

Once a week for a year, the fifth grade class geography lessons were based on *Where in the World Is Carmen Sandiego?* (Mindscape). Students worked in pairs in the computer lab. One student took notes to show how the kids were making decisions to get to the next city. It took them a while to acclimate to the game. They often just guessed at the answers and hit the keys on the keyboard more or less randomly.

I modeled how to play the game by projecting the game onto a big screen. I prepared worksheets for them to keep track of their answers. I gave them databases to help answer the clues and find the criminals. They had a wonderful year. If they caught a villain, they received a certificate. They learned to recognize a host of locations in the world, such as "Where do they have volcanoes and cold temperatures? Iceland." All this was learned through computer technology.

I have also used a computer atlas, *My First Amazing World Explorer* (DK Multimedia). This works in kindergarten and first grade, where students read a lot of stories. We use the atlas to locate places in the stories. When I click on the pictures in the atlas, the students learn the animals of that region and other information. The atlas zooms in or out so that you can start with a world map and zoom in on a city, and then zoom out again. This technique gives a global perspective on each specific location we study.

What advice would you give new teachers?

Try to engage the children. Get their attention with hands-on projects. New teachers might be concerned about finding the time for hands-on projects; they may be worried about all the different things they must teach in a year. I suggest trying to find a theme behind the material that needs to be learned, and incorporating instruction in several disciplines as you explore that theme with the students. For example, our fourth graders need to learn a great deal of information about the history, economy, and geography of New York State. One theme that we've used to integrate much of this material is the importance of rivers. We talk about why Native Americans lived near rivers, why the first European settlers also wanted to live along rivers. Students read literature selections that relate to the river theme. The theme even extends to science, where fourth graders are learning about structures. They can study bridges, hydroelectric dams, and more. Teachers who find a theme like this can help students learn a lot of necessary information and integrate their understanding of a variety of disciplines.

word processing: All students must eventually learn how to spell, choose vocabulary thoughtfully, and check their work for grammatical accuracy without the help of technology. The word processing program is a tool for good writing just as a calculator is a tool for doing mathematical computation. It is one thing to use a calculator or word processor to improve efficiency once the basic skills are well understood; it is another thing to depend on computers and calculators to fill gaps in actual knowledge.

One study examined the effects of using a word processor in a one-year course on holistic writing skills (Dalton & Hannafin, 1987). The course emphasized the writing process rather than the mechanics of writing to a group of 80 seventh graders. Some students used word processors and others used traditional paper and pencil. Word

Name three good uses and three poor uses of computers for high school students, if the goal is enhancing meaningful learning.

SUGGESTION: Good uses: Searching out information related to lesson topics; repetitive drill on those occasions when it is necessary; designing simulated city or other environments that meet teacher-specified criteria. Poor uses: Distributing personal photographs; online shopping; chat rooms on nonacademic topics.

processing helped the low achievers write better compositions by encouraging them to revise their writing, but it did not help the able learners, who were hindered by the mechanics of word processing. Thus we can conclude that expert teachers should vary instruction and assessment to require students to learn and perform both with and without the tools of technology. For example, in-class essays can be completed longhand, and homework compositions can be word processed if the student has access to a computer. It is essential not to become overly awed by technology, and not to allow technology to supplant imagination and real understanding.

Some particularly innovative work focused on using technology to create meaningful learning environments has been done by the Cognition and Technology Group at Vanderbilt University. Their ongoing series of projects, including the well-known Jasper Project, has involved a wide variety of students. For example, their work with young children (kindergarten and first grade) (Cognition and Technology Group at Vanderbilt University, in press) involves a new program integrating literacy, mathematics, and science by anchoring instruction to a complex story presented on video (CD-ROM or Videodisc, as well as tape). The stories end with challenges that invite students to retell the story in their own words and then engage in other comprehension activities that deepen their understanding of important themes in the stories. Theme-related folktales are also available. Such software video supports print-based literacy skills as well as building on the power of video to communicate and stimulate children's desires to communicate.

INTEGRATING COMPUTERS INTO DAILY CLASSROOM LIFE. In planning how to use computers in daily instruction, consider individual differences in the efficacy of computer-based instruction. In a recent study of 1035 students in grades 5 to 10, Bannert and Arbinger (1996) found gender differences in computer use, with boys spending more time than girls on the computer. Another study (Owens & Waxman, 1998) of over 15,000 tenth-grade students again found boys using computers more than girls in science and mathematics classrooms. Obviously, you must remain aware of different patterns of computer use among students of different groups. Some students possess a learning style that is well adapted to learning from a computer terminal, and others do not; computers are not a panacea for all students.

Kindergarten students use a computer to practice both math and reading. Expert teachers are aware both of the benefits and the liabilities of computer-assisted learning in the classroom. Computers should be regarded as one of many components of an effective learning system. (Stone)

Computers can also be used effectively as part of student-centered learning situations (Newell, 1996). Newell's study looked at the effects of a cross-age tutoring program on computer literacy learning of second graders. Seventeen fourth-grade students tutored 17 second graders on three computer programs: a keyboarding program, a problem-solving program, and a word processing program. Observations of the second-grade tutees were conducted before and after the tutoring program to determine the effects of the tutoring program on their computer literacy learning. The results indicated that prior to the tutoring, only five second graders could play a game, and three of them could use a simulation program. The observations following the program indicated that all 17 tutees could use and interact with the three programs, a game, and a simulation program. Thus peer tutoring was an effective approach for increasing computer literacy in these students.

LIMITATIONS OF COMPUTER-ASSISTED LEARNING. Researchers are also analyzing the limitations of learning from computers. Charles Brainerd and Valerie Reyna (Brainerd, Reyna, & Kneer, 1995; Reyna & Brainerd, 1993) have studied computer-based learning in children—especially how computer-based learning affects memory. Through experiments, they have shown that when material is presented in a form that produces especially vivid verbatim memories, children do better on rote memory tests, but they do worse on reasoning and inference tests of their ability to transfer material to new domains. Computer-based learning relies heavily on strong visuals, which may improve children's verbatim memories at the expense of their reasoning ability. The data show that younger children are particularly sensitive to such interference. By middle elementary years, most children can compensate, but their reasoning ability is never helped by computer-based visual images. More research on the role of computers in learning is clearly needed. As we learn more and more about the inappropriate versus appropriate uses of computers in the classroom, expert teachers should view computers as one part of an effective learning system, not as the central focus of that system.

■**LIMITATIONS OF STUDENT-CENTERED APPROACHES** Critics of student-centered instruction point out that some teachers become so enamored with the activities and techniques of student-centered instruction that they lose sight of the main goal of education: meaningful learning. Group discussions, project work, and inquiry methods can be far more fun than traditional forms of instruction—for students and teachers alike. Traditional teacher-centered methods can seem boring by comparison. Thus you may be tempted to abandon traditional approaches and allow students to spend too much time engaged in fun activities. The students may be happy and compliant, but they may not be learning essential material. The bottom line is that student-centered approaches should be used when they help meet the goals of meaningful learning, and not simply to make school more pleasant.

Another criticism of student-centered instruction is that it is easy to lose control of students and their learning experiences. Goals may take a backseat to the performance of the activities. The focus can too easily shift from performing activities in service of learning to performing activities for their own sake, regardless of whether any meaningful learning is taking place. In addition, student-centered instruction takes more time than teacher-centered instruction, and it is therefore more difficult to ensure coverage of the required material and curriculum.

Student-centered approaches are better for some types of educational objectives than others. But for some teachers, every educational goal or objective can become a vehicle for using a student-centered approach, regardless of the appropriateness of these objectives for student-centered methods. In general, the effectiveness of student-centered teaching approaches depends on the quality and insight of the teacher. Expert teachers know how to incorporate student-centered approaches into their teaching— with exceptional results.

WHO SHOULD BE AT THE CENTER?

Are teacher-centered approaches the best way to teach? Or are student-centered, constructivist approaches the most effective way to reach students?

FIRST VIEW: *Students learn more from traditional, teacher-centered approaches.* Proponents of traditional techniques of instruction cite the long-term success and proven track record of these techniques. Advocates cite the effectiveness of repeated drilling and repetition in helping children learn and remember basic facts and concepts. These basic facts are seen as the foundation for all other learning; thus they must be learned accurately and thoroughly for students to progress and not be derailed by a lack of basic knowledge. Teacher-centered approaches have the advantage of maximizing students' time on academic tasks, which maximizes learning per unit time. Students learn to discipline themselves, an important life skill. The teacher, not other students, is seen as the natural and appropriate leader of student learning.

SECOND VIEW: *Students learn the most from constructivist approaches.* Advocates of constructivist approaches believe that meaningful learning occurs when students are deeply involved in their learning. Hands-on techniques and activities teach knowledge more deeply and result in a more mature and useful level of understanding. Constructivist techniques mirror real-world situations that students will participate in throughout their lives—cooperating rather than always competing, solving real-world problems, working with others from different backgrounds, generating and evaluating alternative hypotheses, asking fruitful questions, and completing extensive projects. The student is a leader rather than a follower in the teaching process, and consequently becomes a more engaged and active learner.

A THIRD VIEW: A SYNTHESIS: *Students benefit most from the combination of different teaching techniques.* Both teacher-centered and student-centered techniques are useful. The key for the teacher is to recognize the strengths and weaknesses of each approach, as well as the types of students for whom each approach is best suited. The best teaching approach often consists of using traditional techniques to teach basic skills, facts, and concepts, and using constructivist techniques to encourage students to integrate their knowledge and use this knowledge to solve real-world problems. Some students need more basic instruction than others. Other students may be ready quickly to move past basic instruction, and for these students, project work under student control may encourage the greatest intellectual growth. By combining techniques, teachers can customize their approaches to meet the needs of every student. The key is to combine techniques effectively to provide a range of learning experiences to all students.

Implications for Teaching

- **Take steps to ensure active student involvement in learning.** The constructivist movement in education has helped expert teachers to understand the student's central role in learning and to design instruction to create an active learning experience. Hands-on, active, compelling lessons working from the principle that students create their own knowledge become easier with the tools of constructivist approaches.

- **Familiarize yourself with the different student-centered teaching methods.** These include individualized instruction, discovery, group discussion, groupwork, cooperative learning, and reciprocal teaching. From research in educational psychology you can learn the details about what works for different types of students and why. Be willing to try different approaches to see which ones are most effective.

- ■ ***Consider the increasingly important role of computers and technology in the classroom and use this technology as appropriate.*** Computers can serve both meaningful and meaningless (and even harmful) ends, depending on how they are used. Effective teachers speak to other teachers, read magazines and journals, and consult other sources of information about computer programs before making their selections. They also preview programs to ensure their appropriateness for classroom use.

CONSTRUCTING YOUR OWN LEARNING

Choose a subject you hope to teach someday, and choose one age-range of student on which to focus (elementary, middle school, or high school). Select one topic you believe might be difficult for the students to understand. Now, create five brief lesson plans portraying five distinct ways to teach the topic. For example, one way to teach fractions to fourth graders is to review several examples from the textbook on the chalkboard, asking students to chime in when they know the right answer. Another way to teach fractions would be to bring a pie or a pizza to class and cut it into many small pieces. Once you have sketched out five different ways to teach the same topic, describe the strengths and weaknesses of each approach. What types of students would be likely to do best with each approach, and why? Which approach do you like best, and why?

SUMMING IT UP

WHY UNDERSTANDING CLASSROOM TEACHING IS IMPORTANT TO TEACHERS

- ■ Expert classroom teachers are more knowledgeable, more efficient, and more insightful than novice teachers. Experts' teaching plans tend to be more flexible and fluid than the plans of novices.

PRINCIPLES OF TEACHER-CENTERED TEACHING

- ■ Teacher-centered teaching consists of techniques for direct, teacher-led instruction. Learning objectives are clear descriptions of educational goals. They can be action oriented and specific (referring to individual behaviors), or they can be general. If they are general, they should be tied to specific behaviors that indicate when the objectives are met.

- ■ Taxonomies are systematic hierarchical classifications of learning objectives. Bloom sorted educational objectives into three categories: cognitive, affective, and psychomotor. Bloom's six levels of cognitive objectives have been very influential in education.

- ■ Methods of direct instruction include lecturing, recitation and questioning, and seatwork and homework. Lectures should begin with a thorough introduction to the topic that gives relevant con-

text. They should end with a review and an opportunity for teacher-supervised practice followed by independent practice. Recitation and questioning are effective when teachers choose good questions representing a variety of types of thinking, and wait for students to think before calling on anyone. The rules for seatwork and homework should be clearly specified. Teachers should provide help during seatwork. Homework, recommended as a normal part of instruction, should reinforce what was learned in class and should be graded promptly. Both homework and seatwork should stress meaningful learning.

- ■ Aptitude-treatment interaction refers to the fact that students learn different things and in different amounts from the same instruction. Students have different personalities, abilities, and backgrounds; teachers must vary approaches to meet the needs of all students.

PRINCIPLES OF STUDENT-CENTERED OR CONSTRUCTIVIST TEACHING

- ■ Student-centered or constructivist teaching gives the student a central and active role in instruction. The constructivist view sees students as constructing their own understanding. The American Psychological Association's learner-centered principles define many of the objectives of student-centered teaching.

- Planning is very important for student-centered teaching: Activities need concrete goals and methods of assessment so students' learning can be documented. Activities should not become merely excuses to have fun in the classroom.

- Among the several methods for teaching constructively, individualized instruction is a process in which teacher and students customize what the students learn, decide the time frame, and specify the method and approach. In discovery approaches, and especially guided discovery, the teacher assists students in discovering concepts, ideas, and principles on their own, often using props and manipulatives.

- Also a constructivist approach, group discussion requires teachers to keep the students on-track and focused; these discussions foster the students' development of interpersonal skills. Inquiry methods involve students testing alternative hypotheses in order to answer a question posed by the teacher. Groupwork consists of small groups of students working together on tasks in informal settings.

- Cooperative learning is a constructivist approach in which structured groups of students use strategies for enhancing learning and interpersonal development; groups of four are ideal. One type of cooperative learning approach uses Student Teams Achievement Divisions (STAD); another is called Jigsaw. Another constructivist approach, reciprocal teaching, is a method for reading instruction in which students learn four strategies to enhance understanding and then take turns leading the class or a small group in using the strategies.

- Computers can either assist in meeting educational goals through computer-assisted instruction or take students off-track. The key is the precise activity the computer is being used for; teachers and parents should supervise. Computers should not take the place of learning essential writing and mathematical skills.

KEY TERMS AND DEFINITIONS

- **Affective domain** Domain in which educational objectives are focused on feeling and emotion. Page 429

- **Aptitude-by-treatment interaction** Effect of instruction in which individual students learn different things from the same instruction depending on their personalities, abilities, and backgrounds. Page 441

- **Cognitive domain** Domain in which educational objectives are focused on thinking. Page 429

- **Computer-assisted instruction** Individualized instruction administered by a computer. Page 456

- **Constructivism** View of learning that sees students as constructing their own understanding. Page 444

- **Cooperative learning** Teaching approach in which structured groups of students use specific strategies for enhancing learning and interpersonal development. Page 452

- **Direct instruction** Teaching methods including lecturing, recitation and questioning, and seatwork and homework. Page 432

- **Discovery learning** Learning process in which students use information supplied to them to construct their own understanding. Page 450

- **Expository teaching** Ausubel's approach, designed to encourage meaningful verbal learning. Page 434

- **Group discussions** Conversations among students in which students pose and answer their own questions and in which the teacher does not play the dominant role. Page 444

- **Group instruction** Instruction in which students learn, process, and discuss material in groups. Page 444

- **Guided discovery** Learning process in which the teacher assists the students in making discoveries. Page 450

- **Individualized instruction** Form of instruction modified to meet the needs of individual students. Page 449

- **Inquiry method** Dewey's method, in which teachers first ask students a question. Students then formulate various hypotheses that represent possible answers to the question, gather actual information to evaluate the rival hypotheses, and come to appropriate conclusions. Finally, students revisit the processes they followed and evaluate them. Page 452

- **Jigsaw** Cooperative learning approach in which groups of students are assigned topics on which to become expert, compare notes with other experts in their topic area, and then teach members of other groups about their topic. Page 453

- **Learning objectives** Clear descriptions of educational goals. Page 427

- **Open schools** Schools in which students are actively involved in deciding what and how they will learn and study. Page 444

- **Programmed instruction** Structured lessons that students work on by themselves and at their own pace. Page 437

- **Psychomotor domain** Domain in which educational objectives are focused on physical action. Page 429

- **Reciprocal teaching** Approach that attempts to increase students' understanding of what they read by teaching students four strategies: summarize, question, clarify, predict. Page 454

- **Recitation** Teaching methods in which teachers ask questions and students provide answers. Page 435

- **Seatwork** Quiet, independent work students do at their desks. Page 437
- **Student-centered approach** Teaching that gives a central and active role to the student. Page 444
- **Student groupwork** Small groups of students working together on tasks in relatively informal settings. Page 452
- **Student Teams Achievement Divisions (STAD)** Formalized system for cooperative learning that creates learning situations most likely to result in desired outcomes. Page 453
- **Taxonomies** Systematic or hierarchical classifications of learning objectives. Page 429
- **Teacher-centered approach** Teaching centered on, or led by, the teacher. Page 426
- **Unstructured discovery** Learning process in which students make discoveries on their own. Page 450
- **Wait time** Period of silence before and after a student answers a question that gives all students an opportunity to think. Page 436

BECOMING AN EXPERT: QUESTIONS AND PROBLEMS

IN ELEMENTARY SCHOOL

1. You teach a class of 15 first graders. How important do you believe general versus specific learning objectives are with such young students? Which type of objective would be more successful with this group, and why?

2. You are a new third-grade teacher preparing for your first year of teaching. Do you believe learning taxonomies could be useful in planning your teaching? How might you use a learning taxonomy to prepare a basic science lesson?

3. Your class of fourth graders seems to tune you out whenever you give a lecture, even if only for 10 minutes. What steps can you take to hold the students' interest more effectively? What other teaching techniques might work better?

4. Do you believe that students should be given homework in first through fourth grade? Why or why not? Describe what types of homework might be appropriate versus inappropriate for such young students.

5. Your class of second graders is socioeconomically, culturally, and ethnically diverse. You are concerned that instruction must reach every student in this widely varying group. What can you do to ensure that students from very different backgrounds relate to your teaching?

IN MIDDLE SCHOOL

1. Your eighth-grade math and science classroom is about to receive a gift of six new computers from a local business. How can you best utilize these computers to improve your science and math instruction?

2. Describe a situation in your teaching of seventh-grade social studies when a handout containing a learning taxonomy would be a useful teaching aid. What could the students learn from such a handout? How might this mode of presentation help the students understand the material?

3. You are leading an eighth-grade math class, and you often find it necessary to use lecture and recitation to cover all of the material. What other teaching techniques could you use to help broaden your style? What about reciprocal teaching?

4. How much homework should teachers assign in grades 6 through 8? What types of homework might be appropriate for students of this age? How would you know if you are assigning too much homework?

5. In what ways can social and cultural issues interfere with students' learning as they enter adolescence? How can you use different instructional techniques to help students learn during this challenging period in their lives?

IN HIGH SCHOOL

1. You teach twelfth-grade biology and chemistry. How important are general versus specific learning objectives with students of this age? How can you use learning objectives to help students organize their studying and assimilation of the material?

2. How might you encourage eleventh-grade students to use learning taxonomies on their own to organize their couse work and, especially, their homework? How would you convince them that taxonomies could help?

3. When is direct lecturing most effective with high school language arts students? How about recitation? How can these techniques be made more effective for use with high school students? What other techniques should teachers try with high school students?

4. You are concerned that many teachers do not assign enough homework to their tenth-grade students because they are afraid of overburdening these students. How can you determine what amount of homework is optimal for your own students?

5. You are a twelfth-grade foreign language teacher. What steps can you take to tailor your instruction to each student's personal needs?

Connecting Theory and Research to Practice

How many technical resources are available to help teachers teach effectively and creatively within their classrooms? Hundreds? Thousands? There are literally too many resources available on the Internet to count. Many sites offer comprehensive help when it comes to designing integrative, interactive, and interesting lessons that foster student involvement, interest, and lifelong learning. Many of the educational sites on the Internet contain, as described in this chapter, student-centered or constructivist instructional strategies.

One such site was developed with the support of the U.S. Department of Education's READ*WRITE* NOW program. The Alphabet Superhighway (ASH), located at *http://www.ash .udel.edu/ash/index.html,* was developed to promote student learning at all ability and grade levels of communication skills via student-centered approaches such as guided discovery and cooperative learning. The site features a multitude of user-friendly tools for students, teachers, and parents.

On this site, K–12 students can search for information, take practice quizzes, receive tutoring, or participate in learning activities that promote writing and reading skills. One of the most interesting features of the Alphabet Superhighway is a K–12-

generated student magazine called *Cyberzine* that features student poems, jokes, cartoons, and news stories. "The Exhibit Hall" is a collection of collaborative projects that are created by students at different schools throughout the United States. Teachers can visit the "Teacher's Lounge" to search an index of lesson plans, view student work for lesson ideas, get tips for effective teaching, find links to other education Web sites, and read suggestions for using the Alphabet Superhighway in their classrooms. "Parents' Place" offers an educational resource where parents can search for thematic activities to do with their children, provide feedback to the project administrators, or post their child's work.

Building Your Self-Portrait as an Educator

While many teachers know of the benefits of using collaboration as an instructional strategy, they rarely think about collaboration as a way to learn about or improve their own teaching. Available at *http://www .thejournal.com/features/ rdmap/hs154c.cfm* is a listing of resources for teachers to collaborate with educators around the nation and the world.

One Internet resource is "The Viking Network,"

located at *http://viking.no/ index.html.* Designed by Yngve Skråmm, this site is bilingual (Dutch and English) and includes information and lesson plans about the Vikings that is appropriate for ages 9–13. Students and teachers have access to a great deal of information, maps, and projects and activities about the Vikings. At a discussion board about the Vikings, students can exchange ideas and comments with other students around the world. The site also lists the different schools participating in Viking projects. This is just one example of how the Internet can contribute to collaborative learning in the world community.

Communities of Learners/Teachers

A technology tool connecting classrooms all over the world is called E*Pals *(http://www.epals .com).* On E*Pals, students and teachers can connect with others to share ideas, participate in collaborative projects, and search for collaborators from other countries. Also included are listings of curricular resources (text and Web based), maps, weather, and special E*Pal events. One event, the Space Day Talk, featured an online student discussion with guest moderators from NASA and the Johnson Space Center.

One of the most interesting features of this site is the

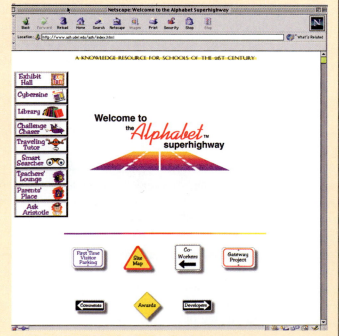

instant translation feature, which will translate pages into five different languages (English, French, Spanish, Dutch, and Portuguese) or written text into several languages (seventeen different combinations are offered). This helpful feature allows teachers to connect to a global community of learners and allows students to pair up with others who may not speak their language. Like many other technological tools used by children, E*Pal offers monitored e-mail and discussion boards in order to provide a safe, respectful environment for student interaction.

Online Resources

The Global Schoolhouse (*www.gsn.org*) and Lightspan.com (*www.lightspan.com*) have collaborated to provide teachers and parents with an online resource for collaborative projects. With their "Internet Project Registry" *(http://k12.bilkent.edu.tr/www.gsn.org/pr/),* teachers can search for online collaborative projects that are age- and content area-specific or that start during a particular month. A search of projects for 5–7-year-olds resulted in 438 hits and a search of projects starting in March, 2001 resulted in 16 hits. Projects are posted by teachers seeking to collaborate with other teachers in the United States and around the world.

"The Education Index," created by Cincinnati soft-

ware company College-View, gives educators a searchable index of educational Web sites. Located at *http://www.educationindex.com,* it offers a variety of technological resources pertinent to classroom teaching. One of the most impressive features is the index, searchable by subject or by age-appropriateness, of over 3,000 education related sites. The subject index organizes sites by 56 categories including agriculture, chemistry, ethnic and cultural studies, marketing, and music. Users can also search for age-appropriate sites by clicking on the Lifestages

menu and selecting from the 11 options that break down into the traditional K–12 divisions, but also includes distance learning, parenting, and career indexes. The site has two additional features: "Weasel World" and the "Coffee Shop." While the "Coffee Shop" is a traditional teacher chat room and discussion area, "Weasel World" highlights fun activities and games for students and teachers.

Online technological tools can help classroom teachers incorporate technology into their teaching. "The Learning Space: Evolving Tools for Evolving

Minds" *(www.learningspace.org)* provides a variety of tools for integrating technology in K–12 classrooms, including technology help, online lesson plans, and information regarding assessment and evaluation. Another site containing valuable information regarding technology and education is hosted by the International Society for Technology in Education (ISTE) *(www.iste.org).* This professional organization provides a variety of resources and information for both teachers and researchers interested in the role of technology in teaching and learning.

13

Standardized Testing

CHAPTER OUTLINE

THE BIG PICTURE

To help you see the big picture, keep the following questions in mind as you read this chapter:

■ What is a standardized test? How do standardized tests differ from tests that are not standardized? What are the main types of standardized tests?

■ What statistical concepts do you need to know to interpret test scores? What types of scores can tests yield?

■ When should students be compared to other students, to themselves, and to some objective standard of performance? What are the advantages and disadvantages of each test approach, and when should you use each one?

■ How can you assess the fairness and quality of a standardized test?

■ What are the main issues to consider in giving and interpreting tests?

◄ *A grade-school teacher monitors a standardized test.*
(Tony Freeman, PhotoEdit)

Tonight was Jolene Johnson's first parent-teacher conference night, and she was nervous about presenting the basic skills test scores. At Southside Elementary School, third graders were required to take the California Achievement Test, the first major standardized test of their school careers. Teachers presented the score reports at parent-teacher conferences as a way of encouraging attendance at the twice-a-year event.

Jolene confided her concerns to McKinley Phillips, the other third-grade teacher at Southside. McKinley had been teaching third grade for seven years, and Jolene had relied on her expert advice frequently during the first few weeks of school.

"I read the booklet that came with the score reports, but I am afraid the parents are going to ask me to explain something that I don't fully understand myself," admitted Jolene.

"I worried quite a bit about the same thing," McKinley confirmed. "Let me tell you what works for me. The first thing I cover," said McKinley, "is the percentile score. Parents are always interested in finding out how their child compares to third graders around the country. It is a pretty natural instinct, I guess, and because our students usually do well in comparison to the national average, most of the time we begin on a positive note."

"Then, I point out the graph of scores on all the different subtests," McKinley continued. "The graph gives a picture of a child's strengths and weaknesses on the test, and this helps some parents. One thing I try to make very clear is that what they are seeing is only the strengths and weaknesses on one particular test. I mention some things that might affect a test score, and I emphasize that at our school we are not going to base anybody's future on a single test. This observation usually alleviates any tension that may have arisen.

"I always make it a point to share my own perceptions—whether I agree or disagree with the picture the test scores are showing," McKinley advised. "Sometimes this sharing is a good introduction to my showing parents some of the student's work from the sample folders. We usually finish by discussing what the next steps will be for the student, and how the parents can help," she finished.

"That sounds like a good plan," agreed Jolene, feeling reassured, "but what do you tell them about grade equivalents? One of my students has scored at the fifth-grade level in math. Won't her parents ask why she is not in fifth grade rather than third, if her tests show she is already working at a fifth-grade level?"

"Yes, I get that question every year," smiled McKinley. "I explain to the parents that grade equivalents can be misleading. A fifth-grade equivalent actually means the score their child got was the score that a fifth grader who was taking the third graders' test would get, and not what their third grader would get if she tried to do fifth-grade work. See the difference?"

"I think I finally comprehend it myself," laughed Jolene. "Thanks, McKinley, I am feeling much better."

From your own experiences as a student, you are probably familiar with taking standardized tests, including a college entrance exam such as the *SAT* or *ACT*. As Jolene's experience makes clear, standardized tests will continue to be important to you in your role as a teacher. In this chapter, we define what standardized tests are and how they are used, and assess what types of tests are available and what results on these tests mean. We also discuss how you can assess the fairness and quality of a standardized test, and we consider some of the issues associated with testing in general.

Why Understanding Standardized Testing Is Important to Teachers

Standardized tests are a part of the educational experience of nearly every U.S. student. Over 40 states require standardized tests as part of their annual assessment of students. Standardized tests are also very important in American society. For example, they are used to help decide a student's academic placement, such as for college admissions. Standardized tests also are used to compare the performance of teachers, schools, districts, states, and even nations, with one another. In recent years, some educators and researchers have argued that standardized tests are overemphasized (Gardner, 1999; Madaus & Kellaghan, 1993); other commentators are pushing for even more standardized tests. In 1997 President Clinton proposed a national standardized test for all students in fourth and eighth grades. More recently, President Bush has also proposed expansion of standardized testing.

Whatever your opinion about the future of standardized tests, their current prevalence and importance demands that teachers know how to use them. Expert teachers understand the strengths and weaknesses of standardized tests in order to use them fairly and effectively (Linn & Gronlund, 2000). They also know how and when to use a specific test. Understanding why some standardized tests are better and more nearly fair than others will help you recognize which tests meet the needs of both schools and students. After students take a standardized test, you must then know what to do with the scores. Part of being an expert teacher is understanding the confusing array of standardized test scores and being able to interpret these scores for others. Expert teachers are able to interpret test scores while taking into account students' cultural background, native language, and socioeconomic status. Finally, they understand some of the pitfalls of standardized testing, so they can avoid them to the extent possible. The Forum: "Costs and Benefits of Standardized Testing" explores different opinions about the use of standardized testing.

FORUM

COSTS AND BENEFITS OF TESTING

Standardized test scores have become enormously powerful in American society and in other societies as well. In the United States, standardized tests are used for evaluation and placement in the elementary and secondary schools. They also are used for admission to college; law school, medical school, dental school, education school, business school, and other advanced educational institutions; and many other kinds of programs. Many people have begun to question America's use of standardized tests.

FIRST VIEW: *Tests can help teachers and admissions officers make informed decisions.* For example, a test such as the *SAT* or *ACT* can help compare students who come from different parts of the country, different high schools, and different family backgrounds. Comparing students on other factors, such as grades, is not as fair, because some teachers or schools may grade unusually easily or unusually hard. A student who gets B's and C's at a "hard school" may be just as capable as one who gets all A's at an "easy school." Standardized test scores can be a reliable way of comparing students' achievement. In addition, such tests have been shown to predict performance, such as grades, in the first year of college.

SECOND VIEW: *Standardized tests can be, and at times have been, used irresponsibly.* Such use occurs because there is a natural human tendency to value quantitative precision, often without considering whether the quantitatively precise information is valid for the purposes for which it is being used. For example, Sternberg and

Williams (1997) reported that the standardized test used as a factor in graduate school admissions decisions actually could not well predict any other measure of success in one graduate school except first-year grades.

There is also the danger that test scores will become self-fulfilling prophecies (Rosenthal & Jacobson, 1968), a situation in which test scores can create an expectation on the part of a teacher for a student, which then materializes only because the expectation was there. For example, a teacher might place students with low scores on a reading aptitude test in the slow reading group. The students in the slow group may get less challenging reading assignments and homework than the students in the faster groups. Eventually, the reading levels of students in the slow group may indeed fall behind those of the fast groups. Are the lower reading levels caused by the students' ability levels, or by the teacher's low expectations, based on the test scores?

THIRD VIEW: A SYNTHESIS: *Tests can be a blessing or a curse, and it is up to all of us— teachers and researchers alike—to use them productively.* Tests should be used only when they have been demonstrated to be reliable and valid for the purposes for which they are being proposed, and only in conjunction with other information. For example, a multiple-choice test may not provide a fully valid assessment of science knowledge. New forms of standardized tests, including essay exams or tests that actually require students to demonstrate hands-on task performance, may give better estimates of mastery and the ability to succeed in some areas of endeavor.

Tests should always be used together with other information. In elementary and secondary schools, placement should be based on class performance and teacher evaluations as well as test scores. The weighting of various factors in admissions decisions, including test scores, grades, admissions essays, and interviews, should be balanced so as to yield the best possible validity for decisions.

What Are Standardized Tests?

A **standardized test** is a test given to many individuals, often across the nation, to develop appropriate content and scoring comparisons, and it is administered and scored according to uniform procedures. Uniform, or standardized, procedures are the key to the definition of a standardized test. Constructors of these tests try to assure that every student taking the test has a similar experience. Standardized tests are usually purchased from test publishers, who sell the tests only to those qualified to use them.

Each of these fourth-graders experiences the same test conditions as the other students. (Bob Daemmrich, Stock Boston)

Not all tests purchased from publishers are standardized. For example, textbook publishers often offer banks of test questions. The publisher, in this case, does not try to standardize the experience of every student who is tested. Teacher-made tests are not standardized, because they are created by or for individual teachers who use them on only a limited number of students and because each teacher scores the tests he or she creates in an individual way. Ideally, all tests of achievement should be closely tied to the learning that students have done (Dochy & McDowell, 1997), in part because the way you test can affect the way students decide to learn (Airasian, 1997).

Standardized tests are of two types: norm referenced and criterion referenced (Gregory, 2000). **Norm-referenced tests** compare each test taker's scores with the performance of all the test takers (Haynes & O'Brien, 2000). Remember that standardized tests are given to large numbers of students to establish standards for scoring and content. Giving a test to many students allows test developers to develop **norms,** or **normative scores,** test scores that reflect the performance of individuals in the population of interest. For example, the population of interest to Jolene Johnson and McKinley Phillips is all the third graders in the nation. Typically, students, teachers, administrators, and parents are interested in finding out how test scores in their school compare with the national norms for the test. Although norms are often based on national samples, they do not have to be. Sometimes, they are based on scores across a state (as in a statewide mastery test), across a school district, or even in a classroom. As we see later in the chapter, it is important to know who constituted the normative sample.

Criterion-referenced tests measure a student's performance relative to what the student should know, rather than to the performance of other students (Haynes & O'Brien, 2000). In an arithmetic test on fractions, for example, it is helpful for a teacher to know not only how well a student has done in comparison to others, but also exactly which operations the child does and does not understand. Criterion-referenced tests are developed differently from norm-referenced tests. Emphasis is placed on being able to compare students' understanding of the knowledge required by a given curriculum, rather than on being able to compare students' scores to each other. Publishers of some tests provide both normative and criterion-based information as part of their score reports.

Recall from Chapter 2 the difference between *maximal performance*—the very best you can perform under optimal circumstances—and *typical performance*—how well you perform under ordinary, everyday circumstances. Most of the standardized tests students take in school are designed to elicit maximal performance. To do well, students typically have to work as quickly and as hard as they can to finish some fairly difficult problems within a limited time period: In other words, they have to work their fastest and be at their best. For example, students might be asked to do a difficult arithmetic problem or to read a passage and then answer challenging questions on the material in the passage.

Many factors can prevent a student from giving a maximal performance. A student who wants to give a maximal performance may not be able to do so if he or she has a cold or is distracted in the testing room. Some students simply may not be interested in performing at their maximal level because they do not regard the test as important.

Expert teachers know that people's maximal performance is not necessarily a good predictor of their typical performance, and vice versa. Some students perform phenomenally well when they set their minds to doing well. On ordinary school tasks, such as homework, however, these same students might put in much effort and not do well. Other students might not do well on maximal performance tests, yet they give each task their all, such that their performance is actually better on a day-to-day basis than that of the student who excelled in the maximal performance test.

Researchers and expert teachers recommend several techniques to encourage and help students give their best performance on standardized tests:

1. **Make the importance and purpose of the test clear.** Today, many decisions about student and teacher placement and even school funding hinge on test scores. Teachers who try to reassure students by telling them "the scores really do not matter that much" are doing students a disservice by providing inaccurate information. They also inadvertently may lower students' motivation to do well. Give students a realistic idea of the uses and importance of test scores, but avoid placing so much emphasis on the test that students become nervous about the outcomes.

2. **Take the mystery out of standardized tests.** Spend some time preparing students for the test. In general, students who are well prepared for the testing experience

THINKING PRACTICALLY

Teacher-made tests are usually not standardized. What is one advantage to measuring achievement via teacher-made rather than standardized tests bought from a publisher?

SUGGESTION: The teacher-made test is targeted to the material the teacher actually taught.

THINKING ANALYTICALLY

Normative and criterion-referenced scores are largely complementary. What is one obvious advantage of each type of score over the other?

SUGGESTION: Normative scores facilitate comparisons between students. Criterion-referenced scores make clearer what skills students have and have not mastered.

THINKING ANALYTICALLY

What kind of task would you give students that involves typical performance? What kind of task involves maximum performance?

SUGGESTION: A typical performance task is stating an opinion. A maximal performance task is writing an essay justifying an opinion.

are better able to focus their attention on the content of the test questions without being distracted by the directions or form of the questions. Use the practice tests provided by test publishers to acquaint students with the testing experience and with the types of questions they are likely to encounter. Help students become familiar with the way questions are phrased and learn to spot words that can mislead them. Brainstorm and practice strategies for understanding what typical standardized-test directions are actually asking the student to do. Encourage students to develop effective strategies for handling various types of items, such as "fill-in-the-blanks" or "identify the incorrect sentence."

3. **Provide good testing conditions.** If students are to be tested in a room other than their classroom, assure them of the comfort of the testing site: adequate climate control and lighting; few distracting features; sufficient supplies; and a seating pattern that gives all students a clear view of the clock and the ability to hear the test monitor. To prevent distraction or illness, some schools even provide snacks during breaks in long testing sessions.

4. **Prepare yourself.** Expert teachers know that monitoring standardized tests involves more than reading the directions and watching the clock. They also know the different types of tests available, so they are able to adjust their facilitation to meet the needs of the test. Test monitors should know how to reduce distractions and help students stay focused during the tests. They should ensure that all students understand the directions. Test monitors also must be prepared to cope with problems, such as cheating, student illness or anxiety, or interruptions.

CONSTRUCTING YOUR OWN LEARNING

Consider how you will apply the guidelines listed above when you help your own students prepare to take standardized tests. Use a statewide criterion-referenced test as an example. Write out what you would tell students to describe the importance of the test. How would you fit into your regular lessons time for practice with typical test question types and directions? Plan what you would do if a student suddenly became ill during the testing session. It may help you to think back to standardized tests you may have taken yourself. How did your teachers help you prepare for those tests? For example, was anything they said especially motivating or reassuring? Did any of your teachers respond especially well when unusual situations arose during testing? Try to adapt some of the best strategies as you make your own plans.

Types of Standardized Tests

As a teacher, you will probably have occasion to use many different types of standardized tests—reading tests, math tests, general ability tests, general achievement tests, and even occupational-preference tests. Expert teachers ensure that a particular standardized test is the most appropriate test for the purpose it is being used. For example, a test of reading comprehension may not be the most appropriate test for helping some high school students determine their career direction. Consider the major types of tests so you will know what standardized tests you can use to assess students in a range of situations and for a range of purposes. One of several sources in which you can find formal reviews is the Buros Institute's *Mental Measurements Yearbook*, which is revised regularly.

Julie Young's approach to teaching math and writing is in sync with the requirements of a state-wide standardized test. It allows her students to feel prepared for a demanding week of testing.

What is the state-wide standardized test?

The test, which is three days each for math and for language arts, is required of all fourth-grade students in our state. The expectations on the standardized tests are high. The tests concentrate on higher level thinking skills—in my opinion, a good thing. The test is a true assessment of what we *should* be teaching and what the students *should* be learning.

The language arts test involves one day of writing in response to a writing prompt. The next day students read an excerpt and write about it. On the third day students interpret many passages for meaning and grammar.

The first day of math testing the students work on concepts and skills in math. The second and third days the students show their process in solving problems.

How did you prepare your students for the math portion of the test?

Problem solving is a significant part of the test. My background is in math, and I believe that problem solving is an important skill for the students. Problem solving used to mean a word problem with a definite answer. Today, students are given a problem that may have more than one right answer. They must show their thinking and write why their answer makes sense. I believe that it is important to know the reasons why you're doing things in math, not just to memorize the steps to get the right answer.

Our school has just adopted a new math series this year. As part of using that series, we are focusing on students' being able to explain what they do,

and being able to solve problems in different ways. This move, away from the past emphasis on computation and memorization, matches my own beliefs.

It also fits in well with the emphasis on problem solving that is part of the statewide standardized tests, so, in a sense, I use the entire year to prepare the students. We start every morning with problem solving. Some problems we work on cooperatively, and other problems, students solve on their own. To prepare specifically for the statewide test, my students took practice tests one month prior to the real test.

How do you prepare students for the language arts portion of the test?

For the most part, the language arts test is in line with the approach I use to teach writing. We have writers' workshops and readers' workshops. These really help the students with the test. I didn't cater to the test—it just happened to be the way I taught writing.

I often start with a mini-lesson based on what I see as their needs—for example, how to write an interesting beginning. Students practice by cutting and pasting new beginnings onto their stories. Then they write, and they conference with each other. They revise and have another conference. Finally, they share their writing with the class. They all have experience in writing a draft, revising it, and getting feedback. The test allows them to write a first draft, edit, and revise.

Is there anything about the standardized tests that you would like to see changed?

The writing assessment was problematic. Doing the writing test in one undertaking is unrealistic. In real life

> I believe that it is important to know the reasons why you're doing things in math, not just to memorize the steps to get the right answer.

you ask others to read your writing, and you get their comments. In a test, you can't talk and you have to write the piece in one day. As a result, the students can't reflect on what they've written. It's not true to the real-life process of writing. It's not how we teach writing.

Another drawback of these tests is that they are timed, a practice that is hard for students who work more slowly.

We often hear about the problems with standardized testing. Do you see any positive aspects of standardized testing?

Standardized test scores provide a way to see if you and your students are moving in a positive direction. You can use the test scores to spot weaknesses, or areas for improvement, in your instruction.

Also, the focus that our standardized test places on higher-level thinking skills may help some teachers who want to include more thinking and problem-solving activities in their curricula.

What advice about standardized testing would you give to new teachers?

Make sure you're aware of the expectations for students, that you know what will be asked of them on the tests. Use the school resources available to you. When I was a new teacher, I relied heavily on an experienced fourth-grade teacher at our school to tell me what the students needed to be able to do at the end of the year and what they needed to do on the tests. You'll find that testing goes a lot more smoothly if you know what's expected.

Tests of intelligence were first developed by Frenchman Alfred Binet in the early 1900s to distinguish children who needed special education from those who were simply having behavior problems in school. Binet's test was very successful in making this distinction, and a version of the test is still in use, along with many other intelligence tests.

Today, there are two basic types of intelligence tests, individual tests and group tests (Gregory, 2000). Like Binet's original test, intelligence tests are used as diagnostic tools to help determine whether children should receive special education. They can also be used as predictive tools, to suggest how students are likely to perform in school.

■ **INDIVIDUAL TESTS** The Stanford-Binet Intelligence Scales (Thorndike, Hagen, & Sattler, 1986) are the modern version of Alfred Binet's original intelligence test (Binet & Simon, 1905/1916). These scales can be used for children as young as 2 years up to adults to measure intelligence according to Binet's conception. The test is given individually and must be administered by a trained psychologist. In its current version, it offers an overall score, as well as subscores. There are 15 subtests in all, 6 of which are given at all age levels: vocabulary, comprehension, pattern analysis, quantitative ability, remembering the order of a string of beads, and memory for sentences.

A similar set of tests prepared by David Wechsler is also used (see Matarazzo, 1972; Wechsler, 1939, 1974). Rather than developing a single, multiaged scale, Wechsler used different but related scales for different age ranges. These scales, with different names at different levels, are the Wechsler Adult Intelligence Scale—(WAIS III), the Wechsler Intelligence Scale for Children (WISC-III) (Wechsler, 1991), and the Wechsler Preschool and Primary Scale of Intelligence (WPPSI). The Wechsler scales yield an overall score, as well as separate verbal and performance scores. Examples of items from the Stanford-Binet and Wechsler scales are shown in Figure 13.1.

Other kinds of individual intelligence tests are used as well (Kaufman, 2000), such as Kaufman and Kaufman's (1983) Kaufman Assessment Battery for Children, which is loosely based on a biological theory of intelligence (Luria, 1966). Another test, the Differential Abilities Scales, provides a large number of subtests as options, from which the examiner decides which tests to administer. An innovative kind of individual intelligence test is Reuven Feuerstein's (1979) Learning Potential Assessment Device, or LPAD. This test measures not children's developed potential, but rather their zone of proximal development (Vygotsky, 1978) (see Chapter 3)—that is, the difference between their underlying capacity and their developed ability, as measured by their ability to profit from guided instruction.

THINKING ANALYTICALLY

Referring to Figure 13.1, name one similarity and one difference between the Stanford-Binet and Wechsler tests.

SUGGESTION: A major similarity is that both tests use many verbal items. A difference is that the Wechsler series places a greater emphasis on nonverbal performance-based tasks.

THINKING ANALYTICALLY

As you examine the test items in Figure 13.1, which do you think are most dependent on cultural background for their solution? Why?

SUGGESTION: Vocabulary is an example of a type of item highly dependent on cultural background.

A first-grade student takes an individual intelligence test, administered by a trained psychologist. (Bob Daemmrich, Stock Boston)

FIGURE 13.1

Examples of Items Appearing on the Stanford–Binet and Wechsler Scales. The sample questions here are not actual questions from the scales. The questions only illustrate the kind of questions that would appear in the main content areas of the tests.

Types of Questions Seen on the Stanford-Binet Intelligence Scales		
Content area	**Explanation of question**	**Example of possible question**
Verbal reasoning	Describe how one word is different from three other words.	Select the word from the following word list that is not like the others. mug fork straw cup (Note that you cannot drink from a *fork,* but you can drink from a *mug, straw,* and *cup.*)
Quantitative reasoning	Complete a number series.	What number seems most likely to come next in the following series of numbers: 3, 10, 17, 24, __ ?
Figure/abstract reasoning	Combine geometric pieces to form a particular geometric shape.	Use the pieces below to form a pyramid.
Short-term memory	The examiner will say a sentence. Repeat the sentence back exactly.	Repeat this sentence back to me: "Allison jumped over a bush and ran down to the lake."

Types of Questions Seen on the Wechsler Adult Intelligence Scale		
Content area	**Explanation of question**	**Example of possible question**
Verbal scale	Define a word's meaning.	What does *orthodontics* mean? What does *conspicuous* mean?
Content area	**Explanation of question**	**Example of question**
Performance scale	Use patterned blocks to create a design that looks like the design provided by the examiner.	Put the blocks on the left together to copy the pattern on the right:

Source: Table 11.2, p. 358 from *In Search of the Human Mind,* 2nd edition by Robert J. Sternberg. Copyright © 1998 by Harcourt, Inc. Reprinted by permission.

■**GROUP TESTS** It is sometimes not practical to test each student individually. In these cases, schools may decide to use group tests of intelligence, typically paper-and-pencil measures of intelligence that can be administered in an hour or two. These tests, unlike individual tests, do not require extensive professional training to administer. The main functions of the examiner are to read directions and to enforce time limits. Because they do not require each student to meet with a trained psychologist, group tests of intelligence tend to be faster and less costly to administer. However, the results of individual tests are often more accurate. In some states, use of group tests is restricted. For example, the state of California does not allow use of group tests of intelligence in schools.

FIGURE **13.2**

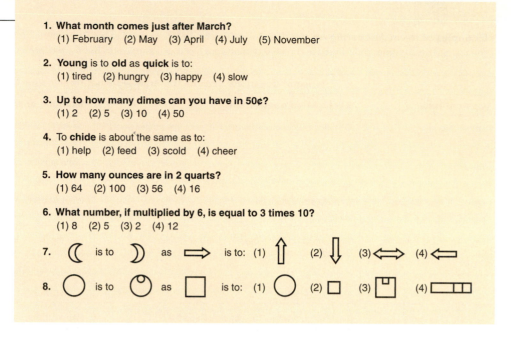

1. **What month comes just after March?**
   (1) February   (2) May   (3) April   (4) July   (5) November

2. **Young** is to **old** as **quick** is to:
   (1) tired   (2) hungry   (3) happy   (4) slow

3. **Up to how many dimes can you have in 50¢?**
   (1) 2   (2) 5   (3) 10   (4) 50

4. To **chide** is about the same as to:
   (1) help   (2) feed   (3) scold   (4) cheer

5. **How many ounces are in 2 quarts?**
   (1) 64   (2) 100   (3) 56   (4) 16

6. **What number, if multiplied by 6, is equal to 3 times 10?**
   (1) 8   (2) 5   (3) 2   (4) 12

Group tests of intelligence generally are of two main kinds. In the first kind, an *omnibus test,* such as the Otis-Lennon School Ability Test and the Henmon-Nelson Test of Mental Abilities, multiple kinds of test items are intermixed. For example, a series-completion item may follow immediately after a vocabulary item. In the second kind, tests are divided into parts, or subtests, in which each part is typically timed separately. Each item in a part is the same kind (e.g., vocabulary). A well-known example of such a test is the Cognitive Abilities Test. Figure 13.2 shows examples of items that frequently appear on group tests of intelligence.

INTELLIGENCE TEST SCORES

What kinds of scores are used to interpret the results of intelligence tests? Here, we discuss two possibilities.

1. **Mental age.** Binet suggested that we can assess children's intelligence on the basis of their *mental age,* or MA—their level of intelligence compared to an average person of the same physical age (also called *chronological age,* or CA). If, for example, a person performs on a test at a level comparable to that of an average 10-year-old, we say the person's mental age is 10. People with very different chronological ages can all have the same mental age. Thus if an 8 year-old, a 10-year-old, and a 12-year-old all have the same score on a test of intelligence, their mental ages are the same, despite the differences in their chronological, or physical, ages.

2. **Intelligence quotient.** The German psychologist William Stern suggested that mental age is a problematical measure, because it is difficult to compare scores of people of different ages. How do you compare the mental age of 10 achieved by an 8-year-old with that achieved by a 12-year-old? In order to deal with this difficulty, Stern suggested the **intelligence quotient (IQ),** a measure of intelligence comparing mental age (MA) to chronological age (CA) times 100. Because of the use of a ratio of MA to CA in calculating the IQ, an IQ calculated in this way is sometimes referred to as a *ratio IQ.* Thus:

ratio IQ = (MA/CA) × 100.

Ratio IQs are rarely used today, because a weak link was discovered in their calculation, namely, the construct of mental age.

There are several problems with the concept of mental age. First, whereas chronological age increases indefinitely throughout a person's lifetime, mental age does not. Usually, people's mental age stops increasing, or starts to increase only slowly, at a chronological age of roughly 16. In old age, mental age often actually starts to decline. This decline typically is due to decreases in scores on tests of rapid and flexible abstract thinking. These facts suggest that the ratio of mental age to chronological age takes on a meaning different for adults from that for children; it can even mean different things for adults of varying ages. For example, an average adult of 40 would have a mental age not of 40, but of around 16 or so. Although compensations in scoring systems have been made to account for this fact, the problem has never been resolved in a fully satisfactory way.

A second problem is that although mental age implies a continuous distribution of intellectual development, we know that intellectual development is not wholly continuous. Whether we see it as occurring in stages or in relation to the acquisition of domain-specific knowledge at certain ages, the fits and starts of mental development are not reflected in the mental-age construct.

Today, therefore, people generally use what are called **deviation IQ scores,** calculated on the basis of how high a person's score is relative to that of other people of his or her age. The average score for either a ratio or deviation IQ is 100. Scores below 100 are "below average." Scores above 100 are "above average." Using common statistical calculations, roughly two-thirds of all IQ scores fall between 85 and 115 and roughly 19 out of 20 scores fall between 70 and 130.

TESTS OF APTITUDES AND INTERESTS

Aptitudes are abilities developed over a period of years that predict success in particular areas of endeavor, such as music, writing, or reading. Among the most widely used aptitude tests are the **Differential Aptitude Tests,** designed to measure such aptitudes as verbal reasoning, numerical ability, abstract reasoning, clerical speed and accuracy, mechanical reasoning, space relations, spelling, and language usage. Such tests are used to help students with curriculum or vocational planning.

Tests of specific aptitudes, such as the Bennett Mechanical Comprehension Test and the Seashore Tests of Musical Aptitudes, are used for narrower purposes, such as selection or vocational placement. For example, a student who wishes to be in the vocal music program at a performing arts high school might be given the Seashore tests as part of the admissions process.

Counselors and teachers often recommend that students engaged in career planning take not only an aptitude test, but also a **vocational interest test,** such as the Strong Vocational Interest Blank. The goal of such tests is to help students decide where their vocational interests lie. The tests do not indicate ability for these vocations, which is why teachers often recommend taking both an interest test and an aptitude test. Unlike most of the other tests mentioned here, interest tests are designed to measure typical, rather than maximal performance. Students are asked to describe or behave in ways that exemplify how they usually think or behave. For example, students are asked to rate statements such as "I enjoy working with others" and "I like to travel." A person rating each of these statements high might be encouraged to become a travel agent, tour guide, or scientific field researcher, depending on the person's other interests, skills, and abilities.

TESTS OF ACHIEVEMENT

An **achievement test** measures accomplishments in either single or multiple areas of endeavor, such as reading comprehension, mathematics, social studies, and science (Cohen & Swerdlik, 1999; Gregory, 2000). Five of the most commonly administered achievement tests are the Iowa Tests of Basic Skills, the SRA Achievement Series, the

THINKING PRACTICALLY

Suppose that someone were to receive an extremely low IQ score on a hypothetical test. Would the very low score mean the person has a very low level of intelligence? If not, what else might it mean?

SUGGESTION: The person might have decided he or she does not want to engage with the test and thus deliberately does not do well.

THINKING ANALYTICALLY

Why do people today generally prefer deviation IQs to ratio IQs, even though the former are not, strictly speaking, intelligence *quotients?*

SUGGESTION: Deviation IQs are not susceptible to statistical problems such as interpretations of ratios of MA to CA for older individuals.

FIGURE 13.3

Examples of Types of Items Found in Some Achievement Tests

The *SAT* is in part an achievement test frequently taken by high school juniors and seniors who are planning to attend college. It includes the types of questions shown here. The *SAT* emphasizes reasoning with the material one has learned and thus has a strong critical-thinking component. Other achievement tests use similar formats, adjusted for the grade level of students who will take the test.

Content Area	Explanation of Task/Question	Example Task/Question
Sentence Completion	Show knowledge of meanings of words and their uses and relations.	Choose the word or set of words that best fits into a whole sentence, such as, "The most common use for a ____ , of course, is to lock and unlock doors." (Correct answer choice would be "key.")
Verbal Analogies		Choose the pair of words with the same relationship as a given pair (analogies). For example: plumber: sink = mechanic: engine
Reading Comprehension	Demonstrate understanding of a text passage.	Correctly answer multiple-choice questions about a text passage, such as "What did the main character of this story hope to achieve?"
Quantitative Skills	Make calculations involving geometry, algebra, fractions, arithmetic, exponential numbers, etc.	Choose the correct answer from several possible answers in a multiple-choice format. For example, after viewing a picture of a polygon with some angles and sides labeled and others left blank, students might be asked to identify the correct number for one of the missing side measurements.

California Achievement Test, the Metropolitan Achievement Test, and the Stanford Achievement Test. All of these tests contain measures of achievement in multiple academic subjects. For example, the California Achievement Test contains measures of achievement in vocabulary, reading comprehension, language mechanics, language expression, mathematical computation, mathematical concepts and applications, spelling, study skills, science, and social studies. In all cases, these tests can be used at multiple levels throughout the elementary and secondary grade levels. Examples of typical items from one test are shown in Figure 13.3.

Implications for Teaching

■ *Take into account the purpose of each type of score.* Expert teachers use both norm-referenced and criterion-referenced information. For example, if a new student joins Jolene Johnson's third-grade class, and Jolene knows that the student scored better than 78 percent of the students in the country on a standardized reading comprehension test, she can use that information in various ways. One way is to compare the student to others in her class. Another way is to use the information as an initial indicator of the work Jolene should assign the student.

■ *Pinpoint strengths and weaknesses.* Use achievement tests that provide diagnostic information as tools to determine what students still need to learn to attain mastery of a body of knowledge. You can use the information in score reports to diagnose the strengths and weaknesses of a student's performance by comparing the scores on individual subtests or parts of the test to the student's overall average score. Areas in which the student scored below his or her own average may be targets for improvement.

■ *Combine test scores with other evaluations to better assess performance.* Compare test performance to work samples and everyday observa-

IN EACH CHAPTER OF THE TEXT, WE INTRODUCE YOU TO A FEW SPECIFIC STRATEGIES—
ANALYTICAL, CREATIVE, AND PRACTICAL—USED BY BOTH EXPERT TEACHERS AND EXPERT STUDENTS.

THE ANALYTICAL TEACHER: Lily puts together a spreadsheet on her computer to help her compare her own classroom objectives with the objectives covered by the standardized tests required in her school so that, later, she can decide which scores are most meaningful to her and her students.

THE CREATIVE TEACHER: Lily tells a few jokes to help her students relax during breaks in the standardized testing session.

THE PRACTICAL TEACHER: One of Lily's students feels bad because his percentile scores on the standardized achievement test are below the national average. Lily helps the student see that he is making progress by pointing out the scores that show how much of the material covered by the test the student has actually mastered.

She also pulls his scores from the previous year from his file to show him how much he has improved in just one year.

THE ANALYTICAL STUDENT: Ethan uses the practice test session to develop a list of possible hazards for misreading the instructions on the upcoming standardized test.

THE CREATIVE STUDENT: Ethan substitutes several key words that clarify standardized test directions for the words of a popular song. During the test, he silently sings the song to himself as a reminder to look for key words in the test instructions.

THE PRACTICAL STUDENT: When Ethan looks at his score report, he realizes it shows areas in which he is strong and areas in which he can improve his performance.

tions. For example, Jolene Johnson noticed the incoherent book reports turned in by one of her third-grade students. The student's test scores on reading comprehension and language expression, however, were well above average. Jolene realized that the student was waiting until the night before the paper was due to read the book and then slap together a book report. Jolene can now work with the student on the true problem: time management.

■ *Evaluate the performance of the class as a whole.* Suppose an elementary school teacher notices that his or her class does much better on the science subtests than on the English ones. If the class has many students whose first language is not English, the teacher may wish to request help from the school's ESL program. If the students are mostly native English speakers, however, the teacher may wish to look closely at his lessons and the time spent on science relative to English. He could look for ways to add enjoyment, as well as rigor, to English lessons.

Assessing Test Quality

Most of the standardized tests that teachers give their students are mandated by the school, school district, or state in which the school is located. Teachers may even encounter nationally mandated standardized tests. In such cases, teachers have little or no say over what tests are given or whether the tests are to be given at all. Sometimes, however, teachers and administrators have the opportunity to choose the standardized tests their students will take. After deciding what type of test they need, a group assigned to choose a standardized test must determine the quality of the various tests available. How do teachers and administrators pick a high-quality test?

Assessing the quality of a standardized test is a fairly involved procedure. It usually is done by school psychologists or others with advanced training in assessment. These professionals assess the test in a number of ways, such as whether the test predicts what it is supposed to predict. They also consider the appropriateness of the test for the students who will be taking it. To assess the fit of the test, professionals must understand the population to which test results are intended to apply and the samples, or members of that population, who help construct the test.

 ## POPULATIONS AND SAMPLES

The **population** is the complete set of individuals to which a set of results will be generalized (Rosnow & Rosenthal, 1999). For example, if test constructors are interested in constructing a test for third graders, the (imaginary) Whiz-Bang Intelligence Scale, the population would be all third graders to which they wish to generalize their results. It is important that they think carefully about this group. Are they talking about all third graders in a school, a school district, a state, a country, or even the world? There is a difference in how one interprets the results. Countries vary drastically in the educational expectations they hold for schoolchildren.

When state departments of education construct tests for pupils in their state, they are usually interested in generalizing only to pupils in their state. The goal is to understand what pupils in that state have learned, and to compare pupils and school districts within that state to each other. When a test publisher creates a standardized test, the publisher is usually concerned with national comparisons. But if the test is used in another country, the population will change, and the standardization that held for the one country will almost certainly *not* apply to the other country.

A *sample* is a subset of a population (Kish, 2000). Test constructors are almost never able to try out their test on all the members of the population of interest. For example, it is not feasible to try out a test for third graders on every third grader in the United States. Thus test constructors have to content themselves with a sample, or portion of the population.

Suppose test constructors want to standardize the Whiz-Bang test for third graders in the United States. They can sample in two basic ways: In the first, called a *random sample,* every member of the population has an equal chance of being drawn for the sample. Thus, for the Whiz-Bang test, a truly random sample is one in which any third grader in the country has an equal chance of being included in the tryout. Such sampling is not practical, because test constructors do not have complete access to every third grader in the country that they would need to generate a truly random sample.

In the second way of sampling, called a *stratified random sample,* the test constructors make sure they proportionately take into account, in the group on which they try out the test, all of the characteristics that might be relevant to the scores that people receive. The sample is random within each stratified group (Rosnow & Rosenthal, 1999). What are some of the likely characteristics along which a test constructor might want to stratify the Whiz-Bang test? One is likely to be gender. Assuming the population consists of roughly one-half boys and one-half girls, they will want their sample to reflect this distribution of boys and girls. A second characteristic may be ethnic group. The test constructors will want to sample members of diverse ethnic groups, about in proportion to their appearance in the third-grade population of the country. A third characteristic may be type of community, such as urban, suburban, and rural. A fourth characteristic may be socioeconomic level. The goal is to ensure that the sample on which the test constructors build their test adequately reflects the population to which they wish to generalize.

A good stratified sample—in which the balance of relevant attributes in the sample is the same as that in the population—is called a *representative sample.* A representative sample is one that takes into account the distribution of relevant characteristics of the

THINKING CREATIVELY

Why is it important to specify the population to which you wish to generalize results from a test?

SUGGESTION: If the population is not specified, you cannot determine whether a test is applicable to a given individual.

population as a whole. Test publishers generally stratify their samples, although they do not always achieve fully representative samples.

If the population and sampling of a test seem appropriate, teachers and administrators must then assess two other important measures of test quality: reliability and validity.

RELIABILITY

Reliability is the consistency of test results (Anastasi & Urbina, 1997; Fekken, 2000; Johnson & Christensen, 2000; Megargee, 2000). If, for example, one of Jolene Johnson's students takes the Whiz-Bang test repeatedly, and (assuming the student's ability remains the same) keeps getting exactly the same score, Jolene can conclude that the test measurements are highly reliable. However, if the student's scores are very different each time he or she takes the test, Jolene will conclude that the test measurements are not very reliable. Reliability is usually expressed as a proportion, on a scale that ranges from 0 to 1, with decimal numbers near 0 indicating low reliability, and numbers nearer 1 indicating high reliability.

There are several different ways to measure reliability, each relying on a somewhat different aspect of consistency (Gliner & Morgan, 2000). For example, test constructors may give the same test to the same group of students more than one time, to determine *test-retest reliability*. Test constructors may also wish to determine whether measurements from two or more slightly different versions of the same test are consistent with one another, that is, to find *alternate-forms reliability*. To determine this, they administer the different versions to a group of students and compare the results on each version.

Another way to calculate reliability is to compare students' performance on one part of the test with their performance on another part. This kind of *internal-consistency reliability* is often determined simply by dividing the test questions in half and comparing the two halves of the test, known as *split-half reliability*. Finally, for tests such as essay tests, in which a subjective judgment is required by graders, test constructors try to determine *interrater reliability*, or the extent to which two or more evaluators of a given response (such as an essay) rate the response in the same way.

The reliability of standardized tests varies according to the method used, but it is generally high. One team of researchers suggested that well-constructed standardized tests used to make decisions about individuals should have a test-retest reliability of about .90, alternate-forms reliability of about .85, and split-half reliability of about .95. There is somewhat more variation in internal-consistency reliabilities, such as split-half reliability, across standardized tests than there is in test-retest and alternate-forms reliabilities. Standardized tests divided into subtests generally have high split-half reliabilty for the test as a whole, but not necessarily for each of the subtests.

On average, longer tests tend to be more reliable in the measurement they provide than do shorter tests because the more items there are, the better the estimate of the level a person shows on the construct or attribute being assessed. To pick an extreme example, suppose you attempted to measure a person's achievement in the sciences with a five-item test. You would not expect much consistency across different forms of five-item tests, for they are just too short to provide any kind of adequate measurement. If even one item were a bad item susceptible to error of measurement, it would have a substantial effect on reliability. On the other hand, with 500 items, you would expect the errors of measurement to cancel each other out, so you would get a fairly consistent measure of science knowledge. One bad item would have little effect.

A second major factor affecting reliability of the test results often is the variation of the individuals being tested in terms of the construct being assessed. Here, too, test results from a large range of people in terms of the construct being measured also tend

THINKING CREATIVELY

If you were developing a standardized test, what attributes of the school population would you take into account to ensure a representative sample of students?

SUGGESTION: Examples are sex and grade.

THINKING CREATIVELY

Name at least three common sources of nonability-related effects in standardized testing that may distort the accuracy of the scores obtained.

SUGGESTION: Examples are distracting noises, poor lighting, and poor temperature regulation in the testing room.

to be more reliable than those from a small one. To take an extreme example, suppose everyone you plan to test has almost the same level of achievement. It will be extremely difficult to develop a test that consistently distinguishes among them, because they are hardly different at all. For example, try consistently measuring differences in height between people, all of whom are between 5 feet 6 inches and 5 feet 6 $\frac{1}{2}$ inches! It is difficult to distinguish among people within such a narrow range. It is not hard to construct a test that consistently distinguishes among people with broad ranges of abilities or achievements—in our example, analogous to heights ranging from 5 feet to 6 feet.

 VALIDITY

Whereas reliability refers to how confident you can be in a test as you use it from time to time, **validity** refers to the degree to which a test provides measurements that are appropriate for its intended purpose (Anastasi & Urbina, 1997; Krueger & Kling, 2000; Megargee, 2000). There are several different kinds of validity. We discuss three that are especially important to teaching and learning.

■ **PREDICTIVE VALIDITY** **Predictive validity** refers to the extent to which a test predicts a performance that will be demonstrated after the test has been taken (Gliner & Morgan, 2000). When such a prediction is made, the test is referred to as the *predictor*, that is, the thing doing the forecasting of future results, and the outcome to be predicted is referred to as the *criterion*. For example, tests of intelligence are often used as predictors of later school achievement, in general. Tests of readiness for reading are used as predictors of how well a child will be able to learn how to read. School achievement and reading ability are the criteria being predicted in these two examples.

Predictive validities are expressed using a correlation coefficient, which ranges from –1 (perfect inverse relation) to 0 (no relation) to 1 (perfect positive relation). A perfectly predictive test has a predictive validity of 1 (or –1) with respect to the criterion. For example, if a perfectly valid test provides results predicting a measure of school achievement, such as grades, as the criterion, you can forecast with absolute accuracy the grades each student will achieve. The correlation coefficient in this example is 1. Such tests, of course, do not really exist. A test with no predictive value at all in its measurements has a predictive validity of 0 with respect to the criterion; in this case, knowing the test score will tell you absolutely nothing about what grades students will achieve. A test for which higher scores are perfectly predictive of lower scores on the criterion has a predictive validity of –1. For example, a high score on a particular test might accurately predict a poor grade in the class.

Realistically, most predictive validities are greater than 0 but less than 1. What constitutes a good validity coefficient is largely a measure of subjective judgment: Anything significantly greater than 0 indicates some level of prediction. Typical ability tests predict school grades with validity coefficients ranging from about .3 to .6, but many tests fall outside this range.

The closer in time one measurement is to another, the higher the two measurements are likely to correlate. For example, achievement in fourth grade is likely to be a better predictor of achievement in fifth grade than it is a predictor of achievement in eleventh grade.

Predictive validities are lowered when there is *restriction of range,* the difference between the highest and lowest scores. Consider the case of students applying to a competitive college. If only students with *SAT* scores of 1350 or higher are admitted, by definition most students admitted will have *SAT*s that are roughly comparable, because the *SAT* only goes up to 1600. However, some of the students at the competitive college are bound to get poor grades. It is difficult to use the *SAT* to predict who these students will be, because the *SAT* scores are all roughly comparable. Even though the *SAT* might pre-

THINKING CREATIVELY

What factor might increase the predictive validity of measurements from a test for predicting some kind of criterion? What factor might undermine predictive validity?

SUGGESTION: Predictive validity tends to increase as a test is more similar in its content to what it is supposed to predict. Predictive validity tends to go down as the test becomes less similar to what it is supposed to predict. Say, for example, that a test is intended to measure reading comprehension. The test's predictive validity will be higher if the students are required to read passages from a work of literature. The test's predictive validity will be lower if the students are required to read mathematical word problems written in a language the students do not understand.

Two middle school students share excitement at their friend's good report card grades. Intelligence tests are often used as predictors of future school achievement, in general. (David Young-Wolff, Stone)

dict freshman-year college grades for a wide range of students, the *SAT* will not be able to predict college grades as well for students at this school.

■ **CONTENT VALIDITY** **Content validity** is the extent to which the content of a test actually measures the knowledge or skills the test is supposed to measure (Gliner & Morgan, 2000). If, for example, a general test of mathematical achievement for high school juniors were to include only plane geometry items, it would be seen as having relatively low content validity. A more valid test would include algebra as well, and probably arithmetical operations, too. Content validity is typically judged by a panel of experts. It is not expressed in terms of a single number, but rather as a consensus judgment that a test's content is either appropriate or not.

Content validity must also be considered in terms of the particular curriculum used in a classroom, school, or district. Teachers should play an important role in evaluating the content validity of an achievement test, because they are the ones who best know what they teach (or should be teaching). Teachers should also assess the content validity of the tests they develop themselves. Thus we return to the issue of how the test fits the students who will be taking it. Consider, for example, teachers and administrators in a school that embraces a curriculum emphasizing expressiveness and creativity in writing over the mechanical skills of writing, such as spelling and punctuation. These teachers and administrators might decide that an English achievement test composed primarily of multiple-choice questions about writing mechanics lacks content validity for evaluating their students.

■ **CONSTRUCT-RELATED VALIDITY** All the kinds of validity just discussed are subsets of construct-related validity. **Construct-related validity,** sometimes called simply **construct validity,** is the extent to which a test completely and accurately captures the theoretical construct or attribute it is designed to measure (Cohen & Swerdlik, 1999; Gliner & Morgan, 2000).

Suppose, for example, you want to develop a test of memory abilities. Your test will be construct valid to the extent that it fully and fairly measures the various aspects of memory. These aspects will depend on the theory of memory you accept. Recall from Chapter 8 that there are various alternative theories of memory. Exactly how you test memory depends on which of these theories you accept. Whatever the theory, you will almost certainly want to use a variety of kinds of memory items in your test. For example, you might include items requiring students to recall lists of words, or recognize which items of a set of words were presented earlier. The goal is to ensure that you have captured your particular idea of memory as completely as possible.

Once an appropriate test has been chosen and administered to students, teachers and other professionals such as guidance counselors and school psychologists are faced with the task of deciding what the test scores mean to them and their students.

Interpreting Standardized Test Scores

Teachers are expected to know how to interpret the results of standardized tests for students, parents, and even other teachers and administrators. Often, students' scores are mailed to schools by the testing companies or scoring agencies to which the completed tests were sent for scoring. For some standardized tests, teachers themselves must know how to score the tests, using scoring keys and answer guidelines distributed with the tests. Many times, several types of scores are calculated for the same test. Expert teachers understand how different types of scores are calculated, what each type of score means, and the implications of each type of score for teaching and learning.

STATISTICAL CONCEPTS UNDERLYING TEST SCORES

To understand standardized tests and to use and interpret these tests effectively, expert teachers must also understand several basic statistical concepts that underlie these tests, including frequency distributions, measures of central tendency and dispersion, the relationship of scores to the normal distribution, and the statistical significance of scores.

■ **FREQUENCY DISTRIBUTIONS AND GRAPHS**   Values obtained on a test are sometimes shown via a **frequency distribution,** a numerical display of the number or proportion of student scores at each score level or interval. An example of a frequency distribution appears in Table 13.1. The table shows, for example, that 10 students received a score of 45 on a hypothetical test.

The frequency distribution enables us to distinguish between two kinds of numbers at each score level. The *relative frequency* represents the number of students who receive a given score. In Table 13.1, for example, the relative frequency of a score of 45 is 10 percent—that is, 10 percent of the test takers scored 45. The *cumulative frequency* represents the number of students who received scores up to that level—in other words, at that level or lower. Thus, as shown in Table 13.1, the cumulative frequency for a score of 45 is 90 percent. A student who scored 45 did the same as or better than 90 percent of all the students who took the test.

TABLE **13.1**   A Sample Frequency Distribution

Score	Frequency	Relative Frequency	Cumulative Frequency
40	5	5%	5%
41	10	10%	15%
42	15	15%	30%
43	25	25%	55%
44	25	25%	80%
45	10	10%	90%
46	3	3%	93%
47	2	3%	95%
48	2	2%	97%
49	2	2%	99%
50	1	1%	100%

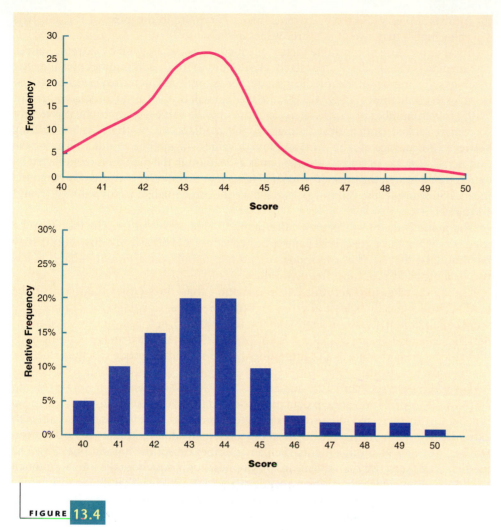

FIGURE 13.4

Graphing Frequency Distribution

Scores on standardized tests can also be represented graphically. Figure 13.4 illustrates the two main kinds of graphic distributions, bar graphs and line graphs. The bar graph shows frequencies as a set of usually vertical (but occasionally horizontal) bars, and the line graph shows frequencies as a series of connected line segments. In addition to frequencies, both kinds of graphs can also display levels of performance achieved on different tests or subtests. For example, a bar graph can show the number of correct answers on each of seven tests of knowledge.

■**MEASURES OF CENTRAL TENDENCY**   In addition to knowing the frequencies of various scores, teachers who want to evaluate their students need to know what constitutes a typical score. Measures of central tendency show the most typical value or score for the population. There are three major measures of central tendency: the mean, the median, and the mode.

The **mean** is the arithmetic average of a set of numbers. To compute the mean, add up all the values of interest and divide by the number of values added. For example, consider the mean of the numbers 2, 3, and 4. Here, we compute the mean by finding that $2 + 3 + 4 = 9$; $9 / 3 = 3$; thus the mean of the values 2, 3, and 4 is 3. The mean is a measure of central tendency that takes into account all the information about the values in a sample. But the mean is also very affected by extreme values. For example, the mean of 1, 1, and 10 is 4, a value higher than two of the three values in the sample.

Another measure of central tendency, the median, is less affected by extreme values. The **median** is the middle of an ordered set of values. With an odd number of values, the median is the number in the middle in value. For example, if you have five values ranked from lowest to highest (2, 5, 9, 12, 18), the median will be the third (middle) value (9). With an even number of values, there is no one middle value. For example, if you have six values ranked from lowest to highest, the median will be the number halfway between (the average of) the third and fourth values—again, the middle. Thus for the numbers 2, 6, 8, 14, 18, and 20, the median is 11. Although the median is less affected by extreme values than the mean, the median takes into account less information than the mean. For example, the values 1, 1, and 2 have the same median as the values 1, 1, and 10 (namely 1).

The **mode** is the most frequent value of an ordered set of values. The mode can be used only when there are at least some repeated values. On occasion, a distribution may be **bimodal**—that is, it has two modes; or, more generally, **multimodal**—that is, it has two or more modes, or most frequent values.

The mode takes into account less information than does either the mean or the median, and typically is least affected by extreme values. Consider, for example, the scores of eight individuals on a hypothetical test: 2, 3, 3, 3, 4, 4, 5, 6. In this set of numbers, the mean is 3.75, or $(2 + 3 + 3 + 3 + 4 + 4 + 5 + 6) / 8$; the median is 3.5, or the middle value between the fourth and fifth values (3 and 4); and the mode is 3, the value that occurs most frequently.

The mean has a substantial advantage over the other two measures: It fully takes into account the information at each data point—each individual test score. Thus the mean is generally the preferred measure of central tendency. But the mean is also sensitive to extremes. For example, in our sample set of scores, if an additional value is 33, the mean will be 7 (or 63 / 9), a value higher than any number except the highest one (33). The median is less sensitive than the mean to extremes, but it does not take into account all the information in the values. The main advantage of the mode is that it is an easily computed measure of central tendency; the main disadvantage is that it takes into account the least information of all.

■ **MEASURES OF DISPERSION**   It is also useful to understand how scores are dispersed or distributed; for example, students' scores may be widely scattered—that is, some students may have scored high and others low; or tightly clustered—that is, all students may have scored roughly the same. It generally is easier to interpret differences between scores when they are more widely distributed than when they are tightly clustered around the mean. Here, we discuss two commonly used measures of dispersion.

The first measure of dispersion is the **range,** the distance between the lowest and the highest values in a distribution. For example, the range of the scores 2, 3, 4, 5, 6 is 4. Other measures take more information into account.

A second measure of dispersion is the **standard deviation,** the adjusted average dispersion of values around the mean. The standard deviation, unlike the range, takes into account all information in the distribution of scores. To compute the standard deviation, you must know the mean of a group of scores. You then use the following steps:

1. Compute the difference between each value and the mean;

2. Square (multiply by itself) each difference (to eliminate negative signs);

3. Sum, or add up, all the squared differences;

4. Find the average, or mean, of the sum of squared differences by dividing the total from step 3 by the number of scores; and

5. Take the square root of this average, in order to bring the final value back to the original scale.

Let's compute the standard deviation of 2, 3, 4, 5, and 6. The mean of the scores 2, 3, 4, 5, 6 is 4. The differences between each value and the mean are 2, 1, 0, 1, and 2. Thus the squared differences of each value from the mean are 4, 1, 0, 1, and 4. The sum of the squared differences is 10. Dividing by 5, the number of scores, gives an average of 2. But this value is still one in squared units. Hence we must compute the square root of the value. The square root of 2 is about 1.41, which is the standard deviation.

The standard deviation is a measure of variability, telling us how much scores differ from the mean, on average. At one extreme, if all values are equal to the mean, the standard deviation is 0. At the opposite extreme, the maximum value of the standard deviation is half the value of the range (for numerical values that are maximally spread apart).

Sometimes dispersion among scores is measured by an index called the **variance,** the value of the standard deviation squared. This measure is particularly useful when various statistical analyses need to be carried out.

■**NORMAL DISTRIBUTION** Many standardized tests have patterns of scores that fall roughly into what is called a normal distribution. In a **normal distribution,** most data values cluster around the average value of the distribution. (In a truly normal distribution, the mean, median, and mode are all the same; thus any of them can be used as the average.) Figure 13.5 shows an example of a normal distribution. The normal distribution of scores is symmetrical; half the scores fall below the average, and the other half above. In general, measured values rapidly decline on each side of the center of the distribution and then tail off more slowly as scores get more extreme. Most people have scores relatively close to the center of the distribution and relatively few people have scores at the extremes. If the scores on a standardized test fall into a normal distribution, roughly 68 percent of the scores in the distribution are between plus or minus one standard deviation of the mean, and roughly 95 percent are between plus or minus two standard deviations of the mean.

TYPES OF SCORES

Many different types of scores are used to describe students' performance. Expert teachers are aware not only of the different types of scores, but also of how these scores compare to one another in terms of the information they provide.

Figure 13.6 on page 488 shows a score report from an achievement test, the Terra Nova California Achievement Test (2nd ed.), for Ken Jones, a hypothetical fourth-grade student. The figure makes it clear that you are likely to encounter several different types of scores, even for the same standardized test. Refer to Figure 13.6 as we discuss the most common scores.

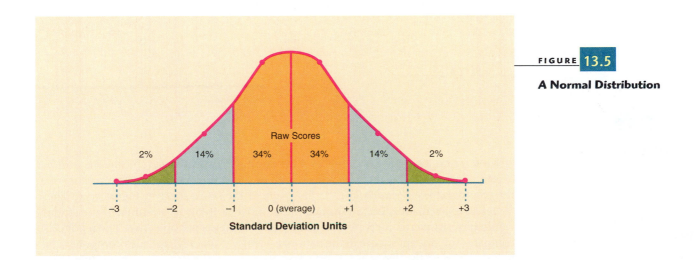

FIGURE 13.5

A Normal Distribution

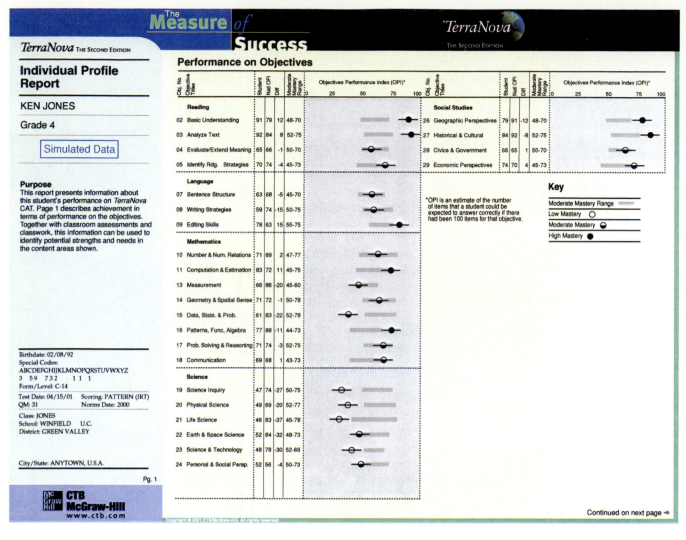

Continued on next page ➡

CAT COMPLETE BATTERY

Individual Profile Report

Simulated Data

Norm-Referenced Scores	Scale Score	Grade Equiv.	National Stanine	National Percentile	NP Range	National Percentile Scale
Reading	677	5.8	6	65	55–75	
Language	657	4.3	5	53	43–60	
Mathematics	699	6.8	7	82	74–89	
Total Score**	681	5.8	6	72	60–81	
Science	671	4.4	5	55	45–66	
Social Studies	669	4.7	5	58	48–68	

**Total Score consists of Reading, Language, and Mathematics.

National Stanine Scale

FIGURE 13.6

A Typical Score Report
Individual Profile Report from TERRANOVA, The Second Edition. Copyright © 2001 by CTB/McGraw-Hill. All rights reserved. Reprinted by permission.

■ **RAW SCORES** The first score to understand is the **raw score,** typically the number of items correctly answered. The raw scores for each performance objective are shown in the column labeled *Student* on the first page of the score sheet in Figure 13.6. These scores have been adjusted to estimate the number of items it is estimated the student would have answered correctly had there been 100 items per objective. The report also compares the student's score to the national average (Natl OPI) and also computes a difference between the two scores (Diff). For example, on the Basic Understanding objective of reading, Ken's score was 91, which was 12 points above the national average. Because raw scores are hard to interpret on standardized tests, these scores are often converted into other types of scores, such as percentile scores.

■**PERCENTILE SCORES** Sometimes we wish to have a direct comparison of a person's performance with that of other people—to make a normative comparison. A useful kind of score for this purpose is the **percentile score,** which is the proportion of other students' scores that equal or fall below a given student's score, multiplied by 100. The percentile scores for Ken Jones shown in the column labeled *National Percentile.* Ken's percentile score for the language section is in the 53rd percentile. Thus 53 percent of the fourth graders across the nation who took this test scored at or below Ken's raw score. Ken is very slightly above average in language compared with his peers.

Just as practice improves musical abilities, so can practice improve student performance on standardized tests. (Bob Daemmrich Photos, Inc.)

Note the difference between raw scores, especially when they are expressed in percentages and percentile scores. The percentage score pertains to the proportion of items on a test that are answered correctly. The percentile score pertains to an individual's standing on a given test relative to other individuals. Thus percentile scores are a measure of comparison against other students, rather than of direct performance. Expressed in terms used earlier in the chapter, percentile scores are based on norms rather than criteria.

■**TRUE SCORES** A useful distinction to make is that between two different kinds of scores: *observed scores* and *true scores* (Cohen & Swerdlik, 1999; Gregory, 2000). An **observed score** is the score someone actually receives on a test. For example, Ken's percentile score on the mathematics section is 82.

Suppose that Ken takes the test again. Chances are he will not receive a percentile score of exactly 82. Maybe he will get a score of 78, or 85. Maybe his score will change more dramatically. Test constructors differentiate between the observed score and the **true score,** the hypothetical score someone would get if he or she took a test an infinite number of times with no practice effects in taking the test. Earlier in the chapter we described some of the factors that can keep an observed score from being a measure of a student's true abilities. The student can get a cold or be unmotivated to try hard on the test. A student might also receive a higher observed score than his or her true score. For example, the student may have just finished studying a book that includes the passage that tests reading comprehension.

Although you might want to determine the true score by giving a test many times, in reality, when people take a test multiple times, they begin to show *practice effects.* Practice effects are changes in score that occur as a result of increasing familiarity with the particular items, the test as a whole, and the experience of taking the test. For the purposes of thinking about true scores, we ignore practice effects.

A true score is obviously a hypothetical construct: We can never know what a person's true score would be, because no one is able to take a test an infinite number of times. However, it is possible to estimate how likely it is that a student's observed score is similar to his or her true score. Whenever a person gets a score, it actually represents a range of scores that the person

THINKING ANALYTICALLY

What *is* the difference between a score of 75 percent and a score in the 75th percentile? Can a score of 75 percent be in the 75th percentile?

SUGGESTION: The 75 percent is calculated on the total number of test items. The 75th percentile is calculated with respect to other individuals. A score of 75 percent can be, but need not be, in the 75th percentile.

A teacher confers with parents to explain a student's results on a standardized test. The expert teacher plans nontechnical explanations for parents, practices the explanations to make sure that they are clear, and always makes clear how the test scores will be used by the school. (Mark Burnett, Stock Boston)

might plausibly receive. Sometimes teachers and test developers use the concept of a **confidence interval** to determine the likely range of scores within which a person's true score lies. A confidence interval is the probability that a person's true score falls within a certain range of the observed score. The measure used to express a confidence interval is called the **standard error of measurement.** In Ken's score report, there is a column labeled *NP Range.* This column shows the range of observed scores within which Ken's true score is likely to fall. The chances are about two out of three that his true score falls within this range.

To be a bit more precise, if we assume a normal distribution of test scores, the chances that a person's true score will lie within plus or minus one standard error of measurement of the observed score are about 68 percent, and the chances that the score will lie within plus or minus two standard errors are about 95 percent. There is a 95 percent chance that Ken's true score lies between these two scores. For Ken, the chances are about 68 percent that his true reading percentile score falls between 55 and 75, and about 95 percent that his true math percentile score falls between 45 and 85.

■ **STANDARD SCORES** Standard scores, also called *z*-scores, derive from converting a raw score into units of standard deviation. Standard scores are arbitrarily defined to have a mean of 0 and a standard deviation of 1. If the scores fall into a normal distribution, roughly 68 percent of the scores will be between −1 and 1, and roughly 95 percent of the scores will be between −2 and 2.

Standard scores are useful because they make it possible to compare results that initially are on different scales. For example, a teacher using standard scores can compare a student's scores for two tests, one on a 100-point scale and one on a 30-point scale. If

THINKING ANALYTICALLY

Sometimes college admissions officers take scores from several administrations of a given test, such as the *SAT* or *ACT,* and use only the highest of the scores in evaluating a candidate for admission. Which do you think will give a better estimate of a person's true score—the highest score obtained or the average score obtained? Why?

SUGGESTION: The average score is a better estimate because it is based on more information.

the mean on the first test is 75 points and the mean on the second test is 20 points, both of these scores will correspond to a *z*-score of 0, the mean value for *z*-scores. To compute a standard score for a student, you need to know the mean and the standard deviation of the distribution of raw scores. Then, you:

1. Subtract the mean raw score from the student's raw score;

2. Divide the difference (the number found in step 1) by the standard deviation of the distribution of raw scores.

Thus, the formula for a *z*-score is:

(observed score − mean raw score)/standard deviation

The *z*-score tells teachers how many standard deviations above or below the mean a raw score is. For example, a raw score that is one standard deviation above the mean yields a *z*-score of 1. A raw score that is two standard deviations below the mean translates into a *z*-score of −2. Even if one test is harder than another test, translating two raw scores from two tests into standard scores is comparable because the scores are phrased in common terms: standard deviations from the mean.

Many standardized tests use variants on standard scores. For example, the College Board scores many of its tests, such as the *SAT*, on a scale that has a range of 200 to 800, with a mean of 500 and a standard deviation of 100. Thus a *z*-score of 0 corresponds to an *SAT* score of 500, a *z*-score of 1 corresponds to an *SAT* score of 600, and so on. A variant of the College Board–type score is the **T-score,** which has a mean of 50 and a standard deviation of 10. Unfortunately, these two kinds of scores can lead users falsely to interpret small and insubstantial differences as meaningful.

Another type of standard score, the **stanine,** has a range of 1 to 9, a mean of 5, and a standard deviation of 2. The advantage of stanines is that they are relatively simple and make no pretense of being highly precise. The disadvantage of stanines is that their imprecision may blur meaningful differences in scores. The Terra Nova California Achievement Test uses stanine scores. The stanine score for Ken Jones is shown in Figure 13.6 in the column marked *National Stanine.* The stanine score of 6 on reading shows that Ken's raw score was about one-half of one standard deviation below the average for all students who took the test. Note that all the kinds of scores derived from *z*-scores are interchangeable through mathematical formulas.

■**GRADE EQUIVALENT SCORES**   Achievement tests also can be scored using the **grade equivalent score,** a measure of grade-level achievement compared with the normative sample for a given test. Say a student in the second month of the third grade scores at the same level on a test of mathematical computation as an average student in the sixth month of the fifth grade is expected to score on that test. Her grade equivalent will be 5 years, 6 months, sometimes abbreviated 5-6.

Teachers often like grade equivalents because they are used to thinking in terms of grade levels. Grade equivalents are often misleading, however (Campbell, 1994). Use them cautiously; even avoid them when possible. For example, Ken Jones's grade equivalent score, shown in Figure 13.6, is 6.8 in mathematics. Keep in mind, though, that the fact that a fourth grader receives a grade equivalent of sixth to seventh grade on a fourth-grade test does not mean the fourth grader can do sixth to seventh grade math. In fact, many of the tests for elementary school have grade equivalents going up to high school for tests that cover none of the algebra, geometry, or trigonometry covered in high school math classes. The same problem applies across the curriculum. These grade equivalents refer to how well students at these grades would be expected to do on the elementary school test, were they given this test: Because students in the higher grades typically take grade-appropriate tests but do not usually take elementary school tests, the grade equivalents are often misleading.

Implications for Teaching

- **Be prepared to explain the scores.** Make sure you fully understand each type of score included on test reports provided for students and parents. Plan nontechnical explanations for parents and students, and consider practicing the explanations to make sure they are clear. Explain norm-referenced versus criterion-referenced scores and describe how scores will be used by you or your school.

- **Explain errors of the measurement.** If a student's percentile score changes from a 97 to a 94, some students and parents may become alarmed. Point out the standard error of measurement, explaining that any score has a confidence interval and may actually reflect a true achievement above or below the actual number on the score sheet.

- **Focus on the entire student.** Avoid overemphasizing a single set of test scores. Scores reflect only one day's performance. If possible, combine news about test scores with information about students' work in class, to determine true patterns of achievement and ability. Teachers can use test scores as feedback to students to challenge them to set higher goals for themselves.

- **Use tests to set teaching and learning goals.** Comparisons of a student's overall average with scores on various subtests suggest areas in which the student needs improvement. Combining test scores with other performance evaluations, work with students and parents to target ways to improve in upcoming months. Teachers may choose to work with students to improve their test-taking skills.

- **Use achievement tests to build self-esteem.** Norm referencing can help build self-esteem when the student scores high in relation to other students who took the test. If unaddressed, lower norm-referenced scores may undermine students' motivation. However, even students with low norm-referenced scores are likely to show increases in their learning from year to year. Examine criterion-referenced scores or compare current test scores with previous scores to demonstrate these improvements.

Issues and Concerns in Standardized Testing

As the discussion of the challenges involved in presenting test scores points out, there are several potential pitfalls in using standardized tests. But some new developments in standardized testing show promise for overcoming some of the pitfalls. What are some of the larger issues involved in standardized testing?

Standardized tests, like most technology, can be helpful to teachers and students alike if they are used properly. But standardized tests can also be harmful if they are misused—for example, if they are biased in favor of one group of students at the expense of another group or if they do not work for students of certain cultural backgrounds. Even high-quality tests can be harmful if they are used for invalid purposes.

THINKING PRACTICALLY

What might be the costs to society of using biased standardized tests in the schools?

SUGGESTION: The society may deprive worthy individuals of opportunities they deserve.

Test bias refers to a test's being unfair for members of some groups but not for others. Whether a test is considered biased or not, however, depends in large part on exactly how bias is defined (Anastasi & Urbina, 1997; Cronbach, 1990).

The most naive way of defining test bias is to state that a test is biased if there is a difference between groups in scores. For example, some groups have challenged the use of standardized college entrance examinations on the basis of the fact that African American and Hispanic American students consistently score lower on these tests than do white and Asian American students. Courts have occasionally ruled in favor of such challenges, but such legal views can be based on a false assumption that groups will not differ in the construct being measured. For instance, as different ethnic groups differ in average height, weight, hair color, eye color, and many other features, there is no reason to assume in principle that they could not differ in whatever is being tested.

A second way to define test bias is to view a test as biased if the content is judged by a panel of experts to favor certain groups over others. Most test publishers have panels of experts read test items carefully in order to search for bias against women, minorities, and members of other groups. The problem here is that the experts may be wrong. For instance, saying an item will discriminate against women does not necessarily make it so. And, of course, the experts may miss items that actually *are* discriminatory.

A third and more sophisticated view of test bias is that a test is biased if it either over-predicts or underpredicts some criterion or set of criteria for members of one group versus members of another. In overprediction, the test predicts a *higher* level of performance than a student actually achieves. In underprediction, the test predicts a *lower* level of performance than the student actually achieves. In other words, the predictive validity of the test varies between groups. Such a conception of test bias is illustrated in Figure 13.7. If scores on the fictional Whiz-Bang intelligence test described earlier predict school grades quite well for girls, but consistently underestimate the grades of boys, the test is biased in favor of girls (or, equivalently, against boys). As a result of the biased results, boys with low scores might not be admitted to advanced classes or other special programs in school, despite the fact that they can probably do as well as girls who had higher test scores.

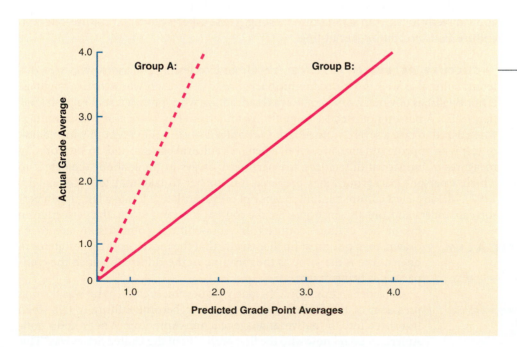

FIGURE 13.7

A Biased Test
These two line graphs show how the relationship between scores and performance measures would differ for a hypothetical test that more accurate predicts perform-ance for Group B than it does for Group A.

A kindergartner shows his anxiety as he works on a test. Many researchers and educators are strongly opposed to the use of readiness tests for grade placement, such as entering first grade. (Bob Daemmrich, Stock Boston)

By this definition of test bias, the tests most frequently used to measure abilities typically are not statistically biased (Reynolds, 1994). In other words, when members of a given group score lower on the tests—for example, tests of various abilities—their performance on the criteria to be predicted, such as school grades, is generally lower. Not everyone accepts this definition, however. Some people believe we need to view bias as part of a larger system, in which it is possible for the criteria (e.g., school grades) as well as the predictor test to be biased.

THE CULTURAL CONTEXT OF TESTING

Although we discussed cultural issues in general in Chapter 6, certain aspects of culture apply directly to issues in standardized testing. These aspects are called culture-relevant, culture-fair, and culture-free testing.

■ **CULTURE-RELEVANT TESTING** People go into testing situations with very different cultural as well as socioeconomic backgrounds. A person whose native language is not English is obviously going to be at a disadvantage when given a test in English (Sattler, 1992). A person not used to doing things under time pressure is at a disadvantage when asked to take a severely timed test. *Cultural relevance* is the extent to which a task or test is an appropriate measure, given a person's cultural background. In interpreting measures of individual differences, teachers need always to think about the extent to which a person's background has prepared him or her to take that test (Greenfield, 1997). Making a test culture relevant means not only translating it into a language a person can understand, but also ensuring that the content is meaningful to the person, given his or her cultural contexts. If cross-cultural comparisons are to be drawn, then one must further ensure that the meaning of the test items in one culture is the same as the meaning in the culture to which the comparison is being drawn.

Consider an example. Obviously, a question such as "Who was the first president of the United States?" does not become culturally fair when translated into the native language of a non-American. Why would a non-American even know who the first president of the United States was? This

THINKING ANALYTICALLY

Can you ever free a test completely of cultural influence? Why or why not?

SUGGESTION: Probably not. The very act of taking a test is culturally influenced.

person would be far more likely to know the first leader of his or her own country. However, changing the test item to read, "Who was the first president of your country?" does not achieve equivalence either. Why not? First, because the country may never have had a president, and second, because even if it has, the importance of the presidency in another country (e.g., one that also has a prime minister) may be different from that in the other country. (For more on these issues, see Ogbu, 1994).

■ **CULTURE-FAIR TESTING**   A **culture-fair test** has the same meaning for members of all cultures. This idea is different from that of culture relevance, where a test is designed to work for a particular culture, or occasionally, more than one culture.

True culture fairness is virtually impossible to achieve because people in different cultures have different language and educational backgrounds, different social backgrounds, different experience with and attitudes toward tests, and even different notions of how to perform in a testing situation.

■ **CULTURE-FREE TESTING**   A **culture-free test** is unaffected by culture or cultural context. It is hard to imagine constructing a test wholly unaffected by culture, because the very act of taking a test is a cultural act, and people bring to the testing situation their cultural background. Moreover, scores on tests always are interpreted in a cultural context by people who have grown up with certain cultural expectations.

Even tests that lack bias or achieve cultural relevance can be harmful if used for purposes for which they are not valid, as we discuss next.

 MISUSES OF STANDARDIZED TESTS

Two of the more common ways in which standardized test scores are misused in American schools are (1) their use as the sole basis for selection or placement decisions, and (2) their use as the primary way of judging the performance of a school, district, state, or even nation. Why are these inappropriate uses of standardized tests?

■ **HIGH-STAKES TESTING**   The use of test scores as the sole basis for making important decisions about a student's placement or admission to educational programs is sometimes called **high-stakes testing.** This use of tests was the concern parents often raised in conferences with McKinley Phillips, the teacher described at the beginning of the chapter. The pressure on students resulting from high-stakes testing has led many students to spend a great deal of time, effort, and money on test preparation courses in order to gain a competitive advantage on the tests. Some students have even resorted to cheating. As we have emphasized in this chapter, test scores alone cannot be expected to provide a complete picture of a student's achievements or abilities. Thus high-stakes testing practices may lead to mistakes in placement. Ideally, standardized test scores are combined with other methods of evaluation, such as grades, interviews, or observations, to make important decisions. Too often, however, this is not the case.

As most college students know, standardized tests such as the *SAT* and *ACT* often play a large part in the college admissions process. Test scores become even more important in the admissions process for graduate school, law school, and medical school. Standardized test scores also have been used to indicate placement along various tracks at the middle school or high school level. Many school districts and states even use **readiness tests** to measure the extent to which a student is prepared to learn something, such as reading, or the extent to which a child is ready for a grade placement, such as entering first grade. Many researchers and educators are strongly opposed to the use of readiness tests (see also Engel, 1991; Meisels, 1989; Shepard & Smith, 1989), because (1) very young children are generally not prepared for the kind of paper-and-pencil tests typically used to measure readiness; (2) delaying entrance into first grade on the basis of a readiness test is a gross overinterpretation of a single source of information; and (3) it is not clear that the tests accurately measure readiness.

Another kind of high-stakes standardized test is the **minimum-competency test,** which measures whether a student has attained the minimum level of overall achievement necessary for a particular purpose. Such tests are used, for example, to determine whether a student is eligible to graduate from high school. Forty U.S. states use minimum-competency tests, although not all of those states base graduation decisions on test scores. Opponents of minimum-competency tests believe that no one test should be of such great importance that a monumental decision, such as whether to graduate a student from high school, is based on that test score alone.

As an aspiring teacher, you may be exposed to a series of evaluations that may feel like high-stakes testing to you, the Praxis Series (Dwyer & Villegas, 1993). Three tests are included in the Praxis battery. States may require any or all of them as part of their teacher certification processes. The first, Praxis I, is taken early in your college career, to assess basic skills in reading, writing, and mathematics. Praxis II is taken at the end of your undergraduate studies and assesses mastery of your major subject and basic principles of teaching. The first two tests are the typical paper-and-pencil standardized tests described throughout most of this chapter, with which you are probably quite familiar. The third test in the Praxis battery, Praxis III, varies from state to state, but it generally consists of classroom observations of your teaching skills, made by trained local evaluators. The Praxis tests are an important requirement for teacher certification in many states, and it would certainly be wise for you to use all the methods you would recommend to your students to achieve your best performance on these tests.

■**OVERUSE OF TESTS IN MEASURING ACCOUNTABILITY** The Praxis tests may be popular among many states because they support the goal of a growing movement to hold teachers and schools accountable for meeting measurable educational outcomes. One of the factors many observers relate to the growth in the use of standardized tests in recent decades is an increasing interest among politicians, parents, and taxpayers in **accountability** from schools (Darling-Hammond & Snyder, 1992). These people believe that schools should set measurable goals for the education of children. Teachers and schools are then held responsible for the extent to which they meet their stated goals. The quantitative measurements provided by standardized tests, particularly those that pro-

Taking part in an authentic assessment, a fourth-grade student displays her portfolio project to her teacher and her classmates. Authentic assessments also include performance tests, which require students to solve problems hands-on, such as doing a physics experiment. Several states have adopted authentic assessments as either part or all of their statewide assessments. (Brian Smith)

vide criterion-referenced scores, have made the tests valuable tools to those who wish to measure and state the achievements of teachers and schools in numerical terms.

As we have emphasized, there are several problems with using standardized tests as the basis for judging teachers and schools. First, if the objectives measured by the standardized test in use do not fully match those of the school or school district, students may score low on objectives because they are not emphasized by the students' teachers. Teachers may then experience pressure from parents or administrators to raise test scores in an effort to prove they are providing quality education (Berliner & Biddle, 1997; Bracey, 1994; Herman, Abedi, & Golan, 1994). Some teachers can succumb to a temptation to change their learning objectives and lesson content so they coincide with the objectives and question content of the test their students must take, a phenomenon known as *teaching to the test*.

Another problem is that, in many cases, a movement that began with the goal of discovering, by means of criterion-referenced scores, exactly what content students were learning has evolved into a race for the best normative scores. A misplaced fixation on normative scores can have some destructive results. Schools and school districts in many areas have found themselves competing for students with the highest percentile scores. Property values in school districts with high test scores may rise as affluent parents move into the area, seeking what they perceive as the best education for their children, often meaning higher budgetary allotments for cash-strapped schools. Teachers and administrators in schools under financial and social pressure to keep normative scores high have, in some cases, resorted to unethical methods for raising school averages. An example is encouraging students with learning disabilities to avoid taking standardized tests solely to give the impression that the schools are doing better than they really are on the tests.

Just as no student's achievements or abilities can be judged fairly by his or her performance on a single standardized test, neither can the performance of a school be fairly judged in the way just described. The multiple-choice, norm-referenced standardized tests commonly used to evaluate school performance may not be able to measure some educational outcomes that are valued by society. For example, a school that emphasizes constructive learning based on experience and group discovery may have low scores on a standard multiple-choice test of accumulated knowledge (Taylor & Walton, 1997). Concerns about the limitations of some of the most commonly used standardized tests have led to the development of some new kinds of tests.

 ## NEW DIRECTIONS IN STANDARDIZED TESTING

Today, a number of new kinds of tests are being developed. One of the most important trends in standardized testing is the development of what are known as **authentic assessments,** tests designed to allow students to show their achievements or abilities in a real-life context (Wiggins, 1993, 1996–1997; Wolf, Bixby, Glenn, & Gardner, 1991; Worthen, 1993).

Different forms of authentic assessments have been developed, including performance tests, which require students to solve problems hands on, as in doing a science experiment, and portfolios, which require students to assemble their best work into a collection, much as an artist would (Hambleton, 1996). Several states have adopted authentic assessments, for either part or all of their statewide assessments. For example, Kentucky passed an Educational Reform Act in 1990 that identifies application of school-based knowledge to everyday life as an objective for students (National Commission on Testing and Public Policy, 1990).

An example of an authentic assessment is to ask students to plan and possibly carry out a simple science experiment. Another example is to ask a student to read a historical document and comment on why it is or is not a credible source. In the first instance, the goal is to assess the extent to which the student can think as a scientist does. In the second instance, the assessment is the extent to which the student can think like a historian. Such assessments are quite different from multiple-choice tests of factual recall or inferences from facts.

Performance assessments are often scored by means of *rubrics,* or formal specifications of criteria for evaluation (Mabry, 1999; Stiggins, 1997). For example, the evaluation of a historical document might use a rubric such as the following:

High = 5. The response is accurate, focused, coherent, and clearly articulated. The student shows firm understanding of bases for evaluating the credibility of a historical document, and of relating the document content to the historical context in which it was written. The response is insightful and draws connections among facts and ideas.

Medium = 3. The response is generally accurate and fairly coherent. The argument is focused but not necessarily compelling. Connections among ideas and between facts and ideas are not always well articulated. The response is at least somewhat insightful but generally does not contain any breakthrough ideas.

Low = 1. The response is often inaccurate and largely unfocused. Arguments are not clearly supported. Connections are either absent or weak. The response shows little grasp of the historical context in which the document was written.

We cover the use of authentic assessment in individual classrooms in some detail in Chapter 14, but special concerns arise when attempts are made to standardize authentic assessment (Worthen, 1993). The uniformity of experience for each student that is the hallmark of a standardized test is difficult to achieve in performance tests or portfolio evaluations. You must take special care to achieve interrater reliability, as discussed earlier in the chapter, if such assessments are to be useful in comparing ratings of students' performance from widely varying schools. In addition, you must take as much care as you have with traditional tests to assure that authentic assessments are valid. A performance test that requires a student to graph sets of numbers, for example, may lack content validity in just the same way as the math test we described earlier in the chapter that only tested plane geometry. As you will learn in detail in Chapter 14, authentic assessments, when they are carefully chosen, developed, and used, can be a useful addition to the present selection of ways to assess and compare students.

WHAT ARE STANDARDIZED TESTS?

- Standardized tests are measurement devices that have been given to many individuals, often across the nation, to develop appropriate content and scoring comparisons. They are administered and scored according to uniform procedures.

- Norm-referenced tests report scores in relation to a set of normative scores. Criterion-referenced tests report students' levels of mastery of a specific body of knowledge. In this chapter, we have primarily focused on maximal performance tests, although typical performance tests also are used in assessment.

TYPES OF STANDARDIZED TESTS

- Various types of standardized tests are available. Some of the most commonly used are intelligence tests, aptitude tests, vocational interest tests, and achievement tests.

- Intelligence tests yield a score known as the intelligence quotient, or IQ. Ratio IQs are formed by comparing a person's mental age with the person's chronological age. In contrast, deviation IQs compare performance with that of an average person of the same chronological age.

- Achievement tests are the most commonly used standardized tests in schools. Omnibus tests combine items of several types in one large test. Other tests divide items into groups of similar item types, or subtests.

ASSESSING TEST QUALITY

- Test quality can be assessed in many ways. One is to consider the samples of people used to develop the test, as well as the population for whom test scores are relevant. Random samples are very difficult for test developers to achieve. Test norms are instead based on stratified samples, including representative samples.

- Tests vary in their consistency of measurement, or reliability, and in the extent to which they measure what they are supposed to measure, or validity. Types of validity include content validity, predictive validity, and construct-related validity.

INTERPRETING STANDARDIZED TEST SCORES

- A number of statistics are used in interpreting group data from tests. These statistics include frequency distributions and measures of relative frequency and cumulative frequency; measures of central tendency (the mean, median, and mode); and measures of dispersion (range, standard deviation, and variance).

- A variety of kinds of scores can be used on standardized tests, such as raw scores, standard scores, including T-scores and stanine scores, percentile scores, or grade equivalents. We can distinguish between true and observed scores, but can only estimate the former, using confidence intervals and the standard error of measurement.

ISSUES AND CONCERNS IN STANDARDIZED TESTING

- Test bias means a test is unfair to members of certain groups. Cultural backgrounds of groups of students often are related to issues of test bias. It is possible, although difficult, to make tests culturally relevant. Culture fairness is often regarded as an ideal to be strived for rather than something that can be achieved, and many believe a truly culture-free test is simply impossible to construct.

- Tests are also used in the pursuit of accountability on the part of teachers and students. High-stakes testing and readiness scores can be misused, to the detriment of the students. Authentic assessments have been developed, in part, to address some of the potential misuses of traditional multiple-choice standardized tests.

Accountability Practice of evaluating teachers and schools for the extent to which they meet measurable educational goals. Page 496

Achievement test Test that measures accomplishments in either single or multiple areas of endeavor. Page 477

Authentic assessments Tests designed to allow students to show their achievements or abilities in a real-life context. Page 497

Bimodal (or **multimodal**) **distribution** Distribution that has two (or more) modes, or most frequent values. Page 486

Confidence interval Probability that a person's true test score falls within a certain range of the observed score. Page 489

Construct-related validity (or **construct validity**) Extent to which a test completely and accurately captures the theoretical construct or attribute it is designed to measure. Page 483

Content validity Extent to which the content of a test actually measures the knowledge or skills the test is supposed to measure. Page 483

Criterion-referenced tests Tests that measure a student's performance relative to what the student should know. Page 471

Culture-fair test Test that, in theory, would have the same meaning for members of all cultures. Page 494

Culture-free test Test that, in theory, would be completely unaffected by culture or cultural context. Page 494

Deviation IQ scores Intelligence test scores calculated on the basis of how high a person's score is relative to that of other people of his or her age. Page 477

Differential Aptitude Tests Tests designed to measure abilities developed over a period of years that predict success in particular areas of endeavor. Page 477

Frequency distribution Numerical display of the number or proportion of student scores at each score level or interval. Page 484

Grade equivalent score Measure of grade-level achievement in comparison with the normative sample for a given test. Page 491

High-stakes testing Use of test scores as the sole basis for making decisions important to the lives of students. Page 495

Intelligence quotient (IQ) Measure of intelligence comparing mental age to chronological age, multiplied by 100. Page 476

Mean Arithmetical average of a set of numbers. Page 485

Median Middle of an ordered set of values. Page 486

Minimum-competency test Test that measures whether a student has attained the minimum level of overall achievement necessary for a particular purpose. Page 496

Mode Most frequent value of an ordered set of values. Page 486

Normal distribution Commonly occurring distribution of test scores in which most data values cluster around the average value. Page 487

Norm-referenced tests Tests that compare test takers' scores with the average performance of the test takers. Page 470

Norms, or **normative scores** Test scores that reflect the performance of individuals in the population of interest. Page 471

Observed score Score someone actually receives on a test. Page 489

Percentile score Proportion of other students' scores that equal or fall below a given student's own score. Page 488

Population Complete set of individuals to which a set of results will be generalized. Page 480

Predictive validity Extent to which a test predicts a performance that will be demonstrated after the test has been taken. Page 482

Range Difference between the lowest and the highest values in a distribution, or group of test scores. Page 486

Raw score Number of test items correctly answered. Page 488

Readiness tests Tests intended to measure the extent to which a student is prepared to learn something. Page 495

Reliability Consistency of test results. Page 481

Standard deviation Measure indicating the adjusted average dispersion of values, such as test scores, around the mean, or average, value. Page 486

Standard error of measurement Measure used to express a confidence interval. Page 490

Standard scores (or **z-scores**) Test scores that derive from converting a raw score into units of standard deviation. Standard scores are arbitrarily defined to have a mean of 0 and a standard deviation of 1. Page 490

Standardized test Test that has been given to many individuals, often across the nation, to develop appropriate content and scoring comparisons and that is administered and scored according to uniform procedures. Page 470

Stanine score Standard test score that has a range of 1 to 9, a mean of 5, and a standard deviation of 2. Page 491

Test bias Tendency for a test to be unfair for members of some groups but not others. Page 492

True score Hypothetical test score a person would get if he or she took a test an infinite number of times with no practice effects. Page 489

T-score Type of standard score that has a mean of 50 and a standard deviation of 10. Page 491

Validity Degree to which a test provides measurements that are appropriate for its intended purpose. Page 482

Variance Value of the standard deviation squared, an index that measures dispersion among scores. Page 487

Vocational interest test Test designed to help students decide where their vocational interests lie. Page 477

Apply the concepts you have learned in this chapter to the following problems of classroom practice.

IN ELEMENTARY SCHOOL

1. How would you explain the importance of sitting through an entire standardized testing session to a fourth grader who is hyperactive? What are some strategies you might use to help the student complete the test?

2. What are some ways you could ensure that your second graders understand the instructions for a standardized test?

3. How would you adjust your fifth-grade reading lessons if you noticed that nearly all your students had low scores on the vocabulary portion of a standardized test, although they scored well on the other reading objectives?

4. How would you respond to the parents of a kindergartner who did not score well on the first-grade readiness test? What could you do if you were convinced the low test score did not truly reflect the student's readiness for first grade?

5. Nearly all of your third-grade class scored below average on the statewide achievement test last year. You are now under pressure from the principal to bring up this year's scores. What are some ways you could improve scores, without teaching to the test?

IN MIDDLE SCHOOL

1. Your seventh graders have taken so many standardized tests that they are thoroughly bored with practice test sessions. How can you motivate them to pay attention to yours?

2. Without specifically teaching to the test, or targeting test content, what are some general principles or activities you can include in a sixth-grade science class in hopes of improving the students' scores on the annual achievement test?

3. The parents of one of your eighth-grade English students have expressed concern because the student's grade-equivalent score in reading is at the sixth-grade level. They ask, "Are you really giving students hard enough books to read?" How will you explain the meaning of the student's score?

4. One of your students disagrees with your comments about her math test scores. "I scored better than 91

percent of kids in the country," she says. "What do you mean I have not fully mastered geometry?" How can you explain the difference between norm-referenced and criterion-referenced scores to her?

5. One of your eighth-grade math students has come to you in tears. She has just learned that a low math score on the standardized placement test will put her in the slow track next year at high school. You believe the placement would be an error. What steps do you think she (or you) can take to change her placement?

IN HIGH SCHOOL

1. One of your junior year students wonders about his chances of getting into college. "African Americans always score lower on those tests," he says. "They are never going to let me in." What can you say to reassure this student?

2. Some of your seniors are worried they will not be able to graduate. They always have scored below average on standardized tests and they are not sure they can pass the state-required minimum competency test. How can you help them?

3. You know one of your students works until late most nights as a nurse's aide. The student is trying to gain experience for a career in physical therapy, but you are concerned that a lack of sleep and preparation time will hurt her performance on the college entrance exam. What will you tell her?

4. You teach a world history class that emphasizes problem solving, critical thinking, and creativity, and includes lots of group projects. During the past few years, however, you have heard complaints from students and parents that, although fun and instructive, your class does nothing to help students excel in the multiple-choice college entrance and minimum-competency tests. How can you better prepare students for these high-stakes tests without compromising your approach to teaching?

5. What kinds of standardized tests would you include in a junior-level life skills unit on career planning? What other information would you ask the students to collect about themselves as part of their career planning process?

Connecting Theory and Research to Practice

As discussed in this chapter, standardized tests may be misused if they are the sole criterion by which individual students and schools are judged. One Web site that highlights this debate, "Fair Test: The National Center for Fair and Open Testing," can be found at *http://www.fairtest.org/*. It was created by an advocacy group to halt the use of standardized tests for high stakes and argues for the elimination of cultural, gender, and socioeconomic bias in standardized tests.

This site revolves around four key goals and princi-ples: (1) that tests should be fair and valid; (2) that researchers and others should have access to standardized tests; (3) that standardized tests should not be the sole criteria by which students and schools are judged; and (4) that alternative forms of assessment should be developed, promoted, and utilized. While providing information and many resources on the issue of standardized testing, this site also features its own newsletter *(The Examiner)*; several fact lists pertaining to standardized testing; materials and information for students, teachers, and parents; contact information for various educational organizations; and current legislation that impacts educational practice.

"Teaching to a Higher Standard: Forget Standardized Testing and the SAT II," by Diane Walker, which can be found at *http://7-12educators.about.com/education/7-12educators/library/weekly/aa092100a.htm* illustrates the impact that standardized testing has had on classroom practice. This article chronicles the relationship between science instruction and learning in Florida and the use of standardized tests for high stakes. Included in this site are the testimonials of one science teacher, Bob Jacobs of Wilson High School, about his efforts to get around "teaching to the test."

Communities of Learners/Teachers

To what degree does standardized testing used for high stakes affect classroom teachers? This question was investigated in a series of articles on education written by journalist Alan J. Borsuk for the *Journal Sentinel* in Milwaukee, Wisconsin. In a 15-part series, available on the Internet, Borsuk examined issues facing today's teachers about quality education. For example, the series highlights articles on such topics as the current teacher job market (Part 4), the mentoring of new teachers (Part 6), and the pay and professional treatment of teachers (Part 10). Part 13 of this series addresses the issue of the detrimental effects of standardized testing on quality teaching in "Testing, Testing: Does Standardized Testing Discourage Good Teachers" (available at *http://www.jsonline.com/news/metro/mar00/alfie10030900a.asp*). Other online articles from the *Journal Sentinel* that are related to teaching can be found at *http://www.jsonline.com/news/edu/*.

FairTest:
The National Center for Fair & Open Testing

Visit these FairTest Pages:
[Our Programs ▼] [GO!]

Donate Now

Make a donation of $30 or more and receive the *Examiner* for a year.

ARN
* Find out about the Assessment Reform Network
* Join the on line ARN **Discussion Group**

CARE
Visit our Coalition for Authentic Reform in Education page to see what is happening with MCAS in Massachusetts.

Need Help in Your State?
See ARN's lists of **state coordinators** and **advocacy resources**.

University Page
Find out about FairTest's work to reduce the role of standardized tests

Welcome to FairTest's Web Site!

The National Center for Fair & Open Testing (FairTest) is an advocacy organization working to end the abuses, misuses and flaws of standardized testing and ensure that evaluation of students and workers is fair, open, and educationally sound.

We place special emphasis on eliminating the racial, class, gender, and cultural barriers to equal opportunity posed by standardized tests, and preventing their damage to the quality of education. Based on four **Goals and Principles**, we provide information, technical assistance and advocacy on a broad range of testing concerns, focusing on three areas: **K-12**, **university admissions**, and **employment tests**, including **teacher testing.**

FairTest publishes a quarterly newsletter, *The Examiner*, plus a full **catalog** of materials on both K-12 and university testing to aid teachers, administrators, students, parents and researchers. See our order form on this Web site! FairTest also has numerous **fact sheets** available to educate you on standardized testing and alternative assessment.

FairTest's current projects include the following:

What's New
Click HERE
for the latest updates
-Last Updated June 4

NEW See our **new web page** with reaction to President Bush's Testing Plans and actions you can take to stop it.

NEW FairTest urges College Board President Gaston Caperton, to "Eliminate Contradictions" Between Public Statements and Company Practices with regard to the SAT. See the **Press Release**, the **letter to Caperton**, and a **sampling of schools listed in the College Board Handbook with cut-off scores.**

Online Resources

The Educational Testing Service (ETS) Web site, located at *http://www.ets.org/index.html,* provides information for students, parents, and educators about many standardized tests currently being used across the country. Also available is an exhaustive index of currently available tests, articles, and resources on related topics (e.g., disabilities and testing), and practice test questions and tutorials. To help you learn more about the *Praxis Series: Professional Assessments for Beginning Teachers,* ETS provides information about this series of professional education tests, test dates and locations, and interpretations of test scores at *http://www.teachingandlearning.org/licnsure/praxis/index.html.*

KidSource Online has a Web site devoted to the history of standardized testing located at *http://www.kidsource.com/kidsource/content2/stand.testing.html.* Located on this site are connections to online publications related to standardized testing. One interesting link provides a discussion about and tips for parents on how improve a child's test taking skills. Also connected to this site is the "Education and Kids" forum for conducting online discussions with others about testing and other educational issues.

The Education Resource and Information Center (ERIC) is an online educational resource from pre-school to adult learning. ERIC has a document on its Web site entitled "What Should Parents Know About Standardized Testing in Schools?" (available at *http://www.accesseric.org:81/resources/parent/testing.html).* This online publication gives an overview of standardized testing geared specifically toward parents and parental concerns, and it provides a list of textual resources for parents to learn more about standardized tests. ERIC is also an invaluable resource for investigating many of the educational topics in this textbook. ERIC's main Web page can be found at *http://www.accesseric.org/index.html.*

"The Open Directory Project," an online informational initiative, lists links to other Web sites that provide information about standardized testing *(http://dmoz.org/Society/Issues/Education/Standardized_Testing/).* One Web link connects to *Frontline's* television feature "Secrets of the SAT." Another link takes you to the site called "Test Usage Information Links," which provides articles and resources about the misuse of high-stakes tests.

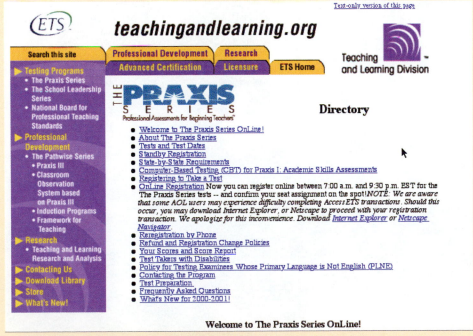

Classroom Assessments

CHAPTER OUTLINE

THE BIG PICTURE

- To help you see the big picture, keep the following questions in mind as you read this chapter:

- What is the role of classroom assessments in today's schools, and why are they important? How do assessments affect student learning and how do they affect instruction?

- What is the difference between using tests to select students for programs or to place them in classes, on the one hand, and using tests to measure what students have learned in a specific course, on the other?

- How can a teacher write fair and appropriate assessments? When is it best to use multiple-choice, fill-in, sentence completion, matching, and essay questions?

- What is the difference between traditional and authentic assessment?

- What are the advantages and disadvantages of each?

- How can a teacher be sure to use the information from assessment to grade students fairly? How can assessment and grading be used most effectively to enhance student motivation and increase learning?

- How can teachers using their own tests ensure they are clear and fair? When should teachers use prepackaged tests?

- How does a teacher accommodate to school-wide grading policies that do not seem to apply to his or her class?

- How can a teacher allow students to do extra work to make up for poor performance while still being fair to other students who scored well the first time around?

◄ *A second grader explains her project to her classmates and teacher.* (Elizabeth Crews)

Jing Xu was trying to put together her American history final exam for her twelfth-grade class. The class had spent the semester doing so many different types of activities—listening to lectures, watching videotapes, breaking into groups for discussions, producing their own play as a final project, and writing three book reports. How could she possibly give a fair test on everything the class had learned? Jing's students had performed well and had exceeded her expectations—by all accounts, her class was a huge success. Because Jing knew that one-third of her students had begun the term with limited proficiency in English, she had based the curriculum on varied formats and presentation styles in order to engage them and give them a chance to do well. Now, she faced the dilemma of testing and grading the students in a way that met the school's uniform assessment goals. She also faced the need to assess the students' factual knowledge of history, although the emphasis of her instruction was not on factual knowledge.

Jing finally settled on a varied format for the test: a selection of multiple-choice, fill-in-the-blank, and matching questions, followed by two essays (the topics for which students could select from a list of five questions). She wrote some of the questions herself, but—because she had trouble recalling exactly what material she had covered in lectures and class activities—she also chose some questions from the sample tests in her teacher's guide. She proofread the test carefully to make sure it was free of typographical errors. Feeling reasonably satisfied, she called it a night.

The next day, Jing noticed the perplexed looks on her students' faces as they worked through the exam. When the bell rang, three-quarters of the class had not finished the test. Several students stayed afterward to tell Jing that the test was unfair and had nothing to do with what they had learned in class. Knowing they had performed poorly on the test, these students asked if they could do an extra project to help raise their averages. Jing did not know how to react. She believed the test was fair: If she let some students do an extra project to make up for their poor performance, her final grades for these students would be higher than the grades students should be getting, based on their knowledge of history. She couldn't give all her students good grades without angering the other history teachers and the principal, as well as the students with high test scores. What should Jing do?

Jing is a dedicated teacher whose goal is to reach her students and excite them about history. Although she succeeded in teaching an interesting and popular course, she failed in her attempt to assess the students fairly. Jing made several mistakes. The test she designed did not cover the same material that she taught: Because she had not followed an explicit teaching plan, when it came time to draw up the final exam, she could not remember what she had covered. She wrote test questions that were sometimes unclear because she did not have time to review the questions, try them out on another teacher, and revise them. She also borrowed questions from sample tests that had little to do with her course. Jing must grade her students in accordance with school policy—one that makes it difficult for every student to get an A or a B in her course. During the semester, however, most students had done well on their projects and reports, and many believed they deserved high grades. In this chapter, we discuss what Jing might do next semester to avoid her mistakes and assess her students more fairly.

Why Understanding Classroom Assessments Is Important to Teachers

What would it be like to be a student in a school with no assessment? Would you learn as much? Would you study as often at home? Freed from the worry of being evaluated, would you blossom in the school environment? Although many students might think the purpose of assessment is to make their lives miserable, research in educational psychology has shown just the opposite: Assessments increase motivation and learning, and as a result, students benefit more from the time they spend in school (Brookhart, 1997; Brookhart & DeVoge, 1999; Crooks, 1988; Dempster, 1991, 1992). Fair assessments help students and teachers measure the students' progress toward their goals; fair assessments also help teachers improve their teaching to better assist students in meeting their goals. Students learn most when they are given brief, frequent assessments instead of longer and less frequent assessments (Bangert-Drowns, Kulik, & Kulik, 1991; Dempster, 1991; Dempster & Perkins, 1993).

What is classroom assessment—is it just the tests a teacher gives every two weeks over the course of the semester or school year? The answer is that it encompasses much more: **Classroom assessment** consists of every type of information you take in about the students in the classroom. It consists of test results, grades on homework and class presentations, and the informal conversations you have with your students over the course of the year. As Jing Xu, the teacher in the opening vignette, realized, classroom assessment is a complex issue that requires a teacher to consider numerous aspects of the students and the instructional environment. Taken as a whole, classroom assessments define student learning: what and how much students have learned, in what time frame. The entire picture of the ways you gather information on your students constitutes your **assessment system.** Often, teachers map out an effective assessment system at the same time they plan instruction. Even in schools that do not give grades, teachers gather information about students' progress so they can guide students and help them develop in their learning.

THINKING PRACTICALLY

What is your personal attitude about taking tests? Do you think that tests make you study harder and learn more? Why or why not?

SUGGESTION: Think about your past experiences with tests, and how an upcoming test tends to influence your behavior. Do you budget your time to prepare for the test, or do you put off studying until the last moment? Does anxiety overwhelm you? Do your results on tests vary from time to time, and from subject to subject? Why might this be?

A student interacts informally with his teacher. Anxious students often do better if asked informal questions by a friendly teacher. The teacher can then use the interchange as part of her total assessment of the student. (Jeff Dunn, Stock Boston)

FORMAL AND INFORMAL ASSESSMENTS

Even though both tests and discussions give you information about what a student has learned, the types of information you get from these two sources are very different from each other. These two sources of information correspond to formal and informal methods of assessment. **Formal assessments** are objective and rigorous methods for obtaining information about student learning, such as tests, quizzes, book reports, and assigned in-class presentations. **Informal assessments** consist of observations you make of students in the classroom, doing work, and talking to you or to other students; such dialogue may include student answers to teacher-initiated questions. Informal assessments also consist of information in written form that you obtain from some students, such as a special letter to you or an extra composition or journal entry that the student asks you to read.

Formal assessment usually results in information collected in a uniform manner on all students, whereas informal assessment consists of information collected opportunistically on some students, but not always on others, as the mechanisms for collecting this information become available to teachers. You gather the information to help plan future instruction and to gauge the success of current instruction. You also use it to evaluate individual students, to form the basis for feedback, and, in general, to help students achieve their maximum potential.

 EVALUATING STUDENT ACHIEVEMENT

What do you do with the results of formal and informal assessments? The assessments themselves represent measurements of student learning. **Measurements** are data on student performance and learning that you collect. You use these measurements to perform an **evaluation,** the process of making judgments about individual student's learning and performance (and effort) based on the measurements, or information, at hand. Consider an example of the difference between measurement and evaluation. Larry Jacobs, an English teacher, has available the following information on two students: Stan received on his tests the grades of B+, A−, B+, and A; he also received a B− on his classroom presentation of his book report project. Susan received the grades of C+, B, B+, and A on the same tests; she also received an A on her classroom book report presentation. These grades, as well as grades on homework and other items, represent the measurements available to Larry on which he will base his decisions regarding final grades.

The process of evaluation is more complex than simply averaging each student's grades to obtain a final grade, however. Consider the impact the following pieces of information might have on the final grades: What if Susan started out the year with an undiagnosed reading disability and then got appropriate help in the middle of the term? What if Stan became terribly nervous when speaking in front of the class? What if Susan's book report project showed evidence of significant parental involvement? What if Stan were caught cheating on the last test of the semester? As you can see, the process of evaluating students' learning often must take into account many factors beyond simply the scores students receive on tests and assignments.

As a footnote, you should remember that evaluation is not the only subjective aspect of the measurement and evaluation process: Measurement itself can have subjective aspects, such as the grade given on an essay— which might be higher if the teacher liked the topic or identified with it— and the grade given on a classroom presentation, which may sometimes reflect the particular preferences and prejudices of a given teacher.

Like Jing Xu, any teacher can become overwhelmed by the responsibility of conducting fair assessments. What is a beginning teacher to do if her or his goal is to assess all students fairly? We begin by discussing how to design and score different types of assessments and how to use the information provided by these scores in final grading decisions. Throughout the chapter, we return frequently to two terms introduced in Chapter 13: *reliability* and *validity,* both of which are important goals of assessment. Remember that *reliability* describes the consistency of a measurement— in other words, the extent to which the method of measurement can be relied on to provide consistent information every time the method is used. *Validity* describes the extent to which an assessment measures what it is supposed to measure. A spelling test is not a valid measure of reading comprehension, for example, nor is a math test on fractions a valid test of everything learned in the sixth-grade curriculum. Assessments can be invalid for many reasons: They might ask the wrong types of questions, given the stated goal of the assessment, or they might ask the right types of questions but cover only a portion of the material they are supposed to cover.

FORMATIVE AND SUMMATIVE ASSESSMENT

Have you ever taken a test to get into a special class, program, or school? Perhaps you have taken a math test to see which math class you belonged in. This type of assessment is called **formative assessment;** its purpose is to discover the strengths and weaknesses in prior learning. Formative assessment reveals a student's developmental stage in the area being tested. Formative assessment is diagnostic—that is, it is often used to assist teachers and others in making decisions about where to place students.

You have undoubtedly been exposed many times in your academic career to the other type of assessment, called **summative assessment.** Summative assessment is the typical final exam type of assessment you are used to—a final test of student learning in a particular area. You can remember the difference between the two different forms of assessment by focusing on the words *form* (as in, to form a decision), and *sum* (as in, to summarize prior learning).

Note that the two types of assessments refer more to the purposes for which the assessments are used than to any defining characteristics of the tests themselves. For example, consider the swimming test given at some colleges. If you take the test during your first week as a freshman and you pass it, you are exempt from a swimming requirement that you would otherwise have to fulfill during your four years in college. Thus the swimming test in this case is a formative assessment, used for making placement decisions. The same test can also be used at the end of the one-semester athletic course in which swimming is taught. Used at this point, the test becomes a summative assessment, or a measure of what you learned in the course. The purpose for which the test is being used is the differentiating aspect.

As a teacher, you will encounter both formative and summative assessments. You may be asked by your school to administer standardized formative assessments early in the school year to help place students into various programs, special classes, or groups within classes. And, of course, you will give many summative assessments to fulfill your school's testing requirements to document student learning.

NORM-REFERENCED VERSUS CRITERION-REFERENCED ASSESSMENTS

Another general concept to understand about assessment is the difference between norm-referenced and criterion-referenced grading (see also Chapter 13). You may not realize it from the terms, but you already know what each expression means. When your teacher in seventh-grade science class announced, "You need to answer 80 percent of the test questions correctly to earn a B," he was using a **criterion-referenced grading system.** In this system, a grade represents a specific set of accomplishments, which can be identified for one student independently of the performances of other students (for example, getting 80 percent of the questions right).

When your teacher in college-level science said, "I grade on a curve, and 20 percent of you will get A's, 40 percent will get B's, and 40 percent will get C's and below," she was using a **norm-referenced grading system** that represents how well a student has done compared with other students. This system involves assigning a student a grade relative to the other students who took the same assessment. Imagine that half of your educational psychology class consists of people who already know the material, but who are taking the course to pad their transcripts with A's. What will this fact mean to you and to your chances for earning an A, if you are not already an expert in educational psychology? Conversely, think of the opposite situation, in which you are better prepared from past experiences and course work for a given course than are the other students.

You might sail through with little effort and receive an A. Thus a norm-referenced system can be unfair and highly influenced by the specific situation and the experiences of the students in a given class.

Criterion-referenced systems, too, can present problems. One teacher complained that he set what he believed were reasonable criteria for an A, a B, a C, and so on. But at the end of the term he found that most of his students had gotten C's. This situation is not likely to satisfy parents or the school principal regarding the teaching and learning that have been taking place. Nor would the opposite situation satisfy the principal or other teachers (although the parents probably would not mind!): a situation in which nearly every student earns an A in one class because that particular teacher set lenient criteria for receiving an A, and other teachers in the same school established more rigorous criteria.

Obviously, both norm-referenced and criterion-referenced grading systems have advantages as well as drawbacks. In practice, many school districts set uniform criteria for teachers to use in assessment and grading, thereby attempting to make the system and the standards uniform. You will probably be given instructions from your principal regarding what type of grading system to use. However, some principals will not supply this information; in this event it is up to the individual teacher to identify the customary procedures. For example, if you are told to use a criterion-based system, ask your principal and fellow teachers what criteria have been established for use in your school, so your practices do not deviate significantly from the practices of other teachers.

THE GOALS OF ASSESSMENT

What are the goals of assessment? Your goals should actively shape the nature of the assessments you use, their frequency, and the types of grading and reporting of grades based on these assessments. At first you may think the only goal of assessment is to determine what students know. However, research has shown that the use of assessments creates an incentive for students to study; thus assessment influences student motivation. The type of assessment given has a direct effect both on how students study and on what they learn (Crooks, 1988; Dempster & Perkins, 1991, 1993; Gronlund, 1993).

■**ASSESSMENT, MOTIVATION, AND LEARNING**   Imagine you are taking an American history course, and you are told you will have a 100-item multiple-choice test on the American Revolution. A friend of yours is told that, in her class, there will be an all-essay exam on the American Revolution. You and she would probably study the same material in different ways, because each of you would be guided by the different uses to which your knowledge will be put. You might be well advised to spend your time on hard-core memorizing of facts and figures. Your friend might be well advised to think in more conceptual terms about the general issues surrounding the Revolution and how she can write about these issues in essays. Although you and your friend might share equal amounts of motivation, the actions you take and the learning you accomplish will probably be differentially shaped by the different types of assessments the two of you were preparing for.

In addition, assessment provides information that serves as a guide to the effectiveness of teaching strategies and as a mechanism for improving teaching. The goal is meaningful learning; if the students do not exhibit such learning on an assessment, you must ask yourself why and attempt to improve the situation.

THINKING ANALYTICALLY

Name two additional drawbacks of both norm-referenced and criterion-referenced grading systems. Consider this question from your own perspective as a student: What seems unfair about each method of grading?

SUGGESTION: Norm: Has no clear standard of performance that can be communicated to the student ahead of time; causes extreme competitiveness among students. Criterion: Teachers can set inappropriate or irrelevant criteria; the best students may feel cheated by overly easy criteria.

THINKING PRACTICALLY

How has the nature of the assessments in your educational psychology course influenced your learning and studying behavior?

SUGGESTION: Ask yourself, first, what types of assessments have been used this term and how you have responded to them. Have any assessments been particularly good at motivating you to study more?

Assessment influences motivation and learning in other ways. Imagine that your goal is to help your students gain confidence in their ability to master tough material in history. Like Jing Xu, the teacher in the opening vignette, you might design assessments that allow the students some choice in which essay questions to complete (in order to help them do as well as possible). Alternatively, you might allow students to grade their own papers, telling them the test will not count toward their grade this time, but rather, will be used to help pinpoint areas in which they are weak. Another common incentive is to tell students that their lowest test grade will be deleted. This technique encourages students to study harder for future assessments, even if they did poorly on one test. Otherwise, the students might surmise that their test grade average had already been destroyed, and not study hard for the next test.

■ **ASSESSMENT AS STUDENT FEEDBACK**   Another important use of assessments is to serve as feedback to students about their progress in learning. In Chapter 10 we discussed the essential role of feedback to students in maintaining their motivation. Students need feedback, preferably frequent, about their progress and about what they are doing right and wrong and how to change (Bardine, 1999). Some ineffective teachers think students know what to do and are simply too lazy to study. Often, this is not the case. Teachers may have been so immersed in the school system they have forgotten what it is like to be new to the task. With feedback, students can chart their progress and gain additional motivation as they move nearer their goals. The more explicit and detailed this feedback—as long as it is constructive—the better. Students who receive written feedback in addition to the more typical letter grades are more likely to believe that effort and hard work, rather than luck and external factors, are responsible for their success (Cross & Cross, 1980, 1981).

As we discussed in Chapter 10, positive feedback consists of praise and encouragement designed to give students confidence about their ability. Constructive feedback is designed to show students specifically what aspects of their performance need improvement, and also to provide specific suggestions for how to improve. Both types of feedback are valuable. Expert teachers often start out with positive feedback to place a student in a receptive and nondefensive mood and then proceed to giving constructive feedback that shows what she or he must do to improve (see Table 14.1).

■ **ASSESSMENT AS TEACHER FEEDBACK**   Assessment of student performance also provides important feedback to teachers about the quality and success of their instruction. A teacher might be very popular with her students; however, if assessments show that the material is not being learned, the teacher must face the fact that her instruction

THINKING CREATIVELY

How can you help students who are unfamiliar with school requirements and tests become more comfortable with the system in use? How can you ensure that students understand the system?

SUGGESTION: Give practice tests with lots of explanation about the testing and grading process; discuss the system openly in class—do not keep it a secret; encourage questions about the system and answer them openly.

TABLE **14.1**   Contrasting Positive and Constructive Feedback with Unhelpful Feedback

Positive Feedback	Constructive Feedback	Unhelpful Feedback
"You worked very hard on this assignment."	"Try to open your composition with a sentence that explains the main idea."	"Do better work next time."
"Excellent job."	"Please do extra math problems each night until you feel more comfortable with fractions."	"Did you even study for this test?"
"This shows real effort."	"Your answers show good thinking but not good organization—try writing from an outline."	"You missed the point of the assignment."
"You are such a good student."	"You subtracted each column perfectly, but you forgot to borrow from the ten's place."	"Poor job."
"I enjoyed reading this."		"Study harder next time."
		"Think before you write!"

A student intently reads her teacher's detailed feedback on a test. Students who receive written feedback in addition to letter grades are more likely to attribute their success to effort and hard work rather than to luck and external factors.
(Frank Siteman, Stock Boston)

is lacking. A teacher who is not popular might point to high student performance in defense of his effectiveness. Feedback on teacher performance, reflected in student assessments, is used widely by principals, other administrators, and school boards, and teachers are held accountable for this information.

Evaluations of students also have a direct effect on parents. Most parents wish to be involved in their children's school experiences, and knowing how well their children are doing is essential to keeping their at-home interactions with the children on target. For example, if a parent institutes a "no television on school nights" rule, the parent needs tangible evidence that her child's test scores have improved. This information will bolster the decision to limit television.

Implications for Teaching

Given the many and varied uses for assessments, how can teachers ensure that assessments are as fair and useful as possible? In the following sections of this chapter, we review specific methods for writing good test items and computing fair grades. However, here are several basic factors to remember about how to use assessments effectively:

- *Make assessments meaningful to students.* Make explicit their role in students' learning and their role in computing final grades. Apply these standards consistently.

- *Ensure that assessments are objective and as fair as possible to all students from all backgrounds.* Assessments should be both reliable and valid—they should consistently measure what they are supposed to measure.

- *Ensure that assessments are neither so easy that all students do well with little effort, nor so difficult that no students do well despite having worked hard.* Assessments must be challenging to students, but always within reasonable limits, so a competent student who works hard will do well.

- *Use methods of assessment frequently enough so that students get practice in being assessed and the assessment process is demystified for them.*

- *Always bear in mind the many and varied influences on students' ability to score well on assessments.* Students' age, developmental level, gender, and cultural background and experiences all impact how an individual student performs on assessments.

Traditional Assessments

Traditional assessments consist of the typical interim and end-of-semester tests that teachers give to measure how much students have learned—much like the final exam prepared by Jing Xu to assess her students' understanding of history. Traditional assessment tests usually contain different types of questions: Multiple-choice, fill-in, sentence completion, matching, and essay forms are commonly used. Traditional types of assessments are not the only way, nor necessarily even the best way, for teachers to evaluate student learning, but they are the most common way. Indeed, well-designed traditional tests provide valuable information about student learning (Linn & Gronlund, 1995). Here, we review how to design and write each type of test item so the tests you design are reliable, valid, and fair. In the next section of this chapter we explore alternative methods of assessing students that go beyond traditional forms of assessment.

WHAT MATERIAL SHOULD THE TEST COVER?

Before considering how to write good items for a particular test, first decide what material the test will cover. What are you testing the students on? What did you cover in your instruction? What activities did the students perform, and what homework and seatwork did you assign? Looking back to the beginning of the term, what were the goals and objectives of your instruction?

■ **CONSULTING PUBLISHED SOURCES** Before designing a test on your own, examine the tests provided with your instructor's manuals and other teaching materials. You may be able to adapt or use as is some of the test questions—or even whole tests—that publishers have developed. The advantage of using these published test questions is that they have often been checked for errors or potential problems in phrasing; it is also much quicker to use these items than to write your own. The disadvantage of using published test questions is that they may not accurately reflect what you taught, because you may have adapted the material in the textbook or used material from more than one textbook or source. Published tests may also have been developed for a population different from yours. You will have to use your judgment both to evaluate the quality and fairness of the published tests, and to see if they contain useful material, given your goals (Airasian, 1996).

■ **USING INSTRUCTIONAL OBJECTIVES** Assuming you have decided to write your own test questions, consider the following pointers. The most important part of designing a good test is to make sure the test reflects what the students were taught—in other words, that the test is valid. The best way to ensure that the material on the test corresponds to the material taught is to return to your set of instructional objectives, discussed at length in Chapter 12 on classroom teaching. If you were following the plan you set forth, your test should cover the same basic content as the instructional objectives, and the number of questions on each concept or topic should correspond to how much time you spent on the topic in class, and how much time students were expected to spend on the topic in homework and out-of-class activities. Some teachers, particularly those at the elementary levels, may have taught several different subjects over the course of the year; these teachers will have to refer back to the units taught within each content area when developing their tests.

A precise way to accomplish the goal of matching assessment to instruction is to use a behavior-content matrix (Berliner, 1987) (see Figure 14.1 on page 514). A behavior-content matrix lists the topics you covered in the left column, and the types of thinking or behaviors that students should be able to engage in across the top row. To design a test, start by summing up how many days (or units of time) you spent on each topic. Next, allocate these totals according to the types of thinking that were encouraged, showing which types of thinking you stressed more or less in your instruction on the various topics.

For example, in a biology course, you have spent 12 days on cells and 8 days on genes. You estimate you used about half your time teaching students how to understand the basic concepts about cells and genes, and the other half teaching students how to apply this information to their own projects. In this case, your test should contain roughly 12

THINKING ANALYTICALLY

What might you do if the material on which you wish to test students was not thoroughly covered in class, but rather was covered by students as home reading? How can you ensure that the test is fair?

SUGGESTION: Make clear to the students that the home reading will be tested; give students classroom time to do extra reading if you suspect some students may get no time to read at home; ask students to tell you beforehand if being tested on home reading presents any problem; vary the content of tests so as not to overly advantage students with parents who are heavily involved in their home reading.

FIGURE 14.1

Example of a Behavior-Content
Matrix—High School Biology
Course

BEHAVIORS

CONTENT	Recall and Recognition	Terminology	Specific Facts	Methodology	Theories and Structures	Knowledge Application	Interpretation of Qualitative Data	Screening of Hypothesis	Identification of Problems	Extrapolation	TOTALS
Cells: Structure											
Functions											
Reproduction											
Genes: Dual Roles											
Macro/Micro Structures											
Inheritance											
Technology											

out of 20, or 60 percent of the questions on cells, and the other 40 percent on genes. Of the cell questions, roughly half—or 30 percent of the entire number of questions on the test—should stress understanding of basic concepts, and the other half should stress applying the information. Similarly, of the 40 percent of the test devoted to genes, about half should be on understanding concepts—20 percent of the entire test's length—and 20 percent should be on applying information. Followed closely, the system ensures that what is tested matches what was stressed in instruction. Although it may seem a bit complex, this type of planning will result in a fairer and more valid test.

 THE WHEN AND HOW OF TESTING

In many schools, the curriculum is dictated by the administration, as are general schedule guidelines for testing students. Sometimes, however, teachers have considerable leeway in deciding if and when to test. When you plan your instruction and assessments for the semester or the year, keep in mind the following guidelines about the best ways to help students benefit from the experience of taking tests.

■**GIVE MORE FREQUENT, SHORTER TESTS** First, schedule frequent and shorter tests rather than infrequent, longer ones. Students tend to leave their studying until just before the test; the more often they are tested, the more they will study. Moreover, the use of many shorter tests helps test-anxious students overcome the paralyzing fear of being given only one opportunity to show what they know. Also, by scheduling frequent tests, you encourage students to actively process and use the material. When you design a test, try to tailor it to the material that has been covered in the recent past. If you give many shorter tests, you will be testing frequently, as the students learn individual topics. Later, give a longer retest in which you integrate material across topics and help students think broadly about what they have learned. As you develop assessments during the term, incorporate questions that require students to reason actively with concepts they learned earlier.

■**CONSIDER TESTING CONDITIONS** When you administer a test, be attentive to the conditions students will face. Poor conditions can depress test performance. For example, noises, music, laughing students in a neighboring room, and other distractions can affect students' ability to concentrate. Give students explicit instructions regarding how long they will have to complete the test, whether you will give them any warnings about elapsed time, and what they should do once their test is handed in so they do not annoy other students still working on the test. Also keep a close watch on students during a test, so you are available to answer questions if students need help with interpreting instructions, and so your presence will discourage cheating. By remaining attentive to students as they take a test, you can also help anxious students with a word of encouragement.

■ **ENSURE CLEAR DIRECTIONS**   To ensure that tests accurately reflect student learning, be certain students understand the test directions. For example, go over a sample test question to demonstrate the task required. Once the students complete the tests and the tests are collected, grade them and return them as soon as possible while the students are still interested in how they did and why. Waiting too long ensures that students will not link learning to performance, or to their level of reward and recognition for that performance. Many teachers find it helpful to discuss right and wrong answers immediately after the test, or even to distribute a list of correct answers or information on where to find these answers. Having students share their correct answers with the class is also a good practice, because it will help you incorporate testing into the curriculum as an instructional activity in itself.

Research has confirmed the importance of frequent, short tests rather than infrequent, long ones; appropriate testing conditions; and clear test directions. Teachers should also grade and return tests as soon as possible, and even distribute a list of correct answers or information on where to find the answers. (David Young-Wolff, Stone)

DEVELOPING OBJECTIVE TEST QUESTIONS

In **objective tests** there is a single, known, correct answer. Contrast objective tests with subjective tests, the most common of which are essay tests. In **subjective tests,** there is no one correct answer; the quality of an answer is open to interpretation, and different teachers may even award different grades for the same response. Objective test items consist of multiple-choice, fill-in-the-blank, short answer, true/false, and matching items. You are probably familiar with all these items. When should you use each type? What testing goals are best served by multiple-choice versus matching items, for example?

■ **MULTIPLE-CHOICE ITEMS**   Research has supported the advantages of the multiple-choice item as the item type of choice in objective tests (Gronlund, 1993). Multiple-choice items let you test a great deal of information in one sitting. Remember that the format of the *SAT* (Scholastic Assessment Test), *ACT* (American College Test), or other standardized tests you may have taken is usually multiple choice. Multiple-choice items are useful for measuring factual knowledge; however, a well-crafted item can also measure higher levels of reasoning and application of knowledge—as is the case with many of the difficult items on the *SAT* and other challenging standardized tests. You are probably familiar with multiple-choice questions. Each multiple-choice question contains a **stem** (consisting of the question or incomplete statement) and a group of options, one of which is the keyed or correct answer. The incorrect options are called **distractors** because they serve to distract students who are not sure which option is the keyed or correct answer. In some multiple-choice questions, there is only one right answer. In other questions, the options represent varying degrees of correctness, and the test taker must choose the best option.

A well-written stem presents one question or problem; the stem must be clear and unambiguous. The distractors also must be clear, grammatically consistent with the question in the stem, and equally technical in their language so the right answer does not leap out because of its technical phrasing compared to the distractors. Vary the position of the right answer amid the group of distractors randomly. All options, whether correct or incorrect, should be comparable in length. Do not use absolutes such as "never" or "always" in distractors because these terms often give away the correct answer to students who are guessing. Similarly, avoid "none of the above" and "all of the above" because they encourage test-taking strategies that are irrelevant to subject matter knowledge—for example, choosing "all of the above" if at least two options are identified as plausible. In addition, two distractors should never have the same meaning, because it is obvious to students that the two distractors must be incorrect answers. Underline negative wording so students see it. (For additional information on writing multiple-choice test items, see Gronlund, 1988; Haladyna, 1999; and Sadler, 2000).

Multiple-choice items can also be used to measure higher order learning and reasoning. Students can be given material to analyze on their own during a test; this material may be new to the students, although the analysis should be related to what the students have learned in class (Gronlund, 1993). Many science tests are designed in this way. For example, the test taker is shown a picture of a group of different types of animals standing at varying distances from one another while drinking from a watering hole in Africa. The question is asked, "Based on this picture, what can you infer about the dietary patterns of the different animals?" The students' task is to analyze which animals are the solitary hunters who eat meat and which are herd-dwelling grazers who eat grass and vegetation. The clues consist of the animals' relative positions at the watering hole, and whether they travel in groups or alone. Animals that travel alone and look like predators are more brazen at the watering hole and thus have a prime spot; herd dwelling grazers are tentative and take safety in numbers at the periphery of the watering hole. As you can see, answering such a question correctly requires higher level reasoning and application of ideas about animal ecology. Table 14.2 provides examples of good and poor multiple-choice items.

TABLE 14.2   Examples of Poor Versus Good Multiple Choice Questions

POOR: 1. Which of the following is not a character in *The Odyssey*?

   A. Telemachus
   B. Penelope
   C. Laertes
   D. Persephone

Why Is It Poor?
By failing to underscore the word "not," a student may read quickly and misunderstand the question.

GOOD: 1. Which of the following is **NOT** a character in *The Odyssey*?

   A. Telemachus
   B. Penelope
   C. Laertes
   D. Persephone

POOR: 2. Which animal is a mammal that can fly?

   A. Spider
   B. Bat
   C. Arachnid
   D. Vulture

Why Is It Poor?
"Arachnid" may be an unfamiliar term for students and it is more technical than the other terms presented.

GOOD: 2. Which animal is a mammal that can fly?

   A. Spider
   B. Bat
   C. Moth
   D. Vulture

POOR: 3. Hemingway has been considered by some critics to be a master of dialogue-writing. Which of the following works did he write?

   A. "Hills Like White Elephants"
   B. *Tender is the Night*
   C. "Maggie, a Girl of the Streets"
   D. *The Grapes of Wrath*

Why Is It Poor?
The information being tested bears no relationship to the opening sentence, which may confuse students.

GOOD: 3. Ernest Hemingway wrote which of the following works?

   A. "Hills Like White Elephants"
   B. *Tender is the Night*
   C. "Maggie, a Girl of the Streets"
   D. *The Grapes of Wrath*

TABLE 14.2   *continued*

POOR: 4. Which of the following terms refers to the tempo of a piece of music?

     A. Forte
     B. Decrescendo poco y poco
     C. Piano
     D. Largo

GOOD: 4. Which of the following terms refers to the tempo of a piece of music?

     A. Forte
     B. Poco
     C. Piano
     D. Largo

Why Is It Poor?
There is an imbalance in the length of choices, with one much longer than the rest.

POOR: 5. What is the definition of bellicose?

     A. War-like
     B. Attractive
     C. Beautiful
     D. Pretty

GOOD: 5. What is the definition of bellicose?

     A. War-like
     B. Attractive
     C. Sensitive
     D. Dishonest

Why Is It Poor?
Three of the choices are so similar that the answer must be the remaining item.

POOR: 6. Which of the following neurotransmitters is most commonly linked with schizophrenia?

     A. Dopamine
     B. Chlorophyll
     C. Platelets
     D. GABA

GOOD: 6. Which of the following neurotransmitters is most commonly linked with schizophrenia?

     A. Acetylcholine
     B. Serotonin
     C. GABA
     D. Dopamine

Why Is It Poor?
Two of the choices (b and c) are not neurotransmitters, thus allowing them to be discarded.

POOR: 7. Which of the following plays did Shakespeare not write?

     A. *Hamlet*
     B. *A Doll's House*
     C. *Timon of Athens*
     D. *The Winter's Tale*

GOOD: 7. Which of the following plays did Shakespeare **NOT** write?

     A. *Hamlet*
     B. *A Doll's House*
     C. *Timon of Athens*
     D. *The Winter's Tale*

Why Is It Poor?
The word "not" should be emphasized so students do not misread the question.

POOR: 8. Schizophrenic disorders affect approximately what percent of the American population?

     A. 1%
     B. 1.5%
     C. 2%
     D. 3%

GOOD: 8. Schizophrenic disorders affect approximately what percent of the American population?

     A. 1%
     B. 8%
     C. 14%
     D. 20%

Why Is It Poor?
The percentages are too similar across the options.

POOR: 9. Which time period is commonly referred to as the *Renaissance*?

     A. 13th–15th centuries
     B. 14th–16th centuries
     C. 15th–17th centuries
     D. 16th–18th centuries

GOOD: 9. Which time period is commonly referred to as the *Renaissance*?

     A. 8th–10th centuries
     B. 11th–13th centuries
     C. 14th–16th centuries
     D. 17th–19th centuries

Why Is It Poor?
The choices are temporally overlapping, thus allowing several partially correct answers.

POOR: 10. The first time a company issues new stock to the public is referred to as an

    A. initial public offering.
    B. price–earnings ratio.
    C. stock split.
    D. interest rate hike.

Why Is It Poor?
The article "an" leads to discarding choices b and c even if a student does not know the answer.

POOR: 11. A varietal wine refers to

    A. a wine that is labeled with the different varieties of grapes used to produce it.
    B. a wine that is labeled with the different years in which its grapes were harvested.
    C. a wine that is labeled with the predominant grape used to produce it.
    D. a wine that is labeled with the different vineyards where it was produced.

Why Is It Poor?
The stem should have included the phrase "a wine that is labeled with the" instead of including this phrase in each option and thus making the options overly wordy.

POOR: 12. The calculated mean of a sample

    A. is never equal to the mean of the population.
    B. is always equal to the mean of the population.
    C. is always equal to the population median.
    D. is an estimate of the population mean.

Why Is It Poor?
Words such as "never" and "always" are seldom true and thus provide clues regarding options to discard. Also, if the item is constructed this way (with the stem and each option forming one complete sentence), the word "is" should be in the stem instead of in each option.

GOOD: 10. The first time a company issues new stock to the public is called

    A. an initial public offering.
    B. their price–earnings ratio.
    C. a stock split.
    D. an interest rate hike.

GOOD: 11. A varietal wine refers to a wine that is labeled with the

    A. different varieties of grapes used to produce it.
    B. years in which its grapes were harvested.
    C. predominant grape used to produce it.
    D. name of the vineyards where it was produced.

GOOD: 12. Which of the following statements best describes the statistical importance of a sample mean?

    A. It cannot equal the mean of the population.
    B. It equals the mean of the population.
    C. It equals the population median.
    D. It represents an estimate of the population mean.

■ **TRUE/FALSE ITEMS** In a true/false item, the test taker is presented with a statement and must judge whether it is true or false. Obviously, with only two possible answers, it is easy for students to guess correctly. In addition, the nature of each statement to be judged as true or false is usually simple and factual. For these reasons, use true/false items only when they are clearly warranted—such as when there are a great number of basic facts students have been taught; even then, there should be only a few such items on a single test (Linn & Gronlund, 1995). True/false items are also good for young students who are not yet adept at writing out their answers.

If you decide to include true/false items on a test, remember to write each statement so it is clear and unambiguous. Be sure each statement contains only one idea to be judged as true or false. When two ideas are represented, a student may become confused, thinking one idea is true and the other is false. If possible, avoid words such as *most, some, sometimes, possibly, may, usually, always, never, all,* and *none;* if you must use these words, scrutinize them carefully because they can often provide clues to the student who guesses (Gronlund, 1993). Some teachers ask students to write a rationale explaining why false items are false, thus increasing the amount of meaningful information being assessed by true/false items. Table 14.3 shows good and poor examples of true/false questions.

■ **MATCHING ITEMS** Matching items are similar to multiple-choice items, except there is both a group of stems and a group of options from which to choose the answers. The best matching items are those in which the same answer can be used several times, and in which the phrasing of the stems, on the one hand, and of the options, on the other

---

THINKING PRACTICALLY

Write four good true/false items on the material you have learned in this chapter.

SUGGESTION: Use the examples in Table 14.3 to write questions about classroom assessment. For example, "Guessing correctly is easier with true/false questions than with multiple-choice questions containing four potential responses . . . true or false?"

TABLE 14.3   **Examples of Poor Versus Good True/False Questions**

POOR: 1. There are 6 stages of moral development. T/F
Why Is It Poor?
Without specifying whose theory is being referred to, one could argue that the statement is either true or false (e.g., Piaget's theory of moral development does not have six stages).

GOOD: 1. According to Kohlberg's theory, there are 6 stages of moral development. T/F

POOR: 2. The automobile was invented before the sewing machine and the phonograph. T/F
Why Is It Poor?
There should be one comparison, not two, for clarity.

GOOD: 2. The automobile was invented before the phonograph. T/F

POOR: 3. There are 12 innings in a baseball game, 4 quarters in a football game, but only 2 periods in a basketball game. T/F
Why Is It Poor?
It contains both true and false choices mixed together.

GOOD: 3. There are 12 innings in a baseball game. T/F

There are 4 quarters in a football game. T/F

There are 2 periods in a basketball game. T/F

POOR: 4. Abraham Lincoln was bigger than Ulysses S. Grant. T/F
Why Is It Poor?
Without specifying that the relevant dimension is height, one could assume some other dimension was being tested (e.g., popularity).

GOOD: 4. In terms of height, Abraham Lincoln was bigger than Ulysses S. Grant. T/F

POOR: 5. The keyboard is composed of eighty-eight keys. T/F
Why Is It Poor?
Keyboards differ for different instruments.

GOOD: 5. The keyboard of a modern piano is composed of eighty-eight keys. T/F

POOR: 6. Judaism and Christianity are monotheistic religions, but Islam believes in many deities. T/F
Why Is It Poor?
It mixes both true and false assertions and the wording is confusing. Also, a religion does not itself believe in one or more deities; people who adhere to the religion may.

GOOD: 6. Judaism, Christianity, and Islam are all monotheistic religions. T/F

POOR: 7. Mozart was a genius. T/F
Why Is It Poor?
Without specifying that the relevant dimension is musical ability, one could argue that Mozart was not a genius.

GOOD: 7. With respect to his musical capabilities, many people consider Mozart a genius. T/F

hand, is consistent. Matching items are useful for measuring students' ability to discern the exact definitions of a group of terms. Well-written items allow students to show what they know more quickly than they would by reading through numerous multiple-choice items. However, to avoid confusion, do not make matching lists longer than roughly ten items. In addition, keep lists of items on the same page because flipping back and forth between two sheets can also be confusing (Linn & Gronlund, 1995). Table 14.4 on page 520 provides examples of good and poor matching questions.

■**FILL-IN-THE-BLANK AND SHORT-ANSWER ITEMS**   Fill-in-the-blank and short-answer items (also called *completion items*) require the test taker to complete a statement by filling in the missing information or to compose a short answer to a question. Teachers often prefer this type of item because it seems easy to write a good item based on statements in a textbook: You can take a statement of fact or a description, remove a key portion, and ask the student to supply the missing portion. Although this procedure seems very straightforward to teachers who know the answer they are seeking, for the student, items requiring the completion of missing information can be very confusing.

First, there are often several potentially correct answers you may not have considered. If a student gives a correct answer that is not what the teacher seeks, the student may inappropriately be marked as wrong. Astute students recognize that their task is not only to think about how to complete the statement, but also to decide what the teacher is looking for before answering. To eliminate such problems, teachers often resort to writing items in a very simple form where there is less opportunity for ambiguity. Avoiding complexity when writing items often leads to items that measure only lower level thinking or basic knowledge. Because of all these potential drawbacks, fill-in-the-blank and short-answer items should be used sparingly (Gronlund, 1993).

TABLE 14.4   Examples of Poor Versus Good Matching Questions

POOR: 1. Match the state in column A with its source of wealth in column B.

Column A	Column B
____ New York	1. agriculture
____ Alaska	2. mining
____ Florida	3. manufacturing
____ Nebraska	4. information processing
____ New Jersey	5. fabrication
____ Wisconsin	6. trucking
____ California	7. insurance
	8. education
	9. endowments

Why Is It Poor?
The question and the options are ambiguous and confusing.

POOR: 2. Match the 2 columns so that the composer is matched with the work he composed.

Column A	Column B
____ Mozart	1. Verdi
____ The Daughter of the Regiment	2. Porgy and Bess
____ Barber of Seville	3. Donizetti
____ Gershwin	4. Marriage of Figaro
____ Aida	5. Rossini

Why Is It Poor?
It mixes composers and works in the same column, thus making it confusing.

POOR: 3. Match the number of the cognitive development stage proposed by Piaget with the developmental achievement given below.

a. During the ____ stage, object permanence is achieved.

b. A child is able to solve abstract problems once s/he reaches the ____ stage.

c. A child is able to perform symbolic play for the first time during the ____ stage.

d. The ____ stage is when the principle of conservation is acquired.

    1. formal operational
    2. sensorimotor
    3. preoperational
    4. concrete operational

Why Is It Poor?
It is overly wordy and confusingly structured.

GOOD: 1. Match the state capital in Column B to the appropriate state in Column A.

Column A	Column B
____ New York	1. Juno
____ Alaska	2. Lincoln
____ Florida	3. Madison
____ Nebraska	4. Tallahassee
____ New Jersey	5. Sacramento
____ Wisconsin	6. Trenton
____ California	7. Albany

GOOD: 2. Match the composer in Column B to his work in Column A.

Column A	Column B
____ The Daughter of the Regiment	1. Rossini
____ Marriage of Figaro	2. Gershwin
____ Porgy and Bess	3. Donizetti
____ Aida	4. Mozart
____ The Barber of Seville	5. Verdi

GOOD: 3. Match the number associated with the cognitive stage of development proposed by Piaget with the developmental achievement given below.

____ Object permanence is achieved.	1. Preoperational
____ Abstract problems can be solved.	2. Sensorimotor
____ Symbolic play is performed.	3. Concrete operational
____ Conservation is acquired.	4. Formal operational

If you do choose to use completion items, keep the following points in mind. First, each question should have one main point and should contain only one blank—or several, in order, if responses comprise a list—for the student to complete. More than one blank separated by portions of a sentence can cause confusion. Second, make all blanks the same length so you do not give students clues about the relative lengths of correct answers. Third, be specific about the form of the answer you seek, without giving the answer away; this way, students will know what is expected of them. Table 14.5 provides examples of good and poor completion questions.

■**EVALUATING OBJECTIVE ITEMS**   Once you have developed an objective test and have proofread it carefully, you may think the test is ready to administer. Before moving forward, however, show the draft of the test to a colleague as an outside check on your thinking, and then pilot the test on a friend, or, ideally, on a student who is not

TABLE 14.5 **Examples of Poor Versus Good Completion Questions**

POOR: 1. Complementary angles _____.

Why Is It Poor?
Without specifying the sum of angles' degrees, one could validly respond in many ways (e.g., "are so-called because they complement each other").

POOR: 2. _____, _____, and _____ have all won the Nobel Prize in chemistry.

Why Is It Poor?
It is confusing to present blanks before the question––the question should come first.

POOR: 3. The _____ War lasted from _____ to 1865.

Why Is It Poor?
It is confusing and poorly worded.

POOR: 4. John Steinbeck received the Pulitzer Prize for _____ _____ ____ _____.

Why Is It Poor?
The length of the lines is proportional to the words that fit them ("The Grapes of Wrath"), thus providing a clue to the correct answer.

POOR: 5. Water is composed of one part _____ and _____ part(s) oxygen.

Why Is It Poor?
The answer called for mixes the name of the element (hydrogen) and the number of parts of the other element (oxygen) and is thus confusing.

POOR: 6. _____ refers to random access memory.

Why Is It Poor?
By failing to limit the question to computer terminology, one could argue for other correct answers.

POOR: 7. _____ are indigenous to Australia.

Why Is It Poor?
Many things are indigenous to Australia besides kangaroos (aborigines, platypuses, koalas, etc.)

POOR: 8. _____ tells the musician to play loudly.

Why Is It Poor?
By failing to specify a musical term, it is possible to give several answers that are valid (e.g., "the audience," "a conductor").

POOR: 9. Plant cells have _____.

Why Is It Poor?
Plant cells have many features that can be listed.

POOR: 10. _____ was assassinated in 1963.

Why Is It Poor?
There may have been other persons assassinated in 1963 besides an American president.

GOOD: 1. Complementary angles add up to _____ degrees.

GOOD: 2. Name 3 people who have received the Nobel Prize in chemistry: _____, _____, and _____.

GOOD: 3. The Civil War began in the year _____ and ended in the year _____.

GOOD: 4. Which of John Steinbeck's literary works received the Pulitzer Prize?

_____

GOOD: 5. Water is composed of one part _____ and two parts _____.

GOOD: 6. The computer term *RAM* stands for _____ _____ _____.

GOOD: 7. Kangaroos are indigenous to _____.

GOOD: 8. *Forte* indicates that a musical selection should be played _____ .

GOOD: 9. Unlike animal cells, plants contain the photosynthesis-related molecule _____ .

GOOD: 10. U.S. president John F. Kennedy was assassinated in the year _____.

in your class and who will not reveal the answers. If you cannot find an outsider to help you evaluate the test, put it aside for a few days and then read it again, with a more critical eye.

Once you have administered a test for which you wrote the items, remain alert to potential problems with individual items. Many student questions about a particular item, for example, indicate a problem. If many students answer an item incorrectly, or if they misread the item (for example, if their answers are consistent for a different reading of the item than the reading you had in mind), the item itself may be flawed. Keep a record (on a clean copy of the test) of the student input you get in response to each item. The best items are clear and discriminate between those students who did well overall on the test and those students who did poorly overall on the test.

As you are grading tests, be alert to unfair items you should rewrite or even eliminate from the test before you use it in the future. With some practice, you will be able to eliminate sources of bias from the objective tests you create.

 DEVELOPING ESSAY TESTS

Now, we consider a more subjective way to assess student learning—the essay test. Essay tests require students to be actively involved in defining a question as they answer it, and in composing and defending their answer. Guessing is no longer an option. Students cannot easily hide behind incomplete knowledge and understanding of the material, although they can answer in generalities. Jing Xu added an essay question to her final exam to complement the multiple-choice and true/false questions. Because of students' different learning styles, vary the types of questions you use on a test to give all students a chance to show what they know. Essays are best used for measuring high-level, complex learning (Gronlund, 1993). Some students naturally gravitate toward essay writing; others have trouble expressing their knowledge in this format. Expert teachers remember these issues when they compose tests.

One study examined the success of students in college if they were either high scoring on essay questions and low scoring on multiple-choice questions, or vice versa (Bridgeman & Morgan, 1996). The authors found that both groups of students were equally successful across different subject areas (history, English, and biology). Both groups had equivalent course grades, although students in the high multiple-choice group performed much better on the multiple-choice portions of tests across subjects (including the verbal portion of the *SAT*), and students in the high essay group performed much better on essay portions of tests across subjects. Obviously, students have differing styles that are reflected in better performance on certain types of test questions; however, in general, students with one style are not smarter nor will they do better in school than students with other styles.

Because essay tests are subjective, different teachers may grade the same response differently. Thus, when they score essays, expert teachers ensure that they follow appropriate guidelines regarding fair grading policies and procedures. In addition, they carefully consider and review their questions before administering an essay test. Well-designed essay tests go much deeper into student learning than objective tests. Essay questions also take longer to answer; thus teachers can cover less content with an essay test than they can with an objective test of the same duration. Often, the best compromise is to have part of a test consist of objective questions and part of it consist of essay questions. Let us review a few suggestions for the best use of the essay format (Gronlund, 1993).

The essay question is the best format for probing student understanding and reasoning at a complex level. A good essay question is clear and unambiguous and defines a specific question or set of questions. When writing essay questions, provide clear input about what the answer should cover, so the essays do not drift from the main point. In deciding how much time to give students to compose their answers, remember that some students may have the appropriate knowledge and understanding but be slow writers. To be sure essay questions do not primarily test the ability to write under pressure, provide ample time. When including more than one question, suggest how students should divide their time among the questions. Finally, avoid making essay tests too long, particularly for younger students, to keep fatigue and writer's block from undermining students' ability to show what they know.

Elementary school students can only begin to answer brief essay questions once they have mastered written language. In their first few years at school, most children need the guidance of true/false, multiple-choice, and fill in questions; an open essay is intimidating. By fourth or fifth grade, students are able to do well on essays if the questions are

THINKING PRACTICALLY

Write three good completion items that test material from this chapter.

SUGGESTION: To get you started, two examples from among many possibilities appear here:

Evaluations of students that focus on real-world performances are known as _____ (authentic assessments).

Three frequently used types of objective test questions are _____, _____, _____ (multiple choice, true/false, matching).

Two basic approaches to grading are _____ and _____ (norm referenced, criterion referenced).

clear, the essay length is specified, and they have been assigned homework and classwork requiring writing essays. As students progress through school, the use of essays becomes more and more appropriate; by high school, most students are well accustomed to writing their answers in essay form.

Essays are often the best way to measure higher order critical thinking. In most cases, for well-crafted questions, students cannot study for and do well on an essay test simply by memorizing vast amounts of information: They must learn how to reason actively and process information. However, be aware of the drawbacks of essay testing. First, scoring essay tests takes far longer than scoring objective tests. Scoring can be highly subjective, although expert teachers take care to eliminate unnecessary bias. In addition, students' writing ability is likely to be a strong contributor to their grades on an essay. If a test seeks also to evaluate writing ability, this is not a problem. But sometimes students with good knowledge and critical-thinking skills do not write well, or they make spelling and grammatical errors that significantly lower their scores, despite their superior understanding. Conversely, students with excellent writing ability may be able to write an immaculate essay that largely misses the point. In general, be careful to use fair scoring procedures that give appropriate weight to both content and form of essays.

THINKING PRACTICALLY

Write three good essay test questions covering material from this chapter.

SUGGESTION: Compare and contrast traditional and authentic assessment; describe the strengths and weaknesses of criterion- versus norm-referenced grading systems; describe three specific methods teachers can use to ensure that their tests are fair.

When writing essay questions, craft the questions carefully and read them over—and have others read them—to spot inconsistencies or areas that can be misread. Stress higher order thinking skills by asking students to compare and contrast, or to analyze the antecedents and consequences of an event. Tell students to list facts to defend their answers. As with objective test items, piloting an essay test is always a good idea. Table 14.6 on page 524 provides examples of good and poor essay questions.

■ **EVALUATING ESSAY TESTS** The most challenging aspect of an objective test is writing good items; the grading is generally simple. The most difficult part of an essay test, however, is ensuring that grading is fair and accurate. Develop criteria for scoring an essay test in advance, unless you have no experience with a particular group of students or a particular grade level, in which case first read the essays and then put them aside while you develop a grading scheme. If you intend to give each essay two grades—one for content and the other for style, for example—inform students of this fact in advance, so they understand the grading scheme you will use.

At least three approaches ensure fair grading (Williams, Blythe, White, Li, Sternberg, & Gardner, 1996). For situations in which there is one long essay rather than multiple short essays, first read through all of the essays and then divide them into piles. Using five piles works well. The first pile should contain the best essays and the fifth pile the worst; the piles in between contain the essays corresponding to intermediate levels of quality. After sorting the essays, skim the piles once again to ensure you have sorted fairly. Finally, award grades that correspond to the piles—A's to the essays in pile 1, B's to the essays in pile 2, and so on.

A second approach to grading essays is to begin by writing a model answer to each question that contains all the facts and main issues you want your students to cover. These model answers should show the point totals a student will earn for each portion of the correct answer. You can allow for good writing to earn more credit by awarding a certain number of points for it. This scoring technique is well suited to grading essays designed to elicit factual recall and direct exposition; however, more complex essay topics do not allow as easily for the use of this technique.

A third approach to grading essays is to begin by developing a scoring key that is generic and can consequently be used for many different types of essays. This scoring key consists of anchors explaining what each score reflects. For example, many teachers use a 1-to-5 scale. A *1* reflects a poor essay that makes few or no appropriate points and is nearly incomprehensible; a *5* reflects an excellent essay that is well argued, well written,

TABLE 14.6   Examples of Poor Versus Good Essay Questions

POOR: 1. What is the general tone of the essays written by Huxley and Snow?

Why Is It Poor?
It is vague with regard to what is being tested; for example, is it "tone" in the sense of affect (optimistic), style (choppy vs. fluid), beliefs (decency of man), etc.

POOR: 2. List all of the differences between Piaget's and Vygotsky's theories of cognitive development.

Why Is It Poor?
The word "list" encourages students simply to make a list without defining or analyzing significant issues; also, the word "all" makes the question potentially impossible to answer and again encourages students to make a list of differences between the two theories with no analysis.

POOR: 3. Describe the life course of an Alzheimer's patient in terms of defining changes.

Why Is It Poor?
It is ambiguous as to what is being sought––life course is a broad concept and a student could write almost anything.

POOR: 4. Why did Harriet Beecher Stowe write *Uncle Tom's Cabin?*

Why Is It Poor?
The question is vague and allows students to respond in numerous ways that have little to do with the most significant aspects of the book. Authors have many potential reasons for writing books—including personal reasons—that are not nearly as important for students to understand as the broader societal impact of the book.

POOR: 5. Describe social mechanisms among chimpanzees.

Why Is It Poor?
It is overly broad and not specific as to which mechanisms are being tested.

GOOD: 1. The essays of Huxley and Snow are both concerned with "the future of man." Do you find these writers generally optimistic or pessimistic? Point out the similarities and differences in their views and present your views of the future of civilization in the context of these two writers.

GOOD: 2. Define, discuss, and defend what you believe to be the three most important differences between Piaget's and Vygotsky's theories of cognitive development.

GOOD: 3. Identify the six stages of the Phase Model with respect to the life course of an Alzheimer's patient. For at least three of the stages, give an example of a defining behavioral and/or physical change seen in a patient in that stage.

GOOD: 4. Describe the social and political atmosphere in the United States when Harriet Beecher Stowe wrote Uncle Tom's Cabin, and state three social and/or political changes that resulted from the publication of this book.

GOOD: 5. Describe social mechanisms among chimpanzees in terms of dependent rank, strategic intelligence, and reciprocity. For two of these give an example of a behavior among chimpanzees that exemplifies that social pattern.

THINKING PRACTICALLY

Have you ever written what you believed was a good response to an essay question and then received a poor grade? Why do you think this happened? What could your teacher have done to help avoid this problem?

SUGGESTION: Sometimes a difference of opinion with a teacher can create such a situation, such as when a student writes a political essay and the teacher opposes the position. Sometimes a teacher may have expected a certain type of response and reacts negatively to other types of responses. Expert teachers take steps to ensure that their grading of essays is not biased by asking other teachers to read essays that seem problematic, or by asking students to discuss and clarify their responses.

and filled with numerous facts that support its arguments. Intermediate numbers correspond to intermediate levels of essay quality. By developing such a scoring key in advance, you can begin grading without reading through all of the essays. However, always shuffle the essays and read a few of them before beginning to get an idea of the range in quality of the responses.

To ensure you are grading the essays fairly, score all students' answers to one question before moving on to score the next question. This procedure prevents bias because of a good or poor first answer on a given student's paper. The student may have done a far better job on the second question than on the first question, and grading all answers to a particular question in a row prevents you from developing a general impression of the student's performance based on answers you read first. Such a general impression may unfairly advantage or disadvantage students whose answers vary in quality. Also try to grade all responses to a particular question at a single sitting. Finally, it is always wise with essay tests—as with all types of tests—to have students place their names on the *backs* of their papers, so you are not biased by knowing the identity of the students during grading. Table 14.7 displays a sample grading scheme for essay tests.

TABLE	14.7	Example of Grading Scheme for Essay Tests

Grading on a 1-to-5 scale:

5   Excellent essay in every respect—well written, clear, well organized, overall excellent use of written English. Excellent understanding and organization of relevant knowledge. Shows level of comprehension, analysis, and synthesis of ideas and concepts that goes beyond simply repeating what was learned in a well-organized way.

4   Very good essay. Some elements may be lacking, but generally a solid effort evidencing good command of written English. Very good understanding and organization of relevant knowledge. (The presence of two or more errors makes a 5 a 4; a 5 should be reserved for excellent essays with only minor errors.)

3   Good essay. It flows and is readable, but it is marked by some flaws in grammar, sentence structure, vocabulary, clarity of expression, and so on. Good understanding and organization of relevant knowledge. (Many serious flaws mean that the essay should be given a 2.)

2   Poor essay. An effort was made, but the quality is generally low. Many errors are apparent; the student could clearly use extra work in writing. Poor command of relevant knowledge.

1   Very poor essay or essentially blank. Nothing much to work with. The student obviously performs very poorly in writing and could clearly use a substantial amount of help. Almost no command of relevant knowledge.

Essay tests measure what students know by asking them to actively demonstrate their knowledge and reasoning ability. Much of what makes essay tests appealing in comparison to objective tests is that, in the real world after graduation from school, students will not be given questions to answer followed by lists of options containing the right answer. Thus essay questions are considered to be a better reflection of the ability to think actively and independently about all information, and to formulate a persuasive argument on one's own.

Implications for Teaching

■ *Count on well-designed traditional assessments to provide valuable information about student learning and progress.* There is a rich history regarding all aspects of traditional assessment, which has been the testing mode of choice in most schools for decades. You can draw on numerous sources of information to refine your understanding and use of traditional assessments.

■ *Plan well-organized lessons and tailor assessment questions to the level and content of classwork and homework.* Tests are effective only when they target the appropriate material at the appropriate level. Careful planning and integration of instruction and assessment are key.

■ *Use frequent, short assessments.* These help students improve and result in greater learning and retention of material. Giving one big test creates intense pressure on students when the big test comes around, but allows for slacking off in the meantime. Expert teachers use tests to motivate good studying behavior, and they prevent single tests from becoming the sole means for a student to show what he or she knows.

■ *Use objective test questions to assess a wide range of student learning in a short time.* Well-written objective questions, especially multiple-choice questions, can be remarkably effective; poorly written questions can be disastrous. Broad coverage of the material is possible with well-written objective questions.

IN EACH CHAPTER OF THE TEXT, WE INTRODUCE YOU TO A FEW SPECIFIC STRATEGIES—
ANALYTICAL, CREATIVE, AND PRACTICAL —USED BY BOTH EXPERT TEACHERS AND EXPERT STUDENTS.

THE ANALYTICAL TEACHER: Raman writes one or two test questions every day in the teacher's lounge after class, to be sure his tests mirror what he taught.

THE CREATIVE TEACHER: To make his assessments more interesting to students, Raman writes essay questions that ask students to take the perspectives of students from different parts of the world.

THE PRACTICAL TEACHER: Raman gives students practice quizzes that he doesn't even collect and then goes over the right answers in class, in order to prepare students for tests.

THE ANALYTICAL STUDENT: Crystal takes practice tests in her textbook under the same conditions that she will face during the actual test (by timing herself, not resting in between questions, and so on).

THE CREATIVE STUDENT: Crystal draws up practice tests for herself to take and hands them in to her teacher for her comments.

THE PRACTICAL STUDENT: Crystal gets together with several of her friends, and they ask themselves what types of test questions the teacher is likely to ask on the next test as they work through the answers together.

■ *In using essay tests, be careful to ensure uniform and fair grading of essays.* Essays sometimes confuse writing skill with knowledge of the subject matter itself—and these do not necessarily always go hand in hand. Writing good essay questions is challenging and takes practice. Ensuring fairness in grading essays requires rigorous application of the techniques discussed in this chapter.

CONSTRUCTING YOUR OWN LEARNING

Write a rough draft of a final exam that reflects the material you have learned in this course. Make sure to write at least two of each of the following types of questions: multiple-choice, fill-in-the-blank, matching, true/false, and essay. Read your test over and try to imagine what it would be like to take the test. Is it fair? Are the questions clear and unambiguous? Now find a friend in the class to whom to give your test. Ask this person to read through the questions and comment on their fairness and appropriateness. Does your friend think the test is clear? How would she or he improve it? What does this demonstration tell you about the process of writing a test for the students you teach?

Authentic Assessments

Many educators believe the entire premise of classroom testing—as well as standardized testing—is flawed: These individuals argue that tests should reflect the types of real-world performances for which schools are preparing students (Wiggins, 1989). Such **authentic assessments** ask students to use skills and knowledge to solve problems in the same manner as if the students were completing real-world tasks. For example, the written test you took to get a driver's license was a typical standardized test, but the road test you took was an authentic assessment. The idea was to observe people actually behind the wheel before giving them driver's licenses, and it makes sense. After all, how comfortable would you be on the road if licenses were awarded solely on the basis of scores on the written test? The goal of authentic assessment is to give a better picture of how students will perform in actual meaningful activities while using their new skills and knowledge (Wolf, 1998; Wolf et al., 1991). Given students' individual differences and the range of learning styles, some students who do not score high on traditional tests perform better on authentic assessments—the nature of the performance required may be a better match to these students' abilities and talents.

TYPES OF AUTHENTIC ASSESSMENTS

Norman Gronlund (1988) describes four types of performance tests that simulate real-world performances to differing degrees. The least like a real-world performance is the paper-and-pencil test, with which we are all familiar. Next is the identification test, in which students are asked to describe things to show their knowledge (for example, the bones in the human body for a medical student, the uses of different tools for a sculpting student, and the parts of an engine for a student of auto mechanics). Next is the simulated performance, in which students perform under conditions created to simulate the real world (for example, learning CPR on a dummy or practicing diving jumps on a trampoline while wearing a harness). Finally, there is the work-sample assessment, in which real-world performances are scored as assessments (for example, a musical performance before an audience or an autopsy performed by a veterinary student on a dead animal).

Perhaps you have taken an authentic assessment. For example, you may have played a musical instrument in a recital, or you may have played on a sports team that entered a competition. In these domains, we are used to thinking in terms of authentic assessments. How much would it mean if you knew the results of a paper-and-pencil test taken by an athlete who wished to join your team or by a music student who wished to play in your band? In other domains, however, we are not used to thinking in terms of authentic assessments. For example, you might not think of the idea of giving grade school children math tests that consisted of their actually buying items with play money and making proper change, their dividing a recipe in half to cook for only two rather than four people, or their using a bus schedule to figure out when they would arrive in a neighboring town. But these are legitimate math tests, because they ask children to apply their math skills to solve real-world problems. Of course, authentic assessments can also be paper-and-pencil tests; teachers can design tests that ask students to complete tasks with real-world relevance, such as writing a persuasive letter to an elected official or developing architectural plans for a house. Thus authentic assessments can take many forms; the key is that such tests assess real-world skills.

THINKING PRACTICALLY

Describe three situations not discussed in the text in which authentic assessments can be used.

SUGGESTION: Screening potential leads for the school play; giving a full in-box to job applicants and asking them to prioritize the work; asking a potential hairdresser to show what he can do (on someone else!) before hiring him.

CHARACTERISTICS OF GOOD AUTHENTIC ASSESSMENTS

What are the characteristics of good authentic assessments? How can teachers be sure that authentic assessments are valid, reliable, and as objective and fair as possible? Often an authentic assessment is open-ended as far as time allotment is concerned. Although the final performance may be timed, in general, ample time to prepare and rehearse is provided. In other words, authentic assessments do not usually involve working against the clock, unless the assessment reflects a naturally speed-related performance (such as jumping horses in a competition or singing a fast song). In addition, authentic assessments often require collaboration with other people in the planning, developing, or enacting of the performance. (One drawback of group performances is the difficulty of evaluating separately the performances of individual team members.) These assessments should mimic as closely as possible the real-world performances students will complete outside of school. They should challenge students to learn, grow, and develop as they push themselves to attain greater levels of ability. Good authentic assessments also give students leeway to customize or select particular aspects of their performances to show their own individual contribution.

Beginning teachers (or any teacher who wishes to learn more) can consult books entirely devoted to the principles and practices of authentic assessment (for example, Khattri, Reeve, & Kane, 1998).

How are authentic assessments graded fairly? The criteria must be well thought through and must match important aspects of the skills on display—handwriting should not matter, for example, in judging the quality of a play script that is being acted out. Authentic assessments are best graded on a criterion-referenced system; grades should be based on independent sets of standards defining good performances. A good authentic assessment is graded on criteria the students themselves perceive as being meaningful to the performance. The types of grades given should reflect multiple aspects of the performance; consequently, the teacher or panel of teachers might give multiple grades for different aspects of the performance. Sometimes, the quality of a performance may not be uniform across the different aspects—the content of the writing on which a speech is based may be good, for example, but the delivery weak. By giving multiple grades, you can reward and acknowledge the aspects of performances that deserve it.

The best authentic assessments allow all students to show what they know. These assessments make it possible for effort to produce a good final product, even if the student lacks natural gifts in the area. In other words, if the goal is to evaluate general understanding of music, an assessment of singing ability is not fair to an unmusical child, whereas an assessment of a general music project is, if this general project consists of a report on a musician along with a live presentation of a recording and an analysis of the person's music. Good authentic assessments energize students about showing what they know. The authentic assessment can particularly provide an opportunity for those students who do not always do well on objective tests or essay tests to display their special gifts. A final quality of good authentic assessments is that they require students to listen to feedback on their performance, and then to react to that feedback and strengthen the performance.

Baxter, Elder, and Glaser (1996) studied the role of performance assessments in making relevant cognitive activity apparent to teachers and students. They found that students' performance on a science authentic assessment showed critical differences between those who could think and reason well, and those who could not. Differences in the quality of explanations, adequacy of problem representation, appropriateness of solution strategies, and frequency and flexibility of self-monitoring all varied among students. Teachers can observe these types of cognitive characteristics of effective performance on an authentic assessment. Expert teachers then use this information for purposes of planning instruction and grading students.

A high school student displays her portfolio to her teacher. Teachers should define the categories a portfolio should contain but allow students to select the exact contents within each category. (H. Dratch, The Image Works)

A **portfolio** is a type of authentic assessment; it is also a method of instruction that assists students in their learning and development. A portfolio is a collection of student work that demonstrates the student's abilities, efforts, accomplishments, and growth in an area or areas. A portfolio can represent the student's own selections of work (influenced by teacher advice), the teacher's selections, or some of both; it should contain a statement regarding the student's goals and progress toward achieving these goals. Collins (1992) recommends that teachers define the categories a portfolio should contain, and allow students to select the exact contents within each category. A portfolio can be changed and adapted as a student moves through a course or semester in order to reflect the student's growth. Often, students are given the task of reflecting on the contents of their portfolio to assess their progress and chart their goals for the future.

■**TYPES OF PORTFOLIOS** Two common types of portfolios you are probably familiar with are artistic portfolios and writing portfolios. For example, when an artist applies to a graduate program, she typically must supply a portfolio she has designed to show the range of her talents and her development as an artist. The portfolio often includes a written statement of her professional goals as well. Similarly, when a fashion model solicits a job, he shows a portfolio of photographs that displays his range of poses and his best physical features. An author's written portfolio consists of a selection of short stories, poems, essays, or critical pieces of work that show that writer's range and strengths. But these artistic and creative arenas are not the only places in which portfolios are appropriate.

A student can prepare a portfolio in any area of study—science, social studies, foreign language, mathematics, or health and nutrition. A portfolio's contents are influenced by the nature of the area being reflected. For example, a portfolio in biology class can include samples of insects and plants with descriptions, as well as laboratory reports and data that have been analyzed. A portfolio in social studies can include copies of old newspaper articles the student has analyzed along with an explanation of the student's analyses, photographs of historical sites with student descriptions of them, and transcripts of interviews with people from different countries—and analyses of these interviews—conducted by the student. A mathematics portfolio can include a record and description of math problems the student attempted and solved at different points in the semester, showing how her methods of analysis became more sophisticated. Portfolio content is also influenced by the age of the students and whether they are grouped with same-age peers or in multi-age teams (Hall & Hewitt-Gervais, 2000).

■**CREATING PORTFOLIOS** When using portfolios to assess and instruct students, remember that students should take primary responsibility for creating their portfolios. Encourage students to include pieces of work that represent self-reflection, improvement, and the ability to learn from criticism. Portfolios should include material that reflects the different activities the students engaged in while doing course work (for example, laboratory reports, library assignments, and foreign language stories). Expert teachers stress that students' portfolios are personal statements and students should be given a substantial say about what to include. However, an expert teacher provides guidelines to ensure that students are including work from a range of areas and of a range of types (in other words, not only their journal entries for the semester, or not only their chemistry lab write-ups). Students must understand that their portfolios should not include everything they have done, but rather a sample of work across several content areas.

Any type of learning task can become the basis for a portfolio collected and managed by the student. One of the advantages of portfolios is that they engender pride in the students who have developed them. Seeing the growth of one's collection provides a feeling

---

THINKING PRACTICALLY

Name three additional situations in which portfolios would be appropriate.

SUGGESTION: A pastry chef displays photos of his creations, a teacher creates a portfolio containing samples of lesson plans and novel approaches to instruction, and a carpenter assembles a photo album showing his past woodworking projects.

of accomplishment that is often lost when the work is never collected and displayed in one place. Also, in their portfolios students can be encouraged to show improvements in their work; this process helps build student confidence by reminding students of their ability to persevere and overcome obstacles. Because of all of these advantages, expert teachers incorporate the use of portfolios into their assessment. Use of portfolios as assessments is most effective if these portfolios are classroom based rather than being assembled solely for large-scale testing and evaluation of students (Freedman, 1993).

 ## EXHIBITIONS

Another type of authentic assessment is a student exhibition or performance. Again, you are probably familiar with exhibitions: Vocal recitals, plays, oral book reports, skits, and other types of exhibitions are common in today's classrooms. An **exhibition** is a public performance before an audience that may involve people who will judge the performance. Exhibitions that represent good authentic assessments will reflect a great deal of time and preparation, and this preparation will have helped the student understand a wide range of material. For example, to earn a graduate degree, a person must often complete an oral qualifying examination that lasts for several days (with breaks for meals and sleep). This authentic assessment is actually an exhibition of what the student has learned, often in a public forum. Because exhibitions can be nervewracking for some students, it is wise to use them with portfolios, which do not entail on-the-spot performances.

 ## EVALUATING PERFORMANCE ON AUTHENTIC ASSESSMENTS

The evaluation of either a portfolio or an exhibition should be criterion based; that is, it should be based on an analysis of whether or not the portfolio or exhibition has met established standards. Points can be assigned for the portions of the work that can be judged as correct or incorrect. Points can also be assigned for the portions requiring written work, such as analyses and essays, following the guidelines already provided for grading essays. For the portions of work that involve artistic displays, either the teacher can be the sole judge, or, preferably, a panel of educators, students, and even parents can make judgments. As with all assessments, the proper use of authentic assessments includes giving students clear feedback and directions regarding how to improve in the future: Students should be told not only what they have done well, but also what they could have done better, why, and how. Authentic assessments can be biased, unreliable, and invalid, just as traditional assessments can be. Develop and enforce rigorous standards for judging the work relative to objective criteria of quality, so all students have an equal chance to do well if they apply themselves.

Herman, Gearhart, and Baker (1993) examined issues of reliability and validity in the scoring of portfolios. They showed that it is possible to score portfolios consistently by giving a single score of overall quality, and to use a common rating scale to score different classroom assignments of a similar type. However, the degree to which these scores are meaningful and can be generalized is questionable. This study showed significant differences in students' performance when judged based on a standard writing assignment, individual student work, and portfolios; the scores depended on the rating and summing procedure used. Because all scoring schemes carry with them value judgments about what is an important and meaningful accomplishment, teachers who use portfolios must recognize that subjectivity in grading can be a significant hurdle to overcome. When experienced raters use well-designed scoring schemes, reliability improves (Herman & Winters, 1994). One way to reduce subjectivity in the scoring of authentic assessments is to develop ahead of time clear and unambiguous scoring guides that are uniformly applied to every student's performance (see Table 14.9 for an example).

THINKING ANALYTICALLY

What factors might bias the grade given to a student for an exhibition?

SUGGESTION: If the teacher likes the student and/or knows her well, if the student has rehearsed the performance for the teacher several times and has gotten the teacher's pledge of approval, if the teacher is in a particularly good or bad mood that day or is angry with the student, for example.

TABLE 14.9 Example of Scoring Protocol for an Authentic Assessment

Task: Writing and performing a skit about preventing teen suicide.

Assign points on a 1-to-5 scale for each of the following aspects of the performance.

1. Displays understanding of nature of problem.

2. Displays knowledge of national statistics.

3. Portrays troubled teens in realistic, convincing manner.

4. Story makes sense and rings true.

5. Performance reaches audience and holds their attention.

6. Performance communicates valuable lessons.

7. Dialogue moves quickly and is well edited.

8. Student actors are convincing.

9. Student actors know their lines and are well rehearsed.

10. Performers look straight ahead and speak clearly and convincingly.

11. Costuming is appropriate.

12. Performance shows effective teamwork.

Another cause of low reliability in the grading of authentic assessments can be uneven student performance—some performances or work samples are often better than others, particularly for those students whose work varies widely from day to day. Consider a broad range of work samples for portfolio inclusion to ensure that the student's best work is represented, and also ensure that every judge (if there are multiple judges) scores the same work samples.

Elementary school students present a Vietnamese musical performance for parents, teachers, and schoolmates. (Bob Daemmrich Photos, Inc.)

Are traditional assessments adequate to evaluate students? Or should schools switch to authentic and performance assessments?

FIRST VIEW: *Traditional assessments are time-honored, reliable, and valid ways to evaluate student learning.* Traditional assessments, consisting mostly of objective and essay classroom tests, are the best way to evaluate the knowledge that students have acquired. It may sometimes be boring or repetitive for students to memorize basic facts and figures, but this basic knowledge provides the foundation for higher-order learning of concepts, principles, and relations among concepts. Regardless of how talented students are, they need this foundation, which is created by hard work and cannot be evaluated as well with authentic assessments as it can be evaluated with traditional assessments. Students must be helped, by their teachers and their parents, to understand that the foundation they create while young will be there to support their intellectual activities for their entire lives. Traditional testing increases student motivation and enhances learning, and it is part of a system that prepares students for the future. Alternative methods of assessment are unreliable and do not provide a clear picture of student learning that is comparable from student to student. Thus evaluations based on authentic assessments are unfair and potentially flawed. Traditional assessments are more objective and represent the most defensible measures of student learning.

SECOND VIEW: *Authentic and performance assessments are the only types of tests that meaningfully evaluate student learning and performance.* Knowledge is fine, but the type of knowledge reflected in traditional assessments is often inert knowledge: Students memorize and then repeat answers under time pressure, but weeks later they have often forgotten the knowledge. Furthermore, when they prepare for traditional tests, students never learn how to apply the knowledge to solve real-world problems. In comparison, authentic assessments map student learning and performance onto real-world performances and challenges that are relevant to students' lives outside of school. Authentic assessments challenge students to use their creative and practical as well as analytical talents to expand their capabilities; these assessments encourage autonomy and self-directedness. Competent performance on authentic assessments means far more than simply getting 50 multiple-choice questions correct.

THIRD VIEW: A SYNTHESIS: *Both traditional and authentic assessments are useful in evaluating students.* It is true that authentic assessments are good learning and development experiences for students, but relying solely on these assessments may allow students to get through school without acquiring the basic facts and figures that form the foundation for later thinking and accomplishments. Furthermore, authentic assessments suffer from a lack of reliability and validity in scoring; it is often difficult or even impossible to identify what a correct answer consists of. Because of this inability to distinguish performances that do or do not show whether a student has learned important information, authentic assessments may result in students progressing through school without learning essential information. Traditional assessments, however, may short-change the types of learning and integration students must do in life after graduation from school.

The answer is that both types of assessments are important and useful. Used in tandem, traditional assessments encourage students to study and learn the basic information they need, and performance-based assessments allow students to apply their knowledge and expand on it to solve real-world problems. Both types of assessments, and the experiences they create, are essential. The goal for teachers is to incorporate both types of assessments into the curriculum, so students display a wide range of performances.

Now that we have discussed at length the use of traditional and authentic assessments for evaluating student learning, we consider how the grades based on students' performance on these assessments should be determined and reported.

Implications for Teaching

- *Use authentic assessments to test students on skills and knowledge required to solve real-world problems and complete real-world tasks.* Like traditional assessments, authentic assessments can be either well or poorly constructed and can reflect either a great deal or very little about student competence. At their best, authentic assessments represent an essential method for evaluating real-world performance.

- *Recognize the diversity of authentic assessment options and take advantage of different testing formats.* Authentic assessments take many forms, from paper-and-pencil tasks to identification tasks to actual performances. Different types of competence can best be evaluated through different types of performances. Students will gravitate toward formats that match their patterns of abilities, preferences, and experiences.

- *Score authentic assessments, including portfolios and exhibitions, as objectively and rigorously as possible.* This care will help ensure that they are fair evaluations of student learning. A frequent criticism is that because authentic assessments are difficult to score, they are good in theory but fall short in practice. Expert teachers recognize and take steps to address this inherent pitfall when using authentic assessment.

Grading and Reporting

Once you have planned your instruction, conducted your classes and activities, and designed and administered fair assessments, you must now master the complex issues of grading and reporting in order to communicate student achievement. As a student yourself, you understand how important grades are to students and their parents. As students develop, grades become essential criteria for selection to specialized programs and schools. Because students agonize over their grades, it is imperative that as a teacher you implement accurate and fair grading policies. Grading is not a task to approach haphazardly: Expert teachers develop grading systems well in advance to ensure that their grading and reporting practices are sound. As Jing Xu learned, students are heavily invested in getting good grades, and they often complain if they perceive unfairness or any lack of carefulness in how grading was conducted.

THE IMPACT OF GRADES

Before choosing a grading system for use in your classrooms, consider the effect of a grading system on student learning and motivation. Remember that the importance you assign during grading to different types of work—tests, quizzes, homework, reports—will directly influence how much importance students assign to these activities. If you emphasize homework's importance by allowing student grades on homework to count 20 percent of their final grade, students will believe their homework assignments are important. But if you verbally emphasize homework by stating how important it is and

EXPERT TEACHER INTERVIEW

FOCUS ON: AUTHENTIC ASSESSMENT, PORTFOLIOS, AND INVOLVING STUDENTS IN ASSESSMENT
CAROL STRICKLAND: EMPORIA HIGH SCHOOL, EMPORIA, KANSAS—GRADES 9–12,
COMMUNICATION, ENGLISH, FORENSICS

Carol Strickland is a 32-year veteran teacher. For the past five years, she has taught a communication class for students with limited English proficiency. She emphasizes preparing students to improve communication skills as they enter the work world. Strickland uses a variety of assessment methods to ensure that each student's strengths emerge.

What are some methods you use to assess your students' progress?

I use a variety of assessment methods. I give students tests, and they write reports. Students are graded on their participation in class discussion. I also try to make my classes as "real-world" as possible through the projects I assign and the way I grade them on their projects.

Can you describe some of these real-world projects?

In the Applied Communication class I teach, students are assigned to work on teams as though they were business teams planning to introduce a new product or service. They must describe the product or service: What is it? How will it be made? How much will it cost? How will they market it? Stu-

dents are graded on the quality of their proposal and on their participation in the process.

In other classes, students conduct mock job interviews. They are graded on their performance, as well their level of preparation and participation. The class participates in the grading, deducting points for poor posture or eye contact. We try to make the grading reflect the things that real employers are judging when they interview candidates.

I've had some wonderful success stories. One Hispanic student, for example, learned interview skills that got him his first job, as a dishwasher in a local restaurant. Like some other Hispanic students, he had some trouble with eye contact. He always looked down out of deference and respect—a reflection of his culture. Many Hispanic kids also don't shake hands and are not accustomed to a strong handshake. I worked with him after school on some of these skills. The employer was impressed with his assertiveness. The successful experience motivated this student to continue to do well. He has

been promoted three times at that restaurant and plans to attend technical college in gourmet cooking or restaurant management.

Do your students create portfolios of their work?

Students in the school-to-work program create a portfolio or notebook. Throughout the term, we work through several drafts to create résumés. Students also have to fill out four or five different types of job application form. They collect their résumés and applications in a notebook. They are graded on how well they followed the directions on the form, as well as grammar and content of their answers.

For my media class, the students keep a weekly notebook on what's happening in the media; they label and annotate the notebook. These annotations get them points every week, and the points go toward their grade for the class.

How do you individualize assessments to encourage success for students at different levels?

I have students with behavioral or

then fail to count it in computing your final grades, students will quickly realize it is less important than you say it is. In addition, if you act as though a grade is a final judgment of a student's ability, rather than simply a reflection of a student's performance at a particular point in time, you will encourage students to view bad grades as an irreparable disaster rather than as evidence of the need for more focused hard work and improvement. Some (but not all) teachers allow students to redo homework or retake tests that led to low grades to emphasize that these poor performances are signs the students must work harder next time.

In general, your grading system should emphasize in varying proportions the types of work and performances you believe are most important to maximize student learning. The right proportions naturally vary for different teachers, classes, and levels of student. In grading, expert teachers remember that words should equal actions; in other words, if they stress conceptual understanding in class, they must also stress it on tests, and give weight to this kind of understanding in computing final grades. The entire system, beginning with what is taught and how different skills are stressed, should lead to an assessment program that evaluates students'

THINKING PRACTICALLY

Based on your experience, describe three ways you could make the grading process less stressful for students.

SUGGESTION: Discuss the grading procedures clearly and fully in advance, answer questions about the grading process thoroughly, and be open to student suggestions for changes to the process.

learning disabilities included in my classes side by side with regular and gifted students. I also have to realize the limits on students' time. They remind me often that they have other classes besides mine! Many of my students are also working or may even have children of their own.

That's why I include a variety of assessment opportunities throughout the term, different ways for students to show they are learning. In addition to tests, projects, and reports, students receive points for taking part in discussions. If a student puts her head down and tunes out, she doesn't get points for the discussion. All the students are able to participate by watching videos and reading daily newspapers and magazines, which we discuss at the beginning of class. In a discussion, if a student has read the material and is willing to take a risk and share ideas, he or she gets points. Even if they say the "wrong" thing, at least they are contributing and

giving ideas to others. Students are motivated to participate because they are rewarded for taking risks.

When I give assignments, we do as much of the work in class as possible, so that all students have time to complete the work and show what they can do. I often give assignments that include multiple levels; students can earn extra points for doing more work or more challenging work.

How do you get students involved in assessments?

Kids should feel some ownership in the assessment. I often ask students to tell *me* what they think should be on a test. As they start to answer this question they may not realize that they are reviewing what they've learned in class.

Students are involved in grading each other during some projects, such as mock job interviews. Sometimes, groups grade themselves on their performance in small group discussions. I provide a checklist and ask each member to

check off the contributions of everyone in the group.

What advice would you offer new teachers?

My general advice to new teachers is to be honest and be yourself. Kids will figure out quickly if you're phony or have a fake attitude. It helps if you really like teaching and you let it show! Many new teachers also need to be more firm with students. Often, they try to make friends with the students, and do not enforce rules consistently. Teachers need to get the respect of their students by being fair and consistent.

My specific advice about assessments focuses on fairness, too. Students should be able to see the fairness of a test, project, or grade, and understand the reason for it. Don't use a test as a threat or punishment for the students. Assessment shouldn't be a barrier. It should be a way to help students learn.

> Assessment shouldn't be a barrier. It should be a way to help students learn.

performance on the skills that have been stressed. Ultimately, grades should be computed in a manner that also emphasizes the same skills stressed in instruction. A smooth and consistently applied teaching, assessment, and grading system is essential to maintaining student enthusiasm and effort.

 GENERAL GRADING GUIDELINES

Expert teachers follow basic guidelines to ensure that the grades they assign are fair. Base grades on multiple sources of information—in other words, performance on different types of test questions, performance on oral reports as well as written ones, and performance on homework as well as on tests. Stressing one source of information biases the grading process in favor of those students who are most competent in that one particular mode of performance. Always check with other teachers and the principal and school administrators to ensure your grading systems comply with school policies.

Grade only when you have determined a grade is really necessary: Perhaps assignments that would normally be graded can sometimes be left ungraded, or can be graded by the students themselves. The form in which feedback on grading is reported

THINKING ANALYTICALLY

Describe three problems that might result if you fail to explain the grading system to students.

SUGGESTION: Misunderstandings can lead to student complaints to other teachers or even to the principal, involvement of students' parents, and students' earning lower grades than they might have if they had understood the system.

to students is also important. A simple B− is not sufficient; students require and deserve more elaborate feedback detailing where and why they made errors, and how they can improve in the future. This feedback may be written or oral.

More generally, help each student feel that he or she is capable of working toward learning goals, by stressing effort and improvement and by being encouraging. Effective teachers also remember that students may not always share the teacher's own views, opinions, or methods. In those circumstances in which there is more than one correct answer, these teachers reward students who disagree as long as the students defend their positions. There will always be some students who are more compliant, but it is important to evaluate skilled performance and not mere compliance.

Regardless of the specific grading system used, explain the system clearly to the students, perhaps by distributing a written guide to the grading system. If the explanation is oral, rehearse it often with the students. New teachers should review their systems with experienced teachers to assess the appropriateness of the system. Evaluate your students at the start of a class to gain an idea of the students' prior level of training and level of understanding. Base all evaluations of students on evidence that can be documented to another teacher, administrator, or parent, if necessary.

Regardless of the grading system in use, expert teachers rarely allow themselves to be argued into raising a student's grade, either by the student or by a parent. (The exception to this rule is if you discover an error in scoring or grading, you missed an answer on the back of a page, or otherwise were in error.) These teachers keep their students informed of their performance relative to the other students in the class; otherwise, students may be surprised to learn they are doing poorly in comparison to classmates. This situation can create problems for you, not only with the student, but also with the administration and parents. Finally, as with any grading system, remember that you may be called on to document individual students' performance. Information on grades and the basis for these grades must be made available to students and parents who request this information, under the terms of the Family Educational Rights and Privacy Act of 1974 and the Educational Amendments Act of 1974 (also called the Buckley amendment). You must be prepared to defend all grading decisions with objective evidence.

RELATIVE IMPROVEMENT VERSUS ABSOLUTE PERFORMANCE

All teachers must determine how to reward improvement in their classes. Say you begin the year with two students: Tim, who performed poorly at the beginning of the term but rose to doing above-average work by the end of the term, and José, who began by doing above-average work and ended by doing the same level of above-average work. The two students' performances on the final examination were equivalent; they ended the year at the same level of competence. However, their averages over the course of the entire term are not equivalent, because Tim started out with lower grades. Tim showed significant improvement over the term, and José basically held firm at a B level of performance. Do the two boys deserve the same grade?

If you have rewarded Tim with a higher final grade, you have been unfair to José, who scored just as high as Tim on the final. However, Tim seems to have worked harder to earn his ultimate level of competence. (Alternatively, Tim may have started out working less hard and ended up working equally hard.) Expert teachers often seek to reward effort in order to encourage further effort—although this practice is certainly not universal among effective teachers. If you give José a higher grade, you may insult Tim, who has worked hard to bring his performance up to the above-average level, despite beginning with a lower level of competence in the class. What should you do in this situation?

THINKING PRACTICALLY

What might be the consequences if you do not document the reasons for failing a student?

SUGGESTION: Students and their parents might take legal action and you would then be called on to document and substantiate your decisions. All records could potentially be made public.

Although individual teachers will have different opinions regarding how to handle this case, one effective way is to assign two grades to each boy. The first grade represents the uncorrected absolute performance grade for the class; therefore, Tim's is a B— and José's is a B. The second grade reflects effort and improvement. For this grade, expressed as a number, Tim receives a 1 (meaning excellent), and José receives a 2 (meaning average) or even a 3 (meaning poor), depending on exactly how much effort the teacher perceives he made. If the school does not offer this type of grading policy, you might assign grades on the basis of absolute performance but couple them with extensive written feedback that details your perceptions about effort expended in achieving the given performance. Some report cards have space for such comments. If not, you can design a comment sheet that you send home with each report card (or at other intervals). You can photocopy these sheets and then write in comments about each student's expenditure of effort and attitude in class. The idea is to provide information that goes beyond that reflected in the basic grade. This information will be useful to students, parents, and to you when it is reviewed at a later time.

In practice, teachers often incorporate an estimate of a student's effort into their calculation of the student's final grade. However, this system can be biased against students the teacher does not know well, or who are quieter and about whom the teacher has little information. A more formal system of separately rewarding absolute levels of performance, on the one hand, and relative improvement, on the other hand, is usually fairer than an often subjective judgment.

CRITERION-REFERENCED AND NORM-REFERENCED GRADING SYSTEMS

Earlier in this chapter, we discussed criterion- and norm-referenced grading. Criterion-referenced grading evaluates the student's performance against a set of success or mastery criteria. Norm-referenced grading compares each student's performance to that of the other students in the class.

■ **CRITERION-REFERENCED SYSTEMS**   Many teachers, particularly teachers in the lower grades, use a criterion-based grading system. In such a system, the teacher describes to the students what levels of competence are associated with individual grades on each test, project, assignment, and in the course in general. For example, the teacher states that 80 percent correct on a test or homework assignment earns a B and then computes final grades based on the students' total progress toward meeting learning goals.

In this type of system, every student theoretically can earn an A if each student works very hard, although it is rare in practice that every student works this hard. For a course as a whole, an A might correspond to overall excellent performance and the completion of every assignment and report; a B might correspond to very good performance and the completion of all except one assignment or report, and so on. It is up to the individual teacher to determine the precise levels of performance that will translate into specific grades. However, teachers must meet schoolwide standards (which they should confirm with the principal), and they must use defensible systems that make sense if questioned by a parent, other teacher, or administrator. One way to handle grading with a criterion-referenced system is to give students specific grades on many individual objectives, rather than one overall grade, to show the extent to which a student has mastered each objective. With this approach, an overall grade in a given subject might not even be computed.

THINKING PRACTICALLY

How can you ensure that your criterion-based grading system is fair?

SUGGESTION: You can look at other teachers' systems and ask them for feedback on your own; ask students for input; consider alternative criteria and defend your choices.

■ **CONTRACT SYSTEMS**   One application of a criterion-referenced grading system is called a **contract system,** in which the teacher creates a contract with the class and establishes specific standards that correspond to specific final grades. The key to a successful contract system is specific guidelines about the quality and quantity of individual pieces of work. The students may be involved in deciding exactly what the contract

A goal of the expert teacher: Totally immersed in the educational process, a classroom of students enthusiastically offer answers to a difficult question. (Kevin Horan, Stock Boston)

will consist of. Once explained completely to the students, the terms of the contract are explicit, and students know exactly what they must accomplish in order to receive a particular grade. Thus the requirements for earning a given grade are demystified, and students tend to have less anxiety about grades and evaluations.

A good contract system should not be so lenient as to make it easy for students to receive the higher grades. Students receiving the highest grades should have completed a substantial amount of high-quality work that demonstrates clear understanding and mastery of the material. Part of the attraction of a contract system is that students feel more in control of their grades and their destiny in a class. Students know that more hard work will pay off; when queried, students working in classes using the contract system report a higher level of ownership of the tasks they must complete. Explicit criteria are essential to make the system work, as is the case with any criterion-referenced grading system. One difficulty with a contract system is its potential to result in disappointment on the part of students who complete all of the work with enthusiasm, but who lack the ability to do high-quality work and thus may receive a lower than expected final grade. Another difficulty is that a teacher may become overwhelmed with a high volume of written work to grade, but this is often considered a measure of success by all but the most overworked teachers.

■ **NORM-REFERENCED SYSTEMS** Norm-referenced grading is more common in high school and college-level courses. With this system, called **grading on the curve,** you grade students in comparison to other students, so that how others do affects a given student's grade. Grade the tests and then determine the average grade (say, a 75 out of 100). Next, sort the papers from highest to lowest, and assign a grade to people scoring within a certain range of this middle grade. For example, the middle one-third of the class receives a C. Then, students with scores above this middle range receive a B if they scored in the group just above the middle third, and an A if they scored in the highest group. Similarly, students scoring below the middle group receive D's or F's.

The statistical principle behind the concept of norm-referenced grading is called the *normal curve.* As we discussed in Chapter 13 on standardized assessments, in a normal curve two-thirds (68 percent) of the distribution of scores falls within 1 standard deviation of the mean. In an exact application of the normal curve to grading, the middle two-thirds of the scores receive grades of C. This can be interpreted as a harsh standard, especially in a class in which many students are working hard and performing well. Thus a more typical use of grading on the curve is to establish a somewhat higher average grade than a C. In the past (the years from 1920 to 1960, for example), average grades of C were common, and a C was not viewed as representing a bad grade. However, grade inflation has pushed up the average grades awarded to students, so that today a C strikes most students as a poor grade indeed.

THINKING CREATIVELY

Design a contract system for your educational psychology class.

SUGGESTION: Ideas include a sampling of student requirements from the following list. Choose four different requirements that will then constitute the contract: four ten-page papers throughout the term, one portfolio of written work, five ten-minute quizzes, three one-hour exams, one performance (teaching a class), three lesson plans, and so on.

One problem with grading on the curve is that often only one point (corresponding to one correct answer) on an entire test may separate students receiving a B− and a C+. Thus teachers often search for better break points between two grades than the arbitrary point determined by the "one-third get the average score" rule. For example, a teacher gives a B to a couple of additional students who score just at the break point between a C and a B, because their scores were four points higher than the next-lowest-scoring student. Another problem with grading on the curve (discussed in Chapter 13) is that sometimes a teacher has a small class or a class whose students are generally excellent or generally poor. In these situations, it is not meaningful to assign grades based on class distribution. For example, a class of all excellent students, if graded on a curve, can result in a student who would have scored a B in a large class of diverse students and might now score a C. In such circumstances, expert teachers do not grade on a curve, or else they use the scores and corresponding performances of students in other classes on the same or closely related tests and assignments to determine a fair way to assign letter grades to the distribution in their class.

THINKING PRACTICALLY

Have you ever been graded on a total-point system? Do you consider the system fair and effective at promoting learning? Why or why not?

SUGGESTION: Many students like such systems because they are clear and straightforward, and encourage students to think in terms of "accumulating points."

TOTAL-POINT GRADING SYSTEMS

One way for teachers to determine final grades is to base them on the total number of points a student has earned in a class. This **total-point system** resembles the contract system described earlier. To establish this system, the teacher decides how many points each test, paper, report, assignment, and so on, is worth. Theoretically, a student earning a perfect score on every assessment then earns every possible point. Some teachers even award some points for attitude, attendance, effort, and other criteria relevant to performance. When using this system, ensure that two tests or assignments worth the same number of points cover the same amount of material and are approximately equal in difficulty.

There are two straightforward approaches for computing final grades by means of a point system. First, add up the total number of points earned by each student, and then rank the students. Assign letter grades based on the percentage of students receiving each letter grade that is customary for your classes and for the school as a whole. Another way to handle the task of assigning grades is to convert each score on each test and assignment to a percentage, and then appropriately weight and then average the percentages, rank the students, and assign letter grades. (The weighting of percentages is discussed further later.)

PERCENTAGE GRADING SYSTEMS

A **percentage grading system** consists of assigning grades on the basis of the percentage of the material a student has learned. The teacher scores each test or assignment on a zero-to-100 percent scale, representing the percentage of the knowledge a student has demonstrated. Thus a student might earn an 85 percent on one test on which she did well, and a 70 percent on a report on which she did less well. Typically, teachers using this system average all the grades they assigned to compute a final average, which they then translate into a letter grade.

Most of us have probably been graded on a percentage system. It is a simple system for teachers to use. However, it too has problems and can be unfair to students. First, some teachers fail to assign appropriate weight to different tests and assignments when they compute a student's overall percentage score. (This same problem plagues other types of grading systems as well: It is a mistake not to assign different weights to different types of tests and assignments when computing grades.) Thus bigger tests carry the same weight as smaller reports or assignments, and doing well on a big test can be offset by doing poorly on one small assignment. Clearly, this is not fair to students who did well on the big test.

Name three ways you can ensure the fairness of a percentage grading system.

SUGGESTION: Make tests all the same general length with the same number, mixture, and level of difficulty of items.

Another potential problem with a percentage system is that it is not possible to know how much total knowledge a student has mastered in a specific area. The percentages look so scientific that some teachers may be fooled into thinking the numbers possess a degree of accuracy they do not. Percentages are just estimates of student learning; when used appropriately, they can be interpreted as indicators of knowledge and can be weighted properly in computing the final grades—but not as the final word on a student's learning. Another problem with percentages concerns the difficulty of the tests on which the percentage grades are based. A test on a given sample of material may be easy or hard, yielding different distributions of scores. Easy tests may yield all grades of 80 percent and above, with most students scoring near the top; hard tests may result in a range of 40 percent correct to 100 percent correct, with students' scores spread out between the extremes.

To be used fairly, average percentages only for assignments or tests that are similar in difficulty and are weighted similarly in computing final grades. (Make decisions on relative weighting of tests and assignments on the basis of the comparative importance, length, and difficulty of the different types of tests and assignments.) Averaging percentages is a popular system because it is simple to use and because teachers, parents, and students are familiar with it and believe it makes intuitive sense. However, the total point system already described is often a fairer and more objective way to evaluate and grade students. Expert teachers are aware of many different types of grading systems, and they often customize their system to fit the characteristics of their students and their classes in a given school year. Figure 14.2 provides an example of one creative expert teacher's grading system, designed to avoid the pitfalls of both criterion-referenced and norm-referenced systems and take advantage of the benefits of both. The system was well received by students, teachers, and administrators alike.

FIGURE 14.2

Example of an Expert Teacher's Creative Grading Scheme

Grading Policy. No grading system that aims to translate the complex processes involved in learning into a single number or letter grade is perfect. Therefore, I use a unique and interesting policy for determining students' grades. I make two assumptions:

1. I assume that some tests are harder than others so individuals with the same level of preparation will do worse on one than they might on another even if both are tests of the same material. Thus, if a test is so difficult that the highest scoring student does not achieve a perfect score (as is nearly always the case), then the highest student's score becomes 100 percent. (In this case we are talking about classes containing numerous gifted students, and so we can be certain that at least some of the students have worked very hard and have the ability to achieve highly.) For example, if the highest student answered only 50 percent of the questions correctly, then 50 percent correct becomes an A+. (Thus, functionally speaking, the highest number of questions answered correctly becomes the total number of questions on the test, for the sake of computing grades.) The scoring system is therefore sensitive to test difficulty and the student is not penalized by an unreasonably difficult test because it is scaled down to the level of the top student's performance.

2. I assume that the lowest passing grade on a test must demonstrate at least half of the knowledge demonstrated by the highest scoring student, after correction for chance guessing. Admittedly, this is an arbitrary cutoff and I might have just as easily decided on a different figure (say, 30 percent or 70 percent). But there is an intuitive appeal to insisting that one demonstrate at least half as much knowledge as the best student in order to pass a test.

An example will help explain my system. Suppose the top student on a particular multiple-choice test answered 30 out of 40 questions correctly. Someone without any knowledge could have answered 10 questions correctly simply by guessing (i.e., if there were four choices for each of the 40 questions). Thus the lowest passing score that reflects at least half of the knowledge of the student who answered 30 correctly (after correction for guessing) is: $1/2 (30 - 10) + 10 = 20$. Someone answering fewer than 20 questions correctly has failed to demonstrate at least half of the knowledge demonstrated by the highest scoring student, after correcting for chance. If you extend this line of reasoning, you will understand how final grades are determined: If you add up all of the questions that were correctly answered on all of the exams by the highest scoring student(s), and correct this score for guessing, then one-half of that figure becomes the lowest passing score for the course.

Implications for Teaching

■ **Take grades as seriously as your students do.** Grades carry enormous significance for students, who prepare for, think about, and worry about them; some critics believe that grades have taken on too much importance in our society. However, you are generally expected to report on your students' achievement through grades, and so you must learn to use grades appropriately and fairly.

■ **Employ defensible, objective criteria when assigning grades.** Taking care with the criteria you use will help ensure fairness for all students. With the responsibility of assigning grades comes power over students' lives, and expert teachers are careful to use this power wisely and constructively.

■ **Assign grades separately to both effort/improvement and absolute performance.** Some teachers believe only absolute performance should matter in grading; others believe that effort is most important. Given these different perspectives, beginning teachers should ensure that their approach is appropriate for the school in which they teach by consulting with other teachers and school administrators.

■ **Review the various grading systems and speak to your principal and colleagues before choosing one.** Do not make such decisions alone and without the input of colleagues and school officials, who can inform a beginning teacher about school policy.

SUMMING IT UP

WHY UNDERSTANDING CLASSROOM ASSESSMENTS IS IMPORTANT TO TEACHERS

■ Classroom assessments provide feedback to teachers and students, increase student motivation and learning, and result in students benefiting more from their time spent in school.

■ Formal assessments consist of information collected in a uniform manner on all students. These assessments include tests, quizzes, book reports, and assigned presentations. Informal assessments include observations teachers make of students in the classroom, doing work, and talking to the teacher or to other students. Both types of assessments are part of a teacher's assessment system. These observations and measurements are collected by teachers and used in making evaluations of students.

■ Formative assessment discovers strengths and weaknesses in prior learning; summative assessment is a final test of student learning in a particular area. Criterion-referenced grades represent a specific set of accomplishments; norm-referenced grades represent how well a student has done compared to other students.

TRADITIONAL ASSESSMENTS

■ Traditional assessments are tests containing multiple-choice, fill-in, true/false, sentence completion, matching, and essay questions. Teachers need to know how to design and write each type of test item to make tests reliable, valid, and fair.

■ In administering tests, coverage and the why and how of testing are all issues. Tests should cover the same material taught in class, with more items devoted to what was stressed more heavily in class. A behavior-content matrix is a table listing the topics the teacher covered and the types of thinking the students should be able to engage in for each topic. Frequent, shorter tests result in more and better learning and retention of material than infrequent, longer tests.

■ Both objective tests and subjective tests are useful. Multiple-choice items are usually preferable to the other types of objective test items. Essay questions are more subjective than the other types of questions used on traditional tests. However, essay questions are best at measuring higher order thinking, and if care is used in grading, they can be fair reflections of learning.

AUTHENTIC ASSESSMENTS

- Authentic assessments are closer to real-world performances than are traditional assessments. Authentic assessments ask students to use skills and knowledge to solve problems in the same manner as if the students were completing real-world tasks.

- Among the types of authentic assessment, a portfolio is a collection of student work that demonstrates the student's abilities, efforts, accomplishments, and growth in an area or areas. An exhibition is a public performance before an audience that may involve people who will judge the performance. Evaluations of portfolios and exhibitions are based on whether established standards have been met.

GRADING AND REPORTING

- Grading should be conducted with great care because of the importance most students place on grades and the effect grades can have on student motivation. Both relative improvement and absolute performance are important considerations in computing grades.

- Contract systems are criterion-referenced grading systems in which students contract to complete a specified amount and type of work in order to earn a specific grade. Grading on the curve is a norm-referenced grading system in which students are graded in comparison with other students.

- Total-point grading systems allow students to earn points on each test, quiz, or assignment toward their final grade. A percentage grading system assigns grades on the basis of the percentage of total material a student has learned, and can often be unfairly used.

KEY TERMS AND DEFINITIONS

- **Assessment system** All of the ways teachers gather information on their students. Page 507

- **Authentic assessments** Assessments that ask students to use skills and knowledge to solve problems in the same manner as if the students were completing real-world tasks. Page 526

- **Classroom assessment** Every type of information a teacher takes in about students in the classroom test results, grades on homework and class presentations, and the informal conversations teachers have with their students over the course of the year. Page 507

- **Contract systems** Criterion-referenced grading system in which the teacher creates with the class a contract that specifies standards that correspond to specific final grades. Page 537

- **Criterion-referenced grading system** System in which a grade represents a specific set of accomplishments, which can be identified for one student independently of the performances of other students (for example, getting 80 percent of the questions right). Page 509

- **Distractors** Incorrect options following the stem in a multiple-choice question. Page 515

- **Evaluation** Uses to which measurements are put by teachers. Page 508

- **Exhibition** Public performance before an audience that may involve people who will judge the performance. Page 530

- **Formal assessments** Objective and rigorous methods for obtaining information about student learning, such as tests, quizzes, book reports, and assigned in-class presentations. Page 507

- **Formative assessment** Assessment with the purpose of discovering the strengths and weaknesses in prior learning that reveal a student's developmental stage in the area being tested. Page 509

- **Grading on the curve** Norm-referenced grading system in which students are graded in comparison with other students; thus how well others do impacts a given student's grade. Page 538

- **Informal assessments** Observations teachers make of students in the classroom, doing work, and talking to the teacher or to other students; and information in written form that teachers obtain from some students. Page 507

- **Measurements** Data on student performance and learning that are collected by teachers. Page 508

- **Norm-referenced grading system** System that represents how well a student has done compared with other students. Page 509

- **Percentage grading system** System in which grades are assigned on the basis of the percentage of the material a student has learned. Page 539

- **Portfolio** Type of authentic assessment consisting of a collection of student work that demonstrates the student's abilities, efforts, accomplishments, and growth in an area or areas. Page 529

- **Objective tests** Tests in which there is a single, known, correct answer. Page 515

- **Stem** Question or incomplete statement that begins a multiple-choice item. Page 515

- **Subjective tests** Tests in which there is no one correct answer and in which different teachers are likely to award different grades for the same response. Page 515

- **Summative assessment** Typical final exam type of assessment, a final test of student learning in a particular area. Page 509

- **Total-point system** Grading system in which final grades are based on the total number of points a student has earned in a class. Page 539

Apply the concepts you have learned in this chapter to the following problems of classroom practice.

IN ELEMENTARY SCHOOL

1. Your first-grade students have never taken a test before. You would like to explain what tests are all about, and you would like to teach these children good test-taking attitudes. What steps can you take to accomplish this?

2. Your third-grade students become extremely anxious about taking tests. At present you give one test every four weeks during the school year. What might you do to reduce student anxiety?

3. A parent of a fifth-grade student has complained to the principal about your unfair testing practices. What should you do to protect your reputation and defend your practices?

4. How can you decide what to include on a science test for your fourth-grade class?

5. At what point (in what grade) can you start asking essay questions of your elementary school–aged students? At what point can you ask a fill-in question? A multiple-choice question?

IN MIDDLE SCHOOL

1. Your seventh-grade class says that your tests are much harder than those given by the other seventh-grade science teacher. Upon doing some detective work, you learn your colleague has in fact been giving much easier tests and awarding much higher grades. What should you do?

2. Your eighth-grade students are obsessed with their test scores, so much so that they tease the low scorers in the class and talk incessantly about their scores. How can you help these students place tests into a healthier perspective?

3. How can you design an authentic assessment for your ninth-grade language arts class? What might the assessment consist of?

4. Some of your seventh-grade students have such severe writer's block that they are virtually unable to complete an essay question. What steps can you take to help them?

5. What steps can you take to ensure that authentic assessments are graded fairly and consistently?

IN HIGH SCHOOL

1. Two of your twelfth-grade biology students claim the last test was scored incorrectly. Upon looking at the test, you see that each of them lost credit for the same answers to a problem that other students were given credit for. What should you do?

2. A tenth-grade math student seems to have lost all motivation. When you speak to him and ask if he is studying hard for the final exam, he says there is no point because he is already doomed to fail, given the way points are totaled to compute the final grade. What should you do to help this student?

3. Your ninth-grade social studies students seem disinterested in their schoolwork. The subject matter just does not come alive for them. How can you use assessment to motivate the students?

4. Describe an effective grading system for a class of disadvantaged—some socially, and some physically—eleventh-grade students.

5. Your high school students never seem to think your tests are fair, regardless of how hard you work on them. What specific steps can you take to change their perception?

Connecting Theory and Research to Practice

As discussed in this chapter, there are two basic types of portfolios: artistic portfolios and writing portfolios. There are also two basic formats in which either type of portfolio can be presented: paper format or electronic format. The lack of classroom storage space for a whole class or several classes (at the secondary level) of portfolios is a practical disadvantage to using portfolios in the "traditional" (paper, binder, or folder) format. One technological innovation is the advent of electronic portfolios, which are stored on floppy disk, CD-ROM, or the Internet.

At Mt. Edgecumbe High School, students create what they call digital or electronic portfolios on the Web. The Mt. Edgecumbe High School Web site offers information for teachers and students on how to construct electronic portfolios as well as a variety of resources on the topic (available at *http://www.mehs.educ.state.ak.us/portfolios/portfolio.html*). One disadvantage in creating electronic portfolios, however, is the time and effort (i.e., to learn the software programs used to construct the portfolios) it takes to create and manage them.

Building Your Self-Portrait as an Educator

Periodic evaluation of your own teaching is necessary to become a reflective practitioner and improve the quality of your own teaching. One way to contribute to your self-portrait as an educator is to construct a teaching portfolio. As noted above, you must make a few decisions regarding the construction and format of your portfolio. The University of Texas at El Paso has a site devoted to the development of teaching portfolios. Located at *http://www.utep.edu/~cetal/portfoli/*, this site provides a rationale for the creation of teaching portfolios, suggestions for creating one, examples of teaching portfolios, and standards and criteria for evaluating teaching portfolios. Additional Web resources to help teachers create their own portfolios are available at:
http:// www.ase.tufts.edu/cte/occasional_papers/portfolio.html
http://transition.alaska.edu/www/portfolios/site98.html
http://curry.edschool.virginia.edu/curry/class/edlf/589_004/sample.html

Communities of Learners/Teachers

The Teacher Pathfinder Community Center, located at *http://teacherpathfinder.org/*, gives teachers a virtual community of educational resources. One such resource is found in "The School House," which provides information and a variety of resources by topic. For instance, *http://teacherpathfinder.org/School/Assess/assessmt.html* provides a list of Web links, online publications, and position pieces on the subject of authentic assessment.

Online Resources

Are you interested in using authentic or performance assessments in your future classroom? One tool to aid in your evaluation of student performance is a grading rubric. While rubrics, or criteria for evaluation, often take time to refine and perfect, an online tool helps teachers create rubrics for a variety of classroom activities and assignments. At RubiStar (*http://rubistar.4teachers.org/*), a teacher can quickly and effectively create a personalized rubric simply by selecting the type of activity that she or he wishes to assess, the type of grading scale (numerical or descriptive), and the categories for evaluation specific to the activity. For example, what if you would like to create a rubric to evaluate your students' ability to effectively prepare for and participate in a class debate? Rubistar offers a variety of evaluation categories to choose from that are activity- or assignment-specific, such as student understanding of the debate topic, presentation style, and the quality of rebuttal. Each specialized rubric is then available for the teacher to print out and use. Also available on this site are K–12 checklists for problem-based learning in a variety of subject areas (such as writing and science) in English and Spanish (*www.4teachers.org/projectbased/checklist.shtml*).

Managing and recording student records and grades can be done in a variety of ways. New technological tools are available for teachers that are designed specifically for this purpose. Some data (i.e., grade) management software is available commercially from vendors and some Web sites offer free demonstrations of their programs (*http://www.ezgrader.com/demos/demos.shtml*), while others offer complete grading packages as freeware on the Web. (Sites that you can search for educational shareware or freeware on a variety of educational

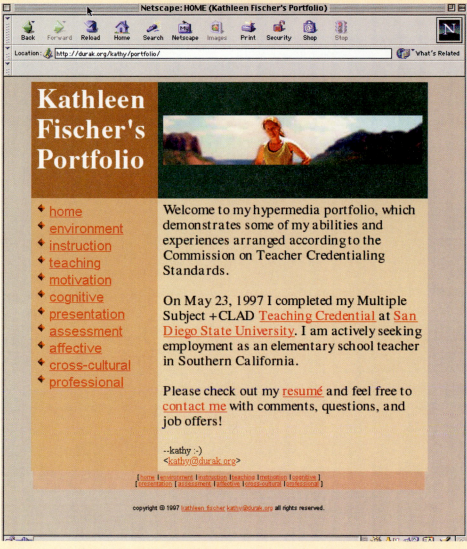

cal Issue: Integrating Assessment and Instruction in Ways That Support Learning." This site, available at *http://www.ncrel.org/sdrs/ areas/issues/methods/ assment/as500.htm,* contains information and resources about the issue of assessment and how it may be used to improve and support student learning. Included on this site are audio file testimonials from classroom teachers using various assessment strategies in their classrooms. Also included are examples of innovative assessment practices in the schools. Highlighted in this site are several essays about assessment, including Vermont's implementation of statewide portfolio assessment for writing and mathematics and the TinkerTools II Project, which developed a performance assessment model for science. (Another site about assessment issues available through the NCRL is located at *http://www .ncrel.org/sdrs/areas/ as0cont.htm.*)

topics, including grade and course information management, are *www .zdnet.com* and *http:// download.cnet.com.*) Classroom Window *(www .classroomwindows.com),* for example, was created by two public school educators and is available free to classroom teachers.

The Alphabet Superhighway (discussed in Chapter 12) also has an informative site about electronic portfolios at *http://www.ash .udel.edu/ash/teacher/ portfolio.html.* Included on this site is general information about electronic portfolios, tips for the creation of an electronic portfolio,

examples of electronic portfolios, and resources (references, bibliography, and glossary of terms) for creating electronic portfolios.

On their Web site, the North Central Regional Laboratory (NCRL) has compiled interesting information about assessment and learning entitled "Criti-

REFERENCES

AAMR Ad Hoc Committee on Terminology and Classification. (1992). *Mental retardation: Definition, classification, and systems of support* (9th ed.). Washington, DC: American Association on Mental Retardation.

Ablard, K.E., & Lipschultz, R.E. (1998). Self-regulated learning in high-achieving students: Relations to advanced reasoning, achievement goals, and gender. *Journal of Educational Psychology, 90*(1), 94–101.

Adams, J.L. (1986). *The care and feeding of ideas: A guide to encouraging creativity.* Reading, MA: Addison-Wesley Publishing Company.

Adams, M.J. (Ed.). (1986). *Odyssey: A curriculum for thinking* (Vol. 106). Watertown, MA: Mastery Education Corporation.

Adelson, B. (1984). When novices surpass experts: The difficulty of a task may increase with expertise. *Journal of Experimental Psychology: Learning, Memory, and Cognition, 10*(3), 483–495.

Ainsworth, M.D.S., Bell, S.M., & Stayton, D.J. (1971). Individual differences in strange-situation behavior in one-year-olds. In H.R. Schaffer (Ed.), *The origins of human social relations.* London: Academic Press.

Ainsworth, M.D.S., Blehar, M., Waters, E., & Wall, S. (1978). *Patterns of attachment.* Hillsdale, NJ: Erlbaum.

Airasian, P.W. (1996). *Assessment in the classroom.* New York: McGraw-Hill.

Airasian, P.W. (1997). *Classroom assessment* (3rd ed.). New York: McGraw-Hill.

Albert, R.S., & Runco, M.A. (1999). A history of research on creativity. In R.J. Sternberg (Ed.), *Handbook of creativity* (pp. 16–31). New York: Cambridge University Press.

Alderman, K.A. (1999). *Motivation for achievement: Possibilities for teaching and learning.* Mahwah, NJ: Erlbaum.

Alexander, P. (1996). The past, present, and future of knowledge research: A reexamination of the role of knowledge in learning and instruction. *Educational Psychologist, 31,* 89–92.

Allen, J.P., & Kuperminc, G.P. (1995, March). *Adolescent attachment, social competence, and problematic behavior.* Paper presented at the meeting of the Society for Research in Child Development, Indianapolis, IN.

Amabile, T.M. (1983). *The social psychology of creativity.* New York: Springer-Verlag.

Amabile, T.M. (1996). *Creativity in context: Update to "The Social Psychology of Creativity."* Boulder, CO: Westview Press.

Amabile, T.M., DeJong, W., & Lepper, M. R. (1976). Effects of externally imposed deadlines on subsequent intrinsic motivation. *Journal of Personality and Social Psychology, 34*(1), 92–98.

American Association for the Advancement of Science (AAAS). (1993). *Benchmarks for science literacy.* Washington, DC: Author.

American Association of University Women Educational Foundation and the Wellesley College Center for Research on Women. (1992). *The AAUW report: How schools shortchange girls—A study of major findings on girls and education.* Washington, DC: Author.

American Psychiatric Association. (1993). Practice guideline for eating disorders. *American Journal of Psychiatry, 150,* 212–228.

Ames, C., & Archer, J. (1988). Achievement goals in the classroom: Students' learning strategies and motivation processes. *Journal of Educational Psychology, 80*(3), 260–267.

Amsel, E., & Renninger, A.K. (Eds.). (1997). *Change and development: Issues of theory, method, and application.* Mahwah, NJ: Erlbaum.

Anastasi, A., & Urbina, S. (1997). *Psychological testing* (7th ed.). Upper Saddle River, NJ: Prentice-Hall.

Anderman, E. M. (1998). The middle school experience: Effects on the math and science achievement of adolescents with LD. *Journal of Learning Disabilitites, 31*(2), 128–138.

Anderman, L. H. (1999). Classroom goal orientation, school belonging and social goals as predictors of students' positive and negative affect following the transition to middle school. *Journal of Research and Development in Education, 32*(2), 89–103.

Anderson, B.F. (1975). *Cognitive psychology.* New York: Academic Press.

Anderson, C.J., & Sawin, D. (1983). Enhancing responsiveness in mother-infant interaction. *Infant Behavior and Development, 6,* 361–368.

Anderson, J.A. (2000). *Cognitive psychology and its implications* (5th ed.). New York: Worth.

Anderson, J.R. (1976). *Language, memory, and thought.* Hillsdale, NJ: Erlbaum.

Anderson, J.R. (1982). Acquisition of cognitive skill. *Psychological Review, 89*(4), 369–406.

Anderson, J.R. (1983). Retrieval of information from long-term memory. *Science, 220,* 25–30.

Anderson, J.R. (1985). *Cognitive psychology and its implications.* New York: Freeman.

Anderson, J.R. (1990). *The adaptive character of thought.* Hillsdale, NJ: Erlbaum.

Anderson, J.R. (1993). Problem solving and learning. *American Psychologist, 48,* 35–44.

Anderson, J.R. (1995). *Learning and memory.* New York: Wiley.

Anderson, J.R., Reder, L.M., & Simon, H.A. (1996). Situated learning and education. *Educational Researcher, 25,* 5–11.

Archer, S.L. (1982). The lower age boundaries of identity development. *Child Development, 53*(6), 1551–1556.

Arlin, M. (1990). What happens to time when you sleep? Children's development of objective time and its relation to time perception. *Cognitive Development, 5*(1), 71–88.

Arlin, P.K. (1975). Cognitive development in adulthood: A fifth stage? *Developmental Psychology, 11,* 602–606.

Arlin, P.K. (1990). Wisdom: The art of problem finding. In R.J. Sternberg (Ed.), *Wisdom: Its nature, origins, and development* (pp. 230–243). New York: Cambridge University Press.

Armsden, G., & Greenberg, M.T. (1987). The inventory of parent and peer attachment: individual differences and their relationship to psychological well-being in adolescence. *Journal of Youth and Adolescence, 16,* 427–454.

Aronson, E., Blaney, N., Stephen, C., Sikes, J., & Snapp, M. (1978). *The jigsaw classroom.* Beverly Hills, CA: Sage.

Atkinson, R.C. (1972). Ingredients for a theory of instruction. *American Psychologist, 27*(10), 921–931.

Atkinson, R.C., & Shiffrin, R.M. (1968). Human memory: A proposed system and its control processes. In K.W. Spence & J.T. Spence (Eds.), *The psychology of learning and motivation: Advances in research and theory* (Vol. 2). New York: Academic Press.

Ausubel, D.P. (1977). The facilitation of meaningful verbal learning in the classroom. *Educational Psychologist, 12*(2) 162–178.

Baddeley, A.D. (1984). Reading and working memory. *Visible Language, 18*(4), 311–322.

Baddeley, A. (1992). Working memory. *Science, 225,* 556–559.

Baddeley, A.D. (1994). The magical number seven: Still magic after all these years? *Psychological Review, 101*(2), 353–356.

Baddeley, A. (1999). Memory. In R.A. Wilson & F.C. Keil (Eds.), *The MIT encyclopedia of the cognitive sciences* (pp. 514–517). Cambridge, MA: MIT Press.

Bahrick, H.P. (1984). Fifty years of second language attrition: Implications for programmatic research. *Modern Language Journal, 68*(2), 105–118.

Bahrick, H.P., Bahrick, L.E., Bahrick, A.S., & Bahrick, P.E. (1993). Maintenance of foreign language vocabulary and the spacing effect. *Psychological Science, 4*(5), 316–321.

Bahrick, H.P., Bahrick, P.O., & Wittlinger, R.P. (1975). Fifty years of memory for names and faces: A cross-sectioned approach. *Journal of Experimental Psychology: General, 104,* 54–75.

Bahrick, H.P., & Phelps, E. (1987). Retention of Spanish vocabulary over eight years. *Journal of Experimental Psychology: Learning, Memory and Cognition, 13,* 344–349.

Bailey, J.M., & Pillard, R.C. (1991). A genetic study of male sexual orientation. *Archives of General Psychiatry, 48*(N12), 1089–1096.

Bailey, S.M. (1993). The current status of gender equity research in American schools. *Educational Psychologist, 28,* 321–339.

Baillargeon, R.L. (1993). The object concept revisited: New directions in the investigation of infants' physical knowledge. In C.E. Granrud (Ed.), *Visual perception and cognition in infancy* (pp. 265–315). Hillsdale, NJ: Erlbaum.

Baker, K. (1985). Research evidence of a school discipline problem. *Phi Delta Kappan, 66,* 482–487.

Baltes, P.B. (1997). On the incomplete architecture of human ontogeny: Selection, optimization, and compensation as foundations of development theory. *American Psychologist, 52,* 366–380.

Baltes, P.B., & Staudinger, U. (2001). *Wisdom: The orchestration of mind and virtue.* Boston: Blackwell.

Banaji, M.P., & Crowder, R.G. (1989). The bankruptcy of everyday memory. *American Psychologist, 44*(9), 1185–1193.

Bandura, A. (1965). Influence of models' reinforcement contingencies on the acquisition of imitative responses. *Journal of Personality and Social Psychology, 1,* 589–595.

Bandura, A. (1969). *Principles of behavior modification.* New York: Holt, Rinehart & Winston.

Bandura, A. (1977a). Self-efficacy: Toward a unifying theory of behavioral change. *Psychological Review, 84,* 181–215.

Bandura, A. (1977b). *Social learning theory.* Englewood Cliffs, NJ: Prentice-Hall.

Bandura, A. (1986a). Fearful expectations and avoidant actions as coeffects of perceived self-inefficacy. *American Psychologist, 41*(12), 1389–1390.

Bandura, A. (1986b). *Social foundations of thought and action: A social cognitive theory.* Englewood Cliffs, NJ: Prentice-Hall.

Bandura, A. (Ed.). (1995). *Self-efficacy in changing societie*s. New York: Cambridge University Press.

Bandura, A. (2000). Social-cognitive theory. In A.E. Kazdin (Ed.), *Encyclopedia of psychology* (Vol. 7, pp. 329–332). Washington, DC: American Psychological Association.

Bandura, A., et al. (1996). Multifaceted impact of self-efficacy beliefs on academic functioning. *Child Development, 67*(3), 1206–1222.

Bandura, A., Ross, D., & Ross, S. (1963). Imitation of film-mediated aggressive models. *Journal of Abnormal and Social Psychology, 66,* 3–11.

Bandura, A., & Schunk, D.H. (1981). Cultivating competence, self-efficacy, and intrinsic interest through proximal self-motivation. *Journal of Personality and Social Psychology, 41*(3), 586–598.

Bangert, R., Kulik, J., & Kulik, C. (1983). Individualized systems of instruction in secondary schools. *Review of Educational Research, 53,* 143–158.

Bangert-Drowns, R. L., Kulik, C.C., & Kulik, J.A. (1991). The instructional effect of feedback in test-like events. *Review of Educational Research, 61 ,* 213–238.

Banks, H.D. (1993). The effect of self-esteem and racial-identity attitudes on academic performance among African-American male college students. *Dissertation Abstracts International, 53*(9-A), 3144.

Banks, J.A. (1993). Multicultural education: Characteristics and goals. In J.A. Banks & C.A.M. Banks (Eds.), *Multicultural education: Issues and perspectives* (2nd ed.). Boston: Allyn & Bacon.

Banks, J.A. (1995). Multicultural education and the modification of students' racial attitudes. In W.D. Hawley & A.W. Jackson, et al. (Eds.), *Toward a common destiny: Improving race and ethnic relations in America.* San Francisco, CA: Jossey-Bass.

Banks, J.A. (1997). *Teaching strategies for ethnic studies* (2nd ed.). Boston: Allyn & Bacon.

Bannert, M., & Arbinger, P.R. (1996). Gender-related differences in exposure to and use of computers: Results of a survey of secondary school students. *European Journal of Psychology of Education, 11*(3), 269–282.

Bardine, B.A. (1999). Students' perceptions of written teacher comments: What do they say about how we respond to them? *High School Journal, 82*(4), 239–247.

Baron, J.B., & Sternberg, R.J. (Eds.). (1987). *Teaching thinking skills: Theory and practice.* New York: Freeman.

Barrera, M.E., Rosenbaum, P.L., & Cunningham, C.E. (1986). Early home intervention with low-birth-weight infants and their parents. *Child Development, 57*(1), 20–33.

Barrett, M., & Boggiano, A.K. (1988). Fostering extrinsic orientations: Use of reward strategies to motivate children. *Journal of Social and Clinical Psychology, 6*(3-4), 293–309.

Barron, F. (1968). *Creativity and personal freedom.* New York: Van Nostrand.

Barron, F. (1988). Putting creativity to work. In R.J. Sternberg (Ed.), *The nature of creativity* (pp. 76–98). New York: Cambridge University Press.

Barsalou, L.W. (1990). Access and inference in categorization. *Bulletin of the Psychonomic Society, 28*(3), 268–271.

Barsalou, L.W. (2000). Concepts: An overview. In A.E. Kazdin (Ed.), *Encyclopedia of psychology* (Vol. 2, pp. 242–248). New York: Oxford University Press.

Bartlett, F.C. (1932). *Remembering: A study in experimental and social psychology.* Cambridge, England: Cambridge University Press.

Bassok, M., & Holyoak, K. (1993). Pragmatic knowledge and conceptual structure: Determinants of transfer between quantitative domains. In D.K. Detterman & R.J. Sternberg (Eds.), *Transfer on trial: Intelligence, cognition, and instruction.* Norwood, NJ: Ablex.

Bates, J.A. (1987). Reinforcement. In M.J. Dunkin (Ed.), *The international encyclopedia of teaching and teacher education.* New York: Pergamon.

Baumrind, D. (1971). Harmonious parents and their preschool children. *Developmental Psychology, 4*(1, Pt. 1), 99–102.

Baumrind, D. (1973). Will a day care center be a child development center? *Young Children, 28*(3) 154–169.

Baumrind, D. (1986). Sex differences in moral reasoning: Response to Walker's (1984) conclusion that there are none. *Child Development, 57,* 511–521.

Baumrind, D. (1989). Rearing competent children. In W. Damon (Ed.), *Child development today and tomorrow. The Jossey-Bass social and behavioral science series.* San Francisco, CA: Jossey-Bass Inc.

Baumrind, D. (1991). Effective parenting during the early adolescent transition. In P.A. Cowan & E.M. Hetherington, (Eds.), *Family transitions. Advances in family research series.* Hillsdale, NJ: Erlbaum.

Baxter, G.P., Elder, A.D., & Glaser, R. (1996). Knowledge-based cognition and performance assessment in the science classroom. *Educational Psychologist, 31*(2), 133–140.

Bean, T.W., & Zulich, J. (1989). Using dialogue journals to foster reflective practice with preservice, content-area teachers. *Teacher Education Quarterly, 16*(1), 33–40.

Bean, T.W., & Zulich, J.L. (1993). The other half: A case study of asymmetrical communication in content-area reading student-professor dialogue journals. *National Reading Conference Yearbook.1993*, No. 42, 289–296.

Beck, A.T. (1967). *Depression: Causes and treatment*. Philadelphia: University of Philadelphia Press.

Beck, A.T. (1985). Cognitive therapy, behavior therapy, psychoanalysis, and pharmacotherapy: A cognitive continuum. In M. Mahoney & A. Freeman (Eds.), *Cognition and psychotherapy*. New York: Plenum Press.

Bedard, J., & Chi, M.T. (1992). Expertise. *Current Directions in Psychological Science, 1*(4), 135–139.

Bee, H.L., Barnard, K.E., Eyres, S.J., Gray, C.A., Hammond, M.A., Speitz, A.L., Snyder, C., & Clark, B. (1982). Prediction of IQ and language skill from perinatal status, child performance, family characteristics, and mother-infant interaction. *Child Development, 53*, 1134–1156.

Bellezza, F.S. (1984). The self as a mnemonic device: The role of internal cues. *Journal of Personality and Social Psychology, 47*(3), 506–516.

Bellezza, F.S. (1992). Recall of congruent information in the self-reference task. *Bulletin of the Psychonomic Society, 32*(4), 275–278.

Belmont, J.M., Butterfield, E.C., & Borkowski, J.G. (1978). Training retarded people to generalize memorization methods across memorization tasks. In M.M. Gruneberg, P.E. Morris, & R.N. Sykes (Eds.), *Practical aspects of memory*. London: Academic Press.

Belmont, J.M., Butterfield, E.C., & Ferretti, R.P. (1982). *To secure transfer of training, instruct self-management skills*. Kansas City, KS: Paper presented at the Education Research Association in Boston (April 10, 1980).

Belsky, J., & Cassidy, J. (1994). Attachment: Theory and evidence. In M. Rutter & D. Hay (Eds.), *Development through life* (pp. 373–402). Oxford: Blackwell.

Bem, D.J. (1996). Exotic becomes erotic: A developmental theory of sexual orientation. *Psychological Review, 81*, 506–520.

Bem, S.L. (1981). Gender schema theory: A cognitive account of sex typing. *Psychological Review, 85*, 485–501.

Bem, S.L. (1985). Androgyny and gender schema theory: A conceptual and empirical integration. In T.B. Sonderegger (Ed.), *Nebraska Symposium on Motivation, 1984. Psychology and gender*. Lincoln: University of Nebraska Press.

Benbow, C.P., & Stanley, J.C. (1980). Sex differences in mathematical ability: Fact or artifact? *Science, 210*(4475), 1262–1264.

Ben-Chaim, D., Lappan, G., & Houang, R.T. (1986). Development and analysis of a spatial visualization test for middle school boys and girls. *Perceptual and Motor Skills, 63*(2, Pt. 1), 659–669.

Bennett, C.I. (1995). *Comprehensive multicultural education: Theory and practice* (3rd ed.). Boston: Allyn & Bacon.

Bennett, M. (Ed.). (1999). *Developmental psychology*. Philadelphia: Psychology Press.

Benware, C.A., & Deci, E.L. (1984). Quality of learning with an active versus passive motivational set. *American Educational Research Journal, 21*(4), 755–765.

Ben-Zeev, T. (1995). The nature and origin of rational errors in arithmetic thinking: Induction from examples and prior knowledge. *Cognitive Science, 19*, 341–376.

Ben-Zeev, T. (1998). Rational errors and the mathematical mind. *Review of General Psychology, 2*, 366–383.

Berenbaum, S.A., & Hines, M. (1992). Early androgens are related to childhood sex-typed toy preferences. *Psychological Science, 3*, 203–206.

Berenbaum, S.A., & Snyder, E. (1995). Early hormonal influences on childhood sex-typed activity and playmate preferences: Implications for the development of sexual orientation. *Developmental Psychology, 31*, 31–42.

Berg, C.A. (2000). Intellectual development in adulthood. In R.J. Sternberg (Ed.), *Handbook of intelligence* (pp. 117–137). New York: Cambridge University Press.

Bergin, T. (1988). Stages of play development. In D. Bergin (Ed.), *Play as a medium for learning and development*. Portsmouth, NH: Heinemann.

Berk, L. (1996). *Infants, children, and adolescents*. Boston: Allyn & Bacon.

Berliner, D. (1987). But do they understand? In V. Richardson-Koehler (Ed.), *Educator's handbook: A research perspective*. New York: Longman.

Berliner, D. (1988). Simple views of effective teaching and a simple theory of classroom instruction. In D. Berliner & B. Rosenshine (Eds.), *Talks to teachers*. New York: Random House.

Berliner, D.C. (1990). What's all the fuss about instructional time? In M. Ben-Peretz & R. Bromme (Eds.), *The nature of time in schools: Theoretical concepts, practitioner perceptions*. New York: Teachers College Press.

Berliner, D.C. (1991). Educational psychology and pedagogical expertise: New findings and new opportunities for thinking about training. *Educational Psychologist, 26*(2), 145–155.

Berliner, D.C., & Biddle, B. (1997). *The manufactured crisis.* White Plains, NY: Longman.

Berliner, D.C., & Calfee, R.C. (Eds.). (1996). *Handbook of educational psychology.* New York: Macmillan Library Reference USA; London: Prentice Hall International.

Berlyne, D.E. (1960). *Conflict, arousal, and curiosity.* New York: McGraw-Hill.

Berlyne, D.E. (1965). Curiosity and education. In J.D. Krumboltz (Ed.), *Learning and the educational process.* Chicago: Rand McNally.

Berndt, T.J. (1982). The features and effects of friendship in early adolescence. *Child Development, 53*(6), 1447–1460.

Berndt, T.J. (1986). Children's comments about their friendships. In M. Perlmutter (Ed.), *Cognitive perspectives on children's social and behavioral development: The Minnesota symposia on child psychology* (Vol. 18, pp. 189–212). Hillsdale, NJ: Erlbaum.

Berndt, T. J. (1996). Friendship quality affects adolescents' self-esteem and social behavior. In W.M. Bukowski, A.F. Newcomb, and W.W. Hartup (Eds.), *The company they keep: Friendship during childhood and adolescence* (pp. 346–365). New York: Cambridge University Press.

Berndt, T.J., & Perry, T.B. (1986). Children's perceptions of friendships as supportive relationships. *Developmental Psychology, 22,* 640–648.

Bernstein, B. (1961). Social class and linguistic development: A theory of social learning. In A.H. Halsey, J. Floud, & C. Anserson (Eds.), *Education, economy, and society.* New York: Free Press.

Bernstein, B. (1971). Language and roles. In R. Huxley & E. Ingram (Eds.), *Language acquisition: Models and methods.* London: Academic Press.

Bernstein, B. (1979). Social class language and socialization. In J. Karabel & A.H. Halsey (Eds.), *Power and ideology in education.* New York: Oxford University Press.

Berscheid, E., & Reis, H.T. (1998). Attraction and close relationships. In D. Gilbert, S. Fiske, & G. Lindzey (Eds.), *Handbook of social psychology* (4th ed.). New York: McGraw-Hill.

Bertenthal, B.I., & Clifton, R.K. (1998). Perception and action. In W. Damon (Series Ed.) & D. Kuhn & R.S. Siegler (Vol. Eds.), *Handbook of child psychology* (5th ed., Vol. 2, pp. 51–101). New York: Wiley.

Bialystock, E., & Hakuta, K. (1994). *In other words: The science and psychology of second-language acquisition.* New York: Basic Books.

Biggs, J. (2000). Enhancing learning: A matter of style or approach? In R.J. Sternberg & L.-F. Zhang (Eds.), *Perspectives on cognitive, learning, and thinking styles.* Mahwah, NJ: Erlbaum.

Binet, A., & Simon, T. (1916). *The development of intelligence in children* (E.S. Kite, Trans.). Baltimore: Williams & Wilkins.

Black, K.A., & McCartney, K. (1995, March). *Associations between adolescent attachment to parents and peer interactions.* Paper presented at the meeting of the Society for Research in Child Development, Indianapolis, IN.

Blau, Z.S. (1981). *Black children/White children: Competence, socialization, and social structure.* New York: Free Press.

Bloom, B.S. (1976). *Human characteristics and school learning.* New York: McGraw-Hill.

Bloom, B.S., & Broder, L.J. (1950). *Problem-solving processes of college students.* Chicago: University of Chicago Press.

Bloom, B.S., Engelhart, M.B., Furst, E.J., Hill, W.H., & Krathwohl, O.R. (1956). *Taxonomy of educational objectives: The classification of educational goals. Handbook 1: The cognitive domain.* New York: Longman.

Bloom, L. (1998). Language acquisition in its developmental context. In D. Kuhn & R.S. Siegler (Eds.), *Handbook of Child Psychology* (5th ed.) (Vol. 2, pp. 309–370). New York: Wiley.

Blustein, D.L., & Palladino, D.E. (1991). Self and identity in late adolescence: A theoretical and empirical investigation. *Journal of Adolescent Research, 6*(4), 437–453.

Boggiano, A.K., Main, D.S., & Katz, P.A. (1988). Children's preference for challenge: The role of perceived competence and control. *Journal of Personality and Social Psychology, 54*(1), 134–141.

Bolin, F.S. (1988). Helping student teachers think about teaching. *Journal of Teacher Education, 39*(2), 48–54.

Bolin, F.S. (1990). Helping student teachers think about teaching: Another look at Lou. *Journal of Teacher Education, 41*(1), 10–19.

Bongiovanni, A. (1977). *A review of research on the effects of punishment in the schools.* Paper presented at the Conference on Child Abuse, Children's Hospital National Medical Center, Washington, DC.

Borko, H., & Livingston, C. (1989). Cognition and improvisation: Differences in mathematics instruction by expert and novice teachers. *American Educational Research Journal, 26*(4), 473–498.

Borko, H., Livingston, C., & Shavelson, R.J. (1990). Teachers' thinking about instruction. *RASE: Remedial and Special Education, 11*(6), 40–49, 53.

Borkowski, J.G., Levers, S., & Gruenenfelder, T.M. (1976). Transfer of mediational strategies in children: The role of activity and awareness during strategy acquisition. *Child Development, 47*(3), 779–786.

Bornstein, M.H., Haynes, O.M., Pascual, L., Painter, K.M., & Galperin, C. (1999). Play in two societies:

Pervasiveness of process, specificity of structure. *Child Development, 70*(2), 317–331.

Borow, L. (1996). The learning-disability scam. *New York, 29*(11), 34–36.

Bouchard, T.J. (1997). IQ similarity in twins reared apart: Findings and responses to critics. In R.J. Sternberg & E.L. Grigorenko (Eds.), *Intelligence, heredity, and environment* (pp. 126–160). New York: Cambridge University Press.

Bouchard, T.J., & McGue, M. (1981). Familial studies of intelligence: A review. *Science, 212,* 1055–1059.

Boulton-Lewis, G.M., Murton, F., & Wilss, L.A. (2000). The lived space of learning: An inquiry into indigenous Australian university students' experiences of studying. In R.J. Sternberg & L.-F. Zhang (Eds.), *Perspectives on cognitive, learning, and thinking styles.* Mahwah, NJ: Erlbaum.

Bower, E.M. (1982). Defining emotional disturbance: Public policy and research. *Psychology in the Schools, 19,* 55–60.

Bower, G.H. (1981). Mood and memory. *American Psychologist, 36,* 129–148.

Bower, G.H. (1983). Affect and cognition. *Philosophical Transaction: Royal Society of London 302,* (Series B), 387–402.

Bower, G.H., Black, J.B., & Turner, T.J. (1979). Scripts in memory for texts. *Cognitive Psychology, 11,* 177–220.

Bower, G.H., Clark, M.C., Lesgold, A.M., & Winzenz, D. (1969). Hierarchical retrieval schemes in recall of categorized word lists. *Journal of Verbal Learning and Verbal Behavior, 8,* 323–343.

Bower, G.H., & Gilligan. (1979). Remembering information related to one's self. *Journal of Research in Personality, 13*(4), 420–432.

Bowlby, J. (1951). *Maternal care and mental health* (World Health Organization Monograph Series No. 2). Geneva, Switzerland: World Health Organization.

(Reprinted by Schocken Books, 1966).

Bowlby, J. (1969). *Attachment: Vol. 1. Attachment and loss.* New York: Basic Books.

Boykin, A.W. (1994). Harvesting culture and talent: African American children and educational reform. In R. Rossi (Ed.), *Schools and students at risk.* New York: Teachers' College Press.

Bozzone, M. (1995). Which is best: Bilingual or English-only? *Instructor, 104*(6), 15.

Bracey, G.W. (1994). Reward and punishment. *Phi Delta Kappan, 75*(6), 494–497.

Braddock, J. (1990). Tracking the middle grades: National patterns of grouping for instruction. *Phi Delta Kappan, 71*(6), 445–449.

Braddock, J.H., & Dawkins, M.P. (1993). Ability grouping, aspirations, and attainments: Evidence from the National Educational Longitudinal Study of 1988. *Journal of Negro Education, 62*(3), 1–13.

Bradley, R.H., & Caldwell, B.M. (1984). 174 Children: A study of the relationship between home environment and cognitive development during the first 5 years. In A.W. Gottfried (Ed.), *Home environment and early cognitive development: Longitudinal research.* San Diego, CA: Academic Press.

Braine, M.D.S., & O'Brien, P.P., (1998). *Mental logic.* Mawah, NJ: Erlbaum.

Brainerd, C.J. (1978). The stage question in cognitive-developmental theory. *Behavioral and Brain Sciences, 1,* 173–182.

Brainerd, C.J., Reyna, V.F., & Kneer, R. (1995). False-recognition reversal: When similarity is distinctive. *Journal of Memory & Language, 34*(2), 157–185.

Branch, M.N. (2000). Operant conditioning: An overview. In A.E. Kazdin (Ed.), *Encyclopedia of psychology* (Vol. 5, pp. 498–502). Washington, DC: American Psychological Association.

Bransford, J.D. (1979). *Human cognition: Learning, understanding, and remembering.* Belmont, CA: Wadsworth.

Bransford, J.D., Burns, M.S., Delclos, V.R., & Vye, N.J. (1986). Teaching thinking: Evaluating evaluations and broadening the data base. *Educational Leadership, 44*(2), 68–70.

Bransford, J.D., & Johnson, M.K. (1972). Contextual prerequisites for understanding: Some investigations of comprehension and recall. *Journal of Verbal Learning and Verbal Behavior, 11,* 717–726.

Bransford, J.D., & Stein, B.S. (1984). *The IDEAL problem solver.* New York: Freeman.

Bransford, J.D., & Stein, B.S. (1993). *The IDEAL problem solver: A guide for improving thinking, learning and creativity* (2nd ed.). New York: W.H. Freeman.

Bretherton, I., & Waters, E. (Eds.). (1985). Growing points of attachment theory research. *Monographs of the Society for Research in Child Development, 50*(1–2, Serial No. 209).

Bridgeman, B., & Morgan, R. (1996). Success in college for students with discrepancies between performance on multiple-choice and essay tests. *Journal of Educational Psychology, 88,* 333–340.

Broadhurst, P.L. (1957). Emotionality and the Yerkes-Dodson Law. *Journal of Experimental Psychology, 54,* 345–352.

Brodkin, A.M., & Coleman, M. (April, 1996). He's trouble with a capital T: What can you do for a child with conduct disorder? *Instructor, 18*–19.

Brody, L.R. (1996). Gender, emotional expression, and parent-child boundaries. In R.D. Kavanaugh, B. Zimmerberg, & S. Fein (Eds.), *Emotion: Interdisciplinary perspectives.* Hillsdale, NJ: Erlbaum.

Brody, N. (1997). Intelligence, schooling, and society. *American Psychologist, 52,* 1046–1050.

Brody, N. (2000). History of theories

and measurement of intelligence. In R.J. Sternberg (Ed.), *Handbook of intelligence* (pp. 16–33). New York: Cambridge University Press.

Bronfenbrenner, U. (1985). Freedom and discipline across the decades. In G. Becker & L. Huber (Eds.), *Ordnung und Unordnung: Hartmut von Hentig* (pp. 326–339). Weinheim, Federal Republic of Germany: Beltz Verlag.

Bronfenbrenner, U. (1986). Ecology of the family as a context for human development: Research perspectives. *Developmental Psychology, 22*(6), 723–742.

Bronfenbrenner, U. & Ceci, S.J. (1994). Nature nuture reconceptualized in developmental perspective: A bioecological model. *Psychological Review, 101*(4), 568–586.

Bronfenbrenner, U., McClelland, P., Wethington, E., & Moen, P. (1996). *The state of Americans: This generation and the next.* New York: Free Press.

Brookhart, S.M. (1997). A theoretical framework for the role of classroom assessment in motivating student effort and achievement. *Applied Measurement in Education, 10*(2), 161–180.

Brookhart, S.M., & DeVoge, J.G. (1999). Testing a theory about the role of classroom assessment in student motivation and achievement. *Applied Measurement In Education, 12*(4), 409–425.

Brophy, J.E. (1979). Teacher behavior and its effects. *Journal of Educational Psychology, 71*(6), 733–750.

Brophy, J. E. (1981). On praising effectively. *Elementary School Journal, 81,* 269–278.

Brophy, J.E. (1982). How teachers influence what is taught and learned in classrooms. *Elementary School Journal, 83*(1), 1–13.

Brophy, J.E. (1983a). Conceptualizing student motivation in the classroom. *Educational Psychologist, 18*(3), 200–215.

Brophy, J.E. (1983b). Research on

the self-fulfilling prophecy and teacher expectations. *Journal of Educational Psychology, 75*(5), 631–661.

Brophy, J.E. (1985a). Teacher student interaction. In J. Dusek (Ed.), *Teacher Expectancies.* Hillsdale, NJ: Erlbaum.

Brophy, J.E. (1985b). Classroom management as instruction: Socializing self-guidance in students. *Theory Into Practice, 24*(4), 233–240.

Brophy, J.E. (1991). I know I can do this, but where's my motivation? *American Journal of Community Psychology, 19*(3), 371–377.

Brophy, J.E. (1998). Failure syndrome students. *ERIC Digest*: ERIC Clearinghouse on Elementary and Early Childhood Education, Champaign, IL.

Brophy, J.E., & Evertson, C.M. (1978). Context variables in teaching. *Educational Psychologist, 12*(3), 310–316.

Brophy, J.E., & Good, T.L. (1970). Teachers' communication of differential expectations for children's classroom performance: Some behavioral data. *Journal of Educational Psychology, 61*(5), 365–374.

Brophy, J.E., & Good, T.L. (1974). *Teacher-student relationships: Causes and consequences.* New York: Holt, Rinehart & Winston.

Brophy, J.E., & Good, T. (1986). Teacher behavior and student achievement. In M. Wittrock (Ed.), *Handbook of research on teaching* (3rd ed.) (pp. 328–375). New York: Macmillan.

Brown, A., & DeLoache, J. (1978). Skills, plans, and self-regulation. In R. Siegler (Ed.), *Children's thinking: What develops?* Hillsdale, NJ: Erlbaum.

Brown, A.L., Bransford, J.D., Ferrara, R.A. , & Campione, J.C. (1983). Learning, remembering and understanding. In J. Flavell & E.M. Markman (Eds.), *Handbook of child psychology,* 4th ed., Vol. 3, (pp. 515–629). New York: Wiley.

Brown, A.L., & Campione, J.C. (1977). Training strategic study time apportionment in educable retarded children. *Intelligence, 1*(1), 94–107.

Brown, A.L., & Campione, J.C. (1981). Inducing flexible thinking: A problem of access. In M. Friedman, J.P. Das, & N. O'Conner (Eds.), *Intelligence and learning.* New York: Plenum Press.

Brown, A.L., & Campione, J.C. (1990). Psychological theory and the design of innovative learning environments: On procedures, principles, and systems. In L. Schauble, & R. Glaser (Eds.), *Innovations in learning: New environments for education.* Mahwah, NJ: Erlbaum.

Brown, A.L., & Campione, J.C. (1994). Guided discovery in a community of learners. In K. McGilly (Ed.), *Classroom lessons: Integrating cognitive theory and classroom practice.* Cambridge, MA: MIT Press.

Brown, A.L., Campione, J.C., Bray, N.W., & Wilcox, B.L. (1973). Keeping track of changing variables: Effects of rehearsal training and rehearsal prevention in normal and retarded adolescents. *Journal of Experimental Psychology, 101,* 123–131.

Brown, A.L., & Ferrara, R.A. (1985). Diagnosing zones of proximal development. In J.V. Wertsch (Ed.), *Culture, communication, and cognition: Vygotskian perspectives.* New York: Cambridge University Press.

Brown, A.L., & Palincsar, A.S. (1989). Guided, cooperative learning and individual knowledge acquisition. In L.B. Resnick, (Ed.), *Knowing, learning, and instruction: Essays in honor of Robert Glaser.* Hillsdale, NJ: Erlbaum.

Brown J.S., & Burton, R.B. (1978). Diagnostic models for procedural bugs in basic mathematical skills. *Cognitive Science, 2,* 155–192.

Brown, J.S., Collins, A., & Duguid, P. (1989). Situated cognition and the culture of learning. *Educational Researcher, 18,* 32–42.

Brown, P., Keenan, J.M., & Potts, G.R. (1986). The self-reference effect with imagery encoding. *Journal of Personality and Social Psychology, 51*(5), 897–906.

Brown, R. (1965). *Social psychology.* New York: Free Press.

Bruer, J. (1993). *Schools for thought: A science of learning for the classroom.* Cambridge, MA: MIT Press.

Bruner, J.S. (1971). *The relevance of education.* New York: Norton.

Bruning, R., Schaw, G., & Ronning, R. (1995). *Cognitive psychology and instruction* (2nd ed.). Upper Saddle River, NJ: Prentice-Hall.

Bryant, P.E., & Trabasso, T. (1971). Transitive inferences and memory in young children. *Nature, 232,* 456–458.

Buckley, K.W. (2000). Watson, John B. In A.E. Kazdin (Ed.), *Encyclopedia of psychology* (Vol. 8, pp. 232–235). Washington, DC: American Psychological Association.

Buss, D.M. (1995). Psychological sex differences: Origin through sexual selection. *American Psychologist, 50,* 164–168.

Buss, D.M. (1996). The evolutionary psychology of human social strategies. In E.T. Higgins & A.W. Kruglarski (Eds.), *Social psychology: Handbook of basic principles.* New York: Guilford.

Buss, D.M., & Kenrick, D.T. (1998). Evolutionary social psychology. In D.T. Gilbert, S.T. Fiske, & G. Lindzey (Eds.), *The handbook of social psychology* (4th ed., Vol. 2, pp. 982–1026). New York: McGraw-Hill.

Butler, R., & Nisan, M. (1986). Effects of no feedback, task-related comments, and grades on intrinsic motivation and performance. *Journal of Educational Psychological Psychology, 78,* 210–224.

Butterfield, E.C., & Belmont, J.M. (1977). Assessing and improving the executive cognitive functions of mentally retarded people. In I. Bialer & M. Sternlicht (Eds.),

Psychological issues in mental retardation. New York: Psychological Dimensions, Inc.

Butterfield, E.C., Wambold, C., & Belmont, J.M. (1973). On the theory and practice of improving short-term memory. *American Journal of Mental Deficiency, 77,* 654–669.

Buyental, D.B., & Goodnow, J.J. (1998). Socialization processes. In W. Damon (Series Ed.) & N. Eisenberg (Vol. Ed.), *Handbook of child psychology* (5th ed., Vol. 3, pp. 389–462). New York: Wiley.

Byrne, B.M., & Worth Gavin, D.A. (1996). The Shavelson model revisited: Testing for structure of academic self-concept across pre-early, and late adolescents. *Journal of Educational Psychology, 88,* 215–229.

Byrne, D. (1961). Anxiety and the experimental arousal of affiliation need. *Journal of Abnormal and Social Psychology, 63,* 660–662.

Byrne, R. (1995). *The thinking ape: Evolutionary origins of intelligence.* Oxford: Oxford University Press.

Callahan, C.M. (2000). Intelligence and giftedness. In R.J. Sternberg (Ed.), *Handbook of intelligence* (pp. 159–195). New York: Cambridge University Press.

Calvert, S.L., & Huston, A.C. (1987). Television and children's gender schemata. In L.S. Liben & M.S. Signorella (Eds.), *Children's gender schemata.* San Francisco: Jossey-Bass.

Campbell, F.A., & Ramey, C.T. (1994). Effects of early intervention on intellectual and academic achievement: A follow-up study of children from low-income families. *Child Development, 65,* 684–698.

Campione, J.C., Brown, A.L., & Ferrara, R. (1982). Mental retardation and intelligence. In R.J. Sternberg (Ed.), *Handbook of human intelligence* (pp. 392–490). New York: Cambridge University Press.

Canter, L. (1989a). Assertive discipline: A response. *Teachers College Record, 90*(4), 631–638.

Canter, L. (1989b). Assertive discipline—More than names on the blackboard and marbles in a jar. *Phi Delta Kappan, 71*(1), 41–56.

Canter, L., & Canter, M. (1992). *Lee Canter's Assertive Discipline: Positive behavior management for today's classroom.* Santa Monica: Lee Carter and Associates.

Cantor, J., & Engle, R.W. (1993). Working memory capacity as long-term memory activation: An individual differences approach. *Journal of Experimental Psychology: Learning, Memory, and Cognition, 19,* 1101–1114.

Carpenter, C.J., Huston, A.C., & Holt, W. (1986). Modification of preschool sex-typed behaviors by participation in adult-structured activities. *Sex Roles, 14*(11–12), 603–615.

Carpenter, C.J., & Huston-Stein, A. (1980). Activity structure and sex-typed behavior in preschool children. *Child Development, 51*(3), 862–872.

Carr, M., Kurtz, B., Schneider, W., Turner, L.A., & Borkowski, J.G. (1989). Strategy acquisition and transfer among American and German children: Environmental influences on metacognitive development. *Developmental Psychology, 25*(5), 765–771.

Carroll, J.B. (1993). *Human cognitive abilities: A survey of factor-analytic studies.* New York: Cambridge University Press.

Carter, L., & Carter, M. (1992). *Assertive discipline.* Santa Monica, CA: Lee Carter & Associates.

Cartledge, G., & Johnson, C.T. (1997). School violence and cultural sensitivity. In A.P. Goldstein & J.C. Conoley (Eds.), et al. (1997). *School violence intervention: A practical handbook.* New York: The Guilford Press.

Case, R. (1984). The process of stage transition: A neo-Piagetian view. In R.J. Sternberg (Ed.), *Mechanisms of cognitive development* (pp. 20–40). New York: Freeman.

Case, R., & Okamoto, Y. (1996). The

role of central conceptual structures in the development of scientific and social thought. In C.A. Havert (Ed.), *Developmental psychology: Cognitive, perceptuomotor and neuropsychological perspectives*. Amsterdam: North-Holland.

Caspi, A., & Silva, P.A. (1995). Temperamental qualities at age 3 predict personality traits in young adulthood. *Child Development, 66,* 486–498.

Cattell, R.B. (1971). *Abilities: Their structure, growth, and action.* Boston: Houghton Mifflin.

Ceci, S.J. (1980). A developmental study of multiple encoding and its relationship to age-related changes in free recall. *Child Development, 51*(3), 892–895.

Ceci, S.J. (1991). How much does schooling influence general intelligence and its cognitive components? A reassessment of the evidence. *Developmental Psychology, 27*(5), 703–722.

Ceci, S.J. (1996a). General intelligence and life success: An introduction to the special theme. *Psychology, Public Policy, and Law, 2*(3–4), 403–417.

Ceci, S.J. (1996b). *On intelligence: A bioecological treatise.* Cambridge, MA: Harvard University Press.

Ceci, S.J., & Bruck, M. (1995). How reliable are children's statements? It depends. *Family Relations, 43*(3), 255–257.

Ceci, S.J., DeSimone, M., & Johnson, S. (1992). Memory in context: A case study of "Bubbles P.," a gifted but uneven memorizer. In D.J. Herrman, H. Weingartner, A. Searleman, & C. McEvoy (Eds.), *Memory improvement.* New York: Springer-Verlag.

Ceci, S.J., & Howe, M.J. (1978). Semantic knowledge as a determinant of developmental differences in recall. *Journal of Experimental Child Psychology, 26*(3), 432–442.

Ceci, S.J., & Leichtman, M.D. (1992). "I know that you know that I know that you broke the toy": A brief report of recursive awareness among 3-year-olds. In S.J. Ceci, M.D. Leitchman & M. Putnick (Eds.). *Cognitive and social factors in early deception.* Hillsdale, NJ: Erlbaum.

Ceci, S.J., Leichtman, M., Nightingale, N., & Putnick, M. (1993). The suggestibility of children's recollections. In D. Cicchetti & S. Toth (Eds.), *Child abuse, child development, and social policy* (pp. 117–138). Norwood, NJ: Ablex.

Ceci, S.J., & Liker, J.K. (1986). A day at the races: A study of IQ, expertise, and cognitive complexity. *Journal of Experimental Psychology: General, 115*(3), 255–266.

Ceci, S.J., & Roazi, A. (1994). Context and cognition: Postcards from Brazil. (pp. 26–49). In R.J. Sternberg & R.K. Wagner (Eds.), *Intellectual development.* New York: Cambridge University Press.

Ceci, S.J., & Williams, W.M. (1997). Schooling, intelligence, and income. *American Psychologist, 52*(10), 1051–1058.

Chance, P. (1992). The rewards of learning. *Phi Delta Kappan, 74*(3), 200–207.

Chance, P. (1993). Sticking up for rewards. *Phi Delta Kappan, 74*(10), 787–790.

Chase, W.G., & Simon, H.A. (1973a). Perception in chess. *Cognitive Psychology, 4,* 55–81.

Chase, W.G., & Simon, H.A. (1973b). The mind's eye in chess. In W.G. Chase (Ed.), *Visual information processing* (pp. 215–281). New York: Academic Press.

Chen, Z., & Siegler, R.S. (2000). Intellectual development in childhood. In R.J. Sternberg (Ed.), *Handbook of intelligence* (pp. 92–116). New York: Cambridge University Press.

Chi, M.T., & VanLehn, K.A. (1991). The content of physics self-explanations. *Journal of the Learning Sciences, 1*(1), 69–105.

Chi, M.T.H., Feltovich, P., & Glaser, R. (1981). Categorization and representation of physics problems by experts and novices. *Cognitive Science, 5,* 121–152.

Chi, M.T.H., Glaser, R., & Farr, M.J. (Eds.) (1988). *The nature of expertise.* Hillsdale, NJ: Erlbaum.

Chi, M.T.H., Glaser, R., & Rees, E. (1982). Expertise in problem solving. In R. Sternberg (Ed.), *Advances in the psychology of human inteligence.* Hillsdale, NJ: Erlbaum.

Chi, M.T.H., & Koeske, R.D. (1983). Network representations of a child's dinosaur knowledge. *Developmental Psychology, 19,* 29–39.

Chomsky, N. (1965). *Aspects of the theory of syntax.* Cambridge, MA: MIT Press.

Chomsky, N. (1972). *Language and mind* (2nd ed.). New York: Harcourt Brace Jovanovich.

Christensen, C.A. (1999). Learning disability: Issues of representation, power, and the medication of school failure. In R.J. Sternberg & L. Spear-Swerling (Eds.), *Perspectives on learning disabilities: Biological, cognitive, contextual* (pp. 227–249). Boulder, CO: Westview Press.

Clark, H.H., & Clark, E.V. (1977). *Psychology and language: An introduction to psycholinguistics.* New York: Harcourt Brace Jovanovich.

Clifford, M.M. (1988). Failure tolerance and academic risk taking in ten- to twelve-year old students. *British Journal of Educational Psychology, 58*(4), 15–27.

Cobb, P. (2000). Constructivism. In A.E. Kazdin (Ed.), *Encyclopedia of psychology* (Vol. 2, pp. 277–279). New York: Oxford University Press.

Cognition and Technology Group at Vanderbilt. (1997). *The Jasper Project: Lessons in curriculum, instruction, assessment, and professional development.* Mahwah, NJ: Erlbaum.

Cohen, D.J., & Volkmar, F.R. (Eds.) (1997). *Handbook of autism and pervasive developmental disorder* (2nd ed.). New York: Wiley.

Cohen, R.J., & Swerdlik, M.E. (1999).

Psychological testing and assessment (4th ed.). Mountain View, CA: Mayfield.

Cohen, R.L., & Squire (1980). Preserved learning and retention of pattern-analyzing skill in amnesia: Dissociation of knowing how and knowing that. *Science, 210*(4466), 207–210.

Cole, M., Gay, J., Glick, J., & Sharp, D.W. (1971). *The cultural context of learning and thinking.* New York: Basic Books.

Cole, M., & Scribner, S. (1974). *Culture & thought: A psychological introduction.* New York: John Wiley & Sons.

Coleman, M.C. (1996). *Emotional and behavioral disorders: Theory and practice.* (3rd ed.). Boston, MA: Allyn & Bacon.

Coleman, S.R. (2000). Skinner, Burrhus Frederic. In A.E. Kazdin (Ed.), *Encyclopedia of psychology* (Vol. 7, pp. 294–297). Washington, DC: American Psychological Association.

Colin, V.L. (1996). *Human attachment.* New York: McGraw-Hill.

Collins, A. (1992). Portfolios for science education: Issues in purpose, structure, and authenticity. *Science Education, 76,* 451–463.

Collins, A., Brown, J.S., & Newman, S.E. (1989). Cognitive apprenticeship: Teaching the crafts of reading, writing, and mathematics. In L.B. Resnick (Ed.), *Knowing, learning, and instruction* (pp. 283–305). Hillsdale, NJ: Erlbaum.

Collins, A., & Stevens, A.L. (1991). A cognitive theory of inquiry teaching. In P. Goodyear (Ed.), *Teaching knowledge and intelligent tutoring.* Norwood, NJ : Ablex Publishing.

Collins, A.M., & Loftus, E.F. (1975). A spreading-activation theory of semantic processing. *Psychological Review, 82,* 407–429.

Collins, A.M., & Qullian, M.R. (1969). Retrieval time from semantic memory. *Journal of Verbal learning and Verbal Behavior, 8,* 240–248.

Collins, M.A., & Amabile, T.M. (1999). Motivation and creativity. In R.J. Sternberg (Ed.), *Handbook of creativity* (pp. 297–312). New York: Cambridge University Press.

Condry, J., & Condry, S. (1976). Sex differences: A study of the eye of the beholder. *Child Development, 47*(3), 812–819.

Condry, J.C. (1984). Gender identity and social competence. *Sex Roles, 11*(5-6), 485–511.

Condry, J.C., & Ross, D.F. (1985). Sex and aggression: The influence of gender label on the perception of aggression in children. *Child Development, 56*(1), 225–233.

Cook, G. (1994). Repetition and learning by heart: An aspect of intimate discourse, and its implications. *ELT Journal, 48*(2), 133–141.

Cooley, C.H. (1982). Human nature and the social order. New York: Scribners. (Originally published 1902).

Cooley, W.W. (1981). Effectiveness in compensatory education. *Educational leadership, 38,* 298–301.

Cooper, E.H., & Pantle, A.J. (1967). The total-time hypothesis in verbal learning. *Psychological Bulletin, 68*(4), 221–234.

Cooper, H.M. (1989a). *Homework.* White Plains, NY: Longman.

Cooper, H.M. (1989b). Synthesis of research on homework. *Educational Leadership, 47*(3), 85–91.

Copeland, W.D., Birmingham, C., de-la-Cruz, E., & Lewin, B. (1993). The reflective practitioner in teaching: Toward a research agenda. *Teaching-and-Teacher-Education, 9*(4), 347–359.

Corno, L. (1992). Encouraging students to take responsibility for learning and performance. *Elementary School Journal, 93*(1): 69–8.

Corno, L. (1994). Student volition and education: Outcomes, influences, and practices. In D. Schunk & B.J. Zimmerman (Eds.), *Self-regulation of learning and performance: Issues and educational applications.* Hillsdale, NJ: Erlbaum .

Corno, L., & Snow, R.E. (1986). Adapting teaching to individual differences among learners. In M.C. Wittrock (Ed.), *Handbook of research on teaching* (3rd ed.). New York: Macmillan.

Costa, A.L. (Ed.). (1985). *Developing minds: A resource book for teaching thinking.* Alexandria, VA: Association for Supervision and Curriculum Development.

Costa, P.T., & McCrae, R.R. (1985). Personality in adulthood: A six-year longitudinal study of self-reports and spouse ratings on the NEO personality inventory. *Journal of Personality and Social Psychology, 54,* 853–863.

Cotton, K., & Cavard, W. (1981). *Instructional grouping: Ability grouping.* Portland, OR: Northwest Regional Laboratory.

Covington, M.V. (2000). Intrinsic versus extrinsic motivation in schools: A reconciliation. *Current Directions in Psychological Science, 9*(1), 22–25.

Covington, M., & Omelich, C. (1987). "I knew it cold before the exam": A test of the anxiety blockage hypothesis. *Journal of Educational Psychology, 79,* 393–400.

Covino, E.A., & Iwanicki, E.F. (1996). Experienced teachers: Their constructs of effective teaching. *Journal of Personnel Evaluation in Education, 10*(4), 325–363.

Craik, F.I.M., & Lockhart, R.S. (1972). Levels of processing: A framework for memory research. *Journal of Verbal Learning and Verbal Behavior, 11,* 671–684.

Craik, F.I.M., & Tulving, E. (1975). Depth of processing and the retention of words in episodic memory. *Journal of Experimental Psychology: General, 104,* 268–294.

Crano, W.D., & Mellon, P.M. (1978). Causal influence of teachers' expectations on children's academic performance: A cross-lagged panel analysis. *Journal of Educational Psychology, 70*(1), 39–49.

Cronbach, L.J., & Snow, R.E. (1977).

Aptitudes and instructional methods: A handbook for research on interactions. New York: Irvington.

Crooks, T.J. (1988). The impact of classroom evaluation practices on students. *Review of Educational Research, 58*(4), 438–481.

Cross, L.H., & Cross, G.M. (1980–1981). Teachers' evaluative comments and pupil perception of control. *Journal of Experimental Education, 49*, 68–71.

Crowder, R.G. (1976). *Principles of learning and memory.* Hillsdale, NJ: Erlbaum.

Crowder, R.G., & Surprenant, A.M. (2000). Sensory stores. In A.E. Kazdin (Ed.), *Encyclopedia of psychology* (Vol. 7, pp. 227–229). New York: Oxford University Press.

Crutchfield, R. (1962). Conformity and creative thinking. In H. Bruber, G. Terrell & M. Wertheimer (Eds.), *Contemporary approaches of creative thinking* (pp. 120–140). New York: Atherton.

Csikszentmihalyi, M. (1988). Society, culture, and person: A systems view of creativity. In R.J. Sternberg (Ed.), *The nature of creativity* (pp. 325–339). New York: Cambridge University Press.

Csikszentmihalyi, M. (1996). *Creativity.* New York: HarperCollins.

Csikszentmihalyi, M. (1997). Intrinsic motivation and effective teaching: A flow analysis. In J.L. Bess, et al. (Ed.), *Teaching well and liking it: Motivating faculty to teach effectively.* Baltimore, MD: Johns Hopkins University Press.

Csikszentmihalyi, M. (1999). Implications of a systems perspective for the study of creativity. In R.J. Sternberg (Ed.), *Handbook of creativity* (pp. 313–335). New York: Cambridge University Press.

Cummins, J. (1976). The influence of bilingualism on cognitive growth: A synthesis of research findings and explanatory hypothesis. *Working Papers on Bilingualism, 9*, 1–43.

Cummins, J. (1987). Bilingualism, language proficiency, and metalinguistic development. In P. Homel & M. Palij, et al. (Eds.), *Childhood bilingualism: Aspects of linguistic, cognitive, and social development.* Hillsdale, NJ: Erlbaum.

Cummins, J. (1996). *Negotiating identities: Education for empowerment in a diverse society.* Ontario, CA: California Association for Bilingual Education, 7.

Cunningham, D.J. (1991). Assessing constructions and constructing assessments: A dialogue. *Educational Technology, 31*, 13–17.

Dalton, D.W., & Hannafin, M.J. (1987). The effects of word processing on written composition. *Journal of Educational Research, 80*(6), 338–342.

Daneman, M., & Carpenter, P.A. (1980). Individual differences in working memory and reading. *Journal of Verbal Learning and Verbal Behavior, 19*, 450–466.

Daneman, M., & Tardif, T. (1987). Working memory and reading skill re-examined. In M. Coltheart (Ed.), *Attention and performance: Vol. 12, The psychology of reading* (pp. 491–508). Hove, England: Erlbaum.

Darley, C.F., Tinklenberg, J.R., Roth, W.T., Hollister, L.E., & Atkinson, R.C. (1973). Influence of marijuana on storage and retrieval processes in memory. *Memory and Cognition, 1*, 196–200.

Darling, N., & Steinberg, L. (1993). Parenting style as context: An integrative model. *Psychological Bulletin, 113*(3), 487–496.

Darling-Hammond, L., & Snyder, J. (1992). Reframing accountability: Creating learner-centered schools. In A. Lieberman (Ed.), *The changing contexts of teaching* (pp. 3–17). Chicago: University of Chicago Press.

Darwin, C.J., Turvey, M.T., & Crowder, R.G. (1972). An auditory analogue of the Sperling partial report procedure: Evidence for brief auditory storage. *Cognitive Psychology, 3*, 255–267.

Dasen, P.R., & Heron, A. (1981). Cross-cultural tests of Piaget's theory. In H.C. Triandis & A. Heron (Eds.), *Handbook of cross-cultural psychology* (Vol. 4). Boston: Allyn & Bacon.

Davidson, J.E. (1995). The suddenness of insight. In R.J. Sternberg & J.E. Davidson (Eds.), *The nature of insight* (pp. 125–155). Cambridge, MA: MIT Press.

Davidson, J.E., & Sternberg, R.J. (1984a). The role of insight in intellectual giftedness. *Gifted Child Quarterly, 28*(2), 58–64.

Davidson, J.E., & Sternberg, R.J. (1984b). The role of insight in giftedness. In R.J. Sternberg & J.E. Davidson (Eds.), *Conceptions of giftedness* (p. 201–222). New York: Cambridge University Press.

Davidson, J.E., & Sternberg, R.J. (1998). Smart problem solving: How metacognition helps. In D.J. Hacker & J. Dunlosky, et al. (Eds.), *Metacognition in educational theory and practice. The educational psychology series.* Mahwah, NJ: Erlbaum.

Davis, J.A., & Smith, T.W. (1994). *General social surveys, 1972–1994: Cumulative codebook.* Chicago: National Opinion Research Center.

Davis, J.K. (1991). Educational implications of field-dependence–independence. In S. Wapner & J. Demick (Eds.), *Field-dependence–independence: Cognitive styles across the life span* (pp. 149–176). Hillsdale, NJ: Erlbaum.

Davis, R.B. (1997). Alternative learning environments. *Journal of Mathematical Behavior, 16*(2), 87–93.

Davison, G.C., & Neale, J.M. (1994). *Abnormal psychology* (6th ed.). New York: Wiley.

Day, J.D., Borkowski, J.G., Dietmeyer, D.L., Howsepian, B.A., & Saenz, D.S. (1994). Possible selves and academic achievement. In L.T. Winegar & J. Valsiner (Eds.), *Research and methodology* (Vol. 2). Hillsdale, NJ: Erlbaum.

Day, J.D., Engelhardt, J.L., Maxwell,

S.E., & Bolig, E.E. (1997). Comparison of static and dynamic assessment procedures and their relation to independent performance. *Journal of Educational Psychology, 89*(2), 358–368.

Deaux, K. (1993). Commentary: Sorry, wrong number: A reply to Gentile's call. *Psychological Science, 4,* 125–126.

DeCasper, A.J., & Fifer, W.P. (1980). Of human bonding: Newborns prefer their mothers' voices. *Science, 208*, 1174–1176.

Deci, E. (1975). *Intrinsic motivation.* New York: Plenum.

Deci, E.L. (1994). Self-determination theory and education. *Ceskoslovenska Psychologie, 38*(5), 420–426.

Deci, E.L. (1996). Making room for self-regulation: Some thoughts on the link between emotion and behavior: Comment. *Psychological Inquiry, 7*(3), 220–223.

Deci, E.L., Koestner, R., & Ryan, R.M. (1999). A meta-analytic review of experiments examining the effects of extrinsic rewards on intrinsic motivation. *Psychological Bulletin, 125*(6), 627–668.

Deci, E.L., & Ryan, R.M. (1985). The general causality orientations scale: Self-determination in personality. *Journal of Research in Personality, 19*(2), 109–134.

Deci, E.L., & Ryan, R.M. (1987). The support of autonomy and the control of behavior. *Journal of Personality and Social Psychology, 53*(6), 1024–1037.

Deci, E.L., Vallerand, R.J., Pelletier, L.G., & Ryan, R.M. (1991). Motivation and education: The self-determination perspective. *Educational Psychologist, 26*(3-4), 325–346.

DeGrandpre, R.J., & Buskist, W. (2000). Behaviorism and neobehaviorism. In A.E. Kazdin (Ed.), *Encyclopedia of psychology* (Vol. 1, pp. 388–392). Washington, DC: Psychological Association.

DeLoache, J.S., Miller, K.F., & Pierroutsakos, S.L. (1998). Reasoning and problem solving. In W. Damon (Series Ed.) & D. Kuhn &

R.S. Siegler (Vol. Eds.), *Handbook of child psychology* (5th ed., Vol. 2, pp. 801–850). New York: Wiley.

Dembo, M.H. (2000). *Motivation and learning strategies for college success: A self-management approach.* Mahwah, NJ: Erlbaum Associates, Inc.

Demetrion, A., Efklides, A., & Platsidou, M. (1993). The architecture and dynamics of developing mind. *Monographs of the Society for Research in Child Development, 58* (5-6), Serial No. 234.

Demetriou, A., & Valanides, N. (1998). A three-level theory of the developing mind: Basic principles and implications for instruction and assessment. In R.J. Sternberg & W.M. Williams (Eds.), *Intelligence, instruction and assessment.* Mahwah, NJ: Erlbaum.

Dempster, F.N. (1991). Synthesis of research on reviews and tests. *Educational Leadership, 48,* 71–76.

Dempster, F.N. (1992). Using tests to promote learning: A neglected classroom resource. *Journal of Research and Development in Education, 25*(4), 213–217.

Dempster, F.N., & Perkins, P.G. (1993). Revitalizing classroom assessment: Using tests to promote learning. *Journal of Instructional Psychology, 20*(3), 197–203.

DeRidder, L.M. (1993). Teenage pregnancy: Etiology and educational interventions. *Educational Psychology Review, 5,* 87–107.

Derry, S., & Lesgold, A. (1996). Toward a situated social practice model for instructional design. In D.C. Berliner & R.C. Calfee (Eds.), *Handbook of educational psychology* (pp. 787–806). New York: Macmillan.

Detterman, D.K., Gabriel, L.T., & Ruthsatz, J.M. (2000). Intelligence and mental retardation. In R.J. Sternberg (Ed.), *Handbook of intelligence* (pp. 141–158). New York: Cambridge University Press.

Detterman, D.K., & Sternberg, R.J. (Eds.). (1993). *Transfer on trial:*

Intelligence, cognition, and instruction. Norwood, NJ: Ablex.

Detterman, D.K., & Thompson, L.A. (1997). What is so special about special education? *American Psychologist, 52*(10), 1082–1090.

Devine, T.G. (1987). *Teaching study skills: A guide for teachers.* Boston: Allyn & Bacon.

DeVries, R., & Zan, B. (1995, April). *The sociomoral atmosphere: The first principle of constructivist education.* Paper presented at the Annual Meeting of the American Educational Research Association, San Francisco.

Dewey, J. (1910). *How we think.* Boston: D.C. Heath.

Diekstra, R.F.W. (1996). The epidemiology of suicide and parasuicide. *Archives of Suicide Research, 2,* 1–29.

Dinkelman, T. (2000). TI: An inquiry into the development of critical reflection in secondary student teachers. *Teaching and Teacher Education, 16*(2), 195–222.

Dochy, F., & McDowell, L. (1997). Introduction: Assessment as a tool for learning. *Studies in Evaluation, 23,* 279–298.

Dochy, F., Segers, M., & Beuhl, M.M. (1999). The relation between assessment practices and outcomes of studies: The case of research on prior knowledge. *Review of Educational Research, 69*(2), 145–186.

Dornbusch, S.M., Ritter, P.L., Leiderman, P.H., & Roberts, D.F., et al. (1987). The relation of parenting style to adolescent school performance. *Child Development, 58*(5), 1244–1257.

Dornbush, S. (1994). *Off the track.* Paper presented at the annual meeting of the Society for Research on Adolescence, San Diego.

Douglas, J.D. (1967). *The social meanings of suicide.* Princeton, NJ: Princeton University Press.

Douvan, E., & Adelson, J. (1966). *The adolescent experience.* New York: Wiley.

DuBois, D.L., & Hirsch, B.J. (2000). Self-esteem in early adolescence: From stock character to marquee attraction. *Journal of Early Adolescence, 20*(1), 5–11.

Duncker, K. (1945). On problem-solving. *Psychological Monographs, 58*(5, Whole No. 270).

Dunn, K., & Dunn, R. (1987). Dispelling outmoded beliefs about student learning. *Educational Leadership, 44*(6), 55–62.

Dunn, L.M. (1968). Special education for the mentally retarded—Is it justified? *Exceptional Children, 35*, 5–22.

Dweck, C.S. (1998). The development of early self-conceptions: Their relevance for motivational processes. In J. Heckhausen & C.S. Dweck, et al. (Eds.), *Motivation and self-regulation across the life span.* New York: Cambridge University Press.

Dweck, C.S. (1999). Caution—Praise can be dangerous. *American Educator, 23*(1), 4–9.

Dweck, C.S. (1999). *Self-theories: Their role in motivation, personality, and development.* Philadelphia, PA: Psychology Press.

Dweck, C.S., & Bempechat, J. (1983). Children's theories on intelligence: Consequences for learning. In S. Paris, G. Olson, & W. Stevenson (Eds.), *Learning and motivation in the classroom* (pp. 239–256). Hillsdale, NJ: Erlbaum.

Dweck, C.S., & Leggett, E.L. (1988). A social-cognitive approach to motivation and personality. *Psychological Review, 95*(2), 256–273.

Dwyer, C.A., & Villegas, A.M. (1993). *Guiding conceptions and assessment principles for the Praxis Series: Professional assessments for beginning teachers.* Princeton, NJ: Educational Testing Services.

Eccles, J.S. (1985a). Why doesn't Jane run? Sex differences in educational and occupational patterns. In F.D. Horowitz & M. O'Brien (Eds.), *The gifted and talented: Developmental perspectives.* Washington, DC: American Psychological Association.

Eccles, J.S. (1985b). Model of students' mathematics enrollment decisions. *Education Studies in Mathematics, 16*(3), 311–314.

Eccles, J.S., Jacobs, J.E., & Harold, R.D. (1990). Gender role stereotypes, expectancy effects, and parents' socialization of gender differences. *Journal of Social Issues, 46*(2), 183–201.

Eccles, J.S., Lord, S., & Buchanan, C.M. (1996). School transitions in early adolescence: What are we doing to our young people? In J.A. Graber & J. Brookes-Gunn (Eds.), *Transitions through adolescence: Interpersonal domains and context.* Mahwah, NJ: Erlbaum.

Eccles, J.S., Lord, S., & Midgley, C. (1991). What are we doing to early adolescents? The impact of educational contexts on early adolescents. *American Journal of Education, 99*(4), 521–542.

Eccles, J.S., Wigfield, A., Harold, R.D., & Blumenfeld, P. (1993). Age and gender differences in children's self- and task perceptions during elementary school. *Child Development, 64*(3), 830–847.

Eccles, J.S., Wigfield, A., & Schiefele, U. (1998). Motivation to succeed. In W. Damon (Series Ed.) & N. Eisenberg (Vol. Ed.), *Handbook of child psychology* (5th ed., Vol. 3, pp. 1017–1095). New York: Wiley.

Egeland, B., & Sroufe, L.A. (1981). Attachment and early maltreatment. *Child Development, 52*, 44–52.

Eiferman, R.R. (1971). Social play in childhood. In R.E. Herton & B. Sutton-Smith (Eds.), *Child's play.* New York: Wiley.

Eisenberg, N. (Ed.). (1998). *Handbook of child psychology* (Vol. 3). New York: Wiley.

Eisenberg, N., & Fabes, R.A. (1998). Prosocial development. In W. Damon (Series Ed.) & N. Eisenberg (Vol. Ed.), *Handbook of child psychology* (5th ed., Vol. 3, pp. 701–778). New York: Wiley.

Eisenberger, R., & Selbst, M. (1994). Does reward increase or decrease creativity? *Journal of Personality and Social Psychology, 66*(6), 1116–1127.

Elam, S.M., & Rose, L.C. (1995). The 27th annual Phi Delta Kappa/Gallup Poll of the public's attitude toward the public schools. *Phi Delta Kappan, 77*(11), 41–59.

Elashoff, J.D., & Snow, R.E. (1971). *Pygmalion reconsidered.* Worthington, Ohio: Charles A. Jones.

Elkind, D. (1981). *The hurried child.* Reading, MA: Addison Wesley.

Elliott, E.S., & Dweck, C.S. (1988). Goals: An approach to motivation and achievement. *Journal of Personality and Social Psychology, 54*(1), 5–12.

Ellis, N.R. (1963). Memory processes in retardates and normals. In N.R. Ellis (Ed.), *International review of research in mental retardation.* New York: Academic Press.

Ellis, N.R. (Ed.). (1979). *Handbook of mental deficiency, psychological theory and research* (2nd ed.). Hillsdale, NJ: Erlbaum.

Emmer, E. (1988). Praise and the instructional process. *Journal of Classroom Interaction, 23*, 32–39.

Emmer, E., Evertson, C., Clements, B., & Worsham, M. (1997). *Classroom management for secondary teachers* (4th ed.). Boston, MA: Allyn & Bacon.

Engel, P. (1991). Tracking progress toward the school readiness goal. *Educational Leadership, 48*(5), 39–42.

Engle, R.W. (1994). Memory. In R.J. Sternberg (Ed.), *Encyclopedia of intelligence* (Vol. 2, pp. 700–704). New York: Macmillan.

Engle, R.W., Cantor, J., & Carullo, J.J. (1992). Individual differences in working memory and comprehension: A test of four hypotheses. *Journal of Experimental Psychology: Learning, Memory, and Cognition, 18*(5), 972–992.

Ennis, R. (1987). A taxonomy of critical thinking dispositions and abilities. In J. Baron & R. Sternberg

(Eds.), *Teaching thinking skills* (pp. 9–26). New York: Freeman.

Entwistle, N., McCune, V., & Walker, P. (2001). Conceptions, styles, and approaches within higher education: Analytical abstractions in everyday experience. In R.J. Sternberg & L.F. Zhang (Eds.), *Perspectives on thinking, learning, and cognitive styles. The educational series* (pp. 103–136). Mahwah, NJ: Erlbaum.

Entwistle, N.J., & Tait, H. (1996). Identifying and advising students with deficient study skills: An integrated computer-based package for staff and students. In M. Birenbaum & F.J. Dochy (Eds.), *Alternatives in assessment of achievements, learning processes, and prior knowledge: Evaluation in education and human services* (pp. 365–380). Boston, MA: Kluwer Academic Publishers.

Ericsson, A. (1999). Expertise. In R.A. Wilson & F.C. Keil (Eds.), *The MIT encyclopedia of the cognitive sciences* (pp. 298–300). Cambridge, MA: MIT Press.

Ericsson, K.A. (1996a). The acquisition of expert performance: An introduction to some of the issues. In K.A. Ericsson (Ed.), *The road to excellence: The acquisition of expert performance in the arts and sciences, sports, and games.* Mahwah, NJ: Erlbaum.

Ericsson, K.A. (Ed.) (1996b). *The road to excellence.* Mahwah, NJ: Erlbaum.

Ericsson, K.A., & Charness, N. (1999). Expert performance: Its structure and acquisition. In S.J. Ceci & W.M. Williams, et al. (Eds.), *The nature–nurture debate: The essential readings. Essential readings in developmental psychology.* Malden, MA: Blackwell Publishers, Inc.

Erikson, E.H. (1950). *Childhood and society.* New York: Norton.

Erikson, E.H. (1968). *Identity, youth, and crisis.* New York: Norton.

Ertmer, P.A., & Newby, T.J. (1996). The expert learner: Strategic, self-regulated, and reflective. *Instructional Science, 24*(1), 1–24.

Estrada, P., Arsenio, W.F., Hess, R.D., & Holloway, S.D. (1987). Affective quality of the mother-child relationship: Longitudinal consequences for children's school-relevant cognitive. *Developmental Psychology, 23*(2), 210–215.

Ethington, C.A. (1992). Gender differences in a psychological model of mathematics achievement. *Journal for Research in Mathematics Education, 23*(2), 166–181.

Etzioni, A. (1993). *The spirit of community: The reinvention of American society.* New York: Touchstone.

Evans, E.D., & Richardson, R.C. (1995). Corporal punishment: What teachers should know. *Teaching Exceptional Children, 27*(2), 33–36.

Evertson, C.M. (1988). Managing classrooms: A framework for teachers. In D. Berliner & B. Rosenshine (Eds.), *Talks to teachers.* New York: Random House.

Evertson, C.M. (1989). Improving elementary classroom management: A school-based training program for beginning the year. *Journal of Educational Research, 83*(2), 82–90.

Evertson, C.M., Emmer, E.T., Clements, B.S., & Worsham, M.E. (1984). *Classroom Management for Elementary School Teachers* (4th ed.). Boston: Allyn & Bacon.

Evertson, C.M., Emmer, E.T., Clements, B.S., & Worsham, M.E. (1997). *Classroom management for elementary teachers* (4th ed.). Boston: Allyn & Bacon.

Exline, R.V. (1962). Need affiliation and initial communication behavior in problem solving groups characterized by low interpersonal visibility. *Psychological Reports, 10,* 405–411.

Eysenck, M., & Keane, M.T. (1990). *Cognitive psychology: A student's handbook.* Hove, England: Erlbaum.

Fagot, B.I., & Hagan, R. (1991). Observations of parent reactions to sex-stereotyped behaviors: Age and sex effects. *Child Development, 62,* 617–628.

Fairburn, C.G., Norman, P.A., Welch, S.L., O'Connor, M.E., Doll, H.A., & Peveler, R.C. (1995). A prospective study of bulimia nervosa and the long-term effects of three psychological treatments. *Archives of General Psychiatry, 52,* 304–312.

Farnham-Diggory, S. (1992). *Cognitive process in education* (2nd ed.). New York: HarperCollins.

Fay, R.E., Turner, D.G., Klassen, A.D., & Gagnon, J.H. (1989). Prevalence and patterns of same-gender sexual contact among men. *Science, 243,* 338–348.

Feingold, A. (1988). Matching for attractiveness in romantic partners and same-sex friends: A meta-analysis and theoretical critique. *Psychological Bulletin, 104,* 226–235.

Feingold, A. (1992a). The greater male variability controversy: Science versus politics. *Review of Educational Research, 62*(1), 89–90.

Feingold, A. (1992b). Sex differences in variability in intellectual abilities: A new look at an old controversy. *Review of Educational Research, 62*(1), 61–84.

Fekken, G.C. (2000). Reliability. In A.E. Kazdin (Ed.), *Encyclopedia of intelligence* (Vol. 7, pp. 30–34). New York: Macmillan.

Feldhusen, J.F. (1986). A conception of giftedness. In R.J. Sternberg & J.E. Davidson (Eds.), *Conceptions of giftedness* (pp. 112–127). New York: Cambridge University Press.

Feldhusen, J.F., & Kolloff, M.B. (1981). A self-concept scale for gifted students. *Perceptual and Motor Skills, 53*(1), 319–323.

Feltovich, P.J. (1981). Knowledge based components of expertise in medical diagnosis. *Dissertation-Abstracts-International, 42*(6-B), 2576.

Fennema, E. (1987). Sex-related differences in education: Myths, realities, and interventions. In V. Richardson-Koehler (Ed.), *Educator's handbook.* New York: Longman.

Fernald, A., Taeschner, T., Dunn, J.,

Papousek, M., DeBoysson-Bardies, B., & Fukui, I. (1989). A cross-cultural study of prosodic modification in mothers' and fathers' speech to preverbal infants. *Journal of Child Language, 16,* 477–501.

Ferrari, M., & Sternberg, R.J. (Eds.) (1998). *Self-awareness: Its nature and development.* New York: Guilford Press.

Fetterman, D.M. (1994). Steps of empowerment evaluation: From California to Cape Town. *Evaluation and Program Planning, 17*(3), 305–313.

Feuerstein, R. (1979). *The dynamic assessment of retarded performers: The Learning Potential Assessment Device, theory, instruments, and techniques.* Baltimore: University Park Press.

Feuerstein, R. (1980*). Instrumental enrichment: An intervention program for cognitive modifiability.* Baltimore: University Park Press.

Fillmore, L.W. (1989). Teachability and second language acquisition. In M.L. Rice & R.L. Schiefelbusch, et al. (Eds.), *The teachability of language.* Baltimore, MD: Paul H. Brookes.

Fillmore, L.W. (1991). Second-language learning in children: A model of language learning in social context. In E. Bialystok, et al. (Ed.), *Language processing in bilingual children.* Cambridge, England: Cambridge University Press.

Fischer, K.W. (1980). A theory of cognitive development: The control and construction of hierarchies of skills. *Psychological Review, 87,* 477–531.

Fischer, K.W., & Grannott, N. (1995). Beyond one-dimensional change: Parallel, concurrent, socially distributed processes in learning and development. *Human Development, 38,* 302–314.

Fischer, K.W., & Pipp, S.L. (1984). Process of cognitive development: Optimal level and skill acquisition. In R.J. Sternberg (Ed.), *Mechanisms of cognitive development* (pp. 45–75). New York: Freeman.

Fischoff, B., Slovic, P., & Lichtenstein, S. (1977). Knowing with certainty: The appropriateness of extreme confidence. *Journal of Experimental Psychology: Human Perception and Performance, 3,* 552–564.

Fisher, J.D., & Fisher, W.A. (1992). Changing AIDS-risk behavior. *Psychological Bulletin, 117,* 455–474.

Fjellstrom, G.G., Born, D., & Baer, D.M. (1988). Some effects of telling preschool children to self-question in a matching task. *Journal of Experimental Child Psychology, 46*(3), 419–437.

Flavell, J.H. (1971). Stage-related properties of cognitive development. *Cognitive Psychology, 2,* 421–453.

Flavell, J.H. (1976). Metacognitive aspects of problem solving. In L. Resnick (Ed.), *The nature of intelligence.* Hillsdale, NJ: Erlbaum.

Flavell, J.H. (1981). Cognitive monitoring. In W.P. Dickson (Ed.), *Children's oral communication skills* (pp. 35–60). New York: Academic Press.

Flavell, J.H., Green, F.L., & Flavell, E.R. (1995). Young children's knowledge about thinking. *Monographs of the Society for Research in Child Development, 60*(1) (Serial No. 243).

Flavell, J.H., & Wellman, H.M. (1977). Metamemory. In R.V. Kail, Jr., & J.W. Hagen (Eds.), *Perspectives on the development of memory and cognition* (pp. 3–33). Hillsdale, NJ: Erlbaum.

Fletcher, A.C., Steinberg, L., & Sellers, E.B. (1999). Adolescents' well-being as a function of perceived interparental consistency. *Journal of Marriage and the Family, 61*(3), 599–610.

Flynn, J.R. (1998). Israeli military IQ tests: Gender differences small; IQ gains large. *Journal of Biosocial Science, 30*(4), 541–553.

Forster, K.I. (1994). Computational modeling and elementary process analysis in visual word recognition. *Journal of Experimental Psychology Human Perception and Performance, 20*(6), 1292–1310.

Forsyth, S., Forbes, R., Scheitler, S., & Schwade, M. (1998). Talk during One-on-One Interactions. *Primary Voices K-6, 7*(1), 9–16.

Frank, S.J., Pirsch, L.A., & Wright, V.C. (1990). Late adolescents' perceptions of their parents: Relationships among deidealization, autonomy, relatedness, and insecurity and implications for adolescent adjustment and ego identity status. *Journal of Youth and Adolescence, 19,* 571–588.

Freedman, S.W. (1993). Linking large-scale testing and classroom portfolio assessments of student writing. *Educational Assessment, 1*(1), 27–52.

Freiberg, P. (1991). Suicide in family, friends is familiar to too many teens. *APA Monitor, 22,* 36–37.

Frensch, P.A., & Buchner, A. (1999). Domain-generality versus domain-specificity in cognition. In R.J. Sternberg (Ed.), *The nature of cognition* (pp. 137–172). Cambridge, MA: MIT Press.

Frensch, P.A., & Sternberg, R.J. (1989). Expertise and intelligent thinking: When is it worse to know better? In R.J. Sternberg (Ed.), *Advances in the psychology of human intelligence* (Vol. 5, pp. 157–188). Hillsdale, NJ: Erlbaum.

Freud, S. (1964). Three essays on the theory of sexuality. *In Standard edition of the complete psychological works of Sigmund Freud* (Vol. 7). London: Hogarth Press— Institute of Psychological Analysis. (Original work published 1905).

Frey, K.S., & Ruble, D.N. (1987). What children say about classroom performance: Sex and grade differences in perceived competence. *Child Development, 58*(4), 1066–1078.

Friedman, L. (1989). Mathematics and the gender gap: A meta-analysis of recent studies on sex differences in mathematical tasks. *Review of Educational Research, 59*(2), 185–213.

Friedrich-Cofer, L., & Huston, A.C. (1986). Television violence and aggression: The debate continues. *Psychological Bulletin, 100*(3), 364–371.

Friend, M., & Bursuck, W. (1996). *Including students with special needs: A practical guide for classroom teachers.* Boston: Allyn & Bacon.

Frith, U. (1993). Autism. *Scientific American, 268*(6), 108–116.

Frombonne, E. (1995). Anorexia nervosa: No evidence of an increase. *British Journal of Psychiatry, 166,* 462–471.

Furman, W., & Bierman, K.L. (1984). Children's conceptions of friendship: A multimethod study of developmental changes. *Developmental Psychology, 20,* 925–931.

Furnham, A., & Skae, E. (1997). Changes in the stereotypical portrayal of men and women in British television advertisements. *European Psychologist, 2,* 44–51.

Gagné, R.M. (1977). *The conditions of learning* (3rd ed.). New York: Holt, Rinehart & Winston.

Gagné, R.M. (1985). *The conditions of learning and theory of instruction* (4th ed.). New York: Holt, Rinehart & Winston.

Gaines, S.O., & Reed, E.S. (1995). Prejudice: From Allport to DuBois. *American Psychologist, 50,* 96–103.

Gall, M.D. (1984). Synthesis of research of teachers' questioning. *Educational Leadership, 41,* 40–47.

Gallagher, J.J., & Courtright, R.D. (1986). The educational definition of giftedness and its policy implications. In R.J. Sternberg & J.E. Davidson (Eds.), *Conceptions of giftedness.* Cambridge, England: Cambridge University Press.

Gallagher, J.J., & Gallagher, S.A. (1994). *Teaching the gifted child* (4th ed.). Boston: Allyn & Bacon.

Gamoran, A., Nystrand, M., Berends, M., & LePore, P.C. (1995). An organizational analysis of the effects of ability grouping. *American Educational Research Journal, 32,* 687–715.

Ganellen, R.J., & Carver, C.S. (1985). Why does self-reference promote incidental encoding? *Journal of Experimental Social Psychology, 21*(3), 284–300.

Garbarino, J. (1999). *Lost boys: Why our sons turn violent and how we can save them.* New York: The Free Press.

Garcia, E.E. (1992). "Hispanic" children: Theoretical, empirical, and related policy issues. *Educational Psychology Review, 4,* 69–94.

Gardner, H. (1983). *Frames of mind: The theory of multiple intelligences.* New York: Basic Books.

Gardner, H. (1991). *The unschooled mind: How children think and how schools should teach.* New York: Basic Books.

Gardner, H. (1993). *Creating minds.* New York: Basic Books.

Gardner, H. (1993). *Multiple intelligences: The theory in practice.* New York: Basic Books.

Gardner, H. (1999). Are there additional intelligences? The case for naturalist, spiritual, and existential intelligences. In J. Kane (Ed.), *Education, information, and transformation* (pp. 111–131). Upper Saddle River, NJ: Prentice-Hall.

Gardner, H., Krechevsky, M., Sternberg, R.J., & Okagaki, L. (1994). Intelligence in context: Enhancing students' practical intelligence for school. In K. McGilly (Ed.), *Classroom lessons: Integrating cognitive theory and classroom practice* (pp. 105–127). Cambridge, MA: MIT Press.

Garland, A.F., & Zigler, E. (1993). Adolescent suicide prevention: Current research and social policy implications. *American Psychologist, 48,* 169–182.

Garner, M., & Engelhard, G., Jr. (1999). Gender differences in performance on multiple-choice and constructed mathematics items. *Applied Measurement in Education, 12*(1), 29–51.

Gayne, E.D., Yekovich, C.W., & Yekovich, F.R. (1993). *The cognitive psychology of school learning.* (2nd ed.). New York: HarperCollins.

Geary, D.C. (1995). Sexual selection and sex differences in spatial cognition. *Learning and Individual Differences, 7,* 289–303.

Gelman, R., & Williams, E. M. (1998). Enabling constraints for cognitive development and learning: Domain specificity and epigenesis. In W. Damon (Ed.-in-chief), D. Kuhn & R.S. Siegler (Vol. Eds.), *Handbook of child psychology* (5th ed.) (Vol. 2, pp. 575–630). New York: Wiley.

Gerrig, R.J., & Banaji, M.R. (1994). Language and thought. In R.J. Sternberg (Ed.), *Thinking and problem solving.* New York: Academic Press.

Getzels, J.W. & Csikszentmihalyi, M. (1967). Scientific creativity. *Science Journal, 3*(9), 80–84.

Ghiselin, B (Ed.). (1985). *The creative process: A symposium.* Berkeley, CA: University of California Press (Originally published in 1952).

Gibbs, J. (Ed.). (1968). *Suicide.* New York: Harper & Row.

Gibbs, J.C., Arnold, K.D., Ahlborn, H.H., & Cheesman, F.L. (1984). Facilitation of sociomoral reasoning in delinquents. *Journal of Consulting and Clinical Psychology, 52,* 37–45.

Gick, M.L. (1986). Problem-solving strategies. *Educational Psychologist, 21,* 99–120.

Gick, M.L., & Holyoak, K.J. (1980). Analogical problem solving. *Cognitive Psychology, 12,* 306–355.

Gick, M.L., & Holyoak, K.J. (1983). Schema induction and analogical transfer. *Cognitive Psychology, 14,* 1–38.

Gigerenzer, G., Todd, P.M., & The ABC Group. (1999). *Simple heuris-*

tics that make us smart. New York: Oxford University Press.

Gilligan, C. (1982). *In a different voice: Psychological theory and women's development*. Cambridge, MA: Harvard University Press.

Gilligan, C., & Attanucci, J. (1988). Two moral orientations: Gender differences and similarities. *Merrill-Palmer Quarterly, 34*, 223–237.

Gilligan, C. Hamner, T., & Lyons, N. (1990). *Making connections*. Cambridge, MA: Harvard University Press.

Ginott, H. (1972). *Teacher and child*. New York: McMillan.

Ginsburg, G. S., & Bronstein, P. (1993). Family factors related to children's intrinsic/extrinsic motivational orientation and academic performance. *Child Development, 64*(5), 1461–1474.

Glaser, R. (1996). Changing the agency for learning: Acquiring expert performance. In K.A. Ericsson (Ed.), *The road to excellence: The acquisition of expert performance in the arts and sciences, sports, and games*. Mahwah, NJ: Erlbaum.

Glaser, R., & Chi, M.T.H. (1988). Introduction: What is it to be an expert? In M.T.H. Chi, R. Glaser, & M.J. Farr (Eds.), *The nature of expertise*. Hillsdale, NJ: Erlbaum.

Gliner, J.A., & Morgan, G.A. (2000). *Research methods in applied settings*. Mahwah, NJ: Erlbaum.

Gobet, F., & Simon, H.A. (1998). Expert chess memory: Revisiting the chunking hypothesis. *Memory, 6*(3), 225–255.

Godden, D.R., & Baddeley, A.D. (1975). Context-dependent memory in two natural environments: On land and underwater. *British Journal of Psychology, 66*, 325–331.

Golann, S. E. (1962). The creativity motive. *Journal of Personality, 30*, 588–600.

Goldenberg, C. (1992). The limits of expectations: A case for case knowledge about teacher expectancy effects. *American*

Educational Research Journal, 29(3), 517–544.

Good, T.L. (1983a). Classroom research: A decade of progress. *Educational Psychologist, 18*, 127-144.

Good, T.L. (1983b). Research on classroom teaching. In L. Shulman and G. Sykes (Eds.), *Handbook of teaching and policy* (pp. 42–80). New York: Longman.

Good, T. (1987). Teacher expectations. In D. Berliner & B. Rosenshine (Eds.), *Talks to teachers* (pp. 159–200). New York: Random House.

Good, T., & Marshall, S. (1984). Do students learn more in heterogeneous or homogeneous groups? In P. Peterson, L.C. Wilkinson, & M. Hallinan (Eds.), *The social context of instruction: Group organization and group processes* (pp. 15–38). New York: Academic Press.

Good, T.L., & Brophy, J.E. (1994). *Looking in classrooms* (6th ed.). New York: HarperCollins.

Goodlad, J.I. (1984). *A place called school*. New York: McGraw-Hill.

Goodrich Andrade, H.L., & Perkins, D.N. (1998). Learnable intelligence and intelligent learning. In R.J. Sternberg & W.M. Williams (Eds.), *Intelligence, instruction, and assessment: Theory into practice* (pp. 67–94). Mahwah, NJ: Erlbaum.

Gordon, E.W. (1985). Social science knowledge production and minority experiences. *Journal of Negro Education, 54*(2), 117–133.

Gordon, T. (1974). *Teachers effectiveness training*. New York: Peter H. Wyden.

Gordon, T. (1981). Crippling our children with discipline. *Journal of Education, 163*, 228–243.

Gorman, C. (1994). Dollars for deeds. *Time, 143*(20), 51.

Goswami, U., & Brown, A.L. (1990). Higher-order structure and rational reasoning: Contrasting analogical and thematic relations. *Cognition, 36*(3), 207–226.

Gottfredson, D.C., & Koper, C.S. (1997). Race and sex differences in the measurement of risk for drug use. *Journal of Quantitative Criminology, 13*(3), 325–347.

Gottfredson, L. (2001). g: Highly general and practical, In R.J. Sternberg & E.L. Grigorenko (Eds.), *The general factor of intelligence: How general is it?* Mahwah, NJ: Erlbaum.

Gottman, J.M. (1983). How children become friends. *Monographs of the Society for Research in Child Development, 48*(Serial No. 201).

Gottman, J.M. (1986). The world of coordinated play: Same- and cross-sex friendship in young children. In J.M. Gottman & J.G. Parker (Eds.), *Conversations of friends: Speculations on affective development* (pp. 139–191). Cambridge, England: Cambridge University Press.

Goyette, K., & Xie, Y. (1999). Educational expectations of Asian American youths: Determinants and ethnic differences. *Sociology of Education, 72*(1), 22–36.

Graham, L., & Wong, B.Y.L. (1993). Comparing two modes of teaching a question-answering strategy for enhancing reading comprehension: Didactic and self-instructional training. *Journal of Learning Disabilities, 26*(4), 270–279.

Greene, R.L., & Crowder, R.G. (1984). Modality and suffix effects in the absence of auditory stimulation. *Journal of Verbal Learning and Verbal Behavior, 23*, 371–382.

Greenfield, P.M. (1997). You can't take it with you: Why assessments of abilities don't cross cultures. *American Psychologist, 52*, 1115–1124.

Greeno, J.G. (1989). A perspective on thinking. *American Psychologist, 44*(2), 134–141.

Greeno, J.G. (1998). The situativity of knowing, learning, and research. *American Psychologist, 53*(1), 5–26.

Greeno, J.G., Collins, A.M., & Resnick, L.B. (1996). Cognition and learning. In D. Berliner & R. Calfee (Eds.), *Handbook of educational psychology* (pp. 15–46). New York: Macmillan.

Greeno, J.G., Moore, J.L., & Smith, D.R. (1993). Transfer of situated learning. In D.K. Detterman & R.J. Sternberg (Eds.), *Transfer on trial: Intelligence, cognition and instruction* (pp. 99–167). Norwood, NJ: Ablex.

Greenwald, A.G., & Banaji, M.R. (1989). The self as a memory system: Powerful but ordinary. *Journal of Personality and Social Psychology, 57*(1), 41–54.

Gregory, R.J. (2000). *Psychological testing: History, principles, and applications* (3rd ed.). Boston, MA: Allyn & Bacon.

Griesson, A. (1999). Expertise. In R.A. Wilson & F.C. Keil (Eds.), *The MIT encyclopedia of the cognitive sciences* (pp. 289–300). Cambridge, MA: MIT Press

Griffin, M.M. (1995). You can't get there from here: Situated learning, transfer, and map skills. *Contemporary Educational Psychology, 20*(1), 65–87.

Grigorenko, E.L. (2000). Heritability and intelligence. In R.J. Sternberg (Ed.), *Handbook of intelligence* (pp. 53–91). New York: Cambridge University Press.

Grigorenko, E.L., & Sternberg, R.J. (1995). Thinking styles. In D.H. Saklofske & M. Zeidner (Eds.), *International handbook of personality and intelligence*. New York: Plenum.

Grigorenko, E.L., & Sternberg, R.J. (1997). Styles of thinking, abilities and academic performance. *Exceptional Children, 63,* 295–312.

Grigorenko, E.L., & Sternberg, R.J. (1998). Dynamic testing. *Psychological Bulletin, 124,* 75–111.

Grissmer, D.W., et al. (1994). *Student Achievement and the Changing American Family*. Santa Monica, CA: Inst. on Education and Training.

Grissmer, D., Flanagan, A., &

Williamson, S. (1998). Why did the Black-White score gap narrow in the 1970s and 1980s? In C. Jencks & M. Phillips, et al. (Eds.), *The Black-White test score gap.* Washington, DC: Brookings Institution.

Grissmer, D.W., Kirby, S.N., Berends, M., & Williamson, S. (1994). *Student Achievement and the Changing American Family*. Santa Monica, CA: Rand.

Grissom, J.B. (1989). Structural equation modeling of retention and overage effects on dropping out of school. *Dissertation Abstracts International, 49*(11-A), 3307.

Groen, G.J., & Parkman, J.M. (1972). A chronometric analysis of simple addition. *Psychological Review, 79,* 329–343.

Groen, G.J., & Patel, V.L. (1988). The relationship between comprehension and reasoning in medical expertise. In M.T.H. Chi, R. Glaser, & M.J. Farr (Eds.), *The nature of expertise.* Hillsdale, NJ: Erlbaum.

Gronlund, N.E. (1988). *How to construct achievement tests* (4th ed.). Englewood Cliffs, NJ: Prentice-Hall.

Gronlund, N.E. (1991). *How to write and use instructional objectives* (4th ed.). Englewood Cliffs, NJ: Prentice-Hall.

Gronlund, N.E. (1993). *How to make achievement tests and assessments* (5th ed.). Boston: Allyn & Bacon.

Grossman, H., & Grossman, S.H. (1994). *Gender issues in education.* Boston: Allyn & Bacon.

Grotzer, T.A., & Perkins, D.N. (2000). Teaching intelligence: A performance conception. In R.J. Sternberg (Ed.), *Handbook of intelligence* (pp. 492–515). New York: Cambridge University Press.

Gruber, H.E., & Wallace, P.B. (1999). The case study method and evolving systems approach for understanding unique creative people at work. In R.J. Sternberg (Ed.), *Handbook of creativity* (pp. 93–115). New York: Cambridge University Press.

Guilford, J.P. (1950). Creativity. *American Psychologist, 5,* 444–454.

Guilford, J.P. (1967). *The nature of human intelligence.* New York: McGraw-Hill.

Guilford, J.P., & Hoepfner, R. (1971). *The analysis of intelligence.* New York: McGraw-Hill.

Guitiérrez, R., & Slavin, R.E. (1992). Achievement effects of the nongraded elementary school: A best evidence synthesis. *Review of Educational Research, 62*(4), 333–376.

Guralnick, M.J. (1986). The peer relations of young handicapped and non-handicapped children. In P.S. Strain, M.J. Guralnick, & H.M. Walker (Eds.), *Children's social behavior: Development, assessment, and modification.* Orlando, FL: Academic Press.

Guralnick, M.J., Connor, R.T., Hammond, M.A., Gottman, J.M., & Kinnish, K. (1996). The peer relations of preschool children with communication disorders. *Child Development, 67*(2), 471–489.

Gustafssson J-E. (1984). A unifying model for the structure of intellectual abilities. *Intelligence, 8,* 179–203.

Gustafsson, J-E., & Undheim, J.O. (1996). Individual differences in cognitive functioning. In D. Berliner & R. Calfee (Eds.), *Handbook of Educational Psychology* (pp. 186–242). New York: Macmillan.

Guthrie, E.R. (1959). Association by contiguity. In S. Koch (Ed.), *Psychology: A study of science* (Vol. 2, pp. 158–195). New York: McGraw-Hill.

Guttmacher Institute. (1994). *Sex and America's teenagers.* New York: Alan Guttmacher Institute.

Hakuta, K. (1986). *Mirror of language.* New York: Basic Books.

Hakuta, K. (1999). The debate on bilingual education. *Journal of Developmental and Behavioral Pediatrics, 20,* 36–37.

Hakuta, K., & Garcia, E.E. (1989). Bilingualism and education. *American Psychologist, 44*(2), 374–379.

Hakuta, K., & Mostafapour, E.F. (1996). Perspectives from the history and politics of bilingualism and bilingual education in the United States. In I. Parasnis, et al. (Ed.), *Cultural and language diversity and the deaf experience.* New York: Cambridge University Press.

Haladyna, T.M. (1999). *Developing and validating multiple-choice test items* (2nd ed.). Mahwah, NJ: Erlbaum.

Hall, B.W., Hewitt-Gervais, C.M. (2000). The application of student portfolios in primary-intermediate and self-contained-multiage team classroom environments: Implications for instruction, learning, and assessment. *Applied Measurement in Education, 13*(2), 209–228.

Hallahan, D.P., & Kauffman, J.M. (1997). *Exceptional learners: Introduction to special education* (7th ed.). Boston: Allyn & Bacon.

Hallahan, D.P., Kauffman, J.M., & Lloyd, J.W. (1995). *Introduction to learning disabilities.* Boston: Allyn & Bacon.

Halpern, D.F. (1992). *Sex differences in cognitive abilities* (2nd ed.). Hillsdale, NJ: Erlbaum.

Halpern, D.F. (1998). Teaching critical thinking for transfer across domains: dispositions, skills, structure, training and metacognitive monitoring. *American Psychologist, 53,* 449–455.

Halpern, D.F. (2000). *Sex differences in cognitive abilities* (3rd ed.) Hillsdale, NJ: Erlbaum.

Hambleton, R.K. (1996). Advances in assessment models, methods, and practices. In D.C. Berliner & R.C. Calfee, *Handbook of educational psychology* (pp. 899–925). New York: Macmillan.

Hampson, E. (1990). Variations in sex-related cognitive abilities across the menstrual cycle. *Brain and Cognition, 14*(1), 26–43.

Hampson, E., & Kimura, D. (1988). Reciprocal effects of hormonal fluctuations on human motor and perceptual-spatial skills. *Behav-ioral Neuroscience, 102*(3), 456–459.

Hampton, J.A. (1995). Testing the prototype theory of concepts. *Journal of Memory and Language, 32,* 686–708.

Hampton, J.A. (1997). Psychological representation of concepts. In M.A. Conway & S.G. Gathercole (Eds.), *Cognitive models of memory* (pp. 81–110). Hove, Gryland: Psychology Press.

Hampton, J.A. (1999). Concepts. In R.A. Wilson & F. C. Keil (Eds.), *The MIT encyclopedia of the cognitive sciences.* Cambridge, MA: MIT Press.

Handley, H.M., & Morse, L.W. (1984). Two-year study relating adolescents' self-concept and gender role perceptions to achievement and attitudes toward. *Journal of Research in Science Teaching, 21*(6), 599–607.

Hannafin, M.J., & Land, S.M. (1997). The foundations and assumptions of technology-enhanced student-centered learning environments. *Instructional Science, 25*(3), 167–202.

Hardman, M.L., Drew, C.J., & Eagan, M.W. (1996). *Human exceptionality: Society, school, and family* (5th ed.). Boston: Allyn & Bacon.

Harris, M.J., & Rosenthal, R. (1985). Mediation of interpersonal expectancy effects: 31 meta-analyses. *Psychological Bulletin, 1985, 97*(3), 363–386.

Harrow, A.J. (1972). *A taxonomy of the psychomotor domain.* New York: David McKay.

Harter, S. (1982). The Perceived Competence Scale for Children. *Child Development, 53*(1), 87–97.

Harter, S. (1990) Self and identity development. In S.S. Feldman & G.R. Elliott (Eds.), *At the threshold: The developing adolescent.* Cambridge, MA: Harvard University Press.

Harter, S. (1998). The development of self-representations. In W. Damon (Series Ed.) & N. Eisenberg (Vol. Ed.), *Handbook of child psychology* (5th ed., Vol. 3, pp. 553–618). New York: Wiley.

Harter, S., & Pike, R. (1984). The pictorial scale of Perceived Competence and Social Acceptance for Young Children. *Child Development, 55*(6), 1969–1982.

Hartup, W.W. (1989). Social relationships and their developmental significance. *American Psychologist, 44*(2), 120–126.

Hartup, W.W. (1996). The company they keep: Friendships and their developmental significance. *Child Development, 67,* 1–13.

Hauser, R.M., & Warren, J.M. (1997). Socioeconomic indexes for occupations: A review, update, and critique. In A.E. Raferty (Vol. Ed.), *Sociological Methodology: Vol. 27* (pp. 177–298). Washington, DC: American Sociological Association.

Hayes, J. (1989). *The complete problem solver* (2nd ed.). Hillsdale, NJ: Erlbaum.

Hayes, J.R., & Simon, H.A. (1974). Understanding written problem instructions. In L.W. Gregg (Ed.), *Knowledge and cognition.* Potomac, MD: Erlbaum.

Haynes, S.N., & O'Brien, W.H. (2000). *Principles and practice of behavioral assessment.* New York: Kluwer/Plenum.

Headden, S. (1995, September 25). Tongue-tied in the schools: bilingual education began as a good idea. Now it needs fixing. *U.S. News & World Report, 119*(12), 44–47.

Heath, S.B. (1982). What no bedtime story means: Narrative skills at home and school. *Language in Society, 11*(1), 49–76.

Heath, S.B. (1983). *Ways with words.* New York: Cambridge University Press.

Hedges, L.V., & Nowell, A. (1995). Sex differences in mental test scores, variability, and numbers of high-scoring individuals. *Science, 269*(5220), 41–45.

Heider, E.R., & Olivier, D.C. (1972). The structure of color space in naming and memory for two language. *Cognitive Psychology, 3,* 337–354.

Heider, F. (1958/1983 reprint). *The psychology of interpersonal relations.* Hillsdale, NJ: Erlbaum.

Heider, F. (1967). On social cognition. *American Psychologist, 22*(1), 25–31.

Heider, F., & Benesh-Weiner, M. (Eds.) (1988). *Fritz Heider: 'The notebooks,' Vol. 5: Attributional and interpersonal evaluation.* Munich, Federal Republic of Germany: Psychologie Verlags Union.

Helmreich, R.L., Spence, J.T., & Wilhelm, J.A. (1981). A psychometric analysis of the Personal Attributes Questionnaire. *Sex-Roles, 7*(11), 1097–1108.

Henderson, A.S. (1992). Social support and depression. In H.O.F. Veiel & U. Baumann (Eds.), *The meaning and measurement of social support* (pp. 85–92). New York: Hemisphere.

Henderson, V.L. & Dweck, C.S. (1990). Motivation and achievement. In S.S. Feldman & G.R. Elliott (Eds.), *At the threshold: The developing adolescent.* Cambridge, MA: Harvard University Press.

Hendry, G.D., & King, R.C. (1994). On theory of learning and knowledge: Educational implications of advances in neuroscience. *Science Education, 78*(3), 223–253.

Henley, N.M. (1969). A psychological study of the semantics of animal terms. *Journal of Verbal Learning and Verbal Behavior, 8,* 176–184.

Herman, J.L., Abedi, J., & Golan, S. (1994). Assessing the effects of standardized testing on schools. *Education and Psychological Measurement, 54,* 471–481.

Herman, J.L., Gearhart, M., & Baker, E.L. Assessing writing portfolios: Issues in the validity and meaning of scores. *Educational Assessment, 1*(3), 201–224.

Herman, J.L., & Winters, L. (1994). Portfolio Research: A Slim Collection. *Educational Leadership, 52,* 48–55.

Hernandez, D.J. (1997). Child devel-

opment and the social demography of childhood. *Child Development, 68*(1), 149–169.

Hernandez, F. (1993). From multiculturalism to mestizaje in world culture. *Visual Arts Research, 19*(2)[38], 1–12.

Hernandez, F. (1997). Mexican gender studies and the American university. *American Behavioral Scientist, 40*(7), 968–974.

Herrnstein, R.J., & Murray, C. (1996). *The bell curve.* New York: Free Press.

Hernnstein, R.J., Nickerson, R.S., de Sanchez, M., & Swets, J.A. (1986). Teaching thinking skills. *American Psychologist, 41,* 1279–1289.

Hetherington, E.M. (1993). A review of the Virginia Longitudinal Study of Divorce and Remarriage: A focus on early adolescence. *Journal of Family Psychology, 7,* 39–56.

Heward, W.L., & Orlansky, M.D. (1980). *Exceptional children.* Columbus, OH: Merrill.

Heyduk, R.G., & Bahrick, L.E. (1977). Complexity, response competition, and preference implications for affective consequences of repeated exposure. *Motivation and Emotion, 1,* 249–259.

Heyman, G.D., Dweck, C.S., & Cain, K.M. (1992). Young children's vulnerability to self-blame and helplessness: Relationship to beliefs about goodness. *Child Development, 63*(2), 401–415.

Heyman, G.D., & Dweck, C.S. (1992). Achievement goals and intrinsic motivation: Their relation and their role in adaptive motivation. *Motivation and Emotion, 16*(3), 231–247.

Hiebert, E., & Raphael, T. (1996). Psychological perspectives on literacy and extensions to educational practice. In D. Berliner & R. Calfee (Eds.), *Handbook of educational psychology* (pp. 550–602). New York: Macmillan.

Hill, D. (1990). Order in the classroom. *Teacher, 1*(7), 70–77.

Hill, J.P. (1987). Research on adolescents and their families: Past and

prospect. In C.E. Irwin, Jr. (Ed.), *Adolescent social behavior and health.* San Francisco: Jossey-Bass.

Hiscock, M., Inch, R., Hawryluk, J., Lyon, P. J., & Perachio, N. (1999). Is there a sex difference in human laterality? III. An exhaustive survey of tactile laterality studies from six neuropsychology journals. *Journal of Clinical and Experimental Neuropsychology, 21*(1), 17–28.

Hittner, J.B. (1997). Alcohol-related outcome expectancies: Construct overview and implications for primary and secondary prevention. *Journal of Primary Prevention, 17,* 297–314.

Ho, D.Y.F. (1986). Chinese patterns of socialization: A critical review. In M.H. Bond, et al. (Eds.), *The psychology of the Chinese people.* New York: Oxford University Press.

Hodapp, R.N. (1994). Mental retardation: Cultural-familial. In R.J. Sternberg (Ed.), *Encyclopedia of human intelligence* (Vol. 2, pp. 711–717). New York: Macmillan.

Hodapp, R.M., & Zigler, E. (1999). Intellectual development and mental retardation: Some continuing controversies. In M. Anderson (Ed.), *Development of intelligence* (pp. 295–308). East Sussex, UK: Psychology Press.

Hoerr, T. (1996). Multiple intelligences update: Apply the theory, avoid the traps. *Learning, 25*(1), 69–70.

Hoffman, A.M. (Ed.). (1996). *Schools, violence, and society.* Westport, CT: Praeger Publishers/ Greenwood Publishing Group, Inc.

Hoffman, L.W., & Youngblade, L.M. (1998). Maternal employment, morale and parenting style: Social class comparisons. *Journal of Applied Developmental Psychology, 19*(3), 389–413.

Hogan, D. (1997). ADHD: A travel guide to success. *Childhood Education, 73*(3), 158–161.

Hogan, K., Nastasi, B.K., & Pressley, M. (1999). Discourse patterns and collaborative scientific reasoning in peer and teacher-guided discussions. *Cognition and Instruction, 17*(4), 379–432.

Hollingshead, A.B., & Redlich, F.C. (1958). *Social class and mental illness.* New York: Wiley.

Holstein, C.B. (1976). Irreversible, stepwise sequence in the development of moral judgment: A longitudinal study of males and females. *Child Development, 47,* 51–61.

Hooker, E. (1993). Reflection of a 40-year exploration: A scientific view on homosexuality. *American Psychologist, 48*(4), 450–453.

Horn, J.L. (1968). Organization of abilities and the development of intelligence. *Psychological Review, 75,* 242–259.

Hornblower, M. (1995). Putting tongues in cheeks. *Time, 146*(15), 40–45.

Horowitz, F., & O'Brien, M. (1986). Gifted and talented children: State of knowledge and directions for research, *American Psychologist, 41*(10), 1147–1152.

How to manage your students with ADD/ADHD. (1997). *Instructor, 106*(6), 63–66.

Howe, M.J.A. (1999). *The psychology of high abilities.* New York: NYU Press.

Howe, M.J.A. (1999). *Genius explained.* Cambridge, UK: Cambridge University Press

Howes, C., & Hamilton, C.E. (1993). The changing experience of child care: Changes in teachers and in teacher-child relationships and children's social competence with peers. *Early Childhood Research Quarterly, 8*(1), 15–32.

Howes, C., Hamilton, C.E., & Matheson, C.C. (1994). Children's relationships with peers: Differential associations with aspects of the teacher-child relationship. *Child Development, 65*(1), 253–263.

Howes, C., & Matheson, C.C. (1992). Sequences in the development of competent play with peers: Social and social pretend play. *Developmental Psychology, 28,* 961–974.

Howes, C., Matheson, C.C., & Hamilton, C.E. (1994). Maternal, teacher, and child care history correlates of children's relationships with peers. *Child Development 65*(1), 264–273.

Hsia, J. (1988). *Asian Americans in higher education and at work.* Hillsdale, NJ: Erlbaum.

Hsai, J., & Peng, S. S. (1998). Academic achievement and performance. In L.C. Lee & N.W.S. Zane, et al. (Eds.), *Handbook of Asian American psychology.* Thousand Oaks, CA: Sage Publications, Inc.

Hsu, L.K.G. (1980). *Eating disorders.* New York: Guilford.

Hudson, J. & Nelson, K. (1986). Repeated encounters of a similar kind: Effects of familiarity on children's autobiographical memory. *Cognitive Development, 1*(3), 253–271.

Hudson, J.A. (1990). Constructive processing in children's event memory. *Developmental Psychology, 26*(2), 180–187.

Huesmann, L.R., Lagerspetz, K., & Eron, L.D. (1984). Intervening variable in the TV violence-aggression relation: Evidence from two countries. *Developmental Psychology, 20,* 746–775.

Huges, R. Jr., & Perry-Jenkins, M. (1996). Social class issues in family life education. *Family Relations: Journal of Applied Family and Child Studies, 45*(2), 175–182.

Hughes, F.P. (1995). *Children, play, and development* (2nd ed.). Boston: Allyn & Bacon.

Humphreys, L.G. (1986). Describing the elephant. In R.J. Sternberg & D.K. Detterman (Eds.), *What is intelligence?* (pp. 97–100). Norwood, NJ: Ablex.

Humphreys, L.G., & Stubbs, J. (1977). A longitudinal analysis of teacher expectation, student expectation, and student achievement. *Journal of Educational Measurement, 14*(3) 261–270.

Hunt, E.B. (1978). Mechanics of verbal ability. *Psychological Review, 85,* 109–130.

Hunt, E.B. (1994). Problem solving. In R.J. Sternberg (Ed.), *Thinking and problem solving: Handbook of perception and cognition* (2nd ed.) (pp. 215–232). San Diego, CA: Academic.

Hunt, E.B., Lunneborg, C., & Lewis, J. (1975). What does it mean to be high verbal? *Cognitive Psychology, 7,* 194–227.

Hyde, J.S. (1997). Gender differences in cognition: Results from meta-analyses. In P.J. Caplan & M. Crawford (Eds.) et al., *Gender differences in human cognition. Counterpoints: Cognition, memory, and language.* New York: Oxford University Press.

Hyde, J.S., Fennema, E., & Lamon, S.J. (1990). Gender differences in mathematics performance: A meta-analysis. *Psychological Bulletin, 107*(2), 139–155.

Hyde, J.S., & Linn, M.C. (1988). Gender differences in verbal ability: A meta-analysis. *Psychological Bulletin, 104*(1), 53–56.

Inhelder, B., & Piaget, J. (1958). *The growth of logical thinking from childhood to adolescence.* New York: Basic Books.

Intelligence and its measurement: A symposium. (1921). *Journal of Educational Psychology, 12,* 621–623.

Jacklin, C.N., Dipietrro, J.A., & Maccoby, E.E. (1984). Sex-typing behavior and sex-typing pressure in child-parent interactions. *Sex Roles, 13,* 413–425.

Jackson, P., & Messick, S. (1965). The person, the product and the response: Conceptual problems in the assessment of creativity. *Journal of Personality, 33,* 309–329.

Jensen, A.R. (1979). *G:* Outmoded theory or unconquered frontier? *Creative Science and Technology, 2,* 16–29.

Jenson, A.R. (1980). *Bias in mental testing.* New York: Free Press.

Jensen, A.R. (1982). Reaction time and psychometric g. In H.J. Eysenck (Ed.), *A model for intelligence.* Heidelberg: Springer-Verlag.

Jensen, A.R. (1985). The nature of

the Blackhite difference on various psychometric tests: Spearman's hypothesis. *Behavioral and Brain Sciences, 8*(2), 193–263.

Jensen, A.R. (1997). Adoption data and two g-related hypotheses. *Intelligence, 25*(1), 1–6.

Jensen, A.R. (1998). *The g factor: The science of mental ability.* Westport, CT: Prager/Greenwood.

Jensen, A.R. (2001). Psychometric g: Definition and substantiation. In R.J. Sternberg & E.L. Grigorenko (Eds.), *The general factor of intelligence: How general is it?* Mahwah, NJ: Erlbaum.

Jensen, A.R., & Munro, E. (1979). Reaction time, movement time and intelligence. *Intelligence, 3,* 121–126.

Johnson, A.K., & Anderson, E.A. (1990). In J.T. Cacioppo & L.G. Tassinary (Eds.). *Stress and arousal. Principles of psychophysiology: Physical, social, and inferential elements.* New York: Cambridge University Press.

Johnson, B., & Christensen, L. (2000). *Educational research: Quantitative and qualitative approaches.* Boston: Allyn & Bacon.

Johnson, D., & Johnson, R. (1985). Motivational processes in cooperative, competitive and individualistic learning situations. In C. Ames & R. Ames (Eds.), *Research on motivation in education. Vol. 2: The classroom milieu.* New York: Academic Press.

Johnson, D.W., & Johnson, R.T. (1991). *A meta-analysis of cooperative, competitive and individualistic goal structures.* Hillsdale, NJ: Erlbaum.

Johnson, M.K., & Hasher, L. (1987). Human learning and memory. *Annual Review of Psychology, 38,* 631–668.

Johnson, W.R. (1994). "Chanting Choristers": Simultaneous recitation in Baltimore's nineteenth-century primary schools. *History of Education Quarterly, 34*(1), 1–23.

Johnson-Laird, P.N. (2000). Reasoning. In A.E. Kazdin (Ed.), *Encyclopedia of psychology* (Vol. 8, pp. 75–79). New York: Oxford University Press.

Johnson-Laird, P.N., & Byrne, R.M.J. (1991). *Deduction.* Hillsdale, NJ: Erlbaum.

Joyce, B., & Weil, M. (1996). *Models of teaching* (5th ed.). Boston: Allyn & Bacon.

Juel-Nielsen, N. (1965). Individual and environment: A psychiatric-psychological investigation of monozygous twins reared apart. *Acta Psychiatrica et Neurologica Scandinavica* (Monograph Supplement, 183).

Jusczyk, P. (1977). *The discovery of spoken language.* Cambridge, MA: MIT Press.

Jussim, L. (1991a). Grades may reflect more than performance: Comment on Wentzel (1989). *Journal of Educational Psychology, 83*(1), 153–155.

Jussim, L. (1991b). Social perception and social reality: A reflection construction model. *Psychological Review, 98*(1), 54–73.

Kagan, J. (1965). Information processing in the child. In P.M. Mussen, J.J. Conger, & J. Kagan (Eds.), *Readings in child development and personality.* New York: Harper and Row.

Kagan, J. (1966). Reflection-impulsivity: The generality and dynamics of conceptual tempo. *Journal of Abnormal Psychology, 71,* 17–24.

Kagan, J. (1998). Biology and the child. In W. Damon (Series Ed.) & N. Eisenberg (Vol. Ed.), *Handbook of child psychology* (5th ed., Vol. 3, pp. 177–235). New York: Wiley.

Kahneman, D. (1973). *Attention and effort.* Englewood Cliffs, NJ: Prentice-Hall.

Kahneman, D., & Tversky, A. (1971). Subjective probability: A judgment of representativeness. *Cognitive Psychology, 3,* 430–454.

Kail, R. (1986). Sources of age differences in speed of processing. *Child Development, 57,* 969–987.

Kanner, L. (1943). Autistic disturbances of effective content. *Nervous Child, 2,* 217–240.

Kaplan, A.S., & Woodside, D.B. (1987). Biological aspects of anorexia nervosa and bulimia nervosa. *Journal of Consulting and Clinical Psychology, 55*(5), 645–653.

Kaplan, C.A., & Davidson, J.E. (1989). *Incubation effects in problem solving.* Unpublished manuscript.

Karpov, Y.V., & Bransford, J.D. (1995). L.S. Vygotsky and the doctrine of empirical and theoretical learning. *Educational Psychologist, 30,* 61–66.

Kashani, J.H., & Carlson, G.A. (1987). Seriously depressed preschoolers. *American Journal of Psychiatry, 144,* 348–350.

Katz, A.N. (1987). Self-reference in the encoding of creative-relevant traits. *Journal of Personality, 55,* 97–120.

Katz, J.J. (1972). *Semantic theory.* New York: Harper & Row.

Katz, J.J., & Fodor, J.A. (1963). The structure of a semantic theory. *Language, 39,* 170–210.

Kaufman, A.S. (2000). *Tests of intelligence.* In R.J. Sternberg (Ed.), Handbook of intelligence (pp. 445–476). New York: Cambridge University Press.

Kaufman, A.S., & Kaufman, N.L. (1983). *Kaufman assessment battery for children: Interpretive manual.* Circle Pines, MN: American Guidance Service.

Kazdin, A.E. (2000). Token economy. In A.E. Kazdin (Ed.), *Encyclopedia of psychology* (Vol. 8, pp. 90–92). Washington, DC: American Psychological Association.

Kearins, J.M. (1981). Visual spatial memory in Australian aboriginal children of desert regions. *Cognitive Psychology, 13*(3), 434–460.

Kee, D.W., Gottfried, A.W., Bathurst, K., & Brown, K.W. (1987). Left-hemisphere language specialization: Consistency in hand preference and sex differences. *Child Development, 58*(3), 718–724.

Keil, F.C. (1989). *Concepts, kinds, and cognitive development.* Cambridge, MA: MIT Press.

Keil, F.C. (1999). Conceptual change. In R.A. Wilson & F.C. Keil (Eds.), *The MIT encyclopedia of the cognitive sciences* (pp. 179–182). Cambridge, MA: MIT Press.

Keil, F.C. (1999). Cognition, content, and development. In M. Bennett (Ed.), *Developmental psychology* (pp. 165–184). Philadelphia, PA: Psychology Press.

Keller, H.R., & Tapasak, R.C. (1997). Classroom management. In A.P. Goldstein & J.C. Conoley, et al. (Eds.), *School violence intervention: A practical handbook.* New York: The Guilford Press.

Kellman, P.J., & Banks, M.S. (1998). Infant visual perception. In W. Damon (Series Ed.) & D. Kuhn & R.S. Siegler (Vol. Eds.), *Handbook of child psychology* (5th ed., Vol. 2, pp. 103–146). New York: Wiley.

Kelly, J.F., Morisset, C.E., Barnard, K.E., Hammond, M.A., et al. (1996). The influence of early mother-child interaction on preschool cognitive/linguistic outcomes in a high-social-risk group. *Infant Mental Health Journal, 17*(4), 310–321.

Kelman, M., & Lester, G. (1997). *Jumping the queue: An inquiry into the legal treatment of students with learning disabilities.* Cambridge, MA: Harvard University Press.

Kember, D., & Gow, L. (1991). A challenge to the anecdotal stereotype of the Asian student. *Studies in Higher Education, 16*(2), 117–128.

Kendall, D.C., Krain, A.L., & Henin, A. (2000). Cognitive-behavioral therapy. In A.E. Kazdin (Ed.), *Encyclopedia of psychology* (Vol. 2, pp. 135–139). Washington, DC: American Psychological Association.

Kendler, K.S., MacLean, C., Neale, M., Kessler, R., Heath, A., & Eaves, L. (1991). The genetic epidemiology of bulimia nervosa. *American Journal of Psychiatry, 49,* 273–281.

Kenrick, D.T., & Trost, M.R. (1993). The evolutionary perspective. In A. Beall & R.J. Sternberg (Eds.), *Perspectives on the psychology of gender.* New York: Guilford.

Khattri, N., Reeve, A.L., & Kane, M.B. (1998). *Principles and practices of performance assessment.* Mahwah, NJ: Erlbaum.

Khouzam, H.R. (1997). Attention deficit hyperactivity disorder in adults: Guidelines for evaluation and treatment. *Consultant, 37*(8), 2159–2168.

Kimball, M.M. (1989). A new perspective on women's math achievement. *Psychological Bulletin, 105*(2), 198–214.

King, C.M., & Johnson, L.M.P. (1999). Constructing meaning via reciprocal teaching. *Reading Research and Instruction, 38*(3), 169–186.

Kinsky-Ceci, W. (2000). Weight fluctuation in suburban versus rural *Felis domesticae. Journal of the American Veterinary Association, 74* (4), 32–45.

Kintsch, W. (1988). The role of knowledge in discourse comprehension: A construction-integration model. *Psychological Review, 95*(2), 163–182.

Kintsch, W. (1998). *Comprehension: A paradigm for cognition.* New York: Cambridge University Press.

Kipling, R. (1937/1985). Workingtools. In B. Ghiselin (Ed.), *The creative process: A symposium* (pp. 161–163). Berkeley: University of California Press. (Original work published 1937).

Kirk, S., Gallagher, J.J., & Anastasiow, N.J. (1993). *Educating exceptional children* (7th ed.). Boston: Houghton Mifflin.

Kish, L. (2000). Sampling. In A.E. Kazdin (Ed.), *Encyclopedia of psychology* (Vol. 7, pp. 139–142). New York: Macmillan.

Klahr, D., & MacWhinney, B. (1998). Information processing. In W. Damon (Series Ed.) & D. Kuhn & R.S. Siegler (Vol. Eds.), *Handbook of child psychology* (5th ed., Vol. 2, pp. 631–678). New York: Wiley.

Knight, G.P., Johnson, L.G., Carlo, G., & Eisenberg, N. (1994). A multiplicative model of the dispositional antecedents of a prosocial behavior: Predicting more of the people more of the time. *Journal of Personality and Social Psychology, 66,* 178–183.

Kobak, R.R., & Sceery, A. (1988). Attachment in late adolescence: Working models, affect regulation, and representations of self and others. *Child Development, 59,* 125–146.

Kohlberg, L. (1963). The development of children's orientations toward a moral order: Pt. 1. Sequence in the development of moral thought. *Vita Humana, 6,* 11–33.

Kohlberg, L. (1983). *The psychology of moral development.* New York: Harper & Row.

Kohlberg, L. (1984). The psychology of moral development: The nature and validity of moral stages. In *Essays on moral development* (Vol. 2). New York: Harper and Row.

Kohlberg, L., & Kramer, R. (1969). Continuities and discontinuities in childhood and adult moral development. *Human Development, 12,* 93–120.

Kohn, A. (1993). Rewards versus learning: A response to Paul Chance. *Phi Delta Kappan, 74,* 783–787.

Kolligian, J. Jr., & Sternberg, R.J. (1987). Intelligence, information processing, and specific learning disabilities: A triarchic synthesis. *Journal of Learning Disabilities, 20,* 8–17.

Kolloff, P.B. (1983). The Center for Global Futures: Meeting the needs of gifted students in a laboratory school. *Roeper Review, 5*(3), 32–33.

Komatsu, L.K. (Ed.). (1993). *Experimenting with the mind: Readings in cognitive psychology.* Pacific Grove, CA: Brooks/Cole.

Korf, R. (1999). Heuristic search. In R.A. Wilson & F.C. Keil (Eds.), *The MIT encyclopedia of the cognitive sciences* (pp. 372–373). Cambridge, MA: MIT Press.

Kosslyn, S.M. (1995). Mental imagery. In S.M. Kosslyn & N.D. Osherson (Eds.), *Visual cognition.* Cambridge, MA: MIT Press.

Kotovsky, K., Hayes, J.R., & Simon, H.A. (1985). Why are some problems hard? Evidence from the Tower of Hanoi. *Cognitive Psychology, 17,* 248–294.

Kounin, J.S. (1941). Experimental studies in rigidity. II. The explanatory power of the concept of rigidity as applied to feeblemindedness. *Character and Personality: A Quarterly for Psychodiagnostic and Allied Studies, 9,* 273–282.

Kounin, J.S. (1970). *Discipline and group management in classrooms.* New York: Holt, Rinehart & Winston.

Kozhevnikov, M., Hegarty, M., & Mayer, R. (1999). Students' Use of Imagery in Solving Qualitative Problems in Kinematics.

Krashen, S., & Biber, D. (1988). *On course: Bilingual education's success in California.* Sacramento: California Association for Bilingual Education.

Krathwohl, D.R., Bloom, B.S., & Masia, B.B. (1964). *Taxonomy of educational objectives. Handbook II: Affective domain.* New York: McKay.

Krechevsky, M., & Seidel, S. (1998). Minds at work: Applying multiple intelligences in the classroom. In R.J. Sternberg and W.M. Williams (Eds.), *Intelligence, instruction, and assessment: Theory into practice* (pp. 17–42). Mahwah, NJ: Erlbaum.

Kremer, H.L. & Tillema, H.H. (1999). Self-regulated learning in the context of teacher education. *Teaching and Teacher Education, 15*(5), 507–522.

Krueger, R.F., & Kling, K.C. (2000). Validity. In A.E. Kadzin (Ed.), *Encyclopedia of psychology* (Vol. 8, pp. 149–153). New York: Oxford University Press.

Kuhn, D., Schauble, L., & Garcia-Mila, M. (1992). Cross-domain development of scientific reasoning. *Cognition & Instruction, 9,* 285–327.

Kuhn, D., Garcia-Mila, M., Zohar, A., & Andersen, C. (1995). Strategies of knowledge acquisition. *Monographs of the Society for Research in Child Development, 60,* Serial No. 245.

Kuhn, D., & Siegler, R.S. (Eds.). (1998). *Handbook of child psychology* (Vol. 2) (5th ed.) New York: Wiley.

Kupersmidt, J.B., & Coie, J.D. (1990). Preadolescent peer status, aggression, and school adjustment as predictors of externalizing problems in adolescence. *Child Development, 61,* 1350–1362.

Kurtines, W., & Greif, E.B. (1974). The development of moral thought: Review and evaluation of Kohlberg's approach. *Psychological Bulletin, 81,* 453–470.

Kyllonen, P. (2001). "g": Knowledge, speed, strategies, or working-memory capacity? A systems perspective. In R.J. Sternberg & E.L. Grigorenko (Eds.), *The general factor of intelligence: How general is it?* Mahwah, NJ: Erlbaum.

LaBerge, D., & Samuels, S.J. (1974). Toward a theory of automatic information processing in reading. *Cognitive Psychology, 6,* 293–323.

Labouve-Vief, G. (1980). Beyond formal operations: Uses and limits of pure logic in life span development. *Human Development, 23,* 141–161.

Labouve-Vief, G. (1990). Wisdom as integrated thought: Historical and developmental perspectives. In R.J. Sternberg (Ed.), *Wisdom: Its nature, origins, and development* (pp. 52–83). New York: Cambridge University Press.

Labov, W. (1971). "Psychological conflict in Negro American language behavior": An invited commentary. *American Journal of Orthopsychiatry, 41*(4), 636–637.

Labov, W. (1997). Some further steps in narrative analysis. *Journal of Narrative and Life History, 7*(1-4), 395–415.

Lamb, M.E. (1996). *The role of the father in child development* (3rd ed.). New York: Wiley.

Landry, S. H., Smith, K. E., Swank, P.R., & Miller-Loncar, C. L. (2000). Early maternal and child influences on children's later independent cognitive and social functioning. *Child Development, 71*(2), 358–375.

Langer, E.J. (1993). A mindful education. *Educational Psychologist, 28,* 43–51.

Langer, E.J. (1997). *The power of mindful learning.* Reading, MA: Addison-Wesley.

Larkin, J.H. (1985). Understanding problem representation and skill in physics. In S.F. Chipman, J.W. Segal, & R.Glaser (Eds.), *Thinking and learning skills* (Vol. 2, pp. 141–159). Hillsdale, NJ: Erlbaum.

Larkin, J.H., McDermott, J., Simon, D.P., & Simon, H.A. (1980a). Models of competence in solving physics problems. *Cognitive Science, 4*(4) 317–345.

Larkin, J.H., McDermott, J., Simon, D.P., & Simon, H.A. (1980b). Expert and novice performance in solving physics problems. *Science, 208,* 1335–1342.

Larkin, J.H., & Rainard, B. (1984). A research methodology for studying how people think. *Journal of Research in Science Teaching, 21*(3), 235–254.

Lask, B., & Bryant-Waugh, R. (1992). Early-onset anorexia nervosa and related eating disorders. *Journal of Child Psychology and Psychiatry, 33,* 281–300.

Lave, J., & Wenger, E. (1991). *Situated learning: Legitimate peripheral participation.* Cambridge, MA: Cambridge University Press.

Lazar, I., & Darlington, R. (1982). Lasting effects of early education: A report from the consortium for longitudinal studies. *Monographs of the Society for Research in Child Development, 47*(2-3, Serial No. 195).

Lederer, J.M. (2000). Reciprocal teaching of social studies in inclusive elementary classrooms. *Jour-*

nal of Learning Disabilities, 33(1), 91–106.

Lee, L.C., & Zane, W.S., et al. (Eds.), (1998). Handbook of Asian American psychology. Thousand Oaks, CA: Sage Publications.

Leinhardt, G. (1987). Development of an expert explanation: An analysis of a sequence of subtraction lessons. Cognition and Instruction, 4(4), 225–282.

Leinhardt, G., & Greeno, J.G. (1986). The cognitive skill of teaching. Journal of Educational Psychology, 78(2), 75–95.

Leinhardt, G., & Greeno, J.G. (1991). The cognitive skill of teaching. In P. Goodyear (Ed.), Teaching knowledge and intelligent tutoring. Norwood, NJ: Ablex Publishing.

Leinhardt, G., & Putnam, R.T. (1987). The skill of learning from classroom lessons. American Educational Research Journal, 24(4), 557–587.

Lepper, M.R. (1988). Motivational considerations in the study of instruction. Cognition and Instruction, 5, 289–309.

Lepper, M.R. (1994). "Hot" versus "cold" cognition: An Abelsonian voyage. In R.C. Schank & E. Langer, et al. (Eds.), Beliefs, reasoning, and decision making: Psycho-logic in honor of Bob Abelson. Hillsdale, NJ: Erlbaum.

Lepper, M.R., & Chabay, R.W. (1985). Intrinsic motivation and instruction: Conflicting views on the role of motivational processes in computer-based education. Educational Psychologist, 20(4), 217–230.

Lepper, M.R., & Cordova, D.I. (1992). A desire to be taught: Instructional consequences of intrinsic motivation. Motivation and Emotion, 16(3), 187–208.

Lepper, M.R., Keavney, M., & Drake, M. (1996). Intrinsic motivation and extrinsic rewards: A commentary on Cameron and Pierce's meta-analysis. Review of Educational Research, 66(1), 5–32.

Lepper, M.R., Sethi, S., Dialdin, D., & Drake, M. (1997). Intrinsic and extrinsic motivation: A develop-

mental perspective. In S.S. Luthar, J.A. Burack, D. Cicchetti, & J.R. Weisz (Eds.), Developmental psychopathology: Perspectives on adjustment, risk, and disorder. New York: Cambridge University Press.

Lesgold, A.M. (1984). Human skill in a computerized society: Complex skills and their acquisition. Behavior Research Methods, Instruments and Computers, 16(2), 79–87.

Lesgold, A.M. (1988). Problem solving. In R.J. Sternberg & E.E. Smith (Eds.), The psychology of human thought (pp. 188–213). New York: Cambridge University Press.

Lesgold, A.M, Rubinson, H., Feltovich, P., Glaser, R., Klopfer, D., & Wang, Y. (1988). Expertise in a complex skill: Diagnosing x-ray pictures. In M.T.H. Chi, R. Glaser, & M.J. Farr (Eds.), The nature of expertise. Hillsdale, NJ: Erlbaum.

Lester, G., & Kelman, M. (1997). State disparities in the diagnosis and placement of pupils with learning disabilities. Journal of Learning Disabilities, 30(6), 599–607.

Levy, D.A. (1997). Tools of critical thinking. Boston, MA: Allyn & Bacon.

Levy, J., Wubbels, T., Brekelmans, M., & Morganfield, B. (1997). Language and cultural factors in students' perceptions of teacher communication style. International Journal of Intercultural Relations, 21(1), 29–56.

Lewinsohn, P.M., Rohde, P., & Seeley, J.R. (1994). Psychological risk factors for future attempts. Journal of Consulting and Clinical Psychology, 62, 297–305.

Liberman, I.Y., Mann, V.A., Shankweiler, D., & Werfelman, M. (1981). Children's memory for recurring linguistic and nonlinguistic material in relation to reading ability. Cortex, 18(3), 367–375.

Licht, B.G. (1992). The achievement-related perceptions of children with learning problems: A developmental analysis. In D.H. Schunk & J.L. Meece (Eds.), Stu-

dent perceptions in the classroom (pp. 247–264). Hillsdale, NJ: Erlbaum.

Liggitt-Fox, D. (1997). Fighting student misconceptions: Three effective strategies. Science Scope, 20(5), 28–30.

Lindow, J.A., Wilkinson, L.C., & Peterson, P.L. (1985). Antecedents and consequences of verbal disagreements during small-group learning. Journal of Educational Psychology, 77(6), 658–667.

Linn, M.C., & Hyde, J.S. (1989). Gender, mathematics, and science. Educational Researcher, 18, 17–27.

Linn, R.L., & Gronlund, N.E. (1995). Measurement and assessment in teaching. Columbus, OH: Merrill.

Linn, R.L., & Gronlund, N. (2000). Measurement and assessment in teaching (8th ed.). Upper Saddle River, NJ: Merrill/Prentice-Hall.

Lipman, M., Sharp, A., & Oscanyan, F. (1980). Philosophy in the classroom. Philadelphia: Temple University Press.

Livingston, C., & Borko, H. (1990). High school mathematics review lessons: Expert novice distinctions. Journal for Research in Mathematics Education, 21(5), 372–387.

Livingston, K. (1997). Ritalin: miracle drug or cop-out? The Public Interest, 3-19. (Serial No. 127).

Locke, E.A., & Latham, G.P. (1990). A theory of goal setting and task performance. Englewood Cliffs, NJ: Prentice Hall.

Locke, J.L. (1994). Phases in the child's development of language. American Scientist, 82, 436–445.

Lockheed, M.E. (1986). Reshaping the social order: The case of gender segregation. Sex Roles, 14(11-12), 617–628.

Loehlin, J.C., Horn, J.M., & Willerman, L. (1997). Heredity, environment, and IQ in the Texas Adoption Project. In R.J. Sternberg & E.L. Grigorenko (Eds.), Intelligence, heredity, and environment (pp. 105–125). New York: Cambridge University Press.

Loftus, E.F. (1975). Leading questions and the eyewitness report. *Cognitive Psychology, 7,* 560–572.

Loftus, E.F. (1977). Shifting human color memory. *Memory and Cognition, 5,* 696–699.

Loftus, E.F., & Ketcham, K. (1991). *Witness for the defense: The accused, the eyewitness, and the expert who puts memory on trial.* New York: St. Martin's Press.

Loftus, E.F., Miller, D.G., & Burns, H.J. (1978). Semantic integration of verbal information into a visual memory. *Journal of Experimental Psychology: Human Learning and Memory, 4,* 19–31.

Loftus, E.F., Miller, D.G., & Burns, H.J. (1987). Semantic integration of verbal information into a visual memory. In L.S. Wrightsman, C.E. Willis, & S.M. Kassin (Eds.), *On the witness stand: Vol. 2. Controversies in the courtroom.* Newbury Park, CA: Sage.

Loftus, E.F., & Pickerall, J. (1995). The formation of false memories. *Psychiatric Annals, 25,* 720–725.

Lohman, D. (1995, April). *Intelligences as an outcome of schooling: Some prescriptions for developing and testing the fluidization of abilities.* Paper presented at the Annual Meeting of the American Educational Research Association, San Francisco.

Lolordo, V.M. (2000). Classical conditioning. In A.E. Kazdin (Ed.), *Encyclopedia of psychology* (Vol. 2, pp. 91–95). Washington, DC: American Psychological Association.

Long, J.D., Biggs, J.C., & Hinson, J.T. (1999). Perceptions of education majors and experienced teachers regarding factors that contribute to successful classroom management. *Journal of Instructional Psychology, 26*(2), 105–110.

Lovaas, O.I. (1987). Behavioral treatment and normal educational and intellectual functioning in young autistic children. *Journal of Consulting and Clinical Psychology, 55,* 3–9.

Lubinski, D., & Benbow, C.P. (1992). Gender differences in abilities and preferences among the gifted: Implications for the math/science pipeline. *Current Directions in Psychological Science, 1*(2), 61–66.

Luchins, A.S. (1942). Mechanization in problem solving. *Psychological Monographs, 54*(6, Whole No. 248).

Luckasson, R. (Ed.)(1992). *Mental retardation: Definition, classification, and systems of support.* Washington, DC: American Association on Mental Retardation.

Lucy, J.A. (1997). Linguistic relativity. *Annual Review of Anthropology, 26,* 291–312.

Luria, A. R. (1966). *The human brain and psychological processes.* New York: Harper & Row.

Lutz, D., & Sternberg, R.J. (1999). Cognitive development. In M.H. Bornstein & M.E. Lamb (Eds.), *Developmental psychology: An advanced textbook* (4th ed.) (pp. 275–311). Mahwah, NJ: Erlbaum.

Lynn, R. (1997). Direct evidence for a genetic basis for black-white differences in IQ. *American Psychologist, 52*(1), 73–74.

Lytton, H., & Romney, D.M. (1991). Parents' sex-related differential socialization of boys and girls: A meta-analysis. *Psychological Bulletin, 109,* 267–296.

Mabry, L. (1999). Writing to the rubric. *Phi Delta Kappan, 80,* 673–679.

Maccoby, E.E. (1990). Gender and relationships. *American Psychologist, 45,* 513–520.

Maccoby, E.E., & Jacklin, C.N. (1987). Gender segregation in childhood. In H.W. Reese (Ed.), *Advances in child development and behavior, Vol. 20.* Orlando, FL: Academic Press.

MacKinnon, D. (1962). The nature and nurture of creative talent. *American Psychologist, 17,* 484–495.

Mackintosh, N.J. (1996). Sex differences and IQ. *Journal of Biosocial Science, 28*(4), 559–571.

MacMillan, D.L., & Knopf, E.D. (1971). Effect of instructional set on perceptions of event outcomes by EMR and nonretarded children. *American Journal of Mental Deficiency, 76*(2), 185–189.

Madaus, G.F., & Kellaghan, T. (1993). Testing as a mechanism of public policy: A brief history and description. *Measurement and Evaluation in Counseling and Development, 26,* 6–10.

Mager, R.F. (1975). *Preparing instructional objectives* (2nd ed.). Belmont, CA: Fearon.

Main, M., & Solomon, J. (1990). Procedures for identifying infants as disorganized/disoriented during the Ainsworth strange situation. In M. Greenberg, D. Ciccheti, & E.M. Cummings (Eds.), *Attachment in the preschool years: Theory, research, and intervention* (pp. 121–160). Chicago: University of Chicago Press.

Malcolm, S. (1984). *Equity and excellence: Compatible goals.* Washington, DC: AAAS Publications.

Mandler, J.M. (1998). Representation. In W. Damon (Series Ed.) & D. Kuhn & R.S. Siegler (Vol. Eds.), *Handbook of child psychology* (5th ed., Vol. 2, pp. 255–308). New York: Wiley.

Manges, C.D., & Wigle, S.E. (1997). Quality schools and constructivist teaching. *Journal of Reality Therapy, 16*(2), 45–51.

Mann, A.R., Miller, D.A., & Baum, M. (1995). Coming of age in hard times. *Journal of Health and Social Policy, 6*(3), 41–57.

Mann, L. (1981). The baiting crowd in episodes of threatened suicide. *Journal of Personality and Social Psychology, 41*(4), 703–709.

Mann, V. (1991). Language problems: A key to early reading problems. In B.Y.L. Wong (Ed.), *Learning about learning disabilities* (pp. 129–162). San Diego, CA: Academic Press.

Manning, B.H. (1988). Application of cognitive behavior modification: First and third graders' self-management of classroom behaviors. *American Educational Research Journal, 25,* 193–212.

Manning, B.H. (1990). Cognitive self-instruction for an off-task fourth-grader during independent academic tasks: A case study. *Contemporary Educational Psychology, 15*(1), 36–46.

Manning, B.H. (1991). *Cognitive self-instruction of classroom processes.* Albany, NY: State University of New York Press.

Marcia, J.E. (1966). Development and validation of ego identity status. *Journal of Personality and Social Psychology, 130*(6), 829–830.

Marcia, J.E. (1980). Identity in adolescence. In J. Adelson (Ed.), *Handbook of adolescent psychology* (pp. 159–187). New York: Wiley.

Marcia, J.E. (1991). Identity and self-development. In R.M. Lerner, A.C. Petersen, & J. Brooks-Gunn (Eds.), *Encyclopedia of adolescence.* New York: Garland Publishing.

Marion, R., Hewson, P.W., Tabachnick, B.R., & Blomker, K.B. (1999). Teaching for conceptual change in elementary and secondary science methods courses. *Science Education, 83*(3), 275–307.

Mark, L.S. (1998). The exploration of complexity and the complexity of exploration. In R.R. Hoffman & M.F. Sherrick, et al. (Eds.), *Viewing psychology as a whole: The integrative science of William N. Dember.* Washington, DC: American Psychological Association.

Markman, E.M. (1977). Realizing that you don't understand: A preliminary investigation. *Child Development, 48,* 986–992.

Markman, E.M. (1979). Realizing that you don't understand: Elementary school children's awareness of inconsistencies. *Child Development, 50,* 643–655.

Markus, H., & Nurius, P. (1986). Possible selves. *American Psychologist 41*(9), 954–969.

Markus, H.R., & Kitayama, S. (1991).

Culture and the self: Implications for cognition, emotion, and motivation. *Psychological Review, 98*(2), 224–253.

Markus, H.R., Kitayama, S., & Heitman, R.J. (1996). Culture and "basic" psychological principles. In E.T. Higgins & A.W. Kruglanski (Eds.), *Social psychology: Handbook of basic principles* (pp. 857–913). New York: Guilford.

Marland, S.P. (1972). *Education of the gifted and talented: Report to the Congress of the United States by the U.S. commissioner of education.* Washington, DC: U.S. Government Printing Office.

Marsh, H.W. (1992). Extracurricular activities: Beneficial extension of the traditional curriculum or subversion of academic goals? *Journal of Educational Psychology, 84*(4), 553–562.

Marsh, H.W., & Craven, R.G. (1991). Self-other agreement on multiple dimensions of preadolescent self-concept: Inferences by teachers, mothers, and fathers. *Journal of Educational Psychology, 83*(3), 393–404.

Marsh, H.W., & Yeung, A.S. (1998). Longitudinal structural equation models of academic self-concept and achievement: Gender differences in the development of math and English constructs. *American Educational Research Journal, 35*(4), 705–738.

Marshall, H.H. (Ed.). (1992). *Redefining student learning: roots of educational change.* Norwood, NJ: Ablex.

Martin, J. (1993). Episodic memory: A neglected phenomenon in the psychology of education. *Educational Psychologist, 28*(2), 169–183.

Martin, N.K., & Baldwin, B. (1996). Helping beginning teachers foster healthy classroom management: Implications for elementary school counselors. *Elementary School Guidance and Counseling, 31*(2), 106–113.

Marton, F., & Booth, S. (1997). *Learning and awareness.* Mahwah, NJ: Erlbaum.

Maslow, A.H. (1970). *Motivation and personality* (2nd ed.). New York: Harper and Row.

Mason, D.A., & Good, T.L. (1993). Effects of two-group and whole-class teaching on regrouped elementary students' mathematics achievement. *American Educational Research Journal, 30*(2), 328–360.

Matazarro, J.D. (1972). *Wechsler's measurement and appraisal of adult intelligence* (5th ed.). Baltimore, MD: Williams & Wilkins.

Matlin, M. (1998). *Cognition* (4th ed.). Ft. Worth, TX: Harcourt.

Matsumoto, D. (1994). *People: Psychology from a cross-cultural perspective.* Belmont, CA: Brooks-Cole.

Matsumoto, D. (1996). *Culture and psychology.* Belmont: Brooks-Cole.

Matthews, D.B. (1991). The effects of school environment on intrinsic motivation of middle-school children. *Journal of Humanistic Education and Development, 30*(1), 30–36.

Maulden, J., & Luker, K. (1996). The effects of contraceptive education on method used at first intercourse. *Family Planning Perspectives, 28,* 19–24, 41.

Mayer, R.E. (1995). The search for insight: Grappling with Gestalt psychology's unanswered questions. In R.J. Sternberg & J.E. Davidson (Eds.), *The nature of insight.* Cambridge, MA: MIT Press.

Mayer, R.E. (2000). Intelligence and education. In R.J. Sternberg (Ed.), *Handbook of intelligence* (pp. 519–533). New York: Cambridge University Press.

Mayer, R.E., & Wittrock, M.C. (1996). Problem-solving transfer. In D. Berliner & R. Calfee (Eds.), *Handbook of educational psychology* (pp. 47–62). New York: Macmillan.

Mayer, R.G. (1999). Fifty years of

creativity research. In R.J. Sternberg (Ed.), *Handbook of creativity* (pp. 449–460). New York: Cambridge University Press.

Mazur, J. (1990). *Learning and behavior* (2nd ed.). Englewood Cliffs, NJ: Prentice-Hall.

McCaslin, M., & Good, T. (1996). The informal curriculum. In Berliner, D., & Calfee, R. (Eds.), *Handbook of educational psychology*, (pp. 622–670). New York: MacMillan.

McClelland, D.C. (1969). *The achieving society*. New York: Free Press.

McClelland, D.C. (1985). How motives, skills, and values determine what people do. *American Psychologist, 40*(7), 812–825.

McClelland, D.C., & Teague, G. (1975). Predicting risk preferences among power related tasks. *Journal of Personality, 43*(2), 266–285.

McClelland, D.C., & Watson, R.I. (1973). Power motivation and risk-taking behavior. *Journal of Personality, 41*(1), 121–139.

McClelland, D.C., & Winter, D.G. (1969). *Motivating economic achievement*. New York: Free Press.

McClelland, J.L. (1953). *The achievement motive*. New York: Appleton-Century-Crofts.

McClelland, J.L., & Rumelhart, D.E. (1985). Distributed memory and the representation of general and specific information. *Journal of Experimental Psychology: General, 114*(2), 159–188.

McClelland, J.L., & Rumelhart, D.E. (1988). *Explorations in parallel distributed processing: A handbook of models, programs, and exercises*. Cambridge, MA: MIT Press.

McCombs, B.L. (1996). Integrating metacognition, affect, and motivation in improving teacher education. In L. Baker & P. Afflerbach, et al. (Eds.), *Developing engaged readers in school and home communities*. Mahwah, NJ: Erlbaum.

McCombs, B.L. (1998). Integrating metacognition, affect, and motivation in improving teacher edu-

cation. In N.M. Lambert & B.L. McCombs, et al. (Eds.), *How students learn: Reforming schools through learner-centered education*. Washington, DC: American Psychological Association.

McCombs, B.L., & Pope, J.E. (1994). *Motivating hard to reach students*. Washington, DC: American Psychological Association.

McCrae, R.R. (1987). Creativity, divergent thinking, and openness to experience. *Journal of Personality and Social Psychology, 52,* 1258–1265.

McEwen, B.S., Alves, S.E., Bulloch, K., & Weiland, N.G. (1998). Clinically relevant basic science studies of gender differences and sex hormone effects. *Psychopharmacology Bulletin, 34*(3), 251–259.

McKeachie, W.J., & Kulik, J.A. (1975). Effective college teaching. In F.N. Kerlinger (Ed.), *Review of research in education* (Vol. 3). Washington, DC: American Educational Research Association.

McKoon, G., & Ratcliff, R. (1986). A critical evaluation of the semantic-episodic distinction. *Journal of Experimental Psychology: Learning, Memory, and Cognition, 12*(2), 295–306.

McKoon, G., & Ratcliff, R. (1992). Spreading activation versus compound cue accounts of priming: Mediated priming revisited. *Journal of Experimental Psychology: Learning, Memory, and Cognition, 18*(6), 1155–1172.

McLanahan, S., & Sandefur, G. (1994). *Growing up with a single parent*. Cambridge, MA: Harvard University Press.

McLaughlin, H.J. (1994). From regulation to negotiation: Moving away from the management metaphor. *Action in Teacher Education, 16*(1), 75–84.

McLaughlin, M.W., & Talbert, J. (1990). Constructing a personalized school environment. *Phi Delta Kappan, 72*(3), 230–235.

McLaughlin, T.F., & Williams, R.L. (1988). The token economy. In

J.C. Witt, S.N. Elliott, & F.M. Gresham (Eds.), *Handbook of behavior therapy in education*. New York: Plenum Press.

McNamara, T.P. (1994). Theories of priming: II. Types of primes. *Journal of Experimental Psychology: Learning, Memory, and Cognition, 20*(3), 507–520.

McNatt, B.D. (2000). Ancient Pygmalion joins contemporary management: A meta-analysis of the result. *Journal of Applied Psychology, 85*(2), 314–322.

McPartland, J.M., Coldiron, J.R., & Braddock, J.H. (1987). *School structures and classroom practices in elementary, middle, and secondary schools* (Tech. Rep. No. 14). Baltimore: Johns Hopkins University, Center for Research on Elementary and Middle Schools.

Medin, D.L., Proffitt, J.B., & Schwartz, H.C., (2000). Concepts: An overview. In A.E. Kazdin (Ed.), *Encyclopedia of psychology* (Vol. 2, pp. 242–245). New York: Oxford University Press.

Meece, J.L., Blumenfeld, P.C., & Hoyle, R.H. (1988). Students' goal orientations and cognitive engagement in classroom activities. *Journal of Educational Psychology, 80*(4), 514–523.

Megargee, E.I. (2000). Testing. In A.E. Kazdin (Ed.), *Encyclopedia of psychology* (Vol. 8, pp. 47–52). New York: Macmillan.

Meichenbaum, D.H. (1977). *Cognitive behavior modification: An integrative approach*. New York: Plenum.

Meichenbaum, D.H., & Goodman, J.B. (1971). Training impulsive children to talk to themselves: A means of developing self-control. *Journal of Abnormal Psychology, 77*(2), 115–126.

Meinschaefer, J., Hausmann, M., & Guentuerkuen, O. (1999). Laterality effects in the processing of syllable structure. *Brain and Language, 70*(2), 287–293.

Meisels, S.J. (1989). High-stakes testing in kindergarten. *Educational Leadership, 46*(7), 16–22.

Messer, B., & Harter, S. (1985). *The self-perception scale for adults.* Unpublished manuscript, University of Denver.

Messick, S. (1984). The nature of cognitive styles: Problems and promises in educational practice. *Educational Psychologist, 19,* 59–74.

Mickler, S.E. (1993). Perceptions of vulnerability: Impact on AIDS-preventative behavior among college adolescents. *AIDS Education and Prevention, 5,* 43–53.

Midgley, C., Feldlaufer, H., & Eccles, J.S. (1989a). Change in teacher efficacy and student self- and task-related beliefs in mathematics during the transition to junior high school. *Journal of Educational Psychology, 81*(2), 247–258.

Midgley, C., Feldlaufer, H., & Eccles, J.S. (1989b). Student/teacher relations and attitudes toward mathematics before and after the transition to junior high. *Child Development, 60*(4), 981–992.

Miller, D., Barbetta, P., & Heron, T. (1994). START tutoring: Designing, training, implementing, adapting, and evaluating tutoring programs for school and home settings. In R. Gardner, D. Sianato, J. Cooper, W. Heward, T. Heron, J. Eshelman, & T. Grossi (Eds.), *Behavior analysis in education: Focus on measurably superior instruction* (pp. 265–282). Pacific Grove, CA: Brooks/Cole.

Miller, G.A. (1956). The magical number seven, plus or minus two: Some limits on our capacity for processing information. *Psychological Review, 63,* 81–97.

Miller, G.A., Galanter, E., & Pribram, K.H. (1986). *Plans and the structure of behavior.* New York: Holt, Rinehart, & Winston.

Miller, L.S. (1995). *An American imperative: Accelerating minority educational achievement.* New Haven, CT: Yale University Press.

Mills, C.J. (1983). Sex-typing and

self-schemata effects on memory and response latency. *Journal of Personality and Social Psychology, 45*(1), 163–172.

Mischel, W., Shoda, Y., & Rodriguez, M.L. (1989). Delay of gratification in children. *Science, 244*(4907), 933–938.

Mitchell, J.J. (1990). *Human growth and development: The childhood years.* Calgary, Alberta: Detselig Enterprises.

Mitchell, P., & Erickson, D.K. (1980). The education of gifted and talented children: A status report. *Exceptional Children, 45,* 12–16.

Miyake, K., Chen, S., & Campos, J.J. (1985). Infant temperament, mother's mode of interaction, and attachment in Japan: An interim report. In I. Bretherton & E. Waters (Eds.), *Growing points of attachment in theory and research* (Monographs of the Society for Research in Child Development, 50, 1-2, Serial No. 209).

Moallem, M. (1998). An expert teacher's thinking and teaching and instructional design models and principles: An ethnographic study. *Educational Technology Research and Development, 46*(2), 37–64.

Morelli, G.A., Rogoff, B., Oppenheim, D., & Goldsmith, D. (1992). Cultural variations in infants' sleeping arrangements: Questions of independence, *Developmental Psychology, 28,* 604–613.

Morgan, M. (1985). Self-monitoring of attained subgoals in private study. *Journal of Educational Psychology, 77*(6), 623–630.

Morrison, F.J. (1985). The nature of reading disablity. In F.J. Morrison, C. Lord, & D.P. Keating (Eds.), *Applied developmental psychology.* San Francisco: Academic Press.

Morison, P., & Masten, A.S. (1991). Peer reputation in middle childhood as a predictor of adaptation in adolescence: A seven-year follow-up. *Child Development, 62,* 991–1007.

Moses, L.J., & Baird, J.A. (1999).

Metacognition. In R.A. Wilson & F.C. Keil (Eds.), *The MIT Encyclopedia of the cognitive sciences* (pp. 533–535). Cambridge, MA: MIT Press.

Moshman, D. (1998). Cognitive development beyond childhood. In D. Kuhn & R.S. Siegler (Eds.), *Handbook of child psychology* (5th ed.) (Vol. 2, pp. 947–978). New York: Wiley.

Mott, F.L., Fondell, M.M., Hu, P.N., Kowalski-Jones, L., & Menaghan, E.G. (1996). The determinants of first sex by age 14 in a high-risk adolescent population. *Family Planning Perspectives, 28,* 13–18.

Mousavi, S., Low, R., & Sweller, J. (1995). Rediscovering cognitive lead by mixing auditory and visual presentation modes. *Journal of Educational Psychology, 87,* 319–334.

Muldoon, O.T. (2000). Social group membership and self-perceptions in Northern Irish children: A longitudinal study. *British Journal of Developmental Psychology, 18*(1), 65–80.

Murphy, G., & Allopena, P. (1994). The locus of knowledge effects in concept learning. *Journal of Educational Psychology, 20*(4), 904–919.

Mwangi, M.W. (1996). Gender roles portrayed in Kenyan television commercials. *Sex Roles, 34,* 205–214.

National Center for Health Statistics (NCHS). (1991). *Vital statistics of the United States (Vol. 2): Mortality —Part A (for the years 1966–1988).* Washington, DC: U.S. Government Printing Office.

National Center for Health Statistics (NCHS). (1993). Advance report of final mortality statistics, 1991. *NCHS Monthly Vital Statistics Report, 42*(2), Hyattsville, MD: U.S. Public Health Service.

National Commission on Testing and Public Policy. (1990). *From gatekeeper to gateway.* Chestnut Hill, MA: Boston College Press.

National Council of Teachers of Mathematics (NCTM). (1989).

Curriculum and evaluation standards for school mathematics. Reston, VA: NCTM.

National Educational Goals Panel. (1991). *The national educational goals report.* Washington, DC: U.S. Government Printing Office.

National Joint Committee on Learning Disabilities (NJCLD). (1999). Available Internet: http://www.ncld.org/ld/info_ld.html.

Needels, M., & Knapp, M. (1994). Teaching writing to children who are underserved. *Journal of Educational Psychology, 86*(3), 339–349.

Neisser, U. (Ed). (1998). *The rising curve: Long-term gains in IQ and related measures.* Washington, DC: American Psychological Association.

Neisser, U., Boodoo, G., Bouchard, T.J. Jr., Boykin, A.W., Brody, N., Ceci, S.J., Halpern, D.F., Loehlin, J.C., Perloff, R., Sternberg, R.J., & Urbina, S. (1996). Intelligence: Knowns and unknowns. *American Psychologist, 51*(2), 77–101.

Nelson, K. (1999). The developmental psychology of language and thought. In M. Bennett (Ed.), *Developmental psychology* (pp. 185–204). Philadelphia, PA: Psychology Press.

Nelson, T.O. (1996). Consciousness and metacognition. *American Psychologist, 51,* 102–116.

Nelson, T.O. (1999). Cognition versus metacognition. In R.J. Sternberg (Ed.), *The nature of cognition* (pp. 625–641). Cambridge, MA: MIT Press.

Newcomb, A.F., & Bagwell, C. (1995). Children's friendship relations: A meta-analytic review. *Psychological Bulletin, 117,* 306–347.

Newcomb, A.F., & Bukowski, W.M. (1984). A longitudinal study of the utility of social preference and social impact sociometric status schemes. *Child Development, 55,* 1434–1447.

Newcomb, M.D., & Bentler, P.M. (1989). Substance use and abuse among children and teenagers. *American Psychologist, 44,* 242–248.

Newcombe, N., & Dubas, J.S. (1992). A longitudinal study of predictors of spatial ability in adolescent females. *Child Development, 63*(1), 37–46.

Newell, A. (1973). Production systems: Models of control structures. In W.G. Chase (Ed.), *Visual information processing.* New York: Academic.

Newell, A., & Simon, H.A. (1972). *Human problem solving.* Englewood Cliffs, NJ: Prentice-Hall.

Newell, F.M. (1996). Effects of a cross-age tutoring program on computer literacy learning of second-grade students. *Journal of Research on Computing in Education, 28*(Spring), 346–358.

Newman, H.H., Freeman, F.N., & Holzinger, K.J. (1937). *Twins: A study of heredity and environment.* Chicago: University of Chicago Press.

Newmann, F.M. (1991). Promoting higher order thinking in social studies: Overview of a study of 16 high school departments. *Theory and Research in Social Education, 19*(4), 324–340.

Nicholls, J.G. (1984). Achievement motivation: Conceptions of ability, subjective experience, task choice, and performance. *Psychological Review, 91*(3), 328–346.

Nickerson, R.S. (1994). The teaching of thinking and problem solving. In R.J. Sternberg (Ed.), *Thinking and problem solving* (pp. 409–449). San Diego, CA: Academic Press.

Nickerson, R.S., Perkins, D.N., & Smith, E.E. (1985). *The teaching of thinking.* Hillsdale, NJ: Erlbaum.

Nickerson, R.S. (1987). Why teach thinking? In J.B. Baron & R.J. Sternberg (Eds.), *Teaching thinking skills: Theory and practice* (pp. 27–37). New York: Freeman.

Nieto, S. (2000). *Affirming diversity: The sociopolitical context of multicultural learning.* New York: Longman.

Nisan, M., & Kohlberg, L. (1982). Universality and variation in moral judgment: A longitudinal and cross-sectional study in Turkey. *Child Development, 53,* 865–876.

Noice, H. (1993). Effects of rote versus gist strategy on verbatim retention of theatrical scripts. *Applied Cognitive Psychology, 7*(1), 75–84.

Nolen-Hoeksema, S., Girgus, J.S., & Seligman, M.E. (1992). Predictors and consequences of childhood depressive symptoms: A 5-year longitudinal study. *Journal of Abnormal Psychology, 101,* 405–422.

Nordvik, H., & Amponsan, B. (1998). Gender differences in spatial abilities and spatial activity among university students in an egalitarian educational system. *Sex Roles, 38*(11-12), 1009–1023.

Norem, J.K., & Cantor, N. (1990). Cognitive strategies, coping, and perception of competence. In R.J. Sternberg & J. Kolligan, Jr. (Eds.), *Competence considered* (pp. 190–204). New Haven, CT: Yale University Press.

Norman, D.A., & Rumelhart, D.E. (1975). *Explorations in cognition.* San Francisco: Freeman.

Novak, J.D., & Musonda, D. (1991). A twelve-year longitudinal study of science concept learning. *American Educational Research Journal, 28,* 117–154.

Nuthall, G., & Alton-Lee, A. (1992). Understanding how students learn in classrooms. In M. Pressley, K.R. Harris, & J.T. Guthrie (Eds.), *Promoting academic competence and literacy in school.* San Diego, CA: Academic Press.

Nuthall, G., & Alton-Lee, A. (1993). Predicting learning from student experience of teaching: A theory of student knowledge construction in classrooms. *American Educational Research Journal, 30*(4), 799–840.

O'Leary, K.D., & O'Leary, S. (Eds.). (1977). *Classroom management: The successful use of behavior modification* (2nd ed.). Elmsford, NY: Pergamon.

Oakes, J. (1992). Can tracking research inform practice? *Educational Researcher, 21*(4), 12–21.

Oakes, J., & Guiton, G. (1995). Matchmaking: The dynamics of high school tracking decisions. *American Educational Research Journal 32*(1), 3–33.

Oakes, J., Quartz, K.H., Gong, J., Guiton, G., & Lipton, M. (1993). Creating middle schools: Technical, normative, and political considerations. *The Elementary School Journal, 93*(5), 461–480.

Ochse, R. (1990). *Before the gates of excellence: The determinants of creative genius.* New York: Cambridge University Press.

Office of the Federal Register. (1994). *Code of Federal Regulations 34. Parts 300 to 399.* Washington, DC: Office of the Federal Register.

Ogbu, J.U. (1994). From cultural differences to differences in cultural frame of reference. In P.M. Greenfield & R.R. Cocking (Ed.), *Cross-cultural roots of minority child development* (pp. 365–391). Hillsdale, NJ: Lawrence Erlbaum.

Okagaki, L., & Sternberg, R.J. (Eds.). (1991). *Directors of development: Influences on the development of children's thinking.* Hillsdale, NJ: Erlbaum.

Okagaki, L., & Sternberg, R.J. (1993). Parental beliefs and children's school performance. *Child Development, 64*, 36–56.

Orton, S.T. (1937). *Reading, writing, and speech problems in children.* New York: Norton.

Owens, E.W., & Waxman, H.C. (1998). Investigating technology use in science and mathematics classrooms across urban, suburban, and rural high schools. *High School Journal, 79*(1), 41–48.

Page, R.N. (1991). *Lower track classrooms: A curricular and cultural perspective.* New York: Teachers College Press.

Paige, J.M., & Simon, H.A. (1966). Cognitive processes in solving algebra word problems. In B.

Kleinmuntz (Ed.), *Problem solving: Research, method, and theory* (pp. 51–118). New York: Wiley.

Paivio, A. (1971). *Imagery and verbal processes.* New York: Holt, Rinehart & Winston.

Paivio, A. (1986). *Mental representations: A dual coding approach.* New York: Oxford University Press.

Palincsar, A.S. (1986). The role of dialogue in providing scaffolded instruction. *Educational Psychologist, 21*(1-2), 73–98.

Palincsar, A.S., & Brown, A.L. (1984). Reciprocal teaching of comprehension-fostering and comprehension-monitoring activities. *Cognition and Instruction, 1*(2), 117–175.

Palinscar, A., & Collins, K. (2000). Learning skills. In A.E. Kazdin (Ed.), *Encyclopedia of psychology* (Vol. 5, pp. 30–33). New York: Oxford University Press.

Pallas, A.M., & Alexander, K. (1983). Sex differences in quantitative SAT performance: New evidence on the differential coursework hypothesis. *American Educational Research Journal, 20*, 165–182.

Palmer, S.E. (1978). Structural aspects of visual similarity. *Memory and Cognition, 6*(2), 91–97.

Papalia, D., & Wendkos-Olds, S. (1989). *Human development* (4th ed.). New York: McGraw-Hill.

Paris, S.G., & Cunningham, A.G. (1996). Children becoming students. In D. Berliner & R. Calfee (Eds.), *Handbook of educational psychology* (pp. 117–146). New York: Macmillan.

Paris, S.G., Lipson, M.Y., & Wixson, K.K. (1983). Becoming a strategic reader. *Contemporary Educational Psychology, 8*, 293–316.

Parke, R.D., Berkowitz, I., Leyens, J.P., West, S.G., & Sebastian, R.J. (1977). Some effects of violent and nonviolent movies on the behavior of juvenile delinquents. In L. Berkowitz (Ed.), *Advances in experimen-*

tal social psychology (Vol. 10). New York: Academic Press.

Parke, R.D., & O'Neil, R. (1997). The influence of significant others on learning about relationships. In S. Duck (Ed.), *Handbook of personal relationships* (2nd ed., pp. 29–60). New York: Wiley.

Parke, R.D., & Walters, R.H. (1967). Some factors influencing the efficacy of punishment training for inducing response inhibition. *Monographs of the Society for Research in Child Development, 32*,(1, Whole No. 109).

Parten, M. (1932). Social participation among preschool children. *Journal of Abnormal and Social Psychology, 27*, 243–269.

Parziale, J., & Fischer, K.W. (1998). The practical use of skill theory in the classrooms. In R.J. Sternberg, & W.M. Williams (Eds.), *Intelligence, instruction and assessment.* Mahwah, NJ: Erlbaum.

Pascual-Leone, J. (1984). Attentional, dialectic, and mental effort. In M.L. Commons, F.A. Richards, & C. Armon (Eds.), *Beyond formal operations.* New York: Plenum.

Pascual-Leone, J. (1990). An essay on wisdom: Toward organismic processes that make it possible. In R.J. Sternberg (Ed.), *Wisdom: Its nature, origins, and development* (pp. 52–83). New York: Cambridge University Press.

Patterson, C.J., & Mischel, W. (1976). Effects of temptation-inhibiting and task-facilitating plans on self-control. *Journal of Personality and Social Psychology, 33*(2), 209–217.

Patterson, G.R., DeBaryshe, B.D., & Ramsey, E. (1989). A developmental perspective on antisocial behavior. *American Psychologist, 44*(2), 329–335.

Paul, R.W. (1987). Dialogical thinking: Critical thought essential to the acquisition of rational knowledge and passions. In J.B. Baron & R.J. Sternberg (Eds.), *Teaching thinking skills: Theory and practice* (pp. 127–148). New York: Freeman.

Pavlov, I.P. (1955). *Selected works.* Moscow: Foreign Languages Publishing House.

Pellegrini, A.D. (1988). Elementary-school children's rough-and-tumble play and social competence. *Developmental Psychology, 24,* 802–806.

Peplau, L.A. (1983). Roles and gender. In H.H. Kelley (Ed.), *Close relationships.* New York: Freeman.

Perkins, D.N. (1987). Thinking frames: An integrative perspective on teaching cognitive skills. In J.B. Baron & R.J. Sternberg (Eds.), *Teaching thinking skills: Theory and practice* (pp. 41– 61). New York: Freeman.

Perkins, D.N. (1995). Insight in minds and genes. In R.J. Sternberg & J.E. Davidson (Eds.), *The nature of insight* (pp. 495–533). Cambridge, MA: MIT Press.

Perkins, D.N., & Grotzer, (1997). Teaching intelligence. *American Psychologist, 52,* 1125–1133.

Perkins, P.N., & Salomon, G. (1989). Are cognitive skills context-bound? *Educational Researcher, 18,* 16–25.

Perlmutter, M., & Lange, G. (1978). A developmental analysis of recall-recognition distinctions. In P.A. Ornstein (Ed.), *Memory development in children.* Hillsdale, NJ: Erlbaum.

Perner, J. (1999). Theory of mind. In M. Bennett (Ed.), *Developmental psychology* (pp. 231–252). Philadelphia, PA: Psychology Press.

Petersen, A.C., Compas, B.E., Brooks-Gunn, J., Stemmler, M., Ey, S., & Grant, K.W. (1993). Depression in adolescence. *American Psychologist, 48,* 155–168.

Petre, M., & Blackwell, A.F. (1999). Mental imagery in program design and visual programming. *International Journal of Human Computer Studies, 51*(1), 7–30.

Petrill, S.A. (2001). The case for general intelligence: A behavioral genetic perspective. In R.J. Stern-berg & E.L. Grigorenko (Eds.), *The general factor of intelligence: How general is it?* Mahwah, NJ: Erlbaum.

Petrus, J.A. (1997). Bringing the shadow child into the light. *Learning, 26*(1), 36–40.

Phillipps, B.K. (1995). Improving school attendance through an incentive system. *NASSP Bulletin, 79,* 111–115.

Phillips, D.A. (1984). The illusion of incompetence among academically competent children. *Child Development, 55*(6), 2000–2016.

Phillips, D.A. (1987). Socialization of perceived academic competence among highly competent children. *Child Development, 58*(5), 1308–1320.

Phillips, D.A., & Zimmerman, M. (1990). The developmental course of perceived competence and incompetence among competent children. In R. Sternberg & J. Kolligian (Eds.), *Competence considered* (pp. 41–66). New Haven, CT: Yale University Press.

Piaget, J. (1965). *The moral judgment of the child* (M. Gabain, Trans.). New York: Harcourt. (Original work published 1932).

Piaget, J. (1969). *The child's conception of physical causality.* Totowa, NJ: Littlefield, Adams.

Piaget, J. (1972). *The psychology of intelligence.* Totowa, NJ: Littlefield, Adams.

Pinker, S. (1994). *The language instinct.* New York: William Morrow.

Pinker, S. (1998). *How the mind works.* New York: Norton.

Pintozzi, F. J., & Valeri-Gold, M. (2000). Teaching English as a second language (ESL) students. In R.F. Flippo & D.C. Caverly, et al. (Eds.), *Handbook of college reading and study strategy research.* Mahwah, NJ: Erlbaum.

Pintrich, P.R., Marx, R.W., & Boyle, R.A. (1993). Beyond cold conceptual change: The role of motivational beliefs and classroom contextual factors in the process of conceptual change. *Review of Educational Research, 63*(2), 167–199.

Pintrich, P.R., & Schrauben, B. (1992). Students' motivational beliefs and their cognitive engagement in academic tasks. In D. Schunk & J. Meece (Eds.), *Students' perceptions in the classroom: Causes and consequences* (pp. 149–183). Hillsdale, NJ: Erlbaum.

Pintrich, P.R., & Schunk, D.H. (1996). *Motivation in education: Theory, research and application.* Columbus, OH: Merrill.

Piran, N., Kennedy, S., Garfield, P.E., & Owens, M. (1985). Affective disturbance in eating disorders. *Journal of Nervous and Mental Disease, 173*(7), 395–400.

Plomin, R. (1997). Identifying genes for cognitive abilities and disabilities. In R.J. Sternberg & E.L. Griorenko (Eds.) *Intelligence, heredity, and environment* (pp. 89–104). New York: Cambridge University Press.

Plucker, J.A., & Renzulli, J.S. (1999). Psychometric approaches to the study of human creativity. In R.J. Sternberg (Ed.), *Handbook of creativity* (pp. 35–61). New York: Cambridge University Press.

Policastro, E., & Gardner, H. (1999). From case studies to robust generalizations: An approach to the study of creativity. In R.J. Sternberg (Ed.), *Handbook of intelligence* (pp. 213–225). New York: Cambridge University Press.

Polivy, J., & Herman, C.P. (1993). Etiology of binge eating: Psychological mechanisms. In C.E. Fairburn & G.T. Wilson (Eds.), *Binge eating: Nature, assessment, and treatment.* New York: Guilford.

Polk, T.A., & Newell, A. (1995). Deduction as verbal reasoning. *Psychological Review, 102,* 533–566.

Pollard, A. (Ed.). (1996). *Readings for reflective teaching in the primary school.* London, England: Cassell.

Popper, K.R. (1959). *The logic of scientific discovery.* London: Hutchinson.

Premack, D. (1959). Toward empirical behavior laws: I. Positive reinforcement. *Psychological Review, 66,* 219–233.

Pressley, M. (1979). Increasing children's self-control through cognitive interventions. *Review of Educational Research, 49*(2), 319–370.

Pressley, M. (1995). More about the development of self-regulation: Complex, long-term, and thoroughly social. *Educational Psychologist, 30*(4), 207–212.

Pressley, M., & Afflerbach, P. (1995). *Verbal protocols of reading: The nature of constructively responsive reading.* Hillsdale, NJ: Erlbaum.

Pressley, M., Levin, J.R., Ghatala, E.S. (1988). Strategy-comparison opportunities promote long-term strategy use. *Contemporary Educational Psychology, 13*(2), 157–168.

Pressley, M., Ross, K.A., Levin, J.R., & Ghatala, E.S. (1984). The role of strategy utility knowledge in children's strategy decision making. *Journal of Experimental Child Psychology, 38*(3), 491–504.

Price, J. (1996). DEA restless about Ritalin: Doctors sounding the alarm about a popular drug used to combat attention disorders in kids. *Insight on the News, 12*(25), 39.

Pring, R. (1971). Bloom's taxonomy: A philosophical critique. *Cambridge Journal of Education,1,* 83–91.

Pritchard, R. (1990). The evolution of introspective methodology and its implications for studying the reading process. *Reading Psychology,11*(1), 1–13.

Pullen, P.L., & Kaufman, J.M. (1987). *What should I know about special education? Answers for classroom teachers.* Austin, TX: Pro-Ed.

Qian, Z., & Blair, S. L. (1999). Racial/ethnic differences in educational aspirations of high school seniors. *Sociological Perspectives, 42*(4), 605–625.

Qin, Z., Johnson, D.W., & Johnson, R.T. (1995). Cooperative versus competitive efforts and problem solving. *Review of Educational Research, 65*(2), 129–143.

Ramey, C.T., & Landesman Ramey, S. (2000). Intelligence and public policy. In R.J. Sternberg (Ed.), *Handbook of intelligence* (pp. 534–548). New York: Cambridge University Press.

Ramirez, C.M. (1986). Bilingual education and language interdependence: Cummins and beyond. *Dissertation Abstracts International, 46*(11-B), 4039.

Range, L.M. (1993). Suicide prevention: Guidelines for schools. *Educational Psychology Review, 5,* 135–154.

Rapoport, J.L., et al. (1980). Dextroamphetamine: Its cognitive and behavioral effects in normal and hyperactive boys and normal men. *Archives of General Psychiatry, 37*(8), 933–943.

Rath, S. (1998). Verbal self-instructional training: An examination of its efficacy, maintenance, and generalisation. *European Journal of Psychology and Education, 13*(3), 399–409.

Raudenbush, S. W. (1984). Magnitude of teacher expectancy effects on pupil IQ as a function of the credibility of expectancy induction: A synthesis of findings from 18 experiments. *Journal of Educational Psychology, 76*(1), 85–97.

Rawson, H.E. (1992). Effects of intensive short-term remediation on academic intrinsic motivation of "at-risk" children. *Journal of Instructional Psychology, 19*(4), 274–285.

Redl, F., & Wattenberg, W.W. (1959). *Mental hygiene in teaching* (2nd ed.). New York: Harcourt Brace Jovanovich.

Reed, S.K. (2000). *Cognition: Theory and applications* (5th ed.). Belmont, CA: Wadsworth.

Reed, S.K., (2000). Problem solving. In A.E. Kazdin (ed.), *Encyclopedia of psychology,* (Vol. 8, pp. 71–75). New York: Oxford University Press.

Reeder, G.D., McCormick, C.B., & Esselman, E.D. (1987). Self-referent processing and recall of prose. *Journal of Educational Psychology, 79*(3), 243–248.

Reisberg, D. (1997). *Cognition: Exploring the science of the mind.* New York: Norton.

Reisberg, D. (1999). Learning. In R.A. Wilson & F.C. Keil (Eds.), *The MIT encyclopedia of the cognitive sciences* (pp. 460–461). Cambridge, MA: MIT Press.

Reitman, J.S. (1971). Mechanisms of forgetting in short-term memory. *Cognitive Psychology, 2,* 185–195.

Reitman, J.S. (1974). Without surreptitious rehearsal, information in short-term memory decays. *Journal of Verbal Learning and Verbal Behavior, 13,* 365–377.

Reitman, J.S. (1976). Skilled perception in Go: Deducing memory structures from inter-response times. *Cognitive Psychology, 8*(3), 336–356.

Render, G.F., Padilla, J.N., & Krank, H.M. (1989). Assertive Discipline: A critical review and analysis. *Teachers College Record, 90*(4), 607–630.

Renzulli, J.S. (1977). The enrichment triad model: A plan for developing defensible programs for the gifted and talented: II. *Gifted Child Quarterly, 21*(2), 227–233.

Renzulli, J.S. (1986). The three ring conception of giftedness: A developmental model for creative productivity. In R.J. Sternberg & J.E. Davidson (Eds.), *Conceptions of giftedness* (pp. 53–92). New York: Cambridge University Press.

Renzulli, J.S. (1994). Research related to the Schoolwide Enrichment Triad Model. *Gifted Child Quarterly, 38*(1), 7–20.

Renzulli, J.S. (1994). *Schools for talent development.* Mansfield Center, CT: Creative Learning Press.

Renzulli, J.S., Smith, L., & Reis, S. (1982). Curriculum compacting: An essential strategy for working with gifted students. *Elementary School Journal, 82*(3), 185–194.

Rescorla, R.A. (1967). Pavlovian conditioning and its proper control procedures. *Psychological Review, 74*, 71–80.

Rest, J.R. (1979). *Development in judging moral issues*. Minneapolis: University of Minnesota Press.

Rest, J.R. (1983). Moral development. In P.H. Mussen (Ed.), *Handbook of child psychology* (4th ed.) (Vol. 3, pp. 556–629).

Reyna, V.F., & Brainerd, C.J. (1993). Fuzzy memory and mathematics in the classroom. In R. Logie & G. Davies (Eds.), *Everyday memory*. Amsterdam: North-Holland.

Reynolds, C.R. (1994). Test bias and the assessment of intelligence and personality. In D.H. Saklofske & M. Zeidner, *International handbook of personality and intelligence: Perspectives on individual differences* (pp. 545–573). New York: Plenum Press.

Rholes, W.S., Jones, M., & Wade, C. (1980). A developmental study of learned helplessness. *Developmental Psychology, 16*, 616–624.

Ricciardelli, L.A. (1992). Bilingualism and cognitive development: Relation to threshold theory. *Journal of Psycholinguistic Research, 21*, 301–316.

Richards, T. (1999). Brainstorming. In M.A. Runco & S.R. Pritzker (Eds.), *Encyclopedia of creativity* (Vol. 1, pp. 219–227). San Diego, CA: Academic Press.

Richardson-Klavehn, A., & Bjork, R.A. (1988). Measures of memory. *Annual Review of Psychology, 39*, 475–543.

Riegel, K.F. (1973). Dialectical operations: The final period of cognitive development. *Human Development, 16*, 346–370.

Ringel, B.A., Springer, C.J. (1980). On knowing how well one is remembering: The persistence of strategy use during transfer. *Journal of Experimental Child Psychology, 29*(2), 322–333.

Rips, L.J. (1994). *The psychology of proof*. Cambridge, MA: MIT Press.

Rips, L.J. (1999). Deductive reasoning. In R.A. Wilson & F.C. Keil (Eds.), *The MIT encyclopedia of the cognitive sciences* (pp. 225–226). Cambridge, MA: MIT Press.

Rist, M.C. (1992). Learning by heart. *Executive Educator, 14*(11), 12–19.

Rist, R. (1970). Student social class and teacher expectations: The self-fulfilling prophecy in ghetto education. *Harvard Educational Review, 40*, 411–451.

Rochelle, J. (1998). Beyond romantic versus skeptic: A microanalysis of conceptual change in kinematics. *International Journal of Science Education, 20*(9), 1025–1042.

Rocklin, T. (1987). Defining learning: Two classroom examples. *Teaching of Psychology, 14*, 228–229.

Rodriguez, M.L., Mischel, W., & Shoda, Y. (1989). Cognitive person variables in the delay of gratification of older children at risk. *Journal of Personality and Social Psychology, 57*(2), 358–367.

Rodriguez, R. (1996). The politics of language. *Hispanic, 9*(4), 53–57.

Roe, A. (1953). A psychological study of eminent psychologists and anthropologists, and a comparison with biological and physical scientists. *Psychological Monographs: General and Applied, 67*, 352.

Roediger, H.L., III. (1980). Memory metaphors in cognitive psychology. *Memory and Cognition, 8*(3), 231–246.

Rogers, C.R., & Freiberg, H.J. (1994). *Freedom to learn* (3rd ed.). New York: Merrill/Macmillan College Publishing.

Rogers, S.M., & Turner, C.F. (1991). Male-male sexual contact in the U.S.A.: Findings from five sample surveys, 1970–1990. *Journal of Sex Research, 28*(4), 491–519.

Rogers, T.B., Kuiper, N.A., & Kirker, W. S. (1977). Self-reference and the encoding of personal information. *Journal of Personality and Social Psychology, 35*, 677–688.

Rogoff, B. (1986). The development of strategic use of context in spatial memory. In M. Perlmutter (Ed.), *Perspectives on intellectual development*. Hillsdale, NJ: Erlbaum.

Rogoff, B. (1990). *Apprenticeship in thinking: Cognitive development in social context*. New York: Oxford University Press.

Rogoff, B. (1998). Cognition as a collaborative process. In D. Kuhn & R.S. Siegler (Eds.), *Handbook of child psychology* (5th ed.) (Vol. 2, pp. 679–744). New York: Wiley.

Rogoff, B., Ellis, S., & Gardner, W. (1984). Adjustment of adult/child instruction according to child's age and task. *Developmental Psychology, 20*(2), 193–199.

Romaine, S. (1996). Bilingualism. In W.C. Ritchie & T.K. Bhatia, et al. (Eds.), *Handbook of second language acquisition*. San Diego, CA: Academic Press, Inc.

Roopnarine, J.L., Ahmeduzzaman, M., Donnely, S., Gill, P., Mennis, A., Arry, L., Dingler, K., McLaughlin, M., & Talukder, E. (1992). Social-cognitive play behaviors and playmate references in same-age and mixed-age classrooms over a 6-month period. *American Educational Research Journal, 29*, 757–776.

Rosch, E.H. (1973). On the internal structure of perceptual and semantic categories. In T.E. Moore (Ed.), *Cognitive development and the acquisition of language*. New York: Academic Press.

Rosch, E.H., & Mervis, C.B. (1975). Family resemblances: Studies in the internal structure of categories. *Cognitive Psychology, 7*, 573–605.

Rosenberg, M., Schooler, C., & Schoenbach, C. (1989) Self-esteem and adolescent problems: Modeling reciprocal effects. *American Sociological Review, 54*, 1004–1018.

Rosenshine, B. (1979). Content, time and direct instruction. In P. Peterson & H. Walberg (Eds.), *Research on teaching: Concepts, findings and implications*. Berkley, CA: McCutchan.

Rosenshine, B. (1986). Synthesis of research on explicit teaching. *Educational Leadership, 43*(7), 60–69.

Rosenshine, B.V. (1978). Academic engaged time, content covered, and direct instruction. *Journal of Education, Boston, 160*(3), 38–66.

Rosenshine, B.V., & Stevens, R.J. (1986). Teaching functions. In M.C. Wittrock (Ed.), *Third handbook of research on teaching.* Chicago: Rand McNally.

Rosenshine, B., & Meister, C. (1992) The use of scaffolds for teaching higher-level cognitive strategies. *Educational Leadership, 49*(7), 26–33.

Rosenshine, B., & Meister, C. (1994). Reciprocal teaching: A review of the research. *Review of Educational Research, 64,* 479–530.

Rosenthal, R. (1984). Interpersonal expectancy effects and psi: Some communalities and differences. *New Ideas in Psychology, 2*(1), 47–50.

Rosenthal, R. (1995). Critiquing Pygmalion: A 25-year perspective. *Current Directions in Psychological Science, 4*(6), 171–172.

Rosenthal R., & Jacobson, L. (1968). *Pygmalion in the classroom.* New York: Holt, Rinehart & Winston.

Rosnow, R.L., & Rosenthal, R. (1999). *Beginning behavioral research: A conceptual primer* (3rd ed.). Upper Saddle River, NJ: Prentice-Hall.

Ross, B.H. (2000). Concepts: Learning. In A.E. Kazdin (Ed.), *Encyclopedia of psychology* (Vol. 2, pp. 248–251). New York: Oxford University Press.

Ross, B.H., & Saplding, T.L. (1994). Concepts and categories. In R.J. Sternberg (Ed.), *Handbook of perception and cognition: Thinking and problem solving* (pp. 119–148). San Francisco: Academic Press.

Rotter, J.B. (1966). Generalized expectancies for internal versus external control of reinforcement. *Psychological Monographs, 80*(1, Whole No. 609).

Rotter, J.B. (1971). External control and internal control. *Psychology Today, 5*(1), 37–42, 58–59.

Rotter, J.B. (1975). Some problems and misconceptions related to the construct of internal versus external control of reinforcement. *Journal of Consulting and Clinical Psychology, 43*(1), 56–67.

Rotter, J.B. (1990). Internal versus external control of reinforcement: A case history of a variable. *American Psychologist, 45*(4), 489–493.

Rubenstein, C. (1993, November 18). Child's play, or nightmare on the field? *New York Times,* pp. C1, C10.

Rubin, K.H. (1980). Fantasy play: Its role in the development of social skills and social cognition. In K.H. Rubin (Ed.), *Children's play: New directions for child development.* San Francisco: Jossey-Bass.

Rubin, K.H., Bukowski, W., & Parker, J. (1998). Peer interactions, relationships, and groups. In W. Damon (Series Ed.) & N. Eisenberg (Vol. Ed.), *Handbook of child psychology* (5th ed., Vol. 3, pp. 619–700). New York: Wiley.

Rubin, K.H., Coplan, R.J., Nelson, L.J., Cheah, C.S.L., & Lagace-Seguin, D.G. (1999). Peer relationships in childhood. In M.H. Bornstein & M.E. Lamb (Eds.), *Developmental psychology: An advanced textbook* (4th ed., pp. 451–501). Mahwah, NJ: Erlbaum.

Ruble, D.N., & Martin, C.L. (1998). Gender development. In W. Damon (Series Ed.) & N. Eisenberg (Vol. Ed.), *Handbook of child psychology* (5th ed., Vol. 3, pp. 933–1016). New York: Wiley.

Runco, M.A., & Pritzker, S.R. (Eds.)(1999). *Encyclopedia of creativity.* San Diego, CA: Academic Press.

Rushton, J.P. (1997a). Race, IQ, and the APA report on The Bell Curve. *American Psychologist, 52*(1), 69–70.

Rushton, J.P. (1997b). More on political correctness and race differ-

ences. *Journal of Social Distress and the Homeless, 6*(2), 195–198.

Rushton, J.P. (1997c). Cranial size and IQ in Asian Americans from birth to age seven. *Intelligence, 25,* 7–20.

Rutter, M. (1983). School effects on pupil progress: Research findings and policy implications. *Child Development, 54*(1), 1–29.

Rutter, M., Maughan, B., Mortimore, P., Ousten, J., & Smith, A. (1979). *Fifteen thousand hours: Secondary schools and their effects on children.* Cambridge, MA: Harvard University Press.

Sabers, D.S., Cushing, K.S., & Berliner, D.C. (1991). Differences among teachers in a task characterized by simultaneity, multidimensionality, and immediacy. *American Educational Research Journal, 28*(1), 63–88.

Sadker, M., & Sadker, D. (1994). *Failing at fairness: How America's schools cheat girls.* New York: Charles Scribner's Sons.

Sadker, M., Sadker, D., & Klein, S. (1991). The issue of gender in elementary and secondary education. *Review of Research in Education, 17,* 269–334.

Sadler, P.M. (2000). The relevance of multiple-choice testing in assessing science understanding. In J.J. Mintzes & J.H. Wandersee, et al. (Eds.), *Assessing science understanding: A human constructivist view.* San Diego, CA: Academic Press, Inc.

Saloman, G., & Perkins, D.N. (1989). Rocky roads to transfer: Rethinking mechanisms of a neglected phenomenon. *Educational Psychologist, 24*(2), 113–142.

Salthouse, T.A. (1996). The processing-speed theory of adult age differences in cognition. *Psychological Review, 103,* 403–428.

Salthouse, T.A., & Somberg, B.L. (1982). Skilled performance: Effects of adult age and experience on elementary processes. *Journal of Experimental Psychology: General, 111,* 176–207.

SAMSHA. (1995). Survey shows youth drug abuse up. *SAMSHA News, 3,* 11, 20.

Samuels, S. (1988). Decoding and automaticity: Helping poor readers become automatic at word recognition. *Reading Teacher, 41*(8), 756–760.

Samuels, S.J. (1999). Developing reading fluency in learning-disabled students. In R.J. Sternberg & L. Spear-Swerling (Eds.), *Perspectives on learning disabilities* (pp. 176–189). Boulder, CO: Westview-HarperCollins.

Sanchex, G. & Valcarcel, M.V. (1999). Science teachers' views and practices in planning for teaching. *Journal of Research in Science Teaching, 36*(4), 493–513.

Sansone, C., Sachau, D.A., & Weir, C. (1989). Effects of instruction on intrinsic interest: The importance of context. *Journal of Personality and Social Psychology, 57*(5), 819–829.

Sapir, E. (1964). *Culture, language and personality.* Berkeley: University of California Press. (Original work published 1941).

Sapp, M. (1996). Three treatments for reducing the worry and emotionality components of test anxiety with undergraduate and graduate college students: Cognitive-behavioral hypnosis, relaxation therapy, and supportive counseling. *Journal of College Student Behavior, 37*(1), 79–87.

Sattler, J. (1992). *Assessment of children* (3rd ed. revised). San Diego: Jerome M. Sattler.

Sax, R., & Kohn, A. (1994). Bribes for behaving: Why behaviorism doesn't help children become good people. *NAMTA Journal, 19*(2), 71–94.

Scardamalia, M., & Bereiter, C. (1993). Computer support for knowledge-building communities. *Journal of the Learning Sciences, 3*(3), 265–283.

Scardamalia, M., & Bereiter, C. (1996). Computer support for knowledge-building communities. In T. Koschmann (Ed.), *CSCL: Theory and practice of an emerging paradigm. Computers, cognition, and work.* Mahwah, NJ: Erlbaum.

Scarr, S. (1997). Behavior-genetic and socialization theories of intelligence: Truce and reconciliation. In R.J. Sternberg & E.L. Grigorenko (Eds.), *Intelligence, heredity, and environment* (pp. 3–41). New York: Cambridge University Press.

Schaie, K.W. (1996). *Intellectual development in adulthood: The Seattle longitudinal study.* New York: Cambridge University Press.

Schank, R.C. (1972). Conceptual dependency: A theory of natural language understanding. *Cognitive Psychology, 3,* 552–631.

Schank, R.C., & Abelson, R.P. (1977). *Scripts, plans, goals, and understanding.* Hillsdale, NJ: Erlbaum.

Schank, R.C., & Joseph, D.M. (1998). Intelligent schooling. In R.J. Sternberg & W.M. Williams (Eds.), *Intelligence, instruction, and assessment* (pp. 43–65). Mahwah, NJ: Erlbaum.

Schliemann, A.D. & Magalhäes, V.P. (1990). Proportional reasoning: From shopping, to kitchens, laboratories, and, hopefully, schools. In G. Booker, P. Cobb., & T. Mendicuti (Eds.), *Proceedings of the XIV PME Conference, vol. III* (pp. 67–73). International Group for the Psychology of Mathematics Education, Oaxtepec, Mexico.

Schneider, W. (1999). TI: Working memory in a multilevel hybrid connectionist control architecture (CAP2). In A. Miyake & P. Shah, et al. (Eds.), *Models of working memory: Mechanisms of active maintenance and executive control.* New York: Cambridge University Press.

Schneider, W. (2000). Giftedness, expertise, and (exceptional) performance: A developmental perspective. In K.A. Heller, F.J. Monks, R.J. Sternberg, & R.F. Subotnik (Eds.), *International handbook of giftedness and talent* (2nd ed.). London: Elsevier.

Schneider, W., & Bjorklund, D.F. (1992). Expertise, aptitude, and strategic remembering. *Child Development, 63,* 416–473.

Schneider, W., & Bjorklund, D.F. (1998). Memory. In D. Kuhn & R.S. Siegler (Eds.), *Handbook of child psychology* (5th ed.) (Vol. 2, pp. 467–521). New York: Wiley.

Schneider, W., & Shiffrin, R.M. (1985). Categorization, restructuring, and automatization: Two separable factors. *Psychological Review, 92*(3), 424–428.

Schneider, W., & Sodian, B. (1997). Memory strategy development: Lessons from longitudinal research. *Developmental Review, 17*(4), 442–461.

Schoenfield, A.H. (1979). Explicit heuristic training as a variable in problem solving performance. *Journal for Research in Mathematics Education, 10,* 173–187.

Schofield, J.W., Eurich-Fulcer, R., & Britt, C.L. (1994). Teachers, computer tutors, and teaching: The artificially intelligent tutor as an agent for classroom change. *American Educational Research Journal, 31,* 579–607.

Schon, D. (1983). *The reflective practitioner.* New York: Basic Books.

Schraw, G., & Moshman, D. (1995). Metacognitive theories. *Educational Psychology Review, 7,* 351–371.

Schukar, R. (1997). Enhancing the middle school curriculum through service learning. *Theory into Practice, 36*(3), 176–183.

Schultz, G.F., & Switzky, H.N. (1993). The academic achievement of elementary and junior high school students with behavior disorders and their nonhandicapped peers as a function of motivational orientation. *Learning and Individual Differences, 5*(1), 31–42.

Schultz, T.R., Wright, K., & Schleifer, M. (1986). Assignment of moral responsibility and punishment. *Child Development, 57,* 177–184.

Schunk, D.H. (1987). Peer models and children's behavioral change. *Review of Educational Research, 57,* 149–174.

Schunk, D.H. (1990). Goal setting and self-efficacy during self-regulated learning. *Educational Psychologist, 25*(1), 71–86.

Schunk, D.H. (1991a). Self-efficacy and academic motivation. *Educational Psychologist, 26*(3-4), 207–231.

Schunk, D.H. (1991b). *Learning theories: An educational perspective.* New York: Macmillan Publishing.

Schunk, D.H. (1996a). Goal and self-evaluative influences during children's cognitive skill learning. *American Educational Research Journal, 33*(2), 359–382.

Schunk, D.H. (1996b). *Learning theories: An educational perspective.* New York: Merrill.

Schunk, D.H. (1998). Goal and self-evaluative influences during children's cognitive skill learning. *American Educational Research Journal, 33*(2), 359–382.

Schwartz, D.L., Lin, X., Brophy, S., & Bransford, J.D. (1999). Toward the development of flexibly adaptive instructional designs. In C.M. Reigeluth, et al. (Ed.), *Instructional-design theories and models: A new paradigm of instructional theory, Vol. II.* Mahwah, NJ: Erlbaum.

Seddon, G.M. (1978). The properties of Bloom's taxonomy of educational objectives for the cognitive domain. *Review of Educational Research, 48,* 303–323.

Selman, R. (1981). The child as friendship philosopher. In J.M. Gottman (Ed.), *The development of children's friendships.* Cambridge, England: Cambridge University Press.

Sensales, G., & Greenfield, P.M. (1995). Attitudes toward computers, science, and technology: A cross-cultural comparison between students in Rome and Los Angeles. *Journal of Cross Cultural Psychology, 26*(3), 229–242.

Separate and unequal: bilingual education. (1997, August 30). *The Economist, 344,* 16–18.

Sera, M.D. (1992). To be or not to be: Use and acquisition of the Spanish copulas. *Journal of Memory and Language, 31,* 408–427.

Serpell, R. (2000). Intelligence and culture. In R.J. Sternberg (Ed.), *Handbook of intelligence* (pp. 549–577). New York: Cambridge University Press.

Serpell, R., & Boykin, A.W. (1994). Cultural dimensions of cognition: A multiplex, dynamic system of constraints and possibilities. In R.J. Sternberg (Ed.), *Thinking and problem solving handbook of perception and cognition* (2nd ed.) (pp. 369–408). San Diego, CA: Academic Press.

Sethi, S., Drake, M., Dialdin, D.A., & Lepper, M.R. (1995, April). *Developmental patterns of intrinsic and extrinsic motivation: A new look.* Paper presented at the annual meeting of the American Educational Research Association, San Francisco.

Shade, B.J. (1982). Afro-American cognitive style: A variable in school success? *Review of Educational Research, 52*(2), 219–244.

Shakeshaft, C., Mandel, L., Johnson, Y.M., Sawyer, J., Hergenrother, M.A., & Barker, E. (1997). Boys call me cow. *Educational Leadership, 55*(2), 22–25.

Shavelson, R.J. (1987). Teacher planning. In M.J. Dunkin (Ed.), *International encyclopedia of teaching and teacher education.* Oxford: Pergamon Press.

Shaver, P.R., Collins, N., & Clark, C. (1996). Attachment styles and internal working models of self and relationship partners. In G.J.O. Fletcher & J. Fitress (Eds.), *Knowledge structures in close relationships: A social psychological approach.* Mahwah, NJ: Erlbaum.

Shaver, P., Hazan, C., & Bradshaw, D. (1988). Love as attachment. In R.J. Sternberg & M.L. Barnes (Eds.), *The psychology of love* (pp. 68–99). New Haven, CT: Yale University Press.

Shaywitz, B.A., Shaywitz, S.E., Sebrechts, M.M., & Anderson, G.M., et al. (1990). Growth hormone and prolactin response to methylphenidate in children with attention deficit disorder. *Life Sciences, 46*(9), 625–633.

She, H.C. (2000). The interplay of a biology teacher's beliefs, teaching practices and gender-based student-teacher classroom interaction. *Educational Research, 42*(1), 100–111.

Shepard, L.A., & Smith, M.L. (1989). Academic and emotional effects of kindergarten retention. In L. Shepard & M. Smith (Eds.), *Flunking grades: Research and policies on retention* (pp. 79–107). Philadelphia: Falmer Press.

Siegler, R.S. (1998). *Children's thinking* (3rd ed.). Upper Saddle River, NJ: Prentice-Hall.

Shields, J. (1962). *Monozygotic twins brought up apart and brought up together.* London: Oxford University Press.

Shiffrin, R.M., & Schneider, W. (1977). Controlled and automatic human information processing: II. Perceptual learning, automatic attending and a general. *Psychological Review, 84*(2), 127–190.

Shook, S.C., LaBrie, M., Vallies, J., McLaughlin, T.F., & Williams, R.L. (1990). The effects of a token economy on first grade students' inappropriate social behavior. *Reading Improvement, 27*(2), 96–101.

Shulman, L.S. (1987). Knowledge and teaching: foundations of the new reform. *Harvard Educational Review, 57*(1), 1–32.

Siegler, R.S. (1984). Mechanisms of cognitive growth: Variation and selection. In R.J. Sternberg (Ed.), *Mechanisms of cognitive development* (pp. 142–162). New York: Freeman.

Siegler, R.S. (1996). *Emerging minds: The process of change in children's thinking.* New York: Oxford.

Siegler, R.S., & Shrager, J. (1984). A model of strategy choice. In C. Sophian (Ed.), *Origins of cognitive skills* (pp. 229–293). Hillsdale, NJ: Erlbaum.

Signorelli, N., McLeod, D., & Healy, E. (1994). Gender stereotypes in MTV commercials: The beat goes on. *Journal of Broadcasting and Electronic Media, 38*, 91–101.

Simon, H.A. (1999). Problem solving. In R.A. Wilson & F.C. Keil (Eds.), *The MIT encyclopedia of the cognitive sciences* (pp. 674–676). Cambridge, MA: MIT Press.

Simonton, D.K. (1984). *Genius, creativity, and leadership.* Cambridge, MA: Harvard University Press.

Simonton, D.K. (1988). Creativity, leadership, and chance. In R.J. Sternberg (Ed.), *The nature of creativity* (pp. 386–426). New York: Cambridge University Press.

Simonton, D.K. (1994). *Greatness: Who makes history and why?* New York: Guilford Press.

Simonton, D.K. (1999). Creativity from a historiometric perspective. In R.J. Sternberg (Ed.), *Handbook of creativity* (pp. 116–133). New York: Cambridge University Press.

Simpson, E.J. (1972). *The classification of educational objectives: Psychomotor domain.* Urbana, IL: University of Illinois Press.

Skinner, B.F. (1957). *Verbal behavior.* New York: Appleton-Century-Crofts.

Skrtic, T.M. (1997). Learning disabilities as organizational pathologies. In R.J. Sternberg & L. Spear-Swerling (Eds.), *Perspectives on learning disabilities: Biological, cognitive, contextual* (pp. 193–226). Boulder, CO: Westview Press.

Slavin, R.E. (1987). Ability grouping and student achievement in elementary schools: A best-evidence synthesis. *Review of Educational Research, 57*, 293–336.

Slavin, R.E. (1993). Ability grouping in the middle grades: Achievement effects and alternatives. *The Elementary School Journal 93*(5), 535–552.

Slavin, R.E. (1995). Enhancing intergroup relations in schools: Cooperative learning and other strategies. In W.D. Hawley & A.W. Jackson, et al. (Eds.), *Toward a common destiny: Improving race* and ethnic relations in America. San Francisco, CA: Jossey-Bass.

Slavin, R.E. (1995). *Cooperative learning.* 2nd ed. Boston: Allyn & Bacon.

Slavin, R.E., & Cooper, R. (1999). Improving intergroup relations: Lessons learned from cooperative learning programs. *Journal of Social Issues, 55*(4), 647–663.

Slobin, D.I. (1971). Cognitive prerequisites for the acquisition of grammar. In C.A. Ferguson & D. I. Slobin (Eds.), *Studies of child language development.* New York: Holt, Rinehart & Winston.

Slobin, D.I. (Ed.) (1985). *The cross-linguistic study of language acquisition.* Hillsdale, NJ: Erlbaum.

Slotta, J.D., Chi, M.T.H., & Joram, E. (1995). Assessing students' misclassifications of physics concepts: An ontological basis for conceptual change. *Cognition and Instruction, 13*(3), 373–400.

Small, M.Y., Lovett, S.B., & Scher, M.S. (1993). Pictures facilitate children's recall of unillustrated expository prose. *Journal of Educational Psychology, 85*, 520–528.

Smedler, A.C., & Torestad, B. (1996). Verbal intelligence: A key to basic skills. *Educational Studies, 22*(3), 343–356.

Smelter, R.W., Rasch, B.W., Fleming, J., Nazos, P., & Baranowski, S. (1996). Is attention deficit disorder becoming a desired diagnosis? *Phi Delta Kappan, 77*(6), 429–433.

Smetana, J.G. (1997). Parenting and the development of social knowledge reconceptualized: A social-domain analysis. In J.E. Grusec & L. Kuczynski (Eds.), *Parenting and children's internalization of values* (pp. 162–192). New York: Wiley.

Smith, A.E., Jussim, L., & Eccles, J. (1999). Do self-fulfilling prophecies accumulate, dissipate, or remain stable over time? *Journal of Personality and Social Psychology, 77*(3), 548–565.

Smith, A.E., Jussim, L., Eccles, J., Van-Noy, M., Madon, S., & Palumbo, P. (1998). Self-fulfilling prophecies, perceptual biases, and accuracy at the individual and group levels. *Journal of Experimental Social Psychology, 34*(6), 530–561.

Smith, D.D., & Luckasson, R. (1995). *Introduction to special education.* (2nd ed.). Boston: Allyn & Bacon.

Smith, E.E. (1999). Working memory. In R.A. Wilson & F.C. Keil (Eds.), *The MIT encyclopedia of the cognitive sciences* (pp. 888–890). Cambridge, MA: MIT Press.

Smith, E.E., & Medin, D.L. (1981). *Categories and concepts.* Cambridge, MA: Harvard University Press.

Smith, E.E., Shoben, E.J., & Rips, L.J. (1974). Structure and process in semantic memory: A featural model for semantic decisions. *Psychological Review, 81*, 214–241.

Smith, S.M. (1995). Getting into and out of mental ruts: A theory of fixation, incubation and insight. In R.J. Sternberg & J.E. Davidson (Eds.), *The nature of insight* (pp. 229–252). Cambridge, MA: MIT Press.

Smolensky, P. (2000). Connectionist approaches to language. In R.A. Wilson and F.C.. Keil (Eds.), *The MIT encyclopedia of the cognitive sciences* (pp. 188–190). Cambridge, MA: MIT Press.

Snarey, J.R. (1985). Cross-cultural universality of social-moral development: A critical review of Kohlbergian research. *Psychological Bulletin, 97*, 202–232.

Snarey, J.R., Reimer, J., & Kohlberg, L. (1985a). Development of social-moral reasoning among kibbutz adolescents: A longitudinal cross-cultural study. *Developmental Psychology, 21*, 3–7.

Snarey, J.R., Reimer, J., & Kohlberg, L. (1985b). The kibbutz as a model for moral education: A longitudinal cross-cultural study. *Journal of Applied Developmental Psychology, 6*, 151–172.

Snow, R.E. (1977). Research on aptitude for learning. In L.S. Shulman (Ed.), *Review of research in education* (Vol. 4). Itasca, IL: F.E. Peacock.

Snow, R.E. (1989). Cognitive-conative aptitude interactions in learning. In R. Kanfer, P.L. Ackerman, & R. Cudeck (Eds.), *Abilities, motivation, and methodology: The Minnesota Symposium on Learning and Individual Differences*. Hillsdale, NJ: Erlbaum.

Snow, R.E. (1992). Aptitude theory: Yesterday, today, and tomorrow. *Educational Psychologist, 27*(1), 5–32.

Snow, R.E. (1995). Pygmalion and intelligence? *Current Directions in Psychological Science, 4*(6), 169–171.

Snow, R.E., Corno, L., & Jackson, D. (1996). Individual differences in affective and cognitive functions. In D. Berliner & R. Calfee (Eds.), *Handbook of educational psychology* (pp. 342–310). New York: Macmillan.

Snyder, H. & Sickmund, M. (1999). *Juvenile Offenders and Victims: 1999 National Report*. Washington, DC: Office of Juvenile Justice and Delinquency Prevention, 1999.

Sokolove, S., Garrett, J., Sadker, D., & Sadker, M. (1986). Interpersonal communications skills. In J. Cooper (Ed.), *Classroom teaching skills: A handbook*. Lexington, MA: D.C. Heath.

Solso, R.L. (1995). *Cognitive psychology* (4th ed.). Boston: Allyn & Bacon.

Soriano de Alencar, G.M.L., Blumen, S., & Castellanos-Simons, D. (2000). Programs and practices for identifying and nurturing giftedness and talent in Latin American countries. In K.A. Heller, F.J. Monks, R.J. Sternberg, & R.F. Subotnik (Eds.), *International handbook of giftedness and talent* (2nd ed.). London: Elsevier.

Sowell, E.J., Bergwall, L.K., Zeigler, A.J., & Cartwright, R.M. (1990). Identification and description of mathematically gifted students: A review of empirical research. *Gifted Child Quarterly, 34*(4), 147–154.

Spearman, C. (1904). General intelligence, objectively determined and measured. *American Journal of Psychology, 15*, 201–293.

Spearman, C. (1927). *The abilities of man*. New York: Macmillan.

Spear-Swerling, L., & Sternberg, R. J. (1996). *Off track: When poor readers become learning disabled*. Boulder, CO: Westview Press.

Spear-Swerling, L., & Sternberg, R.J. (1994). The road not taken: An integrative model of reading disability. *Journal of Learning Disabilities, 27*(2), 91–103.

Spence, J.T., & Helmreich, R.L. (1983). Achievement-related motives and behavior. In J.T. Spence (Ed.), *Achievement and achievement motives: Psychological and sociological approaches*. New York: Freeman.

Spoehr, K.T., & Corin, W.J. (1978). The stimulus suffix effect as a memory coding phenomenon. *Memory and Cognition, 6*, 583–589.

Squire, L. R. (1987). *Memory and the brain*. New York: Oxford University Press.

Sroufe, L.A. (1996). *Emotional development: The organization of emotional life in the early years*. New York: Cambridge University Press.

Stack, S. (1987). Celebrities and suicide: A taxonomy and analysis, 1948–1983. *American Sociological Review, 52*, 401–412.

Stahl, S.A., Erickson, L.G., & Rayman, M.C. (1986). Detection of inconsistencies by reflective and impulsive seventh-grade readers. *National Reading Conference Yearbook, 35*, 233–238.

Stainback, S., & Stainback, W. (1992). Schools as inclusive communities. In W. Stainback & S. Stainback (Eds.), *Controversial issues confronting special education: Divergent perspectives* (pp. 29–43). Boston: Allyn & Bacon.

Stanley, J.C. (1978). Radical acceleration: Recent educational innovations at JHU. *Gifted Child Quarterly, 22*(1), 62–67.

Stanley, J.C. (1996). In the beginning: The study of mathematically precocious youth. In C.P. Benbow & D. Lubinski (Eds.), *Intellectual talent* (pp. 225–245). Baltimore, MD: The Johns Hopkins University Press.

Stanley, J.C., & Benbow, C.P. (1982). Educating mathematically precocious youths: Twelve policy recommendations. *Educational Researcher, 11*(5), 4–9.

Stanley, J.C., & Benbow, C.P. (1983). SMPY's first decade: Ten years of posing problems and solving them. *Journal of Special Education, 17*(1), 11–25.

Stanley, J.C., & Benbow, C.P. (1986a). Extremely young college graduates: Evidence of their success. *College and University, 58*, 361–371.

Stanley, J.C., & Benbow, C.P. (1986b). Youths who reason exceptionally well mathematically. In R.J. Sternberg & J.E. Davidson (Eds.), *Conceptions of giftedness*. Cambridge, England: Cambridge University Press.

Steele, C.M. (1997a). Race and the schooling of Black Americans. In L.A. Peplau & S.E. Taylor et al. (Eds.) *Sociocultural perspectives in social psychology: Current readings*. Upper Saddle River, NJ: Prentice-Hall.

Steele, C.M. (1997b). A threat in the air: How stereotypes shape intellectual identity and performance. *American Psychologist, 52*(6), 613–629.

Steele, C.M., & Aronson, J. (1995). Stereotype threat and the intellectual test performance of African Americans. *Journal of Personality and Social Psychology, 69*(5), 797–811.

Steinberg, L. (2000). Punishment: Developmental perspectives. In A.E. Kazdin (Ed.), *Encyclopedia of psychology* (Vol. 6, pp. 484–487). Washington, DC: American Psychological Association.

Steinberg, L., Lamborn, S.D., Dornbusch, S. M., & Darling, N. (1992).

Impact of parenting practices on adolescent achievement: Authoritative parenting, school involvement, and encouragement to succeed. *Child Development, 63*(5), 1266–1281.

Sternberg, R.J. (1977). *Intelligence, information processing, and analogical reasoning: The componential analysis of human abilities.* Hillsdale, NJ: Erlbaum.

Sternberg, R.J. (1981a). The evolution of theories of intelligence. *Intelligence, 5*(3), 209–230.

Sternberg, R.J. (1981b). Intelligence and nonentrenchment. *Journal of Educational Psychology, 73*, 1–16.

Sternberg, R.J. (1981c) Novelty seeking, novelty finding, and the developmental continuity of intelligence. *Intelligence, 5*(2), 149–155.

Sternberg, R.J. (1981d). Reasoning with determinate and indeterminate linear syllogisms. *British Journal of Psychology, 72*(4), 407–420.

Sternberg, R.J. (Ed.). (1984). *Mechanisms of cognitive development.* San Fransisco: Freeman.

Sternberg, R.J. (1985). *Beyond IQ: A triarchic theory of human intelligence.* New York: Cambridge University Press.

Sternberg, R.J. (1986). *Intelligence applied: Understanding and increasing your intellectual skills.* New York: Harcourt Brace Jovanovich.

Sternberg, R.J. (1987a). Most vocabulary is learned from context. In M.G. McKeown & M.E. Curtis (Eds.), *The nature of vocabulary acquisition* (pp. 89–105). Hillsdale, NJ: Erlbaum.

Sternberg, R.J. (1987b). Teaching intelligence: The application of cognitive psychology to the improvement of intellectual skills. In J.B. Baron & R.J. Sternberg (Eds.), *Teaching thinking skills.* New York: Freeman.

Sternberg, R.J. (1988a). A three-facet model of creativity. In R.J. Sternberg (Ed.), *The nature of creativity* (p. 125–147). New York: Cambridge University Press.

Sternberg, R.J. (1988b). *The triarchic mind.* New York: Viking.

Sternberg, R.J. (1989). Domain-generality versus domain specificity: The life and impending death of a false dichotomy. *Merrill-Palmer Quarterly, 35*, 115–130.

Sternberg, R.J. (1990). *Metaphors of mind.* New York: Cambridge University Press.

Sternberg, R.J. (1993). Would you rather take orders from Kirk or Spock? The relation between rational thinking and intelligence. *Journal of Learning Disabilities, 26*(8), 516–519.

Sternberg, R.J. (1994a). Answering questions and questioning answers. *Phi Delta Kappan, 76*(2), 136–138.

Sternberg, R.J. (1994b). Allowing for thinking styles. *Educational Leadership, 52*(3), 36–40.

Sternberg, R.J. (Ed.) (1994c). *Encyclopedia of human intelligence.* New York: Macmillan.

Sternberg, R.J. (1994d). Human intelligence: Its nature, use, and interaction with context. In D.K. Detterman (Ed.), *Current topics in human intelligence* (Vol. 4, pp. 361–407). Norwood, NJ: Ablex.

Sternberg, R.J. (1994e). Thinking styles: Theory and assessment of the interface between intelligence and personality. In R.J. Sternberg & P. Ruzgis (Eds.), *Personality and intelligence* (pp. 169–187). New York: Cambridge University Press.

Sternberg, R.J. (1995). Styles of thinking in the school. *European Journal for High Ability, 6*(2), 201–219.

Sternberg, R. J. (1996a). Educational psychology has fallen, but it can get up. *Educational Psychology Review, 8*(2), 175–185.

Sternberg, R.J. (1996b). IQ counts, but what really counts is successful intelligence. *Bulletin, 18*–23.

Sternberg, R. J. (1996c). Matching abilities, instruction, andassessment: Reawakening the sleeping giant of ATI. In I. Dennis & P. Tapsfield (Eds.), *Human abilities: Their nature and measurement* (pp. 167–181). Mahwah, NJ: Erlbaum.

Sternberg, R.J. (1997a, August 25). Extra credit for doing poorly. *New York Times,* p. A-27.

Sternberg, R.J. (1997b). Fads in psychology: What we can do. *APA Monitor, 28*(7), 19.

Sternberg, R. J. (1997c). Intelligence and lifelong learning: What's new and how can we use it? *American Psychologist, 52*(10), 1134–1139.

Sternberg, R.J. (1998). *Cupid's arrow.* New York: Cambridge University Press.

Sternberg, R.J. (1998a). The dialectic as a tool for the teaching of psychology. *Teaching of Psychology, 25*, 177–180.

Sternberg, R.J. (1998b). A dialectical basis for understanding the study of cognition. In R.J. Sternberg (Ed.), *The nature of cognition.* Cambridge, MA: MIT Press.

Sternberg, R. J. (1998c). Abilities are forms of developing expertise. *Educational Researcher, 27*(3), 11–20.

Sternberg, R. J. (1998d). Metacognition, abilities, and developing expertise: What makes an expert student? *Instructional Science, 26*(1-2), 127–140.

Sternberg, R.J. (1999). Schools should nurture wisdom. In B.Z. Presseeisen (Ed.), *Teaching for intelligence I* (pp. 55–82). Arlington Heights, IL: Skylight.

Sternberg, R.J. (1999). The theory of successful intelligence. *Review of General Psychology, 3,* 292–310.

Sternberg, R. J. (1999a). Ability and expertise: It's time to replace the current model of intelligence. *American Educator, 23*(1), 10–13, 50–51.

Sternberg, R.J. (1999b). *Cognitive psychology* (2nd ed.). Ft. Worth, TX: Harcourt Brace College Publishers.

Sternberg, R.J. (2000). Thinking. In

A.E. Kazdin (Ed.), *Encyclopedia of psychology* (Vol. 8, pp. 68–71). New York: Oxford University Press.

Sternberg, R.J. (Ed.). (2000). *Handbook of intelligence.* New York: Cambridge University Press.

Sternberg, R.J., & Ben-Zeev, T. (1996). *The nature of mathematical thinking.* Mahwah, NJ: Erlbaum.

Sternberg, R.J., & Ben-Zeev, T. (Eds.). (2001). *Complex cognition: The psychology of human thought.* New York: Oxford University Press.

Sternberg, R.J., & Berg, C.A. (Eds.) (1990). *Intellectual development.* New York: Cambridge University Press.

Sternberg, R.J., & Berg, C.A. (Eds.). (1992). *Intellectual development.* New York: Cambridge University Press.

Sternberg, R.J., & Bhana, K. (1986). Synthesis of research on the effectiveness of intellectual skills programs: Snake-oil remedies or miracle cures? *Educational Leadership, 44*(2), 60–67.

Sternberg, R.J., Castejón, J.L., & Prieto, M.D., Hautamäki, J., & Grigorenko, E.L. (2001). Confirmatory factor analysis of the Sternberg triarchic abilities test in three international samples: An empirical test of the triarchic theory of intelligence. *European Journal of Psychological Assessment, 17*(1) 1–16.

Sternberg, R.J., Clinkenbeard, P.R. (1995). A triarchic model of identifying, teaching, and assessing gifted children. *Roeper Review, 17*(4), 255–260.

Sternberg, R.J., & Davidson, J.E. (1982, June). The mind of the puzzler. *Psychology Today,* 37–44.

Sternberg, R.J., & Davidson, J.E. (Eds.). (1986). *Conceptions of giftedness.* New York: Cambridge University Press.

Sternberg, R.J., & Davidson, J.E. (Eds.). (1995). *The nature of insight.* Cambridge, MA: MIT Press.

Sternberg, R.J., & Detterman, D.K. (Eds.). (1986). *What is intelligence? Contemporary viewpoints on its nature and definition.* Norwood, NJ: Ablex.

Sternberg, R.J., Ferrari, M., Clinkenbeard, P.R., & Grigorenko, E.L.(1996). Identification, instruction, and assessment of gifted children: A construct validation of a triarchic model. *Gifted Child Quarterly, 40*(3), 129–137.

Sternberg, R.J., Forsythe, G.B., Hedlund, J., Horvath, J.A., Wagner, R.K., Williams, W.M., Snook, S.A., & Grigorenko, E.L. (2000). *Practical intelligence in everyday life.* New York: Cambridge University Press.

Sternberg, R.J., & Frensch, P.A. (Eds.). (1991). *Complex problem solving: Principles and mechanisms.* Hillsdale, NJ: Erlbaum.

Sternberg, R.J., & Grigorenko, E.L. (Eds.)(1997). *Intelligence, heredity, and environment.* New York: Cambridge University Press.

Sternberg, R.J., & Grigorenko, E.L. (1997). Interventions for cognitive development in children 0–3 years old. In M.E. Young (Ed.), *Early child development programs: Investing in our children's future* (pp. 127–156). Amsterdam: Elsevier.

Sternberg, R.J., & Grigorenko, E.L. (1999). *Our labeled children.* Needham Heights, MA: Perseus.

Sternberg, R.J., & Grigorenko, E.L. (2000). *Teaching for successful intelligence.* Arlington Heights, IL: Skylight.

Sternberg, R.J., & Grigorenko, E.L. (2000a). A capsule history of theory and research on styles. In R.J. Sternberg and L.-F. Zhang (Eds.), *Perspectives on cognitive, learning, and thinking styles.* Mahwah, NJ: Erlbaum.

Sternberg, R.J., & Grigorenko, G.L. (2001). *Intelligence applied* (2nd ed.). New York: Oxford University Press.

Sternberg, R.J., Grigorenko, E.L., Ferrari, M., & Clinkenbeard, P. (1999). A triarchic analysis of an aptitude-treatment interaction.

European Journal of Psychological Assessment, 15, 1–11.

Sternberg, R.J., Grigorenko, E.L., & Nokes, C. (1997). Effects of children's ill health on cognitive development. In M.E. Young (Ed.), *Early child development programs: Investing in our children's future* (pp. 85–125). Amsterdam: Elsevier.

Sternberg, R.J., & Horvath, J.A. (1995). A prototype view of expert teaching. *Educational Researcher, 24*(6), 9–17.

Sternberg, R.J., & Horvath, J.A. (1998). In R.C. Friedman & K.B. Rogers, et al. (Eds.), *Talent in context: Historical and social perspectives on giftedness.* Washington, DC: American Psychological Association.

Sternberg, R.J., & Horvath, J.A. (Eds.). (1999). *Tacit knowledge in professional practice: Researcher and practitioner perspectives.* Mahwah, NJ: Erlbaum.

Sternberg, R.J., & Lubart, T.I. (1991). An investment theory of creativity and its development. *Human Development, 34,* 1–31.

Sternberg, R.J., & Lubart, T.I. (1995). *Defying the crowd: Cultivating creativity in a culture of conformity.* New York: The Free Press.

Sternberg, R.J., & Lubart, T.I., (1996). Investing in creativity. *American Psychologist, 51,* 677–688.

Sternberg, R.J., & Lubart, T.I. (1999). The concept of creativity: Prospects and paradigms. In R.J. Sternberg (Ed.), *Handbook of creativity* (pp. 3–15). New York: Cambridge University Press.

Sternberg, R.J., Okagaki, L., & Jackson, A. (1990). Practical intelligence for success in school. *Educational Leadership, 48,* 35–39.

Sternberg, R.J., & Powell, J.S. (1983). Comprehending verbal comprehension. *American Psychologist, 38,* 878–893.

Sternberg, R.J., & Rifkin, B. (1979). The development of analogical reasoning processes. *Journal of*

Experimental Child psychology, 27, 195–232.

Sternberg, R.J., & Spear, L.C. (1985). A triarchic theory of mental retardation. In N. Ellis & N. Bray (Eds.), *International review of research in mental retardation* (Vol. 13, pp. 301–326). New York: Academic Press.

Sternberg, R.J., & Spear-Swerling, L. (1996). *Teaching for thinking.* Washington, DC: American Psychological Association.

Sternberg, R.J., & Spear-Swerling, L. (Eds.). (1999). *Perspectives on learning disabilities: Biological, cognitive, contextual.* Boulder, CO: Westview Press.

Sternberg, R.J., Torff, B., & Grigorenko, E.L. (1998). Teaching triarchically improves school achievement. *Journal of Educational Psychology, 90*(3), 1–11.

Sternberg, R.J., & Wagner, R.K. (1982). Automatization failure in learning disabilities. *Topics in Learning and Learning Disabilities, 2,* 1–11.

Sternberg, R.J., & Wagner, R.K. (1983). Understanding intelligence: What's in it for educators? In *A nation at risk.* Washington, DC: National Commission on Excellence in Education.

Sternberg, R.J., Wagner, R.K., Williams, W.M., & Horvath, J.A. (1997). Testing common sense. In D.F. Russ-Eft & H.S. Preskill (Eds.), *Human resource development review: Research and implications.* Thousand Oaks, CA: Sage Publications.

Sternberg, R.J., & Williams, W.M. (1996). *How to develop student creativity.* Alexandria, VA: Association for Supervision and Curriculum Development.

Sternberg, R.J., & Williams, W.M. (1997). Does the graduate record examination predict meaningful success in the graduate training of psychologists? A case study. *American Psychologist, 52,* 630–641.

Sternberg, R.J., & Williams, W.M. (Eds.) (1998). *Intelligence, instruc-tion, and assessment.* Mahwah, NJ: Erlbaum.

Sternberg, R.J., & Zhang, L.-F. (Eds.)(2000). *Perspectives on cognitive, learning, and thinking styles.* Mahwah, NJ: Erlbaum.

Sternberg, R.J., & Zhang, L.F. (1995). What do we mean by giftedness? A pentagonal implicit theory. *Gifted Child Quarterly, 39*(2), 88–94.

Stiggins, R. (1997). *Student-centered classroom assessment* (2nd ed.). Upper Saddle River, NJ: Prentice-Hall.

Stipek, D.J. (1984). Sex differences in children's attributions for success and failure on math and spelling tests. *Sex Roles, 11*(11–12), 969–981.

Stipek, D.J., & Gralinski, J.H. (1991). Gender differences in children's achievement-related beliefs and emotional responses to success and failure in mathematics. *Journal of Educational Psychology, 83*(3), 361–371.

Stodolsky, S.S. (1988). *The subject matters: Classroom activity in math and social studies.* Chicago, IL: University of Chicago Press.

Strange, A. (1997). Agency, communion, and achievement motivation. *Adolescence, 32*(126), 299–312.

Strauss, S., Ravid, D., Magen, N., & Berliner, D.C. (1998). Relations between teachers' subject matter knowledge, teaching experience and their mental models of children's minds and learning. *Teaching and Teacher Education, 14*(6), 579–595.

Streitmatter, J. (1997). An exploratory study of risk-taking and attitudes in a girls-only middle school math class. *Elementary School Journal, 98*(1).

Stroh, L.K., & Reilly, A.H. (1999). Gender and careers: Present experiences and emerging trends. In G.N. Powell, et al. (Ed.), *Handbook of gender and work.* Thousand Oaks, CA: Sage Publications, Inc.

Sulzer-Azaroff, B., & Mayer, G. (1986). *Achieving educational excellence using behavioral strategies.* New York: Holt, Rinehart & Winston.

Suzuki, L.A., & Valencia, R.R. (1997). Race-ethnicity and measured intelligence: Educational implications. *American Psychologist, 52*(10), 1103–1114.

Swanson, H.L., O'Connor, J.E., & Cooney, J.B. (1990). An information processing analysis of expert and novice teachers' problem solving. *American Educational Research Journal, 27*(3), 533–556.

Swanson, R.L. (1995). Toward the ethical motivation of learning. *Education, 116*(1), 43–51.

Sylvester, R. (1985). Research on memory: Major discoveries, major educational challenges. *Educational Leadership, 42,* 69–75.

Tanfer, K., Cubbins, L.A., & Billy, J.O.G. (1995). Gender, race, class, and self-reported sexually transmitted disease incidence. *Family Planning Perspectives, 27,* 196–202.

Tannenbaum, A.J. (1986). Reflections and refraction of light on the gifted. *Roeper Review, 8*(4), 212–218.

Tannenbaum, A.J. (2000). A history of giftedness in school and society. In K.A, Heller, F.J. Monks, R.J. Sternberg, & R.F. Subotnik (Eds.), *International handbook of giftedness and talent* (2nd ed.). London: Elsevier.

Tassi, F., & Schneider, B.H. (1997). Task-oriented versus other-referenced competition: Differential implications for children's peer relations. *Journal of Applied Social Psychology, 27*(17), 1557–1580.

Tauber, R.T. (1990). Classical conditioning: Eliciting the right response. *NASSP Bulletin, 74*(5), 90–92.

Taylor, C., & Kokot, S. (2000). The status of gifted child education in Africa. In K.A. Heller, F.J. Monks, R.J. Sternberg, & R.F. Subotnik (Eds.), *International handbook of giftedness and talent* (2nd ed.). London: Elsevier.

Tennyson, R., & Cocchiarella, M. (1986). An empirically based instructional design theory for teaching concepts. *Review of Educational Research, 56,* 40–71.

Tennyson, R., & Park, O. (1980). The learning of concepts: A review of instructional design research literature. *Review of Educational Research, 50,* 55–70.

Terhune, K.W. (1968). Studies of motives, cooperation, and conflict within laboratory microcosms. In G.H. Snyder (Ed.), *Studies in international conflict* (Vol. 4, 29-58). Buffalo, NY: SUNY Buffalo Council on International Studies.

Terman, L.M. (1925). *Genetic studies of genius: Mental and physical traits of a thousand gifted children* (Vol. 1). Stanford, CA: Stanford University Press.

Terman, L.M. (1930). Trails to psychology. In G. Murchison (Ed.), *A history of psychology in autobiography (Vol. 2).* Worcester, MA: Clark University Press.

Thagard, P. (1999). Induction. In R.A. Wilson & F.C. Keil (Eds.), *The MIT encyclopedia of the cognitive sciences* (pp. 399–400). Cambridge, MA: MIT Press.

Tharp, R.G. (1989). Psychocultural variables and constants: Effects on teaching and learning in schools. *American Psychologist, 44*(2), 349–359.

Tharp, R.G., Cutts, R.I., & Burkholder, R. (1970). The community mental health center and the schools: A model for collaboration through demonstration. *Community Mental Health Journal, 6*(2), 126–135.

Thomas, E.L., & Robinson, H.A. (1972). *Improving reading in every class: A sourcebook for teachers.* Boston: Allyn & Bacon.

Thompson, L.P., Herrmann, D.J., Read, J.D., Bruce, D., Payne, D.G., & Toglia, M.P. (Eds.) (1998). *Eyewitness memory: Theoretical and applied perspectives.* Mahwah, NJ: Erlbaum.

Thompson, R.F. (2000). Memory: Brain systems. In A.E. Kazdin (Ed.), *Encyclopedia of psychology* (Vol. 5, pp. 175–178). New York: Oxford University Press.

Thompson, S.K. (1975). Gender labels and early sex role development. *Child Development, 46,* 339–347.

Thorkildsen, T.A., & Schmahl, C.M. (1997). Conceptions of fair learning practices among low-income African American and Latin American children: Acknowledging diversity. *Journal of Educational Psychology, 89*(4), 719–727.

Thorndike, E.L. (1898). Animal intelligence: An experimental study of the associative processes in animals. *Psychological Monographs, 2*(Whole No. 8).

Thorndike, E.L. (1911). *Animal intelligence: Experimental studies.* New York: Macmillan.

Thorndike, R.L., Hagen, E.P., & Sattler, J.M. (1986). *Stanford-Binet Intelligence Scale: Guide for administering and scoring the fourth edition.* Chicago: Riverside.

Thurstone, L.L. (1938). *Primary mental abilities.* Chicago: University of Chicago Press.

Tiedemann, J. (2000). Parents' gender stereotypes and teachers' beliefs as predictors of children's concept of their mathematical ability in elementary school. *Journal of Educational Psychology, 92*(1), 144–151.

Torgeson, J.K. (1977). Memorization processes in reading-disabled children. *Journal of Educational Psychology, 69*(5), 571–578.

Torgesen, J.K. (1999). Phonologically based reading disabilities: Toward a coherent theory of one kind of learning disability. In R.J. Sternberg & L. Spear-Swerling, *Perspectives on learning disabilities: Biological, cognitive, contextual* (pp. 106–135). Boulder, CO: Westview Press.

Torquati, J.C., & Vazsonyi, A.T. (1994, February). *Attachment models and emotionality: Predicting differential coping strategies in late adolescence.* Paper presented at the biennial meeting of the Society for Research on Adolescence, San Diego.

Torrance, E.P. (1974). *The Torrance tests of creative thinking: Technical-norms manual.* Bensenville, IL: Scholastic Testing Services.

Tulving, E. (1966). Subjective organization and effects of repetition in multi-trial free-recall learning. *Journal of Verbal learning and Verbal Behavior, 5,* 193–197.

Tulving, E. (1983). *Elements of episodic memory.* New York: Oxford University Press.

Tulving, E. (2000). Episodic vs. semantic memory. In R.A. Wilson & F.C. Keil (Eds.), *The MIT encyclopedia of the cognitive sciences* (pp. 278–280). Cambridge, MA: MIT Press.

Tulving, E., & Pearlstone, Z. (1966). Availability versus accessibility of information in memory for words. *Journal of Verbal Learning and Verbal Behavior, 5,* 381–391.

Tulving, E., & Thomson, D.M. (1973). Encoding specificity and retrieval processes in episodic memory. *Psychological Review, 80,* 352–373.

Turiel, E. (1973). Stage transitions in moral development. In R. Travers (Ed.), *Second handbook of research on teaching* (pp. 732–758). Chicago: Rand McNally.

Turiel, E. (1998). The development of morality. In W. Damon (Series Ed.) & N. Eisenberg (Vol. Ed.), *Handbook of child psychology* (5th ed, Vol. 3, pp. 863–932). New York: Wiley.

Tversky, A., & Kahneman, D. (1973). Availability: A heuristic for judging frequency and probability. *Cognitive Psychology, 5,* 207–232.

Underwood, B.J., Boruch, R.F., & Mulmi, R.A. (1978). Composition of episodic memory. *Journal of Experimental Psychology: General, 107*(4), 393–419.

United States Department of Education. (1994). *Sixteenth annual report to Congress on the implementation of the Individuals with Disabilities Education Act.* Washington, DC: U.S. Department of Education.

United States Office of Educational Research and Improvement. (1997). *Attaining excellence: A TIMSS resource kit.* Washington, DC: Government Printing Office.

Vandell, D., & Mueller, E.C. (1980). Peer play and friendships during the first two years. In H.C. Foot, A.J. Chapman, & J.R. Smith (Eds.), *Friendship and social relations in children.* New York: Wiley.

Vaughn, B.E., Gove, F.L., & Egeland, B. (1980). The relationship between out-of-home care and the quality of infant-mother attachment in an economically disadvantaged population. *Child Development, 51,* 1203–1214.

Vederhus, L., & Krekling, S. (1996). Sex differences in visual spatial ability in 9-year-old children. *Intelligence, 23*(1), 33–43.

Vellutino, F.R. (1978). Alternative conceptualizations of dyslexia: Evidence in support of a verbal-deficit hypothesis. *Harvard Educational Review, 47*(3), 334–354.

Vernon, P.A. (2000). Brain research related to giftedness. In K.A. Heller, F.J. Monks, R.J. Sternberg, & R.F. Subotnik (Eds.), *International handbook of giftedness and talent* (2nd ed.). London: Elsevier.

Vernon, P.E. (1971). *The structure of human abilities.* London: Methuen.

Volkmar, F.R. (Ed.). (1996). *Psychoses and developmental disorders in childhood and adolescence.* Washington, DC: American Psychiatric Press.

Von Eckardt, B. (1999). Mental representation. In R.A. Wilson & F.C. Keil (Eds.), *The MIT encyclopedia of the cognitive sciences* (pp. 527–529). Cambridge, MA: MIT Press.

Voss, J.F. & Post, T.A. (1988). On the solving of ill-structured problems. In M.T.H. Chi, R. Glaser, & M.J. Farr (Eds.), *The nature of expertise* (pp. 261–285). Hillsdale, NJ: Erlbaum.

Vygotsky, L.S. (1962). *Thought and language.* Cambridge, MA: MIT Press. (Original work published 1934).

Vygotsky, L.S. (1978). *Mind in society: The development of higher psychological processes.* Cambridge, MA: Harvard University Press.

Waddington, C.H. (1956). *Principles of embryology.* London: Macmillan.

Wade, C., & Cirese, S. (1991). *Human sexuality* (2nd ed.). New York: Harcourt Brace Jovanovich.

Wagner, R.K., & Garon, T. (1999). Learning disabilities in perspective. In R.J. Sternberg & L. Spear-Swerling (Eds.), *Perspective on Learning Disabilities* (pp. 83–105). Boulder, CO: Westview Press.

Wagner, R.K., & Sternberg, R.J. (1984). Alternative conceptions of intelligence and their implications for education. *Review of Educational Research, 54,* 179–224.

Wagner, R.K., & Sternberg, R.J. (1985). Practical intelligence in real-world pursuits: The role of tacit knowledge. *Journal of Personality and Social Psychology, 49,* 436–458.

Wagner, R.K., & Sternberg, R.J. (1987). Executive control in reading comprehension. In B.K. Brittin & S.M. Glynn (Eds.), *Executive control processes in reading.* (pp. 1–21). Hillsdale, NJ: Erlbaum.

Walberg, H.J., Harnisch, D.L., & Tsai, S.I. (1986). Elementary school mathematics productivity in twelve countries. *British Educational Research Journal, 12*(3), 237–248.

Walker, J.E., & Shea, T.M. (1991). *Behavior management: A practical approach for educators* (5th ed.). New York: Macmillan.

Walker, L.J. (1989). A longitudinal study of moral reasoning. *Child Development, 60*(1), 157–166.

Walker, L.J., Pitts, R., Hennig, K., & Matsuba, M.K. (1995). Reasoning about morality and real-life moral problems. In M. Killen & D. Hart (Eds.), *Morality in everyday life: Developmental perspectives* (pp. 371–407). New York: Cambridge University Press.

Wallas, G. (1926). *The art of thought.* New York: Harcourt, Brace.

Walters, G.C., & Grusec, J.F. (1977). *Punishment.* San Francisco: Freeman.

Wang, A.Y., Thomas, M.H., & Ouel-lette, J.A. (1992). Keyword mnemonic and retention of second- language vocabulary words. *Journal of Educational Psychology, 84,* 520–528.

Wapner, S., & Demick, J. (Eds.). (1991). *Field dependence-independence: Cognitive style across the life span.* Hillsdale, NJ: Erlbaum.

Ward, T.B. (1994). *Structured imagination: The role of category structure in exemplar generation.* College Station, TX: Academic Press.

Warren, B., & Ogonowski, M. (1998). *From knowledge to knowing: An inquiry into teacher learning in science.* Education Development Center. Newton, MA: Center for the Development of Teaching.

Wason, P.C., & Johnson-Laird, P.N. (1972). *Psychology of reasoning: Structure and content.* London: B.T. Batsford.

Waters, E., Wippman, J., & Sroufe, L.A. (1979). Attachment, positive affect, and competence in the peer group: Two studies in construct validation. *Child Development, 50,* 821–829.

Watkins, D. (2000). Correlates of approaches to learning: A cross-cultural meta-analysis. In R.J. Sternberg & L.F. Zhang (Eds.), *Perspectives on cognitive, learning, and thinking styles.* Mahwah, NJ: Erlbaum.

Watkins, D., Reghi, M., & Astilla, E. (1991). The Asian-learner-as-a-rote-learner stereotype: Myth or Reality? *Educational Psychology, 11*(1), 21–34.

Watson, J.B. (1930). *Behaviorism.* (Rev. ed.) New York: Norton.

Waugh, N.C., & Norman, D.A. (1965). Primary memory. *Psychological Review, 72,* 89–104.

Wechsler, D. (1974). *Wechsler intelligences scale for children—Revised.* New York: Psychological Corp.

Wechsler, D. (1991). *Manual for the Wechsler intelligence scales for children* (3rd ed.)(WISC—III). San Antonio, TX: Psychological Corporation.

Weiner, B. (1982). An attribution

theory of motivation and emotion. *Series in Clinical and Community Psychology Achievement, Stress, and Anxiety,* 223–245.

Weiner, B. (1985). An attributional theory of achievement motivation and emotion. *Psychological Review, 92*(4), 548–573.

Weiner, B. (1992a). Excuses in everyday interaction. In M.L. McLaughlin, M.J. Cody, & S.J. Read (Eds.), *Explaining one's self to others: Reason-giving in a social context.* Hillsdale, NJ: Erlbaum.

Weiner, B. (1992b). *Human motivation: Metaphors, theories, and research.* Newbury Park, CA: Sage Publications.

Weiner, B., & Handel, S.J. (1985). A cognition-emotion-action sequence: Anticipated emotional consequences of causal attributions and reported communication strategy. *Developmental Psychology, 21*(1), 102–107.

Weinstein, C.S., & Mignano, A.J. (1993). *Organizing the elementary school classroom: Lessons from research and practice.* New York: McGraw-Hill.

Weinstein, C.S., & Mignano, A.J. Jr. (1997). *Elementary classroom management: Lessons from research and practice* (2nd ed.). New York: McGraw-Hill.

Weinstein, R.S. (1998). Promoting positive expectations in schooling. In N.M. Lambert & B.L. McCombs (Eds.), *How students learn: Reforming schools through learner-centered education.* Washington, DC: American Psychological Association.

Wellman, H.M., & Gelman, S.A. (1998). Knowledge acquisition in foundational domains. In D. Kuhn & R.S. Siegler (Eds.), *Handbook of child psychology* (5th ed.) (Vol. 2, pp. 523–574). New York: Wiley.

Werner, E.E. (1972). Infants around the world. *Journal of Cross-Cultural Psychology, 3,* 111–134.

Werner, H., & Kaplan, B. (1963). *Symbol formation.* New York: Wiley.

Wheelock, A. (1994). *Alternatives to tracking and ability grouping.* Arlington, VA: American Association of School Administrators.

Whitaker, A., Johnson, J., Shaffer, D., et al. (1990). Uncommon troubles in young people: Prevalence estimates of selected psychiatric disorders in a nonreferred adolescent population. *Archives of General Psychiatry, 47*(5), 487–496.

White, R.W. (1959). Motivation reconsidered: The concept of competence. *Psychological Review, 66,* 297–333.

White, T.L., & Wethington, E. (1996). Youth: Changing beliefs and behaviors. In U. Bronfenbrenner, P. McClelland, E. Wethington, P. Moen, & S.J. Ceci (Eds.), *State of Americans.* New York: Free Press.

Whorf, B.L. (1956). In J.B. Carroll (Ed.), *Language, thought and reality: Selected writings of Benjamin Lee Whorf.* Cambridge, MA: MIT Press.

Wigfield, A., Eccles, J.S., & Pintrich, P.R. (1996). Development between the ages of 11 and 25. In D. Berliner & R. Calfee (Eds.), *Handbook of educational psychology,* (pp. 148–185). New York: Macmillan.

Wiggins, G. (1989). A true test: Toward more authentic and equitable assessment. *Phi Delta Kappan, 70,* 703–713.

Wiggins, G. (1996–1997). Practicing what we preach in designing authentic assessment. *Educational Leadership, 54*(4), 18–25.

Wiggins, G. (1993). Assessment, authenticity, context, and validity. *Phi Delta Kappan, 75,* 200-214.

Wiig, E.H. (1982). Communication disorders. In H. Haring (Ed.), *Teaching and learning through discussion* (pp. 3–24). Springfield, IL: Charles C. Thomas.

Wild, T.C., Enzle, M.E., & Hawkins, W.L. (1992). Effects of perceived extrinsic versus intrinsic teacher motivation on student reactions to skill acquisition. *Personality and Social Psychology Bulletin, 18*(2), 245–251.

Willcutt, E.G., & Pennington, B.F. (2000). Comorbidity of reading disability and attention-deficit/hyperactivity disorder: Differences by gender and subtype. *Journal of Learning Disabilities, 33*(2), 179–191.

Williams, T. (1976). Teacher prophecies and the inheritance of inequality. *Sociology of Education, 49*(3), 223–236.

Williams, W. M. (1998). Are we raising smarter children today? School- and home-related influences on IQ. In U. Neisser (Ed.), *The Rising Curve: Long-term changes in IQ and related measures.* Washington, DC: American Psychological Association Books.

Williams, W.M., Blythe, T., White, N., Li, J., Sternberg, R.J., & Gardner, H.I. (1996). *Practical intelligence for school: A handbook for teachers of grades 5-8.* New York: HarperCollins.

Williams, W.M., & Ceci, S.J. (1997a). Are Americans becoming more or less alike? Trends in race, class, and ability differences in intelligence. *American Psychologist, 52*(11), 1226–1235.

Williams, W.M., & Ceci, S.J. (1997b). "How'm I doing?": Problems with the use of student ratings of instructors and courses. *Change, 29*(5), 12–23.

Willoughby, T., Wood, E., & Khan, M. (1994). Isolating variables that impact on or detract from the effectiveness of elaboration strategies. *Journal of Educational Psychology, 86,* 279–289.

Wilson, J.Q. (1993). *The moral sense.* New York: Free Press.

Winne, P.H. (1995). Inherent details in self-regulated learning. *Educational Psychologist, 30,* 173–188.

Winter, D.G. (1973). *The power motive.* New York: Free Press.

Witkin, H.A. (1973). *The role of cognitive style in academic performance and in teacher-student relations.* Unpublished report, Educational Testing Service, Princeton, NJ.

Witkin, H.A., Dyk, R.B., Faterson, H.F., Goodenough, D.R., & Karp,

S.A. (1962). *Psychological differentiation.* New York: Wiley.

Witkin, H.A., Oltman, P.K., Raskin, E., & Karp, S.A. (1971). *Embedded Figures Test, Children's Embedded Figures Test, Group Embedded Figures Test* [manual]. Palo Alto, CA: Consulting Psychologists Press.

Wittgenstein, L. (1953). *Philosophical investigations.* New York: Macmillan.

Wolf, D. (1998). *Presence of minds, performances of thought.* New York: College Entrance Examination Board.

Wolf, D., Bixby, J., Glenn, J., & Gardner, H. (1991). To use their minds well: New forms of student assessment. *Review of Research in Education, 17,* 31–74.

Woloshyn, V.E., Pressley, M., & Schneider, W. (1992). Elaborative-interrogation and prior-knowledge effects on learning of facts. *Journal of Educational Psychology, 84*(1), 115–124.

Wolraich, M.L. (Ed.). (1996). *Disorders of development and learning: A practical guide to assessment and management* (2nd ed.). St. Louis: Mosby.

Wood, R., & Bandura, A. (1989). Impact of conceptions of ability on self-regulatory mechanisms and complex decision making. *Journal of Personality and Social Psychology, 56*(3), 407–415.

Woodword, A.L., & Markman, E.M. (1998). Early word learning. In D. Kuhn & R.S. Siegler (Eds.), *Handbook of Child Psychology* (5th ed.) (Vol. 2, pp. 371–420). New York: Wiley.

Work Group of the American Psychological Association Board of Educational Affairs (BEA), (1997). *Learner Centered Psychological Principles.* Washington, DC: American Psychological Association.

Worthen, B. (1993). Critical issues that will determine the future of alternative assessment. *Phi Delta Kappan, 74,* 444–454.

Wotors, C.A., & Pintrich, P.R. (1998). Contextual differences in student motivation and self-regulated learning in mathematics, English, and social studies classrooms. *Instructional Science, 26*(1-2), 27–47.

Wright, M.J. (1997). Gifted and learning disabled: Double jeopardy or a winning combination? *Learning, 25*(3), 49–51.

Wright, R. (1994). *The moral animal: The new science of evolutionary psychology.* New York: Pantheon.

Wynn, R.L., & Fletcher, C. (1987). Sex role development and early educational experiences. In D.B. Carter (Ed.), *Current conceptions of sex roles and sex typing.* New York: Praeger.

Yerkes, R.M., & Dodson, J.D. (1908). The relation of strength of stimulus to rapidity of habit formation. *Journal of Comparative Neurology, 18,* 459–482.

Young, M.F. (1993). Instructional design for situated learning. *Educational Technology Research and Development, 41*(1), 43–58.

Yuen-Yee, G.C., & Watkins, D. (1994). Classroom environment and approaches to learning: An investigation of the actual and preferred perception of Hong Kong secondary school students. *Instructional Science, 22*(3), 233–246.

Yzerbyt, V.Y., Rocher, S., & Schadron, G. (1996). Stereotypes as explanations: A subjective essentalistic view of group perception. In R. Spears, P.J. Oakes, N. Ellemers, & S.A. Haslam (Eds.), *The social psychology of stereotyping and group life.* Cambridge, MA: Blackwell.

Zentall, S.S. (1989). Attentional cuing in spelling tasks for hyperactive and comparison regular classroom children. *Journal of Special Education, 23*(1), 83–93.

Zetlin, A., & Murtaugh, M. (1990). Whatever happened to those with borderline IQs? *American Journal on Mental Retardation, 94*(5), 463–469.

Zigler, E. (1982). Development versus difference theories of mental retardation and the problem of motivation. In E. Zigler & D. Balla (Eds.), *Mental retardation: The developmental-difference controversy.* Hillsdale, NJ: Erlbaum.

Zigler, E. (1999). The individual with mental retardation as a whole person. In E. Zigler & D. Bennett-Gates (Eds.), *Personality development in individuals with mental retardation* (pp. 1–16). New York: Cambridge University Press.

Zigler, E., & Berman, W. (1983). Discerning the future of early childhood intervention. *American Psychologist, 38,* 894–906.

Zigler, E., & Hodapp, R. (1986). *Understanding mental retardation.* New York: Cambridge University Press.

Zimmerman, B.J. (1995). Self-efficacy and educational development. In A. Bandura (Ed.), *Self-efficacy in changing societies* (pp. 202–231). New York: Cambridge University Press.

Zimmerman, B.J., Bandura, A., & Martinez-Pons, M. (1992). Self-motivation for academic attainment: The role of self-efficacy beliefs and personal goal setting. *American Educational Research Journal, 29*(3), 663–676.

Zuckerman, D.M., & Zuckerman, B.S. (1985). Television's impact on children. *Pediatrics, 75,* 233–240.

NAME INDEX

Clements, B., 89
Clifford, M.M., 146
Clifton, R.K., 42
Clinkenbeard, P., 133
Clinkenbeard, P.R., 137, 166, 442
Clinton, W.J., 469
Cobb, P., 294
Cocchiarella, M., 314
Cocking, R.R., 305
Cognition and Technology Group at Vanderbilt University, 458
Cohen, R.J., 477, 483, 489
Cohen, R.L., 278
Coie, J.D., 97
Coldiron, J.R., 138
Cole, M., 220
Coleman, M.C., 179
Coleman, S.R., 238
Colin, V.L., 95
Collary, M., 304
Collins, A., 9, 274, 296, 298, 299, 305, 529
Collins, A.M., 277, 286, 294, 296, 298
Collins, M.A., 146
Collins, N., 96, 279
Compas, B.E., 109
Condry, J.C., 211
Condry, S., 211
Cook, G., 274
Cooley, C.H., 373
Cooney, J.B., 15
Cooper, E.H., 272
Cooper, H.M., 438
Cooper, R., 452
Copeland, W.D., 15
Coplan, R.J., 87
Cordova, D.I., 361
Corin, W.J., 271
Corno, L., 27, 28, 140, 143
Costa, A.L., 333
Costa, P.T., 146
Cotton, K., 139
Council for Exceptional Children (CEC), 188
Courtright, R.D., 163
Covington, M., 236
Covington, M.V., 347, 348
Covino, E.A., 384
Craik, F.I.M., 284, 285
Crano, W.D., 364
Craven, R.G., 27
Cronbach, L.J., 442, 493
Crooks, T.J., 507, 510
Cross, G.M., 511
Cross, L.H., 511
Crowder, R.G., 268, 271, 300
Crutchfield, R., 145
Csikszentmihalyi, M., 145, 371, 437
Cubbins, L.A., 111
Cummins, J., 70, 215
Cunningham, A.G., 279
Cunningham, C.E., 59

Cunningham, D.J., 299
Cushing, K.S., 9, 14
Cutts, R.I., 219

Douglas, J.D., 110
Douvan, E., 98
Downey, C., 172–173
Drake, M., 348
Drew, C.J., 168
Dubas, J.S., 213
DuBois, D.L., 373
Duguid, P., 274, 298, 299
Duguid, P., 305
Duncker, K., 327
Dunn, J., 68
Dunn, K., 143
Dunn, L.M., 157
Dunn, R., 143
Dweck, C.S., 24, 26, 82, 346, 369, 370, 371
Dwyer, C.A., 496
Dyck, B., 420

Ey, S., 109
Eysenck, M., 276

F

Fabes, R.A., 80, 98
Fagot, B.I., 91
Fairburn, C.G., 109
Farnham-Diggory, S., 296
Farr, M.J., 8, 9, 328
Faterson, H.F., 141
Fay, R.E., 93
Feingold, A., 90, 93, 210
Fekken, G.C., 481
Felder, R., 152–153
Feldhusen, J.F., 166
Feldlaufer, H., 346
Feltovitch, P., 8, 9
Feng, Y., 305
Fennema, E., 90, 210, 213
Fernald, A., 68
Ferrara, R., 167, 170
Ferrara, R.A., 57, 371
Ferrari, M., 133, 137, 142, 166, 442
Fetterman, D.M., 166
Feuerstein, R., 57, 137, 170, 333, 474
Fifer, W.P., 67
Fillmore, L.W., 215
Fischer, K.W., 50, 52, 130
Fischoff, B., 318
Fisher, J.D., 112
Fisher, W.A., 112
Fjellstrom, G.G., 259
Flanagan, A., 203
Flavell, E.R., 64
Flavell, J.H., 42, 64, 271
Fleming, J., 177
Fletcher, A.C., 200
Fletcher, C., 90
Flynn, J.R., 209
Fodor, J.A., 310
Foehr, R., 381
Fondell, M.M., 111
Forbes, R., 23
Foreso, R., 297
Forster, K.I., 171
Forsyth, S., 23
Freedman, S.W., 530
Freeman, F.N., 135
Freiberg, H.J., 356
Freiberg, P., 110
Frensch, P.A., 43, 146, 328
Freud, S., 91
Frey, K.S., 367, 373
Friedman, L., 213
Friedrich-Cofer, L., 254
Friend, M., 158
Frith, U., 180
Frombonne, E., 108

Frost, E.J., 427
Fukui, I., 68
Furman, W., 98
Furnham, A., 92

G

Gabriel, L.T., 167
Gagné, R.M., 279, 434
Gagnon, G., 304
Gagnon, J.H., 93
Gaines, B., 340
Galanter, E., 362
Gall, M.D., 435
Gallagher, J.J., 163, 182
Gamoran, A., 139, 140
Ganellen, R.J., 285
Garbarino, J., 414
Garcia, E.E., 70, 215, 216
Garcia-Mila, M., 45, 50
Gardner, H., 9, 42, 13, 24, 25, 125–134, 126, 127, 137, 146, 164, 171, 203, 298, 469, 497, 523
Gardner, W., 201
Garfield, P.E., 109
Garland, A.F., 110
Garner, M., 209
Garon, T., 174
Garrett, J., 411
Garwood, P., 357
Gayne, E.D., 275
Gearhart, M., 530
Geary, D.C., 91
Gelman, 90
Gelman, R., 43, 50
Gelman, S.A., 53, 64
Gerrig, R.J., 69
Getzels, J.W., 437
Ghatala, E.S., 23
Ghiselin, B., 146
Gibbs, J., 110
Gibbs, J.C., 105
Gick, M.L., 319, 330
Gigerenzer, G., 316
Gilligan, C., 105, 285
Gilman, B., 128–129
Ginott, H., 407
Ginsburg, G.S., 375
Girgus, J.S., 109
Glaser, R., 8, 9, 328, 528
Glenn, J., 497
Gliner, J.A., 481, 482, 483
Gobet, F., 8
Godden, D.R., 289
Golan, S., 497
Golann, S.E., 145, 146
Goldenberg, C., 364
Goldsmith, D., 96
Gong, J., 138

Good, T.L., 139, 140, 252, 364, 393, 440, 450, 454
Goodenough, D.R., 141
Goodlad, J.I., 138, 140
Goodman, J.B., 259
Goodnow, 91
Goodrich Andrade, H.L., 130, 269
Gordon, E.W., 203
Gordon, T., 407, 409
Gorman, C., 242
Gorsky, P., 228
Goswami, U., 51
Gottfredson, D.C., 203
Gottfredson, L., 123
Gottman, J.M., 97, 184
Gove, F.L., 96
Gow, L., 273
Goyette, K., 220
Graham, L., 259
Gralinski, J.H., 213
Grannott, N., 50
Grant, K.W., 109
Green, F.L., 64
Greenberg, M.T., 96
Greene, R.L., 271
Greenfield, P.M., 51, 219, 494
Greeno, J.G., 9, 10, 286, 294, 296, 298, 331
Greenwald, A.G., 286
Gregory, R.J., 470, 474, 477, 489
Greif, E.B., 106
Griffin, M.M., 299
Grigorenko, E.L., 51, 53, 57, 59, 132, 133, 134, 135, 136, 137, 141, 142, 166, 171, 174, 289, 316, 319, 320, 327, 442
Grissmer, D.W., 197, 203, 204
Groen, G.J., 63
Gronlund, N.E., 427, 469, 510, 513, 515, 516, 518, 519, 521, 522, 527
Grossman, H., 90
Grossman, S.H., 90
Grotzer, T.A., 60, 136, 309, 333
Gruber, H.E., 146
Gruenenfelder, T.M., 22
Grusec, J.F., 247
Guentuerkuen, O., 211
Guilford, J.P., 126, 145
Guitiérrez, R., 139
Guiton, G., 138, 140
Guralnick, M.J., 97, 184
Gustafsson, J-E., 124
Guthrie, E.R., 235
Guttmacher Institute, 111

H

Hagan, R., 91
Hagen, E.P., 121
Hakuta, K., 61, 69, 70, 71, 214, 215, 216
Haladyna, T.M., 516

Hall, B.W., 529
Hallahan, D.P., 176, 181
Halpern, D.F., 90, 91, 208, 209, 211, 212, 213, 309
Hambleton, R.K., 497
Hamilton, C.E., 99
Hammond, M.A., 184, 200
Hamner, T., 105
Hampson, E., 211, 212
Hampton, J.A., 308, 310, 312
Handley, H.M., 212
Hannafin, M.J., 456, 457
Hansen, D.T., 117
Hardman, M.L., 168
Harnisch, D.L., 213
Harold, R.D., 212
Harris, M.J., 364
Harrow, A.J., 431
Harter, S., 82, 87, 373
Hartup, W.W., 87, 97
Hasher, L., 276
Hauser, R.M., 194
Hausmann, M., 211
Hautamäki, , J., 133
Hawkins, W.L., 350
Hawryluk, J., 211
Hayes, J., 146, 321
Hayes, J.R., 326
Haynes, O.M., 213
Haynes, S.N., 470, 471
Hazan, C., 96
Headden, S., 71
Healy, E., 92
Heath, A., 109
Heath, S.B., 163, 219
Hedges, L.V., 209
Hegarty, M., 9
Hegel, G., 335
Heider, E.R., 69
Heider, F., 369
Heiman, R.J., 88
Helmreich, R.L., 242, 350
Henderson, A.S., 110
Henderson, V.L., 24, 26, 346, 371
Hendry, G.D., 283
Henin, A., 232
Henley, N.M., 277
Hennig, K., 105
Herman, J.L., 108, 497, 530
Hernandez, D.J., 194, 204
Hernandez, F., 194, 204
Heron, A., 51
Herrnstein, R.J., 137, 203
Hess, R.D., 200
Hetherington, E.M., 99
Heward, W.L., 181
Hewitt-Gervais, C.M., 529
Heyduk, R.G., 361
Heyman, G.D., 370
Hiebert, E., 298

Hill, J.P., 98
Hill, W.H., 427
Hines, M., 91
Hinson, J.T., 386
Hirsch, B.J., 373
Hiscock, M., 211
Hittner, J.B., 111
Ho, D.Y.F., 367
Hodapp, R.N., 167, 168
Hoerr, T., 130
Hoffman, A.M., 386
Hoffman, L.W., 198
Hogan, D., 177
Hogan, K., 445
Hollingshead, A.B., 194
Hollister, L.E., 111
Holloway, S.D., 200
Holstein, C.B., 106
Holt, W., 212
Holyoak, K.J., 330
Holzinger, K.J., 135
Hooker, E., 93
Horn, J.L., 124
Horn, J.M., 134
Hornblower, M., 71, 72
Horowitz, F., 166
Horvath, J.A., 6
Houang, R.T., 209
Howe, M.J.A., 332, 349
Howes, C., 97, 99
Howsepian, B.A., 26
Hoyle, R.H., 26, 362
Hsia, J., 220, 221
Hu, P.N., 111
Hudson, J.A., 295
Huesmann, L.R., 254
Hughes, F.P., 96
Hughes, R., Jr., 198
Humphreys, L.G., 163, 364
Hunt, E.B., 125, 320
Huston, A.C., 92, 212, 254
Huston-Stein, A., 212
Hyde, J.S., 93, 209, 210, 213

Jarwan, 166
Jemison, M., 202
Jensen, A.R., 123, 124, 133, 163, 203, 210
Johnson, B., 98, 481
Johnson, C.T., 414
Johnson, D.W., 452, 454
Johnson, L.M.P., 454
Johnson, M.K., 269, 276
Johnson, R.T., 452, 454
Johnson, S., 294
Johnson, W.R., 273
Johnson-Laird, P.N., 314, 315
Jones, M., 373
Joram, E., 9
Joseph, D.M., 269
Joyce, B., 314
Juel-Nielsen, N., 135
Jusczyk, P., 67
Jussim, L., 364

Masia, B.B., 431
Maslow, A.H., 356, 365
Mason, D.A., 140
Masten, A.S., 97
Matarazzo, J.D., 474
Matheson, C.C., 97, 99
Matlin, M., 282, 283
Matsuba, M.K., 105
Matsumoto, D., 88
Matthews, D.B., 356
Maulden, J., 112
Maxwell, S.E., 57
Mayer, G., 246, 255–256
Mayer, R., 9
Mayer, R.E., 17, 330, 331, 332, 334
Mayer, R.G. 136, 146
Mazur, J., 232
McCartney, K., 96
McCaslin, M., 454
McClelland, D.C., 146, 365, 366, 367
McClelland, J.L., 282
McClelland, P., 375
McCombs, B.L., 345, 376
McCormick, C.B., 285
McCrae, R.R., 146
McCune, V., 143
McDermott, J., 9, 125, 320
McDowell, L., 470
McEwen, B.S., 211
McGue, M., 135
McKeachie, W.J., 435
McKensie, Walter, 152
McKoon, G., 276, 282
McLanahan, S., 99
McLaughlin, H.J., 248
McLaughlin, M.W., 414
McLaughlin, T.F., 242
McLeod, D., 92
McNamara, T.P., 275, 276
McNatt, B.D., 364
McPartland, J.M., 138, 139
Medin, D.L., 310, 311, 312
Meece, J.L., 26, 362
Megargee, E.I., 481, 482
Meichenbaum, D.H., 257, 259
Meinschaefer, J., 211
Meisels, S.J, 495
Meister, C., 454
Mellon, P.M., 364
Menaghan, E.G., 111
Merseth, K.K., 381
Mervis, C.B., 311
Messer, B., 373
Messick, S., 141, 144
Mickler, S.E., 112
Midgley, C., 346
Mignano, A.J., 388, 400, 436
Miller, D.G., 295
Miller, G.A., 271, 362
Miller, K.F., 49

Miller, L.S., 204, 205, 206, 219, 22
Miller-Loncar, C.L., 200
Mischel, W., 29, 259, 354
Mitchell, J.J., 97
Mitchell, P., 162
Miyake, K., 96
Moallem, M., 9
Moen, P., 375
Moore, J.L., 298, 331
Morelli, G.A., 96
Morgan, G.A., 481, 482, 483
Morgan, M., 363
Morgan, R., 522
Morganfield, B., 219
Morison, P., 97
Morisset, C.E., 200
Morrison, F.J., 112
Morse, L.W., 212
Moses, L.J., 271, 309
Moshman, D., 52, 53, 271
Mostafapour, E.F., 214
Mother Theresa, 105
Mott, F.L., 111
Mousavi, S., 275
Mueller, E.C., 97
Muldoon, O.T., 373
Mulmi, R.A., 287
Munro, E., 124
Murphy, G., 312
Murphy, G., 58–59
Murray, C., 137, 203
Murtaugh, M., 169
Murton, F., 143
Musonda, D., 312
Mwangi, M.W., 92

Nahmias, M.L., 189
Nastasi, B.K., 445
National Center for Health Statistics
    (NCHS), 110
National Commission on Testing and
    Public Policy, 497
National Council of Teachers of
    Mathematics (NCTM), 296, 298
National Education Association (NEA), 36–37
National Education Goals Panel, 309
National Joint Committee on Learning
    Disabilities (NJCLD), 171
Nazos, P., 177
NCHS (National Center for Health
    Statistics), 110
NCTM (National Council of Teachers of
    Mathematics), 296, 298
Neale, J.M., 108, 109
Neale, M., 109
NEA (National Education Association),
    36–37

Needels, M., 299
Neisser, U., 203
Nelson, K., 64, 66, 87, 122, 295
Newby, T.J., 15
Newcomb, A.F., 87, 97
Newcomb, M.D., 111
Newcombe, N., 213
Newell, A., 278, 315, 324
Newell, F.M., 459
Newman, H.H., 135
Newman, S.E., 296
Newmann, F.M., 438
Nicholls, J.G., 370
Nickerson, R.S., 24, 137, 309, 333
Nieto, S., 70
Nightingale, N., 345
Nisan, M., 106, 363
NJCLD (National Joint Committee on
    Learning Disabilities), 171
Noice, H., 274
Nokes, C., 59, 136
Nolen-Hoeksema, S., 109
Nordvik, H., 209
Norem, J.K., 93
Norman, D.A., 270, 282
Norman, P.A., 109
Novak, J.D., 312
Nowell, A., 209
Nucci, L., 117
Nurius, P., 26
Nuthall, G., 444
Nystrand, M., 139, 140

Oakes, J., 138, 139, 140
O'Brien, M., 166
O'Brien, P.P., 315
O'Brien, W.H., 470, 471
Ochse, R., 144
O'Connor, J.E., 15
O'Connor, M.E., 109
Ogbu, J.U., 495
Ogonowski, M., 31
Okagaki, L., 137, 163
Okamoto, Y., 50
O'Leary, K.D., 248
O'Leary, S., 248
Olivier, D.C., 69
Oltman, P.K., 141
Omelich, C., 236
O'Neil, R., 83
Oppenheim, D., 96
Orlanski, M.D., 181
Orton, S.T., 174
Oscanyan, F., 333
Ouellette, J.A., 274
Owens, E.W., 458
Owens, M., 109

Wittrock, M.C., 330, 331, 332, 334
Wixson, K.K., 279
Wolf, D., 497, 527
Woloshyn, V.E., 24
Wolters, C.A., 27
Wong, B.Y.L., 259
Wood, E., 273
Wood, R., 26
Wood-Shuman, 351
Woodside, D.B., 108
Woodward, A.L., 42, 62
Work Group of the American Psychological Association Board of Educational Affairs, 445, 450
Worsham, M., 89, 393
Worthen, B., 497, 498
Wright, K., 102, 106
Wright, M.J., 176

Wubbels, T., 219
Wynn, R.L., 90

 X

Xie, Y., 220

Y

Yekovich, C.W., 275
Yekovich, F.R., 275
Yerkes, R.M., 358
Yeung, A.S., 209
Young, C., 153
Young, J., 473
Young, M.F., 299
Youngblade, L.M., 198

Yuen-Yee, G.C., 274
Yzerbyt, V.Y., 92

Z

Zan, B., 102, 117
Zane, W.S., 193
Zentall, S.S., 259
Zetlin, A., 169
Zhang, L.F., 141, 163
Ziegler, A.J., 203
Zigler, E., 110, 136, 167, 169
Zimmerman, B.J., 26, 256
Zimmerman, M., 318, 367, 373
Zohar, A., 45
Zuckerman, B.S., 92
Zuckerman, D.M., 92
Zulich, J.L., 15

SUBJECT INDEX

Note: Boldface type indicates key terms and the pages on which they are defined.

A

Abilities. *See also* Gifted
  children
  analytical, 130, 442
  beliefs about, 369–372
  creative, 130, 442
  diverse, development of, 442
  exceptional, motivation and, 349–350
  perceptions of, as influences on achievement, 371–372
  perspective-taking, 98–101
  practical, 130, 442
  primary mental abilities, 123
Ability grouping, 53, **138,** 138–140
  advantages and disadvantages of, 139–140
  implications for teaching, 140
  types of groups for, 138–139
Ability OnLine Support Network, 188–189
Absence seizures, 181–182
Abstract thinking, 50
Acceleration for gifted children, 165
Accommodation, 46
Accountability, 496
  overuse of tests in measuring, 496–497
Achievement
  assessment and, 510–511
  motivation and, 375–377, 510–511
  need for, 365
  perceptions of ability as influences on, 371–372
  socioeconomic status and, 201–202
Achievement motivation, 362, 366–367
Achievement tests, 477, 477–478
Acoustic level of processing, 285
Acquired immune deficiency syndrome
  (AIDS), 111, 112

Acquisition and performance phase,
  instructional events supporting, 434
Acquisition in classical conditioning, 236
Acronyms as memory strategy, 21, 290
Acrostics as memory strategy, 21, 290
Active listening, 409, 409–411
Actualizing tendency, 356
Adaptation
  as component of intelligence, 122–123
  in triarchic theory of intelligence, 131
Additive bilingualism, 70, 215
Adolescents
  achievement by, parental styles and, 200–201
  friendship development by, 98
  pregnancy among, 112
Advance organizers, 288
Affective domain, 429, 431
Affiliation, need for, 365
Affirming the consequent, 316
African Americans. *See* Ethnic diversity
Agitated depression, 109
Algorithms, 324
Allocated time, 387, 387–388
The Alphabet Superhighway, 464, 545
Alternate-forms reliability, 481
American College Test (ACT), format of,
  515
American Psychological Association,
  learner-centered psychological principle
  collection developed by, 445–447
Analogical representations, 276
Analytical abilities, 130, 442
Androgyny, 90
Anorexia nervosa, 108
Antecedent stimuli, 246
Antitheses, 53, 335
Anxiety, 358
Aptitude-by-treatment interactions, 441,
  441–442

Aptitude tests, 477
Arbitrariness of language, 66
Arousal, 358, 358–361
  implications for teaching, 361
  optimal levels of, creating, 359–361
  performance and, 358–359
Articulation disorders, 184
Asian Americans. *See also* Ethnic diversity
  motivation of, 220–221
Aspirations of expert students, 26
Assertive discipline, 248, **408,** 408–409
Assessments, 447. *See also* Authentic assessments; Classroom assessments;
  Traditional assessment tests
Assessment systems, 507
Assimilation, 46
Associative play, 97
At-risk children, 157
Attachment, 95, 95–96
  implications for teaching, 99, 100
Attention, social learning and, 254
**Attention-deficit hyperactivity disorder
  (ADHD),** 156, **177,** 177–178
Attitudes, changes in, classroom management and, 385
Attributions, 368, 368–369
Authentic assessments, 497, 497–498, **526,**
  526–533
  characteristics of, 527–528
  evaluating performance on, 530–531
  exhibitions, 530
  implications for teaching, 533
  portfolios, 529–530
  traditional assessments
    versus, 534–535, 543
  types of, 527
Authoritarian parental style, 199, 200
Authoritative parental style, 199, 200
Autistic disorder (autism), **180**
Automaticity, 278, **328**

Automatic mental processes, 11
Automatization, 11, 14, 16
Autonomous morality, 102
Autonomy versus shame and doubt stage, 82, 84
Availability heuristic, 317, 317–318
Aversive stimuli, 236, 236–237
Avoidant attachment, 95

Completion items, 519–520
Componential subtheory of triarchic theory of intelligence, 130–131
Comprehension, verbal, 62
Computer(s)
 effective versus ineffective uses of, 455–458
 integrating into daily classroom life, 458–459
 limitations of computer-assisted learning and, 459
 in student-centered teaching, 454–459
Computer-assisted instruction, 456
 limitations of, 459
Concept(s), 308, **310,** 310–314
 characteristic features of, 311–312
 defining features of, 310–311
 implications for teaching, 312, 314
Concept maps, 312
 Web sites about, 340
Concrete operational stage, 48, 48–49
Condition-action sequences, 278
Conditional knowledge, 275, **279**
Conditional syllogisms, 316
Conditioned emotional responses (CERs), 236, 236–237
Conditioned response (CR), 234, 236
Conditioned stimulus (CS), 234, 235, 236
Conditioning. *See* Classical conditioning; Operant conditioning
Conduct disorders, 179
Confidence intervals, 490
Connectionist model, 281, 281–283
Conscience, moral development and, 105
Conservation, 48
 of liquid quantity, 48
 of mass, 49
Constructivism, 444
Constructivist approaches, 294. *See also* Student-centered approach
 to learning, 296, 298–300
 to memory, 294–296
 Web sites about, 304, 305
Construct-related validity, 483
Content knowledge, 8, 31
Content validity, 483
Context, 268, 269, 446
 constructivist, 444–445
Contextual subtheory of triarchic theory of intelligence, 131–132
Contingency, 235
Contingency contracts, 246
Contingency contract systems, 416
Continuous reinforcement, 244
Contract systems, 537, 537–538
Control
 locus of, 351
 maintaining in classroom. *See* Maintaining control

self-determination and, 367–368
Control groups, 32
Conventional morality, 103, **104,** 104–105
Convergent thinking, 145
Cooing, 67
Cooperative learning, 452, 452–454
 criticisms of, 454
 effective approaches for, 453–454
Cooperative play, 97
The Coordinated Campaign for Learning Disabilities, 189
Correlations, 30
Council for Exceptional Children (CEC) Web site, 188
Creative abilities, 130, 442
Creative-productive giftedness, 163
Creativity, 144, 144–148. *See also* Insight
 confluence approach to, 145–146
 implications for teaching, 146–148
 investment theory of, 145–146
 mystical approach to, 144
 psychometric approach to, 144–145
 social-psychological approaches to, 145
 Web sites on, 153
Criteria, 482
Criterion-referenced grading systems, 509, 510, 537
Criterion-referenced tests, 471
Critical periods, 68
Critical thinking, 309
 Web resources about, 340–341
"Critical Thinking on the Web: A Directory of Quality Online Resources," 341
Criticism
 as component of intelligence, 122–123
 constructive, 393
Crystallized intelligence, 124
Cues, 246
Culture, 193. *See also* Diversity; Multicultural education; Vygotsky's sociocultural theory of cognitive development
 attachment and, 96
 classroom dynamics and, 219–220
 learning styles and, 143
 memory development and, 64
 motivation and, 220–221
 Piaget's theory of cognitive development and, 51
 sex differences related to, 212–213
 thinking and, 220
Culture-fair tests, 495
Culture-free tests, 495
Culture-relevant testing, 494–495
Curriculum and Evaluation Standards for School Mathematics, 296, 298
Curriculum compacting, 165
Cystic fibrosis, 181

Individualism, moral development and, 104
**Individualized education programs (IEPs),
159,** 159–160, 376–377
Individualized instruction, 449, 449–450
Individual rights, moral development and,
105
**Individuals with Disabilities Education
Act (IDEA), 157,** 157–158
definition of emotional and behavioral
disorders in, 178
Inductive reasoning, 315, 316–317
Industry versus inferiority stage, 82, 84
Inert knowledge, 308
Inference, transitive, 51
Informal assessments, 507
Information processing, speed of, 124–125
Information-processing theories, 61–65
comparison with other approaches to cog-
nitive development, 65–66
implications for teaching, 64–65
memory skills and, 64
quantitative skills and, 63–64
verbal skills and, 62
Infused instruction, 333
for teaching thinking, 333–335
Initiative versus guilt stage, 82, 84
Inquiry methods, 452
Insight, 17–19
experts' ways of thinking about problems
and, 17–19
processes key to, 322–323
redefining problems and, 17
Insight problems, 322–323
Instrumental conditioning. *See* Operant
conditioning
Instrumental Enrichment program, 137,
170
Integrity versus despair stage, 83, 83–84
Intelligence, 121, 121–140. *See also* Gifted
children; Mental retardation
ability grouping and, 138–140
contemporary systems theories of,
125–133
crystallized, 124
defining, 121–122
elements occupational therapy, 122–123
emotional, 153
entity view of, 24, 26
fluid, 124
heritability of, 134–135
incremental view of, 24, 26
modifiability of, 135–138
multiple intelligences and, 125–130
programs to improve, 136–137
psychometric theories of, 122–126
triarchic theory of, 5, 130–133
Web sites on, 152
Intelligence Applied program, 137
Intelligence quotient (IQ), 121, **476,**
476–477

giftedness and, 163
mental retardation and, 168–169
Intelligence tests, 474–477
online, 153
Interactive images as memory strategy, 21,
289
Interest tests, 477
Interference theory, 292, 292–293
Intermittent reinforcement, 244
Intermittent support for persons with men-
tal retardation, 169
Internal consistency reliability, 481
Internalization, 56, 256
Internalizing behavior disorders, 179
Internal personality pattern, 28
International Partnership for Service-
Learning, 117
International Society for Technology in
Education (ISTE), 465
"The Internet Encyclopedia of Philosophy,"
117
Interpersonal conformity, moral develop-
ment and, 105
Interpersonal intelligence, 126
Interrater reliability, 481
Interval schedules, 244, 245
Intervention, 59, 59–60
Intimacy versus isolation stage, 83, 84
Intrinsic motivation, 145, 347, 347–350
development of exceptional abilities and,
349–350
implications for teaching, 351
to learn, 446–447
research on, 347–348
Investment theory of creativity, 145,
145–146
Involving students
in assessments, 534–535
for classroom management, 391–392
Iowa Tests of Basic Skills, 477
Isolated children, 97

J

The Jean Piaget Society, 77
Jigsaw, 453, 453–454
Joplin Plan, 139
Judicial cognitive style, 142, 143

K

Kanner's syndrome, 180
Kaufman Assessment Battery for Children,
474
Keywords
to facilitate retrieval, 291
as memory strategy, 21
KidSource Online, 503

Knowledge
conditional, 275, 279
construction of, 446
of expert teachers. *See* Expert knowledge
inert, 308
procedural, 275, 278
Knowledge-acquisition components
in triarchic theory of intelligence,
131
"Knowledge Integration Environment
(KIE)," 77
Kohlberg's theory of moral development,
102–105
evaluating, 106

L

Language acquisition devices (LADs), 68
Language development, 66–72
bilingualism and, 69–72
comparison of theories of, 67–68
implications for teaching, 72
properties of language and, 66
stages of, 67
thought and, 68–69
Language diversity, 214–217
dialects and, 214
implications for teaching, 217
socioeconomic status and, 216–217
Standard English and, 214
teaching non-native speakers of English
and, 214–216. *See also* Bilingual education; Bilingualism
Law of effect, 239
Learning, 41, 232
context of, 268, 269, 446
cooperative, 452–454
discovery, 450
distributed, 274–275
goals of, 446
massed, 274–275
maturation versus, 41–42, 232
nature of process, 446
phases of, instructional events supporting,
434
rote, 273–274
situated, 298
social, 253–256
Learning disabilities (LD), 171, 171–177
defining, 171–172
implications for teaching, 176–177
problems with special services and,
173–174
reading disabilities, 174–175
teaching students with, 175–176
Learning environments, 268, 269, 446
constructivist, 444–445
Learning goals, 370, 371
The Learning Network, 305

criterion-referenced, 471
cultural issues concerning, 494–495
format of, 515
group, 475–476
implications for teaching, 478–479
importance of understanding, 469–470
individual, 474
of intelligence, 474–477
misuses of, 495–497
new directions for, 497–498
norm-referenced, 470–471
omnibus, 476
preparation for, 473
quality of, assessing, 479–483
scores on. *See* Test scores
teaching to the test and, 497
test bias and, 493–494
Web sites about, 502
Standard memory model, 269–281
encoding in, 269, 270–275
implications for teaching, 279–281
long-term storage in, 275–279
retrieval in, 269–270
working-memory model versus, 284
Standards, 447
Standard scores, 490, 490–491
Stanford Achievement Test, 478
Stanford-Binet Intelligence Scales, 474
Stanford University Center for Problem-
Based Learning, 340
Stanines, 491
Static assessment environment, 57
Statistical significance, 30
Stems, 515, 515–516
Stereotypes, gender, 92
Stereotype threat, 372
Sternberg's Seven-Level Model of teacher
responses to student questions,
437–438
Stimulus(i)
antecedent, 246
aversive, 236–237
conditioned, 234, 235, 236
neutral, 233
unconditioned, 234, 235, 236
Stimulus discrimination, 236
Stimulus generalization, 236
Strange situation, 95
Strategic thinking, 446
Stratified random samples, 480
Strong Vocational Interest Bland, 477
Student(s)
challenging, motivating, 375–377
expert. *See* Expert students
helpless, 370–371
involving. *See* Involving students
Student-centered approach, 444, 444–461
computers in, 454–459
constructivism in classroom and, 444
cooperative learning in, 452–454

creating constructivist learning environments for, 444–445
discovery approaches for, 450
group discussion in, 450–452
groupwork in, 452
individualized instruction in, 449–450
inquiry methods for, 452
learner-centered psychological principles
and, 445–447
limitations of, 459
planning for, 448
reciprocal teaching for, 454
teacher-centered approaches versus, 460
Student goals, 361–364
effective, 362–363
enhancement of motivation by, 361–362
implications for teaching, 364
importance of teacher feedback and
expectations and, 363–364
Student groupwork, 452
"Students with Intellectual Disabilities: A
Resource Guide for Teachers," 189
**Student Teams Achievement Divisions
(STAD), 453**
Study skills courses, 22
Stuttering, 183–184
Subject(s), 32
Subjective tests, 515
Substance abuse
by parents, damage caused to children by,
181
by students, 111
Subtractive bilingualism, 70, 215, 215–216
Successive approximations, 251, 251–252
Suicide, 110
Summative assessment, 509
Support, classification of mental retardation
based on level of, 169
Supporting self-control, 412
Surface-processing approach, 143
Surface structures of problems, 9
The Survival Guide for New Teachers, 381
Syllogisms, 315, 315–316
Symbolic representations, 276
Syntax, 67
Syntheses, 53, 335
Syphilis, 112
Systems theories of intelligence, 125–132
critique of, 133
multiple intelligences and, 125–130
triarchic theory of human intelligence,
130–133

T

Task(s), pursuit to completion, 27–28
Task-mastery goals, 362, 362–363
Taxonomies, 429, 429–432
affective domain and, 429, 431

cognitive domain and, 429–430
psychomotor domain and, 429, 431–432
Teacher(s)
challenges faced by, 18
expert. *See* Expert teachers
feedback and expectations of, importance
of, 363–364
Teacher-centered teaching, 426, 426–443
direct instruction methods for. *See* Direct
instruction
planning in. *See* Planning for teacher-centered teaching
student-centered approach versus, 460
Teacher Pathfinder Community Center, 544
"The Teacher's Guide to the U.S.
Department of Education," 37
Teachers.Net, 421
Teacher Talk, 420–421
Teaching, 423–462
importance of understanding, 424–425
reciprocal, 454
student-centered. *See* Student-centered
approach
teacher-centered. *See* Direct instruction;
Planning for teacher-centered teaching
to the test, 497
Teaching context, knowledge about, 10–11
Teaching Exceptional Children magazine,
188
Teaching for thinking, 333–336
group projects for, 336
methods for, 333–336
modeling and explicit teaching for, 336
role playing for, 336
Teaching portfolios, 544
"Teaching to a Higher Standard: Forget
Standardized Testing and the SAT II,"
502
Teachnet classroom management forum, 420
Teen pregnancy, 112
Telegraphic speech, 67
Temporal contiguity, 235
Test(s). *See* Standardized tests; Traditional
assessment tests
Test anxiety, 236–237
Test bias, 493, 493–494
"Testing, Testing: Does Standardized Testing
Discourage Good Teachers," 502
Test-retest reliability, 481
Test scores
ethnic diversity related to, 203–204
grade equivalent, 491
implications for teaching, 492
on intelligence tests, 476–477
normative, 471
percentile, 488–489
raw, 488
standard, 490–491
statistical concepts underlying, 484–487
true, 489–490

Theory, 30. *See also specific theories*
Theory of mental self-government, 142, 142–143
Theory of multiple intelligences, 125, 125–130
  implications for teaching, 129–130
Theory of primary mental abilities, 123
Theses, 53, 335
Think-aloud protocols, 23, 23–24
Thinking, 307–337
  about thinking, 14–16, 446
  abstract, 50
  concept formation and, 310–314
  convergent, 145
  critical, 309
  culture and, 220
  dialectical, 53, 335–336
  dialogical, 335
  divergent, 145
  importance of understanding, 309
  insightful. *See* Insight
  language and, 68–69
  post-formal, 52
  problem solving and. *See* Problem solving
  reasoning and, 314–319
  reflective, 6–7
  reversible, 49
  strategic, 446
  teaching for, 333–336
  transfer and, 329–333
  triarchic, 5
Thinking styles, 141. *See also* Cognitive styles
Third-party perspective taking, 99
Thought, representational, 47
Three-ring model of giftedness, 164
Time
  allocated versus engaged, 387–388
  intelligence and, 124–125
  wait, 436
Time-out, 248
Token reinforcement systems, 242, 415, 415–416
"Tools of the Mind" program, 77
Torrance Tests of Creative Thinking, 144–145
Total-point systems, 539
Total-time hypothesis, 272
Tracking, 139
Traditional assessment tests, 512–526
  authentic assessments versus, 543
  essay, developing, 522–525

  implications for teaching, 525–526
  material to cover with, 513–514
  objective questions for, developing, 515–521
  timing and methods for, 514–515
Transfer, 329, 329–333
  teaching for, 331–333
  types of, 330–331
Transfer of learning phase, instructional events supporting, 434
Transitions, smooth, creating, 391
Transitive inference, 51
Transitive relations, 315–316
Trial and error strategy, 325
Triangle of thinking, 5
Triarchic theory of human intelligence, 5, 130, 130–133
  implications for teaching, 132–133
Triarchic thinking, 5
True/false items, 518
True scores, 489, 489–490
Trust versus mistrust stage, 82, 84
T-scores, 491
Two-word utterances, 67
Type A attachment, 95
Type B attachment, 95
Type C attachment, 95

U

Unconditioned response (UR), 234
Unconditioned stimulus (US), 234, 235, 236
Underconfidence, 318, 318–319
Underextension errors, 67
Undifferentiated perspective taking, 98
Universal principles of justice, 105
Unoccupied children, 97
Unstructured discovery, 450
"The Use of Concept Maps in the Teaching-Learning Process," 341

V

Validity, 482
  of assessments, 508–509
  of tests, 482–483
Variable-interval reinforcement schedule, 245
Variable-ratio reinforcement schedule, 244, 245
Variance, 487

Venereal warts, 112
Verbal comprehension, 62
Verbal skills, development of, 62
Vicarious reinforcement, 255
"The Viking Network," 464
Violence
  increase in, classroom management and, 386
  in schools, coping with, 413–414
Violent behavior, 110–111
Visual impairment, 182, 182–183
Vocational interest tests, 477
Voices project, 228
Voicing problems, 184
Volition, 27, 27–28
Vygotsky's sociocultural theory of cognitive development, 55–61
  comparison with other approaches to cognitive development, 65–66
  evaluating, 60
  implications for teaching, 61
  internalization and, 56
  scaffolding and, 57–60
  Web site on, 77
  zone of proximal development and, 56–57

W

Wait time, 436
Warts, venereal, 112
Wechsler Adult Intelligence Scale (WAIS III), 474
Wechsler Intelligence Scale for Children (WISC-III), 474
Wechsler Preschool and Primary Scale of Intelligence (WPPSI), 474
Well-structured problems, 321
White Americans. *See* Ethnic diversity
Within-class grouping, 138, 138–139, 140
With-it-ness, 389
Word processors, 456–458
Working backward, 325
Working forward, 325
Working-memory model, 283, 283–284
  standard memory model versus, 284

Z

Zone of proximal (potential) development (ZPD), 56, 56–57
z-scores, 490, 490–491